T0260527

The Kimball Group Reader

The Kimball Group Reader

Relentlessly Practical Tools for Data Warehousing and Business Intelligence

Remastered Collection

Ralph Kimball and Margy Ross
with Bob Becker, Joy Mundy, and Warren Thornthwaite

WILEY

The Kimball Group Reader: Relentlessly Practical Tools for Data Warehousing and Business Intelligence, Second Edition

Published by
John Wiley & Sons, Inc.
10475 Crosspoint Boulevard
Indianapolis, IN 46256
www.wiley.com

Copyright © 2016 by Ralph Kimball and Margy Ross

Published simultaneously in Canada

ISBN: 978-1-119-21631-5
ISBN: 978-1-119-23879-9 (ebk)
ISBN: 978-1-119-21659-9 (ebk)

Manufactured in the United States of America

10 9 8 7 6 5 4 3 2 1

No part of this publication may be reproduced, stored in a retrieval system or transmitted in any form or by any means, electronic, mechanical, photocopying, recording, scanning or otherwise, except as permitted under Sections 107 or 108 of the 1976 United States Copyright Act, without either the prior written permission of the Publisher, or authorization through payment of the appropriate per-copy fee to the Copyright Clearance Center, 222 Rosewood Drive, Danvers, MA 01923, (978) 750-8400, fax (978) 646-8600. Requests to the Publisher for permission should be addressed to the Permissions Department, John Wiley & Sons, Inc., 111 River Street, Hoboken, NJ 07030, (201) 748-6011, fax (201) 748-6008, or online at http://www.wiley.com/go/permissions.

Limit of Liability/Disclaimer of Warranty: The publisher and the author make no representations or warranties with respect to the accuracy or completeness of the contents of this work and specifically disclaim all warranties, including without limitation warranties of fitness for a particular purpose. No warranty may be created or extended by sales or promotional materials. The advice and strategies contained herein may not be suitable for every situation. This work is sold with the understanding that the publisher is not engaged in rendering legal, accounting, or other professional services. If professional assistance is required, the services of a competent professional person should be sought. Neither the publisher nor the author shall be liable for damages arising herefrom. The fact that an organization or Web site is referred to in this work as a citation and/or a potential source of further information does not mean that the author or the publisher endorses the information the organization or Web site may provide or recommendations it may make. Further, readers should be aware that Internet Web sites listed in this work may have changed or disappeared between when this work was written and when it is read.

For general information on our other products and services please contact our Customer Care Department within the United States at (877) 762-2974, outside the United States at (317) 572-3993 or fax (317) 572-4002.

Wiley publishes in a variety of print and electronic formats and by print-on-demand. Some material included with standard print versions of this book may not be included in e-books or in print-on-demand. If this book refers to media such as a CD or DVD that is not included in the version you purchased, you may download this material at http://booksupport.wiley.com. For more information about Wiley products, visit www.wiley.com.

Library of Congress Control Number: 2015956232

Trademarks: Wiley, and the Wiley logo are trademarks or registered trademarks of John Wiley & Sons, Inc. and/or its affiliates, in the United States and other countries, and may not be used without written permission. All other trademarks are the property of their respective owners. John Wiley & Sons, Inc., is not associated with any product or vendor mentioned in this book.

About the Authors

Ralph Kimball founded the Kimball Group. Since the mid-1980s, he has been the DW/BI industry's thought leader on the dimensional approach and has trained more than 20,000 IT professionals. Prior to working at Metaphor and founding Red Brick Systems, Ralph co-invented the Star workstation at Xerox's Palo Alto Research Center (PARC). Ralph has a Ph.D. in Electrical Engineering from Stanford University.

Margy Ross is President of the Kimball Group and Decision Works Consulting. She has focused exclusively on data warehousing and business intelligence since 1982. Margy has consulted with hundreds of clients and taught DW/BI best practices to tens of thousands. Prior to working at Metaphor and co-founding DecisionWorks Consulting, she graduated with a B.S. in Industrial Engineering from Northwestern University.

Credits

Project Editor
Tom Dinse

Production Editor
Christine O'Connor

Copy Editor
Kim Cofer

Manager of Content Development & Assembly
Mary Beth Wakefield

Marketing Director
David Mayhew

Marketing Manager
Carrie Sherrill

Professional Technology & Strategy Director
Barry Pruett

Business Manager
Amy Knies

Associate Publisher
Jim Minatel

Project Coordinator, Cover
Brent Savage

Proofreader
Nancy Carrasco

Indexer
Johnna VanHoose Dinse

Cover Designer
Wiley

Cover Image
The Kimball Group

Warren Thornthwaite (1957–2014) ·

The Kimball Group lost Warren to a brain tumor in 2014. He wrote many insightful articles that appear in this Reader. All of us at the Kimball Group miss Warren dearly—his intellect, curiosity, creativity, and most especially, his friendship and sense of humor. As any of you who met Warren will attest, he was truly one of a kind!

Acknowledgments

First, we want to thank the 33,000 subscribers to the Kimball *Design Tips*, and the uncounted numbers who have visited the Kimball Group website to peruse our archive. This book brings the remastered *Design Tips* and articles together in what we hope is a very usable form.

The Kimball Group Reader would not exist without the assistance of our business partners. Kimball Group members Bob Becker, Joy Mundy, and Warren Thornthwaite wrote many of the valuable articles and *Design Tips* included in the book. Thanks to Julie Kimball for her insightful comments. Thanks also to former Kimball Group member Bill Schmarzo for his contributions on analytic applications.

Thanks to our clients and students who have embraced, practiced, and validated the Kimball methods with us. We have learned as much from you as you have from us!

Jim Minatel, our executive editor at Wiley Publishing, project editor Tom Dinse, and the rest of the Wiley team have supported this project with skill, encouragement, and enthusiasm. It has been a pleasure to work with them.

To our families, thank you for your support over the twenty year span during which we wrote these *Design Tips* and articles. Julie Kimball and Scott Ross: We couldn't have done it without you! And, of course, thanks to our children, Sara Kimball Smith, Brian Kimball, and Katie Ross, who have grown into adults over the same time!

Contents

11 Back Room ETL and Data Quality 495

Introduction

The Kimball Group's article and *Design Tip* archive has been the most popular destination on our website (www.kimballgroup.com). Stretching back twenty years to Ralph's original 1995 *DBMS* magazine articles, the archive explores more than 250 topics, sometimes in more depth than provided by our books or courses.

With *The Kimball Group Reader, Second Edition*, we have organized all of the articles in a coherent way. But *The Reader* is more than merely a collection of our past magazine articles and *Design Tips* verbatim. We have trimmed the redundancy, made sure all the articles are written with the same consistent vocabulary, and updated many of the figures. This is a new and improved remastered compilation of our writings.

After considerable discussion, we decided to update many time references and edit content throughout the book to provide the perspective of 2015 rather than leaving old dates or outdated concepts in the articles. Thus an article written in 2007 may use 2015 in an example! When articles refer to the number of years that have passed, we have updated these references relative to 2015. For example, if a 2005 article originally said "during the past five years," the article now reads "during the past fifteen years." Mentions regarding our years of experience, number of books sold, articles written, or students taught have also been updated to 2015 figures. Finally, we occasionally changed references from outmoded technologies such as "modems" to more modern technologies, especially "internet." We trust these changes will not mislead or cause confusion, but rather make your reading experience more natural.

Intended Audience and Goals

The primary reader of this book should be the analyst, designer, modeler, or manager who is delivering a data warehouse in support of business intelligence. The articles in this book trace the entire lifecycle of DW/BI system development, from original business requirements gathering all the way to final deployment. We believe that this collection of articles serves as a superb reference-in-depth for literally hundreds of issues and situations that arise in the development of a DW/BI system.

The articles range from a managerial focus to a highly technical focus, although in all cases, the tone of the articles strives to be educational. These articles have been accessed thousands of times per day on the Kimball Group website over a span of 20 years, so we're confident they're useful. This book adds significant value by organizing the archive, and systematically editing the articles to ensure their consistency and relevance.

Preview of Contents

Following two introductory chapters, the book's organization will look somewhat familiar to readers of *The Data Warehouse Lifecycle Toolkit, Second Edition* (Wiley, 2008) because we've organized the articles topically to correspond with the major milestones of a data warehouse/business intelligence (DW/BI) implementation. Not surprisingly given the word "Kimball" is practically synonymous with dimensional modeling, much of *The Reader* focuses on that topic in particular.

- **Chapter 1: *The Reader* at a Glance.** We begin the book with a series of articles written by Ralph several years ago for *DM Review* magazine. This series succinctly encapsulates the Kimball approach in a cohesive manner, so it serves as a perfect overview, akin to *CliffsNotes*, for the book.

- **Chapter 2: Before You Dive In.** Long-time readers of Ralph's articles will find that this chapter is a walk down memory lane, as many of the articles are historically significant. Somewhat amazingly, the content is still very relevant even though most of these articles were written in the 1990s.

- **Chapter 3: Project/Program Planning.** With an overview and history lesson under your belt, Chapter 3 moves on to getting the DW/BI program and project launched. We consider both the project team's and sponsoring stakeholders' responsibilities, and then delve into the Kimball Lifecycle approach.

- **Chapter 4: Requirements Definition.** It is difficult to achieve DW/BI success in the absence of business requirements. This chapter delivers specific recommendations for effectively eliciting the business's needs. It stresses the importance of organizing the requirements findings around business processes, and suggests tactics for reaching organizational consensus on appropriate next steps.

- **Chapter 5: Data Architecture.** With a solid understanding of the business requirements, we turn our attention to the data (where we will remain through Chapter 11). This chapter begins with the justification for dimensional modeling. It then describes the enterprise data warehouse bus architecture, discusses the agile development approach to support data warehousing, provides rationalization for the requisite integration and stewardship, and then contrasts the Kimball architecture with the Corporate Information Factory's hub-and-spoke.

- **Chapter 6: Dimensional Modeling Fundamentals.** This chapter introduces the basics of dimensional modeling, starting with distinguishing a fact from a dimension, and the core activities of drilling down, drilling across, and handling time in a data warehouse. We also explore familiar fables about dimensional models.

- **Chapter 7: Dimensional Modeling Tasks and Responsibilities.** While Chapter 6 covers the fundamental "what and why" surrounding dimensional modeling, this chapter focuses on the "how, who, and when." Chapter 7 describes the dimensional modeling process and tasks, with the aim of organizing an effective team, whether starting with a blank slate or revisiting an existing model.

■ **Chapter 8: Fact Table Core Concepts.** The theme for Chapter 8 could be stated as "just the facts, and nothing but the facts." We begin by discussing granularity and the three fundamental types of fact tables, and then turn our attention to fact table keys and degenerate dimensions. The chapter closes with a potpourri of common fact table patterns, including null, textual, and sparsely populated metrics, as well as facts that closely resemble dimension attributes.

■ **Chapter 9: Dimension Table Core Concepts.** We shift our focus to dimension tables in Chapter 9, starting with a discussion of surrogate keys and the ever-present time (or date) dimensions. We then explore role playing, junk, and causal dimension patterns, before launching into a thorough handling of slowly changing dimensions, including four new advanced dimension types. Hang onto your hats.

■ **Chapter 10: More Dimension Patterns and Considerations.** Chapter 10 complements the previous chapter with more meaty coverage of dimension tables. We describe snowflakes and outriggers, as well as a significantly updated section on bridges for handling both multi-valued dimension attributes and ragged variable hierarchies. We discuss nuances often encountered in customer dimensions, along with internationalization issues. The chapter closes with a series of case studies covering insurance, voyages and networks, human resources, finance, electronic commerce, text searching, and retail; we encourage everyone to peruse these vignettes as the patterns and recommendations transcend industry or application boundaries.

■ **Chapter 11: Back Room ETL and Data Quality.** We switch gears from designing the target dimensional model to populating it in Chapter 11. Be forewarned: This is a hefty chapter, as you'd expect given the subject matter. This updated edition of the *Reader* has a wealth of new material in this chapter. We start by describing the 34 subsystems required to extract, transform, and load (ETL) the data, along with the pros and cons of using a commercial ETL tool. From there, we delve into data quality considerations, provide specific guidance for building fact and dimension tables, and discuss the implications of real-time ETL.

■ **Chapter 12: Technical Architecture Considerations.** It's taken us until Chapter 12, but we're finally discussing issues surrounding the technical architecture, starting with server oriented architecture (SOA), master data management (MDM), and packaged analytics. A new section on big data features two in-depth Kimball Group white papers written by Ralph. Final sections in this chapter focus on the presentation server, including the role of aggregate navigation and online analytical processing (OLAP), user interface design, metadata, infrastructure, and security.

■ **Chapter 13: Front Room Business Intelligence Applications.** In Chapter 13, we step into the front room of the DW/BI system where business users are interacting with the data. We describe the lifecycle of a typical business analysis, starting with a review of historical performance but not stopping there. We then turn our attention to standardized BI reports before digging into data mining and predictive analytics. The chapter closes by exploring the limitations of SQL for business analysis.

- **Chapter 14: Maintenance and Growth Considerations.** In this penultimate chapter, we provide recommendations for successfully deploying the DW/BI system, as well as keeping it healthy for sustained success.
- **Chapter 15: Final Thoughts.** The *Reader* concludes with final perspectives on data warehousing and business intelligence from each Kimball Group principal. The insights range from the most important hard won lessons we have learned to some glimpses of what the future of data warehousing may hold.

Navigation Aids

Given the breadth and depth of the articles in *The Kimball Group Reader*, we have very deliberately identified over two dozen articles as "Kimball Classics" because they captured a concept so effectively that we, and many others in the industry, have referred to these articles repeatedly over the past twenty years. The classic articles are designated with a special icon that looks like this:

We expect most people will read the articles in somewhat random order, rather than digesting the book from front to back. Therefore, we have put special emphasis on *The Reader's* index as we anticipate many of you will delve in by searching the index for a particular technique or modeling situation.

Terminology Notes

We are very proud that the vocabulary established by Ralph has been so durable and broadly adopted. Kimball "marker words" including dimensions, facts, slowly changing dimensions, surrogate keys, fact table grains, factless fact tables, and degenerate dimensions, have been used consistently across the industry for more than twenty years. But in spite of our best intentions, a few terms have morphed since their introduction; we have retroactively replaced the old terms with the accepted current ones.

- *Artificial keys* are now called *surrogate keys*.
- *Data mart* has been replaced with *business process dimensional model*, *business process subject area*, or just *subject area*, depending on the context.

- *Data staging* is now known as *extract, transform, and load*.
- *End user applications* have been replaced by *business intelligence applications*.
- *Helper tables* are now *bridge tables*.

Since most people won't read this book from cover to cover, we need to introduce some common abbreviations up front:

- *DW/BI* is shorthand for the end-to-end *data warehouse/business intelligence* system. This abbreviation is useful for brevity, but it also explicitly links data warehousing and business intelligence as codependent. Finally, it reflects the shift of emphasis from the data warehouse being an end in itself to business intelligence (BI) really driving everything we do. After all, the data warehouse is the platform for all forms of BI.
- Many figures in *The Reader* include the *DD, FK,* and *PK* abbreviations, which stand for *degenerate dimension, foreign key,* and *primary key*, respectively.
- *ETL* means *extract, transform, and load,* the standard paradigm for acquiring data and making it ready for exposure to BI tools.
- *ER* refers to *entity-relationship*. We frequently use ER when we discuss third normal form (3NF) or normalized data models, as opposed to dimensional data models.
- *OLAP* stands for *online analytical processing*, typically used to differentiate dimensional models captured in a multidimensional database or *cube* from dimensional models in a relational DBMS called *star schemas*. These relational star schemas are sometimes referred to as *ROLAP*.
- *SCD* is the abbreviation for *slowly changing dimension*, referring to the techniques we've established for handling dimension attribute changes.

1 The *Reader* at a Glance

Beginning in late 2007, Ralph wrote a series of articles for *DM Review* magazine (now called *Information Management*). Published over a 16-month time frame, this sequence systematically describes the Kimball approach and classic best practices in a cohesive manner. Rather than scattering these articles topically throughout the book, we opted to present the series nearly in its entirety because it provides an overview of the content that follows in subsequent chapters. You can think of Chapter 1 as *CliffsNotes* for *The Kimball Group Reader. Please note that specific date and contextual references throughout this chapter have been freshened to the perspective of 2015, as explained in the Introduction.*

The chapter begins with several articles encouraging you to practice restraint and establish appropriate boundaries with other stakeholders when embarking on a data warehouse/business intelligence (DW/BI) project. From there, the series turns its attention to bringing operational data into the data warehouse and then leveraging core dimensional modeling principles to deliver robust analytic capabilities to the business users.

In addition to the articles in this chapter, Ralph also wrote a very detailed article on data quality for *DM Review*. Due to its in-depth coverage, this article is presented in Chapter 11 with other back room extract, transform, and load (ETL) topics.

Setting Up for Success

Before diving into implementing the DW/BI system, make sure you assess the complete set of related requirements, while avoiding the risks of overpromising.

1.1 Resist the Urge to Start Coding

Ralph Kimball, DM Review, Nov 2007

The most important first step in designing a DW/BI system, paradoxically, is to stop. Step back for a week, and be absolutely sure you have a sufficiently broad perspective on all the requirements that surround your project. The DW/BI design task is a daunting intellectual challenge, and it is not easy to step far enough back from the problem to protect yourself from embarrassing or career-threatening problems discovered after the project is underway.

Before cutting any code, designing any tables, or making a major hardware or software purchase, take a week to write down thoughtful, high quality answers to the following 10 questions, each of which is a reality that will come to control your project at some point. These define the classic set of simultaneous constraints faced by every DW/BI effort.

1. **Business requirements.** Are you in touch with the key performance indicators (KPIs) your users actually need to make the decisions currently important to their enterprise? Although all 10 questions are important, understanding the business requirements is the most fundamental and far reaching. If you have a positive answer to this question, you can identify the data assets needed to support decision making, and you will be able to decide which measurement process to tackle first.

2. **Strategic data profiling.** Have you verified that your available data assets are capable of supporting the answers to question number one? The goal of strategic data profiling is to make "go/no go" decisions very early in the DW/BI project as to whether to proceed with a subject area.

3. **Tactical data profiling.** Is there a clear executive mandate to support the necessary business process re-engineering required for an effective data quality culture, perhaps even driving for Six Sigma data quality? The only real way to improve data quality is to go back to the source and figure out why better data isn't being entered. Data entry clerks are not the cause of poor data quality! Rather, the fixes require an end-to-end awareness of the need for better quality data and a commitment from the highest levels to change how business processes work.

4. **Integration.** Is there a clear executive mandate in your organization to define common descriptors and measures across all your customer-facing processes? All of the organizations within your enterprise that participate in data integration must come to agreement on key descriptors and measures. Have your executives made it clear that this must happen?

5. **Latency.** Do you have a realistic set of requirements from business users for how quickly data must be published by the data warehouse, including as-of-yesterday, many times per day, and truly instantaneous?

6. **Compliance.** Have you received clear guidance from senior management as to which data is compliance-sensitive, and where you must guarantee that you have protected the chain of custody?

7. **Security.** Do you know how you are going to protect confidential as well as proprietary data in the ETL back room, at the users' desktops, over the web, and on all permanent media?

8. **Archiving.** Do you have a realistic plan for very long term archiving of important data, and do you know what data should be archived?

9. **Supporting business users.** Have you profiled all your user communities to determine their abilities to use spreadsheets, construct database requests in ad hoc query tools, or just view

reports on their screens? Are the users expecting to attach high-end predictive analysis or data mining tools to the underlying data?

10. **IT licenses and skill sets.** Are you prepared to rely on the major technology site licenses your organization has already committed to, and do you have enough staff with advanced skills to exploit the technical choices you make? Do you know which parts of your organization expect to access big data or the Internet of Things, and do you have the skills to support these activities that often arise from outside IT?

Time spent answering these classic DW questions is enormously valuable. Every one of the answers will affect the architecture, choice of approaches, and even the feasibility of your DW/BI project. You dare not start coding before all the team members understand what these answers mean!

The big news is that business users have seized control of the DW. They may not be building the technical infrastructure, but they are quite sure that they own the data warehouse and the BI tools and those tools must meet their needs. This transfer of initiative from IT to the users has been very obvious over the past 15 years. Witness the soul-searching articles and industry speeches exhorting CIOs to show more business leadership and the high CIO turnover as reported in *CIO Magazine* (see the April 1, 2004 issue at www.cio.com).

Many of the 10 questions in this article are brought into much clearer focus by increased user ownership of the DW/BI system. Let's focus on the top five new urgent topics, in some cases coalescing our questions:

- **Business requirements.** The DW/BI system needs a permanent "KPI team" continuously in touch with business users' analytic needs and the consequent demand for new data sources to support new KPIs. Also, the system should increasingly support the full gamut of analytic applications, which include not only data delivery, but alerting the users to problems and opportunities, exploring causal factors with additional data sources, testing what-if scenarios to evaluate possible decisions, and tracking the decisions made. The DW/BI system is not just about displaying reports, but rather must be a platform for decision making in the broadest sense. The oldest label for data warehousing, *decision support*, remains surprisingly apt.
- **Strategic data profiling.** The earlier you tell the users bad news about the viability of a proposed data source, the more they will appreciate you. Develop the ability to assess a data source within a day or two. Elevate the data profiling tool to a strategic, must-have status.
- **Tactical data profiling.** The increased awareness of data quality is one of the most remarkable new DW perspectives, certainly driven by business users. But all is for naught if the business is not willing to support a quality culture and the end-to-end business process re-engineering required.
- **Integration and latency.** The user demand for the 360-degree integrated view of the business has been more like an approaching express train than a shock wave. We have been talking about it for more than a decade. But now the demands of integration, coupled with real-time access to information, have combined these two issues into a significant new architectural challenge.

■ **Compliance and security.** DW/BI folks in IT often don't have the right instincts for protecting data because the system is supposed to be about exposing data. But this new emphasis on compliance and security must be built systematically into the data flows and the BI tools across the entire DW/BI solution.

The purpose of this first article has been to expose the fundamental design issues every DW/BI design team faces and to bring to the surface the urgent new requirements. In this ongoing series of articles, I probe each of these areas in some depth, reminding us of the remarkably unchanging aspects of data warehousing, while at the same time trying to catch the winds of change.

1.2 Set Your Boundaries

Ralph Kimball, DM Review, *Dec 2007*

In article 1.1, *Resist the Urge to Start Coding,* I encouraged you to pause briefly before charging forward on your ambitious DW/BI project. You were supposed to use this pause to answer a checklist of major environmental questions regarding business requirements, quality data, and whether your organization is ready to attack the hard issues of integration, compliance, and security.

While answering the questions, I hope you talked to all your business user clients and sponsors who may have a stake or a responsibility in the DW/BI system. Before the memory of these conversations fades away, I suggest you make a thorough list of all the promises you made as you were selling the concept of the DW/BI system. It wouldn't surprise me if you said, "Yes, we will…"

■ Tie the rolling operational results to the general ledger (GL).

■ Implement effective compliance.

■ Identify and implement all the key performance indicators (KPIs) needed by marketing, sales, and finance and make them available in the executive dashboard.

■ Encourage the business community to add new cost drivers to our system requirements so that they can calculate activity-based costing and accurate profit across the enterprise. And while we are adding these cost drivers, we'll work out all the necessary allocation factors to assign these costs against various categories of revenue.

■ Identify and implement all the customer satisfaction indicators needed by marketing.

■ Seamlessly integrate all the customer-facing operational processes into a single coherent system.

■ Promise to use exclusively the front end, middleware, and back end tools provided by the enterprise resource planning (ERP) vendor whose worldwide license was just signed by our CEO.

■ Be the first showcase application for the new service-oriented architecture (SOA) initiative, and we'll implement, manage, and validate the new infrastructure.

■ Implement and manage server virtualization for the DW/BI system. And this new system will be "green."

■ Implement and manage the storage area network (SAN) for the DW/BI system.

- Implement and manage security and privacy for all data in the DW/BI system, including responsibility for the lightweight directory access protocol (LDAP) directory server and its associated authentication and authorization functions. We'll also make sure that all data accesses by the sales force on their mobile devices in the field are secure.
- Define the requirements for long term archiving and recovery of data looking forward 20 years.

Looking at this list of promises all at once, you might wonder who in their right mind would agree to them. Actually, I am much more sympathetic than it may seem. You must address these topics because they are all key facets of the DW/BI challenge. But if you gave the answers as literally stated, you have lost control of your boundaries. You have taken on far too much, you have made promises you can't deliver, and your business clients and enterprise bosses have abrogated or avoided key responsibilities that they must own. More seriously, even if you think you can deliver all these promises, you are not in a powerful enough position in your enterprise to make all these results happen.

You don't have to be a curmudgeon to be a good DW/BI system manager. This isn't about saying no to every possible responsibility. You will be doing your enterprise a favor by alerting and educating your business users and management to the appropriate boundaries of responsibilities. You can still be an enthusiastic advocate, as long as your boundaries are clear. Let's describe the key boundaries.

- **Boundaries with the business users.** Your job is to find the business users, interview them, and interpret what they tell you into specific DW/BI deliverables. You must assemble a findings document that describes the results of the interviews and how you interpreted what the business users told you. Their responsibility is to be available for the interviews and to put energy into describing how they make decisions. Later in the process, the business users have a responsibility to provide feedback on your findings. You cannot attempt to define business requirements unless the business user community is an equal partner with IT.

  Your job is not over after the first round of interviews. You must encourage ongoing business user feedback and suggestions, and also educate the business users as to the realities of system development. View this as a mutual learning process. In the latter stages of DW/BI system development, you simply cannot add new KPIs and especially new data sources to the project without slipping the delivery date. You cannot suddenly change a batch-oriented system into a real-time pipeline. Your business users must be understanding and trusting partners of the DW/BI system development, and they have to understand the costs of sudden new requirements. Bottom line—business users must become sophisticated observers of the DW/BI development process and know when it is inappropriate to change the scope by adding new KPIs, new data sources, or new real-time requirements.
- **Boundaries with finance.** Of the promises you made, several should be the responsibility of finance. You should never agree to implement cost allocations, even if the "profit system" is your main responsibility. Not only are cost allocations very complex, but the assignment of costs to various revenue-producing departments is bad news politically. In this case, finance

should work out the logical and political implications of the cost allocations, and you can quietly implement them.

You also should never agree to tie rolling operational results to the GL. In dimensional modeling parlance, you can't make this happen because the GL dimensions, such as organization and account, can't be conformed to the operational dimensions, such as customer and product. Also, special GL transactions, such as journal adjustments done at the end of the month, often cannot be put into an operational context. Again, you need to hand this issue back to finance and wait for a solution from them.

- **Boundaries across organizations.** These days it is hard to find anyone who argues against integration of all your data assets under the DW/BI umbrella. But this challenge is 70 percent political and only 30 percent technical. Your executives must establish a corporate culture that sends a very clear message to all the separate departments that they must come together to agree on common dimensional attributes, key performance metrics, and calendars. Your executives must lead the way before you can do your job.

- **Boundaries with legal.** In the early '90s, we often lamented that the data warehouse wasn't seeing widespread use. Well, now we have the opposite problem. A big piece, shall I say headache, of being taken very seriously is providing adequate security, privacy, archiving, and compliance across the DW/BI system. But you can't do anything until you understand your enterprise's policies. You must not define these policies yourself. You can lose your job and go to jail if you get these wrong. Go to your legal department with a list of areas where you need firm guidance.

- **Boundaries with IT.** Strangely, one of the most important boundaries you must maintain is with IT. You should be able to rely on other groups within IT for storage (either SAN or networked attached storage), server virtualization, LDAP server maintenance, authentication technologies, providing new infrastructure such as SOA, and support for big data infrastructure such as Hadoop.

Most of us in the DW/BI business are natural salespeople. We are evangelists for the use of our systems because we really believe they will benefit the business. But we need to be conscious of trying to please the client too much. Ultimately, the DW/BI system will be much more successful if all the other parties described in this article are equal, responsible partners.

Tackling DW/BI Design and Development

This group of articles focuses on the big issues that are part of every DW/BI system design.

1.3 Data Wrangling

Ralph Kimball, DM Review, Jan 2008

In this article, we are ready to design the first stage of the data pipeline leading from the operational sources to the final BI user interfaces. I call this stage "data wrangling" because we must lasso the data and get it under our control. Successful data wrangling includes change data capture, extraction, data staging, archiving, and the first step of data warehouse compliance. Let's examine these narrow data wrangling responsibilities.

The amount of data processed in each data extract should be kept to the bare minimum. You should strive not to download complete copies of source tables, but sometimes you must. Limiting the data extract to the bare minimum is a fascinating challenge and can be harder than it appears. The first architectural choice is whether to perform change data capture on the production source computer or after extraction to a machine owned by the data warehouse. From the data warehousing point of view, the more attractive alternative is doing change data capture at the production source. For this you need cooperation from the production source database administrators (DBAs), adequate processing resources on the production machine, and a very high quality scheme for identifying 100 percent of the changes that have occurred since the previous load.

To design the change data capture system on the production source, you need to have a very candid conversation with the production system DBAs. You need to identify every situation in which a change to source data could happen. These include normal applications posting transactions, special administrative overrides, and emergency scenarios, such as restoration of a data set.

One popular way to look for source data changes is to query a `change_date_time` field in the source table. This is a pretty strong approach if this field is populated by database triggers that are not circumvented by any process. But many production applications prohibit the use of triggers for performance reasons. Also, how does such an approach handle record deletes? If the record simply vanishes, you won't find it by querying the `change_date_time` field. But maybe you can collect the deletes in a separate feed.

Another approach is a special production system daemon that captures every input command by reading the production system transaction log or by intercepting message queue traffic. The daemon approach solves the delete problem but is still vulnerable to special administrative override commands performed manually by the DBAs. Some of you may think such overrides are crazy, but I have seen some very well-run shops resort to doing these overrides occasionally because of weird business rules that are simply too complicated to program into the normal transaction processing applications.

If you have figured out an acceptable scheme for isolating all data changes at the source, you still need to ask for one more favor, if you have any political capital left with the source system DBAs. You need to get a reason code for all changes to the major dimensional entities, such as customer or product. In dimensional modeling parlance, these reason codes will tell you whether the change to an individual dimensional attribute should be treated as a slowly changing dimension (SCD) type 1, 2, or 3. These distinctions are a big deal. The ETL pipelines required to process these three SCD choices are completely different.

If your production system presents too many objections, consider doing change data capture after extraction. Now you must download much larger data sets, perhaps complete dimensions or even complete fact tables. But you are guaranteed to find every change in the source system, as long as you keep a complete prior copy of the source system tables against which to compare.

If you download a complete source table today, you can find all the changes by performing a record-by-record and field-by-field comparison against a copy of yesterday's source table. You will indeed find every change, including the deletes. But in this case, you are probably missing reason codes for dimensional attribute changes. If so, you may need to impose unilaterally a reason code policy crafted for each attribute. In other words, if the package type of an existing product suddenly is changed, you could always assume that manufacturing is correcting a data error, and hence the change is always type 1.

If the table you are comparing is very large, the brute force approach of comparing each field can take too long. You can often improve this comparison step by a factor of 10 using a special hash code, called a *cyclic redundancy checksum (CRC)*. For a discussion of this advanced technique, see the discussion of cyclic redundancy checksums on Wikipedia.

Finally, even if you are sure you have accounted for 100 percent of the source system changes, you should periodically check the DW totals against totals computed directly on the source. This is like balancing your checkbook when you have to manually investigate a discrepancy between the two data sets.

Extraction, whether it occurs before or after change data capture, is the transfer of data from the source system into the DW/BI environment. Besides actually moving the data, you have two main responsibilities in this step. First, you need to rid yourself of all narrowly proprietary data formats during the transfer itself. Change EBCDIC character formatting to ASCII. Unravel all IBM mainframe data formats (e.g., packed decimals and OCCURS statements) into standard relational database management system table and column formats. I also suggest unraveling XML hierarchical structures at this stage, even though XML structures can now be fully supported at a semantic level by relational databases.

Your second responsibility is to direct the flow of incoming data either into simple flat files or relational tables. Both choices are equally valid. You can process flat files very efficiently with sort utilities and sequential processing commands like grep and tr. Of course, you will eventually load everything into relational tables for joining and random access operations.

I recommend immediately *staging* all data received by the DW/BI system. In other words, save the data you just received in the original target format you have chosen before you do anything else to it. I am very conservative. Staging the extracted data means keeping it forever, either offline or online. Data staging is meant to support all the types of backup.

A special form of archiving serves as an important step when you are forced to deal with compliance-sensitive data: proving that the data you received has not been tampered with. In this case, the data staging is augmented with a strong hash code that you use to show that the data has not changed. You should also write this staged data and hash code to permanent media and store this media with a bonded third party who can verify that the data was sent to them on a certain date.

Now that you have wrangled the data into your DW/BI environment, it is time to tame the beast by making the data support the business users' decision making.

1.4 Myth Busters

Ralph Kimball, DM Review, *Feb 2008*

Dimensional modeling is an old discipline, dating from the late 1960s when General Mills and Dartmouth College proposed "data cubes," and from the 1970s when ACNielsen introduced its Inf*Act syndicated data reporting service, organized around dimensions and facts. It is, therefore, surprising that some consultants and industry pundits consistently state myths and misrepresentations about dimensional modeling that have been debunked multiple times. It is time (once again) to address these myths.

Myth: A dimensional view could be missing key relationships that exist only in a true relational view.

Myth buster: This is perhaps the best place to start debunking dimensional modeling misrepresentations and myths. A dimensional model contains all the data relationships that a normalized model contains. There is no data relationship expressible in a normalized model that cannot be expressed in a dimensional model. Note that dimensional models are fully relational. Fact tables are generally in third normal form and dimension tables are generally in second normal form. The major difference between the two approaches is that the many-to-one relationships in the dimensions have been denormalized to flatten the dimensions for user understandability and query performance. But all the data relationships and data content are otherwise identical.

Myth: A very real issue with a dimensional enterprise data model (EDM) is the possibility that the model may not be extensible and easily accommodate changing business needs. Although a logical representation of the business can be achieved using dimensional structures, using these structures could have negative effects on extensibility and industry data integration.

Myth buster: This myth about extensibility is a strange one; dimensional models are significantly more robust than normalized models when data relationships change. From the beginning, we have been teaching the "graceful extensibility" of dimensional models. Five types of change have no effect on the business intelligence applications running on dimensional models:

1. Adding a new dimension to a fact table
2. Adding a new fact to a fact table
3. Adding a new dimension attribute to a dimension table
4. Altering the relationship of two dimension attributes to form a hierarchy (many-to-one relationship)
5. Increasing the granularity of a dimension

In the normalized world, such changes often involve altering the relationship between separate tables. Altering the relationship between tables exposed to the BI tools forces recoding of applications. With dimensional models, the applications keep on running without the need to recode because the dimensional schemas are inherently more robust when confronted with new content and new business rules.

Myth: A dimensional model by its definition is built to address a very specific business need. Relational modeling mimics business processes, while dimensional modeling captures how people monitor their business.

Myth buster: A dimensional model is built in response to a measurement process, never a specific business need or a desired final report for a specific department. A fact record in a dimensional model is created as a 1:1 response to a measurement event in a specific business process. Fact tables are defined by the physics of the real world. Our job as modelers is to carefully understand the grain of the physical measurement event and to faithfully attach facts and dimensions to that event that are "true to the grain." A dimensional model satisfies a business requirement only if the business happens to need the measurement events represented in the fact table. The format and content of a dimensional model has no dependence on a final report desired by the business users because it is determined only by the physics of the measurement process. A dimensional model is never crafted to meet the needs of a specific department, but rather is a single representation of a business process that looks the same to all observers.

Myth: In a dimensional model, usually only one date is associated with time. The other dates (e.g., in an order) are not captured, and, therefore, valuable data can be lost.

Myth buster: If you understand the previous myth buster, then you can appreciate that a measurement involving a line item on an order will naturally expose many dates. Each of these dates is represented by a foreign key to a copy or view of the date dimension. I first described this technique of using dimension "roles" in article 9.11, *Data Warehouse Role Models*. Role playing dimensions are an old standard dimensional modeling technique we have described hundreds of times.

Myth: Relational is preferred because an EDM should capture data at a very low granular level—preferably individual transactions.

Myth buster: From the very beginning, I have urged designers to capture measurement events in fact tables at the lowest possible (e.g., transaction) grain. In my 1996 book, *The Data Warehouse Toolkit*, I wrote, "A data warehouse almost always demands data expressed at the lowest possible grain of each dimension, not because queries want to see individual records, but because queries need to cut through the database in very precise ways." If we have consistently urged dimensional models to be built at the most expressive granular grain for the past 15 years, through 400,000 books, more than 250 articles, and 20,000 students in our classes, where do people come up with myths like this?

Stepping back from these specific myths, I urge you to think critically. When you read or hear strong statements, circle around the issues and educate yourself. Challenge the assumptions. Look for defendable positions, detailed logic, and clear thinking. I expect to be held to such high standards, and I hope you will do the same to others.

1.5 Dividing the World

Ralph Kimball, DM Review, Mar 2008

In the prior four articles in this section, I laid a solid foundation for building a data warehouse. We have done a careful job of gathering all the overlapping design constraints; we have established a good set of boundaries with all the groups we interact with; we have captured a perfect subset of changed data to feed our data extraction; and we have described common misunderstandings about dimensional models.

Our next big task is to divide the data into dimensions and facts. *Dimensions* are the basic stable entities in our environment, such as customers, products, locations, marketing promotions, and calendars. *Facts* are the numeric measurements or observations gathered by all of our transaction processing systems and other systems. Business users instinctively understand the difference between dimensions and facts. When we deliver data to the BI tools, we take great care to make dimensions and facts visible at the user interface level in order to exploit the users' understanding and familiarity with these concepts. Perhaps another way to say this is the dimensional data warehouse is the platform for BI.

Dimensions and facts drive the user interface experience in the BI tools. Dimensions are overwhelmingly the target for constraints and the source of "row headers" in the BI tool results. Facts are overwhelmingly the grist for computations. Separating the dimensions and facts structurally in the data is very helpful because it encourages consistency in application development and the BI tool user interfaces.

Dividing the world of data into dimensions and facts is a fundamental and powerful idea. Ninety-eight percent of all data items are immediately and obviously categorized as one or the other. Discrete textual data items that describe the attributes of our stable entities belong to dimensions. Repeated numeric measurements whose values are not fully predictable are facts. Thus, if we sell a red ballpoint pen for $1.79, then "red" is an attribute in the ballpoint pen row in the product dimension, and $1.79 is an observed fact.

The foundation of the data warehouse is the measurement event that produces a fact record. This is a very physical, tangible result. A fact record exists if and only if a measurement event takes place. This physical result is used by the data warehouse designer to make sure that the design sits on solid rock. When we describe the measurement in physical, real-world terms, we call this the grain of the fact table. If you are quite sure of the grain, you will have a relatively easy time designing the fact table. That is why I keep telling students to "keep to the grain."

When a measurement event creates a fact record, we scramble to attach contemporary versions of all the relevant dimensional entities to this fact record. When we sell the red ballpoint pen for $1.79, the flash bulb goes off, and from this snapshot we assemble an impressive set of dimensional entities, including customer, product, store location, employee (cashier), employee (store manager), marketing promotion, calendar, and maybe even the weather. We are careful to use up-to-date versions of the dimensions so that we are describing this sales measurement event correctly. Notice that the grain of this measurement is the cash register "beep" when the item is scanned. Later in the design process, we implement this grain with various foreign keys connecting to the dimensions, but we don't start the design process with the keys. We start with the physical event.

Once we have the grain of the fact table firmly in mind, we make sure that the only facts introduced into our fact records are defined by the scope of the measurement event. In our cash register example, the instantaneous price of the product and the number of units sold are good facts that are true to the grain. But total sales for the month or the sales on the same day last year are not true to the grain and must not be included in the physical fact record. Sometimes it is hard to resist adding facts that are not true to the grain because they provide a shortcut for a specific query, but these rogue facts always introduce complexities, asymmetries, and confusion for the application developer and the business user. Once again—keep to the grain.

Whenever possible, we strive to make facts additive. In other words, it makes sense to add the fact across records. In our retail sales example, although the price is true to the grain, it is not additive. But if we instead store the extended price (unit price multiplied by quantity sold) and the quantity sold, then both these facts are additive. We can instantaneously recover the unit price with a simple division. Forcing facts to be additive whenever possible seems like a small point, but it is one of the many ways we make our BI platform simple. Like the famous Japanese auto manufacturer example of quality, a thousand little improvements eventually become a sustainable strategic advantage. Conversely, a thousand little "gadgets" shoehorned into a database to make certain queries simpler will produce an unworkable, unmaintainable design.

In a similar vein, we resist taking normalized data models all the way into the BI environment. Normalized data models are essential for efficient transaction processing, and are helpful for storing data after the data has been cleaned. But normalized models are not understandable by business users. Before you lapse into religious wars with your colleagues, please recognize that when correctly designed, normalized models and dimensional models contain exactly the same data and reflect exactly the same business rules. Any and all data relationships can be accurately represented using either methodology. Thus, the reason for using dimensional models is that they form a proven, workable basis for BI.

Earlier in this article, I stated that 98 percent of all data items are immediately and obviously categorized as either a fact or a dimension attribute. What about the remaining 2 percent? Perhaps you have been thinking that in our retail sales example the price of the product should actually be in the product dimension, not in the fact table. In my opinion, upon a little reflection, this is an easy choice. Because the price of a product often varies over time and over location, it becomes very cumbersome to model the price as a dimension attribute. It should be a fact. But it is normal to recognize this rather late in the design process.

A more ambiguous example is the limit on coverage within an automobile insurance policy. The limit is a numerical data item, perhaps $300,000 for collision liability. The limit may not change over the life of the policy, or it changes very infrequently. Furthermore, many queries would group or constrain on this limit data item. This sounds like a slam dunk for the limit being an attribute in the coverage dimension. But the limit is a numeric observation, and it can change over time, albeit slowly. One could pose some important queries summing or averaging all the limits on many policies and coverages. This sounds like a slam dunk for the limit being a numeric fact in a fact table.

Rather than agonizing over the dimension versus fact choice, simply model it both ways! Include the limit in the coverage dimension so that it participates in the usual way as a target for constraints and the content for row headers, but also put the limit in the fact table so it can participate in the usual way within complex computations.

This example allows me to summarize this article with an important principle: Your design goal is ease of use, not methodological correctness. In the final step of building dimensional models that are intended for consumption by business users, we should be willing to stand on our heads to make our BI systems understandable and fast. That often means transferring work into the extract, transform, and load (ETL) back room and tolerating more storage overhead to simplify the final data presentation.

1.6 Essential Steps for the Integrated Enterprise Data Warehouse

Ralph Kimball, DM Review, *Apr 2008 and May 2008*

This content was originally published as two consecutive articles in the DM Review *series.*

In this article, I propose a specific architecture for building an integrated enterprise data warehouse (EDW). This architecture directly supports master data management (MDM) efforts and provides the platform for consistent business analysis across the enterprise. I describe the scope and challenges of building an integrated EDW, and provide detailed guidance for designing and administering the necessary processes that support integration. This article has been written in response to a lack of specific guidance in the industry as to what an integrated EDW actually is and what necessary design elements are needed to achieve integration.

What Does an Integrated EDW Deliver?

The mission statement for the integrated EDW is to provide the platform for business analysis to be applied consistently across the enterprise. Above all, this mission statement demands consistency across business process subject areas and their associated databases. Consistency requires:

- Detailed textual descriptions of entities such as customers, products, locations, and calendars be applied uniformly across subject areas, using standardized data values. This is a fundamental tenet of MDM.
- Aggregated groupings such as types, categories, flavors, colors, and zones defined within entities have the same interpretations across subject areas. This can be viewed as a higher level requirement on the textual descriptions.
- Constraints posed by business intelligence applications, which attempt to harvest the value of consistent text descriptions and groupings, be applied with identical application logic across subject areas. For instance, constraining on a product category should always be driven from a field named "category" found in the product dimension.
- Numeric facts be represented consistently across subject areas so that it makes sense to combine them in computations and compare them to each other, perhaps with ratios or differences. For example, if revenue is a numeric fact reported from multiple subject areas, the definitions of each of these revenue instances must be the same.
- International differences in languages, location descriptions, time zones, currencies, and business rules be resolved to allow all of the previous consistency requirements to be achieved.

- Auditing, compliance, authentication, and authorization functions be applied in the same way across subject areas.
- Coordination with industry standards be adopted for data content, data exchange, and reporting, where those standards impact the enterprise. Typical standards include ACORD (insurance), MISMO (mortgages), SWIFT and NACHA (financial services), HIPAA and HL7 (health care), RosettaNet (manufacturing), and EDI (procurement).

Ultimate Litmus Test for Integration

Even an EDW that meets all of the consistency requirements must additionally provide a mechanism for delivering integrated reports and analyses from BI tools, attached to many database instances, possibly hosted on remote, incompatible systems. This is called *drilling across* and is the essential act of the integrated EDW. When we drill across, we gather results from separate business process subject areas and then align or combine these results into a single analysis.

For example, suppose the integrated EDW spans manufacturing, distribution, and retail sales in a business that sells audio/visual systems. Assume that each of these subject areas is supported by a separate transaction processing system. A properly constructed drill-across report could look like Figure 1-1.

Product Category	Fiscal Period	Manufacturing Finished Inventory (Units)	Distribution Waiting to Return (Units)	Retail Revenue (US Dollars)
Consumer Audio	2015 FP1	14,386	283	$15,824,600
Consumer Audio	2015 FP2	17,299	177	$19,028,900
Consumer Video	2015 FP1	8,477	85	$16,106,300
Consumer Video	2015 FP2	9,011	60	$17,120,900
Pro Audio	2015 FP1	2,643	18	$14,536,500
Pro Audio	2015 FP2	2,884	24	$15,862,000
Pro Video	2015 FP1	873	13	$7,158,600
Pro Video	2015 FP2	905	11	$7,421,000
Storage Media	2015 FP1	35,386	258	$1,380,054
Storage Media	2015 FP2	44,207	89	$1,724,073

Figure 1-1: Drill-across report combining data from three subject area fact tables.

The first two columns are row headers from the product and calendar conformed dimensions, respectively. The remaining three columns each come from separate business process fact tables, namely manufacturing inventory, distribution, and retail sales. This deceptively simple report can only be produced in a properly integrated EDW. In particular, the product and calendar dimensions must be available in all three separate databases, and the category and period attributes within those dimensions must have identical contents and interpretations. Although the metrics in the three fact columns are different, the meaning of the metrics must be consistent across product categories and times.

You must understand and appreciate the tight constraints on the integrated EDW environment demanded by the preceding report. If you don't, you won't understand this article, and you won't have the patience to study the detailed steps described next. Or to put the design challenge in other terms, if you eventually build a successful integrated EDW, you will have visited every issue that follows. With those warnings, read on.

Organizational Challenges

The integrated EDW deliverables I've described are a daunting list indeed. But for these deliverables to even be possible, the enterprise must make a profound commitment, starting from the executive suite. The separate divisions of the enterprise must have a shared vision of the value of data integration, and they must anticipate the steps of compromise and decision making that will be required. This vision can only come from the senior executives of the enterprise, who must speak very clearly on the value of data integration.

Existing MDM projects provide an enormous boost for the integrated EDW, because presumably the executive team already understands and approves the commitment to building and maintaining master data. A good MDM resource greatly simplifies, but does not eliminate, the need for the EDW team to build the structures necessary for data warehouse integration.

In many organizations, a chicken-and-egg dilemma exists as to whether MDM is required before an integrated EDW is possible or whether the EDW team creates the MDM resources. Often, a low profile EDW effort to build conformed dimensions solely for data warehouse purposes morphs into a full-fledged MDM effort that is on the critical path to supporting mainline operational systems. In my classes since 1993, I have shown a backward pointing arrow leading from cleansed data warehouse data to operational systems. In the early days, we sighed wistfully and wished that the source systems cared about clean, consistent data. Now, more than 20 years later, we seem to be getting our wish!

Conformed Dimensions and Facts

Since the earliest days of data warehousing, conformed dimensions have been used to consistently label and constrain separate data sources. The idea behind conformed dimensions is very simple: Two dimensions are conformed if they contain one or more common fields whose contents are drawn from the same domains. The result is that constraints and labels have the same content and meaning when applied against separate data sources.

Conformed facts are simply numeric measures that have the same business and mathematical interpretations so that they may be compared and computed against each other consistently.

Using the Bus Matrix to Communicate with Executives

When you combine the list of EDW subject areas with the notion of conformed dimensions, a powerful diagram emerges, which we call the enterprise data warehouse bus matrix. A typical bus matrix is shown in Figure 1-2.

The business process subject areas are shown along the left side of the matrix and the dimensions are shown across the top. An X marks where a subject area uses the dimension. Note that "subject area" in our vocabulary corresponds to a business process, typically revolving around a transactional data source. Thus, "customer" is not a subject area.

	Date	Raw Material	Supplier	Plant	Product	Shipper	Warehouse	Customer	Sales Rep	Promotion Deal
Raw Material Purchasing		X	X	X		X				
Raw Material Delivery	X	X	X	X		X				
Raw Material Inventory	X	X	X	X						
Bill of Materials	X	X		X	X					
Manufacturing	X	X	X	X	X					
Shipping to Warehouse	X			X	X	X	X			
Finished Goods Inventory	X				X		X			
Customer Orders	X				X	X		X	X	X
Shipping to Customer	X				X	X	X	X	X	X
Invoicing	X				X		X	X	X	X
Payments	X				X		X	X	X	X
Returns	X				X	X		X	X	X

Figure 1-2: Bus matrix for a manufacturer's EDW.

At the beginning of an EDW implementation, this bus matrix is very useful as a guide, both to prioritize the development of separate subject areas and to identify the potential scope of the conformed dimensions. The columns of the bus matrix are the invitation list to the conformed dimension design meeting.

Before the conformed dimension design meeting occurs, this bus matrix should be presented to senior management, perhaps in exactly the form of Figure 1-2. Senior management must be able to visualize why these dimensions (master entities) attach to the various business process subject areas, and they must appreciate the organizational challenges of assembling the diverse interest groups together to agree on the conformed dimension content. If senior management is not interested in what the bus matrix implies, then to make a long story short, you have no hope of building an integrated EDW.

It is worth repeating the definition of a conformed dimension at this point to take some of the pressure off of the conforming challenge. Two instances of a dimension are conformed if they contain one or more common fields whose contents are drawn from the same domains. This means that the individual subject area proponents do not have to give up their cherished private descriptive attributes. It merely means that a set of master, universally agreed upon attributes must be established. These master attributes then become the contents of the conformed dimension and become the basis for drilling across.

Managing the Integrated EDW Backbone

The backbone of the integrated EDW is the set of conformed dimensions and conformed facts. Even if the enterprise executives support the integration initiative and the conformed dimension design meetings go well, there is a lot to the operational management of this backbone. This management can be visualized most clearly by describing two personality archetypes: the dimension manager and the fact provider. Briefly, the dimension manager is a centralized authority who builds and distributes a conformed dimension to the rest of the enterprise, and the fact provider is the client who receives and utilizes the conformed dimension, almost always while managing one or more fact tables within a subject area.

At this point, I must make three fundamental architectural claims to prevent false arguments from arising:

1. The need for dimension managers and fact providers arises solely from the natural reuse of dimensions across multiple fact tables or online analytical processing (OLAP) cubes. Once the EDW community has committed to supporting cross-process analysis, there is no way to avoid all the steps described in this article.
2. Although I describe the handoff from the dimension manager to the fact provider as if it were occurring in a distributed environment where they are remote from each other, their respective roles and responsibilities are the same whether the EDW is fully centralized on a single machine or profoundly distributed across many separate machines in different locations.
3. The roles of dimension manager and fact provider, although obviously couched in dimension modeling terms, do not arise from a particular modeling persuasion. All of the steps described in this article would be needed in a fully normalized environment.

We are now ready to roll up our sleeves and describe exactly what the dimension manager and fact provider do.

The Dimension Manager

The dimension manager defines the content and structure of a conformed dimension and delivers that conformed dimension to downstream clients known as fact providers. This role can definitely exist within a master data management (MDM) framework, but the role is much more focused than just being the keeper of the single truth about an entity. The dimension manager has a list of deliverables and responsibilities, all oriented around creating and distributing physical versions of the dimension tables that represent the major entities of the enterprise. In many enterprises, key conformed dimensions include customer, product, service, location, employee, promotion, vendor, and calendar. As I describe the dimension manager's tasks, I will use customer as the example to keep the discussion from being too abstract. The tasks of the customer dimension manager include:

- **Defining the content of the customer dimension.** The dimension manager chairs the design meeting for the conformed customer dimension. At that meeting, all the stakeholders from the customer-facing transaction systems come to agreement on a set of dimensional attributes that everyone will use when drilling across separate subject areas. Remember that these attributes are used as the basis for constraining and grouping customers. Typical conformed customer attributes include type, category, location (multiple fields implementing an address), primary contact (name, title, address), first contact date, credit worthiness, demographic category, and others. Every customer of the enterprise appears in the conformed customer dimension.

- **Receiving notification of new customers.** The dimension manager is the keeper of the master list of dimension members, in this case, customers. The dimension manager must be notified whenever a new customer is registered.

- **Deduplicating the customer dimension.** The dimension manager must deduplicate the master list of customers. But realistically, customer lists in the real world are nearly impossible to deduplicate completely. Even when customers are registered through a central MDM process, it is often possible to create duplicates, either for individual customers or business entities.

- **Assigning a unique durable key to each customer.** The dimension manager must identify and keep track of a unique durable key for each customer. Many DBAs automatically assume that this is the "natural key," but quickly choosing the natural key may be the wrong choice. A natural key may not be durable! Using the customer example, if there is any conceivable business rule that could change the natural key over time, then it is not durable. Also, in the absence of a formal MDM process, natural keys can arise from more than one customer-facing process. In this case, different customers could have natural keys of very different formats. Finally, a source system's natural key may be a complex, multifield data structure. For all these reasons, the dimension manager needs to step back from literal natural keys and assign a unique durable key that is completely under the control of the dimension manager. I recommend that this unique, durable key be a simple sequentially assigned integer, with no structure or semantics embedded in the key value.

- **Tracking time variance of customers with type 1, 2, and 3 slowly changing dimensions (SCDs).** The dimension manager must respond to changes in the conformed attributes describing a customer. Much has been written about tracking the time variance of dimension members using SCDs. A type 1 change overwrites the changed attribute and therefore destroys history. A type 2 change creates a new dimension record for that customer, properly time stamped as of the effective moment of the change. A type 3 change creates a new field in the customer dimension that allows an "alternate reality" to be tracked. The dimension manager updates the customer dimension in response to change notifications received from various sources. More advanced SCD variations are described by Margy in article 9.25, *Slowly Changing Dimension Types 0, 4, 5, 6 and 7*.

- **Assigning surrogate keys for the customer dimension.** Type 2 is the most common and powerful of the SCD techniques because it provides precise synchronization of a customer description with that customer's transaction history. Because type 2 creates a new record for the same customer, the dimension manager is forced to generalize the customer dimension primary key beyond the unique, durable key. The primary key should be a simple surrogate key, sequentially assigned as needed, with no structure or semantics in the key value. This primary key is separate from the unique durable key, which simply appears in the dimension as a normal field. The unique, durable key is the glue that binds the separate SCD type 2 records for a single customer together.

- **Handling late-arriving dimension data.** When the dimension manager receives late notification of a type 2 change affecting a customer, special processing is needed. A new dimension record must be created and the effective dates of the change adjusted. The changed attribute must be propagated forward in time through existing dimension records.

- **Providing version numbers for the dimension.** Before releasing a changed dimension to the downstream fact providers, the dimension manager must update the dimension version number if type 1 or type 3 changes have occurred or if late arriving type 2 changes have occurred. The dimension version number does not change if only contemporary type 2 changes have been made since the previous release of the dimension.

- **Adding private attributes to dimensions.** The dimension manager must incorporate private departmental attributes in the release of the dimensions to the fact providers. These attributes are of interest to only a part of the EDW community, perhaps a single department.

- **Building shrunken dimensions as needed.** The dimension manager is responsible for building shrunken dimensions that are needed by fact tables at higher levels of granularity. For example, a customer dimension might be rolled up to the demographic category to support a fact table that reports sales at this level. The dimension manager is responsible for creating this shrunken dimension and assigning its keys.

- **Replicating dimensions to fact providers.** The dimension manager periodically replicates the dimension and its shrunken versions to all the downstream fact providers. All the fact providers should attach the new dimensions to their fact tables at the same time, especially if the version number has changed.

- **Documenting and communicating changes.** The dimension manager maintains metadata and documentation describing all the changes made to the dimension with each release.

- **Coordinating with other dimension managers.** Although each conformed dimension can be administered separately, it makes sense for the dimension managers to coordinate their releases to lessen the impact on the fact providers.

The Fact Provider

The fact provider sits downstream from the dimension manager and responds to each release of each dimension that is attached to a fact table under the provider's control. Tasks include:

- **Avoiding changes to conformed attributes.** The fact provider must not alter the values of any conformed dimension attributes, or the whole logic of drilling across diverse business process subject areas will be corrupted.

- **Responding to late-arriving dimension updates.** When the fact provider receives late-arriving updates to a dimension, the primary keys of the newly created dimension records must be inserted into all fact tables using that dimension whose time spans overlap the date of the change. If these newly created keys are not inserted into the affected fact tables, the new dimension record will not tie to the transactional history. The new dimension key must overwrite existing dimension keys in the affected fact tables from the time of the dimension change up to the next dimension change that was already correctly administered.

- **Tying the conformed dimension release to the local dimension.** The dimension manager must deliver to the fact provider a mapping that ties the fact provider's local natural key to the primary surrogate key assigned by the dimension manager. In the surrogate key pipeline (next task), the fact provider replaces the local natural keys in the relevant fact tables with the conformed dimension primary surrogate keys using this mapping.

- **Processing dimensions through the surrogate key pipeline.** The fact provider converts the natural keys attached to contemporary transaction records into the correct primary surrogate keys and loads the fact records into the final tables with these surrogate keys.

- **Handling late arriving facts.** The surrogate key pipeline mentioned in the previous paragraph can be implemented in two different ways. Traditionally, the fact provider maintains a current key lookup table for each dimension that ties the natural keys to the contemporary surrogate keys. This works for the most current fact table data where you can be sure that the contemporary surrogate key is the one to use. But the lookup tables cannot be used for late-arriving fact data because it is possible that one or more old surrogate keys must be used. In this traditional approach, the fact provider must revert to a less efficient dimension table lookup to figure out which old surrogate key applies.

    A more modern approach to the surrogate key pipeline implements a dynamic cache of records looked up in the dimension table rather than a separately maintained lookup table. This cache handles contemporary fact records as well as late-arriving fact records with a single mechanism.

- **Synchronizing dimension releases with other fact providers.** It is critically important for all the fact providers to respond to dimension releases at the same time. Otherwise a client application attempting to drill across subject areas will encounter dimensions with different version numbers. See the description of using dimension version numbers in the next section.

Configuring Business Intelligence (BI) Tools

There is no point in going to all the trouble of setting up dimension managers, fact providers, and conformed dimensions if you aren't going to perform drill-across queries. In other words, you need to "sort merge" separate answer sets on the row headers defined by the values from the conformed dimension attributes. There are many ways to do this in standard BI tools and straight SQL. See articles 13.21, *Simple Drill-Across in SQL*, and 13.22, *An Excel Macro for Drilling Across*.

You should use dimension version numbers when performing drill-across queries. If the requesting application does not include the version number in the select list, erroneous results are possible because dimension attributes may not be consistent across subject areas. If the requesting application does include the version number in the select list, then at least the results from the fact table queries will end up on separate rows of the answer set, properly labeled by the dimension version. This isn't much consolation to the user, but at least the problem is diagnosed in an obvious way.

Figure 1-3 shows a report drilling across the same three databases as in Figure 1-1, but where a dimension version mismatch occurs. Perhaps the definition of certain product categories has been adjusted between product dimension version 7 and version 8. In this case, the retail sales fact table is using version 8, whereas the other two fact tables are still using version 7. By including the product dimension version attribute in the SQL select list, we automatically avoid merging potentially incompatible data. Such an error would be particularly insidious because without the rows being separated, the result would look perfectly reasonable but could be disastrously misleading.

Product Category	Product Dimension Version	Manufacturing Finished Inventory (Units)	Distribution Waiting to Return (Units)	Retail Revenue (US Dollars)
Consumer Audio	7	14,386	283	
Consumer Audio	8			$15,824,600
Consumer Video	7	8,477	85	
Consumer Video	8			$17,120,900

Figure 1-3: Drill-across report with a dimension version mismatch.

Joint Responsibilities

Dimension managers and fact providers must ensure that auditing, compliance, authentication, authorization, and usage tracking functions are applied uniformly for all BI clients. This set of responsibilities is especially challenging because it is outside the scope of the steps described in this article. Even when modern role-enabled authentication and authorization safeguards are in place when using the EDW, subtle differences in the definition of roles may give rise to inconsistency. For example, a role named "senior analyst" may have different interpretations at different entry points to the EDW. The best that can be said for this difficult design challenge is that personnel responsible for defining the LDAP-enabled roles should be invited to the original dimension conforming meetings so that they become aware of the scope of EDW integration.

The integrated EDW promises a rational, consistent view of enterprise data. This promise has been repeated endlessly in the trade literature. But until now, there has been no specific design for actually implementing the integrated EDW. Although this implementation of the integrated EDW must seem daunting, I believe that the steps and responsibilities I have described are basic and unavoidable, no matter how your data warehouse environment is organized. Finally, this architecture represents a distillation of more than 25 years' experience in building data warehouses based on conformed dimensions and facts. If you carefully consider the detailed recommendations in these articles, you should avoid reinventing the wheel when you are building your integrated EDW.

1.7 Drill Down to Ask Why

Ralph Kimball, DM Review, Jul 2008 and Aug 2008

This content was originally published as two separate articles in the series.

Boiled down to its essence, the real purpose of a data warehouse is to be the perfect platform for decision making. Most DW and BI architects accept this view, but how many stop and think carefully about what is decision making, exactly? Every DW/BI architect can describe his or her technical architecture, but how many can describe the architecture of decision making? If there even is an architecture of decision making, how does the DW/BI system interact with its components, and what specific demands does decision making place on the DW/BI system?

In 2002, Bill Schmarzo, a former member of the Kimball Group, proposed a very useful architecture for decision making, which he called the *analytic application process*. According to Bill, an analytic application consists of five stages:

1. **Publish reports.** Provide standard operational and managerial "report cards" on the current state of a business.
2. **Identify exceptions.** Reveal the exceptional performance situations to focus attention.
3. **Determine causal factors.** Seek to understand the "why" or root causes behind the identified exceptions.
4. **Model alternatives.** Provide a backdrop to evaluate different decision alternatives.
5. **Track actions.** Evaluate the effectiveness of the recommended actions and feed the decisions back to both the operational systems and DW, against which published reporting will occur, thereby closing the loop.

I have found these analytic application stages to be very useful when I think about the architecture of a DW/BI system. Publishing reports (stage one) is the traditional legacy view of the data warehouse. We pump out reports and we stack them on the business users' desks. There isn't a lot of interactive BI in stage one! We also have been identifying exceptions (stage two) with thresholds, alerts, and red/green blinking graphics for many years. At least in stage two, the choice of which alerts and thresholds we want on our desktops implies some judgment and involvement by the user.

But it is in stage three, where we determine the causal factors behind the exceptions that life really gets interesting. A good DW/BI system should let the decision maker bring his or her full intellectual capital to bear on understanding what the system is bringing to our attention. This stage can be summarized by one all-important word: *why*.

Suppose that you work for an airline as a fare planner. In this role, a critical key performance indicator (KPI) is the yield, which according to Wikipedia is "the revenue or profits from a fixed, perishable resource such as airline seats or hotel room reservations. The challenge is to sell the right resources to the right customer at the right time for the right price."

This morning, in your job as a fare planner, the DW/BI system produces a yield report (stage one) and highlights a number of airline routes for which the yield has dropped significantly (stage two). So, how does the DW/BI system support the all-important stage three? How does the DW/BI system support the fare planner when you ask, "Why are my yields down?"

Imagine five ways in which the fare planner might ask why. I'll arrange these in order of increasing breadth and complexity:

1. **Give me more detail.** Run the same yield report, but break down the problematic routes by dates, time of day, aircraft type, fare class, and other attributes of the original yield calculation.

   In a dimensional data warehouse environment where all business process subject areas are built as fact tables and dimension tables on the lowest level atomic data, drilling down is easily accomplished by adding a row header (grouping column) to the report query from any of the attached dimensions. In your yield report, if you assume the report is calculated from a database of individual boarding passes, then drilling down by date, time of day, aircraft type, or fare class is simply a user interface gesture that drags the new grouping attribute from the relevant dimension into the query. Note that this general form of drilling down does not require a predetermined or predeclared hierarchy. As I have been pointing out for 20 years, drilling down has nothing to do with hierarchies!

2. **Give me a comparison.** Run the same yield report, but this time compare to a previous time period or to competitive yield data if it is available.

   In the example, if the route is the row header of the yield report, a common comparison mode would be to add one or more numeric columns to the report, each perhaps with a different date. Thus, the yields at different dates could be compared. This can be accomplished in several different ways by your BI tool, but as the comparisons become more complex, a drill-across approach to sort merging separate queries is the most practical and scalable. See article 1.6 *Essential Steps for the Integrated Enterprise Data Warehouse*, for more information on drill-across techniques. Keep in mind that graphical comparisons may be more effective than straight text reports, especially for time series data.

3. **Let me search for other factors.** Jump to non-yield databases, such as a weather database, holiday/special events database, marketing promotions database, or competitive pricing database to see if any of these exogenous factors could have played a role.

   To jump to a separate database, the context of the current report query must be captured and used as input to the new database. When the user selects a specific row or cell in the original report, that detailed context should be used. For instance, if the June 2015 yield on the San Jose to Chicago route is selected by the user, then June 2015, San Jose, and Chicago should be carried as constraints on the next query. Perhaps the next query focuses on weather. This scenario presents some challenges to the DW/BI designer. The user can't jump to another database if it isn't there. Thus, the designer needs to anticipate and provide possible targets for this kind of jump. Also, the BI tool should support the context capture steps described in this section so that the process of jumping to a new database is as effortless as possible. We describe this capability in article 1.11, *Exploit Your Fact Tables*.

4. **Tell me what explains the variance.** Perform a data mining analysis, perhaps using decision trees, examining hundreds of marketplace conditions to see which of these conditions correlates most strongly with the drop in yield ("explaining the variance" in data mining terminology).

   To feed data mining, the DW/BI designer must again anticipate the database resources that will be needed when these kinds of analyses are performed. Practical information about how to build these kinds of data mining interfaces, including decision trees, is available in Michael Berry and Gordon Linoff's *Data Mining Techniques for Marketing, Sales and Customer Relationship Management, 3rd edition,* (Wiley, 2011).

5. **Search the web for information about the problem.** Google or Yahoo! the web for "airline yield 2015 versus 2014."

   Finally, if you have successfully searched for other factors (number three), you need to be able to transfer the context of the exception you have identified into a Google or Yahoo! query. If you are dubious that this would be of much value, search for "airline yield 2015 versus 2014." This can be a paradigm shift kind of experience. What we need is a one-button jump from a report cell to a browser.

Thirty years ago, when we drilled down in a data warehouse to ask why, we rarely provided more than the first capability. I like to think of the longer list of all five capabilities as 2015's definition of drilling down to ask why.

In this article, we have reminded ourselves of the true goal of the data warehouse/business intelligence system: assisting the business user in making decisions. The key capability is providing the most flexible and comprehensive ways to drill down and ask why.

1.8 Slowly Changing Dimensions

Ralph Kimball, DM Review, *Sep 1, 2008 and Oct 1, 2008*

This content was originally published as two separate articles in the series.

The notion of time pervades every corner of the data warehouse. Most of the fundamental measurements we store in our fact tables are time series, which we carefully annotate with time stamps and foreign keys connecting to calendar date dimensions. But the effects of time are not isolated just to these activity-based time stamps. All of the other dimensions that connect to fact tables, including fundamental entities such as customer, product, service, terms, facility, and employee, are also affected by the passage of time. As data warehouse managers, we are routinely confronted with revised descriptions of these entities. Sometimes the revised description merely corrects an error in the data. But many times the revised description represents a true change at a point in time of the description of a particular dimension member, such as customer or product. Because these changes arrive unexpectedly, sporadically, and far less frequently than fact table measurements, we call this topic *slowly changing dimensions* (SCDs).

The Original Three Types of Slowly Changing Dimensions

In more than 30 years of studying the time variance of dimensions, amazingly I have found that the data warehouse only needs three basic responses when confronted with a revised or updated description of a dimension member. I call these, appropriately, types 1, 2, and 3. I'll start with type 1, using the employee dimension to keep the discussion from being too abstract.

Type 1: Overwrite   Suppose we are notified that the home city attribute for Ralph Kimball in the employee dimension has changed from Santa Cruz to Boulder Creek as of today. Furthermore, we are advised that this is an error correction, not an actual change of location. In this case, we may decide to overwrite the home city field in the employee dimension with the new value. This is a classic type 1 change. Type 1 changes are appropriate for correcting errors and for situations where a conscious choice is made not to track history. And of course, most data warehouses start out with type 1 as the default.

Although the type 1 SCD is the simplest and seemingly cleanest change, there are a number of fine points to think about:

1. Type 1 destroys the history of a particular field. In our example, reports that constrain or group on the home city field will change. Business users will need to be aware that this can happen. The data warehouse needs an explicit, visible policy for type 1 fields that says, "We will correct errors" and/or "We do not maintain history on this field even if it changes."

2. Precomputed aggregates (including materialized views and automatic summary tables) that depend on the home city field must be taken offline at the moment of the overwrite and be

recomputed before being brought back online. Aggregates that do not depend on the home city field are unaffected.

3. In financial reporting environments with month-end close processes and in any environment subject to regulatory or legal compliance, type 1 changes may be outlawed. In these cases, the type 2 technique must be used.

4. Overwriting a single dimension field in a relational environment has a pretty small impact but can be disastrous in an OLAP environment if the overwrite causes the cube to be rebuilt. Carefully study your OLAP system reference manual to see how to avoid unexpected cube rebuilds.

5. All distributed copies of the employee dimension in our example, as well as aggregates, must be updated simultaneously across the enterprise when type 1 changes occur, or else the logic of drilling across will be corrupted. In a distributed environment, type 1 (and type 3) changes should force the dimension version number to be updated, and all drill-across applications must include the dimension version number in their queries. This process was described in detail in article 1.6, *Essential Steps for the Integrated Enterprise Data Warehouse*.

6. In a pure type 1 dimension where all fields in the dimension are subject to overwriting, a type 1 change like the home city change for Ralph Kimball will typically affect only one record (the record for Ralph Kimball). But in a more typical complex environment, where some fields are type 1 and other fields are type 2, the act of overwriting the home city field must overwrite all the records for Ralph Kimball. In other words, type 1 affects all history, not just the current perspective.

Type 2: Add a New Dimension Record   Let's alter the previous scenario where I overwrote the home city field in Ralph Kimball's employee record to assume that Ralph Kimball actually moved from Santa Cruz to Boulder Creek on July 18, 2015. Assume our policy is to accurately track the employee home addresses in the data warehouse. This is a classic type 2 change.

The type 2 SCD requires that we issue a new employee record for Ralph Kimball effective July 18, 2015. This has many interesting side effects:

1. Type 2 requires that we generalize the primary key of the employee dimension. If Ralph Kimball's employee natural key is G446, then that natural key will be the "glue" that holds Ralph Kimball's multiple records together. I do not recommend creating a smart primary key for type 2 SCDs that contains the literal natural key. The problems with smart keys become especially obvious if you are integrating several incompatible HR systems with differently formatted natural keys. Rather, you should create completely artificial primary keys that are simply sequentially assigned integers. We call these keys *surrogate keys*. You must make a new surrogate primary key whenever you process a type 2 change in a dimension.

2. In addition to the primary surrogate key, I recommend adding five additional fields to a dimension that is undergoing type 2 processing. These fields are shown in Figure 1-4. The date/times are full time stamps that represent the span of time between when the change became effective and when the next change becomes effective. The end effective date/time stamp of a type 2 dimension record must be exactly equal to the begin effective date/time stamp of the

next change for that dimension member. The most current dimension record must have an end effective date/time stamp equal to a fictitious date/time far in the future. The effective date key links to a standard calendar date dimension table to view dimension changes filtered on attributes such as fiscal period. The change reason text attribute should be drawn from a preplanned list of reasons for a change, in our example, to the employee attributes (such as employee moved, employee left company, etc.). Finally, the current flag provides a rapid way to isolate exactly the set of dimension members that is in effect at the moment of the query. These five administrative fields allow users and applications to perform many powerful queries.

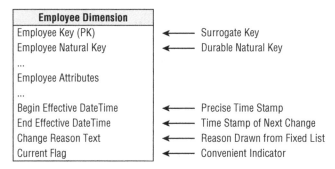

Figure 1-4: Employee dimension designed for type 2 SCD.

3. With a dimension undergoing type 2 processing, great care must be taken to use the correct contemporary surrogate keys from this dimension in every affected fact table. This assures that the correct dimension profiles are associated with fact table activity. The extract, transform, and load (ETL) process for aligning the dimension tables with fact tables at load time is called the *surrogate key pipeline* and is covered extensively in articles 11.27, *Pipelining Your Surrogates*, and 11.28, *Unclogging the Fact Table Surrogate Key Pipeline*.

Type 3: Add a New Field Although the type 1 and 2 SCDs are the primary workhorse techniques for responding to changes in a dimension, we need a third technique for handling alternate realities. Unlike physical attributes that can have only one value at a given point in time, some user-assigned attributes can legitimately have more than one assigned value depending on the observer's point of view. For example, a product category can have more than one interpretation. In a stationery store, a marking pen could be assigned to the household goods category or the art supplies category. Users and BI applications need to be able to choose at query time which of these alternate realities applies.

The requirement for an alternate reality view of a dimension attribute usually is accompanied by a subtle requirement that separate versions of reality be available at all times in the past and in the future, even though the request to make these realities visible arrived at the data warehouse today.

In the simplest variation, there is only one alternate reality. In this case, for the product category example, we add a new field in the dimension, perhaps called Alternate Category. If the primary category of our marking pen used to be household goods and now should be art supplies, then in a type 3 treatment, we push the household goods label into the alternate category field and we update the regular category field with art supplies by overwriting. The overwriting step is similar to a type 1 SCD and provokes all the same earlier caveats.

With type 3 machinery in place, users and BI applications can switch seamlessly between these alternate realities. If the environment requires more than one alternate reality, this approach can be generalized by adding more alternate fields, although obviously this approach does not scale gracefully beyond a few choices.

The three SCD approaches to handling time variance in dimensions have enormous applicability in the real-world situations encountered by the data warehouse. Type 2, in particular, allows us to make good on the data warehouse pledge to preserve history faithfully.

Advanced Slowly Changing Dimensions

In article 9.25, *Slowly Changing Dimension Types 0, 4, 5, 6 and 7*, Margy describes a number of advanced SCD techniques that can be thought of as extensions of types 1, 2, and 3.

1.9 Judge Your BI Tool through Your Dimensions

Ralph Kimball, DM Review, *Nov 1, 2008*

Dimensions implement the user interface (UI) in a BI tool. In a dimensional DW/BI system, the textual descriptors of all the data warehouse entities like customer, product, location, and time reside in dimension tables. My previous articles carefully described three major types of dimensions according to how the DW/BI system responds to their slowly changing characteristics. Why all this fuss about dimensions? They are the smallest tables in the data warehouse, and the real "meat" is actually the set of numeric measurements in the fact tables. But that argument misses the point that the DW/BI system is always accessed through the dimensions. The dimensions are the gatekeepers, the entry points, the labels, the groupings, the drill-down paths and, ultimately, the texture of the DW/BI system. The actual content of the dimensions determines what is shown on the screen of a BI tool and what UI gestures are possible. That is why we say that the dimensions implement the UI.

This article points out what a good BI tool must be able to do with the dimensions in order to implement an expressive, easy-to-use DW/BI system. I invite you to compare this list against your own BI tools. Almost all of the functions described should be accomplished with single UI gestures, such as dragging an item from a list and dropping it onto a target.

- **Assemble a BI query or report request by first selecting dimension attributes and then selecting facts to be summarized.** This requirement is so basic that it is easy to overlook. One has to be able to see the dimensions and the facts in order to use them. Look for a clean, linear list of all the attributes in your dimensions. Do not accept a normalized snowflaked portrayal, which may appeal to data modelers but is notoriously intimidating to business users. The dimension attributes and the numeric facts should be added to a query or report request with simple UI gestures, as suggested by Figure 1-5.

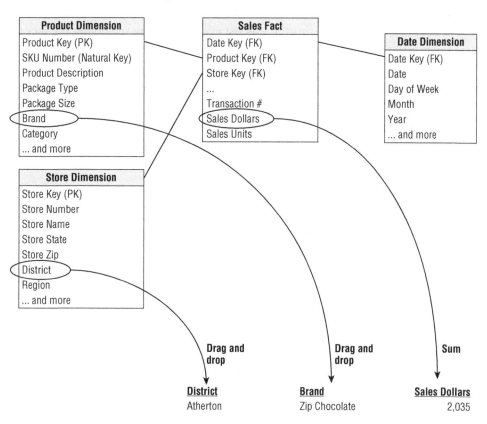

Figure 1-5: Adding dimension attributes and numeric facts through simple user interface gestures.

- **Drill down by adding a row header.** The most fundamental maneuver in a BI tool is drilling down to a more detailed perspective. In almost all cases, drilling down has nothing to do with declared hierarchies. For instance, in Figure 1-5, you can drill down by dragging the promotion type attribute into the results set from the promotion dimension. This would let you see how the individual brands did under different types of promotions. This is drilling down in its most effective form.
- **Browse a dimension to preview permissible values and set constraints.** In Figure 1-5, you should be able to see a list of all the product categories by double-clicking the category attribute in the product dimension. This list should serve both as a preview of what the row labels will be when you use the attribute as a row header, and as a place to set constraints, such as category = "Candy". Make sure you can set multiple picks if you want a short list of simultaneous constraints.

■ **Restrict the results of a dimension browse with other constraints in effect.** Sometimes, the list of dimension attribute values is too long to be useful. Make sure that the list can be shortened by applying the constraints you have already set on other attributes in that dimension. An advanced feature would let you shorten this list even further by traversing the fact table and applying constraints that have been set on other dimensions. For instance, maybe you want a list of product categories that were sold in a particular store in January.

■ **Drill across by "accreting" measures under labels defined by conformed dimension attributes.** In article 1.6, *Essential Steps for the Integrated Enterprise Data Warehouse*, I described the architecture of drill-across reports that delivered integrated results from multiple separate fact tables. Such a report is shown in Figure 1-6, where we are drilling across three separate fact tables: shipments, inventory, and sales.

Product Name	Manufacturing Shipments	Warehouse Inventory	Retail Sales
Frame	2,940	1,887	$761
Toggle	13,338	9,376	$2,448
Widget	7,566	5,748	$2,559

Figure 1-6: Sample drill-across report.

The first column in Figure 1-6 is the product name, which comes from a product dimension that must be attached to each fact table separately. The product name is a conformed attribute because it has the same column name and content in all three product dimensions, which could well be located on physically separate machines. The challenge for a BI tool is to allow the user or report designer to "pin" the product name as a row header and then systematically visit various possible fact tables, dragging separate fact columns into the report.

Stepping back from these BI tool requirements, we can judge the maturity and experience of the BI tool by first asking whether these maneuvers are even possible, and then asking how easy they are to use. I think it is amazing that some BI tools still don't "get it"; I have talked about these capabilities for 30 years, and we had most of these functions in the Metaphor tool suite starting in 1984.

Judge the ease of use with a simple test—count the clicks. A double-click or click-and-drag counts as a single click. To my way of thinking, one click counts as outstanding, two clicks is pretty good, three clicks is marginal, and more than three clicks is unacceptable.

Modern BI tools have lots more features than those I have described in this article, but what good are advanced features if the BI tool can't support the basic maneuvers? Put your tool to the test.

1.10 Fact Tables

Ralph Kimball, DM Review, *Dec 1, 2008*

Fact tables are the foundation of the data warehouse. They contain the fundamental measurements of the enterprise, and they are the ultimate target of most data warehouse queries. Perhaps you are wondering why it took me so long to get to fact tables in this series of articles. Well, there is no point in hoisting fact tables up the flagpole unless they have been chosen to reflect urgent business priorities, have been carefully quality assured, and are surrounded by dimensions that provide a wealth of entry points for constraining and grouping. Now that we have paved the way for fact tables, let's see how to build them and use them.

Stay True to the Grain

The first and most important design step is declaring the fact table grain. The grain is the business definition of what a single fact table record represents. The grain declaration is not a list of dimensional foreign keys that implement a primary key for the fact table. Rather the grain is the description of the measurement event in the physical world that gives rise to a measurement. When the grocery store scanner measures the quantity and the charged price of a product being purchased, the grain is literally the beep of the scanner. That is a great grain definition!

Immediately after declaring the grain, it is possible to list the dimensional foreign keys that exist at that grain. By declaring the grain first, the discussion of foreign keys remains grounded and precise.

The real purpose of the fact table is to be the repository of the numeric facts that are observed during the measurement event. It is critically important for these facts to be true to the grain. The grocery store "beep" measures the quantity and extended price of the product being scanned. We never include other numeric measurements that violate the grain, such as the overall category sales or the sales of this product last month. Even though these other measurements might be narrowly helpful for selected calculations, they cannot be combined across fact records and they introduce weird asymmetries in the design of applications. We let our BI tools compute these off-topic values at query time rather than hard coding them into our fact tables.

We always strive to make the facts additive across the dimensions and exactly consistent with the grain. Notice that we don't store the price of the product being scanned because the price is nonadditive. Rather, we store the extended price (unit price multiplied by quantity sold), which can be added freely across products, stores, times, and all the other dimensions.

Build Up from the Lowest Possible Grain

The data warehouse should always be built on fact tables expressed at the lowest possible grain. In the example, the beep of the grocery store cash register is the lowest possible grain because it cannot be divided any further. Fact tables at the lowest grain are the most expressive because they have the most complete set of possible dimensions for that business process. The beep grain fact table could have date, store, product, cashier, manager, customer, promotion, competition, basket, and even weather if all these data sources can be marshaled when the fact records are created. Higher grain aggregated tables such as category sales by district cannot support all these dimensions and therefore are much less expressive. It is a fundamental mistake to publish only aggregated tables to the business users without making the lowest grain fact tables smoothly accessible by drilling down. Most of the false notions that dimensional tables presuppose the business question come from making this fundamental mistake.

Three Kinds of Fact Tables

If you stay true to the grain, all of your fact tables can be grouped into just three types: transaction grain, periodic snapshot grain, and accumulating snapshot grain, as shown in Figure 1-7. In Figure 1-7, the dimensions are designated by foreign keys (FK) and the numeric facts are italicized.

Transaction Grain	Periodic Snapshot Grain	Accumulating Snapshot Grain
Date Key (FK)	Month Key (FK)	Order Date Key (FK)
Product Key (FK)	Account Key (FK)	Ship Date Key (FK)
Store Key (FK)	Branch Key (FK)	Delivery Date Key (FK)
Customer Key (FK)	Household Key (FK)	Payment Date Key (FK)
Cashier Key (FK)	*Balance*	Return Date Key (FK)
Manager Key (FK)	*Fees Paid*	Warehouse Key (FK)
Promotion Key (FK)	*Interest Earned*	Customer Key (FK)
Weather Key (FK)	*Transaction Count*	Promotion Key (FK)
Transaction # (DD)		Order Status Key (FK)
Quantity		*Quantity*
Extended Price		*Extended List Price*
		Discount
		Extended Net Price

Figure 1-7: The three different types of fact tables.

The transaction grain corresponds to a measurement taken at a single instant. The grocery store beep is a transaction grain. The measured facts are valid only for that instant and event. The next measurement event could happen one millisecond later or next month or never. Thus, transaction grain fact tables are unpredictably sparse or dense. We have no guarantee that all the possible foreign keys will be represented. Transaction grain fact tables can be enormous, with the largest containing many billions of records.

The periodic snapshot grain corresponds to a predefined span of time, often a financial reporting period. Figure 1-7 illustrates a monthly account periodic snapshot. The measured facts summarize activity during or at the end of the time span. The periodic snapshot grain carries a powerful guarantee that all of the reporting entities will appear in each snapshot, even if there is no activity. The periodic snapshot is predictably dense, and applications can rely on combinations of keys always being present. Periodic snapshot fact tables can also get large. A bank with 20 million accounts and a 10-year history would have 2.4 billion records in the monthly account periodic snapshot!

The accumulating snapshot grain fact table corresponds to a predictable process that has a well-defined beginning and end. Order processing, claims processing, service call resolution, and college admissions are typical candidates. The grain of an accumulating snapshot for order processing, for example, is usually the line item on the order. Notice in Figure 1-7 that there are multiple dates representing the standard scenario that an order undergoes. Accumulating snapshot records are revisited and overwritten as the process progresses through its steps from beginning to end. Accumulating snapshot fact tables generally are much smaller than the other two types because of this overwriting strategy.

1.11 Exploit Your Fact Tables

Ralph Kimball, DM Review, *Jan/Feb 2009*

Article 1.10, *Fact Tables*, described the three types of fact tables that are all you will ever need in your data warehouse. The secret to this simple observation is adhering fanatically to the grain. A fact table records measurement events, and as long as we only record one kind of measurement event in a given fact table, we only need the three basic types: transaction grain, periodic snapshot grain, and accumulating snapshot grain. In this article, I describe basic ways to exploit these clean fact table designs in the front room and in the back room.

Front Room: Aggregate Navigation

I've previously described that the most atomic grain of a measurement process is the most expressive. More dimensions can be attached to the atomic grain than can be attached to higher aggregated levels. The DW/BI team should expose the atomic grain of a business process to the business users and application designers, allowing the data warehouse to choose aggregated levels of the data at run time, not design time. Thus, in our grocery store "beep" grain example, if the user's query asks for a category total, the database chooses a category level aggregated fact table silently and behind the scenes at run time. In this way, aggregate tables are like indexes that don't rise to the level of user consciousness. Reports and queries should be designed without specific reference to the aggregate tables. If the user asks for a category total of specific products packaged in glass containers, the database cannot use the simple category aggregate table and must gracefully assemble the answer from the atomic fact table.

Front Room: Drilling across Different Grains

If you are good at visualizing dimensional schemas, you will understand that you can drill across multiple fact tables at different grains as long as you choose conformed dimension attributes for the answer set row headers that exist for all the fact tables in your integrated query. For example, if you have a sales fact table in the grocery store whose grain is every individual transaction, and you also have a monthly brand forecast table whose grain is product brand by month, you can perform a drill-across query on these two tables as long as all the dimensional references in the SELECT list and in the query constraints refer only to brands and months.

Front Room: Exporting Constraints to Different Business Processes

If you have a sophisticated data warehouse, you may be able to support the capabilities in the previous two sections. But there's one absolute bedrock of decision support I bet you can't do. Suppose you have drilled down in the grocery store database and found a product brand that seems to be selling poorly in certain regions. Your instinct is aroused, and you ask, "What were the merchandising deals we did with that manufacturer in those regions and in the time period I am concerned with?" In most data warehouses, you would have to scribble down the brand, region, and time period information on a piece of paper, close the current application, open another user interface, and reenter this information. But why can't you simply select one or more offending rows in the first application and copy/paste them with a single user interface gesture into the second application? The context of the selection would apply the appropriate constraints directly. I know this is possible because I have built query tools that do this.

Back Room: Fact Table Surrogate Keys

Surrogate keys are a staple of dimension table design, but surprisingly, there are times when we want a surrogate key in a fact table. Remember that a surrogate key is just a simple integer key, assigned in sequence as records are created. Although fact table surrogate keys (FSKs) have no business meaning in the front room, they have a number of uses in the back room:

- FSKs uniquely and immediately identify single fact records.
- Because FSKs are assigned sequentially, a load job inserting new records will have FSKs in a contiguous range.
- An FSK allows updates to be replaced by insert-deletes.
- Finally, an FSK can become a foreign key in a fact table at a lower grain.

2

Before You Dive In

Ralph wrote his first article on data warehousing for *DBMS* magazine in September 1995. At the time, he (and many of us who eventually formed the Kimball Group) had already focused on delivering information and analytic capabilities to support business decision making for nearly a decade; however, Ralph's first foray into publishing set the stage for the more than 150 articles that followed. It also helped Ralph catch the attention of Wiley Publishing—subsequently resulting in the sale of more than 400,000 *Toolkit* books. It all began with one article.

The articles selected for this chapter were chosen largely because of their historical significance. Even though many were written in the 1990s, the content is still amazingly relevant.

We kick off the chapter with an overview of Ralph's career prior to data warehousing, followed by his initial submission to *DBMS* magazine (which was subsequently renamed to *Intelligent Enterprise*); the other articles provide additional historical perspective, including Ralph's first description of the data warehouse bus architecture. The chapter continues with one of our favorite analogies about the uncanny parallels between managing a data warehouse/business intelligence (DW/BI) system and running a commercial restaurant. We'll refer back to this analogy elsewhere in the *Reader*. We then talk about how to approach some of data warehousing's most challenging problems in easy, incremental steps, and we finish with some hints about the expanding and non-traditional boundaries of the data warehouse.

NOTE   As we note in the Introduction, we've systematically replaced most references to the term *data mart* in our writings with *business process subject area*. However, they've been retained in this chapter given its role as a history lesson. Ralph originally presented the term to the marketplace in these articles, so it felt appropriate to retain it here.

Before Data Warehousing

This first article chronicles Ralph's career and some of the early developments in the computer world before data warehousing.

2.1 History Lesson on Ralph Kimball and Xerox PARC

Margy Ross, Design Tip #144, *Apr 3, 2012*

If you subscribe to our *Design Tips,* you're likely already well aware of Ralph Kimball's contributions to the field of data warehousing and business intelligence. However, many of you may not know about Ralph's contributions and accomplishments prior to turning his attention to our industry. I recently shared this historical perspective with a client who insisted it be disseminated more broadly.

Ralph's official title is Dr. Kimball. He received his PhD in electrical engineering from Stanford University in 1973 after building a computer-assisted tutor that taught calculus concepts to students, but at the same time learned superior problem-solving techniques from the students themselves. Shortly after earning his doctorate, Ralph went to work at the Xerox Palo Alto Research Center (PARC). PARC was a research think tank that attracted the best and the brightest engineers and computer scientists in the early 1970s. While PARC was never a household word, its pioneering innovations still impact us daily—client-server computing, the Ethernet, laser printing, bitmapped graphical user interfaces (GUIs) including windows and icons, the mouse, object-oriented programming, and the list goes on. The PARC alumni roster reads like a veritable who's who of early Silicon Valley leaders.

While at PARC, Ralph spent four years doing research on user interface design, and then joined a group dedicated to building products based on the research prototypes demonstrated at PARC. Contrary to most product development practices at the time, a guiding principle for Ralph and his colleagues was to focus first on the user experience, then back into the design of the underlying hardware and software. They tried to follow the advice of their PARC colleague, Alan Kay: "The simple things should be simple; complex things should be possible."

With the early adoption of some PARC innovations in Xerox's experimental Alto workstation, Ralph was a principal architect of the Star workstation, the first commercial product that incorporated a bitmapped display for a graphical user interface including icons and windows, Ethernet networking, file and printer servers, and a mouse. The user interface mimicked the office paradigm with a desktop and icons depicting documents, folders, and email so it was intuitive to users. Xerox introduced the Star workstation in 1981, the same year that IBM introduced PC-DOS. Here's a link to a snippet from an early Xerox promotional video for the Star workstation: `http://www.youtube.com/watch?v=zVw86emu-K0`. Ralph was the product manager of the Star workstation; he made his acting debut about 7 minutes from the start of the video.

Steve Jobs and several other Apple engineers saw a demonstration of Xerox's Alto computer in late 1979, and Ralpave Steve Jobs a demo of the Star workstation during its launch announcement in 1981. Needless to say, Steve grasped the commercial potential of PARC's mouse-driven GUI; the concepts were subsequently incorporated in the Apple Lisa, which was released in 1983, followed by the Macintosh in 1984.

In 1982, Ralph and several other Xerox colleagues envisioned leveraging the Star workstation beyond its traditional document creation market to tackle the world of decision support. But Xerox senior management decided not to pursue that opportunity. So in the fall of 1982, Ralph and several research colleagues and business leaders left Xerox to launch a company called Metaphor Computer

Systems to focus on the data access and analysis needs of business professionals. During the product research phase, Ralph conducted interviews with Fortune 500 analysts to better understand their requirements. When speaking with folks in the consumer package goods industry, Ralph was introduced to the syndicated data from A. C. Nielsen, IRI, and SAMI that was used for competitive analysis.

Ralph spent time with the experts at A. C. Nielsen who described their data in terms of dimensions and "fact tables" containing metrics. While Ralph didn't invent dimensional modeling, he was quick to envision the broader applicability of the concepts for decision support across a variety of industries and functional application areas.

Metaphor released an integrated hardware and software product in 1984 with file servers, database servers, and workstations (including unattached keyboards and mice), linked together by the Ethernet. The workstations delivered a graphical user interface with query, spreadsheet, and plotting tools, along with a Capsule tool that Ralph invented. The Capsule, originally called "graphical pipes," was a programming tool that connected the separate icons on the desktop with arrows that directed the flow of data from icon to icon. The Capsule could export the results of a query into a spreadsheet, then into a graph, and finally to an email outbox or a printer. We take these capabilities for granted today, but it was rocket science nearly 30 years ago. The icon flow diagrams, pioneered in the Metaphor workstation as the Capsule, are the default user interfaces of all commercial ETL tools today.

True confessions … I saw a Metaphor demonstration in 1984 just prior to the product's release and was so blown away that I immediately joined Metaphor's initial class of field consultants. Ralph taught star schema design to my fellow new hires and me. The mantra from his formative years at PARC continued to resonate: Focus on the business users' experience by making the data model as understandable as possible, then work backward through the design and development. Fortunately, old habits sometimes die hard.

Historical Perspective

For all that's changed in our industry over the past 20 years, the core concepts and drivers are still remarkably valid. The next article is Ralph's first article published in *DBMS* magazine and its successors.

2.2 The Database Market Splits

Ralph Kimball, DBMS, Sep 1995

In the past year or two, a growing split has occurred in the database market. Similar to a giant iceberg, this split is about to carve off a huge new piece that will have its own identity and direction. We call this new half of the database market *data warehousing*. We call the old half *online transaction processing* (OLTP).

Data warehousing is that part of relational technology that deals with getting the data out. Data warehousing is a direct descendant of what led the industry to relational technology in the first place. Back in the early 1980s, we didn't decide to turn all of our IT shops upside down just because we were in love with transaction processing. We wanted better information. Those of you who still own Chris Date's original book explaining relational databases, *An Introduction to Database Systems* (Addison Wesley, 1977), ought to go back and look at it again. The entire book is about queries and getting the data out! Transaction processing, entity-relationship (ER) diagrams, CASE tools, and all of the other OLTP apparatus came much later.

Once we got hooked on relational databases, most of us realized that we had some serious work to do to make these databases production-ready. So for the past dozen years we have had to put off getting the data out in order to concentrate on getting the data in. We needed systems that could absorb at least 1,000 transactions per second to enable us to store our basic enterprise data. Grafting transaction processing onto relational databases nearly put the lights out. We became fixated on the new mechanisms we created, such as entity-relationship diagrams and distributed database technology, and we came perilously close to forgetting why we bought relational databases in the first place.

Fortunately, the chief executives in most companies have long memories. They remembered the promise that we would be able to "slice and dice" all of our data. These executives have noticed that we have almost succeeded in storing all the corporate data in relational databases. They also haven't forgotten that they have spent several billion dollars. From their point of view, it is now time to get all that data out.

Almost every IT shop experiences significant pressure to make the corporate data accessible. Two or three years ago, we saw a brief flurry of marketing material from relational database management system (RDBMS) vendors trying to reduce this pressure by promoting the use of OLTP systems for querying. This approach didn't work. Anyone who tried to use a major corporate database for both OLTP and querying soon realized some basic truths about systems for getting the data in versus systems for getting the data out.

OLTP systems and data warehouse systems have different end users, managers, administrators, communications interfaces, backup strategies, data structures, processing needs, and access rhythms. Fortunately, DBMS and hardware vendors have stopped talking about one system that does it all. They now understand the profound difference between OLTP systems and data warehouse systems. Well, maybe they understand, and maybe they don't. But they have certainly figured out that if they keep quiet, they will sell two DBMS licenses and two hardware systems.

The little crack in the database market iceberg is widening very rapidly. A large channel of blue water is now visible between OLTP systems and data warehouse systems. Both IT shops and vendors realize that you can benefit from having two systems that are specialized for each task. An OLTP system must specialize in managing rapidly changing data and keeping it safe. OLTP systems must track millions of separate transactions per day and encourage a usage style that peppers the database with tiny atomic processing requests that are all very similar. An OLTP transaction rarely uses a join.

Conversely, a data warehouse system must specialize in managing huge static sets of data copied from production OLTP systems. The average data warehouse query ranges dynamically over wide extremes of processing, and assembles hundreds, thousands, or even millions of separate data elements into small answer sets to be delivered to users. A data warehouse query is very join-intensive. Also, the data warehouse performs only one transaction per day when it loads millions of records from the production system. (We are not outlawing a light sprinkle of transactions restricted to forecasting and planing tables within the data warehouse.)

We don't need systems that are only pretty good at transaction processing and pretty good at querying. To be blunt, today's systems are very good at transaction processing and pretty horrible at querying. A lot of shops are still using 30-year-old B-tree technology to index their databases because B-tree indexes are a compromise between querying and updating. However, we don't need to compromise when we decide to break our database world into two pieces. By specializing in getting the data out, the data warehouse half of the iceberg will yield a 100-fold improvement in query performance over the next few years. (Remember that you read this bold prediction in *DBMS* magazine.)

Some of our cherished notions, such as cost-based optimization, may mean that an optimizer is necessary when our data schemas are too complex—and no one can figure them out. The data warehouse marketplace seems to be adopting very simple data schemas. These schemas—called *dimensional schemas*—have large central "fact" tables surrounded by a single layer of much smaller dimension tables, as illustrated in Figure 2-1. One of the great charms of the dimensional schema is that you can use fixed, deterministic evaluation strategies. You don't need a cost-based optimizer. Horrors!

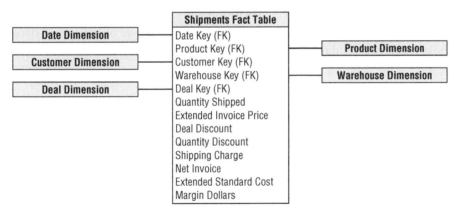

Figure 2-1: Dimensional schema example.

Over the next few years, we'll witness a development in data warehouse-oriented query systems. The wonderful vocabulary for OLTP developed by the hardware and software vendors who are members of the Transaction Processing Performance Council will be mirrored by a new vocabulary specific to data warehousing. Terms like "two-phase commit" and "row-level locking" will have data warehouse counterparts such as "factless fact tables" and "slowly changing dimensions." Hardware and software developers have just begun to turn their attention to data warehousing. Thus, the two icebergs will continue to drift further apart.

2.3 Bringing Up Supermarts

Ralph Kimball, DBMS, Jan 1998

In this article, the term supermart *refers to dimensional data marts built on an architecture of conformed dimensions. While the reference to supermarts was preserved in the article's title, we have updated it within the article to reduce reader distraction.*

One of the most widely debated issues in data warehousing is how to go about planning the warehouse construction. Do we build the whole data warehouse all at once from a central, planned perspective (the monolithic approach) or do we opportunistically build separate subject areas whenever we feel like it (the stovepipe approach)? In this article I set out to demolish two powerful myths. The first myth is that a data warehouse must be built either all at once as a single piece, or as a series of solo, unconnected data marts. Today, nobody believes in a totally monolithic approach, and yet nobody defends a totally stovepipe approach either; most leading data warehouse practitioners use some kind of architectural step-by-step approach to build an enterprise data warehouse. This article describes a specific variation of that step-by-step approach where dimensional business process data marts are carefully built with a disciplined architectural framework.

The second myth I want to demolish is that we have passed out of the phase in data warehouse development where a data mart must be restricted to a highly aggregated subset of a nonqueryable data warehouse; this view of data marts is the source of many problems and misunderstandings. You will see that an architected dimensional data mart is naturally a complete subset of the overall data warehouse and must expose the most granular (atomic) data that can possibly be collected and stored.

The Planning Crisis

The task of planning an enterprise data warehouse is daunting. The newly appointed manager of the data warehousing effort in a large enterprise is faced with two huge and seemingly unrelated challenges. On the one hand, the manager is supposed to understand the content and location of the most complicated asset owned by the enterprise: the legacy data. Somehow (usually overnight) the new data warehouse manager is supposed to become an authority on exactly what is contained in all those VSAM, ISAM, IMS, DB2, and Oracle tables. Every field in every table must be understood. The data warehouse manager must be able to retrieve any such element of data and, if necessary, clean it up and correct it. If all this weren't enough, the data warehouse manager is also supposed to understand exactly what keeps management awake at night. The data warehouse is expected to contain the exact data needed to answer everyone's burning questions. Of course, the data warehouse manager is "free" to drop in on senior management at any time to discuss current corporate priorities. Just make sure you get this data warehouse done pretty soon.

The pressure of this daunting task has built up to the point where it has a name: data mart. Regardless of specific definitions, the phrase "data mart" means avoiding the impossibility of tackling the enterprise data warehouse planning job all at once. Data warehouse planners take refuge in carving off a little piece of the whole data warehouse, bringing it to completion, and calling it a data mart.

Unfortunately, in many cases building separate data marts rather than a single data warehouse has become an excuse for ignoring any kind of design framework that might tie the data marts together. Vendors' marketing claims for a "data mart in a box" and a "15-minute data mart" are pandering to the market's need for a simple solution, but these claims are a real disservice to the data warehousing manager who must make these data marts fit together into a coherent whole.

Isolated stovepipe data marts that cannot be tied together usefully are the bane of the data warehouse movement. They are much worse than a simple lost opportunity for analysis. Stovepipe data marts perpetuate incompatible views of the enterprise. Stovepipe data marts enshrine the reports that cannot be compared with each other. And stovepipe data marts become legacy implementations in their own right, where, by their very existence, they block the development of an integrated enterprise data warehouse. So if building the data warehouse all at once is too daunting, and building it as isolated pieces defeats the overall goal, what is to be done?

Data Marts with an Architecture

The answer to this dilemma is to start the data warehouse planning process with a short overall architecture phase that has finite and specific goals. Next, follow this architecture phase with a step-by-step implementation of separate data marts where each implementation step closely adheres to the architecture. In this way the data warehouse manager gets the best of both worlds. The architecture phase produces specific guidelines that the separate data mart development teams can follow, and the data mart development teams can work fairly independently and asynchronously. As the separate data marts come online, they will fit together like the pieces of a puzzle. At some point, enough architected data marts exist to make good on the promise of an integrated enterprise data warehouse.

To succeed in building an enterprise data warehouse you must inevitably perform the following two steps: First, create a surrounding architecture that defines the scope and implementation of the complete data warehouse, and second, oversee the construction of each piece of the complete data warehouse. Now stop and consider the second step. The biggest task in constructing a data warehouse is designing the extract system. This is the mechanism that gets the data from a specific legacy system and moves it into the data staging area, where it can be transformed into the various load record images needed by the final database that presents the data for querying. Since the implementation of the extract logic is largely specific to each original data source, it really doesn't matter whether you think of the task as a whole or break it into pieces. Either way, you have to put your pants on one leg at a time. You will in effect be implementing your data marts one at a time no matter how you plan your project.

Importance of Conformed Dimensions

In the architecture phase that precedes the implementation of any data mart, the goals are to produce a master suite of conformed dimensions and standardize the definitions of facts. I am assuming you have a proper dimensional design for all the data marts. Any given data mart is assumed to consist of a set of fact tables, each with a multipart key made up of dimension key components (foreign keys joining to the dimension tables). The fact tables all contain zero or more facts that represent measurements taken at each combination of the dimension key components. Every fact table is surrounded by a "halo" of dimension tables, where the dimension keys are primary keys in each respective dimension table. If you are not familiar with dimensional modeling, see article 5.2, *A Dimensional Modeling Manifesto.*

A conformed dimension is a dimension that means the same thing with every possible fact table to which it can be joined. Generally this means that a conformed dimension is identical in each data mart. Examples of obvious conformed dimensions include customer, product, location, deal (promotion), and date, as shown in Figure 2-2. A major responsibility of the central data warehouse design team is to establish, publish, maintain, and enforce the conformed dimensions.

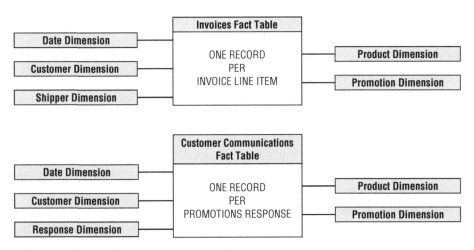

Figure 2-2: Conformed dimensions used by multiple fact tables.

Establishing a conformed dimension is a very significant step. A conformed customer dimension is a master table of customers with a clean customer key and many well-maintained attributes describing each customer. It is likely that the conformed customer dimension is an amalgamation and distillation of data from several legacy systems and possibly outside sources. The address fields in the customer dimension, for instance, should constitute the best mailable address that is known for each customer anywhere within the enterprise. It is often the responsibility of the central data warehouse team to create the conformed customer dimension and provide it as a resource to the rest of the enterprise, both for legacy and data warehouse use. I described this special role for the central data warehouse team in more detail in article 3.4, *What Does the Central Team Do?*

The conformed product dimension is the enterprise's agreed-upon master list of products, including all product attributes and all product rollups such as category and department. A good product dimension, like a good customer dimension, should have at least 50 separate textual attributes.

Ideally, the conformed location dimension should be based on specific points on the map, like specific street addresses or even precise latitudes and longitudes. Specific points in space roll up to every conceivable geographic hierarchy, including city-county-state-country, as well as ZIP codes and idiosyncratic sales territories and sales regions.

The conformed date dimension will almost always be a table of individual days, spanning a decade or more. Each day will have many useful attributes drawn from the legal calendars of the various states and countries the enterprise deals with, as well as special fiscal calendar periods and marketing seasons relevant only to internal managers.

Conformed dimensions are enormously important to the data warehouse. Without a strict adherence to conformed dimensions, the data warehouse cannot function as an integrated whole. If a dimension like customer or product is used in a nonconformed way, then either the separate data marts cannot be used together or, worse yet, attempts to use them together will produce incorrect results. To state this more positively, conformed dimensions make possible a single dimension table to be used against multiple fact tables in the same database space, consistent user interfaces and data content whenever the dimension is used, and a consistent interpretation of attributes and, therefore, rollups across data marts.

Designing Conformed Dimensions

The task of identifying and designing the conformed dimensions should take a few weeks. Most conformed dimensions will naturally be defined at the most granular level possible. The grain of the customer dimension will be the individual customer. The grain of the product dimension will be the lowest level at which products are tracked in the source systems. The grain of the date dimension will usually be the individual day.

Conformed dimensions should almost always have an anonymous (surrogate) data warehouse key that is not a production system key from one of the legacy systems. There are many reasons for the data warehouse keys to be independent from production. The administrative goals of the production systems are not the same as those of the data warehouse. Sooner or later, the production system will step on the data warehouse, either by reusing the same key or by changing the administrative assumptions in some way. Also, the data warehouse has to produce generalized keys for various situations, including the problem of slowly changing dimensions, as discussed in Chapters 1 and 9.

Taking the Pledge

If the central data warehouse team succeeds in defining and providing a set of master conformed dimensions for the enterprise, it is extremely important for the separate project teams actually to use these dimensions. The commitment to use the conformed dimensions is much more than a technical decision. It is a business policy decision that is key to making the enterprise data warehouse function. The use of the conformed dimensions should be supported at the highest executive levels. This issue should be a sound bite for the enterprise CIO.

Using data effectively in a large enterprise is intimately connected to how the enterprise is organized and how it communicates internally. The data warehouse is the vehicle for delivering the data to all the affected parties. Changing the way an enterprise is organized, how it communicates, and how it uses its data assets is mainline business reengineering. The CIO should make all the separate teams "take the pledge" always to use the conformed dimensions.

Permissible Variations of Conformed Dimensions

It is possible to create a subset of a conformed dimension table for certain data marts if you know that the domain of the associated fact table only contains that subset. For example, the master product table can be restricted to just those products manufactured at a particular location if the data mart in question pertains only to that location. We could call this a *simple data subset*, because the reduced dimension table preserves all the attributes of the original dimension and exists at the original granularity.

A *rollup data subset* systematically removes both rows and columns from the original dimension table. For example, it is common to restrict the date table from days down to months. In this case we may only keep the record describing the first or last day of each month, but we must also remove all those attributes like day-of-week and holiday flag that only make sense at a daily grain.

Perhaps you are wondering how to create queries in an environment where the conformed dimensions can be subsetted. Which dimension table should be used where? Actually, it is much simpler than it sounds. Each dimension table is paired with its companion fact table in a particular data mart. Any application that drills across data marts must inevitably use multipass SQL to query each mart separately and in sequence. It is usually the case that a separate SQL query is generated for each column in a drill across report. The beauty of using conformed dimensions is that the report will run to completion if and only if the dimension attributes used in the report are found in each dimension table. Since the dimensions are conformed, the business answers are guaranteed to be consistent. The numbers will also be comparable if we have established standard fact definitions.

Establishing Standard Fact Definitions

I have talked thus far about the central task of setting up conformed dimensions to tie marts together. This is 80 percent of the upfront architectural effort. The remaining 20 percent is establishing standard, conformed fact definitions.

Fortunately, the task of identifying the standard fact definitions is done at the same time as the identification of the conformed dimensions. You need standard fact definitions when you use the same terminology across data marts and when you build single reports that drill across the data marts as described in the previous section.

Examples of facts that must be standardized include revenue, profit, standard price, and standard costs. The underlying equations that derive these measures must be the same if they are to be called the same thing. These standard fact definitions need to be defined in the same dimensional context and with the same units of measurement from data mart to data mart.

Sometimes a fact has a natural unit of measurement in one fact table and another natural unit of measurement in another fact table. For example, the flow of a product down a typical manufacturing value chain may best be measured in shipping cases at the manufacturer but should be measured in scanned units at the retailer. Even if all the dimensional considerations have been correctly taken into account, it would be difficult to use these two incompatible units of measurement in one drill across report. The usual solution to this is to refer the user to a conversion factor buried in the product dimension table and hope the user can find the conversion factor and use it correctly. This is unacceptable overhead in my opinion. The correct solution is to carry the fact in both shipping cases and scanned units in the manufacturer's table or in a view of the manufacturer's table. That way a report can easily glide down the value chain, picking off comparable facts.

If it is difficult or impossible to standardize a fact exactly, then care must be taken to give the different interpretations different names. We must distinguish month end revenue from billing cycle revenue. The most serious mistake is to call both of these facts revenue.

Importance of Granularity

The conformed dimensions will usually be granular (atomic) because each record in these tables most naturally corresponds to a single description of a customer, a product, a promotion, or a day. This makes it quite easy to bring in the associated fact tables at the intersection of all these granular dimensions. In other words, the base level fact tables in each data mart should be at the natural lowest levels of all the constituent dimensions.

There is tremendous power and resiliency in granular, atomic fact table data. By expressing the bedrock data of the data mart at the lowest grain, the data mart becomes almost impervious to surprises or changes. Such a granular fact table can be gracefully extended by adding newly sourced facts, newly sourced dimension attributes, and whole dimensions. When I say "gracefully extended," I mean specifically that all old queries and applications continue to run after a graceful change has been made; no fact tables have to be dropped and reloaded, and no keys have to be changed. This notion of graceful extension is one of the strong characteristics of the dimensional modeling approach.

When the fact tables are granular, they serve as the natural destination for current operational data that may be extracted frequently from the operational systems. The current rolling snapshot of an operational system finds a happy home in the granular fact table defined at the account by transaction level. Two companion tables, transaction and snapshot fact tables, form the bedrock foundation of many data marts.

A new and growing justification for extremely granular data is the desire to do data mining and understand customer behavior. Data mining is generally much less effective on aggregated data. Well, suppose we agree with all this but we don't have enough room on our data mart server to store the big granular fact tables. Does this invalidate the whole approach of this article?

No! This dilemma is simply a matter of terminology. Let us broaden the definition of data mart to include all the fact tables and dimension tables associated with a business process, regardless of where they are physically stored. We are moving so rapidly into a network-oriented view of our data warehouses that tying the definition of a data mart to a specific hardware box is unnecessarily restricting. The queries against our data marts are increasingly being handled by a navigator layer that sorts out the physical location of the data based on the details of the user's request. If the user calls for relatively aggregated data, perhaps that data is on a local server. But if the user calls for more detailed data, we switch to a larger centralized machine at another location. There are many reasons for encouraging this kind of indirection at the physical storage level, because it gives the back room DBAs much more flexibility to mix and match hardware without worrying about tweaking the user's applications.

Higher Level Data Marts

This article has mostly focused on first-level data marts that are recognizable images of legacy applications. In other words, if we have an orders system, then we have an orders data mart. If we have a payments and collections system, then we have a payments and collections data mart.

I recommend starting with these kinds of first-level data marts because I believe this minimizes the risk of signing up to an implementation that is too ambitious. Most of the risk comes from biting off too big an extract programming job. Also, in many cases an efficiently implemented first-level data mart will provide users with enough interesting data to keep them happy and quiet while the data mart teams keep working on harder issues.

After several first-level data marts have been implemented, it is reasonable to combine these data marts into a second-level data mart. The classic example of a second-level data mart is the profitability data mart, where separate components of revenue and cost are combined to allow a complete view of profitability. Profitability data marts at a granular level are tremendously exciting because they can be rolled up through the customer dimension to generate customer profitability. They can be rolled up through the product dimension to generate product profitability. And they can be rolled up through the promotion dimension to generate promotion profitability. The lesson here is to be disciplined and not try to bring up a complete profitability data mart on the first try. Otherwise you will drown in extract programming as you struggle to source all the separate components of revenue and cost. If you are absolutely forced to bring up profitability in your first data mart, then you may need to assign costs with simple rule-of-thumb allocations rather than by doing the complete job of sourcing all the underlying cost detail. Later, when you have time to source the cost detail correctly, you can bring up an activity-based profitability second-level data mart to complement your first-level data mart.

Rescuing Stovepipes

Can you rescue your stovepipes and convert them into architected dimensional data marts? You can do this only if the dimensions used in the stovepipes can be mapped one-to-one or one-to-many with the proper conformed dimensions. If so, then the stovepipe dimension can be replaced with the conformed dimension. In some cases the conformed dimension can gracefully inherit some of the special attributes of the stovepipe dimension. But usually a stovepipe data mart has one or more dimensions that cannot easily be mapped into the conformed dimensions. The stovepipe sales geographies may be incompatible with the conformed sales geographies. Be careful about assuming that you can reengineer simple stovepipe dimensions back into conformed dimensions. As difficult as it is to admit, most of the time the stovepipe data marts must be shut down and rebuilt in the proper conformed dimensional framework.

When You Don't Need Conformed Dimensions

If your customers and products are disjointed and you don't manage your separate business lines together, then there is little point in building a data warehouse that tightly integrates these businesses. For example, if you are a conglomerate business whose subsidiaries span food businesses, hardware businesses, and services, it probably doesn't make sense to think of your customers as leveraging your brand name from product to product or service to service. Even if you tried to build a set of conformed product and customer dimensions in a single data warehouse spanning all the lines of business, most of the reports would end up weirdly "diagonalized" with the data from each business line in rows and columns not shared by the other lines. In this case your data warehouse should mimic your management structure, and you should build separate and self-contained data warehouses for each subsidiary.

Clear Vision

In this article, I have described a rational approach to planning an enterprise data warehouse. We have achieved the best of two worlds. We have created an architectural framework with marts that guides the overall design, but we have divided the problem into bite-sized chunks that can be implemented by real human beings. Along the way, we have adjusted the conventional definitions of the data mart. We see now that an architected data mart is a complete subset of the overall data warehouse, perhaps physically distributed across multiple hardware and software platforms, and always based on the most granular data possible we can extract from our legacy systems. Every architected mart is a family of similar tables sharing conformed dimensions. These conformed dimensions have a uniform interpretation across the enterprise. Finally, we see the overall data warehouse for what it is: a collection of separately implemented marts bound together with a powerful architecture based on conformed dimensions and standardized facts.

Dealing with Demanding Realities

In the late 1990s and early 2000s, Ralph wrote several articles describing the challenges associated with data warehousing, along with suggestions for addressing them.

2.4 Brave New Requirements for Data Warehousing

Ralph Kimball, Intelligent Enterprise, *Oct 1998*

Ten years ago, when we began focusing on data warehousing, we were primarily concerned with defining a data warehouse as something different from an operational system. This view was clear whenever we talked about the requirements for a data warehouse. Ten years ago, we needed to remind everyone that a data warehouse was a centralized, static copy of operational data. We viewed the warehouse as a cross between a historical archive and an archaeological dig. Thou shalt proceed cautiously to assemble a complete data warehouse before releasing anything to the public. Thou shalt not write into the data warehouse.

In the intervening 10 years we've learned a lot. We've built many successful data warehouses, but we've also had some disappointments and failures. Technology has improved enormously. We have spectacularly more powerful computers. We have both online analytical processing (OLAP) and relational database engines that are devoted to getting the data out rather than putting the data in. We have developed powerful data warehouse modeling skills, especially in the area of dimensional modeling. We now have a *bus architecture* for our data marts that lets us connect the data marts together similar to the way that we connect the components of our personal computers to the bus in the computer. As IT consumers, we've survived a whole generation of back end and front end tools, and we now have more informed opinions about tools and their vendors. We have passed out of the best of breed experimentation phase and have come to realize that each of us needs to focus on a small number of end-to-end vendors to keep our data warehouse environments under control.

As businesspeople, we are no longer content to just see the top line view of our enterprises, where we barely drill down from the annual report. Instead, we demand to see detailed customer behavior down to the individual ticket line item and the individual button click at the ATM. Fortunately, in most cases, our data warehouse systems are now big enough to store all the ticket line items and button clicks. It's an interesting chicken and egg debate as to whether this demand for atomic detail begat monster database machines or the other way around.

At the same time that we've been demanding more detailed data, we have also insisted on a broader, more meaningful view. We no longer manage business on volume alone; profitability is now key to our business management. For the data warehouse provider, profitability is much more difficult than volume because profitability almost always requires a fully integrated view of the business, where the costs incurred in all the phases of the business are correctly allocated back to products, customers, geographies, and time periods.

For all these reasons, data warehouse managers and implementers have had a collective allergic reaction to the difficulty of building a monolithic, centralized data warehouse. It just seems too hard and too much work. In many ways, the sheer responsibility and intellectual challenge of taking on the whole enterprise data warehouse has been too much. This allergic reaction has a name: data mart. Somehow we have to cut the data warehouse implementation task down to human proportions.

Looking at all these developments, it becomes clear that the data warehouse game has changed completely from where we started in the 1980s. We really can't keep modifying the old set of requirements anymore. We need to stop, wipe the slate clean, and articulate a new set of requirements. That's where a new set of requirements comes in for the modern data warehouse. It's a pretty daunting set of requirements, but before proposing a solution to all of them, let's try to understand their architectural effects in a little more detail.

- **Decentralized, incremental development.** We're forced to accede to the reality that departments and divisions are going to create their own mini data warehouses to answer urgent business questions. If we admit that we can't stop these developments, we need to provide a discipline and framework for them so the rest of the enterprise can leverage their work. Technically, this means that whatever this common framework is, it must allow an individual data mart team to proceed with its implementation without knowing in detail what the other data mart teams are doing. An individual team must be able to select technology independent of other teams.

- **Anticipation of continuous change as business needs and available data sources evolve.** Our design approach must recognize change as a constant. We want a design approach that has no built-in preferences for the business questions we happen to ask this month versus the business questions we will ask next month. We certainly don't want to adjust our data schemas if we think of new questions to ask. We do not want to adjust our schemas if we add new descriptors to our basic entities such as customer, product, or location. We want to be able to add new numerical measurements to our data environment and add new dimensions—all without having to modify our database schemas. The requirement that we hold our database schemas constant is extremely important. If we can hold to this goal, then existing applications will continue to work, even after we add the new data to the environment.

- **Rapid deployment.** The requirement to build the parts of the data warehouse rapidly probably mandates the first requirement for decentralized and incremental development. It is hard to imagine a rapid deployment of a centralized, monolithic data warehouse where the whole enterprise data warehouse has to be in place before the data warehouse can be used. Beyond this, rapid deployment also means that the techniques for building the parts of the data warehouse are well understood, predictable, and simple. It would help if all the parts of the data warehouse looked the same and had the same structure. Then we would know how to load these parts, index these parts for performance, select tools to access these parts, and query these parts.

- **Seamless drill down to the lowest possible atomic data.** We know we need to expose atomic data in most of our data marts. We know that our users want to see customer behavior, which is often at the individual user transaction level. We also know that our users want to make precise cuts through the data even if they ask for aggregate behavior. How many people use the ATM between 5 and 6 p.m. at ATM locations near their work but not near their homes? As we descend from aggregated to more atomic data, we want our access methods and query tools to function seamlessly. In a proper dimensional framework, drilling down is nothing more than adding a row header to a request. Everything else stays constant. Above all, drilling down must not mean that you leave behind one user interface and change your mindset and training in order to get more detail.

- **The parts (data marts) adding up to the whole (data warehouse).** The requirement that the data warehouse is composed of nothing more and nothing less than the sum of the data marts is largely a consequence of the previous requirements. The separate subject areas are going to be implemented in a distributed fashion. Each data mart is going to contain its underlying atomic data. We don't want to duplicate the numerical measurement data in multiple places around the enterprise; this data is overwhelmingly the largest part of any data mart. The surrounding text-like descriptive dimensions are often a tiny fraction of the overall data storage, so they can afford to be replicated in multiple places around the enterprise. This bimodal view of the world is very important in our brave new architecture.

When the data marts add up to the whole data warehouse, they must function together so we can drill across data marts to assemble integrated views of the enterprise. Drilling across, similar to drilling down, has a very specific technical interpretation. In order to get numeric facts from different data marts to line up across the row of a report, the row header that "controls" the line of the report has to be defined in the context of each data mart. More specifically, the row header has to mean the same thing in each data mart. It doesn't help to have a western zone in one data mart that means something different from the western zone in another data mart. Or maybe there is no western zone in the second data mart. These issues have to be addressed before the data marts are built.

■ **The parts (data marts) implemented on diverse, incompatible technologies.** Because our data warehouse may be built from distributed data mart efforts, it is obvious that the various groups will show up at the finish line with different technologies. The hardware will be different and the database engines will be different. Some may be OLAP and some may be relational online analytical processing (ROLAP). The OLAP and ROLAP systems will differ in small details of access methods. In spite of this, we demand there be an overarching framework that allows robust drilling across the separate data marts by an end user application. Even more aggressively, we would like any end user application to be able to perform this drill across whether or not the application was designed with drill across in mind. Architecturally, this means there needs to be some kind of consolidating layer between an application and the actual database engines in each data mart. We're beginning to sniff out the outlines of our architectural solution.

■ **24 × 7 availability.** We can no longer afford to have our data warehouses offline for extended periods of time while we perform back room cleaning, loading, and indexing chores. Somehow, we need more of a hot switch approach that lets us take our time with these back room activities, while at the same time continuing to support access to yesterday's data. Then we need to switch over to today's data. The downtime should be measured in seconds. The hot switch also needs to be done so that the drilling across operations previously described remain consistent. In other words, if we make a change in the definition of something that might be a row header in a report, we must be careful to replicate this change in a synchronous fashion to all the affected data marts.

■ **Publishing data warehouse results everywhere, preferably over the internet.** Our users are mobile, both on a long and short term basis. They will move from building to building, city to city, and country to country demanding the same user interfaces and the same level of service. The same user may log in from an internal network at headquarters, a remote location in the field, or from home—all on the same day. In the last few years, the internet has grown to provide a ubiquitous transport medium for our communications and data. It's likely to be much cheaper to use the internet in all these situations than it would be to provide dedicated or dial-up telephone lines.

The other factor driving us to internet solutions is the reality that every query and report-writing tool is developing a browser user interface. Vendors are being forced to do this because everyone wants web-based deployment.

- **Securing the data warehouse results everywhere, especially over the internet.** The obvious downside of the ubiquitous internet solutions is the enormous concern over security. Data warehouse results must be handled securely, or we warehouse managers lose our jobs and our companies get sued. At the very least, the data warehouse must reliably authenticate the identity of the requesting user and must handle the interactive sessions in an entirely private, highly secure fashion. This security architecture must be built into the design of the distributed data warehouse. In many cases, end-to-end encryption must be supported.

- **Near instantaneous response to all requests.** There's no such thing as an "acceptable" response time being measured in hours or even minutes. The only truly acceptable response time for a request is instantaneous. Data warehousing as an industry is in the middle of a steep learning curve on which query response times are dropping very rapidly as we learn how to use indexes, aggregations, and new query technology. This rapid set of changes is reminiscent of the rapid changes we experienced in transaction processing performance in the 1980s, but it also means that data warehouse managers must constantly reevaluate the solutions if the response times are not quite instantaneous.

- **Ease of use, especially for computer nonenthusiasts.** The final requirement in our list is actually the most important requirement. Business users simply won't use something that is difficult to use. Or perhaps a tiny subset of technical enthusiasts will use something complicated. Or perhaps we will end up with a priesthood of application developers who are the only true users. In all these scenarios, we've missed the potential of expanding data warehousing to the majority of possible users. Ease of use is more than motherhood. We need user interfaces that are recognizable, memorable, high performance, and are based on templates that can be invoked or modified in a single button click.

The 11 brave new requirements I have described here are both exciting and scary at the same time. They are exciting because if we can achieve them all in a data warehouse implementation, we are likely to have a cost-effective solution that really works and will stand up to the test of time as our environments evolve. They are scary because they are unconventional and because there aren't obvious models in many of our minds for addressing these requirements, especially all at once in a single project. In article 2.5, *Coping with the Brave New Requirements*, I describe the data warehouse bus concept in more detail and show how this concept provides the foundation for addressing all these requirements.

2.5 Coping with the Brave New Requirements

Ralph Kimball, Intelligent Enterprise, Nov 1998

In article 2.4, *Brave New Requirements for Data Warehousing*, I described a set of 11 requirements that data warehouse implementers and owners face. None of these requirements are unfamiliar or unexpected, but they have been gathering force and coherence for several years, and it is appropriate to step back to take a snapshot of the data warehouse state of the art. Glancing back at the list of all the requirements together reveals how much our perspectives have changed over the last 10 years.

Data Marts and Dimensional Modeling

The data warehousing industry is beginning to respond implicitly to all 11 of the requirements. This response does not imply, however, that the industry is going in 11 independent directions. Almost all the requirements are affected by two broad data warehousing themes: data marts and dimensional modeling. If you look at these two themes together, all the requirements I outlined can be addressed simultaneously.

To see how to do this, let's extract two key principles to guide our data warehouse designs:

- Separate your architectures. Draw a very clear line between the back room and the front room. The back room is where you extract, transform, and load the data, and the front room is where you make the data available for presentation.
- Build your presentation-oriented data marts around dimensional models, not normalized entity-relationship (ER) models.

Figure 2-3 shows a typical horizontal cut through an overall data warehouse environment. At the extreme left you see the traditional transaction-oriented legacy systems. The data warehouse responsibility starts when you extract data from the legacy systems and bring it into the back room ETL staging area.

The data staging area is the complete back room operation for the data warehouse in which you clean, prune, combine, sort, look up, add keys, remove duplicates, assemble households, archive, and export. The data arriving in the data staging area is frequently dirty, malformed, and in a flat file format. If you're lucky, the data arrives in pristine third normal form, but that's rare. When you're done cleaning and restructuring the data, you can leave it in flat file form or store it in third normal form. The data staging area is dominated by flat files, simple sorting, and sequential processing. Third normal form relational representations are wonderful, but they're mostly the final result of a lot of hard work done in nonrelational formats.

The key architectural requirement for the data staging area is that it is off limits to the business users. The data staging area is like the back room of a car repair shop. Customers are not allowed in the back room; it isn't safe and the shop doesn't have insurance to cover an injury occurring to a customer in the back room. The mechanics are busy fixing the cars and do not want to be diverted to serving the customers directly. In the same way, the data staging area of the warehouse must be off limits to all forms of user inquiry. We must not distract ourselves by having to provide availability of data, indexes, aggregations, time series, synchronous integration across subject areas, and especially user-level security.

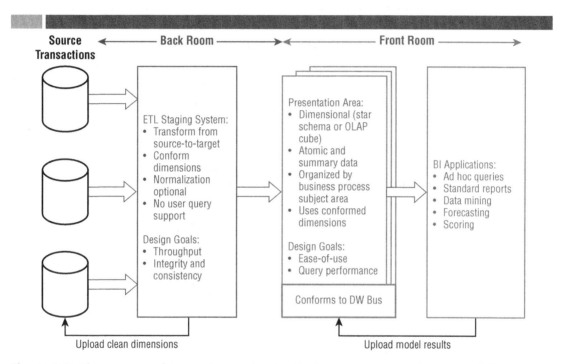

Figure 2-3: The enterprise data warehouse, showing the back room ETL staging area and the front room presentation area.

The presentation area is the complete front room operation for the data warehouse. As its name implies, the presentation area is on stage and available at all times for user inquiry. All forms of inquiry are serviced by the presentation area, including ad hoc querying, drilling down, reporting, and data mining. We don't allow drilling down into an atomic data store located in the back room if that atomic data store is just another name for the ETL staging area.

The presentation area is broken into business process-centric subject areas, which are called data marts. Each data mart is organized entirely around effective presentation, which, in my opinion, means dimensional models. Presenting encompasses all inquiry and analysis activities including ad hoc querying, report generation, sophisticated analysis tools, and data mining. All the dimensional models in all the data marts look somewhat similar, and this suite of dimensional models must share the key dimensions of the enterprise. We call these the *conformed dimensions*.

Plugging Data Marts into the Data Warehouse Bus Architecture

Figure 2-4 shows how to attach several business process data marts (labeled as "subject areas") together with conformed dimensions—a consistently defined set of dimensions that all data marts that wish to refer to these common entities must use. Conformed dimensions typically include such things as calendar (time), customer, product, location, and organization. We also have to consider conformed facts, which involve any measure that exists in more than one data mart. Perhaps revenue, for example, is defined in several data marts. To conform several instances of revenue, we must insist that the technical definitions of each instance be the same so that separate revenues can be compared and added. If two versions of revenue cannot be conformed, they must be labeled differently so users won't compare or add versions.

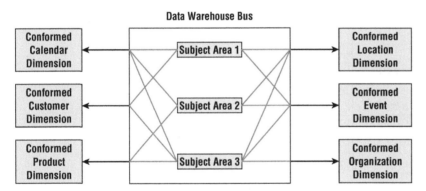

Figure 2-4: The data warehouse bus architecture, showing a series of data marts connecting to the conformed dimensions of the enterprise.

Imagine that the data warehouse bus is like the bus in your computer. The bus in your computer is a standard interface specification that lets you plug in a CD-ROM, a disk drive, or any number of special-purpose cards. Because of the bus standard, these peripherals work together smoothly even though they're manufactured at different times by different vendors.

In the same way, the data warehouse bus is a standard that allows separate data marts to be implemented by different groups in your enterprise at different times. By adhering to the standard (conformed dimensions), the separate data marts can be plugged together. They won't smoke, and they can even share data usefully in a drill across report because the row headers on the report will mean the same thing across each of the data marts.

The data warehouse bus architecture combines the two key concepts I mentioned earlier: data marts and dimensional models. You separate the overall architecture of the data warehouse cleanly so the ETL staging area and the presentation area perform distinctly different functions. The bus architecture, which defines the data presentation area, relies on the predictable similarity of the dimensional models to let the enterprise hook all the data marts together. This approach is a framework for addressing all the brave new requirements in the data warehouse industry.

Given the overall architecture and this new vocabulary, let me comment briefly on each of the 11 brave new requirements.

- **Decentralized, incremental development.** The discipline of defining conformed dimensions and conformed facts before embarking on separate data mart projects is the secret to decentralized and incremental development.
- **Anticipation of continuous change as business needs and available data sources evolve.** The similarity of all dimensional schemas lets us anticipate the effects of unexpected changes. When users start asking questions that are geographically focused rather than focused on product category, nothing much changes in the dimensional data mart. Location and product are simply two dimensions connected symmetrically and equivalently to most of the same fact tables. Queries that constrain and group by location have the same form as queries that constrain and group by product. Query tools and query strategies don't have to be reprogrammed when the user community begins asking new kinds of questions. New data elements can be added to dimensional schemas in such a way that old applications continue to function without modification. You can add new data elements in this graceful way as new dimensional attributes, new additive facts, and entirely new dimensions.
- **Rapid deployment.** Once the conformed dimensions and conformed facts have been established, separate data mart teams can proceed independently of each other. In many cases, it makes sense to build the first tables in each data mart as dimensional images of single underlying sources. The data warehouse bus architecture provides a formula for combining these single source fact tables into higher level combinations involving multiple sources. The charm of building single source fact tables is that this is the fastest possible path to a partial deployment of data warehouse data.
- **Seamless drill down to the lowest possible atomic data.** Drilling down is nothing more than adding a row header to an existing report. In a conformed dimension bus architecture, these row headers are known to be available in the dimensions and will have a consistent meaning as we descend from more aggregated fact tables to less aggregated ones. Remember that the most atomic data is the most naturally dimensional data because most single valued attributes exist for each fact table record at this level.
- **The parts (data marts) adding up to the whole (data warehouse).** This is a direct consequence of defining the data marts as complete logical subsets of the data warehouse. We have added

substance to this definition by showing the structure of each data mart (dimensional) and how to connect them together (the bus architecture).

- **The parts (data marts) implemented on diverse, incompatible technologies.** We can relax and let the data marts be incompatible at the lowest hardware and software levels because we don't insist on making the hardware and software talk to each other directly. By performing separate queries to each data mart (using so-called multipass SQL and its equivalent for OLAP databases), we simply combine the answer sets in a higher level applications layer. This approach also has the significant benefit that the separate queries avoid a host of complex logical problems associated with trying to join fact tables with different cardinalities.

- **24 × 7 availability.** By thinking clearly about the separation of the back room from the front room, we see that the requirement for 24 × 7 availability refers to the data presentation area. The first step to achieving 24 × 7 availability is to implement the data staging area on a separate machine or on a separate process from the data presentation area. The final output of the staging area is a set of load files for the presentation area. However, loading and indexing these files into the final presentation database may be a lengthy process that takes the presentation database offline. To avoid going offline for lengthy periods, you can use a file renaming strategy. Each morning's database load goes into a "temp" file that starts as a complete copy of the normal presentation database. When the temp file has been loaded and indexed, the system goes offline for a few seconds while the current production database table is renamed, and the temp file is named as the production database table. This scenario is important to the data warehouse daily cycle, and it gets more intricate in the presence of partitioned tables and aggregates.

- **Publishing data warehouse results everywhere, preferably over the internet.** Although individual IT data architects and some industry consultants are not completely convinced that simple queries and dimensional approaches are required, the tools vendors have moved heavily toward these approaches because the approaches work. Additionally, the tools vendors nearly all provide web-enabled user interfaces. In some senses, most data warehouse owners will find themselves presenting their data warehouses over intranets or even the internet, whether they plan for it or not.

- **Securing the data warehouse results everywhere, especially over the internet.** The downside of using the ubiquitous internet transport medium is the exposure to security problems. The data warehouse owner is especially vulnerable because of the sensitivity of much of the underlying data, and because, ironically, of the success of the warehouse in publishing the data effectively to all the business users.

- **Near instantaneous response to all requests.** Improving response times for user queries includes disciplining ourselves to use simple, predictable database structures, augmenting the use of database indexes with database aggregations, and using multipass SQL instead of monolithic complex SQL. All these approaches use the dimensional model approach heavily, and there is a growing body of experience and technology in these areas based on dimensional assumptions. It is interesting that (as far as I know) there seems to be no serious scholarly argument for meeting the objectives of very fast response times with normalized entity-relationship data models and traditional cost-based optimizers. No one has proposed a general framework for aggregate navigation in the entity-relation world either.

- **Ease of use, especially for computer nonenthusiasts.** This final requirement completes the circle. The original design motivation for fact tables and dimension tables in the dimensional approach was pioneered by General Mills and Dartmouth College in the 1960s and later commercialized by A.C. Nielsen in the 1970s. Their concern, as I understand it, was first and foremost to represent the data in an understandable way for the benefit of business users. As early as 1980, Nielsen figured out that the way to tie separate data sources together was by using "conformed dimensions."

The 11 brave new requirements for the data warehouse yield a mixture of bad news and good news. The bad news is that the requirements are aggressive and demanding, and they don't fit easily into traditional design techniques and management approaches. The good news is that with a data mart and dimensional design approach, we can make serious progress against all the requirements.

2.6 Stirring Things Up

Ralph Kimball, Intelligent Enterprise, *Jun 22, 1999*

About once a year I feel the need to write a provocative article. This is one of those articles. I don't mind if you say, "Kimball is full of horse feathers"; maybe there are a few horse feathers here. But I hope you will say, "Now that's a different perspective. Maybe there's a grain of truth in that." So here are some topics that are on my mind.

The web challenges the current view of the data warehouse with multiple new requirements. Data warehousing has matured noticeably during the 1990s. We now have a lot of successes, a fair number of failures, and a lot of hard won, accumulated experience. But the bigger story these days is the web revolution. The web revolution represents a fundamental free-fall in communication costs, and every time communication costs drop precipitously, society changes. This phenomenon is happening as we speak.

The data warehouse must play an integral role in the web revolution as the analysis platform for all the wonderful behavior data coming in from the clickstream, as well as for the many websites that rely on the data warehouse to customize and drive the end user's web experience in real time. The data warehouse is taking central stage in the web revolution, and it requires restating and adjusting our data warehouse thinking. This *data webhouse* must:

- Be designed from the start as a fully distributed system with many independently developed nodes contributing to the overall whole. In other words, there is no center to the data webhouse.
- Not be a client/server system, but a web-enabled system. This means a top-to-bottom redesign. A web-enabled system delivers its results and exposes its interfaces through remote browsers

on the web. These browser interfaces should use a strong form of security based on two factors, a password and a physical token, to establish connections through virtual private networks to a network directory server. The directory server authenticates and passes the user to an authorization server, which in turn gives the user permission to use data warehouse resources through one or more web or application servers. The application servers, in turn, connect to various multimedia database engines using private, strong security. The users never connect to the multimedia database engines directly. The web-enabled system is thus a six tier model consisting of the browser and five servers: directory, authorization, web, application, and database.

- Deal equally well with textual, numeric, graphic, photographic, audio, and video data streams because the web already supports this mix of media.

- Support atomic-level behavior data to at least the terabyte level in many business process subject areas, especially those containing clickstream data. Many behavioral analyses must, by definition, crawl through the lowest level of data because the analysis constraints preclude summarizing in advance.

- Respond to a user request in roughly 10 seconds, regardless of the complexity of the request. I know, I know. This is impossible. But the web is setting an expectation, and we can't ignore the tide coming in.

- Include the user interface's effectiveness as a primary design criterion. The only thing that matters in the data webhouse is the effective publication of information on the web. Delays, confusing dialogs, and the lack of the desired choices are all direct failures.

The data webhouse necessitates a well-distributed architecture. Increasingly, web-enabled data warehouses will be sets of lightweight, flexible business process subject areas implemented on a widely heterogeneous mix of incompatible technologies. We need to take seriously the scientific issues of hooking these subject areas together (it can be done), rather than arguing that these independent subject areas shouldn't exist. Welcome to the web.

Centralized, monolithic designs will become more difficult to pursue in these widely distributed data warehouse environments in the same way that centralized designs are difficult in widely distributed computing environments and networks. The problem is that it is too expensive and time consuming to plan a fully centralized database, and these idealistically motivated designs are difficult to keep in synch with dynamically changing real-world environments. Because our data webhouse designs encompass not only our internal operations but also our business partners in the supply chain and even our customers, we simply can't mandate a fully centralized approach. There is no center.

However, in moving more aggressively to a distributed design approach, we can certainly avoid the old stovepipe argument that distributed systems represent out of control separate efforts that can't be connected. The solution to the stovepipe argument is a flexible framework of common definitions (conformed dimensions and conformed facts) that let us stitch the individual data marts together. Interestingly, we need to centralize the actual definition, implementation, and replication of the conformed dimensions and facts out to the working data marts logically only, not physically. In my writings, I have extensively described this distributed framework, as first implemented in the early 1980s by A.C. Nielsen, the syndicated data supplier.

The biggest enterprise resource planning (ERP) vendors need to follow data warehousing rather than take it over. Some of the biggest ERP vendors have declared that they are the data warehouse—probably because they sense the importance of making decisions using enterprise information—and they want to control that part of the market. However, their data warehousing instincts so far have been counterproductive. The scope of the data warehouse will always be larger than any ERP system. The data warehouse—and now the data webhouse—is a publishing platform for information arriving from many sources and many directions. The data webhouse has to be a comfortable home for data from all these different places. The data webhouse must be distributed, flexible, fast, and user oriented. In my opinion, the biggest ERP vendors have not taken these requirements seriously.

If you are a data warehouse project manager and you have been told to use your ERP system as the centralized data warehouse because of the significant investment made in that ERP system, you have my sympathies. I think you should extract data from the ERP system, just like any other data source, and present that data as one or more business process subject areas that participate effectively with other conformed subject areas representing non-ERP sources.

The user interfaces of most data warehousing tools have been designed by vendors' software developers who haven't implemented enough data warehouses. My favorite professional activity is sitting next to business users and watching them use a computer. For me, this goes way back to my roots. My graduate thesis in the late 1960s was a large LISP program that tutored calculus students on a time-shared PDP-10 with a graphics terminal. This program learned superior problem-solving strategies by watching the students. At Xerox PARC, I spent 10 years helping design the user interface for the Star Workstation. Along the way, we set up a laboratory for watching end users struggle with our computers. Since my Xerox days, I have frequently encountered business users who are overwhelmed and nonplussed by unnecessarily complex user interfaces. But all too often there has been no effective, tight feedback loop to get the vendors to change their products. Field support people working for the software vendor collect user suggestions that are transmitted occasionally back through sales channels to product marketing. Product marketing negotiates once or twice a year with development to include features in the next software release. The feature suggestions and usability enhancements have to compete with new tool development, which headquarters executives usually drive. Individual feature suggestions are often rejected because they are too small on their own to seem worthwhile. Or, worse, they are interpreted as requests by "unsophisticated" users who should have read the manual.

In my opinion, this is all going to change. The web is an unforgiving crucible that measures user effectiveness directly. The clickstream supplies the evidence in a way that we can't avoid. We see every gesture the user makes, and some of the gestures aren't pretty. Users arrived at the page and left in 10 seconds. If they didn't click on the page, they didn't see what they needed. If they left the page before it finished painting, it was too slow. If they don't come back to the page, they can't use it. The web is finally making usability important.

Normalized entity-relationship (ER) models are neither unique nor complete. In my opinion, the data warehouse community still has not sorted out the right places to use various forms of modeling. In the spirit of stirring things up this month, I want to focus on one specific issue that fascinates me.

Normalized ER models that drive redundancy out of data sets are a wonderful benefit for transaction processing. Normalized models that serve as targets for cleaned data are useful because they are a goal. But this goal becomes attainable only after the cleaning steps are finished. In my recent thinking about normalized models, I have come to suspect that they are neither unique nor complete. Given a set of data entities—describing, for instance, all the employees and organizations in a complex enterprise—there may be no unique normalized model that describes all the relationships among the data. There are many simultaneously overlapping and alternative, many-to-many and many-to-one relationships, and these can be represented in more than one way—or at least I suspect that this is true. If so, then a given normalized model is only one chosen interpretation of the data. It is not a unique description.

More seriously, a given normalized model makes no claim to be complete; it makes no claim to wring out all the relationships among the data and show them on the diagram. In some sense, a normalized model is only the set of things the modeler happens to think about, discover, or is willing to document.

There is too little critical thinking in the data warehousing field. Authors and speakers aren't judged as critically as they are in other disciplines, and they aren't held accountable for what they say. Don't let it be said that I shrink from tough topics. My wife, Julie, was a professional speech and language specialist in a former career, and she now studies very carefully what people (including me) say. In a recent email to a colleague, she made the following remarks:

> *Do people really think critically about what they read and hear, or do they blindly accept it? Ultimately I believe that critical thinking by any customer base improves the quality of any marketplace. There is a kind of collective leadership and power associated with [this customer base when] they exercise their critical thinking skills. It would be nice to encourage the IT community to be more demanding of those they listen to.*

2.7 Design Constraints and Unavoidable Realities

Ralph Kimball, Intelligent Enterprise, *Sep 3, 2002*

The basic mission of a data warehouse professional, as described in articles 3.1, *Professional Boundaries*, and 3.2, *An Engineer's View*, is to *publish the right data*. Because I am an engineer and try to build practical things that work, the next question for me is: What does a good engineer do when confronted with the task of presenting an organization's data most effectively?

Well, unfortunately, before we can start looking through the engineer's portfolio of tools and techniques, we have to swallow some bitter medicine. We have to face, all at once, the complete list of design constraints and unavoidable realities of designing a modern data warehouse. And it's a daunting list. Perhaps more than any other job in IT, the data warehouse design task combines computer technology, cognitive psychology, business content, and politics.

Whenever I present the following design constraints and unavoidable realities, I worry that I'm encouraging prospective data warehouse professionals to seek another career. But maybe the challenges of the job are what make these techniques so attractive and compelling. We will dig our way out, I promise you, but not until we've faced the full list.

Design Constraints

Design constraints are the requirements that we, as good engineers, seek to place on our design because they're obvious and desirable goals. Unavoidable realities, as the name suggests, are requirements that we wish we could avoid, but dare not if we're being honest. The first two design constraints are, in my opinion, absolutely nonnegotiable requirements of publishing the right data:

- **Understandability.** The final screens presented to the business user must be immediately understandable, simple, recognizable, and intuitive. This is the most challenging constraint in the whole list. As I've often said, we designers are genetically selected because we have an unusual tolerance for complexity. Almost all of our designs are too intricate and too complicated. We put features in front of users and mistake them for solutions. We give demos when we should be listening. We should provide more blank space on our application screens with fewer choices. Intricate, tiny dashboards filled with widgets appeal to only 10 percent of our users. Count the mouse clicks as a measure of complexity. Try to make everything work with three clicks or less.
- **Speed.** From the business user's perspective, the only acceptable delay in presenting the data is zero. One of the biggest false design rules is, "The users will accept a long delay if the results are complicated (or involve processing a lot of data)." This is a mealy mouthed excuse by designers who are unwilling to say, "We know this is slow, and we are working diligently to make it faster."
- **Implementation cost.** There are several costs that a good engineer must be constrained by. Implementation costs include the labor costs and delays during the design phase before any useful result is delivered to end users. The design is probably divided 70 percent between the back room extract, transform, load (ETL) applications and 30 percent for the front room user queries and reports. Implementation costs swell when each data warehouse design starts from a clean slate as a "custom job" without any reusable designs. Implementation costs can't be controlled when the design approach depends on the complexity of the data. A design with

10 tables is controllable. A design with 100 tables is marginal. A design with 1,000 tables is a disaster that will fail.

■ **Hardware and software technology cost.** The hardware and software should be scaled to the requirements at hand and should be easy to extend well beyond the first implementation. Software is the gold coin in the long run for understandable and fast delivery of data to our business users. Hardware is a commodity that should periodically be discarded in favor of more powerful versions. The most serious mistake with hardware and software is choosing a proprietary and closed hardware solution that emphasizes raw computing power on complex production schemas rather than careful software and data design. While such solutions may reduce isolated back room costs, they drive up the costs of application development and increase the chances that users will encounter complexity.

■ **Daily administrative costs.** Daily administration includes the routine loading of data into fact tables and dimension tables through standard ETL applications and includes the production of standard reports distributed to business users. In a dimensional data warehouse, the key ETL application is the "surrogate key pipeline."

■ **Cost of surprises.** Little surprises include late arriving facts, late arriving dimensions, and corrections to existing data. We know they'll happen but we can't respond until we receive the data. We need standard techniques for handling these little surprises. Big surprises include new dimensions, dimension attributes, facts, and granularity of a data source. All the big surprises make us alter our database schemas while we're in production. We demand that that these big surprises are handled "gracefully" so that all existing user applications keep on working without requiring any recoding.

■ **Prevention of irrelevant results.** One of the biggest causes of data warehouse failures is shooting at the wrong target. The data warehouse must be relevant if it is to be successful. Relevance is not an accident; it comes from extensive and continuous business requirements gathering at the beginning and throughout the life of the warehouse. The best data warehouse engineer lives half in IT and half in the business user department. Data warehouse professionals should have desks in the users' department.

■ **Prevention of inappropriate centralization.** A centrally planned data warehouse is as likely to be successful as a centrally planned economy. It sounds great on paper, and it appeals to the controlling instincts of IT, but a centrally planned data warehouse makes the assumptions of perfect information and control. Eventually, the problems with these assumptions, like those of a centrally planned economy, come home to roost. In the long run, a data warehouse should be a decentralized community of data marts, tied together with an architecture that makes them work together effectively, but where true control is ceded to the individual and autonomous remote departments.

Unavoidable Realities

Unavoidable realities are departures from the ideal model of the business world. Anthropologists who study the business world call the ideal model *normative* and the realistic model *descriptive*.

The descriptive model throws away the procedures manual and describes the unavoidable realities of the business world, such as:

- **Decentralized, incremental development.** Very few of us are wise enough and staffed sufficiently enough to complete a perfect design of a data warehouse up front from a centralized position. The rest of us need to rely on designs developed in separate departments and done in an incremental manner as we learn the requirements of the users and the implications of the data. Our data warehouse must be a profoundly decentralized system, in some cases with no physical center at all.

  I can't resist describing my favorite centralized system metaphor. If the telephone system in the United States had been designed as a fully centralized system, then there would be a single massive switching center located somewhere in Iowa, and every telephone with a separate wire running to this location! The telephone system is a great example of a distributed system, and it's thousands of times more complex than any data warehouse.

- **Multiple, incompatible technologies.** Most organizations have a variety of operational systems, database engines, and user analysis and delivery technologies that, below a certain physical level, are profoundly incompatible. To integrate these systems, we need a sophisticated approach to applications and data communications at relatively high levels, divorced from individual data formats.

- **Rapid deployment.** Business users think that six weeks is "about right" for the deployment of a data warehouse. At the other end of the spectrum, you'd better deliver something useful within a year because if not, your budget will go away, your boss will go away, and maybe your company will go away.

- **Continuous change.** The business world continuously changes, making a joke out of long range design assumptions. The only recourse is a kind of design that invites yet is resistant to change. What kind of design is that? You'll see that the secret is symmetry.

- **Data marts.** The term data mart is important because it represents the insistence that individual groups source and publish their own data to meet urgent local needs. The real problem with data marts, of course, is that they're often stovepipes. As engineers, we eliminate the stovepipes and turn the natural energy of data mart development to our advantage. We call the modern dimensional data marts *business process subject areas*. These subject areas must become the central elements of our distributed data warehouse.

- **Atomic, near real-time data.** We need the most atomic data in our data warehouse in order to ask the most precise questions and drill down to the most operational perspective. We also need this atomic data to be as real-time as possible. Real time now is generally understood to mean less than an hour old, although it can often mean virtually zero latency. The data warehouse needs to track the operational systems in lockstep.

- **Seamless history.** As if the previous requirements weren't bad enough, now the data warehouse must connect the real-time data seamlessly to the static historical data to present at least the illusion of a seamless connection from the beginning of time to the present.

Picking Ourselves Up Off the Floor

If you're still with me, stay tuned. In article 2.8, *Two Powerful Ideas*, I'll dig us out of this seemingly impossible set of design constraints and unavoidable realities. We'll separate our physical systems so they perform focused tasks much more efficiently, and we'll use dimensional modeling to attack all these challenges in a predictable, reusable, cost effective way.

2.8 Two Powerful Ideas

Ralph Kimball, Intelligent Enterprise, *Sep 17, 2002*

There are two powerful ideas at the foundation of most successful data warehouses. First, separate your systems. Second, build stars and cubes.

In article 2.7, *Design Constraints and Unavoidable Realities*, I described the challenges facing the data warehouse designer. This was such a daunting list that I worried that you would head for the door. But maybe what kept you reading this far was my promise to dig us out of the morass.

I stated that the nonnegotiable constraints on a data warehouse design are user understandability and query execution speed. A complex, slow data warehouse is a failure no matter how elegant the rest of the design may be because the people for whom it was intended won't want to use it. This is where the two powerful ideas come in.

All the rest of the constraints and unavoidable realities were pragmatic and honest admissions that the data warehouse design space is extremely complex. The source data, source systems, database technologies, and business environments we must deal with are incredibly complicated. So, as good engineers, to dig our way out of the mire, we must decompose the problem into separate manageable parts and emphasize techniques that are predictable, reusable, and robust when our design environment is altered.

Separate Your Systems

The first crucial step in designing a data warehouse across a complex enterprise is to separate your systems logically, physically, and administratively.

I've found it very useful to think of the project as four distinct and different systems, of which a data warehouse manager should be responsible for only two. I won't overwhelm you with the typical block diagram because the issues are simpler than that. The four systems are:

- Production (source) transaction processing systems
- ETL staging systems
- Presentation systems, including client/server and web-based query tools and report writers
- Optional high end analytic tools supporting data mining, forecasting, scoring, or allocating

As a data warehouse manager, you shouldn't be responsible for the source systems that are capturing and processing transactions. That's someone else's job. You don't want to be involved in supporting the legal and financial auditing functions or the rollback and recovery functions of these systems. They are the cash registers of the company, and their priorities are different from those of the data warehouse.

The first system for which the data warehouse is responsible is the data staging area, where production data from many sources is brought in, cleaned, conformed, combined, and ultimately delivered to the data warehouse presentation systems. Much has been written about the crucial extract, transform, and load (ETL) steps in the staging area, but stepping away from this detail, the main requirement for the staging area is that it is off limits to all final data warehouse clients. The staging area is exactly like the kitchen in a restaurant (see article 2.9, *Data Warehouse Dining Experience*). The kitchen is a busy, even dangerous, place filled with sharp knives and hot liquids. The cooks are busy, focused on the task of preparing the food. It just isn't appropriate to allow diners into a professional kitchen or allow the cooks to be distracted with the very separate issues of the fine dining experience. In data warehouse terms, by barring all data warehouse clients from the data staging area, we avoid:

- Guaranteeing uptime service levels for querying or reporting
- Enforcing client-level security
- Building performance-enhancing indexes and aggregations for query performance
- Handling logical and physical conflicts between the querying and data cleaning steps
- Guaranteeing consistency across separate, asynchronous data sources

The two dominant data structures in the data staging area are the flat file and the normalized entity-relationship schema, which are directly extracted or derived from the production systems. Almost all processing in the staging area is either sorting or simple sequential processing.

The second major system under the specific control of the data warehouse is the presentation system. Of course, this system is analogous to the dining area of a fine restaurant. The dining area is organized for the comfort of the diners. The food is delivered promptly and in the most appealing way, and hassles and distractions are avoided as much as possible. In the same way, the data warehouse presentation system is purpose-built to enhance the query and reporting experience. The presentation system needs to be simple and fast and present the right data to meet the analysis needs of the business users. Also, in the presentation system, we can easily handle the foregoing bulleted list of requirements that we excluded from the staging area.

The dominant data structures in the presentation area are the dimensional database schema and the OLAP data cube. Processing in the presentation area must respond to a blizzard of large and small queries coming in from every possible angle on the data. Over time, there will be no predictable pattern to these queries. Some designers call this the *ad hoc attack*.

The fourth system on our list is an optional layer of specific high end analytic tools that often consume data warehouse data in batch quantities. Frequently these data mining, forecasting, scoring, and allocating tools use specialized algorithms outside the normal expertise of the data warehouse designer.

And, honestly, many of these processes have an interpretive or political component that's wisely segregated from the data warehouse. For example, data mining as a discipline is a complex interpretive task involving a whole collection of powerful analytic techniques, many of which the business community doesn't readily understand or trust. Proper data mining requires a professional data mining expert who's equipped to use the tools effectively and represent the data mining results to the community.

In addition, as I've often stated, there's a fundamental impedance mismatch between data mining and the data warehouse. Data mining frequently needs to look at thousands or millions of "observations" over and over again, at extremely high data rates. This just isn't easy to support from the data warehouse directly. Better to hand the observation set over to the data mining team, just once.

Another example of a high end analytic tool the data warehouse should avoid is the allocation system for assigning costs to the various lines of business in your organization so as to compute overall profitability. Not only can this be a complex processing step outside the capabilities of most query and reporting tools, it's also a political hot potato. Let the finance department do the allocations, and you (the data warehouse) will be glad to store the results.

Symmetrical Stars and Cubes

Most presentation areas today are dominated by relational star schemas and multidimensional OLAP data cubes. These data structures have proven over the past 30 years to be the ones business users can understand. Remember that understandability is one of our two nonnegotiable design constraints.

The simplicity of the star schemas and OLAP cubes has allowed smart software designers to focus on very powerful algorithms for rapid query performance. Remember that speed is the other nonnegotiable design constraint.

The symmetry of both the star schema and OLAP cube also makes for:

- Predictable user interfaces that can "learn" what to do at query time
- Predictable administrative scenarios in the ETL staging area because all the data structures have the same familiar look and feel
- Predictable implementation responses whenever new types of data are made available

Of course, the star schema and OLAP cube are intimately related. Star schemas are most appropriate for very large data sets, with many millions or billions of numerical measurements, or many millions of members in a customer entity or a product entity. OLAP cubes are most appropriate for smaller data sets where analytic tools can perform complex data comparisons and calculations. In almost all OLAP cube environments, it's recommended that you originally source data into a star schema structure, and then use wizards to transform the data into the OLAP cube. In that way, all the complex staging area ETL tools that deal with flat files and entity-relationship schemas can be part of the OLAP data pipeline. And, of course, hybrid dimensional schema-OLAP systems allow very large data sets in dimensional formats to be smooth drill down targets from smaller OLAP data cubes, all under a single user interface.

The Big Payoff

The final big payoff for building the presentation system in the data warehouse around symmetrical dimensional schemas and OLAP cubes is the predictable set of points of commonality for linking together data from across the enterprise. These conformed dimensions will be the basis for a data warehouse bus architecture—a set of standard connection points that provide power to your data warehouse, just like the bus bar in a power station provides power to all the transmission lines, and just like the bus in your computer provides data to all the peripherals.

What Have We Accomplished?

So far we've implemented two powerful ideas. First we've logically, physically, and administratively separated the systems in our environment into four distinct types. You really do need four different computer systems, but you're responsible for only two of them! Our two data warehouse systems also allow us to separate the incompatible responsibilities of data staging and user querying. Second, we've populated our data warehouse presentation area with star schemas and OLAP cubes, the only structures that are understandable, fast, and can stand up to the ad hoc attack.

Although we clearly haven't addressed all the complex design constraints and unavoidable realities, we've chipped away at an impressive part of the overall challenge, just by leveraging these two powerful ideas. We've effectively addressed large parts of understandability, query speed, all three types of costs mentioned in that article, the risks of inappropriate centralization, the need for incremental development, handling continuous change consisting of little surprises and big surprises, and how to think about the role of data marts. Maybe there's hope.

2.9 Data Warehouse Dining Experience

Margy Ross, Intelligent Enterprise, Jan 1, 2004

Several members of the Kimball Group worked at a company called Metaphor back in the early 1980s. As part of a startup software company introducing then cutting-edge concepts (such as folders, file drawers, and workflows on a graphical electronic desktop), we appreciated the benefits of using metaphors to represent seemingly complex concepts. Effective verbal and visual metaphors help convert complexity into easily understood and highly memorable images.

One of our favorite metaphors reinforces the importance of separating the overall data warehouse environment into distinct components, as described in article 2.8, *Two Powerful Ideas*. Data warehouses should have an area that focuses exclusively on data staging and extract, transform, and load activities. A separate layer of the warehouse environment should be optimized for presentation of the data to the business constituencies and application developers.

This division is underscored if you consider the similarities between a data warehouse and a restaurant.

The Kitchen

The kitchen of a fine restaurant is a world unto itself. It's where the magic happens. Talented chefs take raw materials and transform them into appetizing, delicious multi-course meals for the restaurant's diners. But long before a commercial kitchen is put into productive use, a significant amount of planning goes into designing the layout and components of the workspace.

The restaurant's kitchen is organized with several design goals in mind. First, the layout must be highly efficient. Restaurant managers are very concerned about kitchen throughput. When the restaurant is packed and everyone is hungry, you don't have time for wasted movement.

Delivering consistent quality from the restaurant's kitchen is the second goal. The establishment is doomed if the plates coming out of the kitchen repeatedly fail to meet expectations. A restaurant's reputation is built on legions of hard work; that effort is for naught if the result is inconsistent. In order to achieve reliable consistency, chefs create their special sauces once in the kitchen, rather than sending ingredients out to the table where variations will inevitably occur.

The kitchen's output, the meals delivered to restaurant customers, must also be of high integrity. You wouldn't want someone to get food poisoning from dining at your restaurant. Consequently, kitchens are designed with integrity in mind. Salad prep doesn't happen on the same surfaces where raw chicken is handled.

Just as quality, consistency, and integrity are major considerations when designing the kitchen layout, they are also ongoing concerns for everyday management of the restaurant. Chefs strive to obtain the best raw material possible. Procured products must meet quality standards. For example, if the produce purveyor tries to unload brown, wilted lettuce or bruised tomatoes, the materials are rejected because they don't meet minimum standards. Most fine restaurants modify their menus based on the availability of quality inputs.

The restaurant kitchen is staffed with skilled professionals wielding the tools of their trade. Cooks manipulate razor sharp knives with incredible confidence and ease. They operate powerful equipment and work around extremely hot surfaces without incident.

Given the dangerous surroundings, the kitchen is off limits to restaurant patrons. It simply isn't safe. Professional cooks handling sharp knives shouldn't be distracted by diners' inquiries. You also wouldn't want patrons entering the kitchen to dip their fingers into a sauce to see whether they want to order an entree or not. To prevent these intrusions, most restaurants have a closed door that separates the kitchen from the area where diners are served.

Even restaurants that boast an open kitchen format typically have a barrier, such as a partial wall of glass, separating the two environments. Diners are invited to watch, but can't wander into the kitchen themselves. But while part of a kitchen may be visible, there are always out-of-view back rooms where the less visually attractive preparation work is performed.

The data warehouse's ETL staging area is very similar to the restaurant's kitchen. The staging area is where source data is magically transformed into meaningful, presentable information. The staging area must be laid out and architected long before any data is extracted from the source. Like the kitchen, the staging area is designed to ensure throughput. It must transform raw source data into the target model efficiently, minimizing unnecessary movement.

Obviously, the data warehouse ETL staging area is also highly concerned about data quality, integrity, and consistency. Incoming data is checked for reasonable quality as it enters the staging area. Conditions are continually monitored to ensure staging outputs are of high integrity. Business rules to consistently derive value added metrics and attributes are applied once by skilled professionals in the staging area, rather than relying on each patron to develop them independently. Yes, that puts an extra burden on the ETL team, but it's done in the spirit of delivering a better, more consistent product to the data warehouse patrons.

Finally, the data warehouse's staging area should be off limits to the business users and reporting/delivery application developers. Just as you don't want restaurant patrons wandering into the kitchen and potentially consuming semi-cooked food, you don't want busy ETL professionals distracted by unpredictable inquiries from data warehouse users. The consequences might be highly unpleasant if users dip their fingers into interim staging pots while data preparation is still in process. As with the restaurant kitchen, activities occur in the staging area that just shouldn't be visible to the data warehouse patrons. Once the data is ready and quality checked for user consumption, it's brought through the doorway into the warehouse's presentation area. Who knows, if you do a great job, perhaps you'll become a data warehouse celebrity chef a la Emeril Lagasse or Wolfgang Puck.

The Dining Room

Now turn your attention to the restaurant's dining room. What are the key factors that differentiate restaurants? According to the popular Zagat Surveys, restaurants around the world are rated on four distinct qualities:

- Food (quality, taste, and presentation)
- Decor (appealing, comfortable surroundings for the restaurant patrons)
- Service (prompt food delivery, attentive support staff, and food received as ordered)
- Cost

Most Zagat Survey readers focus initially on the food score when they're evaluating dining options. First and foremost, does the restaurant serve good food? That's the restaurant's primary deliverable. However, the decor, service, and cost factors also affect the patrons' overall dining experience and are considerations when evaluating whether to eat at a restaurant or not.

Of course, the primary deliverable from the data warehouse kitchen is the data in the presentation area. What data is available? Like the restaurant, the data warehouse provides "menus" to describe what's available via metadata, published reports, and parameterized analytic applications.

Is the data of high quality? Data warehouse patrons expect consistency and quality. The presentation area's data must be properly prepared and safe to consume.

In terms of decor, the presentation area should be organized for the comfort of its patrons. It must be designed based on the preferences expressed by the data warehouse diners, not the ETL staff. Service is also critical in the data warehouse. Data must be delivered, as ordered, promptly in a form that is appealing to the business user or reporting/delivery application developer. Finally, cost is a factor for the data warehouse. The data warehouse kitchen staff may be dreaming up elaborate, albeit expensive meals, but if there's no market at that price point, the restaurant won't survive.

If restaurant diners are pleased with their dining experience, then everything is rosy for the restaurant manager. The dining room is always busy; there's even a waiting list on some nights. The restaurant manager's performance metrics are all promising: high numbers of diners, table turnovers, and nightly revenue and profit, while staff turnover is low. Things look so good that the restaurant's owner is considering an expansion site to handle the traffic. On the other hand, if the restaurant's diners aren't happy, then things go downhill in a hurry. With a limited number of patrons, the restaurant isn't making enough money to cover its expenses (and the staff isn't making any tips). In a relatively short time period, the restaurant shuts down.

Restaurant managers often proactively check on their diners' satisfaction with the food and dining experience. If a patron is unhappy, they take immediate action to rectify the situation. Similarly, data warehouse managers should proactively monitor data warehouse satisfaction. You can't afford to wait to hear complaints. Often, people will abandon a restaurant without even voicing their concerns. Over time, you'll notice that diner counts have dropped, but you may not even know why.

Inevitably, the prior patrons of the data warehouse will locate another "restaurant" that better suits their needs and preferences, wasting the millions of dollars invested to design, build, and staff the data warehouse. Of course, you can prevent this unhappy ending by being an excellent, proactive restaurant manager. Make sure the kitchen is properly organized and utilized to deliver as needed on the presentation area's food, decor, service, and cost.

Ralph and I have been using this analogy for years; it strikes a chord and evolves as we discover more parallels between the restaurant and the data warehouse. The sign of a good metaphor is one that can be expanded and still hold together. Let us know if you have further embellishments to this analogy.

2.10 Easier Approaches for Harder Problems

Ralph Kimball, Design Tip #131, Feb 3, 2011

Data warehouses are under intense architectural pressure. The business world has become obsessed with data, and new opportunities for adding data sources to our data warehouse environments are arriving every day. In many cases analysts within our organizations are discovering "data features" that can be demonstrably monetized by the business to improve the customer experience, or increase the conversion rate to purchase a product, or discover a demographic characteristic of particularly valuable customers. When the analyst makes a compelling business case to bring a new data source into our environment there is often pressure to do it quickly. And then the hard work begins. How do we integrate the new data source with our current environment? Do the keys match? Are geographies and names defined the same way? What do we do about the quality issues in new data sources that are revealed after we do some sleuthing with our data profiling tool?

We often do not have the luxury of conforming all the attributes in the new data source to our current data warehouse content, and in many cases we cannot immediately control the data collection practices at the source in order to eliminate bad data. As data warehouse professionals we are expected to solve these problems without complaining!

Borrowing a page from the agile playbook, we need to address these big problems with an iterative approach that delivers meaningful data payloads to the business users quickly, ideally within days or weeks of first seeing the requirement. Let's tackle the two hardest problems: integration and data quality.

Incremental Integration

In a dimensionally modeled data warehouse, integration takes the form of commonly defined fields in the dimension tables appearing in each of the sources. We call these conformed dimensions. Take for example a dimension called Customer that is attached to virtually every customer-facing process for which we have data in the data warehouse. It is possible, maybe even typical, for the original customer dimensions supplied with each source to be woefully incompatible. There may be dozens or even hundreds of fields that have different field names and whose contents are drawn from incompatible domains. The secret powerful idea for addressing this problem is not to take on all the issues at once. Rather, a very small subset of the attributes in the Customer dimension is chosen to participate in the conforming process. In some cases, special new "enterprise attributes" are defined that are populated in a consistent way across all of the otherwise incompatible sources. For example, a new attribute could be called "enterprise customer category." Although this sounds like a rather humble start on the larger integration challenge, even this one attribute allows drilling across all of the data sources that have added this attribute to their customer dimension in a consistent way.

Once one or more conformed attributes exist in some or hopefully all of the data sources, you need a BI tool that is capable of issuing a federated query. We have described this final BI step many times in our classes and books, but the essence is that you fetch back separate answer sets from the disparate data sources, each constrained and grouped only on the conformed attributes, and then you sort merge these answer sets into the final payload delivered by the BI tool to the business user. There are many powerful advantages to this approach, including the ability to proceed incrementally by adding new conformed attributes within the important dimensions, by adding new data sources that sign up to using the conformed attributes, and being able to perform highly distributed federated queries across incompatible technologies and physical locations. What's not to like about this? See two articles in this *Reader* on techniques for drilling across: Article 13.21, *Simple Drill-Across in SQL*, and Article 13.22, *An Excel Macro for Drilling Across*.

Incremental Data Quality

Important issues of data quality can be addressed with the same mindset that we used with the integration problem. In this case, we have to accept the fact that very little corrupt or dirty data can be reliably fixed by the data warehouse team downstream from the source. The long term solution to data quality involves two major steps: First we have to diagnose and tag the bad data so that we can avoid being misled while making decisions; and second, we need to apply pressure where we can on the original sources to improve their business practices so that better data enters the overall data flow.

Again, like integration, we chip off small pieces of the data quality problem, in a nondisruptive and incremental way, so that over a period of time we develop a comprehensive understanding of where the data problems reside and what progress we're making in fixing them.

The data quality architecture that we recommend is to introduce a series of quality tests, or "screens" that watch the data flow and post error event records into a special dimensional model in the back room whose sole function is to record data quality error events.

Again, the development of the screens can proceed incrementally from a modest start to gradually create a comprehensive data quality architecture suffusing all of the data pipelines from the original sources through to the BI tool layer.

We have written extensively about the challenge of data quality. Please see article 11.19, *An Architecture for Data Quality*.

2.11 Expanding Boundaries of the Data Warehouse

Ralph Kimball, Design Tip #141, Dec 6, 2011

There is never a dull moment in the data warehouse world. In the past decade, we have seen operational data come thundering in, then an enormous growth of interest in customer behavior tracking, and in the past two years, big data. At the same time, there has been a steady stream of software and hardware changes impacting what we have to think about. We have big shifts in RDBMS architectures that include massively parallel processing, columnar store databases, in-memory databases, and database appliances. Data virtualization threatens to change where the data warehouse actually resides physically and where the processing steps occur.

Big data, in particular, has ushered in a whole competing paradigm to traditional RDBMSs named MapReduce and Hadoop, as well as data formats outside of the traditional comfort zone of relational tables. And let's not forget our increased governance responsibilities including compliance, security, privacy, and records retention. Whew! No wonder we get paid so much. Just kidding …

It is fair to ask at this juncture what part of all this IT activity is "data warehouse?"

Whenever I try to answer this question I go back to the data warehouse mission statement, which can be said in four words: Publish the Right Data. "Publish" means to present the data assets of the organization in the most effective possible way. Such a presentation must be understandable, compelling, attractively presented, and immediately accessible. Think of a high-quality conventional publication. "Right Data" means those data assets that most effectively inform decision makers for all types of decisions ranging from real-time tactical to long term strategic.

Taking the mission statement seriously means that the data warehouse must encompass all the components necessary to publish the right data. Yes, this is an expansive view! At the same time, the data warehouse actually has well-defined boundaries. The data warehouse is NOT responsible for original data generation, or defining security or compliance policies, or building storage infrastructure, or building enterprise service oriented architecture (SOA) infrastructure, or implementing the enterprise message bus architecture, or figuring out software-as-a-service (SAAS) applications, or committing all of IT to the cloud, or building the enterprise master data management (MDM) system. Does that make you feel better?

All of the above-mentioned exclusions (shall we say headaches?) are necessary parts of the IT ecosystem that the data warehouse absolutely needs and uses. We data warehousers need to focus on the key pieces that enable us to publish the right data. We must own and control the extraction interfaces to all of the data needed to fulfill our mission. That means considerable influence over the source systems, both internal and external, that provide us with our data. We must own and control the data virtualization specs, even if they sit right on top of operational systems. We must own and control everything that makes up the "platform" for BI, including all final presentation schemas, user views, and OLAP cubes. And finally, it must be clear to management that the new pockets of big data analytic modelers sprouting up in end user departments need to participate in the data warehouse mission. The new big data tools including Flume, Sqoop, Hadoop, Pig, Hive, HBase, Spark, MongoDB, and Cassandra are absolutely part of the data warehouse sphere of influence.

From time to time, vendors try to invalidate tried-and-true approaches so that they can position themselves as doing something new and different. Don't let them get away with that! Data warehousing has an enormous and durable legacy. Keep reminding IT management and senior business management of the natural and expected expanding boundaries of the data warehouse.

Chapter 3

Project/Program Planning

With the historical perspective and grounding from the previous chapter, it's time to get everyone organized to embark on a DW/BI project. We begin this chapter by focusing on the project team, their role as information publishers, and the sometimes insurmountable realities that they confront. We then turn our attention to the all important business stakeholders. Finally, we describe the Kimball Lifecycle approach for tackling your DW/BI initiatives.

Professional Responsibilities

We begin by discussing what the data warehouse/business intelligence manager and team should (and shouldn't) do.

3.1 Professional Boundaries

Ralph Kimball, DBMS, Jul 1998

This article and the next discuss the similarities between a data warehouse manager's job and the responsibilities of an editor in chief.

The data warehouse manager's job is potentially huge, offering many opportunities and just as many risks. The data warehouse manager has been given control of one of the most valuable assets of any organization: the data. Furthermore, the data warehouse manager is expected to interpret and deliver that asset to the rest of the organization in a way that makes it most useful. All eyes are on the data warehouse manager.

In spite of all this visibility, many newly appointed data warehouse managers are simply given their titles without a clear job definition or a clear sense of what is and is not their responsibility. As an industry, we have been groping for a definition of the data warehouse manager position. Perhaps this was appropriate in past years because we needed to define the job. We needed time to get some accumulated experience. We needed to test the boundaries of what being a data warehouse manager means. I think we are somewhat overdue in defining the data warehouse manager's job. It is not sufficient or helpful to just say that a data warehouse manager's job is to "bring all the data into a central place and make it available for management to make decisions." Although such a definition may be correct, it isn't precise enough for anyone to tell if the data warehouse manager has done the job well. In this article I'll begin to tackle the data warehouse manager's job definition. I will suggest a metaphor for the job that, if accurate, may provide a rich set of criteria to judge a "job well done." Furthermore, a clear definition will help senior IT executives understand what the data warehouse manager needs to do and, just as importantly, what things a data warehouse manager should not have to do.

A good metaphor for the job of the data warehouse manager is the job of an editor in chief for a magazine or newspaper. At a high level, the editor in chief:

- Collects input from a variety of sources, including third party authors, investigative reporters, and in-house writers
- Assures the quality of this input by correcting spelling, removing mistakes, and eliminating questionable material
- Applies broad editorial control over the nature of the published material and assures a consistent editorial view
- Publishes on a regular schedule
- Relies on and respects the trust of the readers
- Is named prominently on the masthead to serve as a clear communication as to where the buck stops
- Is driven by continuously changing demographics and reader interests
- Is driven by rapidly changing media technologies, especially the internet revolution that is happening as we speak
- Is very aware of the power of the media and consciously markets the publications

These statements seem a little obvious because we all know, based on experience, what the job title "editor in chief" implies. And most editors in chief understand very clearly that they don't create the content about which they write, report, or publish. They are, rather, the purveyors of content created by others.

I hope that you have been struck by the many parallels between the job of an editor in chief and the job of a data warehouse manager. Perhaps a good way to sum this up is to say that the job of the data warehouse manager is to *publish the enterprise's data*.

Let's examine the parallels between these two jobs. In most cases, the data warehouse manager is aggressively pursuing the same goals as the editor in chief. In some cases, the data warehouse manager could learn some useful things by emulating the editor in chief. At a high level, the data warehouse manager:

- Collects data inputs from a variety of sources, including legacy operational systems, third party data suppliers, and informal sources

- Assures the quality of these data inputs by correcting spelling, removing mistakes, eliminating null data, and combining multiple sources
- Applies broad data stewardship over the nature of the published data and assures the use of conformed dimensions and facts across the disparate business process subject areas (which can be thought of as separate publications). See article 5.14, *Data Stewardship 101: The First Step to Quality and Consistency.*
- Releases the data from the ETL data staging area to the individual data subject areas on a regular schedule
- Relies on and respects the trust of the business users
- Is named prominently on the organizational chart to serve as a clear communication as to where the buck stops
- Is driven by the continuously changing business requirements of the organization and the increasingly available sources of data
- Is driven by rapidly changing media technologies, especially the current internet revolution
- Is very aware of the business significance of the data warehouse and consciously "captures" and takes credit for the business decisions made as a result of using the data warehouse

In addition, the data warehouse manager has a number of responsibilities that most editors do not have to think about. These special data warehouse responsibilities include backing up the data sources and the final, published versions of the data. These backups must be available—sometimes on an emergency basis—to recover from disasters or provide detail that wasn't published the first time around. The data warehouse manager must deal with overwhelming volumes of data and must diligently avoid being stranded by obsolete backups. He or she must replicate published data in a highly synchronized way to each of the downstream "publications" (business process subject areas) and provide a detailed audit trail of where the data came from and what its lineage and provenance is. The data warehouse manager must be able to explain the significance and true meaning of the data and justify each editing step that the ETL may have performed on the data before it was published, and must protect published data from all unauthorized readers. Of all the responsibilities the data warehouse manager has in addition to the classic editorial responsibilities, this security requirement is the most nightmarish; it is also the biggest departure from the editing metaphor. The data warehouse manager must somehow balance the goal of publishing the data to everyone with the goal of protecting the data from everyone. No wonder data warehouse managers have an identity problem.

In the discussion of the editor in chief's responsibilities, we remarked that nearly all editors in chief understand that they are merely the purveyors of content created by others. Most editors don't have a boundary problem in this area. Many data warehouse managers, on the other hand, do. Frequently, the data warehouse manager agrees to be responsible for allocations, forecasts, behavior scoring, modeling, or data mining. This is a major mistake! All these activities are content creation activities. It is understandable that the data warehouse manager is drawn into these activities, because, in many cases, there is no prior model for the division of the new responsibilities between IT and a business user group such as finance. If an organization has never had good allocated costs, for example, and the data warehouse manager is asked to present these costs, then the data warehouse manager is also going to be expected to create these costs.

The data warehouse manager should treat allocations, forecasts, behavior scoring, modeling, and data mining as clients of the data warehouse. These activities should be the responsibilities of various analytic groups in the finance and marketing departments, and these groups should have an arm's length relationship to the data warehouse. They should consume warehouse data as inputs to their analytic activities and, possibly, engage the data warehouse to republish their results when they are done. But these activities should not be mixed into all the mainline publishing activities of the data warehouse.

Creating allocation rules that let you assign infrastructure costs to various product lines or marketing initiatives is a political hot potato. It is easy for a data warehouse manager to get pulled into creating allocations because it is a necessary step in bringing up a profit-oriented subject area. The data warehouse manager should be aware of the possibility of this task being thrust on the data warehouse and should tell management that, for example, the "data warehouse will be glad to publish the allocation numbers once the finance department has created them." In this case, the editorial metaphor is a useful guide.

Beyond the boundaries defined by the editorial metaphor, we must add the responsibilities of backing up data, auditing the extract and transform processes, replicating to the presentation tables of the data warehouse, and managing security. These tasks make the data warehouse manager's job more technical, more intricate, and at the same time, broader than the job of an editor in chief.

Perhaps this article can stimulate the development of criteria for data warehouse manager training and help IT executive management appreciate what data warehouse managers face in doing their jobs. In many ways, the responsibilities discussed in this article have been implicitly assumed, but the data warehouse managers have neither had them spelled out, nor been compensated for them.

Finally, by focusing on boundaries, we can see more clearly some content creation activities the data warehouse manager should leave on the table. Allocating, forecasting, behavior scoring, modeling, and data mining are valuable and interesting, but they are done by the readers (business users) of the data warehouse. Or to put it another way, if the data warehouse manager takes on these activities, then the data warehouse manager (of course) should get two business cards and two salaries. Then the boundaries can be twice as large.

3.2 An Engineer's View

Ralph Kimball, Intelligent Enterprise, *Jul 26, 2002*

This article builds on the preceding one to illustrate the evolution of the publisher metaphor.

Based on reader feedback, I've decided to do something I haven't done for quite some time: go back to lay the foundation for what data warehouse designers do, and why they use certain techniques.

Doing this also lets me restate the assumptions and techniques with the benefit of hindsight and more experience. I hope the results are tighter, more up to date, and more clearly worded.

The Data Warehouse Mission

At the outset, I want to share a perspective that I take very seriously, and in some ways is the foundation for all my work in data warehousing. It's the publishing metaphor.

Imagine that you've been asked to take over responsibility for a high quality magazine. If you approach this responsibility thoughtfully, you'll do the following 12 things:

- Identify your readers demographically.
- Find out what the readers want in this kind of magazine.
- Identify loyal readers who'll renew their subscriptions and buy products from the magazine's advertisers.
- Find potential new readers and make them aware of the magazine.
- Choose the magazine content most appealing to the target readers.
- Make layout and rendering decisions that maximize the readers' pleasure.
- Uphold high quality writing and editing standards and adopt a consistent presentation style.
- Continuously monitor the accuracy of the articles and the advertisers' claims.
- Keep the readers' trust.
- Develop a good network of writers and contributors.
- Draw in advertising and run the magazine profitably.
- Keep the business owners happy.

While these responsibilities may seem obvious, here are some dubious "goals" that you should avoid:

- Build the magazine around the technology of a particular printing press.
- Put most of your management energy into the printing press operational efficiencies.
- Use a highly technical and complex writing style that many readers may not understand.
- Use an intricate and crowded layout style that's difficult to read and navigate.

By building the whole business on the foundation of serving the readers, your magazine is likely to be successful.

The point of this metaphor, of course, is to draw the parallel between being a conventional publisher and being a data warehouse project manager. I'm convinced that the correct job description for a data warehouse project manager is *publish the right data*. Your main responsibility is to serve your readers who are your business users. While you'll certainly use technology to deliver your data warehouse, the technology is at best a means to an end. The technology and the techniques you use to build your data warehouses shouldn't show up directly in your top 12 responsibilities, but the appropriate technologies and techniques will become much more obvious if your overriding goal is to effectively publish the right data.

Now let's recast the 12 magazine publishing responsibilities as data warehouse responsibilities:

- Understand your users by business area, job responsibilities, and computer tolerance.
- Find out what decisions the users want to make with the help of the data warehouse.
- Identify loyal users who will make effective decisions using the data warehouse.
- Find potential new users and make them aware of the data warehouse.
- Choose the most effective, actionable subset of the data to present in the data warehouse, drawn from the vast universe of possible data in your organization.
- Make the user screens and applications much simpler and more template driven, explicitly matching the screens to the cognitive processing profiles of your users.
- Make sure your data is accurate and can be trusted, labeling it consistently across the enterprise.
- Continuously monitor the accuracy of the data and the content of the delivered reports.
- Keep the business users' trust.
- Continuously search for new data sources, and continuously adapt the data warehouse to changing data profiles and reporting requirements.
- Take a portion of the credit for business decisions made using the data warehouse, and use these successes to justify your staffing, software, and hardware expenditures.
- Keep the business users, their executives, and your boss happy.

If you do a good job with all these responsibilities, I think you'll be a great data warehouse project leader! Conversely, go down through the list and imagine what happens if you omit any single item. Ultimately your data warehouse would have problems.

Design Drivers

Let's boil down the data warehouse mission into some simple but specific design drivers, because as engineers we have to build something. Our users will be happy if we publish the "right" data that gives them insight into their key business questions, in a way that they perceive as simple and fast.

These design drivers dominate everything. As an engineer, I know I can't compromise them or my data warehouse will fail. But, assuredly, there are other real-world constraints that I have to pay attention to. I also try to:

- Limit administrative overhead in the design and production phases.
- Limit the total cost of ownership.
- Reduce the risk of no result or an irrelevant result.
- Reduce the risks of centralization.

Design Constraints

As data warehouse designers, we live in an enormously complex world. I'm almost reluctant to make a list of the implicit constraints we have to live with because I worry that the new student will decide on a different career! But here's my list:

- Necessity for decentralized, incremental development because very few organizations are truly, effectively centralized in every function
- Requirement to integrate multiple technologies that are incompatible at various levels because there are many vendors of technology
- Truly unreasonable demands for rapid deployment (business users think that six weeks is a little excessive)
- Need to allow for continuous change (little surprises and big surprises)
- Inevitability of remote independent data marts springing up
- Users' desire for instantaneous system response

And three more requirements that have been added just since 2000:

- The so-called 360 degree view of the customer
- Tracking, storing, and predicting customer behavior
- Access to atomic data, delivered from operational systems in real time, and seamlessly connected to old history

And finally a requirement that has grown explosively since 2010:

- Access to big data in many forms, including machine data from the Internet of Things, streaming event data from the internet, unstructured textual data, and non-textual data such as images

The Engineer's Response

So what does an engineer make of all this? All these requirements and expectations placed on us are beyond overwhelming. Well, building a bridge across the Golden Gate must have seemed pretty impossible in 1930. And how about going to the moon in the 1960s? Data warehouses may not be that hard, but the examples are inspiring.

A good engineer first sorts through all the available mathematics and science, accumulating ideas and possible techniques. Some of the math and science is practical and some isn't. This is the time to be a skeptic. Next, the engineer decomposes the design problem. If it can be broken into pieces that are relatively independent, then the engineer can focus on manageable parts.

Once the design is started, the engineer must continuously choose practical techniques that are reusable, simple, and symmetrical. Idealized designs and assumptions need to be recognized and thrown out. There's no such thing as perfect information or control (especially of people), either at the beginning of a project or after the project is in production. Throughout the project, the engineer must be a good manager. And, finally, the original design goals have to be constantly in view to provide the foundation for all decisions.

3.3 Beware the Objection Removers

Ralph Kimball, Intelligent Enterprise, *Sep 1, 2005*

An *objection remover* is a claim made during the sales cycle intended to counter a fear or concern that you have. Objection removers occupy a gray zone in between legitimate benefits and outright misrepresentations. While an objection remover may be technically true, it's a distraction intended to make you close the door on your concern and move forward in the sales process without careful thinking.

Objection removers crop up in every kind of business, but often the more complex and expensive your problem is, the more likely objection removers will play a role. In the data warehouse world, classic objection removers include:

- You don't need a data warehouse because now you can query the source systems directly. (Whew! That data warehouse was expensive and complicated. Now I don't need it.)
- You can leave the data in a normalized structure all the way to the business user query tools because our system is so powerful that it easily handles the most complex queries. (Whew! Now I can eliminate the step of preparing so-called queryable schemas. That gets rid of a whole layer of application specialists, and my business users can sort out the data however they want. And since I don't need to transform the source data, I can run my whole shop with one DBA!)
- Our "applications integrator" makes incompatible legacy systems smoothly function together. (Whew! Now I don't have to face the issues of upgrading my legacy systems or resolving their incompatibilities.)
- Centralizing customer management within our system makes your customer matching problems go away and provides one place where all customer information resides. (Whew! Now I don't need a system for deduplication or merge-purge, and this new system will feed all my business processes.)
- You don't need to build aggregates to make your data warehouse queries run fast. (Whew! I can eliminate a whole layer of administration and all those extra tables.)
- Leave all your security concerns to the IT security team and their LDAP server. (Whew! Security is a big distraction, and I don't like dealing with all those personnel issues.)
- Centralizing all IT functions lets you establish control over the parts of your data warehouse. (Whew! By centralizing, I'll have everything under my control, and I won't have to deal with remote organizations that do their own thing.)
- Leave your backup worries behind with our comprehensive solution. (Whew! I didn't really have a comprehensive plan for backup, and I have no idea what to do about long term archiving.)

■ Build your data warehouse in 15 minutes. (Whew! Every data warehouse development plan I've reviewed recently has proposed months of development!)

Objection removers are tricky because they are true—at least if you look at your problem narrowly. And objection removers are crafted to erase your most tangible headaches. The relief you feel when you suddenly imagine that a big problem has gone away is so overwhelming that you feel the impulse to rush to the finish line and sign the contract. That is the purpose of an objection remover in its purest form. It doesn't add lasting value; it makes you close the deal.

So, what to do about objection removers? We don't want to throw the baby out with the bathwater. Showing the salesperson to the door is an overreaction. Somehow we have to stifle the impulse to sign the contract and step back to see the larger picture. Here are four steps you should keep in mind when you encounter an objection remover:

1. **Recognize the objection remover.** When your radar is working, spotting objection removers is easy. A startling claim that flies in the face of conventional practice is almost always too good to be true. A sudden feeling of exhilaration or relief means that you have listened to an objection remover. In some cases, the claim is written in black and white and is sitting in plain view on your desk. In other cases, you need to do a little self analysis and be honest about why you're suddenly feeling so good.

2. **Frame the larger problem.** Objection removers work because they narrow the problem to one specific pain, which they decisively nail, but they often ignore the larger complexity of the problem or transfer the hard work to another stage of the process. Once you recognize an objection remover, count to 10 before signing the contract and force yourself to think about the larger context of your problem. This is the key step. You'll be shocked by how these claims lose their luster, if only they are placed in the proper context. Let's take a second look at the objection removers listed earlier.

   ■ **You don't need a data warehouse; you can query the source systems directly.** This is an old and venerable objection remover that has been around since the earliest days of data warehousing. Originally, it was easy to disqualify this objection remover because the source transaction systems didn't have the computing capacity to respond to complex user queries. But with the recent technical advances in grid computing and powerful parallel processing hardware, a good salesperson can argue that the source systems do have the capacity to do the double duty of processing transactions and serving user queries. But in this case there's a larger issue: The data warehouse is the comprehensive historical repository for perhaps your most important company asset—your data. The data warehouse is purpose-built to house, protect, and expose your historical data. Certainly these issues have come sharply into focus with the recent emphasis on compliance and business transparency. Transaction processing systems are virtually never built with the goal of maintaining an accurate historical perspective on your data. For instance, if the transaction system ever modifies a data element by destructively overwriting it, you've lost historical context. You must have a copy of the transaction system because the historical context is structurally different from the volatile data in a transaction system. Thus, you must have a data warehouse.

- **You can leave your data in a normalized structure all the way to the users.** The larger issue: Decision support systems will only work if they seem simple to the business users. Building a simple view is hard work that requires very specific design steps. In many ways, the delivery of data to the business users and their BI tools is analogous to the final delivery made by a restaurant chef from the kitchen through the door to the customers in the dining room. We all recognize the contribution made by the chef in making sure the food is perfect just as it's being taken from the kitchen. The transfer of an (uncooked) complex database schema to business users and their immediate application support specialists is in some ways worse than an objection remover: It's a snare and a delusion. To make this work, all the transformations necessary to create a simple view of the data are still required, but the work has been transferred out of IT to the business user. Finally, if the simple data views are implemented as relational database "views," then the simple queries all devolve into extremely complex SQL that requires an oversized machine to process!

- **Applications integrators make incompatible legacy systems smoothly function together.** The larger issue: Incompatibilities don't come from deficiencies in any technology, but rather from the underlying business practices and business rules that create the incompatible data in the first place. For any application integration technology to work, a lot of hard work must take place up front, defining new business practices and business rules. This hard work is mostly people sitting around a table hammering out those practices and rules, getting executive support for the business process reengineering that must be adopted across the organization, and then manually creating the database links and transformations that make an integrated system work.

- **A centralized customer management system makes your customer data issues go away.** This is a subtle objection remover that's not as blatant as the first three. Probably every company would benefit from a rational single view of their customers. But only a core part of the customer identity should be centralized. Once a single customer ID has been created and deployed through all customer-facing processes, and selected customer attributes have been standardized, there remain many aspects of the customer that should be collected and maintained by individual systems. In most cases, these systems are located remotely from a centralized site.

- **You don't need to build aggregates.** The larger issue: Data warehouse queries typically summarize large amounts of data, which implies a lot of disk activity. Supporting a data warehouse requires that you constantly monitor patterns of queries and respond with all the technical tools possible to improve performance. The best ways to improve query performance in data warehouse applications, in order of effectiveness, have proven to be:

1. Clever software techniques building indexes on the data
2. Aggregates and aggregate navigation
3. Large amounts of RAM
4. Fast disk drives
5. Hardware parallelism

Software beats hardware every time. The vendors who talk down aggregates are hardware vendors who want you to improve the performance of slow queries on their massive, expensive hardware. Aggregates, including materialized views, occupy an important place in the overall portfolio of techniques for improving performance of long-running queries. They should be used in combination with all the software and hardware techniques to improve performance.

- **Leave all your security concerns to the IT security team.** The larger issue: Data warehouse security can only be administered by simultaneously being aware of data content and the appropriate user roles entitled to use that data. The only staff who understands both these domains is the data warehouse staff. Controlling data security is a fundamental and unavoidable responsibility of the data warehouse team.

- **Centralizing all IT functions lets you establish control over the parts of your data warehouse.** This objection remover is a cousin of the earlier application integration claim. But this general claim of centralization is more dangerous because it is less specific and therefore harder to measure. Strong centralization has always appealed to the IT mentality, but in the largest organizations, centralizing all IT functions through a single point of control has about as much chance of succeeding as a centrally planned economy. The grand experiment of centrally planned economies in Eastern Europe lasted most of the 20th century and was a spectacular failure. The arguments for centralization have a certain consistency, but the problem is that it's too expensive and too time consuming to do fully centralized planning, and these idealistically motivated designs are too insular to be in touch with dynamic, real-world environments. These plans assume perfect information and perfect control, and are too often designs of what we'd like to have, not designs reflecting what we actually have. Every data architect in charge of a monolithic enterprise data model should be forced to do business user support.

- **Leave your backup worries behind you.** Developing a good backup and recovery strategy is a complex task that depends on the content of your data and the scenarios under which you must recover that data from the backup media. There are at least three independent scenarios:

1. Immediate restart or resumption of a halted process such as a data warehouse load job
2. Recovery of a data set from a stable starting point within the past few hours or days, as when a physical storage medium fails
3. Very long term recovery of data when the original application or software environment that handles the data may not be available

The larger picture for this objection remover, obviously, is that each of these scenarios is highly dependent on your data content, your technical environment, and the legal requirements, such as compliance, that mandate how you maintain custody of your data. A good backup strategy requires thoughtful planning and a multipronged approach.

■ **Build your data warehouse in 15 minutes.** I've saved the best one for last! The only way you can build a data warehouse in 15 minutes is to narrow the scope of the data warehouse so drastically that there's no extraction, no transformation, and no loading of data in a format meant for consumption by your BI tools. In other words, the definition of a 15-minute data warehouse is one that is already present in some form. Too bad this objection remover is so transparent; it doesn't even offer a temporary feeling of relief.

There's always a letdown after shining a bright light on these objection removers by examining their larger context. Life is complex, after all. Let's finish our list of four steps:

3. **Create the counterargument.** Remember, most objection removers aren't patently fraudulent, but by creating a good counterargument, you'll remove the impulse factor and understand the full context of your problem. This is also an interesting point at which you'll see if the salesperson has a textured, reasonable view of a product or service.
4. **Make your decision.** It's perfectly reasonable to buy a product or service even when you've detected an objection remover. If you've placed it in an objective context or dismissed it altogether yet are still feeling good about the product, then go for it!

3.4 What Does the Central Team Do?

Ralph Kimball, DBMS, Jun 1997

Are you part of the central data warehouse team in your large organization? Do you also work with remote divisional or departmental teams implementing far-flung independent data marts? Do you wonder what your role should be versus the divisional teams' role? If these questions are familiar to you, you may be frustrated because you feel you have an important responsibility in your central role, yet you may not actually own anything. Even worse, perhaps the divisional teams are implementing their own subject area data stores and are charging ahead with their own technologies, vendor selections, and logical and physical database designs.

If you are part of the central data warehouse team, you need to play an active role in defining and controlling your enterprise data warehouse. You should not be content to just be a liaison, a recommender, or some kind of ill-defined glue that holds projects together. You need to be a leader and a provider, and you must be very visible to the separate divisional teams implementing their own subject area data marts.

Conversely, if you are a part of a decentralized divisional data warehouse team, you should expect the central team to provide you with some very valuable services and impose some noticeable structure and discipline on your effort. You are a part of an overall enterprise, and you need to conform to these structures and disciplines so that the data from your division can be usefully combined with the data from other divisions.

The central data warehouse team has three major responsibilities that not only are essential to the integrity of the overall data warehousing effort, but cannot be provided by any of the individual divisions. These responsibilities are defining and publishing the corporate dimensions, providing cross-divisional applications, and defining a consistent data warehouse security architecture for the enterprise.

Defining and Publishing Corporate Dimensions

If your organization has multiple lines of business, and if you have any interest in combining these lines of business into an overall framework, you need to identify four or five dimensions that are common to the multiple lines of business. The most obvious corporate dimensions are customer, product, geography, and date. Since this article was written in 1997, the industry has given a name to defining and publishing corporate dimensions: master data management (MDM).

The customer dimension has one record for each one of your customers (actually, one record for each historical description of each customer). Although this seems obvious, the crucial step is to make sure that each divisional data mart (subject area) uses the same single customer dimension wherever there is a reference to customer. Each division will therefore see the customer the same way. Individual divisions will be able to see the relationship other divisions have with the customer, and the enterprise will, perhaps for the first time, be able to see the whole customer relationship.

The requirement that each division must always use the corporate customer dimension is a strong requirement that will impact everyone. From the central team's perspective, the corporate customer dimension must embrace the complete range of possible customers. The key for corporate customer almost certainly will need to be an artificial customer number defined and created by the central data warehouse team. No individual divisional customer number will be administered and controlled in a way that serves the needs of the entire enterprise. The descriptive attributes for customer will need to be a broad set that includes all of the desired descriptors for all of the divisional groups. Hopefully the central data warehouse team can meet with the divisional groups and try to compress and standardize the various descriptors into a reasonable working set, but in the long run there is no absolute need to force any individual group to give up its idiosyncratic customer descriptors. Because dimension tables are generally much smaller than fact tables in a dimensional data warehouse design, there is room for multiple sets of customer descriptors in the same customer dimension record. In banks, I have often seen the master customer record contain 200 descriptive attributes. I advocate making this customer table a single flat, denormalized table in order to improve user understandability and allow the exciting new bitmap indexing technologies to speed lookup. The leading database vendors all have bitmap indexes that thrive on fat, wide, denormalized dimension tables.

The need to standardize on a corporate definition of customer is a very important central team responsibility. This need will arise whenever management wants to look at overall customer relationships, and it will arise whenever your enterprise makes an acquisition. The good news is that you just acquired your biggest competitor. The bad news is that you must now merge the separate customer dimensions.

Often there will be no individual division willing or able to provide the corporate customer dimension. Yet frequently these same divisions will be eager to receive such a customer dimension from you, the central team. Even the production online transaction processing (OLTP) systems in the division may be willing to upload the central data warehouse's customer dimension if it contains cleaned and corrected customer addresses. In these cases, the central data warehouse team becomes the creator and provider of the master enterprise customer file.

The failure to enforce the use of a corporate customer dimension is a very serious lapse and therefore must be addressed by the central data warehouse team. The ability to "drill across" separate business processes can only be accomplished if all of the shared dimensions in the separate data marts are conformed. In other words, if two data marts have the same dimension, such as customer, these two customer dimensions must share a set of common attribute fields that are drawn from the same domains. The descriptive attributes within these shared dimensions must be defined and populated in a consistent way. Allowing two customer dimensions in different business process subject areas to drift apart means that the two subject areas cannot be used together. Ever.

The product dimension has one record for each one of your products or services. As the central data warehouse team, you must be the judge as to whether your individual divisions have enough in common to warrant building a corporate product dimension. In a tightly integrated business, such as the multiple geographic divisions of a big retailer, it seems obvious that a single master product dimension is called for, even if there are regional variations in the products sold. In such a case, you probably already have a production group that works constantly to define this product master and download its descriptions and price points to the cash registers of the individual stores. The central data warehouse team can easily work with this group to create a proper product dimension for the enterprise. In a financial services organization, such as a bank or insurance company, there is a lot of interest in a core or super-type view of the business that groups all of the products and services into a single hierarchical framework. But there will be lots of special descriptive attributes that only make sense for a single division, such as mortgage loans versus credit card accounts. In this case, the best approach is to create a core product dimension containing only common attributes, and a set of custom or sub-type product dimensions that are different for each division. This *heterogeneous product* design is discussed in article 9.17, *Hot-Swappable Dimensions*. Finally, if your enterprise is so loosely integrated that your products have almost nothing in common, and if your management has never bothered to define a set of hierarchies that group all of the different divisional products into a common framework, then you may not need a corporate product dimension. Just remember, if you don't create a conformed product dimension, you will not be able to combine the separate divisional data marts together.

The geography dimension has one record for each one of your districts, regions, or zones. If your individual divisions have incompatible sales geographies, then the separate division data marts can only be used together at the highest common geographical aggregate. If you are lucky, this highest geographical aggregate will be something useful to all the data marts, such as state.

The date dimension has one record for each calendar time period. Hopefully all of your divisions operate on the same calendar and report on the same fiscal periods. If at all possible, all reporting should be done either at an individual daily grain or at the fiscal period grain, such as month. In this case, days always roll up to the fiscal periods, and the fiscal periods roll up to years. It becomes a monumental headache if the separate divisions have incompatible reporting calendars. Fortunately, the central data warehouse team has a strong ally in the corporate financial reporting group who hopefully is in the process of standardizing the reporting calendars of the divisions. Separate databases denominated in weeks and months should be avoided at all costs because these time dimensions cannot usefully be conformed, and the week databases will always be isolated from the month databases.

Providing Cross-Divisional Applications

The central data warehouse team is in a unique position of being able to provide cross-divisional applications. A value chain of distributed business process subject areas can be assembled from each of the separate divisions. In article 6.2, *Drilling Down, Up, and Across*, I showed six subject areas for a clothing store retailer. These subject areas may have been built at different times, but they share a number of common dimensions. From the previous discussion, it should be clear that the central team should define and enforce the use of these dimensions.

With the proper tools, it is fairly easy to build cross-divisional applications in these environments that are capable of drilling across. I discussed drilling across in some detail in article 13.25, *Features for Query Tools*.

The central team's responsibility is to provide a reporting tool that allows drilling across and to enforce the use of common dimensions.

Defining a Consistent Data Warehouse Security Architecture

The data warehouse team must play a very proactive role in understanding and defining security. The data warehouse team must include a new member: the security architect.

The security architect for the data warehouse should define and enforce a data warehouse security plan for the enterprise and all of the individual subject areas; define consistent user privilege profiles; identify all possible access points in the corporate network, including every modem and every web interface; implement a single logon protocol so that a user is authenticated once for the whole network; track and analyze all attempts to override security or gain unauthorized access to the warehouse; implement a link encryption scheme, or its equivalent, for remote users; implement a remote user authentication scheme, such as a biometric reader at each PC, that is more reliable than typed user passwords; and educate the divisional teams about security issues and consistent administration of the subject areas.

3.5 Avoid Isolating DW and BI Teams

Margy Ross, Design Tip #64, *Feb 8, 2005*

Several people have asked a similar question recently. "Should the DW or BI team gather requirements from the business?" Honestly, this question makes the hair start to stand up on the back of my neck. I'm concerned that too many organizations have overly compartmentalized their data warehouse and business intelligence teams.

Of course, some of this division is natural, especially when the resources allocated to DW/BI grow as the environment expands, creating an obvious span of control issues. Also, separation of labor allows for specialization. Viewing the overall DW/BI environment as analogous to a commercial restaurant—some team members are highly skilled in kitchen food preparation, while others are extremely attentive to the needs of the restaurant patrons, ensuring their return for a subsequent visit. There are likely few waiters who should suddenly don the chef's garb, and vice versa.

Despite the distribution of responsibilities, the kitchen and dining rooms of a restaurant are tightly entwined. Neither can be successful on its own. The best chefs need a well-trained, well-oiled front room machine; the most attractive dining room requires depth and quality from the kitchen. Only the complete package can deliver consistent, pleasurable dining experiences (and sustainability as a restaurant). That's why the chef and wait staff often huddle to educate and compare notes before a meal rush.

In the world of DW/BI, we've observed that some teams take a more isolationist approach. Matters are further complicated by the complexities and realities of organizational culture and politics. There may be a kitchen and dining area, but there's no swinging door between the two. It's like there's a transom (above eye level) where orders and plates are flung back and forth, but the two teams of specialists aren't communicating or cooperating. In this scenario, you end up with data models that can't reasonably be populated; or data models that don't address the diners' needs and/or leverage their tools; or diners' tools that are overtaxed or slow performing because they're repeatedly doing the work that could have been done once in the kitchen and shared throughout the organization. In the worst case, the wall becomes so impenetrable that the BI dining room substitutes a different kitchen (or creates their own) to source meals.

The data warehouse should be the foundation for effective business intelligence. Too many organizations have focused on one without the other. Sure, you can create a data warehouse without concern for business intelligence, and vice versa, but neither situation is sustainable for long. Isolationism is not a healthy approach for building and supporting the DW/BI environment. Even if you don't report into the same management structure, collaboration and communication are critical.

3.6 Better Business Skills for BI and Data Warehouse Professionals

Warren Thornthwaite, Intelligent Enterprise, *May 11, 2008*

Anyone who takes even a cursory glance at the common DW/BI failure points would spot the pattern: The hardest parts for most teams are understanding business issues and handling cross-organizational interactions. The challenges will become even more common as the DW/BI system evolves into a standard component of the IT environment, thus weakening the connection to the business.

Historically, DW/BI projects were driven by visionary people who were conversant in both business and technology. They understood the potential of better business insight and were motivated to help the DW/BI team deliver on it. As DW/BI systems have become commonplace, teams are now often made up of more technically oriented people. This change is not bad in and of itself, but it does mean that DW/BI teams will need to build up skills around understanding business requirements and strengthening relationships with business users.

Let's be clear here: Not everyone on the team needs to get an MBA, but everyone on the team should develop a basic understanding of how their organization works, how to work well with other people, and how to communicate more effectively, both in writing and in business meetings and presentations. This article presents advice on improving in these areas, along with valuable resources for professional development.

Building Business Understanding

To better understand business, the first place to start is with documents from your own organization. Annual reports, strategic plans, marketing plans, and internal vision documents all provide solid insight into your business and its challenges and opportunities. However, without a basic business understanding, you may not get full value from these documents. Fortunately, there are many readily accessible resources to gain this understanding. Start with a book or two. There are at least a dozen good books available that attempt to boil a two-year MBA program down into a short, easy read. Here's a book that offers a good overview of the basics of business:

> *The Ten-Day MBA: A Step-By-Step Guide to Mastering the Skills Taught in America's Top Business Schools, 4th edition*, by Steven A. Silbiger (Collins, 2012)

Once your senior management team has selected its top priorities for the DW/BI system and you want to learn more about it, seek out books that go into detail on those areas, whether it's marketing, sales, finance, promotions, manufacturing, logistics, or other functional areas. At this level, it's probably more valuable to take a course in the particular subject area rather than read a book. A good instructor can bring experience and perspective to the topic, drawing from multiple resources and adding exercises, examples, and anecdotes. You also get the benefit of interaction with classmates. If you can't find relevant courses at local universities, colleges, or community colleges, try looking online. Many major institutions offer online MBA courses. Search the internet and you will find plenty of options.

Building Interpersonal Skills

Some would argue that interpersonal skills are even more important than business acumen. Right from the start, someone on the DW/BI team must be able to persuasively articulate the vision and value of the system if you are to bring the project into existence or realign an existing project. Before any software is installed, someone on the team must ask questions about goals and elicit honest, useful answers without frightening or alienating the business users. Fortunately, these, too, are skills that can be learned. To master the basics of interpersonal and relationships skills, try one of these classics:

> *Crucial Conversations: Tools for Talking When Stakes are High, 2nd edition,* by Kerry Patterson, Joseph Grenny, Ron McMillan, Al Switzler (McGraw-Hill, 2011)
> *How to Win Friends and Influence People* by Dale Carnegie (Simon and Schuster, 1936, revised 1998)
> *The 7 Habits of Highly Effective People* by Stephen R. Covey (Simon and Schuster, 2013)

You will need to translate the advice offered in these books to your situation, but the core principles and recommendations are enduring. Basic principles such as having a sincere interest in others, listening to what they say, and looking for a win-win solution are the foundation of interpersonal success. Employ these principles with the goal of building a positive long term relationship with your business users—a relationship based on openness and trust. Use the techniques described in these books in a sincere fashion; if your intent is to manipulate or deceive, your efforts will backfire in the long run.

Building Public Speaking Skills

Every successful leader must be able to effectively communicate to groups. Public speaking and presentations involve two skill sets: the private act of preparing the content itself and the public act of delivering it to the audience. Both skill sets are addressed at length in these two books:

> *Presentation Zen: Simple Ideas on Presentation Design and Delivery* by Garr Reynolds (New Riders Press, 2011)
> *The Quick and Easy Way to Effective Speaking* by Dale Carnegie (Simon and Schuster, 1990; dated but still useful)

Getting better at speaking and presenting takes practice, but practicing in the work environment can be difficult and intimidating. It may help to take a class or find another venue for practice. One excellent, low cost option for developing public speaking skills is Toastmasters International (http://www.toastmasters.org/). Toastmasters is a nonprofit organization with thousands of local chapters across the globe. Toastmasters clubs typically have 20 to 30 members who meet two to four times per month for one or two hours. Members learn by speaking to the group and working with others in a supportive environment. The Toastmasters site can help you find clubs near you. There are also numerous commercial organizations that provide professional training in public speaking.

Building Written Communication Skills

Written communications are another pillar of the communications skill set. Much of how we interact with others is through the written word. Emails, proposals, requirements documents, and related documentation actually define the DW/BI system to 95 percent of your business user community. Poor or sloppy writing can distract the reader and undermine the value and credibility of the message. Try one or more of these bibles on good writing:

> *The Elements of Style* by William Strunk Jr. and E.B. White (Allyn and Bacon, 2011)
> *Keys to Great Writing* by Stephen Wilbers (Writers Digest Books, 2007)
> *On Writing Well: The Classic Guide to Writing Nonfiction* by William Zinsser (Collins, 2006)

In addition to these books, there are hundreds of web sites that offer writing tips and style guides. Take a look at Purdue University's Online Writing Lab (`http://owl.english.purdue.edu/`).

Most of what you find on the internet is a starting point at best. It's difficult to provide the depth of content available in a book or classroom on the web, but it's an easy place to start.

Practice, Practice, Practice

The internet and books are a good starting point, but they are no substitutes for practice. These are skills like any other; the more you work on them, the more you will improve. Every time you communicate with another person, you have an opportunity to practice your interpersonal skills. Every email, document, or even comments in your code present a chance to work on better writing. Opportunities to practice public speaking are all around you, but they need to be cultivated a bit. Ask for time in your team's weekly meeting to present an educational segment on an interesting problem you've been dealing with and how you solved it. Offer to teach one of the DW/BI system ad hoc tool classes. In fact, if you take it seriously—by preparing well, creating clear graphics, and practicing— even a design review is an opportunity to practice your presentation skills.

Ask your manager or human resources department for additional recommendations on communications resources. While you're at it, have them include the whole area of communications in your performance appraisal. That way, you get credit for doing what you need to do to be successful in your project. You also get a little external motivation.

If you are excited by the prospect of improving your business acumen, interpersonal skills, speaking talent, and writing abilities, then you are half way there! Your enthusiasm and motivation will make it a rewarding endeavor.

3.7 Risky Project Resources Are Risky Business

Margy Ross, Design Tip #173, Mar 9, 2015

Over the years, we've worked with countless exemplary DW/BI project team members: smart, skilled, dedicated, and motivated, coupled with a healthy dose of mutual trust, respect, and camaraderie with their teammates. Teams with members who possess these characteristics tend to fire on all cylinders, with the resulting whole often greater than the sum of the parts. But we've also run into risky project resources; in addition to being individual non-contributors, they can undermine the effectiveness of the entire DW/BI team. Model team members often become short-timers if the team is stacked with unproductive non-performers. We hope your team doesn't include resources that resemble the following profiles:

- Obstructionist debaters are perpetual naysayers who find fault with everything and get more satisfaction from the process of debating than the process of delivering.
- Heat seekers are always anxious to try the latest, greatest technical gadgets and gizmos regardless of whether they align with the DW/BI project's objectives.
- Cookie cutters continue to do exactly what's worked for them in the past, regardless of their latest assignment's nuances.
- Weed dwellers lose sight of the forest for the trees, focusing exclusively on the nitty-gritty details without regard to the bigger picture.
- Perpetual students and researchers want to read, read, and then read some more, but are disinclined to ever take action because there's always more to learn.
- Independent spirits march to their own drummer without regard to rules, standards, or accepted best practices.
- Honesty dodgers and problem hiders are always nodding "yes" and saying "no problem," even when serious issues are lurking just around the corner.
- Dysfunctional incompetents and mental retirees are checked out and unable to perform.
- Self-declared "know it all" experts don't need to listen because they already have all the answers—just ask them!
- Threatened worriers are so paralyzed with fear about what might happen that they respond by doing nothing at all.

Of course, even with superstar teammates, the right team leadership is also necessary. Hopefully your DW/BI project/program manager fits the following bill:

- Establishes a partnership with the business, including joint ownership for the DW/BI project/program, in part because they're respected by the business as being user-oriented rather than technology-focused.
- Demonstrates excellent interpersonal and organizational skills since the DW/BI project/program is a political and cultural animal.
- Recruits and retains resources with the talent to deliver, gets them operating cohesively from a common playbook, and understands that adding more mediocre players won't increase the team's chances of winning. Conversely, they also spot individuals who are slowing down the effort and proactively counsel them (or at least minimize the risk of project derailment).
- Listens keenly, plus communicates effectively and honestly, setting appropriate expectations and having the courage to say "no" when necessary.

- Optimally possesses some DW/BI domain expertise, in addition to strong project management skills. At a minimum, they're staying one chapter ahead of the project team in The Data Warehouse Lifecycle Toolkit …
- Understands that DW/BI success is directly tied to business acceptance. Period.

Inexperienced, ineffective, or indecisive DW/BI project managers who don't demonstrate these characteristics are equally risky project resources.

3.8 Implementation Analysis Paralysis

Bob Becker, Design Tip #66, Apr 11, 2005

Many data warehouse teams lean heavily toward the *doing* side. They leap into implementation activities without spending enough time and energy to develop their data models, identify thorough business rules, or plan their ETL data staging processes. As a result, they charge full speed ahead and end up reworking their processes, delivering bad or incomplete data, and generally causing themselves difficulty.

Other project teams have the opposite challenge. These teams are committed to doing their homework in all the critical areas. They are focused on data quality, consistency, completeness, and stewardship. However, these project teams sometimes bog down on issues that should have been resolved long ago. Of course, this impasse occurs at the worst time—the promised implementation dates are rapidly approaching and design decisions that should be well into implementation remain unresolved.

Naturally, the outstanding issues involve the most difficult choices and the project team disagrees on the best solutions. The easy issues have already been resolved and the solutions for the more difficult issues don't come as easily. Despite copious amounts of time spent in research, data profiling, design meetings, and informal discussions, nothing seems to move the team closer to a decision on the best approach. The project sits at a crossroads unable to move forward. By this time, fear has usually taken hold of the project team. The pressure is on.

One helpful approach is the use of an arbitrator, a trusted individual from outside the project team, to help move the team ahead. The outstanding issues are identified and meetings scheduled with the arbitrator and interested stakeholders. All participants must agree that a final decision will be made during these sessions. The arbitrator should establish a time box to limit discussion on each issue. Discuss the pros and cons of each approach one last time; the arbitrator makes the ultimate decision if the team can't reach consensus.

Another approach is to defer the unresolved issues until a future implementation after further research and discussion have identified an appropriate solution. The downsides to this approach are that the business requirements may not allow the issues to be deferred; postponing resolution may simply delay the inevitable without any significant gain.

There is a delicate balance between planning and doing in the data warehouse world. The goal is to identify reasonable solutions, not necessarily perfect solutions, so the team can transition from planning to implementation. There may still be more to learn, but the implementation process is often more effective at revealing the weak spots in the plan so they can be reinforced than any amount of talking and planning. In fact, for many of the hard choices, much of the information needed to make good choices can only be gained through trial and error.

Clearly, we are not advocating a casual, ad hoc approach to implementing the data warehouse. But we recognize that sometimes you must be pragmatic and move forward with less than ideal solutions that may need to be revisited to achieve your overall goals.

3.9 Contain DW/BI Scope Creep and Avoid Scope Theft

Bob Becker, Design Tip #154, Apr 1, 2013

Keeping tight control over the scope of your data warehouse/business intelligence (DW/BI) program is an important ingredient for success. Surprisingly, in some organizations it's equally important to ensure that the program doesn't suffer the theft of its scope after an otherwise good plan has been developed.

It's nearly impossible to tackle everything at once in a DW/BI program. The DW/BI team should identify subsets of effort based on the organization's business processes (see article 4.7, *Identifying Business Processes*), to phase the overall design, development, and deployment effort. Each phase or iteration should be meaningful and manageable. That is, the scope of effort should be large enough to result in a deliverable that provides meaningful business value, yet the scope should be small enough that the size of the team, the amount of data involved, and the communications requirements are "reasonable," especially given the resources allocated. It's important to avoid a large galactic scope that requires an army of resources and years of effort.

Once the scope for the project is established, there will inevitably be pressures to increase the scope. The most disruptive kind of scope creep is adding a new data source. Such a small incremental change in scope seems innocuous enough: "We are just adding a new cost element" or "We are just adding a weather source to the sales data." However, these so-called small changes add up over time. Often the DW/BI project team is at fault. Most DW/BI teams are very focused on serving the requirements of their business partners and sponsors. But you need to be careful in your enthusiasm to serve not to succumb to scope creep that negatively impacts your ability to meet expectations. While it's important to be flexible, it's necessary to say "no" to maintain scope, especially after the project is underway.

Scope creep also results from overzealous business partners and sponsors. Once they've thrown their support behind the DW/BI initiative, they're eager for quick progress and immediate results. They clamor for a greater scope (more business processes, more history, complex business rules, and so on) delivered more quickly than originally agreed upon. Clearly, the business's enthusiasm and support is positive, but so is sticking to the game plan and delivering the meaningful and manageable scope.

The main business sponsor in a DW/BI project needs to be a sophisticated observer of the technical development, as well as being a good manager.

A strong program/project manager is critical for successfully managing scope creep. The program manager's job will be made easier with a supportive business sponsor, a solid IT/business partnership, and a project team committed to meeting expectations. Frequent frank discussions between the program manager and business sponsor regarding the scope, challenges, progress, timing, and expectations will ensure everyone remains on the same page.

A second concern regarding project scope is scope theft. Scope theft occurs when proponents of other projects/programs within the organization try to attach their agenda to the DW/BI program. Often these efforts support important enterprise needs; however, when they become attached to the DW/BI program, it's usually the DW/BI program that suffers. These other efforts often lack business sponsorship, payback, and most importantly, funding. Supporters of these initiatives want to attach their agendas to the DW/BI program to leverage (i.e., steal) the momentum, senior management visibility, business sponsorship, staffing, and/or funding of the DW/BI initiative. These efforts are often repackaged as prerequisites, companion, and/or complementary efforts to the DW/BI initiative; suddenly the agreed scope of the DW/BI initiative has been usurped to focus on other initiatives.

There are a wide variety of enterprise initiatives that might potentially attach themselves to a DW/BI program. Some common examples include:

- Data quality initiatives focused on the replacement of aging operational systems
- Efforts to solve ongoing operational data integration challenges resulting from ineffective source system integration
- Master data management efforts
- IT projects focused on infrastructure re-platforming
- Implementation of a new role-based security infrastructure
- First deployment of a publish-subscribe style service oriented architecture (SOA)
- Utilization of off-premises cloud-based storage for the DW/BI initiative

There is little argument that these initiatives may be in the best interest of the enterprise (as is the DW/BI program); it's hard to dispute them conceptually. But, be wary. The reason the proponents of these initiatives want to leverage the DW/BI program is because their initiatives are complex, challenging, and expensive—they have likely been unable to secure the funding and sponsorship required to launch as a separate viable initiative. Since the DW/BI program has strong business support and funding, these competing initiatives look to cloak themselves as prerequisites or architectural requirements for the DW/BI program to move under its program umbrella.

The key question is whether these other initiatives become part and parcel of the DW/BI program. Typically not; it is likely best for both initiatives if they stand on their own merits. Otherwise the DW/BI program risks becoming a more IT-driven, galactic effort that delays the planned DW/BI capabilities and fails to meet the business's expectations. These other efforts are almost always clearly distinct from the DW/BI program and should be scoped, funded, sponsored, and governed independently. The DW/BI program manager and business sponsor need to be politically astute, cautious, and fight to ensure the DW/BI program remains independent. The DW/BI business sponsor must typically work through these challenges given that the organizational politics are often beyond the DW/BI program manager's control.

3.10 Are IT Procedures Beneficial to DW/BI Projects?

Joy Mundy, Design Tip #129, *Nov 3, 2010*

Back when the world was young and data warehousing was new, projects were a lot more fun. Kimball Group consultants (before there was a Kimball Group) were usually called in by the business users, and we'd help them design and build a system largely outside the aegis of corporate IT. In the intervening years—decades!—data warehousing has become a mainstream component of most IT organizations. For the most part, this is a good thing: The rigor that formal IT management brings to the DW makes our systems more reliable, maintainable, and performant. No one likes the idea of a BI server sitting under a business user's desk.

However, IT infrastructure is not always helpful to the DW/BI project. Sometimes it gets in the way, or is actively obstructionist. No doubt every little sub-specialty of information technology clamors that it is somehow different or special, but in the case of DW/BI, it's really true.

Specifications

The classic waterfall methodology subscribed to by many IT organizations has you develop a painfully detailed specification that's formalized, agreed to by the business and IT, and then turned over to the developers for implementation. Changes to the specification are tightly controlled, and are the exception rather than the rule.

If you try to apply a waterfall methodology to a DW/BI project, the best you'll end up with is a reporting system. The only things you can specify in sufficient detail are standard reports, so that's what you get: a system to deliver those standard reports. Many specs include a demand to support ad hoc analysis, and sometimes include examples of specific analyses the users would like to be able to do. But within the waterfall methodology it's impossible to clearly specify the boundaries and requirements of ad hoc analyses. So the project team "meets" this requirement by plopping an ad hoc query tool in front of the database.

It's really frustrating for the business users who are asked to write or approve the specification. They know the spec doesn't capture the richness of what they want, but they don't know how to communicate their needs to IT. I was recently in a meeting with a disgruntled business user who glared at the DW manager and said "Just provide me with a system that captures all the relationships in the data." If only that one sentence were sufficient for the poor guy to design a data warehouse.

The data model takes a much more central role in the system design for a data warehouse than for a transaction system. As Bob argued in article 4.12, *Using the Dimensional Model to Validate Business*

Requirements, the data model—developed collaboratively with the business users—becomes the core of the system specification. If the business users agree that any realistic analysis on the subject area can be met through the data in the model, and IT agrees the data model can be populated, the two sides can shake hands over the model. This is quite different from the standard waterfall approach, where the data modeler would take the spec into his cubicle and emerge several weeks later with the fully formed data model.

Naming Conventions

Another place I've seen formal IT processes get in the way is in naming the entities in the data warehouse. Of course, this is much less important an issue than the specifications, but I find myself deeply annoyed by naming dogmatisms. Because the DW database is designed for ad hoc use, business users are going to see the table and column names. They are displayed as report titles and column headers, so extremely long column names are problematic.

That said, naming conventions, the use of case words, and minimizing the use of abbreviations are all good ideas. But like all good ideas, temper them with reason. Taken to an extreme, you can end up with absurdly long column names like (and I'm not making this up) CurrentWorldwideTimezoneAreaIdentifier.

Although they give us something to laugh about, the real problem with absurdly long names is that the users won't tolerate them in their reports. They'll always be changing them in the report display, which means they'll use inconsistent names and introduce a new (and stupid) reason for the "multiple versions of the truth" problem. Please let your naming conventions be tempered by common sense.

Dogma

Unless it's Kimball Group dogma. I have heard all sorts of rules instituted by "someone at corporate IT." These include:

- All queries will be served from stored procedures (clearly someone doesn't understand what "ad hoc" means).
- All ETL will be done in stored procedures (All? Why?).
- All database constraints will be declared and enforced at all times (most of the time—sure; but all the time?).
- All tables will be fully normalized (no comment).
- There will be no transformations to data in the DW (I don't have any response to this one other than a puzzled expression).

Don't get us wrong… As easy as it is to mock some practices, we believe in professionally developed and managed DW/BI systems, which usually mean IT. The advantages are huge:

- Central skills in data modeling, ETL architecture, development, and operations are greatly leveraged from one project to the next.
- Professional development, including code check-ins, code reviews, ongoing regression testing, automated ETL, and ongoing management

- Solid bug tracking, release management techniques, and deployment procedures mean an IT-managed DW/BI system should more smoothly roll out improvements to a system already in production.
- Security and compliance

However, if you're on a project that's suffering under an IT mandate that makes no sense to you, don't be afraid to push back.

Justification and Sponsorship

With the project team roles and responsibilities defined, we shift our focus to the all important business stakeholders of the data warehouse program. We'll describe the habits that make or break a business sponsor, challenge the conventional view of total cost of ownership calculations, then close this section with guidance to boost your skills for interacting with the business.

3.11 Habits of Effective Sponsors

Margy Ross, Intelligent Enterprise, Sep 1, 2003

As data warehouse designers, you know how important a business executive sponsor is to your initiative. After focusing on data warehousing for the past two decades, I'm convinced that strong business sponsorship is the leading make-or-break indicator of data warehouse success. Having the right sponsor can overcome a multitude of shortcomings elsewhere in the project. On the other hand, sponsor turnover is one of the most common causes of data warehouse stagnation; unsponsored data warehouses simply don't survive.

In this article, I explore the characteristics that distinguish highly effective data warehouse sponsors. Sponsors who take their responsibilities seriously seem to naturally crave guidance about doing their job well. They're just as interested in data warehouse success as you are. Of course, the more effective the business sponsor is, the more fun you'll have associating with the data warehouse initiative. Remember that you're both on the same team. So after reading this article, route it to your existing or potential sponsors as this one's for them.

Setting Up for Success

You've volunteered (or perhaps been mildly coerced) to serve as the business sponsor for the data warehouse. You've been successful in most previous ventures, but this is new and different. Then again, it can't be that difficult, can it?

No, it's not difficult, if you're committed. After working with hundreds of data warehouse sponsors, the same patterns of behavior occur repeatedly. I encourage you to learn from others' mistakes and keep these habits in mind as you undertake your new responsibilities.

As a data warehouse sponsor, it's important that you visualize and verbalize the potential effects of improved information on the organization's key initiatives. If you have the authority, but don't truly believe, then you should step aside as the business sponsor because you'll inevitably struggle to be effective. Data warehouse business sponsors need to be passionate about the cause and convey their vision to the organization. If this doesn't sound like you, then you and the data warehouse team need to find an alternate sponsor before plowing full steam ahead; otherwise, you'll be doing a disservice to yourself, the warehouse team, and the entire organization.

Resist the Path of Least Resistance

A common approach to managing the enterprise's data assets is avoidance. Data is managed departmentally rather than across the organization. Each department or organizational function builds its own private data repository, but there's no overall enterprise view. It's initially appealing because every department gets exactly what it wants without contending with organizational consensus. Numerous existing data warehouses have been constructed on this basis.

However, because each department uses slightly different definitions and interpretations, no one's data ties to anyone else's, and the result is anarchy. You lose the ability to look across the enterprise, missing opportunities for cross-functional sharing. Likewise, this mayhem produces significant organizational waste. Partially redundant databases translate into partially redundant data development, administration, and storage expenses. Even more wasteful are the resources devoted to understanding and reconciling this inconsistently defined data.

Of course, you can bring order to the chaos, but you need the political clout, financial means, and inclination to challenge the status quo. Rather than letting everyone build independent, department-centric databases or dashboards, corporate information assets need to be proactively managed. Many CIOs consider this their fiduciary responsibility. As the business sponsor, you'll need to work closely with the CIO to encourage key stakeholders to watch out for the good of the greater whole. The enterprise will need to commit to a common foundation, relying on shared reference information (known as *dimensions* to our regular readers) as the foundation for integration. No one said it would be a cakewalk.

Establishing order begins with a simple underlying premise: Key performance metrics are reused repeatedly across the organization. In a health insurance company, processing claims is a primary business activity, although one department may analyze the insured party's characteristics while another wants to study the health care professional involved. Despite distinct departmental focuses, claims data is a common link.

Rally Those around You

Data warehouse business sponsors need to influence others up, down, and across the organization. You're the internal data warehouse booster. Rallying the troops typically comes naturally to sponsors. You need to create enthusiasm within your organization, without overpromising or setting expectations that the data warehouse team can never fulfill. Don't be surprised if the project manager asks you to send out a friendly reminder conveying the importance of this initiative to key business representatives, encouraging their participation. Predictably, business folks more actively engage in data warehouse requirements or review meetings when it has been strongly suggested by their boss's boss. In the long run, getting business representatives personally involved during the design and development phases is crucial to their acceptance of the ultimate deliverable.

Rallying your peers is equally important, especially if you understand the ultimate costs associated with the easy route and commit to an enterprise approach. Obviously, you'll need your peers' backing, both financially and organizationally, to realize this vision. However, you may need to create awareness first. Perhaps your peers have already written big checks for new transaction processing systems, but don't yet understand that these operationally oriented systems won't address their analytic needs.

Business sponsors also need to build peer consensus on priorities. This consensus must be resilient enough that everyone involved sends consistent messages to the organization, both in words and actions. Attempting to step above the political fray doesn't come naturally. You'll need both a keen awareness of your peers' needs and the ability to empathize, without alienating them or being condescending. Early sponsors of the data warehouse often recruit peers to become cosponsors. You and your cosponsors must agree on and be committed to common goals. Inevitably, you will feel organizational pressure to change course.

Patience Is a Virtue

Successful data warehouses are built incrementally. Business users won't get everything they want in the first phase, when establishing the core shared reference data is the priority. You need to be patient and ensure others follow suit. The data warehouse business sponsor should share the team's desire to balance meaningfulness and manageability when considering project iterations and time frames.

Analytic and reporting alternatives to the data warehouse probably already exist in the organization. Any incremental expenditure to enhance or expand these pre-existing point solutions should be evaluated against the overall goal. In the long run, many of these departmental solutions will be migrated or retired. Obviously, you need peer support to make this happen, especially when the near-term resolution to requests is "no" or "you're next in line."

Serving as a business sponsor for the data warehouse is not a short term assignment, so plan to be involved for the long haul. Your visible participation helps encourage organizational acceptance and maintain momentum and enthusiasm.

Battles will erupt, usually over funding or resources. Business sponsors need to provide ongoing financial support for the foreseeable future. Data warehouses collapse without adequate funding. On the other hand, you can overspend. Although big budgets provide the team with short term euphoria, nothing is sustainable if the costs exceed the benefits. You must expect and assure that the data warehouse team continues to deliver new incremental value to the organization in a timely and consistent manner.

Remain Focused on the Goal

Data warehouses are built to materially improve the organization's decision-making capabilities. As the data warehouse sponsor, you should continually remind all within earshot that business acceptance is the key success metric for the initiative. Everyone involved with the program, both on the business and IT side, needs to recite this pledge daily. That's especially true for those vulnerable to distraction by whiz-bang technology. Remember, nothing in your mission to improve the organization's decision making says anything about technology.

You must understand that building a data warehouse isn't a single project, but an ongoing program. Asking when the data warehouse will be finished is akin to asking, "When will we stop developing and enhancing our operational transaction processing systems?" The data warehouse environment will advance as an organization's core business processes, associated operational systems, and analytic processes mature.

As the business sponsor for the data warehouse, you ensure that the program is in continuous alignment with the business. As the business and its initiatives evolve, so must the vision for the data warehouse. The team can't afford to become complacent and rest on its laurels. The sponsor should ensure the program stays on a trajectory for excellence, without dictating or expecting compliance with unrealistic time frames. Your strategy should focus on those opportunities that translate into the biggest benefit for the overall enterprise.

The habits of highly effective data warehouse business sponsors don't require a degree in rocket science. They're common sense, largely variations on themes that let us be effective in other aspects of our professional and personal lives. So go forth and be an effective sponsor—the organization and data warehouse team are counting on you!

3.12 TCO Starts with the End User

Ralph Kimball, Intelligent Enterprise, *May 13, 2003*

The recent industry preoccupation with calculating the total cost of ownership (TCO) for a data warehouse focuses on minor issues while missing the big picture. Metaphors such as "not seeing the forest for the trees" or even "rearranging the deck chairs on the Titanic" come to mind.

Reading various white papers and listening to industry consultants would make you think that data warehouse TCO is dominated by the costs of hardware, software licenses and maintenance contracts, IT staff expenses, and services.

Some of the more detailed analyses break these categories down to reveal chronically unplanned costs such as hiring and firing, training, tuning, testing, and documentation. One large hardware vendor even bases its TCO advantages on reducing the number of DBAs. With all these categories as a foundation, the various vendors "prove" that their approach is better by claiming to show head-to-head comparisons. Observers like you and me are left to wonder how the conflicting claims could be so dramatically at odds. But all of this muddling misses the big picture. As one of my former colleagues used to say, there is a hippopotamus in the room but nobody is talking about it.

Bad Decisions Are Costs

When I think about data warehouse TCO, I start by asking: Why do we have a data warehouse, and who in the organization judges the cost and the return from a data warehouse? My answer is that the data warehouse publishes the data assets of the company to most effectively facilitate decision making. In other words, the data warehouse is an organization-wide resource, the cost and value of which you must judge by its effect on decision making in the broadest possible sense.

So who are the decision makers in an organization? For the most part, they're not the IT employees! The mainline decision makers of an organization are the business users of the data warehouse, whether they're executives, managers, knowledge workers, analysts, shop floor stewards, customer service representatives, secretaries, or clerks. All these users have a powerful, instinctive need to see data. With the computer revolution of the past half century, a profound cultural shift has taken place in the way businesses are run. Business end users are now quite certain that if they can see their data, they can run their businesses better.

So when I step back to the broader perspective of an entire organization trying to make better decisions with a data warehouse, the traditional IT-centric costs don't even make my top ten costs to be concerned about! The hippopotamus in this room is a set of problems that can destroy the value of a data warehouse. And yes, to avoid these problems entails some real costs.

Here's my list of the real sources of data warehouse costs that come before the traditional hardware, software, staff, and services costs that we've been so fixated on. The list begins with the most important in my opinion, but you can adjust the ranking to your own environment:

- Data needed for decisions is unavailable
- Lack of partnership between IT and business users
- Lack of explicit user-focused cognitive and conceptual models
- Delayed data
- Unconformed dimensions
- Unconformed facts
- Insufficiently verbose data
- Data in awkward formats
- Sluggish, unresponsive delivery of data
- Data locked in a report or dashboard
- Prematurely aggregated data
- Focus on data warehouse return on investment (ROI)
- Creation of a corporate data model
- A mandate to load all data into the warehouse

As you'll see, most of these problems are akin to snatching defeat from the jaws of victory. When these problems raise their heads, they can threaten the entire data warehouse initiative. If the data warehouse fails, the cost analysis is really ugly. Add the traditional IT-centric costs to the cost of running your business without your data.

In all of these types of problems, the potential cost is the failure of the data warehouse. This cost dominates and renders traditional cost analyses meaningless. There's no upper bound on the potential cost of not being able to make the right decision. Your goal is to replace this potentially unbounded cost with finite, knowable costs, and at the same time eliminate the risks of losing the data warehouse. Many of these finite costs are in the numeric range of the less important costs I listed at the start of this article.

A Closer Look at the Costs

Taking a constructive view, let's look at these sources of cost to the data warehouse, how much they affect the overall organization, and what we can do to reduce them.

- **Data needed for decisions is unavailable.** This is the big one. Unavailable data means the data warehouse failed to inform decisions. We want to replace this unbounded and unknowable cost with the predictable costs of gathering business requirements from the users, studying what information users need when making decisions, regularly canvassing business decision makers to understand new requirements, and systematically trawling for new sources of data and new metrics that explain or predict events.

- **Lack of partnership between IT and business users.** When IT and the business users don't have a good partnership, the users will be frustrated because they aren't being served well, and IT will blame the users for complaining, not being computer literate, and not reading the documentation. A failed or underperforming data warehouse results with probably no clear consensus on how to fix it. Decisions will be missed because the system isn't usable. A good partnership means that IT staff live in the user environments, and that there's a flow of personnel across the business/IT organization boundary. I've often said that the best application support person is permanently conflicted as to whether the business or the technology is more appealing. These people (of which I am one) spend their entire careers moving back and forth across the business/IT boundary. The cost to address this problem is an explicit program of tours of duty for IT people to spend a year or longer working directly in the business user department. Business credibility for IT personnel is the "gold coin."

- **Lack of explicit user-focused cognitive and conceptual models.** IT application designers systematically make things too complicated, or assume that business users will be adept at wrangling data from one computer window into another, or assume that users even want to perform analysis. Business end users come in many flavors. A good IT applications delivery team will carefully profile the cognitive and computer sophistication of the users, and at the same time construct conceptual models of how the user performs a task and makes a decision. Then the team can choose or configure the delivery tools to be the best match. The cost of this approach is significant. Multiple tools may be needed. More custom user interfaces and canned reports may have to be built. In my experience, this focus on business users is rare.

- **Data needed for decisions is delayed.** There's been a groundswell of interest recently in providing real-time data warehouse access. The tongue in cheek definition of real time is "any data delivery that is too fast for the current extract, transform, and load system." The demand for real-time data warehousing appears in many market trading, customer support, credit approval, security authorization, medical diagnosis, and process management situations. The killer, of course, is a data delivery system that's too slow to support the decision that must be made in real time. The costs of real-time data delivery can be significant, and there's no single approach. I described one piece of this puzzle in article 11.44, *Real-Time Partitions*.

- **Unconformed dimensions.** If a customer dimension (for instance) is unconformed, it means that two of your data sources have incompatible customer categorizations and labels. The result is that the two data sources can't be used together. Or, more insidiously, the data sources will look like they can be compared but the logic is wrong. The cost, once again, is a lost opportunity to be well informed about your customers, but there are huge unreported costs when managers waste time resolving the data incompatibilities and vent their anger at not having comprehensible data. The more desirable cost in this case is the cost of resolving the categorization and labeling differences up front when designing conformed dimensions, as I describe in article 5.4, *Divide and Conquer*.

- **Unconformed facts.** Unconformed facts are related to unconformed dimensions. They arise when two numeric measures are similar, but cannot be logically combined in a calculation such as a ratio or a difference. For instance, two different revenue numbers may not be put into the same calculation because one is before tax adjustments and one is after. The cost to fix this problem can be combined with the cost of conforming dimensions and can be accomplished by the same people in the same meetings.

- **Insufficiently verbose data.** Providing verbose dimensional descriptions is a basic responsibility of the data warehouse designer. Each attribute in a product or customer dimension is a separate entry point into the data because attributes are the dominant means of constraining and grouping data. The cost of making data more verbose usually comes from finding, cleaning, and merging auxiliary data sources into the database.

- **Data in awkward formats.** There are several categories of poorly formatted data that defeat the business users, even when the data is present. By far, the worst offender is data presented to the business user in a normalized entity-relationship format. These complex normalized schemas are impossible for business users to understand, and they require custom schema-dependent programming to deliver queries and reports. A few vendors actually recommend normalized schemas for data warehouse delivery and then sell extremely expensive hardware solutions to IT that are powerful enough to overcome these inefficient schemas. What these vendors systematically avoid is an honest accounting of the application development costs and lost opportunity costs they have transferred to the business users.

- **Sluggish, unresponsive delivery of data.** Business users have little tolerance for slow user interfaces. The only truly acceptable response time is instantaneous, and the data warehouse designer must always have this as a goal. Business users aren't likely to try ad hoc queries more than once if they take many minutes or hours to return a result. The use of a really fast decision support system is qualitatively different from a system that has to be used in batch job mode. Users of a fast system try far more alternatives and explore more directions than users of a slow system. Fixing a slow system is a multipronged challenge, but it starts with good database design and good software. Dimensional models are fast for querying and normalized models are slow, given the same hardware capacities. After addressing the database design and choice of software, the next relevant performance knobs are lots of real memory (RAM), proper tuning with aggregations and indexes, distributed parallel architectures, and CPU raw speed.

- **Data locked in a report or dashboard.** Data that can't be transferred in tabular format with a single command to a spreadsheet is locked uselessly in an application. Choose applications that allow any visible data to be copied by the user to another tool, especially a spreadsheet.

- **Prematurely aggregated data.** Business process subject areas that consist of aggregated, non-atomic data are dangerous because they anticipate a set of business questions and prohibit the business user from drilling down to needed detail. This was the fatal mistake of the executive information system movement in the late 1980s. The solution to this problem, of course, is not to use the outmoded definition of "data mart" but to base all business process subject areas on dimensional models using the most atomic data. Atomic data is the most naturally dimensional data and is the most able to withstand the ad hoc attack where business users pose unexpected and precise questions.

- **Focus on data warehouse ROI.** It's fashionable to measure return-on-investment with highly analytic-sounding techniques, such as payback period, net present value, or internal rate of return. In my opinion, these miss the main point of evaluating the costs and eventually the value of a data warehouse. A data warehouse supports decisions. After a decision is made, give the data warehouse a portion of the credit, and then compare that retrospectively to the costs of the warehouse. My rule of thumb is to take 20 percent of the monetary value of a decision made and book that to the benefit of the data warehouse. This really drives the point that the only meaningful view of the warehouse is the ability to support business user decisions.

- **Creation of a corporate data model.** In most cases, an a priori effort to model an organization's data is a waste of time. All too often the model is an ideal expression of how data ought to be, and the thousands of entities created are never actually physically populated. It may be fun, and even mildly educational, but the corporate data model is a waste of time that delays the data warehouse. Now, a data model that describes an actual data source, warts and all, is probably a good thing.

- **Mandate to load all data into the warehouse.** Finally, following a mandate to source "all data" in an organization is an excuse to avoid talking to the business users. While it's necessary to have a design perspective that understands the basic dimensionality and content of all your data sources, most IT shops will never be able to address more than a fraction of all their possible data sources. When the preliminary data audit is finished, it's time to go hang out with the business users and understand which of those data sources need to be published in the data warehouse first.

I hope that after reading about all these potential and real costs of the data warehouse you've almost forgotten about hardware, software, and services. Years ago at the Xerox Palo Alto Research Center (now just PARC), I was shocked when Alan Kay, inventor of the personal computer, said, "Hardware is tissue paper. You use it and throw it away." That seemed disrespectful of all the tangible pieces of gear we had at the research center, but he was right. For the data warehouse, the only thing that matters is to effectively publish, in the most pleasing and fulfilling sense, the right data that supports our ability to make decisions.

Kimball Methodology

The final section in this chapter describes the Kimball Lifecycle approach, presents common mistakes made on DW/BI projects, and offers practical advice to reduce project risks.

3.13 Kimball Lifecycle in a Nutshell

Margy Ross, Design Tip #115, Aug 4, 2009

A student in a recent class asked me for an overview of the Kimball Lifecycle approach to share with her manager. Confident that we'd published an executive summary, I was happy to oblige. Much to my surprise, our only published Lifecycle overview was a chapter in a *Toolkit* book, so this *Design Tip* addresses the unexpected content void in our archives.

The Kimball Lifecycle approach has been around for decades. The concepts were originally conceived in the 1980s by members of the Kimball Group and several colleagues at Metaphor Computer Systems. When we first published the methodology in *The Data Warehouse Lifecycle Toolkit* (Wiley, 1998), it was referred to as the Business Dimensional Lifecycle because this name reinforced three fundamental concepts:

- Focus on adding *business* value across the enterprise.
- *Dimensionally* structure the data delivered to the business via reports and queries.
- Iteratively develop the solution in manageable *lifecycle* increments rather than attempting a Big Bang deliverable.

Rewinding back to the 1990s, our methodology was one of the few emphasizing this set of core principles, so the Business Dimensional Lifecycle name differentiated our approach from others in the industry. Fast forwarding to the late 2000s when we published the second edition of the *Lifecycle Toolkit*, we still absolutely believed in these concepts, but the industry had evolved. Our principles had become mainstream best practices touted by many, so we condensed the methodology's official name to simply the Kimball Lifecycle.

In spite of dramatic advances in technology and understanding during the last couple of decades, the basic constructs of the Kimball Lifecycle have remained strikingly constant. Our approach to designing, developing, and deploying DW/BI solutions is tried and true. It has been utilized by thousands of project teams in virtually every industry, application area, business function, and technology platform. The Kimball Lifecycle approach has proven to work again and again.

The Kimball Lifecycle approach is illustrated in Figure 3-1. Successful DW/BI implementations depend on the appropriate amalgamation of numerous tasks and components; it's not enough to have a perfect data model or best of breed technology. The Lifecycle diagram is the overall roadmap depicting the sequence of tasks required for effective design, development, and deployment.

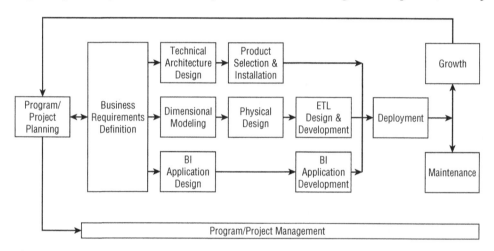

Figure 3-1: The Kimball Lifecycle diagram.

Program/Project Planning and Management

The first box on the roadmap focuses on getting the program/project launched, including scoping, justification, and staffing. Throughout the Lifecycle, ongoing program and project management tasks keep activities on track.

Business Requirements

Eliciting business requirements is a key task in the Kimball Lifecycle because these findings drive most upstream and downstream decisions. Requirements are collected to determine the key factors impacting the business by focusing on what business users do today (or want to do in the future), rather than asking "what do you want in the data warehouse?" Major opportunities across the enterprise are identified, prioritized based on business value and feasibility, and then detailed requirements are gathered for the first iteration of the DW/BI system development. Three concurrent Lifecycle tracks follow the business requirements definition.

Technology Track

DW/BI environments mandate the integration of numerous technologies, data stores, and associated metadata. The technology track begins with system architecture design to establish a shopping list of needed capabilities, followed by the selection and installation of products satisfying those architectural needs.

Data Track

The data track begins with the design of a target dimensional model to address the business requirements, while considering the underlying data realities. The word *Kimball* is synonymous with dimensional modeling where data is divided into either measurement facts or descriptive dimensions. Dimensional models can be instantiated in relational databases, referred to as star schemas, or multidimensional databases, known as OLAP cubes. Regardless of the platform, dimensional models attempt to address two simultaneous goals: ease of use from the users' perspective and fast query performance. The enterprise data warehouse bus matrix is a key Kimball Lifecycle deliverable representing an organization's core business processes and associated common conformed dimensions; it's a data blueprint to ensure top-down enterprise integration with manageable bottom-up delivery by focusing on a single business process at a time. The bus matrix is tremendously important because it simultaneously serves as a technical guide, a management guide, and a forum for communication with executives. The bus matrix is illustrated and described in detail in articles 5.5, *The Matrix,* and 5.6, *The Matrix: Revisited.*

The dimensional model is converted into a physical design where performance tuning strategies are considered, then the extract, transform, and load (ETL) system design and development challenges are tackled. The Lifecycle describes 34 subsystems in the ETL process flow grouped into four major operations: *extracting* the data from the source, performing *cleaning and conforming* transformations, *delivering* the data to the presentation layer, and *managing* the back room ETL processes and environment.

Business Intelligence Track

While some project members are immersed in the technology and data, others focus on identifying and constructing a broad range of BI applications, including standardized reports, parameterized queries, dashboards, scorecards, analytic models, and data mining applications, along with the associated navigational interfaces.

Deployment, Maintenance, and Growth

The three Lifecycle tracks converge at deployment, bringing together the technology, data, and BI applications. The deployed iteration enters a maintenance phase, while growth is addressed by the arrow back to project planning for the next iteration of the DW/BI system. Remember that a DW/BI system is a long term program, not a one-off project!

Throughout the Kimball Lifecycle, there's a recurring theme acknowledging that DW/BI professionals must continuously straddle the business's requirements and the underlying realities of the source data, technology, and related resources. Project teams who focus exclusively on the requirements (or realities) in isolation will inevitably face significant delivery and/or business adoption risks.

Finally, we've said it before, and we'll surely repeat it again. Regardless of your organization's specific DW/BI objectives, we believe your overarching goal should be *business acceptance of the DW/BI deliverables to support decision making.* This target must remain in the bull's eye throughout the design, development, and deployment lifecycle of any DW/BI system.

3.14 Off the Bench

Margy Ross, Design Tip #49, *Sep 15, 2003*

Plenty of folks in the DW/BI industry seem to feel personally qualified to explain the Kimball approach, while further fueling debate about which approach for tackling DW/BI development is best. Unfortunately, they sometimes spread misunderstandings and continue to blur the issues. While we'd never pretend to be an expert on the corporate information factory (CIF), we do feel it's our responsibility to clarify our methods rather than watching from the sidelines.

When we wrote the first edition of *The Data Warehouse Lifecycle Toolkit* (Wiley, 1998), we referred to our approach as the Business Dimensional Lifecycle. In retrospect, we should have probably just called it the Kimball Approach as suggested by our publisher. We chose the Business Dimensional Lifecycle label instead because it reinforced our core tenets about successful data warehousing based on our collective experiences since the mid-1980s:

1. First and foremost, you need to focus on the business. If you're not enabling better business decision making, then you shouldn't bother investing resources in data warehouses and business intelligence. Focusing on the business does NOT imply that we encourage the development of isolated data stores to address specific departmental business needs. You must have one eye on the business' requirements, while the other is focused on broader enterprise data integration and consistency issues.

2. The analytic data should be delivered in dimensional models for ease-of-use and query performance. We recommend that the most atomic data be made available dimensionally so that it can be sliced and diced "any which way." As soon as you limit the dimensional model to pre-summarized information, you've limited your ability to answer queries that need to drill down into more details.

3. While the data warehouse program will constantly evolve, each iteration should be considered a project lifecycle consisting of predictable activities with a finite start and end.

Somewhere along the line, we were tagged as being a "bottom-up" approach. Perhaps this term was associated because of our strong alignment with the business. Unfortunately, the label fails to reflect that we strongly recommend the development of an enterprise data warehouse bus matrix to capture the relationships between the core business processes/events and core descriptive dimensions BEFORE development begins. These linkages ensure that each project iteration fits into the larger enterprise puzzle.

Finally, we believe conformed dimensions, logically defined in the bus matrix and then physically enforced through the ETL staging process, are absolutely critical to data consistency and integration. They provide consistent labels, business rules/definitions, and domains that are reused as we construct more fact tables to integrate and capture the results from additional business processes/events.

So these are the concepts that we hold near and dear. I know I'm biased, but I frankly don't see that they warrant debate.

3.15 The Anti-Architect

Ralph Kimball, Intelligent Enterprise, *Jan 14, 2002*

Data warehousing is interesting because it involves so many different kinds of businesses and because the responsibility is so central to the mission of IT. But, as important as this job is, I have often felt overwhelmed when I listen to someone explain all the data warehouse manager's responsibilities. Be responsive to the business. Be responsive to the business users. Use technology wisely. Don't forget anything. Deliver results on time. Be courteous, kind, thrifty, brave, clean, and reverent.

Sometimes I find that casting data warehouse responsibilities in the negative is an effective way to cut through the vagueness. We've always been told what to do; now let's balance the list with what not to do. I list the mistakes in order of increasing seriousness here. Of course, all of these are showstoppers, so you might order them differently.

- **Mistake 1:** Rely on past consultants or other IT staff to tell you the data warehouse requirements. Don't interview the business users.

    The reality: Nothing substitutes for direct exposure to the business users. Develop and trust your instincts gained from firsthand experience. Develop the ability to listen.

- **Mistake 2:** Live with the assumption that the administrators of the major OLTP source systems of the enterprise are too busy and important to spend a lot of time with the data warehouse team, and they certainly cannot significantly alter their operational procedures for passing data to or from the data warehouse.

    The reality: If your organization really understands and values the data warehouse, then the OLTP source system administrators should be effective partners with you in downloading the data you need and uploading your cleaned data, such as customer names and addresses.

- **Mistake 3:** After the data warehouse has been rolled out, set up a planning meeting to discuss ongoing communications with the business users, if the budget allows.

The reality: Newsletters, training sessions, and ongoing personal support of the user community should all be part and parcel of the first rollout of the data warehouse.

- **Mistake 4:** Make sure all the data warehouse support personnel have nice offices in the IT building, which is only a short drive from the business users. Set up a data warehouse support number with lots of touchtone options, and a guarantee that you will get back to the users as soon as possible. And of course, assure the users that they can email the support team any time, day or night.

    The reality: Data warehouse support people should be physically located in the business user departments, and while on assignment, should spend all their waking hours devoted to the business content of the departments they serve. Such a relationship engenders trust and credibility with the business users, which ultimately is the "gold coin" for IT.

- **Mistake 5:** Declare user success at the end of the first training class. Make sure that the user's business intelligence tools are very powerful and be sure to demonstrate every feature and every command, including building complex reports, in the first training class. Defer training about the content of the data, because you have scheduled the training class on the dummy data you have been using for development, and the real data won't be ready for another few months. Don't bother to schedule follow up training or training for new employees. You've met the milestone.

    The reality: Delay training until your first business process subject area is ready to go live on real data. Keep the first training session short and focus only on the simple uses of the tool. Train 50 percent on the tool and 50 percent on the content of the data. Plan on a permanent series of beginner and follow up training classes. Take credit for the user success milestone when your trained users are still using the data warehouse six months after training.

- **Mistake 6:** Assume that sales, operations, and finance users will naturally gravitate to the good data and will develop their own killer apps.

    The reality: Business users are not application developers. Most will use the data warehouse only if a killer application is waiting to beckon them.

- **Mistake 7:** Make sure that before the data warehouse is implemented you write a comprehensive plan that describes all possible data assets of your enterprise and all the intended uses of information. Avoid the seductive illusion of iterative development, which is only an excuse for not getting it right the first time.

    The reality: Very few organizations or human beings can develop the perfect, comprehensive plan for a data warehouse up front. Not only are the data assets of an organization too vast and complex to describe completely up front, but the urgent business drivers, and even the staff, will change significantly over the life of the first implementation. Start with a lightweight data warehouse bus architecture of conformed dimensions and conformed facts, and build your data warehouse iteratively. You will keep altering and building it forever.

- **Mistake 8:** Don't bother the senior executives of your organization with the data warehouse until you have it up and running and can point to a significant success.

The reality: The senior executives must support the data warehouse effort from the very beginning. If they don't, or can't, then your organization may not be able to use a data warehouse effectively. Get this support at the very beginning.

■ **Mistake 9:** Encourage the business users to give you continuous feedback throughout the development cycle about new data sources and new key performance metrics they would like to see. Make sure to include these requirements in your upcoming release.

The reality: You need to think like a software developer and manage three very visible stages of developing each subject area deliverable:

1. The requirements gathering stage, in which every suggestion is considered seriously
2. The implementation stage, during which changes can be accommodated but must be negotiated and will generally slip the schedule
3. The rollout stage, where the project features are frozen. In the second and third stages you have to stop being a pal to everyone or else fall victim to scope creep.

The trick is to turn around the development cycle as fast as possible, where in each "sprint" you have a clearly defined and achievable set of goals which you implement and test before accepting new input.

■ **Mistake 10:** Agree to deliver a high profile customer-centric dimensional model as your first deliverable. Ideally, choose customer profitability or customer satisfaction as your beginning point.

The reality: These kinds of subject areas are consolidated, "second level" subject areas with serious dependencies on multiple sources of data. Customer profitability requires all the sources of revenue and all the sources of cost, as well as an allocation scheme to map costs onto the revenue! Focus the first deliverable instead on a single source of data and do the more ambitious subject areas later.

■ **Mistake 11:** Define your professional role as the authority on appropriate use of the data warehouse. Educate the business users as to how to think about the data, and what the appropriate uses of computers should be. Systematically raise the sophistication of the user community until most business users can develop their own data access applications, thereby eliminating the need for long term support.

The reality: Your job is to be the publisher of the right data. Your professional role is to listen to the business users, who are always right. The users, not you, define the usability of the computers. You will be successful only if you serve the users' needs, not the other way around.

■ **Mistake 12:** Collect all the data in a physically centralized data warehouse before interviewing any business users or releasing any data marts. Ideally, implement the data warehouse on a single, monolithic machine where you can control and protect everything.

The reality: More power to you if you have the organizational clout and the budget to implement a fully centralized data warehouse. But, in my opinion, a centrally planned data warehouse is as likely to be as successful as a centrally planned economy. It's hard to argue against idealistic inspirational promises made in advance of reality, but the truth is, the centrally planned systems often don't work. Instead, build cost-effective, distributed systems, and add incrementally to the logical and physical design as you learn from your business users. And finally, don't assume that your big, expensive, centralized machine is intrinsically secure because it is big, expensive, and centralized. If anything, such a centralized machine is a single point of failure—a system vulnerability.

3.16 Think Critically When Applying Best Practices

Bob Becker and Ralph Kimball, Intelligent Enterprise, *Mar 26, 2007*

Data warehousing is a mature discipline with well-established best practices. But these best practices are useless or even harmful if they are described inaccurately or incompletely. We have published more than 100 articles describing various aspects of the Kimball method. Yet every year or two we encounter serious misrepresentations made especially by speakers at training organizations where hundreds of students are given misleading information about our approach.

This article addresses major points of misunderstanding and vagueness by providing guidelines that DW/BI professionals can tuck into their project notebooks and refer to as unassailable facts and best practices of the Kimball method.

Take an Enterprise Approach

The Kimball method is specifically intended to deliver large-scale enterprise DW/BI solutions. Occasionally it has been described as a bottom-up approach, but it's more accurately described as a blended approach starting with an enterprise, top-down view. At the same time, it's tempered with the bottom-up realities of real data sources.

We teach an enterprise point of view, starting with horizontal, cross-department requirements gathering. This involves the executive team, senior managers, and data analysts identifying and prioritizing high value needs. The next step is to create the enterprise data warehouse bus matrix, a pivotal design document and powerful tool for understanding and creating the appropriate enterprise data architecture to support the business requirements. As we've said many times, real data sources in their atomic form are the data marts (or business process subject areas) of the enterprise, a definition that differs from other designers who define data marts only as aggregated releases from a centralized data store. When we then say (correctly) that the enterprise data warehouse is the sum of these data marts, other observers sometimes miss the point of our architecture; see article 4.10, *The Bottom-Up Misnomer*, for more details.

Embrace Business Intelligence

Business intelligence is a term that has emerged and evolved over the past few years and is now often used to describe all the systems and processes an enterprise uses to gather, process, provide access to, and analyze business information. The term data warehouse is now used to mean *the platform for all forms of business intelligence.*

Since we have been writing on this topic for more than 20 years, we are beholden to our legacy of books and articles. In fact, "data warehouse" is included in the title of all of our books! Nonetheless, changing industry vernacular does not change the core concepts and methodologies described by the Kimball method. Our approach has always embraced the entire, end-to-end process as critical to an organization's success.

Design Dimensional Schemas

The Kimball method is predicated on the principle that all business user access to data is supported via dimensional schemas. Thus, what we call the presentation area of the overall business intelligence solution is comprised of a number of granular, atomic fact tables decorated with a rich set of descriptive, conformed dimension tables. We specifically avoid summarized, departmental data marts supported by a large, normalized data warehouse providing access to atomic data. We believe that such a centralized and normalized view of a data warehouse is responsible for many of the failures of data warehousing to support business intelligence applications.

Dimensional modeling is a design discipline focused on optimizing the business intelligence platform for business users' ease of use and query performance. To achieve the goals of simple and fast, we describe a set of very specific design recommendations:

- Conformed master dimensions form the bedrock of the enterprise DW/BI system and by themselves address the central issues of integration.
- Fact tables are derived directly from *measurement processes* found in familiar operational transaction applications. A fact table should never be departmentally or functionally bound but rather depends only on the physics of the original measurement process.
- Fact tables should always be populated at the most atomic level possible for maximum flexibility. Atomic data lets business users ask constantly changing, far-ranging, and very precise questions. It also assures the extensibility of additional attributes, metrics, or dimensions without disrupting existing reports and queries.
- Exposing snowflaked or normalized dimension tables directly to business users is strongly discouraged. We have shown repeatedly that properly designed denormalized (flat) dimension tables contain precisely the same information content as normalized schemas. The only difference is complexity, as experienced by the business users. We embrace (and teach) normalized designs in the extract, transform, and load (ETL) phases; however, we avoid normalization in the user accessible presentation area.

Articles 5.16, *Differences of Opinion*, and 6.10, *Fables and Facts*, describe these concepts in greater detail.

Use Conformed Dimensions for Integration

Data integration and consistency are key goals of any enterprise business intelligence effort. Data integration requires organizational consensus to establish and administer common labels and measures enterprise wide. In the Kimball method, these labels and measures reside in *conformed dimensions* and *conformed facts*, respectively. Conformed dimensions are typically built and maintained as centralized, persistent master data during ETL, then reused across dimensional models to enable data integration and ensure consistency.

We enthusiastically support the recent master data management (MDM) and customer data integration (CDI) trends, because they are very consistent with the conformed approach. For more insight, read articles 5.6, *The Matrix: Revisited*, and 5.12, *Integration for Real People*.

Carefully Plan the ETL Architecture

Our approach describes a formal data staging area, much like the kitchen in a restaurant, with detailed ETL processes required to bridge the gap between the production system source data and the presentation area dimensional schema. The approach further defines cleaning and conforming activities as part of the transformation process.

Let there be no doubt, the ETL effort is hard work. The ETL system is often estimated to consume 70 percent of the time and effort of building a business intelligence environment. Too often, little thought goes into architecting a robust ETL system, and it ends up as an uncoordinated, spaghetti-mess of tables, modules, processes, scripts, triggers, alerts, and job schedules. This sort of design approach has unmistakably derailed many business intelligence efforts.

The Kimball method describes a comprehensive set of ETL subsystems that comprise a robust set of ETL best practices, including those required to support real-time requirements as described in article 11.2, *The 34 Subsystems of ETL*.

Be wary of any approach that suggests that ETL is no longer a required architectural component. Some architects believe that a simple intermediate data structure or an integration software layer is all that's needed to perform translation on the fly. Unfortunately, true data integration can only succeed if the textual descriptors in each separate source are physically altered so they have the same label (column name) and content (data domain values). If it sounds too easy, it is.

This article has highlighted five best practices drawn from the Kimball method, which we recommend designers study carefully in order to avoid the misrepresentations sometimes heard in various teaching and writing venues. As a designer, you are free to choose any approach you are comfortable with, but we want you to think critically when you are making these choices.

3.17 Eight Guidelines for Low Risk Enterprise Data Warehousing

Ralph Kimball, Intelligent Enterprise, *Apr 26, 2009*

In today's economic climate, DW/BI projects face two powerful and conflicting pressures. On the one hand, business users want more focused insight from their BI tools into customer satisfaction and profitability. Conversely, these same users are under huge pressure to control costs and reduce risks. The explosion of new data sources and new delivery modes available for BI really makes this dilemma acute.

How can we fail? We could do nothing, thereby overlooking important customer insights and specific areas where we could be more profitable. We could start a task force to produce a grand architectural specification covering the next couple of years, which is just another way of doing nothing. We could implement several high priority spot solutions, ignoring overall enterprise integration. We could start by buying a big piece of iron, believing that it is so powerful that it will handle any type of data, once we decide what that data is.

You get the idea. Even though some of these ways to fail seem obviously dumb, we can nevertheless find ourselves in these positions when we respond with a crisis mentality.

How can we succeed? How can we move forward quickly and decisively while at the same time clamping down on risk? Enterprise data warehousing (EDW) development is never easy, but this article presents eight guidelines for approaching this intimidating task in a flexible, reasonably low risk way.

Work on the Right Thing

We recommend a simple technique for deciding what the right thing is. Make a list of all your potential DW/BI projects and place them on a simple 2 × 2 grid, like the one in Figure 3-2.

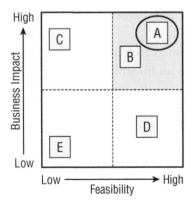

Figure 3-2: Impact versus feasibility prioritization.

Figure out, with your business executives, how valuable each of the potential projects would be, independent of the feasibility. Next, do an honest assessment of whether each project has high quality data and how difficult it will be to build the data delivery pipelines from the source to the BI tool. Remember that at least 70 percent of BI project risks and delays come from problems with the data sources and meeting data delivery freshness (latency) requirements.

Once projects have been placed on the grid, work from the upper-right corner. Project A in Figure 3-2 has high business impact and is eminently feasible. Don't take the easy way out and start with low risk project D. That project may be feasible, but even if you do a great job, it won't have much impact. Similarly, don't start with project C. The users would love to have it, but there are big feasibility issues which translate into big risks.

Give Business Users Control

A few years ago, data warehousing was essentially relabeled as "business intelligence." This relabeling was far more than a marketing tactic, because it correctly signaled the transfer of the initiative and ownership of the data assets to the business users. Everyone knows instinctively that they can do a better job if they can see the right data. Our job in IT is to sort through all the technology in order to give the users what they want.

The transfer of control means having users directly involved with, and responsible for, each DW/BI project. Obviously these users have to learn how to work with IT so as to make reasonable demands. The impact-feasibility grid shown in Figure 3-2 is not a bad place to start.

Proceed Incrementally

In this era of financial uncertainty, it's hard to justify a classic waterfall approach to DW/BI development. In the waterfall approach, a written functional specification is created that completely specifies the sources, the final deliverables, and the detailed implementation. The rest of the project implements this specification, often with a big bang comprehensive release. The origins of the waterfall approach lie in the manufacturing industry, where changes after implementation are prohibitively costly. The problem with the waterfall approach for DW/BI projects is that it takes too long and does not recognize the need to adapt to new requirements or changes in understanding.

Many DW/BI projects are gravitating to what could be called an "agile" approach that emphasizes frequent releases and midcourse corrections. Interestingly, a fundamental tenet of the agile approach is ownership by the business users, not by technical developers.

An agile approach requires tolerating some code rewriting and not depending on fixed price contracts. The agile approach can successfully be adapted to enterprise-wide projects such as master data management and enterprise integration. In these cases, the first few agile releases are not working code but rather architectural guidelines.

Start with Lightweight, Focused Governance

Governance is recognizing the value of your data assets and managing those assets responsibly. Governance is not something that is tacked onto the end of a DW/BI project. Governance is part of a larger culture that recognizes the value of your data assets and is supported and driven by senior executives. At the level of an individual project, governance is identifying, cataloging, valuing, assigning responsibility, securing, protecting, complying, controlling, improving, establishing consistent practices, integrating across subject areas, planning for growth, planning to harvest value, and generally nurturing. Governance doesn't need a waterfall approach, but these issues need to be part of the project from the very start. Failing to think about governance can result in fundamental rework of the DW/BI project.

Build a Simple, Universal Platform

One thing is certain in the BI space: The nature of the user-facing BI tools cannot be predicted. In the future, what's going to be more important: data mining predictive analytics, delivery to mobile devices, batch reporting, real-time alerts, or something we haven't thought of yet? Fortunately, we have a good answer to this question; we must recognize that the enterprise data warehouse is the single platform for all forms of business intelligence. This viewpoint makes us realize that the enterprise data warehouse's interface to all forms of BI must be agnostic, simple, and universal.

Dimensional modeling meets these goals as the interface to all forms of BI. Dimensional schemas contain all possible data relationships, but at the same time can be processed efficiently with simple SQL emitted by any BI tool. Even the flat files preferred by data mining tools are easily delivered from dimensional models.

Integrate Using Conformed Dimensions

Enterprise-wide integration has risen to the top of the list of DW/BI technical drivers along with data quality and data latency. Dimensional modeling provides a simple set of procedures for achieving integration that can be effectively used by BI tools. Conformed dimensions enable BI tools to drill across multiple business process subject areas, assembling a final integrated report. The key insight is that the entire dimension (customer, for example) does not need to be made identical across all subject areas. The minimum requirement for a drill-across report is that at least one field be common across multiple subject areas. Thus, the EDW can define a master enterprise dimension containing a small but growing number of conformed fields. These fields can be added incrementally over time. In this way, we reduce the risk and cost of enterprise integration at the BI interface. This approach also fits well with our recommendation to develop the DW/BI system incrementally.

Manage Quality a Few Screens at a Time

In article 11.19, *An Architecture for Data Quality*, I describe an effective approach to managing data quality by placing data quality screens throughout the data pipelines leading from the sources to the targets. Each data quality screen is a test. When the test fails or finds a suspected data quality violation, the screen writes a record in an error event fact table—a dimensional schema hidden in the back room away from direct access by business users. The error event fact table lets DW/BI administrators measure the volume and source of the errors encountered. A companion audit dimension summarizes the error conditions and is exposed to the business users along with every dimensional fact table.

The data quality screens can be implemented one at a time, allowing development of the data quality system to grow incrementally.

Use Surrogate Keys Throughout

Finally, a seemingly small recommendation to reduce your DW/BI development risk: Make sure to build all your dimensions (even type 1 dimensions) with surrogate primary keys. This insulates you from surprises downstream when you acquire a new division that has its own ideas about keys. What's more, all your databases will run faster with surrogate keys.

Requirements Definition

e firmly believe that business acceptance is the most critical measure of DW/BI success. If the business doesn't embrace the DW/BI deliverables to support its decision making processes, then the DW/BI initiative is an exercise in futility as far as we're concerned, despite potential technical feats of accomplishment. And if you don't learn what the business really needs from the data warehouse, you can't provide it.

This chapter begins by focusing on techniques to effectively elicit requirements from the business stakeholders and representatives. It touches upon the value of data profiling early in your DW/BI project, then describes the importance of organizing the business's needs around the organization's core process subject areas; these building block processes help establish appropriate boundaries for the downstream design and development activities. Finally, the closing article details the activities required to bring the requirements definition process to an orderly conclusion.

Gathering Requirements

The articles in this section provide detailed Dos and Don'ts for gathering requirements from the business. Good listening skills are a critical prerequisite.

4.1 Alan Alda's Interviewing Tips for Uncovering Business Requirements

Margy Ross, Intelligent Enterprise, *May 1, 2005*

Alan Alda is still widely known as "Hawkeye" Pierce from the hit television series *M*A*S*H*, but he's also the long time host of the PBS series *Scientific American Frontiers* in which he interviews research scientists. Discussing his 11-year PBS hosting stint on National Public Radio recently, Alda described his approach for eliciting information from brilliant scientists. His tactics struck a chord because they're similar to the methods we advocate for collecting information from brilliant businesspeople during requirements interviews. Here are a few of Alda's practical techniques with our embellishments for DW/BI professionals.

Be Curious, but Not Too Smart

Skilled interviewers must be curious. Alda has a natural interest in science, but he warns of the "too-smart syndrome" where interviewers think they're nearly as well versed in the subject as interviewees. Alda remarks:

> I found I wasn't asking good enough questions because I assumed I knew something. I would box them into a corner with a badly formed question, and they didn't know how to get out of it. Now, I let them take me through it step by step, and I listen. Then I say, "Well, if that's true, then how could this be true?" or "Tell me more about that."

Perhaps you've observed too-smart interviewers. Their questions tend to be long-winded, often eliciting blank stares or responses like "What was the question again?" Interviewers who try to impress others are missing the point. Ask simple, straightforward questions and you'll have a better chance of understanding complex concepts.

Know-it-all observers are also a potential problem. The observer's behind-the-scenes role during requirements interviews should be self-explanatory. Observers who would rather be in the limelight sometimes jump right in and start answering the questions on behalf of the intended interviewees.

The goal of a requirements interview is to ask questions in order to discover unknown frontiers. Think of it as a one hour immersion to better understand what businesspeople do and why. How do they make decisions today, and how do they want to be making decisions in the future? First ask interviewees about their roles and responsibilities to get them engaged and focused on their spheres. From there, cover the following areas:

- What are the key business objectives? And what are the key performance metrics to determine success?
- What roles do data and analysis play in achieving goals? Alternatively, how would better access and analysis benefit them?
- What are the current analysis challenges?

A good question to get the interview started is "How can people tell when you're doing a great job?" Marketing and salespeople especially like to answer this question.

Take a look at the sample questionnaire on the Kimball Group website under the tools and utilities for *The Data Warehouse Lifecycle Toolkit, 2nd Edition*, (Wiley, 2008) to get a feeling for the process.

Be Conversational

Alda believes *Scientific American Frontiers* is popular because of his conversational approach. Alda sets a tone that makes the interview more enjoyable for his subject:

The conversational element … makes it good. I'm trying to find out what she's doing, what it really means, and how she really does it … and she's trying to make me understand. She's not just giving a lecture. So it's a very personal interaction.

This is a profound subject, well known to office anthropologists. Thirty years ago at the Xerox Palo Alto Research Center, Ralph Kimball was strongly influenced by the well-known researcher David Holtzmann, who said that the procedures in a typical office manual are worthless as indicators about how people acquire information and make decisions. What was needed, in Holtzmann's opinion, were the "shadow functions" that described what really took place. Perhaps the crucial source of information to make a decision came from informal conversations around the water cooler. The interviewer needs to get past the procedures manual and find these shadow functions.

For the DW/BI practitioner, being conversational means putting yourself into a business frame of mind. Learn the language of the business. Don't intimidate users by asking "What do you want in a data warehouse?" Business users aren't systems designers. Acronyms and IT vernacular don't belong in a business requirements interview. Business as a second language is a challenge for some of us; not everyone is cut out to be a lead interviewer.

Tape recorders change meeting dynamics, so don't use them. Users are often uncomfortable being taped and might want segments of the meeting to be "off the record," which makes for awkward transitions. If you rely on recorders, your written notes won't capture the interview's full content, so inevitably you'll have to listen to the recordings again and take supplemental notes. This process is like watching reruns on television; it isn't very interesting, but consumes large chunks of time. It's better for the lead interviewer and a scribe to be actively engaged in the session.

You're not setting the stage for conversation if you hand a list of data elements to interviewees and ask which ones are important. Ask open-ended questions to draw them out. Several techniques can help you establish a more conversational tone:

- Learn a bit about the business beforehand by reviewing the company's website or annual report to understand company-specific vocabulary and hot-button issues.
- Meet with interviewees on their own turf. Go to their offices or conference rooms, rather than IT meeting spaces.
- Prior to the interview, send out an announcement describing the high level discussion topics and confirming the interview time and place. Don't attach a detailed questionnaire to this meeting notice. You can't achieve a conversational flow if you're reviewing questionnaire results (presuming anyone even bothers to complete the survey).
- Interview questions prepared in advance are fallback devices, used only if uncomfortable lulls occur in conversations or to ensure key points are covered before ending sessions.

■ Most good conversations tend to wander, so remember your session goals and steer conversations back on track if you stray too far from core issues. Stay at a relatively high level in the interview's early stages. Don't follow an early comment to a very low level of detail, only to run out of time and discover that you haven't discussed three other major areas of responsibility with important requirements for the DW/BI effort.

Listen and Expect to Be Changed

When you're gathering requirements, your job is to listen intently. According to Alda:

> *There's one skill that I really make use of in a big way, and that is listening. If you don't listen deeply, the connection won't take place.... [You have to be] willing to be changed by the person you're listening to, where you're not just waiting for a pause so you can say your thing, but you're actually letting them have an effect on you if they can.*

Good interviewers should be seen but not heard—well, at least not heard too much. Strong active listening skills are required; don't be surprised if you're exhausted after a full day of requirements interviews. Use physical body language and verbal clues to encourage interviewees and show your interest. Interviewees often understand what information we're looking for during the requirements process; with a little prodding and subtle encouragement, sometimes they essentially interview themselves.

Without a doubt, assumptions regarding the scope, timeline, architecture, and other matters were made before the requirements process was in full swing. It's also inevitable that you'll uncover requirements not accounted for in those pre-existing assumptions. Many times in operational environments, the user will announce that the data warehouse "has to tie to the financial books." That's a classic hidden assumption that may be impossible to address. Pay close attention and actively listen for the unexpected. Of course, once you discover a discrepancy, the DW/BI team needs to correct the assumptions.

As you're gathering requirements from the business users, intersperse some data reality into the process by interviewing key IT personnel, especially those responsible for operational systems. You need to consider the business needs in tandem with the availability of data to support these requirements. It's a balancing act, but failure is inevitable if you consider one without the other. IT meetings tend to be informal discussions, beginning with knowledgeable project team members. Once you start to hear consistent themes from users, it's time to sit down with the data gurus and get into the details of their source systems. During these data audit interviews, try to understand whether complete, reliable data is there to support what users are asking for. You're also trying to understand where to find the data land mines—indicator fields that were never populated, for example. A good data profiling tool is enormously helpful for digging into the actual data records.

Your attitude and approach as an interviewer are more important than the tactical and logistical concerns of setting up and conducting the sessions. A good interview should seem to the business user like an interesting discussion with a touch of flattery, rather than a courtroom cross-examination. We're sure Alan Alda would agree.

QUICK STUDY

Here's a list of Dos and Don'ts for gathering requirements:

- Do talk with a vertical span of businesspeople, including executives, directors/managers, and analysts.
- Don't rely on a single user to represent the business, even if it's less intimidating and easier to schedule.
- Do allow plenty of time to coordinate calendars for scheduling, especially with traveling business management.
- Don't get angry if someone has to reschedule at the last second.
- Do get help from skilled assistants to manage scheduling.
- Don't offload interview coordination to someone unfamiliar with the project or organization.
- Do arrive for the interview on time.
- Don't bring food to the interview, leave your cell phone on, or spill a large latte over the interviewee's conference table and sample reports.
- Do plan on a two-person requirements team in each interview, if possible.
- Don't overwhelm a lone interviewee with six people sitting across from him, Inquisition-style.
- Do designate one person as the lead interviewer with primary responsibility for steering the session.
- Don't turn the interview into a free-for-all, bouncing randomly from one interviewer to the next.
- Do flesh out your scribbled interview notes immediately, or you'll lose much of the interesting detail by the next day.
- Don't schedule more than four interviews per day.
- Do document what you learned during the requirements gathering and feedback results to close the loop with participants.
- Don't lose sight of the scope of your DW/BI requirements process.

4.2 More Business Requirements Gathering Dos and Don'ts

Margy Ross, Design Tip #110, May 4, *2009*

Successful data warehouse and business intelligence solutions provide value by helping the business identify opportunities or address challenges. Obviously, it's risky business for the DW/BI team to attempt delivering on this promise without understanding the business and its requirements. This article covers basic guidelines for effectively determining the business's wants and needs.

First, start by properly preparing for the requirements process:

- Do recruit a lead requirements analyst with the right stuff, including confidence and strong communication and listening skills, coupled with the right knowledge, such as business acumen and vision for BI's potential.
- Do involve the right business representatives representing both vertical (cross-management ranks) and horizontal (cross-department) perspectives. Don't rely solely on the input from a lone power analyst who's a pseudo-IT professional.
- Don't presume you already know what the business wants because you've supported them for the past decade.
- Don't accept a static requirements document from the business that lists general items such as "we need the ability to quickly drill down into a single version of integrated data."
- Do differentiate between project and program requirements. Although the mechanics are similar, there are differences in terms of the participants, breadth and depth of details collected, documentation, and next steps.
- Do get face-to-face with business representatives (or at least voice-to-voice). Don't rely on non-interactive static surveys or questionnaires; don't think producing a 3-inch binder of existing reports equates to requirements analysis.
- Do prepare interviewees in advance so you don't spend the first 30 minutes of every session conceptually explaining DW/BI.

Secondly, spend your time with the business representatives wisely:

- Do show up at the appointed meeting time. Don't allow your cell phone to ring or casually try to determine why it's vibrating.
- Do ask "what do you do (and why)"; don't ask "what do you want" in the data warehouse, or pull out a list of data elements to determine what's needed.
- Do ask unbiased open-ended why, how, what if, and what then questions. Do respect the lead interviewer's or facilitator's role in steering the sessions; don't turn it into a questioning free-for-all.
- Do strive for a conversation flow; don't dive into the detailed weeds too quickly.
- Do listen intently to absorb like a sponge; don't allow the requirements team to do too much talking.
- Do conduct some sessions with source system experts to begin understanding the underlying data realities.
- Don't schedule too many requirements sessions in a day; do allow time between sessions to debrief.

- Do ask the business representatives for measurable success criteria (before thanking them for their brilliant insights).
- Do set reasonable expectations with the business representatives about next steps; don't leave it to their imaginations.

Finally, bring the requirements gathering activities to an orderly conclusion:

- Do synthesize the findings into business process-centric categories. Do review article 4.7, *Identifying Business Processes*, to help identify business processes representing manageable units of design and development effort for the DW/BI team.
- Do write down what you heard (along with who said it and why it's required), but don't attempt to reinvent an alternative Dewey Decimal System for classification and cross-footing. Detailed project requirements can often be classified into three categories (data, BI application/report delivery, and technical architecture requirements) that correspond to downstream lifecycle tasks.
- Don't allow the requirements gathering activities to be overcome by analysis paralysis or process perfection.
- Do present your findings to senior executives to ensure a common understanding, reach consensus about an overall roadmap, and establish next step priorities based on business value and feasibility.

Focusing on business requirements has always been a cornerstone of the Kimball approach; I first delivered a presentation on the topic at an industry conference in 1994. Much has changed in our industry over the past 21 years, but the importance of effective requirements gathering has remained steadfast. Good luck with your requirements gathering initiative!

4.3 Balancing Requirements and Realities

Margy Ross, Design Tip #125, Jun 30, 2010

If you're a long time reader of our articles, *Design Tips*, and books, you know we feel strongly about the importance of understanding the business's data and analytic requirements.

Suffice it to say that we expect more than merely inventorying the existing reports and data files; we encourage you to immerse yourself in the business community to fully appreciate what businesspeople do and why, and what kind of decisions they make today and hope to make in the future. However, as with many things in life, moderation is prudent. You need to temper the business requirements with numerous realities: the available source data realities, the existing architecture realities, the available resource realities, the political landscape and funding realities, and the list goes on.

Balancing the organization's requirements and realities is a never ending exercise for DW/BI practitioners, as shown in Figure 4-1. It takes practice and vigilance to maintain the necessary equilibrium. Some project teams err on the side of becoming overly focused on the technical realities and create over-engineered solutions that fail to deliver what the business needs. At the other end of the spectrum, teams focus exclusively on the business's needs in a vacuum. Taken to an extreme, these requirements-centric teams fail to deliver because what the business wants is unattainable; more often, the result is a silo point solution to address isolated requirements, which perpetuates a potentially inconsistent view of the organization's performance results.

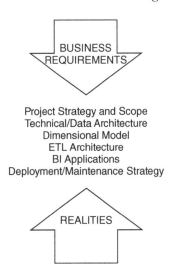

BUSINESS REQUIREMENTS

Project Strategy and Scope
Technical/Data Architecture
Dimensional Model
ETL Architecture
BI Applications
Deployment/Maintenance Strategy

REALITIES

Figure 4-1: The intersection of business requirements and realities.

Throughout the key design, development, and deployment tasks outlined in our Kimball Lifecycle approach, it's a recurring theme to be constantly mindful of this requisite balancing act. You want to keep the pendulum from swinging too far in one direction where you're exposed to significant delivery and/or business adoption risks.

Most would agree that balance is critical for long term DW/BI sustainability. However, there's a trump card for this high wire act. If you can't unequivocally declare that your DW/BI deliverable has improved the business's decision-making capabilities, then straddling the requirements and realities is a moot point. Providing an environment that positively impacts the business's ability to make better decisions must be an overarching, non-negotiable target; delivering anything less is a technical exercise in futility for the organization.

4.4 Overcoming Obstacles When Gathering Business Requirements

Margy Ross, Intelligent Enterprise, *Jun 1, 2007*

For nearly two decades, the Kimball Group has stressed the importance of focusing on the business and its requirements for DW/BI success. We've provided specific requirements-gathering tips and techniques in articles and our *Toolkit* books, but what happens when things don't go according to plan? This article describes seven common challenges you may encounter during the requirements gathering process, along with recommendations for overcoming these obstacles.

- **The abused user.** Uncooperative business executives and managers who claim "we already told IT what we want" are typically abused users. These folks have been interviewed repeatedly in the past for DW/BI initiatives but have yet to see anything result from their efforts. They are frustrated by past false starts and may even refuse to meet with a requirements team again.

  You should proactively determine who was involved and interviewed in earlier DW/BI attempts. Any requirements documentation from the prior project should be reviewed. Unfortunately, documentation is seldom sufficient to take the place of a face-to-face meeting with the business representatives again. When scheduling meetings with these abused users, it's helpful to acknowledge their participation in previous efforts and let them know that you have already reviewed the resulting documentation. The new session can be presented as a validation, rather than as another back-to-the-beginning interview.

  Naturally, users will resist rehashing previously covered territory, but they may be more willing to meet if you are focused on understanding current priorities. Finally, this is probably a good time to select an alternative forum for gathering requirements. If interviews were conducted previously, use the earlier requirements documentation as a baseline for a facilitated session to gather details on changes within their business.

- **The overbooked user.** These disengaged business users are simply too busy to meet anytime soon. They may agree to a scheduled time, but then not show up or send a substitute in their place. An email message from the program sponsor to all the participants about their importance to the initiative will often nip this disorder in the bud. However, if this is a contagious malady and executive management is unwilling or unable to address the condition, stop before you waste more effort. It's a safe bet that business users who don't have time to share their requirements won't have time to attend education sessions and incorporate new information and analyses into their daily jobs, resulting in a constant uphill struggle for the DW/BI team. Get off this slippery slope before further damage is done. You may be able to locate a more cooperative business partner elsewhere in your organization.

- **The comatose user.** These business users respond to your classic, open-ended questions with monosyllabic, one-word responses. Fortunately, this is a relatively rare syndrome. Most often, their apathetic responses are due to external distractions totally unrelated to the DW/BI project. It's sometimes effective to ask these people questions from a more negative perspective. For example, rather than trying to get them to envision life outside the box, these users sometimes find it easier to tell you what's wrong inside the box.

  If you need a crowbar to pry information out of interviewees like this, it's senseless to prolong everyone's pain because these interviews quickly become no fun for anyone involved. Make a valiant attempt, but if it is still not working, abort the interview and schedule a replacement representative if the user is in a critical function or position.

■ **The overzealous user.** You're expecting to interview two business users, but seven people arrive in the designated conference room instead; these overzealous users are excited and want to be heard directly by the DW/BI team. It's great that the users are so engaged and enthused, but that won't last long if you try to interview seven people in a one-hour meeting. Quickly assess the homogeneity of the crowd. Are they all doing the same job and could build off of one another's ideas, or more likely, do they represent different jobs and functions? It's almost always the latter, so you should break them into smaller groups and give them separate slots on the interview schedule. This ensures adequate time is allocated to gather the details needed.

■ **The know-it-all user.** Folks in this category often sit between IT and the real business users. Know-it-all users sometimes act as gatekeepers, rationalizing that there's no need to bother other business folks for their requirements when they already have a thorough understanding and can represent their needs. Sometimes know-it-alls do know it all, but other times, their perspective is skewed. Even if their understanding is 100 percent accurate, bypassing opportunities to bond with the rest of the business community via requirements sessions is a blunder that can be difficult to recover from. You can engage the know-it-alls and even elevate their perceived role and importance, but don't fall into the trap of overdependence. This potential political quagmire may require some finessing and feather smoothing on the part of the business sponsor.

As an aside, be aware that know-it-all users are sometimes IT wannabes. In addition to limiting access to the rest of the business community, they sometimes also want to perform IT's design duties by thoroughly specifying the data layouts for their proposed system solution. In their defense, IT wannabes have sometimes been forced into this role because IT has traditionally underperformed and under delivered.

■ **The clueless user.** Do you have users that just don't get it? Do you feel it's a worthless exercise to schedule requirements interviews with them because they don't have any requirements? From our vantage point, 99.9 percent of the time, clueless users are a figment of an IT professional's imagination. Users may not be able to articulately convey precisely which data elements in which source systems interest them, but nearly all the time, they can clearly describe what they do, why they do it, and what they want to be doing in the future. It's then IT's job to translate this information into data and functional specifications for the DW/BI system. Asking the right questions is critical to obtaining relevant, useful guidance.

■ **The nonexistent user.** The final obstacle is typically fatal to a data warehouse initiative. This condition results when members of the IT organization say they already know what the business users need: "In fact, we know it better than they do." These IT organizations attempt to model their data warehouse based on source data layouts exclusively, and then don't understand why business users aren't clamoring to use their deliverables. The good news is that this obstacle is totally within the ability of the IT organization to overcome.

There you have seven common challenges you may encounter during your requirements gathering initiatives. Hopefully our suggestions will keep these bumps in the road from becoming debilitating program/project showstoppers.

4.5 Surprising Value of Data Profiling

Ralph Kimball, Design Tip #59, Sep 14, 2004

Data profiling is something of a quiet little corner of data warehousing. I suspect most of us think of data profiling as something you do after most of the ETL system has been built. In this view, data profiling checks for small anomalies in the data that may require cleanup before the real production data is delivered. Finding these anomalies would seem to save the data warehouse team from little surprises after going into production.

During the past year I have dug deeply into the back room ETL processes required to build a data warehouse while working on *The Data Warehouse ETL Toolkit* (Wiley, 2004). Perhaps the biggest revelation of the whole project has been discovering how undervalued data profiling is in the average data warehouse project.

What is data profiling?

Data profiling is the systematic analysis of the content of a data source, all the way from counting the bytes and checking cardinalities up to the most thoughtful diagnosis of whether the data can meet the high level goals of the data warehouse. We explore these types of analysis in more detail in article 11.19, *An Architecture for Data Quality*.

Data profiling practitioners divide this analysis into a series of tests, starting with individual fields and ending with whole suites of tables comprising extended databases. Individual fields are checked to see that their contents agree with their basic data definitions and domain declarations. We call these *column screens*, where a "screen" is a test. It is especially valuable to see how many rows have null values, or have contents that violate the domain definition. For example, if the domain definition is "telephone number," then alphanumeric entries clearly represent a problem. The best data profiling tools count, sort, and display the entries that violate data definitions and domain declarations.

Moving beyond single fields, data profiling then describes the relationships discovered between fields in the same table or across tables. We call these *structure screens*. Fields implementing a key to the data table can be displayed, together with higher level many-to-one relationships that implement hierarchies. Checking what should be the key of a table is especially helpful because the violations (duplicate instances of the key field) are either serious errors, or reflect a business rule that has not been incorporated into the ETL design.

Relationships between tables are also checked in the data profiling step, including assumed foreign key to primary key (FK-PK) relationships and the presence of parents without children.

Finally, data profiling can be custom programmed to check complex business rules unique to a business, such as verifying that all the preconditions have been met for granting approval of a major funding initiative. We call these *business rule screens*.

Hopefully as I've been describing the features of data profiling, you have been thinking that data profiling really belongs at the very beginning of a project, where it could have a big effect on design and timing. In fact, I have come to the conclusion that data profiling should be the mandatory "next step" in every data warehouse project after the business requirements gathering. Here are the deliverables of data profiling that I have come to appreciate during my recent ETL research project:

- **A basic "go/no go" decision on the project as a whole!** Data profiling may reveal that the data on which the project depends simply does not contain the information required to make the hoped-for decisions. Although this is disappointing, it is an enormously valuable outcome.
- **Source system data quality issues that must be corrected before the project can proceed.** Although slightly less dramatic than canceling the whole project, these corrections are a huge external dependency that must be well managed for the data warehouse to succeed.
- **Data quality issues that can be corrected in the ETL processing flow after the data has been extracted from the source system.** Understanding these issues drives the design of the ETL transformation logic and exception handling mechanisms. These issues also hint at the manual processing time that will be needed to resolve data problems each day.
- **Unanticipated business rules, hierarchical structures, and FK-PK relationships.** Understanding the data at a detailed level flushes out issues that will permeate the design of the ETL system.

Finally, a big benefit of data profiling that perhaps should be left unstated (at least while justifying the data warehouse to executives) is that data profiling makes the implementation team look like they know what they are doing. By correctly anticipating the difficult data quality issues of a project up front, the team avoids the embarrassing and career-shortening surprises of discovering BIG problems near the end of a project.

Organizing around Business Processes

DW/BI projects typically focus on the data captured by a core operational business process. This section focuses on the value of organizing the business users' requirements around these implementation building blocks sooner rather than later.

4.6 Focus on Business Processes, Not Business Departments!

Margy Ross, Design Tip #3, Jan 30, 2000

One of the most prevalent fallacies in our industry is that dimensional models are defined by business department boundaries. We've seen countless data warehouse architecture diagrams with boxes labeled "Marketing Data Mart," "Sales Data Mart," and "Finance Data Mart." After reviewing business requirements from these departments, you'd inevitably learn that all three organizations want the same core performance information, such as orders data. Rather than constructing a Marketing mart that includes orders, a Sales mart with orders, and so on for Finance, you should build a single detailed orders dimensional model that multiple departments can access.

Focusing on business *processes* rather than business *departments* allows you to more economically deliver consistent information throughout the organization. If you establish departmentally-bound dimensional models, you'll duplicate data. Regardless of whether the source is an operational system or centralized data warehouse, multiple data flows into the multiple models invariably result in data inconsistencies. The best way to ensure consistency is to publish the data once. A single publishing run also reduces the ETL development effort, ongoing data management burden, and disk storage requirements.

We understand that it can be tricky to build a process-centric dimensional model given the departmental funding model typical of most businesses. You can promote the process concept by scrutinizing the unnecessary expense associated with implementing and maintaining the same (or nearly the same) large fact tables in multiple departmental marts. Even if organizational walls exist, management typically responds favorably to savings opportunities.

So how do you go about identifying the key business processes in your organization? The first step is to listen to your business users. The performance metrics that they clamor to analyze are collected or generated by a business process. As you're gathering requirements, you should also investigate key operational source systems. In fact, it's easiest to begin by defining subject area dimensional models in terms of source systems. After you've identified the subject areas based on individual business processes and source systems, then you can focus on those that integrate data across processes, such as a vendor supply chain, or all the inputs to customer profitability or customer satisfaction. We recommend that you tackle these more complex (albeit highly useful) cross-process models as a secondary phase.

Of course, it will come as no surprise to hear that you must use conformed dimensions across the business process subject areas. Likewise, we strongly suggest drafting an enterprise data warehouse bus matrix upfront to establish and communicate your overall development strategy. Just don't let the rows of your matrix read "Marketing," "Sales," and "Finance."

4.7 Identifying Business Processes

Margy Ross, Design Tip #69, Jul 5, 2005

Readers who follow the Kimball approach can often recite the four key decisions when designing a dimensional model: Identify the business process, grain, dimensions, and facts. While this sounds straightforward, teams often stumble on the first step. They struggle to articulate the business process as it's a term that seems to take on different meanings depending on the context. Because the business process declaration is the first stake driven into the ground when designing a dimensional model, we want to eliminate confusion in this context.

First, let's begin by discussing what a business process is not. When designing a dimensional model, the business process does not refer to a business department, organization, or function. Likewise, it shouldn't refer to a single report or specific analysis.

For a dimensional modeler, the business process is *an event or activity that generates or collects metrics*. These metrics are performance measurements for the organization. Business analysts inevitably want to scrutinize and evaluate these metrics by a seemingly limitless combination of filters and constraints. As dimensional modelers, it's our job to present these metrics in an easy-to-understand structure that responds quickly to unpredictable inquiries.

When identifying the business process for dimensional modeling, some common characteristics and patterns often emerge:

1. Business processes are typically supported by an operational system. For example, the billing business process is supported by a billing system; likewise for the purchasing, ordering, or receiving business processes.

2. Business processes generate or collect unique measurements with unique granularity and dimensionality used to gauge organizational performance. Sometimes the metrics are a direct result from the business process. Other times, the measurements are derivations. Regardless, the business processes deliver the performance metrics used by various analytic processes. For example, the sales ordering business process supports numerous reports and analytics, such as customer analysis, sales rep performance, and product penetration.

3. Business processes are frequently expressed as action verbs with the associated dimensions as nouns describing the who, what, where, when, why, and how associated with the process. For example, the billing business process results will be analyzed by date, customer, service/product, and so on.

4. Business processes are usually triggered by an input and result in output that needs to be monitored. For example, an accepted proposal is input to the ordering process, resulting in a sales order and its associated metrics. In this scenario, the business process is sales ordering; you'll have an orders fact table with the sales order as a potential degenerate dimension and the order amounts and counts as facts. Try to envision the general flow from input into a business process, resulting in output metrics. In most organizations, there's a series of business processes where outputs from one process become inputs to the next. In the parlance of a dimensional modeler, these business processes will result in a series of fact tables.

5. Analysts sometimes want to drill across business processes, looking at the result of one process alongside the results of another. Drilling across processes is certainly viable if the dimensions common to both processes are conformed.

Determining your organization's core business processes is critical to establishing your overall framework of dimensional models. The easiest way to determine these processes is by listening to the business users. Which processes generate the performance metrics they're most interested in monitoring? At the same time, the data warehouse team should be assessing the realities of the source environment to deliver the data coveted by the business.

One final comment: It should go without saying that the ever popular dashboard is NOT a business process; it presents the performance results of numerous individual business processes.

4.8 Business Process Decoder Ring

Bob Becker, Design Tip #72, Oct 7, 2005

Focusing on business processes is absolutely critical to successfully implementing a DW/BI solution using the Kimball methods. Business processes are the fundamental building blocks of a dimensional data warehouse. We suggest you build your data warehouse iteratively, one business process at a time. You may wonder, "What's so magical about business processes? How does identifying the business process help in our dimensional modeling activities?" The answer is that correctly identifying the business processes launches the entire dimensional design. It's no secret that each business process will result in at least one fact table. Identifying the business processes essentially identifies the fact tables to be built.

> **NOTE** It's not unusual for a single business process to result in more than one fact table. This occurs most frequently when the process involves heterogeneous products. In this case, several similar but separate fact tables will be spawned. Health care provides a good example. The paid claims business process may result in three fact tables: professional claims (e.g., doctors' office visits), institutional claims (e.g., hospital stays), and drug claims.

The consequences of incorrectly identifying the business process are designs that never come to fruition, or worse, a fact table designed at an inappropriate level of detail. Given the volumes we've written on the topic, it should go without saying (although you wouldn't know it by reading some of the recent analyst reports that have crossed our desks) that we advocate implementing data at its most atomic level of detail in your dimensional data warehouse.

A good test of whether you have accurately identified a business process is to state the fact table's grain. If you can succinctly state the grain, you are in good shape. On the other hand, if there is confusion regarding the level of detail of a single row in the fact table, you're not there yet; most likely you are mixing two or more business processes. You need to step back and look carefully for additional business processes that may be involved.

Listening to your business users' requirements is the best way to develop an understanding of the business processes. Unfortunately, as the business requirements unfold, they don't take the shape of business processes as we describe them. The business users typically describe analytic requirements: the types of analysis and decisions they want to make using data, described in their terms. For example, an actuarial analyst in a health care organization may describe their needs for ratings analysis, utilization trend reporting, and the claim triangles they rely on. But none of these analytic requirements seem to describe a business process. The key is to decode the requirements, decomposing them into the appropriate business processes. This means digging a bit deeper to understand the data and operational systems that support the analytic requirements. Further analysis in our example ultimately shows that all three analytic requirements are served by data from the paid claims business process.

Sometimes the analytic requirements are more challenging to decode. Often the most valuable analytic requirements described by business users cross multiple business processes. Unfortunately, it's not always obvious that multiple business processes are involved. The decoding process is more difficult because it requires decomposing the analytic requirements into all of the unique types and sources of data required. In our health care example, underwriting requires a loss ratio analysis to support renewal decisions. Digging further into the details, we can determine that the loss ratio analysis compares clients' premium revenues against their claim expenses in order to determine the ratio. In this case, two business processes are required to support the analytic requirement: paid claims and premium billing.

After reflecting on this article, you should be able to discern the challenges of creating a corporate dashboard. A dashboard is not a single business process; rather it is a display mechanism for presenting the results of many or most of the business processes in the organization. Unfortunately, the dashboard is usually presented (and accepted) by the DW/BI team as a single analytic requirement.

4.9 Relationship between Strategic Business Initiatives and Business Processes

Bill Schmarzo, Design Tip #47, Jul 10, 2003

One of the questions I frequently field is "What is the relationship between an organization's strategic business initiative (which is where the business is focused) and the business process (which is the foundation upon which I build the data warehouse)?"

Strategic business initiatives are organization-wide plans, championed by executive leadership, to deliver significant, compelling, and distinguishable financial or competitive advantage to the organization. A strategic business initiative typically has a measurable financial goal and a 12- to 18-month delivery time frame. Understanding the organization's strategic business initiatives ensures that the BI project is delivering something of value—or relevance—to the business community.

Meanwhile, a business process is the lowest level of activity that the business performs, such as taking orders, shipping, invoicing, receiving payments, handling service calls, and processing claims. We are particularly interested in the metrics resulting from these business processes because they support a variety of analytics. For example, the business process might be retail sales transactions from the point-of-sale system. From that core business process and resulting data, we could embark on a slew of analytics such as promotion evaluation, market basket analysis, direct marketing effectiveness, price point analysis, and competitive analysis. Business process data is the foundation upon which we build the data warehouse.

So the business is focused on the strategic business initiatives, and the DW/BI team is focused on business processes. Doesn't that cause a huge disconnect? Actually, no. As part of the business requirements gathering process, the DW/BI team needs to break down or decompose the strategic business initiative into its supporting business processes.

Imagine a row/column matrix where you have business processes as the row headers (just like in the enterprise data warehouse bus matrix) and strategic business initiatives as the column headers. The intersection points in the matrix mark where the business process data is necessary to support the strategic business initiatives, as illustrated in Figure 4-2. Instead of adding confusion, the integration of strategic business initiatives and business process provides more clarity as to where to begin the analytics project and why. It maintains the tried and true implementation approach of building your data warehouse one business process at a time, reducing time to delivery and eliminating data redundancy, while delivering the foundation necessary to support those initiatives that the business has deemed important.

Business Process / Event	Strategic Business Initiatives		
	Optimize Supplier Relations	Improve Customer Retention	Reduce Dependency on Major Brands
Purchase Ordering	X		
Supplier Delivery	X		
Warehouse Inventory	X		
Customer Solicitations		X	X
Orders		X	X
Shipments		X	X
Returns	X	X	X
Customer Complaints	X	X	

Figure 4-2: Matrix of business processes mapped to strategic business initiatives.

Wrapping Up the Requirements

After meeting with the business representatives and synthesizing the findings, you need to communicate what you've learned and gain organizational consensus on a roadmap for building the data warehouse. The articles in this final section describe deliverables and techniques for appropriately concluding the requirement definition task.

4.10 The Bottom-Up Misnomer

Margy Ross, Intelligent Enterprise, *Sep 17, 2003*

The Kimball methodology of building a data warehouse is often called a bottom-up approach. This label, along with its associated connotations, is misleading, and misunderstandings about our approach are proliferating. It's time to set the record straight: Although our iterative development and deployment techniques may superficially suggest a bottom-up methodology, a closer look reveals a broader enterprise perspective.

Focus on the Enterprise, Not Departments

The bottom-up terminology originated to distinguish the Kimball approach from other alternatives. Bottom-up is typically viewed as quick and dirty—focused on the needs of a single department rather than the enterprise as a whole. But suggesting that Kimball business process dimensional models are built to serve the needs of a single department or workgroup is a gross misrepresentation. Unfortunately, this perception causes an enormous amount of confusion and consternation, in addition to spawning criticism regarding our techniques. Our dimensional models explicitly embrace an enterprise point of view.

For more than 30 years, we've been helping organizations publish their data assets to enable better strategic and tactical decision making. Our focus on business requirements has remained steadfast. Unfortunately, a business-centric approach is sometimes seen as synonymous with building independent departmental or workgroup solutions. However, we provide very specific recommendations for avoiding that snake pit both in *The Data Warehouse Toolkit, 3rd Edition* and *The Data Warehouse Lifecycle Toolkit, 2nd Edition*, both from Wiley. When gathering business requirements, we encourage you to broaden your perspective both vertically and horizontally.

Rather than solely relying on business data analysts to determine requirements, you should also meet with senior managers to better understand their vision, objectives, and challenges. Ignoring this vertical span leaves the data warehouse team vulnerable to "here-and-now" myopia—a failure to grasp the organization's direction and likely future needs.

Keep in mind that you also need to look horizontally across the organization before designing a data warehouse's dimensional presentation. This suggestion, although somewhat challenging to adopt if a single department is funding the project, is absolutely critical to establishing the enterprise view. Ignoring the horizontal span leaves the team vulnerable to isolated, workgroup-centric databases that are inconsistent and can't be integrated. Obviously, no one expects complete coverage in a large organization; however, you should meet with representatives from related departments, because they often share needs for the same core data.

Draft the Enterprise Data Warehouse Bus Matrix

The enterprise bus matrix reflects the enterprise's core business processes or events, in addition to the common dimensional reference data. Both the rows and columns represent cross-departmental requirements. You can learn more about this technique in article 5.6, *The Matrix: Revisited*.

In the simplified bus matrix in Figure 4-3, the rows identify a subset of the primary business pro-cesses within an insurance company. The rows were uncovered while gathering information about the company's business requirements by asking about strategic business initiatives. The effectiveness of these initiatives is measured by key performance indicators (KPIs) and success metrics, which are collected or generated by the organization's core business processes, such as underwriting, billing, and payment processing. Typically, a single primary data source supports each business process; the resulting KPIs and metrics from each process are used in a variety of analyses.

	Date	Policyholder	Coverage	Covered Item	Agent	Policy	Claim	Claimant	Payee
Underwriting Transactions	X	X	X	X	X	X			
Policy Premium Billing	X	X	X	X	X	X			
Agents Commissions	X	X	X	X	X	X			
Claims Transactions	X	X	X	X	X	X	X	X	X

Figure 4-3: Simplified enterprise data warehouse bus matrix.

The columns are also culled from the requirements gathering sessions. As we explore the business representatives' decision making process, we listen for "by" and "where" phrases to gain insight to natural analytic groupings. For example, business managers may want to look at claims payments *by* policyholder, agent, and coverage; each represents a core dimension or dimension attribute. Or they may want to analyze payments *where* the agents have more than five years of experience and work in the Eastern region. By listening to their word choices, we gather clues about dimensions and their attributes.

Drafting the enterprise bus matrix is an iterative process; after each business requirements gath-ering session, the matrix is fine-tuned to reflect new insights. By the time the requirements process is winding down, we've arrived at a surprisingly complete matrix. In fact, when no changes to the matrix are made following a session, we know the requirements process is likely nearing the end.

Prioritize for an Orderly Conclusion

Although DW/BI teams and their management generally appreciate the need to gather business requirements, they often fail to appreciate the importance of reaching organizational agreement on priorities. One way to help clarify priorities is to create an "opportunity matrix," as shown in Figure 4-4. The rows—as in the bus matrix—list the core processes of the business. But in the oppor-tunity matrix, the columns represent departments or workgroups rather than common dimensions. Each x in the table indicates which groups are interested in the metrics associated with the business process/event rows. In this manner, the opportunity matrix captures shared data needs and interests across the organization. Keep in mind, however, that focusing on the most frequently requested business process and its metrics doesn't necessarily translate into the top organizational priority.

	Underwriting & Actuarial	Marketing & Sales	Customer Service	Finance
Underwriting Transactions	X	X		
Policy Premium Billing	X	X	X	X
Agents Commissions		X		X
Claims Transactions	X	X	X	X

Figure 4-4: Opportunity matrix.

Once all the requirements have been gathered, we conduct a presentation and prioritization session with senior management from various departments and workgroups. The session begins with a playback of the requirements findings—typically a major eye opener for senior management. These managers may have been funding (or trying to fund) their own department-focused analytic data fiefdoms. They're often unaware of the common information needs across departments, in addition to the redundant resources and organizational waste associated with existing departmental solutions.

We then paint the long term picture of integrated analytic data across the enterprise. Rather than presenting a complex diagram with numerous boxes representing various data stores, we share the enterprise data warehouse bus matrix, illustrated in Figure 4-3, with management. It's a wonderful communication tool to ensure a common vision and understanding without getting mired in technical details.

Each business process row of the matrix represents a project within the overall DW/BI program. As such, we subtly focus the senior managers on manageable (and hopefully meaningful) project scope boundaries.

The dimension columns of the matrix provide the common links between the business processes' KPIs and success metrics. Senior managers need to understand the importance of common conformed dimensions for consistent business rules, labels, and data. They should also appreciate that regardless of which data warehouse project (matrix row) is selected, resources are required to construct core dimension tables that subsequent iterations of the data warehouse—future projects—will use.

Once we achieve a common understanding of the current status and desired goals, we then help prioritize the projects. Using the two-by-two grid in Figure 4-5, we ask business management to evaluate each project based on business value, impact, or importance to the organization. Meanwhile, IT representatives have assessed the feasibility of delivering the business process data. In short, for each row of the matrix, business drives the relative vertical placement, while IT drives the relative horizontal placement on the quadrant.

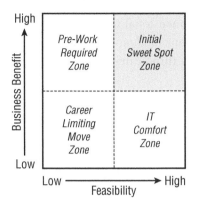

Figure 4-5: Prioritization grid.

This often highly interactive exercise concludes with projects in each of the four quadrants. Those in the upper-right, sweet spot quadrant in Figure 4-5 will be tackled individually as part of the initial phases of the data warehouse program. The metrics associated with the projects in the upper-left quadrant are highly important to the business, so IT resources not assigned to the data warehouse should address the feasibility concerns—most likely data issues, such as inadequate or nonexistent data collection systems—that are deterring those projects.

Projects in the lower-right comfort zone don't warrant immediate attention because they're irrelevant to the business. Finally, those in the lower-left zone should fall to the very bottom of the list.

Achieve an Enterprise Roadmap

We've been involved in dozens of requirements projects that have culminated in this capstone event. Facilitating these sessions is extremely gratifying because the benefits to both the business and data warehouse project team are so significant. By the conclusion of the meeting, there's cross-organizational understanding of the present state of the data, a vision for the ultimate long term enterprise plan, and an agreed-upon roadmap for addressing the gap that's been prioritized by both the business and IT. What more could you ask for?

Now that we've explored our recommended activities and techniques for embarking on a dimensional data warehousing program with iterative projects, you can see why the bottom-up label is a misnomer. We strongly encourage an enterprise orientation, not just from a data perspective but, more important, from a business point of view. Business management buy-in and consensus at this formative stage is critical to the long term acceptance of the enterprise data warehouse environment.

4.11 Think Dimensionally (Beyond Data Modeling)

Margy Ross, Design Tip #160, *Oct 3, 2013*

Our articles and books are loaded with guidance about designing dimensional models for the data warehouse/business intelligence (DW/BI) presentation area. But dimensional modeling concepts go beyond the design of databases that are simple and fast. You should think dimensionally at other critical junctures of a DW/BI project.

When gathering requirements for a DW/BI initiative, you need to listen for and then synthesize the findings around business processes, as described in article 4.7, *Identifying Business Processes*. Sometimes teams get lulled into focusing on a set of required reports or dashboard gauges. Instead you should constantly ask yourself about the business process measurement events producing the report or dashboard metrics. As you are planning the project's scope, you should remain steadfast about focusing on a single business process per project and not sign up to deploy a dashboard that includes a handful of them in a single iteration. Attempting to design dimension models to deliver multiple loosely related metrics is a classic "failure to declare the grain" mistake.

Although it's critical that the DW/BI team concentrates on business processes, it's equally important to get IT and business management on the same process-centric wavelength. Due to historical IT funding policies, the business may be more familiar with departmental data deployments. You need to shift their mindset about the DW/BI rollout to a process perspective, not a department or report perspective. When prioritizing opportunities and developing the DW/BI roadmap, business processes are the unit of work. Fortunately, business management typically embraces this approach since it mirrors their thinking about key performance indicators, and can nudge IT in the right direction. Plus, the business has lived with the inconsistencies, incessant debates, and never ending reconciliations caused by the departmental approach, so they're ready for a fresh tactic. Working with senior business partners, you should rank each business process on business value and feasibility, then tackle processes with the highest impact and feasibility scores first. Although prioritization is a joint activity with the business, your underlying understanding of the organization's business processes is essential to its effectiveness and subsequent actionability.

If tasked with drafting the DW/BI system's data architecture, you need to wrap your head around the organization's processes, along with the associated master descriptive dimension data. The prime deliverable for this activity, the enterprise data warehouse bus matrix, is described in our article 5.6, *The Matrix: Revisited*. The matrix also serves as a useful tool for touting the potential benefits of more rigorous master data management.

Data stewardship or governance programs should focus first on the business's major dimensions. Depending on the industry, the list might include date, customer, product, employee, facility, provider, patient, student, faculty, account, and so on. Thinking about the central nouns used to describe the business translates into a list of data governance efforts to be led by subject matter experts from the business community. Establishing data governance responsibilities for these nouns is the key to eventually deploying dimensions that deliver consistency and address the business's needs for analytic filtering, grouping, and labeling. Robust dimensions translate into robust DW/BI systems.

As you can see, the fundamental motivation for dimensional modeling is front and center long before you descend into the technical world of star schemas or OLAP cubes. Dimensional concepts link the business and technical communities together as they collaboratively specify the DW/BI deliverables.

4.12 Using the Dimensional Model to Validate Business Requirements

Bob Becker, Design Tip #123, May 5, 2010

The Kimball Group has frequently written about the importance of focusing on business requirements as the foundation for a successful DW/BI implementation. Article 4.2, *More Business Requirements Gathering Dos and Don'ts*, provides a crisp set of dos and don'ts for gathering requirements. However, some organizations find it difficult to land on the right level of detail when documenting the requirements, and then leveraging them to define the scope of a DW/BI development iteration.

Many organizations have formalized rules of engagements for major IT development efforts including a set of structured deliverables used in the development process. This often includes a document such as a functional specification for capturing business requirements. Unfortunately, these documents were originally intended to support operational system development efforts and are typically ineffective for capturing the requirements to build a BI system. It's often difficult to translate DW/BI business requirements into the type of scenarios and detail called for in these templates. In addition, DW/BI requirements are often fuzzy rather than specific; they may be captured in statements such as "measure sales volume every which way" or "slice and dice claims at any level of detail."

Sometimes DW/BI requirements are captured as a set of representative analytic questions or a set of predetermined reports with caveats surrounding required flexibility to support ad hoc reporting capabilities. Such requirements make it hard for the business representatives and DW/BI project team to agree on the exact requirements that are in scope or out of scope.

To confront this challenge, organizations should develop the data warehouse bus matrix (see article 5.7, *Drill Down into a Detailed Bus Matrix*) and logical dimensional model as deliverables before looping back to finalize the business requirements and scope sign-off. The bus matrix clearly identifies the business processes and associated dimensions that represent the high-level data architecture required to support the business requirements. The bus matrix alone can help define scope. The logical dimensional model then describes the details of the DW/BI data architecture: dimension tables, columns, attributes, descriptions, and the beginnings of the source to target maps for a single business process. Including the logical model allows the business representatives to concur that their requirements can be met by the proposed data model. Likewise, it is important that the DW/BI project team commit to the business users that they understand the required data, have performed the necessary technical evaluation including data profiling, and agree that they can populate the logical dimensional model with the anticipated data. Gaining this agreement will enable both the business community and DW/BI project team to reach a common understanding of the business requirements and scope as documented by the logical data model. Once the model has been agreed to, then any business requirement that can't be resolved by the data represented by the logical data model is clearly out of scope. Likewise, any business requirements that can be resolved by the logical data model are in scope.

The logical dimensional model should be developed jointly by representatives from all interested groups: business users, reporting teams, and the DW/BI project team. It is critical that the appropriate individuals are represented on the dimensional data model design team as described in article 7.3, *Staffing the Dimensional Modeling Team*, for this strategy to be effective. Be sure to incorporate thorough reviews of the proposed data models with a wide set of business users and DW/BI project team members to assure that all the business and technical requirements and challenges have been identified (see article 7.9, *When Is the Dimensional Model Design Done?*).

5 Data Architecture

With the business requirements in hand, it's time to turn our attention to data architecture. We launch this chapter with a series of historically significant articles in which Ralph lays out the justification for dimensional modeling. From there, we focus on the enterprise data warehouse bus architecture and associated matrix for establishing the data warehouse's integration strategy. We then gather together perspectives on the agile approach and how it supports data warehousing. We provide guidance for achieving integration via stewardship, rather than being distracted by the debate over centralized versus distributed data stores. Finally, we offer a comparison of the Kimball bus architecture to the dominant hub-and-spoke alternative, the Corporate Information Factory.

Making the Case for Dimensional Modeling

The three articles in this section originally referred to data models normalized to third normal form (3NF) as *entity-relationship (ER) models*. Because ER diagrams merely depict the relationship between tables in a relational database management system, they can be used to illustrate both dimensional and third normal form structures. Therefore, we've changed the references from ER models to either 3NF or normalized for greater clarity throughout this section.

5.1 Is ER Modeling Hazardous to DSS?

Ralph Kimball, DBMS, Oct 1995

As mentioned in the section introduction, ER has been systematically changed to either 3NF or normalized, however we've retained the original article title from 1995. DSS is an acronym for decision support systems, the term originally used to describe DW/BI systems.

Normalized modeling is a powerful technique for designing transaction processing systems in relational environments. The normalization of physical data structures has greatly contributed to the phenomenal success of getting large amounts of data into relational databases. However, models normalized to third normal form do not contribute to the users' ability to query the data. I recommend a different technique, called dimensional modeling (DM), to structure data for querying. Now that you have succeeded in getting the data into your operational databases, it is time to get the data out.

The two modeling approaches require different starting assumptions, techniques, and design trade-offs, and yield very different database designs. A dimensional model also produces a database with fewer tables and keys to administer than a normalized database.

In my classes, I explicitly ask students about their perceptions of data normalization. They consistently say that they perform normalization in their modeling "to take the redundancy out of the data." They look for one-to-many or many-to-many relationships among data elements, and separate the data elements into distinct tables joined by keys. They then use the modeling tool to automate the creation of normalized physical data structures directly from the model. The use of normalized tables simplifies update and insert operations because changes to the data affect only single records in the underlying tables.

Dimensional Model versus Normalized Model

Unfortunately, the reliance on 3NF normalization proliferates tables mindlessly. Every IT shop that has built a normalized model of an important business process (such as sales) has a similar looking map that covers most of a wall. There are hundreds of tables connected by an even larger number of join paths. The result is overwhelming, and, from a business user perspective, unusable. No human being or computer software can analyze such a normalized entity-relationship diagram in its entirety. ER diagrams are useful, but they are meant to be viewed in small sections, not all at once.

A dimensional model looks very different. Figure 5-1 shows a dimensional schema for cash register sales in a large retail chain. The central and largest table is called the fact table. It is the only table with a composite key. The rest of the fact table consists of *facts* that you can think of as numerical business measurements taken at the intersection of the dimensions. In an enterprise data warehouse, you can have a number of separate fact tables, each representing a different business process within the organization, such as orders, inventory, shipments, and returns. These separate fact tables will be threaded by as many common dimension tables as possible. Although the surrounding dimension tables have several descriptive text fields, they will always have far fewer rows and take up much less disk space than the fact table. Each dimension table has a single part key. The fields in dimension tables are typically textual and are used as the source of constraints and row headers in reports.

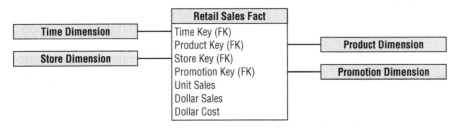

Figure 5-1: A dimensional model for grocery store sales.

Dimensional schemas such as the one shown in Figure 5-1 support two specific kinds of queries: browse and multi-table join. Browse queries operate on only one of the dimension tables and do not involve joins. A typical browse query occurs when the user asks for a pull-down list of all the brand names in the product dimension table, perhaps subject to constraints on other elements in the dimension table. This query must respond instantly because the user's full attention is on the screen. Multi-table join queries occur after a series of browses and involve constraints placed on several of the dimension tables that are all joined to the fact table simultaneously. The goal is to fetch hundreds or possibly thousands of underlying fact records into a small answer set for the user, grouped together by one or more textual attributes selected from the dimension tables. Even so-called table scans fit this second paradigm because there will always be some kind of constraint and grouping action in a decision support query. This second kind of query is rarely instantaneous because of the significant resources required to satisfy the query.

Dimensional modeling is a top-down design process. First you identify the main business processes that act as the sources of the fact tables, and then you populate the fact tables with numeric, additive facts. You describe each fact record by as many business dimensions as you can identify. The resulting fact table records consist entirely of key values that have many-to-many relationships with one another, together with numeric data representing measurements. Overall, the storage of the fact table records is quite efficient. The dimension tables represent the biggest departure from the usual normalization techniques. It is important that the dimension tables remain as flat tables without being further normalized. This is the hardest design step for relational data modelers to accept.

If the dimension tables are normalized into typical *snowflake* structures, as shown in Figure 5-2, two bad things happen. First, the data model becomes too complex to present to the user. Second, linking the elements among the various branches of the snowflake compromises browsing performance. Even when a long text string appears redundantly in the dimension table and can be moved to an *outrigger* table, you won't save enough disk space to justify moving it. The fact table is always overwhelmingly the largest table in a dimensional schema. In many cases, normalization can actually increase the storage requirements. If the cardinality of the repeated dimension data element is high (in other words, there are just a few duplications), the outrigger table may be nearly as big as the main dimension table. But we have introduced another key structure that is now repeated in both tables.

The final argument given for normalizing the dimensions is to improve update performance. This is rarely important in a decision support environment. You update the dimension tables only once per night (typically), and the processing associated with loading perhaps millions of fact records dominates the relatively minor processing associated with inserting or updating dimension records.

A dimensional model has a fixed structure that has no alternative join paths. This greatly simplifies the optimization and evaluation of queries on these schemas. There is only one basic evaluation approach, along with a "bail out" option. First, you evaluate the constraints on all of the dimension tables. Then you prepare a long sorted list of composite keys to the fact table. You scan the fact table composite index in sorted order once, fetching all of the required records into the answer set. Period. The only exception to scanning the fact table index occurs when you notice that your dimensional constraints are so weak that you have an unreasonably long list of composite candidate keys. "Unreasonably long" should be several times the number of actual records in the fact table. At this point—and before attempting to scan the index—you bail out to a relation scan in which you look at every fact table record without using any indexes.

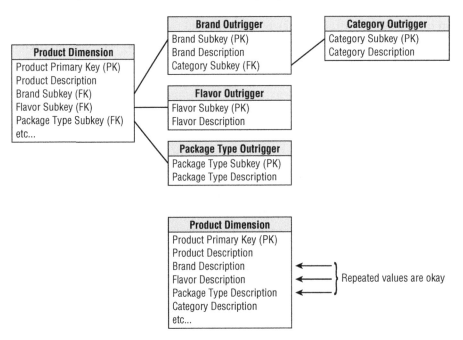

Figure 5-2: Two representations of a product dimension—the top snowflaked version is normalized to 3NF, and the bottom is denormalized into a flat dimension.

Watch closely as your database management system (DBMS) attempts to process a dimensional query. If the query evaluation plan has the fact table part way down the list with the dimension tables mentioned after it, your DBMS doesn't know how to do dimensional schemas. When the fact table is only part way down the list, the DBMS is writing a scratch subset of the fact table to the disk. The DBMS is then testing the resulting records individually against the remaining dimension tables and the result is a query that runs much too long.

A final and somewhat controversial difference between normalized and dimensional models is the degree of judgment left in the hands of the designer. The essence of a good dimensional model is the choice of the set of most natural dimensions from a business user's perspective. There are always two or more alternatives that represent the data in the same way, but package the dimensions differently. Ultimately, the designer's judgment must prevail.

It may be helpful to have a normalized ER diagram before embarking on a dimensional design because the data warehouse team may understand the data better and may be more confident of the governance processes underlying the data. However, the team must set aside the normalized ER diagram during the data warehouse design process because dimensional modeling must proceed from a user perspective, rather than from a data perspective. If you do not already have an ER analysis, I don't recommend taking the time to do it for the purpose of building a data warehouse database. The last 75 percent of a normalization exercise is squeezing redundancy out of the data—especially out of the dimension tables—which does not benefit the dimensional design.

5.2 A Dimensional Modeling Manifesto

Ralph Kimball, DBMS, *Aug 1997*

Dimensional modeling (DM) is the name of a logical design technique often used for data warehouses. It is different from, and contrasts with, normalized modeling, which can have up to five levels of normalization. For the sake of brevity we will choose the most common normalization level (third) and designate all of these approaches as 3NF. This article points out the many differences between the two modeling techniques and draws a line in the sand: DM is the only viable technique for databases that are designed to support business user queries in a data warehouse. 3NF is very useful for the transaction capture and data administration phases of constructing a data warehouse, but it should be avoided for user delivery.

What Is 3NF Normalized Modeling?

3NF normalization is a logical design technique that seeks to remove the redundancy in data. Imagine we have a business that takes orders and sells products to customers. In the early days of computing (long before relational databases) when we first transferred this data to a computer, we probably captured the original paper order as a single wide record with many fields. Such a record could easily have been 1,000 bytes distributed across 50 fields. The line items of the order were probably represented as a repeating group of fields embedded in the master record. Having this data on the computer was very useful, but we quickly learned some basic lessons about storing and manipulating data. One of the lessons we learned was that data in this form was difficult to keep consistent because each record stood on its own. The customer's name and address appeared many times, because this data was repeated whenever a new order was taken. Inconsistencies in the data were rampant because all of the instances of the customer address were independent, and updating the customer's address was a messy transaction.

Even in the early days, we learned to separate out the redundant data into distinct tables, such as a customer master and product master, but we paid a price. Our software systems for retrieving and manipulating the data became complex and inefficient because they required careful attention to the processing algorithms for linking these sets of tables together. We needed a database system that was very good at linking tables. This paved the way for the relational database revolution, where the database was devoted to just this task.

The relational database revolution bloomed in the mid 1980s. Most of us learned what a relational database was by reading Chris Date's seminal book on the subject, *An Introduction to Database Systems* (Addison Wesley), first published in the late 1970s. As we paged through Chris's book, we worked through his parts, suppliers, and cities database examples. It didn't occur to most of us to ask whether the data was completely "normalized" or whether any of the tables could be "snowflaked," and Chris didn't develop these topics. In my opinion, Chris was trying to explain the more fundamental concepts of how to think about tables that were relationally joined. 3NF modeling and normalization were developed in later years as the industry shifted its attention to transaction processing.

The 3NF modeling technique is a discipline used to illuminate the microscopic relationships among data elements. The highest art form of 3NF modeling is to remove all redundancy in the data. This is immensely beneficial to transaction processing because transactions are made very simple and deterministic. The transaction of updating a customer's address may devolve to a single record lookup in a customer address master table. This lookup is controlled by a customer address key, which defines uniqueness of the customer address record and allows an indexed lookup that is extremely fast. It is safe to say that the success of transaction processing in relational databases is mostly due to the discipline of 3NF modeling.

However, in our zeal to make transaction processing efficient, we have lost sight of our original, most important goal. We have created databases that cannot be queried! Even our simple orders example creates a database of dozens of normalized tables linked together by a bewildering spider web of joins, as illustrated in Figure 5-3. All of us are familiar with the big chart on the wall of the IT database designer's cubicle. The 3NF model for the enterprise has hundreds of logical entities! High end systems, such as SAP, have thousands of entities. Each of these entities usually turns into a physical table when the database is implemented. This situation is not just an annoyance, it is a showstopper:

- Business users cannot understand, navigate, or remember a 3NF model. There is no graphical user interface (GUI) that takes a general 3NF model and makes it usable by users.
- Software cannot usefully query a general 3NF model. Cost-based optimizers that attempt to do this are notorious for making the wrong choices, with disastrous consequences for performance.
- Use of the 3NF modeling technique defeats the basic allure of data warehousing, namely intuitive and high performance retrieval of data.

Each box in Figure 5-3 actually represents many entities. Each business process shown is probably a separate legacy application. The equivalent DM design would isolate each business process and surround it with just its relevant dimensions.

Ever since the beginning of the relational database revolution, IT shops have noticed this problem. Many of them that tried to deliver data to business users have recognized the impossibility of presenting these immensely complex schemas to business users, and many of these IT shops have stepped back to attempt "simpler designs." I find it striking that these simpler designs all look very similar! Almost all of these simpler designs can be thought of as dimensional. In a natural, almost unconscious way, hundreds of IT designers have returned to the roots of the original relational model because they know the database cannot be used unless it is packaged simply. It is probably accurate to say that this natural dimensional approach was not invented by any single person. It is an irresistible force in the design of databases that will always appear when the designer places understandability and performance as the highest goals. We are now ready to define the DM approach.

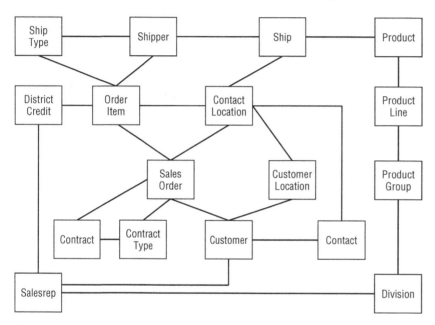

Figure 5-3: A high level 3NF model.

What Is DM?

DM is a logical design technique that seeks to present the data in a standard, intuitive framework that allows for high performance access. It is inherently dimensional, and it adheres to a discipline that uses the relational model with some important restrictions. Every dimensional model is composed of one table with a multipart key, called the fact table, and a set of smaller tables called dimension tables. Each dimension table has a single part primary key that corresponds exactly to one of the components of the multipart key in the fact table, as shown in Figure 5-4. This characteristic star-like structure was originally called a *star join*, but we will refer to it as a dimensional model.

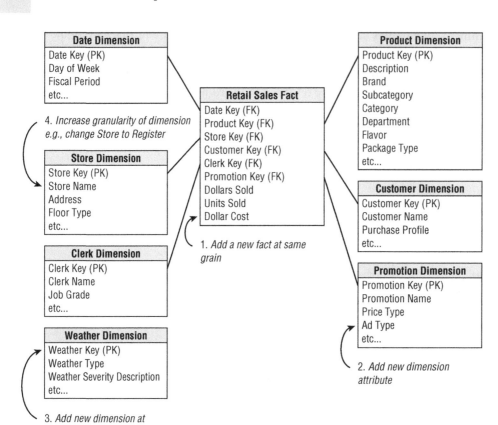

Figure 5-4: A detailed dimensional model for retail point of sales. Numbers 1 through 4 show places where the design may be gracefully extended.

A fact table, because it has a multipart primary key made up of two or more foreign keys, always expresses a many-to-many relationship. The most useful fact tables also contain one or more numerical measures, or facts, that are physical measurements that occur for the combination of keys that define each record. In Figure 5-4, the facts are dollars sold, units sold, and dollars cost. The most useful facts in a fact table are numeric and additive. Additivity is crucial because data warehouse applications almost never retrieve a single fact table record; rather, they fetch back hundreds, thousands, or even millions of these records at a time, and almost the only useful thing to do with so many fact records is to add them up.

Dimension tables, by contrast, most often contain descriptive textual information. Dimension attributes are used as the source of the interesting constraints in data warehouse queries, and are virtually always the source of the row headers in the SQL answer set. In Figure 5-4, we could constrain on the lemon-flavored products via the flavor attribute in the product table, and on radio promotions via the ad type attribute in the promotion table. It should be obvious that the power of the database in Figure 5-4 is proportional to the quality and depth of the dimension tables.

The charm of the database design in Figure 5-4 is that it is highly recognizable to the business users. I have observed literally hundreds of instances where users agree immediately that this is "their business."

DM versus 3NF

Obviously, Figure 5-3 and Figure 5-4 look quite different. Many designers react to this by saying, "There must be less information in the dimensional model," or "The dimensional model is only used for high level summaries." Both of these statements are false.

The key to understanding the relationship between DM and 3NF is that a single 3NF diagram breaks down into multiple DM diagrams. Think of a large 3NF diagram as representing every possible business process in the enterprise. The enterprise 3NF diagram may have sales calls, order entries, shipment invoices, customer payments, and product returns, all on the same diagram. In a way, the 3NF diagram does itself a disservice by representing on one diagram multiple processes that never coexist in a single data set at a single consistent point in time. It's no wonder the 3NF diagram is overly complex. Thus, the first step in converting a 3NF diagram to a set of DM diagrams is to separate the 3NF diagram into its discrete business processes and model each one separately.

The second step is to select the many-to-many relationships in the 3NF model containing numeric and additive nonkey facts and designate them as fact tables. The third step is to denormalize all of the remaining tables into flat tables with single part keys that connect directly to the fact tables. These tables become the dimension tables. In cases where a dimension table connects to more than one fact table, we represent this same dimension table in both schemas, and we refer to the dimension tables as *conformed* between the two dimensional models.

The resulting dimensional model of a data warehouse for a large enterprise will consist of somewhere between 10 and 25 very similar looking dimensional models. Each dimensional model will have four to 20 dimension tables. If the design has been done correctly, many of these dimension tables will be shared from fact table to fact table. Applications that drill down will simply be adding more dimension attributes to the SQL answer set from within a single dimensional model. Applications that drill across will simply be linking separate fact tables together through the conformed, shared dimensions. Even though the overall suite of schemas in the enterprise dimensional model is complex, the query processing is very predictable because each fact table should be queried independently at the lowest level.

The Strengths of DM

The dimensional model has a number of important data warehouse advantages that the 3NF model lacks. First, the dimensional model is a predictable, standard framework. Report writers, query tools, and user interfaces can all make strong assumptions about the dimensional model to make the user interfaces more understandable and processing more efficient. For instance, because nearly all of the constraints come from the dimension tables, a user tool can provide high performance "browsing" across the attributes within a dimension via the use of bitmap indexes. Metadata can use the known cardinality of values in a dimension to guide the user interface behavior. The predictable framework offers immense advantages in processing. Rather than using a cost-based optimizer, a database engine can make very strong assumptions about first constraining the dimension tables and then "attacking" the fact table at once with the Cartesian product of those dimension table keys satisfying the user's constraints. Amazingly, by using this approach, it is possible to evaluate arbitrary n-way joins to a fact table in a single pass through the fact table's index. We are so used to thinking of n-way joins as hard that a whole generation of DBAs doesn't realize that the n-way join problem is formally equivalent to a single sort-merge. Really.

A second strength of DM is that the predictable framework withstands unexpected changes in user behavior. Every dimension is equivalent. All dimensions can be thought of as symmetrically equal entry points into the fact table. The logical design can be done independent of expected query patterns. The user interfaces are symmetrical, the query strategies are symmetrical, and the SQL generated against the dimensional model is symmetrical.

A third strength of DM is that it is gracefully extensible to accommodate unexpected new data elements and design decisions. When we say gracefully extensible, we mean several things. First, all existing fact and dimension tables can be changed in place by simply adding new data rows in the table, or the table can be changed in place with a SQL `ALTER_TABLE` command. Data should not have to be reloaded. Graceful extensibility also means that that no query or reporting tool needs to be reprogrammed to accommodate the change. And finally, graceful extensibility means that all old applications continue to run without yielding different results. In Figure 5-4, numbers 1 through 4 indicate where graceful changes can be made after the data warehouse is up and running by:

1. Adding new additive numeric fields in the fact table, as long as they are consistent with the fundamental grain of the existing fact table
2. Adding new dimensional attributes
3. Adding completely new dimensions, as long as there is a single value of that dimension defined for each existing fact record
4. Breaking existing dimension records down to a lower level of granularity from a certain point in time forward

A fourth strength of DM is that there is a body of standard approaches for handling common modeling situations in the business world. Each of these situations has a well understood set of alternatives that can be specifically programmed in report writers, query tools, and other user interfaces. These modeling situations include:

- Slowly changing dimensions, where a constant dimension such as product or customer actually evolves slowly and asynchronously. Dimensional modeling provides specific techniques for handling slowly changing dimensions, depending on the business environment.
- Heterogeneous products, where a business such as a bank needs to track a number of different lines of business together within a single common set of attributes and facts, but at the same

time needs to describe and measure the individual lines of business in highly idiosyncratic ways using incompatible measures
- Event-handling databases, where the fact table usually turns out to be *factless*

A final strength of DM is the growing body of administrative utilities and software processes that manage and use aggregates. Recall that aggregates are summary records that are logically redundant with base data already in the data warehouse, but are used to enhance query performance. A comprehensive aggregate strategy is required in every medium- and large-sized data warehouse implementation. To put it another way, if you don't have aggregates, then you are potentially wasting millions of dollars on hardware upgrades to solve performance problems that could be otherwise addressed by aggregates.

All of the aggregate management software packages and aggregate navigation utilities depend on a very specific single structure of fact and dimension tables that is absolutely dependent on the dimensional model. If you don't adhere to the dimensional approach, you cannot benefit from these tools.

Myths about DM

A few myths floating around about DM deserve to be addressed. Myth number one is "Implementing a dimensional model will lead to stovepipe decision support systems." This myth sometimes goes on to blame denormalization for supporting only specific applications that therefore cannot be changed. This myth is a short-sighted interpretation of DM that has managed to get the message exactly backwards! First, we have argued that every 3NF model has an equivalent set of dimensional models that contain the same information. Second, we have shown that even in the presence of organizational change and business user adaptation, the dimensional model extends gracefully without altering its form. It is in fact the 3NF model that whipsaws the application designers and users!

A source of this myth, in my opinion, is the designer who is struggling with fact tables that have been prematurely aggregated. For instance, the design in Figure 5-4 is expressed at the individual sales ticket line item level. This is the correct starting point for this retail database because this is the lowest possible grain of data. There just isn't any further breakdown of the sales transaction. If the designer had started with a fact table that had been aggregated up to weekly sales totals by store, there would be all sorts of problems in adding new dimensions, new attributes, and new facts. However, this isn't a problem with the design technique; this is a problem with the database being prematurely aggregated.

Myth number two is "No one understands DM." This myth is absurd. I have seen hundreds of excellent dimensional designs created by people I have never met or had in my classes. A whole generation of designers from the packaged goods retail and manufacturing industries has been using and designing dimensional databases for the past 15 years. I personally learned about dimensional models from A.C. Nielsen and IRI applications that were installed in such places as Procter & Gamble and The Clorox Company as early as 1982.

Incidentally, although this article has been couched in terms of relational databases, nearly all of the arguments in favor of the power of dimensional modeling hold perfectly well for proprietary multidimensional OLAP databases.

Myth number three is "Dimensional models only work with retail databases." This myth is rooted in the historical origins of DM, but not in its current day reality. DM has been applied to many different businesses including retail banking, commercial banking, property and casualty insurance, health insurance, life insurance, brokerage, telephone company operations, newspaper advertising, oil company fuel sales, government agency spending, and manufacturing shipments.

Myth number four is "Snowflaking is an alternative to DM." Snowflaking is the removal of low cardinality textual attributes from dimension tables and the placement of these attributes in secondary dimension tables. For instance, a product category can be treated this way and physically removed from the low level product dimension table. I believe this method compromises cross-attribute browsing performance and may interfere with the legibility of the database, but some designers are convinced that this is a good approach. Snowflaking is certainly not at odds with DM. A designer can snowflake with a clear conscience if this technique improves user understandability and overall performance. The argument that snowflaking helps the maintainability of the dimension table is specious. Maintenance issues are indeed leveraged by normalization disciplines, but all of this happens in the back room of the data warehouse, before the data is loaded into the final dimensional schema.

The final myth is "DM only works for certain kinds of single subject data marts." This myth is an attempt to marginalize DM by individuals who do not understand its fundamental power and applicability. DM is the appropriate technique for the overall design of a complete enterprise-level data warehouse. Such a dimensional design consists of families of business process subject areas, each implemented via one or more dimensional models. The families are linked together in an effective way by insisting on the use of conformed dimensions.

In Defense of DM

Now it's time to take off the gloves. I firmly believe that DM is the only viable technique for designing end user delivery databases. 3NF modeling defeats end user delivery and should not be used for this purpose.

3NF modeling does not really model a business; rather, it models the micro relationships among data elements. 3NF modeling does not have "business rules," it has "data rules." Few if any global design requirements in the 3NF modeling methodology speak to the completeness of the overall design. For instance, does your CASE tool try to tell you if all of the possible join paths are represented and how many there are? Are you even concerned with such issues in a 3NF design? What does 3NF have to say about standard business modeling situations such as slowly changing dimensions?

3NF models are wildly variable in structure. Tell me in advance how to optimize the querying of hundreds of interrelated tables in a big 3NF model. By contrast, even a big suite of dimensional models has an overall deterministic strategy for evaluating every possible query, even those crossing many fact tables. (Hint: You control performance by querying each fact table separately. If you actually believe that you can join many fact tables together in a single query and trust a cost-based optimizer to decide on the execution plan, then you haven't implemented a data warehouse for real business users.)

The wild variability of the structure of 3NF models means that each data warehouse needs custom, handwritten, and tuned SQL. It also means that each schema, once it is tuned, is very vulnerable to changes in the user's querying habits, because such schemas are asymmetrical. By contrast, in a dimensional model all dimensions serve as equal entry points to the fact table. Changes in users' querying habits don't change the structure of the SQL or the standard ways of measuring and controlling performance.

3NF models do have their place in the data warehouse. First, the 3NF model should be used in transaction processing applications based on relational technology. This is the best way to achieve the highest transaction performance and the highest ongoing data integrity. Second, the 3NF model can be used very successfully in the back room data cleaning and combining steps of the data warehouse.

However, before data is packaged into its final queryable format, it must be loaded into a dimensional model. The dimensional model is the only viable technique for achieving both user understandability and high query performance in the face of ever changing user questions.

5.3 There Are No Guarantees

Ralph Kimball, Intelligent Enterprise, *Aug 2000*

As database designers, we talk frequently about business rules. Business rules, after all, are the heart and soul of our applications. If our systems obey the business rules, then the data will be correct, our applications will function, and our users and management will be happy.

But what exactly is a business rule? Where do we declare business rules and where do we enforce them? Let's propose four levels of business rules, starting with the simplest local definitions of data that are clearly enforced at the database level:

1. **Single field format definitions, enforced directly by the database:**
   - The payment field is an amount interpreted as dollars and cents.
   - The surname field is a text field expressed in the UNICODE character set.

2. **Multiple field key relationships, enforced by key declarations residing in the database:**
   - The brand name field in the brand table has a many-to-one relationship with the manufacturer name field in the manufacturer table.
   - The product foreign key in the sales fact table has a many-to-one relationship to the product primary key in the product dimension table.

3. **Relationships between entities, declared on a third normal form (3NF) entity-relationship (ER) diagram, but not directly enforced by the database because the relationship is many-to-many:**
   - Employee is a sub-type of person.
   - Supplier supplies customer.

4. Complex business logic, relating to business processes, and enforced perhaps only at data entry time, by a complex application:

   ■ When an insurance policy has been committed but has not yet been approved by the underwriter, the administration date can be NULL, but when the policy has been under-written, the administration date must be present and must always be more recent than the agreement date.

Looking at these four kinds of business rules makes it clear that the core database software manages only the first two levels, single field format definitions and multiple field key relationships. While these first two levels are a kind of bedrock of any proper database environment, we would hope to enforce level 3, relationships between entities, and level 4, complex business logic, because there is much more valuable business content at these levels.

Does 3NF Modeling Handle Business Rules?

3NF normalized modeling is something of a Holy Grail among database designers. At first blush it appears to be a comprehensive language for describing relationships between entities. But what does 3NF modeling really guarantee?

3NF modeling is a diagramming technique for specifying one-to-one, many-to-one, and many-to-many relationships among data elements. While in a pure sense a 3NF model is only a logical model, powerful tools such as Computer Associates' ERwin convert a 3NF diagram into data definition language (DDL) declarations that appropriately define key definitions and join constraints among tables that enforce the various flavors of relationships.

This all sounds wonderful. What's the problem? What is missing from this picture provided by 3NF modeling?

In my opinion, while 3NF modeling is a useful technique for beginning the process of understanding and enforcing business rules, it falls far short of providing any kind of completeness or guarantee. Worse, it has been drastically overblown as a platform for all forms of business rules. Here is my list of practical and theoretical issues with 3NF modeling:

■ **3NF modeling is incomplete.** The entities and relationships on any given diagram represent only what the designer decided to emphasize, or was aware of. There is no test of a 3NF model to determine if the designer has specified all possible one-to-one, many-to-one, or many-to-many relationships.

■ **3NF modeling is not unique.** A given set of data relationships can be represented by many 3NF diagrams.

■ **Most real data relationships are many-to-many.** This is a kind of catch-all declaration that doesn't provide any discipline or value. "Enforcing" a many-to-many relationship is a kind of oxymoron. There are many flavors of many-to-many relationships involving various conditions and degrees of correlation that would be useful to include as business rules, but 3NF modeling provides no extensions to the basic many-to-many declaration.

■ **3NF models are sometimes ideal, not real.** Nearly all the large corporate data models I have seen are an exercise in "how things ought to be." Up to a point, such a model is a useful exercise in understanding the business, but if that model is not physically populated with real data, I have never found it worthwhile to use the corporate data model as the basis for a pragmatic data warehouse implementation.

■ **3NF models are rarely models of real data.** A close corollary to the previous point is that we don't have tools for crawling over real data sets and making 3NF models. We almost always make the 3NF model and then try to shoehorn the data into the model. This fact leads to the odd realization that when dirty data arrives at the data staging area after we've extracted it from a primary production source, we cannot put it into a 3NF model as a prelude to cleaning! We can only put it into the 3NF model after we've cleaned it. And, given the first two points in this section, even if we eventually place the data into a 3NF framework, there is no guarantee that the cleaning step is complete, unique, or has captured many of the interesting data relationships.

■ **3NF models lead to absurdly complex schemas that defeat the primary objectives of information delivery.** Every designer is aware of how complex an enterprise-level normalized model can become. The models underlying Oracle Financials can easily require 2,000 tables, and SAP's model can easily require 10,000 of them. These huge schemas thwart the basic data warehouse objectives of understandability and high performance. Only a few high end hardware vendors still try to deliver data warehouse services against large 3NF schemas, while most of the rest of us have sought simpler design techniques that we can implement far more cost effectively.

At this point, you are probably thinking: "Kimball is at it again. People who really understand data modeling use the E/R technique as their primary tool."

Well, I have always thought of Chris Date as someone who really understands modeling. In many ways, he invented the important concepts of relational database modeling. The seventh edition of his seminal book, *An Introduction to Database Systems* (Addison Wesley, 2000) has just been released, and I was paging through my copy, reminiscing about my own first exposure to these ideas through a much earlier version of the book.

In Chapter 13, "Semantic Modeling," his comments about E/R modeling caught my eye. We have preserved his terminology using "E/R" rather than "3NF" in the following three paragraphs in order to be faithful to his exact wording. I quote:

> *It is not even clear that the E/R 'model' is truly a data model at all, at least in the sense we have been using that term in this book … (page 435).*

> *A charitable reading of [Chen's original paper defining E/R modeling] would suggest that the E/R model is indeed a data model, but one that is essentially just a thin layer on top of the basic relational model (page 436).*

> *The E/R model is completely incapable of dealing with integrity constraints or 'business rules,' except for a few special cases (admittedly important ones) … Declarative rules are too complex to be captured as part of the business model and must be defined separately by the analyst/developer (page 436).*

Although Chris and I come to the database world from very different origins, we appear to agree on the relative importance of E/R modeling. E/R modeling is useful for transaction processing because it reduces redundancy in the data, and it is useful for a limited set of data cleaning activities, but it falls far short of being a comprehensive platform for data warehouse business rules, and it is very difficult to use for data delivery.

Early Dimensional Modeling

I have always been fascinated by the way Chris introduced the relational model in the original editions of his book with his classic suppliers and parts database. To my surprise, the recent edition of his book uses the same original data model as its foundation. In fact, the data model is the book's frontispiece. Study this model, which I cast as Figure 5-5, for a moment.

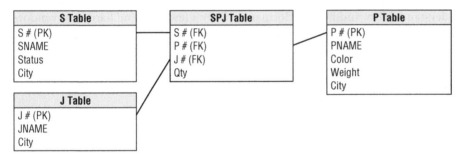

Figure 5-5: The suppliers and parts database.

Doesn't this model look familiar? It's a perfect star schema! The SPJ table is a fact table. It has a multipart key consisting of foreign keys linking to the individual supplier table, parts table, and projects table. The remaining field in the SPJ table is an additive numeric fact that is clearly a measurement.

The S (supplier) table is a perfect dimension table with a single primary key, the S#. The remaining fields are all text, or text-like. The P (parts) and J (projects) tables are also perfect dimension tables and are organized in the same way. The primary keys in all the dimensions are beautiful surrogate keys, devoid of any content found elsewhere in the dimension tables.

A subtle point: Chris could have normalized all three of the dimension tables further by creating a snowflaked City table. But these tables have been left in the classic denormalized form favored by dimensional modelers.

I consider a student to be a "graduate" when they produce dimensional models as perfect as Chris' model. And yet Chris' model is the one we all cut our teeth on starting in the 1970s.

This fact tells me that the classic dimensional model has a profound symmetry and simplicity that are very close to that expressed in the classic view of relational systems. 3NF modeling is effectively an offshoot of this classic view of the relational world that solved some problems and created others.

Enterprise Data Warehouse Bus Architecture

The four articles in this section focus on the bus architecture as an enterprise data integration framework based on a foundation of conformed dimensions.

5.4 Divide and Conquer

Ralph Kimball, Intelligent Enterprise, *Oct 30, 2002*

In article 2.8, *Two Powerful Ideas*, I described two ideas that are the basis for data warehouse design: The first was about separating your systems logically, physically, and administratively into a back room ETL data staging area and a front room data presentation area. The second was about building dimensional schemas and cubes in the presentation area. I left you with the thought that the symmetrical dimensional schemas and cubes in the presentation area gave us a set of predictable points of commonality for linking together data from across the enterprise.

Common Labels Wanted?

Not every enterprise wants or needs a system of common labels for disparate data sources enforced across the enterprise. An umbrella organization that owns a broad portfolio of manufacturing businesses probably doesn't want a common set of labels across all the different product types. The suppliers are different, the product categories are incompatible, the sales channels are distinct, and the customers are varied. Most important, the senior managers of the umbrella organization don't manage the details of the individual businesses and don't treat the businesses monolithically. Similarly, the separate lines of business in a large financial organization may not have much motivation to adopt a set of common labels if their lines of business are quite different.

But many enterprises have a strong desire to enforce a set of common labels across disparate data sources. If these labels are to drive the design of the data warehouse, the enterprise must meet two conditions:

1. The most senior management of the enterprise must be strongly committed to using the common labels.
2. One of the business executives must be available as a forceful sponsor of the effort to define the common labels.

The data warehouse architect, no matter how energetic and persuasive, cannot single-handedly create and enforce a set of common labels for an enterprise. The senior management and the sponsoring business executive must periodically cut through the politics of the enterprise to make sure all the parties stick to the task of defining the common labels.

Business Process Subject Areas Are Not Departmental

Whether or not you put a system of common labels for disparate data sources into place, it's mandatory that you present each single data source to the users with a single set of labels.

Another way to say this is that subject areas are defined by business process data sources, not by departments. If an enterprise has an orders subject area, then there should be exactly one such subject area, which serves to present that data source to all the business users. This subject area should have one set of labels that everyone uses. The enterprise must not have orders data in a sales department data mart, orders data in a marketing department data mart, and orders data in a finance department data mart. Having three different, incompatible views of the same data is poor data warehouse design and a recipe for disaster.

Conformed Dimensions and Facts

Theoretically, the effort of establishing a set of common labels across an enterprise is independent of the data modeling approach you take. But in practice, dimensional modeling forces the issue of establishing common labels, whereas normalized modeling provides no support or inducement for this task. A big normalized model of inconsistent data across an organization is just that: a big model of inconsistent data. Oddly, dimensional modeling is sometimes criticized as being difficult because it strongly invites you to define conformed dimensions. Yes, the difficult part is reaching agreement on common labels in your enterprise, but it has nothing to do with the storage model implied by the choice of modeling technique!

Dimensional modeling divides the world of data into two major types: measurements and descriptions of the context surrounding those measurements. The measurements, which are typically numeric, are stored in fact tables, and the descriptions of the context, which are typically textual, are stored in the dimension tables. Every dimensional design is boringly similar. For example, if the notion of product is found in many places across a large enterprise, the structure of the product dimension in each of these places is likely to be similar, even before you attack the issue of common labels.

If a large enterprise decides it can't or won't create a set of common labels (in all the product dimensions, for instance), the enterprise will have separate data warehouses that aren't intended to be linked together.

But, more likely, when the enterprise decides to create a set of common labels across all the sources of data, the separate subject area teams (or, equivalently, a single centralized team) must sit down to create master dimensions that everyone will use for every data source. These master dimensions are called conformed dimensions. A single, centralized dimension authority creates, administers, and periodically releases each conformed dimension. There would normally be separate dimension authorities for the conformed calendar, product, vendor, employee, and customer dimensions, to name some typical examples.

Conformed dimensions are agreed to by an interdisciplinary team representing all the interests of the enterprise. This is a hard job. It's expected that the team will get stuck from time to time trying to align the incompatible original vocabularies of different groups. This is why the high level business executive sponsor is necessary. The executive must periodically approve these tough vocabulary compromises or even force them to be made.

At the same time the team is defining the conformed dimensions, it's natural to discuss the various kinds of measured facts that exist in the various separate data sources. For instance, if several parts of the enterprise report revenue, then the assembled team is in a good place to discuss the exact definition of these different revenue measurements. If the definitions are highly consistent, the team can combine the revenues mathematically in sums and ratios. We call these highly consistent facts *conformed facts*. Facts that can't be conformed must be labeled differently so that they are not used in computations that could be misleading.

The Data Warehouse Bus Architecture

You can think of the conformed dimensions and facts of an enterprise as a standard set of connection points for applications—in other words, as a data warehouse bus architecture. The term *bus* comes from the bus in an electrical power system or the backplane of a computer, both of which define a set of common connection points and a methodology for making the connections.

By using the data warehouse bus architecture, a set of very simple query applications can retrieve results from separate data sources, all with the same row labels on the answer sets, and then combine the sets by sort-merging these identical row headers in a process called *drilling across* (also called *multi-pass SQL*). The row labels are guaranteed to be drawn from the same domain because they're drawn from the same dimension table! This seemingly obvious and trivial result is immensely powerful. These consistent row headers, because they allow us to divide and conquer the overall data warehouse problem, make possible:

- Distributed systems
- Incremental, adaptive designs
- High performance querying
- Cost-effective hardware solutions

Only for Highly Distributed Systems?

You might ask, is the bus architecture only for highly distributed systems? The bus architecture approach, with its conformed dimensions and facts, has nothing to do with the issue of centralization! The bus architecture is all about using a set of common labels that have been defined across separate data sources. A highly centralized data warehouse with a single design team and physical installation faces exactly the same issues of creating and then using a master set of common labels.

In fact, even in a highly centralized data warehouse, the separate data sources will appear as separate physical tables. Even in a normalized environment, the tables containing measurements and the tables describing the context of the measurements are pretty distinct. In order to perform queries across these separate tables, all the issues addressed by the bus architecture must be attacked in a centralized, normalized environment as well.

Netting Out the Benefits

Using conformed dimensions and conformed facts to build a data warehouse bus architecture is a kind of predictable cookbook approach to building a data warehouse in our complex enterprises. It allows us to divide the problem into separate chunks and arrive at the final solution gradually and incrementally. The upfront investment required with the bus architecture is defining the conformed dimensions and facts. Once that is done, new subject areas can be added as opportunity dictates, as long as they observe the bus architecture rules consistently.

The bus architecture also allows an autonomous development style, where loosely coupled teams cooperate to build an overall distributed system. The bus architecture is therefore a blueprint for separate organizations to share data effectively, even if they have different IT departments and different technologies. In fact, OLAP and ROLAP can coexist gracefully in a bus architecture environment because they only need to be compatible along their row headers at query results time.

 ## 5.5 The Matrix

Ralph Kimball, Intelligent Enterprise, *Dec 7, 1999*

Over the years, I have found that a matrix depiction of the data warehouse plan is a pretty good planning tool once you have gathered the business requirements and performed a full data audit. This matrix approach has been exceptionally effective for distributed data warehouses without a center.

The matrix is simply a vertical list of business process subject areas and a horizontal list of dimensions. Figure 5-6 is an example matrix for the enterprise data warehouse of a large telecommunications company. You start the matrix by listing all the first-level subject areas that you could possibly build over the next three years across the enterprise. A first-level subject area is a collection of related fact tables and dimension tables that is typically:

- Derived from a single data source
- Based on the most atomic data possible to collect from the source
- Conformed to the data warehouse bus

First-level subject areas should be the smallest and least risky initial implementations of an enterprise data warehouse. They form a foundation on which a larger implementation can be brought to completion in the least amount of time, but they are still guaranteed to contribute to the final result without being incompatible stovepipes.

Business Process/Event	Date	Customer	Service	Rate Category	Local Svc Provider	Calling Party	Called Party	Long Dist Provider	Internal Organization	Employee	Location	Equipment Type	Supplier	Item Shipped	Weather	Account Status
1ST LEVEL SUBJECT AREAS																
Customer Billing	X	X	X	X	X			X			X					X
Service Orders	X	X	X		X			X	X	X	X	X			X	X
Trouble Reports	X	X	X		X	X		X	X	X	X	X	X	X	X	X
Yellow Page Ads	X	X		X		X			X	X	X					X
Customer Inquiries	X	X	X	X	X	X		X	X	X	X				X	X
Promotions & Communication	X	X	X	X	X	X		X	X	X	X	X	X	X		X
Billing Call Detail	X	X	X	X	X	X	X	X	X		X	X	X	X	X	X
Network Call Detail	X	X	X	X	X	X	X	X	X		X	X	X	X	X	X
Customer Inventory	X	X	X	X	X			X	X		X	X	X	X		X
Network Inventory	X		X						X	X	X	X	X	X		
Real Estate	X								X	X	X	X				
Labor & Payroll	X								X	X	X					
Computer Charges	X	X	X		X			X	X	X	X	X	X	X		
Purchase Orders	X								X	X	X	X	X	X		
Supplier Deliveries	X								X	X	X	X	X	X		
2ND LEVEL SUBJECT AREAS																
Combined Field Ops	X	X	X	X	X	X		X	X	X	X	X	X	X	X	X
Customer Relationship Mgmt	X	X	X	X	X	X	X	X	X	X	X	X	X	X	X	X
Customer Profit	X	X	X	X	X	X	X	X	X	X	X	X	X	X	X	X

Figure 5-6: Enterprise data warehouse bus matrix for a telecommunications company.

You should try to reduce the risk of implementation as much as possible by basing the first-level subject areas on single production sources. In my experience, the cost and complexity of data warehouse implementation, once the "right" data has been chosen, turns out to be proportional to the number of data sources that must be extracted. Each separate data source can be as much as a six month programming and testing exercise. You must create a production data pipeline from the legacy source through the data staging area to the fact and dimension tables of the presentation part of the data warehouse.

In Figure 5-6, the first-level subject areas for the telecommunications company are many of the major production data sources. An obvious production data source is the customer billing system, listed first. This row in the matrix is meant to represent all the base-level fact tables you expect to build in this subject area. Assume this subject area contains one major base-level fact table, the grain of which is the individual line item on a customer bill. Assume the line item on the bill represents the class of service provided, not the individual telephone call within the class of service. With these assumptions, you can check off the dimensions this fact table needs. For customer bills, you need date, customer, service, rate category, local service provider, long distance provider, location, and account status.

Continue to develop the matrix rows by listing all the possible first-level subject areas, based on known, existing data sources. Sometimes I am asked to include a first-level subject area based on a production system that does not yet exist. I usually decline the offer. I try to avoid including "potential" data sources, unless there is a very specific design and implementation plan in place. Another dangerously idealistic data source is the grand corporate data model, which usually takes up a whole wall of the IT department. Most of this data model cannot be used as a data source because it is not real. Ask the corporate data architect to highlight with a red pen the tables on the corporate data model that are currently populated with real data. These red tables are legitimate drivers of subject areas in the planning matrix and can be used as sources.

The planning matrix columns indicate all the dimensions a subject area might need. A real enterprise data warehouse contains more dimensions than those in Figure 5-6. It is often helpful to attempt a comprehensive list of dimensions before filling in the matrix. When you start with a large list of dimensions, it becomes a kind of creative exercise to ask whether a given dimension could possibly be associated with a subject area. This activity could suggest interesting ways to add dimensional data sources to existing fact tables. The weather dimension in Figure 5-6 is an example of such a creative addition. If you study the details of Figure 5-6, you may decide that more X's should be filled in, or that some significant dimensions should be added. If so, more power to you! You are using the matrix as it was intended.

Inviting Subject Area Groups to the Conforming Meeting

Looking across the rows of the matrix is revealing. You can see the full dimensionality of each subject area at a glance. Dimensions can be tested for inclusion or exclusion. But the real power of the matrix comes from looking at the columns. A column in the matrix is a map of where the dimension is required.

The first dimension, date, is required in every subject area. Every subject area is a time series. But even the date dimension requires some thought. When a dimension is used in multiple subject areas, it must be conformed. Conformed dimensions are the basis for distributed data warehouses, and using conformed dimensions is the way to avoid stovepipe subject areas. A dimension is conformed when two copies of the dimensions are either exactly the same (including the values of the keys and all the attributes), or else one dimension is a perfect subset of the other. So using the date dimension in all the subject areas implies that the subject area teams agree on a corporate calendar. All the subject area teams must use this calendar and agree on fiscal periods, holidays, and workdays.

The grain of the conformed date dimension needs to be consistent as well. An obvious source of stovepipe subject areas is the reckless use of incompatible weeks and months across the subject areas. Get rid of awkward time spans such as quad weeks or 4-4-5-week quarters.

The second dimension in Figure 5-6, customer, is even more interesting than date. Developing a standard definition for customer is one of the most important steps in combining separate sources of data from around the enterprise. The willingness to seek a common definition of the customer is a major litmus test for an organization intending to build an enterprise data warehouse. Roughly speaking, if an organization is unwilling to agree on a common definition of the customer across all subject areas, the organization should not attempt to build a data warehouse that spans these subject areas. The subject areas should remain separate forever.

For these reasons, you can think of the planning matrix columns as the invitation list to the conforming meeting! The planning matrix reveals the interaction between the subject areas and the dimensions.

Communicating with the Boss

The planning matrix is a good communication vehicle for senior management. It is simple and direct. Even if the executive does not know much about the technical details of the data warehouse, the planning matrix sends the message that standard definitions of calendars, customers, and products must be defined, or the enterprise won't be able to use its data.

A meeting to conform a dimension is probably more political than technical. The data warehouse project leader does not need to be the sole force for conforming a dimension such as customer. A senior manager such as the enterprise CIO should be willing to appear at the conforming meeting and make it clear how important the task of conforming the dimension is. This political support is very important. It gets the data warehouse project manager off the hook and puts the burden of the decision making process on senior management's shoulders, where it belongs.

Second-Level Subject Areas

After you have represented all the major production sources in the enterprise with first-level subject areas, you can define one or more second-level areas. A second-level subject area is a combination of two or more first-level areas. In most cases, a second-level subject area is more than a simple union of data sets from the first-level areas. For example, a second-level profitability subject area may result from a complex allocation process that associates costs from several first-level cost-oriented subject areas onto products and customers contained in a first-level revenue subject area. I discuss the issues of creating these kinds of profitability subject areas in article 10.27, *Not So Fast*.

The matrix planning technique helps you build an enterprise data warehouse, especially when the warehouse is a distributed combination of far-flung subject areas. The matrix becomes a resource that is part technical tool, part project management tool, and part communication vehicle to senior management.

5.6 The Matrix: Revisited

Margy Ross, Intelligent Enterprise, Dec 1, 2005

With the current industry buzz focused on master data management (MDM), it's time to revisit one of the most critical elements of the Kimball method. Back in 1999, Ralph Kimball wrote article 5.5, *The Matrix*. The 1999 movie of the same name spawned two sequels, but we haven't devoted an article to our matrix in more than six years.

Dimensional modelers strive to deliver information in a way that's easily understood. The same objectives apply when representing an organization's breadth of performance information and associated descriptive reference data. That sounds like a formidable task, but the tabular row-and-column orientation of a matrix lends itself beautifully to the challenge. The data warehouse bus matrix is akin to a Swiss Army pocketknife for DW/BI professionals; it's one tool that serves multiple purposes, including architecture planning, data integration coordination, and organizational communication.

Matrix Columns for Reference Data

Delving into bus matrix fundamentals, let's start with the matrix columns, which address the demands of master data management and data integration head-on. Each column of the bus matrix corresponds to a natural grouping of standardized, descriptive reference data. The matrix's columns are conformed dimensions containing the textual attributes used for filtering, constraining, grouping, or labeling. Each attribute has an agreed-upon name, definition, and domain values to ensure consistent data presentation, interpretation, and content. The bus matrix includes separate columns to identify the "who, what, where, when, why, and how," such as date, customer, product, and employee associated with each business event or transactional activity.

Much is being said and written lately about the importance and value of master data management and data integration. We wholeheartedly agree; the Kimball Group has been talking about conformed dimensions since our first use of the terminology in 1984. We're thrilled others are jumping on the bandwagon and embracing the concepts. It's simply unacceptable to build separate data stores (whether warehouses, marts, or cubes) without a framework to tie the data together. Reusable conformed dimensions supply potent integration glue, letting businesses drill across core processes with consistent, unified views.

Data Stewardship

Unfortunately, you can't purchase a wonder product to create conformed dimensions and miraculously solve your organization's master data management issues. Defining master conformed dimensions to be used across the enterprise is a cultural and geopolitical challenge. Technology can facilitate and enable data integration, but it doesn't fix the problem. Data stewardship must be a key component of your solution.

In our experience, the most effective data stewards come from the business community. As with technology, the data warehouse team facilitates and enables stewardship by identifying problems and opportunities and then implementing the agreed-upon decisions to create, maintain, and distribute "gold standard" dimensions. But the subject matter experts in the business are the ones rationalizing the diverse business perspectives and driving to common reference data. To reach a consensus, senior business and IT executives must openly promote and support the stewardship process and its outcomes, including the inevitable compromises.

Over the years many have criticized the concept of conformed dimensions as being too hard. Yes, it's difficult to get people in different corners of the business to agree on common attribute names, definitions, and values, but that's the crux of unified, integrated data. If everyone demands their own labels and business rules, there's no chance of delivering the single version of the truth DW promises.

Process-Centric Rows

While the matrix columns refer to the business's nouns, the matrix rows are typically expressed as verbs. Each row of the bus matrix corresponds to a business process within the organization. A business process is simply an activity that the business performs, such as taking orders, shipping, invoicing, receiving payments, and handling service calls. In most cases, measurements or metrics are generated each time one of these actions or events occurs. When the order is taken, the source system captures the order quantities and amounts. At shipping and customer invoicing, you again deal with quantities and amounts, albeit different from the order metrics. Each customer payment has an amount associated with it. Finally, as the business receives service calls from customers, metrics such as call duration are captured.

Each business process is typically supported by an operational system, which can introduce complexity. Some of you may deal with large, monolithic source systems that support a handful of business processes; conversely, others may have several order source systems in their environments. Insert a row in the matrix for each business process that collects or generates unique performance metrics with unique dimensionality.

After listing the core business process rows, you might also identify more complex cross-process or consolidated rows. These consolidated rows can be extremely beneficial analytically, but they are typically much more difficult to implement given the need to combine and potentially allocate performance metrics from multiple source systems; they should be tackled after the underlying processes have been built.

Associate Columns and Rows

Once you've determined several dozen core processes and dimensions, shade the matrix cells to indicate which columns are related to each row. Presto! You see the logical relationships and complex interplay between the organization's conformed reference dimensions and key business processes. By looking across a row, you quickly understand its dimensionality. Looking down a column gives immediate feedback about conformed dimension opportunities and obstacles, visually highlighting dimensions that warrant special attention given their participation in multiple matrix rows.

The number of data warehouse bus matrix rows and columns varies by organization. For many, the matrix is surprisingly square, with approximately 25 to 40 rows and a comparable number of columns. However, there are some interesting industry-specific anomalies, such as in insurance and health care, where matrices typically have many more columns than rows.

It's relatively straightforward to lay out the matrix's rows and columns, and you're essentially defining the overall data architecture in the process. The matrix delivers the big picture perspective, regardless of database or technology platform preferences, while also identifying reasonably manageable development efforts. Separate development teams can work on components of the matrix fairly independently, with confidence that the puzzle pieces will fit together.

The matrix is a succinct and effective communication tool. It lets you visually convey the entire plan within and across development teams, as well as upward and outward throughout the organization, including directly with senior IT and business management. The matrix isn't intended to be a static document that's created and then gathers dust. It will evolve as you delve more deeply into the requirements of the business and realities of your operational source systems.

Common Matrix Mishaps

When drafting a bus matrix, people sometimes struggle with the level of detail expressed by each column or row. Row mishaps commonly fall into the following two categories:

- **Departmental or overly encompassing rows.** The matrix rows shouldn't correspond to the boxes on your corporate organization chart, which represent functional groups, not business processes. Sure, some departments may be responsible or acutely interested in a single business process, but the matrix rows shouldn't look like a list of direct reports to your CEO.
- **Report-centric or too narrowly defined rows.** At the opposite extreme, your bus matrix shouldn't resemble a laundry list of requested reports. A single business process, such as shipping orders, often supports numerous analyses such as customer ranking, sales rep performance, and product movement analysis. The matrix row should reference the business process, not the derivative reports or analytics.

When defining the matrix columns, architects naturally fall into the similar traps of defining columns that are either too broad or too narrow:

- **Overly generalized columns.** A person column on the bus matrix may refer to a wide variety of people, from internal employees to external suppliers and customer contacts. Because there's virtually zero overlap between these populations, it adds confusion to lump them into a single, generic dimension. Similarly, it's not beneficial to put internal and external addresses referring to corporate facilities, employee addresses, and customer sites into a generic location column in the matrix.

■ **Separate columns for each level of a hierarchy.** The columns of the bus matrix should refer to dimensions at their most detailed level. Some business process rows may require an aggregated version of the detailed dimension, such as sales forecast metrics at the brand level. But rather than creating separate matrix columns, such as product, brand, category, and department, for each level of the product hierarchy, we advocate a single column for product. Because the cell is shaded to show participation with a business process row, you can denote the level of detail in the cell (if it's not at the most granular level). An even more extreme example of this mishap is to list each individual descriptive attribute as a separate column; this defeats the concept of dimensions and results in a completely unruly matrix.

Matrix Extensions

One of the beauties of the bus matrix is its simplicity. You can reuse the familiar tabular format to convey other DW/BI relationships. These extensions aren't a substitute for the DW bus matrix, but are intended as complementary opportunities to reuse the framework.

■ **Opportunity matrix.** Once the bus matrix rows have stabilized, replace the dimension columns with business functions, such as marketing, sales, and finance. Based on the business requirements gathering activities, shade the cells to indicate which business functions (columns) are interested in which business process rows. This is a useful tool to assist with the prioritization of matrix rows.

■ **Analytics matrix.** While numerous analyses focus on the results of a single business process, more sophisticated analytics and data presentation tools, such as dashboards, require metrics from multiple business processes. In this case, reference the stable bus matrix rows but list the complex analytic applications as columns, shading the boxes to indicate which business processes are needed by each application to convey the prerequisite building blocks.

■ **Strategic business initiatives matrix.** As a variation of the analytics matrix just described, you can list the organization's key initiatives or executive hot buttons as columns mapped to the underlying process metric rows. This clarifies the need to tackle the underlying components in order to support the broader business initiatives.

■ **Detailed implementation bus matrix.** A single business process matrix row sometimes spawns multiple fact tables or OLAP cubes. For example, this occurs when there's a need to view the metrics at both atomic and summarized levels of detail or with both transactional and snapshot perspectives. In this scenario, the matrix rows are expanded to list individual fact tables or

OLAP cubes, along with their specific granularity and captured or derived metrics, as further described in article 5.7, *Drill Down into a Detailed Bus Matrix*. In this situation the standard dimension columns are reused.

We've described the benefits of creating a data warehouse bus matrix, but what happens if you're not starting with a blank data warehousing slate? Have several data stores already been constructed without regard to common master reference data? Can you rescue these stovepipes and convert them to the bus architecture with conformed dimensions? We discuss these issues in article 14.10, *Four Fixes for Legacy Data Warehouses*.

5.7 Drill Down into a Detailed Bus Matrix

Margy Ross, Design Tip #41, Nov 6, 2002

Many of you are already familiar with the data warehouse bus architecture given its central role in building architected data warehouses. The corresponding bus matrix identifies the key business processes of an organization, along with their associated dimensions. In a single document, the data warehouse team has a tool for planning the overall data warehouse, identifying the shared dimensions across the enterprise, coordinating the efforts of separate implementation teams, and communicating the importance of shared dimensions throughout the organization. We firmly believe drafting a bus matrix is one of the key initial tasks to be completed by every data warehouse team after soliciting the business' requirements.

While the matrix provides a high level overview of the data warehouse presentation layer "puzzle pieces" and their ultimate linkages, it is often helpful to provide more detail as each matrix row is implemented. Multiple fact tables often result from a single business process. Perhaps there's a need to view business results in a combination of transaction, periodic snapshot, or accumulating snapshot perspectives. Alternatively, multiple fact tables are often required to represent atomic versus more summarized information or to support richer analysis in a heterogeneous product environment.

We can alter the matrix's "grain" or level of detail so that each row represents a single fact table (or cube) related to a business process, as illustrated in Figure 5-7. Once we've specified the individual fact table, we can supplement the matrix with columns to indicate the fact table's granularity and corresponding facts (actual, calculated, or implied). Rather than merely marking the dimensions that apply to each fact table, we can indicate the dimensions' level of detail.

The resulting embellished matrix provides a roadmap to the families of fact tables in your data warehouse. While many of us are naturally predisposed to dense details, we suggest you begin with the more simplistic, high level matrix and then drill down into the details as each business process is implemented. Finally, for those of you with an existing data warehouse, the detailed matrix is often a useful tool to document the "as is" status of a more mature warehouse environment.

Business Process	Fact Tables	Granularity	Facts	Date	Policyholder	Coverage	Covered Item	Employee	Policy	Claim	Claimant	3rd Party
Policy Transactions	Corporate Policy Transactions	1 row for every policy transaction	Policy Transaction Amount	X Trxn Eff	X	X	X	X	X			
	Auto Policy Transactions	1 row per auto policy transaction	Policy Transaction Amount	X Trxn Eff	X	X Auto	X Auto	X	X			
	Home Policy Transactions	1 row per home policy transaction	Policy Transaction Amount	X Trxn Eff	X	X Home	X Home	X	X			
Policy Premium Snapshot	Corporate Policy Premiums	1 row for every policy, covered item, and coverage each month	Written Premium Revenue Amount, Earned Premium Revenue Amount	X	X	X	X	X Agent	X			
	Auto Policy Premiums	1 row per auto policy, covered item, and coverage each month	Written Premium Revenue Amount, Earned Premium Revenue Amount	X	X	X Auto	X Auto	X Agent	X			
	Home Policy Premiums	1 row per home policy, covered item, and coverage each month	Written Premium Revenue Amount, Earned Premium Revenue Amount	X	X	X Home	X Home	X Agent	X			
Claim Transactions	Claim Transactions	1 row for every claim transaction	Claim Transaction Amount	X Trxn Eff	X	X	X	X	X	X	X	X
	Claim Accumulating Snapshot	1 row per covered item and coverage on a claim	Original Reserve Amount, Assessed Damage Amount, Reserve Adjustment Amount, Current Reserve Amount, Open Reserve Amount, Claim Amount Paid, Payments Received, Salvage Received, Number of Transactions	X	X	X	X	X Agent	X	X	X	
	Accident Event	1 row per loss party and affiliation in an auto claim	Implied Accident Count	X	X	X Auto	X Auto		X	X Auto	X	X

Figure 5-7: A detailed implementation bus matrix.

Agile Project Considerations

The agile methodology has been used by many development organizations to combat the typical cumbersome "waterfall" approach that emphasizes formal documentation, and a lengthy, often political process where everything must be specified far in advance of implementation. Although the agile approach was developed independently from data warehousing, it fits beautifully with the flexible, distributed, and incremental approach that the Kimball approach advocates.

5.8 Relating to Agile Methodologies

Margy Ross, Design Tip #73, Nov 17, 2005

As an aside, someone forwarded this article to Scott Ambler, who was referenced in the Design Tip. Scott responded by asking for our permission to republish it to the Agile Modeling and Agile Unified Process subscriber lists.

I've fielded several questions recently regarding agile development methodologies. People seem to want a quick binary response: Do we support and approve of agile methods or not? Unfortunately, our reaction is not so clearly black-and-white. One thing for certain is that the agile approach has enthusiastic supporters. Tackling the topic might be akin to discussing someone's religion after having read a bit about it on the internet, likely a foolhardy proposition, but we'll jump in regardless.

First of all, what is agile software development? As with most things related to information technology, agile development takes on slightly different meanings depending on who you talk to or what you read. In general, it refers to a group of methodologies, including Extreme Programming (XP), SCRUM, Adaptive Software Development, and others, which share a common focus on iterative development and minimizing risk by delivering new functionality in short time frames, often measured in weeks. These approaches were initially referred to as "lightweight methodologies" in contrast to more regimented, documentation-intensive traditional methods. The term *agile* was adopted in 2001 when a group of prominent thought leaders convened to discuss the common threads of their methodologies. The group published the Agile Manifesto (www.agilemanifesto.org) to encapsulate their shared beliefs and the nonprofit Agile Alliance was established. Scott Ambler, author of several books on the subject, sums it up in a sound bite: "Agile is an iterative and incremental (evolutionary) approach to software development which is performed in a highly collaborative manner with 'just enough' ceremony."

There are many principles or tenets of the agile approach that resonate and tightly align with the Kimball method's standard techniques:

- Focus on the primary objective of delivering business value. This has been our mantra for decades.
- Value collaboration between the development team and stakeholders, especially business representatives. Like the agile camp, we strongly encourage a close relationship and partnership with the business.

- Stress the importance of ongoing face-to-face communication, feedback, and prioritization with the business stakeholders. While the Kimball method encourages some written documentation, we don't want the burden to be overly onerous (or pointless).
- Adapt quickly to inevitably evolving requirements.
- Tackle development of reusable software in an iterative, incremental manner with concurrent, overlapping tasks. As an aside, standardizing on the "agile" nomenclature was a marketing triumph; wouldn't you rather be agile than spiraling or stuck in a waterfall (methodology)?

So what's the bottom line? In reality, one size seldom fits all, despite what the label claims. From my vantage point, there's a time and place for agile techniques when creating a DW/BI system. They seem to naturally fit with the business intelligence application layer. Designing and developing the analytic reports and analyses involves unpredictable, rapidly changing requirements. The developers often have strong business acumen and curiosity, allowing them to communicate effectively with the business users. In fact, we suggest that BI team members cohabitate with the business so they're readily available and responsive; this in turn encourages more business involvement. It's reasonable to deliver functionality in a matter of weeks. At the other end of the spectrum, the real-world wrangling of the data is inherently more complex and dependent on order. While we support reducing ETL development time, the essential tasks realistically take months, not weeks, in our experience.

One final word of caution: Some DW/BI development teams have naturally fallen into the trap of creating analytic or reporting solutions in a vacuum. In most of these situations, the team worked with a small set of users to extract a limited set of source data and make it available to solve their unique problems. The outcome is often a standalone data stovepipe that can't be leveraged by others or worse yet, delivers data that doesn't tie to the organization's other analytic information. We encourage agility, when appropriate; however, building isolated data sets must be avoided. As with most things in life, moderation and balance between extremes is almost always prudent.

5.9 Is Agile Enterprise Data Warehousing an Oxymoron?

Ralph Kimball, Design Tip #111, *Apr 1, 2009*

In today's economy the data warehouse team is caught between two conflicting pressures. First, we need more immediate, impactful results about our customers and our products and services across the enterprise. In other words, integrate the enterprise's data NOW! But second, we need to allocate our scarce people and money resources more wisely than ever before. In other words, make sure that all our designs are extensible and universal, and avoid any future rework. We can't waste a dime!

If we yield to the first pressure to deliver results too quickly, then we deliver one-off spot solutions that pretty quickly get us in trouble. For example, suppose we show the marketing department a prototype application written by one of our developers that provides new demographic indicators on some of our existing customers. Suppose that the application is based on a server-side implementation driven through a web interface that calls PHP to pull data from a MySQL database on a small development server. At the time of the demo to marketing, anyone can access the application via a browser if they know the URL. Furthermore the testing was done through Internet Explorer. It doesn't seem to work quite correctly under Firefox, but "we'll fix that soon." In spite of the fact that you got marketing's attention, you are asking for trouble. What's wrong with this picture? If you slow down and count to ten, you will realize that you are about to have a "success disaster." Your application has little or no data quality, governance, security, or extensibility. It also doesn't help that the person who wrote the PHP program has left the company.

On the other hand, if we revert to the safe IT tradition of using a waterfall design to propose a comprehensive system architecture, write a functional specification, evaluate vendors, and design an enterprise data model, we won't deliver useful results in time to help the business. If IT management is competent, we won't be allowed to start such a project!

Is there a middle ground that we might call an "agile enterprise data warehouse?" Remember that agile development calls for small teams, a succession of closely spaced deliverables, acceptance of a cut-and-try mentality, delivery of code rather than documentation, and intensive interaction throughout the project from business users who effectively control the project. For more on the "agile development" movement, read the previous article 5.8, *Relating to Agile Methodologies*, or check out the topic on Wikipedia.

If organized effectively and in the right cultural environment, perhaps any IT initiative can be a candidate for agile development, but let's not get carried away. Here's my recommendation for a very useful project that will yield measurable results quickly, and is designed not to be politically controversial. Best of all, this is a "stealth project" that when successful, will lay the foundation for an architectural revolution in your environment. The acronym for this stealth project is LWDS-MDM: Light Weight DownStream Master Data Management!

In article 12.1, *Can the Data Warehouse Benefit from SOA?*, I describe the typical downstream master data management (MDM) function that exists within most data warehouse environments, given that few of us have a full-fledged centralized MDM driving our operational systems. The downstream MDM gathers incompatible descriptions of an entity such as customer and publishes the cleaned, conformed, and deduplicated dimension to the rest of the data warehouse community. The subscribers to this dimension are almost always owners of fact tables who want to attach this high quality conformed dimension to their fact tables so that BI tools around the enterprise can do drill-across BI reports and dashboards on the conformed contents of the dimension.

Your job is to assemble a small team of developers and business users to start building the conformed customer dimension. This is an ideal target for incremental, adaptive development. Remember that the essential content of a conformed dimension is a small set of "enterprise attributes" that have a consistent interpretation across all the members of the dimension and can be used for constraining and grouping by all forms of BI. Furthermore, the agile development team can start by cleaning and conforming customer records from a limited set of original sources around the enterprise. Don't try to design the cosmic solution for customer metadata! Instead, concentrate on making the first set of attributes and sources produce a usable result in two to four weeks! If you read about agile development, you will be shocked and amazed that you are expected to give a working demo of your system to the business users at the end of every such two to four week sprint!

Hopefully you see how this stealth project should be able to grow to become really powerful. Over time, each sprint adds more attributes and more sources. You are chipping away at the big issues of enterprise data integration, including an understanding of user requirements, data quality, and the need for data governance.

5.10 Going Agile? Start with the Bus Matrix

Margy Ross, Design Tip #155, *May 1, 2013*

Many organizations are embracing agile development techniques for their DW/BI implementations. While we strongly concur with agile's focus on business collaboration to deliver value via incremental initiatives, we've also witnessed agile's "dark side." Some teams get myopically focused on a narrowly defined set of business requirements. They extract a limited amount of source data to develop a point solution in a vacuum. The resultant standalone solution can't be leveraged by other groups and/or integrated with other analytics. The agile deliverable may have been built quickly, so it's deemed a success. But when organizations lift their heads several years down the agile road, they often discover a non-architected hodgepodge of stovepipe data marts. The agile approach promises to reduce cost (and risk), but some organizations end up spending more on redundant, isolated efforts, coupled with the ongoing cost of fragmented decision making based on inconsistent data.

It's no surprise that a common criticism of the agile approaches for DW/BI development is the lack of planning and architecture, coupled with ongoing governance challenges. We believe the enterprise data warehouse bus matrix (described in article 5.6, *The Matrix: Revisited*) is a powerful tool to address these shortcomings. The bus matrix provides a master plan for agile development, plus it identifies the reusable common descriptive dimensions that provide both data consistency and reduced time-to-market delivery in the long run.

With the right mix of business and IT stakeholders in a room, along with a skilled facilitator, the bus matrix can be produced in relatively short order (measured in days, not weeks). Drafting the bus matrix depends on a solid understanding of the business's needs. Collaboration is critical to identifying the business's core processes. It's a matter of getting the team members to visualize the key measurement events needed for analyses. Involving business representatives and subject matter experts will ensure the team isn't paralyzed by this task. You'll likely discover that multiple business areas or departments are interested in the same fundamental business processes. As the business is brainstorming the list of measurement events, IT representatives are bringing a dose of reality about the available operational source data and any known limitations.

Once the matrix has been drafted, the team can then adopt agile development techniques to bring it to life. Business and IT management need to identify the single business process matrix row that's both a high priority for the business, and highly feasible from a technical perspective. Focusing on just one matrix row minimizes the risk of signing up for an overly ambitious implementation. Most implementation risk comes from biting off too much ETL system design and development; focusing on a single business process, typically captured by a single operational source system, reduces this risk. Incremental development can produce the descriptive dimensions associated with the selected matrix row until sufficient functionality is available and then the dimensional model is released to the business community.

5.11 Conformed Dimensions as the Foundation for Agile Data Warehousing

Margy Ross, Design Tip #135, *Jun 1, 2011*

Some clients and students lament that while they want to deliver and share consistently defined master conformed dimensions in their data warehouse/business intelligence (DW/BI) environments, it's "just not feasible." They explain that they would if they could, but with senior management focused on using agile development techniques to deliver DW/BI solutions, it's "impossible" to take the time to get organizational agreement on conformed dimensions. I want to turn this argument upside down by challenging that conformed dimensions enable agile DW/BI development, along with agile decision making.

Whether a Kimball specialist or not, many of you are conceptually familiar with conformed dimensions. A conformed dimension is descriptive master reference data that's referenced in multiple dimensional models. Conformed dimensions are a fundamental element of the Kimball approach. Conformed dimensions allow DW/BI users to consistently slice-and-dice performance metrics from multiple business process data sources. Conformed dimensions allow data from different sources to be integrated based on common, unified dimension attributes. Finally, conformed dimensions allow a dimension table to be built and maintained once rather than re-creating slightly different versions during each development cycle.

Reusing conformed dimensions across projects is where you get the leverage for more agile DW/BI development. As you flesh out your portfolio of master conformed dimensions, the development crank starts turning faster and faster. The time-to-market for a new business process data source shrinks as developers reuse existing conformed dimensions. Ultimately, new ETL development will focus almost exclusively on delivering more fact tables as the associated dimension tables are already sitting on the shelf ready to go.

Defining a conformed dimension requires organizational consensus and commitment to data stewardship. But you don't need to get everyone to agree on every attribute in every dimension table. At a minimum, you should identify a subset of attributes that have significance across the enterprise. These commonly referenced descriptive characteristics become the starter set of conformed attributes, enabling drill across integration.

Over time, you can expand from this minimalistic starting point iteratively. Any special dimensional attributes unique to a single business process do not have to be discarded during the conforming process, so there are very few serious compromises. And finally, if your organization has already implemented a master data management (MDM) capability to support the transactional source systems, the work to create conformed dimensions for the enterprise data warehouse just got much easier.

If you fail to focus on conformed dimensions because you're under pressure to deliver something yesterday, the various departmental analytic data silos will likely have inconsistent categorizations and labels. Even more troubling, data sets may look like they can be compared and integrated due to similar labels, but the underlying business rules may be slightly different. Business users waste inordinate amounts of time trying to reconcile and resolve these data inconsistencies, which negatively impacts their ability to be agile decision makers.

The senior IT managers who are demanding agile systems development practices should be exerting even greater organizational pressure, in conjunction with their peers in the business, on the development of consistent conformed dimensions if they're interested in both long term development efficiencies and long term decision making effectiveness across the enterprise.

Integration Instead of Centralization

Over the years, the pendulum has swung between centralized versus distributed data storage. Rather than focusing on this debate, we encourage organizations to allocate resources, including data stewards, to the challenges and opportunities associated with data integration instead.

5.12 Integration for Real People

Ralph Kimball, Intelligent Enterprise, *Aug 1, 2006*

Integration is one of the older terms in data warehousing. Of course, almost all of us have a vague idea that integration means making disparate databases function together in a useful way. But as a topic, integration has taken on the same fuzzy aura as metadata. We all know we need it; we don't have a clear idea of how to break it down into manageable pieces; and above all, we feel guilty because it is always on our list of responsibilities. Does integration mean that all parties across large organizations agree on every data element or only on some data elements?

This article decomposes the integration problem into actionable pieces, each with specific tasks. We'll create a centralized administration for all tasks, and we'll publish our integrated results out to a wide range of consumers. These procedures are almost completely independent of whether you run a highly centralized shop on one physical machine, or whether you have dozens of data centers and hundreds of database servers. In all cases, the integration challenge is the same; you just have to decide how integrated you want to be.

Defining Integration

Fundamentally, *integration* means reaching agreement on the meaning of data from the perspective of two or more databases. Using the specific notion of agreement, as described in this article, the results of two databases can be combined into a single data warehouse analysis. Without such an accord, the databases will remain isolated stovepipes that can't be linked in an application.

It's very helpful to separate the integration challenge into two parts: reaching agreement on labels and reaching agreement on measures. This separation, of course, mirrors the dimensional view of the world. Labels are normally textual, or text-like, and are either targets of constraints or are used as row headers in query results, where they force grouping and on-the-fly summarization. In a pure dimensional design, labels always appear in dimensions. Measures, on the other hand, are normally numeric, and, as their name implies, are the result of an active measurement of the world at a point in time. Measures always appear in fact tables in dimensional designs. The distinction between labels and measures is very important for our task of integration because the steps we must perform are quite different. Taken together, reaching agreement on labels and on measures defines integration.

Integrating Labels

To get two databases to relate to each other, at least some of the labels in each database must have the same name and domain. For instance, if we have a notion of product category in both databases, we can use category as a point of integration if and only if the category field in the product dimension in the two databases has the same contents (as when drawn from the same domain). With this simple criterion, we are astonishingly close to achieving integration! If we issue separate but similar queries to the two databases, such as:

```
Database-1: select category, sum(private_measure1)
    from fact1 ... group by category

Database-2: select category, sum(private_measure2)
    from fact2 ... group by category
```

then in virtually all BI tools we can sort-merge the two answer sets returned from the separate databases on the category row header to get a multi-row results set with the column headers category, sum_private_measure1, and sum_private_measure2.

It's crucial that you appreciate the importance of this simple result. We have successfully aligned measures from two separate databases on the same rows of a report and at the same level of granularity; because the category label has been carefully integrated across the two databases, at a certain level the report makes sense regardless of the value of measure1 and measure2. Even without integrating the measures across the two databases, we have achieved a powerful, valid integration result.

This method of assembling results from two databases in a single result set, often called *drill across*, has some other powerful advantages. Because the queries are launched to the two databases separately, the databases can be on separate data servers, or even hosted by separate database technologies. Both databases can manage performance independently. But even in the most centralized environment, we almost always have to execute this drill across against two independent fact tables. This approach has nothing to do with dimensional modeling; regardless of your modeling persuasion, it simply isn't possible to put multiple data sets of different granularity and dimensionality into a single table.

Integrating the labels of an enterprise is a huge and important step, but it's not easy and the main challenge isn't technical.

Integrating Measures

After studying the drill-across query in the previous section, you might think that integrating measures between databases is not necessary. You would be right, with one big exception. You dare not do arithmetic combining the two numeric results (sum_ private_measure1 and sum_private_measure2) unless you have first carefully vetted the business rules defining these two measures. For instance, if private_measure1 is month end actual revenue after taxes, and private_measure2 is rolling accrued revenue before taxes, then it is probably misleading to add, subtract, or ratio these two quantities, even though the drill-across query yielded measures at the same granularity.

For disparate measures to be combined analytically, the data warehouse design team must identify all measures to be conformed at the same time the labels are being negotiated. If the back room ETL can modify the measures so they can be combined analytically, then they should be named in such a way to alert analysts that cross-database arithmetic makes sense. These specially vetted measures are conformed facts. If facts that are similar cannot be conformed, then they need to be named appropriately to warn the analysts.

You now understand the full gamut of integration. Using dimensional terminology as shorthand, integration consists of conforming the dimensions and facts, or, to be more pragmatic, conforming enough of the labels and measures to support useful drill across.

Note that building a pre-integrated physical database in the back room that avoids the drill-across approach adds nothing new to the integration discussion. All you will have done is push these integration steps back into ETL processing, although the pre-integrated database may provide performance advantages.

Responsibilities of the Dimension Manager

Suppose that a large enterprise with many data sources commits to building an integrated view of its data. The crucial step is building a centralized set of conformed dimensions. This responsibility must be centralized because the definition, maintenance, and publishing of these dimensions must be precisely coordinated down to the individual keys. A big organization will have many conformed dimensions. Theoretically, each conformed dimension could be administered independently and asynchronously, but it makes most sense if all the *dimension managers* work together and coordinate their efforts.

So what do dimension managers do? These individuals update and maintain the master dimension on behalf of the enterprise, and they periodically copy it into all of the destination database environments that use the dimension with one or more of their fact tables. Taking a step-by-step technical view, the dimension manager:

1. Periodically adds fresh new records to the conformed dimension, generating new surrogate keys, but at the same time embedding the natural keys from the sources as ordinary fields in the dimension

2. Adds new records for type 2 changes to existing dimension entries (true physical changes at a point in time), generating new surrogate keys

3. Modifies records in place for type 1 changes (overwrites) and type 3 changes (alternate realities), without changing the surrogate keys, and updates the version number of the dimension if either of these changes are made

4. Supplies a dimension version number with the dimension reflecting minor (type 2) and major (types 1 and 3 and postdated entries) alterations

5. Replicates the revised dimension simultaneously to all fact table providers

The fact table provider mentioned in step 5 is the consumer of the dimension. In tightly run centralized shops, the dimension manager and fact provider could be the same person. But that changes nothing. The dimension must still be replicated to the destination databases and attached to the fact tables. Furthermore, this replication should occur simultaneously across all such destinations. If it is not simultaneous, a drill-across query could return a well-structured result that is wrong if different definitions of category coexist in different versions of the master product dimension. Thus, coordination among fact providers is essential.

Responsibilities of the Fact Provider

The fact providers have a rather complex task when they receive the updated dimension. They must:

1. Process dimension records marked as new and current by attaching them to current fact table records, replacing natural keys with surrogate keys (so you now appreciate the significance of the natural keys being supplied by the dimension manager).

2. Process dimension records marked as new postdated entries. This requires adjusting existing foreign keys in the fact table.

3. Recalculate aggregates that have become invalidated. An existing historical aggregate becomes invalidated only when a type 1 or type 3 change occurs on the attribute that is the target of the aggregation or if historical fact records have been modified in step 2. Changes to other attributes do not invalidate an aggregate. For instance, a change in the flavor attribute of a product does not invalidate aggregates based on the category attribute.

4. Bring updated fact and dimension tables online.

5. Inform users that the database has been updated, notifying them of major changes including dimension version changes, postdated records being added, and changes to historical aggregates.

The version number supplied by the dimension manager is an important enforcement tool for ensuring correct drill-across applications. For example, if the version number is embedded as a constant field in every dimension record, this field can be added to the select list of queries in a drill-across app so the BI tool can't align the rows of results inappropriately.

This article has described the data integration task in a specific, actionable way. Hopefully some of the mystery surrounding integration has been reduced, and you can take this task off your to-do list so you don't have to feel guilty.

5.13 Build a Ready-to-Go Resource for Enterprise Dimensions

Ralph Kimball, Design Tip #163, *Feb 5, 2014*

Although dimension tables are typically much smaller than fact tables, the dimension tables are the true drivers of the data warehouse. Dimension tables provide the descriptive context for all the measurements recorded in the fact tables. Although it's something of an obvious point, without the dimensions the data warehouse would be a meaningless ocean of numbers.

Dimensions should not be built on an individual, case-by-case basis for each data source coming into the data warehouse because dimensions are a strategic resource that provide coherence and consistency across the data warehouse. The descriptions of typical enterprise entities including calendars, customers, locations, products, services, providers, and competitors should be attached wherever possible to each data source available for querying and analysis across the enterprise.

This strategic view of enterprise dimensions has powerful architecture and governance implications. Let's summarize these powerful ideas. Be warned that in the rest of this short design tip, we'll be reminding you of the standard dimensional modeling techniques, about which we have written extensively. See especially Chapter 1 of this book, *The* Reader *at a Glance*, for introductions to all these topics.

Enterprise dimensions should be logically centralized and available on a publish/subscribe basis. Each enterprise dimension should have a single authoritative source that makes that dimension available to "fact table providers" across the enterprise. This guarantees that all queries and reports that use an enterprise dimension automatically constrain and group that dimension in a consistent way. Merely providing a centralized dimension is a big data governance step. Don't get too bogged down in implementing a high tech publish/subscribe architecture. The point is to have everyone using the same data, even if it is based on simple file transfers.

Enterprise dimensions should track time variance using the slowly changing dimension Type 2 (SCD2) technique: Add a new row. Any dimension that has changeable content should be built around the standard SCD machinery: 1) single column surrogate primary key; 2) surrogate natural key (sometimes called the durable key); 3) administrative fields describing the reason and time stamps for each change; and 4) original raw natural keys from each data source contributing to the dimension. (For instance, in a bank, the customer dimension may be built from multiple lines of business, each with its idiosyncratic version of the natural key for the same customer.) If the concepts of this paragraph are unfamiliar, please follow up by reading Chapter 1 because SCD techniques are part of the bedrock of modern data warehouses.

Build similar data pipelines for each fact table. Once the enterprise dimensions are available, you should build identical ETL pipelines for processing incoming fact table data. Using the dimension tables themselves, look up the raw natural keys in each dimension, and replace the fact table keys with the correct dimension table surrogate primary keys. Although different ETL environments may code this processing step differently, all the data warehouse teams should have this logic as part of their basic skill set and vocabulary.

Maintain shrunken rollup dimensions as part of the logically centralized enterprise dimension resource. Shrunken rollup dimensions must be physically separate tables apart from the corresponding atomic base dimensions. In general, it is impossible to implement a rollup dimension as a dynamic view on a base dimension. Shrunken rollup dimensions must have their own surrogate primary keys.

Merge enterprise dimension content with local dimension content at the time of publishing. Having an enterprise dimension does not mean that the dimension is a suffocating replacement of local dimension content. For instance, a line of business in a bank, such as credit cards, may have private descriptive attributes of each customer that are not exposed as part of the overall enterprise description of that customer. When the credit card data warehouse team receives periodic updates of the enterprise dimension, they merge their local descriptive attributes into the enterprise dimension by matching on the raw natural key, as described above. These steps are at the root of processing "conformed dimensions" in the data warehouse. Please see article 1.6, *Essential Steps for the Integrated Enterprise Data Warehouse.*

I hope with these perspectives you see the power and leverage of building a ready-to-go resource for enterprise dimensions. It gets easier and easier to add data sources from across the enterprise as you build up your dimension "library" because so much of the hard work in each dimension has already been done. As an extra bonus, you have made good progress on establishing data governance, everyone's favorite topic.

5.14 Data Stewardship 101: The First Step to Quality and Consistency

Bob Becker, Intelligent Enterprise, Jun 1, 2006

Consistent data is the Holy Grail for most data warehouse initiatives, and data stewards are the crusaders who fearlessly strive toward that goal. An active data stewardship program identifies, defines, and protects data across the organization. Stewardship ensures the initial effort to populate the data warehouse is done correctly, while significantly reducing the amount of rework necessary down the road. Data stewards enforce discipline and serve as a conduit between the business and IT.

The primary focus of a stewardship team is determining an organization's data warehouse content, defining common definitions, assuring data quality, and managing appropriate access. They help create and enforce firm vocabularies and associated business rules. In many organizations, the same words are often used to describe different things, different words are used to describe the same thing, and the same descriptor or value may have several different meanings. A stewardship team can reach across the organization to develop consistently defined business terminology.

Why Stewardship Is Essential

An active stewardship program lets organizations improve their understanding of corporate data assets, discover the relationships among the data, consolidate metadata describing the data, and ultimately transform data into actionable information.

An enterprise data warehousing effort committed to dimensional modeling must commit to conformed dimensions to ensure consistency across multiple business processes. An active data stewardship program can help large enterprises tackle the difficult task of agreeing upon conformed dimensions, which is more of a communication than technical challenge. Various groups across the enterprise are often committed to their own proprietary business rules and definitions. Data stewards must work closely with and cajole all interest groups to develop and embrace common business rules and definitions across the enterprise.

The primary goal of a data stewardship program is to provide the enterprise with legible, consistent, accurate, documented, and timely information about its data resources. Stewardship also ensures that authorized individuals use corporate data correctly and to its fullest potential.

Data stewardship also demystifies the corporate unknowns about the analytic process and provides resources to resolve data-related questions such as:

- Where do I get this information?
- What does the data mean?
- How does it relate to other data?
- Where did this data come from?
- How frequently is this data updated?
- How reliable is this data?
- How much history do we have for this data?

A key goal is ensuring that data warehousing efforts align with the business strategy. Stewards spend a great deal of time working outside the data warehouse team. They should be available to business users, offering a one-stop source for analytic knowledge. They are the primary resource for business users starting a new analytic process, and they can ensure that these users are going in the right direction, potentially saving hours or days of unproductive effort. The data warehouse team can more quickly deliver new iterations of the data warehouse by relying on steward knowledge. Stewards ensure that the organization can develop consistent fact-based analytic applications.

Stewardship Responsibilities

Roles and responsibilities may vary depending on whether the steward is responsible for dimension tables, fact tables, or both. In general, a data steward must:

- Become familiar with the business users and their various usage profiles to convey requirements and ease-of-use concerns to the data warehouse project team.
- Understand business requirements and how the data supports those requirements to help users leverage corporate data.

- Develop in-depth knowledge of the structure and content of the data warehouse, including tables, views, aggregates, attributes, metrics, indexes, primary and foreign keys, and joins, to answer data-related questions and enable a broader audience to analyze the data directly.

- Interpret new and changing business requirements to determine their impact on data warehouse design and propose enhancements and changes to meet these new requirements.

- Analyze the potential impact of data definition changes proposed by the business and communicate related requirements to the entire data warehouse team.

- Get involved early in source system enhancement or content changes to ensure that the data warehouse team is prepared to accept these changes.

- Comply with corporate and regulatory policies to verify data quality, accuracy, and reliability, including establishing validation procedures to be performed after each data load and prior to its release to the business. Stewards must withhold new data and communicate status if significant errors are identified.

- Establish and perform data certification processes and procedures while exercising proper due diligence in ensuring compliance with related corporate and regulatory requirements.

- Provide metadata that describes the data with a business description/definition and identifies the source data element(s) and any business rules or transformations used to deliver the data.

In addition to all of the above, data stewards who are specifically responsible for conformed dimensions for the enterprise must help forge agreement on their definition and use in downstream analytic environments. They also must determine departmental interdependencies and ensure that the conformed dimensions meet business needs across business processes and departments. In some large organizations, developing consensus on conformed dimensions can be a significant political challenge, so data stewards need to communicate and coordinate with the other stewards, reach agreement on data definitions and domain values, and minimize conflicting or redundant efforts. When conflicts arise, stewards must get data warehouse executive sponsors involved to resolve cross-departmental issues.

Stewards who support fact tables must ensure that conformed dimensions are used in their creation to avoid redundant or nonconforming tables. They must also ensure that any metrics used in multiple fact tables are conformed across business events. Finally, they must understand any consolidated or aggregate tables built on their fact tables, and must put processes in place to remove aggregated tables that may be invalidated by slowly changing dimensions.

Right Stuff for Stewardship

Data stewards should be well-respected, experienced subject matter experts with a solid understanding of the business area supported and a commitment to working through the inevitable cross functional challenges. Data stewards need strong communications skills to talk to the business users in their language while translating their requirements to the data warehouse team. Stewardship typically involves more cultural than technical challenges, so these individuals need to be organizationally and politically savvy. An effective data steward needs a mature attitude toward interpersonal relationships and organizational wrangling in order to deal with the inevitable conflict, and they should be comfortable with technologies and have a working knowledge of database concepts. Depending on the complexity of the source systems, the industry, and the breadth of the data warehouse environment, it may take one or two years before a new data steward becomes truly productive.

Communication Tools and Techniques

Stewards need to foster an open, approachable atmosphere so business users are at ease approaching them for assistance in framing an analytic request. Stewards also need more formal communications approaches, such as maintaining an email distribution list and relaying the "state of the data," including known issues and inconsistencies, to interested business users. Many data warehouse teams use websites to communicate with business constituencies, in which case stewards should help determine and provide the site content.

Data stewards should also participate and present at meetings and educational venues provided by peers in the business community, taking advantage of any chance to increase corporate awareness and knowledge of the data warehouse and its capabilities. They also can use these opportunities to gather feedback, including suggestions for warehouse improvement and requests for future warehouse iterations.

How to Get Started

Every organization, whether successful or not in their data warehousing efforts, has individuals fulfilling the roles and responsibilities of data stewardship. To develop a formal stewardship program, identify the individuals handling these responsibilities and organize their activities.

Establishing an effective stewardship program requires a strong leader with a solid vision of potential benefits. Gaining senior management support for the initiative is critical. In the early stages of the program, it may be necessary to involve senior management to help arbitrate and ensure consensus across the enterprise. Your organization's unique circumstances will drive the strategy; however you get there, your data warehousing efforts will be much more successful with a solid data stewardship program in place.

5.15 To Be or Not To Be Centralized

Margy Ross, Intelligent Enterprise, Feb 1, 2003

Contrary to William Shakespeare and some data warehouse industry pundits, centralization is not the question. As the data warehouse market matures, the cause of data warehouse pain (otherwise known as vendor growth opportunity) within the IT organization is bound to evolve. Vendors promote centralization as a miracle elixir to treat data warehouse ailments. They claim it spins independent, disparate "data marts" into gold by reducing administrative costs and improving performance. Physical centralization may deliver some efficiency; however, you can't afford to bypass the larger, more important issues of integration and consistency.

If your data warehouse environment has been developed without an overall architecture or strategy, you're probably dealing with multiple, independent islands of data with the following characteristics:

- Multiple, uncoordinated extracts from the same operational sources
- Multiple variations of similar information using inconsistent naming conventions and business rules
- Multiple business analyses delivering inconsistent metrics

Some have tried to implicate data marts as the root cause of these problems. That's a generalization that fails to acknowledge the benefits many organizations have realized with properly designed data marts, which we call business process subject areas. The problems just listed result from a nonexistent, poorly defined, or inappropriately executed strategy and can crop up with any architectural approach, including the enterprise data warehouse, the hub-and-spoke data warehouse, and distributed or federated data marts.

All That Glitters Is Not Gold

We can all agree that independent, isolated sets of data warrant attention, because they're inefficient and incapable of delivering on the business promise of data warehousing. These standalone databases may be easier to implement initially, but without a higher level enterprise integration strategy, they're dead ends that perpetuate incompatible views of the organization. Merely moving these renegade data islands onto a bigger, better centralized platform to give the appearance of centralization is no silver bullet: Data integration and consistency are the true targets. Any approach that aims elsewhere treats the symptoms rather than the disease. While it may be simpler to just brush integration and consistency under the carpet to avoid the political or organizational challenges they pose, doing so will keep you from realizing the true business benefit of the data warehouse.

I can't stress enough the importance of logical centralization and integration in the data warehouse, regardless of the physical implementation. In the vernacular of dimensional modeling, using this objective means focusing on the enterprise data warehouse bus architecture and conformed dimensions and facts. The enterprise data warehouse bus architecture is a tool to establish and enforce the overall data integration strategy for the warehouse. It provides the framework for integrating the analytic information in your organization. The result is a powerful centralized architecture that you can implement either as a distributed system on multiple hardware platforms and technologies or on a single, physically centralized technology. The enterprise data warehouse bus architecture is nondenominational and technology independent.

The enterprise's bus architecture is documented and communicated via the data warehouse bus matrix. The matrix rows represent the core business events or processes of the organization, while the columns reflect the common, conformed dimensions. Conformed dimensions are the means for consistently describing the core characteristics of your business. They're the integration points between the disparate processes of the organization, ensuring semantic consistency. There may be valid business reasons for not conforming dimensions—for example, if your organization is a diversified conglomerate with subsidiaries that sells unique products to unique customers through unique channels. However, for most organizations, the key to integrating disparate data is organizational commitment to the creation and use of conformed dimensions throughout the warehouse architecture, regardless of whether data is physically centralized or distributed.

As I warned earlier, physical centralization without integration may only throw more fuel on the fire of preexisting problems. Management may be convinced that buying a new platform to house the myriad existing data marts and warehouses will deliver operational efficiency and performance enhancements. Depending on the budget, these largely IT-centric benefits might be realized. However, they're insignificant compared to the business potential from truly integrated data. Physical centralization without data integration and semantic consistency will distract an organization from focusing on the real crux of the problem. Inconsistent data will continue to flummox the organization's decision making ability.

Be Not Afraid of Greatness

Moving to an enterprise data warehouse bus architecture will of course require organizational willpower and the allocation of scarce resources. No one said it would be easy. The issues brought to the surface when establishing a bus architecture are the generic, unavoidable issues all organizations face when trying to build an integrated view of their data.

Let's examine some of the typical activities involved in migrating disparate data to a bus architecture with conformed dimensions. Of course, because each organization's preexisting environment varies, you'll need to modify these steps to reflect your specific scenario.

- **Step 1: Identify the existing data marts/warehouses in your organization, as well as those under development.** You'll probably be surprised by the sheer number lurking in nooks and crannies. (And don't forget the data cubes sitting on your analysts' desktops.) Note the level of detail or granularity for the data in each of these existing data warehouse deliverables, as well as the inevitable data overlaps. Overlaps in the descriptions of entities will drive the design of conformed dimensions, while overlaps in the calculation of metrics will drive the design of conformed facts.
- **Step 2: Understand the organization's unmet business requirements for the data warehouse at a high level.** Although the enterprise bus architecture needs to keep an eye on the outer

boundaries of future data requirements in your organization, the initial implementation must practically focus on the most urgently needed data.

- Step 3: Gather key stakeholders to develop a preliminary enterprise data warehouse bus matrix for your organization. These stakeholders include back room DBAs and source system experts, as well as front room business analysts. The first stakeholder meeting should be kicked off by a senior executive of the organization who stresses the business importance of reaching agreement on the conformed dimensions and facts. (Then the executive can leave!) Senior level business commitment is critical to moving beyond the inevitable organizational obstacles.

- Step 4: Identify a dimension authority or stewardship committee for each dimension to be conformed and subsequently released to the community. Design the core conformed dimensions by integrating and reconciling the existing, disparate dimension attributes. Realistically, it may be overwhelming to get everyone to agree on every attribute, but don't let that bring this process to a crashing halt. You've got to start walking down the path toward integration in order to gain organization-wide agreement and final sign off on the master conformed dimensions.

- Step 5: Devise realistic, incremental development and administration plans for implementing and deploying or converting to the new conformed dimensions. Ultimately, the conformed dimensions should be used across all data sources to which they connect; however, you can't expect to get there in one fell swoop.

All's Well That Ends Well

These steps focus on the true, core issues of achieving logical integration across your data warehouse. Formulating the bus architecture and deploying conformed dimensions will result in a comprehensive data warehouse for your organization that's integrated, consistent, legible, and well-performing. You'll be able to add data naturally, with confidence that it will integrate with existing data.

Of course, you have the option to implement either a physically distributed system or a classic centralized system. In both cases, using the enterprise bus architecture and conformed dimensions, you'll deliver integrated business results to your users, which is the whole point of a data warehouse. Your organization's decision making capabilities will be turbocharged with consistent data, rather than diverting inordinate attention to data inconsistencies and reconciliations.

Contrast with the Corporate Information Factory

In this final section, we compare the Kimball bus architecture to the hub-and-spoke architecture of the Corporate Information Factory (CIF). The CIF has evolved over the years, so comparisons are a moving target.

5.16 Differences of Opinion

Margy Ross, Intelligent Enterprise, *Mar 6, 2004*

Based on recent inquiries, many of you are in the midst of architecting (or rearchitecting) your data warehouse. There's no dispute that planning your data warehouse from an enterprise perspective is a good idea, but do you need an enterprise data warehouse? It depends on your definition. In this article, we clarify the similarities and differences between the two dominant approaches (Kimball bus architecture and Corporate Information Factory) to enterprise warehousing.

Common Ground

We all agree on some things related to data warehousing. First, at the most rudimentary level, nearly all organizations benefit from creating a data warehouse and analytic environment to support decision making. Maybe it's like asking your barber if you need a haircut, but personal bias aside, businesses profit from well-implemented data warehouses. No one would attempt to run a business without operational processes and systems in place. Likewise, complementary analytic processes and systems are needed to leverage the operational foundation.

Second, the goal of any data warehouse environment is to publish the right data and make it easily accessible to decision makers. The two primary components of this environment are staging and presentation. The staging (or acquisition) area consists of extract, transform, and load (ETL) processes and support. Once the data is properly prepared, it is loaded into the presentation (or delivery) area where a variety of query, reporting, business intelligence, and analytic applications are used to probe, analyze, and present data in endless combinations.

Both approaches agree that it's prudent to embrace the enterprise vantage point when architecting the data warehouse environment for long term integration and extensibility. Although subsets of the data warehouse will be implemented in phases over time, it's beneficial to begin with the integrated end goal in mind during planning.

Finally, standalone "data marts" or warehouses such as those in Figure 5-8 are problematic. These independent silos are built to satisfy specific needs without regard to other existing or planned analytic data. They tend to be departmental in nature, often loosely dimensionally structured. Although often perceived as the path of least resistance because no coordination is required, the independent approach is unsustainable in the long run. Multiple, uncoordinated extracts from the same operational sources are inefficient and wasteful. They generate similar, but different variations with inconsistent naming conventions and business rules. The conflicting results cause confusion, rework, and reconciliation. In the end, decision making based on independent data is often clouded by fear, uncertainty, and doubt.

So we all see eye to eye on some matters. Before turning to our differences of opinion, we'll review the two dominant approaches to enterprise data warehousing.

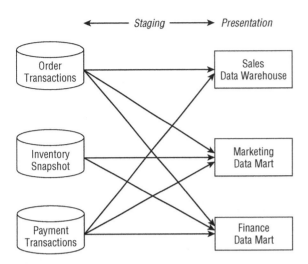

Figure 5-8: Independent data marts/warehouses.

Kimball Bus Architecture

If you've been regularly reading the last 100 or so articles we've written, you're familiar with the Kimball approach in Figure 5-9. As we described in article 2.9, *Data Warehouse Dining Experience*, raw data is transformed into presentable information in the staging area, ever mindful of throughput and quality. Staging begins with coordinated extracts from the operational source systems. Some staging "kitchen" activities are centralized, such as maintenance and storage of common reference data, while others may be distributed.

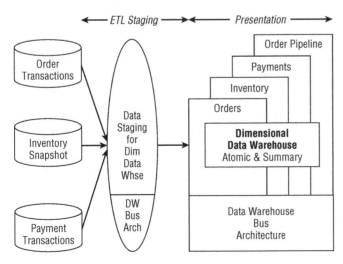

Figure 5-9: Dimensional data warehouse.

The presentation area is dimensionally structured, whether centralized or distributed. A dimensional model contains the same information as a normalized model, but packages it for ease-of-use and query performance. It includes both atomic detail and summarized information (aggregates in relational tables or multidimensional cubes) as required for performance or geographic distribution of the data. Queries descend to progressively lower levels of detail, without reprogramming by the user or application designer.

Dimensional models are built by business processes corresponding to business measurements or events, not business departments. For example, orders data is populated once in the dimensional data warehouse for enterprise access, rather than being replicated in three departmental marts for marketing, sales, and finance. In order to be clear that we are not talking about departmental data marts in the Kimball approach, we consistently relabel them as *business process subject areas*. Once foundation business processes are available in the warehouse, consolidated dimensional models deliver cross-process metrics. The enterprise data warehouse bus matrix identifies and enforces the relationships between business process metrics (facts) and descriptive attributes (dimensions).

Corporate Information Factory

Figure 5-10 illustrates the Corporate Information Factory (CIF) approach, once known as the EDW approach. Like the Kimball approach, there are coordinated extracts from the source systems. From there, a third normal form (3NF) relational database containing atomic data is loaded. This normalized data warehouse is used to populate additional presentation data repositories, including special purpose warehouses for exploration and data mining, as well as data marts.

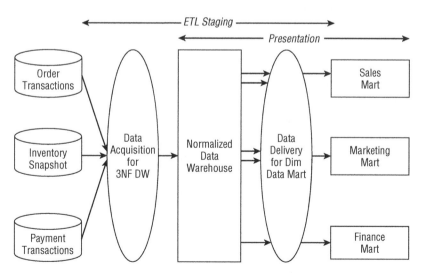

Figure 5-10: Normalized data warehouse with departmental data marts.

In this scenario, the marts are often tailored by business department or function with dimensionally structured summary data. Atomic data is typically accessible via the normalized data warehouse or a logical layer on top of the normalized structures.

Fundamental Differences

There are two fundamental differences between the CIF and Kimball approaches. The first concerns the need for a normalized data structure before loading the dimensional models. Although this is a requisite underpinning of the CIF, the Kimball approach says the data structures required prior to dimensional presentation depend on the source data realities, target data model, and anticipated transformation. Although we don't advocate centrally normalizing the atomic data prior to loading the dimensional targets, we don't absolutely admonish it, presuming there's a real need, financial willpower for both the redundant ETL development and data storage, and clear understanding of the two-step throughput.

In the vast majority of the cases, we find that duplicative storage of core performance measurement data in both normalized and dimensional structures is unwarranted. Advocates of the normalized data structures claim it's faster to load than the dimensional model, but what sort of optimization is really achieved if the data needs to undergo ETL multiple times before being presented to the business?

The second primary difference between the two approaches is the treatment of atomic data. The CIF says atomic data should be stored in the normalized data warehouse. The Kimball approach says atomic data must be dimensionally structured. Of course, if you only provide summary information in a dimensional structure, you've "presupposed the questions." However, with the Kimball approach, if you make atomic data available in dimensional structures, you always have the ability to summarize the data any which way. We need the most finely grained data in our presentation area so that users can ask the most precise questions possible.

Business users may not care about the details of a single atomic transaction, but we can't predict the ways they'll want to summarize the transaction activity (perhaps for all customers of a certain type living in a range of ZIP codes that have been customers for more than two years). Anyone who's worked side by side with a business analyst knows the questions asked are unpredictable and constantly changing. Details must be available so that they can be rolled up to answer the questions of the moment, without encountering a totally different data structure. Storing the atomic data in dimensional structures delivers this fundamental capability. If only summary data is dimensional with the atomic data stored in normalized structures, then drilling into the details is often akin to running into a brick wall. Skilled professionals must intervene because the underlying data structures are so different.

Both approaches advocate enterprise data coordination and integration, but the implementations differ. CIF says the normalized data warehouse fills this role. While normalized models communicate data relationships, they don't inherently apply any pressure to resolve data integration issues. Normalization alone doesn't begin to address the common data keys and labels required for integration.

From the earliest planning activities, the Kimball approach uses the enterprise data warehouse bus architecture with common, conformed dimensions for integration and drill-across support. Common, conformed dimensions have consistent descriptive attribute names, values, and meanings. Likewise, conformed facts are consistently defined; if they don't use consistent business rules, then they're given a distinct name.

Conformed dimensions are the backbone of any enterprise approach because they provide the integration glue. Conformed dimensions are typically built and maintained as central persistent master data in the staging area, then reused across the enterprise's presentation databases to ensure data integration and semantic consistency. It may not be practical or useful to get everyone to agree to everything related to a dimension; however, conformity directly correlates to an organization's ability to integrate business results. Without conformity, you end up with isolated data that cannot be tied together. This situation perpetuates incompatible views of the enterprise, diverting attention to data inconsistencies and reconciliations while degrading the organization's decision making ability.

Hybrid Approach?

Some organizations adopt a hybrid approach, theoretically marrying the best of both the CIF and Kimball methods. As shown in Figure 5-11, the hybrid combines Figures 5-9 and 5-10. There's a normalized data warehouse from the CIF, plus a dimensional data warehouse of atomic and summary data based on the Kimball bus architecture.

Given the final presentation deliverable in Figure 5-11, this hybrid approach is viable. If you have already built a normalized data warehouse and now recognize the need for robust presentation capabilities to deliver value, then the hybrid approach lets you leverage your preexisting investment. However, there are significant incremental costs and time lags associated with staging and storing atomic data redundantly. If you're starting with a fresh slate and appreciate the importance of presenting atomic data to avoid presupposing the business questions, then why would you want to ETL, store, and maintain the atomic details twice? Isn't the value proposition more compelling to focus the investment in resources and technology into appropriately publishing additional key performance metrics for the business?

Success Criteria

When evaluating approaches, people often focus strictly on IT's perception of success, but it must be balanced with the business' perspective. We agree that data warehouses should deliver a flexible, scalable, integrated, granular, accurate, complete, and consistent environment; however, if it's not being leveraged by the business for decision making, then it's impossible to declare it successful. Does the business community use the data warehouse? Is it understandable to them (including nontechnical users)? Does it answer their business questions? Is the performance acceptable from their vantage point?

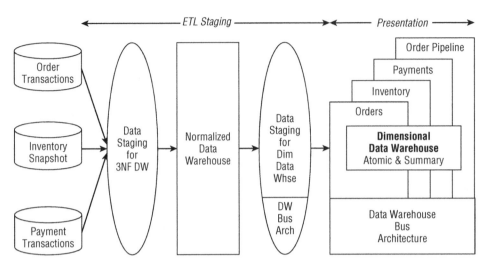

Figure 5-11: Hybrid of normalized data warehouse and dimensional data warehouse.

In our opinion, the success of any data warehouse is measured by the business's acceptance of the analytic environment and their benefits realized from it. You should choose the data warehouse architecture that best supports these success criteria, regardless of the label.

5.17 Much Ado about Nothing

Margy Ross, Design Tip #139, Oct 5, 2011

After years of dormancy, there have been renewed rumblings in the DW/BI industry about the Kimball versus Inmon approaches. When I mentioned the resurrected debate to a former colleague who's been away from our industry for nearly 15 years, she replied, "Again?!" I'm experiencing a serious case of déjà vu.

In fact, we've been contacted by several folks looking for us to jump into the fray in a public event. As far as we're concerned, this supposed controversy is a non-topic. We're not interested in further stirring the pot, especially when the motivation is commercial gain. We have written and presented our views consistently for more than 20 years, focusing on understandable, fast dimensional delivery of data for the enterprise, integrated via conformed dimensions. There are no secrets about our approach. Everything's been documented and available in the public domain.

The recent criticism lobbed at the Kimball approach and dimensional modeling seems largely based on misunderstandings of our long-standing messages. I wrote a white paper in January 2008, which is summarized in article 6.10, *Fables and Facts*. Unfortunately, some people making unfounded charges about the Kimball methodology and architecture apparently haven't read it.

Article 5.16, *Differences of Opinion*, was written in 2003. At the time, I tried to fairly contrast the Kimball bus architecture approach versus the Corporate Information Factory. I had several clients who were struggling to make a decision between the two dominant schools of thought, so I attempted to summarize the similarities and differences. As industry thinking has morphed over time, some of the differences have softened.

I'll admit I have a biased opinion about the Kimball approach. We've seen our methods work time after time in client situations. We've received feedback from the thousands of students we've trained that our practical techniques work. However, I'm also willing to admit that organizations can be successful leveraging the approaches advocated by others. Whatever approach you choose, embrace it; read the books and go to training so you can fully adopt the methodology as it is intended.

Rather than devoting more consternation to the philosophical differences between the Kimball and Inmon approaches, the industry would be far better off devoting energy to ensure that whatever we deliver to the business from our DW/BI systems is broadly accepted by the business to make better, more informed business decisions. Allowing ourselves to be distracted by religious debates may interest some, but it doesn't contribute to what I see as our industry's true objectives.

5.18 Don't Support Business Intelligence with a Normalized EDW

Ralph Kimball, Design Tip #34, *Feb 28, 2002*

This article was originally published as "You Don't Need an EDW."

Although normalized data models are useful for transaction processing, these models should not be used as the platform for business intelligence. The normalized enterprise data warehouse (EDW) approach differs materially from the data warehouse bus architecture approach. Normalized EDWs embody a number of related themes that need to be contrasted individually from the DW bus approach. It may be helpful to separate logical issues from physical issues for a moment.

Logically, both approaches advocate a consistent set of definitions that rationalize the different data sources scattered around the organization. In the case of the DW bus, the consistent set of definitions takes the specific form of conformed dimensions and conformed facts. With the normalized EDW, the consistency seems much more amorphous. You must take it on faith that if you have a single highly normalized model of all the enterprise's information, you then know how to administer hundreds or thousands of tables consistently. But, overlooking this lack of precision, one might argue that the two approaches are in agreement up to this point. Both approaches strive to apply a unifying coherence to all the distributed data sources.

A side issue of the normalized enterprise data model is that frequently these models are idealized models of information rather than real models of data sources. Although the exercise of creating the idealized information model is useful, I have seen a number of these big diagrams that never get populated. I have also written a number of articles trying to shed a harsh light on the related claim that the big normalized models encapsulate an organization's "business rules." At best, the normalized models enforce SOME of the data rules (mostly many-to-one relationships), and almost NONE of what a business procedures expert would call business rules. The explanatory labeling of the join paths on a normalized model rarely if ever is carried into the code of the back room ETL processes or the front room query and report writing tools.

Even if we have a tenuous agreement that both approaches have the same goal of creating a consistent representation of an organization's data, as soon as you move into physical design and deployment issues, the differences between the normalized EDW and the DW bus become really glaring. As most of you know, the conformed dimensions and conformed facts take on specific forms in the bus architecture. Conformed dimensions are dimensions that have common fields, and the respective domains of the values in these fields are the same. That guarantees that you can perform separate queries on remote fact tables connected to these dimensions, and you will be able to merge the columns into a final result. This is, of course, drill across. I have written extensively on the steps required to administer conformed dimensions and conformed facts. I have never seen a comparable set of specific guidelines for the normalized EDW approach. I find that interesting because even in a physically centralized normalized EDW, you have to store the data in physically distinct table spaces, and that necessitates going through the same logic as the replication of conformed dimensions. But I have never seen systematic procedures described by normalized EDW advocates for doing this. Which tables do you synchronously replicate between table spaces and when? The DW bus procedures describe this in great detail.

The flat 2NF (second normal form) nature of the dimensions in the DW bus design allows us to administer the natural time variance of a dimension in a predictable way (slowly changing dimension types 1, 2, and 3). Again, in the highly normalized EDW world, I have never seen a description of how to do the equivalent of slowly changing dimensions. But it would seem to require copious use of time stamps on all the entities, together with a lot more key administration than the dimensional approach requires. By the way, the surrogate key approach I have described for administering SCDs actually has nothing to do with dimensional modeling. In a normalized EDW, the root table of a snowflaked "dimension" would have to undergo exactly the same key administration (using either a surrogate key or a natural key plus a date) with the same number of repeated records if it tracked the same slowly changing time variance as the DW bus version.

The flat 2NF nature of dimensions in the DW bus design allows a systematic approach to defining aggregates, the single most powerful and cost-effective way to increase the performance of a large data warehouse. The science of dimensional aggregation techniques is intimately linked to the use of conformed dimensions. The "shrunken" dimensions of an aggregate fact table are perfectly conformed subsets of the base dimensions in the DW bus architecture. The normalized EDW approach, again, has no systematic and documented approach for handling aggregates in the normalized environment or giving guidance to query tools and report writers for how to use aggregates. This issue interacts with *drilling down* described next.

The normalized EDW architecture is both logically and physically centralized, something like a planned economy. Maybe this is unfair, but I think this approach has the same subtle but fatal problem that a planned economy has. It sounds great up front, and the idealistic arguments are hard to refute before the project starts. But the problem is that a fully centralized approach assumes perfect information a priori and perfect decision making afterward. Certainly, with planned economies, that was a major reason for their downfall. The DW bus architecture encourages a continuously evolving design with specific criteria for graceful modification of the data schemas so that existing applications continue to function. The symmetry of the dimensional design approach of the DW bus allows us to pinpoint exactly where new or modified data can be added to a design to preserve this graceful character.

Most importantly, a key assumption built into most normalized EDW architectures is that the centralized EDW releases "data marts." These data marts are often described as "built to answer a business question." Almost always this comes from inappropriate and premature aggregation. If the data mart is only aggregated data, then of course there will be a set of business questions that cannot be answered. These questions are often not the ones asking for a single atomic record, but rather questions that ask for a precision slice of large amounts of data. A final, unworkable assumption of the normalized EDW is that if the user wants to ask any of these precise questions, they must leave the aggregated dimensional data mart and descend into the 3NF atomic data located in the back room. Everything is wrong with this view, in my opinion. All of the leverage we developed in the DW bus is defeated by this hybrid architecture: drilling down through conformed dimensions to atomic data; uniform encoding of slowly changing dimensions; the use of performance enhancing aggregates; and the sanctity of keeping the back room data staging area off limits to query services.

5.19 Complementing 3NF EDWs with Dimensional Presentation Areas

Bob Becker, Design Tip #148, Aug 1, 2012

Some organizations have adopted a data warehouse architecture that includes an atomic third normal form (3NF) relational data warehouse. This architecture, often called the hub-and-spoke or Corporate Information Factory (CIF), includes a data acquisition ETL process to gather, clean, and integrate data from various sources. Atomic data is loaded into third normal form data structures, typically called the enterprise data warehouse (EDW) in this architecture. Another ETL data delivery process then populates downstream reporting and analytic environments supporting business users.

Organizations that have adopted this architecture often find some business users developing reporting and analytic applications directly against the atomic 3NF data structures. Ideally, these users would leverage an architected downstream analytic platform. Unfortunately, many organizations either populate the downstream environments with summary rather than atomic data, or worse, never get around to building the user assessable environments. Inevitably this results in a set of frustrated business users. The 3NF data structures are difficult to understand, the required queries tend to be very complex and difficult to develop, and the query response times can be abysmal. As a result, business units resort to pulling complete sets of data from the atomic 3NF warehouse to populate their own shadow reporting and analytic platform. Clearly, this is undesirable and leads the organization down a path to non-integrated and inconsistent results.

To overcome these challenges, a popular modification to the Kimball Architecture has evolved. This hybrid architecture leverages the existing 3NF data warehouse as a primary source of clean, integrated data to feed a dimensionally structured enterprise presentation area. The resulting dimensional presentation area would consist of a number of atomic, business process-centric fact tables integrated via a set of conformed dimensions.

The key advantages of enhancing the 3NF environment with a dimensional presentation area are to present an atomic, integrated, consistent environment to the business community that is significantly less complex. As a result, the data is easier to understand, users can more readily create the queries they require, and the queries themselves are less complex. In addition, the query response from the underlying dimensional structures will be significantly quicker.

The majority of organizations will implement the dimensional presentation layer physically. Some organizations may look to leverage other technical solutions to implement the dimensional presentation layer logically rather than physically. In this scenario, the business users would interact directly against some logical dimensional layer and the technologies involved would resolve the required queries directly against the 3NF table structures. Options for implementing this logical layer would include dimensional designs implemented via:

- Logical database views, sometimes called dimensional views
- Semantic layer of a BI tool
- Data virtualization tool

The effectiveness of a logical layer versus physical instantiation is relatively unproven for large-scale production use in most environments. There are several considerations to weigh carefully before committing to a logical dimensional implementation:

- While the logical presentation area relieves the ease of use/understandability issues, it does nothing to improve the performance of the underlying queries. The technology supporting the logical layer will ultimately need to resolve the query against the same underlying 3NF table structures. If query performance against the 3NF environment is already a challenge, then the logical presentation layer is not likely a viable option.
- The use of conformed dimensions is critical in any dimensional presentation area. Often the ETL processing to deliver the integration, deduplication, survivorship, and slowly changing dimension logic necessary for an effective conformed dimension will defeat the use of logical presentation and strongly favor a physical presentation area.

In either case, organizations utilizing a 3NF data warehouse environment can often improve their ease of use and performance characteristics by enhancing their environment to include a well-designed, properly architected dimensional presentation area.

6 Dimensional Modeling Fundamentals

Building on the bus architecture foundation established in Chapter 5, it's time to delve into the basics of dimensional modeling. This chapter begins with an overview of fact and dimension tables, along with the fundamental activities of drilling down, drilling across, and handling time in the data warehouse. Graceful modifications to existing dimensional models are also described.

We then turn our attention to dimensional modeling Dos and Don'ts. Finally, we discuss common myths and misunderstandings about dimensional modeling.

Basics of Dimensional Modeling

This first set of articles describes the fundamental constructs of a dimensional model.

6.1 Fact Tables and Dimension Tables

Ralph Kimball, Intelligent Enterprise, *Jan 1, 2003*

Dimensional modeling is a design discipline that straddles the formal relational model and the engineering realities of text and number data. Compared to third normal form entity-relationship modeling, it's less rigorous (allowing the designer more discretion in organizing the tables), but more practical because it accommodates database complexity and improves performance. Dimensional modeling has an extensive portfolio of techniques for handling real-world situations.

Measurements and Context

Dimensional modeling begins by dividing the world into measurements and context. Measurements are usually numeric and taken repeatedly. Numeric measurements are *facts*. Facts are always surrounded by mostly textual context that's true at the moment the fact is recorded. Facts are very specific, well-defined numeric attributes. By contrast, the context surrounding the facts is open ended and verbose. It's not uncommon for the designer to add context to a set of facts partway through the implementation.

Although you could lump all context into a wide, logical record associated with each measured fact, you'll usually find it convenient and intuitive to divide the context into independent logical clumps. When you record facts—dollar sales for a grocery store purchase of an individual product, for example—you naturally divide the context into clumps named product, store, time, customer, clerk, and several others. We call these logical clumps *dimensions* and assume informally that these dimensions are independent. Figure 6-1 shows the dimensional model for a typical grocery store fact.

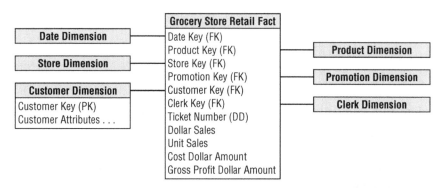

Figure 6-1: A dimensional model for grocery store sales.

In truth, dimensions rarely are completely independent in a strong statistical sense. In the grocery store example, customer and store clearly will show a statistical correlation. But it's usually the right decision to model customer and store as separate dimensions. A single, combined dimension would likely be unwieldy with tens of millions of rows. And the record of when a given customer shopped in a given store would be expressed more naturally in a fact table that also showed the date dimension.

The assumption of dimension independence would mean that all the dimensions, such as product, store, and customer, are independent of time. But you have to account for the slow, episodic change of these dimensions in the way you handle them. In effect, as keepers of the data warehouse, we have taken a pledge to faithfully represent these changes. This predicament gives rise to the technique of slowly changing dimensions.

Dimensional Keys

If the facts are truly measures taken repeatedly, you find that fact tables always create a characteristic many-to-many relationship among the dimensions. Many customers buy many products in many stores at many times.

Therefore, you logically model measurements as fact tables with multiple foreign keys referring to the contextual entities. And the contextual entities are each dimensions with a single primary key, e.g., for the customer dimension, as in Figure 6-1. Although you can separate the logical design from the physical design, in a relational database fact tables and dimension tables are most often explicit tables.

Actually, a real relational database has two levels of physical design. At the higher level, tables are explicitly declared together with their fields and keys. The lower level of physical design describes the way the bits are organized on the disk and in memory. Not only is this design highly dependent on the particular database, but some implementations may even "invert" the database beneath the level of table declarations and store the bits in ways that are not directly related to the higher level physical records. What follows is a discussion of the higher level physical design only.

A fact table in a dimensional star schema consists of multiple foreign keys, each paired with a primary key in a dimension, together with the facts containing the measurements. In Figure 6-1, the foreign keys in the fact table are labeled FK, and the primary keys in the dimension tables are labeled PK, as shown for the customer dimension. (The field labeled DD, special degenerate dimension key, is discussed later in this article.)

I insist that the foreign keys in the fact table obey referential integrity with respect to the primary keys in their respective dimensions. In other words, every foreign key in the fact table has a match to a unique primary key in the respective dimension. Note that this design allows the dimension table to possess primary keys that aren't found in the fact table. Therefore, a product dimension table might be paired with a sales fact table in which some of the products are never sold. This situation is perfectly consistent with referential integrity and proper dimensional modeling.

In the real world, there are many compelling reasons to build the FK-PK pairs as surrogate keys that are just sequentially assigned integers. It's a major mistake to build data warehouse keys out of the natural keys that come from the underlying operational data sources.

Occasionally a perfectly legitimate measurement will involve a missing dimension. Perhaps in some situations a product can be sold to a customer in a transaction without a store defined. In this case, rather than attempting to store a null value in the store FK, you build a special record in the store dimension representing "No Store." Now this condition has a perfectly normal FK-PK representation in the fact table.

Theoretically, a fact table doesn't need a primary key because, depending on the information available, two different legitimate observations could be represented identically. Practically speaking, this is a terrible idea because normal SQL makes it very hard to select one of the records without selecting the other. It would also be hard to check data quality if multiple records were indistinguishable from each other.

Relating the Two Modeling Worlds

Dimensional models are full-fledged relational models, where the fact table is in third normal form and the dimension tables are in second normal form, confusingly referred to as *denormalized*. Remember that the chief difference between second and third normal forms is that repeated entries are removed from a second normal form table and placed in their own "snowflake." Thus the act of removing the context from a fact record and creating dimension tables places the fact table in third normal form.

I resist the urge to further snowflake the dimension tables and am content to leave them in flat second normal form because the flat tables are much more efficient to query. In particular, dimension attributes with many repeated values are perfect targets for bitmap indexes. Snowflaking a dimension into third normal form, while not incorrect, destroys the ability to use bitmap indexes and increases the user perceived complexity of the design. Remember that in the presentation area of the data warehouse, you don't have to worry about enforcing many-to-one data rules in the physical table design by demanding snowflaked dimensions. The ETL staging system has already enforced those rules.

Declaring the Grain

Although theoretically any mixture of measured facts could be shoehorned into a single table, a proper dimensional design allows only facts of a uniform grain (the same dimensionality) to coexist in a single fact table. Uniform grain guarantees that all the dimensions are used with all the fact records (keeping in mind the "No Store" example) and greatly reduces the possibility of application errors due to combining data at different grains. For example, it's usually meaningless to blithely add daily data to yearly data. When you have facts at two different grains, place the facts in separate tables.

Additive Facts

At the heart of every fact table is the list of facts that represent the measurements. Because most fact tables are huge, with millions or even billions of rows, you almost never fetch a single record into your answer set. Rather, you fetch a very large number of records, which you compress into digestible form by adding, counting, averaging, or taking the min or max. But for practical purposes, the most common choice, by far, is adding. Applications are simpler if they store facts in an additive format as often as possible. Thus, in the grocery example, you don't need to store the unit price. You merely compute the unit price by dividing the dollar sales by the unit sales whenever necessary.

Some facts, like bank balances and inventory levels, represent intensities that are awkward to express in an additive format. You can treat these semi-additive facts as if they were additive—but just before presenting the results to the business user, divide the answer by the number of time periods to get the right result. This technique is called *averaging over time*.

Some perfectly good fact tables represent measurement events with no facts, so we call them *factless fact tables*. The classic example of a factless fact table is a record representing a student attending a class on a specific day. The dimensions are day, student, professor, course, and location, but there are no obvious numeric facts. The tuition paid and grade received are good facts, but not at the grain of the daily attendance.

Degenerate Dimensions

In many modeling situations where the grain is a child, the natural key of the parent header winds up as an orphan in the design. In the Figure 6-1 grocery example, the grain is the line item on a sales ticket, but the ticket number is the natural key of the parent ticket. Because you have systematically stripped off the ticket context as dimensions, the ticket number is left exposed without any attributes of its own. You model this reality by placing the ticket number by itself right in the fact table. We call this key a *degenerate dimension*. The ticket number is useful because it's the glue that holds the child records together.

6.2 Drilling Down, Up, and Across

Ralph Kimball, DBMS, Mar 1996

In data warehouse applications we often talk about drilling down, and occasionally we talk about reversing the process and drilling up. It is time for us as an industry to be more consistent and more precise with our vocabulary concerning drilling.

Drilling Down

Drilling down is the oldest and most venerable kind of drilling in a data warehouse. Drilling down means nothing more than "give me more detail." In our standard dimensional schema, the attributes in the dimension tables play a crucial role. These attributes are textual (or behave like text), take on discrete values, and are the source of application constraints and grouping columns in the final reports. In fact, you can always imagine creating a grouping column in a report by opportunistically dragging a dimension attribute from any of the dimension tables down into the report, thereby making it a grouping column, as shown in Figure 6-2. The beauty of the dimensional model is that all dimension attributes can become grouping columns. The process of adding grouping columns can be compounded with as many grouping columns from as many dimension tables as the user wishes. The great strength of SQL is that these grouping columns simply get added to the SELECT list and the GROUP BY clause and the right thing happens. Usually you add these grouping columns to the ORDER BY clause also so that you get the grouping in a prescribed order.

From this discussion, you can see that the precise definition of drilling down is "add a grouping column." A few query tool vendors have tried to be overly helpful and implemented a drill-down command in their user interfaces that adds specific grouping columns, usually from the "product hierarchy." For instance, the first time you press the drill-down button, you add a category attribute. The next time you use the button, you add the subcategory attribute, and then the brand attribute. Finally, you add the detailed product description attribute to the bottom of the product hierarchy. This is very limiting and often not what the user wants. Not only does real drill down mix both hierarchical and nonhierarchical attributes from all the available dimensions, but there is no such thing as a single obvious hierarchy in a business in any case.

It may happen that there is more than one well-defined hierarchy in a given dimension. In some companies, marketing and finance have incompatible and different views of the product hierarchy. Although you might wish that there was only a single product hierarchy, all the marketing defined attributes and all the financially defined attributes are included in the detailed master product table illustrated in Figure 6-3. The user must be allowed to traverse any hierarchy and choose unrelated attributes that are not part of the hierarchy.

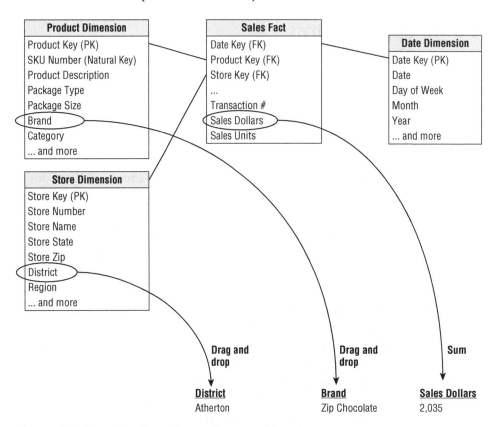

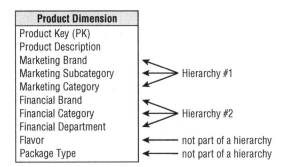

Figure 6-2: Dragging dimension attributes and facts into a report.

Figure 6-3: A product dimension table with both marketing and finance attributes.

Large customer dimension tables often have three simultaneous hierarchies. If the grain of the customer table is the ship-to location, you automatically have a geographic hierarchy defined by the customer's address. You probably also have a hierarchy that is defined by the customer's organization, such as division and corporation. Finally, you may have your own sales hierarchy based on the sales rep assignment to the customer ship-to address. This sales hierarchy could be organized by sales territory, sales zone, and sales region. A richly defined customer table could have all three hierarchies happily coexisting, and awaiting all possible flavors of user drill down.

Drilling Up

If drilling down is adding grouping columns from the dimension tables, then drilling up is subtracting grouping columns. Of course, it is not necessary to subtract the grouping columns in the same order that they were added. In general, each time the user adds or subtracts a grouping column, a new multi-table join query must be launched. If you have an aggregate navigator, as described in article 12.17, *The Aggregate Navigator*, then each multi-table join query smoothly seeks its proper level in the space of explicitly stored aggregates. In a properly tuned data warehouse, there is little difference in performance between bringing back 1000 answer set rows at a high level of aggregation and bringing back 1000 answer set rows at a low level of aggregation.

Drilling Across

If drilling down is requesting ever finer and more granular data from the same fact table, then drilling across is the process of linking two or more fact tables at the same granularity, or, in other words, tables with the same set of grouping columns and dimensional constraints. Drilling across is a valuable technique whenever a business has several fundamental business processes that can be arranged in a value chain. Each business process gets its own separate fact table. For example, almost all manufacturers have an obvious value chain representing the demand side of their businesses consisting of finished goods inventory, orders, shipments, customer inventory, and customer sales, as shown in Figure 6-4. The product and time dimensions thread through all of these fact tables. Some dimensions, such as customer, thread through some, but not all of the fact tables. For instance, customer does not apply to finished goods inventory.

A drill-across report can be created by using grouping columns that apply to all the fact tables used in the report. Thus in our manufacturing value chain example, attributes may be freely chosen from the product and time dimension tables because they make sense for every fact table. Attributes from customer can only be used as grouping columns if we avoid touching the finished goods inventory fact table. When multiple fact tables are tied to a dimension table, the fact tables should all link to that dimension table. When we use dimensions that share common fields with each of the fact tables, we say that these dimensions are *conformed* across the fact tables in our value chain.

After building the grouping columns and additive fact columns, you must launch the report's query one fact table at a time, and assemble the report by performing an outer join of the separate answer sets on the grouping columns. This outer join must be performed by the requesting client tool, not the database. You must never try to launch a single SQL SELECT statement that refers to more than one fact table. You will lose control of performance to our friend, the cost-based optimizer. Note that the necessary outer join assembles the final report, column by column. You cannot solve this with SQL UNION, which assembles reports row by row.

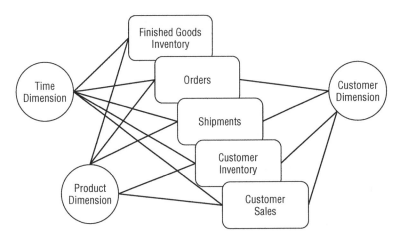

Figure 6-4: Separate fact tables for each business process share common dimensions.

Some of you may be wondering why each business process is modeled with its own separate fact table. Why not combine all of the processes together into a single fact table? Unfortunately, this is impossible for several reasons. Most important, the separate fact tables in the value chain do not share all the dimensions. You simply can't put the customer ship-to dimension on the finished goods inventory data. A second reason is that each fact table possesses different facts, and the fact table records are recorded at different times along the value chain.

Once you have set up multiple fact tables for drilling across, you can certainly drill up and down at the same time. In this case, you take the whole value chain and simultaneously ask all the fact tables for more granular data (drill down) or less granular data (drill up).

6.3 The Soul of the Data Warehouse, Part One: Drilling Down

Ralph Kimball, Intelligent Enterprise, *Mar 20, 2003*

Although data warehouses come in many shapes and sizes and deal with many different subject areas, every data warehouse must embody a few fundamental themes. The three most important are drilling down, drilling across, and handling time. Modern data warehouses so deeply embed these three themes that I think an "if-and-only-if" relationship has developed between them and a real data warehouse. If a system supports drilling down, drilling across, and handling time, then as long as it's easy to use and runs fast, it automatically qualifies as a data warehouse. But as simple as these three themes might seem, they give rise to a set of detailed and powerful architectural guidelines that should not be compromised.

In this article, I drill down into drilling down, starting with a precise operational definition. Then, as a good engineer should, I lay out practical guidelines for building systems that do a good job of drilling down.

Drilling down in a relational database means "adding a row header" to an existing SELECT statement. For instance, if you're analyzing the sales of products at a manufacturer level, the select list of the query reads SELECT MANUFACTURER, SUM(SALES). Of course the rest of the query contains join specifications and constraints on other parts of the database, such as time and geography. If you wish to drill down on the list of manufacturers to show the brands sold, you add the brand row header: SELECT MANUFACTURER, BRAND, SUM(SALES). Now each manufacturer row expands into multiple rows listing all the brands sold. This is the essence of drilling down.

Incidentally, we often call a row header a "grouping column" because everything in the select list that's not aggregated with an operator such as SUM must be mentioned in the SQL GROUP BY clause. So the GROUP BY clause in the second query reads GROUP BY MANUFACTURER, BRAND. Row headers and grouping columns are the same thing.

This example is particularly simple because it's very likely that, in a dimensional schema, both the manufacturer and brand attributes exist in the same product dimension table. So, after running the first query at the manufacturer level, you look at the list of attributes in the product dimension and opportunistically drag the brand attribute into the query. Then you run it again, thereby drilling down in an ad hoc way. If the brand attribute is indeed in the same dimension table as the manufacturer attribute, then the only adjustments to the original SQL are to add brand to the select list and the GROUP BY clause.

You could just as well have selected the color attribute for drilling down rather than the brand attribute. In fact, if you substitute the color attribute for brand in the preceding paragraphs, they would be just as valid. This exercise powerfully illustrates the fact that drilling down has nothing to do with descending a predetermined hierarchy. In fact, once you understand this concept, you see that you can drill down using any attribute drawn from any dimension! You could just as well have drilled down on the weekday from the time dimension; the preceding discussion of the select list and the GROUP BY clause would still be identical.

The idea that you can expand any report row to show more detail simply by adding a new row header is one of the powerful ideas that form the soul of a data warehouse. A good data warehouse designer should always be thinking of additional drill-down paths to add to an existing environment. An example of this out-of-the-box thinking is to add an audit dimension to a fact table, as described in article 11.20, *Indicators of Quality: The Audit Dimension*. The audit dimension contains indicators of data quality in the fact table, such as "data element out of bounds." But this audit dimension can be part of the drill-down process! Now you can devise a standard report to drill down to issues of data quality, including the proportion of questionable data. By drilling down on data quality, each row of the original report would appear as multiple rows, each with a different data quality indicator. Hopefully, most of the report results should cluster under the "normal" row headers.

Finally, it's even possible to drill down with a calculation, as long as you're careful not to use an aggregate operator such as SUM in the calculated quantity. You could drill down on the price point of the manufacturer's sales by adding SALES/QUANTITY to the select list, where this price point calculation contains no aggregate operator. SALES and QUANTITY are both numeric facts in the fact table. The select list now reads SELECT MANUFACTURER, SALES/QUANTITY, SUM(SALES). You must also add SALES/QUANTITY to the GROUP BY clause. This expression replaces each original manufacturer row with the sales of each manufacturer's products at each observed price in the marketplace. Each row shows the price point as well as the total sales at that price point.

I can now make some precise technical comments about drilling down:

1. Drilling down is the most basic user maneuver in the data warehouse, which must support it in as general and flexible a manner as possible because there's no way to predict the user's drill-down path. In other words, every drill-down path must be available and supported with the same user interface gestures because the users see little conceptual difference between the various forms of drilling down described in the preceding examples.

2. The data warehouse must therefore support drilling down at the user interface level, at all times, with the most atomic data possible because the most atomic data is the most dimensional. The most atomic data is the most expressive; more dimensions are attached to atomic data than to any form of aggregated or rolled-up data.

3. Combining the first two points means that for all practical purposes, the atomic data must be in the same schema format as any aggregated form of the data; the atomic data must be a smoothly accessible target for drill-down paths using standard ad hoc query tools. Failure in this area is the showstopper for an architecture in which atomic data is hidden in the back room in a normalized physical format and somehow is accessed after "drilling through" aggregated dimensional data marts. The proponents of this architecture have never explained how this magic occurs. Fortunately, this crisis evaporates if you use the same data structures at all levels of aggregation including the atomic level.

4. To build a practical system for drilling down, you want standard ad hoc query tools to present the drill-down choices without special schema-dependent programming, and you want these tools to emit the correct resulting SQL without schema-dependent programming. Schema-dependent programming is the kiss of death for a data warehouse shop because it means that each schema requires custom-built applications. This problem was a crisis in the 1980s; there's no excuse for it to remain a problem now. Avoiding schema-dependent programming means choosing a standard schema methodology for all user-facing data sets in the presentation layer of the data warehouse.

5. Only one standard schema methodology exists that's capable of expressing data in a single, uniform format that looks the same at the atomic layers as in all aggregated layers, and at the

same time requires no schema dependent programming: the star schema, otherwise known as the dimensional model. Dimensional models support all forms of drilling down described in this column. All possible many-to-one and many-to-many data relationships are capable of representation in a dimensional model; thus, the dimensional model is the ideal platform for ad hoc querying.

6. The dimensional design in the presentation layer smoothly supports prebuilt aggregation tables. An *aggregated fact table* is a mechanically derived table of summary records. The most common reason to build aggregated fact tables is that they offer immense performance advantages compared to using the large, atomic fact tables. But you get this performance boost only when the user asks for an aggregated result! The first example query asking for the manufacturer sales of products was a good example of an aggregated result.

A modern data warehouse environment uses a query rewrite facility called an *aggregate navigator* to choose a prebuilt aggregate table whenever possible. Oracle's materialized views and IBM DB2's automatic summary tables are examples of aggregate navigators. Each time the user asks for a new drill-down path, the aggregate navigator decides in real time which aggregate fact table will support the query most efficiently. Whenever the user asks for a sufficiently precise and unexpected drill down, the aggregate navigator gracefully defaults to the atomic data layer.

Drilling down is probably the most basic capability that a data warehouse needs to support. Drilling down most directly addresses the natural business user need to see more detail in an interesting result.

6.4 The Soul of the Data Warehouse, Part Two: Drilling Across

Ralph Kimball, Intelligent Enterprise, *Apr 5, 2003*

If drilling down is the most fundamental maneuver in a data warehouse, drilling across is a close second. From the perspective of an answer set, drilling across *adds more data to an existing row.* Note that this result isn't what you get from a UNION of rows from separate queries. It's better described as the column accretion from separate queries.

Drilling across by adding another measured fact to the SELECT list from the existing fact table mentioned in the query is a trivial accomplishment. What's more interesting and important is adding another measured fact from a new fact table. The issues raised by this simple view of drilling across are at the heart of data warehouse architecture. These issues boil down to an observation and a choice.

The observation about drill across is that the new fact table called for in the drill-across operation must share certain dimensions with the fact table in the original query. Certain dimensions will be named in the original query because they contribute row headers. Remember that these row headers are the basis of the grouping that creates the answer set row. These dimensions will appear in the FROM clause of the SQL code and will be joined to the fact table through the relationship of a foreign key to the primary key. The new fact table must also support exactly these same row headers, or the context of the answer set row is meaningless.

The drill-across choice is that you can either send a single, simultaneous SQL request to the two fact tables or send two separate requests. Although sending a single SQL request to the two fact tables seems cleaner, this choice can become a showstopper. Sending a single request means mentioning both fact tables in the FROM clause of the SQL code and joining both fact tables in some way to the common dimension tables I just discussed. This commingling of two fact tables in the same SQL statement causes these problems:

- Because the two fact tables will be joined together either directly or through the common dimensions, the query must specify whether the many-to-many relationship between the two fact tables is handled with inner or outer joins. This fundamental challenge arises from the relational model. It's effectively impossible to get this right, even if you're an expert SQL programmer. Depending on the relative cardinality of the two fact tables, your aggregated numeric totals can either be too low or too high, or both! Even if you don't believe me, you have to deal with the next bullet point.

- The vast majority of queries the relational database receives are generated by powerful query tools and report writers, and you have no direct control over the SQL they emit. You don't *want* control over the SQL. Some of these tools generate mind-boggling reams of SQL, and you can't effectively intervene.

- Emitting a single SQL statement precludes you from requesting data from separate table spaces, separate machines, or separate database vendors. You're stuck in the same table space on the same machine talking to one database vendor. If you can easily avoid this problem, why take on these restrictions?

- Finally, if you emit a single SQL statement involving both fact tables, you'll almost certainly be unable to use any of the powerful query-rewrite tools that perform aggregate navigation. Aggregate navigation is the most cost-effective way to make dramatic gains in data warehouse performance. For more on aggregate navigation, see article 12.18, *Aggregate Navigation with (Almost) No Metadata*.

Implementing Drill Across

If you've followed the logic of the observation and the choice, the architecture to support drill across begins to emerge.

1. All fact tables in a drill-across query must use *conformed dimensions*.
2. The actual drill-across query consists of a *multi-pass* set of separate requests to the target fact tables followed by a simple sort-merge on the identical row headers returned from each request.

The simplest definition of conformed dimensions is that two instances of a conformed dimension are identical. So if two fact tables have a customer dimension, then customer is conformed if the two dimensions are exactly the same. But this definition is unnecessarily restrictive. Here's the precise definition of conformed dimensions: *Two dimensions are conformed if the fields that you use as common row headers have the same domains.*

When you bring two separate queries together in a drill-across operation, both queries must have the same number of row headers, arranged from left to right in the same order. All the rest of the columns (the computed facts) in the two queries, by definition, are not row headers. In other words, an independent examination of both queries shows that neither query has rows that duplicate the same row headers. To put it another way, the row headers form a unique key for each row of the answer set.

To sort-merge (also called merge-sort) the two queries, you must sort them the same way. At this point, it becomes possible to merge the rows of the two queries together in a single pass. The resulting merged answer set has a single set of row headers plus the combined set of computed facts returned from both queries. Because traditional sort-merge is the same as an outer join, it is possible for a row in the final merged answer set to have nulls for either the first set of computed facts or the second set, but not both!

Once you've visualized the sort-merge step in drilling across, you really understand conformed dimensions. With conformed dimensions, the only thing you care about is matching row headers. If the contents of the respective fields you're using for the sort-merge are drawn from the same domains, then the match makes sense. If you try to match row headers from two dimensions that aren't conformed, you're guaranteed to get garbage. The sort-merge will fail, and the SQL engine will post the results from the two queries on separate lines—and probably in separate sorting locations in the merged answer set.

Amazing Magic

In my classes, I sometimes describe conformed dimensions as either dimensions that are exactly equal (the trivial case) or dimensions where "one is a subset of the other." For example, a brand dimension may be a subset of a more detailed product dimension. In this case, you can drill across two fact tables, one at the brand level with a brand dimension (such as a forecast), and the other at a detailed product level with a product dimension (such as sales transactions). Assume that the product dimension is a nice flat table containing the low cardinality brand attribute.

If the row header of the two queries is simply "brand," then some amazing magic takes place. The engine automatically aggregates both data sets to the brand level, which is exactly the right level for the drill across. If the names of the brands are drawn from the same domain, you can complete the drill across (of forecast versus actual) by confidently merging the rows with the same brand names. Many commercial query and report writing tools perform this drill-across operation. Please see the rather technical articles 13.21, *Simple Drill-Across in SQL*, and 13.22, *An Excel Macro for Drilling Across*, for deeper dives into implementing drill-across.

You can see that it's possible to conform two dimensions even when they have some incompatible fields. You just need to be careful to avoid using these incompatible fields as row headers in drill-across queries. Not avoiding it lets a dimension contain some private fields that are meaningful only to a local user group.

Finally, it's worth pointing out that the decision to physically centralize a data warehouse has very little to do with conformed dimensions. If you combine two data sets in a drill-across operation, you have to label them the same way, whether the data sets are tightly administered on a single piece of hardware by one DBA or are loosely administered by remote IT organizations that merely agree to create a set of overlapping labels.

6.5 The Soul of the Data Warehouse, Part Three: Handling Time

Ralph Kimball, Intelligent Enterprise, *Apr 22, 2003*

The three most fundamental maneuvers in every data warehouse are drilling down, drilling across, and handling time. The third, handling time, makes good on a pledge that every data warehouse provider implicitly takes: *The data warehouse shall preserve history.* In practice, this pledge generates three main requirements for the data warehouse:

First, every piece of data in the data warehouse must have clearly understood time validity. In other words, when did the data become valid, and when did it cease to be valid?

Second, if the detailed description of a data warehouse entity has changed over time, you must correctly associate each version of that entity with the contemporary versions of other measurements and entities in the data warehouse. In other words, if a customer made a purchase a year ago, the description of the customer attached to that purchase must be correct for that time frame.

Last, the data warehouse must support the natural ways people have of viewing data over time. These natural ways include seeing instantaneous events, regular periodic reports, and latest status.

Dimensional modeling provides a convenient framework for dealing with each of these requirements. Remember that dimensional models are organized around measurements. Measurements, which are usually numeric, occupy fact tables in a dimensional model. The contexts of the measurements are in dimension tables, which surround the fact tables and connect to them through a series of simple relationships between foreign keys and primary keys.

Time Validity

A measurement is usually a physical act that takes place at a specific time, so it's natural, even irresistible, to attach a time stamp to each fact table record. Every fact table has a time dimension.

Time stamps are commonly recorded at a daily grain because many legacy systems don't record time of day when posting a measurement. In a dimensional schema, the daily time stamp consists of a surrogate integer foreign key in the fact table joined to a corresponding primary key in the daily time dimension table. You want the time stamp in the fact table to be a surrogate key rather than a real date for three reasons: First, the rare time stamp that is inapplicable, corrupted, or hasn't happened yet needs a value that cannot be a real date. Second, most user calendar navigation constraints, such as fiscal periods, end-of-periods, holidays, day numbers, and week numbers aren't supported by database time stamps. Therefore, they need to come from a table with a verbose time dimension, rather than computed in the requesting query tool. Third, integer time keys take up less disk space than full dates.

When the source system provides a detailed time stamp for the measurement down to the minute or the second, the time of day needs to be a separate dimension or a full date/time stamp. Otherwise, a combined day and time-of-day dimension would be impractically large.

In multinational applications, there are often two time stamp perspectives: the remote party's and home office's. Certainly, when recording the time of day, it usually makes sense to include two pairs of time stamps (calendar day and full date/time stamp for both remote and local) rather than leaving it up to the query tool to work out time zones. Mainly because of daylight savings time rules, the calculation of time zone differences is horrendously complicated.

Correct Association

Dimensional modeling assumes that dimensions are largely independent. This assumption, combined with the fact that time is its own dimension, implies that other entities, such as customer and product, are independent of time. In the real world, this inference isn't quite true. Entities such as customer and product slowly change over time, usually in episodic, unpredictable ways.

When the data warehouse encounters a legitimate revised description of, for example, a customer, there are three fundamental choices for handling this slowly changing dimension (SCD):

1. Overwrite the changed attribute, thereby destroying previous history. This approach is justifiable when correcting an error, if you're living by the pledge.
2. Issue a new record for the customer, keeping the customer natural key, but creating (by necessity) a new surrogate primary key.
3. Create an additional field in the existing customer record, and store the old value of the attribute in the additional field. Overwrite the original attribute field. This strategy is called for when the attribute can have simultaneous "alternate realities."

All three choices need at least one embedded time stamp stating when the record was updated, as well as a companion field describing that change. For the primary type 2 SCD, where a new record is created, you need a pair of time stamps as well as a change description field. The pair of time stamps define a span of time from the begin effective time to end effective time when the complete customer description remains valid. The most sophisticated treatment of a type 2 SCD record involves five fields:

- Begin effective date/time stamp (not a surrogate key pointer)
- End effective date/time stamp
- Effective date surrogate key (daily grain) connecting to date dimension as a snowflake
- Change description field (text)
- Most recent flag

The first two fields are what conventional BETWEEN constraints use to profile the dimension at specific points in time. They need to be single fields with full date and time stamps in order to make the BETWEEN machinery work. The third field constrains specific records in the dimension that changed on days that can be described only via the organization's calendar date table (such as employee demotions that occurred the day before payday). The fourth field lets you find all changes in the dimension meeting a particular description. The fifth field is a quick way to find all the current records in a dimension without using BETWEEN.

Natural Grains

In 30 years of analyzing and modeling data, I've found that fact table measurements all fall into just three classes. These types correspond to instantaneous events, regular periodic reports, and latest status. In dimensional modeling, these three fact table types are the transaction grain, the periodic snapshot grain, and the accumulating snapshot grain.

The *transaction grain* represents a point in space and time, and is meant for a measurement event defined at a particular instant. A scanner event at a grocery store is the classic example of a transaction event. In this case, the time stamp in the fact table is very simple. It's either a single daily grain foreign key or a pair consisting of a daily grain foreign key together with a time-of-day date/time stamp, depending on what the source system provides. The facts in this transaction grain table must be true to the grain and should describe only what took place in that instant.

The *periodic snapshot grain* represents a regular repeating measurement, like a bank account monthly statement. This fact table also has a single time stamp, representing the overall period. Usually the time stamp is the end of the period, and often is expressed at the daily grain, even if it's understood to represent a month or a fiscal period. The facts in this periodic snapshot grain table must be true to the grain and should describe only measures appropriate to the specific period.

The *accumulating snapshot grain* represents the current evolving status of a process that has a finite beginning and end. Usually these processes are of short duration and therefore don't lend themselves to the periodic snapshot. Order processing is the classic example of an accumulating snapshot.

The design and administration of the accumulating snapshot is quite different from the first two fact table types. All accumulating snapshot fact tables have a set of as many as four to 12 dates describing the typical scenario of the process being modeled. For instance, an order has a set of characteristic dates: original order date, actual ship date, delivery date, final payment date, and return date. In this example, these five dates appear as five separate foreign (surrogate) keys. When the order record is first created, the first of these dates is well defined, but perhaps none of the others have yet happened. This same fact record is subsequently revisited as the order wends its way through the pipeline. Each time something happens, the accumulating snapshot fact record is destructively modified. The date foreign keys are overwritten, and various facts are updated. Often the first date remains inviolate because that describes when the record was created, but all the other dates may well be overwritten, sometimes more than once.

Have You Lived Up to Your Pledges?

This article has been a brief overview of the central techniques of handling time in a data warehouse. If you've systematically employed surrogate keys for all your connections to your master time dimensions, faithfully tracked changes in dimension entities with the three types of SCDs, and supported your users' reporting needs with transaction grain, periodic snapshot grain, and accumulating snapshot grain fact tables, then you have indeed lived up to your pledges.

6.6 Graceful Modifications to Existing Fact and Dimension Tables

Ralph Kimball, Design Tip #29, *Oct 15, 2001*

Despite the best plans and intentions, the data warehouse designer must often face the problem of adding new data types or altering the relationships among data after the data warehouse is up and running. In an ideal world we would like such changes to be graceful so that existing query and reporting applications continue to run without being recoded, and existing user interfaces "wake up" to the new data and allow the data to be added to queries and reports.

Obviously, there are some changes that can never be handled gracefully. If a data source ceases to be available and there is no compatible substitute, then the applications depending on this source will stop working. But can we describe a class of situations where changes to our data environment can be handled gracefully?

The predictable symmetry of our dimensional models comes to our rescue. Dimensional models are able to absorb some significant changes in the source data without invalidating existing applications. Let's list as many of these changes as we can, starting with the simplest.

1. **New dimensional attributes.** If, for example, we discover new textual descriptors of a product or customer, we add these attributes to the dimension as new fields. All existing applications will be oblivious to the new attributes and will continue to function. Most user interfaces should notice the new attributes at query time. Conceptually, the list of attributes available for constraining and grouping should be displayed in a query or reporting tool via an underlying query of the form SELECT COLUMN_NAME FROM SYS_TABLES WHERE TABLE_NAME = 'PRODUCT'. This kind of user interface will continuously adjust when new dimension attributes are added to the schema. In a slowly changing dimension environment, where slightly changed versions of the dimension are being maintained, care must be taken to assign the values of the new attributes correctly to the various versions of the dimension records. If the new attributes are available only after a specific point in time, then "NA" (not available) or its equivalent must be supplied for old dimension records.

2. **New types of measured facts.** Similarly, if new measured facts become available we can add them to the fact table gracefully. The simplest case is when the new facts are available in the same measurement event and at the same grain as the existing facts. In this case, the fact table is altered to add the new fact fields, and the values are populated into the table. In an ideal world, an ALTER TABLE statement can be issued against the existing fact table to add the new fields. If that is not possible, then a second fact table must be defined with the new fields and the records copied from the first. If the new facts are only available from a point in time forward, then true null values need to be placed in the older fact records. If we have done all of this, old applications will continue to run undisturbed. New applications using the new facts

should behave reasonably even if the null values are encountered. The users may have to be trained that the new facts are only available from a specific point in time forward.

A more complex situation arises when new measured facts are not available in the same measurement event as the old facts, or if the new facts occur naturally at a different grain. If the new facts cannot be allocated or assigned to the original grain of the fact table, it is very likely that the new facts belong in their own fact table. It is a mistake to mix grains of measurements or disjoint kinds of measurements in the same fact table. If you have this situation, you need to bite the bullet and find a query tool or report writer that is capable of drill-across SQL so that it can access multiple fact tables in the same user request.

3. **New dimensions.** A dimension can be added to an existing fact table by adding a new foreign key field and populating it correctly with values of the primary key from the new dimension. For example, a weather dimension can be added to a retail sales fact table if a source describing the weather is available at each selling location each day. Note that we are not changing the grain of the fact table. If the weather information is only available from a point in time forward, then the foreign key value for the weather dimension must point to a record in the weather dimension whose description is "weather unavailable."

4. **More granular dimension.** Sometimes it is desirable to increase the granularity of a dimension. For instance, a retail sales fact table with a store dimension could be modified to replace the store dimension with an individual cash register dimension. If we had 100 stores, each with an average of 10 cash registers, the new cash register dimension would have 1000 records. All of the original store attributes would be included in the cash register dimension because cash registers roll up perfectly in a many-to-one relationship to stores.

5. **Addition of a completely new data source involving new and existing dimensions.** Almost always, a new source of data has its own granularity and its own dimensions. All of you dimensional designers know the answer to this one. We sprout a brand new fact table. Because any existing fact tables and dimension tables are untouched, by definition, all the existing applications keep chugging along. Although this case seems almost trivial, the point here is to avoid cramming the new measurements into the existing fact tables. A single fact table always owns a single kind of measurement expressed with a uniform grain.

This article has tried to define a taxonomy of unexpected changes to your data environment to give you a way to sort through various responses, and recognize those situations where a graceful change is possible. Because redoing queries and reports is hugely expensive and probably disruptive to the business users, our goal is to stay on the graceful side of the line.

Dos and Don'ts

In this section, we provide dimensional modeling guidelines to follow, as well as common traps to avoid.

6.7 Kimball's Ten Essential Rules of Dimensional Modeling

Margy Ross, Intelligent Enterprise, *May 29, 2009*

A student recently asked me for a list of "Kimball's Commandments" for dimensional modeling. Due to the religious connotations, we'll refrain from calling these commandments, but the following is a checklist of not-to-be-broken Kimball rules, along with less stringent rule-of-thumb recommendations.

Rule #1: Load detailed atomic data into dimensional structures. Dimensional models should be populated with bedrock atomic details to support the unpredictable filtering and grouping required by business user queries. Users typically don't need to see a single record at a time, but you can't predict the somewhat arbitrary ways they'll want to screen and roll up the details. If only summarized data is available, then you've already made assumptions about data usage patterns that will cause users to run into a brick wall when they want to dig deeper into the details. Of course, the atomic details can be complemented by summary dimensional models that provide performance advantages for common queries of aggregated data, but the business users cannot live on summary data alone; they need the gory details to answer their ever-changing questions.

Rule #2: Structure dimensional models around business processes. Business processes are the activities performed by your organization; they represent measurement events, like taking an order or billing a customer. Business processes typically capture or generate unique performance metrics associated with each event. These metrics translate into facts, with each business process represented by a single atomic fact table. In addition to single process fact tables, consolidated fact tables are sometimes created that combine metrics from multiple processes into one fact table at a common level of detail; consolidated fact tables are a complement to the detailed single process fact tables, not a substitute for them.

Rule #3: Ensure every fact table has a date dimension table associated with it. The measurement events described in rule #2 always have a date stamp of some variety associated with them, whether it's a monthly balance snapshot or a monetary transaction captured to the hundredth of a second. Every fact table should have at least one foreign key to an associated date dimension table, whose grain is a single day, with calendar attributes and nonstandard characteristics about the measurement event date, such as the fiscal month and corporate holiday indicator. Sometimes multiple date foreign keys are represented in a fact table.

Rule #4: Ensure that all facts in a single fact table are at the same grain or level of detail. There are three fundamental grains to categorize all fact tables: transactional, periodic snapshot, or accumulating snapshot. Regardless of its grain type, every measurement within a fact table must be at the exact same level of detail. When you mix facts representing multiple levels of granularity in the same fact table, you are setting yourself up for business user confusion and making the BI applications vulnerable to overstated or otherwise erroneous results.

Rule #5: Resolve many-to-many relationships in fact tables. Because a fact table stores the results of a business process event, there's inherently a many-to-many (M:M) relationship between its foreign keys, such as multiple products being sold in multiple stores on multiple days. These foreign key fields should never be null. Sometimes dimensions can take on multiple values for a single measurement event, such as the multiple diagnoses associated with a health care encounter or multiple customers with a bank account; in these cases, it's unreasonable to resolve the many-valued dimensions directly in the fact table because this would violate the natural grain of the measurement event, so we use a many-to-many dual keyed bridge table in conjunction with the fact table.

Rule #6: Resolve many-to-one relationships in dimension tables. Hierarchical, fixed depth many-to-one (M:1) relationships between attributes are typically denormalized or collapsed into a flattened dimension table. If you've spent most of your career designing normalized entity-relationship models for transaction processing systems, you'll need to resist your instinctive tendencies to normalize or snowflake the M:1 relationship into smaller subdimensions; dimension denormalization is the name of the game in dimensional modeling. It is relatively common to have multiple M:1 relationships represented in a single dimension table. One-to-one relationships, like a unique product description associated with a product code, are also handled in a dimension table. Occasionally many-to-one relationships are resolved in the fact table, such as the case when the detailed dimension table has millions of rows and its roll up attributes are frequently changing; however, using the fact table to resolve M:1 relationships should be done sparingly.

Rule #7: Store report labels and filter domain values in dimension tables. The codes and, more importantly, associated decodes and descriptors used for labeling and query filtering should be captured in dimension tables. Avoid storing cryptic code fields or bulky descriptive fields in the fact table itself; likewise, don't just store the code in the dimension table and assume that users don't need descriptive decodes or that they'll be handled in the BI application. If it's a row/column label or pull-down menu filter, it should be handled as a dimension attribute. While we stated in rule #5 that fact table foreign keys should never be null, it's also advisable to avoid nulls in the dimension tables' attribute fields by replacing the null value with "NA" (not applicable) or another default value determined by the data steward to reduce user confusion, if possible.

Rule #8: Make sure dimension tables use a surrogate key. Meaningless, sequentially assigned surrogate keys (except for the date dimension where chronologically assigned and even more meaningful keys are acceptable) deliver a number of operational benefits, including smaller keys, which mean smaller fact tables, smaller indexes, and improved performance. Surrogate keys are absolutely required if you're tracking dimension attribute changes with a new dimension record for each profile change; even if your business users don't initially visualize the value of tracking attribute changes, using surrogates will make a downstream policy change less onerous. The surrogates also allow you to map multiple operational keys to a common profile, plus buffer you from unexpected operational activities, like the recycling of an obsolete product number or acquisition of another company with its own coding schemes.

Rule #9: Create conformed dimensions to integrate data across the enterprise. Conformed dimensions (otherwise known as common, master, standard, or reference dimensions) are essential for enterprise data warehousing. Managed once in the ETL system and then reused across multiple fact tables, conformed dimensions deliver consistent descriptive attributes across dimensional models and support the ability to drill across and integrate data from multiple business processes. The enterprise data warehouse bus matrix is the key architecture blueprint for representing the organization's core business processes and associated dimensionality. Reusing conformed dimensions ultimately shortens the DW/BI system's time-to-market by eliminating redundant design and development efforts; however, conformed dimensions require a commitment and investment in data stewardship and governance, even if you don't need everyone to agree on every dimension attribute to leverage conformity.

Rule #10: Continuously balance the requirements and realities to deliver a DW/BI solution that's accepted by the business users and supports their decision making. Dimensional modelers must constantly straddle the business users' requirements along with the underlying realities of the associated source data to deliver a design that is both reasonably implementable, and more importantly, stands a reasonable chance of business adoption. The requirements versus realities balancing act is a fact of life for DW/BI practitioners, whether you're focused on the dimensional model, project strategy, technical/ETL/BI architectures, or deployment/maintenance plan.

If you've read our *Intelligent Enterprise* articles regularly or our *Toolkit* books and monthly *Design Tips* (all of which are included in this Kimball Reader!), the rules discussed in this article shouldn't be news to you; however, we've tried to consolidate them into a single rulebook that you can easily reference as you're gathered to design (or review) your own models. Good luck!

6.8 What Not to Do

Ralph Kimball, Intelligent Enterprise, *Oct 24, 2001*

In nearly all the articles I have written for *Intelligent Enterprise* and its predecessor, *DBMS*, I described design techniques needed to build a data warehouse. But despite all those columns, something is missing. The tone of the columns has almost always been imperative: "In situation A, use design techniques X, Y, and Z." I realize that data warehouse designers also need boundaries, so this column is devoted to dimensional modeling design techniques NOT to use.

The 12 dimensional modeling techniques to avoid are listed in reverse order of importance. But even the first few mistakes I list can be enough to seriously compromise your data warehouse.

Mistake 12: Place text attributes in a fact table if you mean to use them as the basis of constraining and grouping. Creating a dimensional model is a kind of triage. Start by identifying the numeric measurements delivered from an operational source; those go in the fact table. Then identify the descriptive textual attributes from the context of the measurements; these go in the dimensions. Finally, make a case-by-case decision about the leftover codes and pseudo numeric items, placing them in the fact table if they are more like measurements, and in the dimension table if they are more like physical descriptions of something. But don't lose your nerve and leave true text in the fact table, especially comment fields. Get these text attributes off the main runway of your data warehouse and into dimension tables.

Mistake 11: Limit the use of verbose descriptive attributes in dimensions to save space. You might think that you're being a good, conservative designer by keeping the size of your dimensions under control. But in virtually every data warehouse, the dimension tables are geometrically smaller than the fact tables. So what if you have a 100MB product dimension table, if the fact table is 100 times as large! To design an easy-to-use data warehouse, you must supply as much verbose descriptive context in each dimension as you can. Make sure every code is augmented with readable descriptive text. Remember that the textual attributes in the dimensions "implement" the user interface for browsing your data, provide the entry points for constraining, and supply the content for the row and column headers in the final reports.

Mistake 10: Split hierarchies and hierarchy levels into multiple dimensions. A hierarchy is a cascaded series of many-to-one relationships. Many products roll up to a single brand. Many brands roll up to a single category, and so on. If your dimension is expressed at the lowest level of granularity (such as product), then all the higher levels of the hierarchy can be expressed as unique values in the product record. Users understand hierarchies, and your job is to present them in the most natural and efficient way. A hierarchy belongs in a single, physical flat dimension table. Resist the urge to "snowflake" a hierarchy by generating a set of progressively smaller subdimension tables. Don't confuse back room data cleaning with front room data presenting! And finally, if you have more than one hierarchy existing simultaneously, in most cases it makes sense to include all the hierarchies in the same dimension, if the dimension has been defined at the lowest possible grain.

Mistake 9: Delay dealing with a slowly changing dimension (SCD). Too many data warehouses are designed to regularly overwrite the most important dimensions, such as customer and product, from the underlying data sources. This goes against a basic data warehouse oath: The data warehouse will represent history accurately, even if the underlying data source does not. SCDs are an essential design element of every data warehouse.

Mistake 8: Use smart keys to join a dimension table to a fact table. Beginning data warehouse designers tend to be somewhat too literal minded when designing the primary keys in dimension tables that must necessarily connect to the foreign keys of the fact table. It is counterproductive to declare a whole suite of dimension attributes as the dimension table key and then use them all as the basis of the physical join to the fact table. All sorts of ugly problems eventually arise. Replace the smart physical key with a simple integer surrogate key that is numbered sequentially from 1 to N (the number of records in the dimension table).

Mistake 7: Add dimensions to a fact table before declaring its grain. All dimensional designs should start with the numeric measurements and work outward. First, identify the source of the measurements. Second, specify the exact granularity and meaning of the measurements. Third, surround these measurements with dimensions that are true to that grain. Staying true to the grain is a crucial step in the design of a dimensional data model.

Mistake 6: Declare that a dimensional model is "based on a specific report." A dimensional model has nothing to do with an intended report! A dimensional model is a model of a measurement process. A numeric measurement is a solid physical reality. Numeric measurements form the basis of fact tables. The dimensions appropriate for a given fact table are the physical context that describe the circumstances of the measurements. A dimensional model is solidly based on the physics of a measurement process and is quite independent from how a business user chooses to define a report.

Mistake 5: Mix facts of differing grain in the same fact table. A serious error in a dimensional design is to add "helpful" facts to a fact table, such as records that describe totals for an extended time span or rolled up geographic area. Although these extra facts are well known at the time of the individual measurement and would seem to make some applications simpler, they cause havoc because all the automatic summations across dimensions double and triple count these higher level facts, producing incorrect results. Each different measurement grain demands its own fact table.

Mistake 4: Leave lowest level atomic data in normalized format. The lowest level data is the most dimensional and should be the physical foundation of your dimensional design. Aggregated data has been deprived of some of its dimensions. If you build a dimensional model from aggregated data and expect your user query tools to drill down to normalized atomic data that you have left in your staging area, then you're dreaming. Build all your dimensional models on the most atomic data. Make all atomic data part of the presentation portion of your data warehouse. Then your user tools will gracefully resist the "ad hoc attack."

Mistake 3: Eschew aggregate fact tables and shrunken dimension tables when faced with query performance concerns; solve performance problems by adding more parallel processing hardware. Aggregates (such as Oracle's materialized views and IBM DB2's automatic summary tables) are the single most cost-effective way to improve query performance. Most query tool vendors explicitly support aggregates, and all of these depend on dimensional modeling constructs. The addition of parallel processing hardware, which is expensive, should be done as part of a balanced program that consists also of building aggregates, choosing query-efficient DBMS software, building lots of indexes, increasing real memory size, and increasing CPU speed.

Mistake 2: Fail to conform facts across separate fact tables. It would be a shame to get this far and then build stovepipes. This is called snatching defeat from the jaws of victory. If you have a numeric measured fact called, for example, revenue, in two or more of your dimensional models sourced from different underlying systems, then you need to take special care to make sure that the technical definitions of these facts match exactly. You want to be able to add and divide these separate revenue facts freely in your applications. This act is called *conforming the facts*.

Mistake 1: Fail to conform dimensions across separate fact tables. This is the biggest mistake because the single most important design technique in the dimensional modeling arsenal is conforming your dimensions. If two or more fact tables have the same dimension, you must be a fanatic about making these dimensions identical or carefully chosen subsets of each other. When you conform your dimensions across fact tables, you will be able to drill across separate data sources because the constraints and row headers will mean the same thing and match at the data level. Conformed dimensions are the secret sauce needed for building distributed data warehouses, adding unexpected new data sources to an existing warehouse, and making multiple incompatible technologies function together harmoniously.

Myths about Dimensional Modeling

The final articles in this chapter will help you differentiate between dimensional modeling truths versus fiction.

6.9 Dangerous Preconceptions

Ralph Kimball, DBMS, Aug 1996

We've retained the references to data marts in this early article rather than substituting the more current business process dimensional model nomenclature because Ralph addressed common misunderstandings surrounding the Kimball definition of a data mart.

This month I look at some preconceptions about data warehouses that are not only false, but are dangerous to the success of your projects. By eliminating these preconceptions, you simplify the design of your data warehouse and reduce the implementation time. The first set of dangerous preconceptions concerns a current hot topic: data marts.

Dangerous Preconceptions: The data mart is a quick and dirty data warehouse. You can bring up a data mart without going to the trouble of developing an overall architectural plan for the enterprise. It's too much trouble to develop an overall architecture, and there is no way that you have the perspective to try that now.

The Liberating Truth: The data mart must not be a quick and dirty data warehouse; rather it should focus on a business process subject area implemented within the framework of an overall plan. A data mart can be loaded with data extracted directly from legacy sources. A data mart does not have to be downloaded formally from a larger centralized enterprise data warehouse.

The key to a successful data mart strategy is simple. For any two data marts or business process dimension models in an enterprise, the common dimensions must be conformed. Dimensions are conformed when they share attributes (fields) that are based on the same underlying values. Thus in a grocery store chain, if the "back door" purchase orders database is one data mart and the "front door" retail sales database is another data mart, the two dimensional models will form a coherent part of an overall enterprise data warehouse if their common dimensions (say, time and product) conform.

The beauty of conformed dimensions is that the two data marts don't have to be on the same machine and don't need to be created at the same time. Once both data marts are running, an overarching application can request data simultaneously from both (in separate queries) and the answer set is likely to make sense. Logically, the only valid "row headers" in a joint report must come from common dimensions such as time and product in our grocery store example. But we have guaranteed that at least some of the row headers from these two data marts will be in common because the dimensions are conformed. Any of these common row headers can produce a valid report, as shown in Figure 6-5. In this example, the purchase order data is at the individual day level, but the sales forecast data is at the week level. Because days roll up to weeks, the two date dimensions are conformed since they share all the attributes that roll upward from individual weeks.

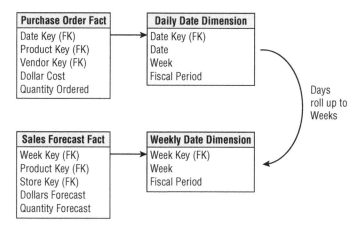

Figure 6-5: Two fact tables with conformed dimensions.

The idea of developing an overall data warehouse architecture is daunting, but the key step in that architecture plan is simple: Identify the common dimensions. In virtually every company, the most important common dimensions are customers, products, geographies, and time frames.

Once the common dimensions have been identified, the development of separate data marts must be managed under this common dimensional framework. When two data marts use the same dimension (for example, customer), they must share a set of attributes that are based on the same values.

The second set of dangerous preconceptions concerns dimensional models and whether they are "robust."

Dangerous Preconceptions: The dimensional data model is a specific high level summary type of design that is not extensible and cannot readily accommodate changes in database design requirements.

The Liberating Truth: The dimensional data model is extremely robust. It can withstand serious changes to the content of the database without requiring existing applications to be rewritten. New dimensions can be added to the design. Existing dimensions can be made more granular. New unanticipated facts and dimensional attributes can also be added, as shown in Figure 6-6.

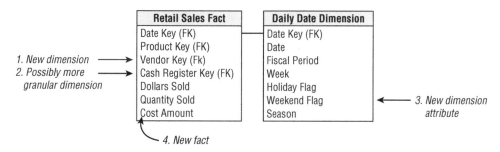

Figure 6-6: Potential changes to an existing dimensional model.

The secret of an extensible dimensional database is building the fact table at the most granular level. In Figure 6-6, the fact table represents daily sales of individual products in individual stores. Because all three primary dimensions (date, product, and store) are expressed in low level atomic units, they can roll up to any conceivable grouping requested by a user in the future. If you had already aggregated the database up to weeks, you cannot provide reliable monthly data without returning to a primary database extract and building a new database incompatible with the old. With daily data, however, you can accommodate both the weekly view and the monthly view without compatibility problems and without re-extracting the original data.

Figure 6-6 shows how the dimensional schema provides standard, convenient hooks for extending the database to meet new requirements. You can add new dimensions, add new facts, add new attributes to a dimension, and even make a dimension more granular. All of the extensions shown can be implemented without changing any previous application. No SQL must be rewritten. No applications must be rebuilt. This is the essence of extendibility.

6.10 Fables and Facts

Margy Ross, Intelligent Enterprise, Oct 16, 2004

According to Merriam-Webster, fables are fictitious statements. Unfortunately, fables about dimensional modeling circulate throughout our industry. These false claims and assertions are a distraction, especially if you're trying to align a team. In this article, we describe the root misunderstandings that perpetuate these myths so you understand why they're as unfounded as fairy tales about two-headed creatures.

Not All Dimensional Models Are Created Equal

We review a lot of dimensional models in our work. They often illustrate best practice design principles from our *Toolkits* and articles. However, not all supposed dimensional models are designed appropriately. Some blatantly violate core dimensional modeling tenets. Given the abysmal sample star schemas found in seemingly authoritative books and training presentations, this comes as no surprise. However, you shouldn't lump all dimensional models into a "bad" category based on misguided imposters.

Most of the fabled assertions are rooted in several basic mistakes regarding dimensional modeling best practices. Dimensional modeling can't be blamed if its fundamental concepts aren't embraced. Likewise, criticisms lobbed by individuals who don't understand its key premises need to be taken with a grain of salt. Once we clarify these misunderstandings, you'll be prepared to distinguish fables from facts for yourself.

Focus on Measurement Processes, Not Departmental Reports

We advocate a four-step approach for designing dimensional models. The first step is to identify the business process, followed by declaring the grain, then selecting the dimensions and facts. Nowhere do we recommend specifying the business's top 10 reports or queries.

If requirements are gathered by focusing exclusively on report or query templates, you're susceptible to modeling data to produce a specific report, rather than capturing the key metrics and related dimensions for analysis. Obviously, it's important to consider business usage when designing dimensional models. The dimension attributes must support the BI environment's filtering and labeling requirements. Robust dimension attributes translate into nearly endless analytic slicing and dicing combinations. However, don't blindly focus on a top 10 list in isolation because priorities and hot reports will inevitably evolve.

Instead of concentrating on specific reports or departmental needs in a vacuum, we suggest focusing the dimensional design on the most critical performance measurement process. In doing so, you can put the following fables to rest.

> **FABLE:** *Dimensional databases are built to address a specific business report or application. When the business needs a new report, another dimensional star schema is built.*
>
> FACT: Dimensional models should be built around physical measurement processes or events. A fact table row is created when a measurement occurs. The associated dimension attributes reflect contextual characteristics and hierarchies. If the business identifies a new report based on the same measurement process, there's no need to build a new mart, model, or schema. Measurement processes are relatively stable in most organizations; the analytics performed against these metrics are more fluid.

> **FABLE:** *Dimensional models are departmental solutions. When a different department needs access to the data, a new model is built and labeled with the department's vocabulary. Dimensional models require multiple extracts from the same source data repeatedly.*
>
> FACT: Dimensional models shouldn't be departmentally bound. A fact table representing a fundamental measurement process need only have one physical instance that's shared across business functions or departments. There's no reason to create multiple extracts from the same source. Metrics resulting from the invoicing business process, for example, are made available in a single dimensional model for access across the enterprise; there's no reason to replicate invoice performance metrics in separate departmental solutions for finance, marketing, and sales. Even if these departmental solutions were sourced from the same repository, they likely use similar, but slightly different naming conventions, definitions, and business rules, defeating the promise of a single version of the truth. The departmental approach is highly vulnerable to inconsistent, nonintegrated point solutions. We've never advocated this approach.

> **FABLE:** *You can't incorporate new data sources without rebuilding the original star schema or creating separate fact tables or data marts.*
>
> FACT: If the new data source is another capture system for an existing measurement process in the BI environment, then the new data can be gracefully combined with the original data without altering any existing reporting applications, presuming the granularity is the same. If the new data source is at a different grain representing a new measurement process, then a new fact table must be created. This has nothing to do with dimensional modeling. Any data representation would create a new entity when a new table with different keys is introduced.

FABLE: *With dimensional modeling, the fact table is forced to a single grain that is inflexible.*
FACT: Having the discipline to create fact tables with a single level of detail assures that measurements aren't inappropriately double-counted. A table with mixed grain facts can only be queried by a custom application knowledgeable about the varying levels of detail, effectively ruling out ad hoc exploration. If measurements naturally exist at different grains, then the most foolproof design establishes a fact table for each level. Far from being inflexible, this approach protects existing applications from breaking or recoding as changes occur.

Begin with Atomic Details, Not Summarized Data

Some claim that dimensional models are intended for managerial, strategic analysis and, therefore, should be populated with summarized data, not operational details. We strongly disagree. Dimensional models should be populated with atomic data so business users can ask very precise questions. Even if users don't care about the details of a single transaction, their question of the moment involves summarizing the details in unpredictable ways. Database administrators may presummarize some information, either physically or via materialized views, to avoid on-the-fly summarization with every query. However, these aggregates are performance tuning complements to the atomic level, not replacements. If you create dimensional models with atomic details, the following fables are nonissues.

FABLE: *Star schemas and dimensional models presuppose the business question. When the requirements change, the model must be modified.*
FACT: When you presummarize information, you've presupposed the business question. However, dimensional models with atomic data are independent of the business question because users can roll up or drill down ad infinitum. They answer new, previously unspecified questions without database changes.

FABLE: *Star schemas and dimensional models are only appropriate when there's a predictable pattern of usage. Dimensional models aren't appropriate for exploratory queries.*
FACT: Both normalized and dimensional models contain the same information and data relationships; both are capable of answering exactly the same questions, albeit with varying difficulty. Dimensional models naturally represent the physics of a measurement event; fact tables contain the measurements, and dimension tables contain the context. A single dimensional model based on the most atomic data is capable of answering all possible questions against that data.

FABLE: *Dimensional models aren't scalable. If detailed data is stored in a dimensional data mart, performance will be degraded. Data marts only contain recent information and are restricted from storing history.*
FACT: Dimensional star schemas are extremely scalable. It isn't unusual for modern fact tables to have billions of rows corresponding to the billions of measurement transactions captured. Million row dimension tables are common. Dimensional models should contain as much history as required to address the business requirements. There's nothing about dimensional modeling that prohibits the storage of substantial history.

FABLE: *Dimensional models aren't extensible and are unable to address future needs of the data warehouse.*

FACT: Dimensional models that express data at the lowest level of detail deliver maximum flexibility and extensibility. Users can summarize the atomic data any which way. Likewise, atomic data can be extended with additional attributes, measures, or dimensions without disrupting existing reports and queries.

FABLE: *A dimensional model can't support complex data. It eliminates many-to-many relationships between entities, allowing only many-to-one relationships.*

FACT: The logical content of dimensional models and normalized models are identical. Every data relationship expressed in one model can be accurately expressed in the other model. Dimensional models are always based on fact tables, which are completely general many-to-many relationships. A dimensional model is a form of an entity-relationship model with unnecessary snowflaking (normalization of dimension attributes) suppressed.

Integration Is the Goal, Not Normalization

Some people believe normalization solves the data integration challenge. Normalizing data contributes nothing to integration, except forcing data analysts to confront the inconsistencies across data sources.

Data integration is a process apart from any specific modeling approach. It requires identifying incompatible labels and measures used by the organization, then reaching consensus to establish and administer common labels and measures enterprise-wide. In dimensional modeling, these labels and measures reside in conformed dimensions and conformed facts, respectively. As represented in the enterprise data warehouse bus architecture, conformed dimensions are the integration glue across measurement business processes. Conformed dimensions are typically built and maintained as centralized persistent master data during ETL, then reused across dimensional models to enable data integration and ensure semantic consistency.

FABLE: *Dimensional modeling concepts like conformed dimensions put an undue burden on the ETL effort.*

FACT: Data integration depends on standardized labels, values, and definitions. It's hard work to reach organizational consensus and implement the corresponding ETL system rules, but you can't dodge the effort, regardless of whether you're dealing with a normalized or dimensional model.

FABLE: *Dimensional modeling isn't appropriate when there are more than two unique source systems due to the complexities of integrating data from multiple sources.*

FACT: The challenges of data integration have nothing to do with the modeling approach. Paradoxically, dimensional modeling and the bus architecture reveal the labels and measures of a business so clearly that an organization has no choice but to address the integration problems directly.

FABLE: *Changes to dimension attributes are only an issue for dimensional models.*

FACT: Every data warehouse must deal with time variance. When the characteristic of an entity like customer or product changes, we need a systematic approach for recording the change. Dimensional modeling uses a standard technique known as slowly changing dimensions (SCDs). When normalized models step up to the issue of time variance, they typically add time stamps to the entities. These time stamps serve to capture every entity change (just like a type 2 SCD does), but without using a surrogate key for each new row, the query interface must issue a double-barreled join that constrains both the natural key and time stamp between every pair of joined tables, putting an unnecessary, unfriendly burden on every reporting application or query.

FABLE: *Multiple dimensional models can't be integrated. They're built bottoms up, catering to the needs of an individual department, not the needs of an enterprise. Data mart chaos is the inevitable outcome.*

FACT: It's definitely a struggle to integrate databases of any flavor that have been built as departmental, standalone solutions that haven't been architected with conformed dimensions. That's precisely why we advise against this approach! Chaos won't result if you use the bus architecture for the enterprise framework of conformed dimensions, then tackle incremental development based on business measurement processes. Organizational and cultural obstacles are inevitable as consistent definitions, business rules, and practices are established across the enterprise. The technology is the easy part.

7

Dimensional Modeling Tasks and Responsibilities

With a basic understanding of dimensional modeling concepts in hand, we turn our attention to focus on the dimensional modeling process itself—how do we go about tackling a design, who's involved, and what do we need to worry about during the design activities? This chapter is divided into two sections; the first deals with issues surrounding an initial design starting from a blank sheet of paper, and the second half deals with the tasks surrounding the review of an existing dimensional model or system implementation.

Design Activities

The articles in this section focus on the tasks and players involved during the design of a new dimensional model, beginning with a historical perspective that is still remarkably valid.

7.1 Letting the Users Sleep

Ralph Kimball, DBMS, Dec 1996 and Jan 1997

This content was originally published as two consecutive articles.

The job of a data warehouse designer is a daunting one. Often the newly appointed data warehouse designer is drawn to the job because of the visibility and importance of the data warehouse function. In effect, management says to the designer: "Take all of the enterprise data and make it available to management so that they can answer all of their questions and sleep at night. And please do it very quickly, and we're sorry but we can't add any more staff until the proof of concept is successful."

This responsibility is exciting and very visible, but most designers feel overwhelmed by the sheer enormity of the task. Something real needs to be accomplished, and fast. Where do you start? Which data should be brought up first? Which management needs are most important? Does the design depend on the details of the most recent interview, or are there some underlying and more constant design guidelines that you can depend on? How do you scope the project down to something manageable, yet at the same time build an extensible architecture that will gradually let you build a comprehensive data warehouse environment?

These questions are close to causing a crisis in the data warehouse industry. Much of the recent surge in the industry toward "data marts" is a reaction to these very issues. Designers want to do something simple and achievable. No one is willing to sign up for a galactic design. Everyone hopes that in the rush to simplification, the long term coherence and extendibility of the design will not be compromised.

Fortunately, a pathway through this design challenge achieves an implementable immediate result, and at the same time, continuously augments the design so that eventually a true enterprise data warehouse is built. This divide-and-conquer approach is based on business process subject areas (originally referred to as data marts). Thus, an enterprise data warehouse is revealed as the union of a set of separate business process subject areas implemented over a period of time, possibly by different design teams, and possibly on different hardware and software platforms.

Each business process subject area is designed using a nine-step design methodology:

1. Choose the process.
2. Choose the grain.
3. Identify and conform the dimensions.
4. Choose the facts.
5. Store precalculations in the fact table.
6. Round out the dimension tables.
7. Choose the duration of the database.
8. Determine the need to track slowly changing dimensions.
9. Decide the physical design.

As a result of interviewing marketing users, finance users, sales force users, operations users, middle management, and senior management, a picture emerges of what is keeping these people awake at night. You can list and prioritize the primary business issues facing the enterprise. At the same time, you should conduct a set of interviews with the operational systems' DBAs who will reveal which data sources are clean, which contain valid and consistent data, and which will remain supported over the next few years.

Preparing for the design with a proper set of interviews is crucial. Interviewing is also one of the hardest things to teach people. I find it helpful to reduce the interviewing process to a tactic and an objective. Crudely put, the tactic is to make the business users talk about what they do, and the objective is to gain insights that feed the nine design decisions. The tricky part is that the interviewer can't pose the design questions directly to the users. Business users don't have opinions about data warehouse system design issues; they have opinions about what is important in their business lives. Business users are intimidated by system design questions, and they are quite right when they insist that system design is IT's province, not theirs. Thus, the challenge of the data warehouse designer is to meet the users far more than halfway.

In any event, armed with the top-down view (what keeps management awake) and the bottom-up view (which data sources are available), the data warehouse designer is ready to tackle the nine design decisions:

1. **Choose the process.** By process, I mean the content of a particular operational activity. The first business process subject area you build should be the one with the most bang for the buck. It should simultaneously answer the most important business questions and be the most accessible from a data extraction point of view. A great place to start in most enterprises is to model the process consisting of customer invoices or monthly statements, as shown in Figure 7-1. This data source is probably fairly accessible and of fairly high quality. One of Kimball's laws is that the best data source in any enterprise is the record of "how much money they owe us." Unless costs and profitability metrics are readily available, it's best to avoid adding these items to this first project; nothing drags down a data warehouse implementation faster than a heroic or impossible mission to provide activity-based costing as part of the first deliverable.

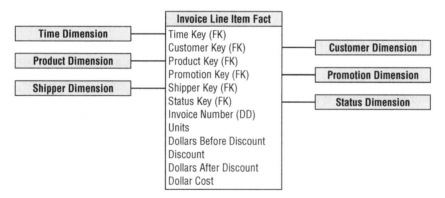

Figure 7-1: Customer invoice line item fact table.

2. **Choose the grain.** This second step seems like a technical detail at this early point, but it is actually the secret to making progress on the design. Choosing the grain means deciding exactly what a fact table record represents. Recall that the fact table is the large central table in the dimensional design that has a multipart key. Each of the components of the multipart key is a foreign key to an individual dimension table. In the customer invoices example in Figure 7-1, the grain of the fact table is the individual line item on the customer invoice. In other words, a line item on an invoice is a single fact table record, and vice versa. Only when you have chosen the grain can you have a coherent discussion of the business process's corresponding dimensions.

3. **Identify and conform the dimensions.** The dimensions are the source of both the query constraints and row headers in the user's reports; they carry the enterprise's vocabulary to the users. A well-architected set of dimensions makes the model understandable and easy to use. A poorly presented or incomplete set of dimensions robs the model of its usefulness.

   Dimensions should be chosen with the enterprise data warehouse in mind. This choice presents the primary moment at which the data warehouse architect must lift up his or her gaze from the project details and consider the longer range plans. If any dimension occurs in two business processes, they must contain an overlapping set of attributes (fields) that are drawn from the same domains. Only in this way can two processes share such a dimension in the same application. When a dimension is used in two business process subject areas, this dimension is said to be *conformed.* Good examples of dimensions that absolutely must be conformed are the customer and product dimensions in an enterprise. If these dimensions are allowed to drift out of synchronization across processes, the overall data warehouse will fail because the business process subject areas will not be able to be used together.

   The requirement to conform dimensions across business processes is very strong. Careful thought must be given to this requirement before the first business process is implemented. The DW/BI team must figure out what an enterprise customer ID is and what an enterprise product ID is. If this task is done correctly, successive business processes can be built at different times, on different machines, and by different development teams, and these process subject areas will merge coherently into an overall data warehouse. In particular, if the dimensions of two processes are conformed, it is easy to implement drill across by sending separate queries to the two subject areas, and then sort-merging the two answer sets on a set of common row headers. The row headers can be made to be common only if they are drawn from a conformed dimension common to the two processes, as shown in Figure 7-2.

4. **Choose the facts.** The grain of the fact table determines which facts you can use for the given business process. All of the facts must be expressed at the uniform level implied by the grain. In other words, if the grain of the fact table is an individual line item on a customer bill, then all of the numerical facts must refer to this particular line item. Also, as I have said many times before, the facts should be as additive as possible.

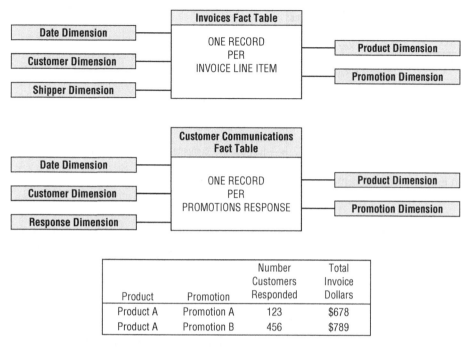

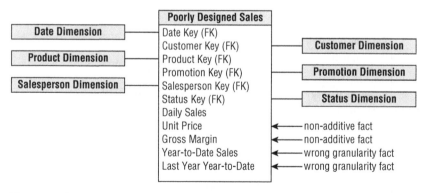

Figure 7-2: Two subject areas with conformed dimensions.

Figure 7-3 shows a "bad" fact table with a horrible mixture of non-numeric facts, non-additive facts, and facts at the wrong grain. This design is unusable.

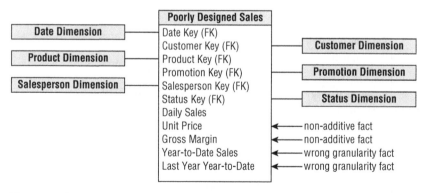

	Poorly Designed Sales
Date Dimension	Date Key (FK)
	Customer Key (FK)
Product Dimension	Product Key (FK)
	Promotion Key (FK)
Salesperson Dimension	Salesperson Key (FK)
	Status Key (FK)
	Daily Sales
	Unit Price
	Gross Margin
	Year-to-Date Sales
	Last Year Year-to-Date

Customer Dimension

Promotion Dimension

Status Dimension

← non-additive fact
← non-additive fact
← wrong granularity fact
← wrong granularity fact

Figure 7-3: An example of a "bad" fact table.

Figure 7-4 shows a "good" fact table in which all of the data elements in the first design have been correctly recast so that they are as numeric and additive as possible.

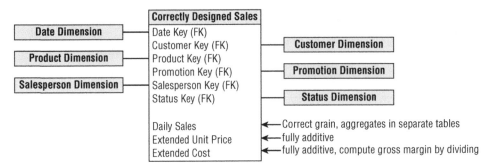

Figure 7-4: An example of a "good" fact table addressing the issues in Figure 7-3.

Notice that additional facts can be added to the fact table at any time, as long as they are consistent with the grain of the table. These additional facts do not invalidate any previously functioning applications.

5. **Store precalculations in the fact table.** A common example of the need to store precalculations occurs when the facts comprise a profit and loss statement. This situation will often arise when the fact table is based on a customer bill. Figure 7-5 shows the fact table starting off with the quantity sold and extended list price. Both are beautiful additive quantities from which you can always derive the average unit list price after you have added up some number of fact table records. Of course, the customer doesn't usually pay the list price. You need to subtract any allowances and discounts to arrive at the extended net price. Because the extended net price can always be derived from the extended list price minus the allowances and discounts, do you need to store the extended net price explicitly?

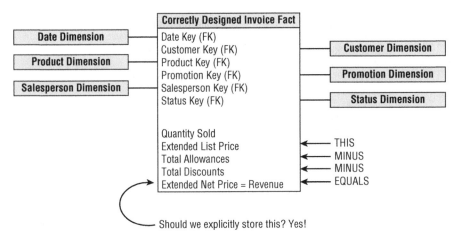

Figure 7-5: A customer billing fact table.

The answer is a resounding YES! This example is complicated enough that if there is even the smallest chance that a user will derive the extended net price incorrectly, you should put it into the underlying physical schema, even though it takes up space. The cost of a user incorrectly representing the extended net price, which after all is the primary revenue number of your whole enterprise, overwhelms the minor cost of a little redundant data storage. Note that a view that simply calculates the extended net price is somewhat dangerous if there is any chance that a user with an ad hoc query tool can sneak around the view to get at the physical table. In the long run, views are a good way to achieve a balance between eliminating user blunders and saving on storage, but the DBA must allow no exceptions to the users always accessing the data through the view.

6. **Round out the dimension tables.** At this point the fact table is complete, and you understand the roles of the dimension tables in providing the entry points into the fact table through constraints on the dimensional attributes. The grain decision in step 2 also determined the grain of each dimension table. For instance, if the grain is an individual customer bill line item, then the customer dimension grain is probably the customer bill-to address, and the product/service dimension grain is the lowest level of the product/service hierarchy at which you do billing. In step 3, you should have identified the dimensions in sufficient detail to describe such things as customers and products at the correct grain.

   In this step, you can return to the dimension tables and exhaustively add as many text-like descriptors to the dimensions as possible. In my data warehouse design consulting, I insist that clients identify a minimum of 50 text-like attributes for such important dimensions as customer and product. Even inherently small dimensions such as transaction type should be graced with good text descriptions of what each transaction type means. Chances are these transactions can also be arranged in groups. The transaction group should be another text attribute.

   All of the text attributes should consist of real words. Cryptic abbreviations are extremely undesirable. Remember that these text attributes are both the user interface to the application and the row and column headers in printed reports. IT shops must do a very professional job of quality assurance on the dimension table attributes.

7. **Choose the duration of the database.** The duration measures how far back in time the fact table goes. In many businesses, there is a natural need to look at the same time period a year ago. This need usually mandates at least five calendar quarters of data. Near the end of a calendar year, this implies two full years' worth of data. These arguments can be repeated with less intensity for two-year-old data, three-year-old data, and so on.

   Insurance companies and organizations with regulatory reporting requirements may have very long fact table durations, often extending back seven or more years. These long duration fact tables raise at least two very significant data warehouse design issues. First, it is often increasingly difficult to source old data as you go backward in time. The older the data, the more likely there will be problems in reading and interpreting the old files. Second, it is mandatory that the old versions of the important dimensions be used, not the most current versions.

8. **Determine the need to track slowly changing dimensions.** The proper description of the old product and old customer must be used with the old transaction history. The data warehouse must assign a generalized key to these important dimensions in order to distinguish multiple snapshots of customers and products over a span of time. I discussed these design issues in article 1.8, *Slowly Changing Dimensions*.

9. **Decide the physical design.** After the first eight steps, you have a complete logical design of your business process subject area. You are ready to turn your attention to physical design issues. In this step, I restrict attention to the biggest physical design issues affecting the user's perception of the subject: the physical sort order of the fact table on the disk and the presence of pre-stored summaries or aggregations. Beyond these issues, there are a host of additional physical design issues affecting administration, backup, indexing performance, and security.

   The physical sort order on the disk can be a significant design tool in a data warehouse. In my data warehouse design classes, I discuss a "headquarters sort" and a "field sales sort." The data warehouse designer usually must choose one of these sorts at the expense of the other. In extreme circumstances, the designer can affect performance by a factor of four or more, depending on this choice.

If you systematically perform the nine steps, you will not only end up with a complete and detailed design that drives the implementation, but you will understand how to tie your separate business process subject areas together with conformed dimensions so that over time you will end up with an enterprise data warehouse.

7.2 Practical Steps for Designing a Dimensional Model

Margy Ross, Intelligent Enterprise, *Sep 29, 2008*

The Kimball Group has written hundreds of articles and *Design Tips* about dimensional modeling techniques, but we haven't written much about the dimensional modeling process itself. What are the tasks and deliverables required to create a robust design?

Before embarking on a dimensional design project, you need a solid understanding of the business's requirements along with a reasonable assessment of the underlying source data. It's tempting to skip the requirements review, but resist this urge because doing so increases the risk of developing a source-driven model that falls short of business needs in numerous small but significant ways. Optimally, the requirements have been thoroughly researched and documented in a user-approved requirements finding document with the top priority needs clearly identified. This deliverable often also includes a preliminary data warehouse bus matrix, as described in article 5.6, *The Matrix: Revisited*.

In addition to the business requirements and bus matrix, you'll also want to review any source data profiling insights uncovered by the project team to date. The final item on your required reading list is your organization's naming convention standards document. If you don't already have naming conventions to adapt for data warehousing and business intelligence, you'll need to establish them as you develop the dimensional model (see article 7.7, *The Naming Game*).

Join the Party

Everyone knows that the key to a successful party is inviting the right people. The same holds true for the dimensional modeling festivities. Unfortunately, too many data modelers view the development of a dimensional model as a solo, independent activity; they retreat to their ivory cubicle to ponder the pros and cons of modeling alternatives on their own, emerging weeks later to unfurl their masterpiece for others to review. While the data modeler should be leading the charge and retain primary responsibility for the deliverables, the best way to arrive at a sound dimensional design is through a collaborative team effort because no one person likely has detailed knowledge of both the business requirements and source system idiosyncrasies.

The modeling team should include people who can accurately represent the business users' analytic needs, such as the business analyst, power user, BI application developer, or all of the above. In particular, power user involvement is valuable as they've likely already identified business rules to convert source data into more meaningful information for decision making; their insights often result in a richer, more analytically complete design. The designated data stewards should be involved in the modeling process to drive to organizational agreement on names, definitions, and business rules. If you haven't already established a data stewardship program, there's no time like the present to do so.

It's also beneficial to have some source experts at least intermittently involved in the process to quickly answer questions and resolve issues regarding data timing and content nuances. Finally, you should invite members of the ETL team to the party to gain early insights about the model and its source-to-target mapping. ETL team members typically have more to gain than to contribute to the modeling process, but getting their buy-in to the design saves time and avoids tire spinning down the road. For the same reason, you should also invite the DBAs who will implement the physical design.

With the team assembled and prerequisite reading completed, you'll need to briefly introduce dimensional modeling so everyone on the team understands its core principles (and appreciates that denormalization is not always evil).

The team's first objective is to reach agreement on a high level model diagram, or bubble chart, as illustrated in Figure 7-6. The bubble chart represents a fact table corresponding to a single business process; it includes a clearly articulated grain declaration and identification of core dimensions. The bubble chart can often be derived largely from the preliminary bus matrix. It serves to get everyone on the same page regarding the scope of the model without getting unnecessarily mired in the details. Because it's easy to understand, the high level diagram also facilitates discussion between the design team and business partners.

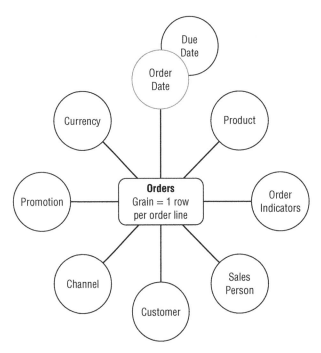

Figure 7-6: Example high level bubble chart diagram.

Dive into the Details

With consensus on the bubble chart, the team then launches into table-by-table and column-by-column discussions, drilling into more detail about the requisite attributes and metrics, including definitions, transformation rules, and data quality concerns. The dimensional model will unfold through a series of design sessions, with each pass producing a more detailed design that's been repeatedly tested against your understanding of the business needs.

Don't attempt to schedule all-day design meetings; plan for a number of two hour morning and afternoon sessions so the lead modeler has time to update the documentation before the next meeting (and so team members can deal with the demands of their day jobs). Your initial sessions should focus on a more straightforward dimension table so the team experiences a quick win before dealing with the more controversial dimensions.

As you're iteratively fleshing out the design, team members will need to further interrogate the data. Thus, ongoing access to a profiling tool (or less sophisticated method) will be critical. Ferreting out the good, bad, and ugly realities of your source data during the design process will minimize the surprises and corresponding overruns during the ETL design and development activity.

Throughout the design sessions, the data modeler or designated scribe should be filling in a detailed worksheet for each table with information such as the attribute or fact name, column description, sample values and decodes, change tracking rules for dimension attributes, and preliminary transformation business rules. These worksheets form the basis for the source-to-target mapping, which is further embellished by the physical designer and then ultimately handed off to the ETL team. In addition to the detailed worksheets, a member of the design team should also be logging open issues so they're captured in a single document to facilitate review and assignment at the end of every session.

Review the Results

The last phase of the modeling process involves reviewing and validating the model with interested parties, starting with the project team, extending to those in IT with intimate knowledge of the source systems, and concluding with the broader business community. Approval from this last group is critical before time and money are invested in the data implementation. Plan to devote much of this review to illustrating how the model will address sample questions from the requirements findings.

A typical design effort usually takes three to four weeks for a single business process dimensional model, but the time required will vary depending on the complexity of the business process, availability of preexisting conformed dimensions, experience of the modeling team, existence of well documented business requirements, and the difficulty of reaching consensus.

Designing a dimensional model with interested parties representing diverse skills requires commitment and cooperation, but the end result is a robust model that has been rigorously tested against both the business needs and data realities. That's exactly what you want before you move ahead with the implementation.

7.3 Staffing the Dimensional Modeling Team

Bob Becker, Design Tip #103, Jul 1, 2008

It's surprising the number of DW/BI teams that confine the responsibility for designing dimensional models to a single data modeler or perhaps a small team of dedicated data modelers. This is clearly shortsighted. The best dimensional models result from a collaborative team effort. No single individual is likely to have the detailed knowledge of the business requirements and the idiosyncrasies of all the source systems to effectively create the model themselves.

In the most effective teams, a core modeling team of two or three people does most of the detailed work with help from an extended team. The core modeling team is led by a data modeler with strong dimensional modeling skills and excellent facilitation skills. The core team should also include a business analyst who brings a solid understanding of the business requirements, the types of analysis to be supported, and an appreciation for making data more useful and accessible. Ideally, the core team will include at least one representative from the ETL team with extensive source systems development experience and an interest in learning.

We recommend including one or more analytic business users as part of the core modeling team. These power users add significant insight and help speed the design process. They are particularly valuable to the modeling process because they understand the source systems from a business point of view.

The core modeling team needs to work closely with source system developers to understand the contents, meaning, business rules, timing, and other intricacies of the source systems involved in populating the dimensional model. If you're lucky, the people who actually built or originally designed the source systems are still around. For any given dimensional model, there are usually several source system people you need to pull into the modeling process. There might be a DBA, a developer, and someone who works with the data input process. Each of these folks does things to the data that the other two don't know about.

The DBA implementing the physical database, the ETL architect/developer, and the BI architect/developer should also be included in the modeling process. Being actively engaged in the design process will help these individuals better understand the business reasons behind the model and facilitate their buy-in to the final design. Often the DBA comes from a transaction system background and may not understand the rationale for dimensional modeling. The DBA may naturally want to model the data using more familiar normalization design rules, physically defeating your dimensional design. ETL designers often have a similar tendency. Without a solid appreciation of the business requirements and justification for the dimensional design, the ETL designer will want to streamline the ETL process by shifting responsibility for calculations to the BI tool, skipping a description lookup step, or taking other shortcuts. Though these changes may save ETL development time, the trade-off may be an increase in effort or decrease in query performance for hundreds of business users. BI designers can often provide important input into the models that improve the effectiveness of the final BI applications.

Before jumping into the modeling process, take time to consider the ongoing management and stewardship implications of the DW/BI environment. If your organization has an active data stewardship initiative, it is time to tap into that function. If there is no stewardship program, it's time to initiate the process. An enterprise DW/BI effort committed to dimensional modeling as an implementation approach must also be committed to a conformed dimension strategy to assure consistency across business processes. An active data stewardship program can help an organization achieve its conformed dimension strategy.

Although involving more people in the design process increases the risk of slowing down the process, the improved richness and completeness of the design is well worth the additional overhead.

7.4 Involve Business Representatives in Dimensional Modeling

Bob Becker, Design Tip #157, *Jun 28, 2013*

The Kimball Group has always stressed the importance of keeping a keen eye on the business requirements when designing dimensional data models for the data warehouse/business intelligence (DW/BI) environment. Gathering business requirements is typically undertaken just prior to beginning the dimensional data model design process. Article 4.2, *More Business Requirements Gathering Dos and Don'ts*, is a reminder of requirements gathering dos and don'ts. We also believe it's extremely important to include key business representatives in the design process itself. Unfortunately, many organizations balk at including business representatives in the design activities. They view dimensional modeling as a technical exercise focused on modeling data elements and fail to appreciate the value of involving business subject matter experts.

My manta regarding the dimensional data modeling process is "Remember—data warehousing is not about the data. It's about serving the business requirements!" Okay, I'll admit that data warehousing is about the data to a significant extent, but when it comes to the design process, I'll stand by my mantra. Worrying primarily about the data and failing to focus on the business requirements is a critical mistake. Including business representatives in the design process and keeping them engaged will result in a significantly better design. Often it's hard to appreciate the value of business involvement until you are deep into the design process. But at the end of the day, the resultant data model must support the business requirements or the DW/BI initiative will fail. Article 4.12, *Using the Dimensional Model to Validate Business Requirements*, describes how to leverage the dimensional data model to validate and capture business requirements.

To effectively leverage the participation of business users, it is important to constantly keep them engaged. If discussions turn away from modeling the requirements and turn to detailed ETL design topics or other technical issues, the business users will tune out and ultimately stop participating. To keep them involved, maintain the focus on the design and how it supports the business requirements. The technical discussions can wait for another time.

Business users will actively participate in the design process if given half a chance. At the beginning they won't be sure about how to participate as this is new to them. Fortunately, there are countless opportunities during a design session to engage the business. Every key dimensional attribute or metric is ripe for discussion. Key questions include: "Why is this data element important? How do you use it? What will you do with it in a report or analysis? What other attributes or metrics do you combine it with? Why?" Typically, these discussions lead to a deeper understanding of the business requirements that may not have surfaced earlier.

For example, many business processes (such as tracking call segments in a call center) result in transaction fact tables that include Begin Time and End Time dimensions. An inexperienced data-oriented design team that does not include business representation will be satisfied with a fact table with both these dimensions. A more experienced design team might query their business partners regarding the use of these time dimensions and discover they are used to calculate the call's duration. With this newly understood requirement, the design team will enhance the fact table to include call duration as a metric. This enhancement results in a more compelling design for the business users who can now measure average call durations by any of the associated dimension attributes, enabling them to understand service levels without performing the duration calculations at query time. From a business perspective, this represents a significant usage improvement over the initial design.

Continued discussions with the business users regarding this metric might uncover the existence of standard service levels that have been defined by the business. For example, you may discover the business has recently established a new baseline for classifying call durations: a call duration of 2 to 5 minutes is considered "Normal," 1 to 2 minutes is considered "Normal – Short," less than 1 minute is considered "Abnormal – Short," and likewise for "Normal – Long" and "Abnormal – Long." The users explain that this classification will serve as the basis for several planned dashboards and scorecards based on the new data warehouse environment. Aha! Here is another opportunity to embellish the design to better support the business requirements. Clearly, you will want to create a Duration Type dimension that includes this classification, plus a rollup attribute to aggregate all "Normal" durations and "Abnormal" durations.

Due to the active participation of your business partners, the resulting design will better support their underlying business requirements. While the initial design would have included all the data elements required to support the requirements, it would have fallen short on ease of use and richness from a business perspective. Thus, the mantra that data warehousing is not just about the data; it's about serving the business requirements. The active, engaged participation of your business partners in the design process will result in a design that is far more effective than solely focusing on modeling the data.

7.5 Managing Large Dimensional Design Teams

Bob Becker, Design Tip #161, Nov 5, 2013

Regular readers know we stress the importance of focusing on business requirements when designing dimensional data models to support the data warehouse/business intelligence (DW/BI) environment. It is critical to include business partners in the dimensional design process.

But including business representatives on the design team obviously increases the size of the group. In many organizations, the resulting team will be a small group of four to eight individuals. In these situations, managing the design process is relatively straightforward. The team needs to gather on a regular basis, focus on the effort at hand, and follow a defined process to complete the modeling effort.

However, in larger organizations, especially when the scope includes tackling enterprise-wide conformed dimensions, the design team may be considerably larger. In recent years we've participated in design projects with over 20 participants representing different departments. Large design teams introduce several additional complications that need to be overcome.

The first obstacle is ensuring the consistent participation of team members in all the design sessions. Everyone involved has normal day-to-day job responsibilities, in addition to their design team involvement. Inevitably participants will face pressing issues outside the design process that require their presence. The larger the group, the more frequently these absences will occur. When an individual misses important deliberations regarding key issues, the team will need to circle back with the individual, revisit the discussion and design options, and then perhaps reconsider earlier decisions. This discourse may be important to the overall design, but it negatively impacts the team's productivity. Excessive backtracking and rehashing is frustrating and draining to the group.

With large design teams, you should avoid overly aggressive scheduling to ensure the highest level of consistent participation. Don't schedule full weeks or even full days for design sessions. We suggest limiting design sessions to no more than three days in a week; Tuesday through Thursday seems to work best. Instead of full-day sessions, schedule two sessions per day, each two and a half hours in duration. Start the morning session a little later than the normal start time, take a two-hour midday break, and finish before the normal end time. In addition to Mondays and Fridays, this schedule gives participants time at the beginning, middle, and end of each day to schedule meetings, deal with email, and other daily responsibilities. Each participant only needs to allocate fifteen hours per week to the design sessions. In exchange, each participant is expected to firmly commit this time to the design team. The goal is full participation in all design sessions resulting in greater overall productivity and minimal backtracking.

When the focus of the design effort is on core conformed dimensions, it is important that all the business representatives participate since the goal is enterprise agreement on the key attributes that must be conformed across the organization. However, once the team's attention turns to specific business processes and the associated fact table designs, it is often possible to excuse some of the business representatives not involved/interested in a particular business process for several design sessions.

Remember that any effort to define core conformed dimensions across business processes requires a clear and urgent message from senior management that they expect the effort to produce results. IT by itself cannot "herd the cats through the door." Make sure you have clear and visible guidance from senior management before you start the dimension conforming process or you will be wasting your time.

Occasionally, gnarly design challenges will arise. Often these issues are relevant or only thoroughly understood by a small group of participants. Trying to work through these very specific issues may be counterproductive for most members of the larger design team. In these situations, it makes more sense to table the discussions during the general design sessions and assign a smaller workgroup to work through the issues and then bring the conclusions/recommendations back to the larger group.

Effective facilitation is often another large design team challenge. Ideally, the lead dimensional data modeler has the required skills to facilitate the group. However, it is sometimes necessary to team a skilled facilitator alongside the dimensional data modeler. In either case, make sure the facilitator and/or modeler possess the key skills required to guide a large team effort:

- Deep knowledge of dimensional data modeling concepts and techniques, including the pros and cons of design alternatives
- Understanding of the organization's business processes and the associated business requirements surrounding those processes within the design effort's scope
- Self-confidence to appreciate when to remain neutral on an issue and when to push back. Occasionally, the facilitator/modeler needs to take a contrary position to help participants clearly articulate their requirements and concerns.

- Keen listening skills. Some participants will not be well versed in dimensional modeling, yet will be communicating key requirements which they're unable to express in modeling terms.
- Strong facilitation skills to draw out participants, adequately debate key issues, control wandering discussions, retain focus on the goal, and ultimately, ensure success

We also suggest that one team member be assigned to documenting the design and outstanding issues during the sessions. In large group designs, the facilitator/modeler is primarily focused on understanding the requirements and translating those requirements into an optimal dimensional model. Their work requires considerable discussion and evaluation of design options. It's a productivity gain if the facilitator/modeler doesn't need to slow down the process to capture design decisions.

7.6 Use a Design Charter to Keep Dimensional Modeling Activities on Track

Bob Becker, Design Tip #138, Sep 7, 2011

The logical dimensional model should be developed jointly by representatives from all interested groups: business users, reporting teams, and the DW/BI project team. It is important that the appropriate individuals are represented on the dimensional data model design team as described in article 7.3, *Staffing the Dimensional Modeling Team*, in order to achieve an effective design. The best dimensional models result from a collaborative team effort. No single individual is likely to have the detailed knowledge of the business requirements and the idiosyncrasies of all the source systems to effectively create the model themselves.

However, involving more people in the design process increases the risk of slowing down the process. With so many individuals involved, it's important that the lead designer/facilitator keeps the group on track. The team may find itself spiraling into deep, complex discussions of data elements only to determine that the data element in question isn't within the design scope or perhaps isn't a reasonable candidate to be included in the design.

A helpful strategy for limiting long resource-draining discussions is to establish a "design charter" early in the design process. The goal of the design charter is to keep the team focused on the key issues and avoid runaway discussion on ancillary topics. The design charter is simply the mantra the design team looks to when in doubt to help guide the process. As data elements are discussed and it is not readily apparent whether the item is in scope or out of scope, the design team can run the data element through the project's design charter. While each design team should develop its own specific charter, the following are examples of charters we've used in the past:

- Does the data element help support the business requirements that are in scope?

    For example, one insurance client's core business requirements included supporting the organizations' financial, management, and regulatory reporting requirements. All proposed data elements were passed through that filter.

Another client's goal was to build an analytic platform enabling the business to support world class analytics. In that case the filter became: Is the data element analytically interesting? Will it be used to support analytic requests? Or does it exist only to support a need of the operational system?

- What does the data element describe? Is it a dimension attribute used for slicing/dicing/ grouping/constraining? Or is it a metric? If the data element is an amount, is it a metric or dimensional attribute? If it is an amount that behaves like an attribute, can it be range valued?
- If it is a dimension attribute, can it change? If it can change, will analysis based on the value at the time of the measurement be required? If it can change, will analysis based on the current value be required? Or both?

It is easy for the design team to get bogged down trying to incorporate the seemingly endless data elements available. To stay on track, keep the design charter in mind at all times during the design process. The first bullet is critical: Does the data element support the business requirements? Always keep in mind that the goal is not to "model the data." The goal is to create a data model that will support the business need. It's okay to leave data elements behind. Be especially leery of data elements that primarily support operational capabilities. Constantly ask "How will the data element be used analytically? What value does it provide?" in an effort to fully understand the data in question. Often it's not enough to merely include the data element in the design; it may need to be tweaked, enriched, or ranged to make it as valuable as possible to the business community.

7.7 The Naming Game

Warren Thornthwaite, Design Tip #71, Sep 2, 2005

The issue of field naming rears its ugly head while you're creating the dimensional data model. Naming is complex because different people have different meanings for the same name, and different names with the same meaning. The difficulty comes from human nature: Most of us don't want to give up what we know and learn a new way. The unenviable task of determining names typically falls on the data steward. If you are responsible for dealing with this political beast, you will find the following three-step approach helpful. Steps 1 and 2 generally happen before the model is presented to the business users. Step 3 usually happens after business users have seen and understand the model.

Step 1: Preparation

Begin by developing skills at thinking up succinct, descriptive, unique names for data elements. Learn your organization's (and team's) naming conventions. Study the table and column names in the various systems. If you don't have established naming conventions, now's a good time to create them. A common approach is to use a column name standard with three parts: PrimeWord_ ZeroOrMoreQualifiers_ClassWord. The prime word is a categorization word that often corresponds to the entity the column is from, and in some cases, qualifiers may not be necessary. So the field in the sales fact table that represents the amount sold might be `Sales_Dollar_Amount`. You can research different data naming conventions and standards on the internet.

Step 2: Creating an Initial Name Set

During the modeling process, work with the modeling team (including a representative or two from the business) to draft an initial set of names and the rationale. Once the model is near completion, hold a review session with the modeling team to make sure the names make sense.

In addition to the review session, it helps to have meetings with the key stakeholders. This typically includes the core business users and any senior managers whom you have a sense might have an opinion. If their preferred name for any given column is different from your suggested name, try to figure out why. Help them be clear on their definition of the data element by asking them to explain what the term means to them. Look for missing qualifiers and class words to clarify the meaning. For example, a sales analyst would be interested in sales numbers, but it turns out that this sales number is really `Sales_Commissionable_Amount`, which is different from `Sales_Gross_Amount` and `Sales_Net_Amount`.

The resulting name set should be used by the data modeling team to update the current version of the data model. Keep track of the alternative names for each field and the reasons people offered for their preferred choices. This will be helpful in explaining the derivations of the final name set.

Step 3: Building Consensus

Once you have a solid, tested name set, and the core users have seen the data model presentation, gather all the stakeholders in a conference room for at least half a day (count on more if you have a lot of columns or a contentious culture) and work through it. Start from the high level model and progress through all the columns, table by table. Generally, there have been enough model reviews and naming discussions so that many of the issues have already been resolved and the remaining issues are reasonably well understood.

The goal of this session is to reach consensus on the final name set. Often this means someone has to accept the will of the majority and let go of their favorite name for a given column. It is surprising how emotional this can be. These names represent how we view the business, and people feel pretty strongly about getting them "right." Don't let people get out of the room without reaching agreement if it is at all possible. If you have to reconvene on the same issues, it will take extra time to rehash the various arguments.

Once you have reached agreement on the final name set, document it carefully and take it back to the data modelers so they can work it into the final data model.

7.8 What's in a Name?

Joy Mundy, Design Tip #168, Jul 21, 2014

It seems like a small thing, but names are important. Good names for tables and columns are particularly important for ad hoc users of the DW/BI system who need to find the objects they're looking for. Object names should be oriented to the business users, not the technical staff.

As much as possible, strive to have the names in the DW/BI system be unchanged in the semantic layer and unchanged by report designers. More challenging, your users should be discouraged from changing object names once they've pulled the information to their desktop. We usually can't prevent them from doing that, but attractive and sensible names will reduce the temptation.

Here are my top ten suggestions for naming objects in your DW/BI system:

1. **Follow naming conventions.** If you don't have them, create (and document!) naming conventions that follow the rules in this Design Tip. If your organization already has naming conventions, you may be faced with a problem: Most existing naming conventions were developed for technical people. But names in the DW/BI environment should be oriented to the business users. They become row and column names in ad hoc analyses and predefined reports. We will return to this issue later.

2. **Each object has one name.** Let's not perpetuate the confusion around data definitions that already exists in our organizations. It is not OK to say that the sales team can call a column Geography and the marketing group calls the same entity Region. If it's the same column, with the same content, it has to have the same name. If you can't get agreement organization-wide on object names, enlist the help of your business sponsor.

3. **Object names are descriptive.** Users should not need 20 years' tenure at your organization to decipher what a name means. This rule forbids a lot of silliness, like RBVLSPCD (we have more than 8 characters to work with!). It also forbids column names like NAME, which is non-descriptive outside the context of the table you are examining.

4. **Abbreviations and acronyms are discouraged.** Abbreviations and acronyms are endemic in the corporate world, and the non-corporate world is even worse. A lot of information can be encoded in an acronym, but it places a huge burden on newcomers. The most effective approach is to maintain a list of approved abbreviations, and try not to add to them without a good reason. You may even want to document that reason in the list. Examples include:

Abbreviation	Replaces	Reason
Amt	Amount	Extremely common
Desc	Description	Extremely common
Corp	Corporation	Common
FDIC	Federal Deposit Insurance Corporation	Common; familiar to all users

For most organizations, a reasonable list has dozens of approved abbreviations, not hundreds.

5. **Object names are pretty.** Remember that object names become headers in reports and analyses. Although beauty is in the eye of the beholder, I find all caps to be particularly annoying. The object names should contain a visual clue for where the words end:

Spaces: [Column Name]
Camel case: ColumnName
Underscore: Column_Name or COLUMN_NAME

I recommend using spaces. They look the best when displayed in reports. And I scoff at the argument that developers have to type square brackets when they type the column name. I am confident that any developer who actually types SQL can figure out where the brackets keys are located, and they can develop the requisite finger muscles.

6. **Object names are unique.** This rule is a corollary to the rule that each object has one name. If two objects are different, they should have different names. This rule forbids column names such as [City]. A better name is [Customer Mailing Address City]. This rule is especially important for ad hoc use of the DW/BI system. Although the context of [City] may be obvious during the analytic process, once that analysis is saved and shared, that context is lost. Are we looking at the customer's city or the store's city, the mailing address or the shipping address? Although we can't prevent users from changing object names once they export to Excel, we don't want to force them to do so in order to be clear.

7. **Object names are not too long.** This rule conflicts with rules 3, 4, and 6. If we have unique, unabbreviated, descriptive object names, the odds are that some column names will be very long. Consider [Mandatory Second Payer Letter Opt Out Code] or [Vocational Provider Referral Category]. These are reasonably descriptive column names for someone in the insurance business, but what will happen when the user or report designer drags that column into the body of a report or analysis? The name will wrap unattractively, making the header row very fat. Or it will shrink down to a font so tiny that no one can read it. And then the user will rename the column, violating our key rule that each object has one name.

   I try to limit column names to 30 characters, though sometimes I go to 35. In order to achieve this goal, I have to register more abbreviations or acronyms than I would like.

8. **Consider prepending column names with an abbreviated table name.** I hate to make this recommendation, because it violates several of my previous rules about abbreviations and short names. But I am finding myself following this practice with increasing frequency in order to guarantee consistency and uniqueness.

9. **Change names in the view layer if needed.** We have always recommended a set of views in the DW/BI system which sit atop the physical tables and to which all queries are directed. The primary purpose of the view layer is to provide a layer of insulation between the BI applications and the physical database, providing a bit of flexibility to smoothly migrate change to a system already in production. Additionally, the view layer can also provide a place to put the business-oriented names into the database:

   ■ Our first recommendation is always to name the physical tables and columns with business-oriented names. Failing that, use the view layer. We dislike changing the names in the BI tools for several reasons:
      ■ Most organizations have several BI tools; the names should be consistent across all BI tools.

- The more business logic you put into the BI tool, the more challenging it will be to migrate to a different tool.
- If the names are only in the BI tool, there is a barrier to communication between users, front room support team, and back room database people.

10. **Be consistent!** It's only a foolish consistency that's the hobgoblin of little minds. Consistency in naming is hugely valuable to your users.

7.9 When Is the Dimensional Design Done?

Bob Becker, Design Tip #108, *Dec 3, 2008*

There is a tendency for data warehouse project teams to jump immediately into implementation tasks as the dimensional data model design is finalized. But we'd like to remind you that you're not quite done when you think you might be. The last major design activity that needs to be completed is a review and validation of the dimensional data model before moving forward with implementation activities.

We suggest you engage in a review and validation process with several successive audiences, each with different levels of technical expertise and business understanding. The goal is to solicit feedback from interested people across the organization. The entire DW/BI team benefits from these reviews because they result in a more informed and engaged business user community. At a minimum, the design team should plan on talking to three groups:

- Source system developers and DBAs who can often spot errors in the model very quickly
- Core business or power users who were not directly involved in the model development process
- Broader user community

Typically the first public design review of the detailed dimensional model is with your peers in the IT organization. This audience is often comprised of reviewers who are intimately familiar with the target business process because they wrote or manage the system that runs it. Likely, they are partly familiar with the target dimensional model because you've already been pestering them with source data questions.

The IT review can be challenging because the reviewers often lack an understanding of dimensional modeling. In fact, most of them probably fancy themselves as proficient third normal form modelers. Their tendency will be to apply transaction processing-oriented modeling rules to the dimensional model. Rather than spending the bulk of your time debating the merits of different modeling disciplines, it is best to be prepared to provide some dimensional modeling education as part of the review process.

When everyone has the basic dimensional modeling concepts down, begin with a review of the bus matrix. This will give everyone a sense for the project scope and overall data architecture, demonstrate the role of conformed dimensions, and show the relative business process priorities. Next, illustrate how the selected row on the matrix translates directly into the dimensional model. Most of the IT review session should then be spent going through the individual dimension and fact tables.

Often, the core business users are members of the modeling team and are already intimately knowledgeable about the data model, so a review session with them is not required. However, if they have not been involved in the modeling process, a similar, detailed design review should be performed with the core business users. The core users are more technical than typical business users and can handle more detail about the model. Often, especially in smaller organizations, you can combine the IT review and core user review into one session. This works if the participants already know each other well and work together on a regular basis.

Finally, the dimensional data model should be shared with the broader community of business users. Often, this is a relatively large audience. In such cases a representative subsection of the users can be selected. This session is as much education as it is design review. You want to educate people without overwhelming them, while at the same time illustrating how the dimensional model supports their business requirements. In addition, you want them to think closely about how they will use the data so they can help highlight any shortcomings in the model.

Create a presentation that starts with basic dimensional concepts and definitions, and then describe the bus matrix as your enterprise DW/BI data roadmap. Review the high level model, and finally, review the important dimensions, like customer and product.

During the broader user review, you should allocate about a third of the time to illustrate how the model can be used to answer a range of questions about the business process. Pull some interesting examples from the requirements documentation and walk through them. More analytical users will get this immediately. Reassure the rest of your audience that most of this complexity will be hidden behind a set of structured reports. The point is to show you can answer just about every question they might ask about this business process.

There are usually only minor adjustments to the model once you get to this point. After working so hard to develop the model, the users may not show what you consider to be appropriate enthusiasm. The model may seem obvious to the users and makes sense; after all, it is a reflection of their business. This is a good thing; it means you have done your job well!

Design Review Activities

The second half of the chapter focuses on the review and assessment of existing dimensional models and dimensional DW/BI systems.

7.10 Design Review Dos and Don'ts

Margy Ross, Design Tip #120, *Feb 2, 2010*

Over the years, we've described common dimensional modeling mistakes, such as the next article, 7.11, *Fistful of Flaws*. And we've recommended dimensional modeling best practices countless times; article 6.7, *Kimball's Ten Essential Rules of Dimensional Modeling*, has been widely read.

While we've identified frequently observed errors and suggested patterns, we haven't provided much guidance about the process of conducting design reviews on existing dimensional models. Kimball Group consultants perform numerous design reviews like this for clients as it's a cost-effective way to leverage our experience; here are some practical dos and don'ts for conducting a design review yourself.

Before the design review…

- **Do invite the right players.** Obviously, the modeling team needs to participate, but you'll also want representatives from the BI development team (to ensure that proposed changes enhance usability) and ETL development team (to ensure that the changes can be populated). Perhaps most importantly, it's critical that folks who are really knowledgeable about the business and their needs are sitting at the table. While diverse perspectives should participate in a review, don't invite 25 people to the party.

- **Do designate someone to facilitate the review.** Group dynamics, politics, and the design challenges themselves will drive whether the facilitator should be a neutral resource or involved party. Regardless, their role is to keep the team on track to achieving a common goal. Effective facilitators need the right mix of intelligence, enthusiasm, confidence, empathy, flexibility, assertiveness, and the list goes on. Don't forget a sense of humor.

- **Do agree upon the scope of the review (e.g., dimensional models focused on several tightly coupled business processes).** Ancillary topics will inevitably arise during the review, but agreeing in advance on the scope makes it easier to stay focused on the task at hand.

- **Do block off time on everyone's calendar.** We typically conduct dimensional model reviews as a focused 2-day effort. The entire review team needs to be present for the full two days. Don't allow players to float in and out to accommodate other commitments. Design reviews require undivided attention; it's disruptive when participants leave intermittently.

- **Do reserve the right space.** The same conference room should be blocked for the full two days. Optimally, the room has a large white board; it's especially helpful if the white board drawings can be saved or printed. If a white board is unavailable, have flip charts on hand. Don't forget markers and tape; drinks and food never hurt.

- **Do assign homework.** For example, ask everyone involved to make a list of their top five concerns, problem areas, or opportunities for improvement with the existing design. Encourage participants to use complete sentences when making their list so it's meaningful to others. These lists should be emailed to the facilitator in advance of the design review for consolidation. Soliciting advance input gets people engaged and helps avoid "group think" during the review.

During the design review…

- **Do check attitudes at the door.** While it's easier said than done, don't be defensive about prior design decisions. Do embark on the review thinking change is possible; don't go in resigned to believing nothing can be done to improve the situation.
- **Do check laptops and smartphones at the door (at least figuratively), unless needed to support the review process.** Allowing participants to check email during the sessions is no different than having them leave to attend an alternative meeting.
- **Do exhibit strong facilitation skills.** Review ground rules. Ensure that everyone is participating and communicating openly. Do keep the group on track; ban side conversations and table discussions that are out of scope or spiral into the death zone. There are tomes written on facilitation best practices, so we won't go into detail here.
- **Do ensure a common understanding of the current model before delving into potential improvements.** Don't presume everyone around the table already has a comprehensive perspective. It may be worthwhile to dedicate the first hour to walking through the current design and reviewing objectives. Don't be afraid to restate the obvious.
- **Do designate someone to act as scribe, taking copious notes about both the discussions and decisions being made.**
- **Do start with the big picture.** Just as when you're designing from a blank slate, begin with the bus matrix, then focus on a single high priority business process, starting with the granularity then moving out to the corresponding dimensions. Follow this same "peeling back the layers of the onion" method with your design review, starting with the fact table, then tackling dimension-related issues. Do undertake the meatiest issues first; don't defer the tough stuff to the afternoon of the second day.
- **Do remind everyone that business acceptance is the ultimate measure of DW/BI success; the review should focus on improving the business users' experience.**
- **Do sketch out sample rows with data values during the review sessions to ensure everyone has a common understanding of the recommended changes.**
- **Do close the meeting with a recap; don't let participants leave the room without clear expectations about their assignments and due dates.** Do establish a time for the next follow-up.

Following the design review…

- **Do anticipate that some open issues will remain after the 2-day review.** Commit to wrestling these issues to the ground, even though this can be challenging without an authoritative party involved. Don't fall victim to analysis paralysis.

- **Don't let your hard work gather dust.** Do evaluate the cost/benefit for the potential improvements; some changes will be more painless (or painful) than others. Then develop action plans for implementing the improvements.
- **Do anticipate similar reviews in the future.** Plan to reevaluate every 12 to 24 months. Do try to view inevitable changes to your design as signs of success, rather than failure.

Good luck with your review!

7.11 Fistful of Flaws

Margy Ross, Intelligent Enterprise, *Oct 10, 2003*

People often engage the Kimball Group to conduct dimensional model design reviews. In this article, we provide a laundry list of common design flaws to scout for when performing a review. We encourage you to use this list to critically review your own schemas in search of potential improvement opportunities.

What's the Grain?

When a data warehouse team proudly unrolls its draft dimensional modeling masterpiece, one of our first questions is "What's the grain of the fact table?" We need to know the specific level of detail captured in the fact table. Surprisingly, we often get inconsistent answers to this inquiry. Declaring a clear and concise definition of the fact table grain is critical to a productive modeling effort. Without agreement, the design team and business liaisons will spin in circles.

For maximum flexibility and extensibility, you should build your fact table at the lowest level of granularity possible. You can always roll up the granular details. On the other hand, there's no way to drill down into the details if you've only loaded pre-aggregated, summary information. Obviously, the lowest level of granularity depends on the business process being modeled.

Mixed Grain or Textual Facts?

Once you have established the fact table granularity, identify the facts that are consistent with this grain. If some facts are line item level metrics, while others exist only at the header level, you must either allocate the header facts to the line item grain or create a separate fact table with the granularity of one row per header.

Fact tables typically consist of foreign keys plus numeric counts and amounts measuring business performance. Optimally, the facts are additive, meaning they can be summed across any dimension. In an effort to improve performance or reduce query complexity, aggregated facts such as year-to-date totals sometimes sneak into the fact row. These totals are dangerous because they aren't perfectly additive. A year-to-date total may reduce the complexity and run time of a few queries, but having it in the fact table invites other queries to double count the year-to-date column (or worse) when more than one date is included.

You should also prohibit text fields, including cryptic indicators and flags, from entering the fact table. They almost always take up more space in the fact table than a surrogate key. More important, business users generally want to query, constrain, and report against these text fields. You can provide quicker responses and more flexible access by handling these textual values in a dimension table, along with additional descriptive roll-up attributes often associated with the indicators or flags.

Dimension Descriptors and Decodes?

Any identifiers and codes in the dimension tables should be accompanied by descriptive decodes. It's time for us to dismiss the misperception that business users prefer to work with codes. If you need to convince yourself, just stroll down to their offices to see the decode listings filling their bulletin boards or lining their monitors. Adding descriptive names makes the data more legible to business users. If deemed appropriate by the business, operational codes can accompany the descriptors as dimension attributes, but they shouldn't be the dimension table primary keys.

Design teams sometimes opt to embed complex filtering or labeling logic in the data access application rather than supporting it via a dimension table. Although query and reporting tools may let you decode within the application, we recommend that decodes be stored as data instead. Applications should be data-driven in order to minimize the impact of decode additions and changes. Placing decodes in the dimensions ensures greater report labeling consistency.

Handling of Hierarchies?

Each dimension associated with a fact table should take on a single value with each fact row. Similarly, each dimension attribute should take on one value for each dimension row. If the attributes have a many-to-one relationship, then this hierarchical relationship can be represented within a single dimension. You generally should look for opportunities to collapse dimension hierarchies whenever possible, except in the case of really large dimensions with highly volatile attribute changes. It isn't uncommon to represent multiple hierarchies in a single dimension.

Designers sometimes attempt to deal with the dimension hierarchies within the fact table. For example, rather than having a single foreign key to the product dimension, they include fact table foreign keys for the key elements of the product hierarchy, such as brand, category, and department. Before you know it, a compact fact table turns into an unruly monster, joining to dozens of dimension tables. This example is a severe case of having "too many dimensions." If the fact table has more than 20 foreign keys, you should look for opportunities to combine or collapse them into dimensions.

In general, we discourage snowflaking, or normalizing, dimension tables. Snowflaking may reduce the disk space needed for dimension tables, but the savings are usually insignificant when compared with the entire data warehouse storage needs and seldom offset the disadvantages in ease of use or query performance.

Outriggers are a variation of the snowflake theme. Rather than normalizing the entire dimension, a cluster of relatively low cardinality or frequently reused attributes is placed in an outrigger joined to the dimension. In most cases, dimensions should be a single join away from the fact table.

Be careful to avoid abusing the outrigger technique; outriggers should be the exception rather than the rule. Similarly, if your design is riddled with bridge tables to capture many valued dimension relationships, you need to go back to the drawing board. Chances are that you have an issue with the fact table's granularity.

Explicit Date Dimension?

Every fact table should have at least one foreign key to an explicit date dimension. The SQL date function doesn't support date attributes such as fiscal periods, seasons, and holidays. Rather than trying to determine these nonstandard calendar calculations in a query, you should store them in a date dimension table.

Designers sometimes avoid a date dimension altogether by representing a series of monthly buckets of facts on a single fact table row. These fixed time slots often become an access and maintenance nightmare; the recurring time buckets should be presented as separate rows in the fact table instead.

Control Numbers as Degenerate Dimensions?

In transaction-oriented fact tables, treat the operational control numbers (such as the purchase order or invoice number) as degenerate dimensions. They reside as dimension keys on the fact table, but don't join to a corresponding dimension table.

Teams are sometimes tempted to create a dimension table with information from the operational header record, such as the transaction number, transaction date, transaction type, or transaction terms. In many cases, you'd end up with a dimension table that has nearly as many rows as the fact table. A dimension table growing at nearly the same pace as the fact table is a warning sign that a degenerate dimension may be lurking within it.

Surrogate Keys?

Instead of relying on operational keys or identifiers, you should use meaningless surrogate keys for all the dimension primary keys and fact table foreign keys. The administrative overhead to manage surrogate keys is minor, while the benefits are multifold. They isolate the warehouse from operational changes (such as recycling closed account numbers), while letting the warehouse handle "not applicable" or "to be determined" conditions. Because surrogate keys are typically 4-byte integers, performance is improved due to the smaller fact keys, smaller fact tables, and smaller indices.

Surrogate keys also let you integrate data with multiple operational keys from multiple sources. Finally, they are required to support the dominant technique for tracking changes to dimension table attributes.

Slowly Changing Dimension Strategies?

Your dimensional design isn't complete until you have identified a slowly changing dimension strategy for each dimension attribute. You may opt to overwrite the column, add a new row, add a new column, or even add a new dimension to track changes.

It's important that the strategy, or combination of strategies, is well thought out before development occurs.

Well Understood Business Requirements?

Not to sound like a broken record, but there's no way to effectively conduct a design review without first having a solid understanding of your business requirements. You need to be keenly aware of both the business requirements and data realities to review a dimensional model with any sense of confidence. Business subject matter experts or liaisons are typically excellent guides along this path; you can't expect to take any shortcuts.

7.12 Rating Your Dimensional Data Warehouse

Ralph Kimball, Intelligent Enterprise, *Apr 28, 2000 and May 15, 2000*

This content was originally published as two consecutive articles.

Over the past two decades, data warehouses have evolved their own design techniques distinct from transaction processing systems. Dimensional design has emerged as the dominant theme for most of our data warehouses. For some years we have had a fairly stable vocabulary that includes slowly changing dimensions, surrogate keys, aggregate navigation, and conformed dimensions and facts. Yet in spite of the growing awareness of this body of practice, we still don't have good metrics for what makes a system more dimensional or less dimensional.

This article attempts to fill this gap. I'll propose 20 criteria for what makes a data warehouse system dimensional. Besides naming each of the 20 criteria, I will define the criteria in decisive ways that let you decide whether your system complies. I want you to assign a 0 (non-compliant) or a 1 (compliant) to each criterion, and then add up the zeros and ones. Your data warehouse system should then measure somewhere between a score of zero, representing a system completely unsupportive of a dimensional approach, and 20, representing a system as completely supportive as I can imagine.

Architecture Criteria

The architecture criteria are fundamental characteristics of the overall system that are not only "features" but are central to the whole way the system is organized. Architectural criteria usually extend from the back room, through the DBMS, all the way to the front room and the user's desktop.

1. **Explicit declaration.** The system provides explicit database declarations that distinguish a dimensional entity from a measurement (fact) entity. These declarations are stored in the system metadata. The declarations are visible to administrators and users and affect query strategy, query performance, grouping logic, and physical storage. Facts can be declared as fully additive, semi-additive, and nonadditive. Default (automatic) aggregation techniques other than summation can be associated with facts. The default association between dimensions and facts is declared in the metadata so that the user can omit specifying the link between them.

A dimension attribute included in a query is automatically the basis of a dynamic aggregation. A fact included in a query is by default summed within the context of all aggregations. Semi-additive facts and nonadditive facts are prohibited from being summed across the wrong dimensions.

2. **Conformed dimensions and facts.** The system uses conformed dimensions and facts to implement drill-across queries where answer sets from different databases, different locations, and possibly different technologies can be combined into a higher level answer set by matching on the row headers supplied by the conformed dimensions. The system detects and warns against the attempted uses of unconformed facts. *This is the most fundamental and profound architecture criterion.* It is the basis for implementing distributed data warehouses.

3. **Dimensional integrity.** The system guarantees that the dimensions and the facts maintain referential integrity. In particular, a fact may not exist unless it is in a valid framework of all its dimensions. However, a dimensional entry may exist without any corresponding facts.

4. **Open aggregate navigation.** The system uses physically stored aggregates as a way to enhance performance of common queries. These aggregates, like indexes, are chosen silently by the database if they are physically present. Users and application developers do not need to know what aggregates are available at any point in time, and applications are not required to explicitly code the name of an aggregate. All query processes accessing the data, even those from different application vendors, realize the full benefit of aggregate navigation.

5. **Dimensional symmetry.** All dimensions allow comparison calculations that constrain two or more disjoint values of a single attribute from a dimension in computations such as ratios or differences. Also, the underlying database engine supports an indexing scheme that allows a single indexing strategy to efficiently support query constraints on an arbitrary and unpredictable subset of the dimensions in a highly dimensional database.

6. **Dimensional scalability.** The system places no fundamental constraints on either the number of members or the number of attributes within a single dimension. Dimensions with 100 million members or 1,000 textual attributes are practical. Dimensions with a billion members are possible.

7. **Sparsity tolerance.** Any single measurement can exist within a space of many dimensions. Such a space can be viewed as extraordinarily sparse. The system imposes no practical limit on the degree of sparsity. A 20-dimension fact table, each of whose dimensions has a million or more members, is practical.

Administration Criteria

Administration criteria are certainly more tactical than architectural criteria, but have been chosen for this list because they are showstoppers if they are missing from a dimensional data warehouse. Administration criteria generally affect IT personnel who are building and maintaining the data warehouse.

8. **Graceful modification.** The system must allow the following modifications to be made in place without dropping or reloading the primary database:

   - Adding an attribute to a dimension
   - Adding a new kind of fact to a measurement set, possibly beginning at a specific point in time
   - Adding a whole new dimension to a set of existing measurements
   - Splitting an existing dimension into two or more new dimensions

9. **Dimensional replication.** The system supports the explicit replication of a conformed dimension outward from a dimension authority to all the relevant dimensional models, in such a way that you can perform drill-across queries on business process subject areas if they have consistent versions of the dimensions. Aggregates that are affected by changes to the content of a dimension are automatically taken offline until you can make them consistent with the revised dimension and atomic fact table.

10. **Changed dimension notification.** The system delivers upon request all the records from a production source of a dimension that have changed since the last such request. In addition, a reason code is supplied with this dimension notification that allows the data warehouse to distinguish between type 1 and type 3 slowly changing dimensions (overwrites) and type 2 slowly changing dimensions (true physical changes at a point in time).

11. **Surrogate key administration.** The system implements a surrogate key pipeline process for: a) assigning new keys when the system encounters a type 2 slowly changing dimension; and b) replacing the natural keys in a fact table record with the correct surrogate keys before loading into the fact table. In other words, the cardinality of a dimension can be made independent from the definition of the original production key. Surrogate keys, by definition, must have no semantics or ordering that makes their individual values relevant to an application. Surrogate keys must support not applicable, nonexistent, and corrupted measurement data. A surrogate key may not be visible to a user application.

12. **International consistency.** The system supports the administration of international language versions of dimensions by guaranteeing that a translated dimension possesses the same grouping cardinality as the original dimension. The system supports the UNICODE character set, as well as all common international numerical punctuation and formatting alternatives. Incompatible, language-specific collating sequences are allowed.

Expression Criteria

The final eight expression criteria are common analytic capabilities needed in most real life data warehouse situations. The business user community experiences all expression criteria directly. These expression criteria for dimensional systems are not the only features users look for in a data warehouse, but they are all capabilities needed to exploit the power of a dimensional system.

13. **Multiple dimension hierarchies.** The system allows a single dimension to contain multiple independent hierarchies. No practical limit exists to the number of hierarchies in a single dimension. Hierarchies may be complete (encompassing all the members of a dimension) or partial (encompassing only a select subset of the members of a dimension). Two hierarchies may have common levels or common attributes (fields), and may have different numbers of levels. Two hierarchies may also share one or more common levels, but otherwise have no correlation.

14. **Ragged dimension hierarchies.** The system allows dimension hierarchies of indeterminate depth, such as organization charts and parts explosions, where records in the dimension can play the roles of parents as well as children. Using this terminology, a parent may have any number of children, and these children may have other children, to an arbitrary depth limited only by the number of records in the dimension. A child may have multiple parents, where these parents' "total ownership" of the child is explicitly represented and adds up to 100 percent. With a single command the system must be able to summarize a numeric measure from a fact table (or cube) on a ragged hierarchy for all members:

    ■ Starting with a specified parent and descending to all the lowest possible levels summarizing all intermediate levels

    ■ Starting with a specified parent and summarizing only children exactly N levels down from the parent or N levels up from the lowest child of any branch of the hierarchy, where N is equal to or greater than zero

    ■ Starting with a specified child and summarizing all the parents from that child to the supreme parent in that child's hierarchy

    ■ Starting with a specified child and summarizing all the parents exactly N levels upward in the hierarchy from that child.

    ■ Starting with a specified child and summarizing only that child's unique supreme parent

    A given ragged dimension hierarchy may contain an arbitrary number of independent families (independent supreme parents with no common children). Conversely, independent supreme parents may share some children, as stated when discussing total ownership.

15. **Multiple valued dimensions.** A single atomic measure in a fact table (or cube) may have multiple members from a dimension associated with that measure. If more than one member from a dimension is associated with a measure, an explicit allocation factor is provided that optionally lets the numeric measure spread across the dimension's associated members. In such a case, the allocation factors for a given atomic measure and a given multiple-valued dimension must add up to 100 percent.

16. **Slowly changing dimensions.** The system must explicitly support the three basic types of slowly changing dimensions: type 1, where a changed dimension attribute is overwritten;

type 2, where a changed dimension attribute causes a new dimension member to be created; and type 3, where a changed dimension attribute causes an alternate attribute to be created so that both the old and new values of the attribute are simultaneously accessible in the same dimension member record. Support for slowly changing dimensions must be system wide, as the following requirements imply:

- Changes to a dimension that invalidate any physically stored aggregate must automatically disqualify that aggregate from use.
- A type 2 change must trigger the automatic assignment of a new surrogate key for the new dimension member, and that key must apply for all concurrent fact records loaded into the system. In other words, the creation of a new type 2 dimension member must automatically link to the associated concurrent facts without the user or application developer needing to track beginning and ending effective dates.
- If the system supports ragged hierarchy dimensions and/or multiple-valued dimensions, then these types of dimensions must support all three types of slowly changing dimensions.

17. **Multiple dimension roles.** A single dimension must be associated with a set of facts via multiple roles. For instance, a set of facts may have several independent time stamps that you can simultaneously apply to the facts. In this case, a single underlying time dimension must be able to attach to these facts multiple times, where each instance is semantically independent. A given set of facts may have several different kinds of dimensions, each playing multiple roles.

18. **Hot-swappable dimensions.** The system must allow an alternate instance of a dimension to swap in at query time. For example, if two clients of an investment firm wish to view the same stock market data through their own proprietary "stock ticker" dimensions, then the two clients must be able to use their versions of the dimension at query time, without requiring the fundamental fact table (or cube) of stock market facts to be duplicated. Another example of this capability would let a bank attach an extended account dimension to a specific query if the user restricts the query to a cluster of accounts of the same type.

19. **On-the-fly fact range dimensions.** The system provides direct support for dynamic value banding queries on numeric measures in a fact table (or cube). In other words, at query time the user can specify a set of value ranges and use these ranges as the grouping criteria in a query. All the normal summarizing functions (count, sum, min, max, and average) can apply within each group. The sizes of the value bands needn't be equal.

20. **On-the-fly behavior dimensions.** The system supports constraining a dimension via a simple list of that dimension. For the sake of vocabulary, this list of members is called a "behavior dimension." The support of behavior dimensions must be system wide, as the following requirements imply:

- A behavior dimension can be captured from a report showing on the user's screen; from a list of keys or attributes appearing in a file extracted from a production source;

directly from a constraint specification; or from a union, intersection, or set difference of other behavior dimensions.

- A user may have a library of many behavior dimensions and can attach a behavior dimension to a fact table (or cube) at query time.
- The use of a behavior dimension in a query restricts the fact table (or cube) to the members in the study, but in no way otherwise limits the ability to select and constrain attributes of any regular dimension, including the one the behavior dimension affects directly.
- A behavior dimension may be of unlimited size.
- A behavior dimension may have an optional date stamp associated with each element of the list in such a way that two behavior dimensions can be merged where membership in the combined behavior dimension requires a specific time ordering.

Are You Dimensional?

A system that supported most or all these dimensional criteria would be adaptable, easier to administer, and able to address many real-world analytic challenges. The whole point of dimensional systems is that they are business issue and business user driven. I urge you to apply these criteria against your data warehouse to see how it does.

8 Fact Table Core Concepts

imensional models are directly tied to the measurement activities performed by an organization as the metrics captured or generated by these activities are unveiled in corresponding fact tables. This chapter focuses on the central figure of any dimensional model—the fact table.

Every fact table should have a single, explicitly stated granularity; we begin the chapter by encouraging you to tackle the most atomic details available from an operational source system. We then describe a relatively remarkable dimensional modeling phenomenon: All fact tables are either transactional, periodic snapshots, or accumulating snapshots. The treatment of transaction header versus line item details is further explored.

From there, we turn our attention to the pros and cons of fact table surrogate keys and the role of degenerate dimensions. Techniques to help reduce the width of voluminous fact tables are described. Finally, we close the chapter by discussing the handling of null, textual, and sparsely populated facts, along with metrics that sometimes more closely resemble dimension attributes.

Granularity

This first set of articles stresses the importance of precisely establishing the grain of a fact table early in the design process. They also argue that the fact table's granularity should correspond to the most detailed, atomic data captured in the operational source system for maximum analytic flexibility and extensibility.

8.1 Declaring the Grain

Ralph Kimball, Intelligent Enterprise, *Mar 1, 2003*

In debugging literally thousands of dimensional designs from my students over the years, I have found that the most frequent design error by far is not declaring the grain of the fact table at the beginning of the design process. If the grain isn't clearly defined, the whole design rests on quicksand. Discussions about candidate dimensions go around in circles, and rogue facts that introduce application errors sneak into the design.

Declaring the grain means saying *exactly* what a fact table record represents. Remember that a fact table record captures a measurement event. Example grain declarations include:

- An individual line item on a customer's retail sales ticket as measured by a scanner device
- An individual transaction against an insurance policy
- A line item on a bill received from a doctor
- A boarding pass used by someone on an airplane flight
- An inventory measurement taken every week for every product in every store

In Business Terms

Notice that most of these grain declarations are expressed in business terms. Perhaps you were expecting the grain to be a traditional declaration of the fact table's primary key. Although the grain ultimately is equivalent to the primary key, it's a mistake to list a set of dimensions and then assume that this list is the grain declaration. This is the most common mistake in my students' designs. In a properly executed dimensional design, the grain is first anchored to a clear business process and a set of business rules. Then, the dimensions that implement that grain become obvious.

So, when you make a grain declaration, you can then have a very precise discussion of which dimensions are possible and which are not. For example, a line item of a doctor's bill likely would have the following dimensions:

- Date (of treatment)
- Doctor (or provider)
- Patient
- Procedure
- Primary Diagnosis
- Location (such as the doctor's office)
- Billing Organization (an organization the doctor belongs to)
- Responsible Party (either the patient or the patient's legal guardian)
- Primary Payer (often an insurance plan)
- Secondary Payer (maybe the responsible party's spouse's insurance plan)

And quite possibly others.

Powerful Effects

As you've been following this example, I hope you've noticed some powerful effects from declaring the grain. First, you can visualize the dimensionality of the doctor bill line item very precisely, and you can therefore confidently examine your data sources, deciding whether or not a dimension can be attached to this data. For example, you probably would exclude "treatment outcome" from this example because most medical billing data doesn't tie to any notion of outcome.

This is my main gripe with many of the current offerings of "standard schemas" in books and CDs. Because they have no grain discipline, they often combine entities that don't coexist in real data sources. Every fact table design must be rooted in the realities of available physical data sources.

A second major insight from the doctor bill line item grain declaration is that this very atomic grain gives rise to many dimensions! I listed 10 dimensions, and experts in health care billing probably know of a few more. It's an interesting realization that the smaller and more atomic the measurement (fact table record), the more things you know for sure, and the more dimensions you have. This phenomenon is another way of explaining why atomic data resists the ad hoc attack by business users. Atomic data has the most dimensionality and so it can be constrained and rolled up in every way possible for that data source. Atomic data is a perfect match for the dimensional approach.

In the doctor bill line item example with 10 dimensions, you wouldn't expect the primary key of the fact table to consist of all 10 dimensional foreign keys. Logically from a business rules perspective, perhaps we know that the combination of date, doctor, patient, and procedure are enough to guarantee a unique record. So these fields could implement the fact table primary key. Or, it is possible that we have extra degenerate keys for the patient bill number and the line item number that would implement an acceptable physical fact table key. But we are confident that we can add these degenerate dimensions to the design because they are consistent with our grain declaration. The grain declaration is like a contract!

The grain declaration lets us think creatively about adding dimensions to a fact table design that may not obviously be present in the source data. In retail sales data, marketplace causal factors like promotions and competitive effects may be very important to understanding the data, but this information may not be present in a literal sense in the data extract. The grain definition (see the first example grain declaration) tells us that we can indeed add a causal "store condition" dimension to the fact table as long the store condition descriptions vary appropriately by time, product, and store location. A weather dimension can be added to many fact table designs using the same logic. Once such a new dimension is identified, it is incumbent on the data warehouse designer to find the appropriate store condition or weather data source and insert it into the back room ETL staging applications that build the fact tables.

All of the grain declarations listed in this article represent the lowest possible granularity of their respective data sources. These data measurements are "atomic" and cannot be divided further. But it is quite possible to declare higher level grains for each of these data sources that represent aggregations of atomic data, such as:

- All the sales for a product in a store on a day
- Insurance policy transaction totals by month by line of business
- Billed amount totals by treatment by diagnosis by month

- Counts of passengers and other flight metrics by route by month
- Average inventory levels by quarter by region

These higher levels of aggregation will usually have fewer, smaller dimensions. The health care billing example might end up with only the dimensions:

- Month
- Doctor
- Procedure
- Diagnosis

It would be nonsensical in an aggregated fact table to try to include all the original dimensions of the atomic data, because you would find yourself recapitulating the atomic level of the data!

Useful aggregations necessarily shrink dimensions and remove dimensions; therefore, aggregated data always needs to be used in conjunction with its base atomic data because aggregated data has less dimensional detail. Some developers get confused on this point, and after declaring that dimensional models necessarily consist of aggregated data, they criticize the dimensional model for "anticipating the business question." All these misunderstandings disappear when aggregated data is made available along with the atomic data from which it's derived.

Keep Facts True to the Grain

The most important result of declaring the grain of the fact table is anchoring the discussion of the dimensions. But declaring the grain lets you be equally clear about the measured numeric facts. Simply put, the facts must be true to the grain. In the health care example, the most obvious measured fact would be "billed amount," relating to the specific line item.

Other facts relating to the treatment that patient received at that time may also exist. But helpful facts, such as the amount billed year-to-date to this patient for all treatments, aren't true to the grain. When a reporting application combines fact records arbitrarily, these untrue-to-the-grain facts produce nonsensical, useless results. Viewed in this way, these facts are dangerous because they invite the business user to make mistakes. Omit them from the design and calculate such aggregate measures in your application.

8.2 Keep to the Grain in Dimensional Modeling

Ralph Kimball, Intelligent Enterprise, Jul 30, 2007

The power of a dimensional model comes from a careful adherence to "the grain." A clear definition of the grain of a fact table makes the logical and physical design possible; a muddled or imprecise definition of the grain poses a threat to all aspects of the design, from the ETL processes that fetch the data all the way to the reports that try to use the data.

What, exactly, is the grain? The grain of a fact table is the *business definition of the measurement event that creates a fact record*. The grain is exclusively determined by the physical realities of the source of the data.

All grain definitions should start at the lowest, most atomic grain and should describe the physical process that collects the data. Thus, in our dimensional modeling classes, when we start with the familiar example of retail sales, I ask the students "what is the grain?" After listening to a number of careful replies listing various retail dimensions such as product, customer, store, and time, I stop and ask the students to visualize the physical process. The salesperson or checkout clerk scans the retail item and the register goes "BEEP." The grain of the fact table is BEEP!

Once the grain of the fact table is established with such clarity, the next steps of the design process can proceed smoothly. Continuing with our retail example, we can immediately include or exclude possible dimensions from the logical design of the retail fact table. Benefiting from the very atomic definition (BEEP), we can propose a large number of dimensions including date, time, customer, product, employee (perhaps both checkout clerk and supervisor), store, cash register, sales promotion, competitive factor, method of payment, regional demographics, the weather, and possibly others. Our humble little BEEP turns into a powerful measurement event with more than a dozen dimensions!

Of course, in a given practical application, the design team may not have all these dimensions available. But the power of keeping to the grain arises from the clarity that the grain definition supplies to the design process. Once the logical design has been proposed, the design team can systematically investigate whether the data sources are rich enough to "decorate" the BEEP event with all these dimensions in the physical implementation.

The BEEP grain illustrates why the atomic data is the place to start all designs. The atomic data is the most expressive data because it is the most precisely defined. Aggregated data, for example, store sales by product by month, can easily be derived from the atomic data, but necessarily must truncate or delete most of the dimensions of the atomic data. Aggregated data is NOT the place to start a design!

This article was motivated in part by one that appeared recently in a trade magazine discussing the design of dimensional star schemas. The author stated "a star needs to be defined by a set of business questions and [metrics are assigned] to stars based on common reporting and queries." This is terrible advice! A dimensional model that is designed around business questions and reports has no clear grain. It has lost its connection to the original data source and is hostage to the "report of the day" mentality that causes the database to be tweaked and altered until no one can explain why a record is in the table or not.

When a dimensional design has lost its connection to the grain, it becomes vulnerable to a subtle problem called *mixed granularity* that is nearly impossible to fix. In this case, records in the same fact table may represent different physical measurement events that are not comparable or may even overlap. A simple example deviating from the BEEP grain would be a fact table containing "combo-pack" sales records in addition to the sales records of the individual items comprising the combo-pack.

This is dangerous because without a careful constraint in the query tool or report, the sales of these items would be double counted. A corollary to keeping to the grain is "don't require the BI user tools to correct problems with the grain."

Keeping to the grain means building physical fact tables around each atomic business process measurement event. These tables are the least difficult to implement and they provide the most durable and flexible foundation for addressing business questions and reports-of-the day.

8.3 Warning: Summary Data May Be Hazardous to Your Health

Margy Ross, Design Tip #77, Mar 9, 2006

An overarching false statement about dimensional models is that they're only appropriate for summarized information. Some people maintain that data marts and dimensional models are intended for managerial, strategic analysis and therefore should be populated with summarized data, not operational details.

We strongly disagree! Dimensional models should be populated with the most detailed, atomic data captured by the source systems so business users can ask the most detailed, precise questions possible. Even if users don't care about the particulars of a single transaction or line item, their "question of the moment" requires summarizing these details in unpredictable ways. Of course, database administrators may pre-summarize information, either physically or via materialized views, to avoid on-the-fly summarization in every case. However, these aggregate summaries are performance tuning *complements* to the atomic level, not replacements.

If you restrict your dimensional models to summarized information, you will be vulnerable to the following shortcomings:

- **Summary data naturally presupposes the typical business questions.** When the business requirements change, as they inevitably will, both the data model and ETL system must change to accommodate new data.
- **Summary data limits query flexibility.** Users run into dead ends when the pre-summarized data can't support an unanticipated inquiry. Although you can roll up detailed data in unpredictable ways, the converse is not true—you can't magically explode summary data into its underlying components.

When critics authoritatively state that "dimensional models presuppose the business question, are only appropriate for predictable usage, and are inflexible," they're conveying the hazards of pre-summarization, not dimensional modeling. If dimensional models contain atomic data, as we advocate, business users can roll up or drill down in the data ad infinitum. They can answer previously unexpected questions without any change to the database structures. When new attribute or measure details are collected by the source system, the atomic data model can be extended without disrupting any existing BI applications.

Some people advocate an approach where the atomic data is stored in a normalized data model, while summary data is stored dimensionally. The atomic details are not completely ignored in this scenario; however, accessing them for user consumption is inherently restricted. Normalized structures remove data redundancies to process transactional updates/inserts more quickly, but the resulting complexity causes navigational challenges and typically slower performance for BI reports and queries. While normalization may save a few bytes of storage space, it defeats the users' ability to seamlessly and arbitrarily traverse up, down, and across the detailed and summary data in a single interface. In the world of DW/BI, query functionality/performance trumps disk space savings.

As the architect Mies van der Rohe is credited with saying, "God is in the details." Delivering dimensional models populated with the most detailed data possible ensures maximum flexibility and extensibility. Delivering anything less in your dimensional models undermines the foundation necessary for robust business intelligence, and is hazardous to the health and well being of your overall DW/BI environment.

8.4 No Detail Too Small

Margy Ross, Intelligent Enterprise, *Oct 30, 2003*

Atomic fact tables are the core foundation of any analytic environment. Business analysts thrive on atomic details because they can be rolled up "any which way" by grouping on one or more dimension attributes. The robust dimensionality of atomic data is extremely powerful because it supports a nearly endless combination of inquiries. However, business analysts can't always live happily ever after on atomic details alone.

Accumulating the Atoms

In addition to atomic fact tables, you'll probably also build aggregated dimensional models. Aggregations and indexes are the most common tools for improving query performance. Summary aggregations may be structured as an OLAP cube or another relational star schema. Because the granularity is no longer atomic, you'll need a different fact table for the aggregated data, which typically exhibits the following characteristics:

1. **Business process.** Focused on a single business process or event, just like the atomic fact tables
2. **Granularity.** Specified as a roll up of the atomic facts
3. **Dimensions.** Detail and/or summary conformed dimension foreign keys corresponding to the level of detail. When atomic data is aggregated, some dimensions may be completely eliminated. In other cases, the relevant dimension tables are shrunken, subset versions of the more detailed dimension tables.
4. **Facts.** Aggregated performance metrics consistent with the stated granularity

Consolidating across Processes

In addition to aggregated fact tables that roll up facts from a single atomic fact table, we sometimes construct fact tables that combine data from multiple atomic fact tables. These cross-process or cross-event tables are referred to as *second-level* or *consolidated* fact tables. The consolidated fact tables are identified as separate enterprise data warehouse bus matrix rows, but are typically listed after the single process or first level matrix rows they are dependent upon. Consolidated fact tables exhibit slightly different characteristic patterns:

1. **Business process.** As the name implies, these fact tables look across discrete business processes or events.
2. **Granularity.** Represents the lowest level of detail common to the set of processes. In the case of consolidated accumulating snapshots, the grain is typically one row per "object" moving through a pipeline of discrete processes.
3. **Dimensions.** Often multiple dates corresponding to the major events or milestones, plus "least common denominator" conformed dimensions and degenerate dimensions from each underlying process
4. **Facts.** Key metrics from each of the individual business process fact tables. Calculated metrics such as differences or lag metrics are also common.

More Performance, Less Dimensionality

In article 6.4, *The Soul of the Data Warehouse, Part Two: Drilling Across*, Ralph discusses drilling across fact tables. Facts from distinct fact tables are grouped based on common dimension attributes as row headers in a multi-pass request using a robust query or reporting tool. Although joining on common row header values is powerful (assuming your query tool has multi-pass capabilities), it may not deliver the ease of use or query performance demanded by the business users.

Wouldn't it be even easier if users just pointed their query tool at a single fact table that already combined the metrics? Similarly, if the metrics are frequently compared to one another, rather than repeatedly drilling across and comparing on the fly, it likely makes more sense to physically combine the data into a single fact table once during the ETL staging process.

Of course, you make trade-offs with this technique. When we bring facts together in a consolidated table, we sometimes lose dimensionality. All the facts in the consolidated table must live at the same granularity; the consolidated fact table grain is the "least common denominator" of shared dimensions across the discrete, atomic fact tables. Another consolidation cost is the ETL staging burden because the effort to extract, transform, load, and maintain data from multiple sources may be significant.

Consolidated Fact Table Example

Fact tables supporting actual to forecast comparisons are a common example of consolidated fact tables. Most organizations forecast business performance at a more summarized level than transactions are processed. Sales projections may be generated monthly by sales rep and product group. Meanwhile, sales transactions identify each unique product sold by a sales rep to a given customer. We could roll up the transactions into an aggregated fact table with one row per month, sales rep, and product group, and then compare it to the projected forecast.

However, if this side-by-side comparison is frequently requested, physically creating a fact table that brings together both actual and forecast facts at a common grain will likely deliver more timely results with fewer analytic back flips. Of course, the business user's next question will be, "What's the difference between the forecasted and actual performance?" Because that's a simple intra-row computation, we could easily make it available as a calculated fact, either physically or via a view.

Profitability fact tables, which combine revenue and all the elements of cost, are another classic, albeit nontrivial, example of consolidated fact tables.

Accumulating Snapshot Example

Fact tables come in three standard flavors. The most common are *transaction* fact tables with grains such as one row per transaction or transaction line. *Periodic snapshot* fact tables are also frequently encountered where a predictable set of fact rows is appended to the fact table following each regularly scheduled snapshot.

Less frequently encountered fact tables are *accumulating snapshots*. They behave very differently from the other two flavors of fact tables. Accumulating snapshots capture the results from the key events in a related series of processes. Fact table rows are loaded when the first event or milestone occurs. Unlike other fact tables, accumulating snapshot fact tables are revisited and overwritten; we update existing fact table rows to reflect the current or accumulated results of each event.

Perhaps the business users want to analyze their procurement pipeline. They already have individual atomic fact tables capturing the rich details associated with each transactional event in the pipeline, such as submitting purchase requisitions, issuing purchase orders, receiving deliveries, receiving invoices, and issuing payments. Although each of these events shares many common dimensions, such as product, vendor, and requester, the individual fact tables have unique dimensionality and metrics.

Suppose someone in the business wants to know how quickly purchase orders are issued after requisitions are submitted. Or what's the discrepancy between the quantities ordered versus what was received? Or what's the duration or time lag between invoice receipt and payment? The accumulating snapshot comes to the rescue, as illustrated in Figure 8-1.

We have five date keys in the procurement accumulating snapshot corresponding to the key milestones in the pipeline. The other dimensions would be limited to those that are common to all the underlying processes, plus the degenerate dimensions generated along the way. Accumulating snapshots often have a status dimension to easily determine the current "state." Finally, there's a series of quantities, amounts, and lag or velocity calculations, again capturing the core cross-process performance metrics.

As we describe the accumulating snapshot, it's obvious that we're really talking about another variation of a consolidated fact table. Imagine how much easier it would be to answer the questions posed earlier if you had a consolidated accumulating snapshot, rather than trying to put together the procurement puzzle pieces by drilling across five transaction fact tables.

Procurement Accumulating Snapshot
Requisition Date Key (FK)
Purchase Order Date Key (FK)
Delivery Receipt Date Key (FK)
Invoice Date Key (FK)
Payment Date Key (FK)
Requester Key (FK)
Product Key (FK)
Vendor Key (FK)
Status Key (FK)
Purchase Requisition Number (DD)
Purchase Order Number (DD)
Delivery Receipt Number (DD)
Invoice Number (DD)
Payment Check Number (DD)
Requisition Quantity
Requisition Dollar Amount
Purchase Order Quantity
Purchase Order Dollar Amount
Received Quantity
Invoice Quantity
Invoice Amount

Figure 8-1: Example procurement accumulating snapshot.

Details Always Come First

Because consolidated fact tables deliver ease of use and query performance, perhaps you're thinking that you'll start there. It's especially tempting if you're chartered with creating a flashy scorecard or dashboard for the executive team. However, don't be lured onto this supposedly easy street. You need to focus on the atomic details before pursuing either aggregated or consolidated dimensional models. If you start at the more macro level without the detailed foundation, there's nothing to drill into when a business user wants to probe into an exceptional condition or anomaly in the consolidated data. Remember, you can always roll up, but you can only drill down if the lower level details are available.

Types of Fact Tables

As discussed in the following articles, all the measurement events captured by operational business processes fit into three types of fact tables; this remarkably simple pattern reliably holds true regardless of the industry or business function. Factless fact tables are also described in detail at the end of this section.

8.5 Fundamental Grains

Ralph Kimball, Intelligent Enterprise, *Mar 30, 1999*

A powerful theme in data warehouse design is measurement publication. We can decompose many of the meaningful transactions captured by our OLTP systems into two main components: a context for the transaction and an amount. We view the amount as a measurement. When an insurance agent modifies the amount of collision insurance on a customer's car, the context of the transaction consists of the date and time, policy, customer and agent identification, coverage in question (collision), covered item (the customer's car), and nature of the transaction. The amount of the transaction is the new collision coverage limit, and it's what we measure. Usually, we know all the ingredients of a transaction's context in advance. We already have descriptions of the customer, agent, policy, car, types of coverage, and types of possible transactions. We don't know, however, what the new coverage limit is going to be, which is why we think of the transaction amount as a measurement.

Our duty as data warehouse designers is to publish these measurements for all the managers and analysts in our organization so they can make sense of the pattern of transactions. Ultimately, revenue, costs, profit, and much of the important customer behavior should be understandable from this series of measurements.

This view leads directly to the dimensional design perspective shown in Figure 8-2. The context of a transaction is modeled as a set of generally independent dimensions. Figure 8-2 shows seven such dimensions. The measured transaction amount is in a fact table that refers to all the dimensions by foreign keys pointing outward to their respective dimension tables. The clean removal of all the context detail from the transaction record is an important normalization step and is why I often refer to fact tables as "highly normalized."

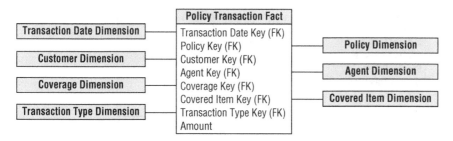

Figure 8-2: A transaction grained insurance fact table.

As compelling as the transactional view of the world is, there's more to life than transactions. Although we can always reconstruct a complete picture of a business from the transaction history, it is often grossly impractical to do so. Typically we need to augment the transactions with an alternate view of the world: the snapshot.

A snapshot is a measurement of status at a specific point in time. In the data warehouse world, there are two different snapshots of status, both equally important. The *periodic snapshot*, the most common type, is a regular, predictable statement of status. Some of these snapshots are instantaneous measurements at the end of the period, and some are measurements accumulated throughout the period. The *periodic snapshots* focus on the activity that occurred during the time interval between snapshots.

The other important kind of snapshot is the *accumulating snapshot*, which shows us the latest status. If we ask for the current status an hour from now, it may be different. The accumulating snapshot often combines the most recent volatile status with measures that accumulate from the beginning of history.

Fundamental Grains

The three kinds of measurements—transaction, periodic snapshot, and accumulating snapshot—are the choices for the grain of any given fact table. All three are useful, and you often need a minimum of two to get a complete picture of a business. In Figure 8-3, I've lined up all three to point out their similarities and differences.

Transaction Grain Fact	Periodic Snapshot Grain Fact	Accumulating Snapshot Grain Fact
Transaction Date Key (FK)	Reporting Month Key (FK)	Snapshot Date Key (FK)
Policy Key (FK)	Policy Key (FK)	Effective Date Key (FK)
Customer Key (FK)	Customer Key (FK)	Expiration Date Key (FK)
Agent Key (FK)	Agent Key (FK)	First Claim Date Key (FK)
Coverage Key (FK)	Coverage Key (FK)	Last Payment Date Key (FK)
Covered Item Key (FK)	Covered Item Key (FK)	Policy Key (FK)
Transaction Key (FK)	Status Key (FK)	Customer Key (FK)
Amount	Earned Premium	Agent Key (FK)
	Incurred Claims	Coverage Key (FK)
	Change in Reserve	Covered Item Key (FK)
	Reserve Balance	Status Key (FK)
	Number Transactions	Earned Premium to Date
		Number Claims to Date
		Claim Payments to Date

Figure 8-3: Three fact table grains in insurance.

The first thing to note is that many of the dimensions (indicated by the key fields in Figure 8-3) are the same across the three fact tables. Whenever the same key is listed in separate fact tables, we insist that the definitions of the keys be exactly the same and that they point to exactly the same dimension tables. These *conformed dimensions* are the secret behind building separate business process subject areas that you can use together and that aren't isolated, incompatible stovepipes. But although the dimensions are similar, the administration and rhythms of the three tables are different.

The transaction grained fact table represents an atomic action that occurs at an instantaneous point in time. There is often no guarantee that a record for a given policy or customer exists in the transaction fact table; a record exists only if a transaction occurs. Conversely, there is no upper limit to the number of records for a given policy or customer. The date key is accurate to the calendar day, and may be augmented with a date/time stamp accurate to the hour and minute. Sometimes there is only a single fact generically called "amount." Its meaning depends on the value of the transaction key. After posting it, we don't usually revisit a transaction grained fact record for any type of update.

The periodic snapshot grained fact table represents a predefined time span. There is often a strong guarantee that a record exists in this fact table as long as the policy is in effect—or as long as any claims against the policy are open. Usually, exactly one record exists for each combination of significant keys. The time stamp on the periodic snapshot is only the name of the period and usually denotes the end of the period. Periodic snapshots can have any number of facts, depending on what measures are possible or useful to calculate. Some of these facts may be extraordinarily difficult to calculate directly from the transactions. In Figure 8-3, earned premium is the fraction of the total policy premium that the insurance company can book as revenue during the particular reporting period. The calculation of earned premium may be very complex. In such cases, it is often better to let the OLTP system provide this calculation as part of its production processing, and treat this result as data simply to be loaded into the data warehouse. Finally, once it's posted, we do not normally revisit a periodic snapshot fact record for any type of update unless we decide to add a completely new periodic snapshot metric to the table.

The accumulating snapshot grained fact table represents an indeterminate time span, covering the entire history starting when the collision coverage was created for the car in our example and ending with the present moment. There is a strong guarantee that a single record exists in the fact table if the customer's car was ever covered. Accumulating snapshot fact tables almost always have multiple time stamps. One time stamp represents the last time the snapshot was updated, and the others represent generic or predictable events that may have taken place in the life of the coverage. Note that some of these time stamps may have to handle null values because, for example, the first claim date will not have a real value unless a claim has been filed. The correct treatment of null date keys requires using integer-valued surrogate keys that point to a specially crafted row in the date dimension corresponding to "No Date." Accumulating snapshots can have any number of facts depending on what measures are possible or useful to calculate. In dramatic contrast to the other fact table types, we frequently revisit accumulating snapshot fact records to update the facts. Remember that in this table there is generally only one fact record for the collision coverage on a particular customer's car. As history unfolds, we must revisit the same record several times to revise the accumulating status.

How Do We Use Each Fact Table Type?

The transaction grained fact table is the only table that can answer detailed questions about unpredictable behavior. In our insurance example, the transaction grained fact table can tell us the length of time between an agent's preliminary approval of a coverage and the underwriter's final signoff. This time period is a useful measure of the efficiency of policy processing.

The periodic snapshot fact table is often the only table that can easily generate a regular, predictable view of the important measures of a business. Calculating basic measures, such as revenue and cost, may be impractical if starting from any sort of transactional view of the business. So we publish such measures once each month at a low level of granularity and let all the company's managers and analysts roll these measures upward into different combinations from our periodic snapshot table.

The accumulating snapshot fact table is appealing when we are tracking pipelines that have a finite lifetime, such as insurance policy coverages or line items on orders. If the coverage or order line item exists for a finite period of time, there is a flurry of updating activity on those fact records when they are "open," and then the record quiets down. It remains in the fact table as a summary of the activity surrounding that coverage or line item. The advantage of the accumulating snapshot is that we can do a great deal of useful reporting without complex constraints on the time dimension and without double counting across the multiple records of a periodic snapshot.

It would be somewhat unusual to implement all three fact tables for a single business process; however, transactions and snapshots are the yin and yang of an enterprise data warehouse. Transactions give us the fullest possible view of detailed behavior, and snapshots allow you to measure the status of the enterprise quickly. You need them both because there is no simple way to combine these two contrasting perspectives. Used together, transactions and snapshots provide a full, immediate view of the business, and when they are part of the overall data warehouse, they blend gracefully into the larger views across time and across the other main dimensions.

Although there is some theoretical information redundancy between the transaction and snapshot tables, we don't object to such redundancy as data warehouse providers. Our mission is to publish data effectively for the business organization, and these separate types of fact tables speak in their own ways to different audiences.

8.6 Modeling a Pipeline with an Accumulating Snapshot

Ralph Kimball, Design Tip #37, Jun 13, 2002

In all the thousands of fact table designs I have studied, they all have sorted themselves into three fundamental grains:

1. The transaction grain that represents a point in space and time
2. The periodic snapshot grain that represents a regular span of time repeated over and over
3. The accumulating snapshot grain that represents the entire life of an entity that has a well defined beginning and ending

The accumulating snapshot fact table is unusual in a number of ways. Unlike the other grains, the accumulating snapshot usually has a number of date dimensions, representing when specific steps in the life of the "accumulating entity" take place. For example, an order is created, committed, shipped, delivered, paid for, and maybe returned.

So the design for an orders accumulating snapshot fact table could start off with six date keys, all being foreign keys to views on a single physical date dimension table. These six views of the date table are called *roles* played by the date table, and they are semantically independent as if they were separate physical tables because we have defined them as separate views.

The other unusual aspect of the accumulating snapshot fact table is that we revisit the same records over and over, physically changing both foreign keys and measured facts, as the (usually short) life of the entity unfolds. The orders process is a classic example.

Now that we have reminded ourselves of the salient design issues for accumulating snapshot fact tables, let's apply this design technique to a pipeline process. We'll use the student admissions pipeline, but those of you interested in sales pipelines should be able to apply this design to your situation easily.

In the case of admissions tracking, prospective students progress through a standard set of admissions hurdles or milestones. We're interested in tracking activities around 15 key steps in the process, including:

1. Receipt of preliminary admissions test scores
2. Information requested
3. Information sent
4. Interview conducted
5. On-site campus visit
6. Application received
7. Transcript received
8. Test scores received
9. Recommendations received
10. First pass review by admissions
11. Application reviewed for financial aid
12. Final decision from admissions
13. Student accepted
14. Student admitted
15. Student enrolled

At any point in time, the admissions department is interested in how many applicants are at each stage in the pipeline. It's much like a funnel where many applicants enter the pipeline, but far fewer progress through to the final stage. They also want to analyze the applicant pool by a variety of characteristics. In this admissions example, we can be confident that there is a very rich applicant dimension filled with interesting demographic information.

The grain of the accumulating snapshot is one row per applicant. Because this is an accumulating snapshot, we revise and update each applicant's unique record in the fact table whenever one of the steps is completed.

A key component of the design is a set of 15 numeric facts, each a 0 or 1 corresponding to whether the applicant has completed one of the 15 steps listed. Although technically these 15 facts could be deduced from the 15 date keys, the additive numeric zeros and ones make the application elegant and easy to use with almost any query or reporting tool.

As an extra goodie, we add four more numeric additive facts representing "lags" or time gaps between particularly important steps in the process. These include:

- Information requested => information sent lag
- Application submitted => application complete lag
- Application submitted => final decision lag
- Final decision => accept or decline lag

Imagine how easy it would be to summarize the state of the pipeline at any point in time using the fact table in Figure 8-4. Although the records are obviously wide, this is not an especially big table. If you are a big state university with 100,000 applicants per year, you would only have 100,000 records per year. Assume the 17 foreign keys are all 4-byte integers (nice surrogate keys), and the 21 quantities and lags are 2-byte tiny integers. Our fact table records are then $(17 \times 4) + (21 \times 2) = 110$ bytes wide. This makes about 11 MB of data per year in this fact table. Check my math. Actually this is a common outcome for accumulating snapshot fact tables. They are the smallest of the three types of fact tables, by far.

8.7 Combining Periodic and Accumulating Snapshots

Ralph Kimball, Design Tip #42, *Jan 7, 2003*

Normally we think of the accumulating snapshot and periodic snapshot as two different styles of fact tables that we must choose between when we are building a fact table around a data source. Remember that a periodic snapshot (like the monthly summary of a bank account) is a fact table that records activity during a repeating predictable time period. Periodic snapshot records are generally repeated each reporting period as long as the thing being measured (like the account) is in existence. Periodic snapshots are appropriate for long-running processes that extend over many reporting periods.

Accumulating snapshots, on the other hand, are used for short processes that have a definite beginning and end, such as an order being filled. For an order, we would usually make a record for each line on the order, and we would revisit the record making updates as the order progressed through the pipeline. The accumulating snapshot is by definition a snapshot of the most recent state of something and therefore the dimensional foreign keys and the facts are, in general, overwritten as time progresses.

The simplest implementation of an accumulating snapshot does not give you intermediate points in the history of an order pipeline, for example.

There are at least three ways to capture this intermediate state:

1. **Freeze the accumulating snapshots at regular intervals such as month end.** These periodic snapshots should probably be in a separate fact table by themselves to keep applications from getting too complicated. Ironically, this approach comes in the back door to mimic a real-time interpretation of a periodic snapshot (where you create a hot rolling current month), but that's

another story. The frozen snapshots of the orders can now reflect the use of type 2 slowly changing dimensions. As in any periodic snapshot, the good news is that you know you have a record for that order each month the order is active. The bad news is that you only see the snapshots of the order at month ends.

Student Admissions Accumulating Snapshot Fact
Preliminary Test Score Receipt Date Key (FK)
Information Requested Date Key (FK)
Information Sent Date Key (FK)
Interview Conducted Date Key (FK)
On-site Campus Visit Date Key (FK)
Application Submitted Date Key (FK)
Transcript Received Date Key (FK)
Test Scores Received Date Key (FK)
Recommendations Received Date Key (FK)
Admissions First Pass Review Date Key (FK)
Reviewed For Financial Aid Date Key (FK)
Admissions Final Decision Date Key (FK)
Applicant Decision Received Date Key (FK)
Admitted Date Key (FK)
Enrolled Date Key (FK)
Applicant Key (FK)
Admissions Decision Key (FK)
Preliminary Test Score Receipt Quantity
Information Requested Quantity
Information Sent Quantity
Information Requested-Sent Lag
Interview Conducted Quantity
On-site Campus Visit Quantity
Application Submitted Quantity
Transcript Received Quantity
Test Scores Received Quantity
Recommendations Received Quantity
Application Complete Quantity
Application Submitted-Complete Lag
Admissions First Pass Review Quantity
Reviewed For Financial Aid Quantity
Admissions Final Decision Quantity
Application Submitted-Final Decision Lag
Accepted Quantity
Decline Quantity
Final Decision-Accepted/Decline Lag
Admitted Quantity
Enrolled Quantity

Figure 8-4: Accumulating snapshot for the student admissions pipeline.

2. **Freeze the accumulating snapshot and store it in a second fact table if and only if a change to the order occurs.** This gives the complete history of an order. It has the same number of records as option 3.

3. **Maintain a full transaction grain fact table on the order lines.** Add a transaction dimension to this fact table to explain each change. This is "fully general" in that you can see every action that has occurred on an order, but be careful. Some of the transactions are not additive over time. For instance, if a line item on an order is cancelled and two other line items are substituted for the original one, it is a complex calculation to correctly reconstruct the order at an arbitrary point in time after these transactions. That's why option 2 may be the best if you need to see every intermediate state of a complete order.

8.8 Complementary Fact Table Types

Bob Becker, Design Tip #167, Jun 17, 2014

There are three fundamental types of fact tables in the data warehouse presentation area: transaction fact tables, periodic snapshot fact tables, and accumulating snapshot fact tables. Most DW/BI design teams are very familiar with transaction fact tables. They are the most common fact table type and are often the primary workhorse schema for many organizations. Many teams have also incorporated periodic snapshot fact tables in their presentation areas. Fewer organizations leverage the accumulating snapshot fact table. Design teams often don't appreciate how an accumulating snapshot fact table can complement transaction and/or periodic snapshot fact tables.

Each of the fact table types is a design response to the wide variety of requirements posed by the business community. Often the best design response is a combination of two, or even all three, fact table types. The multiple fact tables complement one another, each supporting a unique view of the business processes that would be difficult to achieve with only one fact table type.

A logistics supply chain is an excellent scenario to illustrate all three fact table types working together to support a rich set of business requirements. We'll use a simplified view of the finished goods logistics pipeline of a large auto manufacturer to help understand the strengths and appropriate use of each fact table type.

Our auto manufacturer has plants where vehicles are assembled. The finished vehicles eventually find their way to dealers where they will be sold to the ultimate owners. Our fictitious auto manufacturer maintains finished goods inventory in a large parking lot—really a warehouse—located just outside the assembly plant doors. Vehicles (inventory) are shipped from the finished goods warehouse via freight train to one of several regional parking lots. From these regional warehouses, the inventory is shipped via carrier truck to dealer locations. Once the vehicle arrives at the dealer, it is prepped and put on the dealer lot (store inventory) for final sale.

The logistics business users need to understand the number of vehicles flowing out of final assembly, in and out of each warehouse, and the final customer demand for various vehicle types, colors, models, and so on. The company also needs to understand and analyze the inventory levels at each stage of the logistics chain. Logistics management wants to understand the time it takes for a vehicle to move from the assembly plant to the final customer, depending on vehicle type, warehouses, and carriers. Moving vehicles more quickly and efficiently through the logistics pipeline helps the company minimize inventory levels and reduce carrying costs.

A robust design to support our auto manufacturer's finished goods logistics pipeline illustrates all three fact table types.

Transaction Fact Table

A key component of the logistics pipeline is the flow of inventory from one location to another. The flow of vehicles is captured in a series of inventory movement transactions. An assembly plant releases a vehicle into the finished goods inventory via an inventory movement transaction. The vehicle is then shipped via rail to the regional warehouse where it is received into its inventory; later it is removed from inventory and shipped via truck to the dealer where it is received into the dealer inventory. For each of these inventory moves, an inventory movement or shipping/receiving transaction is generated. The inventory flow is a great opportunity for a transaction fact table. The grain of this fact table is one row for each inventory movement transaction for each vehicle. Similarly, the final sale of the vehicle should be captured in a sales transaction fact table with one row for each vehicle sold.

Transaction fact tables are an appropriate design response to business requirements that look for an understanding of the intensity or quantity of a business process. Transaction fact tables help answer the "how many?" question. For example, how many white sports utility vehicles (SUVs) were sold last week? What were the dollar sales? How many all-wheel drive vehicles were released by assembly into salable inventory? How many vehicles did we ship with a given carrier? How many vehicles were received by our dealers this month? Compared to last month, last quarter, or last year? There's a reason transaction fact tables are the workhorse fact table type: They support critically important business requirements. On the other hand, transaction fact tables are less effective in answering questions regarding the state of our inventory levels or the speed/efficiency of the logistics pipeline. To support these business requirements, we look to other fact table types to complement transaction fact tables.

Periodic Snapshot Fact Table

The second requirement is understanding the total amount of inventory at any point in the pipeline. Supporting analysis of inventory levels is a task well suited for a periodic snapshot fact table. At any point in time, each vehicle is in a single physical location such as finished goods inventory at the plant, in a regional distribution center, on a dealer lot, or in-transit on a railcar or truck. To support inventory analysis, the periodic snapshot fact table has a grain of one row per vehicle each day. A location dimension will support the analysis of inventory in each point of the pipeline.

The periodic snapshot fact table does an excellent job of helping understand the volume of vehicles in our pipeline. It answers the "how much?" question. How much total inventory do we have? How much inventory is available in white vehicles? SUVs? Four doors? Sport models? In California? On dealer lots? Compared to prior months, quarters, or years? The periodic snapshot supports trending of inventory levels over time. The inventory movement transaction fact table and inventory periodic snapshot together support a wide range of the business requirements surrounding the logistics pipeline. However, even with both of these fact tables, it will be difficult to address the pipeline efficiency requirements. To complete the picture, an accumulating snapshot fact table will complement the transaction and periodic snapshot fact tables.

Accumulating Snapshot Fact Table

The third set of requirements for the logistics pipeline is supporting analysis of the speed at which vehicles travel through the pipeline (no pun intended). Each vehicle will pass through a series of milestones during its travels to the final owner. To support the analytic requirements for measuring and understanding the efficiencies of our logistics pipeline, an accumulating snapshot fact table will be populated with one row per vehicle. As each vehicle moves through the pipeline, the accumulating snapshot will be updated with the date of each movement and current location of the vehicle. The accumulating snapshot will have numerous date keys, such as date released by assembly, date shipped to distribution center, date received at distribution center, and so on until date of final sale. Fact table metrics will include a series of date lags that measure the time it took for a vehicle to move between pipeline steps.

The accumulating snapshot fact table supports the key efficiency measures of velocity. How quickly do vehicles move through the pipeline? What's the average length of time from assembly release to final customer sale? Is it different for autos than SUVs? Hybrids versus non-hybrids? White versus red vehicles? Which carriers/railroads are most effective? The accumulating snapshot will be updated daily for vehicles currently in the logistics pipeline. Thus, the accumulating snapshot can also be used to look at the current state of the pipeline to identify "stuck" vehicles, such as find all the vehicles that have been at a regional distribution center or on a dealer lot for more than "n" days. How many vehicles have been in transit via rail or truck for more than "n" days? Where are all the SUVs? This fact table can help the logistics team identify and move the vehicles in highest demand, identify efficiency improvement opportunities, and identify preferred shipping partners.

In the case of our auto manufacturer, it is clear that the three fact table types complement one another. Implementing all three fact table types is an appropriate response to the rich set of business requirements. Implementing only one or even only two of the fact table types would have made it very difficult, if not impossible, to support all the requirements.

8.9 Modeling Time Spans

Ralph Kimball, Design Tip #35, Mar 27, 2002

In the past couple of years I have seen an increased demand for applications that need to ask questions about time spans. One person captured it nicely when he said "each record in my fact table is an episode of constant value over a region of time." Time spans can start and stop at arbitrary points in time. In some cases, time spans link together to form an unbroken chain. In other cases, the time spans are isolated, and in the worst cases, the time spans overlap arbitrarily. But each time span is represented in the database by a single record. To make these variations easier to visualize, imagine that we have a database filled with atomic transactions, such as deposits and withdrawals from bank accounts. We'll also include open account and close account transactions.

Each transaction implicitly defines an episode of constant value over a region of time. A deposit or a withdrawal defines a new value for the account balance that is valid until the next transaction. This time span could be one second or it could be many months. The open account transaction defines the status of the account as continuously active over a time span until a close account transaction appears.

Before we propose a database design, let's remind ourselves of some of the time span questions we want to ask. We'll start off by limiting our questions to a granularity of individual days, rather than parts of days like minutes and seconds. We'll return to minutes and seconds at the end. The easy questions we have always been good at answering include:

- What transactions occur within a given time span?
- Does a selected transaction occur within a given time span?
- How are time spans defined using complex calendar navigation capabilities including seasons, fiscal periods, day numbers, week numbers, pay days, and holidays?

For these cases all we need is a single time stamp on the transaction fact table record. The first question picks up all the transactions whose time stamp is in an interval specified in the user's query. The second question retrieves the time stamp from a selected transaction and compares it to the interval. The third set of questions replaces the simple time stamp with a calendar date dimension key associated with lots of helpful calendar attributes. This date dimension is connected to the fact table through a standard foreign key-primary key join. This is all vanilla dimensional design and only requires a single time key in the fact table record to represent the required time stamp. So far, so good.

By the way, when using complex calendar navigation, the queries become much easier if the verbose date dimension includes first day and last day markers for each defined span of time, such as "last day of quarter." This field would have the value "N" for all the days except the last day of the applicable quarter, which would have the value "Y." These markers allow the complex business time spans to be easily specified in the queries. Note that the use of a verbose date dimension means the application is not navigating a time stamp on the fact table. More about this in the last section.

A second moderately hard category of time span questions include:

- Who are customers at a particular point within a time span?
- What was the last transaction for a given customer within a time span?
- What was the balance of an account at a particular point in time?

We'll continue to make the simplifying assumption that all the time spans are described by calendar days, not by minutes and seconds. It is possible to answer all these questions with the single time stamp design given earlier, but this approach requires complex and inefficient queries. For instance, to answer the last question, we would need to search the set of account transactions for the latest transaction at or prior to the desired point in time. In SQL, this would take the form of a correlated sub-SELECT embedded in the surrounding query. Not only is this probably slow, but the SQL is not readily produced by user BI tools.

For all of these moderately hard time span questions, we simplify the applications enormously by providing twin time stamps on each fact record, indicating the beginning and end of the time span implicitly defined by the transaction.

With the twin time stamp design, we knock off the preceding three example questions easily:

1. Search for all the open account transactions whose begin date occurs on or prior to the end of the time span, and whose end date occurs on or after the beginning of the time span.
2. Search for the single transaction whose begin date is on or before the end of the time span and whose end date is on or after the end of the time span.
3. Search for the single transaction whose begin date is on or before the arbitrary point in time and whose end date is on or after the arbitrary point in time.

In all these cases, the SQL uses a simple BETWEEN construct. The "value between two fields" style of this SQL is indeed allowable syntax. When we use the twin time stamp approach, we have to be honest about one major drawback. In almost all situations, we have to visit each fact table record twice: once when we first insert it (with an open-ended end time stamp), and once more when a superseding transaction occurs that actually defines the real end time stamp. The open-ended end time stamp probably should be a real value somewhere out in the future, so that applications don't trip over null values when they try to execute the BETWEEN clause.

We have saved the hardest questions to the end: time spans to the second. In this case we ask the same basic questions as in the first two sections, but we allow the time span boundaries to be defined to the nearest second. In this case, we'll put the same two twin time stamps in the fact record, but we have to give up our connection to a robust date dimension. Both our beginning and ending time stamps must be conventional RDBMS date/time stamps. We must do this because we usually cannot create a single time dimension with all the minutes or all the seconds over a significant period of time. Dividing the time stamp into a day dimension and a seconds-in-a-day dimension would make the BETWEEN logic horrendous. So for these ultra precise time spans, we live with the limitations of SQL date/time semantics and give up the ability to specify seasons or fiscal periods to the nearest second. With time spans accurate to the second, we make the end time span of a record exactly equal to the begin time stamp of the next record. We then constrain a desired moment in time greater than or equal to the begin time and strictly less than the end time. This guarantees that we find exactly one time span and that there are no gaps between time spans.

If you are really a diehard, you could consider four time stamps on each transaction record if your time spans are accurate to the second. The first two would be RDBMS date/time stamps as described in the preceding paragraph. But the third and fourth would be calendar day (only) foreign keys connecting to a verbose calendar date dimension as in the first two sections of this article. That way you can have your cake and eat it too. You can search for ultra precise time spans, but you can also ask questions like "Show me all the power outages that occurred on a holiday."

8.10 A Rolling Prediction of the Future, Now and in the Past

Ralph Kimball, Design Tip #23, May 2, 2001

Here's a message that I received from a reader describing a fun design puzzle:

Hi Ralph & Co,

Help! I'm really stuck on an interesting design question for anyone who feels up to the challenge: How do I predict the future?

I have an account table that has a status field and a status effective date. Let's say the status is "Overdue" effective May 2, 2001.

The business user wants to know the following: For the next rolling month, how many days will the account have been at the overdue status? If today is May 5, 2001, the user wants to see the following report:

> *May 5, 2001: 4 days*
> *May 6, 2001: 5 days*
> *May 7, 2001: 6 days*
> *… up to June 4, 2001 as this is a rolling month into the future starting today.*

They then want to count all the accounts in the account table and group them by day bands at status "Overdue" like the following:

> *May 5, 2001: 100 accounts at 4 to 6 days Overdue*
> *May 6, 2001: 78 accounts at 4 to 6 days Overdue*
> *…*
> *May 5, 2001: 200 accounts at 7 to 9 days Overdue*
> *May 6, 2001: 245 accounts at 7 to 9 days Overdue*
> *…*

I also need to travel back in time and do the same for any point in time + 1 month, however many accounts will have the status ineffective date then set and will no longer be at a status of "Overdue," although they will have a historical record in the account table to preserve that they were at this status at a point in time.

If anyone has similar experience with such a problem or knows of a design that could support this, please let me know. . . my brain hurts.

Regards,
Richard

Here's my response to Richard:

Hi Richard,

Assume your account dimension table has the following fields (as you described):

```
ACCOUNT_KEY
STATUS
STATUS_EFFECTIVE_DT
```

Now build another table with the following fields:

```
STATUS_EFFECTIVE_DT
STATUS_REPORTING_DT
DELTA
```

where `DELTA` *is just the number of days between the effective date and reporting date. You need a record in this table for every combination of* `EFFECTIVE` *date and* `REPORTING` *date your users could possibly be interested in. If you have* `EFFECTIVE` *dates going back one year (365 dates) and you want to report forward one year, then you would need about 365*365 rows in this table, or about 133,000 rows.*

Join this second table to the first on the `STATUS_EFFECTIVE_DT`. *Then your first query should be satisfied with:*

```
SELECT STATUS_REPORTING_DT, DELTA
FROM ...
WHERE STATUS = 'OVERDUE'
AND STATUS_REPORTING_DT BETWEEN 'May 5, 2001' and 'June 4, 2001'
ORDER BY STATUS_REPORTING_DT
```

To get your banding report, maybe you can build a third table (a banding table) with fields:

```
BAND_NAME
UPPER_DELTA
LOWER_DELTA
```

You join this table to the second where:

```
DELTA <= UPPER_DELTA
DELTA > LOWER_DELTA
```

Your SQL is something like:

```
SELECT BAND_NAME, COUNT(*)
FROM (all three tables joined as described)
WHERE STATUS_REPORTING_DT BETWEEN 'May 5, 2001' and 'June 4, 2001'
AND DELTA <= UPPER_DELTA
AND DELTA > LOWER_DELTA
ORDER BY UPPER_DELTA
GROUP BY BAND_NAME
```

Good luck,
Ralph Kimball

And finally, here's Richard's follow up response after trying my advice:

Hi Ralph,

I'm very pleased to say that your recommendations worked! Thank you. I tried it out on a few sample rows in SQL Server 7 and the results look good. I've now taken it to the next level to include a `Status_Ineffective_Date` *so we can exclude accounts that stopped the "Overdue" status somewhere within the reporting period.*

Firstly, I slightly modified your SQL to the following:

```
SELECT
COUNT(account.Account_Id),
```

```
days_overdue.reporting_date
FROM
account,
days_overdue
WHERE
( account.Status_Effective_Date=days_overdue.effective_date )
AND (
days_overdue.reporting_date BETWEEN '05/05/2001' AND '06/04/2001'
AND days_overdue.delta >= 10 {an arbitrary number or banding that the
user decides at run time}
)
GROUP BY
days_overdue.reporting_date
```

The key to the preceding SQL is to constrain on DELTA (which we call days_overdue) or else the query pulls back every account for every day that the reporting period is for, and the COUNT is always the same number. The constraint can be =, <, > or BETWEEN, but must be present.

Secondly, to exclude accounts that are no longer overdue, we simply include a status_ineffective_date in the account table and can do the following:

```
SELECT
COUNT(account.Account_Id),
days_overdue.reporting_date
FROM
account,
days_overdue
WHERE
( account.Status_Effective_Date=days_overdue.effective_date )
AND (
days_overdue.reporting_date BETWEEN '05/05/2001' AND '06/04/2001'
AND days_overdue.delta >= 10
AND account.Status_Ineffective_Date > days_overdue.reporting_date
)
GROUP BY
days_overdue.reporting_date
```

Of course, you would have to set the ineffective_date for all currently overdue accounts to something in the future like 01/01/3000. This also fits perfectly with the SCD type 2 where we are creating a new row in the account dimension each time the status changes to give us a complete historical comparison!!

Thank you very much for your help and I wish you all the best,
Richard

8.11 Timespan Accumulating Snapshot Fact Tables

Joy Mundy, Design Tip #145, May 1, 2012

In article 8.12, *Is it a Dimension, a Fact, or Both?*, I discuss the challenges of designing dimensional schemas for processes of indeterminate length such as a sales pipeline or insurance claims processing. We concluded they are best represented as accumulating snapshot fact tables characterized by one row per pipeline occurrence where each row is updated multiple times over its lifetime. However, because each row is updated, we have an imperfect recording of history. The accumulating snapshot does a great job of telling us the pipeline's current state, but it glosses over the intermediate states. For example, a claim may move in and out of states multiple times: opened, denied, protested, re-opened, re-closed. The accumulating snapshot is hugely valuable, but there are several things that it cannot do:

- It can't tell us the details of when and why the claim looped through states multiple times.
- We can't re-create our "book of business" at any arbitrary date in the past.

To solve both of these problems, we'll need two fact tables. A transaction fact table captures the details of individual state changes. Then we'll add effective and expiration dates to the accumulating snapshot fact table to capture its history.

The transaction fact table is straightforward. As described in the cornerstone article 8.5, *Fundamental Grains*, we often pair the accumulating snapshot fact table with a transaction fact table that contains a row for each state change. Where the accumulating snapshot has one row per pipeline process such as a claim, the transaction fact table has one row per event. Depending on your source systems, it's common to build the transaction fact table first, and derive the accumulating snapshot from it.

Now let's turn our attention to the timespan accumulating snapshot fact table. First of all, not everyone needs to bother with retaining these time-stamped snapshots. For most organizations, a standard accumulating snapshot representing the current state of the pipeline, combined with the transaction fact table to show the event details, is ample. However, we've worked with several organizations that need to understand the evolution of a pipeline. While it's technically possible to do that from the transaction data, it's not child's play.

One solution to the historical pipeline tracking requirement is to combine the accumulating snapshot with a periodic snapshot: Snap a picture of the pipeline at a regular interval. This brute force method is overkill for pipelines that are relatively long in overall duration, but change infrequently. What works best in this case is to add effective and expiration change tracking to the accumulating snapshot.

Here's how it works:

- Design a standard accumulating snapshot fact table.
- Instead of updating each row as it changes state, add a new row. Our recent designs have been at the daily grain: add a new row to the fact table any day in which something about that pipeline (e.g., claim, sales process, or drug adverse reaction) has changed.

■ You need some additional metadata columns, similar to a type 2 dimension:

■ **Snapshot start date:** the date this row became effective.
■ **Snapshot end date:** the date this row expired, updated when a new row is added.
■ **Snapshot current flag:** updated when we add a new row for this pipeline occurrence.

Most users are only interested in the current view, i.e., a standard accumulating snapshot. You can meet their needs by defining a view (probably an indexed or materialized view) that filters the historical snapshot rows based on snapshot current flag. Alternatively, you may choose to instantiate a physical table of current rows at the end of each day's ETL. The minority of users and reports who need to look at the pipeline as of any arbitrary date in the past can do so easily by filtering on the snapshot start and end dates.

The timespan accumulating snapshot fact table is slightly more complicated to maintain than a standard accumulating snapshot, but the logic is similar. Where the accumulating snapshot will update a row, the time stamped snapshot updates the row formerly-known-as-current and inserts a new row. The big difference between the standard and time stamped accumulating snapshots is the fact table row count. If an average claim is changed on twenty days during its life, the time stamped snapshot will be twenty times bigger than the standard accumulating snapshot. Take a look at your data and your business's requirements to see if it makes sense for you. In our recent designs, we've been pleasantly surprised by how efficient this design is. Although a few problematic pipeline occurrences were changed hundreds of times, the vast majority were handled and closed with a modest number of changes.

8.12 Is it a Dimension, a Fact, or Both?

Joy Mundy, Design Tip #140, Nov 1, 2011

For most subject areas, it's pretty easy to identify the major dimensions: Product, Customer Account, Student, Employee, and Organization are all easily understood as descriptive dimensions. A store's sales, a telecommunication company's phone calls, and a college's course registrations are all clearly facts.

However, for some subject areas, it can be challenging—especially for the new dimensional modeler—to identify whether an entity is a dimension or a fact. For example, an insurance company's claims processing unit wants to analyze and report on their open claims. "Claim" feels like a dimension, but at the same time, it can behave like a fact table. A similar situation arises with software companies with extended sales cycles: Is the sales opportunity a dimension, a fact, or both?

In most cases, the design puzzle is solved by recognizing that the business event you're trying to represent in the fact table is actually a long-lived process or lifecycle. Often, the business users are most interested in seeing the current state of the process. A table with one row per process—one row per claim or sales opportunity, for example—sounds like a dimension table. But if you distinguish between the entity (claim or sales opportunity) and the process (claim settlement or sales pipeline), it becomes clearer. We need a fact table to measure the process. And many dimension tables to describe the attributes of the entity measured in that process.

This type of schema is implemented as an accumulating snapshot. The accumulating snapshot is less common than transactional and periodic snapshot fact tables. The grain of this type of fact table is one row per step in a process that has a well defined beginning and end; the table exposes many roles of the date dimension; and the fact table rows are updated multiple times over the life of the process (hence the name accumulating snapshot).

Many of the core dimensions of an accumulating snapshot schema are easy to identify, but there are some challenges to these designs. Long-lived processes tend to have a lot of little flags and codes from the source system that signal various statuses and conditions in the process. These are great candidates for junk dimensions. Expect your accumulating snapshot schema to have several junk dimensions.

I try to avoid creating a dimension with the same number of rows as the accumulating snapshot fact table. This can happen if you have not separated your junk dimensions into logically correlated groupings. In the earlier examples, I also resist designing a Claim or Sales Opportunity text description dimension for as long as I can. Realistically, though, there is usually some bit of detail that the business users absolutely need to see, such as the accident report or description of the sales opportunity. Although such a dimension may be huge, it is likely to be accessed by the business users only after other dimensions have been tightly constrained since there may be no predictable structure to the text entries.

8.13 Factless Fact Tables

Ralph Kimball, DBMS, *Sep 1996*

Fact tables contain the numeric, additive fields that are best thought of as the measurements of the business, measured at the intersection of all of the dimension values. There has been so much talk about numeric additive values in fact tables that it may come as a surprise that two kinds of very useful fact tables don't have any facts at all! They may consist of nothing but keys. These are called *factless* fact tables.

The first type of factless fact table is a table that records an event. Many event tracking tables in dimensional data warehouses turn out to be factless. One good example is shown in Figure 8-5, which tracks student attendance at a college. Imagine that you have a modern student tracking system that detects each student attendance event each day. You can easily list the dimensions surrounding the student attendance event, including date, student, course, teacher, and facility.

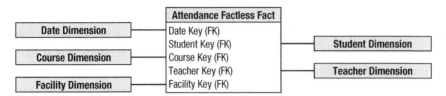

Figure 8-5: Daily student attendance is recorded in a factless fact table.

The grain of the fact table in Figure 8-5 is the individual student attendance event. When the student walks through the door into the lecture, a record is generated. It is clear that these dimensions are all well defined and that the fact table record, consisting of just the five keys, is a good representation of the student attendance event. Each of the dimension tables is deep and rich, with many useful textual attributes on which you can constrain and from which you can form row headers in reports.

The only problem is that there is no obvious fact to record each time a student attends a lecture or suits up for physical education. Tangible facts such as the grade for the course don't belong in this fact table. This fact table represents the student attendance process, not the semester grading process or even the midterm exam process. You are left with the odd feeling that something is missing.

Actually, this fact table consisting only of keys is a perfectly good fact table and probably ought to be left as is. A lot of interesting questions can be asked of this dimensional schema, including:

- Which classes were the most heavily attended?
- Which classes were the most consistently attended? Which teachers taught the most students?
- Which teachers taught classes in facilities belonging to other departments?
- Which facilities were the most lightly used?

My only real criticism of this schema is the unreadability of the SQL. Most of the preceding queries end up as counts. For example, the first question starts out as:

```
SELECT COURSE, COUNT(COURSE_KEY) FROM FACT_TABLE, COURSE_DIMENSION, ETC.
WHERE ... GROUP BY COURSE
```

In this case you are counting the course keys non-distinctly. It is an oddity of SQL that you can count any of the keys and still get the same correct answer. For example:

```
SELECT COURSE, COUNT(TEACHER_KEY) FROM FACT_TABLE, COURSE_DIMENSION, ETC.
WHERE ... GROUP BY COURSE
```

would give the same answer because you are counting the number of keys that fly by the query, not their distinct values. Although this doesn't faze a SQL expert, it does make the SQL look odd. For this reason, data designers will often add a dummy "Attendance" field at the end of the fact table in Figure 8-5. The attendance field always contains the value 1. This doesn't add any information to the database, but it makes the SQL much more readable. Of course, select count (*) also works, but most query tools don't automatically produce the select count (*) alternative. The attendance field gives users a convenient and understandable place to make the query.

Now your first question reads:

```
SELECT COURSE, SUM(ATTENDANCE) FROM FACT_TABLE, COURSE_DIMENSION, ETC.
WHERE ... GROUP BY COURSE
```

You can think of these kinds of event tables as recording the collision of keys at a point in space and time. Your table simply records the collisions that occur. Automobile insurance companies often literally record collisions this way. In this case, the dimensions of the factless fact table could be:

Date of Collision
Insured Party
Insured Auto
Claimant
Claimant Auto
Witness
Claim Type

A second kind of factless fact table is called a coverage table. A typical coverage table is shown in Figure 8-6. Coverage tables are frequently needed when a primary fact table in a dimensional data warehouse is sparse. Figure 8-6 also shows a simple sales fact table that records the sales of products in stores on particular days under each promotion condition. The sales fact table does answer many interesting questions but cannot answer questions about things that didn't happen. For instance, it cannot answer the question, "Which products were on promotion that didn't sell?" because it contains only the records of products that did sell. The coverage table comes to the rescue. A record is placed in the coverage table for each product in each store that is on promotion in each time period. Notice that you need the full generality of a fact table to record which products are on promotion. In general, which products are on promotion varies by all of the dimensions of product, store, promotion, and time. This complex many-to-many relationship must be expressed as a fact table. Every many-to-many relationship is a fact table, by definition.

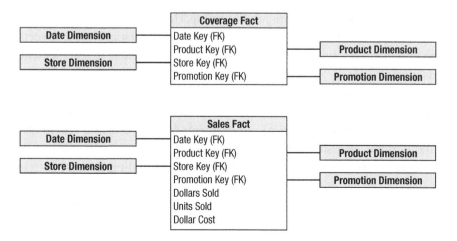

Figure 8-6: Factless coverage fact table for promotion events.

Perhaps some of you would suggest just filling out the original fact table with records representing zero sales for all possible products. This is logically valid, but it would expand the fact table enormously. In a typical grocery store, only about 10 percent of the products sell on any given day. Including all of the zero sales could increase the size of the database by a factor of ten. Remember, too, that you would have to carry all of the additive facts as zeros. Because many big grocery store sales fact tables approach a billion records, this would be a killer. Besides, there is something obscene about spending large amounts of money on disk drives to store zeros.

The coverage factless fact table can be made much smaller than the equivalent set of zeros described in the previous paragraph. The coverage table must only contain the items on promotion; the items not on promotion that also did not sell can be left out. Also, it is likely for administrative reasons that the assignment of products to promotions takes place periodically, rather than every day. Often a store manager will set up promotions in a store once each week. Thus we don't need a record for every product every day. One record per product per promotion per store each week will do. Finally, the factless format keeps us from storing explicit zeros for the facts as well.

Answering the question, "Which products were on promotion that did not sell?" requires a two-step application. First, query the coverage table for the list of products on promotion on that day in that store. Second, query the sales table for the list of products that did sell. The desired answer is the set difference between these two lists of products.

Coverage tables are also useful for recording the assignment of sales teams to customers in businesses in which the sales teams make occasional very large sales. In such a business, the sales fact table is too sparse to provide a good place to record which sales teams were associated with which customers. The sales team coverage table provides a complete map of the assignment of sales teams to customers, even if some of the combinations never result in a sale.

8.14 Factless Fact Tables? Sounds Like Jumbo Shrimp?

Bob Becker and Bill Schmarzo, Design Tip #50, *Oct 16, 2003*

Factless fact tables appear to be an oxymoron, similar to jumbo shrimp. How can you have a fact table that doesn't have any facts? A factless fact table captures the many-to-many relationships between dimensions, but contains no numeric facts. In this article, we use a factless fact table to complement our slowly changing dimension strategies.

Imagine we are working on a design for a large business-to-consumer company, such as an airline, insurance, credit card, banking, communications, or web retailer. The company does business with tens of millions of customers. In addition to the typical requirements for a transaction schema to track consumer behavior and periodic snapshot schema to trend our consumer relationships over time, our business users need the ability to see a customer's exact profile (including dozens of attributes) at any point in time.

Ralph discusses a similar situation in article 8.27, *When a Fact Table Can Be Used as a Dimension Table*. He outlines a technique where the dimension itself captures profile change events as a slowly changing dimension type 2, rather than creating a fact table to capture the profile transactions.

However, we are not likely to use that technique in the current scenario given the huge data volumes (millions of customer rows) and potentially volatile changes (dozens of attributes).

Let's assume we design a base customer dimension (with minimal type 2 attributes), along with four "mini" dimensions to track changes to customer credit attributes, customer preferences, market segmentation/propensities, and customer geography. The five foreign keys are included in the transaction grained fact table, as well as the monthly snapshot. These foreign keys represent the customer's "state" when the fact row is loaded. So far so good, but we still need to support customer profiling at any point in time. We consider using another periodic snapshot fact table, loaded daily for every customer to capture the point-in-time relationship of the customer dimension and associated mini dimensions. This translates into loading tens of millions of snapshots nightly with several years of history. We quickly do the math and decide to evaluate other alternatives.

About now you're thinking, "That's great, but what about the jumbo shrimp?" We can use a factless fact table to capture the relationship between the customer dimension and mini dimensions over time. We load a fact row in the factless fact table whenever there is a type 2 change to the base customer dimension or a change in the relationship between the base dimension and mini dimensions. The factless fact table contains foreign keys for the base customer dimension and each of the four mini dimensions when the row is loaded. We then embellish this design with two dates, row effective and row expiration, to locate a customer's profile at any point in time. We might also add a simple dimension to flag the current customer profile, in addition to a change reason dimension to indicate what caused a new row to be loaded into the factless fact table.

8.15 What Didn't Happen

Ralph Kimball, Intelligent Enterprise, *Feb 1999*

Our data warehouses are filled with data telling us what happened in our businesses. Frequently the lowest level in each of our business process dimensional models is the most atomic data we can gather from our production systems. Each button click, transaction, and product sale is a record. When an event takes place, we create a fact record.

We are very good at formulating queries to find out what did happen. These are the directed queries that constitute nearly all our data warehouse use. But how do we ask our data warehouses what *didn't* happen?

How do we ask our data warehouse what didn't sell today or which combinations of products didn't sell together in the market basket? How do we ask for mixtures of events that did happen together with events that didn't happen, such as what was on promotion that didn't sell or which products had options 1, 5, and 9 but not 2, 7, or 29?

Modeling the nonexistence of events is interesting because, in some cases, we can explicitly make records for the nonevents. But in many cases, it's ridiculous to make records for things that didn't happen. If we are tracking frequent flyer flights on an airline, we certainly don't build records for each of the flights not taken by each frequent flyer.

Let's examine the main techniques for modeling what didn't happen.

Coverage Tables

A classic sales fact table in a retail environment might have foreign keys representing the calendar day, product, store, and promotion. We assume that the grain of the sales fact table is daily sales totals for each product in each store. We place a record in this fact table at the end of each day only if a particular product has been sold. We almost never put records in the fact table for zero sales of a product on a day because, in most retail settings, only a small fraction of the total product portfolio sells in each store each day.

When we ask, "What products didn't sell?" we have to decide whether we are asking, "What products were in the store that didn't sell?" or, "What products should have been in the store but are out of stock?" To answer either of these questions, we need an accurate inventory measure for each product in each store on that day.

We may not have a physical inventory table for each product in each store on each day. Perhaps we must calculate daily inventory levels by starting with a known physical inventory at the start of the month and then working forward by taking into account sales, shrinkage, and deliveries. In any case, we end up with either a real or virtual inventory fact table with the dimensions of calendar day, product, and store.

To answer the question "What products were in the store but didn't sell?" we must perform a set difference between this inventory table and the sales table. This takes the form:

```
{select all products with nonzero inventory today}
MINUS
{select any products that sold today}.
```

The MINUS operation in relational systems is simply the set difference operation. In this applica-tion, the inventory table plays the role of a *coverage* table because it's effectively a foundation for all events that could take place on that inventory. In this case, we have subtracted the sales events to answer the question of what products didn't sell.

Explicit Records for Non-Behavior

The coverage table we built in the previous example was separate from the main fact tables that recorded actual measurement events. But in some cases, it is appropriate to record nonevents in the same table as event measurements. This is a matter of designer discretion, but usually this approach is appropriate if the final fact table does not grow alarmingly and if the nonevents have the same dimensionality as the events. A good example is student attendance.

If we are tracking student attendance in each course each day, then the dimensions of each event record in the attendance fact table might be calendar day, student, professor, course, and location. However, if we make a fact called "attendance," the value of which is either one or zero, then we can easily ask which students didn't attend the class. This approach is appropriate in this case because the extra records showing what didn't happen are (you hope) a small fraction of the total.

Now, our query asking which students didn't attend the class is a simple single query:

```
{select student_name where Attendance = 0}.
```

Searching for Nonexistent Facts with NOT EXISTS

Both of the previous approaches required a degree of preplanning. Either we built a coverage table describing inventory levels or promotion coverage, or we explicitly put zeros into an attendance fact. But usually, we can't anticipate the "what didn't happen" query.

The NOT EXISTS construct in SQL is a powerful, general-purpose mechanism for identifying records that don't exist in a database. However, it's still not a panacea. Even though we can ask what doesn't exist, paradoxically we must ask *very specifically* what doesn't exist by framing the NOT EXISTS within a larger query. We have no good way to ask what things unknown to us don't exist. To see this general statement illustrated, study the following example.

To generate a single query using NOT EXISTS to determine what products were on promotion in the San Antonio outlet on January 15, 2015, that didn't sell, you would have to issue SQL such as:

```
SELECT P1.PRODUCT_DESCRIPTION
FROM SALES_FACT F1, PRODUCT P1, STORE S1, CALENDAR_DATE D1, PROMOTION R1
WHERE F1.PROD_KEY = P1.PROD_KEY
AND F1.STORE_KEY = S1.STORE_KEY
AND F1.DATE_KEY = D1.DATE_KEY
AND F1.PROMO_KEY = R1.PROMO_KEY
AND S1.STORE_LOCATION = 'San Antonio Outlet'
AND D1.MONTH = 'January, 2015'
AND NOT EXISTS
(SELECT R2.PROMO_KEY
FROM SALES_FACT F2, PROMOTION R2, CALENDAR_DATE D2
WHERE F2.PROMO_KEY = P2.PROMO_KEY
AND F2.PROD_KEY = F1.PROD_KEY
AND F2.STORE_KEY = F1.STORE_KEY
AND F2.DATE_KEY = F1.DATE_KEY
AND F2.DATE_KEY = D2.DATE_KEY
AND R2.PROMOTION_TYPE = 'Active Promotion'
AND D2.FULL_DATE = 'January 15, 2015')
```

The first six lines in the WHERE clause define the products that were on sale in the San Antonio outlet in January 2015. The last nine lines specifying the query inside the NOT EXISTS construct asks for each of those products sold on promotion on January 15, 2015. The ones that don't exist (that is, that were sold sometime in January but not sold on promotion on January 15) are returned by the overall query. This is a SQL correlated subquery. Although this approach avoids the necessity for an inventory or promotions coverage table, it may still miss some products that didn't sell at all in January, and the query probably runs slowly because of its complexity.

Using NOT EXISTS to Find Non Attributes

A final challenging variation of the "what didn't happen" problem is finding a set of products that have some options but don't have other options, where each product's option list is open ended. Suppose we sell cars, each of which has many options drawn from a list of 100 possibilities. How do we ask for all the cars with options 1, 11, and 21 but not options 2, 12, 22, or 32?

We start by building a fact table with one record for each option on each car. The dimensions of this fact table are Car and Option. For simplicity, we will assume a CAR_KEY identifies a unique car, and an OPTION_KEY is the option number. Using NOT EXISTS, we can ask the question posed in the previous paragraph:

```
SELECT F1.CAR_KEY
FROM FACT F1
WHERE
(SELECT COUNT(F2.CAR_KEY)
FROM FACT F2
WHERE F2.CAR_KEY = F1.CAR_KEY
AND F2.OPTION_KEY IN (1, 11, 21))
= 3
AND NOT EXISTS
(SELECT *
FROM FACT F3
WHERE F3.CAR_KEY = F1.CAR_KEY
AND F3.OPTION_KEY IN (2, 12, 22, 32))
```

In this case, we can use the MINUS operation to write the equivalent logic:

```
{select cars with all the options 1, 11, and 21}
  as in the first clause of the preceding query...
MINUS
{select cars with any of the options 2, 12, 22, or 32}.
```

Notice that asking for cars with all the options 1, 11, and 21 is a little tricky. You cannot just ask for the cars with options 1, 11, or 21 because that won't get the cars with all the options simultaneously.

8.16 Factless Fact Tables for Simplification

Bob Becker, Design Tip #133, Apr 5, 2011

We talked about factless fact tables in article 8.14, *Factless Fact Tables? Sounds Like Jumbo Shrimp?*. You may recall that a factless fact table is "a fact table that has no facts but captures the many-to-many relationship between dimension keys."

We've previously discussed factless fact tables to represent events or coverage information. An event-based factless fact table is student attendance information; the grain of the fact table is one row per student each day. A typical coverage factless fact table in retail includes one row for every item being promoted during the time it is promoted; it is used to help answer the "what didn't happen?" question identifying items being promoted but not sold.

Factless fact tables can simplify the overall design. Think of a property and casualty insurance company providing automobile coverages. It's reasonable to create a transaction fact table that captures the written premiums resulting from a new sale or change to an existing policy. Likewise, it makes perfect sense to implement a monthly snapshot fact table to capture the earned premium associated with every policy by customer, by named insured, by household, by vehicle, by driver, and so on.

But real-life complications jump up and the design seems to get horribly complex in an effort to capture the relationships between dimensions and the changes in these relationships over time. For example, a single driver can relate to multiple vehicles, policies, and households. Of course, in a similar manner there can be multiple drivers on a single vehicle, single policy, or single household.

This complexity can cause the design team significant headaches. The next thing they know the design is littered with bridge tables. Even then, many of the design challenges are not well suited for a bridge table solution as they require three, four, or more dimensions. In the end, the designs get too complex, too hard to understand, and provide poor query performance.

The key to avoiding this situation is recognizing there are multiple business processes at play and designing a solution to include additional fact tables. The problem is many design teams fail to understand there are multiple business processes involved as they cannot visualize the "facts" that would result, forgetting about the factless fact table. Tracking drivers associated to vehicles is not the same business process as recognizing the earned premium related to a policy each month. Recognizing multiple business processes will result in a simplified design for the core transaction and snapshot fact tables surrounded by several factless fact tables that help track the relationship between other dimension tables.

To finish our example, a property and casualty design might include factless fact tables to support:

- **Household involved parties.** One row per household and insured party with begin and end effective dates
- **Policy involved parties.** One row per policy, household, insured item, and insured party with begin and end effective dates
- **Vehicle involved parties.** One row per policy, driver, and vehicle with begin and end effective dates

On the claims side of the business, complex claims may result in several to dozens of claim handlers involved in the resolution of a claim. Another factless fact table can capture the relationship of each claim handler, their role, the coverage, and other details of the claim.

Other industry examples that can benefit from utilizing this design pattern include financial services where it is common to have multiple accounts and multiple individuals moving in and out of households over time. Similarly in long running, complex sales situations, a factless fact table may be helpful to identify all the sales support resources involved with various clients and products.

It's important to remember that the use of factless fact tables does not make the complexity of our examples go away. The complexity is real! But the factless fact tables allow us to package the complexity in clean, understandable ways. BI users will find these factless fact tables natural and intuitive.

Parent-Child Fact Tables

The two articles in this section discuss a pattern commonly encountered in operational systems: a transaction header parent record with multiple line item children records.

8.17 Managing Your Parents

Ralph Kimball, Intelligent Enterprise, Sep 18, 2001

The parent-child data relationship is one of the fundamental structures in the business world. An invoice (the parent), for instance, includes many line items (the children). Other examples include orders, bills of lading, insurance claims, and retail sales tickets. Basically, any business document with an embedded repeating group qualifies as a parent-child application, especially when the embedded line items contain interesting numerical measurements such as dollars or physical units. Parent-child applications are extremely important to data warehousing because most of the basic control documents that transfer money and goods (or services) from place to place take the parent-child form.

But a parent-child source of data presents a classic design dilemma. Some of the data is available at only the parent level and some at only the child level. Do you need two fact tables in your dimensional model, or can you do with just one? And what do you do with the data that is available at only the parent level when you want to drill down to the child level?

Imagine a typical product sales invoice. Each line item on the invoice represents a different product sold to the customer.

The parent-level data includes:

- **Four standard dimensions:** date of overall invoice, sales agent, customer, and payment terms
- **One degenerate dimension:** invoice number (more on this later)
- **Five additive facts:** total extended net price from the line items, total invoice promotional discount, total freight charges, total tax, and grand total

The child-level data includes:

- **Two dimensions:** product and promotion
- **Four additive facts:** number of units, extended gross price (units x price), extended net price [units x (unit price – promotional discount)], and unit price of product and promotional discount for this specific product (more on this later)
- **Context from the overall invoice consisting of the five parent dimensions**

With the dimensions and facts spelled out, you might think you are done. You have two nice fact tables. The parent invoice fact table has five dimensions and five facts, and the child line item fact table has seven dimensions and three facts.

But this design is a failure. You can't roll up your business by product! If you constrain by a specific product, you don't know what to do with invoice-level discounts, freight charges, and tax. All of the business's higher level rollups are forced to omit the product dimension.

In most businesses, this omission is unacceptable. There is only one way to fix this problem. You have to take the invoice-level data and allocate down to the line item level. Yes, this allocation is somewhat controversial and yes, you must force some business decisions in the process. But the alternative is not being able to analyze your business in terms of your products.

Replace the two fact tables with a single fact table whose grain is the invoice line item. In other words, you will consistently drop to the most atomic child level when you create a parent-child dimensional design.

When you design a fact table around a specific type of measurement, you "decorate" the measurement with everything you know to be true at that time. The measurements in this case are found in the context of individual line items. Everything at the line item and invoice levels is true at the time of the measurement. So your single line item grain fact table has the following dimensions:

- Invoice date
- Sales agent
- Customer
- Payment terms
- Product
- Promotion

What do you do with the invoice number? It is certainly single valued, even at the line item level, but you have already "exposed" everything you know about the invoice in your first six dimensions. You should keep the invoice number in the design. But you don't need to make a dimension out of it because that dimension would turn out to be empty. We call this characteristic result a *degenerate dimension*.

Now your facts for this child fact table include:

- Number of units of product (additive fact)
- Gross extended product price (additive fact)
- Net extended product price (additive fact)
- *Allocated* promotional discounts (additive fact)
- *Allocated* freight charges (additive fact)
- *Allocated* tax (additive fact)

You don't include the unit prices or unit discounts as physical facts because you can always divide the extended amounts by the number of units in your reporting application to get these non-additive quantities.

You can instantly recover the exact invoice-level amounts by adding up all the line items under a specific invoice number. You don't need the separate invoice parent fact table because now it is only a simple aggregation of the more granular line item child fact table. You have in no way compromised the invoice totals by performing the allocations down to the line item.

And, best of all, you can now smoothly roll up your business to the highest levels of geography, time, and products, including the allocated amounts, to get a complete picture of your revenue.

Conflicting Allocation Theories

Sometimes an organization will agree that allocating invoice-level costs is necessary, but still can't agree on which allocation method to use. A few years ago I designed a data warehouse for a large fulfillment house that shipped all sorts of household items. A single shipment could contain an inexpensive pillow and a heavy, expensive small object like a silver candleholder. The disagreement was whether to allocate the shipment cost by volume, weight, or value.

Allocating by volume assigned most of the shipment cost to the pillow, but allocating by either weight or value assigned most of the cost to the candleholder. This became a political argument, of course, because the product divisions looked more profitable if they could avoid responsibility for the shipment charges!

Because, as a data warehouse architect, I couldn't resolve this political conflict, I proposed that we include three different shipment costs at the line item level:

- Volume-allocated shipment cost
- Weight-allocated shipment cost
- Value-allocated shipment cost

This solution lets anyone roll up the business using any one of the three allocation methods. When there is no constraint or grouping by product line, the results are the same. But any analysis by product reflects the allocation method chosen.

Tough Allocation Environments

Product shipment invoices are good candidates for this allocation scheme. Many of the invoice-level costs and other costs are "activity based." Although you have to make some compromises and estimates when deciding the allocations, everyone usually agrees that the allocations should be done. In this kind of business, *activity based costing* (ABC) is a methodology often used as a foundation for exactly the kind of analysis this management of parents makes possible.

But in other businesses, the allocation process is excruciating and maybe impossible. Typically, a business with large infrastructure costs that are not directly related to the products or services sold has trouble agreeing on allocations and ABC. For example, a large telecommunications company with billions of dollars of infrastructure costs in its equipment, employees, and real estate has great difficulty allocating these costs down to individual phone calls. For the same reason, a large bank has trouble allocating its infrastructure costs down to individual checking accounts. If you are told to allocate costs in one of these environments in order to calculate "product profitability," I suggest you ask the finance department to actually perform the allocations, which you will be glad to store in your data warehouse. Stay off the hot seat!

But for most businesses, the technique of descending to the line item level and building a single granular fact table is at the heart of data warehouse modeling. It is our way of making good on the promise that we can "slice and dice the enterprise data every which way."

8.18 Patterns to Avoid When Modeling Header/Line Item Transactions

Margy Ross, Design Tip #95, *Oct 2, 2007*

Many transaction processing systems consist of a transaction header "parent" with multiple line item "children." Regardless of your industry, you can probably identify source systems in your organization with this basic structure. In this article, we describe two common, albeit flawed, approaches for modeling header/line item information, using invoicing data as a case study. Sometimes visualizing flawed designs can help you more easily identify similar problems with your own schemas.

Bad Idea #1: Retain the Header as a Dimension

In this scenario, illustrated in Figure 8-7, the transaction header file is virtually replicated in the dimensional model as a dimension. The transaction header dimension contains all the data from its operational equivalent. The natural key for this dimension is the transaction number itself. The grain of the fact table is one row per transaction line item, but there's not much dimensionality associated with it because most descriptive context is embedded in the transaction header dimension.

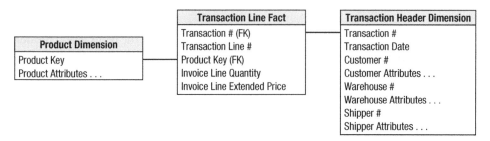

Figure 8-7: Bad idea #1—The transaction header is a dimension table.

Although this design accurately represents the parent-child relationship, there are obvious flaws. The transaction header dimension is likely very large, especially relative to the fact table itself. If there are typically five line items per transaction, then the dimension is 20 percent as large as the fact table. Usually there are orders of magnitude differences between the size of a fact table and its associated dimensions. Also, dimensions don't normally grow at nearly the same rate as the fact table. With this design, you'd add one row to the dimension table and an average of five rows to the fact table for every new transaction. Any analysis of the transaction's interesting characteristics, such as the customer, warehouse, or shipper involved, would need to traverse this large dimension table.

Bad Idea #2: Line Items Don't Inherit Header Dimensionality

In this example, shown in Figure 8-8, the transaction header is no longer treated as a monolithic dimension but as a fact table instead. The header's associated descriptive information is grouped into dimensions surrounding the header fact. The line item fact table (identical in structure and granularity as the first diagram) joins to the header fact based on the transaction number.

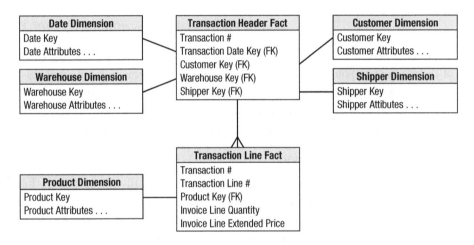

Figure 8-8: Bad idea #2—None of the header dimensionality is directly joined to the line items.

Once again, this design accurately represents the parent-child relationship of the transaction header and line items, but there are still flaws. Every time the user wants to slice and dice the line facts by any of the header attributes, he'll need to join a large header fact table to an even larger line fact table.

Recommended Structure for Header/Line Item Transactions

The second scenario more closely resembles a proper dimensional model with separate dimensions uniquely describing the core descriptive elements of the business, but it's not quite there yet. Rather than holding onto the operational notion of a transaction header "object," we recommend that you bring all the dimensionality of the header down to the line items, as shown in Figure 8-9.

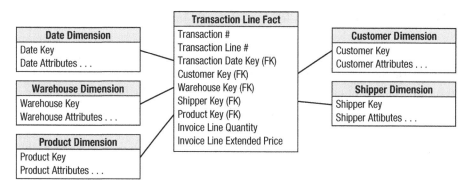

Figure 8-9: Recommended structure for modeling header/line item transactions.

Once again, this model represents the data relationships from the source system's transaction header/line constructs. But we've abandoned the operational mentality surrounding a header file. The header's natural key, the transaction number, is still present in our design, but it's treated as a degenerate dimension.

Fact Table Keys and Degenerate Dimensions

This section explores the scenarios where a surrogate key on a fact table would be useful. The appropriate handling of degenerate dimensions is also discussed.

8.19 Fact Table Surrogate Keys

Bob Becker, Design Tip #81, Jul 6, 2006

Meaningless integer keys, otherwise known as surrogate keys, are commonly used as primary keys for dimension tables in data warehouse designs. But should a unique surrogate key be assigned for every row in a fact table? For the logical design of a fact table, the answer is no; however, we find a fact table surrogate key may be helpful at the physical level. We only recommend creating surrogate keys for fact tables under special circumstances, such as those described in this article.

As a quick reminder, surrogate keys are meaningless keys, typically defined as an integer data type, and sequentially assigned by the data warehouse team to serve as the primary keys of the dimension tables. Surrogate keys provide a number of important benefits for dimensions including avoiding reliance on awkward "smart" keys made up of codes from the dimension's source, protecting the data warehouse from changes in the source systems, enabling integration of data from disparate source systems, support for type 2 slowly changing dimensions attributes, space savings in the fact tables when the dimension keys are embedded as foreign keys, and improved indexing and query performance.

But in a fact table, the primary key is almost always defined as a subset of the foreign keys supplied by the dimensions. In most environments this composite key will suffice as the primary key to the fact table; there is typically no advantage of assigning a surrogate key to the fact rows at a logical level because we have already defined what makes a fact table row unique. And, by its nature, the surrogate key would be worthless for querying.

However, there are a few circumstances when assigning a surrogate key to the rows in a fact table is beneficial:

1. Sometimes the business rules of the organization legitimately allow multiple identical rows to exist for a fact table. Normally as a designer, you try to avoid this by searching the source system for some kind of transaction time stamp to make the rows unique. But occasionally you are forced to accept this undesirable input. In these situations it will be necessary to create a surrogate key for the fact table to allow the identical rows to be loaded.

2. Certain ETL techniques for updating fact rows are only feasible if a surrogate key is assigned to the fact rows. Specifically, one technique for loading updates to fact rows is to insert the rows to be updated as new rows, and then delete the original rows as a second step in a single transaction. The advantages of this technique from an ETL perspective are improved load performance, recovery capability, and audit capabilities. The surrogate key for the fact table rows is required because multiple identical primary keys will often exist for the old and new versions of the updated fact rows between the time of the insert of the updated row and the delete of the old row.

3. A similar ETL requirement is to determine exactly where a load job was suspended, either to resume loading or back out the job entirely. A sequentially assigned surrogate key makes this task straightforward.

Remember, surrogate keys for dimension tables are a great idea. Surrogate keys for fact tables are not logically required but can be very helpful, especially in the back room ETL processing.

8.20 Reader Suggestions on Fact Table Surrogate Keys

Ralph Kimball and Bob Becker, Design Tip #84, *Oct 3, 2006*

A number of readers wrote to us regarding article 8.19, *Fact Table Surrogate Keys*, suggesting additional clever ways in which fact table surrogate keys can be exploited. The reader should note that these concepts primarily provide for behind-the-scenes improvements in query performance or ETL support.

Reader Larry pointed out that his experience in Oracle was that a fact table surrogate key can make the database optimizer happier in a situation where declaring the key (the combination of fields that guarantee a row is unique) of the fact table otherwise would require enumerating a large number of foreign keys to dimensions. Some optimizers complain when a large number of B-Tree indexes are defined. With a surrogate key, a single B-Tree index could be placed on that field, and separate bitmap indexes placed on all the dimension foreign keys.

Another reader, Eric, similarly reports that in Microsoft SQL Server "Another reason to use a surrogate key with a clustered index on a fact table is to make the primary key of each fact table row smaller, so that the nonclustered indexes defined on the fact table (which contain these primary key values as row identifiers) will be smaller."

Larry also reports, "If I have a user who complains about a report or query being wrong, I can often simply add in the surrogate key column to the report or query, forcing the results to show EVERY row that contributes to it. This has proven useful for debugging." In a similar vein, he also uses the surrogate key as an efficient and precise way to identify a specific fact record that he may wish to point out to the ETL development team as an example of a problem.

And finally Larry reports that "In healthcare (payers), it seems that there is a lot of late-arriving dimension data, or changes to dimension data. This always seems to happen on a type 2 dimension. Often this has caused me to need to update the dimension rows, creating new rows for a prior period forward. A simple query of the fact table can return a list of the surrogate keys for affected rows. Then this can be used to limit the retroactive update to fact rows to only those that need to be touched. I have seen this technique improve this kind of update substantially."

Reader Norman offers an interesting query application depending on fact table surrogate keys. He writes "I wanted to offer up an additional reason for having surrogate keys in the fact tables. This is in cases where it is necessary to join two fact records together in a single query for the purpose of performing calculations across related rows. The preference would be to do these calculations in the ETL and then store them in the fact records, but I have had some requirements where the possible number of stored calculations could have been immense (and thus would have greatly increased the size of the fact tables) and/or the calculations were important yet infrequently performed by the query application, thus needing to be supported with relatively high query speeds, but not at the expense of calculating and storing the calculations. Storing "next record" surrogate keys in the fact table supports these types of requirements."

Following Norman's interesting insight, we would assume a fact table row contains a field called NextSurrogateKey, which contains the surrogate key of the desired companion record. Constraining on this value immensely simplifies the SQL, which otherwise would have to repeat all the dimension constraints of the first record. You would just have an embedded SELECT statement, which you would use in a computation as if it were a variable, like:

```
(SELECT additional_fact from fact table b
  where b.surrogatekey = NextSurrogateKey).
```

And finally reader Dev writes about a similar applications technique where instead of using a fact table surrogate key to link to an adjacent record in the same fact table, he embeds the surrogate key of a related record that resides in another fact table. His example linked a monthly-grained fact table that records health care plan measures to a second fact table that records client group benchmarks.

Like Norman's example, embedding the surrogate key of the second fact table in the first allowed the applications to be far simpler. We recommend that, like Norman's example, the link from one fact table to another be handled with an explicit SELECT clause rather than a direct join between fact tables. All too often, we have seen correct but weird results from SQL when two fact tables are joined directly because of tricky differences in cardinality between the two tables. The explicit SELECT statement should eliminate this issue.

Clearly, although these last two examples enable joins between fact table rows, we are NOT advocating creating surrogate keys for your fact tables to enable fact table to fact table joins. In most circumstances, delivering results from multiple fact tables should use drill-across techniques described in article 13.21, *Simple Drill Across in SQL*. Keep in mind that in this article we are discussing advanced design concepts to support unique business requirements. These concepts need to be carefully considered and tested before being implemented in your environment.

8.21 Another Look at Degenerate Dimensions

Bob Becker, Design Tip #46, Jun 4, 2003

Degenerate dimensions cause confusion because they don't look or feel like normal dimensions. It's helpful to remember that according to Webster, "degenerate" refers to something that's 1) declined from the standard norm, or 2) is mathematically simpler.

A degenerate dimension (DD) acts as a dimension key in the fact table; however, it does not join to a corresponding dimension table because all its interesting attributes have already been placed in other analytic dimensions. Sometimes people want to refer to degenerate dimensions as textual facts; however, they're not facts because the fact table's primary key often consists of the DD combined with one or more additional dimension foreign keys.

Degenerate dimensions commonly occur when the fact table's grain is a single transaction (or transaction line). Transaction control header numbers assigned by the operational business process are typically handled as degenerate dimensions, such as order, ticket, credit card transaction, or check numbers.

Even though there is no corresponding dimension table of attributes, degenerate dimensions can be quite useful for grouping together related fact table rows. For example, retail point-of-sale transaction numbers tie all the individual items purchased together into a single market basket. In health care, degenerate dimensions can group the claims items related to a single hospital stay or episode of care.

We sometimes encounter more than one DD in a fact table. For example, an insurance claim line fact table typically includes both claim and policy numbers as degenerate dimensions. A manufacturer could include degenerate dimensions for the quote, order, and bill of lading numbers in the shipments fact table, as long as these numbers take on single values in the target fact table.

Degenerate dimensions also serve as a helpful tie back to the operational world. This can be especially useful during ETL development to align fact table rows to the operational system for quality assurance and integrity checking.

We typically don't implement a surrogate key for a DD. Usually the values for the degenerate dimension are unique and reasonably sized; they don't warrant the assignment of a surrogate key. However, if the operational identifier is an unwieldy alphanumeric value, a surrogate key might conserve significant space, especially if the fact table has a large number of rows. Likewise, a surrogate key is necessary if the operational ID is not unique over time or facilities. Of course, if you join this surrogate key to a dimension table, then the dimension is no longer degenerate.

During design reviews, we sometimes find a dimension table growing proportionally with the fact table. As rows are inserted into the fact table, new rows are also inserted into a related dimension table, often at the same rate as rows were added to the fact table. This situation should send a red flag waving. Usually when a dimension table is growing at roughly the same rate as the fact table, a degenerate dimension was missed in the design.

8.22 Creating a Reference Dimension for Infrequently Accessed Degenerates

Bob Becker, Design Tip #86, Dec 15, 2006

This article introduces a concept called the *reference dimension* where we stash rarely used fact table elements, such as degenerate dimension reference numbers, in a separate table that's linked to the fact table either through a regular dimension surrogate key or the fact table's surrogate key. The recommendations in this article apply to "row-major" databases where each fact table record is stored as a contiguous set of bytes on the storage device; it does not apply to "columnar databases" where each column in the schema is stored separately on the storage device.

Degenerate dimensions often play an important role in supporting reporting and analytic requirements. However, some degenerate dimensions are not analytically valuable; they are included in the schema for reference purposes only. They help provide occasional ties back to the operational source systems, support audit, compliance, or legal requirements, or are included simply because "we might need it someday." The result can be a fact table that contains a large number of degenerate dimensions with perhaps only two or three that are truly important and interesting. In health care, for example, the degenerate dimensions might reference the provider network contract number, fee schedule number, and claim microfiche number. Because fact tables are the largest tables in our schema, often containing hundreds of millions or billions of rows, we'd like to keep them as tight as possible. It certainly seems wasteful to populate the fact table with ten or more large alphanumeric degenerate dimensions, especially if they are not typically used for reporting or analytics. This is where the reference dimension can be helpful.

The concept of the reference dimension is to break the fact table apart, moving the seldom used degenerate dimension values to a separate reference dimension table with the fact table or reference dimension surrogate key preserving the relationship between the tables. The analytically valuable degenerate dimensions should not be moved to the reference dimension; they need to be retained in the fact table where they can be used most effectively. It is very important to move only the degenerate dimensions that are not used to support analytic or reporting requirements. Though it is generally not considered good dimensional modeling practice to create a dimension with a potential one-to-one relationship with the fact table, in this situation we will accept it as a reasonable trade-off.

The important advantage we gain is dramatically reducing the length of the fact table row resulting in a tighter design that will perform better. This design trade-off works because the reference dimension should very seldom actually join back to the fact table. If the design assumptions were correct and the degenerate dimensions that moved to the reference dimension are not required to support reporting and analytics, most users will never use the reference dimension. There should be just a few occasional investigatory requirements that need to access this information.

In the rare occasion when some component of the reference table is required, it will be necessary to join it to the fact table, which may be an expensive and slow-running query. User expectations when using the reference dimension need to be carefully managed. Frequent complaints about the performance of the reference dimension likely means some date element needs to migrate back to the fact table because it's important for supporting reporting or analytic needs.

Caution: This article should not to be construed as granting design teams permission to build large dimensions with potentially one-to-one relationships with the fact table. Rather, the reference dimension is a specific design response to a particular situation that a design team may confront. We would not expect to see reference dimensions in most dimensional designs. They should be the rare exception rather than the rule.

Miscellaneous Fact Table Design Patterns

This final section is a catchall for additional fact table nuances, including techniques for reducing the width of a fact table, handling textual, null, and sparsely populated facts, and adapting the accumulating snapshot fact table to complex workflows.

8.23 Put Your Fact Tables on a Diet

Ralph Kimball, Design Tip #30, Nov 3, 2001

In the middle of the 1990s, before the internet, it appeared that the data explosion might finally abate. At that time we were learning how to capture every telephone call, every item sold at a cash register, every stock transaction on Wall Street, and every policy transaction in huge insurance companies. It's true that we often didn't store a very long time series of some of these data sources in our data warehouses, but there was a feeling that maybe we had reached a kind of physical limit to the granularity of the data. Maybe we had at last encountered the true "atoms" of data.

Well, that view was obviously wrong. We now know that there is no limit to the amount of data we can collect. Every measurement can be replaced by a whole series of more granular sub-measurements. In web logs, we see every gesture made by a visitor BEFORE they check out and purchase a product. We have now replaced the single product purchase record with a dozen or a hundred behavior tracking records. The worst thing is that our marketing people love these behavior tracking records, and want to do all sorts of analysis on them. Just wait until GPS data capture systems get embedded in our cars, credit cards, and telephones. Every human being could eventually generate one or more records every second, 24 hours per day!

Although we cannot stop this avalanche of data, we have to try to control it, or we will spend too much money on disk storage. Many of our current data sizing plans are based on quick estimates. In many cases, these estimates seriously overstate our storage needs. The result may be either a decision to buy far too much storage, or to cancel our plans for analyzing available data. In a dimensional modeling world, it is easy to see that the culprit is always the fact table. The high frequency, repeated measurements in our businesses are stored in the fact table. The fact table is surrounded by geometrically smaller dimension tables. Even a huge customer dimension table with millions of records will be much smaller than the biggest fact table.

By paying fanatic attention to the design of your fact tables, you can often slim them down significantly. Here are the guidelines:

1. Replace all natural foreign keys with the smallest integer (surrogate) keys possible.
2. Replace all date/time stamps with integer surrogate keys.
3. Combine correlated dimensions into single dimensions where possible.
4. Group tiny low cardinality dimensions together, even if uncorrelated.
5. Take all text fields out of the fact table and make them dimensions, especially comment fields.
6. Replace all long integer and floating point facts with scaled integers, wherever possible.

As an example suppose we are a large telephone company processing 300 million calls per day. We could easily do a data-sizing plan for tracking all these calls over a 3-year period based on the following assumptions:

- Date/time = 8 byte date/time stamp
- Calling party phone number = 10-byte string
- Called party phone number = 15-byte string (to handle international numbers)
- Local provider entity = 10-byte string
- Long distance provider entity = 10-byte string
- Added value service provider entity = 10-byte string
- Dialing status = 5-byte string (100 possible values)

- Termination status = 5-byte string (100 possible values)
- Duration fact = 4-byte integer
- Rated charge fact = 8-byte float

Each call is an 85-byte record in this design. Storing three years of this raw data, with no indexes, would require 27.9 terabytes. Obviously, there is wasted fat in the preceding record. Let's really turn the screws on this one and see how well we can do. Using the preceding guidelines, we can code the same information as follows:

- Date = 2-byte tiny integer
- Time of day = 2-byte tiny integer
- Calling party phone number = 4-byte integer surrogate key
- Called party phone number = 4-byte integer surrogate key
- Local provider business entity = 2-byte tiny integer surrogate key
- Long distance provider entity = 2-byte tiny integer surrogate key
- Added value service provider = 2-byte tiny integer surrogate key
- Status = 2-byte tiny integer surrogate key (combination of dialing and termination status)
- Duration fact = 4-byte integer
- Rated charge fact = 4-byte scaled integer

We have made a few assumptions about the data types supported by our particular database. We have assumed that the 65,536 possible 2-byte tiny integer keys are enough to support each of the dimensions where listed.

With this design, the raw data space required by our fact table becomes 9.2 terabytes, a saving of 67 percent! Be a fanatic about designing your fact tables conservatively. Put them on a diet.

8.24 Keeping Text Out of the Fact Table

Bob Becker, Design Tip #55, *Jun 9, 2004*

This article was originally titled Exploring Text Facts.

In this article, we return to a fundamental concept that perplexes numerous dimensional modelers: text facts. Some of you may be rightfully saying that text facts are a dimensional modeling oxymoron. However, we frequently field questions from clients and students about indicator, type, or comment fields that seem to belong in the fact table, but the fields are not keys, measurements, or degenerate dimensions.

Generally, we recommend not modeling these so-called text facts in the fact table, but rather attempt to find an appropriate home for them in a dimension table. You don't want to clutter the fact table with several mid-sized (20- to 40-byte) descriptors. Alternatively, you shouldn't just store cryptic codes in the fact table (without dimension decodes), even though you are quite certain everyone knows the decodes already.

When confronted with seemingly text facts, the first question to ask is whether they belong in another dimension table. For example, customer type likely takes on a single value per customer and should be treated as a customer dimension attribute.

If they don't fit neatly into an existing core dimension, they should be treated as either separate dimensions or separate attributes in a junk dimension. It would be straightforward to build small dimension tables that assigned keys to all the payment or transaction types, and then reference those keys in the fact table. If you get too many of these small dimension tables, you should consider creating a junk dimension. There are several considerations when evaluating whether to maintain separate dimensions or to lump the indicators together in a junk dimension:

- **Number of existing dimension foreign keys in the fact table.** If you're nearing 20 foreign keys, you'll probably want to lump them together.
- **Number of potential junk "combination" rows, understanding that the theoretical combinations likely greatly exceed the actual encountered combinations.** Ideally you want to keep the size of the junk dimension to less than 100,000 rows.
- **Business relevance or understanding of the attribute combinations.** Do the attributes have so little to do with each other that users are confused by the forced association in a junk dimension?

Finally, what should you do when the supposed "fact" is a verbose, freeform text field that takes on unlimited values, such as a 240-byte comment field? Profiling the field, then parsing and codifying would make it most useful analytically, but that's almost always easier said than done.

It's been our experience that if the field is truly freeform, it is seldom accessed analytically. Usually these comment fields are only valuable to support a detailed investigation into suspicious transactions on an occasional basis. In this event, you'll want to put the text into a separate "comment" dimension rather than carrying that extra bulk on every fact record.

8.25 Dealing with Nulls in a Dimensional Model

Warren Thornthwaite, Design Tip #43, *Feb 6, 2003*

Most relational databases support the use of a null value to represent an absence of data. Nulls can confuse both data warehouse developers and users because the database treats nulls differently from blanks or zeros, even though they look like blanks or zeros. This article explores the three major areas where we find nulls in our source data and makes recommendations on how to handle each situation.

Nulls as Fact Table Foreign Keys

We encounter this potential situation in the source data for several reasons: Either the foreign key value is not known at the time of extract, is (correctly) not applicable to the source measurement, or is incorrectly missing from the source extract. Obviously, referential integrity is violated if we put a null in a fact table column declared as a foreign key to a dimension table, because in a relational database, null is not equal to itself.

In the first case, especially with an accumulating snapshot fact table, we sometimes find columns tracking events that have not yet occurred. For example, in an orders tracking accumulating snapshot, a business might receive an order on the 31st, but not ship until the next month. The fact table's ship date will not be known when the fact row is first inserted. In this case, ship date is a foreign key to the date dimension table, but will not join as users expect if we leave the value as null. That is, any fact reporting from the date table joined on ship date will exclude all orders with a null ship date. Most of our users get nervous when data disappears, so we recommend using a surrogate key that joins to a special record in the date dimension table with a description like "Data not yet available."

Similarly, there are cases when the foreign key is simply not applicable to the fact measurement, such as when promotion is a fact table foreign key, but not every fact row has a promotion associated with it. Again, we'd include a special record in the dimension table with a value such as "No promotion in effect."

In the case where the foreign key is missing from the source extract when it shouldn't be, we have a few options. We can assign a specific record such as "Missing key for source code #1234," or write the row out to a suspense file. In both cases, we will need to troubleshoot the offending row.

Nulls as Facts

In this case, the null value has two potential meanings. Either the value did not exist, or our measurement system failed to capture the value. Either way, we generally leave the value as null because most database products will handle nulls properly in aggregate functions including SUM, MAX, MIN, COUNT, and AVG. Substituting a zero instead would improperly skew these aggregated calculations.

Nulls as Dimension Attributes

We generally encounter dimension attribute nulls due to timing or dimension subsetting. For example, perhaps not all the attributes have been captured yet, so we have some unknown attributes for a period of time. Likewise, there may be certain attributes that only apply to a subset of the dimension members. In either case, the same recommendation applies. Putting a null in these fields can be confusing to the user, because it will appear as a blank on reports and pull-down menus, and require special query syntax to find. Instead, we recommend substituting an appropriately descriptive string, like "Unknown" or "Not provided."

Note that many data mining tools have different techniques for tracking nulls. You may need to do some additional work beyond the preceding recommendations if you are creating an observation set for data mining.

8.26 Modeling Data as Both a Fact and Dimension Attribute

Ralph Kimball, Design Tip #97, Dec 11, 2007

In the dimensional modeling world, we try very hard to separate data into two contrasting camps: numerical measurements that we put into fact tables, and textual descriptors that we put into dimension tables as attributes. If only life were that easy.

Remember that numerical facts usually have an implicit time series of observations, and usually participate in numerical computations such as sums and averages, or more complex functional expressions. Dimension attributes, on the other hand, are the targets of constraints, and provide the content of "row headers" (grouping columns) in a query.

While probably 98 percent of all data items are neatly separated into either facts or dimension attributes, there is a solid 2 percent that don't fit so neatly into these two categories. A classic example is the price of a product. Is this an attribute of the product dimension or is this an observed fact? Because the price of a product often varies over time and over location, it becomes very cumbersome to model the price as a dimension attribute; it should be a fact.

A more ambiguous example is the limit on a coverage within an automobile insurance policy. The limit is a numerical data item, say $300,000 for collision liability. The limit may not change over the life of the policy, or it changes very infrequently. Furthermore, many queries would group or constrain on this limit data item. This sounds like a slam dunk for the limit being an attribute of the coverage dimension.

But the limit is a numeric observation, and it can change over time, albeit slowly. One could pose some important queries summing or averaging all the limits on many policies and coverages. This sounds like a slam dunk for the limit being a numeric fact in a fact table.

Rather than agonizing over the dimension versus fact choice, simply model it both ways! Include the limit in the coverage dimension so that it participates in the usual way as a target for constraints and the content for row headers, but also put the limit in the fact table so it can participate in the usual way within complex computations.

This example illustrates some important dimensional modeling themes:

- Your design goal is ease of use, not elegance, or methodological correctness. In the final step of preparing data for consumption by business users, we should be willing to stand on our heads to make our BI systems understandable and fast. That means 1) transferring work into the ETL back room, and 2) tolerating more storage overhead in order to simplify the final data presentation.

- In correctly designed models, there is never a meaningful difference in data content between two opposing approaches. Stop arguing that "you can't do the query if you model it that way." That is almost never true. The issues that you should focus on are ease of application development, and understandability when presented through a user interface.

8.27 When a Fact Table Can Be Used as a Dimension Table

Ralph Kimball, Design Tip #13, Sep 15, 2000

Fact tables come in three main flavors, as described in article 8.5, *Fundamental Grains*. The grain of a fact table can be an individual transaction, where a fact table record represents an instant in time. Or the grain can be a periodic snapshot, representing a predictable duration of time like a week or a month. Finally, the grain can be an accumulating snapshot, representing the entire history of something up to the present.

The first fact table type, the instantaneous transaction, may give us an opportunity to capture the description of something at an exact moment. Suppose that we have a series of transactions against the customer information in your bank account. In other words, an agent in the bank periodically makes changes to your name, address, phone number, customer classification, credit rating, risk rating, and other descriptors. The relational table that captures these transactions is shown in Figure 8-10. Fundamentally it looks like a dimension table, but it has characteristics of a fact table, too!

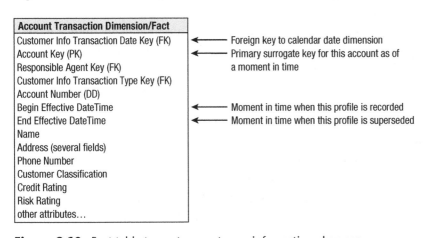

Figure 8-10: Fact table to capture customer information changes.

This is a typical design for data where the "measurements" recorded by the customer information transactions are changes made to textual values, such as the name, address, and other textual fields already listed. Such a table blurs the distinction between a fact table and a dimension table because this table is filled with discrete textual values and non-additive numeric values that cannot be summarized, but are instead the targets of query constraints. Perhaps it's a stretch to even call this table a fact table, but business users will certainly think that this table records account profile transactions.

Three of the four keys to this table are simple foreign keys (FKs) connecting to conventional dimension tables. These include the transaction date, the responsible agent, and the type of the transaction itself. The production account number is not a data warehouse join key, but rather is the bank's constant identifier for this customer account.

The remaining key is the surrogate account key. In other words, it is simply a sequentially assigned number that uniquely identifies this transaction against this account. But here is the subtle point that is the secret of this whole design. This account surrogate key therefore uniquely represents this snapshot of this account at the moment of the customer info transaction, and continues to accurately describe the account until the next customer info transaction occurs at some indeterminate time in the future.

So to make a long story short, we can use the account surrogate key as if it was a typical type 2 slowly changing dimension key, and we can embed this key in any other fact table describing account behavior. For example, suppose that we also are collecting conventional account transactions like deposits and withdrawals, as shown in Figure 8-11. We'll call these *balance transactions* to distinguish them from the customer information transactions.

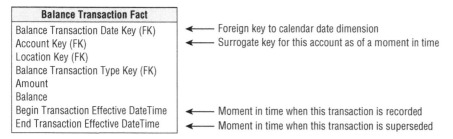

Figure 8-11: Balance transactions that reference the account surrogate key.

When we make one of these balance transaction fact records, we carefully consult our account transaction table and pick out the right surrogate key to use. Normally when we process today's records, we just use the most recent surrogate key for the account. This design then perfectly links every balance transaction to the right account profile described in our first fact table. Or is it a dimension table?

Well, I hope this has got you thinking. Article 10.25, *Human Resources Dimensional Models*, describes a similar design approach.

8.28 Sparse Facts and Facts with Short Lifetimes

Ralph Kimball, Design Tip #20, *Feb 27, 2001*

Fact tables are built around numerical measurements. When a measurement is taken, a fact record comes into existence. The measurement can be the amount of a sale, the value of a transaction, a running balance at the end of a month, the yield of a manufacturing process run, or even a classic laboratory measurement. If we record several numbers at the same time, we can often put them together in the same fact record.

We surround the measurement(s) with all the things we know to be true at the precise moment of the measurement. Besides a time stamp, we often know things like customer, product, market condition, employee, status, supplier, and many other entities depending on the process supplying us the measurement.

We package all the things we know into descriptive text-laden dimension records and connect the facts to the dimension records through a foreign key-primary key (FK-PK) relationship. This leads to the classic organization of a fact table (shown here with N dimensions and two facts called dollars and units):

> dimkey1 (FK)
> dimkey2 (FK)
> dimkey3 (FK)
> ...
> dimkeyN (FK)
> dollars
> units

The dollars and units fields are reserved placeholders for those specific measurements. This design carries the implicit assumptions that:

1. These two measures are usually present together.
2. These are the only measures in this process.
3. There are lots of measurement events; in other words, it is worthwhile to devote this fixed format table to these measures.

But what happens when all three of these assumptions break down? This happens frequently in complex financial investment tracking where every investment instrument has idiosyncratic measures. It also happens in industrial manufacturing processes where the batch runs are short and each batch type has a host of special measures. And finally, clinical and medical lab environments are dominated by hundreds of special measurements, none of which occur very frequently. All three of these examples can be described as *sparse facts*.

You can't just extend the classic fact table design to handle sparse facts. You would have an unworkably long list of fact fields, most of which would be null in a given record. The answer is to add a special *fact dimension* and shrink the list of actual numeric facts down to a single amount field:

> dimkey1 (FK)
> dimkey2 (FK)
> dimkey3 (FK)
> ...
> dimkeyN (FK)
> factdimkey (FK) <== additional dimension
> amount

The "fact dimension" describes the meaning of the measurement amount. It contains what used to be the field name of the fact, as well as the unit of measure, and any additivity restrictions. For instance, if the measurement is a balance fact, then it may be fully additive across all the dimensions except time. But if it is a full-blown intensity measurement like temperature, then it is completely non-additive. Summarizing across non-additive dimensions requires averaging, not summing.

This approach is elegant because it is superbly flexible. You add new measurement types just by adding new records in the fact dimension, not by altering the structure of the table. You also eliminate all the NULLs in the classic design because a record only exists if the measurement exists. But there are some significant trade-offs. You may be generating a LOT of records. If some of your measurements give you 10 numeric results, now you have 10 records rather than the single record you had in the classic design. For extremely sparse situations, this is a great compromise. But as the density of the facts grows in the dimensional space you have created, you start papering the universe with records. At some point you have to return to the classic format.

This approach also makes applications more complicated. Combining two numbers that have been taken as part of a single measurement event is more difficult because now you have to fetch two records. SQL makes this awkward because SQL likes to do arithmetic within a record, not across records. And you have to be very careful that you don't mix incompatible amounts in a calculation, because all the numeric measures exist within the single amount field.

8.29 Pivoting the Fact Table with a Fact Dimension

Joy Mundy, Design Tip #82, *Aug 2, 2006*

The article was originally titled Turning the Fact Table on its Head.

The grain of the fact table most often comes directly from the grain of the transaction table from which the data is sourced. Occasionally it makes sense to pivot the facts so that we actually create *more* fact table rows than there are rows in the source.

This counterintuitive occurrence is most likely when the source system isn't a transaction system, such as one that captures sales events, but an analytic system like a forecasting, promotion, or financial analysis system. For example, let's say we're building a fact table to hold budget and actual data. Our source table was designed to support the budget process; it contains financial information by month, account, and department with actual and budget amount facts. The beginning data modeler starts to create a similar structure in the data warehouse database. But interviews with the business community help us understand that there are several versions of budget. We need for the data warehouse to track several drafts of the budget during the budget development process.

The solution here is to create a fact table with four dimensions: month, account, department, and scenario. Please see the preceding article 8.28, *Sparse Facts and Facts with Short Lifetimes*. The new scenario dimension would have a handful of rows, including Actual, Budget Draft 1 FY07, and Final Budget FY07. Our fact table contains only one measure, Amount. The fact table is normalized to be "long and skinny" rather than "short and fat." The new structure is more flexible and easily accommodates an arbitrary number of draft and final budgets.

It's easy for an outsider to see this solution. It's surprising how difficult it can be, while in the trenches, to pull your mind away from the structure you've been handed and think about creative alternatives. Here are some hints that you should think about this approach to pivot the fact table and add a new dimension:

1. **Excessive number of facts.** What does excessive mean? A hundred facts in a fact table is excessive; ten is not. Somewhere in the middle, perhaps around thirty measures, you cross into the grey area toward excessive.
2. **Naming conventions to group measures.** If you have a ton of facts, your fact column names probably use prefixes and suffixes to help users find the facts they're looking for.
3. **Many measures in a row are null.** Of the, say, 100 facts that could apply to a row, only a subset of them tend to be populated at any one time.

If all these conditions are true, consider normalizing the fact table by creating a fact dimension. The fact dimension could contain several columns that would help users navigate the list of facts. Admittedly, our long skinny fact table will have a lot more rows than the short fat one. It will use somewhat more disk space as well, though depending on the sparsity of facts, it may not be all that much bigger. The biggest downside is that many users want to see the facts on a row. It would require pretty good SQL skills to formulate the query to unpivot the data back to get several measures on the same row in a report. If we use an OLAP database as the user presentation layer, this notion of a fact dimension is entirely natural.

8.30 Accumulating Snapshots for Complex Workflows

Margy Ross, Design Tip #130, *Dec 1, 2010*

As Ralph described in article 8.6, *Modeling a Pipeline with an Accumulating Snapshot,* accumulating snapshots are one of the three fundamental types of fact tables. We often state that accumulating snapshot fact tables are appropriate for predictable workflows with well-established milestones. They typically have five to ten key milestone dates representing the workflow/pipeline start, completion, and the key event dates in between.

Our students and clients sometimes ask for guidance about monitoring cycle performance for a less predictable workflow process. These more complex workflows have a definite start and end date, but the milestones in between are often numerous and less stable. Some occurrences may skip over some intermediate milestones, but there's no reliable pattern.

Be forewarned that the design for tackling these less predictable workflows is not for the faint of heart! The first task is to identify the key dates that will link to role-playing date dimensions. These dates represent key milestones; the start and end dates for the process would certainly qualify. In addition, you'd want to consider other commonly occurring, critical milestones. These dates (and their associated dimensions) will be used for report and analyses filtering. For example, if you want to see cycle activity for all workflows where a milestone date fell in a given work week, calendar month, fiscal period, or other standard date dimension attribute, then it should be identified as a key date with a corresponding date dimension table. The same holds true if you want to create a time series trend based on the milestone date. While selecting specific milestones as the critical ones in a complex process may be challenging for IT, business users can typically identify these key milestones fairly readily. But they're often interested in a slew of additional lags, which is where things get thorny.

For example, let's assume there are six critical milestone dates, plus an additional 20 less critical event dates associated with a given process/workflow. If we labeled each of these dates alphabetically, you could imagine analysts being interested in any of the following date lags:

> A-to-B, A-to-C, …, A-to-Z (total of 25 possible lags from event A)
> B-to-C, …, B-to-Z (total of 24 possible lags from event B)
> C-to-D, …, C-to-Z (total of 23 possible lags from event C)
> …
> Y-to-Z

Using this example, there would be 325 (25 + 24 + 23 + … + 1) possible lag calculations between milestone A and milestone Z. That's an unrealistic number of facts for a single fact table! Instead of physically storing all 325 date lags, you could get away with just storing 25 of them, and then calculate the others. Since every cycle occurrence starts by passing through milestone A (workflow begin date), you could store all 25 lags from the anchor event A, then calculate the other 300 variations.

Let's take a simpler example with actual dates to work through the calculations:

> Event A (process begin date) – Occurred on November 1
> Event B – Occurred on November 2
> Event C – Occurred on November 5
> Event D – Occurred on November 11
> Event E – Didn't happen
> Event F (process end date) – Occurred on November 16

In the corresponding accumulating snapshot fact table row for this example, you'd physically store the following facts and their values:

> A-to-B days lag = 1
> A-to-C days lag = 4
> A-to-D days lag = 10
> A-to-E days lag = null
> A-to-F days lag = 15

To calculate the days lag from B-to-C, you'd take the A-to-C lag value (4) and subtract the A-to-B lag value (1) to arrive at 3 days. To calculate the days lag from C-to-F, you'd take the A-to-F value (15) and subtract the A-to-C value (4) to arrive at 11 days. Things get a little trickier when an event doesn't occur, like E in our example. When there's a null involved in the calculation, like the lag from B-to-E or E-to-F, the result needs to also be null because one of the events never happened.

This technique works even if the interim dates are not in sequential order. In our example, let's assume the dates for events C and D were swapped: Event C occurred on November 11, and D occurred on November 5. In this case, the A-to-C days lag is 10, and the A-to-D lag is 4. To calculate the C-to-D lag, you'd take the A-to-D lag (4) and subtract the A-to-C lag (10) to arrive at a −6 days.

In our simplified example, storing all the possible lags would have resulted in 15 total facts (5 lags from event A, plus 4 lags from event B, plus 3 lags from event C, plus 2 lags from event D, plus 1 lag from event E). That's not an unreasonable number of facts to just physically store. This tip makes more sense when there are dozens of potential event milestones in a cycle. Of course, you'd want to hide the complexity of these lag calculations under the covers from your users, like in a view declaration.

As I warned earlier, this design pattern is not simplistic; however, it's a viable approach for addressing a really tricky problem.

9 Dimension Table Core Concepts

Building on your solid understanding of fact tables from Chapter 8, it's time to turn your attention to dimension tables, whose descriptive attributes allow the business users to filter and group information in nearly countless ways. Robust dimension tables filled with interesting attributes enable robust analytics.

The chapter begins by discussing the importance of replacing a dimension's natural operational keys with meaningless integer surrogate keys during the ETL process. From that basic concept, the second section focuses on the time (or date) dimension that you'll find with virtually every fact table.

We then describe other common dimension table patterns, including role-playing, junk, and causal dimensions. We close out the chapter with a deep dive into more advanced techniques for handling slowly changing dimension (SCD) attributes.

There are lots of additional topics to discuss when it comes to dimensions; hang onto your hats for more coverage in Chapter 10.

Dimension Table Keys

The first two articles in this chapter focus on the value of using meaningless surrogate keys as the primary keys of your dimension tables.

 ### 9.1 Surrogate Keys

Ralph Kimball, DBMS, May 1998

According to the *Webster's Unabridged Dictionary*, a surrogate is an "artificial or synthetic product that is used as a substitute for a natural product." That's a great definition for the surrogate keys we use in data warehouses. A surrogate key is an artificial or synthetic key that is used as a substitute for a natural key.

Actually, a surrogate key in a data warehouse is more than just a substitute for a natural key. In a data warehouse, a surrogate key is a necessary generalization of the natural production key and is one of the basic elements of data warehouse design. Let's be very clear: Every join between dimension tables and fact tables in a data warehouse environment should be based on surrogate keys, not natural keys. It is up to the ETL logic to systematically look up and replace every incoming natural key with a data warehouse surrogate key each time either a dimension record or a fact record is brought into the data warehouse environment.

In other words, when we have a product dimension joined to a fact table, or a customer dimension joined to a fact table, or even a date dimension joined to a fact table, as shown in Figure 9-1, the actual physical keys on either end of the joins are not natural keys directly derived from the incoming data; rather the keys are surrogate keys that are just anonymous integers. Each one of these keys should be a simple integer, starting with 1 and going up to the highest number that is needed. The product key should be a simple integer, the customer key should be a simple integer, and even the date key should be a simple integer (allowing the format of a date-valued key to be yyyymmdd). None of the keys should be:

- Smart where you can tell something about the record just by looking at the key (with the exception of a date-valued key)
- Composed of natural keys glued together
- Implemented as multiple parallel joins between the dimension table and the fact table, so-called double- or triple-barreled joins

If you are a professional DBA, I probably have your attention. If you are new to data warehousing, you are probably horrified. Perhaps you are saying, "But if I know what my underlying key is, all my training suggests that I make my key out of the data I am given." Yes, in the production transaction processing environment, the meaning of a product key or a customer key is directly related to the record's content. In the data warehouse environment, however, a dimension key must be a generalization of what is found in the record.

As the data warehouse designer, you need to keep your keys independent from the natural keys. The production operational system has different priorities from you. Natural keys, such as product or customer keys, are generated, formatted, updated, deleted, recycled, and reused according to the dictates of production. If you use natural keys as your keys, you will be whipsawed by changes that can be, at the very least, annoying, and at the worst, disastrous. Here's a list of some of the ways that production may step on your toes:

- Production may reuse keys that it has purged but that you are still maintaining in the data warehouse.
- Production may make a mistake and reuse a key, even when it isn't supposed to. This happens frequently in the world of universal product codes (UPCs) in the retail world, despite everyone's best intentions.

- Production may legitimately overwrite some part of a product or customer description with new values, but not change the product or customer key to a new value. You are left holding the bag and wondering what to do about the revised attribute values. This is the slowly changing dimension crisis, which I explain in a moment.

- Production may generalize its key format to handle some new situation in the transaction system. Now the production keys that used to be integers become alphanumeric. Or perhaps the 12-byte keys you are used to have become 20-byte keys.

- Your company has just made an acquisition, and you need to merge more than a million new customers into the master customer list. You will now need to extract from two production systems, but the newly acquired system has nasty customer keys that don't look remotely like the others.

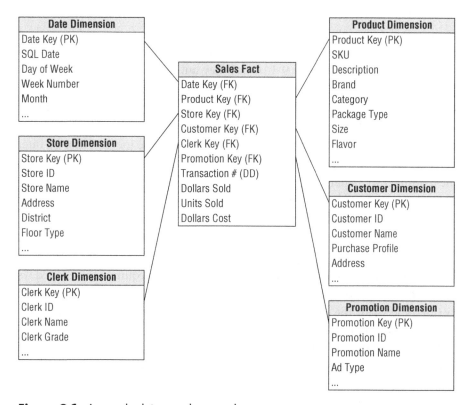

Figure 9-1: A sample data warehouse schema.

The slowly changing dimension crisis I mentioned earlier is a well known situation in data warehousing. It is constructive to recognize that this is an area where the interests of operational production systems and the interests of the data warehouse legitimately diverge. Usually when the data warehouse administrator encounters a changed description in a dimension record, the correct response is to issue a new dimension record. But to do this, the data warehouse must have a more general key structure; hence, the need for a surrogate key.

There are still more reasons to use surrogate keys. One of the most important is the need to encode uncertain knowledge. You may need to supply a customer key to represent a transaction, but perhaps you don't know for certain who the customer is. This would be a common occurrence in a retail situation where cash transactions are anonymous, like most grocery stores. What is the customer key for the anonymous customer?

If you think carefully about the "I don't know" situation, you may want more than just this one special key for the anonymous customer. You may also want to describe the situation where "the customer identification has not taken place yet." Or maybe "there was a customer, but the transaction system failed to report it correctly." And also, "no customer is possible in this situation." All of these meta-situations call for a data warehouse customer key that cannot be composed from the natural customer keys. Don't forget that in the data warehouse you must provide a key for every dimension referenced in a fact record shown in Figure 9-1. A null key automatically turns on the referential integrity alarm in your data warehouse because a foreign key (as in the fact table) can never be null.

Maybe one of the reasons you are holding on to your smart natural keys is that you think you want to navigate the keys directly with an application, avoiding the join to the dimension table. It is time to forget this strategy. If the fifth through ninth alpha characters in the join key can be interpreted as a manufacturer's ID, then copy these characters and make them a field in the dimension table. Better yet, add the manufacturer's name in plain text as a field. As the final step, consider throwing away the alphanumeric manufacturer ID, unless it is needed to loop back to production. In most cases, the only reason the business users know these IDs is that they have been forced to use them for query requests.

We recommend a special exception to sequentially assigned integer surrogate keys for the calendar date dimension since this dimension has unique characteristics and requirements. The days of the calendar are obviously fixed and predetermined. You never delete or create new days. We recommend creating integer primary keys for the calendar date dimension using the yyyymmdd format. We do this not for the business user, but for the convenience of the DBA who frequently needs to look at individual fact table records without a full dimensional context. The yyyymmdd format lets the DBA understand the context of an isolated fact record. Yes, with the yyyymmdd format, you could navigate date keys with straight SQL in a BI application, thereby avoiding the join to the dimension table, but you have left all your special calendar attributes marooned in the date table. If you navigate these date keys with an application, you will inevitably begin embedding calendar logic in your application. Calendar logic belongs in a dimension table, not in your application code.

You may be able to save substantial storage space with integer-valued surrogate keys. Suppose you have a big fact table with a billion rows of data. In such a table, every byte wasted in each row is a gigabyte of total storage. The beauty of a 4-byte integer key is that it can represent more than 2 billion different values. That is enough for any dimension, even the so-called monster dimensions that represent individual human beings. So we compress all our long customer IDs, product IDs, and date stamps down to 4-byte keys. This saves many gigabytes of total storage.

The final reason for surrogate keys is that replacing big, ugly, alphanumeric natural keys and composite keys with beautiful, tight, integer surrogate keys is bound to improve join performance. The shorter rows mean more fact records fit in a block, and the index lookups will be simpler.

Having made the case for surrogate keys, we now are faced with creating them. Fundamentally, every time we see a natural key in the incoming data stream, we must look up the correct value of the surrogate key and replace the natural key with the surrogate key. Because this is a significant step in the routine extract and transformation processing, we need to tighten down our techniques to make this lookup simple and fast, as I describe in article 11.27, *Pipelining Your Surrogates*.

9.2 Keep Your Keys Simple

Ralph Kimball, Design Tip #100, Apr 3, 2008

In 2008 a student emailed me with a design dilemma concerning dimension surrogate keys. He said:

> I was told by my client that their method to assign surrogate keys to type 2 slowly changing dimensions (SCDs) was the "industry standard." They are maintaining a one-to-one relationship between the natural keys and the surrogate keys in the dimension table. Their type 2 SCD in their enterprise data warehouse (EDW) looks as follows:

dim_key	nat_key	color	start_dt	end_dt
1	ABC	Blue	1/1/2008	3/31/2008
1	ABC	Red	4/1/2008	12/31/1999
2	DEF	Green	1/1/2008	2/29/2008
2	DEF	Yellow	3/1/2008	12/31/1999

> I expected to see a unique surrogate key for each record, not reusing the same surrogate key for each natural key with differing row start and end dates.

Here's my response to the student:

I've seen this story a few times before! All of your dimension keys should be simple integers assigned by the data warehouse during the ETL. It is definitely wrong to make the dimension key be a combination of a fixed key (one-to-one with the natural key) plus a date range for several reasons:

1. Performance will be compromised with a multi-field join from the dimension table to the fact table, especially if the fields involved are complex alphanumeric fields or date/time stamps.

The best join performance is achieved by using single field integer keys between dimension tables and fact tables.

2. User/application developer understandability will definitely be compromised with the need to constrain the dates correctly. This point is expanded in several of the following points.

3. The date ranges in the dimension for each natural key presumably implement an unbroken overall span with no gaps. That is hard and sometimes nearly impossible to do correctly. If the end effective date of one record is exactly equal to the begin effective date of the next record, then you can't use BETWEEN in order to pick a specific dimension record because you could land on the exact dividing line and get two records. You must use greater-than-or-equal for the begin date and less-than for the end date, which will further compromise performance. You can't make an end date/time one "tick" less than a begin date/time of the next record in order to use BETWEEN because the "tick" is machine/DBMS-dependent, and you can get situations in busy environments with data arriving from multiple sources where you lose transactions that fall into the gap. For example, one of my students gets 10,000 financial transactions in the last second of a fiscal period from 40 separate (and incompatible) source systems with varying formats for the exact transaction times.

4. In situations where the begin and end effective stamps are actually date/time stamps, you have a serious issue of how accurately the user/application developer needs to constrain the dimension. You must have a detailed understanding of intra-day business rules to do this correctly. Also, date/time stamps could be very unwieldy, depending on the DBMS.

5. Explicit date/time stamps are machine- and DBMS-dependent and therefore do not port cleanly from one environment to another.

6. In product movement situations, the begin and end stamps may not straddle the activity date of the fact record. For example, a specific product profile may be valid from January 1 to February 1, and hence those are the dates in the dimension, but the product may be sold February 15. Try explaining that to the users. Even worse, try building an application that requires two different date constraints. Using simple surrogate keys eliminates this objection, because the correct correspondence between dimension and fact records is resolved during the ETL steps.

7. The user/developer must always constrain the dimension (actually every dimension simultaneously) to an exact instant in time in every query for the rest of his/her life. Eight dimensions equal eight time constraints. And if one of the dimensions has date/time fields, whereas the others have only date fields, you will get wrong answers if you constrain only to a date. Dates are dangerous because SQL is too "smart." A constraint on a day works on values within a day and the system doesn't warn you.

8. The style of embedding date ranges in every dimension record hints at a normalized style of modeling in which every many-to-one relationship is encumbered with date ranges in order to handle time variance. Thus the objection raised in the previous paragraph is much worse if these normalized tables are actually exposed to the application developer or business user.

Now the date constraints would need to appear in every intermediate pair of tables, not just in the final dimension tables attached to fact tables.

9. Finally, any explicit dependence on the content of natural keys coming from a source system fails to anticipate the challenge of integrating data from multiple source systems, each with their own notion of natural keys. The separate natural keys could be of bizarrely different data types or could even overlap!

9.3 Durable "Super-Natural" Keys

Warren Thornthwaite, Design Tip #147, *Jul 10, 2012*

One of the tasks of the ETL system's customer dimension manager is to "assign a unique durable key to each customer." By durable key, we mean a single key value that uniquely and reliably identifies a given customer over time. In most cases, this unique durable key is the natural business key from the operational systems, and all we have to do is copy it over as an attribute in the dimension table. However, there are cases where the natural key changes, and when it does, the dimension manager has to step in.

Some common causes for natural key changes include business reasons, duplicate entries, and integration of data from multiple sources. All of these require the creation and management of a unique durable key, also known as a super-natural key, during the ETL process.

A good example of a natural key change for business reasons comes from the credit card industry. Credit card account numbers are natural keys; they appear in transactions, and are mapped to surrogate keys in the dimension table. If a credit card is stolen, a new account number is issued. Without awareness of this change, the new account number would look like a totally new account and be entered as a new entity in the account dimension. The full history of the account would be lost because it now has two natural keys.

When this kind of business-driven change happens, the transaction system must generate a notification record telling the ETL process that a new account has been created to replace an old account. This could be as simple as a table with the old account number, the new account number, and the effective date. The ETL system must then create a new row with the new account number and a separate durable key column that ties the old and new accounts together. Figure 9-2 shows how this durable key would look in an account dimension.

Account_Key	Account_ID	Durable_Account_ID	Account Holder	State	Eff_Date	End_Date
3	8765	3	Smith	CA	2011-02-01	2011-05-10
7	8765	3	Smith	OR	2011-05-11	2011-10-23
23	9251	3	Smith	CA	2011-10-24	2011-12-31
55	9251	3	Smyth	CA	2012-01-01	9999-12-31

Figure 9-2: A durable key in an account dimension.

In Figure 9-2, the Account_Key is the surrogate key assigned by the ETL system to uniquely identify each row. The Account_ID is the ETL substitute for the natural key from the transaction system because you would not usually load a sensitive element such as a credit card account number directly into the data warehouse. The third key column, called the Durable_Account_ID, is the durable key assigned by the ETL system to tie all related rows together. Figure 9-2 shows four rows for the same account because there were two Type 2 changes to track, one state change and one last name change, in addition to the Account_ID change.

Another useful design pattern is to add the durable account key to the fact table in addition to the dimension's surrogate key. This joins back to the current rows in the dimension to make it easier to report all of history by the current dimension attributes. See article 9.24, *Slowly Changing Dimensions Are Not Always as Easy as 1, 2, and 3*, for more information.

Dealing with duplicate entries in a dimension, or integrating disparate sources into a single dimension, involves more complex business logic that relies on durable keys. The end result is similar to Figure 9-2, but the integration process has to generate the list of related items rather than relying on the transaction system. Figure 9-3 shows the integration of products from multiple source systems. The MDM subsystem in the ETL process has identified these three products as the same and assigned them to the same durable key.

Product_ Key	Product_ID	Durable_ Product_ Key	Product_ Name	Product_ Group	Match_ Date	Match_ Score
5	37285	5	Wrench	Tools	2011-02-01	1.00
9	39101	5	Wrench	Hand Tools	2011-10-24	0.93
25	17195	5	Wrench	Tools	2012-05-11	1.00

Figure 9-3: Duplicate product entries.

In this case, you might need to mark the natural keys from the different sources so they don't collide with each other. Try using a character data type for the source natural key, prepended by a source code. For example, if the products in Figure 9-3 came from SAP or the CRM system, the Product_ID column might contain the following values: SAP|37285, CRM|39101, and SAP|17195. This table then becomes input to the dimension and fact managers.

Durable keys are mandatory for dealing with ambiguities in the source system natural keys. Creating and assigning durable keys allows you to work around business changes to the natural keys, or to integrate duplicate or disparate data. But durable keys are just the start; there is a lot more to deduplicating and data integration.

Date and Time Dimension Considerations

Every fact table should have at least one date and/or time dimension associated with it. This section focuses on these most common dimensions. Historically, calendar or time centric dimensions were generically called time dimensions, as reflected in articles 9.4, *It's Time for Time*, and 9.5, *Surrogate*

Keys for the Time Dimension. More recently, we have referred to daily grained dimensions as date dimensions, whereas time dimensions imply time of day granularity.

9.4 It's Time for Time

Ralph Kimball, DBMS, *Jul 1997*

This article includes discussion of facts that are not additive across time periods. Although it's a tangential topic, it's not covered elsewhere in The Kimball Group Reader, *so we opted to retain the original content in this article.*

The time dimension is a unique and powerful dimension in every data warehouse. Although one of the tenets of dimensional modeling is that all dimensions are created equal, the truth is that the time dimension is very special and must be treated differently from the other dimensions.

Basic Time Issues

Virtually every business process subject area is a time series. Figure 9-4 is a familiar basic dimensional design where the fact table contains orders received by a manufacturing company. The first dimension is the time dimension. In this case, the time dimension represents the order date.

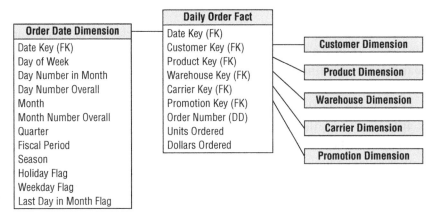

Figure 9-4: A basic dimensional design for order tracking.

Data architects in my design class ask, "Why can't I just leave out the time dimension? The foreign key in the fact table can easily be a SQL date value, and I can just constrain on calendar periods through the mechanisms of standard SQL. This way I avoid an expensive join!" They also ask, "If I have to have a time dimension, where do I get it?"

The first question is answered by recalling the fundamental reason for wanting dimension tables in a data warehouse. The dimension tables serve as the source of constraints and report row headers. A dimensional model is only as good as its dimension tables. Figure 9-4 shows a recommended time dimension table expressed at a daily grain. If you don't have lots of good descriptive attributes in your dimensions, then you have a crippled data warehouse; you won't be able to constrain on inadequate dimensions, and you won't be able to construct the reports you want. Although it is true in the case of the time dimension that SQL provides some minimal assistance in navigating dates, standard SQL functionality isn't nearly complete enough to support the needs of a typical organization. SQL certainly doesn't know anything about your corporate calendar, your fiscal periods, or your seasons. It is so easy to add these attributes to a time table that the data warehouse architect should never consider having this calendar logic embedded in users' applications.

The second data architect question is answered by saying, "Build it in a spreadsheet." Unlike nearly any other dimension in a data warehouse, the time dimension can be built once on the architect's PC and then uploaded into the data warehouse. The time dimension in Figure 9-4 can be built in half a day of fussing with spreadsheet cells and studying the official corporate calendar. It would be reasonable for this time dimension to contain at least 20 or 30 years' worth of days, perhaps extending from 1990 to 2020 and beyond.

Some subject areas additionally track time of day to the nearest minute or even the nearest second. For these cases, presuming no grouping is done on time-of-day attributes, I recommend separating the time of day measure out as a separate "numeric fact" expressed as a full SQL date/time stamp. It should not be combined into one key with the calendar day dimension because this would make for an impossibly large dimension table.

Intermediate Time Issues

Time is a dimension that invites incompatible rollups; the most obvious are weeks and months. You should start with the daily time grain. Daily data rolls up to virtually every possible calendar. If your company operates on calendar month reporting, then you should organize around days, months, quarters, and years. If your company operates on artificial fiscal periods that roll up from weeks, such as a five-week, four-week, four-week quarter, then you should organize around days, weeks, fiscal periods, quarters, and years. It is okay to overlay incompatible seasonal periods based on specific spans of days onto either one of these schemes, but seasonal periods such as Christmas or Easter will not roll up to any of the other calendar periods. Adding seasonal interpretations to the calendar is easy if you start at a daily time grain. This is one of the advantages of the dimensional approach. It is very robust in the face of changing business requirements, as long as you start at the lowest atomic grain of data—in this case daily.

It is common to have dates embedded in other dimensions, such as product or customer. In these cases, it is permissible to embed these dates as foreign keys to the calendar date dimension in order to give the business user access to complex calendar constraints. This snowflake dimension can be hidden in a view so that the business user sees the calendar date attributes at the same level as the surrounding dimension. Some care must be taken to use this snowflaking approach only for date values that fall within the range of your time dimension. Sometimes dates embedded in a dimension occur before the beginning of the date dimension, in which case you should just use a SQL date stamp and forego some of the calendar attribution that your date dimension offers.

Another intermediate level design issue involving time is the very common issue of aggregating non-additive measures of intensity across time. The most common examples are inventory levels and account balances. The problem is that in most cases you want to aggregate these measures across time by computing the "average over time." This is not the same calculation as SQL AVG, which is the average over all of the records returned to the answer set for a particular SQL SELECT statement. The application designer must calculate "average over time" by first determining the cardinality of the constraint on the time dimension by itself, saving this number away, then adding the intensity measure across time, and finally dividing out by the time cardinality that has been saved away. Although this is trivial mathematics, it is a significant pain in a standard SQL environment that has no AVGPERIODSUM operator to handle this case automatically. Standard ad hoc query tools that emit single SQL SELECT statements simply cannot perform "average daily balance" calculations, although some sophisticated application development environments know how to do it.

I have tried to provide some perspective on the main time issues confronting the data warehouse designer and how to tackle each of them. Although the dimension table for time is one of the simplest and most obvious tables in any data warehouse, the surrounding design issues for handling time are very challenging. In my classes, when I ask the students, "What is the first dimension we might choose for this particular business process?" they soon learn to yell in unison: "TIME!"

9.5 Surrogate Keys for the Time Dimension

Ralph Kimball, Design Tip #5, *Mar 19, 2000*

Here's a data warehouse design question I received recently:

Our consultant proposed a time dimension that looks rather different from the ones you suggest. His time dimension structure was:

```
Key (varchar2 (8))
StartDate (date)
EndDate (date)
```

Here's some sample data from his proposed time dimension:

Key	StartDate	EndDate
xmas99	25Nov99	06Jan00
1qtr99	01Jan99	31Mar99
newyrsdy	01Jan00	01Jan00
01Jan00	01Jan00	01Jan00

What is your view on a time dimension with this structure? For what type of scenario/ business would you find this a good viable alternative?

Here's what I wrote back to the student:

I don't like the time dimension proposed by your consultant very much. I expect a time dimension to describe the time context of a measurement expressed in a fact table. In database terms, there needs to be a time-valued foreign key in every fact table record that points out to a specific record in the time dimension.

It is very important for an application's simplicity that the fact table is of uniform granularity. In other words, all the records in the fact table should represent measurements taken at either a daily, weekly, or monthly level, for instance.

Your proposal has time dimension records of varying grain and it appears that they overlap. If you have a measurement record that occurs on a particular date, and these "time dimension" records overlap, which one of the records do you choose for a particular fact table record?

In a uniform grain fact table, you can use the associated time dimension to constrain in a simple way on many different spans of time. A time dimension table with entries for every discrete day is very flexible because in this table you can simultaneously represent all the useful time groupings.

A typical daily grain time table with a U.S. perspective could have the following structure:

Time Key (surrogate key of simple integers in the format yyyymmdd)
Time Type (Normal, Not Applicable, Hasn't Happened Yet, Corrupted)
SQL Time Stamp (8-byte date stamp for `type=Normal`, null otherwise)
Day Number in Month (1...31)
Day Number in Year (1...366)
Day Number in Epoch (an integer, positive or negative)
Week Number in Year (1...53)
Week Number in Epoch (an integer, positive or negative)
Month Number in Year (1...12)
Month Number in Epoch (an integer, positive or negative)
Month Name (January, ..., December, can be derived from SQL time stamp)

Year (can be derived from SQL time stamp)

Quarter (1Q, ... ,4Q)

Half (1H, 2H)

Fiscal Period (names or numbers, depending on your finance department)

Civil Holiday (New Years Day, July 4, Thanksgiving, Christmas)

Workday Indicator (Workday, Non Workday)

Selling Season (Winter Clearance, Back to School, Christmas Season)

In this daily time table, you make a record for each day of the year and you populate each field (as shown in the preceding list) with the relevant values for that day. All the special navigation fields like fiscal period and selling season let you define arbitrary spans of time for these special items. For example, you can constrain Selling Season = "Back to School" *and would automatically get all the days from August 15 to September 10.*

In the design proposed by your consultant, the keys of the time dimension table have values like xmas99 *and* 1qtr99. *These are smart keys. Smart keys are dangerous in a data ware-house dimension table for several reasons. The generation of these keys is held hostage to the rules for their syntax. It is tempting to write applications and user interfaces that would make these keys visible to someone. If there is a* 1qtr99, *are you guaranteeing that there is a* 2qtr99? *And what do you do when you need one of the not applicable situations for a date stamp?*

9.6 Latest Thinking on Time Dimension Tables

Ralph Kimball, Design Tip #51, *Feb 1, 2004*

Virtually every fact table has one or more time-related dimension foreign keys. Measurements are defined at specific points of time and most measurements are repeated over time.

The most common and useful time dimension is the calendar date dimension with the granularity of a single day. This dimension has surprisingly many attributes. Only a few of these attributes (such as month name and year) can be generated directly from a SQL date/time expression. Holidays, work days, fiscal periods, week numbers, last day of month flags, and other navigational attributes must be embedded in the calendar date dimension; all date navigation should be implemented in applications by using the dimensional attributes.

The calendar date dimension has some very unusual properties. It is one of the only dimensions that is completely specified at the beginning of the data warehouse project. It also doesn't have a conventional source. The best way to generate the calendar date dimension is to spend an afternoon with a spreadsheet and build it by hand. Ten years' worth of days is less than 4000 rows.

Every calendar date dimension needs a date type attribute and a full date attribute. These two fields comprise the natural key of the dimension table. The date type attribute almost always has the value "date," but there must be at least one record that handles the special non-applicable date situation where the recorded date is inapplicable, corrupted, or hasn't happened yet. The foreign key references in the fact table in these cases must point to a non-date date in the calendar date table! You always need at least one of these special records in the calendar date table, but you may want to distinguish several of these unusual conditions. For the inapplicable date case, the value of the date type is "inapplicable" or "NA." The full date attribute is a full relational date stamp, and it takes on the legitimate value of null for the special cases described previously. Remember that the foreign key in a fact table can never be null because by definition that violates referential integrity.

The calendar date primary key ideally should be a meaningless surrogate key, but many ETL teams can't resist the urge to make the key a readable quantity such as 20150718, meaning July 18, 2015. However, as with all smart keys, the few special records in the calendar date dimension will make the designer play tricks with the smart key. For instance, the smart key for the inapplicable date would have to be some nonsensical value, like 99999999, and applications that tried to interpret the date key directly without using the dimension table would always have to test against this value because it is not a valid date.

In some fact tables, time is measured below the level of calendar day, down to minutes or even seconds. One cannot build a time dimension with every minute or second of every day represented. There are more than 31 million seconds in a year! We want to preserve the powerful calendar date dimension and simultaneously support precise querying down to the minute or second. We may also want to compute very precise time intervals by comparing the exact time of two fact table records. For these reasons, we recommend a design with a calendar date dimension foreign key and a full SQL date/time stamp, both in the fact table. The calendar day component of the precise time remains as a foreign key reference to our familiar calendar day dimension. But we also embed a full SQL date/time stamp directly in the fact table for all queries requiring the extra precision. Think of this as a special kind of fact, not a dimension. In this interesting case, it is not useful to make a dimension with the minutes or seconds component of the precise time stamp, because the calculation of time intervals across fact table records becomes too messy when trying to deal with separate day and time-of-day dimensions. Previously, we have recommended building such a dimension with the minutes or seconds component of time as an offset from midnight of each day, but we have come to realize that the resulting user applications became too difficult, especially when trying to compute time spans. Also, unlike the calendar day dimension, there are very few descriptive attributes for the specific minute or second within a day.

If the enterprise has well-defined attributes for time slices within a day, such as shift names or advertising time slots, an additional time-of-day dimension can be added to the design where this dimension is defined as the number of minutes (or even seconds) past midnight. Thus, this time-of-day dimension would either have 1440 records if the grain were minutes or 86,400 records if the grain were seconds. The presence of such a time-of-day dimension does not remove the need for the SQL date/time stamp described earlier.

9.7 Smart Date Keys to Partition Fact Tables

Warren Thornthwaite, Design Tip #85, Nov 1, 2006

I've recently had two people ask if it's OK to use a meaningful key for the date dimension: an integer of the form yyyymmdd. In one case, my recommendation was no; in the other it was yes. In the "no" case, the designer's goal was to provide users and applications with a key in the fact table they could recognize and query directly thereby bypassing the date dimension. We describe why this actually reduces usability in article 9.6, *Latest Thinking on Time Dimension Tables*. This approach could also hurt performance in some database platforms.

The "yes" case involved partitioned fact tables. Partitioning allows you to create a table that is segmented into smaller tables under the covers, usually by date. Thus, you can load data into the current partition and re-index it without having to touch the whole table. Partitioning dramatically improves load times, backups, archiving old data, and even query performance. It makes it possible to physically manage terabyte data warehouses.

So why does partitioning lead us to consider a smart surrogate key in the date dimension? It turns out updating and managing partitions is a fairly tedious, repetitive task that can be done programmatically. These programs are much easier to write if the table is partitioned on date and the date key is an ordered integer. If the date key follows a date style pattern, you can also take advantage of date functions in the code.

In SQL Server 2005, for example, the initial definition of a simple partitioned table that holds the first three months of sales data for 2015 might look like this:

```
CREATE PARTITION FUNCTION SalesPartFunc (INT)  AS RANGE RIGHT
FOR VALUES (10000000, 20150101, 20150201, 20150301, 20150401)
```

The values are breakpoints and define six partitions, including a partition to hold the non-date entries in the table (DateKey<10000000), and empty partitions on either side of the data to make it easier to add, drop, and swap partitions in the future.

Prior to loading the fourth month of 2015, we would add another partition to hold that month's data. This hard-coded version splits the empty partition by putting in the next breakpoint, in this case, 20150501:

```
ALTER PARTITION FUNCTION PFMonthly () SPLIT RANGE (20150501)
```

The following Transact SQL code automatically generates the command using a variable called @CurMonth. It is a bit convoluted because it converts the integer into a date type for the DATEADD function, then converts it to VARCHAR(8) to concatenate it into the SQL statement string. Finally, the EXEC command executes the string.

```
DECLARE
  @CurMonth INT, @DateStr Varchar(8), @SqlStmt VARCHAR(1000)
SET @CurMonth = 20150401
SET @DateStr = CONVERT(VARCHAR(8),DATEADD(Month, 1, CONVERT(datetime,
```

```
                    CAST(@CurMonth AS varchar(20)), 112)),112)
    SET @SqlStmt = 'ALTER PARTITION FUNCTION PFMonthly () SPLIT RANGE (' + _
                    @DateStr + ')'
    EXEC (@SqlStmt)
```

So by using a smart yyyymmdd key, you still get the benefits of the surrogate key and the advantage of easier partition management. We recommend using your BI tool's metadata to hide the foreign keys in the fact table to discourage your users from directly querying them.

As a final note, remember that this logic surrounding the date key cannot be replicated for any other dimension such as customer or product. Only the date dimension can be completely specified in advance before the database is created. Calendar dates are perfectly stable: They are never created or deleted!

9.8 Updating the Date Dimension

Joy Mundy, Design Tip #119, Dec 2, 2009

Most readers are familiar with the basic date dimension. At the grain of a calendar day, we include various labels for calendar and fiscal years, quarters, months, and days. We include both short and long labels for various reporting requirements. Even though the labels in the basic date dimension could be constructed at the time we design a report, we always build the date dimension in advance so that report labels are consistent and easy to use.

The date dimension gets new rows as time marches forward, but most attributes are not subject to updates once a row has been added. December 1, 2015 will, of course, always roll up to December, calendar Q4, and 2015.

However, there are some attributes you may add to the basic date dimension that will change over time. These include indicators such as IsCurrentDay, IsCurrentMonth, IsPriorDay, IsPriorMonth, and so on. IsCurrentDay obviously must be updated each day. The attribute is particularly useful for generating reports that always run for today—or, even better, a report which defaults to today but which can be run for any day in the past. A nuance to consider is the day that IsCurrentDay refers to. Most data warehouses load data daily, so IsCurrentDay should refer to yesterday (or more accurately, the most recent day of data in the system).

You might also want to add attributes to your date dimension that are unique to your business processes or corporate calendar. These are particularly valuable because they cannot be derived using SQL calendar functions. Examples include IsFiscalMonthEnd, IsCloseWeek, IsManagementReviewDay, and IsHolidaySeason.

Some date dimension designs include lag columns. The LagDay column would take the value 0 for today, –1 for yesterday, +1 for tomorrow, and so on. This attribute could easily be a computed column rather than physically stored. It might be useful to set up similar structures for month, quarter, and year.

Many reporting tools, including all OLAP tools, include functionality to do prior period kinds of calculations, so the lag columns are often not required. Developers are sometimes skeptical of the date dimension's value since many of the attributes can be derived by the report developer. There are many excellent reasons to have a date dimension, but by including valuable attributes that cannot be computed, you may avoid the argument altogether.

9.9 Handling All the Dates

Bob Becker, Design Tip #61, Oct 28, 2004

It's not unusual to identify dozens of different dates, each with business significance that must be included in a dimensional design. For example, in a financial services organization you might be dealing with deposit date, withdrawal date, funding date, check written date, check processed date, account opened date, card issued date, product introduction date, promotion begin date, customer birth date, row effective date, row load date, and statement month.

The first thing to know is not all dates are created equal and handled the same way. Many dates end up as date dimension foreign keys in the fact tables. Some end up as attributes in a dimension table, while others become date dimension foreign keys in dimension tables. Finally, some dates are introduced in the design to facilitate ETL processing and auditing capabilities.

Assume our financial services company is designing a fact table integrating checking account transactions, such as deposit, ATM, and check transactions. Each fact row includes a transaction type dimension to identify the transaction it represents, as well as a transaction date dimension. The business meaning of the date (such as check transaction date, ATM transaction date, or deposit transaction date) is defined by the transaction type dimension. In this case, we would not include three separate date keys in the fact table because only one would be valid for a given row, as shown in Figure 9-5.

Financial Services Transaction Fact
Transaction Date Key (FK)
Transaction Type Key (FK)
Account Key (FK)
Branch Key (FK)
Household Key (FK)
Transaction Amount

Figure 9-5: The specific meaning of the transaction date depends on the transaction type dimension.

In other situations, a single transaction represented by one row in the fact table can be defined by multiple dates, such as the transaction event date and transaction posted date. In this case, both dates will be included as uniquely named dimension foreign keys. We would use role playing (described in article 9.11, *Data Warehouse Role Models*) to physically build one date dimension with views to present logically unique transaction event and transaction post date dimensions.

Obviously, we also include a date dimension in periodic snapshot schema reflecting the time period for the row, such as snapshot month. Month dimensions are shrunken subset date dimensions that conform with our core daily date dimension.

Many business-significant dates will be included as attributes in dimension tables. Account open date would be included in the account dimension, along with the primary account holder's birth date. When dates are dimension table attributes, we need to consider their reporting and analysis usage. Is it enough to know the actual date an account was opened, or should we also include attributes for account opened year and account opened fiscal month? These additional attributes improve the business users' ability to ask interesting analytic questions by grouping accounts based on the year and/or month the account was opened.

In order to support more extensive date-related analysis of these dimension attributes, you can incorporate a robust date dimension as an outrigger to the dimension table, as illustrated in Figure 9-6. In this case, we include the surrogate key for the applicable date in our dimension rather that the date itself, then use a view to declare unique business-appropriate column labels. This technique opens up all of the rich attributes of our core date dimension for analysis. However, remember that extensive use of outrigger dimensions can compromise usability and performance. Also, be careful that all outrigger dates fall within the date range stored in the standard date dimension table.

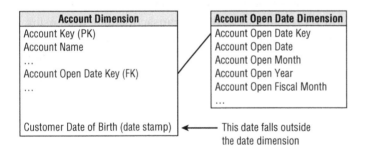

Figure 9-6: A dimension table with a date foreign key, as well as a date stamp attribute.

There are additional dates to help the data warehouse team manage the ETL process and support auditability of the data. Dates such as row effective date, row expiration date, row loaded date, or row last updated date should be included in each dimension table. Though these dates may not need to be user accessible, they can prove invaluable to the data warehouse team.

Miscellaneous Dimension Patterns

This section addresses several common dimension table patterns, including role-playing dimensions, junk dimensions, and causal dimensions. We also discuss hot-swappable dimensions, as well as the dangers of using abstract generic dimensions.

9.10 Selecting Default Values for Nulls

Bob Becker, Design Tip #128, *Oct 6, 2010*

The first scenario where nulls should be avoided is when we encounter a null value as a foreign key for a fact table row during the ETL process. We must do something in this case because an actual null value in a foreign key field of a fact table will violate referential integrity; the DBMS may not allow this situation to happen. There are a number of reasons why we have no foreign key:

- There is a data quality issue because the key value provided by the source system is invalid or incorrect.
- The dimension itself is not applicable for the particular fact row.
- The foreign key value is missing from the source data. In some cases, this missing data is another data quality issue. In other cases, the foreign key legitimately is not known because the event being tracked has not yet occurred as frequently happens with accumulating snapshot fact tables.
- When dealing with null foreign keys, we suggest applying as much intelligence in the ETL process as possible to select a default dimension row that provides meaning to the business users. Do not simply set up a single default row and point all default scenarios to the same row. Consider each condition separately and provide as many default rows as needed to provide the most complete understanding of the data as possible. At a minimum consider the following default rows:
    - **Missing Value.** The source system did not provide a value that would enable looking up the appropriate foreign key. This could indicate a missing data feed in the ETL process.
    - **Not Happened Yet.** The missing foreign key is expected to be available at a later point in time.
    - **Bad Value.** The source provided bad data or not enough data to determine the appropriate dimension row foreign key. This may be due to corrupted data at the source, or incomplete knowledge of the business rules for this source data for this dimension.
    - **Not Applicable.** This dimension is not applicable to this fact row.

■ Every dimension needs a set of default rows to handle these cases. Usually the ETL team assigns specific values such as 0, –1, –2, and –3 to the keys that describe these alternatives. The choice of the specific key value generally makes no difference, but there is one weird special case. When the calendar date dimension is used as the basis for partitioning a large fact table (say, on the Activity Date of a set of transactions), care must be taken that the Activity Date always has a real value, not one of the exceptional values, since such an exceptional record will get partitioned off to Siberia in the oldest partition if it has a key value of 0!

Handling Null Attribute Values in Dimension Tables

Nulls should also be avoided when we can't provide a value for a dimension attribute in a valid dimension row. There are a several reasons why the value of a dimension attribute may not be available:

■ **Missing Value.** The attribute was missing from the source data.
■ **Not Happened Yet.** The attribute is not yet available due to source system timing issues.
■ **Domain Violation.** Either we have a data quality issue, or we don't understand all the business rules surrounding the attribute. The data provided by the source system is invalid for the column type or outside the list of valid domain values.
■ **Not Applicable.** The attribute is not valid for the dimension row in question.

Text attributes in dimension tables usually can contain the actual values that describe the null conditions. Try to keep in mind the effect on BI tools downstream that have to display your special null value description in a fixed format report. Avoid tricks we've seen, such as populating the default attributes with a space or meaningless string of symbols like @@@ as these only confuse the business users. Consider the default values for each dimension attribute carefully and provide as much meaning as possible to provide context to the business users.

Numeric attributes in dimension tables will need to have a set of special values. A value of zero often is the best choice because it is usually obvious to the users that it is artificial. Some numeric attributes will present you with a difficult choice if the business users combine these values in numeric computations. Any actual numeric value used to stand in for null (say, zero) will participate in the computation but give misleading results. An actual null value participates gracefully in simple sums and averages, but may cause an error in a computation, which is annoying but at least does not produce a falsely confident result. Perhaps you can program your BI tool to display null numeric dimension attributes with "null" so that you can both report and compute on these attributes without worrying about distorted data.

Finally, these default value choices should be re-used to describe common null conditions across business processes and dimension tables in your dimensional data warehouse.

9.11 Data Warehouse Role Models

Ralph Kimball, DBMS, *Aug 1997*

Given the title, you may expect this article to be about stalwart IT citizens who play inspirational roles in making their data warehouses successful. Sorry, but yours truly is a modeler to the end. So what this article is really about is how "roles" arise in a data warehouse design and how we model them.

A *role* in a data warehouse is a situation in which a single dimension appears several times in the same fact table. This can happen in a number of ways. In certain kinds of fact tables, the date dimension can appear repeatedly. For instance, we may build a fact table to record the status and final disposition of a customer order as an accumulating snapshot fact table, illustrated in Figure 9-7.

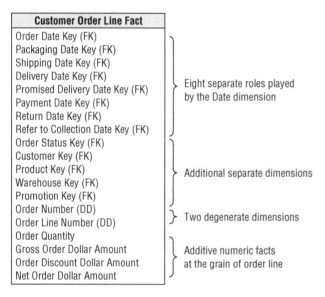

Customer Order Line Fact
Order Date Key (FK)
Packaging Date Key (FK)
Shipping Date Key (FK)
Delivery Date Key (FK)
Promised Delivery Date Key (FK)
Payment Date Key (FK)
Return Date Key (FK)
Refer to Collection Date Key (FK)
Order Status Key (FK)
Customer Key (FK)
Product Key (FK)
Warehouse Key (FK)
Promotion Key (FK)
Order Number (DD)
Order Line Number (DD)
Order Quantity
Gross Order Dollar Amount
Order Discount Dollar Amount
Net Order Dollar Amount

Eight separate roles played by the Date dimension

Additional separate dimensions

Two degenerate dimensions

Additive numeric facts at the grain of order line

Figure 9-7: Multiple dates on an accumulating snapshot of orders data.

The first eight dimensions in the design are all dates! However, we cannot join these eight foreign keys to the same table. SQL would interpret such an eight-way simultaneous join as requiring that all of the dates be the same. That doesn't seem very likely.

Instead of an eight-way join, we need to fool SQL into believing that there are eight independent date dimension tables. We even need to go to the length of labeling all of the columns in each of the tables uniquely. If we don't label the columns uniquely, we get into the embarrassing position of not being able to tell the columns apart if several of them have been dragged into a report.

Even though we cannot literally use a single time table, we still want to build and administer a single time table behind the scenes. For the user, we can create the illusion of eight independent time tables in a couple of ways. We can either make eight identical physical copies of the time table, or we can create eight virtual copies of the time table with the SQL SYNONYM command. Regardless of the approach, once we have made these eight clones, we still have to define a SQL view on each copy in order to make the field names uniquely different.

Now that we have eight differently described date dimensions, they can be used as if they were independent. They can have completely unrelated constraints, and they can play different roles in a report. This is a classic example of data warehouse role models. Although the other examples I am about to describe have nothing to do with time, they are handled in exactly the same way.

A second example was developed in article 10.24, *Traveling Through Databases*. We saw that voyage dimensional models representing journeys all needed to have at least four port dimensions to properly describe the context of a journey segment, as illustrated in Figure 9-8.

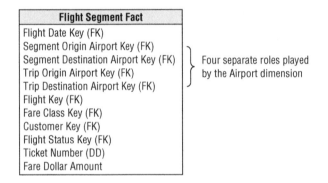

Figure 9-8: Multiple airports on a flight segment fact table.

The four airport dimensions are four different roles played by a single underlying airport table. We build and administer these exactly the way we handled the eight time tables in the previous example.

The telecommunications industry has many situations requiring the use of role models. With the advent of deregulation, a number of competing entities may all extract revenue from a single phone call. On a single call, these entities might include source system provider, local switch provider, long distance provider, and added value service provider.

These four entities need to be dimensions on every call. In the complex and evolving telecommunications industry, it may be very difficult and confusing to maintain four different partially overlapping tables of business entities; some business entities will play several of these roles. It will be far easier to keep a single business entity table and use it repeatedly within a data warehouse role model framework.

Actually, in building a full blown call revenue analysis fact table, we would also recognize that there are at least two more business entity roles that should be added to the design: calling party and called party. Figure 9-9 associates all six roles with the business entity dimension.

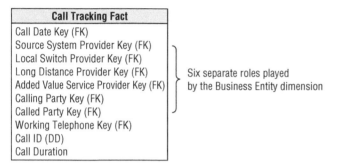

Call Tracking Fact
Call Date Key (FK)
Source System Provider Key (FK)
Local Switch Provider Key (FK)
Long Distance Provider Key (FK)
Added Value Service Provider Key (FK)
Calling Party Key (FK)
Called Party Key (FK)
Working Telephone Key (FK)
Call ID (DD)
Call Duration

Six separate roles played by the Business Entity dimension

Figure 9-9: Multiple business entities associated with a phone call.

The telecommunications industry also has a very well-developed notion of location. Many telecommunications dimensions have a precise geographic location as part of their description. This location may be resolved to a physical address, or even to a highly precise latitude and longitude. Using our role modeling skills, we can imagine building a master location table in the back room and then using it as the basis for populating selected attributes in all the dimensions that contain location information. These dimensions would typically include working telephone number, billing telephone number, equipment inventory, network inventory (including poles and switch boxes), real estate inventory, service location, dispatch location, right of way, and even business entity. Each record in the location table should define a point in space. Points in space are great because they roll up to every conceivable geography. Points in space roll up to counties, census tracts, and sales territories. The back room location records should probably include all of these rollups simultaneously.

To finish off, although it might be a stretch to implement such a table, imagine a single fact table that combines three of the examples in this article into one design. Imagine that we are capturing switch traffic at an internal node of a large telecommunications company. We want a very detailed view of this switch traffic so that we can make investments in new alternative routes for calls, new capacity for the current switch, and new features for the current switch. To make these decisions, we want to go all the way down to a microanalysis of who is using the switch for what purpose. We further imagine that after capturing the raw call traffic though the switch, we come back later in the billing cycle and correctly rate the revenue of each call, as illustrated in Figure 9-10.

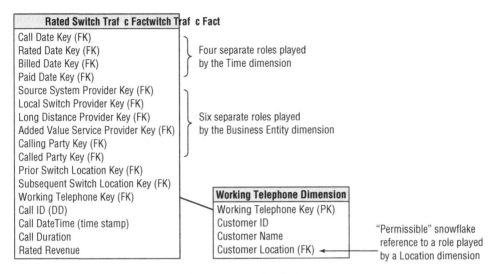

Figure 9-10: Sample schema with extensive role playing.

Here we have time playing four roles in the first four dimensions, business entity playing six roles, and location playing a role by being embedded in the last several dimensions. Although there is tremendous expressive power in all these dimensions, most of the work in creating the dimensions is focused on just three underlying tables. Any data warehouse designer who pulled off a design like this would be considered a good role model indeed.

9.12 Mystery Dimensions

Ralph Kimball, Intelligent Enterprise, *Mar 20, 2000*

In this article, junk dimensions are referred to as mystery dimensions.

Often, data warehouse architects derive a fact table's design from a specific data source. A typical complex example might be a set of records describing investment transactions. A recent example I studied had more than 50 fields in the raw data, and the business users assured me that all the fields were relevant and valuable.

Because every record in the data represented an investment transaction, and all the investments were somewhat similar, I hoped that the data source would generate only one fact table, where the grain was the individual transaction. But the 50 fields intimidated me. What on earth was all that stuff?

Investment transactions are good examples of complex, messy data. The complexity isn't the database designer's fault. These transactions are complex because there are a lot of context descriptors and special parameters describing modern financial investments. When a design challenge such as this confronts me, I try to stand back from the details and perform a kind of triage.

Find the Obvious Dimension-Related Fields

For the first step of triage, I find fields in the source data that are obviously parts of dimensions. Time stamps are straightforward. Maybe four separate time stamps describe our investment transaction. Each of these can be a time dimension, where we ask a single underlying calendar dimension to play four roles. We can accomplish this task by creating four views on the single underlying calendar table, as described in article 9.11, *Data Warehouse Role Models.*

Other straightforward dimension-related fields in our investment transaction include account numbers, account types, portfolio numbers, transaction types and codes, customer names and numbers, broker names and numbers, and location-specific information. A typical raw source data record is likely to be a kind of flat record containing both keys for these entities as well as descriptive text such as account type and customer name.

In the case of the 50 investment transaction fields I've described, we can quickly identify no fewer than 20 of the fields as dimension-related. We need to place a lot of redundant textual information in conventional dimensions, but after the dust clears, there are still 12 independent dimensions, of which four were roles the time dimension played, as shown in Figure 9-11.

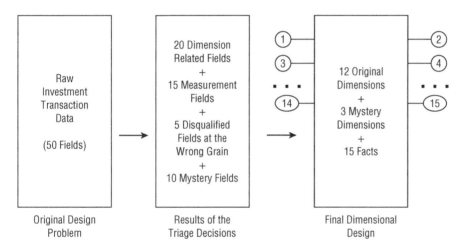

Figure 9-11: The logical progression of transforming complex source data into its corresponding dimensional model.

Find the Fact Related Fields

The second step of the triage is to look for the numeric measurements. Anything that is a floating point number or a scaled integer (such as a currency value) is likely to be a measurement. If the value varies in a seemingly random way between records and takes on a very large number of different values, then it is almost surely a measurement.

In the case of the 50 investment transaction fields, 20 of the fields clearly fit the characteristics of measurements. But five of the fields turned out to be cumulative measures that are not appropriate to the grain of an individual transaction. We excuse these five fields from the design and keep the remaining 15 fields, which we model as facts.

Now you may be thinking, what kind of weird transaction could possibly have 15 simultaneous facts? That's a good question because none of the source data transaction records actually had all 15 facts. Certain kinds of transactions gave rise to one set of facts and other transactions gave rise to an overlapping, but different set of facts. Most important, there was no disjoint partitioning of all the transactions that would separate the clumps of facts into nice groups. There were many transaction types and many investment account types; the pattern of measurements across these types and accounts was too complex to describe or neatly segment. In this sense, we could vindicate the raw data's design because it had to be flexible enough to handle many different investment transaction situations, including future types of investments that the records had not yet described.

Decide What to Do with the Rest

So far we have accounted for 40 of the 50 fields in our original data. But there are still 10 mystery fields left over, as shown in Figure 9-11. These fields aren't obvious textual dimension attributes or obvious foreign key values, so they may not feel like dimensions. The fields do not appear to be numeric measurements. When the fields are present, they seem to take on a small range of discrete values. Some of them are designated as codes, but no one is entirely sure of their significance. At this point, I ask an obligatory, but pointless question: If we don't know what the field means, why don't we leave it out of the design? The answer, of course, is that someone may need it, so we will leave it in. Actually, in spite of this frustrating third step of the triage, we have proceeded correctly. The value of the triage approach is to quickly identify the easy choices (in this case the obvious dimensions and facts) and to isolate a hopefully small subset of difficult data elements that require individual attention.

Also, perhaps at this point you are thinking that if we had a proper enterprise data model, then all these problems would have been sorted out and we wouldn't have to pursue such an ad hoc approach. Well, I couldn't agree more. If an enterprise data model is a model of real data, then I am its biggest fan. In that case, this article probably describes a specific episode in building that very useful enterprise data model. But if the enterprise data model describes a kind of abstract, ideal data world, describing how data should be if only it were designed correctly, then I have very little patience. Idealized enterprise data models are of only marginal use when we try to take real data and deliver it to business users on a tight budget and time frame. Idealized enterprise data models aren't populated with data.

Transform Mystery Fields Into Mystery Dimensions

Returning to our problem of 10 rogue fields that seem to be neither dimensions nor facts, we may be tempted to just leave them in the fact table. This is almost certainly a bad idea. Our goal should be to make these fields into dimensions. Many of the codes or alphanumeric fields would otherwise take up too much room, and we could drastically compress them if we could make them into dimensions.

Another easy approach is to just make 10 more dimensions, one for each mystery field. While this does place these low cardinality codes and textual values in dimension tables where we can easily index and constrain upon them, we now have 22 dimensions in our design, and that should raise a warning flag.

Should we just make one huge mystery dimension for all these remaining fields? That would seem to solve a number of problems. All the fields would be replaced by a single key. But this approach is likely to produce a dimension with as many records as the fact table itself. If the dimension contains several uncorrelated fields, there will be very few repeated values for the whole dimension record, and every transaction would produce a new mystery dimension record.

The secret to this last step of the design is to group the mystery fields together into correlated groups. Each of these correlated groups becomes a new dimension. It is wise to be flexible when searching for these correlations. Suppose fieldX has 100 discrete values and fieldY has 1,000 discrete values. The key question is: How many unique fieldX + fieldY combinations exist in the data? If there are exactly 1,000 such combinations, then fieldX is a hierarchical parent of fieldY, and they should absolutely be in the same dimension table. If the number of fieldX + fieldY combinations approaches 100,000, then the two fields are virtually independent and we would gain very little by placing them in the same dimension. But the situation is rarely so extreme. The number of fieldX + fieldY combinations might be 5,000 or 10,000. Even this correlation is pretty interesting, and the two fields should be part of the same dimension. To discover this case, you may have to comb the data, counting combinations of values in order to figure out what to do.

Finally, try to keep perspective. If you have five uncorrelated fields, but they each have only three values, it would be reasonable to package them all in a single mystery dimension. Yes, we end up with the Cartesian product of the fields, but there are only 35 = 243 possible combinations, a small and convenient mystery dimension. Ultimately, you should not be striving for mathematical elegance; rather you should be making pragmatic packaging decisions that best fit your data and your tools.

9.13 De-Clutter with Junk Dimensions

Bob Becker, Design Tip #48, *Aug 7, 2003*

When developing a dimensional model, we often encounter miscellaneous indicators and flags that don't logically belong to the core dimension tables. These unattached attributes are usually too valuable to ignore or exclude. Designers sometimes want to treat them as facts (supposed textual facts) or clutter the design with numerous small dimension tables. A third, less obvious but preferable solution is to incorporate a junk dimension as a holding place for these flags and indicators.

A junk dimension is a convenient grouping of flags and indicators. It's helpful, but not absolutely required, if there's a positive correlation among the values. The benefits of using a junk dimension include:

- Providing a recognizable, user-intuitive location for related codes, indicators, and their descriptors in a dimensional framework

- Cleaning up a cluttered design that already has too many dimensions. There might be five or more indicators that could be collapsed into a single 4-byte integer surrogate key in the fact table.
- Providing a smaller, quicker point of entry for queries compared to performance from constraining directly on these attributes in the fact table. If your database supports bitmap indices, this third potential benefit may be irrelevant, although the others are still valid.

An interesting use for a junk dimension is to capture the context of a specific transaction. While our common, conformed dimensions contain the key dimensional attributes of interest, there are likely attributes about the transaction that are not known until the transaction is processed.

For example, healthcare insurance providers may need to capture the context surrounding their claims transactions. The grain for this key business process is one row for each line item on a claim. Due to the complexities of the healthcare industry, similar claims may be handled quite differently. They may design separate junk dimensions to capture the context of how the claim was processed, how it was paid, and the contractual relationship between the healthcare providers at the time of the claim.

There are two approaches for creating junk dimensions. The first is to create the junk dimension table in advance. Each possible, unique combination generates a row in the junk dimension table. The second approach is to create the rows in the junk dimension on the fly during the ETL process. As new unique combinations are encountered, a new row with its surrogate key is created and loaded into the junk dimension table.

If the total number of possible rows in the junk dimension is relatively small, it is probably best to create the rows in advance. On the other hand, if the total number of possible rows in the junk dimension is large, it may be more advantageous to create the junk dimension as unique rows are encountered. One of the junk dimensions encountered in the recent healthcare design had more than one trillion theoretical rows, while the actual number of observed rows was tens of thousands. Obviously, it did not make sense to create all the theoretically possible rows in advance. If the number of rows in the junk dimension approaches or exceeds the number of rows in the fact table, the design should be clearly reevaluated.

Finally, because a junk dimension includes all valid combinations of attributes, it will automatically track any changes in dimension attributes. Therefore slowly changing dimension strategies do not need to be considered for junk dimensions.

9.14 Showing the Correlation between Dimensions

Ralph Kimball, Design Tip #6, Apr 10, 2000

One of the questions I get asked frequently is "How can I represent the correlation between two dimensions without going through the fact table?" Often the designer follows up with the question

"Can I create a little joiner table with just the two dimension keys and then connect that table to the fact table?"

Of course, in a classic dimensional model, we only have two choices. Either the dimensions are modeled independently and the two dimension keys occur together only in the fact table, or else the two dimensions are combined into a single super dimension with a single key. So when does the designer choose separate dimensions and when does the designer combine the dimensions?

To be more concrete, imagine that the two dimensions are product and market in a retail setting. The fact table records actual sales of products in the various markets over time. Our desire to represent the correlation between the product and market dimensions is based on the suspicion that "products are highly correlated with markets in our business." This sentence is the key to the whole design question.

If products are very highly correlated with markets, then there may be a one-to-one or a many-to-one relationship between products and markets. In this case, combining the two dimensions makes eminent sense. The combined dimension is only as big as the larger of the two dimensions. Browsing (looking at the combinations of values) within the combined dimension would be useful and fast. Interesting patterns would be apparent.

But rarely do product and market have such a nice relationship. At least three factors intrude that eventually make us pull these two dimensions apart:

1. The one-to-one or many-to-one relationship may not literally be true. We may have to admit that the relationship is really many-to-many. In the extreme case when most products are sold in most markets, it becomes obvious that we need two dimensions because otherwise our combined dimension becomes huge and starts to look like a Cartesian product of the original dimensions. Browsing doesn't yield much insight.
2. If the relationship between product and market varies over time, or under the influence of a fourth dimension, like promotion, then we have to admit that the combined dimension is, in reality, some kind of fact table itself!
3. There are more relationships between product and market than simply the retail sales. Each business process involving product and market will result in its own fact table. Good candidates include promotion coverage, advertising, distribution, and inventory. Creating a combined product-market dimension exclusively around retail sales would make some of these other processes impossible to express.

The point of this article is to encourage you to visualize the relationship between the entities you choose as dimensions. When entities have a fixed, time-invariant strongly correlated relationship, they should be modeled as a single dimension. In most other cases, your design will be simpler and smaller when you separate the entities into two dimensions.

Don't avoid the fact table! Fact tables are incredibly efficient. They contain only dimension keys and measurements. They contain only the combinations of dimensions that occur in a particular process. So when you want to represent the correlation between dimensions, remember that the fact table was created exactly for this purpose.

9.15 Causal (Not Casual) Dimensions

Ralph Kimball, DBMS, *Nov 1996*

One of the most interesting and valuable dimensions in a data warehouse is one that explains why a fact table record exists. In most data warehouses, you build a fact table record when something happens. For example:

- When the cash register rings in a retail store, a fact table record is created for each line item on the sales ticket. The obvious dimensions of this fact table record are product, store, customer, sales ticket, and date, as shown in Figure 9-12.
- At a bank ATM, a fact table record is created for every customer transaction. The dimensions of this fact table record are financial service, ATM location, customer, transaction type, and time.
- When the telephone rings, the phone company creates a fact table record for each "hook event." A complete call tracking data warehouse in a telephone company records each completed call, busy signal, wrong number, and partially dialed call.

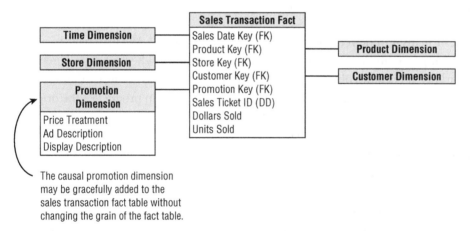

Figure 9-12: A typical dimensional schema for a set of retail sales transactions with a "causal" promotion dimension.

In all three of these cases, a physical event takes place, and the data warehouse responds by storing a fact table record. However, the physical events and the corresponding fact table records are more interesting than simply storing a small piece of revenue. Each event represents a conscious decision by the customer to use the product or the service. A good marketing person is fascinated by these events. Why did the customer choose to buy the product or use the service at that exact moment? Our data warehouses could answer almost any marketing question if we only had a dimension called "why did the customer buy my product just now?" We call a dimension like this a "causal" dimension because it explains what caused the event.

Surprisingly, in many cases the available data can build a good approximation of a causal dimension. This data masquerades under headings such as promotion, store condition, deal, contract, rate card, or reason. For instance, in a retail environment, a number of management decisions are in effect at any time for a product, including temporary price reduction, on ad, or on display. Each of these management decisions arguably affects the volume of sales. Most of these decisions are viewed as retail promotions.

At a bank ATM, there may be a new account drive, a promotional mailing, or a branch teller surcharge. Again, each of these management decisions affects the volume and the patterns of ATM usage. There may also be exogenous effects on ATM usage that are not the result of a human management decision, such as a national holiday or bad weather.

The telephone company hook events are similarly "explained" by causal dimensions such as reduced rate dialing specials, lifeline rates, and off-peak usage incentives. Some of these descriptors can be found in legacy data in the form of contracts, deals, or rate cards.

One of the best things a data warehouse designer can do is search for and build causal dimensions. Data for causal conditions, such as promotions, store conditions, or contracts, is often available somewhere in the corporate environment, but is rarely linked in a clean way to the primary transaction data feed. Retail transaction systems are the most likely to have a link to causal data, largely because retail transaction systems must keep track of price reductions and markdowns. Less commonly, the retail transaction system also keeps track of whether an item is on display or being advertised. In some cases, the data warehouse team can ask the production point-of-sale programming staff to add an advisory data field to the legacy data. The store manager can fill in the field on a regular basis to record whether an item is being promoted through displays or advertisements. This kind of business reengineering greatly simplifies data extraction for the data warehouse team and improves the power of the data warehouse.

ATM transaction and telephone switch usage data almost never contain links to causal data. In these cases, causal data needs to be merged into the transaction data from an entirely separate source, such as a marketing promotion system.

A useful causal dimension need not describe every minor variation in a promotion or store condition. It may be most useful to build a causal dimension at a reasonably high level, gradually building up a few hundred types of promotion descriptions or store conditions. Figure 9-12 shows a useful causal dimension for a retail store point of sale fact table. The new causal dimension key is simply inserted into the existing fact table without violating the grain of the fact table or changing any existing applications. In this case, the relevant causal conditions being measured include price treatment, ad description, and display description. Any given promotion for a product in a store on a given day will consist of some combination of these factors. For example, orange juice may be discounted today in all of the stores, but only some of the stores may accompany the discount with a special in-store display. Notice that one of the most important records in this promotion dimension is the record describing "no promotion." Most of the products in a store on a given day are probably sold under the "no promotion" causal condition.

A causal dimension is a kind of advisory dimension that should not change the fundamental grain of a fact table. Recall that the grain of a fact table identifies the meaning of a single fact table record. In Figure 9-12, the grain of the fact table is the individual line item on a particular customer's sales ticket. I stated earlier in this article that the natural dimensions of this fact table are product, store, customer, sales ticket, and time. If you decide that you can describe each sale more specifically by a set of promotion conditions, store conditions, and exogenous conditions, then you can add a special key into the fact table that points to the relevant combined causal description for each sales record. The addition of such a key does not change the number of fact table records. All of the old applications continue to work, continue to produce exactly the same results, and do not require recoding. This is an example of the robustness of the dimensional database organization as described in article 6.9, *Dangerous Preconceptions*. In this case, the dangerous preconception is that you cannot add additional information, such as a causal dimension, to the design after the data warehouse becomes operational. As this example illustrates, you can add new dimensions at any time, as long as you are careful to preserve the original grain. As I pointed out in article 6.9, it is easy to preserve the original grain if you start with the lowest level transactions in the business, because in a very fundamental sense it is not possible to create a more granular view of the business. A sales transaction is a sales transaction, whether or not you accompany it with fancy causal descriptors.

Some of you may be bothered by the assumption that the causal dimension "explains" why the customer bought the product. Obviously, you never know for sure why anyone buys anything. In some cases, you can't even be sure whether the presumed stimulus (the ad or display) was even noticed by the customer. For these reasons, causal factors are usually classified as "absolute" or "suspected." An absolute causal factor, such as a price reduction, is a factor you know affected some aspect of the sale, such as the price. A suspected causal factor, such as a newspaper ad or bad weather, is simply a causal factor that existed at the same time as the sale but may not have been visible to or even noticed by the customer at the time of purchase. In the long run, it is up to advanced techniques such as data mining to determine if a correlation exists between these suspected causal factors and any change in sales.

The link between causal factors and business performance leads to the most important business question surrounding a causal dimension, namely "Was my promotion profitable?" Equivalently we ask, "Did the promotion (or other causal factor) make any difference?" There are at least three increasingly sophisticated ways to ask this question. The most basic form of the question is: Was I profitable while the promotion or other causal factor was happening? The intermediate form of the question is: What was the lift of the promotion compared to the baseline sales? And the most advanced form of the question is: What were the patterns of cannibalization and time shifting as a result of the promotion? Which other products were affected, and which other products showed no effect?

Finally, the existence of a causal dimension often provokes the "what didn't happen?" question. For example, what was on promotion that did not sell? Even with a causal dimension, you cannot answer these questions with a fact table that records what did happen. A companion fact table, called a factless fact table, is needed in this case. The set difference between the factless fact table and the primary sales event fact table provides the answer. In article 8.13, *Factless Fact Tables*, I describe the structure of coverage factless tables that help show where causal factors did not produce the results we had hoped for.

9.16 Resist Abstract Generic Dimensions

Margy Ross, Design Tip #83, *Sep 8, 2006*

Childhood guessing games sometimes rely on the distinction of "person, place, or thing" for early mystery solving clues. Some modelers use these same characterizations in their data models by creating abstract person, place, and/or thing (typically referred to as product) tables. Although generalized tables appeal to the purist in all of us and may provide flexibility and reusability advantages for a data modeler, they often result in larger, more complicated dimension tables in the eyes of the business user.

Consider a generic person or party dimension. Because our employees, customers, and supplier contacts are all people, we should store them in the same dimension, right? Similarly, the same argument could be made for the geographic locations where our internal facilities, customers, and suppliers reside. Though a single table approach might seem clean and logical to data modelers and IT application developers, this abstraction often appears completely illogical to most business analysts for several reasons:

1. We collect and know vastly different information about our own internal entities than we do about external entities. Using a generic model means that some attributes are either nonsensical and/or unpopulated.
2. Generic attribute labels don't supply adequate meaning and context for the business users and BI applications. For example, if a report illustrates sales by state, it's unclear whether that refers to the state where the store is located or the state where the customer is located. It's far preferable if the attribute is clearly labeled to denote its full meaning.
3. Lumping all varieties of people, places, or products that our business interacts with inevitably results in larger dimension tables than if they were divided into more discrete logical entities.

Some of you might be familiar with a technique called *role playing,* described in article 9.11, *Data Warehouse Role Models*, where the same physical dimension table simultaneously serves multiple logical roles in the same fact table, such as the date dimension appearing as two uniquely labeled dimensions for the ship date and request date in a single fact table. Other role playing examples might include the origin and destination airports, or the servicing and authorizing employees, or the dealer that sold the car versus the dealer maintaining it. In each of these examples, a single row in the dimension table could serve in multiple capacities. Role playing is a very different concept than creating a generic dimension table that's potentially the Cartesian product of all possible parties.

It's worth noting that while generic dimensions are not appropriate for the dimensional model viewed by the business, we're certainly not opposed to their usage in operational systems where they're behind the scenes and not visible to the business. However, in most legacy situations, the operational source systems do not treat persons, places, or things homogenously. It's more likely that descriptive information about our facility locations, customer locations, and supplier locations comes from a variety of different source systems and have different attributes. Attempting to create a generic dimension table from these various sources may create onerous integration challenges for the ETL team without any payback from a business user perspective.

Finally, let's not forget the dimensional modelers' mantra—easy to use and fast query performance. In most cases, abstract dimension tables fail to deliver on either front because the abstraction process reduces clarity for the business users and inevitably creates a larger table. They should be avoided in the dimensional models that are presented to the business in your DW/BI architecture.

9.17 Hot-Swappable Dimensions

Ralph Kimball, Design Tip #16, *Dec 8, 2000*

In article 7.12, *Rating Your Dimensional Data Warehouse*, criterion #18 in the list of dimensionally friendly criteria defines a *hot-swappable dimension*, which is a dimension with two or more alternative versions. If the dimension is hot-swappable, any of the alternative versions of the dimension can be chosen at query time.

There are a number of situations where alternative versions of the same dimension can be very useful. Here are three interesting scenarios:

1. An investment banking house makes available to its clients a large fact table that tracks stocks and bonds on a daily basis over a several year period. The investment dimension in this fact table provides information about each stock and bond. But this investment dimension is customized to each client accessing the fact table so that they can each describe and group the investments in interesting and proprietary ways. The different versions of the investment dimension may be completely different, including incompatible attribute names and different hierarchy schemes. All clients use the same fact table (hence it only needs to be stored in one place), but each client uses their own investment dimension table as the basis for analyzing the price movements of the stocks and bonds. Viewed from the database server, the clients are busily hot-swapping the investment dimension with each query.

2. A retail bank creates a single large fact table that records the month end balances of all the account types in the bank, including checking, savings, mortgage, credit card, personal loans, small business loans, certificates of deposit, student loans, and others. This is a classic case of *heterogeneous products* because the detailed descriptions of each of these account types are wildly different. There is no single description template that can adequately deal with the complexities of all these account types. Therefore we build a simplified account dimension that is

meant to join to all the accounts uniformly. We use this simplified account dimension when we are doing cross-selling and up-selling analyses and are looking at the overall portfolio of a customer. But when we restrict our attention to a single account type (e.g., mortgages), we swap in a drastically wider (more fields) dimension that only contains mortgage-related attributes. We can do this when we are confident that we have restricted the analysis to just one kind of account. If we have 20 lines of business, we have 21 account dimensions: one simplified dimension describing all the accounts and 20 extended dimensions describing disjoint sets of similar accounts.

3. A manufacturer wishes to make its shipments fact table available to its trading partners, but needs to shield the orders of the partners from each other. In this case, each partner gets their own version of the partner dimension with only their own name appearing in plain text. All the other partners show as "Other." Additionally, a mandatory weighting factor field in the dimension is set to one for the intended partner and is set to zero for all others. This weighting factor is uniformly multiplied against all facts in the fact table. In this way, a single shipments fact table can be used to support competitive trading partners in a secure way.

Hot swapping dimensions is straightforward in a standard relational database because the joins between tables can be specified at query time. But if referential integrity is required between the dimension tables and the fact table, then every swappable version of the dimension must contain the full key set and hence the full set of dimension records. In this case if the swappable dimension is being used to restrict the access to the fact table (as in examples 2 and 3), the restricted rows of the dimension table must contain dummy or null values. Hot swapping of dimensions is more of a challenge for OLAP systems where the identity of the dimension is built deeply into the fabric of the OLAP data cube.

9.18 Accurate Counting with a Dimensional Supplement

Warren Thornthwaite, Design Tip #12, *Aug 27, 2000*

We can obviously perform counts on a dimension table in the absence of fact metrics. Sometimes we're asked to provide dimension counts relative to supplemental information that intersects with the dimension table.

We recently loaded a simple example of this kind of supplemental table that maps zip code to Media Market Areas (MMA). Marketing folks were interested in seeing how our customers break out by MMA compared to the overall population. In other words, they want to know where are we getting strong geographical penetration, and where are we not doing as well. If this supplemental data proves valuable to the organization, we would go ahead and add it into the customer dimension as an additional attribute. But first, marketing asked us to do some initial queries to make sure it is worth the effort.

To run these queries, we join the supplemental table to our customer table and do customer counts by MMA. However, we have to be careful because the two sets do not overlap 100 percent. There are some zip codes in the MMA table with no corresponding customers, and there are some customers whose zip codes have no corresponding MMA. An inner join will undercount both sides of the query. We can use the following two tables to illustrate this:

Zip	MMA	Customer_Key	Zip
94025	SF-Oak-SJ	27	94303
94303	SF-Oak-SJ	33	94025
97112	Humboldt	47	24116
98043	Humboldt	53	97112
00142	Gloucester	55	94025

If we'd like to see how many customers we have by MMA, an inner join gives us the following:

MMA	Count(Customer_Key)
Humboldt	1
SF-Oak-SJ	3

The inner join is an equal join. Because there is no MMA for zip 24116, the query undercounts our subscriber base, giving us 4 customers when we really have 5. We also lose information on the other side of the join because the results don't tell us the MMAs where we have zero penetration (e.g., Gloucester). Rewriting the query with a full outer join gives us the following:

MMA	Count(Customer_Key)
NULL	1
Gloucester	0
Humboldt	1
SF-Oak-SJ	3

Now we are counting all 5 of our customers, and we see we have no customers in Gloucester. We could use an IFNULL function on the character column to replace those NULLs with friendlier values, like "MMA Unknown." Note that what you count makes a big difference in your results. In our case, we counted Customer_Key. If we had counted(*), we would have gotten a total of 7 items, because the * counts rows, and the full results set has 7 rows. If we had counted (MMA_to_Zipcode.Zip_Code), we would have returned a count of 6 because 94025 is counted twice.

You need to be cautious using outer joins because you can easily undermine the logic by putting a constraint on one of the participating tables. A constraint on Customer_Age < 25 would yield a report with exactly the same structure and headings but reduced counts. If the report is not explicitly labeled, it would be misleading.

We've discovered that combining the CASE statement with the SUM function is a great trick to get counts of various subsets of the full results set from both sides of the outer join in a single pass. Using the preceding data, we could create a query that gives us total counts for all three areas of the data set. In the SELECT list you could write:

```
SUM(CASE WHEN Media_Market_Area.Zip IS NULL THEN 1 ELSE 0 END) AS
Customer_Count_with_No_MMA,
SUM(CASE WHEN COUNT(customer_key) = 0 THEN 1 ELSE 0 END) AS
    MMA_Count_with_No_Customers,
SUM(CASE WHEN NOT(Media_Market_Area.Zip IS NULL
    OR COUNT(customer_key) = 0) THEN 1
    ELSE 0 END AS Count_MMAs_with_Customers)
```

This gives you three columns: the count of customers with no MMAs, the count of MMAs with no customers, and a count where they match. Essentially, the constraints are built into the CASE statement, so they don't limit the results of the outer join.

Slowly Changing Dimensions

We introduced the concept of slowly changing dimensions (SCDs) in article 1.8, *Slowly Changing Dimensions*, but this section delves deeper into the nuances, complexities, and alternative approaches for tracking attribute changes in a dimension table.

9.19 Perfectly Partitioning History with Type 2 SCD

Ralph Kimball, Design Tip #8, May 21, 2000

The type 2 SCD approach provides a different kind of partitioning. You could call this a logical partitioning of history. In the type 2 approach, whenever we encounter a change in a dimension record, we issue a new record, and add it to the existing dimension table. A simple example of such a change is a revised product attribute where something about the product, such as the packaging type, changes but the product stock number does not change. As keepers of the data warehouse, we have taken a pledge to perfectly track history and so we must track both the new product description, as well as the old.

The type 2 SCD requires special treatment of the dimension key. We must assign a generalized key because we can't use the same product stock number as the key. This gives rise to the whole discussion of assigning anonymous surrogate keys. Stop and think for a moment about how we have been using the dimension key up to the point where we make the new dimension record described previously. Before today, we have been using the "old" surrogate key whenever we created a fact table record describing some product activity. Today, two things happen. First, we assume that the changed packaging type goes into effect with the new fact table data that we receive today. Second, this means that after we create the new dimension record with its new surrogate key, we then use that surrogate key with all of today's new fact records. But we don't go back to previous fact records to change the product key!

The old product dimension record still points correctly to all the previous historical data, and the new product dimension record will now point to today's records and subsequent records, until we are forced to make another type 2 change.

This is what we mean when we say that the type 2 SCD perfectly partitions history. If you visualize this, you really understand this design technique.

Notice that when you constrain on something in the dimension like the product name, which is unaffected by the change in the packaging type attribute, you automatically pick up both the old and new dimension records, and you automatically join to all of the product history in the fact table. It is only when you constrain or group on the packaging type attribute that SQL smoothly divides the history into the two regimes.

9.20 Many Alternate Realities

Ralph Kimball, Intelligent Enterprise, *Feb 9, 2000*

Data warehouse designers take an implicit oath to represent the past correctly. We promise our users that if the definition of a customer or product changes slowly over time, we will be very careful to keep the old definitions in the database and apply them to history correctly. If we work for an insurance company and we are looking backward in time to see why we approved insurance for a particular cluster of customers, we must have the correct descriptions of those customers at the moments in the past when we approved their insurance, not the descriptions that are valid in the present. These customers are now older and presumably wealthier, wiser, and have larger families. We don't want these revised descriptions when evaluating an old decision.

Data warehouse designers have long recognized the need for describing the past accurately. In the dimensional data warehouse, the world divides into fact tables and dimension tables. Fact table data, by its nature, represents a time series of measurements and is always augmented with an explicit time dimension. Finding old fact table data is easy and is one of the standard queries in the data warehouse. Just constrain the time dimension to the appropriate previous time interval.

But dimension table data requires more thought. Dimensions don't change in predictable ways. Individual customers and products evolve slowly and episodically. Some of the changes are true physical changes. Customers change their addresses because they move. A product is manufactured with different packaging. Other changes are actually corrections of mistakes in the data. And finally, some changes are changes in how we classify a product or customer and are more a matter of opinion than physical reality.

Over the past decade, data warehouse designers have sorted out three major approaches to SCDs, called type 1, type 2, and type 3.

- *A type 1 SCD* **is an overwrite of a dimensional attribute.** History is definitely lost. We overwrite when we are correcting an error in the data or when we truly don't want to save history.
- *A type 2 SCD* **creates a new dimension record with a new surrogate key.** We create surrogate keys when a true physical change occurs in a dimension entity at a specific point in time, such as the customer address change or the product packaging change. We often add effective and expiration time stamps and a reason code in the dimension record to precisely describe the change.
- *A type 3 SCD* **adds a new field in the dimension record, but does not create a new record.** We add a new field when we have a new classification for the customer or product that is a matter of opinion rather than physical reality. Maybe we change the designation of the customer's sales territory because we redraw the sales territory map, or we arbitrarily change the category of the product. In both cases, we augment the original dimension attribute with an "old" attribute so we can switch between these alternate realities. Type 3 is distinguished from type 2 because we could regard both the old and new descriptions of a type 3 change as true simultaneously.

These three types of slowly changing dimensions handle most of the situations faced by the data warehouse designer. But a few weird situations remain that seem to be a hybrid of type 2 and type 3; I refer to them as *many alternate realities*.

Predictable Multiple Realities

Consider a situation where a sales organization continually revises the map of its sales districts. Perhaps it adjusts its sales districts each year to try to adapt to changing market conditions. Over a 10-year period, the sales organization accumulates no fewer than 10 different maps. On the surface, this organization would seem like a candidate for the type 2 slowly changing dimension. But as the database designer, you discover during the user interviews that this sales organization has a much more complex set of requirements. It wants to:

- Report each year's sales using the approved district map for that year.
- Report each year's sales using a district map from an arbitrary different year.
- Report an arbitrary span of years' sales using a single district map from any chosen year.

The most common version of the third requirement would be to report the complete span of years using today's map.

You cannot serve this set of requirements with the type 2 model because type 2 perfectly partitions history, and a year can only be reported using its assigned unique map. The requirements cannot be met with a type 3 model because type 3 only allows a single "alternate reality," and in this case, we have 10 alternate realities.

In this example, we can take advantage of the regular nature of these 10 alternate realities by generalizing the type 3 model to have not one, but 10, versions of the district attribute for each sales team. The sales team dimension would then look something like:

> Sales Team Key
> Sales Team Name
> Sales Team Physical Address (stays constant)
> Current District
> District2015 (the district assignment for the team in 2015)
> District2014
> District2013
> District2012
> District2011
> District2010
> District2009
> District2008
> District2007
> … plus other unrelated sales team attributes.

Each sales team record would have all 10 district interpretations, and the user could choose to roll up all sales teams with any of the 10 district maps. In this design, there is one record for each sales team, and the addition of more realities merely requires the addition of more district attributes in the original dimension records.

Unpredictable Multiple Realities

Now let's make the problem harder. Suppose that the assignment of each sales team to a district is not synchronized to calendar years, but occurs at random and unpredictable times, and each sales team is different. Now we will restate the reporting requirements a little. The users want to:

- Report district sales at any past instant in time using the assignments that were valid at that instant
- Report all sales over all time using today's district map
- Report all sales over all time using a selected obsolete district map

This design requires a hybrid of type 2 and type 3. We issue a new record for a sales team whenever its district assignment changes, but we also carry along a Current District attribute in all the versions of each sales team record that is overwritten whenever the current district map is altered. The sales team record now looks like:

> Sales Team Key
> Sales Team Name
> Sales Physical Address (remains unchanged)

District (the district assignment valid between the following dates)

Begin Effective Date (the first date this record is valid)

End Effective Date (the last date this record is valid)

Obsolete District (a selected obsolete definition)

Current District (the most current district assignment; periodically overwritten)

… plus other unrelated sales team attributes.

We administer this design differently. When a sales team is deemed to be part of a new district, we issue a new record for that sales team. This is a straightforward type 2 SCD response. We bookkeep the begin and end dates correctly. We assume here that the end effective date for one assignment of a district is exactly one day less than the begin effective date of the next assignment. We keep the same value in a given obsolete definition across all the records that describe a specific sales team. Finally, we also sweep back through all previous instances of this sales team's records and overwrite the Current District attribute. The obsolete and current attributes are a variation of the type 3 SCD. Now we can meet all of the reporting objectives given to us by the users. When we report all district sales at a particular instant in time, we must constrain the query in the following way:

```
Reporting_date >= Begin_effective_date AND Reporting_date
<= End_effective_date
```

Or you can write this:

```
Reporting_date BETWEEN Begin_ effective_date AND End_effective_date
```

9.21 Monster Dimensions

Ralph Kimball, DBMS, May 1996

In today's data warehouses, a medium size dimension, such as a master product list for a retailer, may have 500,000 records. Serious DBMSs are capable of browsing among the textual attributes such as flavor and package type in a 500,000-row table and giving the user good interactive performance. The biggest customer dimensions, however, are at least 10 times bigger than the biggest product dimensions. All large companies that deal with individual human customers have customer lists ranging from a few million to more than 100 million records. This dimension cannot be compressed or summarized. The customer list dimension drives just about every interesting fact table in these businesses and needs to be available at the lowest level of granularity in order to subset the business based on detailed customer characteristics.

Unfortunately, big customer lists are even more likely to "slowly change" than the medium size product lists. Retailers are anxious to periodically update their customer information. Insurance companies must update their information about their customers, their insured automobiles, and their insured homes because it is critical to have an accurate description of these items at the time a policy is approved and when a claim is made. Figure 9-13 shows a typical customer list, with "hot" demographic fields that are especially interesting to track as they change. However, it would seem like you are between a rock and a hard place. You must track the slowly changing nature of the customer list, but you don't dare create a new dimension record every time something changes because of the table size.

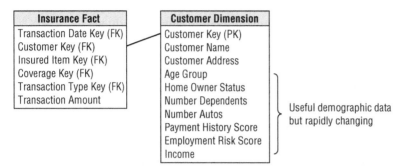

Figure 9-13: Customer dimension with rapidly changing demographic attributes.

The solution to this dilemma is to break off the hot customer attributes into their own separate "demographics" mini-dimension table as shown in Figure 9-14. You leave behind more stable information in the original customer table and gain the advantage of being able to track the changing nature of the customer descriptions.

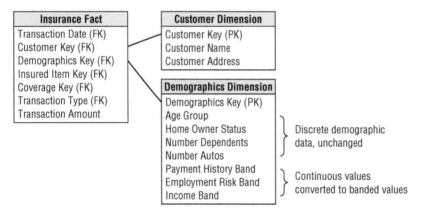

Figure 9-14: Separating frequently changing customer attributes in a demographics mini-dimension.

First, you need to make a subtle change in order to successfully create this new demographics dimension. All of the continuously variable demographic measures, such as income, must be converted to banded values. In other words, you force the attributes in this new dimension to have a relatively small number of discrete values. You then build the dimension with all possible discrete attribute combinations. For example, in Figure 9-14, if each of the seven attributes has 10 possible values, then the demographics dimension theoretically could have a very large number of records. But in practice the number is much smaller since we build these dimension records as we encounter them in the real data.

Now every time something interesting happens with one of your customers, such as a sales event or an insurance claim event, you put a record into the appropriate fact table describing this event. Two of the surrogate keys will be customer and demographics, as shown in Figure 9-14. Because the decision to associate the demographics key with the customer key occurs whenever you place a record into the fact table, you can change the demographics description of the customer as frequently as you wish. There is little added overhead in the dimension tables with this approach because at load time you reuse existing demographics combinations and only build new ones as needed.

The big advantage of this approach is that you can support very frequent snapshotting of customer profiles with little increase in data storage or complexity as you increase the number of snapshots. But there are some trade-offs. First, you are forced to clump the demographic attributes into banded ranges of discrete values. This places a limit on the specificity of the data (such as income), and makes it impractical to change to a different set of value bands at a later time. Once you decide on your bands, you are stuck with them.

Second, the demographics dimension itself cannot be allowed to grow too large. There are certainly some cases in which you will have more than a million possible combinations of demographics attributes. Surprisingly, a workable solution to this problem is to build a second demographics dimension. At a large retailer recently, I faced the problem of two sets of demographics measures. One set related to traditional income, family, and education measures of the customer and the other related to volatile purchase and credit behavior measured while buying the retailer's products. All of these attributes combined together resulted in several million possible combinations. I was worried that the demographic dimension approach was not going to work. Somewhat reluctantly, I proposed a two demographics dimensions approach. To my surprise, the resulting data warehouse was very successful. The retailer was very pleased with the flexibility of the data model and the ability to track the changes both in family demographics and behavior very responsively.

A third potential drawback to this approach is that we have separated the hot demographics data from the more constant descriptors of the customer, such as geographic location and birth date. Now it is harder to browse the data as if it were a single dimension implemented as a flat file. The demographics data can now only be browsed along with the more constant customer data by linking through the fact table. This will usually be a slower and more expensive browse than if all the data were in a single dimension table. I don't think this is a killer criticism, however. Relational systems will give the correct answer to the browse; they simply may be a little slow. This seems like a reasonable price to pay for the freedom to track the customers so responsively.

Finally, sharp-eyed readers may point out that when using this approach you can associate demographics with the customer only when you actually generate a fact table record, such as a sales event or an insurance claim event. Theoretically, if there are no sales, the fact table is empty. If the fact table is empty, then you will never be able to link the demographics to the customer. Though this is technically true, there are easy ways around this dilemma. If sales are so sparse that you actually are in danger of missing a demographics measurement, then all you need to do is define a demographics transaction event. This event has no sales dollars associated with it, but it serves as a good place to register a new demographics profile of the customer. Fact table records are cheap. There are billions of them in fact tables anyway.

9.22 When a Slowly Changing Dimension Speeds Up

Ralph Kimball, Intelligent Enterprise, *Aug 3, 1999*

Slowly changing dimensions are one of the hallmarks of dimensional modeling. They have become so well recognized as a standard data warehousing design problem that they now have their own acronym. Once I saw a discussion on a list server about "SCDs" and I was wondering what an SCD was. Then I realized they were talking about slowly changing dimensions.

The data warehouse has a responsibility to track history accurately, so we can't afford to overwrite the prior customer description with the new one. Similarly, we can't overwrite the old product description. So whenever a dimension record undergoes a change, we issue a new dimension record. This is the heart of the type 2 SCD logic, and it has significant implications. The grain of our dimension is no longer the individual customer or the individual product; rather it's the individual customer snapshot or the individual product snapshot. Also, we are forced to generalize the dimension key if we haven't already done so. Obviously, we cannot use the simple customer ID or product ID as the physical key for the dimension; this situation drives the use of surrogate keys.

Now that data warehousers have been using type 2 SCDs for several years, what have we learned? What are the refinements of this technique, and what are the limits of this approach? What happens when a slowly changing dimension isn't slow after all?

Date Stamps in Slowly Changing Dimensions

It certainly feels natural to include a date (or time) stamp in an SCD record. Date stamps represent the moment in time when the current description in the record becomes valid. It is important to realize, however, that the stamp does not participate as a normal constraint on the dimension when it is connected to a fact table. Suppose, for example, we are talking about a product dimension record. The date stamp refers to the moment when the product description became valid, but this stamp may have little to do with the date and time dimensions attached to the main fact table. It's often incorrect to constrain the date stamp in the dimension record to coordinate with the date and time in the fact table. A company may sell an old product well after a new version has superseded it. In that case, the fact table date has little to do with the date stamp in the dimension.

Nevertheless, the date stamp in the dimension has its own uses, and using such stamps in a dimension is an advanced SCD technique. It is possible, with a little careful SQL, to perform very precise time slicing of the dimension by itself. If, for example, you are asking for all the customer dimension records as of September 13, 2015, at 1:00 p.m., you must ask for all the records that have distinct customer IDs and whose date stamps are the latest ones less than or equal to September 13, 2015, at 1:00 p.m. I'll leave it to you to work out the SQL.

An alternate date stamping technique places two date stamps in the dimension, the first representing the date of the change and the second representing the date of the next change. This requires more ETL work, but makes the SQL for retrieving a dimension record as of a specific date much simpler.

Precision time slicing of a dimension using the technique just described is particularly powerful in human resources applications, in which you may want to ask such questions as, "how many employees of a particular job grade did we have at a precise moment in the past?"

SCDs That Aren't Slowly Changing

SCDs live on a continuum. The records in some product dimensions change less than once per year. A small dimension of less than 100,000 records that seldom change—less than once a year—is an ideal candidate for the type 2 SCD approach. But other dimensions, such as customer dimensions or organization entity dimensions, may change several times per year. The worst combination for an SCD approach is a very large dimension (such as a multimillion row customer dimension) where the average record changes many times per year.

There is no hard and fast rule that says the type 2 SCD approach of creating a new dimensional record is no longer practical. It's just a matter of to what degree. When a dimension table gets too large and is changing with such frequency that administration and query performance are getting ridiculous, it is time to do something.

If a dimension table is changing too rapidly, one powerful technique is to break off and make one or more new dimensions out of these rapidly changing parts. For example, if we have a large customer dimension in which we have embedded various behavior scores or classifications, we may find that these behavior attributes are driving the dimension crazy. Each customer's behavior score might change every month. This is a pretty obvious example of needing to take these attributes out of the dimension. If the attributes are largely textual (such as premium customer, new customer, chronic product returner, or overdrawn customer) and are usually the basis for constraints and report breaks, then these metrics need to be in their own dimension.

We collect all the combinations of these textual behavior metrics into an abstract "behavior" mini-dimension, make a surrogate key for this new dimension, and attach the new key to each fact table where we also have a regular dimension key. The compromise, of course, is that in order to associate a customer with his or her behavior labels, you must have a fact table context in which you can expose both customer and behavior keys simultaneously. But the alternative is likely to be unthinkable. The biggest customer dimensions built by national retailers and web businesses routinely have more than 100 million distinct customers, so you don't want to multiply this dimension by anything.

If the behavior metrics are not textual and discrete, but are numeric and continuous, you should place them in a fact table. The kinds of operations we perform on these numeric measurement-like fields are quite different from the constraints and report breaks we do on dimension tables. For numeric, continuously valued facts:

- We trend the facts numerically over time. We may graph them, average them over time, and use predictive techniques to guess the next few measurements we will encounter in the future.
- We count the number of facts falling within various ranges of values. We call this a *value banding report*.
- We almost never constrain on a specific value, especially if the fact is truly continuously valued.

If you have a business in which you send your customers a monthly statement, you already have a fact table tailor-made to hold these behavior scores. Take them out of your rapidly changing SCD, and append them to your monthly statement fact table if you are comfortable with monthly snapshots of these scores.

If you do not have a reliable, periodic fact record waiting to receive these scores, consider making a special behavior tracking fact table that will store and publish these behavior scores. A monthly snapshot of every customer that is complete is attractive from an applications point of view because you can easily profile your entire customer base.

Whether you have rapidly changing textual attributes or rapidly changing numeric attributes, the techniques discussed in this article will give your big, important, slowly changing dimensions a well deserved breather. Somehow, somewhere, you have to draw a line between your SCDs and your rapidly changing dimensions (RCDs).

9.23 When Do Dimensions Become Dangerous?

Ralph Kimball, Design Tip #79, May 10, 2006

Given the inevitable technology improvements in hardware platforms, database engines, including columnar databases, indexing techniques and other factors impacting performance, the practical boundaries of a very large dimension table will continue to be pushed out. On the other hand, our data is growing at least as fast as the advances.

In many organizations, either the customer or product dimensions can have millions of members. Especially in the early days of data warehousing, we regarded these large dimensions as very dangerous because both loading and querying could become disastrously slow. But with the latest 2015 technology, fast processors, and gigabytes of RAM, do we have to worry any more about these large dimensions, and if so, when does a dimension become dangerous?

How big can a dimension get? Consider a typical wide customer dimension describing account holders in a large bank. Suppose there are 30 million account holders (customers) and we have done a good job of collecting 20 descriptive and demographic attributes for each customer. Assuming an average width of 10 bytes for each field, we start with 30 million $\times$ 20 $\times$ 10 = 6 GB of raw data as input for the ETL data loader. Of course, if we collect 100 attributes instead of 20, our dimension is five times as big, but let's avoid that one for now.

Although OLAP vendors may disagree, I think a 30 million row dimension puts us solidly in dangerous territory for multidimensional OLAP deployments. Remember that usually any type 1 or type 3 changes to a dimension in an OLAP system forces all OLAP cubes using that dimension to be rebuilt. Be careful with type 1 and type 3 changes, if you can even build a cube with such a large dimension!

Relational systems do not have this sensitivity to type 1 and type 3 changes, but a properly supported ROLAP system needs to place an index (typically a bitmap index) on every field in the dimension. In most relational systems, this level of indexing adds as much as a factor of three to the storage size of the dimension. Now we are up to as much as 18 GB for our customer dimension.

Most serious relational deployments should be able to support this 18 GB dimension at query time if the dimension is not also being updated. But two danger scenarios lurk close by: update frequency and slowly changing dimensions.

If your 30 million member dimension requires thousands of insertions, deletions, and updates per week, you need to plan this administration very carefully. The problem is that you can't afford to drop all the indexes every time you load, and you probably can't find a way to partition the dimension in order to make the dimension updating more efficient. So you have to perform these administrative actions in the presence of all your indexes. Perhaps if you are lucky, you can get your database to defer index updates until after a batch load process runs to completion. You need to study these options carefully, and consider batching certain kinds of updates together.

Perhaps the biggest threat to our dimension, however, comes from type 2 tracking of attribute changes. Remember that this means every time any attribute in a customer record is updated, we do not overwrite; rather we issue a new record with a new surrogate key. If the average customer record undergoes two updates per year, then in three years, our 30 million rows become 180 million rows, and the 18 GB of storage becomes 108 GB. All the preceding discussions get worse by a factor of six. In this case, I would try very hard to split the customer dimension into at least two pieces, isolating the "rapidly changing" attributes (such as demographics) into an abstract demographics mini-dimension. This takes most of the type 2 pressure off of the original customer dimension. In a financial reporting environment, this is an effective approach because our fact tables are normally periodic snapshots, where we can guarantee that the customer key and the demographics key have a target record in the fact table every reporting period.

 ## 9.24 Slowly Changing Dimensions Are Not Always as Easy as 1, 2, and 3

Margy Ross, Intelligent Enterprise, Mar 1, 2005

Unlike most OLTP systems, a major objective of the data warehouse is to track history; accounting for change is one of the data warehouse designer's most important responsibilities. The three fundamental techniques for handling slowly changing dimension attributes, types 1, 2, and 3, are adequate for most situations. However, what happens when you need variations that build on these basics to serve more analytically mature data warehouse users? Business folks sometimes want to preserve the historically accurate dimension attribute associated with a fact (such as at the time of sale or claim), but maintain the option to roll up historical facts based on current dimension characteristics. That's when you need hybrid variations of the three main types, as we describe next.

Mini-Dimension with Current Overwrite

When you need historical tracking but are faced with semi-rapid changes in a large dimension, pure type 2 tracking is inappropriate. If you use a mini-dimension, as originally described in article 9.21, *Monster Dimensions*, you can isolate volatile dimension attributes in a separate table rather than track changes in the primary dimension table directly. The granularity of the mini-dimension is one row per "profile" or combination of attributes, while the grain of the primary dimension might be one row per customer. The number of rows in the primary dimension may be in the millions, but the number of mini-dimension rows should be a fraction of that. You capture the evolving relationship between the mini-dimension and primary dimension in a fact table. When a business event (transaction or periodic snapshot) spawns a fact row, the row has one foreign key for the primary dimension and another for the mini-dimension profile in effect at the time of the event.

Profile changes sometimes occur outside of a business event, for example when a customer's geographic profile is updated without a sales transaction. If the business requires accurate point-in-time profiling, a supplemental factless fact table with effective and expiration dates can capture every relationship change between the primary and profile dimensions. One more embellishment with this technique is to add a "current profile" key to the primary dimension. This is a type 1 attribute, overwritten with every profile change, that's useful for analysts who want current profile counts in the absence of fact table metrics or want to roll up historical facts based on the current profile. You'd logically represent the primary dimension and profile outrigger as a single table to the presentation layer if doing so doesn't harm performance, as shown in Figure 9-15. To minimize user confusion and potential error, the current attributes should have column names that distinguish them from the mini-dimension attributes. For example, the labels should indicate whether a customer's marketing segment attribute is the current assignment or the segmentation that was effective when the fact occurred—such as "historical marital status at time of event" in the profile mini-dimension and "current marital status" in the primary customer dimension.

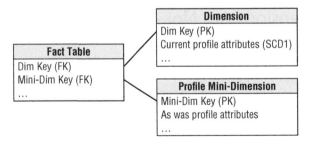

Figure 9-15: A mini-dimension for capturing profile changes with type 1 overwrite in the primary dimension table.

Type 2 with Current Overwrite

Another variation for tracking unpredictable changes while supporting the rollup of historical facts to current dimension attributes is a hybrid of type 1 and type 2. In this scenario, you capture a type 2 attribute change by adding a row to the primary dimension table. In addition, you have a "current" type 1 attribute on each row that you overwrite for the current and all previous rows; the historical attribute value is retained in a separate column, as shown in Figure 9-16. When a change occurs, the most current dimension row has the same value in the uniquely labeled current and historical ("as was" or "at time of event") columns. A recent student suggested that we refer to this as a type 6 because we're creating new rows to capture change (type 2), adding attributes to reflect an alternative view of the world (type 3), which are overwritten for all earlier dimension rows for a given product (type 1). Both $2 + 3 + 1$ or $2 \times 3 \times 1$ equate to 6.

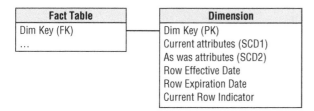

Figure 9-16: Tracking both "as was" and current profile attributes in a single dimension table.

You can expand this technique to cover not just the historical and current attribute values, but also a fixed, end of period value as another type 1 column. Although it seems similar, the end of period attribute may be unique from either the historical or current perspective. Say a customer's segment changed on January 5 and the business wants to create a report on January 10 to analyze the last period's data based on the customer's December 31 designation. You could probably derive the right information from the row effective and expiration dates, but providing the end of period value as an attribute simplifies the query. If this query occurs frequently, it's better to have the work done once during the ETL process, rather than every time the query runs. You can apply the same logic to other fixed characteristics, such as the customer's original segment, which never changes. Instead of having the historical and current attributes reside in the same physical table, the current attributes could sit in an outrigger table joined to the dimension natural key. The same natural key, such as customer ID, likely appears on multiple type 2 dimension rows with unique surrogate keys. The outrigger contains just one row of current data for each natural key in the dimension table; the attributes are overwritten whenever change occurs. To promote ease of use, the core dimension and outrigger of current values should appear to the user as one table, unless this hurts query performance.

Type 2 with Durable Keys in the Fact Table

If you have a million-row dimension table with many attributes requiring historical and current tracking, the last technique described becomes overly burdensome. In this situation, consider including the dimension natural key (assuming it's durable) as a fact table foreign key, in addition to the surrogate key for type 2 tracking, as illustrated in Figure 9-17. This technique gives you two dimension tables associated with the facts, but for good reason. The type 2 dimension has historically accurate attributes for filtering or grouping based on the effective values when the fact table was loaded. The dimension natural key joins to a table with just the current type 1 values. Again, the column labels in this table should be prefaced with "current" to reduce the risk of user confusion. You use these dimension attributes to summarize or filter facts based on the current profile, regardless of the attribute values in effect when the fact row was loaded. Of course, if the natural key is unwieldy or ever reassigned, you should use a durable surrogate reference key instead.

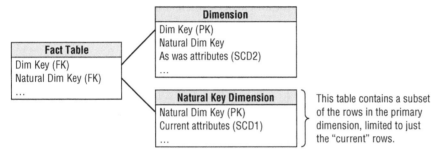

Figure 9-17: One foreign key in the fact table joins to a SCD2 dimension table, while the natural/durable key joins to only the most current version of the dimension.

This approach delivers the same functionality as the "type 2 with current overwrite" technique discussed earlier; that technique spawns more attribute columns in a single dimension table, while this approach relies on two foreign keys in the fact table. This approach inevitably requires less ETL effort because the table of current type 1 attributes could just be delivered via a view of the type 2 dimension table, limited to the most current row. In terms of performance, the incremental cost of this last technique is the additional column carried in the fact table, however queries based on current attribute values would be filtering on a smaller dimension table than previously discussed in the "type 2 with current overwrite" technique.

Of course, you could avoid storing the natural or durable key in the fact table by joining the type 1 view of the table with current attributes to the durable or natural key attribute in the type 2 dimension table itself. However, in this case, queries that are only interested in current rollups would need to traverse from this type 1 outrigger through the more voluminous type 2 dimension table before finally reaching the facts which would likely negatively impact query performance.

Although it's uncommon, we're sometimes asked to roll up historical facts based on any specific point-in-time profile, in addition to reporting by the attribute values when the fact measurement occurred or by the current dimension attribute values. For example, perhaps the business wants to report three years of historical metrics based on the attributes or hierarchy in effect on December 1 of last year. In this case, you can use the dual dimension keys in the fact table to your advantage. You first filter on the type 2 dimension table's row effective and expiration dates to locate the attributes in effect at the desired point in time. With this constraint, a single row for each natural or durable surrogate key in the type 2 dimension has been identified. You can then join to the natural or durable surrogate dimension key in the fact table to roll up any facts based on the point-in-time attribute values. It's as if you're defining the meaning of "current" on the fly. Obviously, you must filter on the type 2 row dates or you'll have multiple type 2 rows for each natural key, but that's fundamental in the business's requirement to report any history on any specified point-in-time attributes. Finally, only unveil this capability to a limited, highly analytic audience; this embellishment is not for the faint of heart.

Series of Type 3 Attributes

If you have a dimension attribute that changes with a predictable rhythm, such as annually, sometimes the business needs to summarize facts based on any historical value of the attribute (not just the historically accurate and current, as we've primarily been discussing). For example, imagine the product line is re-categorized at the start of every fiscal year and the business wants to look at multiple years of historical product sales based on the category assignment for the current year or any prior year.

This situation is best handled with a series of type 3 dimension attributes, as illustrated in Figure 9-18. On every dimension row, have a "current" category attribute that can be overwritten, as well as attributes for each annual designation, such as "2015 attribute", "2014 attribute" and "2013 attribute." You can then group historical facts based on any annual categorization.

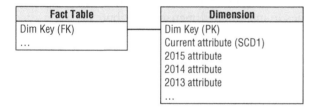

Figure 9-18: A dimension table with a series of type 3 attributes to track predictable changes.

This seemingly straightforward technique isn't appropriate for the unpredictable changes we described earlier. Customer attributes evolve uniquely. You can't add a series of type 3 attributes to track the prior attribute values ("prior-1," "prior-2," and so on) for unpredictable changes because each attribute would be associated with a unique point in time for nearly every row in the dimension table.

Balance Power against Ease of Use

Before using any of these hybrid techniques to support sophisticated change tracking, remember to maintain the equilibrium between flexibility and complexity. Users' questions and query answer sets will vary depending on which dimension attributes are used for constraining or grouping. Given the potential for error or misinterpretation, you should hide the complexity (and associated capabilities) from infrequent users. Hybrid SCDs can sometimes take you for a dizzying ride.

9.25 Slowly Changing Dimension Types 0, 4, 5, 6 and 7

Margy Ross, Design Tip #152, *Feb 5, 2013*

Ralph introduced the concept of slowly changing dimension (SCD) attributes in 1996. Dimensional modelers, in conjunction with the business's data governance representatives, must specify the data warehouse's response to operational attribute value changes. Most Kimball readers are familiar with the core SCD approaches: type 1 (overwrite), type 2 (add a row), and type 3 (add a column). Since legibility is a key component of the Kimball mantra, we sometimes wish Ralph had given these techniques more descriptive names, such as "overwrite" instead of "type 1." But at this point, the SCD type numbers are part of our industry's vernacular.

We have written about more advanced SCD patterns, such as article 9.24, *Slowly Changing Dimensions Are Not Always as Easy as 1, 2, and 3*. However, we've not consistently named the more advanced and hybrid techniques. In the third edition of *The Data Warehouse Toolkit* (Wiley, 2013), we decided to assign "type numbers" to several techniques that had been described, but not precisely labeled in the past.

Type 0: Retain Original

With type 0, the dimension attribute value never changes, so facts are always grouped by this original value. Type 0 is appropriate for any attribute labeled "original," such as a customer's original credit score, or any durable identifiers. Type 0 also applies to most date dimension attributes.

Type 4: Add Mini-Dimension

The type 4 technique is used when a group of dimension attributes are split off into a separate mini-dimension, as shown in Figure 9-19. This approach is useful when dimension attribute values are relatively volatile. Frequently used attributes in multi-million row dimension tables are also mini-dimension design candidates, even if they don't change frequently. A surrogate key is assigned to each unique profile or combination of attribute values in the mini-dimension. The surrogate keys of both the base dimension and mini-dimension profile are captured as foreign keys in the fact table.

The following type 5, 6, and 7 techniques are hybrids that combine the basics to support the common requirement to both accurately preserve historical attribute values, plus report historical facts according to current attribute values. The hybrid approaches provide more analytic flexibility, albeit with greater complexity.

Type 5: Add Mini-Dimension and Type 1 Outrigger

The type 5 technique builds on the type 4 mini-dimension by embedding a "current profile" mini-dimension key in the base dimension that's overwritten as a type 1 attribute, as shown in Figure 9-20.

This approach, called type 5 because 4 + 1 equals 5, allows the currently assigned mini-dimension attribute values to be accessed along with the base dimension's others without linking through a fact table. Logically, we typically represent the base dimension and current mini-dimension profile outrigger as a single table in the presentation layer. The outrigger attributes should have distinct column names, like "Current Income Level," to differentiate them from attributes in the mini-dimension linked to the fact table. The ETL team must update/overwrite the type 1 mini-dimension reference whenever the current mini-dimension changes over time. If the outrigger approach does not deliver satisfactory query performance, then the mini-dimension attributes could be physically embedded (and updated) in the base dimension.

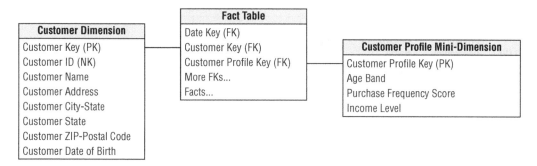

Figure 9-19: Add a mini-dimension to make SCD type 4.

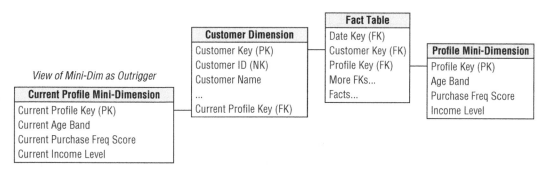

Figure 9-20: Add a mini-dimension and type 1 outrigger to make SCD type 5.

Type 6: Add Type 1 Attributes to Type 2 Dimension

Type 6 builds on the type 2 technique by also embedding current attributes in the dimension so that fact rows can be filtered or grouped by either the type 2 value in effect when the measurement occurred or the attribute's current value. The type 6 moniker was suggested by an HP engineer in

2000 because it's a type 2 row with a type 3 column that's overwritten as a type 1; both 2 + 3 + 1 and 2 x 3 x 1 equal 6. With this approach, the current attributes are updated on all prior type 2 rows associated with a particular durable key, as illustrated by the sample rows in Figure 9-21.

Product Key	SKU (NK)	Product Description	Historic Department Name	Current Department Name	Row Effective Date	Row Expiration Date	Current Row Indicator
12345	ABC922-Z	IntelliKidz	Education	Education	2012-01-01	9999-12-31	Current

Rows in Product dimension following first department reassignment:

Product Key	SKU (NK)	Product Description	Historic Department Name	Current Department Name	Row Effective Date	Row Expiration Date	Current Row Indicator
12345	ABC922-Z	IntelliKidz	Education	Strategy	2012-01-01	2012-12-31	Expired
25984	ABC922-Z	IntelliKidz	Strategy	Strategy	2013-01-01	9999-12-31	Current

Rows in Product dimension following second department reassignment:

Product Key	SKU (NK)	Product Description	Historic Department Name	Current Department Name	Row Effective Date	Row Expiration Date	Current Row Indicator
12345	ABC922-Z	IntelliKidz	Education	Critical Thinking	2012-01-01	2012-12-31	Expired
25984	ABC922-Z	IntelliKidz	Strategy	Critical Thinking	2013-01-01	2013-02-03	Expired
31726	ABC922-Z	IntelliKidz	Critical Thinking	Critical Thinking	2013-02-01	9999-12-31	Current

Figure 9-21: Add type 1 attributes to type 2 dimension to make SCD type 6.

Type 7: Dual Type 1 and Type 2 Dimensions

With type 7, the fact table contains dual foreign keys for a given dimension: a surrogate key linked to the dimension table where type 2 attributes are tracked, plus the dimension's durable supernatural key linked to the current row in the type 2 dimension to present current attribute values, as shown in Figure 9-22.

Type 7 delivers the same functionality as type 6, but it's accomplished via dual keys instead of physically overwriting the current attributes with type 6. Like the other hybrid approaches, the current dimension attributes should be distinctively labeled to minimize confusion.

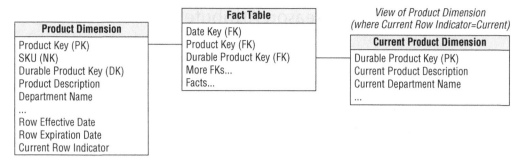

Figure 9-22: Add dual type 1 and type 2 dimensions to make SCD type 7.

Finally, Figure 9-23 highlights the implications of each slowly changing dimension technique on the analysis of fact table performance metrics. As we've warned in the past, there's more to consider than simply 1, 2, and 3!

SCD Type	Dimension Table Action	Impact on Fact Analysis
Type 0	No change to attribute value	Facts associated with attribute's original value
Type 1	Overwrite attribute value	Facts associated with attribute's current value
Type 2	Add new dimension row for profile with new attribute value	Facts associated with attribute value in effect when fact occurred
Type 3	Add new column to preserve attribute's current and prior values	Facts associated with both current and prior attribute alternative values
Type 4	Add new mini-dimension table containing rapidly changing attributes	Facts associated with rapidly changing attributes in effect when fact occurred
Type 5	Type 4 mini-dimension, plus overwrite current mini-dimension key in base dimension	Facts associated with rapidly changing attributes in effect when fact occurred plus current rapidly changing attribute values
Type 6	Type 2 new dimension row with new attribute value, plus overwrite dual attributes on all prior dimension rows	Facts associated with attribute value in effect when fact occurred, plus current values
Type 7	Type 2 new dimension row with new attribute value, plus view limited to current rows and/or attribute values	Facts associated with attribute value in effect when fact occurred, plus current values

Figure 9-23: Slowly changing dimension techniques summary.

9.26 Dimension Row Change Reason Attributes

Warren Thornthwaite, Design Tip #80, Jun 1, 2006

We are firm believers in the principle that business requirements drive the data model. Occasionally, we'll work with an organization that needs to analyze type 2 changes in a dimension. They need to answer questions like "How many customers moved last year?" or "How many new customers did we get by month?" which can be difficult with the standard type 2 control columns. When this happens, we add a control column called "row change reason" to the design. I was recently approached by someone who realized their business could use a row change reason column and asked if it was possible to add one onto an existing dimension. In this article, we describe a bulk update technique for retroactively adding a row change reason column to any of your dimensions.

In its simplest version, the row change reason column contains a two-character abbreviation for each type 2 column that changed in a given row. For example, if last name and zip code changed, the row change reason would be "LN ZP." You can certainly use more characters if you like, but make sure to put a space between the abbreviations. Although this is not meant to be a user queryable column, it does let us easily identify and report on change events. A question like "How many people changed zip codes last year?" could be answered with the following SELECT statement:

```
SELECT COUNT(DISTINCT CustomerBusinessKey)
FROM Customer
WHERE RowChangeReason LIKE '%ZP%'
AND RowEffectiveDate BETWEEN '20150101' AND '20151231'
```

The LIKE operator and wildcards make the order of the entries unimportant. The row change reason column allows us to answer a lot of interesting questions about behaviors in the dimension table.

We'll use the simple customer dimension shown in Figure 9-24 as our example. In this dimension table, first name is tracked as type 1, and the other business attributes are tracked as type 2. Because the table has type 2 attributes, it also has the necessary type 2 control columns: row effective date, row end date, and row current indicator (which we realize is redundant, but we like the convenience). It also includes the new column we are adding on called row change reason.

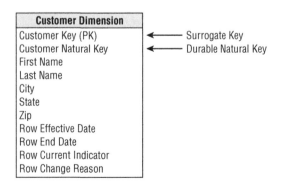

Figure 9-24: Customer dimension table with type 2 administration control columns.

The process to bulk update the new row change reason column takes two passes: one for the new row for each business key, and one for all subsequent changed rows. The first pass joins the dimension to itself using an outer join, treating the table as the current row and the alias as the prior row. The query then finds all the new rows by constraining on all those entries that don't have prior rows using the IS NULL limit in the WHERE clause.

```
UPDATE Customer
SET RowChangeReason = 'NW'
FROM Customer LEFT OUTER JOIN
     Customer PE ON    -- Prior Entry Customer table alias
     Customer.CustomerBusinessKey =
         PE.CustomerBusinessKey
     AND
     Customer.RowEffectiveDate = PE.RowEndDate+1
WHERE PE.CustomerBusinessKey IS NULL
```

The second pass is a bit more complicated because it needs to create a row change reason for all the rows that have been added to the dimension due to a change in a type 2 attribute. In this case, we use an inner join between the current row and the prior row, which automatically excludes the new rows. We'll also use a CASE statement to generate the string of abbreviations which identifies each of the four type 2 columns that actually had a change from their prior values. Finally, we'll concatenate the abbreviations together to make the entry for the row change reason column.

```
UPDATE Customer
SET RowChangeReason = Query1.RowChangeReason
FROM
  (SELECT NE.CustomerBusinessKey, NE.RowEffectiveDate,
     (CASE WHEN NE.LastName <> PE.LastName
        THEN 'LN ' ELSE '' END) +
     (CASE WHEN NE.City <> PE.City
        THEN 'CT ' ELSE '' END) +
     (CASE WHEN NE.State <> PE.State
        THEN 'ST ' ELSE '' END) +
     (CASE WHEN NE.Zip <> PE.Zip
        THEN 'ZP ' ELSE '' END) RowChangeReason
  FROM Customer NE INNER JOIN   -- NE for new entry
        Customer PE ON    -- PE for prior entry
        NE.CustomerBusinessKey = PE.CustomerBusinessKey AND
        NE.RowEffectiveDate = PE.RowEndDate + 1
  ) Query1
INNER JOIN Customer ON
     Customer.CustomerBusinessKey = Query1.CustomerBusinessKey AND
     Customer.RowEffectiveDate = Query1.RowEffectiveDate
```

This SQL will work for the one-time process of adding on a row change reason column if you left it off your initial design. Of course, you will still need to add the appropriate comparison logic to your ETL programs to fill the row change reason column moving forward.

10

More Dimension Patterns and Considerations

So you thought you knew everything you needed to know about dimension tables after reading Chapter 9. Not so fast! There is much more where Chapter 9 leaves off.

We begin this chapter by discussing snowflaked versus outrigger dimension tables, plus bridge tables for handling both multi-valued dimension attributes as well as variable-depth hierarchical relationships. From there, we turn our attention to several patterns often observed with customer-centric dimension tables. We also describe approaches for handling the challenges presented by the internationalization of dimensional models.

The final section of this chapter provides a series of case studies from a variety of industries and application areas—insurance, voyage, human resources, finance, electronic commerce, text searching, and retail. Even if you don't work in one of these arenas, we encourage you to peruse these articles because the patterns and recommendations transcend industry or application boundaries.

Snowflakes, Outriggers, and Bridges

We begin by exploring the distinctions between snowflaked, outrigger, and bridge tables in dimensional modeling. In this section, bridge tables are described as a technique for modeling multi-valued dimension attributes; in the next section, we look at bridges to address variable-depth ragged hierarchies.

Several articles in this section originally referred to bridge tables as helper tables; the original references have been updated to reflect the more current bridge terminology.

10.1 Snowflakes, Outriggers, and Bridges

Margy Ross, Design Tip #105, *Sep 3, 2008*

Students often blur the concepts of snowflakes, outriggers, and bridges. In this article, we try to reduce the confusion surrounding these embellishments to the standard dimensional model.

When a dimension table is snowflaked, the redundant many-to-one attributes are removed into separate dimension tables. For example, instead of collapsing hierarchical rollups such as brand and category into columns of a product dimension table, the attributes are stored in separate brand and category tables, which are then linked to the product table. With snowflakes, the dimension tables are normalized to third normal form. A standard dimensional model often has 15 to 20 denormalized dimension tables surrounding the fact table in a single-layer halo; this exact same data might easily be represented by 100 or more linked dimension tables in a snowflake schema.

We generally encourage you to handle many-to-one hierarchical relationships in a single dimension table rather than snowflaking. Snowflakes may appear optimal to an experienced OLTP data modeler, but they're suboptimal for query performance. As you see in Figure 10-1, the linked snowflaked tables create complexity and confusion for users directly exposed to the table structures; even if users are buffered from the tables, snowflaking increases complexity for the optimizer, which must link hundreds of tables together to resolve queries. Snowflakes also put a burden on the ETL system to manage the keys linking the normalized tables, which can become grossly complex when the linked hierarchical relationships are subject to change. Though snowflaking may save some space by replacing repeated text strings with codes, the savings are negligible, especially in light of the price paid for the extra ETL burden and query complexity.

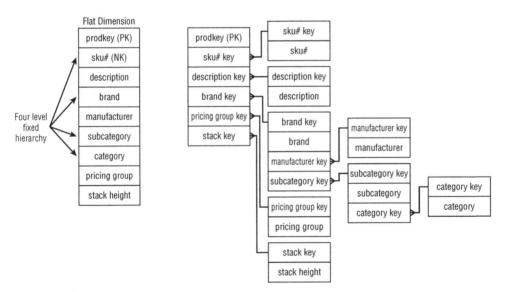

Figure 10-1: Denormalized and snowflaked versions of the same dimension table.

Outriggers are similar to snowflakes in that they're used for many-to-one relationships; however, they're more limited. Outriggers are dimension tables joined to other dimension tables, but they're just one more layer removed from the fact table, rather than being fully normalized snowflakes. Outriggers are most frequently used when a standard dimension table is referenced in another dimension, such as a hire date attribute in the employee dimension table (illustrated in Figure 10-2). If the users want to slice and dice the hire date by non-standard calendar attributes such as the fiscal period or fiscal year, then a date dimension table (with unique column labels such as hire date fiscal year) could serve as an outrigger to the employee dimension table joined on a date key.

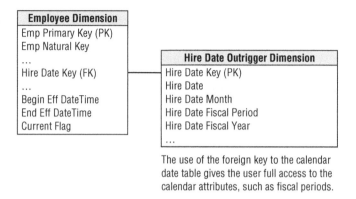

The use of the foreign key to the calendar date table gives the user full access to the calendar attributes, such as fiscal periods.

Figure 10-2: A date dimension outrigger joined to the employee dimension.

Like many things in life, outriggers are acceptable in moderation, but they should be viewed as the exception rather than the rule. If outriggers are rampant in your model, it's time to return to the drawing board given the potentially negative impact on ease of use and query performance.

Bridge tables are used in two more complicated scenarios. As shown in Figure 10-3, the first is where a many-to-many relationship can't be resolved in the fact table itself because a single fact measurement is associated with multiple occurrences of a dimension, such as multiple customers associated with a single bank account balance. Placing a customer dimension key in the fact table would require the unnatural and unreasonable divvying of the balance among multiple customers on an account, so a bridge table with dual keys to capture the many-to-many relationship between customers and accounts is used in conjunction with the measurement fact table.

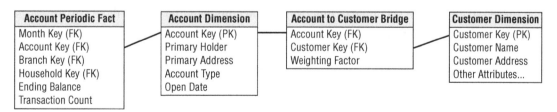

Figure 10-3: A bridge table resolves a many-valued dimension attribute.

Bridge tables are also used to represent a ragged or variable-depth hierarchical relationship, which cannot be reasonably forced into a simpler fixed-depth hierarchy of many-to-one attributes in a dimension table, as shown in Figure 10-4. This technique is further described in article 10.10, *Help for Hierarchies.*

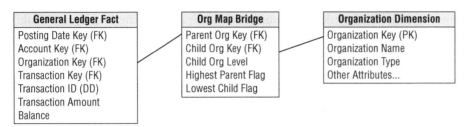

Figure 10-4: A bridge table models a hierarchical variable-depth relationship.

In these isolated situations, the bridge table comes to the rescue, albeit at a price. Sometimes bridges are used to capture the complete data relationships, but compromises, such as including the primary account holder or top rollup level as dimension attributes, help avoid paying the toll for navigating the bridge on every query.

10.2 A Trio of Interesting Snowflakes

Ralph Kimball, Intelligent Enterprise, Jun 29, 2001

This article refers to snowflakes, but the examples would more accurately be described as outriggers because none of the dimensions have been fully normalized into third normal form.

"When can I use a snowflake?" is a question data warehouse designers have asked me hundreds of times. I usually answer that it's a bad idea to expose the users to a physical snowflake design because it almost always compromises understandability and performance. But in certain situations a snowflake design is not only acceptable, but recommended.

Classic Snowflake

The way to create a classic snowflake is to remove low cardinality attributes from a dimension table and place these attributes in a secondary dimension table connected by a snowflake key. In cases where a set of attributes form a multilevel hierarchy, the resulting string of tables looks a little like a snowflake—hence the name.

A classic physical snowflake design may be useful in the back room ETL area as a way to enforce the many-to-one relationships in a dimension table. But in the front room presentation part of your data warehouse, you have to demonstrate to me that the business users find the snowflake easier to understand and, moreover, that queries and reports run faster with the snowflake, before I am comfortable with the snowflake design.

But having issued this warning, I have found three cases where variations on a snowflake are not only acceptable, but are the keys to a successful design. These three cases are large customer dimensions, financial product dimensions, and multi-enterprise calendar dimensions.

Large Customer Dimensions

The customer dimension is probably the most challenging dimension in a data warehouse. In a large organization, the customer dimension can be huge, with millions of records, and wide, with dozens of attributes. To make matters worse, the biggest customer dimensions commonly contain two categories of customers, which I will call "visitor" and "customer."

Visitors are anonymous. You may see them more than once, but you don't know their names or anything else about them. On a website, the only knowledge you have about visitors is a cookie indicating they have returned. In a retail operation, a visitor with a physical shopper tag engages in an anonymous transaction.

Customers, conversely, are reliably registered with your company. You know customers' names, addresses, and as much demographic and historical data as you care to elicit directly from them or purchase from third parties.

Let us assume that at the most granular level of your data collection, 80 percent of the fact table measurements involve visitors and 20 percent involve customers. You accumulate just two simple behavior scores for visitors consisting only of recency (when they last visited you) and frequency (how many times they have visited).

On the other hand, let us assume you have 50 attributes and measures for a customer, covering all the components of location, payment behavior, credit behavior, directly elicited demographic attributes, and purchased demographic attributes.

Now you combine visitors and customers into a single logical dimension called shopper, as shown in Figure 10-5. You give the visitor or customer a single, permanent shopper ID, but make the key to the table a surrogate key so that you can track changes to the shopper over time.

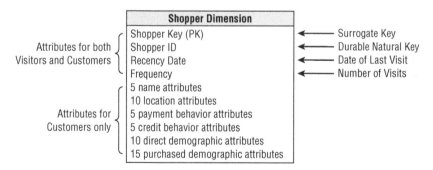

Figure 10-5: Shopper dimension with both visitor and customer attributes.

Note the importance of including the recency and frequency information as dimensional attributes rather than as facts and overwriting them as time progresses. This decision makes the shopper dimension very powerful. You can do classic shopper segmentation directly off the dimension without navigating a fact table in a complex application.

Assuming that many of the final 50 customer attributes are textual, you could have a total record width of 500 bytes or more. Suppose you have 20 million shoppers (16 million visitors and four million registered customers). Obviously, you are worried that in 80 percent of your records, the trailing 50 fields contain no data! In a 10 GB dimension, this condition gets your attention.

This is a clear case where, depending on the database, you may wish to introduce a snowflake. In databases with variable-width records, or in columnar databases, you can simply build a single shopper dimension with all the preceding fields, disregarding the empty field issue. The majority of the shopper records that are simple visitors remain narrow because in these databases, the null fields take up zero disk space.

But in fixed-width databases, you probably don't want to live with the empty fields for all the visitors, and so you break the dimension into a base dimension and a snowflaked subdimension, as shown in Figure 10-6. All the visitors share a single record in the subdimension, which contains special null attribute values, as shown in Figure 10-6.

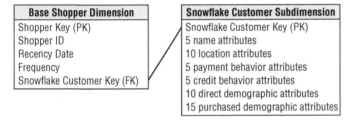

Figure 10-6: A shopper dimension with a snowflake for customer attributes.

In a fixed-width database, using our previous assumptions, the base shopper dimension is 20 million × 25 bytes = 500 MB, and the snowflake dimension is 4 million × 475 bytes = 1.9 GB. You save 8 GB by using the snowflake. If you have a query tool that insists on a classic star schema with no snowflakes, then you can hide the snowflake under a view declaration.

Financial Product Dimensions

Banks, brokerage houses, and insurance companies all have trouble modeling their product dimensions because each of the individual products has a host of special attributes not shared by other products. Except for a set of common "core" attributes, a checking account doesn't look very much like a mortgage or certificate of deposit. They even have different numbers of attributes. If you try to build a single product dimension with the union of all possible attributes, you end up with hundreds of attributes, most of which are empty in a given record.

A possible answer in this case is to build a context-dependent snowflake. You isolate the core attributes in a base product dimension table, and include a snowflake key in each base record that points to its proper extended product subdimension, illustrated in Figure 10-7.

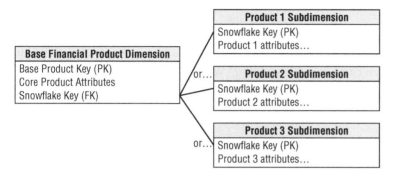

Figure 10-7: A financial product dimension with a subdimension for each product type.

This solution is not a conventional relational join! The snowflake key must connect to the particular subdimension table that a specific product type defines. Usually you can accomplish this task by constructing a relational view for each product type that hardwires the correct join path.

Multi-Enterprise Calendar Dimensions

Building a calendar dimension in a distributed data warehouse spanning multiple organizations is difficult because each organization has idiosyncratic fiscal periods, seasons, and holidays. Although you should make a heroic effort to reduce incompatible calendar labels, many times you want to look at the overall multi-enterprise data through the eyes of just one of the organizations.

Unlike the financial products dimensions, each of the separate calendars can have the same number of attributes describing fiscal periods, seasons, and holidays. But there may be hundreds of separate calendars. An international retailer may have to deal with a calendar for each foreign country.

In this case you modify the snowflake design to let the snowflake key join to a single calendar subdimension, as in Figure 10-8. But the subdimension has higher cardinality than the base dimension! The key for the subdimension is both the snowflake key and the organization key.

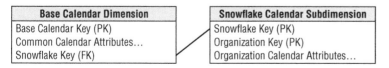

Figure 10-8: A calendar dimension with a higher cardinality subdimension.

In this situation, you must specify a single organization in the subdimension before evaluating the join between the tables. When done correctly, the subdimension has a one-to-one relationship with the base dimension as if the two tables were a single entity. Now the entire multi-enterprise data warehouse can be queried through the calendar of any constituent organization.

Permissible Snowflakes

These three examples show useful variations of snowflake designs. I hope you feel more confident about answering the question, "When can I use a snowflake?" When you are thinking about design alternatives, you should separate the issues of physical design from those of logical design. Physical design drives performance; logical design drives understandability. You can use snowflake designs if you maximize both of these goals.

10.3 Help for Dimensional Modeling

Ralph Kimball, DBMS, Aug 1998

The goal of dimensional modeling is to represent a set of business measurements in a standard framework. Think of the fact table as a set of measurements made in the marketplace. These measurements are usually numeric and taken before the creation of a given fact table. A fact table record may represent an individual transaction, such as a customer withdrawal made at an ATM as shown in Figure 10-9, or the fact table record may represent some kind of aggregated total, such as the sales of a given product in a store on a particular day.

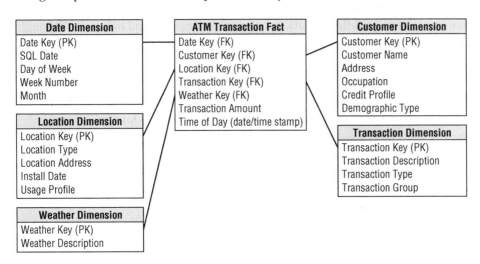

Figure 10-9: A typical dimensional model for ATM transactions.

The secret of choosing dimensions for a given fact table is to identify any description that has a single value for an individual fact table record. In this way, you can work outward from the grain of the fact table and "decorate" the fact table with as many dimensions as you can imagine, as illustrated in Figure 10-9.

Strict adherence to the grain definition lets you disqualify dimensions that do not have a single value for a given fact record. You are more likely to disqualify a dimension if you are dealing with an aggregated or summarized table. The more the fact table is summarized, the fewer the number of dimensions you can attach to the fact records. The converse of this is eye opening. The more granular the data, the more dimensions make sense.

Having made a pretty tidy argument for single-valued dimensions, perhaps we should consider whether there are ever legitimate exceptions. Are there situations where you might need to attach a multi-valued dimension to a fact table? Is this even possible, and what problems might arise?

Consider the following example from healthcare billing. You are handed a data source for which the grain is the individual line item on a doctor bill. The data source could be patient visits to doctor offices or individual charges on a hospital bill. These individual line items have a rich set of dimensions that we show in Figure 10-10.

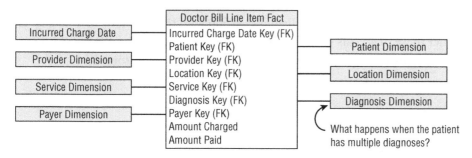

Figure 10-10: A healthcare billing fact table.

So far, this design seems to be pretty straightforward with obvious single values for all of the dimensions. But there is a sleeper. In many healthcare situations, there may be multiple values for the diagnosis. What do you do if a given patient has three separate diagnoses at the moment the service was performed? How about really sick people in hospitals that might have up to 10 diagnoses? How do you encode the diagnosis dimension if you wish to represent this information?

Database designers usually take one of four approaches to this kind of open-ended, multi-valued situation:

- Disqualify the diagnosis dimension because it is multi-valued.
- Choose one value (the "primary" diagnosis) and omit the other values.
- Extend the dimension list to have a fixed number of diagnosis dimensions.
- Put a bridge table in between this fact table and the diagnosis dimension table.

Let's not take the easy way out by disqualifying the diagnosis dimension from the design.

Frequently, designers go with the second alternative by choosing a single value. In healthcare, this often shows up as the primary, or admitting, diagnosis. In many cases, your hands are tied because you are given the data in this form by the production system. If you take this approach, the modeling problem goes away, but you are left doubting whether the diagnosis data is useful.

The third approach of creating a fixed number of additional diagnosis dimension slots in the fact table key list is a hack, and you should avoid it. Inevitably, there will be some complicated example of a very sick patient who exceeds the number of diagnosis slots you have allocated. Also, you cannot easily query the multiple separate diagnosis dimensions. If "headache" is a diagnosis, which diagnosis dimension should be constrained? The resulting OR constraints across dimensions are notorious for running slowly on relational databases. For all these reasons, you should avoid the multiple dimensions style of design.

If you insist on modeling this multi-valued situation, then a "bridge" table placed between the diagnosis dimension and the fact table is the best solution, as shown in Figure 10-11. The diagnosis key in the fact table is changed to be a diagnosis group key. The bridge table in the middle is the diagnosis group table. It has one record for each diagnosis in a group of diagnoses. If I walk into the doctor's office with three diagnoses, then I need a diagnosis group with three records in it. It is up to the modeler to build either these diagnosis groups for each individual patient or a library of known diagnosis groups. Perhaps my three diagnoses would be called "Kimball's Syndrome."

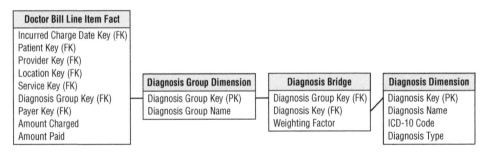

Figure 10-11: A bridge table to handle multiple diagnoses.

The diagnosis group table is joined to the original diagnosis dimension on the diagnosis key. The diagnosis group table in Figure 10-11 contains a very important numeric attribute: the weighting factor. The weighting factor allows reports to be created that don't double count the billed amount in the fact table. For instance, if you constrain some attribute in the diagnosis dimension such as "contagious indicator," then you can group by the contagious indicator and produce a report with the correct totals by multiplying the billed amount by the associated weighting factor. This is a correctly weighted report.

You can assign the weighting factors equally within a diagnosis group. If there are three diagnoses, then each gets a weighting factor of 1/3. If you have some other rational basis for assigning the weighting factors differently, then you can change the factors, as long as all the factors in a diagnosis group always add up to one.

You can, interestingly enough, deliberately omit the weighting factor and deliberately double count the same report grouped by contagious indicator. In this case, you have produced an "impact report" that shows the total billed amount implied partially or fully by each of the values of contagious indicator. Though the correctly weighted report is the most common and makes the most sense, the impact report is interesting and is requested from time to time. Such an impact report should be labeled so that the reader is not misled by any summary totals.

Although the bridge table clearly violates the classic dimensional design where all the dimension tables have a simple one-to-many relationship to the fact table, there is no avoiding the issue of what to do with multi-valued dimensions that designers insist on attaching to a fact table. When you attach a bridge table to a fact table, you can preserve the dimensional illusion in your user interfaces by creating a view that prejoins the fact table to the bridge table. The resulting view then appears to have a simple diagnosis key that joins to our diagnosis table in the healthcare example. The view can also predefine the multiplication of the weighting factor with any additive facts in the fact table.

I have seen other situations where a multi-valued dimension makes sense, including the following examples:

- **Retail banking.** There are often cases where the account dimension is "inhabited" by one or more human customers. If the bank wants to associate individual customers with account balances, then the account dimension must play the same role as the diagnosis group dimension in the healthcare example. Banks are quite interested in both correctly weighted reports and impact reports.
- **Standard Industry Classifications (SICs).** SIC codes are assigned to a commercial enterprise to describe what industry segment they are in. The problem with SIC codes is that all big enterprises are represented by multiple SIC codes. If you encode a fact table with an SIC dimension, you have the same problem as with the multiple diagnoses. SIC codes are really quite useful, however. If you want to summarize all the business you do selling to manufacturers and retailers by using their SIC code, you will need an SIC group bridge table. Here's a case where with some careful thought you may assign unequal weighting factors if you believe the enterprise is mostly a manufacturer and only a little bit a retailer.

10.4 Managing Bridge Tables

Ralph Kimball, Intelligent Enterprise, *Aug 10, 2001*

This article was originally titled Managing Helper Tables.

Multi-valued dimensions are normally illegal in a dimensional design. We usually insist that when the grain of a fact table is declared, the only legal dimensions that can be attached to that fact table are those that take on a single value for that grain.

But for every rule there have to be exceptions. Sometimes even when a dimension takes on multiple values in the presence of the fact table grain, it nevertheless is compelling and natural to attach the multi-valued dimension to the fact table without changing the grain. It is very desirable, for example, to attach a customer dimension to a banking fact table whose grain is account by month.

The problem is that the number of customers associated with each account is open-ended. I may have a checking account in my own name, but my wife and I have a joint savings account. Perhaps we also have a family trust account with five or six customer names.

The preferred way to handle this multi-valued dimension is with a bridge table, as shown in Figure 10-12, where it is called the Account to Customer Bridge. Since article 10.3, *Help for Dimensional Modeling* was written, I have discussed with designers and students many times the details of constructing and using these bridge tables. Let's take a careful look at bridge tables and extend the design.

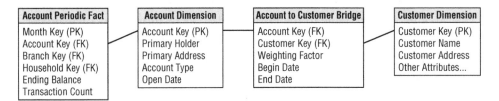

Figure 10-12: Resolving the relationship of multiple customers associated with an account using a bridge table.

Using Surrogate Keys

The account to customer bridge is a kind of fact table whose primary key (PK) is composed of multiple foreign keys (FK). The primary key in this example consists of the account key, customer key, and begin date key. An individual record in this table shows that a particular customer was part of a specific account during the interval defined by the begin date and end date. But this definition requires a careful look.

It is very important that the customer and account foreign keys are surrogate keys referring to their respective dimensions, both of which are type 2 slowly changing dimensions (SCDs). In other words, you carefully track changes in both the customer dimension and account dimension, and continuously issue new versions of records in those dimensions to reflect changes.

The bridge table needs the surrogate keys so that the record of the customer belonging to the account refers to the correct, contemporary descriptions of the customer and the account during the designated time interval. But this necessary precision comes with a price: Each time either the customer or the account undergoes a type 2 change, you need to issue a new record in the bridge table to reflect the new key combinations. So you can see that the begin time and end time in the bridge record actually refer to the time span when the customer was part of the account *and* both the customer description and the account description were unchanged. Although this sounds complicated, you will see in the next section that by using twin time stamps, you can perform interesting queries without having to be an expert logician.

Using Twin Time Stamps

The twin time stamps shown in Figure 10-12 didn't appear in the earlier written article 10.3, *Help for Dimensional Modeling*. In retrospect, I have seen these time stamps prove very useful for querying. A list of the customers in an account named ABC123 at a particular point in time can be expressed with a very simple SQL query, where "map" is the name of the bridge table:

```
SELECT customer.name
FROM account, map, customer
WHERE account.accountkey = map.Accountkey
AND customer.customerkey = map.Customerkey
AND account.naturalid = 'ABC123'
AND '7/18/2015' BETWEEN map.begindate AND map.enddate
```

The disadvantage of using twin time stamps is that it complicates updating the bridge table. Any bridge table record still valid as of today has to have an open-ended end date, which is ugly. When a new record supersedes this one, the end date has to be adjusted to the real value. We assume here that customer transactions have the grain of an individual day. In spite of this administrative complexity, the alternative of storing only the begin date makes querying far too complex. You would have to change the preceding query to look for the largest begin date less than or equal to the requested date. This embedded SELECT statement is inefficient and may be hard to set up in standard query tools, especially by business users.

The twin time stamps also make a time span query fairly simple. Suppose you wanted the list of all customers who were part of an account at any time between two dates. You would need to test only (1) whether the begin date falls in the requested span or (2) whether the requested span completely surrounds the begin and end dates. Now the query looks like this:

```
SELECT DISTINCT customer.name
FROM account, map, customer
WHERE account.accountkey = map.Accountkey
AND customer.customerkey = map.Customerkey
AND account.naturalid = 'ABC123'
AND (map.begindate BETWEEN '7/18/2014' and '7/18/2015'
OR ('7/18/2014' < map.begindate AND '7/18/2015' > map.enddate))
```

The last field in the bridge table is the weighting factor. The weighting factor is used to allocate additive numeric facts in the main fact table against the separate values of the multi-valued dimension in correctly weighted reports. In the banking example, you can report bank balances against individual customers in account ABC123 by multiplying the weighting factor against the balance:

```
SELECT customer.name, fact.balance*weightingfactor
FROM fact, account, map, customer, month
WHERE fact.accountkey = account.Accountkey
AND fact.monthkey = month.Monthkey
```

```
AND account.accountkey = map.Accountkey
AND customer.customerkey = map.Customerkey
AND account.naturalid = 'ABC123'
AND month.monthdate = 'July, 2015'
```

The sum of all the balances this query finds will be the correct balance in account ABC123 for July 2015, which is how you know this is a correctly weighted report. If you remove the weighting factor from this query, it yields an impact report that associates the full balance of each account with each of its customers. Although the impact report deliberately overcounts the aggregate balance, it provides a true assessment of the potential control each customer may exercise over the balance in the account.

At any point in time, all the weighting factors in an account have to add up to exactly 1. Therefore, if a customer is added to an account, it makes the most sense to adjust all the weighting factors and introduce a complete set of customer records in the bridge table. More complex scenarios are possible, but they probably make the updating process too messy.

Updating the Bridge Table

The bridge table must be updated whenever:

- Anything in the account record changes
- Anything in the customer record changes
- Any customers are added to, or deleted from, an account
- The weighting factors are adjusted

To keep the updating application as simple as possible, the entire set of customers should be added with identical begin and end dates whenever one of these changes takes place. For current records, the end date should probably be a fictitious date far into the future so that the SQL given in our examples stays simple.

When you add a new set of customer records for an existing account to the bridge table, the previous set of customer records must all have their end dates adjusted. All the begin and end dates for a given account must connect seamlessly over all time so there are no gaps.

If you introduce postdated changes to either the account dimension or customer dimension, you need to add a new set of bridge table records as well. Presumably you need to split some existing time span defined by begin and end dates to make room for the postdated changes. Doing this can trigger some messy additional processing because a postdated change to a customer record (for instance) may require you to propagate a brand new customer surrogate key forward in time in the mapping table beyond the affected interval. I explore these complex processing issues in article 11.34, *Backward in Time*.

If you got this far, and followed all this, you are definitely entitled to a cup of coffee.

10.5 The Keyword Dimension

Ralph Kimball, Intelligent Enterprise, *Oct 20, 2000*

I had the opportunity to design a data warehouse for a massive archive of historical letters on behalf of an auction house in New York City that auctions rare letters, autographs, and postage stamps. The archive was fascinating, consisting of hundreds of thousands of letters from the 1500s through World War II. The archive mostly consisted of well preserved envelopes, showing the origins and destinations of this "postal history." But perhaps 15 percent of the letters actually retained their original contents, ranging from simple business correspondence to family letters to mail from soldiers on the front lines.

At first glance, this archive did not seem to be an obvious candidate for a data warehouse, especially using the familiar dimensional approaches. But after some study, a number of compelling similarities among all the letters emerged that began to look like descriptive dimensions and measured facts. The list of candidate dimensions included:

- Letter posting date (90 percent clearly determined, 10 percent guessed)
- Letter delivery date (20 percent clearly determined, 80 percent guessed)
- Archive acquisition date (when the archive acquired the letter)
- Appraisal date (the last date on which a value for the letter was assigned)
- Restoration date (the last date on which the letter was cleaned or repaired)
- Presentation date (the last date on which this letter was publicly displayed)
- Divestment date (the date, if applicable, when the letter was sold or traded)
- Origin post office (for example, post office, town, state, and country)
- Destination post office
- Sender (name, title, and affiliation)
- Recipient
- Postal rate (for example, ordinary mail, airmail, or registered letter)
- Postal franking (the postage stamps used)
- Condition (for example, extremely fine, age spots, torn, or repaired)
- Archive storage location
- Keywords

Each letter had a number of pretty obvious measured facts including:

- Appraisal value (a specific value or not applicable)
- Acquisition value (always present)
- Divestment value (a specific value or not applicable)
- Restoration cost (a specific value or not applicable)

- Width
- Height
- Weight
- Number of enclosure pages
- Number of enclosure drawings or illustrations

The natural grain for this postal history archive was one fact table record per letter. Because a letter could go through a number of stages (acquisition, appraisal, restoration, presentation, and divestment), the fact table's most natural form was an accumulating line item grain as described in article 8.5, *Fundamental Grains*. The previous list of dimensions clearly shows the characteristic "accumulating" list of dates corresponding to the various stages of the item being described on the fact record.

The seven dates associated with each letter are represented by a single underlying date table. Note that a number of the dates may be undefined for a given letter. You may only have estimates for the posting date and delivery date. You give these dates real values in the date table, but the date record itself needs to be of a special type like "estimated to the nearest year." Other dates like the restoration date, presentation date, and divestment date may be inapplicable, and these date keys in the fact table need to point to special "not applicable" records in the date dimension table, not records representing actual dates.

Designing the Keyword Dimension

As it turns out, the last item in the list of dimensions is the most interesting part of the design. Each letter had one or more keywords that an expert examiner had added. The keywords described much of the interesting content of the postal history archive. Because the letters ranged over thousands of situations and subjects, there was no significant predictability or structure to the keywords. Some keywords described the subjects of the letter (Civil War, Charleston, or traveling in a covered wagon), while other keywords described special markings on the letter (posted at sea or delayed in a train wreck). The expert examiners were good at applying keywords in a disciplined way, but literally hundreds of interesting keywords drawn from different domains served as targets for queries in the final database.

Because each letter could have a variable number of keywords, the keyword dimension seemed like a good candidate to be a multi-valued dimension, as described in article 10.3, *Help for Dimensional Modeling*. I show the simplest form of a multi-valued dimension for handling the keywords in Figure 10-13. The tricky part of a multi-valued dimension design is the many-to-many join between the fact table and the dimension table. The keyword group key appears many times in the fact table and dimension table. In the dimension table, the keyword group key is repeated for each keyword in the particular list of keywords for a given letter. Some data modeling tools balk at letting you define this many-to-many join, and these tools may try to force you to place an associative "bridge" table in between the fact table and the keyword dimension table.

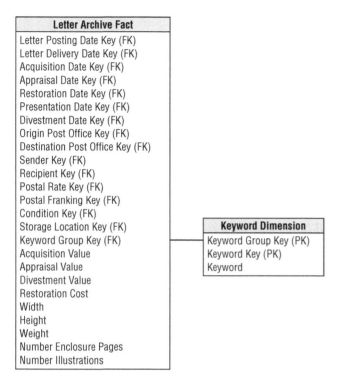

Figure 10-13: The fact table for a letter archive data warehouse showing the keyword bridge dimension table.

Assuming you have worked around your data modeling tool and built the schema as I've shown in Figure 10-13, you are still left with a serious query problem.

The AND/OR Dilemma

User requests against the keywords in the postal history archive fell into two equally important categories. The OR queries (Civil War OR Spanish American War) could be satisfied by a simple OR constraint on the keyword field in the dimension table. But AND queries (Civil War AND train wreck) were difficult because an AND constraint is really a constraint across two records in the keyword dimension table. SQL is notoriously poor at handling constraints across records. Using this design, probably the best you could do is issue a SQL constraint such as:

```
SELECT K1.kwgroupkey
FROM keywordtable K1
WHERE (select COUNT(K2.kwgroupkey)
FROM keywordtable K2
```

```
WHERE K1.kwgroupkey = K2.kwgroupkey
AND K2.keyword in ('Civil War', 'train wreck')
GROUP BY K2.kwgroupkey)
= 2
```

The final "2" in the query is the count of the number of target keywords in this particular search. This approach is awkward and probably slow. It certainly requires a custom user interface that hides the complex SQL from the end user.

Searching for Substrings

It is possible to simultaneously remove the many-to-many join and the complex embedded SELECT constraint by changing the design of the keyword dimension to the simpler form shown in Figure 10-14. Now the records in the keyword dimension each contain one big text string with all the keywords for that letter, one after the other. You should use a special delimiter character like a backslash at the beginning of the keyword field and after every keyword in the list. Thus the keyword text string containing "Civil War" and "train wreck" would look like:

```
\Civil War\train wreck\
```

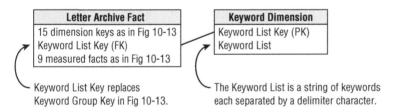

Figure 10-14: The same fact table showing the keyword dimension containing a variable-length text string keyword list.

Those of you more detail oriented and experienced in the ways of text string searching may be worrying about the ambiguity of searching on upper- and lowercase. Is it "Civil War" or "civil war"? You can resolve this either by morphing all the keywords in the database to one case or by using a special database text string search function that is case insensitive.

With the design I've shown in Figure 10-14, the AND/OR dilemma goes away. The OR constraint looks like:

```
kwlist like '%\Civil War\%' OR keyword like '%\Spanish American War\%'
```

while the AND constraint has exactly the same structure:

```
kwlist like '%\Civil War\%' AND keyword like '%\train wreck\%'.
```

The % symbol is a wildcard pattern-matching character defined in SQL that matches zero or more characters. We use the backslash delimiter character explicitly in these constraints to exactly match the desired keywords and not get bogus matches like "uncivil warfare."

High Performance Substring Indexes

Before the year 2000 SQL text constraints that used a leading wildcard were notoriously slow, and were disallowed by many database designers. But in recent years the performance of these queries has improved so dramatically that this has become a preferred technique. Additionally most relational databases now support very large text fields, as much as 64K bytes or even larger.

10.6 Potential Bridge (Table) Detours

Margy Ross, Design Tip #166, May 14, 2014

Dimensional designs often need to accommodate multi-valued dimensions. Patients can have multiple diagnoses. Students can have multiple majors. Consumers can have multiple hobbies or interests. Commercial customers can have multiple industry classifications. Employees can have multiple skills or certifications. Products can have multiple optional features. Bank accounts can have multiple customers. The multi-valued dimension challenge is a natural and unavoidable cross-industry dilemma.

A common approach for handling multi-valued dimensions is to introduce a bridge table as shown in Figure 10-15. This figure shows a bridge table to associate multiple customers with an account. In this case, the bridge contains one row for each customer associated with an account. Similarly, a bridge table might have one row for each skill in an employee's group of skills. Or one row for each option in a bundle of product features. Bridge tables can sit between fact and dimension tables, or alternatively, between a dimension table and its multi-valued attributes (such as a customer and his or her hobbies or interests).

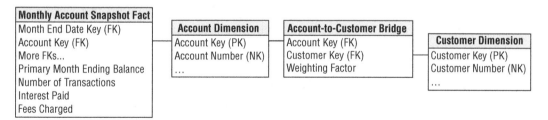

Figure 10-15: A banking example showing an account-to-customer bridge table.

The bridge table is a powerful way to handle dimensions that take on multiple values when associated with the grain of a fact table's measurement event. It's both scalable and flexible to handle an open ended number of values. For example, you can easily associate many diagnoses with a patient's hospital stay, and new diagnoses are easily accommodated without altering the database design. However, bridge tables have their downsides. Ease of use is often compromised, especially since some BI tools struggle to generate SQL that successfully crosses over the bridge. Another unwanted outcome is the potential over-counting that occurs when grouping by the multi-valued dimension because a single fact row's performance metrics can be associated with multiple dimension rows unless an allocation/weighting factor is assigned to each row in the bridge table.

Here are several potential techniques to avoid bridge tables. However, be aware that each comes with its own potential downsides, too:

1. **Alter the fact table's grain to resolve the many-valued dimension relationship, allocating the metrics accordingly.** Many-to-many relationships are typically best resolved in fact tables. For example, if multiple representatives are associated with a sales transaction, you might be able to declare the fact table's grain to be one row per rep per sales transaction, and then allocate the sales quantity and dollars to each row. While a more natural grain might be one row per sales transaction, the subdivided grain may seem logical to the business users in this scenario. In other situations, a subdivided grain would be nonsensical. For example, if you need to represent the customers' multi-valued hobbies, it wouldn't make sense to declare the grain to be one row per customer hobby per sales transaction. That's an unnatural grain!

2. **Designate a "primary" value.** Declaring a primary diagnosis, primary account holder, primary major, etc. with either a single foreign key in the fact table or single attribute in the dimension table eliminates the multi-valued challenge. In this scenario, all the attribute column names would be prefaced with "primary." Of course, coming up with the business rules to determine the primary relationship may be impossible. And subsequent analyses based solely on the primary relationship will be incomplete and/or misleading as the other multi-valued dimensions and their attributes are ignored.

3. **Add multiple named attributes to the dimension table.** For example, if you sold pet supplies, you might include flags in the customer dimension to designate dog buyers, cat buyers, bird buyers, etc. We're not suggesting that you include ten generically labeled columns, such as animal buyer 1, animal buyer 2, etc. The named attribute positional design is attractive because it's easy to query in virtually any BI tool with excellent, predictable query performance. However, it's only appropriate for a fixed, limited number of options. You wouldn't want to include 150 distinct columns in a student dimension, such as art history major, for each possible major at a university. This approach isn't very scalable, plus new values require altering the table.

4. **Add a single concatenated text string with delimited attribute values to the dimension.** For example, if courses can be dual taught, you might concatenate the instructors' names into a single attribute, such as |MRoss|RKimball|. You'd need a delimiter such as a backlash or vertical bar at the beginning of the string and after each value. This approach allows the concatenated value to be easily displayed in an analysis. But there are obvious downsides. There may be ambiguity surrounding upper- and lowercase values in the concatenated string. It wouldn't be appropriate for a lengthy list of attributes. Finally, you can't readily count/sum by one of the concatenated values or group/filter by associated attributes, such as the instructors' tenure status.

Multi-valued dimension attributes are a reality for many designers. The bridge table technique and the alternatives discussed in this *Design Tip* have their pluses and minuses. There's no single right strategy; you'll need to determine which compromises you can live with. Finally, these techniques are not mutually exclusive. For example, dimensional models often include a "primary" dimension with a single foreign key in the fact table, coupled with a bridge table to represent the multi-valued dimensions.

10.7 Alternatives for Multi-Valued Dimensions

Joy Mundy, Design Tip #124, Jun 2, 2010

The standard relationship between fact and dimension tables is many-to-one: Each row in a fact table links to one and only one row in the dimension table. In a detailed sales event fact table, each fact table row represents a sale of one product to one customer on a specific date. Each row in a dimension table, such as a single customer, usually points back to many rows in the fact table.

A dimensional design can encompass a more complex multi-valued relationship between fact and dimension. For example, perhaps our sales order entry system lets us collect information about why the customer chose a specific product (such as price, features, or recommendation). Depending on how the transaction system is designed, it's easy to see how a sales order line could be associated with potentially many sales reasons.

The robust, fully featured way to model such a relationship in the dimensional world is similar to the modeling technique for a transactional database. The sales reason dimension table is normal, with a surrogate key, one row for each sales reason, and potentially several attributes such as sales reason name, long description, and type. In our simple example, the sales reason dimension table would be quite small, perhaps ten rows. We can't put that sales reason key in the fact table because each sales transaction can be associated with many sales reasons. The sales reason bridge table fills the gap. It ties together all the possible (or observed) sets of sales reasons: {Price, Price and Features, Features and Recommendation, Price and Features and Recommendation}. Each of those sets of reasons is tied together with a single sales reason group key that is propagated into the fact table.

For example, Figure 10-16 shows a dimensional model for a sales fact table that captures multiple sales reasons.

Figure 10-16: A sales fact table capturing multiple sales reasons.

If we have ten possible sales reasons, the Sales Reason Bridge table will contain several hundred rows.

The biggest problem with this design is its usability by ad hoc users. The multi-valued relationship, by its nature, effectively "explodes" the fact table. Imagine a poorly trained business user who attempts to construct a report that returns a list of sales reasons and sales amounts. It is absurdly easy to double count the facts for transactions with multiple sales reasons. The weighting factor in the bridge table is designed to address that issue, but the user needs to know what the factor is for and how to use it.

In the example we're discussing, sales reason is probably a very minor embellishment to a key fact table that tracks our sales. The sales fact table is used throughout the organization by many user communities, for both ad hoc and structured reporting. There are several approaches to the usability problem presented by the full featured bridge table design. These include:

- Hide the sales reason from most users. You can publish two versions of the schema: the full one for use by structured reporting and a handful of power users, and a version that eliminates sales reason for use by more casual users.
- Eliminate the bridge table by collapsing multiple answers. Add a row to the sales reason dimension table: "Multiple reasons chosen" or concatenate the sales reasons each surrounded by a unique separator character such as a backslash, and then use leading and trailing wildcard searches, as described in article 10.5, *The Keyword Dimension*.

One way to make this approach more palatable is to have two versions of the dimension structure, and two keys in the fact table: the sales reason group key and the sales reason key directly. The view of the schema that's shared with most casual users displays only the simple relationship; the view for the reporting team and power users could also include the more complete bridge table relationship.

- Identify a single primary sales reason. It may be possible to identify a primary sales reason, either based on some logic in the transaction system or by way of business rules. For example, business users may tell you that if the customer chooses price as a sales reason, then from an analytic point of view, price is the primary sales reason. In our experience it's relatively unlikely that you can wring a workable algorithm from the business users, but it's worth exploring. As with the previous approach, you can combine this technique with the bridge table approach for different user communities.
- Pivot out the sales reasons as shown in Figure 10-17. If the domain of the multi-choice space is small—in other words, if you have only a few possible sales reasons—you can eliminate the bridge table by creating a dimension table with one column for each choice. In the example we've been using, the sales reason dimension would have columns for price, features, recommendation, and each other sales reason. Each attribute can take the value yes or no.

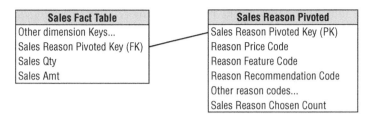

Figure 10-17: Multiple sales reasons modeled as a pivoted sales reason dimension.

This approach solves the fact table explosion problem, but does create some issues in the sales reason dimension. It's only practical with a relatively small number of domain values, perhaps 50 or 100. Every attribute in the original dimension shows up as an additional column for each domain value. Perhaps the biggest drawback is that any change in the domain (adding another sales reason) requires a change in the data model and ETL application.

Nonetheless, if the multi-valued dimension is important to the broad ad hoc user community, and you have a relatively small and static set of domain values, this approach may be more appealing than the bridge table technique. It's much easier for business users to construct meaningful queries.

Clearly the pivoted dimension table doesn't work for all multi-valued dimensions. The classic example of a multi-valued dimension—multiple diagnoses for a patient's hospital visit—has far too large a domain of possible values to fit in the pivoted structure.

The bridge table design approach for multi-valued dimensions, which Kimball Group has described many times over the past decades, is still the best. But the technique requires an educated user community, and user education seems to be one of the first places the budget cutting axe is applied. In some circumstances, the usability problems can be lessened by presenting an alternative, simpler structure to the ad hoc user community.

10.8 Adding a Mini-Dimension to a Bridge Table

Ralph Kimball, Design Tip #136, *Jun 28, 2011*

Experienced dimensional modelers are familiar with the challenge of attaching a many-valued dimension to an existing fact table. This occurs when the grain of the fact table is compelling and obvious, yet one of the dimensions possesses many values at that grain. For example, in the doctor's office a line item on the doctor bill is created when a procedure is performed. The grain of an individual line item is the most natural grain for a fact table representing doctor bills. Obvious dimensions include date, provider (doctor), patient, location, and procedure. But the diagnosis dimension is frequently many-valued.

Another common example is the bank account periodic snapshot, where the grain is month by account. The obvious dimensions in this case are month, account, branch, and household. But how do we attach individual customers to this grain since there may be "many" customers on a given account?

The solution in both cases is a bridge table that contains the many-to-many relationship needed as shown in Figure 10-18.

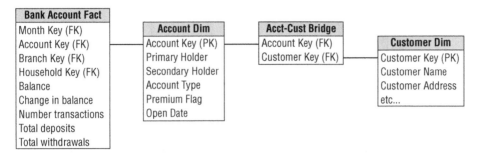

Figure 10-18: The account-to-customer bridge table without the mini-dimension.

The account-to-customer bridge table is what relational theorists call an "associative" table. Its primary key is the combination of the two foreign keys to the account dimension and the customer dimension. On close examination, we discover that all these bridge table examples turn out to be associative tables linking two dimensions.

In the bank account example, this bridge table can get very large. If we have 20 million accounts and 25 million customers, the bridge table can grow to hundreds of millions of rows after a few years, if both the account dimension and the customer dimension are slowly changing type 2 dimensions (where we track history in these dimensions by issuing new records with new keys whenever there is a change).

Now the experienced dimensional modeler asks "what happens when my customer dimension turns out to be a so-called rapidly changing monster dimension?" This could happen when rapidly changing demographics and status attributes are added to the customer dimension, forcing numerous type 2 additions to the customer dimension. Now the 25 million row customer dimension threatens to become several hundred million rows.

The standard response to a rapidly changing monster dimension is to split off the rapidly changing demographics and status attributes into a mini-dimension, which we will call the demographics dimension. This works great when this dimension attaches directly to the fact table along with a dimension like customer, because it stabilizes the large customer dimension and keeps it from growing every time there is a demographics or status change. But can we get this same advantage when the customer dimension is attached to a bridge table, as in the bank account example?

The solution is to add a foreign key reference in the bridge table to the demographics dimension, as shown in Figure 10-19.

The way to visualize the bridge table is that for every account, the bridge table links to each customer and each customer's demographics for that account. The key for the bridge table itself now consists of the account key, customer key, and demographics key.

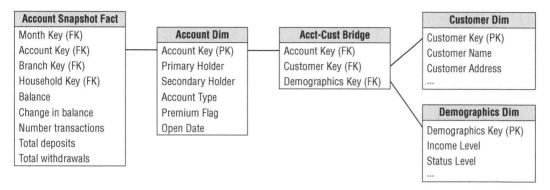

Figure 10-19: The account-to-customer bridge table with the demographics mini-dimension.

Depending on how frequently new demographics are assigned to each customer, the bridge table will grow, perhaps significantly. In Figure 10-19, since the grain of the root bank account fact table is month by account, the bridge table should be limited to changes recorded only at month ends. This will take some of the pressure off the bridge table. In my classes, as designs become more complex, I usually say at some point that "it's not Ralph's fault." The more meticulously we track changing customer behavior, the bigger our tables get. It always helps to add more RAM…

Dealing with Hierarchies

Hierarchical many-to-one relationships are found in most dimension tables. Fortunately, most hierarchies are fixed depth, so they can be denormalized into columns on a flattened dimension table. Things get much more interesting (and complicated) when the hierarchical relationships are ragged with variable depths, as we explore in this section.

10.9 Maintaining Dimension Hierarchies

Joy Mundy, Intelligent Enterprise, *Oct 27, 2008*

Dimensions are key to navigating the data warehouse, and hierarchies are the key to navigating dimensions. Often business users want to drill up or down into the data; they are implicitly referring to a dimension hierarchy. In order for those drill paths to work properly, those hierarchies must be correctly designed, cleaned, and maintained.

Hierarchies are important not just for usability. They play a huge role in query performance for a modern DW/BI system: Aggregations are often precomputed and stored for intermediate hierarchy levels and transparently used in queries. Precomputed aggregations are one of the most valuable tools to improve query performance, but in order for them to work, your hierarchies have to be clean.

Start with the Design

The solution to the problem of maintaining hierarchies begins during the design phase. For every substantial dimension, spend time thinking through the hierarchical relationships. Business user input is absolutely imperative, as is time spent exploring the data.

The first question to resolve is what are the drilldown paths or hierarchies in each dimension? Most dimensions have a hierarchy, even if it's not coded in the transaction system. A core dimension such as customer, product, account, or even date may have many hierarchies. Date provides a good example that we all understand.

The date dimension often has three or more hierarchies. Novice dimensional modelers will try to create a single hierarchy that goes from day to week, month, quarter, and year. But that just doesn't work! Weeks do not roll up smoothly to months or even years. There is usually a separate fiscal calendar, and sometimes several others.

Display the hierarchies graphically to review them with the business users. Figure 10-20 shows clearly the different hierarchies and levels that will be available. Notice the attributes that apply at different levels. This picture is a graphical display suitable for communicating with users and among the DW/BI team; it does not represent the table's physical structure. Get user buy-in on the hierarchies, levels, and names. Equally important, test how much transformation you need to apply to the actual data in order to populate these hierarchical structures.

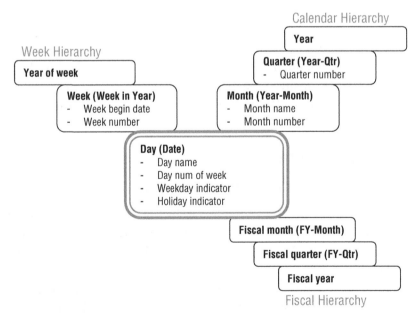

Figure 10-20: Graphical representation of multiple date hierarchies.

The familiar date dimension contains lessons that are applicable to the administration of all dimensions:

- You can have multiple hierarchies. Most interesting dimensions have several alternative hierarchies. Work with business users to name columns and hierarchies so that the meaning of each is clear.

- You must have many-to-one referential integrity between each level: A day rolls up to one and only one month, month to quarter, and quarter to year.

- If the ETL system (as opposed to the original source) maintains referential integrity with explicit physical tables for each level, then a unique primary key must be identified at each level. If these keys are artificial surrogate keys, they should be hidden from the business users in the final single, flat denormalized dimension table in the presentation layer of the data warehouse. A common error is to think of the key for the month level as month name (January) or month number. The correct primary key is year and month. Likewise, in a location dimension, for example, city name alone is not an identifier column; it needs to be some combination of city, state, and perhaps country.

- Think carefully during the design phase about whether columns can be reused between hierarchies. You might think that the week hierarchy could share the year column with the calendar hierarchy, but what about the first and last weeks of the year? If our business rule is to have week 1 for a new year start on the first Monday of the year, week 1 of 2015 starts on January 5. January 1–4 will fall in 2014 for the week hierarchy. You need a separate year-of-week column. Sometimes you do want hierarchies to intersect, but you must be certain that the data will support that intersection.

Load Normalized Data

The date dimension hierarchies are easy to load and maintain. Nothing is more predictable than the calendar, and no user intervention is required.

If your source systems are imperfect, managing the hierarchies over time is painful. Optimally, hierarchies should be maintained before the data warehouse in the transaction system or a master data management (MDM) system. With good source data, the data warehouse will never see malformed data. In the real world, we're not always so lucky. Data warehouse teams have been managing master data for decades and in many organizations will continue to do so.

Consider a product dimension for a retail store, with a hierarchy that goes from product to brand, category, and department. In this example, the product hierarchy isn't officially part of the transaction systems, but instead is managed by business users in the marketing department. When we initially load the data warehouse, our incoming data is as illustrated in Figure 10-21.

SKU	Product Name	Brand Name	Category Name	Department Name	Dept Sq Foot
101	Baked Well Sourdough	Baked Well	Bread	Bakery	150
102	Fluffy Sliced Whole Wheat	Fluffy	Bread	Bakery	150
103	Fluffy Light Whole Wheat	Fluffy	Bread	Bakery	150
951	Fat Free Mini Cinnamon Rolls	Light	Sweeten Bread	Bakery	150
952	Diet Lovers Vanilla	Coldpack	Frozen Desserts	Frozen Foods	200
953	Strawberry Icy Creamy	Icy Creamy	Frozen Desserts	Frozen Foods	200
954	Icy Creamy Sandwiches	Icy Creamy	Frozen	Frozen Foods	200

Figure 10-21: Sample source data for a product dimension.

The scenario described here is not ideal: This product dimension is not well maintained by the source systems. Most of it is fine, but notice the last two rows of data: We have a typo in the category, which breaks referential integrity. The "Icy Creamy" brand in one row rolls up to the Frozen Desserts category, and in another row to Frozen. This is forbidden.

You should find and fix problems like these early on before you even start building the ETL system. Your ETL system must implement checks to confirm that each category rolls to one department, and each brand to one category. But by the time you're actually loading the historical data, you should have worked with the source systems and business users to fix the data errors.

The real challenge lies with ongoing updates of the dimension table. We don't have time during nightly processing to have a person examine a suspect row and make an intelligent determination about what to do. If the data arriving at the ETL system's door is suspect, the ETL system can't distinguish between bad data and intentional changes. This is one of the hazards of developing a prototype or proof of concept. It's easy to fix up the data on a one-time basis; keeping it clean over time is hard.

Maintain True Hierarchies

Clean source data is essential. True hierarchies are often maintained in normalized tables, as illustrated in Figure 10-22. Optimally, this maintenance occurs before the data warehouse proper, either in the source transaction system or a master data management system.

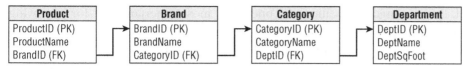

Figure 10-22: Normalized hierarchies in the source or ETL staging area.

You can write an ETL process to move this nicely structured data into the dimension table; it's a two-step process. Start at the top of the hierarchy (department), and perform inserts and updates into normalized tables in the staging area. Work down to the leaf level (product). Your staging tables will look similar to the structures in the sample product hierarchy table presented earlier. Once you've performed the extract step and have staged all the hierarchical data, write a query to join these tables together and perform standard dimension processing from the staging area into the data warehouse dimension.

The product dimension in the data warehouse should be denormalized into a single flattened dimension table. The normalization illustrated previously is the design pattern for the source system and ETL staging areas, not the actual dimension table that users query.

Address Dirty Sources

Not everyone has a well designed source system with normalized hierarchies as described in the preceding section. It's common in the DW/BI world for hierarchies to be managed by business users. Transaction systems tend to have only enough information to do their job, and business users often have a legitimate need for alternative, richer rollups and attributes. What can you do?

- **Modify the source systems.** This is extraordinarily unlikely, unless your organization wrote those systems.
- **Buy and implement a master data management (MDM) system that manages the process of defining and maintaining hierarchies.** This is the best solution, though MDM is expensive in terms of the software license, and even more so in management commitment and attention.
- **Write an applet to manage a specific user hierarchy.** Keep your design simple, solving only the problem in front of you, such as the product hierarchy. If you get carried away, you'll find yourself developing what amounts to an MDM solution.

A true hierarchy has referential integrity between each of its levels. Remember that this is fundamentally a data quality issue that is enforced in the ETL back room or source systems; it's typically not carried into the presentation area as separate tables or snowflakes of tables. When a dimension has a true hierarchy, you gain two huge benefits:

- **You will be able to define and maintain precomputed aggregations at intermediate levels of the hierarchy.** In other words, you can precompute and store an aggregate at the month or brand level. Precomputed aggregations are one of the most important tools for improving query performance in the DW/BI system.

- **You will be able to integrate data at different levels of granularity.** Sometimes data naturally exists at an aggregate level. For example, our store might develop a long term sales forecast by month and category. We can create a subset dimension at the category level to associate with the forecast facts, and then join together actual and forecast sales, if and only if the product hierarchy is a true hierarchy.

Make It Perform

Those with large data warehouses, especially those with large dimensions, need to worry about dimension hierarchies. The performance benefits of precomputed aggregations are tremendous, and they will make or break the usability of the DW/BI system. To realize these benefits, you must implement procedures to maintain hierarchical information correctly in the source or master data management system.

In the meantime, users can benefit from navigation paths that look like hierarchies but really aren't. Business users have legitimate reasons for wanting to group information together, and it's our job to make that not just possible, but also easy and highly responsive.

 ## 10.10 Help for Hierarchies

Ralph Kimball, DBMS, *Sep 1998*

In article 10.3, *Help for Dimensional Modeling*, I discussed using a bridge table to handle the situation where one dimension takes on multiple values for each fact table record. In this article, I tackle another real-world modeling situation where we'll turn to another bridge table between the fact table and the dimension table. In this case, however, it is not because of a many-to-many relationship. This time the dimension has a complex hierarchical structure of variable depth.

Consider the simple business situation shown in Figure 10-23. You can imagine that the fact table represents the revenue from consulting services that a fictitious company called Big Nine Consultants sells to various corporate clients. The grain of the fact table is the line item on each consulting invoice sent to one of the corporate clients.

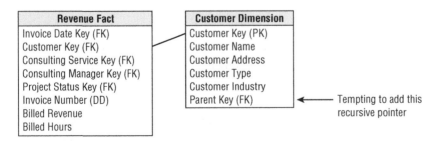

Figure 10-23: A fact table whose grain is the individual invoice line item.

The invoice number is degenerate because when you try to make a normal dimension from this key, you discover that you have already used all the interesting information in the other dimensions that might otherwise have been stored with this key. You want these keys in the design because they are the basis for grouping line items on a particular invoice or ticket, but you don't need to bother creating a dimension when there are no attributes for such keys.

In Figure 10-23, the main attention is focused on the customer dimension. With this schema design you can run all sorts of interesting queries by constraining and grouping various attributes in the customer dimension. You can add up consulting revenue and hours billed for any configuration of customer.

Perhaps, as you are working on the design of this invoicing business process, a user interview participant points out that the consulting services for the largest and most complex customers are sold at several different organizational levels. This user would like to create reports that show total consulting sold not only to individual customers, but also to divisions, subsidiaries, and overall enterprises; the report still must correctly add up the separate consulting revenues for each organization structure. Figure 10-24 shows a simple organizational structure, where each node in the tree is a customer who buys consulting services.

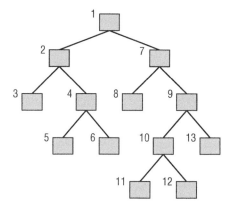

Figure 10-24: A schematic diagram of customer organizations that Big Nine Consultants sells consulting services to.

The first figure, Figure 10-23, does not contain any information about how these separate customers relate to each other. A simple computer science approach to storing such information would add a parent key field to the customer dimension. The parent key field would be a recursive pointer that would contain the proper key value for the parent of any given customer. A special null value would be required for the topmost customer in any given overall enterprise. Although this simple recursive pointer lets you represent an arbitrary organizational tree structure of any depth, there is a killer problem that defeats its use in your data warehouse.

The problem is that you cannot use the recursive pointer with SQL to join the dimension table with the fact table and add up the consulting revenues or hours for a set of organizations, as in

Figure 10-24. The widely used 1998 ANSI-standard SQL made no attempt to deal with recursive pointers (although this was corrected in the 1999 standard) and even such facilities as Oracle's `CONNECT BY` do not let you use a join in the same SQL statement as `CONNECT BY`. Thus in Oracle, although you can enumerate an organizational hierarchy defined via a recursive pointer field in a dimension table, you cannot add anything up by joining that dimension table to a fact table.

Instead of using a recursive pointer, you can solve this modeling problem by inserting a bridge table between the dimension table and fact table, as shown in Figure 10-25. Amazingly enough, you don't have to make any changes to either the dimension or fact table; you just rip the join apart and insert the bridge table.

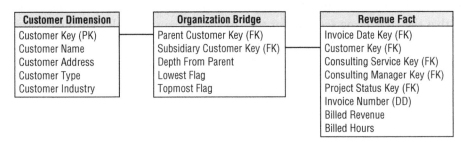

Figure 10-25: A bridge table between the fact and dimension table to navigate the organizational hierarchy.

The bridge table contains one record for *each separate path from each node in the organization tree to itself and to every node below it.* There are, then, more records in the bridge table than there are nodes in the tree. For the organization shown in Figure 10-24, we need a total of 43 records in Figure 10-25's bridge table. See if you can work this out.

If you are descending the tree from certain selected parents to various subsidiaries, you join the dimension table to the bridge table and the bridge table to the fact table with the joins as shown in Figure 10-25. The depth from parent field counts how many levels the subsidiary is below the parent. The lowest flag field is true only if the subsidiary has no further nodes beneath it. The topmost flag field is true only if the parent has no further nodes above it.

The beauty of this design is that you can place any normal dimensional constraint against the customer dimension table that selects a single customer and the bridge table will cause all the fact table records for that customer and all its subsidiaries to be correctly summarized. In other words, you can use your standard relational databases and your standard query tools to analyze the hierarchical structure.

If the field depth from parent is equal to one, only the immediate subsidiaries of the directly constrained customers will be summarized. If the lowest flag is true, only the lowest subsidiaries of the directly constrained customers will be summarized.

The joins shown in Figure 10-25 let you summarize an organizational structure downward from the directly constrained nodes. By reversing the sense of the joins (for example, connecting the customer dimension primary key to the subsidiary customer key), you can move up the organizational structure instead. When the depth from parent is equal to one, you are referring to the immediate parent of a directly constrained customer. When the topmost flag is true, you have selected the supreme parent of a directly constrained customer.

You can generalize this scheme by adding begin effective date and end effective date to each record in the bridge table. In this way, you can represent changing organizational structures. If you add these begin and end effective dates in the bridge table, you must always constrain the bridge table to a single specific date between the effective dates to avoid nonsensical double counting. In this way, you freeze the organization map to a single well-defined snapshot. When a group of nodes is moved from one part of an organizational structure to another, such as with an acquisition, only the records that refer to paths from outside parents into the moved structure need to be changed. All records referring to paths entirely within the moved structure are unaffected. This is an advantage over other tree representation schemes where all the nodes in the tree need to be numbered in a global order. Also, these other representation schemes generally do not preserve the ability of standard SQL to summarize the results in an associated fact table the way this scheme does.

If you have an organization where a subsidiary is jointly owned by two or more parents, you can add a weighting factor field to the bridge table. Strictly speaking this is no longer a tree. I call this an irregular tree. In irregular trees with joint ownership situations, you identify those nodes with two or more direct parents. The fraction of ownership by each parent is identified, and the sum of the fractions for that jointly owned node must be equal to one. Now every bridge table record from any parent that terminates at the jointly owned node or crosses through the jointly owned node must use the proper weighting factor. The weighting factor, if present in the design, must then be multiplied at query time against all additive facts being summarized from the fact table. In this way, the correct contributions to consulting revenue and total hours (in the original example) will be added up through the tree.

You can also use this approach, up to a point, to model manufacturing parts explosions. The tree structures of manufacturing parts explosions can be manipulated to fit the examples discussed in this article. You can even represent a repeated subassembly in the same way as a jointly owned subsidiary, although in this case you don't need a weighting factor because the subassembly is really repeated, not shared. The main limitation in using this approach for manufacturing parts explosions is the sheer number of subassemblies and parts present in a big example. A huge parts explosion with hundreds of thousands or millions of parts could result in a bridge table with "more records than there are molecules in the universe." At some point, this bridge table becomes infeasible.

10.11 Five Alternatives for Better Employee Dimensional Modeling

Joy Mundy, Intelligent Enterprise, *Aug 17, 2009*

Most enterprise data warehouses will eventually build an employee dimension. An employee dimension can be richly decorated, including not only name and contact information, but also job related attributes such as job title, departmental cost codes, hire dates, even salary related information.

One very important attribute of an employee is the identity of the employee's manager. For any manager, we'd like to work down the "reports-to" hierarchy, finding activity for her direct reports or her entire organization. For any employee, we'd like to work up the hierarchy, identifying his entire management chain. This reports-to hierarchy presents significant design and management challenges to the unwary. This article describes approaches for including this relationship in a dimensional model.

The basic structure of the employee dimension is illustrated in Figure 10-26. The unique feature of a reports-to hierarchy is that a manager is also an employee, so employee has a foreign key reference to itself, from manager key to employee key.

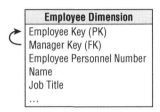

Employee Dimension
Employee Key (PK)
Manager Key (FK)
Employee Personnel Number
Name
Job Title
...

Figure 10-26: Basic structure of the employee dimension and reports-to hierarchy.

Someone new to dimensional modeling might leave the table as it is currently designed, because the manager/employee relationship is fully described. Assuming you can populate the table, the current design will work if an OLAP environment is used to query the data. Popular OLAP tools contain a parent-child hierarchy structure that works smoothly and elegantly against a variable-depth hierarchy modeled as in Figure 10-26. This is one of the strengths of an OLAP tool.

However, if you want to query this table in the relational environment, you have to use the Oracle CONNECT BY syntax. This is very unattractive and probably unworkable:

- Not every SQL engine supports CONNECT BY.
- Even SQL engines that support CONNECT BY may not support a GROUP BY in the same query.
- Not every ad hoc query tool supports CONNECT BY.

Alternative 1: Bridge Table Using Surrogate Keys

The classic solution to the reports-to or variable-depth hierarchy problem is illustrated in Figure 10-27. The same employee dimension table shown in Figure 10-26 relates to the fact table through a bridge table.

The reports-to bridge table contains one row for each pathway from a person to any person below him in the hierarchy, both direct and indirect reports, plus an additional row for his relationship to himself. This structure can be used to report on each person's activity, the activity of their entire organization, or activity down a specified number of levels from the manager.

There are several minor disadvantages to this design:

- The bridge table is somewhat challenging to build.
- The bridge table has many rows in it, so query performance can suffer.
- The user experience is somewhat complicated for ad hoc use, though we've seen many analysts use it effectively.
- In order to drill up, aggregating information up rather than down a management chain, the join paths have to be reversed.

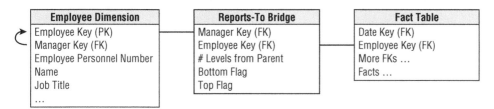

Figure 10-27: Classic relational structure for a reports-to hierarchy.

The major challenge comes when we want to manage the employee dimension and the reports-to hierarchy as a slowly changing type 2 dimension. This bridge table would still work in theory; the problem is the explosion of employee and bridge records to track the changes.

To understand the problem, look back at Figure 10-26 and think about it as a type 2 dimension for a medium-sized company with 20,000 employees. Imagine that the CEO has 10 senior VPs reporting to her. Let's give her a type 2 change that generates a new row and hence a new employee key. Now, how many employees are pointing to her as their manager? It's a brand new row, so of course no existing rows point to it; we need to propagate 10 new type 2 rows for each of the senior VPs. The change ripples through the entire table. We end up replicating the complete employee table because of one attribute change in one row. Even aside from the obvious implication of data volume explosion, simply teasing apart the logic of which rows need to be propagated is an ETL nightmare.

Alternative 2: Bridge Table with Separate Reports-To Dimension

Tracking the history of changes in a variable-depth hierarchy such as an employee reporting hierarchy is especially challenging when the hierarchy changes are intermingled with other type 2 changes in the dimension. An obvious solution is to separate the employee dimension from the reports-to relationship. Simplify employee by removing the self-referencing relationship, and create a new reports-to dimension, as illustrated in Figure 10-28.

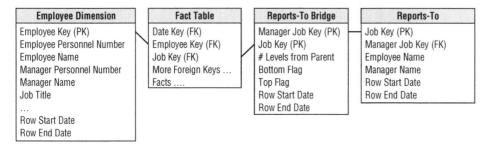

Figure 10-28: Separate employee and reports-to (or job) dimensions.

The key elements that distinguish this design from the classic structure shown in Figure 10-27 are:

- It eliminates the surrogate key for manager from the employee dimension, and hence the recursive foreign key relationship.
- The reports-to dimension has very few columns: surrogate keys, personnel numbers, and names.
- If you're exclusively using OLAP to query the schema, the bridge table is unnecessary.

If the business users don't need to track changes in the full reports-to hierarchy, this solution works neatly. Employee is a type 2 dimension. We see the name of each employee's manager. If manager name in the employee dimension is managed as type 2 we can easily see the names of all past bosses from the employee dimension. If reports-to is managed as type 1, it is no more difficult to populate and maintain than in the classic solution.

If the business users absolutely must see the history of the reporting relationship, this solution will be challenging. We've simplified the management problem by separating out the reports-to and employee dimensions, but if we get a major organizational change we're still going to have to propagate a lot of new rows in both reports-to and the bridge table.

Alternative 3: Bridge Table with Natural Keys

In order to track changes in a reports-to hierarchy for anything other than trivial data volumes, we need a solution that does not use surrogate keys. The classic structure described in Figure 10-27 works fine at query time, but it's a maintenance challenge. Our natural key alternative is illustrated in Figure 10-29.

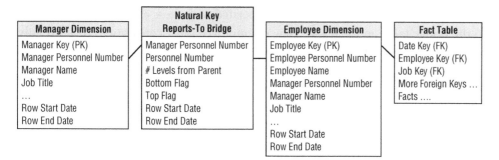

Figure 10-29: Tracking history in the reports-to relationship with a natural key bridge table.

The key elements of this design relative to the classic structure of alternative 1 are:

- Eliminates the surrogate key for manager from the employee dimension, and hence the recursive foreign key relationship
- Includes the employee dimension twice in the schema, once as the employee (linked directly to the fact table), and once as the manager (linked via the bridge table). The manager dimension table is simply a database view of the employee dimension.
- The bridge table is built on employee numbers—the natural key carried in the source systems—rather than the data warehouse surrogate keys. It's like the classic bridge table except that we need start and end dates to uniquely identify each row.
- The propagation of new rows in the bridge table is substantially fewer than before because new rows are added when reporting relationships change, not when any type 2 employee attribute is modified (as in Figure 10-27). A bridge table built on natural keys is an order of magnitude easier to manage, though still quite challenging.

A primary design goal is to be able to find all the fact rows associated with a manager and her entire organization, as the organization was structured at the time of the event measured in the fact table. This is a complicated query:

- From the manager view of the employee dimension, find the manager we're interested in.
- Join to the bridge table to find the personnel numbers and row dates for the employees in her organization.
- Join again to the employee dimension to find the surrogate employee key for the people in the organization.

■ Finally, join to the fact table to pick up all facts associated with these employees.

■ The joins to the bridge table and manager view of employee must constrain to pick up only the one row that's in effect as of the time of the fact transaction.

```
SELECT Manager.ManagerName, Employee.EmployeeName,
    SUM(FactTable.SomeFact) AS OrganizationalSum
FROM FactTable
INNER JOIN Employee  -- standard dimensional join
    ON (FactTable.EmployeeKey = Employee.EmployeeKey)
INNER JOIN NKBridge  -- needs a date constraint
    ON (Employee.PersonnelNum = Bridge.PersonnelNum
    AND Fact.DateKey BETWEEN Bridge.RowStartDate and
    Bridge.RowEndDate)
INNER JOIN Manager  -- needs a date constraint
    ON (Bridge.MgrPersonnelNum = Manager.MgrPersonnelNum
    AND Fact.DateKey BETWEEN Manager.RowStartDate AND
    Manager.RowEndDate)
WHERE Manager.ManagerName = 'Name of specific person'
GROUP BY Manager.ManagerName, Employee.EmployeeName
```

The natural key bridge table approach is unwieldy. Its main advantage is that it's feasible to maintain. It also avoids breaking out the reporting relationship into a separate dimension, as in alternative 2. Any queries that don't involve the reports-to structure can drop the bridge table and manager dimension view. Disadvantages include:

■ Query performance is a concern because the queries are complex and the bridge table will grow quite large over time.

■ The technique is not appropriate for broad ad hoc use. Only a tiny percentage of power users could ever hope to master the complex query structure.

■ The technique relies on dynamic "date-bracketed" joins between the tables, and hence cannot be implemented in OLAP technology.

Alternative 4: Forced Fixed-Depth Hierarchy Technique

It is tempting to force the structure into a fixed-depth hierarchy. Even a very large company probably has fewer than 15–20 layers of management, which would be modeled as 15–20 additional columns in the employee dimension. You'll need to implement a method of handling the inevitable future exceptions. A fixed-depth employee dimension table is illustrated in Figure 10-30.

The employee org level number tells us at what level from the top of the hierarchy we'll find this employee. Usually we fill in the lower levels with the employee's name.

At query time, the forced fixed-depth hierarchy approach as shown in Figure 10-30 will work smoothly with both relational and OLAP data access. The biggest awkwardness is to train the users to query the org level number first to find out the level where the employee is located—for example level 5—and then constrain on that column (level05 manager name). A design that uses this approach must very carefully evaluate whether this two-step query procedure is actually workable with a particular query tool and consider the training costs for the business users. Query performance should be substantially better than designs that include a bridge table.

Employee Dimension
Employee Key (PK)
Employee Personnel Number
Employee Name
Manager Personnel Number
Manager Name
Job Title
...
Employee Org Level Number
Level 10 Manager Name
Level 09 Manager Name
...
Level 01 Manager Name
Row Start Date
Row End Date

Figure 10-30: Forced fixed-depth reports-to hierarchy.

The forced fixed-depth approach is maintainable, but you will see a lot of propagation of type 2 rows. If the entire fixed-depth hierarchy is managed as type 2, then a new CEO (level01 manager) would result in a new row for every employee. Some organizations compromise by managing the top several levels as type 1.

Alternative 5: The PathString Attribute

Two years ago, a clever student in a Kimball University modeling class described an approach that allows complex ragged hierarchies to be modeled without needing to use a bridge table. Furthermore, this approach avoids the type 2 SCD explosion described in alternative 1, and it works equally well in both OLAP and ROLAP environments.

The "pathstring" attribute is a field in the employee dimension that contains an encoding of the path from the supreme top level manager down to the specific employee as shown in Figure 10-31. At each level of the hierarchy, the nodes are labeled left to right as A, B, C, D, etc. and the entire path from the supreme parent is encoded in the pathstring attribute. Every employee has a pathstring attribute. The supreme top level manager has a pathstring value of "A." The "A" indicates that this employee is the leftmost (and only) employee at that level. Two additional columns would hold the level number, and an indicator of whether the employee is a manager or an individual contributor. Figure 10-31 shows a sample organization chart with pathstring values for each node.

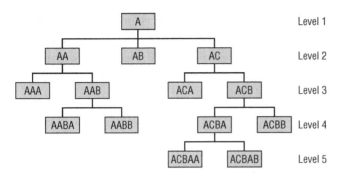

Figure 10-31: Sample org chart with pathstring values.

Users query the tree by creating a filter condition on the pathstring column in the employee dimension. For example, we can find all the people who report (directly or indirectly) to the employee with pathstring ACB by filtering with `WHERE pathstring LIKE 'ACB%'` where % is the wildcard search character. We can find direct reports by adding a clause such as `AND OrgLevel = 4`.

The advantage of the pathstring approach is its maintainability. Because of this clever structure, you will see substantially fewer type 2 rows cascading through the dimension. An organizational change high in the tree—such as creating a new VP organization and moving many people from one node to another—will result in a substantial restatement of the tree. If you're tracking the organizational structure itself as type 2, this would mean many new rows in the employee dimension. But it's still fewer rows than the alternative approaches.

The main disadvantage of the pathstring approach is the awkwardness of the business user query experience. This solution will require substantial marketing and education of the user community for it to be palatable.

Recommendation

Hopefully when you study these alternatives, you will see one that meets your needs. A type 2 reports-to or variable-depth hierarchy is a challenging beast to include in your design. This is particularly true if you want to support ad hoc use of the structure, because you'll need to balance ease of use and query performance against some very difficult maintenance problems. The decision matrix is complicated by the different capabilities of alternative storage engines, especially the differences between relational and OLAP.

The sad conclusion is that there is no universally great solution to the problem. In order to craft the best solution, you need to have a deep understanding of both your data and your business users' requirements. We always strive for that understanding, but in this case, it's imperative.

10.12 Avoiding Alternate Organization Hierarchies

Joy Mundy, Design Tip #114, *Jul 8, 2009*

Most organizations have one or several organizational hierarchies used by sales, finance, and management to roll up data across the enterprise. These organizational hierarchies become key conformed dimensions in the enterprise data warehouse, used for drilling up and down, slicing and dicing, performance-based aggregations, and even security roles. Despite their central position in management reporting, organization hierarchies are often managed—or un-managed—in a haphazard fashion.

You should manage your organization hierarchies centrally and professionally. There should be a clearly defined process for making changes to the organizational structure. Disciplined companies may try to limit major hierarchical changes only at fiscal year boundaries; changing the org structure as seldom as possible helps people mentally track those changes.

Professional management of hierarchies delivers roll-ups that are officially blessed as the truth. The more effective the official hierarchies, the less likely some business users will need to create alternative hierarchies. Unfortunately, in the real world we often see demand for alternative hierarchies: Mid-level managers want to see their organization structured differently than the official rollup. In the data warehouse, we're often asked to bring in those alternative hierarchies, to enable hands-on managers to view information in a way that matches their business. It is easy and common to bring in multiple hierarchies, but a better solution—if possible—is to embellish the official hierarchies.

Senior management typically focuses on the top few levels of an organizational hierarchy—typically, the level of detail exposed in external reporting—and unsurprisingly those top levels work well. However, lower rank managers sometimes perceive two types of problems with official hierarchies:

- Small internal organizations that don't need all the levels available to them. You can address this problem by filling in the lowest levels of the hierarchy with meaningful defaults, and designing drillable reports that make it easy for analysts to hide the repetitive structures.
- Large internal organizations that can't fit everything into the available levels. For example, a recent client has 60 percent of its business in the United States, and the US sales organization had a more complex organization than the non-US business. This situation may be solved by adding one or two levels to the official hierarchy. This obvious solution of adding more levels to the official hierarchy will only be effective if you don't make it too painful for smaller organizations that don't need more levels.

Managing the hierarchies professionally means that one organization—ideally a data administration or data management organization—is in charge of making changes to the rollup structures. Although the central organization is the only one to actually make changes, let the people who will use a piece of the hierarchy be the ones to design its structure. Design a system that distributes ownership broadly across the organization, but still keeps everyone marching to the same drummer.

A good master data management (MDM) system that includes workflow components is the ideal tool to facilitate this process. Assign owners at each node of the hierarchy, and designate additional people who must sign off on any change:

- Owners of immediate parent and child nodes
- Representative(s) from finance
- Representative(s) from data management organization

In addition, designate a larger group of people who are notified of a proposed change which may affect them. If you don't have an MDM tool to manage this process, email works too.

The management of the organizational hierarchies is really not a data warehouse function; all these changes, and the communication required, must be managed upstream of the data warehouse.

If you have distributed management of the hierarchical structures throughout the organization, and included enough levels for all parts of the organization, you will see a greatly reduced demand for alternative hierarchies. Many organizations will get by with one to three official hierarchies. With strong management encouragement to use only official hierarchies, you may be able to eliminate the need for other local structures.

10.13 Alternate Hierarchies

Warren Thornthwaite, Design Tip #62, Dec 7, 2004

Different users often want to see data grouped in different ways. In the simplest case, one department, like marketing, wants to see customers grouped into one hierarchy and another department, like sales, wants to see it grouped into an alternate hierarchy. When it really is this simple, it makes sense to include both hierarchies in the customer dimension table and label them appropriately. Unfortunately, there are only so many alternate hierarchies you can build into a dimension before it becomes unusable.

The need to more flexibly accommodate alternate hierarchies occurs when several departments want to see things their own way, plus they want to see multiple versions of their own way. In this case, we generally work with the users to define the most common way data will be grouped. This becomes the standard or default hierarchy in the base dimension. Any other commonly used hierarchies are also built into the dimension to maintain simplicity for the users.

We then provide an alternate hierarchy table that allows users to roll the data up based on their choice of the available alternate hierarchies. Figure 10-32 shows an example alternate hierarchy bridge table called customer region hierarchy for rolling up geographical regions.

Each hierarchy in the alternate hierarchies bridge table must include the entire hierarchy from its starting point where it joins to its associated dimension up to the top. In this case, the customer region hierarchy table starts at the state level and goes up from there. It is certainly possible to start from a lower level of detail, zip postal code for example, but it would make the bridge table larger and might not add any benefit. On the other hand, if there's a requirement to create alternative groupings of zip codes within states, the bridge hierarchy table obviously has to start at the zip level.

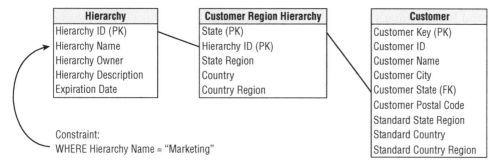

Hierarchy	Customer Region Hierarchy	Customer
Hierarchy ID (PK)	State (PK)	Customer Key (PK)
Hierarchy Name	Hierarchy ID (PK)	Customer ID
Hierarchy Owner	State Region	Customer Name
Hierarchy Description	Country	Customer City
Expiration Date	Country Region	Customer State (FK)
		Customer Postal Code
		Standard State Region
Constraint:		Standard Country
WHERE Hierarchy Name = "Marketing"		Standard Country Region

Figure 10-32: Using a bridge table to support multiple alternate hierarchies.

To simplify reporting and analysis, the bridge table includes the definition of the standard hierarchy. This choice then becomes the default in all structured reports, allowing users to switch between the standard and alternative hierarchies. The creation of a separate hierarchy table helps simplify maintenance with one row for each hierarchy, but increases the visual complexity. This table could be denormalized back into the bridge table.

The customer region hierarchy table should be used in structured reports or by expert users. Joining it to the customer table will cause overcounting unless the hierarchy name is constrained to a single hierarchy. All structured reports that provide access to an alternate hierarchies table should be built using the default hierarchy and should require the selection of a single hierarchy.

Customer Issues

This section describes patterns that we often observe with customer dimension tables. Of course, many of the patterns discussed more generically in Chapter 9 and elsewhere in Chapter 10, like handling rapidly changing monster dimensions, outrigger tables, or variable-depth hierarchies, are also relevant to customer-centric dimension tables.

10.14 Dimension Embellishments

Bob Becker, Design Tip #53, Mar 24, 2004

When developing dimensional models, we strive to create robust dimension tables decorated with a rich set of descriptive attributes. The more relevant attributes we pack into dimensions, the greater the users' ability to evaluate their business in new and creative ways. This is especially true when building a customer dimension.

We encourage you to embed intellectual capital in dimensional models. Rather than applying business rules to the data at the analytical layer (often using Excel), derivations and groupings required by the business should be captured in the data so they're consistent and easily shared across analysts regardless of their tools. Of course, this necessitates understanding what the business is doing with data above and beyond what's captured in the operational source. However, it's through this understanding and inclusion of derived attributes (and metrics) that the data warehouse adds value.

As we deliver a wide variety of analytic goodies in the customer dimension, we sometimes become victims of our own success. Inevitably, the business wants to track changes for all these interesting attributes. Assuming we have a customer dimension with millions of rows, we need to use mini-dimensions to track customer attribute changes, as described in article 9.21, *Monster Dimensions*. Our old friend, the type 2 slowly changing dimension technique, isn't effective due to the large number of additional rows required to support all the changes.

The mini-dimension technique uses a separate dimension(s) for the attributes that frequently change. We might build a mini-dimension for customer demographic attributes, such as own/rent home, presence of children, and income level. This dimension would contain a row for every unique combination of these attributes observed in the data. The static and less frequently changing attributes are kept in our large base customer dimension. The fact table captures the relationship of the base customer dimension and demographic mini-dimension as the fact rows are loaded.

It is not unusual for organizations dealing with consumer level data to create a series of related mini-dimensions. A financial services organization might have mini-dimensions for customer scores, delinquency statuses, behavior segmentations, and credit bureau attributes. The appropriate mini-dimensions along with the base customer dimension are tied together via their foreign key relationship in the fact table rows. The mini-dimensions effectively track changes and also provide smaller points of entry into the fact tables. They are particularly useful when analysis does not require consumer-specific detail.

Users often want to analyze customers without analyzing metrics in a fact table, especially when comparing customer counts based on specific attribute criteria. It's often advantageous to include the currently assigned surrogate keys for the customer mini-dimensions as a type 1 attribute in the base customer dimension to facilitate this analysis without requiring joins to the fact table. A simple database view or materialized view provides a complete picture of the current view of the customer dimension. In this case, be careful not to attempt to track the mini-dimension surrogate keys as type 2 slowly changing dimension attributes. This will put you right back at the beginning with a large customer dimension growing out of control with too frequent type 2 changes.

Another dimension embellishment is to add aggregated performance metrics to the customer dimension, such as total net purchases last year. Though we normally consider performance metrics to be best handled as facts in fact tables (and they should certainly be there!), we are additionally populating them in the dimension to support constraining and labeling, not for use in numeric calculations. Business users will appreciate the inclusion of these metrics for analyses. Of course, populating these attributes in our dimension table places additional demands on the ETL system. We must ensure these aggregated attributes are accurate and consistent.

An alternative and/or complementary approach to storing the actual aggregated performance metrics is grouping the aggregated values into range buckets or segments, such as identifying a credit card customer as a balance revolver or transactor. This is likely to be of greater analytic value than the actual aggregated values and has the added benefit of assuring a consistent segment definition across the organization. This approach works particularly well in combination with the mini-dimension technique.

10.15 Wrangling Behavior Tags

Ralph Kimball, Intelligent Enterprise, *May 9, 2002*

In article 13.5, *Behavior: The Next Marquee Application*, I argue that behavior was the new marquee application of the 2000s. As we entered the third decade of data warehousing, we progressed beyond the shipments and share applications of the '80s, past the customer profitability applications of the '90s, to this new focus on individual customer behavior.

The granularity of the data has increased by roughly a factor of 1,000 each decade. The megabyte databases of the '80s gave way to gigabytes in the '90s. Gigabytes are clearly giving way to terabytes in the 2000s, and petabytes in the 2010s. Our databases are still growing without bounds because we're recording more and more subtransactions in advance of the sales transaction. Even if the customer eventually makes only a single purchase, we might capture all the behavior that led up to it. When we extract data from all the customer-facing processes of the business, we see physical visits to brick and mortar stores, website page requests from electronic commerce store visits, calls to support lines, responses to mailings, receipt records of HTML emails containing web bugs that report back the display of the email on the user's screen, product deliveries, product returns, and payments made either by regular mail or online. The flood of data from all the customer-facing processes surrounds and explains the final solitary sales transaction. The scary thing about all these subtransactions is that there's no obvious barrier or limit to the amount of data you might collect.

Well, it's nice that we have all this data available for describing customer behavior, but how can we boil the terabytes down to simple, understandable behavior tracking reports?

In article 13.5, I describe how our data mining colleagues can assign behavior tags to complex patterns of subtransactions. Three standard customer behavior metrics are recency, frequency, and intensity (RFI). *Recency* is a measure of how recently you've interacted with the customer in any transaction or subtransaction. The metric of recency is the number of days elapsed since the last interaction. Similarly, *frequency* is a measure of how often you've interacted with the customer. And finally, *intensity* is a numeric measure of how productive the interactions have been. The most obvious measure of intensity is the total amount of purchases, but you might decide that the total number of web pages visited is a good measure of intensity, too. All the RFI measures can be subdivided into separate measures for each customer-facing process, but I'll keep this example simple.

Now for every customer, we compute the RFI metrics for a rolling time period, such as the latest month. The result is three numbers. Imagine plotting the RFI results in a three-dimensional cube with the axes recency, frequency, and intensity.

Now you call in your data mining colleagues and ask them to identify the natural clusters of customers in this cube. You really don't want all the numeric results; you want the behavioral clusters that are meaningful for your marketing department. After running the cluster identifier data mining step, you might find eight natural clusters of customers. After studying where the centroids of the clusters are located in your RFI cube, you're able to assign behavior descriptions to the eight behavior clusters:

> A: High volume, repeat customer, good credit, few product returns
> B: High volume, repeat customer, good credit, but many product returns
> C: Recent new customer, no established credit pattern
> D: Occasional customer, good credit
> E: Occasional customer, poor credit
> F: Former good customer, hasn't been seen recently
> G: Frequent window shopper, mostly unproductive
> H: Other

Imagine that you're developing a time series of behavior tag measurements for a customer over time with a data point each month, such as John Doe: C C C D D A A A B B. This time series shows that the business successfully converted John Doe from a new customer, to an occasional customer, and then to a very desirable high volume repeat customer. But in recent months, you've seen a propensity for John to start returning products. Not only is this recent behavior costly, but you worry that John will become disenchanted with your products and end up in the F behavior category!

How can you structure your data warehouse to pump out these kinds of reports? And how can you pose interesting constraints on customers to see only those who've gone from cluster A to cluster B in some recent time period?

You can model this time series of textual behavior tags in several different ways. Each approach has identical information content, but they differ significantly in ease of use. Here are three approaches:

1. Fact table record for each customer for each month with the behavior tag as a textual fact
2. Slowly changing type 2 customer dimension record with the behavior tag as a single attribute (field). A new customer record is created for each customer each month, yielding the same number of new records each month as approach 1.
3. Single customer dimension record with a 24-month time series of behavior tags as 24 type 3 attributes

Approaches 1 and 2 both have the problem that each successive behavior tag for a given customer is in a different record. Although simple counts will work well with these first two schemes, comparisons and constraints are difficult. For instance, finding the customers who had crossed from cluster A to cluster B in the last time period would be awkward in a relational database because there's no simple way to perform a straddle constraint across two records.

In this example, we're influenced very much by the predictable periodicity of the data. Every customer is profiled each month. So, even though the behavior tag is a kind of fact, approach 3 looms as very effective. Placing the time series of behavior tags in each customer record has three big advantages. First, the number of records generated is greatly reduced because a new behavior tag measurement doesn't by itself generate a new record. Second, complex straddle constraints are easy because the relevant fields are in the same record. And third, you can easily associate the complex straddle constraints with the complete portfolio of customer-facing fact tables by means of a simple join to the customer dimension.

Of course, modeling the time series as a specific set of positional fields in the customer dimension has the disadvantage that once you exhaust the 24 fields, you probably need to alter the customer dimension to add more fields. But, in today's fast changing environment, perhaps that will give you an excuse to add to the design in other ways at the same time! At least this change is "graceful" because the change doesn't affect any existing applications.

Even though you've packed the 24-month time series of behavior tags into each customer record, you may still have other reasons for administering the customer record as a true type 2 slowly changing dimension (SCD). In other words, you would still introduce another customer record for a specific customer if something else significant in that customer's profile changed. In this case, you would copy the 24 behavior tag attributes with their contents over to the new record. And when you developed a behavior tag for a new month, you would visit all the records for a given customer, filling in that field, even in the old records. This is an example of a hybrid SCD, where you're both partitioning history (type 2) and supporting alternate realities with the succession of behavior tags (type 3).

Using the techniques outlined in this article, you can boil down terabytes of subtransactional behavior data into a simple set of tags, with help from your data mining colleagues. You can then package the tags into a very compact and useful format that supports your high level ease of use and ease of application development objectives. You're now ready to pump out all sorts of interesting behavior analyses for your marketing users.

10.16 Three Ways to Capture Customer Satisfaction

Ralph Kimball, Intelligent Enterprise, *Feb 4, 2008*

For most businesses, the most compelling application of business intelligence is the 360 degree view of the customer—in other words, a comprehensive record of every transaction made through customer-facing processes. The 360 degree view is particularly potent if causal dimensions can be attached to these transactions. In its purest form, a causal dimension explains what the customer was experiencing at the moment of the transaction or as a result of the transaction. Obviously that is difficult to measure! Because we can't peer into the customer's head, we do the next best thing by collecting as many measures of customer satisfaction as we can. A good marketing analyst will be quite satisfied to know what probably satisfies, or doesn't satisfy, the customer.

Let's discuss three common design approaches for capturing customer satisfaction indicators: the standard fixed list; the list of indicators that are simultaneously dimension attributes and fact table measures; and the unpredictable, chaotic list that grows constantly over time.

Standard Fixed List

In some businesses, a reliable set of data sources can be accessed to create a stable, standard set of satisfaction attributes attached to a set of transactions. For example, for an airline, where the transactions come from boarding passes used by frequent flyers, it may be possible to collect satisfaction indicators including:

- Cancelled flight
- Delayed arrival
- Diversion to other airport
- Lost luggage
- Failure to get upgrade
- Middle seat
- Lavatory problem
- Personnel problem
- Other

These indicators are not exclusive. Any or all of them can occur, and several of them have more texture than just a simple yes/no flag. The recommended design in this case is a standalone satisfaction dimension with each of the preceding indicators as explicitly named columns. The data in the dimension records should be descriptive words, even when the choice could be yes/no. Remember that dimension attributes are used as the source of constraints as well as the labels of answer set rows. Descriptive words improve the user interface when building reports or posing queries, and descriptive words make final reports more readable. Finally, descriptive words are much more flexible than yes/no flags because new choices for particular satisfaction indicators can more gracefully be added.

Note that this style of dimension design is typical of causal dimensions, which we have used for many years to describe the exogenous conditions in a store such as media ads, price promotions, and competitive effects. This style of causal dimension is always wide, with individual columns reserved for each condition. Unless the Cartesian product of conditions is small and bounded, the dimension records are normally created on the fly as new combinations of conditions are encountered in the marketplace.

Finally, the "Other" attribute at the end of the list is a safety valve for handling unusual satisfaction situations, perhaps involving a free text description. In this case, a separate comment dimension, also attached to the transaction fact record, should be made available. This dimension contains a record for no comment, which is used most of the time, but has separate unique rows for each idiosyncratic comment that is recorded.

Simultaneous Dimension Attributes and Facts

A common dilemma arises in shipment tracking fact tables. We often have a set of standard satisfaction indicators including on time description (on time or late), order complete description (complete or partial), and damage free description (damage free or damaged). These are handled by a simple satisfaction dimension as shown in Figure 10-33.

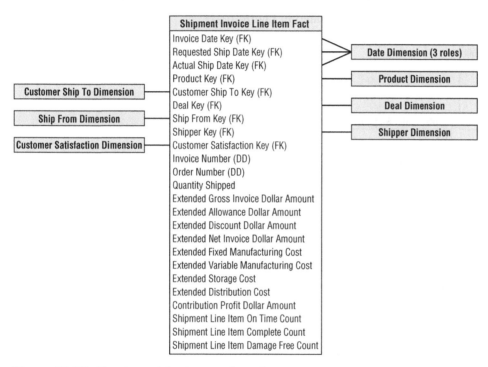

Figure 10-33: Treating satisfaction metrics as facts.

But in these situations it is also traditional to compute numeric measures of satisfaction such as percent on time, which would be awkward to compute from the satisfaction dimension. In this case, we confidently add counts consisting of ones and zeros to the fact table itself, as illustrated with the last three fact fields in Figure 10-33. Admittedly these ones and zeros are completely redundant with the contents of the satisfaction dimension, but they serve a different purpose. These ones and zeros are the grist for computations, not constraints or row labels. It's okay to use the extra disk space for this design by modeling satisfaction both ways! These kinds of binary satisfaction measures that straddle the world of facts and dimension attributes are relatively rare, but they are powerful when they can be used.

The Unpredictable, Chaotic List

In some businesses, a standard set of reliable satisfaction indicators is not available, but there may be a wealth of incompatible information from various sources. We can't use the fixed-column causal dimension approach described in the first section because there might be hundreds of columns, most of which aren't filled in for a given transaction event. For example, suppose that we are capturing mortgage loan application information. These applications could include a mind-boggling array of demographic and financial context information, with the available content of this information changing rapidly over time. In this case, the preferred model uses a bridge table between the transaction fact table and a satisfaction dimension, illustrated in Figure 10-34.

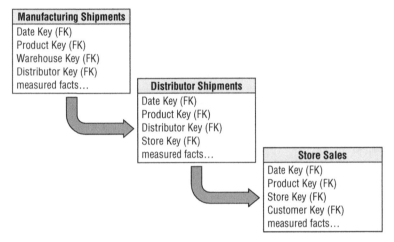

Figure 10-34: Using a bridge table between the transaction fact table and a satisfaction dimension.

The foreign key to foreign key join shown in Figure 10-34 is not a mistake. This is perfectly legal and well defined in relational databases and SQL. In this case, we assemble a potentially unique set of satisfaction indicators for a given mortgage loan transaction and give this set a satisfaction group primary key in our back room ETL processes. There are as many records in the bridge table for a specific satisfaction group as there are indicators that we have assembled for this specific (loan approval) transaction instance. This style of design has powerful advantages and powerful caveats. It's powerful because it is incredibly flexible. New satisfaction indicators and sets of indicators can be introduced constantly without changing the schema design and without having any NULL satisfaction entries. But this schema is awkward to query. For instance, if we are looking for satisfaction groups that involved a multi-unit condominium, federal loan assistance, and no former bankruptcy, we would need SQL like the following:

```
SELECT B1.GROUP_KEY
FROM SATISFACTION_BRIDGE B1
WHERE
```

```
(SELECT COUNT(B2.SET_KEY)
    FROM SATISFACTION_BRIDGE B2, SATISFACTION D2
    WHERE B2.INDICATOR_KEY = D2.INDICATOR_KEY
    AND B1.GROUP_KEY = B2.GROUP_KEY
    AND (D2.DESCRIPTION = 'Multi-Unit Condominium' or
        D2.DESCRIPTION = 'Federal Loan Assistance' or
        D2.DESCRIPTION = 'No Former Bankruptcy'))
= 3
```

We need the count to be 3 because we are only interested in satisfaction sets that contain all three conditions. Also note that we must test for "No Former Bankruptcy" explicitly rather than searching for sets that do not contain a record of bankruptcy. This is because we may not be sure that the lack of a bankruptcy indicator is a reliable record that no bankruptcy occurred. It may just mean that the information was not collected.

This SQL is far beyond the reach of an ad hoc business user, so we must package such queries under a user interface application that gives the user various choices of possible satisfaction indicators and lets them point and click.

This article has described three powerful designs for capturing customer satisfaction indicators and attaching them to low level transaction fact records. Marketing analysts often find these indicators useful for teasing out the real reasons customers engage our businesses.

10.17 Extreme Status Tracking for Real-Time Customer Analysis

Ralph Kimball, Intelligent Enterprise, *Jun 21, 2010*

We live in a world of extreme status tracking, where our customer-facing processes are capable of producing continuous updates on the transactions, locations, online gestures, and even the heartbeats of customers. Marketing folks and operational folks love this data because real-time decisions can be made to communicate with the customer. They expect these communications to be driven by a hybrid combination of traditional data warehouse history and up-to-the-second status tracking. Typical communications decisions include whether to recommend a product or service, or judge the legitimacy of a support request, or contact the customer with a warning.

As designers of integrated enterprise data warehouses (EDWs) with many customer-facing processes, we must deal with a variety of source operational applications that provide status indicators or data-mining-based behavioral scores we would like to have as part of the overall customer profile. These indicators and scores can be generated frequently, maybe even many times per day; we want a complete history that may stretch back months or even years. Though these rapidly changing status indicators and behavior scores are logically part of a single customer dimension, it is impractical to embed these attributes in a type 2 slowly changing dimension. Remember that type 2 perfectly captures history, and requires you to issue a new customer record each time any attribute in the dimension changes. The Kimball Group has long pointed out this practical conflict by calling this situation a "rapidly changing monster dimension." The solution is to reduce the pressure on the primary customer dimension by spawning one or more mini-dimensions that contain the rapidly changing status or behavioral attributes. We have talked about such mini-dimensions for at least a decade.

In our real-time, extreme status tracking world, we can refine the tried-and-true mini-dimension design by adding the following requirements. We want a "customer status fact table" that is…

- a single source that exposes the complete, unbroken time series of all changes to customer descriptions, behavior, and status;
- minutely time-stamped to the second or even the millisecond for all such changes;
- scalable, to allow new transaction types, new behavior tags, and new status types to be added constantly, and scalable to allow a growing list of millions of customers each with a history of thousands of status changes;
- accessible, to allow fetching the current, complete description of a customer and then quickly exposing that customer's extended history of transactions, behavior, and status; and
- usable as the master source of customer status for all fact tables in the EDW.

Our recommended design is the Customer Status Fact table approach shown in Figure 10-35.

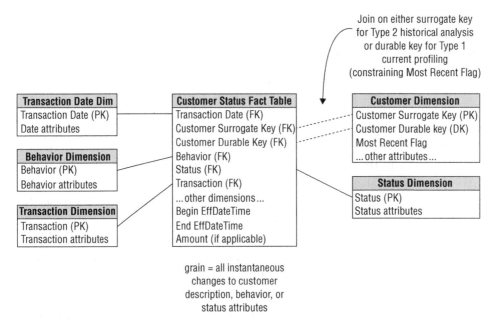

Figure 10-35: Design for real-time customer status tracking with historical and current perspectives.

The Customer Status Fact table records every change to customer descriptions, behavior tags, and status descriptions for every customer. The transaction date dimension is the calendar date of the change and provides access to the calendar machinery that lets an application report or constrain on complex calendar attributes such as holidays, fiscal periods, day numbers, and week numbers.

The customer dimension contains relatively stable descriptors of customers, such as name, address, customer type, and date of first contact. Some of the attributes in this dimension will be type 2 SCD (slowly changing dimension) attributes that will add new records to this dimension when they change, but the very rapidly changing behavior and status attributes have been removed to mini-dimensions. This is the classic response to a rapidly changing monster dimension. The Most Recent Flag is a special type 1 field that is set to True only for the current valid customer record. All prior records for a given customer have this field set to False.

The customer durable key is what we normally designate as the natural key, but we call it durable to emphasize that the EDW must guarantee that it never changes, even if the source system has a special business rule that can cause it to change (such as an employee number that is re-assigned if the employee resigns and then is rehired). The durable key can be administered as a meaningless, sequentially assigned integer surrogate key in those cases where more than one source system provides conflicting or poorly administered natural keys. The point of the durable key is for the EDW to get control of the customer keys once and for all.

The customer surrogate key is definitely a standard surrogate key, sequentially assigned in the EDW back room every time a new customer record is needed, either because a new customer is being loaded or because an existing customer undergoes a type 2 SCD change.

The double-dashed join lines shown in the figure are a key aspect of extreme status processing. When a requesting application sets the most recent flag to True, only the current profiles are seen. The customer surrogate key allows joining to the status fact table to grab the precise current behavior tags and status indicators. In a real-time environment, this is the first step in determining how to respond to a customer. But the customer durable key can then be used as an alternate join path to instantly expose the complete history of the customer we have just selected. In a real-time environment, this is the second step in dealing with the customer. We can see all the prior behavior tags and status indicators. We can compute counts and time spans from the customer status fact table.

The behavior dimension can be modeled in two ways. The simpler design is a wide dimension with a separate column for each behavior tag type. Perhaps these behavior tags are assigned by data mining applications that monitor the customer's behavior. If the number of behavior tag types is small (less than 100), this design works very well because query and report applications can discover and use the types at run time. New behavior tag types (and thus new columns in the behavior dimension) can be added occasionally without invalidating existing analysis applications.

A more complex behavior dimension design is needed when a very large and messy set of behavior descriptors is available. Perhaps you have access to a number of demographic data sources covering complicated overlapping subsets of your customer base. Or perhaps you have account application data containing financial asset information that is very interesting but can be described in many ways. In this case, you will need a dimensional bridge table.

The status dimension is similar to the behavior dimension but can probably always be a wide dimension with a separate column for each status type, simply because this dimension is more under your internal control than the behavior dimension.

The transaction dimension describes what provoked the creation of the new record in the customer status fact table. Transactions can run the gamut from conventional purchase transactions all the way to changes in any of the customer-oriented dimensions, including customer, behavior, and status. The transaction dimension can also contain special priority or warning attributes that alert applications to highly significant changes somewhere in the overall customer profile.

The begin and end effective date/times are ultra-precise, full-time stamps for when the current transaction became effective and when the next transaction became effective (superseding the current one). We have given a lot of thought to these ultra-precise time stamps and we recommend the following design:

- The grain of the time stamps should be as precise as your DBMS allows, at least down to the individual second. Some day in the future, you may care about time stamping some behavioral change in such a precise way.
- The end effective time stamp should be exactly equal to the begin time stamp of the next (superseding) transaction, not "one tick" less. You need to have a perfect unbroken set of records describing your customer without any possibility of miniscule gaps because of your choice of a "tick."
- In order to find a customer profile at a specific point in time, you won't be able to use BETWEEN syntax because of the preceding point. You will need something like:

```
#Nov 2, 2015: 6:56:00# >= BeginEffDateTime and #Nov 2, 2015: 6:56:00# <
EndEffDateTime
```

as your constraint, where Nov 2, 2015, 6:56am is the desired point in time.

The customer status fact table is the master source for the complete customer profile, gathering together standard customer information, behavior tags, and status indicators. This fact table should be the source for all other fact tables involving customer. For example, an orders fact table would benefit from such a complete customer profile, but the grain of the orders fact table is drastically sparser than the customer status fact table. Use the status fact table as the source of the proper keys when you create an orders fact record in the back room. Decide on the exact effective date/time of the orders record, and grab the customer, behavior, and status keys from the customer status fact table and insert them into the orders table. This ETL processing scenario can be used for any fact table in the EDW that has a customer dimension. In this way, you add considerable value to all these other fact tables.

This article has described a scalable approach for extreme customer status tracking. The move toward extreme status tracking has been coming on like an express train, driven both by customer-facing processes that are capturing micro-behavior, and by marketing's eagerness to use this data to make decisions. The customer status fact table is the central switchboard for capturing and exposing this exciting new data source.

Addresses and International Issues

The articles in this section focus on issues related to physical addresses, as well as considerations for including global data in the dimensional model and delivering the dimensional model to a multinational audience of business users.

10.18 Think Globally, Act Locally

Ralph Kimball, Intelligent Enterprise, *Dec 1998*

This article was written in 1998 just as the euro was being adopted. Some of the business rules in the "Dealing with the Euro" section are now only of historical interest.

As soon as the geographic spread of our data warehouse crosses a time zone or national boundary, a whole host of design issues arise. For the sake of a label, let's call such a warehouse a global data warehouse, and let's collect all these design issues in one place. From a designer's perspective, once the code is open for change, we might as well consider all the design changes for the global data warehouse at once.

Synchronizing Multiple Time Zones

Many businesses measure the exact time of their basic transactions. The most common measured transactions include retail transactions at conventional stores, telephone inquiries at service desks, and financial transactions at bank teller machines. When a business spans multiple time zones, it is left with an interesting conflict. Does it record the times of these transactions relative to an absolute point in time, or does it record the times relative to local midnight in each time zone? Both of these perspectives are valid. The absolute time perspective lets us see the true simultaneous nature of the transactions across our entire business, whereas the local time perspective lets us accurately understand the transaction flow relative to the time of day.

It's tempting to store each underlying transaction with an absolute time stamp and leave it up to the application to sort out issues of local times. Somehow this seems to be a conservative and safe thing to do, but I don't support this design. The database architect has left the downstream application designer with a complicated mess. Doing a coordinated local time of day analysis across multiple time zones is nightmarish if all you have is a single absolute time stamp. Transaction times near midnight will fall on different days. Some states, such as Indiana and Arizona, do not observe daylight savings time everywhere in the state. Reversing the design decision and storing the transaction times as relative to local midnight just recasts the same application problem in a different form. What we need instead is a more powerful design.

The time stamp design I recommend for businesses with multiple time zones is shown in Figure 10-36. The time stamp is recorded simultaneously in both absolute and relative formats. Additionally, I recommend separating the calendar day portions of the time stamps from the time of day portions of the time stamps. We end up with four fields in a typical transaction fact table. The two calendar day fields should be surrogate keys pointing to two instances of a calendar date dimension table. These key entries in the fact table should not be actual SQL date stamps. Rather, these keys should be simple integers, in a yyyymmdd format, that point to the calendar date dimension table. We split the time of day from the calendar date because we don't want to build a dimension table with an entry for every minute over the lifetime of our business. Instead, our calendar date dimension table merely has an entry for every day. The two time-of-day fields are not keys that join to dimension tables, but are simply numerical facts in the fact table.

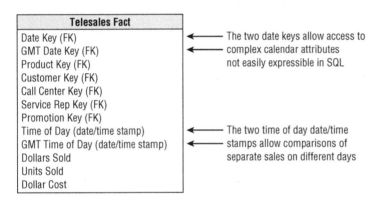

Figure 10-36: A typical fact table recording sales made in different time zones, with GMT as the absolute time stamp.

Although this design uses a bit more storage space (three extra fields) in the fact table, the application designers will be delighted. Both absolute and relative time analyses will "fall out" of the database, regardless of how many time zones your business spans.

Supporting Multiple National Calendars

A multinational business spanning many countries can't easily keep track of an open-ended number of holidays and seasons across many different countries. As happens so often in database design, there are two different perspectives that we need to address. We need the calendar from the perspective from a single country (e.g., is today a holiday in Singapore?), as well as across collections of countries all at once (e.g., is today a holiday anywhere in Europe?).

Figure 10-37 shows the design I recommend for an open ended number of calendars. The primary calendar dimension contains generic entries independent of any particular country. These entries include weekday names, month names, and other useful navigational fields such as day, week, and month numbers. If your business spans major basic calendar types such as Gregorian, Islamic, and Chinese calendars, then it would make sense to include all three sets of major labels for days, months, and years in this single table.

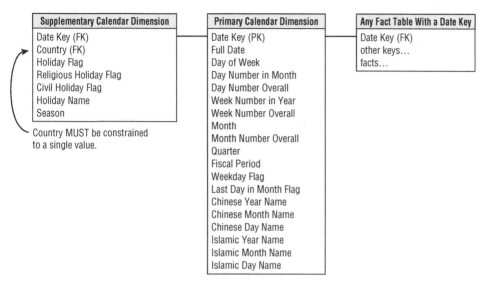

Supplementary Calendar Dimension	Primary Calendar Dimension	Any Fact Table With a Date Key
Date Key (FK)	Date Key (PK)	Date Key (FK)
Country (FK)	Full Date	other keys...
Holiday Flag	Day of Week	facts...
Religious Holiday Flag	Day Number in Month	
Civil Holiday Flag	Day Number Overall	
Holiday Name	Week Number in Year	
Season	Week Number Overall	
	Month	
Country MUST be constrained	Month Number Overall	
to a single value.	Quarter	
	Fiscal Period	
	Weekday Flag	
	Last Day in Month Flag	
	Chinese Year Name	
	Chinese Month Name	
	Chinese Day Name	
	Islamic Year Name	
	Islamic Month Name	
	Islamic Day Name	

Figure 10-37: Primary and supplementary calendar dimensions for organizations that must track multiple national calendars.

The calendar dimension provides the basic framework for all calendars, but each country has a small number of unique calendar variations. I like to handle this with a supplementary calendar dimension whose key is the combination of the calendar key from the main calendar dimension together with the country name. As shown in Figure 10-37, you can join this table to the main calendar dimension or directly to the fact table. If you provide an interface that requires the user to specify the country, then the attributes of the supplementary table can be viewed logically as being appended to the main calendar table, which lets you view the calendar through the eyes of any single country at a time.

You can use the supplementary calendar table to constrain groups of countries. The grouping can be geographic or by any other affiliation you choose for a country (such as Supplier Business Partners). If you choose a group of countries, you can use the EXISTS clause of SQL to determine if any of the countries has a holiday on a particular date.

Collecting Revenue in Multiple Currencies

Multinational businesses often book transactions, collect revenues, and pay expenses in many different currencies. See Figure 10-38 for a basic design for these situations. The primary amount of the transaction is represented in the local currency. In some sense, this is always the correct value of the transaction. For easy reporting purposes, a second field in the transaction fact record expresses the same amount in a single global currency, such as United States dollars. The equivalency between the two amounts is a basic design decision for the fact table, and is probably an agreed upon daily spot rate for the conversion of the local currency into the global currency. Now a business can easily add up all transactions in a single currency from the fact table by constraining the reporting country currency to a single value. It can easily add up transactions from around the world by summing the global currency field.

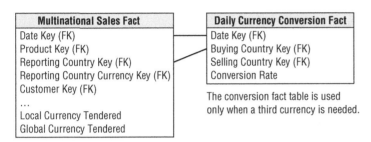

Figure 10-38: A fact table simultaneously recording sales in many different currencies. The currency conversion table is only used when converting to a third currency.

But what happens if we want to express the value of a set of transactions in a third currency? For this, we need a currency exchange table, also shown in Figure 10-38. The currency exchange table typically contains the daily exchange rates both to and from each of the local currencies and one or more global currencies. Thus, if there are 100 local currencies and three global currencies, we would need 600 exchange rate records each day. It is probably not practical to build a currency exchange table between each possible pair of currencies because for 100 currencies, there would be 10,000 daily exchange rates.

Dealing with the Euro (from the 1998 perspective)

As most of you know, many of the European nations (known as the European Union or EU) are standardizing on a single European currency known as the euro. The euro is significant from a data warehouse point of view; don't look at it as just another currency. The euro brings with it some specific financial reporting and data warehousing requirements. The most significant requirements are the three currency conversion requirement and the six decimals of precision requirement.

For all currency conversion calculations performed between EU countries, a currency must first be converted into the euro, and then the euro value converted into the second currency. Every currency conversion among EU countries must take this two-step process; you can't convert directly between currencies. These conversions in the data warehouse, of course, can be implemented from the design of the previous section, where the global currency is assumed to be the euro.

The second mandate is that you must perform all currency conversion calculations with six decimals of precision to the right of the decimal point. The purpose of this requirement is to place a maximum bound on the rounding error of currency conversion calculations. The big issue here is not the exchange factor, but rather the precision of any numeric field that stores a currency valued amount. If any such field truncates or rounds to less than six decimals of precision to the right of the decimal point for any EU currency, then this field cannot be used as a source field for a currency conversion to euros. (Ouch!) You have to make sure that your databases and spreadsheets don't perform this rounding or truncation implicitly if they have native support for European currencies.

10.19 Warehousing without Borders

Ralph Kimball, Intelligent Enterprise, *Mar 30, 1999*

In article 10.18, *Think Globally, Act Locally*, I looked at representing calendars, times, and currencies in international data warehouses. I deferred the issue of representing names and addresses, however, because of their complexity. To begin, let me give you an example. Suppose you have a name and address such as the following:

Sándor Csilla
Nemzetközi Kiadó Kft
Rákóczi u. 73
7626 PÉCS

Are you prepared to store this sort of address in a database? Is this a valid postal address? Does it represent a person or a company? Male or female? Would the recipient be insulted by anything about the way we've presented the address? Can your system parse it to determine the precise geographic locale? What salutation would be appropriate if you were greeting this entity in a letter or on the telephone? What is going to happen to the various special characters when it is printed? Can you even enter these characters from your various keyboards?

If your data warehouse contains information about people or businesses located in multiple countries, you need to plan carefully for a complete system spanning data input, transaction processing, address label and mailing production, real-time customer response systems, and your data warehouse. Actually, we should remove the "if" at the beginning of the sentence. You can't escape dealing with this problem. Virtually every business must deal with international names and addresses somewhere, whether the business has international suppliers or customers or the human resources department records places of birth or foreign business references.

Before we dive into recommended systems and database structures, let's step back and decide on some goals for our international names and addresses.

- **Universal and consistent representation.** As they say, in for a penny, in for a pound. If we are going to design a system for representing international names and addresses, we want it to work for every country in the world. Our design must not depend on the vagaries of any single country, but it should handle even the weird cases. Our design should be consistent from country to country so that similar data elements appear in predictable, similar places in the database.
- **End-to-end data quality and downstream compatibility.** The data warehouse cannot be the only step in the data pipeline that worries about the integrity of international names and addresses.

A proper design requires support from the first step of capturing the name and the address, through the data cleaning and storage steps, to the final steps of performing geographic and demographic analysis, printing reports, printing letters to customers, and printing postally valid mailing labels. When we hand off a document or report to our foreign subsidiary, we want the names and addresses to be rendered in the correct original form.

■ **Cultural correctness.** In many cases, our foreign customers and partners will see the results from our data warehouse in some form. If we don't understand which is a first and which is a last name, and if we don't understand how to refer to a person, we run the risk of insulting these individuals, or at the very least, looking stupid. When our written output is punctuated improperly or misspelled, our foreign customers and partners will wish they were doing business with a local company rather than us.

■ **Duplication removal and householding.** It is important to remove duplicates from large customer lists. Not only do we save money by removing duplicates, but we also eliminate redundant communications and misleading customer counts. A sophisticated form of duplication removal is householding, in which we identify different customers who share the same domestic or commercial household. When we understand the household as an economic unit, we can plan marketing initiatives more effectively. The secret to duplicate removal and householding is effectively parsing the names and addresses into correctly identified name and address components.

■ **Geographic and demographic analysis.** Geographic and demographic analysis is a kind of "macro householding." Again, to categorize and analyze a large list of customers correctly, we need to parse lists of names and addresses into fine grained detail.

■ **Real-time customer response.** Many data warehouses are playing an operational role by supporting real-time customer response systems. A customer service representative may answer the telephone and have to wait five seconds or less for a greeting to appear on the screen that the data warehouse recommends using with the customer. The greeting may include a proper salutation and the proper use of the customer's title and name.

■ **Foreign mailing, domestic mailing, and package service delivery.** The data warehouse may play an important role in the production of mailing lists for marketing campaigns, customer service, or informational mailings. The data warehouse may have to meet at least three separate requirements. The foreign mailing requirement means that the data warehouse can produce a postally valid mailing address from the country of origin to the destination country. This includes meeting international mailing standards, such as presenting the city and the country in all capital letters and placing the postal code in the right location within the address. The domestic mailing requirement means that the data warehouse can produce a postally valid mailing address within the destination country. This address format frequently differs from the international format, and the data warehouse may have to present it in the foreign country's character set and language. The package service delivery may require that the data warehouse produce a physical address to which they can deliver a package. Such an address often cannot be a post office box.

- **Other kinds of addresses.** We all know that we are in the middle of a communication and networking revolution. If you are designing a system for identifying international names and addresses, you must anticipate the need to store electronic names, security tokens, and internet addresses.

Designing for an International Name and Address Environment

The first and most important step is to tackle the language, font, and character set problem head on. You simply cannot patch together half solutions out of ASCII, EBCDIC, incompatible terminals, incompatible word processing packages, and incompatible printers. Your best efforts to capture a name and address can be thwarted by the next system down the pipe if it remaps your character set or discards all the accents. To solve this problem, you must build a Unicode system from end to end. Unicode is the international multi-byte standard for representing the character sets of all international languages. When your system supports Unicode, a character will be represented permanently with the correct symbols. Unicode is not a font. It is a character set, and therefore is more deeply embedded in your system than a simple font.

Your data capture terminals at the beginning of the pipeline must be capable of creating all the special characters needed at the time of entry. This does not mean that every data capture terminal must handle every language; rather, in a particular data capture location, the terminals must be capable of entering all the special characters they may encounter. It also means that the immediate result of the data capture is a Unicode formatted file.

Support for Unicode must continue from the data capture terminals through intermediate extract file formats, all the way to the data warehouse DBMS. Reporting, analysis, and address list programs must all support Unicode and display and print all special characters the same way. Note that even when you do this, the same character, such as an *a-umlaut*, will sort differently in such countries as Norway and Germany. Even though you can't solve all the variations in international collating sequences, at least both the Norwegians and the Germans will agree that the character is an a-umlaut.

The second necessary step is to do a complete job of parsing and storing the names and addresses. Resist the urge to cram everything into a few generic fields such as name1, name2, name3, address1, address2, and address3.

For guidance on how to build a robust set of descriptors for international names and addresses, I am indebted to Toby Atkinson for his remarkable book, the *Merriam-Webster's Guide to International Business Communications* (Merriam-Webster, 1999). Atkinson has written a truly useful guide for dealing with the specifics of names and addresses in nearly every foreign country with which you interact. The address example at the beginning of the article is from his book. To get the detailed explanation of that example, you'll have to read Atkinson's book. (Hint: Look in the chapter on Hungarian addresses.)

Based on Atkinson's elaborate examples of name and address variations, we can construct a file layout for names and addresses that will handle nearly every international situation, and at the same time serve as a proper target for parsing and duplicate removal. An international name and address to be used in a commercial context could consist of the following fields:

- Salutation
- First name
- Middle names
- Last name
- Degrees (such as M.S., Ph.D., and other honorary titles)
- Ethnicity
- Company name
- Department name
- Job title
- Building
- Floor
- Mail stop
- Address type (such as headquarters office, secondary field office, and parcel delivery address)
- Intended use (such as domestic or foreign mail)
- Street number
- Street name
- Street direction
- Post office box
- Locality
- City
- State
- Postal code
- Region
- Country
- Assembled address block
- Written greeting
- Verbal greeting
- Unique personal individual identifier
- Unique commercial individual identifier
- Unique commercial entity identifier

Create a record with this content for each variation of address you have for each individual. I don't recommend trying to cram all the variations of addresses into a single long record. You may have a single address for a customer in some cases and half a dozen addresses for customers in other cases. Sometimes the same individual may play multiple roles with different titles and addresses, and hence the individual needs more than one record.

The assembled address block is a long text field with a complete and correct address for the intended use, rendered in the proper order according to the regulations of the destination country and including the line breaks. Having this field simplifies address list creation applications because they don't have to contain the country-by-country rules for correct address formulation.

The written and verbal greetings resolve the issue of what the individual's first and last names are and whether custom demands that these name parts be used. Early in my own career, when I was director of applications for a small company, I remember receiving a letter addressed to "Dir of Apps," and then, "Dear Dir."

The unique identifiers at the end of the record provide the means for you to manage duplicate names and roles. It is possible that you may wish to count a given individual multiple times in different commercial roles. The identifiers give you several options for correctly counting and managing such overlapping entries.

Telephone numbers should not be appended to the previous record layout because an open ended set of such numbers exists for any given individual. A separate record layout for telephone numbers should have at least the following structure:

- Salutation
- Title
- First name
- Middle names
- Last name
- Country code
- City code
- Telephone number
- Internal extension
- Phone number type (including main office, direct line, secretary, home, pager, and fax)
- Secretary name
- Secondary dialing instructions (such as for a pager)
- Complete foreign dialing sequence
- Complete domestic dialing sequence
- Complete local dialing sequence
- Company name
- Department name
- Job title
- City
- State
- Country
- Verbal greeting

- Unique personal individual identifier
- Unique commercial individual identifier
- Unique commercial entity identifier

You can use these record designs for foreign and local address labels, real-time greetings, duplication removal, householding, and demographic analysis. When combined with end-to-end Unicode support, you should have a foundation for effectively dealing with international names and addresses well into the next millennium.

10.20 Spatially Enabling Your Data Warehouse

Ralph Kimball, Intelligent Enterprise, *Jan 1, 2001 and Jan 30, 2001*

This content was originally published as two consecutive articles. The second article in the series was titled Address Space. *Some original content has been deleted from these articles as we deemed it too vendor/tool specific. Also, as you read this article, remember that it was written in 2001, before the widespread use of GPS, Google Earth, and other widely available computer mapping tools. On the other hand, from the perspective of 2015, the gap between data warehouses and geographic information systems persists even today.*

I have always been puzzled by the chasm separating the data warehouse community and the geographic information systems (GIS) community. Very few conventional data warehouses exploit their data with a map-driven approach, yet these same data warehouses are rich with geographic entities including addresses, point locations, sales districts, and higher level political geographies.

Conversely, I have heard the mainline GIS community talking about "geographic data warehouses," but these rarely bear any similarity to the data warehouse world with which I am familiar. GIS data warehouses certainly have a lot of data, but the concerns of the GIS data warehouse revolve around such unfamiliar terms as shape files, vector data sets, cadastral databases, spatio-temporal information systems, and helical hyperspatial codes.

I have always instinctively believed that the conventional data warehouse community could gain a great deal by taking advantage of some GIS tools and user interfaces. A map can be very compelling. For example, a two-dimensional portrayal of data can show patterns that other kinds of analysis simply can't reveal. Presumably, if you GIS-enable one of your conventional data warehouses, it should be easier for you to answer questions such as:

- Do your customers come to your store because it is located near their home or near their work? What does that mean to you in terms of hours of operation and reducing in-store queues?
- Have you located your distribution center optimally between your suppliers and your customers, taking into account expected growth in the next five years?
- What factors explain the obvious disparities in profitability and customer retention that you see when you plot these factors against a national map of all U.S. counties?

Investigating a GIS Vendor

I chose ESRI as the target of my investigation because it is currently (in 2001) the leading GIS provider. In its literature, ESRI defines GIS as "taking the spatial components that already exist in our customers' databases such as store locations, telephone pole locations, and transportation routes and connecting these components to a physical location somewhere on the surface of the earth." That definition is pretty much what was on my mind when I began researching the GIS data warehouse dilemma. I am constantly advising my data warehouse clients about how to carefully parse and store data about locations, yet I don't often see them using a GIS tool for that data.

Furthermore, I was intrigued when I read a comment attributed to ESRI's founder, Jack Dangermond. He said that the maps produced by ESRI's software are really "just the door prize." In other words, the maps, as compelling and necessary as they may be, are simply a means to deliver the information and insights contained in the spatially oriented data.

I agree with the tone of Dangermond's comment. Many times over the years, I have seen dazzling technology distract the customer from the business value contained in the product. The maps and the colorful user interfaces are a necessary component of GIS, but the real point of the exercise is to be able to make decisions from the underlying data. It is at this point that the motivations of the conventional and GIS data warehouses overlap exactly.

Going to Boot Camp

Keeping all this in mind, I decided to learn first hand what barriers existed to attaching GIS user interfaces to our conventional data warehouses. I wanted to see what it would be like to enter the GIS world as both a data warehouse expert and as a GIS novice. Would I be lost? Would I come away frustrated because I would still not know how to make the GIS connection?

So in 2000 I purchased a developer's license for ESRI's MapObjects 2.1 Visual Basic (VB) product, and I signed up and paid for a spot in ESRI's MapObjects boot camp training in Redlands, California.

I came away from my week of training at ESRI very pleased. I got exactly what I expected. The MapObjects OCX is a full-featured driver for GIS capabilities. From the point of view of a conventional data warehouse implementer, MapObjects provides an easy way to GIS-enable almost any data warehouse whose dimensions contain information about locations and routes.

Using GIS tools, we can clean up and effectively use the millions of addresses we already store for all our customers. We can invoke new graphical presentation tools that allow us to see two-dimensional patterns that simply can't be detected in spreadsheets and conventional reports. And we can attach some new verbs to our existing SQL and OLAP databases *without modifying the underlying data* that let us ask spatially-enabled questions, such as "Find all the customers that are within or near a group of counties."

Under the covers of most GIS tools, there is a lot of necessary machinery for attaching ordinary dirty data. The two most interesting pieces of machinery are the address standardizing piece and the geographic query extensions piece. Let's take a look at what it takes to actually use these capabilities and also at the other serious players in this game besides ESRI. Although the specific product details described here are a snapshot of ESRI's early MapObjects offering and certainly have changed greatly since then, these basic capabilities have a generic appeal that makes these descriptions useful even today.

Automatic Address Standardizing

MapObjects provides two objects that work together to let an application interpret ordinary street addresses. The *standardizer object* applies user-specified patterns to a single street address or a table of street addresses, converting the raw addresses into its best guess as to the fully parsed form. A simple pattern for street addresses within a city might look like the following:

```
HN 12: House Number
PD 2: Pre-direction
PT 6: Pre-type
SN 30: Street Name
ST 6: Suffix type
SD 2: Suffix direction
ZN 20: Zone
```

The two-character abbreviations at the beginning of each line are the parse tokens of possible address contents. The number is the maximum byte count for each parse token, and the English text after the semicolon is the meaning of the token. This format represents the maximum generality recognizable in an address if the analyst decides to use this pattern.

A street address fits this pattern if some or all of the tokens can be assigned to the address, in the order given previously. Studying this pattern makes it clear that the more the street addresses fit this pattern, the more accurate the address standardizing will be.

After you have standardized the addresses in MapObjects, it passes them to the *geocoder object*, which attempts to match each parsed address to a standard street network database. In MapObjects, a suitable street network database would be an ESRI *shapefile* attributed with road names. An ESRI shapefile is a presentation-ready database, in this case consisting of line segments, with an open-ended number of textual and numeric attributes associated with each segment. The shapefile describes a complex closed polygon representing a boundary.

Shapefiles are one of the main formats for representing a map layer and can be created in many ways. In the case of a standard street network covering the whole United States, you would expect to purchase the required shapefiles from a geographic data supplier. Look up "TIGER line files" on www.google.com for a lot of leads on data suppliers that add value to the TIGER Census Department data on U.S. streets. (The Census Department itself has a long list of vendors that add value to this data and supply an impressive array of address matching and geocoding products. ESRI is not the only vendor in this space!)

When you run the geocoder object, it returns a set of candidate real locations on its street network that map each of your candidate addresses with varying degrees of certainty. Remember that your candidate addresses may be incomplete, have variant spellings, or be corrupt. Just because you have parsed the address doesn't mean you have a good address. Normally you would accept the geocoder's match if a single address on the street network matches your candidate, and the confidence score the geocoder returned is sufficiently high. If no location on the street network has an acceptable confidence score or if multiple locations match your candidate, then you need to think about improving the quality of your original data.

After passing a whole table of parsed and tokenized addresses to the geocoder, if all goes well, you get back a set of location objects that you can immediately plot on the visual map or write back into a text-and-number geographic data set as "the answer."

I described in some detail the ESRI MapObjects procedure for handling real customer addresses in order to give you a feel for what it takes to translate typical dirty customer addresses into a useful, standardized form for presentation and analysis. The architecture I described is typical of most of the products that perform address matching.

Geographic Query on Standard Databases

It is possible to add spatial analysis semantics to your existing relational databases. ESRI is capable of placing a geographic interpretation layer between the user and any of these databases with its Spatial Database Engine (SDE) product. The charm of SDE is that you don't need to buy a separate database for geographic processing.

SDE can be configured in a variety of modes. The SDE server can directly manage geo-specific tables such as street maps and shapefiles, and at the same time provide virtual links to your own underlying, unmodified tables residing on one of the conventional relational databases. Or SDE can physically alter and populate your underlying tables with geo-specific attributes such as points, lines, and polygons.

SDE exposes an enhanced SQL API to clients, including MapObjects. So within MapObjects, you can construct queries effectively against your normal warehouse data that can determine the relationship between geographic features. Such relationships might be crossings or intersections, shared boundaries or points, or the containment of one feature within another. References to SDE-managed data attributes can be mixed freely within a single SQL expression that is otherwise referring to your normal data. SDE's SQL extensions let you ask complex distance questions, such as the distance between a point location and some other extended boundary defined area. Another difficult distance question is how far a complex, extended area is from a line feature such as a road or a pipeline.

SDE can impose constraints on geographic features such as lines to guarantee at all times that they form a properly constructed network of a certain topology. SDE also manages what ESRI calls *dynamic spatial overlay*, which splits the spatial analysis operations away from the data retrieval operations while pipelining these operations so that SDE can overlay two data sets without first fully extracting both of them.

SDE defines an architecture as well as a set of spatial query operations. Other vendors, such as IBM and Oracle, have implemented the full set of ESRI SDE query operations while proposing their own software architectures, or in some cases, mixing their own products with ESRI's.

The Right Fit?

If you are a GIS professional sitting on top of oceans of geospatial data, then the approach I've described is probably not for you. You need to start with a mainline GIS solution. But if you are a text-and-numbers data warehouse manager already storing millions of addresses and other attributes of physical locations, then consider the techniques shown in this article to pick the low hanging fruit that our GIS colleagues have generously provided for us, without modifying your existing data architecture and without changing your other data warehouse applications.

10.21 Multinational Dimensional Data Warehouse Considerations

Ralph Kimball, Design Tip #24, Jun 1, 2001

If you are managing a multinational data warehouse you may have to face the problem of presenting the data warehouse content in a number of different languages. What parts of the warehouse need translating? Where do you store the various language versions? How do you deal with the open-endedness of having to provide more and more language versions?

There are many design issues in building a truly multinational data warehouse. In this article, we focus only on how to present "language switchable" results to the business users. Our goal will be to switch cleanly among an open-ended number of language representations, both for ad hoc querying and viewing of standard reports. We also want to drill across a distributed multinational data warehouse that has implemented conformed dimensions.

Clearly, the bulk of our attention must focus on our dimensions. Dimensions are the repositories of almost all the text in our data warehouses. Dimensions contain the labels, the hierarchies, and the descriptors of our data. Dimensions drive the content of our user interfaces, and dimensions provide the content of the row and column headers in all of our reports.

The straightforward approach is to provide 1-to-1 translated copies of each dimension in each supported language. In other words, if we have a product dimension originally expressed in English, and we want French and German versions, we copy the English dimension row by row and column by column, preserving the keys and numeric indicators, while translating each textual attribute. But we have to be careful. In order to preserve the user interfaces and final results of the English version, both the French and German product dimensions would have to also preserve the same one-to-one and many-to-one relationships, and grouping logic, both for ad hoc reports and building aggregates.

The explicitly understood one-to-one and many-to-one relationships should definitely be enforced by an entity-relationship model in the back room ETL area. That part is easy. But a subtle problem arises when doing the translations to make sure that no two distinct English attributes end up being translated into the same French or German attribute. For example, if the English words scarlet and crimson were both translated to the German word "rot," certain report totals would be different between the English and German versions. So we need an extra ETL step that verifies we have not introduced any duplicate translations from distinct English attributes.

The big advantage of this design is scalability because we can always add a new language version without changing table structures, and without reloading the database. We can allow the

French or German user to drill across a far-flung distributed data warehouse if we replicate the translated versions of the dimensions to all the remote databases.

When a French or German user launches a drill-across query, each remote database must use the correct translated dimensions. This will be handled easily enough by the original French/German application that formulates the request. Notice that each remote database must support "hot-swappable dimensions" that allow this dimension switching to take place from query to query as different language requests are made. This is easy in a relational environment and may be tough in an OLAP environment.

Although we have accomplished a lot with this design, including a scalable approach to implementing a distributed multi-language data warehouse, we still have some unsolved issues that are just plain hard:

1. We cannot easily preserve sort orders across different language versions of the same report. Certainly we cannot make the translated attributes sort in the same order as the root language. If preserving sort order is required, then we would need a hybrid dimension carrying both the root language and the second language, so that the SQL request could force the sort to be preserved in the root language, but show the second language as unsorted row labels. This is messy and results in double-size dimensions, but probably could be made to work.

2. If the root language is English, we probably will find that almost every other language results in translated text that is longer than the English. Don't ask me why. But this presents problems for formatting user interfaces as well as finished reports.

3. Finally, if our set of languages extends beyond English and the main European languages, then even the 8-bit Extended ASCII character set will not be enough. All of the participating data marts would need to support the 16-bit UNICODE character set. Remember that our design needs the translated dimensions to reside on the target machines.

Finally, a solution that avoids building new dimensions simply waits until the report is completely finished in the root language (perhaps English) and then translates the report face field by field.

Industry Scenarios and Idiosyncrasies

The final section in this chapter provides a series of case study vignettes written by Ralph, Margy, and Bob from their experiences with a variety of clients.

10.22 Industry Standard Data Models Fall Short

Margy Ross, Intelligent Enterprise, *Sep 13, 2010*

Industry-standard data models are an appealing concept at first blush, but they aren't the time savers they are cracked up to be. What's more, these prebuilt models may inhibit data warehouse project success.

Vendors and proponents argue that standard, prebuilt models allow for more rapid, less risky implementations by reducing the scope of the data model design effort. Every manufacturer takes orders and ships products to fulfill the orders. Every insurance company sells policies and processes claims. Every transportation company moves cargo between an origin and a destination. The list goes on across other industries. Why bother "re-creating the wheel" by designing custom data models to support these common business processes when you can buy an industry-standard model instead?

Yes, most businesses in a given industry perform common functions. But if everyone's approach to these business functions was so similar, then why are there so many alternative organizations? Don't most organizations do things slightly differently than their industry peers? And if so, how do these "competitive advantages" get addressed by a pre-defined industry model? True business intelligence requires the injection of an organization's own intellectual capital. Would you really want to use the identical industry solution as your peers? In virtually every data warehouse design and delivery project, the vocabulary used by the operational source system's data model needs to be translated into business vernacular. Some might argue that the source system speaks "geek" rather than Greek. Embracing an industry-standard model introduces the need for yet another pocket dictionary.

First, the data in the source system's language needs to be translated and transformed into the industry model's generic language. This is no small feat; while some data will translate without too much compromise, other data will need to be wrestled and coerced into the pre-defined model and invariably some source data just won't fit.

Once the source has been manipulated into the model's supposedly universal language, the data then needs to go through a second translation so that the vocabulary used in the final presentation layer makes sense to the business users. The challenges surrounding these multiple transformations, and the opportunity to lose something in the translations between three languages—source system, industry model, and business usage—are extensive but often overlooked when considering a standardized model.

Of course, the transformation effort is less onerous if the source data capture system and industry model are supplied by the same vendor. But there are still some sharp corners lurking even in this scenario. First, you'll need to incorporate any custom extensions or flex field data elements from your implementation into the vendor's generic model. Secondly, you'll need to worry about the integration of any source data that's outside the vendor's domain. Can you readily conform the industry model's dimensions with other internally available master data? If not, the industry model is destined to become another isolated stovepipe dataset. Clearly, this outcome is unappealing, but it may be less of an issue if all your operational systems are supported by the same ERP vendor or you're a very small organization without an IT shop doing independent development.

What can you realistically expect to gain from an industry-standard model? A pre-built generic model can help identify core business processes and associated common dimensions for a given industry. That provides some comfort for data warehouse project teams feeling initially overwhelmed by design tasks. However, is this knowledge worth six figures? Alternatively, you could likely gain this same insight by spending a few weeks with the business users; you'd not only improve your understanding of the business's needs, but you'd also begin "bonding" business users to the DW/BI initiative.

Ultimately, the business's ownership and stewardship of the effort are critical to its long term success. Even if you buy an industry-standard model, you're still going to need to spend time with the business to understand the final translations required to address their requirements. There's no dodging this necessary step. In the Kimball Group's experience, after a few days or weeks studying the standard model, most teams typically gain enough confidence to want to customize the schema extensively for "their data" and the desire for an industry-standard model evaporates.

It's also worth mentioning that just because you spend thousands of dollars on a standard model doesn't mean it exhibits generally accepted dimensional modeling best practices. Unfortunately, some pre-built models embody common dimensional modeling design flaws; this isn't surprising if the model's designers have focused more on best practices for source system data capture rather than those required for business reporting and analytics.

Under the heading of full disclosure, the Kimball Group helps clients design dimensional models; but given that we're a six-person organization, the overall demand for customized dimensional models far exceeds our capacity, with or without broad adoption of industry-standard models. I'll also acknowledge that we've worked with several source system vendors on their complementary industry model solutions; we appreciate that it's much harder than you would imagine to design a pre-defined generic model—even when you own the data capture source code.

Based on our experience and observations, business-centric custom models are more likely to be adopted by the business users than vendor-supplied pre-built standard models which appeal more to IT teams less attuned to the business's nuances.

10.23 An Insurance Data Warehouse Case Study

Ralph Kimball, DBMS, *Dec 1995*

This article was originally titled Data Warehouse Insurance.

Insurance is an important and growing sector for the data warehousing market. Several factors have come together in the last year or two to make data warehouses for large insurance companies both possible and extremely necessary. Insurance companies generate several complicated transactions that must be analyzed in many different ways. Until recently, it wasn't practical to consider storing hundreds of millions—or even billions—of transactions for online access. At the same time, the insurance industry is under incredible pressure to reduce costs. Costs in this business come almost entirely from claims or "losses," as the insurance industry more accurately describes them.

In this article, I use ABC123Insurance as a case study to illustrate common issues and show how to resolve them in a data warehouse environment. ABC123Insurance is the pseudonym of a major insurance company that offers automobile, homeowner's, and personal property insurance to about two million customers. ABC123Insurance has annual revenues of more than $2 billion. My company designed ABC123Insurance's corporate data warehouse for analyzing all claims across all its lines of business, with history in some cases stretching back more than 15 years.

The first step at ABC123Insurance was to spend two weeks interviewing prospective users in claims analysis, claims processing, field operations, fraud and security management, finance, and marketing. We talked to more than 50 users, ranging from individual contributors to senior management. From each group of users we elicited descriptions of what they did in a typical day, how they measured the success of what they did, and how they thought they could understand their businesses better. We did not ask them what they wanted in a computerized database. It was our job to design, not theirs.

From these interviews we found three major themes that profoundly affected our design. First, to understand their claims in detail, the users needed to see every possible transaction. This precluded presenting summary data only. Many end user analyses required the slicing and dicing of the huge pool of transactions.

Second, the users needed to view the business in monthly intervals. Claims needed to be grouped by month, and compared at month end to other months of the same year, or to months in previous years. This conflicted with the need to store every transaction because it was impractical to roll up complex sequences of transactions just to get monthly premiums and monthly claims payments. Third, we needed to deal with the heterogeneous nature of ABC123Insurance's lines of business. The facts recorded for an automobile accident claim are different than those recorded for a homeowner's fire loss claim or burglary claim.

These data conflicts arise in many different industries, and are familiar themes for data warehouse designers. The conflict between the detailed transaction view and the monthly snapshot view almost always requires that you build both kinds of tables in the data warehouse. We call these the transaction grain and periodic snapshot grains of a business. Note that we are not referring to SQL views here, but to physical tables. The need to analyze the entire business across all products (lines of business in ABC123Insurance's case) versus the need to analyze a specific product with unique measures is called the "heterogeneous products" problem. At ABC123Insurance, we first tackled the transaction and monthly snapshot grains of the business by carefully dimensionalizing the base-level claims processing transactions. Every claims processing transaction was able to fit into the dimensional schema shown in Figure 10-39.

This structure is characteristic of transaction-level data warehouse schemas. The central transaction-level fact table consists almost entirely of keys. Transaction fact tables sometimes have only one additive fact, which we call amount; the interpretation of the amount field depends on the transaction type, which is identified in the transaction dimension. The time dimension is actually two instances of the same dimension table connecting to the fact table to provide independent constraints on the transaction date and the effective date. This design for ABC123Insurance has 11 dimensions, each of which is known at the time a claims transaction is processed. Each of the 11 dimensions represents a valid and interesting entry point into the vast sea of claims processing transactions.

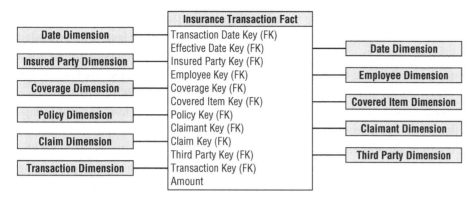

Figure 10-39: A claims transaction dimensional model.

This transaction-level dimensional schema provided an extremely powerful way for ABC123Insurance to analyze claims. The number of claimants, the timing of claims, the timing of payments made, and the involvement of third parties such as witnesses and lawyers, were all easily derived from this view of the data. Strangely enough, it was somewhat difficult to derive "claim-to-date" measures, such as monthly snapshots, because of the need to crawl through every detailed transaction from the beginning of history. The solution was to add to ABC123Insurance's data warehouse a monthly snapshot version of the data. The monthly snapshot removed some of the dimensions, while adding more facts, as illustrated in Figure 10-40.

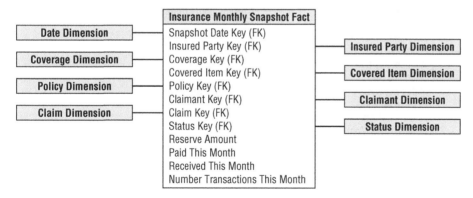

Figure 10-40: A claims monthly snapshot dimensional model.

The grain of this snapshot fact table was the monthly activity of each claimant's claim against ABC123Insurance's insured party. Several of the transaction schema dimensions were suppressed in this monthly snapshot, including effective date, employee, third party, and transaction type. However, it was important to add a status dimension to the monthly snapshot so that ABC123Insurance could quickly find all open, closed, and reopened claims. The list of additive, numeric facts was expanded to include several useful measures. These include the amount of the reserve set aside to pay for a claim, amounts paid and received during the month, and an overall count of the monthly transaction activity for this claim. This monthly snapshot schema was extremely useful at ABC123Insurance as a way to rapidly analyze the month-to-month changes in claims and exposure to loss. Monthly snapshot tables were very flexible because interesting summary metrics could be added as facts, almost at will. Of course, we could never add enough summary buckets to do away with the need for the transaction schema itself. There are hundreds of less frequently requested measures, representing combinations and counts and timings of interesting transactions, which would be rendered inaccessible if we didn't preserve the detailed transaction history.

After dispensing with the first big representation problem, we faced the problem of how to deal with heterogeneous products. This problem arose primarily in the monthly snapshot fact table, in which we wanted to store additional monthly summary measures specific to each line of business. These additional measures included automobile coverage, homeowner's fire coverage, and personal article loss coverage. After talking to the insurance specialists in each line of business, we realized that there were at least 10 custom facts for each line of business. Logically, our fact table design could be extended to include the custom facts for each line of business as shown in Figure 10-41, but physically we had a disaster on our hands.

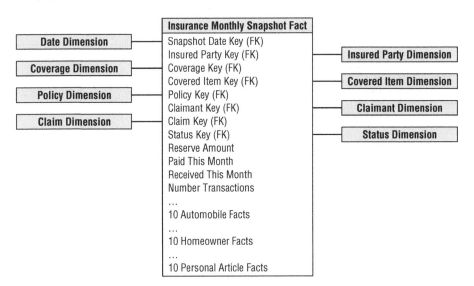

Figure 10-41: Inappropriate way to handle the facts unique to each line of business.

Because the custom facts for each line of business were incompatible with each other, for any given monthly snapshot record, most of the fact table was filled with nulls. Only the custom facts for the particular line of business were populated in any given record. The answer to this dilemma was to physically separate the monthly snapshot fact table by coverage type. We ended up with a single core monthly snapshot schema, which was exactly the same as Figure 10-40, and a series of custom monthly snapshot schemas, one for each line of business. The custom monthly snapshot schema for automobile coverages is shown in Figure 10-42. The core schema can be thought of as a super-type and the customer schemas can be thought of as sub-types that inherit the characteristics of the common super-type.

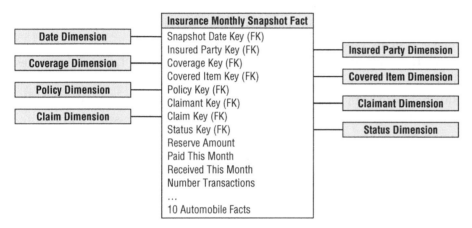

Figure 10-42: Monthly snapshot for automobile coverages.

A key element of this design was the repetition of the core facts in each of the custom schemas. This is sometimes hard for a database designer to accept, but it is very important. The core schema, shown in Figure 10-40, is the one ABC123Insurance uses when analyzing the business across different coverage types. Those kinds of analyses use only the core table. ABC123Insurance uses the automobile custom schema, shown in Figure 10-42, when analyzing the automobile segment of the business. When performing detailed analyses within the automobile line of business, for example, it is important to avoid linking to the core fact table to get the core measures such as amounts paid and amounts received. In these large databases, it is very dangerous to access more than one fact table at a time. It is far better, in this case, to repeat a little of the data in order to keep the users' queries confined to single fact tables.

The data warehouse we built at ABC123Insurance is a classic example of a large data warehouse that has to accommodate the conflicting needs for detailed transaction history, high level monthly summaries, companywide views, and individual lines of business. We used standard data warehouse design techniques, including transaction views and monthly snapshot views, as well as heterogeneous product schemas to address ABC123Insurance's needs. This dimensional data warehouse gives the company many interesting ways to view its data.

10.24 Traveling through Databases

Ralph Kimball, DBMS, May 1997

An interesting design theme that has come up in many data warehouses I have designed is the business application where a person or thing goes on a voyage. Although ship voyages come to mind most readily, I am really talking about any situation where the person or thing travels from a beginning to an end with some stops in the middle. There are many examples of voyage situations: ocean container cargo shipping, ocean cruises, airline passenger travel, airline cargo shipping, rail transport, truck transport, package delivery services, United States mail (any postal system, really), distribution systems, material movement systems, business travel credit card tracking (including car rentals and hotel stays), and, surprisingly, telephone company network inventory tracking (all of the switches and lines in the network).

All of these voyage situations can be thought of as networks. The network is the map of every possible voyage between ports. Although it took a while to dawn on me, the design issues for network-oriented business data warehouses are often the same as the design issues for classic voyage data warehouses. Think about the telephone company network inventory example as a map of the possible voyages a telephone call could make between an origin "port" telephone number and a destination port telephone number.

Walking through the Design

Voyage and network databases raise a number of unique design issues not found in other data warehouses. But voyage databases contain an inherent trap. The most straightforward and obvious dimensional design easily contains all possible information about voyages taken, but it may fail miserably to answer the most basic business questions about the voyages. These questions include "Why did the person or thing take the voyage?" and "Where are they going?"

To understand this dilemma and see how to fix it, suppose that you want to build a frequent flyer activity dimensional model for a major airline. First we identify the business process for this subject area. The business process is the system for generating passenger tickets. You will extract directly from the production ticketing system into the frequent flyer dimensional model. The second step is to decide on the "grain" of the main fact table in the dimensional model.

In voyage databases, it is inevitable that the grain of the fact table must be the individual voyage segment taken. In the frequent flyer case, this means that there is a record in the main fact table for each segment flown by a frequent flyer. You must use the segment as the grain because all of the interesting information about what happened to the frequent flyer is uniquely available at the segment level. This information includes the origin airport for the segment, the destination airport for the segment, the fare class flown, whether an upgrade was purchased or claimed, the type of aircraft, the location of the passenger's seat, whether the flight was late, the actual miles flown, and the miles awarded.

The third and fourth steps in the design are deciding on the specific dimensions and facts. It is fairly easy to arrive at the design shown in Figure 10-43. At first glance, this design seems to be very satisfactory. The dimensionality is clean and obvious, and it seems that there would be many useful "entry points" into this fact table through the dimension tables that would let you construct all sorts of interesting business queries.

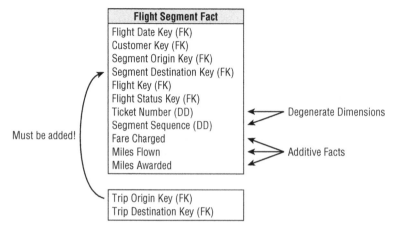

Figure 10-43: The flight segment dimensional model.

Strangely enough, this schema fails miserably. It is nearly impossible for business users to ask why the frequent flyers bought a ticket in the first place! The grain of the individual segment masks the nature of the voyage. On a real business flight, I may leave from San Jose and fly to Detroit with an intermediate hub transfer stop in Dallas. After staying in Detroit for two days, I go on to Atlanta. Then I return to San Jose, again though Dallas. My five segments look like:

- San Jose to Dallas
- Dallas to Detroit
- Detroit to Atlanta
- Atlanta to Dallas
- Dallas to San Jose

I would have to study the flight times closely to realize that my real purpose was to travel between these cities:

- San Jose to Detroit
- Detroit to Atlanta
- Atlanta to San Jose

Adding Dimensions

No query tool—or SQL that I am aware of—will deliver this answer from the basic design in Figure 10-43. There is no reasonable way to determine what a meaningful "business destination" is in this sequence of segments, and any query that tries to constrain across disparate records in the database is the kiss of death for SQL.

Fortunately, there is a simple solution to his dilemma. If you add two more airport dimensions to Figure 10-43, suddenly the design becomes very responsive to business users. These added dimensions are shown with the arrow in Figure 10-43. These new trip origin and trip destination dimensions can be thought of as providing the context for the voyage segment. They augment the original segment origin and segment destination dimensions. Now the users can perform a simple SQL query such as:

```
SELECT COUNT(DISTINCT TICKET_NUMBER) ...
WHERE TRIP_ORIGIN = 'San Jose' AND TRIP_DESTINATION = 'Detroit'.
```

The trip origin and trip destination dimensions are identified during the production data extract process. An airline would normally identify a stopover of more than four hours as a meaningful stop at a destination. While the ticket is being processed during the data extract, the trip origin and destination are easily identified and entered as fields on the individual segment records.

The theme of providing two additional context dimensions for the voyage segment is the secret of the voyage and network schema designs. All of these schemas need these two additional dimensions. Armed with these two additional dimensions, users can ask many interesting questions, including:

- Where are my frequent flyers actually intending to go?
- How many hub stops did we force them to make?
- How many trips are there in a typical overall ticket?

An analogous question for a telephone network that needs the two context dimensions might be: What are the ultimate origins and destinations of the high volume of traffic we are seeing on this particular line between switching points?

The four airport dimensions must be logically independent in this design so that they can be constrained in random and uncorrelated ways. However, you only need to build a single physical airport table to support all four logical dimensions. Although the SQL SYNONYM construct will work to create the illusion of four independent logical tables, the SYNONYM approach by itself is awkward for the users. The four independent logical tables will end up having identical field names. This makes report building and ad hoc querying confusing. The airport name would be found in all four logical tables, and it becomes cosmetically difficult to tell the four roles apart. A better approach might be to also define four SQL views on these four SYNONYMs, where each view relabels all the fields to names such as trip origin airport name and trip destination airport name.

Voyage schemas often have a large number of dimensions. A schema for a container shipping business could easily have 12 or more dimensions, such as original shipper, ultimate consignor, foreign consolidator, domestic consolidator, carrier, voyage origin, voyage destination, segment origin, segment destination, commodity shipped, container vessel, and bill of lading number (degenerate).

The first five of these dimensions are commercial business entities that play roles in shipping the commodity from the original shipper to the ultimate consignor. Like the airport dimension in the previous example, these five dimensions could be implemented in a single commercial entity physical table, but five SYNONYMs and five SQL views should be used to separate the five business roles.

Images and Maps

It is very compelling to combine graphic images and maps in a voyage database. Voyages and networks are inherently physical, and businesses often have rich sources of graphics and maps that fit nicely with the grain of the voyage or network segment. For instance, in your frequent flyer database, you could have images of airplanes, cabin layouts, cities, and airports to accompany each segment record. Maps of flight segments, trips, and overall passenger tickets would be very useful. Maps could be available for gate layouts in airports showing the distance between gates.

Even an ordinary relational database can support extensions to maps and graphic images. For graphic images, the name of a JPEG file in the dimension record for the aircraft or the airport is enough for an application to open the image while using the database. Similarly, latitudes and longitudes can be passed to mapping software, which can display a map in a window alongside the query results (see article 10.20, *Spatially Enabling Your Data Warehouse*).

10.25 Human Resources Dimensional Models

Ralph Kimball, DBMS, Feb 1998

This article was originally titled Human Resources Data Marts.

It is easy in dimensional modeling to get lulled into a kind of "additive complacency," where every data source looks like retail sales. In the simple world of retail sales all the transactions are little pieces of revenue that always add up across all the dimensions, and the dimensions themselves are tangible, physical things like product, store, and date.

I frequently get asked, "Well, what about something like human resources? Most of the facts aren't additive. Most of the facts aren't even numbers, but they are clearly changing all the time, like numeric facts. How do I model that?" Actually, human resources dimensional models are a very good application for dimensional modeling. With a single design we can address just about all the major analysis and reporting needs. We just have to be careful about what is a dimension and what is a fact.

To frame the problem, let's describe a typical human resources environment. Assume that we are the human resources department for a large enterprise with more than 100,000 employees. Each employee has a complex human resources profile with at least 100 attributes. These attributes include all the standard human resources descriptions including date of hire, job grade, salary, review dates, review outcomes, vacation entitlement, organization, education, address, insurance plan, and many others. In our large organization, there is a constant stream of transactions against this employee data. Employees are constantly being hired, transferred, promoted, and having their profiles adjusted in various ways.

In our design, we will address three fundamental kinds of queries run against this complex human resources data. In our first kind of query, we want to report summary statuses of the entire employee base on a regular (monthly) basis. In these summaries, which will be modeled as periodic snapshots, we want counts, instantaneous totals, and cumulative totals, including such things as number of employees, total salary paid during the month, cumulative salary paid this year, total and cumulative vacation days taken, vacation days accrued, number of new hires, and number of promotions. Our reporting system needs to be extremely flexible and accurate. We want these kinds of reports for all possible slices of the data, including time slices, organization slices, geographic slices, and any other slices supported in the data. Remember the basic tenet of dimensional modeling: If you want to be able to slice your data along a particular attribute, you simply need to make the attribute appear in a dimension table. By using the attribute as a row header (with SQL GROUP BY) you automatically "slice." We demand that this database support hundreds of different slicing combinations.

The hidden reporting challenge in this first kind of query is making sure that we pick up all the correct instantaneous and cumulative totals at the end of each month, even when there is no activity in a given employee's record during that month. This prohibits us from merely looking through the transactions that occurred during the month.

In our second kind of query, we want to be able to profile the employee population at any precise instant in time, whether or not it is at the end of a month. We want to choose some exact date and time at any point in our organization's history and ask how many employees we have and what their detailed profiles were on that date. This query needs to be simple and fast. Again, we want to avoid sifting through a complex set of transactions in sequence to construct a snapshot for a particular date in the past.

Although in our first two queries we have argued that we cannot depend directly on the raw transaction history to give us a rapid response, in our third kind of query we demand that every employee transaction be represented distinctly. In this query, we want to see every action taken on a given employee, with the correct transaction sequence and timing. This detailed transaction history is the "fundamental truth" of the human resource data and should provide the answer to every possible detailed question, including questions not anticipated by the original team of designers. The SQL for these unanticipated questions may be complex, but we are confident the data is there, waiting to be analyzed.

In all three cases, we demand that the employee dimension is always a perfectly accurate depiction of the employee base for the instant in time specified by the query. It would be a huge mistake to run a report on a prior month with the current month's employee profiles.

Now that we have this daunting set of requirements, how on earth can we satisfy all of them and keep the design simple? Amazingly, we can do it all with a single dimensional schema with just one fact table and an employee dimension table that is updated whenever an employee status transaction takes place. Take a moment to study Figure 10-44.

The human resources dimensional model consists of a fairly ordinary looking fact table with three dimensions: employee, month, and organization. The month table contains the usual descriptors for the corporate calendar, at the grain of the individual month. The organization dimension contains a description of the organization that the employee belongs to at the close of the relevant month.

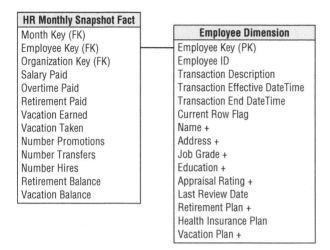

HR Monthly Snapshot Fact
Month Key (FK)
Employee Key (FK)
Organization Key (FK)
Salary Paid
Overtime Paid
Retirement Paid
Vacation Earned
Vacation Taken
Number Promotions
Number Transfers
Number Hires
Retirement Balance
Vacation Balance

Employee Dimension
Employee Key (PK)
Employee ID
Transaction Description
Transaction Effective DateTime
Transaction End DateTime
Current Row Flag
Name +
Address +
Job Grade +
Education +
Appraisal Rating +
Last Review Date
Retirement Plan +
Health Insurance Plan
Vacation Plan +

Figure 10-44: A human resources monthly snapshot with a type 2 slowly changing employee dimension table.

The employee dimension table is a type 2 slowly changing dimension that contains a complete snapshot of the employee record for each individual employee transaction. The employee dimension key is an artificial key made during the extraction process, and should be a sequentially assigned integer, starting with 1. Resist the urge to make this a smart key consisting of employee ID, transaction code, and effective date/time stamp. All these attributes are valuable, but they are simply attributes in the employee record where they participate in queries and constraints like all the other attributes.

The employee ID is the normal human resources "EMP ID" that is used in the production system. The transaction description refers to the transaction that created this particular record, such as promotion or address change. The transaction effective date/time stamp is the exact date and time of the transaction. We assume that these time stamps are sufficiently fine grained that they guarantee uniqueness of the transaction record for a given employee. Therefore, the true primary key for this dimension table is employee ID plus transaction date/time stamp.

A crucial piece of the design is the second time stamp entry: transaction end date/time stamp. This date/time stamp is exactly equal to the date/time of the next transaction to occur on this employee record, whenever that may be. In this way, these two time stamps in each record define a span of time during which the employee description is exactly correct. The two time stamps can be one second apart (if a rapid sequence of transactions is being processed against an employee profile) or the two time stamps can be many months apart.

The last transaction made against an employee profile is identified by the current row flag being set to true. This approach allows the most current or final status of any employee to be quickly retrieved. If a new transaction for that employee needs to be entered, the flag in this particular record needs to be set to false. The transaction end date/time in the most current transaction record should be set to an arbitrary time far in the future.

Some of you may object to the storage overhead of this design. Even in a pretty large organization, this approach doesn't lead to ridiculous storage demands. Assume we have 100,000 employees and perform 10 human resources transactions on them each year. Assume further that we have a relatively verbose 2,000-byte employee profile in the employee dimension record. Five years' worth of data adds up to $5 \times 100,000 \times 10 \times 2,000$ bytes, or just 10 GB of raw data. If your definition of employee transaction is much more fine grained so that a job promotion requires dozens of tiny low level transactions, you should consider creating a small set of super transactions like job promotion in order to make the data sizing realistic. The low level transactions may simply be artifacts of the HR system, rather than being real events. Admittedly, this makes the extraction task more complex, but at the same time the changes in the dimension correspond more realistically to events.

This compact design satisfies our three categories of queries beautifully. The first kind of query for fast high level counts and totals uses the fact table. All the facts in the fact table are additive across all the dimensions except for the facts labeled as balances. These balances, like all balances, are semi-additive and must be averaged across the time dimension after adding across the other dimensions. The fact table is also needed to present additive totals like salary earned and vacation days taken.

The particular employee dimension key used in a fact table record is the precise employee dimension key associated with the stroke of midnight on the last day of the reporting month. This guarantees that the month end report is a correct depiction of all the employee profiles. This means that you don't have to worry about surrogate keys in the employee dimension that came and went during the month. It's only the keys at the end of the month that you need.

The second query is addressed by the employee dimension table. You can make a time-based cut through the employee database by choosing a specific date and time and constraining this date and time to be equal to or greater than the transaction effective date/time stamp and less than the transaction end date/time stamp. This is guaranteed to return exactly one employee profile for each employee whose profile was in effect at the requested moment. The query can perform counts and constraints against all the records returned from these time constraints.

The third kind of query can use the same employee dimension table to look in detail at the sequence of transactions against any given employee.

Some of you may be wondering if the employee dimension table isn't really a kind of fact table because it seems to have a time dimension. While technically this may be true, this employee dimension table mainly contains textual values and is certainly the primary source of constraints and row headers for query and report writing tools. So it is proper to think of this table as a dimension table that serves as the entry point into the human resources fact table. The employee dimension table can be used with any fact table in any subject area that requires an employee dimension. The important idea that makes this human resources database fit into our familiar dimensional framework is making each type 2 dimension record correspond to an individual employee transaction and then tying these records to precise moments in time.

10.26 Managing Backlogs Dimensionally

Bob Becker, Design Tip #118, Nov 4, 2009

Certain industries need the ability to look at a backlog of work, and project that backlog into the future for planning purposes. The classic example is a large services organization with multi-month or multiyear contracts representing a large sum of future dollars to be earned and/or hours to be worked. Construction companies, law firms, and other organizations with long term projects or commitments have similar requirements. Manufacturers that ship against standing blanket orders may also find this technique helpful.

Backlog planning requirements come in several flavors supporting different areas of the organization. Finance needs to understand future cash flow in terms of expenditures and cash receipts, and properly project both invoiced and recognized revenue for management planning and expectation setting. There are operational requirements to understand the flow of work for manpower, resource management, and capacity planning purposes. And the sales organization will want to understand how the backlog will ultimately flow to understand future attainment measures.

Dimensional schemas can be populated when a new contract is signed, capturing the initial acquisition or creation of the contract and thus the new backlog opportunity. In addition, another schema can be created that captures the work delivered against the contract over time. These two schemas are interesting and useful, but by themselves are not enough to support the future planning requirements. They show that the organization has "N" number of contracts worth "X" millions of dollars with "Y" millions of dollars having been delivered. From these two schemas, the current backlog can be identified by subtracting the delivered amount from the contracted amount. Often it is worthwhile to populate the backlog values in another schema as the rules required to determine the remaining backlog may be relatively complex. Once the backlog amount is understood, it then needs to be accurately projected into the future based on appropriate business rules.

The use of another schema we call the "spread" fact table is helpful in supporting the planning requirements. The spread fact table is created from the backlog schema just discussed. The backlog and remaining time on the contract are evaluated and the backlog is then spread out into the appropriate future planning time buckets and rows are inserted into the fact table for each time bucket. For this discussion we'll assume monthly time periods, but it could just as easily be daily, weekly, or quarterly. Thus the grain of our spread fact table will be at the month by contract (whatever is the lowest level used in the planning process). This schema will also include other appropriate conformed dimensions such as customer, product, sales person, and project manager. In our example, the interesting metrics might include the number of hours to be worked, as well as the amount of the contract value to be delivered in each future month.

In addition, we include another dimension called the scenario dimension. The scenario dimension describes the planning scenario or version of the spread fact table's rows. This may be a value such as "2015 October Financial Plan" or "2015 October Operational Plan." Thus, if we plan monthly, there will be new rows inserted into the spread fact table each month described by a new row in the scenario dimension. The secret sauce of the spread fact table is the business rules used to break down the backlog value into the future spread time buckets. Depending on the sophistication and maturity of the planning process, these business rules may simply spread the backlog into equal buckets based on the remaining months in the contract. In other organizations, more complex rules may be utilized that evaluate a detailed staffing and work plan incorporating seasonality trends using a complex algorithm to calculate a very precise amount for each future time period in the spread fact table.

By creatively using the scenario dimension, it is possible to populate several spreads each planning period based on different business rules to support different planning assumptions. As indicated in the scenario descriptions discussed earlier in this article, it may be possible that the financial planning algorithms are different than the operational planning algorithms for a variety of reasons.

The spread fact table is not just useful for understanding the backlog of actual work. Similar planning requirements often surface with other business processes. Another example is planning for sales opportunities that are proposed but have not yet been signed. Assuming the organization has an appropriate source for the future sales opportunities, this would be another good fit for a spread fact table. Again, appropriate business rules need to be identified to evaluate a future opportunity and determine how to spread the proposed contract amounts into the appropriate future periods. This schema can also include indicators that describe the likelihood of winning the opportunity, such as forecast indicators and percent likely to close attributes. These additional attributes will enable the planning process to look at best case/worst case future scenarios. Typically, the sales opportunities spread fact table will need to be populated as a separate fact table than the actual backlog spread as the dimensionality between the two fact tables is typically quite different. A simple drill across query will enable the planning process to align the solid backlog along with the softer projected sales opportunities to paint a more complete picture of what the future may hold for the organization.

10.27 Not So Fast

Ralph Kimball, Intelligent Enterprise, *Oct 26, 1999*

Profitability is a central theme in many data warehouse designs. Just the existence of the data warehouse implies a desire to understand the business in a fine-grained, analytic way—and if you've gone that far, you're surely interested in profitability analysis. However, although concern with profitability might be foremost among your priorities, an attempt to start there is jumping the gun. You need to complete the intermediary steps before you can deliver a profitability dimensional model, and there are a few ways to go about it.

For the past 10 years, I have started almost every speech and class with the observation that data warehouses are usually initiated by the twin, interwoven themes of: *understand the customer* and *measure profitability every which way.* I have seen a number of data warehouse projects start with just one "simple" requirement: Show customer profitability. Gee, maybe after doing customer profitability, we can tackle billings, and then maybe service calls.

But it is almost impossible to start with profitability, customer or otherwise, as the first dimensional model. You can achieve a view of profitability only after all the components of revenue and cost have been separately sourced and brought into the data warehouse. I call these separate components of revenue and cost *first-level* dimensional models. Profitability is definitely a second-level dimensional model and can be built only after the first-level data sources are complete and available.

Let's explore some of the issues you face when building a profitability dimensional model, with an eye toward satisfying the anxious business managers who want to get started measuring the profitability of their business every which way.

Find the Components of Profitability

The first step in building a profitability dimensional model is to determine the profit equation. Then you must find all the individual sources of revenue and cost. A profitability model should present its results in a standard little income statement. The simplest view of an income statement is:

> Revenue − Costs = Profit.

Typically the revenue and costs are broken down into a number of standard buckets that make sense across as many of the product or service lines of the business as possible. Generally you would expect an income statement to fit on one side of a sheet of paper. To be more specific, take the familiar example of a large packaged goods manufacturer that ships its products to commercial customers. The manufacturer's shipment invoice provides a starting point for a typical income statement:

> Gross Revenue at List Price
> > Minus invoice adjustments for finance terms
> > Minus invoice adjustments for marketing promotions such as discounted prices
> = Net Revenue
> > Minus manufacturing costs
> > Minus storage costs
> > Minus freight costs
> > Minus cost of returns
> > Minus allocated marketing costs
> = Profit

The first thing you should notice is that the true revenue target is the net revenue, shown on the fourth line, because that may be the revenue reported to stockholders; the gross revenue on line one is based on list prices. But you'll usually want to look at both.

Second, you'll see that although you've listed some important costs, you're not building the complete income statement as shown in the company's annual report. The income statement shown here is activity-based and omits general costs such as R&D and the CEO's salary. The marketing and finance departments, likely users of the profitability dimensional model, usually are willing to see this activity-based subset of the total company profit. That's fortunate, because an activity-based income statement is a more practical goal for the data warehouse team.

As soon as you define the income statement, which I call the profit equation, you must source all the data, which requires the data warehouse team to do a lot of sleuthing. You'll find some of the revenue and cost data in operational transactional form, but some of it may show up only in accounts payable. Maybe you periodically write a bonus check to your large customers whose contracts call for a certain threshold of purchases. Such an expenditure is certainly a cost, but it won't show up in the invoice transaction system.

Marketing and Finance Need to Help

After establishing the profit equation and identifying the sources of revenue and cost data, you can design all the first-level dimensional models representing these sources. Conformed dimensions, such as calendar, customer, location, and product, are used with every dimensional model. Conformed facts, such as revenue and costs, must be mathematically combinable across the separate business processes.

It is essential to involve both marketing and finance in the conforming step. Through their involvement in this conforming exercise, these groups will deepen their commitment to an enterprise-wide definition of the data warehouse. What's more, you will be covertly warming up these groups for an even more controversial exercise that lies ahead: the dreaded allocations.

Allocations: The Heart of the Profitability Challenge

As soon as you have established the bus architecture of conformed dimensions and facts, data warehouse teams can begin building the separate first-level dimensional models around each of the components of revenue and cost. As these first-level fact tables become available to the community, they will be useful for restricted analyses within each of these business processes. But you don't have a profitability dimensional model yet!

The central truth is that in order to present a view of customer profitability, or product line profitability, or geographic profitability, or promotions profitability, you have to assign all the components of cost down to an atomic level. To continue the manufacturer example, you have to assign them down to the line item on the shipment invoice.

Yes, I know that freight costs, for instance, pertain to the shipment as a whole and are not assigned to the individual line item. This is where it gets hard. You *must* assign the costs all the way down to the lowest level. If you don't, in the manufacturing example, you will be unable to build even product line profitability because the freight costs won't be represented anywhere against products. It doesn't help to try rolling up individual products to some higher level and then assigning the costs. Either the costs are at the lowest level, or they don't participate in the roll up.

Remember that your strong implicit goal is to see profitability every which way. In other words, you want the income statement, which is a list of numerical facts, to be surrounded by a rich set of dimensions, including customer, product, time, location, promotion, and others. Then you just constrain on your favorite dimension and see that version of profitability. The most dimensional piece of data you have is the lowest piece of data, the invoice line item. Hence, you must build the complete income statement at that level.

Once your marketing and finance partners have dealt with conformed dimensions and facts, it is time to give them a harder assignment: deciding on the allocations. Doing so entails apportioning costs down to the lowest level of granularity in your base profitability fact table.

If You're in a Hurry

It should be obvious at this point that you can't release the profitability dimensional model until you've physically sourced all the components of revenue and cost and defined all the allocation rules. Hence, a properly implemented profitability subject area could take years to release, especially if many separate data sources underlie the revenue and (especially) costs.

If you don't have the luxury of this kind of time, there *is* an interesting alternate path of development, as long as all parties understand and agree.

At the outset, get marketing and finance to agree on rules of thumb for the costs, before the underlying cost driver fact tables are available. Therefore, for instance, you decide that each product's manufacturing costs are 27 percent of the list price, and freight costs are $1.29 per pound. By using rules of thumb, and by carefully sourcing the revenue components, you can build a complete income statement.

Of course, it isn't very accurate at first. Everyone knows that. But you put enough work into the rules of thumb that people are willing to live with "release 1.0" of the profitability dimensional model. Now you progressively upgrade the model as the separate sources of cost data come online in their own first level fact tables and are incorporated into the profit equation through the allocation rules you defined.

Another advantage is that users become familiar with the concepts of customer profitability, as well as the other slices of profitability, at an early point in your data warehouse. The users will think of new interpretations and requirements as their experience grows. As you are building the separate cost-driver fact tables one at a time and making new releases of the profitability dimensional models, you can incorporate some of these new perspectives. Whoever said the data warehouse is a static thing, anyway?

10.28 The Budgeting Chain

Ralph Kimball, Intelligent Enterprise, *Jun 1, 1999*

The value chain is one of the most powerful ways to use dimensional models. Most of us are familiar with the traditional, product value chain in which a product moves from the manufacturer's finished goods inventory down through the distribution pipeline all the way to the retailer. There are usually operational systems at every point in this flow recording static inventory levels and dynamic product movement past particular points. Each of these operational systems can be the source of a business process dimensional model.

When we design dimensional models for the successive steps of the value chain, we take great care to recognize the common dimensions shared by the various steps of the chain. In a product value chain, such as the one shown in Figure 10-45, the obvious common dimensions are product, time, and store. Notice that all the business processes share the product and time dimensions, but only some share the store dimension.

A properly designed value chain with conformed dimensions is immensely powerful. Not only can we implement the separate business process dimensional models at different times, but query tools and report writers can combine them at any time into integrated views of the whole value chain, as long as the dimensions have been carefully conformed.

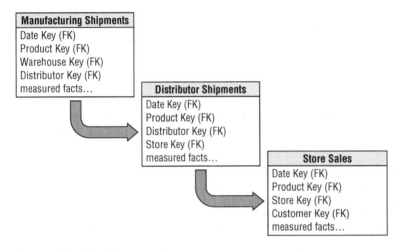

Figure 10-45: This value chain represents a product flow where each process is a fact table.

I have used the example of the product value chain so many times that it may come as a surprise that there is a more common value chain lurking in all our businesses: the budgeting chain.

We are all familiar with the process of creating organizational budgets. Typically, prior to a fiscal year, each department manager creates a budget, broken down by line items. The budget is approved before the year starts, but there are usually adjustments to the budget as the year progresses, reflecting changes in business conditions or the realities of how the spending matches the original budget. Department managers want to see the current budget's status, as well as how the budget has been altered since the first approved version.

As shown in Figure 10-46, I will start the budgeting chain with a fact table called budget, which records what a department is allowed to spend. The second fact table in our budgeting chain, the commitment table, records the department's budget spending commitments, such as purchase orders, work orders, and various forms of contracts. Department managers want to compare commitments to the budget frequently in order to manage their spending. In our design, we will accomplish this by drilling across the budget and commitments fact tables.

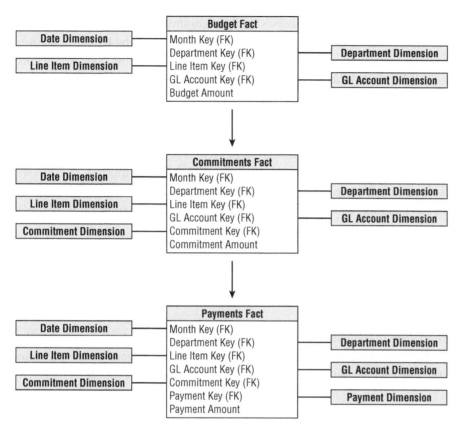

Figure 10-46: The budget chain showing the budget, commitments, and payments fact tables.

The third fact table in the budgeting value chain is called payments. A payment is the actual cash transfer to the party named in a commitment. Department managers are less concerned with these actual payments than accountants, but are concerned about spending within their budget constraints. From a practical point of view, the money is gone from the budget when the commitment is made. But the finance department is intensely interested in the relationship between commitments and payments because it must manage the company's cash.

The Grain of the Budgeting Chain Fact Tables

To flesh out the details of our budgeting chain, we will follow a simple four-step methodology that I have discussed many times before:

1. Identify the business process.
2. Declare the grain of the fact table.
3. Choose the dimensions.
4. Choose the facts.

I have already identified the three business processes: budget, commitments, and payments. We could choose the grain to be every detailed transaction posted separately to the budget, commitment, and payment operational systems. If we were frequently interested in drilling down to specific transactions as an auditor would, we would choose this grain.

Alternatively, we could choose the grain to be the current status of each line item in each budget each month. Although this grain has a familiar ring to it (because it feels like a manager's report), it is a poor choice as the grain of a fact table. The facts that we need to store in such a "status report" are all semiadditive balances, rather than fully additive facts. Also, such a grain makes it difficult to determine how much has changed since the previous month or the previous quarter, because we have to obtain the records from several time periods and then subtract them from each other. Finally, this grain choice requires the fact table to contain many duplicated records when nothing changes in successive months for a given line item.

The grain we will choose is the net change of the line item (of the budget, commitments, or payments) in a department that occurred solely during the current month. We break this down further to the specific general ledger account affected.

The Budgeting Chain Dimensions and Facts

The third step of our methodology is choosing the dimensions for each fact table. If we have made the grain statement carefully, choosing the dimensions is easy. Given the grain statement of the previous paragraph, we can state the dimensions of the budget fact table shown in Figure 10-46:

- Effective month
- Department
- Line item
- GL (general ledger) account

The effective month is when the budget changes are posted to the system. The first entries for a given budget year would show effective months in the preceding year when the budget is first approved. If the budget is updated or modified as the budget year gets underway, the effective months would occur during the budget year. If we don't adjust a budget at all throughout the year, then the only entries would be the first ones when the budget is first approved. This is the meaning of the net change requirement given in the grain definition. Make sure you understand this point, or you won't understand what is in this database.

The line item identifies the purpose of the proposed spending, such as employee salaries, computer equipment, or office supplies. The line item also identifies the budget year by name. The department is the name of the organization subdivision overseen by a particular manager. The GL account is the general ledger account against which budgets are created, commitments are made, and payments are issued. In general, there may be more than one GL account affected by a budget line item. The data warehouse team either needs to allocate budgets, commitments, or payments into the individual GL accounts with a simple proration scheme, or it must be able to identify the specific GL account from the underlying operational systems.

We can state the commitments dimensions easily: all the budget process dimensions, plus commitment. The commitment dimension identifies the type of commitment (purchase order, work order, or contract) together with the party to whom the commitment is owed. Similarly, the payments fact table dimensions are: all the commitments dimensions, plus payment. The payment dimension identifies the type of the payment (such as a check) and the party to whom the payment was actually made. In the budgeting chain, we expand the list of dimensions as we move down the chain from budget to commitments to payments.

Our grain statement makes choosing facts very simple. Each fact is a single fully additive amount. The budget fact is "budget amount," the commitment fact is "commitment amount," and the payment fact is "payment amount."

Applications across the Budget Chain

With this design, we can create a number of analysis applications including all the obvious standard reports a manager needs. To look at the current budgeted amount by department and line item, we constrain on all times up to the present, adding the amounts by department and line item. Because the grain of all the tables is the net change of the line items, adding up all the entries over time does exactly the right thing. We end up with the current approved budget amount, and we get exactly those line items in the given departments that have a budget. Line items in the chart of accounts that have no budget in a department do not appear in the report nor do they occupy any records in the database.

To ask for all the changes to the budget for various line items, we simply constrain on a single month. We'll report only those line items that experienced a change during the month.

To compare current commitments to the current budget, we separately sum the commitment amounts and budget amounts from the beginning of time to the current date (or any date of interest). We then combine the two answer sets on the row headers with a simple sort merge process. This is a standard drill-across application using multipass SQL.

To compare cash payments to commitments, we perform the same kind of drill-across application as the preceding, but this time we use the commitments and payments tables.

By extracting the original transactions from the budget, commitments, and payments operational systems and loading these monthly snapshot fact tables, we have constructed a powerful value chain of interest to the departmental manager as well as the finance department. Amazingly, we should be able to create this value chain in every imaginable organization.

10.29 Compliance-Enabled Data Warehouses

Ralph Kimball, Design Tip #74, Dec 16, 2005

I often describe compliance in the data warehouse as "maintaining the chain of custody" of the data. In the same way a police department must carefully maintain the chain of custody of evidence in order to argue that the evidence has not been changed or tampered with, the data warehouse must also carefully guard the compliance-sensitive data entrusted to it from the moment it arrives. Furthermore the data warehouse must always be able to show the exact condition and content of such data at any point in time that it may have been under the control of the data warehouse. Finally when the suspicious auditor is looking over your shoulder, you need to link back to an archived and time-stamped version of the data as it was originally received, which you have stored remotely with a trusted third party. If the data warehouse is prepared to meet all these compliance requirements, then the stress of being audited by a hostile government agency or lawyer armed with a subpoena should be greatly reduced.

The big impact of these compliance requirements on the data warehouse can be expressed in simple dimensional modeling terms. Type 1 and type 3 changes are dead. Long live type 2. In other words, all changes become inserts. No more deletes or overwrites.

In plain English, the compliance requirements mean that you cannot actually change any data, for any reason. If data must be altered, then a new version of the altered records must be inserted into the database. Each record in each table therefore must have a begin time stamp and an end time stamp that accurately represents the span of time when that record was the "current truth."

Figure 10-47 shows a compliance-enabled fact table connected to a compliance-enabled dimension table. The fields shown in bold italics in each table are the extra fields needed for compliance tracking. The fact table and the dimension table are administered similarly.

Compliance Enabled Transaction Grain Fact Table	Compliance Enabled Type 2 Customer Dimension Table
Fact Table Surrogate Key (PK)	Customer Key (PK)
Begin Version DateTime (SQL)(PK)	***Begin Version DateTime (SQL)(PK)***
End Version DateTime (SQL)	***End Version DateTime (SQL)***
Change Reference (FK)	***Change Reference (FK)***
Source Reference (FK)	***Source Reference (FK)***
Activity Date (FK)	Customer ID (NK)
Activity DateTime (SQL)	Customer Name
Customer (FK)	Customer Address Block
Service (FK)	Attribute 1 (Type 1)
Gross Dollars (fact)	Attribute 2 (Type 2)
Discount Dollars (fact)	SCD2 Change Date (FK)
Net Dollars (fact)	SCD2 Begin Eff DateTime (SQL)
	SCD2 End Eff DateTime (SQL)
	SCD2 Change Reason Code
	SCD2 Current Flag

Figure 10-47: Compliance-enabled fact and dimension tables.

The begin version date/time and end version date/time stamps describe the span of time when the record in question was the "current truth." The change reference field is a foreign key pointing to a change reference dimension (not shown) that describes the change status of that record. The source reference field is a foreign key pointing to a source reference dimension (not shown) that shows the offsite trusted third party location where the hash-encoded and time-stamped version of this record has been stored since the moment when it was created.

The first time that records are loaded into either of the tables, the begin version date/time stamp is set to the time of the load, and the end version date/time is set to an arbitrary date far in the future, such as midnight, December 31, 9999. The change reference would describe the change status as "initial load." If and when a type 1 correction needs to be made to either facts in the fact table or type 1 or 3 attributes in the dimension table, a new record is inserted into the respective table with the same surrogate key, but a new pair of version date/time stamps. Thus, the true primary key of the tables has become the combination of the original primary key field and the end version date/time stamp, as shown in Figure 10-47. When the new record is inserted, the prior most recent end version date/time stamp must be changed to this new load date/time stamp. This two step dance of adjusting the begin and end date/time stamps is familiar to data warehouse architects from the normal type 2 dimension processing.

The presence of existing type 2 attribute processing in the dimension does not change anything. Only type 1 and type 3 updates invoke the special steps described in this article. Type 2 processing proceeds as it always has, by introducing new dimension member records with new surrogate primary keys, and by administering the familiar SCD type 2 metadata fields shown in the bottom portion of the dimension in Figure 10-47.

If you are uncomfortable with the seeming introduction of a two-part key in the dimension table (a violation of the standard dimensional design that insists on a single field surrogate key), then think about it in the following way. Although technically one must view the tables as now having two-part primary keys, think about this schema as still behaving like typical one-part key designs after the version has been constrained. That's the point of this article. First, you choose a version as of a certain date, then you run your typical queries with the same old keys as always.

Before concluding this article, let's not overlook the big benefit of this approach! When the hostile government agency or lawyer armed with a subpoena demands to see what has happened to the data, your tables are fully instrumented to comply. If you must reveal the exact status of the data as of, say, January 1, 2014, then you just constrain this date to be between the begin and end version date/time stamps of all the tables. Presto—the database reverts to that moment in history. And, of course, any subsequent changes made to that data are fully explained by the change reference. Finally, you can prove that the evidence (oops, I mean data) hasn't been tampered with by using the source reference.

10.30 Clicking with Your Customer

Ralph Kimball, Intelligent Enterprise, *Jan 5, 1999*

The web is pummeling the data warehouse marketplace on all sides. The web's presence is changing our clients' and servers' architecture by forcing the front end tool vendors to move the bulk of their technologies toward the server. This shift is taking place because the vendors can no longer control the software content and because everyone is demanding that a web browser, not a dedicated application, must paint the bits on the screen.

End user application developers are increasingly building applications around web pages. The user interface development environment of choice is now a web page development environment. Just set up a web page and embed various data-aware objects in it. Endow the web page's user interface with a few data warehouse gestures, and you have a sophisticated drag and drop, drill up and down, pivoting application. An interesting side effect of this forced migration of user interfaces to web technology is that it's as easy to deliver an application over the web as it is to deliver one to a dedicated single user.

As a result, our data warehouses are becoming data *webhouses*. The medium is not only our delivery vehicle, but our business. Increasingly, we mix the fundamental business content of what we sell with web services and capabilities. An interesting part of the emerging data webhouse is the business process subject area that stores and presents the web activity for later analysis. Fundamentally, we want to analyze all the hits on our website. We want to build a comprehensible view of the immense stream of clicks arriving at our sites, whether we're dealing with our intranet users or with customers on our public website. We call this the *clickstream business process*.

The Goals of the Clickstream Dimensional Model

Clickstream activity can tell us a great deal about detailed customer behavior. If we have information on our customers' every click, gesture, and trajectory through our website, we should be able to answer such questions as:

- What parts of our website get the most visitors?
- What parts of the website do we associate most frequently with actual sales?
- What parts of the website are superfluous or visited infrequently?
- Which pages on our website seem to be session killers where the remote user stops the session and leaves?
- What is the new visitor click profile on our site?
- What is the click profile of an existing customer? A profitable customer? A complaining customer that all too frequently returns our product?
- What is the click profile of a customer about to cancel our service, complain, or sue us?
- How can we induce the customer to register with our site so we learn some useful information about that customer?
- How many visits do unregistered customers typically make with us before they are willing to register? Before they buy a product or service?

These questions involve analysis at a detailed, behavioral level. We describe much of this behavior as a series of sequential steps; because nearly all websites are organized as a hierarchical tree branching out from the home page, these steps necessarily describe the steps of traversing a tree—actually, a huge tree. The biggest websites have several hundred thousand pages.

Given this information, can we imagine building the clickstream subject area using conventional slice and dice dimensional models? And if we manage to build it, how can we hope to analyze the clickstream data to answer all these questions?

To tackle the clickstream business process, let's use a simple, four-step methodology to build the dimensional model. In sequence, we will define the source of our data, choose the grain of our fact table, choose the dimensions appropriate for that grain, and choose the facts appropriate for that grain. I have used this simple four-step methodology hundreds of times over the past 20 years when designing dimensional models for data warehouses.

The Clickstream Data Source

We need to go after the most granular and detailed data possible describing the clicks on our web server. Each web server will potentially report different details, but at the lowest level we should be able to obtain a record for every page hit with the following information: precise date and time of page click; remote client's (requesting user's) IP address; page requested (with path to page starting at the server machine); specific control downloaded; and cookie information, if available.

This level of detail is both good and bad. Like many transactional data sources, this one provides exquisite detail. But in many ways, there is too much detail, and it may be difficult to see the forest with all the trees in the way. The most serious problem, which permeates all analyses of web-clicking behavior, is that the page hits are often stateless. Without surrounding context, a page hit may just be a random isolated event that is difficult to interpret as part of a user session. Perhaps the user linked to this page from some remote website and then left the page five seconds later without returning. It is difficult to make much sense out of such an event, so our first goal is to identify and label complete sessions.

The second serious problem is whether we can make any sense out of the remote client's IP address. If the only client identification is the IP address, we cannot glean much. Most internet users come through an internet service provider (ISP) that assigns IP addresses dynamically. Thus, remote users will have a different address in a later session than they have at the moment. We can probably track the individual session reliably, but we can't be sure when the user returns to the site in a different session.

We can significantly reduce these problems if our web server creates cookies on the requesting user's machine. A *cookie* is a piece of information that the requesting user "agrees" to store and may agree to send to your web server each time his browser opens one of your pages. A cookie usually does not contain much information, but it can identify the requesting user's computer unambiguously. Furthermore, it provides a way to link page hits across a complete user session. A cookie may contain significant information if the user has voluntarily registered with your web server and provided other information, such as a name and company affiliation. In such a case, the cookie provides a link to data you have stored in one of your own databases.

In order to make the raw clickstream data usable in our data webhouse, we need to collect and transform the data so it has a session perspective. This process will be a significant step in the back room. We assume that we have some kind of cookie mechanism that lets us transform our data source into the following format:

- Precise date and time of page hit
- Identity of requesting user (consistent from session to session)
- Session ID
- Page and event requested

The Fundamental Grain of Clickstream Data

We now see that each event an individual user invokes in a special session is the grain of our clickstream fact table. Each event is an individual record, and each record is an event on a web page. Note that the web server may not notice events within the user interface of a downloaded web page unless we have programmed the web page to specifically alert the server when the event occurs. In the back room ETL, we filter out automatic events and focus on ones more related to page formatting than to user actions. These kinds of filtered events include the download of graphic images, such as GIFs adorning a requested page. So if we have 100,000 user sessions per day on our website, and if each session involves an average of eight meaningful events, then we will collect 800,000 records per day.

Identifying the Clickstream's Dimensions and Facts

The clickstream event dimensional model is shown in Figure 10-48. We provide two versions of the date and time—universal and local—that let us align clickstream events in absolute time as well as relative to the user's wall clock. The analyst's query tool can perform this alignment, but this extra logic imposes an unreasonable burden on the application. Therefore, we prefer to provide two hard-wired entry points into each event's date/time stamp. Note that you must take special care if you are merging page events from the web logs of separate physical servers because you then must align the clocks on these servers to within a second or less!

The user dimension should contain some useful information about who the user is, other than just a consistent machine ID. However, this will depend on whether we have coaxed the user into revealing facts about his or her identity.

The page dimension is important because it contains the meaningful context that tells the analyst the user's website location. Each web page must contain some simple descriptors identifying the location and type of page. A complete path name is not nearly as interesting as such basic attributes as "Product Info," "Company Info," "Frequently Asked Questions," and "Order Form." A large website should have a hierarchical description associated with each page that gives progressively more detail about what the page is. This information needs to be stored in the page dimension and be maintained consistently as we update and modify the website. In other words, we have to update the production transaction system (the web server) responsively to meet the needs of the data webhouse analysts.

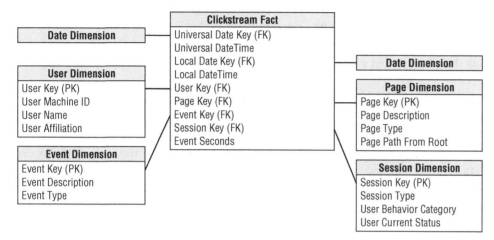

Figure 10-48: The dimensional model for clickstream events.

Finally, the session dimension is more than just a tag that groups together all the page events that constitute a single user's session. This dimension is also where we label the session and trace its activity. We might characterize sessions as "Searching for Information," "Random Browsing," "Price and Feature Shopping," or "Placing an Order." We may be able to create these tags with simple criteria regarding what the user does during the session, or we may turn over the session record to a full-blown link analysis data mining package. In either case, the result is a set of descriptive tags we can put in the session dimension. The session should also be characterized by what we currently know about the customer, such as "Recent Large Purchaser," "Not Yet a Customer," or "Chronic Product Returner."

Our clickstream fact table only contains one fact, event seconds, which is an estimate. We try to accurately record the length of time the user spent on the page after the last click and before moving on. Because page browsing is basically stateless, we can never be completely sure whether the user has perhaps minimized the window or clicked on an unrelated site. We can only make an accurate estimate of the time spent on the page if we have a following event that is part of the session, but we have to be careful not to overinterpret long event seconds.

Analyzing Clickstream Events

This dimensional design lets us perform many powerful queries. It is fairly easy to find the most frequently visited parts of the website and identify the most frequent users. We can also correlate pages and users to our more valuable customers because we know who places the order on the website.

The analysis of clicking histories and clicking trajectories through our website depends heavily on how we have built the session dimension. If we have good descriptive labels on each session and on the current state of the customer, we can perform all the necessary behavioral analyses.

The good news about this design is that we have successfully established a framework for collecting and analyzing all the clicks on our website. The bad news is that we really haven't shed much light on whether we are selling products or web services. That confusion is quite deeply rooted and is one of the reasons that the internet revolution is so interesting and important.

10.31 The Special Dimensions of the Clickstream

Ralph Kimball, Intelligent Enterprise, *Jan 20, 2000*

The most exciting new data source in the data warehouse is the clickstream: the river of clicks on our websites. The clickstream contains a record for every page request from every visitor to our site. In many ways, we can imagine that the clickstream is a record of every gesture each visitor makes, and we are beginning to realize that these gestures add up to descriptions of behavior we have never been able to see before.

We can wrangle and bring the clickstream data source into a dimensional model for analysis just like every other data source in our environment. Of course, any time we bring up a new business process, we are very careful to hook it to the conformed dimensions and facts of the overall enterprise. If we do that with the clickstream, then the clickstream will participate gracefully in the overall distributed data warehouse.

But the clickstream data in its raw form only gives us some of the dimensions we need for our most powerful analyses. If we aren't careful, we will be disappointed in our ability to analyze the behavior of our website visitors. A raw entry in the page event log from the web server only gives us:

- Date/time stamp of the page request
- IP address and possibly cookie ID of the visitor (if they accept cookies)
- Page object being requested (the whole page or an object on the page)
- Type of request (almost always "Get" or "Submit")
- Context from where the page request was made (the so-called referrer)
- Browser version making the request (usually Netscape or Internet Explorer)

This data doesn't tell us very much. We are a long way from inferring behavior just by staring at this bare bones description of the individual page event. We need to clean this low level data and augment it with additional dimensions:

- Date of the page request
- Time of the page request
- Visitor
- Page object

- Request
- Session type
- Session ID (a degenerate dimension tying all the records of a given session together)
- Referrer
- Product/service

Several of these dimensions were already described in article 10.30, *Clicking with Your Customer,* but we'll elaborate on the others in this article.

Visitor Dimension

The visitor dimension is challenging because you probably have three kinds of visitors: first, a huge pool of completely anonymous visitors identified only by their IP addresses. The IP address is only of moderate value because it identifies only an outbound port on the visitor's internet service provider. These ports may be dynamically reassigned, so we cannot track such visitors from session to session, or sometimes even from within a session. A second and more useful type of visitor is one who has agreed to store a cookie we have provided. This cookie then becomes a reliable identifier for a visitor machine, because we ask to see the cookie on every page request. With a cookie, we can be pretty sure that a given machine is responsible for a session, and we can determine when the machine will visit us again, assuming the user hasn't deleted the cookie file. Finally, the third and most valuable level of visitor is the human-identified visitor who not only has accepted our cookie but sometime in the past has revealed their name and other information to us. Realistically, we may not be certain that the same human being is sitting at the remote PC, but at least we know that person's "representative" is there.

This visitor dimension is, of course, huge. We may want to collect visitors of the first IP-only type into pools defined by the visitor's domain and subdomain just to cut down on the mindless proliferation of these visitor records. We then encourage such visitors to accept cookies so we can sort out individual behavior. Maybe some of our pages aren't accessible without a cookie. For the third kind of visitor, we have to merge the cookie ID with our visitor name and demographic data during the ETL process.

Page Object Dimension

The page object dimension is one of two dimensions that the data warehouse team must really work on if the clickstream source is going to be useful. The program must describe the page by more than its location in the web server's file system. In some cases, the path name to the file is moderately descriptive of the page's content and purpose, but it is a classic mistake to try to use a file system both for uniquely locating files and describing their content. Instead, any given page must be associated with a set of textual attributes that describe and classify the page, regardless of where it is stored in the web server's file system or how it is generated. The attributes should be drawn from structured lists whose rules the data warehouse team creates, so that the attributes can most usefully drive analyses. For instance, the attributes of a given page could be

Type='Introductory Product Information' and Product='Datawhack 9000'. Some group needs to take responsibility for assigning these attributes. If the web page designers understand the importance of clickstream analysis, then they can assign attributes to all the pages. If the website team won't pay attention to the needs of the data warehouse analysis, then the data warehouse team must assign the attributes. This may be a challenge, of course, in really huge websites with tens of thousands of pages.

Ideally, the raw clickstream log hands back these page attributes, but the data warehouse team may have to merge these attributes into the clickstream later in the ETL cycle.

The object part of the page object description will become much more interesting as XML-enabled pages become more widely used. Again, we hope that the web server logs reveal the page objects' XML tags.

Session Type

The session type is the other important clickstream dimension that the data warehouse team must really work on. The session type is a high level diagnosis of the complete session. Plausible types include "Product Ordering," "Quick Hit and Gone," and even more interesting diagnoses such as "Unhappy Visitor," or "Recent, Frequent, Intense Return Shopper." Perhaps we have both local and global session descriptors for parts of complex sessions.

How on earth do we assign these session labels? In this case, we can't expect the web server to provide this context. The data warehouse team must figure out the diagnosis in the ETL process. But maybe it's not as hard as it seems. Here's an edited snippet from a web visitor's session on our own site, www.kimballgroup.com. (I plead guilty to using file names to describe content, but cut me a little slack. I'm the entire IT department at my company, and I have an applications backlog.) I have modified the IP address for confidentiality:

```
suborg.company.com session of 10/19/14:
09:27:29 /index.html
referrer = Google, search = 'Data Warehouse Classes'
09:27:30 /kimballgroup.gif
09:27:48 /class.htm
09:27:55 /dwd-class.htm
09:28:37 /register.htm
09:28:50 /dwd-schedule.htm
11:15:12 /index.html
11:15:20 /kimballgroup.gif
11:20:55 /startrak.htm
```

Someone at "Company.com" (a fictitious name) found my site from a search for "Data Warehouse Classes" on Google. So my home page, index.html, was effective in drawing this qualified visitor to my site. In the first second the visitor requested our company logo, kimballgroup.gif. Nineteen seconds after the initial page hit, the visitor had found a link to the class description page. That's pretty good. It means the home page was presented quickly and the navigation choices were clear. After spending only seven seconds on the main class description page, the visitor requested a detailed description of our regular class, Data Warehousing in Depth (dwd-class.html). The visitor studied this page for 42 seconds and then went to my How-To-Register page, which at that time contained an 800 telephone number. I like this session. After 13 seconds on the How-To-Register page, the visitor went to the class schedule page.

We can't be sure how long the visitor spent on the class schedule page because the next entries are more than an hour and 45 minutes later. We can only be sure the visitor did something else in the intervening time. In fact, unless we have a cookie identifier with this session, we cannot be completely sure the same person made the last three page requests, although I would guess that this is the case here. If so, then the return session is very significant. It represents a return visitor, or someone who found the website useful and maybe even bookmarked it.

Building a session diagnosis tool for the ETL process is clearly an interesting challenge. It is a blend of data extract, pattern recognition, and link analysis. When you look at your own session logs, presented like the one here, you will come up with many ideas for diagnosing sessions. This requirement will turn into a complex and evolving one. Rather than committing at the start to a single major data mining approach, it would be better, in my opinion, to write a few simple heuristic rules in your ETL data flow for diagnosing sessions and then accumulate experience over time with the different kinds of sessions. Then you'll be in a better position to choose a sophisticated tool to help you diagnose sessions.

Focus on Page Object and Session Dimensions

The point of this article is to make sure that you put effort into providing page object and session dimensions for your clickstream. Yes, both of these dimensions are a lot of work, but if you leave them out, you can't tell what pages the user visited, or whether they had a productive session. These dimensions are the keys to analyzing web behavior. Hang on to your seat. We're on internet time now.

10.32 Fact Tables for Text Document Searching

Ralph Kimball, Intelligent Enterprise, *Nov 10, 2000*

In article 10.5, *The Keyword Dimension*, I dipped my toe into the large lake of text string searching by describing two approaches for handling a list of keywords describing an archive of documents. But a keyword-based approach to accessing a large number of documents makes some strong assumptions. A really good set of keywords may require human reviewers, a fact that certainly restricts the scale of the document archive. There aren't enough human reviewers to index millions of documents. Some interesting progress has been made in automatically generating keywords for documents, much like you can automatically generate book indexes. But even if you have a pretty good set of keywords describing documents, your business users are still left with some tricky query issues.

The problem with keyword lookups and with most web search engines is that the user only types in a few target words to initiate the search. In both relational databases and web search engines, the hits are generated with a far too literal lookup of the target words. Indeed, even my favorite search engine doesn't know about plurals and alternate word endings; it either matches words exactly or misses them.

The use of a small number of target words to initiate the lookup leaves the user with two very serious problems that, in my opinion, more clever search engines cannot overcome. First, the short list of words simply doesn't carry enough context by itself to really say what the user wants. And second, merely finding some or all of the words in the target document carries no guarantee that the subject matter is relevant.

Similarity Metrics

Many researchers have recognized these problems with keyword-based systems and have been investigating more powerful techniques for allowing a user to search very large collections of documents. Although some of the early seminal papers (for example, that of Cornell's Professor Salton) date back to the 1960s, the advent of the web has more recently lit a brush fire under the text searching community. Text searching is rapidly moving out of the academic realm and into the commercial realm.

In my opinion, the most promising approaches to searching large document archives are based on measuring the similarity between two documents. If you can say that two documents are "similar," and if you can quantify this similarity, then you can avoid more serious problems with keywords. Imagine that one "document" is really the user's request for information. This request document can be a few sentences long or much longer. Of course, there is probably an optimal length for the request document, so that it doesn't contain too many separate subjects that would make the search unfocused.

You can regard the second document as the target. If you have an accurate quantitative measure of the similarity between the request document and the target document, and if you can rapidly process a large archive of target documents with the same request document, then you are well on your way to building an effective text retrieval system.

The creation of robust document similarity metrics is an active research topic today, in both academic and commercial settings. To sample a few of the many approaches, go to Google and search for "text distance metric," "topic spotting metric," "document relevance," and especially, "latent semantic analysis." I hope you appreciate the irony of this recommendation. Your search would be more fruitful if you had a similarity-based search engine!

Latent semantic analysis (LSA) is an approach that analyzes word-word, sentence-sentence, and passage-passage relationships. LSA generalizes the exact words and sentences in a candidate document precisely in order to avoid the problems of literal word matching. LSA is an interesting blend of a cognitive model of how humans think, and rigorous mathematical matrix techniques that capture the "dimensionality" of freeform text. A companion technique, latent semantic indexing (LSI), can generate exactly the kind of document similarity measurements that I have thus far discussed in this article.

LSA is probably not the final word on text searching, but it is likely that developers will build the next generation of text searching systems on document similarity measures like LSA, rather than on keyword searches.

Fact Tables for Similarity Measures

If you have access to a large archive of documents, then for certain applications you can build a very powerful document search system. Suppose you have millions of medical records describing symptoms, treatments, and outcomes for a large number of patients. This archive of medical records may be extremely complex. Many of the patients may have multiple diagnoses, multiple treatments, or multiple environmental and lifestyle factors. An interesting approach to querying this archive would be to define a few hundred single subject queries (request documents) that would individually generate similarity scores for every patient record. You could store the results of testing the candidate request queries against the archive in a fact table whose grain is: target document × request subject × request document.

In other words, the fact table contains one record for each patient record (target document) for each possible request subject and for each request document that "implements" the query subject. Adding the request document to the grain allows the fact table to contain more than one request document for the same request subject.

Using this grain and generalizing the field names so as not to be medical-records specific, you only need two keys: target document key and request document key.

The target document dimension contains the title, author, creation date, and storage location of each target document. The request document dimension contains the name of the request subject and possibly some hierarchical grouping labels (for example, diseases, treatments, or environmental factors) to help organize and search for request subjects. This dimension table also contains the specific title, creation date, author, and storage location of each request document. Note that there may be more than one request document for a specific request subject. This would allow you to use more than one similarity methodology for document matching.

The numeric measured facts include similarity score and target document length.

Keep in mind that although this design looks very symmetrical between target documents and request documents, you can assume that there are a much larger number of target documents (for example, medical records) than request documents, and these target documents may have very heterogeneous contents. You can also assume that there is a smaller set of request documents, and that these documents have been carefully prepared to adequately express the intended requests.

Although you have prepared the request documents and calculated the similarity scores in advance, you hope to preserve considerable ad hoc flexibility so that the user can pose complex and unanticipated requests. In article 10.5, *The Keyword Dimension*, I described the AND/OR dilemma that is typical of these kinds of requests. The user may want to see all the patients who have had treatment A AND treatment B, or conversely, treatment A OR treatment B.

The OR query is the simpler of the two because we don't have to jointly constrain two records from our fact table. Let's assume that a document passes the similarity test if the similarity score is greater than 0.8 on a scale of 0 to 1. The SQL looks something like:

```
Select T.target_doc_title, T.target_doc_location
From archive_fact F, target_doc T, request_doc R
```

```
Where F.target_doc_key = T.target_doc_key
And F.request_doc_key = R.request_doc_key
And ((R.subject = 'Treatment A' and F.similarity > 0.8)
OR (R.subject = 'Treatment B' and F.similarity > 0.8))
```

The AND query is more complex:

```
SELECT T.target_doc_title, T.target_doc_location
FROM archive_fact F, target_doc T
WHERE F.target_doc_key = T.target_doc_key
AND (SELECT COUNT(G.target_key)
FROM archive_fact G, request_doc R
WHERE G.target_doc_key = R.target_doc_key
AND G.target_key = F.target_key
AND ((R.Subject = 'Treatment A'
AND G.similarity > 0.8)
OR (R.Subject = 'Treatment B' AND G.similarity > 0.8))
= 2)
```

Don't be confused by the OR in between the requests for treatment A and treatment B in this code. Here your goal is to look for target documents having a count of 2 for the two joint requests you are making. This code finds the target documents correlating with both treatment A and treatment B!

Powerful Applications

Although I have descended into the implementation details in this article, it is worthwhile to step back and remind yourselves of the powerful applications that you can support with this approach. Because this approach depends on pre-categorizing and preprocessing the requests, you can look for situations where this is appropriate. Applications that come to mind include:

- Medical records analysis where the established categories of requests include diagnoses, treatments, lifestyle, and environmental factors
- Customer responses, customer requests, customer emails, and any kind of questionnaire that includes freeform responses where the established categories include product interest, quality complaints, and payment issues
- Technical support archives where a user's questions can be matched against a large body of other users' experiences
- Research projects, case studies, laboratory results, and environmental impact reports of all kinds where you know the research topics in advance and where there is value in examining many different systematic and correlated requests

The design I have just described is very extensible. You can add new target documents, new request documents, and new similarity measurement methodologies in a graceful fashion that extends the power of the archive but does not invalidate previous lookups or require the fact table to be dropped or reloaded. A search engine like Google whose spider actually saves all the target documents in readable form (see Google's "cache" command) offers the interesting possibility of being able to continuously compute new similarity measures for new requests in a background process without needing to go back to the remotely stored documents.

10.33 Enabling Market Basket Analysis

Ralph Kimball, Intelligent Enterprise, *Apr 20, 1999*

This article was originally titled The Market Basket Data Mart. *While other contemporary data mining approaches may be more powerful and desirable today, this article does describe a powerful architecture for market basket analysis that features a top down approach, an adjustable relevance threshold, the ability to find meaningful market basket correlations at heterogeneous levels of the product hierarchy, where each iteration is progressively more relevant, and an algorithm that is guaranteed to stop.*

Data warehouse architects have long been recording retail store purchases in large atomic fact tables. With the increasing use of customer loyalty cards and in-house credit cards, these fact tables would seem to contain everything our marketing and merchandising managers need to know about customer behavior.

It is certainly true that our atomic fact table tells us in exquisite detail what the stores sold, which stores sold it, when they sold it, and who the customer was. The large atomic fact table is great for promotion analysis. But one of the most interesting analyses of customer behavior—market basket analysis—is served very poorly by this table.

The most basic form of market basket analysis seeks to understand what meaningful product combinations were sold together in individual market baskets. When the store manager or headquarters merchandising manager understands the meaningful market baskets, that manager can make some interesting decisions, including:

- Placing products near each other in the store for shopper convenience and to increase the likelihood that customers will purchase multiple products
- Conversely, placing products far apart from each other to force the customer to traverse certain aisles or go past certain displays
- Pricing and packaging combinations of products, perhaps to piggyback a new brand with an established brand

The primary goal of market basket analysis is to understand the "meaningful combinations" of products sold together. On closer examination, however, this goal often becomes much more complicated. More sophisticated forms of the market basket goal include:

- Understanding combinations of brands, subcategories, and categories, rather than focusing just on lowest level stock keeping units (SKUs) at the bar coded level
- Looking for mixed aggregate results that are more meaningful than results at the same hierarchical level. For instance, maybe an interesting result is that Coca-Cola's 12-ounce cans sell well with frozen pasta dinners. In this case, we have matched an SKU with a subcategory.

- Looking for groups of three—or even more—products sold together
- Understanding which items don't sell well together. This is the so-called missing market basket.
- Looking for products (or brands or categories) that characteristically sell together, but not always in the same specific market basket. In this case, we continue to focus on the individual customer, but we relax the definition of the market basket to include purchase events within a span of time. If the customer buys peanut butter, we would expect to see a jelly purchase at some point in time close by. At this point, we are asking for full-fledged affinity grouping, as described by data mining specialists.

We cannot easily use the basic atomic fact table describing purchases to perform any of these analyses. Part of the problem is the near impossibility of constraining and grouping across records in SQL. Each item in a given basket is in a separate record, and SQL was never designed to express cross-record constraints. Another problem is the combinatorial explosion of products. If a big retail store has 100,000 low level products, then just enumerating all the two-way combinations involves 10 billion possibilities.

The solution for the market basket analysis problem is to create a new fact table, as shown in Figure 10-49, and to populate this fact table in a very specific, disciplined way. We will see that much of the hard work of market basket analysis takes place in the ETL processes, thus simplifying the query and presentation phases of the analysis.

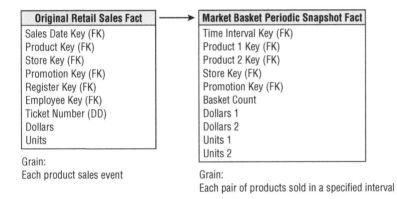

Figure 10-49: A market basket fact table based on atomic retail sales data.

The market basket fact table in Figure 10-49 is a periodic snapshot representing the important pairs of products sold in various market baskets. The time key represents the end-of-period marker.

There are two generalized product keys in this design that must be able to represent individual products (SKUs), brands, subcategories, categories, and departments—all in the same fact table. These choices would come from the traditional merchandise hierarchy in the retail business.

Other generalized product key choices could represent flavors or package types, although in my experience, most market basket analysis takes place only across the levels of the traditional merchandise hierarchy.

The facts include the total number of market baskets with the named combinations of products: the total number of dollars and units sold of product one in this set of baskets, and the total number of dollars and units sold of product two in this set of baskets.

Now if this table in Figure 10-49 were magically filled in for all possible combinations of generalized products, we could navigate this table to answer most of the questions we posed earlier. We would probably first look for records with high basket counts. After all, these are the frequently observed baskets and should be the most meaningful. Second, we would look for baskets where the dollars or units were in reasonable balance; finding baskets where the dollars or units were far out of balance would be rather dull because all we've done is find high selling products coupled with insignificant second products. We probably wouldn't base major merchandising or promotion decisions around such findings.

Realistically, we can't expect the market basket table in Figure 10-49 to be magically filled in. We still haven't dealt with the combinatorial explosion. Somehow, we have to fill in the market basket fact table, generating all the records we hoped to see in the previous paragraph, but nimbly avoiding the generation of billions of bogus records we never want to analyze.

Progressive Pruning Algorithm

The solution is a top-down progressive pruning algorithm, implemented during the ETL phase in the back room. We start from the atomic sales fact table shown on the left of Figure 10-49. and run a series of queries that extract data into the market basket fact table shown on the right. The logic goes like this:

1. Start at the top of the merchandise hierarchy by enumerating all the combinations of department-to-department market baskets. If there are 20 departments, this first step yields 400 records.

2. Prune this list severely by choosing only records with a threshold number of baskets and where the dollars or units are within a specified balance. Experimentation will tell you what the threshold should be and what the criteria for the specified balance should be. (I recommend starting with 20 percent of the total basket count and with products that are balanced within 30 percent of each other.) Stop the algorithm if the pruning step removes all the records or if you run out of storage space or patience.

3. Drill down on product one by descending the merchandise hierarchy one step and enumerating all the new combinations, say category (product one) by department (product two). Repeat similarly by drilling one step down on product two, as long its level is equal to or higher than the level of product one. Go to step 2.

This algorithm is guaranteed to stop because each step that descends the hierarchy necessarily produces records with smaller basket counts. Eventually, the system finds no records with basket counts greater than the minimum threshold for relevance. Also, it is permissible to stop at any time. At each point, the records found thus far are the records that could have the most impact on the analysis. Notice that this top-down approach is superior to a bottom-up approach in several ways. A bottom-up approach starting with individual atomic products could easily miss important patterns. If a store frequently sells Coca-Cola 12-ounce cans with the pasta dinner subcategory, we probably would miss this result if we paired Coca-Cola directly with individual pasta dinner SKUs. And as I stated earlier, the top-down progressive pruning algorithm starts finding relevant results immediately without generating an astronomical number of records. Running the pruning algorithm progressively provides more focus to already relevant results.

Perhaps the most subtle design step in setting up this market basket data mart is choosing the generalized product keys. If we have set up the original sales fact table in Figure 10-49 with standard dimensional modeling techniques, the product keys are integer surrogate keys with no structure and no recognizable semantics. Aggregate fact tables built for query performance reasons accompanying this sales fact table would have one or more shrunken dimensions representing the degrees of aggregation. Typically, a shrunken product dimension would exist at the category level—and possibly other levels as well. The interesting twist to the design of the market basket data mart is that for the first time in our data warehouse, we have to build a single product dimension that contains entries at multiple levels of the hierarchy. This procedure requires creating a special variant of the product dimension table with a smaller number of rather generic attributes (because, for example, none of the most detailed product attributes would exist except at the lowest SKU level) and assigning the keys from the various levels so that they do not overlap.

We can generalize the progressive pruning algorithm to handle three items in the basket in a straightforward way. The market basket fact table now needs three generalized product keys, three dollar sums, and three unit sums. If the first step of the algorithm is computed with the same rules, it creates 8,000 department combinations. We handle the pruning steps in a way analogous to the recipe given earlier.

We can also generalize the progressive pruning algorithm to handle market baskets that extend over several purchase events. We only need to process all the baskets for a given customer within a specified time span as if these baskets actually were one big basket.

It is difficult to use the techniques described in this article to answer what was not in the market basket. Much of the problem is the sheer logical weirdness of the question. After all, every market basket is missing most of the items in the store. Also, if an item is missing, it doesn't contribute to the dollar impact or the units' impact of the basket, making it difficult to use our progressive pruning logic. However, there are a few variations on the question of what didn't happen that are probably worth answering with special queries on the sales fact table. These include: What items are sold most often in single-item market baskets? In two-item market baskets? Which combinations of items occur less often in a statistically significant way than you would expect from their overall presence in all possible market baskets?

Although the preparation and ETL processing for the market basket analyses are significant steps, the resulting market basket fact table and the associated special product dimension let us perform nearly all the interesting and useful types of market basket analysis in a bounded and controllable way.

Back Room ETL and Data Quality

With the target dimensional models designed, it's time to turn our attention to the back room. Designing and developing behind the scenes extract, transform, and load (ETL) systems consumes the lion's share of effort during a DW/BI project.

This chapter begins with guidance for planning the ETL system, including an overview of the 34 subsystems required to extract, clean, conform, and finally deliver the data to the data warehouse's front room, along with the requisite system management infrastructure. These subsystems must be considered whether you're using an ETL tool or not.

The second section of this chapter dives into data quality concerns. We begin by describing the business benefits of clean data, and then describe a comprehensive architecture for capturing and monitoring quality defects. Specific techniques for cleaning substandard data are discussed.

From there, we focus on building the dimension and fact tables, from surrogate key pipelines to dealing with late-arriving facts and dimensions. Finally, we describe the implications of moving to more real-time ETL processing.

Planning the ETL System

The first two articles in this section were written in late 2004 as *The Data Warehouse ETL Toolkit* (Kimball and Caserta, Wiley, 2004) was being released; subsequent articles in this section address the data structures in the back room, the pros and cons of using a commercial ETL tool, as well as techniques for change data capture and integrating data from external parties.

11.1 Surrounding the ETL Requirements

Ralph Kimball, Intelligent Enterprise, *Nov 13, 2004*

Ideally, the design of your ETL system begins with one of the toughest challenges: surrounding the requirements. By this we mean gathering in one place all the known requirements, realities, and constraints affecting the ETL system. The list of requirements is pretty overwhelming, but it's essential to lay them on the table before launching a DW/BI project.

The requirements are mostly things you must live with and adapt your system to. Within the framework of your requirements, you'll have many places where you can make your own decisions, exercise your judgment, and leverage your creativity, but the requirements are just what they're named. They are *required*.

Business Needs

The business needs are the information requirements of the data warehouse's users. We use the term *business needs* somewhat narrowly here to mean the information content that business users need to make informed business decisions. Subsequently listed requirements broaden the definition of business needs, but this requirement is meant to identify the extended set of information sources that the ETL team must introduce into the data warehouse.

Taking, for the moment, the view that business needs directly drive the choice of data sources, it's obvious that understanding and constantly examining the business needs are the ETL team's core activities. The result is a set of expectations the users have about what data will do for them.

In many cases, the original interviews with the business users and the original investigations of possible sources don't fully reveal the data's complexities and limitations. The ETL team often makes significant discoveries that affect whether the user's business needs can be addressed as originally hoped for. And, of course, the ETL team often discovers additional capabilities in the data sources that expand the users' decision making capabilities. The lesson here is that even during the most technical back room development steps of building the ETL system, you must maintain a dialog among the ETL team, data warehouse architects, business analysts, and business users. In a larger sense, the business needs and the content of the data sources are both moving targets that constantly need to be reexamined and discussed.

Compliance

In recent years, especially with the passage of the Sarbanes-Oxley Act of 2002, organizations have been forced to seriously tighten up what they report and provide proof that the reported numbers are accurate, complete, and not tampered with. Of course, data warehouses in regulated businesses such as telecommunications have complied with regulatory reporting requirements for many years. But certainly the whole tenor of financial reporting has become much more serious for everyone.

Some of the financial reporting issues will be outside the scope of the data warehouse, but many others will land squarely within its scope. Typical due diligence requirements for the data warehouse include the following:

- Saving archived copies of data sources and subsequent stagings of data
- Proof of the complete transaction flow that changed any data results
- Fully documented algorithms for allocations, adjustments, and derivations
- Proof of security of the data copies over time, both online and offline

Data Quality via Data Profiling

As Jack Olson explains so clearly in his book *Data Quality: The Accuracy Dimension* (Morgan Kaufmann, 2003), data profiling is a necessary precursor to designing any kind of system to use that data. As he puts it: Data profiling "employs analytic methods for looking at data for the purpose of developing a thorough understanding of the content, structure, and quality of the data. A good data profiling [system] can process very large amounts of data, and with the skills of the analyst, uncover all sorts of issues that need to be addressed."

This perspective is especially relevant to the ETL team who may be handed a data source with content that hasn't really been vetted. For example, Jack points out that a data source that perfectly handles the needs of the production system, such as an order taking system, may be a disaster for the data warehouse, because the ancillary fields the data warehouse hoped to use weren't central to the success of the order taking process and were revealed to be unreliable and too incomplete for data warehouse analysis.

Data profiling is a systematic examination of the quality, scope, and context of a data source to allow an ETL system to be built. At one extreme, a very clean data source that has been well maintained before it arrives at the data warehouse requires minimal transformation and human intervention to load directly into final dimension tables and fact tables.

And at the other extreme, if data profiling reveals that the source data is deeply flawed and can't support the business' objectives, the data warehouse effort should be cancelled. The profiling step not only gives the ETL team guidance as to how much data cleaning machinery to invoke, but protects the ETL team from missing major milestones in the project because of the unexpected diversion to build a system to deal with dirty data. Do the data profiling upfront! Use the data profiling results to prepare the business sponsors for the realistic development schedules, the limitations in the source data, and the need to invest in better data capture practices in the source systems.

Security

The general level of security awareness has improved significantly in the past few years across all IT areas, but security remains an afterthought and an unwelcome additional burden to most data warehouse teams. The basic rhythms of the data warehouse are at odds with the security mentality. The data warehouse seeks to publish data widely to decision makers, whereas the security interests assume that data should be restricted to those with a need to know.

Throughout the *Toolkit* series of books, we've recommended a role-based approach to security where the ability to access the results from a data warehouse is controlled at the final applications' delivery point. Security for business users isn't controlled with grants and revokes to individual users at the physical table level, but is controlled through roles defined and enforced on a lightweight directory access protocol (LDAP) based network resource called a *directory server*. It is then incumbent on the users' applications to sort out what the authenticated role of a requesting user is and whether that role permits the user to view the particular screen that's being requested.

Additionally, security must be extended to physical backups. If a tape or disk pack can easily be removed from the backup vault, then security has been compromised as effectively as if the online passwords were compromised.

Data Integration and the 360 Degree View

Data integration is a huge topic for IT because, ultimately, it aims to make all systems work together seamlessly. The "360 degree view of the customer" is a familiar name for data integration. In many cases, serious data integration must take place among the organization's primary transaction systems before any of that data arrives at the data warehouse. But rarely is that data integration complete, unless the organization has settled on a single enterprise resource planning (ERP) system, and even then it's likely that other important transaction processing systems exist outside the main ERP system.

Data integration usually takes the form of conforming dimensions and conforming facts in the data warehouse. *Conforming dimensions* means establishing common dimensional attributes across separated databases so that "drill across" reports can be generated using these attributes. *Conforming facts* means making agreements on common business metrics such as key performance indicators (KPIs) across separated databases so that these numbers can be compared mathematically by calculating differences and ratios.

Data Latency

The data latency requirement describes how quickly the data must be delivered to the business users. Data latency obviously has a huge effect on the architecture and system implementation. Up to a point, more clever processing algorithms, parallel processing, and more potent hardware can speed up most of the traditional batch-oriented data flows. But at some point, if the data latency requirement is sufficiently urgent, the ETL system's architecture must convert from batch-oriented to streaming. This switch isn't a gradual or evolutionary change; it's a major paradigm shift in which almost every step of the data delivery pipeline must be re-implemented.

Archiving and Lineage

We hinted at these requirements earlier in the compliance and security sections. But even without the legal requirements for saving data, every data warehouse needs various copies of old data, either for comparisons with new data to generate change capture records or reprocessing.

We recommend staging the data at each point that a major transformation has occurred. These staging points occur after all four steps: extract, clean, conform, and deliver. So, when does staging (writing the data to disk) turn into archiving (keeping the data indefinitely on some form of permanent media)?

Our simple answer is a conservative answer. *All staged data should be archived unless a conscious decision is made that specific data sets will never be recovered in the future.* It's almost always less of a headache to read the data back in from permanent media than it is to reprocess the data through the ETL system at a later time. And, of course, it may be impossible to reprocess the data according to the old processing algorithms if enough time has passed.

And while you are at it, each staged/archived data set should have accompanying metadata describing the origins and processing steps that produced the data. Again, the tracking of this lineage is explicitly required by certain compliance requirements, but should be part of every archiving situation.

BI User Delivery Interfaces

The final step for the ETL system is the handoff to the BI user applications. We take a strong and disciplined position on this handoff. We believe the ETL team, working closely with the modeling team, must take responsibility for the content and structure of the data that, as much as we can control, makes the user applications simple and fast. This attitude is much more than a vague motherhood statement. We believe it's irresponsible to hand the data off to the user application in such a way as to increase the complexity of the application, slow down the final query or report creation, or make the data seem unnecessarily complex to the business users. The most elementary and serious error is to hand across a full-blown normalized physical model and walk away from the job. This is why we go to such lengths to build dimensional structures that comprise the actual final handoff.

In general, the ETL team and data modelers need to work closely with the application developers to determine the exact requirements for the final data handoff. Each BI tool has certain sensitivities that should be avoided and certain features that can be exploited if the physical data is in the right format. The same considerations apply to data prepared for OLAP cubes.

Available Skills

Some of the big design decisions when building an ETL system must be made on the basis of available resources to build and manage the system. You shouldn't build a system that depends on critical C++ processing modules if those programming skills aren't in-house and you can't reasonably acquire and keep those skills. You may be much more confident in building your ETL system around a major vendor's ETL tool if you already have those skills in-house and you know how to manage such a project.

You need to look in depth at the big decision of whether to hand code your ETL system or use a vendor's package. Technical issues and license costs aside, you shouldn't go off in a direction that your employees and managers find unfamiliar without seriously considering the long term implications.

Legacy Licenses

Finally, in many cases, major design decisions will be made for you implicitly by senior management's insistence that you use existing legacy licenses. In many cases, this requirement is one you can live with and for which the advantages in your environment are pretty clear to everyone. But in a few cases, the use of a legacy system for your ETL development is a mistake. This is a difficult position to be in, and if you feel strongly enough about it, you may need to bet your job. If you must approach senior management and challenge the use of an existing legacy system, be well prepared in making your case; you'll either need to accept their final decision or possibly seek employment elsewhere.

The combined impact of all these requirements is overwhelming. Perhaps for that reason, many ETL implementations don't have a coherent set of design principles below the basic E and T and L modules. Many ETL systems seem to be the union of a thousand reactions to individual requirements.

11.2 The 34 Subsystems of ETL

Ralph Kimball, Intelligent Enterprise, *Dec 4, 2004*

This article was originally published as The 38 Subsystems of ETL. *The updated version includes content from Bob Becker's* The Subsystems of ETL Revisited *article written in Oct 2007.*

The ETL system, or more informally the back room, is often estimated to consume 70 percent of the time and effort of building a data warehouse. But there hasn't been enough careful thinking about just why the ETL system is so complex and resource intensive. Everyone understands the three letters: You get the data out of its original source location (E), you do something to it (T), and then you load it (L) into a final set of tables for the users to query.

When asked about breaking down the three big steps, many designers say, "Well, that depends." It depends on the source, it depends on funny data idiosyncrasies, it depends on the scripting languages and ETL tools available, it depends on the skills of the in-house staff, and it depends on the BI query and reporting tools the users have.

The "it depends" response is dangerous because it becomes an excuse to roll your own ETL system, which in the worst case scenario results in an undifferentiated spaghetti mess of tables, modules, processes, scripts, triggers, alerts, and job schedules. Maybe this kind of creative design approach was appropriate a few years ago when everyone was struggling to understand the ETL task, but with the benefit of thousands of successful data warehouses, a set of best practices is ready to emerge.

I have spent the past 18 months intensively studying ETL practices and products. I have identified a list of 34 subsystems that are needed in almost every data warehouse back room. That's the bad news; no wonder the ETL system takes such a large fraction of the data warehouse resources. But the good news is that if you study the list, you'll recognize almost all of them, and you'll be on the way to leveraging your experience in each of these subsystems as you build successive data warehouses.

Extracting: Getting Data into the Data Warehouse

To no surprise, the initial subsystems of the ETL architecture address the issues of understanding your source data, extracting the data, and transferring it to the back room environment where the ETL system can operate on it independent of the operational systems. The extract related ETL subsystems include:

1. **Data profiling system.** Column property analysis including discovery of inferred domains; and structure analysis including candidate foreign key/primary key relationships, data rule analysis, and value rule analysis

2. **Change data capture system.** Source log file readers, source date and sequence number filters, and record comparisons based on cyclic redundancy checksum (CRC) algorithms

3. **Extract system.** Source data adapters, push/pull/dribble job schedulers, filtering and sorting at the source, proprietary data format conversions, and data staging after transfer to the ETL environment

Cleaning and Conforming Data

The ETL system adds value to the data during these critical steps. These cleaning and conforming subsystems should be architected to create metadata for diagnosing source system problems. Such diagnoses can eventually lead to business process reengineering initiatives to address the root causes of dirty data and improve data quality over time.

The ETL data cleaning process is often expected to fix dirty data, yet at the same time, the data warehouse is expected to provide an accurate picture of the data as it was captured by the organization's production systems. It's essential to strike the proper balance between these conflicting goals. The key is to develop an ETL system capable of correcting, rejecting, or loading data as is, and then highlighting with easy-to-use structures the modifications, standardizations, rules, and assumptions of the underlying cleaning apparatus so the system is self-documenting.

The five major subsystems in the cleaning and conforming step include:

4. **Data cleaning and quality screen handler system.** Typically a dictionary-driven system for complete parsing of names and addresses of individuals and organizations, possibly also products or locations. "Surviving" using specialized data merge logic that preserves specified fields from certain sources to be the final saved versions. Maintains back references (such as natural keys) to all participating original sources. Inline ETL tests applied systematically to all data flows checking for data quality issues

5. **Error event handler.** Comprehensive system for reporting and responding to all ETL error events. Includes branching logic to handle various classes of errors, and real-time monitoring of ETL data quality

6. **Audit dimension assembler.** Assembly of metadata context surrounding each fact table load in such a way that the metadata context can be attached to the fact table as a normal dimension

7. **Deduplication system.** Includes identification and removal, usually of individuals and organizations, possibly products or locations. Often uses fuzzy logic

8. **Data conformer.** Identification and enforcement of special conformed dimension attributes and conformed fact table measures as the basis for data integration across multiple sources

Delivering: Preparing for Presentation

The ultimate mission of the ETL system is the delivery of the dimension and fact tables. There is considerable variation in source data structures and cleaning and conforming logic, but the delivery processing techniques are more defined and disciplined. The delivery subsystems in the ETL architecture consist of:

9. **Slowly changing dimension (SCD) processor.** Transformation logic for handling dimension attribute time variance: type 1 (overwrite), type 2 (create new record), and type 3 (create new field)

10. **Surrogate key creation system.** Robust mechanism for producing surrogate keys, independently for every dimension. Independent of database instance, able to serve distributed clients

11. **Hierarchy dimension builder for fixed, variable, and ragged hierarchies.** Data validity checking and maintenance system for all forms of many-to-one hierarchies in a dimension. Variable hierarchy dimension builder. Data validity checking and maintenance system for all forms of ragged hierarchies of indeterminate depth

12. **Special dimension builder.** Creation and maintenance of dimensions consisting of miscellaneous low cardinality flags and indicators found in most production data sources

13. **Fact table loader for transaction, periodic snapshot, and accumulating snapshot grains.** System for updating fact tables including manipulation of indexes and partitions. Transaction grain: normally append mode for most recent data. Periodic snapshot grain: includes frequent overwrite strategy for incremental update of current period facts. Accumulating snapshot grain: includes manipulation of indexes and partitions, and updates to both dimension foreign keys and accumulating measures

14. **Surrogate key pipeline.** Pipelined, multithreaded process for replacing natural keys of incoming data with data warehouse surrogate keys

15. **Multi-valued dimension bridge table builder.** Creation and maintenance of associative bridge table used to describe a many-to-many relationship between dimensions. May include weighting factors used for allocations and situational role descriptions

16. **Late-arriving data handler.** Insertion and update logic for fact records and/or dimension records that have been delayed in arriving at the data warehouse

17. **Dimension manager system.** Administration system for the dimension manager who replicates conformed dimensions from a centralized location to fact table providers

18. **Fact table provider system.** Administration system for the fact table provider who receives conformed dimensions sent by the dimension manager. Includes local key substitution, dimension version checking, and aggregate table change management

19. **Aggregate builder.** Creation and maintenance of physical aggregate database structures that are used in conjunction with a query rewrite facility to improve query performance. Includes standalone aggregate tables and materialized views

20. **Multidimensional cube builder.** Creation and maintenance of star schema foundation for loading multidimensional (OLAP) cubes, including special preparation of dimension hierarchies as dictated by the specific cube technology

21. **Data integration manager.** System for transfer of large data sets between production applications and to the data warehouse

Managing the ETL Environment

A data warehouse will not be a success until it can be relied upon as a dependable source for business decision making. The ETL management subsystems are the architectural components that help achieve the goals of reliability, availability, and manageability. Operating and maintaining a data warehouse in a professional manner is not much different than other systems operations. Many of you will be familiar with the following subsystems:

22. **Job scheduler.** System for scheduling and launching all ETL jobs. Able to wait for a wide variety of system conditions including dependencies of prior jobs completing successfully. Able to post alerts

23. **Backup system.** Backup data and metadata for recovery, restart, security, and compliance requirements

24. **Recovery and restart system.** Common system for resuming a job that has halted, or for backing out a whole job and restarting. Significant dependency on backup system

25. **Version control system.** Consistent "snapshotting" capability for archiving and recovering all the metadata in the ETL pipeline. Check-out and check-in of all ETL modules and jobs. Source comparison capability to reveal differences between different versions

26. **Version migration system from development to test to production.** Move a complete ETL pipeline implementation out of development, into test, and then into production. Interface to version control system to back out a migration. Single interface for setting connection information for entire version. Independence from database location for surrogate key generation

27. **Workflow monitor.** Dashboard and reporting system for all job runs initiated by the job scheduler. Includes number of records processed, summaries of errors, and actions taken

28. **Sort system.** Standalone high performance sort package

29. **Lineage and dependency analyzer.** Display the ultimate physical sources and subsequent transformations of any selected data element, chosen either from the middle of the ETL pipeline or on a final delivered report (lineage). Display all affected downstream data elements and final report fields affected by a potential change in any selected data element, chosen either in the middle of the ETL pipeline or in an original source (dependency).

30. **Problem escalation system.** Automatic plus manual system for raising an error condition to the appropriate level for resolution and tracking. Includes simple error log entries, operator notification, supervisor notification, and system developer notification

31. **Parallelizing/pipelining system.** Common system for taking advantage of multiple processors or grid computing resources, and common system for implementing streaming data flows. Highly desirable (eventually necessary) that parallelizing and pipelining be invoked automatically for any ETL process that meets certain conditions, such as not writing to the disk or waiting on a condition in the middle of the process

32. **Security system.** Administer role-based security on all data and metadata in the ETL pipeline.
33. **Compliance reporter.** Comply with regulatory statutes to prove the lineage of key reported operating results. Prove that the data and the transformations haven't been changed. Show who has accessed or changed any such data.
34. **Metadata repository manager.** Comprehensive system for capturing and maintaining all ETL metadata, including all transformation logic. Includes process metadata, technical metadata, and business metadata

If you've survived to the end of this list, congratulations! Here is the important observation I'd like you to carry away: It's really difficult to argue that any of these subsystems are unnecessary as this list makes it clear that without dividing up the task (perhaps 34 ways), the descent into chaos is inevitable. The industry is ready to define best practices goals and implementation standards for each of these 34 subsystems, and it would be a tremendous contribution for the ETL tool vendors to provide wizards or serious templates for each of these 34 subsystems. We have a lot to talk about. Maybe 34 more articles!

11.3 Six Key Decisions for ETL Architectures

Bob Becker, Intelligent Enterprise, Oct 9, 2009

This article describes six key decisions that must be made while crafting the ETL architecture for a dimensional data warehouse. These decisions have significant impacts on the upfront and ongoing cost and complexity of the ETL solution and, ultimately, on the success of the overall BI/DW solution.

1. Should We Use an ETL Tool?

One of the earliest and most fundamental decisions you must make is whether to hand code your ETL system or use a vendor-supplied package. Technical issues and license costs aside, you shouldn't go off in a direction that your employees and managers find unfamiliar without seriously considering the decision's long term implications. This decision will have a major impact on the ETL environment, driving staffing decisions, design approaches, metadata strategies, and implementation timelines for a long time.

In today's environment, most organizations should use a vendor-supplied ETL tool as a general rule. However, this decision must be made on the basis of available resources to build and manage the system. ETL tools are really system building environments that use icons, arrows, and properties to build the ETL solution rather than writing code. Be careful; if your proposed ETL development team is comprised of a number of old-school hand coders, they might not adapt well to an ETL tool. For this reason alone, some organizations find that custom ETL development is still a reasonable solution.

If you decide to use an ETL tool, don't expect a huge payback in your first iteration. The advantages will become more apparent as you traverse additional iterations and begin to leverage the development advantages of using a tool during subsequent implementations. You'll also experience the benefits of enhanced maintenance capabilities, more complete documentation, and improved metadata support over time. Article 11.8, *Should You Use an ETL Tool?*," provides an in-depth look at the pros and cons of using an ETL tool.

2. Where And How Should Data Integration Take Place?

Data integration is a huge topic for IT because, ultimately, it aims to make all systems work together seamlessly. The "360 degree view of the enterprise" is a commonly discussed goal that really means data integration. In many cases, serious data integration should take place among an organization's primary transaction systems before data arrives at the data warehouse. However, rather than dealing with integration in the operational environment, these requirements are often pushed back to the data warehouse and the ETL system.

Most of us understand the core concept that integration means making disparate databases function together in a useful way. We all know we need it; we just don't have a clear idea of how to break it down into manageable pieces. Does integration mean that all parties across large organizations agree on every data element or only on some data elements? This is the crux of the decision that must be made. At what level in the data does business management agree/insist integration will occur? Are they willing to establish common definitions across organizations and to abide by those definitions?

Fundamentally, integration means reaching agreement on the meaning of data from the perspective of two or more databases. With integration, the results of two databases can be combined into a single data warehouse analysis. Without such an accord, the databases will remain isolated stovepipes that can't be linked in an application. For the context of our ETL environment, data integration takes the form of conforming dimensions and conforming facts in the data warehouse. Conforming dimensions means establishing common dimensional attributes across separated fact tables so that "drill across" reports can be generated using these attributes. Conforming facts means making agreements on common business metrics such as key performance indicators (KPIs) across separated databases so that these numbers can be compared mathematically for calculating differences and ratios.

3. Which Change Data Capture Mechanisms Should We Choose?

During the data warehouse's initial historic load, capturing source data content changes is not important since you are loading all data from a point in time forward. However, most data warehouse tables are so large that they cannot be refreshed during every ETL cycle. You must have a capability to transfer only the relevant changes to the source data since the last update. Isolating the latest source data is called change data capture (CDC). The idea behind change data capture is simple enough: Just transfer the data that has been changed since the last load.

But building a good change data capture system is not as easy as it sounds. Realize that the mechanism selected must be absolutely fool proof—all changed data must be identified. Finding the most comprehensive strategy can be elusive; many times updates to source system tables can occur outside the application itself. A mistake here will result in inconsistent results that can't be easily explained; often it takes significant data reconciliation to identify the culprit. Problems can be very costly in terms of rework—not to mention embarrassing. In short, capturing data changes is far from a trivial task, and you must clearly understand the source data systems. This knowledge will help the ETL team evaluate data sources, identify change data capture problems, and determine the most appropriate strategy.

4. When Should We Stage the Data?

In today's data warehousing environment, it's quite possible for ETL tools to establish a direct connection to the source database, extract and stream the data through the ETL tool to apply any required transformation in memory, and finally write it, only once, into the target data warehouse table. From a performance viewpoint, this is a great capability as writes, especially logged writes into the RDBMS, are very expensive; it's a good design goal to minimize them. However, despite the performance advantages, this may not be the best approach. There are several reasons an organization might decide to physically stage the data (i.e., write it to disk) during the ETL process:

- The most appropriate CDC method requires a compare of the current copy of the source table to the prior copy of the same table.
- The organization has elected to stage the data immediately after extract for archival purposes—possibly to meet compliance and audit requirements.
- A recovery/restart point is desired in the event the ETL job fails in midstream—potentially due to a break in the connection between the source and ETL environment.
- Long running ETL processes may open a connection to the source system that creates problems with database locks and that stresses the transaction system.

Article 11.7, *Staging Areas and ETL Tools*, describes this process in greater detail.

5. Where Should We Correct Data?

Business users are aware that data quality is a serious and expensive problem. Thus most organizations are likely to support initiatives to improve data quality. But most users probably have no idea where data quality problems originate or what should be done to improve data quality. They may think that data quality is a simple execution problem for the ETL team. In this environment, the ETL team needs to be agile and proactive: Data quality cannot be improved by ETL alone. The key is for the ETL team to partner with the business and the IT teams that support the source systems.

The key decision is where to correct the data. Clearly, the best solution is to have the data captured accurately in the first place. Of course, this isn't always the case, but nonetheless, in most cases, the data should be corrected back in the source system. Unfortunately, it is inevitable that poor quality data will reach the ETL system. In this event, there are three choices:

- Halting the entire load process
- Sending the offending record(s) to a suspense file for later processing
- Merely tagging the data and passing it through

The third choice is by far the best choice, whenever possible. Halting the process is obviously a pain because it requires manual intervention to diagnose the problem, restart or resume the job, or abort completely. Sending records to a suspense file is often a poor solution because it is not clear when or if these records will be fixed and reintroduced to the pipeline. Until the records are restored to the data flow, the overall integrity of the database is questionable because records are missing. I recommend not using the suspense file for minor data transgressions. The third option of tagging the data with the error condition often works well. Bad fact table data can be tagged with an audit dimension that describes the overall data quality condition of the offending fact row. Bad dimension data can also be tagged using the audit dimension or, in the case of missing or garbage data, can be tagged with unique error values in the field itself. From this point, data quality reporting capabilities can flag the offending fact and dimension rows, indicating a need for resolution and ideally repair of the date in the source system.

6. How Quickly Must Source Data Be Available via the DW/BI System?

Data latency describes how quickly source system data must be delivered to the business users via the DW/BI system. Data latency obviously has a huge effect on the costs and complexity of your ETL environment. Clever processing algorithms, parallelization, and potent hardware can speed up traditional batch-oriented data flows. But at some point, if the data latency requirement is sufficiently urgent, the ETL system's architecture must convert from batch to streaming oriented. This switch isn't a gradual or evolutionary change; it's a major paradigm shift in which almost every step of the data delivery pipeline must be re-implemented.

Typically, ETL streams for most organizations require a data latency which matches the natural rhythm of the business. We find in most organizations this typically results in daily updates for most ETL streams and weekly or monthly updates for other ETL streams. However, in some circumstances, more frequent updates or even real-time updates best suit the rhythm of the business. The key is to recognize that only a handful of business processes within any organization are appropriate for real-time updating. There's no compelling reason to convert all ETL processing to real time. The rhythm of most business processes simply doesn't demand real-time treatment.

Be careful: Asking business users if they want "real-time" delivery of data is an open invitation for trouble. Of course, most business users will respond positively to having data updated more frequently, regardless of whether they understand the impact of their request. Clearly this kind of data latency requirement could be dangerous. We recommend dividing the real-time challenge into three categories: daily, frequently, and instantaneous. You need to get your end users to describe their data latency requirements in similar terms and then design your ETL solution appropriately to support each set of requirements:

▪ **Instantaneous** means that the data visible on the end user's screen represents the true state of the source transaction system at every instant. When the source system status changes, the online screen must also respond instantly.

- **Frequently** means that the data visible to the end user is updated many times per day but is not guaranteed to be the absolute current truth as of this instant.
- **Daily** means that the data visible on the screen is valid as of a batch file download or reconciliation from the source system at the end of the previous working day.

In article 11.45, *The Real-Time Triage*, Ralph describes the impacts and implementation alternatives for each of these capabilities in more detail.

In this article we discussed a number of key decisions that must be evaluated during the creation of an ETL architecture to support a dimensional data warehouse. There is seldom a single correct choice for any of these decisions; as always, the correct choice should be driven by the unique requirements and characteristics of your organization.

11.4 Three ETL Compromises to Avoid

Bob Becker, Intelligent Enterprise, Mar 1, 2010

Whether you are developing a new dimensional data warehouse or replacing an existing environment, the ETL implementation effort is inevitably on the critical path. Difficult data sources, unclear requirements, data quality problems, changing scope, and other unforeseen problems often conspire to put the squeeze on the ETL development team. It simply may not be possible to fully deliver on the project team's original commitments; compromises will need to be made. In the end, these compromises, if not carefully considered, may create long term headaches.

In the previous article I described the decisions ETL teams face when implementing a dimensional data warehouse. This article focuses on three common ETL development compromises that cause most of the long term problems around dimensional data warehouses. Avoiding these compromises will not only improve the effectiveness of your ETL implementation, but will also increase the likelihood of overall DW/BI success.

Compromise 1: Neglecting Slowly Changing Dimension Requirements

Kimball Group has written extensively on slowly changing dimension (SCD) strategies and complementary implementation alternatives. It's important that the ETL team embrace SCDs as an important strategy early in the initial implementation process. A common compromise is to put off to the future the effort required to properly support SCDs, especially type 2 SCDs where dimension changes are tracked by adding new rows to the dimension table. The result is often a total rework disaster.

Deferring the implementation of proper SCD strategies does save ETL development time in the immediate phase. But as a result, the implementation embraces only type 1 SCDs, where all history in the data warehouse is associated with current dimension values. Initially, this seems to be a reasonable compromise. However, it's almost always more difficult to "do it right" when you have to circle back in a later phase. The unfortunate realities include the following:

- Following a successful initial implementation, the team faces pressure to roll out new capabilities and additional phases without time to revisit prior deliverables and add the required change-tracking capabilities. Thus, the rework ultimately required to support SCD requirements continues to expand.

- Once the ETL team finally has the bandwidth to address SCD, the ugly truth becomes apparent. Adding SCD type 2 capabilities into the historical data requires rebuilding every dimension that contains type 2 attributes; each dimension will have to have its primary key rekeyed to reflect the new historically appropriate type 2 rows. Rebuilding and rekeying even one core conformed dimension will unavoidably require reloading all impacted fact tables due to the new dimension key structures.

- Facing a possible rebuild of much of the data warehouse environment, many organizations will back away from the effort. Rather than reworking the existing historical data to restate the dimension and fact tables in their correct historical context, they implement the proper SCD strategies from a point-in-time forward. By compromising the implementation of proper SCD techniques in the initial development process, the organization has lost possibly years of important historic context.

Compromise 2: Failing to Embrace a Metadata Strategy

DW/BI environments spin off copious amounts of metadata. There is business metadata, process metadata, and technical infrastructure metadata that all needs to be vetted, captured, and made available. The ETL processes alone generate significant amounts of metadata.

Unfortunately, many ETL implementation teams do not embrace metadata early in the development process, putting off its capture to a future phase. This compromise typically is made because the ETL team does not "own" the overall metadata strategy. In fact, in the early stages of many new implementation efforts, it's not uncommon for there to be no designated owner of the metadata strategy.

Lack of ownership and leadership makes it easy to defer dealing with metadata, but that's a short-sighted mistake. Much of the critical business metadata is identified and captured, often in spreadsheet form, during the dimensional modeling and source-to-target mapping phases. What's more, most organizations use ETL tools to develop their environment, and these tools have capabilities to capture the most pertinent business metadata. Thus, the ETL development phase presents an opportune moment—often squandered—to capture richly described metadata. Instead, the ETL development team only captures the information required for their development purposes, leaving valuable descriptive information on the cutting room floor. Ultimately, in a later phase, much of this effort ends up being redone in order to capture the required information.

At a minimum, the ETL team should strive to capture the business metadata created during the data-modeling and source-to-target mapping processes. Most organizations find it valuable to focus initially on capturing, integrating, flowing, and, ultimately, surfacing the business metadata through their BI tool; other metadata can be integrated over time.

Compromise 3: Not Delivering a Meaningful Scope

The ETL team is often under the gun to deliver results under tight time constraints. Compromises must be made. Reducing the scope of the initial project can be an acceptable compromise. If, for example, a large number of schemas were included in the initial scope, one time-honored solution is to break that effort up into several phases. It's a reasonable, considered compromise assuming the DW/BI project team and sponsors are all fully, if not grudgingly, on board.

But it's a problem when the ETL team makes scope compromises without proactively communicating with the DW/BI project team and sponsors. Clearly, this is a recipe for failure and an unacceptable compromise.

This situation is often a symptom of deeper organizational challenges. It can start innocently enough, with shortcuts taken under pressure in the heat of the moment. In retrospect, however, these compromises would never have been made in the full light of day. In an effort to achieve overly ambitious deadlines, the ETL team might fail to handle data quality errors uncovered during the development process, fail to properly support late arriving data, neglect to fully test all ETL processes, or perform only cursory quality assurance checks on loaded data. These compromises lead to inconsistent reporting, an inability to tie into existing environments, and erroneous data, and often lead to a total loss of confidence among business sponsors and users. The outcome can be total project chaos and failure.

Make Compromises Openly and Honestly

Compromises may be necessary. The most common concession is to scale back an overly ambitious project scope; but key stakeholders need to be included in this decision. Other, less intrusive changes can be considered, such as reducing the number of years of back history used to seed a new environment, reducing the number of dimension attributes or number of metrics required in the initial phase (while being careful about SCD type 2 requirements), or reducing the number of source systems integrated in the initial phase. Just keep everyone informed and on the same page. The key is to compromise in areas that do not put the long term viability of the project at risk.

11.5 Doing the Work at Extract Time

Ralph Kimball, Intelligent Enterprise, *Feb 21, 2002*

Your mission as data warehouse designers is to publish data effectively. Fulfilling this mission means placing the data in the format and framework that is easiest for business users and application developers to use. Perhaps an apt analogy is a well-equipped kitchen. Ideally all the ingredients and tools needed to cook a meal are within easy reach. The ingredients are exactly what the recipe calls for, and the tools are meant for the job. Great cooks are notorious for using elaborate procedures out of view in the kitchen to produce just the right effect when the plate is served, so by analogy the back room chefs in the data warehouse should do much the same.

In the back room of your data warehouse, you must counter your natural minimalist tendencies when preparing the data for business users' and application developers' final consumption. In many important cases, you should deliberately trade off increased back room processing and increased front room storage requirements in exchange for symmetrical, predictable schemas that are understood by users, reduce application complexity, and improve query performance.

Making these trade-offs should be an explicit design goal for the data warehouse architect. But of course you must choose these trade-offs judiciously. A little sugar may make the recipe better, but a lot more sugar produces an inedible mess. Let's look at half a dozen situations where you'll do just enough work at extract time to really make a difference at query time. I'll also draw some boundaries so you'll know when not to overdo it and spoil the final result. Let's start with some rather narrow examples and gradually expand our scope.

Modeling Events across Multiple Time Zones

Virtually all measurements recorded in data warehouses have one or more time stamps. Sometimes these time stamps are simple calendar dates, but increasingly, we record the exact time to the minute or second. Also, most enterprises span multiple time zones, whether in the United States, Europe, Asia, or around the world.

You therefore have a natural dilemma. Either you standardize all your time stamps to a single well-identified time zone or the correct local wall clock time when the local measurement event occurred. You might be tempted to say, OK, so what's the big deal? If we want to convert from Greenwich Mean Time to local time, we just figure out which time zone the measurement was taken in, and we apply a simple offset.

Unfortunately, this doesn't work. In fact, it fails spectacularly. The rules for international time zones are horrendously complicated. There are more than 500 separate geographic regions with distinct time zone rules. Moral of the story: Don't compute time zones in your BI application. Rather add an extra time foreign key and put both standard and local times in your data. In other words, do the work at extract time, not query time, and give up a little data storage.

Verbose Calendar Dimensions

All fact tables should eschew native calendar date stamps in favor of integer-valued foreign keys that connect to verbose calendar dimensions. This recommendation is not based on a foolish dimensional design consistency, but rather it recognizes that calendars are complicated and applications typically need a lot of navigation help. For example, native SQL date stamps do not identify the last day of the month. Using a proper calendar date dimension, the last day of the month can be identified with a Boolean flag, making applications simple. Just imagine writing a query against a simple SQL date stamp that would constrain on the last day of each month. Here is an example where adding the machinery for an explicit calendar date dimension simplifies queries and speeds up processing by avoiding complex SQL.

There are some situations where you actually want to keep the native date stamp without creating a join to a dimension. If the date stamp in question, such as an employee birth date, falls outside the range of your enterprise date dimension, it may be nonsensical to extend the date dimension to encompass the date in question.

Keeping the Books across Multiple Currencies

The multiple time zone perspective discussed in the first example often occurs with the related issue of modeling transactions in multiple currencies. Again, there are two equal and legitimate perspectives.

If the transaction took place in a specific currency (say, Japanese yen) you obviously want to keep that information exactly. But if you have a welter of currencies, you'll find it hard to roll up results to an international total. Again, take the similar approach of expanding every currency-denominated field in the data warehouse to be two fields: local and standard currency value. In this case, you also need to add a currency dimension to each fact table to unambiguously identify the local currency.

Product Pipeline Measurements

Most of us think that product pipeline measurements are pretty simple, but complications become quickly apparent if you spend some time with manufacturing, distribution, and retail people, all talking about the same products in the same pipe. The manufacturing people want to see everything in carload lots or pallets. The distribution people want to see everything in shipment cases. The retail people can see things only in individual scan units.

So what do you put in the various fact tables to keep everyone happy? The wrong answer is to publish each fact in its local unit of measure context and leave it to the applications to find the right conversion factors in the product dimension tables! Yes, this is all theoretically possible, but this architecture places an unreasonable burden on the business users and application developers. Instead, present all the measured facts in a single standard unit of measure and then, in the fact table itself, provide the conversion factors to all the other desirable units of measure. That way, applications querying the pipeline data from any perspective have a consistent way to convert all the numeric values to the user's specific, idiosyncratic perspective.

Physical Completeness of the Profit and Loss

A profit and loss (P&L) fact table is powerful because you can usually count on it to present all the components of revenue and cost at a low level of granularity. After providing this wonderful level of detail, designers sometimes compromise their design by failing to provide all the intermediate levels of the P&L. For instance, the bottom line profit is calculated by subtracting the costs from the net revenue. This bottom line profit should be an explicit field in the data, even if it is equal to the algebraic sum of other fields in the same record. It would be a real shame if the user or application developer got confused at the last step and calculated the bottom line profit incorrectly.

Heterogeneous Products

In financial services, such as banking and insurance, a characteristic conflict often arises between the need to see all the account types in a single household view of the customer and the need to see the detailed attributes and measures of each account type. In a big retail bank, there may be 25 lines of business and more than 200 special measures associated with all the different account types. You simply cannot create a giant fact table and giant account dimension table that can accommodate all the heterogeneous products. The solution is to publish the data twice. First, create a single core fact table with only the four or five measures, such as balance, that are common to all account types. Then publish the data a second time, with the fact table and account dimension table separately extended for each of the 25 lines of business. Although this technique may seem wasteful because the huge fact table is effectively published twice, it makes the separate householding and line of business applications simple unto themselves.

Aggregations in General

Aggregations are like indexes: They are specific data structures meant to improve performance. Aggregations are a significant distraction in the back room. They consume processing resources, add complexity to the ETL applications, and take up a lot of storage. But aggregations remain the single most potent tool in the arsenal of the data warehouse designer to improve performance cost effectively.

Dimensional Modeling in General

By now I hope it is obvious that the most widely used back room trade-off made for the benefit of the business user is the practice of dimensional modeling. A dimensional model is a second normal form version of a third (or higher) normal form model. Collapsing the snowflakes and other complex structures of the higher normal form models into the characteristic flat dimension tables makes the designs simple, symmetrical, and understandable. Furthermore, database vendors have focused their processing algorithms on this well understood case to make dimensional models run really fast. Unlike most of the other techniques discussed in this article, the dimensional model approach applies across all horizontal and vertical application areas.

11.6 Is Data Staging Relational?

Ralph Kimball, DBMS, Apr 1998

The ETL data staging area is the back room of the data warehouse. It is the place where raw data is brought in, cleaned, combined, archived, and eventually exported to one or more dimensional schemas representing a business process subject area. The purpose of the back room is to get data ready for loading into a presentation server (a relational DBMS or an OLAP engine). We assume that the data staging area is not a query service. In other words, any database that is used for querying is assumed to be physically downstream from the back room.

Perhaps you don't even realize you have an ETL data staging area. Maybe your data just does a "touch and go" landing in between the legacy operational system and the presentation server. (That's an airplane metaphor.) You bring the data in briefly, assign a surrogate key, check the records for consistency, and send them on to the DBMS loader that is the presentation database.

If the legacy data is already available in a relational database, then it may make sense to perform all the processing steps within the relational framework, especially if the source relational database and the eventual target presentation database are from the same vendor. This makes even more sense when the source and target databases are on the same physical machine, or when there is a convenient high speed link between them.

However, there are many variations on this theme, and in many cases it may not make sense to load the source data into a relational database. In the detailed descriptions of the processing steps, we will see that almost all the processing consists of sorting, followed by a single, sequential pass through either one or two tables. This simple processing paradigm does not need the power of a relational DBMS. In fact, in some cases, it may be a serious mistake to divert resources into loading the data into a relational database when what is needed is sequential flat file processing.

Similarly, we will see that if the raw data is not in a normalized entity-relationship (ER) format, in many cases it does not pay to load it into a normalized physical model simply to check data relationships. The most important data integrity steps involving the enforcement of one-to-one and one-to-many relationships can be performed, once again, with simple sorting and sequential processing. Keeping these thoughts in mind, let's tease apart as many of the data transformation steps as we can.

Dimension Processing

In order to enforce referential integrity in our dimensional schemas, we almost always process the dimensions before processing the facts. We take the point of view that we always create a surrogate key for a dimension record before loading it into the dimensional schema. We will see in the next section that the identification of the correct surrogate key is a simple sequential file lookup.

A significant dimension processing problem is deciding what to do with a dimension description that does not match what is already stored in the data warehouse. If the revised description is taken to be a legitimate and reliable update to previous information, then you must use the techniques of slowly changing dimensions. If the revised description is merely an informal entry, the changed fields are ignored.

We need to recognize what has changed in the input data and generate the correct surrogate dimension key. Every data warehouse key should be a surrogate key because the data warehouse designer must have the flexibility to respond to changing descriptions and abnormal conditions in the raw data. If the actual physical join key between a dimension table and a fact table is a direct derivation of a natural key, sooner or later the designer is going to face an impossible situation. Natural keys can be reused or reformatted. Sometimes the dimension value itself must be "unknown." The most common need for a generalized key is when the data warehouse attempts to track a revised dimensional description and the natural key has not been changed.

Deciding What Has Changed

The first step in preparing a dimension record is to decide if we already have the record. The raw data will usually have a natural key value. This natural key value must be matched to the same attribute field in the current dimension record. The current dimension record can be found quickly with an updatable flag in the dimension record that identifies whether or not that record is the current one.

This matching of the incoming natural key to its partner in the current dimension record can be accomplished with a simple sequential pass over the raw data and the dimension table data, both sorted on the natural key. If the incoming dimensional information matches what we already have, then no further action is required. If anything in the incoming dimensional information has changed, we must apply a type 1, type 2, or type 3 change to the dimension.

- **Type 1: Overwrite.** We take the revised description in the raw data and overwrite the dimension table contents.
- **Type 2: Create a new dimension record.** We take the previous version of the dimension record and copy it, creating a new dimension record with a new surrogate key. The new surrogate key is the next sequential integer that represents max(surrogate key)+1 for the dimension under consideration. In order to speed processing, the max(surrogate key) value can be explicitly stored as metadata rather than computed each time it is needed. We then update this record with those fields that have changed and any other fields that are needed.
- **Type 3: Push down the changed value into an "old" attribute field.**

Regardless of which type change we make in processing the incoming dimension data, our choice will always devolve into a single-pass sequential file-processing step.

Combining from Separate Sources

Complex dimensions are usually derived from several sources. We may need to merge customer information from several lines of business and outside sources. There will usually not be a universal key that makes this merge operation easy. The raw data and the existing dimension table data may need to be sorted at different times on different fields in order to attempt a match. Sometimes a match may be based on fuzzy criteria; names and addresses may match except for minor spelling differences. In these cases, a sequential processing paradigm is more natural than an equijoin in a relational database. Fuzzy matches are not directly supported in a relational context in any case.

Another common merging task in data preparation is looking up text equivalents for production codes. In many cases, the text equivalents are sourced informally from a nonproduction source. Again, the task of adding the text equivalents can be done in a single pass by first sorting both the raw data and the text lookup table by the production code.

Data Cleaning

Data cleaning may also involve checking the spelling of an attribute or checking the membership of an attribute in a list. Once again, this is best accomplished by sorting the raw data and the permissible target values and processing them in a single comparison pass.

A useful data quality check, even when there isn't a defined membership list, is simply sorting the raw data on each text attribute; minor variations in spelling or punctuation will jump out. A sorted list can easily be made into a frequency count; the spellings with low frequencies can be checked and corrected.

Processing Names and Addresses

Incoming name and address fields are often packed into a small number of generic fields such as address1, address2, and address3. The contents of these generic fields need to be parsed and separated into all their constituents. Once names and addresses have been cleaned and put into standardized formats, they can be more easily deduplicated. What appears to be two customers at first turns out to be one; perhaps one has a P.O. box and the other has a street address, but the rest of the data clearly reveals that it is the same customer. This kind of duplication is best seen when the customer file is sorted repeatedly by different attributes.

A more powerful form of deduplicating is householding. In this case, an "economic unit" consisting of several individuals is linked under a single household identifier. The most common case would be a husband and wife who have various single and joint accounts with various slight differences in name spellings and addresses.

Validating One-to-One and One-to-Many Relationships

If two attributes in a dimension are supposed to have a one-to-one relationship, you can check it easily by sorting the dimension records on one of the attributes. A sequential scan of the data will show whether any violations exist. Each attribute value in the sorted column must have exactly one value in the other column. The check must then be reversed by sorting on the second column and repeating. Note that you don't put this data into a normalized schema to enforce the one-to-one mapping. You would have to fix any problems before you loaded the data, which is the whole point of this discussion.

A one-to-many relationship can similarly be verified by sorting on the "many" attribute and verifying that each value has only one value on the "one" attribute. Like most of the other processing steps, the paradigm is to first sort and then scan the files sequentially exactly once.

Fact Processing

The incoming fact records will have natural keys, not surrogate keys. The current correspondence between a natural key and the surrogate key must be looked up at load time. The fast lookup of surrogate keys can be facilitated by keeping a two-column table that maps all incoming natural keys to current surrogate keys. If the fast lookup table can be kept in memory during the key substitution, the fact table may not need to be sorted. If not, the quickest procedure would be to sort the incoming fact records in turn on each natural key and then perform the lookups of the surrogate keys in a single sequential scan.

Aggregate Processing

Each load of new fact records requires that aggregates be calculated or augmented. It is very important to keep the aggregates synchronous with the base data at every instant. If the base data is updated and placed online, but a delay ensues before the aggregates are updated, then the aggregates must be taken offline until they are ready. Otherwise, the aggregates will not correctly mirror the base data. In this situation, the DBA has a choice between delaying the entire publishing of the data until both the base data and aggregates are ready, or releasing the revised base data in a performance degraded mode while the aggregates are being updated offline.

The creation of aggregates is equivalent to the creation of break rows in a report. If aggregates representing product category totals are needed, then the incoming data must be sorted by product category. Several passes may be required to produce all the category aggregates.

The Bottom Line: Is Data Staging Relational?

Most ETL activities are actually not relational, but rather they are sequential processing. If your incoming data is in a flat file format, you should finish your ETL processes as flat files before loading the data into a relational database for presentation.

Don't be fooled by the ability to sequentially process a relational table with a relational cursor and programming language. Perhaps all you have done is turn your relational database into a kind of flat file. This is a little like driving an army tank down to the corner grocery store. You will be stunned by the speed of flat file sorting and sequential processing.

11.7 Staging Areas and ETL Tools

Joy Mundy, Design Tip #99, *Mar 4, 2008*

The majority of the data warehouse efforts we've recently worked with use a purchased tool to build the ETL system. A diminishing minority write custom ETL systems, which usually consist of SQL scripts, operating system scripts, and some compiled code. With the accelerated use of ETL tools, several of our clients have asked, does the Kimball Group have any new recommendations with respect to data staging?

In the old days, we would extract data from the source systems to local files, transfer those files to the ETL server, and sometimes load them into a staging relational database. That's three writes of untransformed data right there. We might stage the data several more times during the transformation process. Writes, especially logged writes into the RDBMS, are very expensive; it's a good design goal to minimize writes.

In the modern era, ETL tools enable direct connectivity from the tool to the source database. You can write a query to extract the data from the source system, operate on it in memory, and write it only once: when it's completely clean and ready to go into the target table. Although this is theoretically possible, it's not always a good idea, for the following reasons:

- The connection between source and ETL can break midstream.
- The ETL process can take a long time. If we are processing in stream, we'll have a connection open to the source system. A long-running process can create problems with database locks and stress the transaction system.
- You should always make a copy of the extracted, untransformed data for auditing purposes.

How often should you stage your data between source and target? As with so many issues associated with designing a good ETL system, there is no single answer. At one end of the spectrum, imagine you are extracting directly from a transaction system during a period of activity—your business is processing transactions all the time. Perhaps you also have poor connectivity between your source system and ETL server. In this scenario, the best approach is to push the data to a file on the source system, and then transfer that file. Any disruption in the connection is easily fixed by restarting the transfer.

At the other end of the spectrum, you may be pulling from a quiet source system or static snapshot. You have a high bandwidth and a reliable connection between snapshot and ETL system. In this case, even with large data volumes, it may be perfectly plausible to pull directly from the snapshot source and transform in stream.

Most environments are in the middle: Most current ETL systems stage the data once or twice between the source and the data warehouse target. Often that staging area is in the file system, which is the most efficient place to write data. But don't discount the value of the relational engine in the ETL process, no matter which ETL tool you're using. Some problems are extremely well suited to relational logic. Although it's more expensive to write data into the RDBMS, think about (and test!) the end-to-end cost of staging data in a table and using the relational engine to solve a thorny transformation problem.

11.8 Should You Use an ETL Tool?

Joy Mundy, Intelligent Enterprise, *Apr 6, 2008*

The ETL system is the most time-consuming and expensive part of building a data warehouse and delivering business intelligence to your user community. A decade ago the majority of ETL systems were hand crafted, but the market for ETL software has steadily grown and the majority of practitioners now use ETL tools in place of hand-coded systems.

Does it make sense to hand code an ETL system in 2015, or is an ETL tool a better choice? The Kimball Group generally recommends using an ETL tool, but a custom-built approach might still make sense. This article summarizes the advantages and disadvantages of ETL tools and offers advice on making the choice that's right for you.

Advantages of ETL Tools

There are numerous advantages associated with using an ETL tool:

- **Visual flow and self-documentation.** The single greatest advantage of an ETL tool is that it provides a visual flow of the system's logic. Each tool presents these flows differently, but even the least appealing of these user interfaces compare favorably to custom systems consisting of stored procedures, SQL and operating system scripts, and a handful of other technologies. Ironically, some ETL tools have no practical way to print the otherwise attractive self-documentation.

- **Structured system design.** ETL tools are designed for the specific problem of populating a data warehouse. Although they are only tools, they do provide a metadata-driven structure to the development team. This is particularly valuable for teams building their first ETL system.
- **Operational resilience.** Many of the home-grown ETL systems I've evaluated are fragile: They have too many operational problems. ETL tools provide functionality and practices for operating and monitoring the ETL system in production. You can certainly design and build a well-instrumented hand-coded ETL application, and ETL tool operational features have yet to mature. Nonetheless, it's easier for a DW/BI team to leverage the management features of an ETL tool to build a resilient system.
- **Data lineage and data dependency functionality.** We would like to be able to right-click on a number in a report and see exactly how it was calculated, where the data was stored in the data warehouse, how it was transformed, when the data was most recently refreshed, and what source system or systems underlay the numbers. Dependency is the flip side of lineage: We'd like to look at a table or column in the source system and know which ETL modules, data warehouse tables, OLAP cubes, and user reports might be affected by a structural change. In the absence of ETL standards that hand-coded systems could conform to, we must rely on ETL tool vendors to supply this functionality, though unfortunately, few have done so to date.
- **Advanced data cleaning functionality.** Most ETL systems are structurally complex with many sources and targets. At the same time, requirements for transformation are often fairly simple, consisting primarily of lookups and substitutions. If you have a complex transformation requirement, for example, if you need to deduplicate your customer list, you should use a specialized tool. Most ETL tools either offer advanced cleaning and deduplication modules (usually for a substantial additional price) or integrate smoothly with other specialized tools. At the very least, ETL tools provide a richer set of cleaning functions than are available in SQL.
- **Performance.** You might be surprised that performance is listed last under the advantages of the ETL tools. It's possible to build a high performance ETL system whether you use a tool or not. It's also possible to build an absolute dog of an ETL system whether you use a tool or not. I've never been able to test whether an excellent hand-coded ETL system outperforms an excellent tool-based ETL system; I believe the answer is that it's situational. But the structure imposed by an ETL tool makes it easier for an inexperienced ETL developer to build a quality system.

Disadvantages of ETL Tools

There are some downsides to using an ETL tool:

- **Software licensing cost.** The greatest disadvantage of ETL tools in comparison to handcrafted systems is the licensing cost for the ETL tool software. Costs vary widely in the ETL space, from several thousand dollars to hundreds of thousands of dollars.

- **Uncertainty.** We've spoken with many ETL teams that are uncertain and sometimes misinformed about what an ETL tool will do for them. Some teams undervalue ETL tools, believing they are simply a visual way to connect SQL scripts together. Other teams unrealistically overvalue ETL tools, imagining that building the ETL system with a tool will be more like installing and configuring software than developing an application.
- **Reduced flexibility.** A tool-based approach limits you to the tool vendor's abilities and scripting languages.

Build a Solid Foundation

There are some overarching themes in successful ETL system deployments regardless of which tools and technologies are used. Most important, and most frequently neglected, is the practice of designing the ETL system *before* development begins. Too often we see systems that just evolved without any initial planning. These systems are inefficient and slow, they break down all the time, and they're unmanageable. A solid system design should incorporate the concepts described in detail in article 11.2, *The 34 Subsystems of ETL.*

Good ETL system architects will design standard solutions to common problems, such as surrogate key assignment. Excellent ETL systems will implement these standard solutions most of the time but offer enough flexibility to deviate from those standards where necessary. There are usually half a dozen ways to solve any ETL problem, and each one may be the best solution in a specific set of circumstances. Depending on your personality and fondness for solving puzzles, this can be either a blessing or a curse.

One of the rules you should try to follow is to write data as seldom as possible during the ETL process. Writing data, especially to the relational database, is one of the most expensive tasks that ETL systems perform. ETL tools contain functionality to operate on data in memory and guide the developer along a path to minimize database writes until the data is clean and ready to go into the data warehouse table. However, the relational engine is excellent at some tasks, particularly joining related data. There are times when it is more efficient to write data to a table, even index it, and let the relational engine perform a join than it is to use the ETL tool's lookup or merge operators. We usually want to use those operators, but don't overlook the powerful relational database when trying to solve a thorny performance problem.

Whether your ETL system is hand coded or tool based, it's your job to design the system for manageability, auditability, and restartability. Your ETL system should tag all rows in the data warehouse with some kind of batch identifier or audit key that describes exactly which process loaded the data. Your ETL system should log information about its operations, so your team can always know exactly where the process is now and how long each step is expected to take. You should build and test procedures for backing out a load, and, ideally, the system should roll back transactions in the event of a midstream failure. The best systems monitor data health during extraction and transformation, and either improve the data or issue alerts if data quality is substandard. ETL tools can help you with the implementation of these features, but the design is up to you and your team.

Should you use an ETL tool? Yes. Do you have to use an ETL tool? No. For teams building their first or second ETL system, the main advantages of visual tools are self-documentation and a structured development path. For neophytes, these advantages are worth the cost of the tool. If you're a seasoned expert who has built dozens of ETL systems by hand, it's tempting to stick to what has worked well in the past. With this level of expertise, you can probably build a system that performs as well, operates as smoothly, and perhaps costs less to develop than a tool-based ETL system. But many seasoned experts are consultants, so you should think objectively about how maintainable and extensible a handcrafted ETL system might be once the consultant has moved on.

Don't expect to reap a positive return on investment in an ETL tool during the development of your first system. The advantages will come as that first phase moves into operation, as it's modified over time, and as your data warehouse grows with the addition of new business process models and associated ETL systems.

11.9 Call to Action for ETL Tool Providers

Warren Thornthwaite, Design Tip #122, *Apr 7, 2010*

Let me start by stating this article is an observation on the general state of ETL tools, not any specific ETL product, some of which are better or worse than average.

As I was recently walking through the steps to create a fully functional type 2 slowly changing dimension in one of the major ETL tools, it occurred to me that the ETL tools in general have stopped short of achieving their potential. Certainly they continue to add functionality, such as data profiling, metadata management, real-time ETL, and master data management. But for the most part, they are weak on the core functionality required to build and manage a data warehouse database. They haven't completed the job.

Let's look at the slowly changing dimension example that got me started on this topic. The product in question has a wizard that does a reasonable job of setting up the transformations needed to manage both type 1 and type 2 changes on attributes in the target dimension table. It even offers the choice of updating only the current row or all historical rows in the case of a type 1 change. What it doesn't do is manage the type 2 change tracking columns in the way we recommend. When a row changes, you need to set the effective date of the new row and the expiry date of the old row. I also like to update a current row indicator to easily limit a query to just current rows; I realize it's redundant with the value used as the expiration date on the current row (all rows with some distant future expiry date, such as 12/31/9999, are current rows by definition), but the current row indicator is commonly used for convenience and clarity. Unfortunately, this particular wizard will update either the dates or the current row indicator, but not both. So I have to add a step after the wizard to update the current rows.

Another problem with this specific wizard is that it doesn't provide any way to determine which type 2 columns changed to trigger the creation of a new row. This row reason information can be useful to audit the change tracking process; it can also be useful to answer business questions about the dynamics of the dimension. For example, if I have a row reason on a customer dimension, it's easy to answer the question "How many people moved last year?" Without the row reason, I have to join the table back on itself in a fairly complex way and compare the current row to the previous row and see if the zip code column changed. This is frustrating because I know the wizard knows which columns changed, but it's just keeping it secret.

I realize other ETL tools do a better job of automatically handling slowly changing dimensions. What's disappointing about the general state of ETL tools today is not the shortcomings of this particular SCD processing example, but the lack of effective support for most of the other 33 ETL subsystems, many of which we see in use in almost every data warehouse.

For example, junk dimensions are common dimensional modeling constructs. By combining multiple small dimensions into a single physical table, we simplify the model and remove multiple foreign key columns from the fact table. Creating and maintaining a junk dimension is not conceptually difficult, but it is tedious. You either create a cross-join of the rows in each dimension table if there aren't too many possible combinations, or you add combinations to the junk dimension as they occur in the incoming fact table. An ETL tool vendor that really wants to help their ETL developer customers should provide a wizard or transformation that automatically creates and manages junk dimensions, including the mapping of junk dimension keys to the fact table.

The same issue applies to mini-dimensions, which are column subsets extracted out of a large dimension and put into a separate dimension, which is joined directly to the fact row. Like junk dimensions, mini-dimensions are not conceptually difficult, but they are tedious to build from scratch every time. Unfortunately, I know of no ETL tool that offers mini-dimension creation and maintenance as a standard component or wizard.

ETL vendors are often enthusiastic about demonstrating that their tools can address the 34 subsystems we describe and teach in our design classes. Unfortunately the vendors' responses are typically either PowerPoint slides or demo-ware implemented by an analyst at headquarters, rather than by an ETL developer working in a production environment.

I could go on down the list of subsystems, but you get the idea. Please see article 11.2, *The 34 Subsystems of ETL*. Take a look and see how much time you spend coding these components by hand in your ETL environment. Then ask your ETL vendor what their plans are for making your job easier.

11.10 Document the ETL System

Joy Mundy, Design Tip #65, Mar 8, 2005

Whether you use an ETL tool or hand code your ETL system, it's a piece of software like any other and needs to be documented. As your data warehouse evolves, the ETL system evolves in step; you and your colleagues need to be able to quickly understand both the entire system architecture and the gritty details.

There's a widespread myth that ETL tools are self-documenting. This is true only in comparison with hand-coded systems. Don't buy into this myth: You need to develop an overall, consistent architecture for your ETL system. And, you need to document that system. Yes, that means writing a document.

The first step in building a maintainable ETL system is to stop and think about what you're doing. How can you modularize the system? How will those modules fit together into an overall flow? Develop your system so that you use a separate package, flow, module (or whatever your tool calls it) for each table in the data warehouse. Write a document that describes the overall approach; this can be a few pages, plus a screenshot or two.

Design a template module and group like activities together. The template should clearly identify which widgets are associated with extracts, transformations, lookups, conformation, dimension change management, and final delivery of the target table. Then, document this template flow in painstaking detail, including screenshots. The documentation should focus on what's going on, not on the detailed properties of each step or task.

Next, use the templates to build out the modules for each dimension and fact table. If you can control layout within your ETL tool, make the modules look similar, so people can look in the top left for the extract logic, and can more easily understand the squiggly mess in the middle. The modules for each dimension table should look really similar to each other; likewise for fact tables. Remember, it's only a *foolish* consistency that's the hobgoblin of small minds. The table-specific documentation should focus on what's different from the standard template. Don't repeat the details; highlight what's important. Pepper your ETL system with annotations, if your ETL tool supports them.

Finally, your ETL tool may support some form of self-documentation. Use this feature, but consider it an appendix to the real document because it's either relatively lame (screenshots) or overwhelmingly detailed (all the properties of all the objects); it's not, in our experience, particularly useful.

11.11 Measure Twice, Cut Once

Warren Thornthwaite, Intelligent Enterprise, *Dec 10, 2003*

Almost every major task in the lifecycle of a data warehouse project begins with a planning step. Unfortunately, it's human nature to skip the planning and jump right to the task at hand. With ETL, this goes something like "Let's just get some data loaded, then we'll figure out what we have to do to it." In this article, we describe a simple tool to help the ETL team focus on the big picture, while documenting the major events in moving data from source systems into the target dimensional model.

Objective: High Level ETL Plan

Our goal is to create a conceptual diagram that succinctly captures the ETL process. Figure 11-1 shows a simplified high level ETL plan for a fictitious utility company. It illustrates source-to-target data flows at the table level, along with the major transformations for the entire target dimensional model on a single page. In the real world, ETL plans often require several pages, depending on the complexity of the target model. Regardless, a graphical representation similar to Figure 11-1 is the desired result.

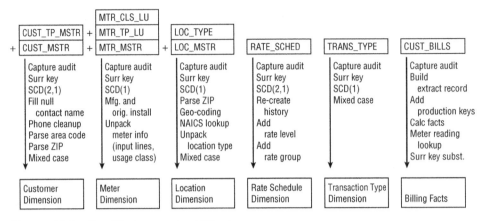

Figure 11-1: Simplified conceptual ETL plan.

The standard template for an ETL plan shows source tables at the top of the page, target tables at the bottom, and data flows, transformations, and processing notes in between. Let's work through an example by delving into the customer dimension table.

Inputs and Data Flows

There are several critical inputs to the ETL plan: the target dimensional model, source system data model, source-to-target mapping, and data content and quality information from the relevant sources. Figure 11-2 shows the target customer dimension.

Customer Dimension
Customer Key (PK)
Cust ID
Customer Name
Customer Contact Name
Customer Phone
Customer Area Code
Customer Address 1
Customer Address 2
Customer City
Customer State
Customer Full Zip Code
Customer 5 Digit Zip Code
Customer Type Description
Row Effective Date
Row End Date
Current Row Flag
Row Change Reason

Figure 11-2: Target customer dimension table.

Figure 11-3 shows sample data rows from two source tables. Access to the source system itself is particularly helpful. Directly querying the source tables to see the exact contents almost always reveals interesting issues.

Sample rows from CUST_MSTR table:

CUST_ID	NAME	CONTACT_NAME	CUST_PHN	ADDR1	CITY	STATE	ZIP	CUST_TYPE
MRN 64 28041-6	JOHN SAMPLE		415-999-9999	50 OAK STREET	SF	CA	94083-4425	R
QBS 71 34042-9	JEFFERSON DRY CLE	TOM JEFFER	510999-9999	120 MAIN ST	BERKELEY	CA	94123	B
DAG 21 10998-3	HEALTHY FARMS	JANE FARMER	707.999.9999	303 NAPA HWY	CALISTOGA	CA	94515	AG

Sample rows from CUST_TP_MSTR table:

CUST_TP	DSC
R	RESIDENTIAL
B	BUSINESS
AG	AGRICULTURE
X	UNKNOWN

Figure 11-3: Sample source rows.

The customer dimension data flow is fairly simple. We need to join the CUST_MSTR table with the CUST_TP_MSTR table to decode the customer type description called DSC in CUST_TP_MSTR. (We just read the source systems; we don't name them.) We draw a line straight from CUST_MSTR to the customer dimension and another line joining the CUST_TP_MSTR as shown in Figure 11-1. This join conveys standard denormalization, which is a common task when processing dimensions.

The plus sign on the CUST_TP_MSTR join line in Figure 11-1 is notational shorthand. Shocking as it may seem, sometimes the source system can't be trusted to enforce referential integrity. We may have CUST_MSTR rows with CUST_TYPE codes that do not have entries in the CUST_TP_MSTR table. In this case, we need outer join logic to find the rows in the CUST_MSTR that do not have corresponding entries in CUST_TP_MSTR, enter a default value for them, and notify the appropriate person to fix this data problem.

Transformation Notes

Once the data flow lines are drawn, we make notes along the line describing the transformations needed to get the data ready for loading into the target. The initial tasks noted along the data flow line apply to every dimension: capturing audit and data quality information, adding the surrogate key, and relaying the slowly changing dimension rules.

Capturing audit data can be as simple as saving the job name, start time, stop time, row counts, and system variables. Most ETL tools do this as a standard part of their logging process. We may want to include supplemental data quality measures.

The next notes inform the ETL team about surrogate keys and slowly changing dimensions (SCDs). The customer dimension will deal with attribute changes using a combination of type 2 (additional rows) and type 1 (attribute overwrite). We communicate this in the ETL plan with a simple notation like SCD (2,1).

We continue working through each column of the target dimension. The first one is simple; the Cust_ID is the transaction system key, so we just copy it over.

The customer name attribute in the target dimension table should be a straightforward copy of the NAME field in the source. However, the sample data in Figure 11-3 highlights potential transformations. We could split NAME into its individual elements: first name, middle name, and last name. But it also appears that the NAME field contains business entity names, not just individual names. Elementizing is particularly important if we need to integrate data from multiple sources. Separate elements are also important if the dimension supports customer contact, like direct mail or call center contact. Apparently we don't have either of these needs because NAME was not split out in the target model. Another possible NAME transformation would be to convert uppercase to title case. Because dimension values appear as row and column headers, cleaning up their appearance makes for more legible reports. Many of the data quality tools have special functions to help with case conversion.

The next column, CONTACT_NAME, is similar to NAME, although it has some null values. In general, we prefer values in every dimension attribute so users understand the meaning. In this case, we might substitute a default value like N/A during the extract process. Or we might copy the NAME field because CONTACT_NAME consistently contains the name of a person. Whatever choice we make is ultimately a business decision and needs to support the business requirements.

The next column in the target table is the customer phone number, and it has a few formatting problems. In this case, we will standardize the format so users can query it in a single, consistent fashion. We'll use the common area code, phone number pattern: (###) ###-####. The next column in the target table is the customer's area code. There must be a business reason for separating out the area code. The good news is it will be easy to do after standardizing the phone number.

The rest of the address fields in the source through state can be copied over fairly directly. Potential problems, such as mixed case and null values, may also need to be resolved with these fields, as we already discussed.

The ZIP field in Figure 11-3 is a mix of five-digit and nine-digit ZIP codes. In this case, the target dimension table gives us guidance on what we need to do because there are two target ZIP code fields: the full ZIP code and the 5-digit ZIP code. The full ZIP code field might be a direct copy of ZIP, or it might be a fully resolved nine-digit ZIP, depending on the requirements. The 5-digit ZIP field is just what we'd expect. Interestingly, significant demographic data is available at the five-digit ZIP code level. If you create a separate five-digit field, it's easy to join it with a five-digit demographic table to better understand your customer base profiles.

Finally, we do the customer type description lookup by joining to the CUST_TP_MSTR table as described earlier. Again, we may want to do a mixed case transformation on the description itself.

Finish Planning before Cutting

We follow the same process for the other target tables—gathering inputs, drawing data flows, and noting transformations. The goal is a compact, visually understandable model to plan and document the overall ETL process. It captures enough information so that a competent ETL professional could complete the detailed design and begin construction. A picture is worth a thousand words; however, we need to spend much more time doing our homework relative to the contents of Figure 11-1 rather than beautifying the graphical representation.

11.12 Brace for Incoming

Warren Thornthwaite, Intelligent Enterprise, *Aug 31, 2001*

Pressure to include external data in our data warehouses bears on us now from a combination of forces that have arisen in the past few years. First, we want to leverage the wealth of information we have about our customers. Second, much more data is available: We work more closely with business partners and third parties who provide us with data about our products, customers, and markets that we are unable to generate in-house. The third driver is the internet. The ready availability of data transfer tools for the internet has lowered the barriers to exchanging data with outside partners.

But don't think using external data is just another data extract and loading task. In reality, managing external data involves special awareness and procedures that may not be needed for data within the confines of your organization.

Typical Data Integration Process

So what does integrating data from a business partner typically involve? This new data source has to go through the full design and development cycle, except you probably do not have access to the source system or its developers. Plus, you have to find (or set up) a secure, reliable landing site for the data that both you and your business partner can access. Even worse, for those of us who feel data warehouse dependability is critical, you now have to manage a process in which someone else, outside your organization, owns half of the process.

First, you need to negotiate the nature of the extract. Will it be a snapshot at a point in time or a set of transactions? Will each file you receive be a full refresh or an incremental load? What is the time increment if it is incremental?

Next, you need to negotiate the file's format and contents. In this case, because you are the recipient of data from a source system you can't access directly, you need to ask lots of questions: What are the names and meanings of all the file's elements? What is the file's natural key? What are the relationships among the different fields? Can a field be null? When is it null? What does that mean?

Dust off your data warehouse naming conventions to make sure the field names make sense. For example, what does the field called "date" mean? Is it the subscription start date, or the last billed date, or the extract batch date? If it is the subscription start date, is it the original subscription start date, or the most recent subscription start date? If the file will be used as a dimension table, you may need to manage it as a slowly changing dimension.

Make sure the data includes lookup tables that provide descriptions of any codes in the main integration table. Refreshed copies of these lookup tables should be included with each load to ensure referential integrity with the main data set. Finally, it's also useful to add a unique batch identifier to each record in case you need to pull it back out of the database. You may want to manage this on the receiving end.

In addition to the contents, you will need to decide on file naming conventions. These should include a descriptive name, extract date, and source.

Your process needs to handle a test load. Distinguishing a test load from a production load could be done at the file level, either in the metadata or file name itself.

Your process may also need to handle versioning. Data sources often change how they define an element or the list of elements included in the extract. Your data integration partner should include a version number in the metadata so your process can handle the incoming data set appropriately. You should also make sure you've agreed on a process to resynchronize the two data sets. If you miss a load or receive bad data, you need a way to get back on track.

Once you agree on the nature and contents of the data set, you need to capture this information in a schema definition and associated documentation. XML is emerging as the ideal tool for this. A single XML file can contain multiple tables, along with the schema definition itself. Your data partner can send you a fully self-contained data set that has the schema, the metadata, any lookup tables, and the data set.

Architecture

Once you have specified the contents, you have to negotiate the architecture. This negotiation involves deciding who will provide the host site. You may find out that your company policy forbids inbound data access for security reasons. You may have to set up a special machine to host the process. This machine will need to be accessible to your data integration partner and to you. You also need to decide on the transport layer. FTP is the most common choice, but alternatives such as email, HTTP, and secure copy are becoming more popular. Figure 11-4 shows a typical architecture to support FTP-based integration.

Setup Process

Many companies use two firewalls, as shown in Figure 11-4, to provide a double layer of defense. In this example, the FTP server resides between these firewalls in an area network engineers call the DMZ, named after the military term *demilitarized zone*. Internet security is best left to the experts. Make sure you involve one in setting up your server.

Once you get the FTP server set up, create a user account and password. Limit the user account to the directory assigned to this partner. Securely send the name and password to your data partner.

At this point, your data partner can create a test file and send it over to the directory. Note that your data partner will have to create a complete, robust extract program with error and exception handling to generate the proper set of data on schedule. Their part of the process is very much like the standard extract portion of a typical data warehouse ETL process, along with the added complexity of cross-organizational data transfer.

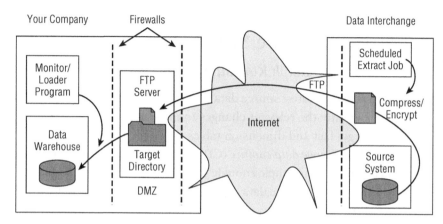

Figure 11-4: Typical architecture to support FTP-based integration.

Meanwhile, you need to set up a process that will monitor the directory to see when the file shows up. You can improve the monitoring process by agreeing on a verbose notification system with your data partner. When the file arrives, your process will need to run the file through data validation before it gets loaded. This validation includes making sure the file format is correct and the contents are as expected. It is a good idea to send a checksum along with the file to verify that you received the entire data set.

Exception Handling

Your process has to handle all kinds of potential problems. If the file doesn't arrive within a certain time period, the process should begin to send out notifications, both to you and your data partner. There should be an escalation procedure in place if the data doesn't arrive within a specified interval. Next, the process needs to deal with any content validation failures by either stopping the load or writing reject rows out to a suspense file. Finally, after the load is complete, you need to update the log files and send a success notification both internally and to your data partner.

Deceptive Simplicity

This kind of data integration can be extremely valuable in improving your users' understanding of their business. It can also make the data warehouse the sole source of information to be found anywhere by both partners.

However, do not be fooled by the innocent simplicity of the FTP `get` command. For data integration to work reliably, it needs to be a full system effort that involves multiple independent organizations, with its own infrastructure and control systems. Because the value of external information is so great, and all this processing can be a bit sticky, in the future you should keep an eye open for new companies that may provide secure, scalable platforms that let you start your data integration process without having to build everything from scratch.

11.13 Building a Change Data Capture System

Ralph Kimball, Design Tip #63, Jan 11, 2005

The ETL data flow begins with transferring the latest source data into the data warehouse. In almost every data warehouse, you must transfer only the relevant changes to the source data since the last transfer. Completely refreshing your target fact and dimension tables is usually undesirable.

Isolating the latest source data is called *change data capture* (CDC) on high level architecture diagrams. The idea behind change data capture seems simple enough: Just transfer the data that has been changed since the last load. But building a good change data capture system is not as easy as it looks.

Here are the goals I have for capturing changed data:

- Isolate the changed source data to allow selective processing rather than a complete refresh.
- Capture all changes (deletions, edits, and insertions) made to the source data including changes made through nonstandard interfaces.
- Tag changed data with reason codes to distinguish error corrections from true updates.
- Support compliance tracking with additional metadata.
- Perform the change data capture step as early as possible, preferably before bulk data transfer to data warehouse.

The first step in change data capture is detecting the changes! There are four main ways to detect changes:

1. **Audit columns.** In most cases, the source system contains audit columns. Audit columns are appended to the end of each table to store the date and time a record was added or modified. Audit columns are usually populated via database triggers that are fired off automatically as records are inserted or updated. Sometimes, for performance reasons, the columns are populated by the operational application instead of database triggers. When these fields are loaded by any means other than database triggers, you must pay special attention to their integrity. You must analyze and test each of the columns to ensure that is a reliable source to indicate changed data. If you find any NULL values, you must find an alternative approach for detecting change. The most common environment situation that prevents the ETL process from using audit columns is when the fields are populated by the application and the DBA team allows

"back end" scripts to modify data. If this is the situation in your environment, you face a high risk that you will eventually miss changed data during your incremental loads.

2. **Database log scraping.** Log scraping effectively takes a snapshot of the database redo log at a scheduled point in time (usually midnight) and scours it for transactions that affect the tables you care about for your ETL load. Sniffing involves a polling of the redo log, capturing transactions on the fly. Scraping the log for transactions is probably the messiest of all techniques. It's not rare for transaction logs to "blow out," meaning they get full and prevent new transactions from occurring. When this happens in a production transaction environment, the knee-jerk reaction for the DBA is to empty the contents of the log so the business operations can resume, but when a log is emptied, all transactions within them are lost. If you've exhausted all other techniques and find log scraping is your last resort for finding new or changed records, persuade the DBA to create a special log to meet your specific needs.

3. **Timed extracts.** With a timed extract you typically select all of the rows where the date in the create or modified date fields equals `SYSDATE-1`, meaning you've got all of yesterday's records. Sounds perfect, right? Wrong. Loading records based purely on time is a common mistake made by most new ETL developers. This process is horribly unreliable. Time-based data selection loads duplicate rows when it is restarted from mid-process failures. This means that manual intervention and data cleanup is required if the process fails for any reason. Meanwhile, if the nightly load process fails to run and misses a day, there's a risk that the missed data will never make it into the data warehouse.

4. **Full database "diff compare."** A full diff compare keeps a full snapshot of yesterday's database, and compares it, record by record against today's database to find what changed. The good news is that this technique is fully general: You are guaranteed to find every change. The obvious bad news is that in many cases this technique is very resource intensive. If you must do a full diff compare, try to do the compare on the source machine so that you don't have to transfer the whole database into the ETL environment. Also, investigate using cyclic redundancy checksum (CRC) algorithms to quickly tell if a complex record has changed.

This article offers only a teaspoon sip of the issues surrounding change data capture. To dig deeper, read *The Data Warehouse ETL Toolkit* for more detail on each of the preceding alternatives.

11.14 Disruptive ETL Changes

Ralph Kimball, Design Tip #126, Aug 3, 2010

Many enterprise data warehouses are facing disruptive changes brought about by increased usage by operations and the exploding interest in customer behavior. My impression is that many shops have implemented isolated adaptations to these new forces but haven't lifted their gaze to the horizon to realize that the data warehouse design landscape has changed in some significant ways, especially in the ETL back room.

The overarching change is modifying the EDW to support mixed workload operational applications where low latency data coexists with historical time series and many other customer facing applications and data sources. The early operational data store (ODS) implementations were restricted to tiny answer set fetches of highly constrained transactional questions such as "was the order shipped?" Today's operational users are drastically more demanding.

Here are seven disruptive changes coming from operational requirements. I wouldn't be surprised if you were facing all seven of these at once:

1. **Driving data latency toward zero.** The urge to see the status of the business at every instant is hard to resist. Not everyone needs it, but for sure someone will claim they do. But as you approach zero latency data delivery, you have to start throwing valuable ETL processes overboard, until finally you only have the vertical retrace interval on your display (1/60th of a second) in which to perform useful ETL work. Although this extreme is admittedly ridiculous, now I have your attention. And keep in mind, if you have true zero latency data delivery, the original source application has to provide the computing power to refresh all the remote BI screens. The lesson here is to be very cautious as your users tighten their requirements to approach zero latency delivery.

2. **Integrating data across dozens, if not hundreds, of sources.** Customer behavior analytics is the rage in the operational/BI world, and there is a lot of money chasing behavior data. Operational and marketing people have figured out that almost any data source reveals something interesting about customer behavior or customer satisfaction. I have seen a number of shops struggling to integrate dozens of not-very-compatible customer facing data collection processes.

3. **Instrumenting and actively managing data quality.** After talking idealistically about data quality for fifteen years, the data warehouse community is now turning actively to do something about it. Within the data warehouse, this takes the form of data quality filters that test for exceptional conditions, centralized schemas that record data quality events, and audit dimensions attached to final presentation schemas. Things get really interesting when you try to address this requirement while simultaneously driving data latency toward zero.

4. **Tracking custody of data for compliance.** Maintaining the chain of custody for critical data subject to compliance means that you can no longer perform SCD type 1 or type 3 processing on dimension tables or fact tables. Check out article 10.29, *Compliance-Enabled Data Warehouses*, to understand how to solve this problem.

5. **Retrofitting major dimensions for true type 2 tracking.** Organizations are revisiting earlier decisions to administer important dimensions, such as customer, with type 1 (overwrite) processing when changes are reported. This provokes a significant change in the ETL pipeline, as well as a serious commitment to the use of surrogate keys. Surrogate keys, of course, simplify the creation of conformed dimensions that combine data from multiple original sources.

6. **Outsourcing and moving to the cloud.** Outsourcing offers the promise of having someone else handle the administration, backing up, and upgrading of certain applications. Outsourcing may also be combined with a cloud implementation, which may be an attractive alternative for storing operational data that is subject to very volatile volume surges. The right cloud implementation can scale up or down on very short notice.

7. **Harvesting light touch data that cannot be loaded into an RDMS.** Finally, a number of organizations that have significant web footprints are capable of collecting tens or hundreds of millions of web page events per day. This data can grow into petabytes (thousands of terabytes) of storage. Often, when these "light touch" web events are first collected as stateless micro-events, their useful context is not understood until much later. For instance, if a web visitor is exposed to a product reference, and then days or weeks later actually buys the product, then the original web page event takes on much more significance. The architecture for sweeping up and sessionizing this light touch data often involves MapReduce and Hadoop technology. Check out Wikipedia for more on these new technologies.

I think that this list of what are today disruptive changes to your ETL pipelines are actually a glimpse of the new direction for enterprise data warehousing. Rather than being exotic outliers, these techniques may well become the standard approaches for handling customer oriented operational data.

11.15 New Directions for ETL

Ralph Kimball, Design Tip #169, *Sep 8, 2014*

This article reflects on the remarkable durability of the basic ETL paradigm, while at the same time recognizing some profound changes that must be addressed. These changes are due to new data demands, new classes of users, and new technology opportunities.

Extreme Integration

Most organizations are realizing that they have dozens, if not hundreds of potential data sources, especially those that are customer facing. The established best practices of manual data conforming are becoming unscalable. A new class of software startups are offering statistical data conforming that can provide usable matching of entities, such as customers, that approach the accuracy of manual data conforming, but at drastically higher speeds. The standard notion of a human dimension manager may give way to a "robot dimension manager!"

Extreme Variety

The big data revolution has trumpeted the four V's: volume, velocity, variety, and value. In my opinion, the most interesting and challenging V is variety. Standard relational databases and standard ETL pipelines are ill-equipped to handle unstructured text, hyper-structured machine data, graph relationships (think Facebook and LinkedIn), or images. As the value of these data types grows, ETL must change with new pipelines and new logic.

Huge Volumes

The lid has been off of data volumes for some time but it has reached a ridiculous point where even normal Main Street organizations want to access petabytes of data. Even when this data consists of conventional text and numbers (think log data), the data is a whale trapped in a swimming pool. You don't dare move or copy the data to a new place for processing.

Real-Time Delivery

Reports and ad hoc queries remain important but the new phrase is operational analytics, which combine high performance data ingestion, real-time data quality checking and data conforming, and finally sophisticated analytics. All of this requires forgoing conventional batch processing and slow periodic updates of the available data.

Rise of the Analyst and Monetization of Data Insights

Data scientist is the new name for analysts who mine data for insights and propose experiments in marketing strategies (often in real time) that can affect revenue, profitability, and customer satisfaction. These data scientists, frequently working in business departments, are often skilled at communicating directly with senior management, effectively bypassing IT. The challenge is whether IT can become a participant in this process, understanding the ETL pipelines, and creating a stable data infrastructure beyond the prototypes built by the data scientists.

New Analytic Tools

Data scientists and others are employing advanced analytic tools that can take several forms. Some of these tools are statistical algorithms found in advanced packages such as MadLib that can be loaded into some DBMS systems. Others are custom user defined functions (UDFs) typically programmed in C. Finally, others are separate BI tools that consume the data warehouse data.

Columnar Data Stores and In-Memory Databases

The sweet spot for high performance dimensional databases is a combination of columnar data stores and in-memory processing. Columnar data stores are typically excellent at processing many simultaneous joins against a fact table and tolerating very wide dimension tables. As the cost of memory continues to decline, it becomes feasible to stand up terabytes of RAM in a distributed shared-nothing environment. Taking advantage of this physical RAM is still a work in progress, and this balancing is a key aspect of the ETL pipeline architecture. The MapReduce processing framework typically found in Hadoop clusters addresses this problem for certain kinds of "relation-scan" analyses, but MapReduce relies on a shuffle step that moves the data from node to node to achieve balancing. Expect to see much more progress that will affect ETL in order to take advantage of the huge performance advantages offered by columnar in-store architectures.

Data Virtualization on Steroids

Finally, the venerable approach of defining simple SQL views to present tables in more usable formats, has given way to data virtualization, which now has become a major tool that in some cases replaces conventional ETL. In its basic form, data virtualization replaces physical data transformations with equivalent computations every time the data is accessed. Data virtualization becomes a classic trade-off between query performance and speed of deployment. Data virtualization is great for prototyping and data exploration, and when the prototyping phase is over, data virtualization can be replaced with true conventional ETL where the data is permanently moved and transformed.

Summary

If anything, ETL has become a bigger part of the data warehouse mission. We used to say that ETL consumed 50 to 70 percent of the data warehouse costs, risks, and implementation time. That number may now be more like 70 to 80 percent, especially considering the challenges described in this article. We can expect many new ETL innovations in the years ahead.

Data Quality Considerations

Many data warehouses wring their hands and lament about data quality problems, but don't do anything about them. This section takes the attitude that not only can you measure data quality but you can return to the source to correct the problems, and then measure your successes. Warren and Joy frame the problem of facing the data quality problem head on, then we follow with one of Ralph's early articles on the business need for quality data. After that we take an in-depth look at an overall architecture for managing data quality. Subsequent articles provide guidance on assessing quality and addressing shortfalls.

11.16 Dealing With Data Quality: Don't Just Sit There, Do Something!

Warren Thornthwaite, Design Tip #117, Sep 30, 2009

Most data quality problems can be traced back to the data capture systems because, historically, they have only been responsible for the level of data quality needed to support transactions. What works for transactions often won't work for analytics. In fact, many of the attributes we need for analytics are not even necessary for the transactions, and therefore capturing them correctly is just extra work. By requiring better data quality as we move forward, we are requiring the data capture system to meet the needs of both transactions and analytics. Changing the data capture systems to get better data quality is a long term organizational change process. This political journey is often paralyzing for those of us who didn't expect to be business process engineers in addition to being data warehouse engineers!

Do not let this discourage you. You can take some small, productive steps in the short term that will get your organization on the road to improving data quality.

Perform Research

The earlier you identify data quality problems, the better. It will take much more time if these problems only surface well into the ETL development task, or worse, after the initial rollout. And it will tarnish the credibility of the DW/BI system (even though it's not your fault).

Your first pass at data quality research should come as part of the requirements definition phase early in the lifecycle. Take a look at the data required to support each major opportunity. Initially, this can be as simple as a few counts and ratios. For example, if the business folks wanted to do geographic targeting, calculating the percentage of rows in the customer table where the postal code is NULL might be revealing. If 20 percent of the rows don't have a postal code, you have a problem. Make sure you include this information in the requirements documentation, both under the description of each opportunity that is impacted by poor data quality, and in a separate data quality section.

The next opportunity for data quality research is during the dimensional modeling process. Defining each attribute in each table requires querying the source systems to identify and verify the attribute's domain (the list of possible values the attribute can have). You should go into more detail at this point, investigating relationships among columns, such as hierarchies, referential integrity with lookup tables, and the definition and enforcement of business rules.

The third major research point in the lifecycle is during the ETL system development. The ETL developer must dig far deeper into the data and often discovers more issues.

A data quality/data profiling tool can be a big help for data quality research. These tools allow you to do a broad survey of your data fairly quickly to help identify questionable areas for more detailed investigation. However, if you don't have a data quality tool in place, don't stop your research until you find the best tool and the funds to purchase it. Simple SQL statements like:

```
SELECT PostalCode, COUNT(*) AS RowCount
FROM Dim_Customer GROUP BY PostalCode ORDER BY 2 DESC;
```

will help you begin to identify anomalies in the data immediately. You can get more sophisticated later, as you generate awareness and concern about data quality.

It's a good idea to include the source systems folks in the research process. If they have a broader sense of responsibility for the data they collect, you may be able to get them to adjust their data collection processes to fix the problems. If they seem amenable to changing their data collection processes, it is a good idea to batch together as many of your concerns as possible while they are in a good mood. Source systems folks often aren't happy at updating and testing their code too frequently. Don't continuously dribble little requests to them!

Share Findings

Once you have an idea of the data quality issues you face, and the analytic problems they will cause, you need to educate the business people. Ultimately, they will need to redefine the data capture requirements for the transaction systems and allocate additional resources to fix them. They won't do this unless they understand the problems and associated costs.

The first major chance to educate on data quality problems is as part of the opportunity prioritization session with senior management. You should show examples of data quality problems, explain how they are created, and demonstrate their impact on analytics and project feasibility. Explain that you will document these in more detail as part of the modeling process, and at that point you can reconvene to determine your data quality strategy. Set the expectation that this is work and will require resources.

The dimensional modeling process is the second major education opportunity. All of the issues you identify during the modeling process should be discussed as part of documenting the model, and an approach to remedying the problem should be agreed upon with key business folks.

At some point, you should have generated enough awareness and concern to establish a small scale data governance effort, which will become the primary research and education channel for data quality.

Conclusion

Improving data quality is a long, slow educational process of teaching the organization about what's wrong with the data, the cost in terms of accurate business decision making, and how best to fix it. Don't let it overwhelm you. Just start with your highest value business opportunity and dive into the data.

11.17 Data Warehouse Testing Recommendations

Joy Mundy, Design Tip #134, May 4, 2011

A DW/BI system is challenging to test. Standard testing methodology tests one little thing at a time, but a DW/BI system is all about integration and complexity, not to mention large data volumes. Here are my top five recommendations for building and executing a testing environment for your DW/BI project:

1. **Create a small static test database, derived from real data.**

   You want it to be small so tests can run quickly. You want it to be static so that the expected results are known in advance. And you want it to be derived from real data because there's nothing like real data to give you a realistic combination of scenarios, both good and bad. You will need to "cook" additional rows into the test database to test any branch of your ETL code that covers a data scenario not included in the original test data.

2. **Test early and often.**

   Start testing as soon as you write a line of code (or connect two boxes in your ETL tool's user interface). Developers do this all the time, of course, developing and running unit tests to ensure their code does what it's supposed to do. Many developers aren't as good about keeping track of all those tests, and running them often. Daily. Every time you check in code. If you run your tests daily, and prioritize fixing any tests that broke yesterday, it will be easy to determine what went wrong.

Unit testing assures that a developer's code works as designed. System testing ensures that the entire system works, end to end, according to specifications. System testing should also begin early. There's an official test phase before you go live; this test phase is for running tests and fixing problems, not for identifying what the tests should be and how to run them. Start system testing early in the development process, so all the kinks are worked out long before the pressure-cooker system testing phase begins.

3. **Use testing tools and automate the test environment.**

The suggestion to test early and often is practical only if you automate the process. No developer is going to spend the last hour of the work day babysitting unit tests! And few teams can afford a full time tester to do that work on the developers' behalf.

To automate testing, you need tools. Many organizations will already have system quality assurance testing tools in place. If you don't, or if you're convinced your tools won't meet the needs of the DW/BI system testing, try googling "software quality assurance tools" for an overwhelming list of products and methodologies available at a wide range of costs.

All commercial software test tools will allow you to enter tests, execute tests, log the results of test runs, and report on those results. For unit testing and data quality testing, define tests to run a query in the source and target data warehouse. You're looking for row counts and amounts to match up.

A testing tool used for DW/BI testing must be able to run a script that sets up the test environment before the tests are run. Tasks you may need to execute include:

- Restoring a virtual machine environment with clean test data
- Modifying the static test data with special rows to test unusual conditions
- Running your ETL program

After the tests are executed and logged, end with a cleanup script, which may be as simple as dropping the VM environment.

Standard testing methodology has you change one thing, run a test, and log results. In the DW/BI world, you should expect to group together many tests into a test group. Even with a tiny test database, you don't want to execute your ETL code for each of the hundreds of unit tests that you should be running.

4. **Enlist the business users to define system tests.**

We need the business users' expertise to define good system tests. How do we know the data is correct? How do we know that query performance meets their expectations? Enlisting business users in the test specification process will ensure better testing than if the DW/BI team just made up tests based on what they think is interesting. Engaging key business users in the quality assurance process also provides a huge credibility boost.

5. **The test environment must be as similar as possible to the production environment.**

It is vitally important that the test environment be similar to production. Ideally, it's exactly the same hardware, software, and configuration. In the real world, relatively few organizations have the budget for two big DW servers. But any organization can, and should, make the following elements match up:

- **Drive configuration (relative names for drives).** Disk is cheap and you should be able to duplicate your disk for testing. But if you can't, at least make the drive letters and database file layout the same. Many people have whined at me that this is so much work to change the environment and make them the same. Yes it is! And so much better to do it now than in the final testing phase of your project.
- **Software versions from the operating system to the database to the users' desktops, and everywhere in between**
- **Server layout.** If the reporting system software will be on its own server in production, test it that way.
- **Security roles and privileges for back room service accounts.** Your deployment is virtually guaranteed to fail if you don't test security roles first. I don't know why, but it always seems to go wrong.

If you follow these suggestions, especially the suggestion for continuous testing, you are likely to have a smooth, crisis-free test phase and move into production on schedule. If not, you're running a serious risk of having an otherwise fabulous project be delayed interminably in QA hell, with business users and management rattling the doors.

11.18 Dealing with Dirty Data

Ralph Kimball, DBMS, Sep 1996

As you read Ralph's comments regarding the data cleaning tool marketplace, remember this article was written in 1996. In spite of that, this article remains surprisingly apt.

A theme in data warehousing that is universally recognized, but far too often ignored, is the cleanliness of the warehouse data. From hundreds of meetings with IT staff, I have identified three consistent themes. Although these three themes stand out dramatically as the biggest problems in corporate data access, the same IT staffs that identify them are only attacking the first two. The three themes can be expressed by the following comments:

- **The data access issue.** "We have one of the world's largest sets of data but we can't get access to it."
- **The query tool issue.** "I want the system to show me what is important and then I want to ask why."
- **The data integrity issue.** "We know that some of our data isn't very good. For instance, we don't have a single, centrally maintained customer list."

Given the universality of these comments, it is strange that entire industries are being organized around the first two issues, but the third issue seems to be something that we don't want to talk about.

The database marketplace has responded to the need for data access with client/server architectures, dedicated data warehouse hardware and software, and whole families of communications schemes to connect users to their data. The query tool marketplace is an embarrassment of riches. There are dozens of ad hoc query tools, report writers, and application development environments. We are well into the second generation of powerful tools for data warehousing user applications with dimensional OLAP/ROLAP tools and the hot new data mining tools. Yet the third issue, data integrity, languishes in the backwater of data warehousing. It is talked about briefly and then the door is closed. There is a definite avoidance of the topic and very few plans in place to address data integrity at the same level as those that address data access or query tools.

Applications Where Good Data Is Critical

One of the reasons for the lack of attention to data integrity is that IT staffs don't adequately consider the business impact of bad data. To put it more positively, we must better appreciate our opportunities for really powerful data warehouse applications that vitally depend on good data. Following is a sampler of such applications, starting with a whole series of customer-based applications:

- **Marketing communications.** If you want to understand who your customers are, and if you want to communicate effectively with them on the phone and via mail, you must have an extraordinarily clean customer list. You destroy your credibility by using nonsensical or misspelled addresses or by sending multiple letters to the same person. Even worse, if the address is invalid in some way, the letter never arrives.

- **Customer matching.** You want to find the same customer when the customer buys a second or a third product from you. Customer matching is a major issue in banking and healthcare where separate customer (or patient) encounters are often listed separately. The average bank has great difficulty listing all of the separate accounts of a given individual, although the reverse process of listing all the individuals in a specific account causes no trouble.

- **Retail householding.** You want to find a group of people who comprise a family, each of whom is a customer. When you correctly identify the household, you can communicate coherently with its members. At that time you can identify the overall needs of the household and suggest an effective consolidation or expansion of products. This process is called "cross-selling." Cross-selling your own customer base is recognized as one of the most effective ways to increase sales.

- **Commercial householding.** You want to look at your customers to find multiple commercial organizations that turn out to be part of a larger parent organization. Many times you may not be aware that you are dealing with various "parts of a whole."

- **Targeted marketing.** You want to generate a mailing list by sifting through the demographic and behavioral attributes of a large customer list. The completeness and correctness of the attributes is crucial.

- **Combining information systems after an acquisition.** An increasingly common problem is merging customer and product lists from incompatible information systems after an acquisition. Organizationally, it may be easy to imagine combining staffs and moving everything to the corporate system after an acquisition, but what do you do with the data itself? Sometimes the customer list is the most valuable asset of the acquired organization.
- **Merging external data with internal data.** This problem is structurally very similar to combining data after an acquisition. Although the external data might be syndicated and cleaner than average, it will still probably not match internal data, such as product names, customer names, or geographic names.
- **Tracking product sales.** In large retail environments with hundreds of stores and hundreds of thousands of products, it is crucial to have a centrally maintained master product file with clean descriptors. A good retail product file will have at least 50 separate descriptors for each product. These descriptors are used by managers and analysts throughout the organization to group and dissect the various kinds of product data, all the way from purchasing at the back door to sales at the front door. I recently designed a comprehensive data warehouse for a large drugstore chain. A major product category in this chain was "lozenges," and the word "lozenge" was spelled 20 different ways in the product file!
- **Medical records.** All of us are affected by the quality of data in medical records. We want the diagnosis and procedure to be correct and readable, both for our medical safety and for billing and insurance purposes. A major headache in the medical insurance industry is the correct identification of the provider physician, clinic, or hospital. This is a variant of the earlier customer matching application.

The preceding list is, in actuality, endless. Every meaningful data warehouse application needs good data. William Weil of Innovative Systems, Inc. recently performed an interesting analysis of the cost of bad data. He assumes that a given customer list for a company is 90 percent accurate. Of the 10 percent of the customers with inaccuracies, 5 percent (0.5 percent of the overall file) have unusable addresses that could have been repaired. In my experience, these numbers seem reasonable, perhaps even low.

Weil goes on to assume that the annual value of cross-selling or retaining each customer is between $100 and $1000. In a big business with a million customers, 0.5 percent (or 5000 customers) will be lost because you can't find them in your database. Multiplying the 5000 affected customers by $100 to $1000 results in a direct cost of $500,000 to $5,000,000 annually for bad data. Although the detailed numbers are debatable, there is a fundamental and compelling ring to this argument. Bad data is expensive, and it is time we face the data cleaning problem head on.

The Science of Data Cleaning

Although data cleaning can take many forms, most of the important data cleaning examples from the previous application list arise from the need for good descriptions of tangible things such as customers, products, procedures, and diagnoses. The current marketplace and technology for data cleaning are heavily focused on customer lists, so I will use them to talk about the underlying science.

Data cleaning is much more than simply updating a record with good data. Serious data cleaning involves decomposing and reassembling the data. You can break down the cleaning into six steps: elementizing, standardizing, verifying, matching, householding, and documenting.

To illustrate these six steps, consider the following fictitious address:

Ralph B and Julianne Kimball Trustees for Kimball Fred C
Ste. 116
13150 Hiway 9
Box 1234 Boulder Crk
Colo 95006

Perhaps this address has been entered in five fields called address_1 through address_5. There may be no reliable ordering of the parts of the address. A critical part of this address has been entered incorrectly; we will find this mistake in a minute.

The first step in cleaning this address is to elementize it: data cleaners' jargon for parsing it correctly. Elementizing the address could produce a result such as:

Addressee First Name(1): Ralph
Addressee Middle Initial(1): B
Addressee Last Name(1): Kimball
Addressee First Name(2): Julianne
Addressee Last Name(2): Kimball
Addressee Relationship: Trustees for
Relationship Person First Name: Fred
Relationship Person Middle Name: C
Relationship Person Last Name: Kimball
Street Address Number: 13150
Street Name: Hiway 9
Suite Number: 116
Post Office Box Number: 1234
City: Boulder Crk
State: Colo
Five Digit ZIP: 95006

This list of standard elements is dependent on what is found when the address is analyzed. Ralph and Julianne could have been trustees for an organization rather than an individual, in which case some of the element types would have been different.

The second step is to standardize the elements. At least four of the elements must be put in a more standard form. We have already dropped "Ste" because we have recognized it as suite. We may suspect that "Hiway 9" should actually read "Highway 9." Make this a provisional change, and in the verification pass make sure that the actual street is called "Highway 9." Also, change "Boulder Crk" to "Boulder Creek" and "Colo" to "Colorado."

The third step is to verify the consistency of the standardized elements. In other words, are there any mistakes in content? Although it may not be obvious, there is a glaring content error in the address. Boulder Creek in ZIP code 95006 is in California, not Colorado. Because two of the three pieces of data point to California, change the state name to California. You should probably also flag this record for further verification. For example, if you have another address instance for either Ralph Kimball or Julianne Kimball, you could verify the correct state. This would be even more urgent if you discovered a legitimate Boulder Creek in Colorado.

Now that you have elementized, standardized, and verified the address, you are in a good position to perform the fourth and fifth steps: matching and householding. Matching consists of finding either Ralph Kimball or Julianne Kimball in other customer records and ensuring that all of the elements of all the addresses are identical.

Householding consists of recognizing that Ralph and Julianne constitute a household because they share the same address, although you must be careful to exclude people who live in different apartments in a single large building. You may have information in another internal or external data source that indicates that Ralph and Julianne are married.

The sixth step of data cleaning consists of documenting the results of elementizing, standardizing, verifying, matching, and householding in metadata. This helps ensure that subsequent cleaning episodes will be better able to recognize addresses and that user applications will be better able to slice, dice, and understand the customer database.

All of the leading data cleaning vendors interviewed for this article noted that these six data cleaning steps require sophisticated software and extensive embedded expert knowledge. The expert knowledge is embedded in fuzzy matching algorithms, address parsing algorithms, and large multi-million entry lookup tables that provide synonyms for parts of names and addresses. In other words, a serious data cleaning system is a large software system.

Marketplace Opportunity for Data Cleaning

I wonder whether current data cleaning companies realize how huge this marketplace may be. I also wonder whether they are prepared for an explosive growth of demand for multiple hardware and operating system platforms and application areas other than name and address list processing. The data warehouse marketplace has tremendous vitality; thousands of IT organizations worldwide feel driven to build data warehouses. Countless IT organizations realize they have a data cleaning problem but defer facing this issue in their haste to bring up their first warehouse. All that is needed to grow this marketplace exponentially is someone with a potent, widely applicable product for data cleaning and the ability to convince the marketplace that it is easy to use.

It seems very possible that the whole marketplace might suddenly decide that it needs a data cleaning capability that:

- Plugs into the overall data extract pipeline as a module
- Reads and writes metadata from the extract tools and provides query tools with additional metadata
- Is available on UNIX and has native interfaces to relational and desktop DBMSs
- Provides data cleaning support for product lists, medical procedures and diagnoses, and unanticipated customer-defined dimensions
- Provides comprehensive multilingual support suitable for multinational companies
- Is fully driven from modern desktop graphical user interfaces
- Is technically and economically scalable from a standalone PC environment to a clustered UNIX SMP data warehouse environment
- Sells for $10,000 over the phone as a utility package that any data warehouse manager can evaluate and install if it proves to live up to its claims

I suspect that all of the current data cleaning companies would give their eyeteeth to address this market opportunity and that they are moving in this direction. However, data cleaning has been a somewhat quiet backwater of data warehousing. The fierce stimulation of the mainline marketplace has not been applied to these companies yet. To put it another way, there may still be room for one or more new players to enter this marketplace.

The traditional data extract providers have largely left advanced data cleaning to specialist data cleaning companies. Although the extract providers talk about data cleaning, they have not yet seized upon advanced data cleaning as a proprietary strength of their products. I would not be surprised to see all of the data extract providers move into this area.

There are additional market forces at work that will make the value of data cleaning more obvious. The year 2000 crisis has everyone trying to analyze how their information systems may have dependencies on date processing. The data cleaning companies have begun to suggest that their tools can be used to ferret out dates from all types of legacy data and thereby give a heads up warning to IT about all of the places where date problems may arise.

Data mining, the hot new trend in data warehousing, is the scanning of large amounts of data to reveal unexpected patterns or correlations. The analysis of demographic or behavioral descriptions of customers is an important part of data mining. Obviously, all of the arguments in this article directly drive the quality of a data mining analysis. Increasingly, the data mining companies are talking publicly about the value of clean data. Perhaps one or more of these companies will try to enter the data cleaning marketplace as well. In a way, when a data miner finds something exciting, it's either a valuable insight into the business or a bogus finding from bad data.

Data Integrity Drives Business Reengineering

It is worthwhile to step back from this close look at data cleaning to get some perspective. Why is data dirty in the first place? Much of the time it is because of poor systems or poor practices at the moment of data capture. Often someone such as a salesperson, field adjuster, or buyer is stuck with the job of entering critical data. That person may have an awkward system with no built-in support for data integrity. For example, a buyer may simply have a product description field in which to enter the characteristics of the product he just acquired. No wonder there were 20 spellings of the word "lozenge" in the drugstore.

At the same time, the person responsible for data entry may not be motivated to drive data quality to the 100 percent level. If your job is to drop data down a pipe and no one ever tells you that your efforts are worthwhile, then you aren't going to do a perfect job for very long. You probably won't even know what a perfect job entails.

The answer to the problem of data entry quality is a kind of business reengineering, which requires multiple steps such as:

- Providing well-engineered data entry systems that are easy and compelling for professionals to use and that restrict the data entry to valid rules as much as possible
- Creating a single set of business rules for data validation of each kind of data
- Providing executive-level support for making data entry quality a high priority
- Providing explicit and regular feedback to the front line professionals in the form of newsletters, contests, or rewards for superior data entry performance
- Providing a corporate culture that admires and values attention to detail and data quality

The data warehouse and data cleaning tools play a unique role in defining the need for this type of business reengineering. The data warehouse is the perfect place to see the value of good data. Sometimes, paradoxically, the data warehouse must make imperfect data available in order to show the organization how valuable perfect data would be.

Data cleaning tools alert IT to the exact issues involved in clean data. The final architecture for data delivery will ideally be balanced between data originally entered as accurately as possible and powerful data cleaning systems operating downstream in the extract process to bring data up to the shining goal of being 100 percent correct.

 ## 11.19 An Architecture for Data Quality

Ralph Kimball, DM Review, *Oct 2007*

In this article, I propose a comprehensive architecture for capturing data quality events as well as measuring and ultimately controlling data quality in the data warehouse. This scalable architecture can be added to existing data warehouse and data integration environments with minimal impact and relatively little upfront investment. Using this architecture, it is even possible to progress systematically toward a Six Sigma level of quality management. This design is in response to the current lack of a published, coherent architecture for addressing data quality issues.

Three powerful forces have converged to put data quality concerns near the top of the list for organization executives. First, the long term cultural trend that says, "If only I could see the data, then I could manage my business better" continues to grow. Most knowledge workers believe instinctively that data is a crucial requirement for them to function in their jobs. Second, most organizations understand that they are profoundly distributed, typically around the world, and that effectively integrating myriad disparate data sources is required. And third, the sharply increased demands for compliance mean that careless handling of data is not going to be overlooked or excused.

These powerful converging forces illuminate data quality problems in a harsh light. Fortunately, the big pressures are coming from the business users, not just from IT. The business users have become aware that data quality is a serious and expensive problem. Thus, the organization is more likely to support initiatives to improve data quality. But most business users probably have no idea where data quality problems originate or what an organization can do to improve data quality. They may think that data quality is a simple execution problem in IT. In this environment, IT needs to be agile and proactive: Data quality cannot be improved by IT alone. An even more extreme view says that data quality has almost nothing to do with IT.

It is tempting to blame the original source of data for any and all errors that appear downstream. If only the data entry clerk were more careful and really cared! We are only slightly more forgiving of typing-challenged salespeople who enter customer and product information into their order forms. Perhaps we can fix data quality problems by imposing better constraints on the data entry interfaces. This approach provides a hint of how to think about fixing data quality, but we must take a much larger view before pouncing on technical solutions. At a large retail bank I worked with, the Social Security number fields for customers were often blank or filled with garbage. Someone came up with the brilliant idea to require input in the 999-99-9999 format, and to cleverly disallow nonsensical entries such as all 9s. What happened? The data entry clerks were forced to supply valid Social Security numbers in order to progress to the next screen, so when they didn't have the customer's number, they typed in their own!

Michael Hammer, in his revolutionary book *Reengineering the Corporation* (originally Harper Collins, 1993, updated in 2006), struck at the heart of the data quality problem with a brilliant insight that I have carried with me throughout my career. Paraphrasing Hammer, seemingly small data quality issues are, in reality, important indications of broken business processes. Not only does this insight correctly focus our attention on the source of data quality problems, but it also shows us the way to the solution.

Establish a Quality Culture and Reengineer the Processes

Technical attempts to address data quality will not function unless they are part of an overall quality culture that must come from the very top of an organization. The famous Japanese car manufacturing quality attitude permeates every level of those organizations, and quality is embraced enthusiastically by all levels, from the CEO down to the assembly line worker. To cast this in a data context, imagine a company like a large drugstore chain where a team of buyers contracts with thousands of suppliers to provide the drugstore inventory. The buyers have assistants whose job it is to enter the detailed descriptions of everything purchased by the buyers. These descriptions contain dozens of attributes. But the problem is that the assistants have a deadly job. They are judged on how many items they enter per hour. The assistants have almost no visibility about who uses their data. Occasionally the assistants are scolded for obvious errors. But more insidiously, the data given to the assistants is itself incomplete and unreliable. For example, there are no formal standards for toxicity ratings, so there is significant variation over time and over product categories for this attribute. How does the drugstore improve data quality? Here is a nine-step template, not only for the drugstore, but for any organization addressing data quality:

1. Declare a high level commitment to a data quality culture.
2. Drive process reengineering at the executive level.
3. Spend money to improve the data entry environment.
4. Spend money to improve application integration.
5. Spend money to change how processes work.
6. Promote end-to-end team awareness.
7. Promote interdepartmental cooperation.
8. Publicly celebrate data quality excellence.
9. Continuously measure and improve data quality.

At the drugstore, money needs to be spent to improve the data entry system so that it provides the content and choices needed by the buyers' assistants. The company's executives need to assure the buyers' assistants that their work is very important and their efforts affect many decision makers in a positive way. Diligent efforts by the assistants should be publicly praised and rewarded. And end-to-end team awareness and appreciation of the value of data quality is the final goal.

Once the executive support and the organizational framework are ready, specific technical solutions are appropriate. The rest of this article describes how to marshal technology to support data quality. Goals for the technology include:

- Early diagnosis and triage of data quality issues
- Specific demands on source systems and integration efforts to supply better data
- Specific descriptions of data errors expected to be encountered in the ETL
- Framework for capturing all data quality errors
- Framework for precisely measuring data quality metrics over time
- Quality confidence metrics attached to final data

Role of Data Profiling

Data profiling is the technical analysis of data to describe its content, consistency, and structure. In some sense, any time you perform a `SELECT DISTINCT` investigative query on a database field, you are doing data profiling. Today there are a variety of tools purpose-built to do powerful data profiling. It probably pays to invest in a tool rather than build your own, because the tools allow many data relationships to be explored easily with simple user interface gestures.

Data profiling plays distinct strategic and tactical roles. At the beginning of a data warehouse project, as soon as a candidate data source is identified, a quick data profiling assessment should be made to provide a "go/no go" decision about proceeding with the project. Ideally this strategic assessment should occur within a day or two of identifying a candidate data source. Early disqualification of a data source is a responsible step that will earn you respect from the rest of the team, even if it is bad news. A very late revelation that the data source cannot support the mission can have a fatal career outcome if this revelation occurs months into a project.

Once the basic strategic decision is made to include a data source in the project, a lengthy tactical data profiling effort should be made to identify as many data problems as possible. Issues that show up in this phase result in detailed specifications that either are: 1) sent back to the originator of the data source as requests for improvement; or 2) are the grist for processing in the data warehouse ETL pipeline every time data is extracted from the source. I firmly believe that most problems can only effectively be addressed at the source.

Quality Screens

The heart of the data warehouse ETL architecture is a set of quality screens that act as diagnostic filters in the data flow pipelines. A quality screen is simply a test implemented at any point in the ETL or data migration processes. If the test is successful, nothing happens and the screen has no side effects. But if the test fails, then every screen must:

- Drop an error event record into the error event schema.
- Choose to halt the process, send the offending data into suspension, or merely tag the data.

Although all quality screens are architecturally similar, it is convenient to divide them into three types, in ascending order of scope. Here we follow the categorizations of data quality as defined by Jack Olson in his seminal book *Data Quality: The Accuracy Dimension* (Morgan Kaufmann, 2003):

- **Column screens test the data within a single column.** These are usually simple, somewhat obvious tests, such as testing if a column contains unexpected null values, if a value falls outside of a prescribed range, or if a value fails to adhere to a required format.
- **Structure screens test the relationship of data across columns.** Two or more fields may be tested to verify that they implement a hierarchy (e.g., a series of many-to-one relationships). Structure screens include testing foreign key-primary key relationships between fields in two tables and also include testing whole blocks of fields to verify that they implement postally valid addresses.

■ **Business rule screens implement more complex tests that do not fit the simpler column or structure screen categories.** For example, a customer profile may be tested for a complex time-dependent business rule, such as requiring that a lifetime platinum frequent flyer has been a member for at least five years and has more than 2 million frequent flyer miles. Business rule screens also include aggregate threshold data quality checks, such as checking to see if a statistically improbable number of MRI examinations have been ordered for minor diagnoses. In this case, the screen only throws an error after a threshold of such MRI exams is reached.

Error Event Schema

The error event schema, shown in Figure 11-5, is a centralized dimensional schema whose purpose is to record every error event thrown by a quality screen anywhere. This approach obviously can be used in a general data integration application, where data is being transferred between legacy applications.

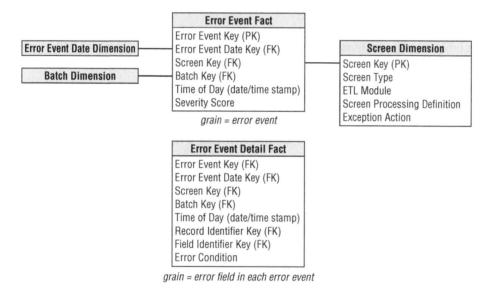

Figure 11-5: The error event schema.

The main table is the error event fact table. Its grain is every error thrown by a quality screen anywhere in the ETL or data migration system. Remember that the grain of a fact table is the physical description of why a fact table record exists. Thus, every quality screen error produces exactly one record in this table, and every record in the table corresponds to an observed error.

The dimensions of the error event fact table include the calendar date of the error, the batch job in which the error occurred, and the screen that produced the error. The calendar date is not a minute and second time stamp of the error; rather, it provides a way to constrain and summarize error events by the usual attributes of the calendar, such as weekday or last day of a fiscal period. The time_of_day fact is a full relational date/time stamp that specifies precisely when the error occurred. This format is useful for calculating the time interval between error events because one can take the difference between two date/time stamps to get the number of seconds separating events.

The batch dimension can be generalized to be a processing step in cases where data is streamed, rather than batched. The screen dimension identifies precisely what the screen criterion is and where the code for the screen resides. It also defines what to do when the screen throws an error (e.g., halt the process, send the record to a suspense file, or merely tag the data).

The error event fact table also has a single column primary key, shown as the error event key. This, like the primary key of the dimension tables, is a surrogate key consisting of a simple integer assigned sequentially as records are added to the fact table. This key field is necessary in those situations where an enormous burst of error records is added to the error event fact table all at once. Hopefully, this won't happen to you.

The error event schema includes a second error event detail fact table at a lower grain. Each record in this table identifies an individual field in a specific data record that participated in an error. Thus, a complex structure or business rule error that triggers a single error event record in the higher level error event fact table may generate many records in this detail fact table. The two tables are tied together by the error event key, which is a foreign key in this lower grain table. The error event detail table identifies the table, record, field, and precise error condition and likewise could inherit the date, screen, and batch dimensions from the higher grain error event fact table. Thus, a complete description of complex multi-field, multi-record errors is preserved by these tables. The error event detail table could also contain a precise date/time stamp to provide a full description of aggregate threshold error events where many records generate an error condition over a period of time. The error event detail fact table does not need to be implemented in a first rollout of this architecture since it is more important to get early experience in seeing the flow of errors. In many cases, the location of the bad data can be determined from higher level error event schema.

We now appreciate that each quality screen has the responsibility for populating these tables at the time of an error.

Responding to Quality Events

I have already remarked that each quality screen has to decide what happens when an error is thrown. The choices are: 1) halting the process, 2) sending the offending record(s) to a suspense file for later processing, and 3) merely tagging the data and passing it through to the next step in the pipeline. The third choice is by far the best choice, whenever possible. Halting the process is obviously a pain because it requires manual intervention to diagnose the problem, restart or resume the job, or abort completely. Sending records to a suspense file is often a poor solution because it is not clear when or if these records will be fixed and reintroduced to the pipeline. Until the records are restored to the data flow, the overall integrity of the database is questionable because records are missing. I recommend not using the suspense file for minor data transgressions. The third option of tagging the data with the error condition often works well. Bad fact table data can be tagged with the audit dimension described in the next section. Bad dimension data can also be tagged using the audit dimension or, in the case of missing or garbage data, can be tagged with unique error values in the field itself.

Audit Dimension

The audit dimension is a normal dimension that is assembled in the back room by the ETL process for each fact table. A sample audit dimension attached to a shipments invoice fact table is shown in Figure 11-6.

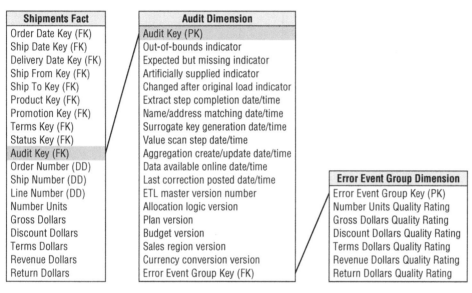

Shipments Fact	Audit Dimension	Error Event Group Dimension
Order Date Key (FK)	Audit Key (PK)	
Ship Date Key (FK)	Out-of-bounds indicator	
Delivery Date Key (FK)	Expected but missing indicator	
Ship From Key (FK)	Artificially supplied indicator	
Ship To Key (FK)	Changed after original load indicator	
Product Key (FK)	Extract step completion date/time	
Promotion Key (FK)	Name/address matching date/time	
Terms Key (FK)	Surrogate key generation date/time	
Status Key (FK)	Value scan step date/time	
Audit Key (FK)	Aggregation create/update date/time	
Order Number (DD)	Data available online date/time	**Error Event Group Dimension**
Ship Number (DD)	Last correction posted date/time	Error Event Group Key (PK)
Line Number (DD)	ETL master version number	Number Units Quality Rating
Number Units	Allocation logic version	Gross Dollars Quality Rating
Gross Dollars	Plan version	Discount Dollars Quality Rating
Discount Dollars	Budget version	Terms Dollars Quality Rating
Terms Dollars	Sales region version	Revenue Dollars Quality Rating
Revenue Dollars	Currency conversion version	Return Dollars Quality Rating
Return Dollars	Error Event Group Key (FK)	

Figure 11-6: A sample audit dimension attached to a shipments invoice fact table.

In this figure, the shipments fact table contains a typically long list of dimensional foreign keys each labeled with FK, three degenerate dimensions labeled with DD, and six additive numeric facts. The audit dimension in Figure 11-6 contains typical metadata context recorded at the moment when a specific fact table record is created. One might say that we have elevated metadata to real data! The designer of the data quality system can include as much or as little metadata as is convenient to record at the time of an error. To visualize how audit dimension records are created, imagine that this shipments fact table is updated once per day from a batch file. Suppose that today we have a perfect run with no errors flagged. In this case, we would generate only one audit dimension record and it would be attached to every fact record loaded today. All of the error conditions and version numbers would be the same for every record in this morning's load. Hence, only one dimension record would be generated. The foreign key in the audit dimension pointing to an error event group table would have a single value corresponding to an error event group showing "normal" fact quality ratings for each of the six fact fields.

Now let us relax the strong assumption of a perfect run. If we had some fact records whose discount dollars triggered an out-of-bounds error, then one more audit dimension record would be needed to handle this condition. The error conditions and version numbers would have appropriate values, and the foreign key to the error event group table would point to a record containing the normal quality indicators for all the fields except the discount dollars, which would be flagged as out-of-bounds. The power of the audit dimension becomes most apparent when the dimension attributes are used in a user report as shown in Figure 11-7.

Normal Report

Product	Ship From	Qty Shipped	Revenue
Axon	East	1438	$235,000
Axon	West	2249	$480,000

Instrumented Report (add Out of Bounds Indicator to SELECT)

Product	Ship From	Out of Bounds Indicator	Qty Shipped	Revenue
Axon	East	Abnormal	14	$2,350
Axon	East	OK	1423	$232,650
Axon	West	Abnormal	674	$144,000
Axon	West	OK	1574	$336,000

Figure 11-7: Normal and instrumented reports using the audit dimension.

The top report in Figure 11-7 is a normal report showing product sales in two geographic regions. The lower report is the same report with the out-of-bounds indicator added to the set of row headers with a simple user interface command. This produces an instant data quality assessment of the original report, and shows that a significant portion of the West region's sales are suspect.

The audit dimension described here is very complete and detailed, as we are trying to describe all the ways it can be used. However, it may be best to start with a reduced set of dimensional attributes, perhaps just including Out of Bounds Indicator, Missing Data, Quality Problem, and perhaps one or two of the environment version numbers. Don't let perfection be the enemy of good enough!

Six Sigma Data Quality

The data warehouse community can borrow some useful experience from the manufacturing community by adopting parts of their quality culture. In the manufacturing world, the Six Sigma level of quality is achieved when the number of defects falls below 3.4 defects per million opportunities. The error event fact table is the perfect foundation for making the same Six Sigma measurement for data quality. The defects are recorded in the error event schema and the opportunities are recorded in the organization's workflow monitor tool that records total number of records processed in each job stream.

The data quality architecture described in this article can be incrementally added to an existing data warehouse or data integration environment with very little disruption. Once the error event schema is established, the library of quality screens can grow indefinitely from a modest start. The screens need only obey the two simple requirements: logging each error into the error event schema and determining the system response to the error condition. Error screens can be implemented in multiple technologies throughout the ETL pipeline, including standalone batch jobs as well as data flow modules embedded in professional ETL tools.

Of course, the error event schema provides a quantitative basis for managing data quality initiatives over time because it is a time series by definition. The dimensionality of the error event data allows studying the evolution of data quality by source, software module, key performance indicator, and type of error.

The industry has talked about data quality endlessly, but there have been few unifying architectural principles. This article describes an easily implemented, nondisruptive, scalable, and comprehensive foundation for capturing data quality events as well as measuring and ultimately controlling data quality in the data warehouse.

11.20 Indicators of Quality: The Audit Dimension

Ralph Kimball, Intelligent Enterprise, *Apr 10, 2000*

As data warehouse managers, we always have an eye on data quality. Because our users trust us implicitly, we worry whether our data is accurate and complete. We occasionally have nightmares that the auditors will ask us *how* the data got into the database, and what exactly our assumptions were when we computed a certain number.

Certainly as data warehouses move closer to the operational interfaces of our web-enabled businesses, they are more likely to become "systems of record." For instance, are you computing salesperson commissions from the data warehouse? If you are, then you need to speak to data quality and lineage when the first legal dispute arises over the calculation of a large commission. The data warehouse industry uses the term *lineage* to describe the traceable origins and ownership of something. Other endeavors, such as art collecting and stamp collecting, use the word *provenance* to describe the same thing.

Let's make a list of data quality and lineage descriptors that we would like to have available when we face the auditors, or maybe when we are just running a report and are curious about the underlying assumptions.

- Quantitative data quality measures:
  - Overall data quality score
  - Completeness of the data collection relative to maximum possible
  - Number of underlying data elements
  - Number of not-applicable data elements encountered in the input
  - Number of corrupt data elements encountered in the input
  - Number of out-of-bounds data elements encountered in the input
  - Number of unknown data elements treated as zero (or mean value)

Number of data elements changed manually in the load process

Number of data elements not classified in regular aggregates

Number of corrections posted since original data load

■ **Data quality processing indicators:**

Extract step completion date/time

Name and address matching step completion date/time

Surrogate key generation date/time

Value scan step date/time

Aggregation create/update date/time

Data available online date/time

Last correction posted date/time

■ **Environmental descriptors:**

ETL system master version number

Allocation logic version

Plan version

Budget version

Sales region version

Currency conversion version

Although very useful, this list seems a bit too idealistic. For example, it raises a number of tough questions: How do we actually use these data quality and lineage indicators? Where do we store them? Is this list data or metadata? If it is metadata, how do we keep all these indicators tightly coupled to the real data? What is the granularity of these indicators? How can we apply these useful indicators to high level data that comes from many different sources?

Start with the Lowest Possible Grain

Let's try to answer several of these questions with a single compact design. Things become a little clearer when we remember that the most expressive and flexible data is always the lowest level data. A fact table record that represents a *single* transaction or a *single* snapshot at a point in time has the most dimensions because more of the surrounding descriptors take on a single value. When you aggregate data, you are forced to prune off your dimension list. Aggregated data becomes less focused.

We take the aggressive approach of attaching data quality indicators directly to the data itself, as shown in Figure 11-6 from article 11.19, *An Architecture for Data Quality*. All you have to do is add a simple audit key to the original data record at the lowest level of granularity. A 4-byte key should be sufficient for any variation on our data quality tracking theme.

The audit key is a meaningless integer key that serves only to join to an audit dimension that contains the immediate data quality and lineage context for the particular fact table record. Besides the key, the above-referenced figure contains many useful fields for tracking data quality and data confidence.

Every field in our example audit dimension has a single well-defined meaning for each fact record. The first four indicators are text values. For instance, the artificially supplied indicator could have the values of not applicable, zero, estimated mean value, or estimated zero variance value. Data miners will find these choices familiar because filling in estimated values to cause the least disruption to the overall data set is an important technique for addressing missing or corrupt data.

The seven date/time stamps usually have legitimate date/time values, but must be capable of representing null values in order to handle situations where a step is not performed.

The ETL master version number is a key to the current description of the ETL software suite. The ETL software librarian, whose job it is to maintain a complete list of all ETL components, including storage location, individual version numbers, and backup status, should be maintaining the master version number. The full description of the ETL software suite is a large record in a separate table (not shown here) that could easily consist of hundreds of items. In article 12.21, *Meta Meta Data Data*, I list approximately 80 of the metadata components in such a suite. Whenever we change any aspect of the ETL software suite, the low order digits of the ETL system master version number must change as well. If we administer this ETL metadata correctly, not only will the audit trail be very specific, but we will be able to restore a consistent, complete set of ETL components. This view of an ETL system mimics the responsibilities of a software librarian in a product software development shop.

Perhaps you are wondering whether you could supply a companion BI tool master version number into this audit record, but in my opinion, this isn't the place for such a key. While such a BI tool master version number might be created with the same kind of process as the ETL master version number, the data itself can't guarantee that a user is viewing the data through a specific version of the BI tools, and therefore such a master version number would be meaningless in understanding the lineage of a particular report.

The final five version fields in our audit dimension are all text entries that describe the overall business assumptions you use to allocate, map, and combine the data.

Our resulting audit dimension record should be of low cardinality compared to the fact table. All the fact table records loaded in the same batch run of the ETL system will probably have the same audit key, except for the few exceptional records that you have to modify or artificially supply. These exceptional records will generate only a few more audit keys.

In this article, we are building a framework for describing the quality and lineage of measurement-oriented fact table records. If we wish to describe the quality and lineage of dimension table records such as customer descriptions, then we can use many of the same techniques, but we would add the new audit fields into the existing dimension records themselves.

Reporting Aggregate Data Quality

The audit dimension lets a conventional query tool report on the data quality, ETL environment, and business logic assumptions of any set of data. Just use the audit dimension as you would any other dimension. You can group by or constrain on any of the audit attributes, and you can use your normal query and reporting tools to display the results. You don't need a custom metadata reporting tool to do any of this.

We can explore many of the interesting data quality and lineage issues just by using the audit dimension. But there are some questions that are defined only for aggregate data sets. The overall data quality score and the completeness of the data collection relative to the maximum possible measures we included in our original requirements list are good examples.

When you are reporting on the completeness of a set of data at an aggregate level, you can't mark a data element as missing if that means the record isn't in the database. This dilemma is an example of representing "what didn't happen" in a database. In all analyses of what didn't happen, somewhere in the database you have to describe two things: 1) What did happen, and 2) what is the universe of all possibilities. You then subtract #1 from #2 to find out what didn't happen. For a more complete perspective on this issue, see article 8.15, *What Didn't Happen*.

In our example, you need to decide how to encode #2, the universe of all possibilities. Sometimes you can do this by adding only a few records to the database, especially when you know the records exist but somehow your data delivery pipeline failed to deliver them in a timely way. For example, if you are a retail operation with 600 stores, and in this morning's load you received only 598 sets of data, then in your daily store totals aggregate fact table, you should include artificially generated records for the two missing stores. You will need an audit key and a shrunken audit dimension for the aggregate fact table. In this shrunken audit dimension, or possibly in the fact table, you can include completeness indicators. Now you can easily generate reports at various aggregate levels that include a measure of data completeness.

Building the Audit Dimension

I hope I've made a compelling case for an audit dimension's usefulness. But like so many interesting designs in data warehousing, the hard part is actually supplying the data for the audit record. We need to actually build most of the quality and lineage indicators into the ETL pipeline. We need to augment each data flow in the ETL pipeline with exception handling routines that diagnose each record as it is being built. In addition, the environment variables, including the date/time stamps and version descriptions, need to be waiting to be put into the current audit record. This goal implies, of course, that we must carefully log all the required date/time stamps and version descriptions. How does the saying go? "If we had some ham, then we could have some ham and eggs, if we had some eggs."

11.21 Adding an Audit Dimension to Track Lineage and Confidence

Ralph Kimball, Design Tip #26, Aug 1, 2001

Whenever we build a fact table containing measurements of our business, we surround the fact table with "everything we know to be true." In a dimensional model, this everything-we-know is packaged in a set of dimensions. Physically we insert foreign keys, one per dimension, into our fact table, and connect these foreign keys to the corresponding primary keys of each dimension. Inside each dimension (like product or customer) is a verbose set of highly correlated text-like descriptors representing individual members of the dimension (like individual products or customers).

We can extend this everything-we-know approach to our fact table designs by including key pieces of metadata that are known to be true when an individual fact record is created. For instance, when we make a fact table record, we should know such things as:

1. what source system supplied the fact data (multiple descriptors if multiple source systems).
2. what version of the extract software created the record.
3. what version of allocation logic (if any) was used to create the record.
4. whether a specific "N.A. encoded" fact field actually is unknown, impossible, corrupted, or not-available-yet.
5. whether a specific fact was altered after the initial load, and if so, why.
6. whether the record contains facts more than 2, 3, or 4 standard deviations from the mean, or equivalently, outside various bounds of confidence derived from some other statistical analysis.

The first three items describe the lineage (provenance) of the fact table record. In other words, where did the data come from? The last three items describe our confidence in the quality of data for that fact table record.

Once we start thinking this way, we can come up with a lengthy list of metadata items describing data lineage and data quality confidence. But for the purpose of this design tip, we'll stop with just these six. A more elaborate list can be found in the discussion of Audit Dimensions in the Data Warehouse Lifecycle Toolkit.

Although these six indicators could be encoded in various ways, I prefer text encoding. Ultimately we are going to constrain and report on these various audit attributes, and we want our user interfaces and our report labels to show as understandable text. So, perhaps the version of the extract software (item #2) might contain the value "Informatica release 6.4, Revenue extract v. 5.5.6." Item #5 might contain values such as "Not altered" or "Altered due to restatement."

The most efficient way to add the lineage and confidence information to a fact table is to create a single Audit foreign key in the fact table. A 4-byte integer key is more than sufficient, since the corresponding Audit dimension could have up to 4 billion records. We won't need that many!

We build the Audit dimension as a simple dimension with seven fields:

    Audit Key (primary key, 4 byte integer)
    Source System (text)
    Extract Software (text)
    Allocation Logic (text)
    Value Status (text)
    Altered Status (text)
    Out of Bounds Status (text)

In our backroom ETL (extract-transform-load) process, we track all of these indicators and have them ready at the moment when the fact table record is being assembled in its final state. If all six of the Audit fields already exist in the Audit dimension, we fetch the proper primary key from the Audit dimension and use it in the Audit dimension foreign key slot of the fact table. If we have no existing Audit dimension record applicable to our fact table record, we add one to the maximum value of the Audit dimension primary key, and create a new Audit dimension record. This is just standard surrogate key processing. Then we proceed as in the first case. In this way, we build up the Audit dimension over a period of time.

Notice that if we are loading a large number of records each day, almost all of the records will have the same Audit foreign key, since presumably nearly all of the records will be "normal". We can modify the processing in the previous paragraph to take advantage of this by caching the Audit key of the "normal" record, and skipping the lookup for all normal records.

Now that we have built the Audit dimension, how do we use it?

The beauty of this design is that the lineage and confidence metadata has now become regular data, and can now be queried and analyzed along with the other more familiar dimensions. There are two basic approaches to decorating your queries and reports with Audit dimension indicators.

The "poor man's" approach simply adds the desired Audit attributes directly to the Select list of a SQL query. In other words in a simple sales query like:

```
SELECT PRODUCT, SUM(SALES)
```

you augment the query to read:

```
SELECT PRODUCT, VALUE_STATUS, SUM(SALES), COUNT(*)
```

Now your report will sprout an extra row whenever an anomalous data condition arises. You will get a count that lets you judge how bad the condition is. Notice that before you did this design, the NA (null) encoded data values just dropped silently out of your report without raising an alarm, because SUM ignores null values.

The "rich man's" approach performs full fledged drill across queries producing separate columns (not separate rows) with more sophisticated indicators of lineage or quality. For instance, our simple sales query in the above example could be embellished to produce report headings across each row like:

```
PRODUCT >> SUM(SALES) >> PERCENT OF DATA FROM OLD SOURCE SYSTEM >>
PERCENT OF DATA CORRUPTED
```

and so on. Modern business intelligence tools like Cognos, Business Objects, and MicroStrategy are capable of these drill across reports, using "stitch queries" or "multi-pass SQL."

11.22 Add Uncertainty to Your Fact Table

Ralph Kimball, Design Tip #116, *Sep 2, 2009*

We always want our business users to have confidence in the data we deliver through our data ware-houses. Thus it goes against our instincts to talk about problems encountered in the ETL back room, or known inaccuracies in the source systems. But this reluctance to expose our uncertainties can ultimately hurt our credibility and lessen the business users' confidence in the data if a data quality problem is revealed and we haven't said anything about it.

More than thirty years ago when I was first exposed to A.C. Nielsen's pioneering data warehouse solution, the Inf*Act data reporting service for grocery store scanner data, I was surprised to see critical key performance indicators in their reports occasionally marked with asterisks indicating a lack of confidence in the data. In this case, the asterisk meant "not-applicable data encountered in the computation of this metric." The key performance indicator nevertheless appeared in the report, but the asterisk warned the business user not to overly trust the value. When I asked Nielsen about these asterisks, they told me the business users appreciated the warning not to make a big decision based on a specific value. I liked this implied partnership between the data provider and business user because it promoted an atmosphere of trust. And, of course, the reminders of data quality issues motivated the data provider to improve the process so as to reduce the number of asterisks.

Today I rarely see such warnings of uncertainty in the final BI layer of our data warehouses. But our world is far more wired to data than it was in 1980. I think it is time we reintroduced "uncer-tainty" into our fact tables. Here are two places we can add uncertainty into any fact table without changing the grain or invalidating existing applications.

Using property and casualty insurance as an example, one of the fact table's key performance indicators is the exposure dollars for a group of policies with certain demographics. This is an esti-mate of total liability for the known claims against the chosen set of policies. Certainly the insurance company management will pay attention to this number!

In Figure 11-8, we accompany the exposure dollar value with an exposure confidence metric, whose value ranges between 0 and 1. An exposure confidence value of 0 indicates no confidence in the reported exposure dollars and a value of 1 indicates complete confidence. We assign the expo-sure confidence value in the back room ETL processes by examining the status of each claim that contributes to the aggregated record shown in Figure 11-8. Presumably a claim associated with a very large exposure but whose claim status is "preliminary estimate" or "unverified claim" or "claim disputed" would lower the overall exposure confidence on the summary record in this fact table. If the doubtful claim's individual reserve value is given a weight of zero, then the overall reserve con-fidence metric could be a weighted average of the individual reserve values.

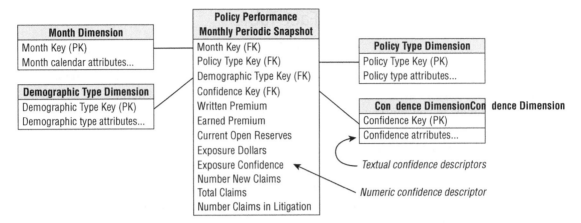

Figure 11-8: An insurance fact table augmented with an exposure confidence fact and uncertainty dimension.

Figure 11-8 also shows a confidence dimension containing textual attributes describing the confidence in one or more of the values in the fact table. A textual attribute for the exposure confidence would be correlated with the exposure confidence metric. An exposure confidence between 0.95 and 1 might correspond to "Certain." An exposure confidence between 0.7 and 0.94 might correspond to "Less Certain," and an exposure confidence of less than 0.7 might correspond to "Unreliable." The combination of numeric and textual confidence information in our example allows BI tools to display numeric values in various ways (e.g., using italics for data less than Certain), and allows the BI tool to constrain and group on ranges of confidence.

This example should be a plausible template for providing confidence indicators on almost any fact table. I have found it to be a useful exercise just to imagine what the confidence is for various delivered metrics. And there is no question that the business users will find that exercise useful too.

11.23 Have You Built Your Audit Dimension Yet?

Ralph Kimball, Design Tip #164, Mar 3, 2014

One of the most effective tools for managing data quality and data governance, as well as giving business users confidence in the data warehouse results, is the audit dimension. We often attach an audit dimension to every fact table so that business users can choose to illuminate the provenance and confidence in their queries and reports. Simply put, the audit dimension elevates metadata to the status of ordinary data and makes this metadata available at the top level of any BI tool user interface.

The secret to building a successful audit dimension is to keep it simple and not get too idealistic in the beginning. A simple audit dimension should contain environment variables and data quality indicators, shown in Figure 11-9.

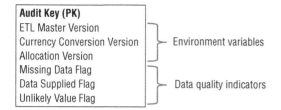

Audit Key (PK)
ETL Master Version
Currency Conversion Version
Allocation Version
Missing Data Flag
Data Supplied Flag
Unlikely Value Flag

Environment variables

Data quality indicators

Figure 11-9: A simple audit dimension.

The audit dimension, like all dimensions, provides the context for a particular fact row. Thus when a fact row is created, the environment variables are fetched from a small table containing the version numbers in effect for specific ranges of time. The data quality indicators are fetched from the error event fact table that records data quality errors encountered along the ETL pipeline. We have written extensively about the error event fact table and the audit dimension. See article 11.19, *An Architecture for Data Quality,* for more details. This short article is really just a reminder for you to build your audit dimension if you have been putting it off!

The environment variables in Figure 11-9 are version numbers that change only occasionally. The ETL master version number is a single identifier, similar to a software version number, that refers to the complete ETL configuration in use when the particular fact row was created. The currency conversion version is another version number that identifies a specific set of foreign currency conversion business rules in effect when the fact table row was created. The allocation version is a number that identifies a set of business rules for allocating costs when calculating profitability. All of these environment variables are just examples to stimulate your thinking. But again, keep it simple.

The data quality indicators are flags that show whether some particular condition was encountered for the specific fact row. If the fact row contained missing or corrupt data (perhaps replaced by null), then the missing data flag would be set to true. If missing or corrupt data was filled in with an estimator, then the data supplied flag would be true. If the fact row contained anomalously high or low values, then the unlikely value flag would be true. Note that this simple audit dimension does not provide a precise description of the data quality problem, rather it only provides a warning that the business user should tread cautiously. Obviously, if you can easily implement more specific diagnostic warnings, then do so. But keep it simple. Don't try to win the elegance award.

Article 11.19 does a deep dive into more sophisticated versions of the audit dimension, but I have been concerned that the really advanced audit dimension designs are daunting. Hence this article.

Finally, if you build an audit dimension, show it to your business users. Figure 11-10 shows a before and after portion of a simple tracking report using an out of bounds indicator with values "Abnormal" and "OK" that provides a useful warning that a large percentage of the Axon West data contains unlikely values. The instrumented report is created just by dragging the out of bounds indicator into the query. Business users are surprisingly grateful for this kind of information, since not only are they curious as to why the data has been flagged, but they appreciate not making business decisions based on too little information.

Normal Report:

Product	Ship From	Qty Shipped	Revenue
Axon	East	1438	$235,000
Axon	West	2249	$480,000

Instrumented Report (add Out of Bounds Indicator to SELECT):

Product	Ship From	Out of Bounds Indicator	Qty Shipped	Revenue
Axon	East	Abnormal	14	$2,350
Axon	East	OK	1424	$232,650
Axon	West	Abnormal	675	$144,000
Axon	West	OK	1574	$336,000

Figure 11-10: Normal and instrumented reports using the audit dimension.

11.24 Is Your Data Correct?

Ralph Kimball, Intelligent Enterprise, *Dec 5, 2000*

One common problem in the data warehouse back room is verifying that the data is correct before you release it to your users. Is the warehouse an accurate image of the production system? Was this morning's download complete? Could some of the numbers be corrupted?

There is no single technique for validating a data load because so much variability exists in the data sources. If you are downloading an unchanged image of a production source (preserving the original granularity), you can probably run a flash report on the production system with up-to-the-minute totals, then recapitulate the same report on the data warehouse. In this case, you know the answer before running the report, and the two results should match to the last decimal place.

But more often you will not have a known baseline of data. For example, perhaps you are receiving the individual sales transactions from 600 retail stores every night. You can certainly perform a gross count on the number of stores reporting, but how can you apply some additional judgment to determine the probability that the data is correct?

Continuing with 600 stores as an example, let's look at the sales totals for each department within each store for each morning and ask if today's new numbers are reasonable. We will decide that today's sales total is reasonable if it falls within three standard deviations of the mean of the previous sales totals for that department in that store.

I chose three standard deviations because in a normal distribution, 99 percent of the values lie within three standard deviations above or below the mean. If all the data values are valid, approximately one percent of them will still fail our test. Perhaps after reviewing these outliers, we will decide that the overall data load seems reasonable.

I'll describe the process of checking the data using this simple technique just in words. After that I'll include some SQL, but you can skip the SQL and still get the basic idea.

In order to make this process run quickly, you want to avoid looking at the complete time history of old data when you are calculating the standard deviation. You can do this by keeping three accumulating numbers for each department in each store in a special table used only in the data validity pass. You need to keep the number of days you are accumulating, the accumulating sum of each day's sales (by department in each store), and the accumulating sum of the square of each day's sales (again by department within store). These could be kept in a small, standalone accumulating department table. The grain of this table is department by store, and the three numeric fields, NUMBER_DAYS, SUM_SALES, and SUM_SQUARE_SALES, are overwritten each day. You can update all three of these fields just by adding the next day's values to the ones already present. So if you have 600 stores and 20 departments in each store, this table has 12,000 rows but does not grow over time. The table also carries the store names and department names in each row.

Using this accumulating department table, look at all 12,000 department totals in the morning's data load, and kick out the morning's numbers that are more than three standard deviations from the mean. You can choose to examine the specific numbers with unusual values if there aren't too many, or you can reject the entire load if you see much more than one percent of the data values being flagged as out of bounds.

If the morning's load passes muster, release the data to your business users and update the accumulating department table to get ready for the next day's load.

Here's some untested SQL that might work in this scenario. Recall that the standard deviation is the square root of the variance. The variance is the sum of the squares of the differences between each of the historical data points and the mean of the data points, divided by $N - 1$, where N is the number of days of data. Normally the calculation of the variance requires you to look at the entire time history of sales, which although possible, makes the computation unattractive. But if you have been keeping track of SUM_SALES and SUM_SQUARE_SALES, you can write the variance as

```
(1/(N-1))*(SUM_SQUARE_SALES-(1/N)*SUM_SALES*SUM_SALES).
```

So if you abbreviate your variance formula with VAR, your data validity check looks like this:

```
SELECT s.storename, p.departmentname, sum(f.sales)
FROM fact f, store s, product p, time t, accumulatingdept a
WHERE
```

First, take care of joins between tables:

```
f.storekey = s.storekey and
f.productkey = p.productkey and
f.timekey = t.timekey and
s.storename = a.storename and
p.departmentname = a.departmentname and
```

Then, constrain the time to today to get the newly loaded data:

```
t.full_date = #December 13, 2000#
```

Finally, invoke the standard deviation constraint:

```
HAVING ABS(sum(f.sales)-(1/a.N)*a.SUM_SALES > 3*SQRT(a.VAR)
```

Expand VAR as in the previous explanation and use the `a.` prefix on N, SUM_SALES, and SUM_SQUARE_SALES. I have assumed that departments are groupings of products and hence are available as a rollup in the product dimension.

Embellishments on this scheme could include running two queries: one for the sales more than three standard deviations above the mean, and another for sales less than three standard deviations below the mean. Maybe there is a different explanation for these two situations. Running two queries would also get rid of the `ABS` function if your SQL doesn't like this in the HAVING clause.

If you normally have significant daily fluctuations in sales (let's say Monday and Tuesday are very slow compared to Saturday), you could add a DAY-OF-WEEK to the accumulating department table and constrain to the appropriate day. Although doing this expands the accumulating department table by a factor of seven, it may remove a significant source of variance and make your test more accurate. Adding this bit of SQL is a kind of poor man's way of handling known daily fluctuations. I describe a high power way to deal with "trading day" and seasonal fluctuations in the last section of this article.

Judging Data Quality with No History

There are some special situations in which you can calculate the expected mean and variance of incoming data even if you have not been accumulating history. Suppose you are collecting data from a large number of individual respondents within the age range of 40 to 49 years. If you have no reason to believe that there is a bias that preferentially selects one gender over another, you can use the ratio of males in the population at large (assume 47/100) and the ratio of females (therefore 53/100) as the basis of your statistics. A statistician would say that your data represents a set of Bernoulli trials, and the resulting data should fit a binomial distribution. Consulting your statistics textbooks, you know that if you have recorded 1,000 respondents, you would expect the mean number of males to be $N \times P$ where $N = 1,000$ and $P = 47/100$. This works out to 470 males in your sample. Seems reasonable. From the textbooks, the variance is $N \times P \times (1-P)$, which is $1,000 \times 0.47 \times 0.53 = 249.1$. The standard deviation is the square root of the variance, which in this case is 15.78.

Again, applying the three standard deviation criteria, you will worry about any data element that is more than three standard deviations away from the mean. In other words, if you see that the number of males reported in a sample of 1,000 is less than $470 - 3 \times 15.78 = 422.6$ or is greater than $470 + 3 \times 15.78 = 517.3$, stop to ask if the reported data is reasonable.

Consider whether you are comfortable assuming that your data is generated with a constant probability. If you are, you can use this technique without accumulating a complex past history. Other examples in which the constant probability assumption is plausible might include the yield percentages of manufacturing processes such as wafer fabrication, paper production, or steel mills.

Compensating for Predictable Changes

Many of the measures (facts) that occur in a data warehouse come from marketplaces that exhibit predictable seasonal fluctuations. The holiday season and summer are predictable, high volume periods. Remove this seasonality as a source of variance when you judge your incoming data. Similarly, maybe business has been growing at an accelerating rate for the past several years; this acceleration could even be nonlinear. Finally, there may be specific days in the week or month during which you know your business volume is predictably high or low.

You can remove these sources of variance in your data in order to judge whether your data is reasonable, but you need some high powered statistical help. You will want to project your previous data forward in time to today, then compare this projection with the data that has just come in.

Professional statisticians for many years have used a technique known as X-11-ARIMA to remove these effects from time series data. ARIMA is an acronym for *auto-regressive integrated moving average*. The X-11 algorithm takes your existing data and projects it forward. In other words, it tells you what it expects today's data value to be.

The venerable X-11 algorithm, which statisticians have been using in various forms for more than 30 years, has been superseded recently by X-13-ARIMA, which offers more flexibility for dealing with constant (non-seasonal) trends and short term effects such as trading day fluctuations. All the serious statistics software vendors will have X-13 modules that you can use to filter out unreasonable data values.

Most of the serious ETL vendors offer "transform" modules with advanced statistics processing, including X-11-ARIMA, X-12-ARIMA and X-13-ARIMA. Have a talk with your ETL vendor and ask them how to attach one of the serious statistics packages to your back room data flow.

11.25 Eight Recommendations for International Data Quality

Ralph Kimball, Intelligent Enterprise, *Aug 1, 2008*

Cultural and technical challenges of international data are also discussed in articles 10.18, Think Globally, Act Locally, *and 10.19,* Warehousing without Borders.

Thomas Friedman's wonderful book, *The World is Flat* (Farrar, Straus, and Giroux, 2007), chronicles a revolution that most of us in IT are well aware of. Our enterprises collect and process data from around the world. We have hundreds or even thousands of suppliers, and we have millions of customers in almost every country. Our employees, with their attendant names and addresses, come from every conceivable culture. Our financial transactions are denominated in dozens of currencies. We need to know the exact time in remote cities. And above all, even though thanks to the web we have a tight electronic connection to all of our computing assets, we are dealing with a profoundly distributed system. This, of course, is the point of Friedman's book.

Data quality is enough of a challenge in an idealized mono-cultural environment, but it is inflamed to epic proportions in a flat world. But strangely, the issues of international data quality are not a single coherent theme in the IT world. For the most part, IT organizations are simply reacting to specific data problems in specific locations, without an overall architecture. Is an overall architecture even possible? This article examines the many challenges surrounding international data quality and concludes with eight recommendations for addressing the problem.

Languages and Character Sets

Beyond America and Western Europe there are hundreds of languages and writing systems that cannot be rendered using a single-byte character set such as ASCII. The Unicode standard, of course, is the internationally agreed upon multi-byte encoding intended to handle all the writing systems on the earth. The latest release, Unicode 8.0.0, encodes more than 100,000 characters in virtually every modern language. It is important to understand that Unicode is not a font. It is a character set. The architectural challenge for the data warehouse is to ensure that there is end-to-end support for Unicode all the way from data capture, through all forms of storage, DBMSs, ETL processes, and finally the BI tools. If any one of these stages cannot support Unicode, the final result will be corrupted and unacceptable.

Cultures, Names, and Salutations

The handling of names is a sensitive issue, and doing it incorrectly is a sign of disrespect. Consider the following examples from different cultures:

> **Brazil:** Mauricio do Prado Filho
> **Singapore:** Jennifer Chan-Lee Bee Lang
> **USA:** Frances Hayden-Kimball

Are you confident that you can parse these names? Where does the last name start? Is Frances male or female? Some years ago, my title was Director of Applications. I received a letter addressed to Dir of Apps, which began with Dear Dir. I didn't take that letter very seriously!

Geographies and Addresses

Addresses in different countries are notoriously difficult to parse without detailed local knowledge. Consider the following examples:

> **Finland:** Ulvilante 8b A 11 Pl 354 SF-00561 Helsinki
> **Korea:** 35-2 Sangdaewon-dong Kangnam-ku Seoul 165-010

Again, do you have any idea how to parse these addresses?

Privacy and Information Transfer

Even if the data you collect is properly parsed and of high quality, you need to be very careful with how you store, transport, and expose that data. France's Act of 6 January 1978 on Data Processing, Files, and Individual Liberties, amended August 2004 and March 2007, states, "The collection and processing of personal data that reveals, directly or indirectly, the racial and ethnic origins, the political, philosophical, religious opinions or trade union affiliation of persons, or which concern their health or sexual life, is prohibited. (8 paragraphs of exceptions follow)." Search the term "privacy law" on Google for much more on this topic.

International Compliance

Compliance is another migraine headache for the data warehouse whenever revenue or profitability data is exposed through BI tools. Be careful! The European Union has 25 member states, each with potentially varying financial responsibility guidance.

Currencies

Transaction systems normally capture detailed financial transactions in the true original currency at the location of the transaction. Different currencies, of course, cannot be directly added. Exchange rates change every day, in some cases rapidly. Foreign currency symbols are essential in final reports, but may not be available in the fonts you use.

Time Zones, Calendars, and Date Formats

Contrary to popular belief, there are not just 24 time zones around the world, but hundreds! The complexity comes from daylight savings time rules. For example, although the state of Indiana is entirely in the Eastern time zone, part of Indiana observes daylight savings time and part does not. You need a list of Indiana counties to know what time it is in Kokomo! In some areas of the world, there are dozens of jurisdictions with different time zone rules.

In western countries, most of us use the Gregorian calendar, but there are several other important calendars. For example, July 8, 2008 in the Gregorian calendar is 6-6-4705 in the Chinese calendar; 6-6-2668 in the Japanese calendar; Rajab 4, 1429 in the Muslim calendar; and Tammuz 5, 5768 in the Talmudic calendar. Can your data warehouse handle these? And if a European writes "7-8-2008," is this July 8 or August 7?

Numbers

One might think that at least with simple numbers, nothing could go wrong. But in India and other parts of central Asia the number "12,12,12,123" is perfectly legitimate and corresponds to "121,212,123" in the United States. Also, in many European and South American countries, the role of the period and the comma for designating the decimal point is reversed from the United States. You'd better get that one right!

Architectures for International Data Quality

Here, in condensed form, are my recommendations for addressing international data quality:

1. Ninety percent of data quality issues can be addressed at the source, and only 10 percent further downstream. Addressing data quality at the source requires an enterprise data quality culture, executive support, financial investment in tools and training, and business process reengineering.

2. The master data management (MDM) movement is hugely beneficial for establishing data quality. Build MDM capabilities for all your major entities including customers, employees, suppliers, and locations. Make sure that MDM creates the members of these entities upon demand, rather than cleaning up the entities downstream. Use MDM to establish master data structures for all your important entities. Make sure the deployment lets you correctly parse these entities at all stages of the DW/BI pipeline, carrying the detailed parsing all the way to the BI tools.

3. Actively manage and report data quality metrics with data quality screens, error event schemas, and audit dimensions, as described in article 11.19, *An Architecture for Data Quality*.

4. Standardize and test Unicode capability through your DW/BI pipelines.

5. Use `www.timezoneconverter.com` at the time of data capture to determine the actual time of day of every transaction that occurs in a remote foreign location. Store both universal time stamps and local time stamps with every transaction.

6. Choose a single universal currency (dollars, pounds, euros, etc.) and store both the local value of a financial transaction together with the universal currency value in every low level financial transaction record.

7. Don't translate dimensions in your data warehouse. Settle on a single, master language for dimensional content to drive querying, reporting, and sorting. Translate final rendered reports, if desired, in place. For hand-held device reporting, be aware that most non-English translations result in longer text than English.

8. Don't even think about establishing privacy and compliance best practices. That is a job for your legal and financial executives, not for IT. You do have a CPO and a CCO (Privacy and Compliance, respectively), don't you?

11.26 Using Regular Expressions for Data Cleaning

Warren Thornthwaite, Intelligent Enterprise, *Jan 19, 2009*

Data quality is one of the biggest challenges for many DW/BI system managers. One common problem, especially with freeform entry data, is that the structure of the data is not in a standard form. For example, telephone numbers in the USA are often standardized to the pattern (999) 999-9999. You typically standardize the contents of a column in order to increase the likelihood of a match when users query or when you are doing data integration comparisons. This article describes an approach you can program directly into your ETL processing for simple to moderately complex data cleaning and standardization tasks.

I recently worked on a web-based, freeform entry registration system for an educational organization. The system works fine for processing the organization's registration transactions. As long as the person's name is on the registration list, they have a badge and course materials. However, freeform entry data is not so good for analytics. In this case, one useful analysis involves seeing how many students have been to more than one class. When new data is loaded into the data warehouse from the class registration system, the ETL system compares columns in the incoming records with existing records to see if any of the new registrants may have registered for a previous class. If the contents of these columns have not been standardized, they are less likely to match. The following examples of the company name column shown in Figure 11-11 from the source registration data illustrate this problem.

RegID	First_Name	Last_Name	Company_Name	Reg_Date
507	Craig	Nelson	Bisontronics, Inc.	6/7/2008
515	Danny	Davinci	Daridune, Inc.	6/14/2008
516	Jenny	Smith	Daridune, Inc.	6/14/2008
580	Tim	Little	Synbis, Inc.	7/31/2008
591	Matthew	Adams	Inclander Incorporated	9/8/2008
596	Candy	Graham	Vencinc,Inc.	8/15/2008
617	Jenny	Smith	Daridune	9/14/2008

Figure 11-11: Sample source data.

Regular Expressions to the Rescue

A regular expression (RegExp) is a string matching pattern based on the regular expression syntax. A fairly short RegExp pattern can be used to match many variations of a given pattern. In the preceding example, we'd like to clean up company name so we are more likely to find matches as new registrations are loaded. Of course, the first approach to take when dealing with this problem is to try and get the source system to capture correct data in the first place. When this doesn't work, you will need to deal with the problem in your ETL system.

Matching is all about probabilities. You can never be 100 percent certain that two entries are the same people. In Figure 11-11, the last record is for a student who had registered before. In this case, we can match on first and last name, but there may be more than one person named Jenny Smith in the database. In order to improve our confidence in this comparison, we'll also match company name. In this case, our match won't be exact because Jenny left off the "Inc." when she registered the second time.

Basic Operators

Regular expressions have a full set of matching operators and abbreviations that work like the simple search string operators in SQL (%, ?, and *) or in Windows Search. Here are the RegExp operators we will use to clean up the company name:

Operator	Function
*	Optional—match zero or more occurrences of the preceding string
|	Or (Alternation)—match the string on one side of the operator or the other (can have multiple ORs in a group)
\	Escape—when used with an operator means treat the next character as a literal; e.g., * means match the "*" character. When used with certain normal characters such as t or b represents a control character
\t	Tab character
\b	Word boundary
( )	Substring grouping

Finding the Occurrences of "Inc"

Because there are several versions of "Inc," we need a RegExp that is flexible enough to find them all without including any false matches. RegExp engines always move in a forward direction from the beginning to the end of the string being searched. If we start our expression based on the first example, our initial RegExp looks like this (not including the quotes):

```
", Inc"
```

This won't match the second row because it doesn't start with a comma and it has a period at the end. By making the comma and period optional, RegExp now looks like this:

```
",* Inc\.*"
```

This combination of operators looks for zero or more commas followed by a space followed by the letters Inc followed by zero or more periods. The period character itself is a RegExp operator meaning "match anything," hence the backslash, which is an escape character changing the meaning to "match the literal period character."

At this point, our RegExp will match the first four rows, but not the next two. We can extend it to match the fifth row by adding the full string " Incorporated" onto the front of our RegExp with an OR operator like so:

```
" Incorporated|,* Inc\.*"
```

The order of this is important. The full word "Incorporated" needs to come first, otherwise the RegExp engine will only match the "Inc" substring to the first three letters of Incorporated. The space in front of "Incorporated" means the pattern will match with the example, but it will not pick up a leading comma. We'll fix this next.

Now we are left with one final challenge in the test data: the "Inc" with the missing space after the comma in the sixth row. In our current pattern, the comma is optional, but the space is not. If we make the space optional as well, the pattern will over-match and return hits like the "inc" in the company name "Vencinc." A more targeted pattern needs to include an OR between the comma and space sub-pattern and the comma only, like this:

```
" (,* |,)(Incorporated|Inc\.*)"
```

We moved things around a bit in this version. The pattern is now in two sections, marked by parentheses. The first looks for the start of the target string: a comma and space, a space, or just a comma. The second section looks for either "Incorporated" or "Inc" followed by an optional period.

The Final Results

This simple expression will match six different ways to type *incorporated*, plus differences in spacing. The ETL process would use it in a regular expression Replace function to add a standardized version, like ", Inc.", or replace it with an empty string, like the results set in Figure 11-12.

Company_Name	Company_Name_Standardized
Bisontronics, Inc.	Bisontronics
Daridune, Inc.	Daridune
Daridune, Inc.	Daridune
Synbis, Inc.	Synbis
Inclander Incorporated	Inclander
Vencinc, Inc.	Vencinc
Daridune	Daridune

Figure 11-12: Standardized company names for the sample source data.

Not only does this standardization increase the likelihood of a match, it also improves the analytics. A count of registrations by the standardized company name is much closer to reality. This result is still not perfect; you might be combining companies that are not the same. Remember, matching is all about probabilities.

Where Can You Use RegExps?

Regular expressions can be used to help standardize any text or number column. You can also use them to extract substrings, like the search string component of a complex URL. There are examples of regular expressions to standardize or parse out most common data entry problems. This one works on United States phone numbers (d stand for any digit):

```
(d{3})([- )]|.)*(*(d{3})([- )]|.)*(d{4})
```

You can find regular expression engines in most development toolkits, such as Microsoft's .NET regular expressions library (System.Text.RegularExpressions class); the Java JDK; and in many scripting languages like PHP, Python, and PowerGREP. Many UNIX utilities have regular expression engines built in as well. Your ETL tool may even offer direct access to regular expressions as part of its toolkit. The free version of EditPad Pro is a nice tool for interactive development and testing of your RegExp patterns.

If you have big data integration problems, there are more sophisticated tools to do matching, including name and address lookups, fuzzy matching algorithms, and standardization libraries. However, if you have a relatively small data cleaning or standardization problem, or need to parse out complex string patterns, regular expressions can be a big help.

Populating Fact and Dimension Tables

The articles in this section describe tips and techniques for building the tables in your target dimensional model.

11.27 Pipelining Your Surrogates

Ralph Kimball, DBMS, Jun 1998

Every join key between a fact table and dimension table should be a surrogate or anonymous integer, not a natural key or a smart key. Once you have created dimension records with surrogate keys, any fact table that references these dimensions must be appointed with the right surrogate key values. In this case, the surrogate key in the fact table is a foreign key, which means that the value of the surrogate key exists in the corresponding dimension table. Think of the dimension table as the "key master" for the dimension. The dimension table controls whether the surrogate key is valid because the surrogate key is the primary key in the dimension table.

When every surrogate key in the fact table is a proper foreign key connecting to its respective primary key in one of the dimension tables, the fact table and dimension tables obey referential integrity. Fact tables with foreign keys connecting outward to a halo of dimension tables present an interesting challenge during data extraction: You must intercept all the incoming fact records and replace all their key components with the correct surrogate key values at high speed.

Let's tackle the challenge of creating the primary surrogate keys in the dimension tables first and then deal with fast fact table key substitution.

Keys for the Dimension Tables

When we think about creating the keys for dimension tables, we can distinguish the dimension table's original load from all subsequent loads. The original load probably creates a dimension table with exactly the same number of records as the incoming production data. Assume that the incoming production data is clean and valid and no further deduplicating of the incoming data is needed. Given this assumption, simply assign sequential numbers for the surrogate key as you load the dimension for the very first time. This simple process is just a sequential read of the incoming data, as shown in Figure 11-13.

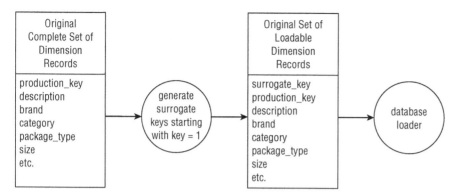

Figure 11-13: The original loading of a dimension where surrogate keys are assigned sequentially to every input record and the natural key becomes an ordinary attribute.

Things get much more interesting after the dimension's original load. The second, and any subsequent, time you read the production data defining the dimension, you must make some complicated decisions. The easiest decision is to recognize new records that have been added to the dimension in the production system and assigned new production keys. For simplicity's sake, imagine that the production data has a clean, well-maintained single field called the natural key. (This discussion doesn't really change if the uniqueness of a production dimension record is defined by several separate fields.) Each time you extract the production dimension information, you must check all the natural keys to see if you've encountered them before. Conceptually, you could just look in the data warehouse dimension table where the natural key is stored as an ordinary field. Momentarily, however, I will recommend a separate lookup table for this purpose, rather than using the real dimension table. (Note: Some ETL tools now allow incremental caching of the dimension tables when this lookup is performed, which is a powerful approach. If this caching is available, then the following discussion of key lookup tables can be skipped.)

When reading the incoming production data that defines the dimension, a more difficult decision comes if you've seen the natural key before but some other attributes in the dimension record have been legitimately changed. This is the classic slowly changing dimension situation; for example, a product might have a minor change in its packaging or ingredients, but the underlying natural key, the stock keeping unit (SKU) number, hasn't changed, or a customer keeps the same customer ID, but some descriptor, such as marital status, has changed. To resolve these problems, you must have a slowly changing dimension policy. This policy says that if certain descriptive fields in a dimension change, the data in the record is destructively overwritten (type 1 change). But if other descriptive fields change, a new data warehouse dimension record is issued (type 2 change). The policy identifies which fields are overwritten or reissued, and the policy is implemented in the transformation logic of the ETL pipeline.

The fastest way to decide if you've seen an incoming natural key before is to have a special table of previously recognized production keys, preferably sorted and indexed for the fastest possible reference, as shown in Figure 11-14. This table has fewer rows than the dimension table because it only has one row for each recognized natural key. Along with the natural key, the lookup table contains the most recent surrogate key associated with this natural key.

production_key	current_surrogate_key
SKU43MFR072	2347
SKU67MFR0064a	4563
SKU112XMfr9	5477
SKU1288MFR13	5432
SKU12-4MFR12	446
SKU34MFR6667	7612
PRODabcSUPPL7	4512

Figure 11-14: The lookup table for a typical dimension with as many rows as there are unique natural keys.

As the incoming production data for the dimension is processed, use the lookup table to decide whether you have seen each natural key before. If you haven't seen the natural key, then you immediately know you must create a new data warehouse dimension record. If you keep track of the highest surrogate key value previously used in this dimension, you can just add one to this value, creating the new dimension record. Conversely, if you've seen the natural key before, then grab the surrogate key from the lookup table and use it to get the most current version of the dimension record. Then compare the current data warehouse version with the incoming production version of the record. If everything matches, then you don't have a slowly changing record, and can go on to the next record in the input. If one or more fields have been changed, use your slowly changing dimension policy to decide whether to overwrite or create a new record. If you create a new record, you must change the lookup table, because now you have a more recent surrogate key that represents your natural key. This decision logic is illustrated in Figure 11-15.

If you're lucky enough to have production data for which the changes have been marked and time stamped, you can avoid the fairly expensive comparison step I just described. However, the rest of the logic probably remains unchanged.

Keys for the Fact Tables

You must process the dimension tables before you even think of dealing with the fact tables. When you're finished updating your dimension tables, not only are all the dimension records correct, but your lookup tables that tie the natural keys to the current surrogate keys have been updated correctly. These little lookup tables are essential for fast fact table processing.

Your task for processing the incoming fact table records is simple to understand. Grab each natural dimension key in the fact table record and replace it with the correct current surrogate key. Notice that I said "replace." Don't keep the natural key value in the fact record itself. If you care what the natural key value is, you can always find it in the associated dimension record.

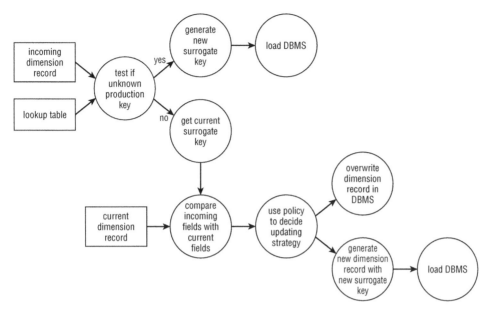

Figure 11-15: Dimension processing logic for all refreshes of a dimension table after the original load.

If you have between four and 20 natural keys, then every incoming fact record requires between four and 20 separate lookups to get the right surrogate keys. Figure 11-16 shows my favorite way to do this quickly. First set up a multi-threaded application that streams all the input records through all the steps shown in Figure 11-16. When I say multi-threaded, I mean that as input record #1 is running the gantlet of successive key lookups and replacements, record #2 is simultaneously behind record #1, and so on. Do not process all the incoming records in the first lookup step and then pass the whole file to the next step. For fast performance, it is essential that the input records are not written to disk until they have passed through all the processing steps. They must "fly" through memory without touching ground (the disk) until the end.

If possible, all the required lookup tables should be pinned in memory so that they can be randomly accessed as each incoming fact record presents its natural keys. This is one of the reasons for making the lookup tables separate from the real dimension tables. Suppose you have a million row lookup table for a dimension. If the natural key is 20 bytes and the surrogate key is 4 bytes, then you need roughly 24 MB of RAM to hold the lookup table. In an environment where you can configure the data staging machine with plenty of RAM, you should be able to get all the lookup tables in memory.

In some important large fact tables, you may have a monster dimension, such as residential customer, with tens of millions of rows. With just one such huge dimension, you can still design a fast pipelined surrogate key system, even though the huge dimension lookup table may need to be read off the disk as it is being used. The secret is to presort both the incoming fact data and the lookup table on the natural key. Now the surrogate key replacement is a single-pass sort merge through the two files. This should be pretty fast, although nothing beats in-memory processing. If you have two such monster lookup tables in your pipeline, you need a consultant!

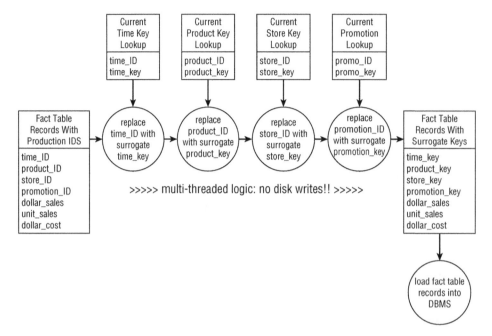

Figure 11-16: The pipelined fact table processing logic for replacing all natural keys (designated as IDs) with surrogate keys.

Although the design of a good fast surrogate key system obviously takes a little thought, you will reap many useful benefits. Surrogate keys will reduce space in the big expensive fact table, eliminate administrative surprises coming from production, potentially adapt to big surprises like a merger or acquisition, have a flexible mechanism for handling slowly changing dimensions, and represent legitimate states of uncertainty for which no natural keys exist.

11.28 Unclogging the Fact Table Surrogate Key Pipeline

Joy Mundy, Design Tip #171, *Jan 5, 2015*

We characterize the ETL system as a back room activity that users should never see nor touch. Even so, the ETL system design must be driven from user requirements. This article looks at the design of one bit of ETL plumbing—the fact table surrogate key pipeline—from the perspective of business users' needs.

The surrogate key pipeline is #14 of the subsystems described in article 11.2, *The 34 Subsystems of ETL*. The surrogate key pipeline is usually the last step of the fact table processing in which the ETL system exchanges source system keys for data warehouse surrogate keys.

For the most part, implementation of the pipeline is a detail safely left to the ETL team. They will decide whether to stage the fact data first, and whether to use an ETL tool widget, lookups, or database joins to do the work of exchanging source system keys for surrogate keys. But the ETL design team needs input from the business user community about how to handle problematic rows described in the following scenarios.

Missing Source System Key

The simplest situation is when an incoming fact row is completely missing a key for one of the dimensions. Sometimes a dimension just doesn't apply to some of the fact rows. For example, consider the scenario of a fact table that describes the sale of products in stores. This dimensional model may include a promotion dimension that describes the marketing promotions and coupons associated with the sale of an item. But many sales are not associated with any promotion at all: The source system promotion code is blank or null.

It is absolutely imperative that each fact table key has a corresponding row in every dimension table. It would be a mistake to handle this missing key problem by inserting a fact row with a null promotion key. A null foreign key in the fact table would automatically violate referential integrity, and no solution involving outer joins would make business sense.

The missing source system key scenario has a simple solution: Put a missing row in the dimension table. It's common to use a surrogate key of –1, and then fill in the other dimension columns with some attractive version of missing, unknown, or not available. Make sure you ask the business users how they want the user-visible attributes in the missing member dimension row to look. Special consideration is needed for missing date keys, as a default value of –1 may affect the overall sort order of the fact table if the leading component of the sorting sequence is a date that might be null. The default value for the "missing date" dimension record should probably be a special very large value to avoid the possibility that such a record would be lumped in the oldest partition of the fact table.

Bad Source System Key

A harder design problem is to handle an incoming source system key that the data warehouse has never seen before. Dimensions should be processed before facts, so under normal circumstances there should be a row in each dimension table for every key in a fact row. But the ETL process must account for the unexpected. We have seen many solutions, none of which is perfect.

Option 1: Throw away the bad fact row.

There are few scenarios in which it would make sense to the business users for the ETL system to throw away incoming fact rows. Throwing away the row would distort overall totals and counts, and there may be salvageable content in the row.

Option 2: Log the bad fact row to an error table.

This is probably the most common solution. It's easy to implement and keeps the fact table and dimension tables clean. However, if your ETL system simply writes the bad rows to an error table and never reviews them, it's functionally equivalent to throwing away the bad fact row. The correct system design should include two processes:

- An automated process that sends the error table rows through the surrogate key pipeline to see if the dimension member has shown up
- A person-based process to evaluate aged errors and communicate with the operational systems for correction or resolution

The biggest downside of this design solution is that the fact data does not get into the fact table. This may be fine for some scenarios, but highly problematic for others, such as finance subject areas which need numbers to balance.

Option 3: Map all bad fact rows to one dimension row.

This solution is very similar to the suggestion for handling a missing source system key: All the bad fact rows get mapped to a single dimension row, let's call it the –2 row. Like the missing or –1 dimension row, this unknown dimension row has attractive default values for all attributes, clarifying the row's purpose.

There are two advantages to this approach: It's extremely simple to implement. It gets the bad fact row into the fact table. In reports, the bad facts all show up associated with the unknown dimension member.

However, there are two significant problems with this approach: 1) Several bad fact rows may get lumped into a single super-row, which makes no business sense; and 2) it is difficult to fix the data if tomorrow's ETL receives the dimension member's details. If it's possible to receive late arriving information about the dimension, the business users may want the ETL to fix up the bad fact row to point to the correct dimension member. But all the bad fact rows have been mapped to –2, no matter what the incoming source system dimension identifier is.

If the business users want the fact rows re-mapped, you will need to capture the source system dimension identifier somewhere. You can either:

- Put the source system identifiers in the fact table, which may add significant width to the fact table and hence degrade query performance.
- Put a surrogate primary key on the fact table, and log the error condition in a separate table which contains both the source system identifiers and the fact table primary key. Use the fact table primary key to find the correct fact rows to update when you learn about a late-arriving dimension member.

In either case, you will need to issue an UPDATE statement against the appropriate fact rows, remapping them from –2 to the correct new dimension key. The primary argument for this approach is simplicity of implementation; but if you need to correct the fact data, this approach isn't simple.

Option 4: Put a unique placeholder row in the dimension (recommended technique).

The final solution to the problem of a bad source system key is to create a placeholder row in the dimension. If the ETL encounters a bad source system key during the fact table processing, it should pause, run over to the dimension table, create a row, get its surrogate key, and hand that key back to the fact table surrogate key pipeline.

These placeholder rows are similar to missing and unknown dimension rows, but they are not exactly the same. We do know one attribute: the source system key.

With this approach, the ETL system is in a great position to fix up the data when it learns about the dimension member. The standard dimension processing will see the dimension attributes change from unknown to their true values. The fact table won't require any updating because the fact rows for this dimension member already had their own surrogate key.

The risk with the placeholder row approach is if there's a high noise-to-signal ratio. Many bad fact rows each of which create a new dimension member, but only a few of those dimension members actually get fixed up in future loads. This is one of the reasons that in real-time ETL systems, where dirty data is arriving every few minutes or seconds, the real-time data is often replaced by a conventional batch load at the end of the day which may have better data quality including complete transaction detail.

Business Requirement Implications

Your design decision about which technique to use for handling problematic fact rows should be driven by the following business user needs:

- Do the business users want the "bad" fact rows in the fact table so the numbers balance? If not, then redirect the problem rows to an error table. Make sure you build processes for getting them out of jail.
- Do the business users want to associate fact rows with late arriving corrections to dimension members? If not, mapping all bad facts to the unknown (–2) member is a possible choice.
- If the business users want the problematic facts in the fact table, and they want to update the dimension members as soon as better information arrives, then the placeholder row approach is a better bet.
- In all cases, someone from the business user community should weigh in on how the placeholder and dummy rows look and behave. Consider sort order too—usually the business users want these dummy rows to show up at the bottom of any list.

This detailed example about the surrogate key pipeline is indicative of how the best ETL system designs follow the Kimball mantra: It's all about the business.

11.29 Replicating Dimensions Correctly

Ralph Kimball, Design Tip #19, *Feb 5, 2001*

The secret of building a distributed data warehouse is using conformed dimensions. The real payoff of using conformed dimensions is being able to drill across separate business process fact tables. If you can constrain and group on the same attributes in each separate subject area, you can then line up the separate answer sets using the row headers from the common dimension table. On one report line you can show metrics from multiple sources side by side.

But administering a conformed dimension requires special discipline. The overall organization needs a dimension manager. This dimension manager is responsible for maintaining the dimension and replicating it successfully to all the business process subject areas that use the dimension in their fact tables. You need to take seriously the task of replicating the dimension and enforcing its consistent use.

It would be a disaster if you drilled across several business processes accumulating results for a report, when half of the subject areas had yesterday's version of the dimension and half had today's. The results would be insidiously wrong. The row labels would not mean the same thing if any of the definitions of any of the reporting attributes had been adjusted. For example, if a category manager had changed the definition of one of the item categories, the reported results across these out-of-sync row headers would be wrong.

A similar issue arises with aggregate fact tables and associated compressed dimension tables. If the dimension manager has released a new dimension table, then all the aggregate tables affected by changes made in the table must be adjusted. For example, if some low level items were moved from one existing category to another, then not only is the item table changed, but any fact table at the category level would have to be adjusted.

We can summarize the two big responsibilities for correctly replicating dimensions:

1. All business process subject areas must deploy the replicated dimension simultaneously so that any user drilling across these subject areas will be using a consistent set of dimension attributes.
2. All subject areas must remove aggregates affected by changes in the dimension, and only make these aggregates available to the users when they have been made completely consistent with the base fact tables and new rollup logic.

11.30 Identify Dimension Changes Using Cyclic Redundancy Checksums

Ralph Kimball, Design Tip #4, Feb 21, 2000

The original title of this article was Super Fast Change Management of Complex Customer Dimensions.

Many data warehouse designers have to deal with a difficult customer dimension that is both wide and deep with 100 or more descriptive attributes and millions of rows. Often the data warehouse receives a complete updated copy of the customer dimension as frequently as once per day. Of course, it would be wonderful if only the deltas (changed records) were delivered to the data warehouse, but more typically the data warehouse has to find the changed records by carefully searching the whole file. This comparison step of each field in each record between yesterday's version and today's version is messy and slow.

Here's a technique that accomplishes this comparison step at blinding speeds and has the added bonus of making your ETL program simpler. The technique relies on a simple cyclic redundancy checksum (CRC) code that is computed for each record (not each field) in the incoming customer file. More on CRCs in a moment. Here are the processing steps:

1. Read each record of today's new customer file and compute the record's CRC code.
2. Compare this record's CRC code with the same record's CRC code from yesterday's run, which you saved. You will need to match on the source system's natural key (customer ID) to make sure you are comparing the right records.
3. If the CRC codes are the same, you can be sure that the entire 100 fields of the two records exactly match. You don't have to check each field!
4. If the CRC codes differ, you can immediately create a new surrogate customer key and place the updated record in the customer dimension. This is a type 2 slowly changing dimension. Or a more elaborate version could search the 100 fields one by one in order to decide what to do. Maybe some of the fields trigger a type 1 overwrite of the dimension attribute instead.

If you have never heard of a CRC code, don't despair. Your ETL programmer knows what it is. CRC is a mathematical technique for creating a unique code for every distinguishable input. The CRC code can be implemented in any programming language. Most introductory computer science textbooks describe the CRC algorithm, or look on Google for "CRC code" or "checksum utility."

11.31 Maintaining Back Pointers to Operational Sources

Ralph Kimball, Design Tip #67, *May 4, 2005*

Our data warehouses are increasingly oriented toward tracking detailed customer transactions in near real time. And as Patricia Seybold points out in her wonderful book, *Customers.com* (Times Business, 2010), managing customer relationships means having access to the data from all the customer-facing processes in an organization.

The combination of keeping the detail behind all the customer-facing processes, but at the same time providing an integrated view, presents an interesting challenge for the ETL architect. Suppose we have a typically complex customer-oriented business with fifteen or more customer-facing systems including store sales, web sales, shipments, payments, credit, support contracts, support calls, and various forms of marketing communications. Many of these systems create their own natural key for each customer, and some of the systems don't do a particularly good job of culling out duplicated entries referring to the same customer. There may be no reliable single customer ID used across all customer-facing source systems.

The ETL architect faces the daunting task of deduplicating customer records from each separate source system, matching the customers across the systems, and surviving the best and most reliable groups of descriptive attributes "cherry picked" from each of the systems.

The dilemma for the ETL architect is that even after producing a perfect final single record for the customer, the business user analyst may be unable to trace backward from the data warehouse to a set of interesting transactions in just one of the source systems. The deduplication and survival steps of preparing the final clean customer master may make subtle changes in names, addresses, and customer attributes that decouple the data warehouse from the original dirty transactions back in the source systems.

The recent demand by the business community to make all customer transaction detail available in the data warehouse means that we need somehow to carry forward all the original source IDs for the customer into the final customer master dimension. Furthermore, if the source systems have generated duplicate records for the same customer (which we find and fix in the ETL pipeline), we need to store all of the original duplicate source system IDs in the customer master dimension. Only by maintaining a complete set of back pointers to the original customer IDs can we provide the level of trace back service that the business analysts are demanding.

I recommend creating a single cross-reference table to hold all the original customer IDs. This table has the following fields:

> Data Warehouse Durable Customer Key
> Source System Name
> Source System Customer ID

The data warehouse natural customer key is a special durable key created by the data warehouse! We need such a permanent, unchanging key in the data warehouse master customer dimension to unambiguously identify slowly changing type 2 versions of a given customer.

This table can be queried directly, constraining the data warehouse durable customer key, or by joining this field to the same field in the master customer dimension. In both cases, the source system fields will give the complete list of back pointers.

This design has the advantage that simply by adding data rows to our little cross-reference table, it flexes gracefully to handle messy duplicated versions of customer IDs in the source systems, as well as the incorporation of new source systems at various points in time.

11.32 Creating Historical Dimension Rows

Warren Thornthwaite, Design Tip #112, May 5, 2009

The business requirement for tracking dimension attribute changes over time is almost universal for DW/BI systems. Tracking attribute changes supports accurate causal analysis by associating the attribute values that were in effect when an event occurred with the event itself. You need a set of ETL tasks to assign surrogate keys and manage the change tracking control fields for this type 2 tracking of historical changes.

One big challenge many ETL developers face is re-creating historical dimension change events during the initial historical data load. This is often a problem because the operational system may not retain history. In the worst case, attribute values are simply overwritten with no history at all.

You need to carefully search the source systems for evidence of historical values. If you can't find all the historical data, or the effort to re-create it is significant, you will need to discuss the implications of incomplete history with business folks. Once the decisions are made, you will need to load what you have and properly set the effective date and end date control columns. We'll talk more about each of these three steps next.

Dig for History

First look at the source tables that directly feed your dimension along with any associated tables. You may find some change tracking system for audit or compliance purposes that isn't obvious from the direct transaction source tables. We worked on one system that wrote the old customer row into a separate history table anytime a value changed. Once we found that table, it was fairly straightforward to re-create the historical dimension rows.

You may need to broaden your search for evidence of change. Any dates in the dimension's source tables might be helpful. Your customer dimension source tables may have fields like registration date, cancel date, or contact date. Transaction events might also be helpful. Sometimes the shipment or customer service systems keep a copy of the customer address in their records each time a fact event occurs.

In the worst case, you may need to pull data from the backup system. Pulling daily backups for a set of tables for the last five years is usually not feasible. Explore the possibility of pulling one backup per month, so you will at least be able to identify changes within a 30-day window of when they actually occurred.

Discuss the Options and Implications

The business folks often don't comprehend the implications of incomplete dimension history without careful explanation and detailed examples. You need to help them understand so they can help make informed decisions. In the worst case, you may not have any change history. Simply associating current dimension values with historical fact events is usually not acceptable from the business perspective. In a case like this, it's not uncommon to only load data from the point where dimension history is available.

Build the Dimension

You may have to pull several different change events for a given dimension together from several sources. Combine all these rows into a single table and order them by the customer transaction key and the dimension change date, which becomes the effective date of the row. The expiration date of each row will depend on the effective date of the next row. You can accomplish the expiration date assignment with a looping function in your language of choice. It's also possible to do it in your database with a cursor or other control structures. Don't worry too much about performance because this is a one-time effort.

Choose a Daily or Minute-Second Grain

For years we have recommended augmenting a type 2 dimension with begin and end effective time stamps to allow for precise time slicing of history as described in this article. But there is a fussy detail that must be considered when creating these time stamps. You must decide if the dimension changes must be tracked on a daily grain (i.e., no more than one change per day) or on a minute-second grain where many changes could occur on a given day. In the first case, you can set the end expiration time stamp to be one day less than the time stamp of the next dimension change, and your BI queries can constrain a candidate date BETWEEN the begin and end time stamps. But if your dimension changes are to be tracked on a minute-second basis, you don't dare set the end time stamp to be "one tick" less than the next dimension change's time stamp because the "tick" is machine and DBMS dependent, and you could end up with gaps in your time sequence. In this case, you must set the end time stamp to be exactly equal to the time stamp of the next change, and forgo the use of the BETWEEN syntax in your BI queries in favor of GREATER-THAN-OR-EQUAL and LESS-THAN.

Here is a set-based example to assign the expiration date for a daily grain customer dimension table that uses the ROW_NUMBER function in Oracle to group all the rows for a given customer in the right order:

```
UPDATE Customer_Master T
SET T.Exp_Date =
    (SELECT NVL(TabB.Real_Exp_Date, '31-DEC-9999')
 FROM
    (SELECT ROW_NUMBER() OVER(Partition by Source_Cust_ID
Order by Eff_Date) AS RowNumA, Customer_Key, Source_Cust_ID,
Eff_Date, Exp_Date
FROM Customer_Master ) TabA    -- target row
LEFT OUTER JOIN
(SELECT ROW_NUMBER() OVER(Partition by Source_Cust_ID
Order by Eff_Date) AS RowNumB, Source_Cust_ID,
Eff_Date -1  AS
    Real_Exp_Date, Exp_Date --  assumes day grain
FROM Customer_Master) TabB    -- next row after the target row
ON TabA.RowNumA = TabB.RowNumB - 1
AND TabA. Source_Cust_ID = TabB. Source_Cust_ID
WHERE T.Customer_Key = TabA.Customer_Key);
```

Here is a set-based example of how to assign the expiration data for a minute-second grain customer dimension table, again using the ROW_NUMBER function. Note that date field references in the first example have been replaced with date/time field references here:

```
UPDATE Customer_Master T
SET T.Exp_Date_Time =
    (SELECT NVL(TabB.Real_Exp_Date_Time,
        '31-DEC-9999 0:0:0')
```

```
FROM
   (SELECT ROW_NUMBER() OVER(Partition by Source_Cust_ID
Order by Eff_Date_Time) AS RowNumA, Customer_Key, Source_Cust_ID,
Eff_Date_Time, Exp_Date_Time
FROM Customer_Master ) TabA   -- The target row
LEFT OUTER JOIN
(SELECT ROW_NUMBER() OVER(Partition by Source_Cust_ID
Order by Eff_Date_Time) AS RowNumB, Source_Cust_ID,
Eff_Date_Time AS
   Real_Exp_Date_Time,
   Exp_Date_Time --  assumes minute-second grain
FROM Customer_Master) TabB   -- next row after the target row
ON TabA.RowNumA = TabB.RowNumB - 1
AND TabA. Source_Cust_ID = TabB. Source_Cust_ID
WHERE T.Customer_Key = TabA.Customer_Key);
```

This article gives you detailed guidance to instrument your slowly changing dimensions with precise time stamps during an initial historical load or routine batch load of large numbers of records.

11.33 Facing the Re-Keying Crisis

Joy Mundy, Design Tip #149, *Oct 2, 2012*

Have you been updating type 1 dimension attributes to reflect current values when the business declares accurate historical context must be preserved (including retroactively for the existing data already loaded into the data warehouse)? How do you tackle the re-keying of an existing dimensional model?

Imagine you're a bank with a mature, dimensional data warehouse. Your current customer dimension has an attribute for credit score, which is initially populated when the customer begins their relationship with your bank. Credit score is managed as type 1 (restate history by updating in place), and updates trickle in sporadically as customers apply for new loans or other credit products.

There are some problems with this design that gradually turn into a crisis. Analysts can't tell whether the credit score is up to date or 10 years old, because it's managed as type 1. Users point out they sometimes want to know the original credit score, and other times they want to know the current credit score, and some of them even want a history of customers' movement from one credit score band to another. The good news, if you can call it that, is that 5 years of detailed historical data is available.

A revised design for the customer dimension could include three new attributes:

- Original credit score (no longer type 1 but unchanged from the original application)
- Current credit score (type 1 updated quarterly from the new data source)
- Credit score band (poor, fair, good, excellent; type 2 updated quarterly from the new data source. Propagate a new row only if the customer moves from one band to another.)

Populating the dimension isn't trivial. The current credit score is easy, because you have a nice clean source from the credit history source. Original credit score could be surprisingly difficult, because most of the bank's systems have overwritten that score, but some sleuthing may uncover an adequate source.

Obtaining the data for the credit score band is easy, but integrating that information into the customer dimension is challenging. You don't want to propagate a new row for each customer every quarter, but only if the customer moved from one credit score band to another. And you need to interweave these new rows propagated by credit score band changes with the existing type 2 customer dimension rows, potentially making many adjustments to the begin and end effective dates in the dimension records.

Finally we come to the problem that is the heart of this article: all the fact tables that refer to the customer dimension need to be altered. You've rebuilt your dimension table, adding new rows for historical changes in credit score band, but the production fact tables have keys pointing to the old customer dimension. All the keys are different now. And remember that most fact tables have orders of magnitude more rows than dimension tables, so any UPDATE operation is extremely unattractive.

Rather than updating a fact table in place, we create a new empty fact table with exactly the same structure as the old fact table. The only thing that's different is the contents of the customer key column. Intellectually the problem is simple: Write a query that joins the old fact table to the new dimension table on the transaction system account number and transaction date, picking up the new surrogate key. You're just pouring water from a full bucket to an identical empty bucket. You may be surprised at how fast your RDBMS can perform this operation: Loading an empty, un-indexed table is extremely fast.

Best practice is to have a test system that's as identical as possible to the production system. Re-key on the test system, which may take several days, then run incremental loads to catch up to real time. When the weekend comes, backup and restore from test to production. If that's not feasible, you'll have to do a table-by-table truncate and simple unload/reload from test to production.

If your data warehouse is currently under development, or in production but small in scope, it makes sense to build an ETL job to re-key each fact table. As already described, the target fact table structure is unchanged; you simply need a job to efficiently load data into an empty table in the test system, using a query that joins the fact table to the dimension table being changed. And of course you need a procedure to test the results and move the new data into production. Moving forward, the exit criteria for releasing a new fact table should include a template job to re-key that fact table.

If your data warehouse is in production and large—dozens or even hundreds of fact tables—it will seem overwhelming to develop a custom ETL job for each fact table. It would be much more cost effective to figure out how to automate the process, by writing a single template job that can be extended to any fact table via metadata or system catalogs. Remember that a fact table can join to a dimension table multiple times. Finally, most data warehouses have one or two fact tables that are much larger than the rest. You will probably develop a custom solution for your very largest fact tables, even if you automate most of the work.

Quite frequently, we see the DW team decide to change an attribute from type 1 to type 2, but only track the type 2 changes moving forward. In effect, the DW team is telling the business users that they need to wait months or years before they can do the historical analysis they're interested in. Or, the business users need to pull down a bunch of data locally, building their own local mart that tracks history the way they want—not a solution that we want to encourage!

Of course in an ideal world the DW team should make copious use of type 2 attributes so this re-keying crisis doesn't occur. It can be seductive to think that "we can make it a type 2 in the future" but as this article shows, doing it in the future is harder than getting it right at the beginning.

11.34 Backward in Time

Ralph Kimball, Intelligent Enterprise, *Sep 29, 2000*

As a data warehouse practitioner, you have been developing powerful techniques for accurately capturing the historical flow of data from your enterprises. Your numeric measurements go into fact tables, and you surround these fact tables with dimension tables containing contemporary descriptions of what you know is true at the time of the measurements.

You allow the descriptions of the customer, product, and store to evolve in the data warehouse whenever these entities change their descriptions. You can distinguish three ways to handle slowly changing dimensions (SCDs). With type 1 and type 3 SCDs, you destructively overwrite the changed value. The type 1 change obliterates the past history, and the type 3 change provides an "alternate reality."

Your main technique for accurately tracking history is the type 2 SCD. With type 2, you issue a new record in the affected dimension that contains an updated description of the customer, product, or store. This updating also forces you to generalize the dimension record key, because now you have more than one record for a single physical entity. When you have assigned the correct surrogate keys for a type 2 SCD, you then must take care to use these surrogate keys in the fact table as you load each day's facts. This process is called the *surrogate key pipeline* and is an important architectural element of the back room ETL system in many data warehouses.

I believe a modern data warehouse needs to possess all the structures that I've described thus far in order to accurately fulfill its mission of correctly describing the historical flow of data. But in many enterprises, a nasty situation arises that violates this surrogate key logic.

What do you do when you receive late-arriving data that should have been loaded into the data warehouse weeks or months ago? There are two interesting cases of this scenario that I'll discuss separately.

Late-Arriving Fact Records

Using my customer purchase scenario, suppose you receive a purchase record today that is several months old. In most operational data warehouses, you are willing to insert this late-arriving record into its correct historical position, even though your sales summary for this prior month will now change. But you must carefully choose the old contemporary dimension records that apply to this purchase. If you have been time stamping the dimension records in your type 2 SCDs, then your processing will involve the following steps:

1. For each dimension, find the corresponding dimension record whose time stamp is the latest time stamp less than or equal to the date of the purchase.
2. Using the surrogate keys found in each of the dimension records from step 1, replace the natural keys of the late-arriving fact record with the surrogate keys.
3. Insert the late-arriving fact record into the correct physical partition of the database containing the other fact records from the time of the late arriving purchase.

Let me make a few subtle points here.

First, I've assumed that dimension records only contain a simple time stamp that indicates when that particular detailed description became valid. You could have assumed that the dimension record contained two time stamps, indicating the beginning and end of the period of validity of the detailed description. An objection to the twin time stamps is that updating a dimension is complicated because you need to be careful to have an unbroken chain of non-overlapping begin and end dates for each customer, product, and store. You avoid these problems with a single time stamp approach, even though it makes certain lookup queries less efficient.

A second subtle point goes back to my assumption that you have an operational data warehouse that is willing to insert these late-arriving records into old months. If your data warehouse has to tie to the books, you can't change an old monthly sales total, even if the old sales total was incorrect. Now you have a tricky situation in which the date dimension on the sales record is for a booking date, which may be today, but the other customer, store, and product dimensions should nevertheless refer to the old descriptions in the way I've described previously. If you are in this situation, you should have a discussion with your finance department to make sure that they understand what you are doing. An interesting compromise I have used in this situation is to carry two date dimensions on purchase records; one refers to the actual purchase date, and the other refers to the booking date.

The third subtle point is that you must insert the late-arriving purchase record into the correct physical partition of the database containing its contemporary "brothers and sisters." This way, when you move a physical partition from one form of storage to another or you perform a backup or restore operation, you will be affecting all the purchase records from a particular span of time. In most cases this is what you want to do. You can guarantee that all fact records in a time span occupy the same physical partition if you declare the physical partitioning of the fact table to be based on the date dimension. Because you should be using surrogate keys for the date dimension, this is the one case when the surrogate keys of a dimension should be assigned in a particular logical order.

To make this point more clearly, let's isolate the following as a design recommendation: *You should assign the time dimension's surrogate keys in sequence so that both the time dimension table and any associated fact table will be in the correct chronological date order when sorted on that surrogate key.*

Late-Arriving Dimension Records

A late-arriving dimension record presents an entirely different set of issues that in some ways are more complex than those in a late-arriving fact record. Suppose you have a fictitious product called Zippy Cola. In the product dimension record for Zippy Cola 12 oz. cans, there is a formulation field that has always contained the value "Formula A." You have a number of records for Zippy Cola 12 oz. cans because this is a slowly changing dimension and other attributes like the package type and subcategory for Zippy Cola 12 oz. cans have changed over the past year or two.

Let's say today you are notified that on July 15, 2015, the formulation of Zippy Cola 12 oz. cans actually was changed to "Formula B" and has been Formula B ever since. To add this new information to the data warehouse requires the following steps:

1. Insert a fresh new record for Zippy Cola 12 oz. cans into the product dimension with the formulation field set to "Formula B" and the effective date set to July 15, 2015. You must create a new surrogate key for this record.

2. Scan forward in the product dimension table from July 15, 2015, finding any other records for Zippy Cola 12 oz. cans, and destructively overwrite the formulation field to "Formula B" in all such records.

3. Find all fact records involving Zippy Cola 12 oz. cans from July 15, 2015, to the first next change for that product in the dimension after July 15, 2015, and destructively change the product foreign key in those fact records to be the new surrogate key you created in step 1.

This is a fairly messy change, but you should be able to automate these steps in a good programmable ETL environment.

There are some subtle issues in this case, too. First, you need to check to see if some other change took place for Zippy Cola 12 oz. cans on July 15, 2015. If so, then you only need to perform step 2.

Second, you can see that using a single date stamp in the slowly changing product dimension simplifies the logic. If you are using a pair of date stamps in each product dimension record, then you need to find the closest previous-to-July-15 product record for Zippy Cola 12 oz. cans and change its end date to July 15, 2015, and you also need to find the closest subsequent-to-July-15 product record for Zippy Cola 12 oz. cans and set the end date for the July 15, 2015 entry to the begin date of that next record. Got it?

Finally, you can see from this example why the surrogate keys for all dimensions, except time, cannot be ordered in any way. You never know when you are going to have to assign a surrogate key for a late-arriving record.

In most of your data warehouses, these late-arriving fact and dimension records are unusual, hopefully. If nothing else, they are bothersome because they change the counts and totals for prior history. But we have taken a pledge as keepers of the data warehouse to present the history of our enterprise as accurately as possible, so we should welcome the old records because they are making our databases more complete.

Some industries, like health care, have huge numbers of late-arriving records. In those cases, these techniques, rather than being specialized techniques for the unusual case, may be the dominant mode of processing.

11.35 Early-Arriving Facts

Ralph Kimball, Design Tip #57, Aug 2, 2004

Data warehouses are usually built around the ideal normative assumption that measured activity (fact records) arrives in the data warehouse at the same time as the context of the activity (dimension records). When we have both the fact records and the correct contemporary dimension records, we have the luxury of bookkeeping the dimension keys first, and then using these up-to-date keys in the accompanying fact records.

Three things may happen when we bookkeep the dimension records:

1. If the dimension entity (say customer) is a new member of the dimension, we assign a fresh new surrogate dimension key.
2. If the dimension entity is a revised version of a customer, we use the type 2 slowly changing dimension technique of assigning a new surrogate key and storing the revised customer description as a new dimension record.
3. Finally if the customer is a familiar, unchanged member of the dimension, we just use the dimension key we already have for that customer.

For several years, we have been aware of special modifications to these procedures to deal with late-arriving facts, namely fact records that come into the warehouse very much delayed. This is a messy situation because we have to search back in history within the data warehouse to decide how to assign the right dimension keys that were in effect when the activity occurred at the right point in the past.

If we have late-arriving facts, is it possible to have early-arriving facts? How can this happen? Are there situations where this is important?

An early-arriving fact takes place when the activity measurement arrives at the data warehouse without its full context. In other words, the statuses of the dimensions attached to the activity measurement are ambiguous or unknown for some period of time. If we are living in the conventional batch update cycle of one or more days' latency, we can usually just wait for the dimensions to be reported to us. For example, the identification of the new customer may come in a separate feed delayed by several hours. We may just be able to wait until the dependency is resolved.

But if we are in a real-time data warehousing situation in which the fact record must be made visible now, and we don't know when the dimensional context will arrive, we have some interesting choices. Our real-time bookkeeping needs to be revised, again using customer as the problem dimension.

1. If the natural customer key on the incoming fact record can be recognized, then we provisionally attach the surrogate key for the existing most recent version of that customer to the fact

table, but we also hold open the possibility that we will get a revised version of this customer reported to us at a later time.

2. If we receive a revised customer record, we add it to the dimension with a new surrogate key and then go in and destructively modify the fact record's foreign key to the customer table.

3. Finally, if we believe that the customer is new, we assign a new customer surrogate key with a set of dummy attribute values in a new customer dimension record. We then return to this dummy dimension record at a later time and make type 1 (overwrite) changes to its attributes when we get more complete information on the new customer. At least this step avoids destructively changing any fact table keys.

There is no way to avoid a brief provisional period where the dimensions are not quite right. But these bookkeeping steps try to minimize the impact of the unavoidable updates to keys and other fields. If these early-arriving records are all housed in a hot partition pinned in memory, then aggregate fact table records should not be necessary. Only when the hot partition is conventionally loaded into the static data warehouse tables at the end of the day (and when the dimensions have caught up with the facts) do you need to build the aggregates.

11.36 Slowly Changing Entities

Ralph Kimball, Design Tip #90, Apr 30, 2007

From time to time we get asked whether the techniques for handling time variance in dimensions can be adapted from the dimensional world to the normalized world. In the dimensional world we call these techniques slowly changing dimensions or SCDs. In the normalized world we might call these slowly changing entities or SCEs. We'll show in this article that while it is possible to implement SCEs, in our opinion it is awkward and impractical to do so.

Consider, for example, an employee dimension containing 50 attributes. In a dimensional schema, this employee dimension is a single flat table with 56 columns. Fifty of the columns are copied from the original source. We assume that these source columns include a natural key field, perhaps called employee ID, which serves to reliably distinguish actual employees. The six additional columns are added to support SCDs in the dimensional world, including a surrogate primary key, change date, begin effective date/time, end effective date/time, change reason, and most recent flag.

Now let's review what we do when we are handed a changed record from the source system. Suppose that an individual employee changes office location, affecting the values of five attributes in the employee record. Here are the steps for type 2 SCD processing:

1. Create a new employee dimension record with the next surrogate key (adding 1 to the highest key value previously used). Copy all the fields from the previous most current record, and change the five office location fields to the new values.

2. Set the change date to today, the begin effective date/time to now, the end effective date/time to December 31, 9999 11:59 pm, the change reason to Relocation, and the most recent flag to true.

3. Update the end effective date/time of the previously most current record for that employee to now, and change the most recent flag to false.

4. Begin using the new surrogate key for that employee in all subsequent fact table record entries.

A slightly more complicated case arises if a hierarchical attribute affecting many employees is changed. For example, if an entire sales office is deemed to be assigned to a new division, then every employee in that sales office needs to undergo the type 2 steps just described, where the sales division fields are the target of the change.

Now what if we have a fully normalized employee database? Remember that normalization requires that every field in the employee record that does not depend uniquely on the employee natural key must be removed from the base employee record and placed in its own table. In a typical employee record with 50 fields, only a small number of high cardinality fields will depend uniquely on the natural key. Perhaps 40 of the fields will be low cardinality fields "normalized out" of the base employee record into their own tables. Perhaps 30 of these fields will be independent of each other and cannot be stored together in the same entity. That means the base employee record must have 30 foreign keys to these entities! There will be additional physical tables containing lower cardinality fields two or more levels away from the base employee table. Instead of maintaining one natural key and one surrogate primary key as in the dimensional world, the DBA and application designer must maintain and be aware of more than 30 pairs of natural and surrogate keys in order to track time variance in the normalized world.

We'll assume that every entity in the normalized database contains all six SCE navigation fields, analogous to the SCD design.

To make the office location change described previously to an individual employee profile, we must perform all the administrative steps listed earlier, for each affected entity. But even worse, if there is a change to any field removed more than one level from the base employee record, the DBA must make sure that the SCE processing steps are propagated downward from the remote entity through each intermediate entity all the way to the base employee table. The base employee table must also support the primary surrogate key for joining to the fact table, unless the normalized designer opts to omit all surrogate keys in favor of only constraining on the begin and end effective date/time stamps. (We think that eliminating all surrogate keys is a performance and applications mistake of the first magnitude.) All of these comments are also true for the second change we described, for the division reassignment of the sales office.

Processing time variance in a fully normalized database involves other nightmares too complicated to describe in detail in this article. For example, if you are committed to a correctly normalized physical representation of your data, then if you discover a business rule that changes a presumed many-to-one relationship in your data to many-to-many, you must undo the key administration and physical table design of the affected entities. These changes also require user queries to be reprogrammed! These steps are not needed in the dimensional world. A second serious problem for handling time variance in the normalized world is how to administer late-arriving dimensional data. Instead of creating and inserting one new dimension record as in the SCD case, we must create and insert new records in every affected entity and all of the parents of these entities back to the base employee record.

As we often remark, a clever person who is a good programmer can do anything. You can make SCEs work in both the ETL back room and the BI front room if you are determined, but because the final data payload is identical to the simpler dimensional SCDs, we respectfully suggest that you win the Nobel prize on a different topic.

11.37 Using the SQL MERGE Statement for Slowly Changing Dimensions

Warren Thornthwaite, Design Tip #107, *Nov 6, 2008*

Most ETL tools provide some functionality for handling slowly changing dimensions. Every so often, when the tool isn't performing as needed, the ETL developer may use the database to identify new and changed rows, and apply the appropriate inserts and updates using standard INSERT and UPDATE statements. A few months ago, my friend Stuart Ozer suggested the new MERGE command in SQL Server 2008 might be more efficient, both from a code and an execution perspective. His reference to a blog by Chad Boyd on MSSQLTips.com gave me some pointers on how it works. MERGE is a combination insert, update, and delete that provides significant control over what happens in each clause.

This example handles a simple customer dimension with two attributes: first name and last name. We are going to treat first name as a type 1 overwrite and last name as a type 2 change.

Step 1: Overwrite the Type 1 Changes

I tried to get the entire example working in a single MERGE statement, but the function is deterministic and only allows one update statement, so I had to use a separate MERGE for the type 1 updates. This could also be handled with an update statement because type 1 is an update by definition.

```
MERGE INTO  dbo.Customer_Master AS CM
USING Customer_Source AS CS
ON (CM.Source_Cust_ID = CS.Source_Cust_ID)
WHEN MATCHED AND -- Update all existing rows for type 1 changes
   CM.First_Name <> CS.First_Name
THEN UPDATE SET CM.First_Name = CS.First_Name
```

This is a simple version of the MERGE syntax that says merge the customer source table into the customer master dimension by joining on the natural key, and update all matched rows where first name in the master dimension table does not equal the first name in the source table.

Step 2: Handle the Type 2 Changes

Now we'll do a second MERGE statement to handle the type 2 changes. This is where things get a little tricky because there are several steps involved in tracking type 2 changes. Our code will need to:

1. Insert new customer rows with the appropriate effective date and end date.
2. Expire the old rows for those that have a type 2 attribute change by setting the appropriate end date and current row flag = 'n'.
3. Insert the changed type 2 rows with the appropriate effective date, end date, and current row flag = 'y'.

The problem with this is it's one too many steps for the MERGE syntax to handle. Fortunately, the merge can stream its output to a subsequent process. We'll use this to do the final insert of the changed type 2 rows by inserting into the customer master table using a SELECT from the MERGE results. This sounds like a convoluted way around the problem, but it has the advantage of only needing to find the type 2 changed rows once, and then using them multiple times.

The code starts with the outer INSERT and SELECT clause to handle the changed row inserts at the end of the MERGE statement. This has to come first because the MERGE is nested inside the INSERT. The code includes several references to getdate; the code presumes the change was effective yesterday (getdate()−1), which means the prior version would be expired the day before (getdate()−2). Finally, following the code, there are comments that refer to the line numbers:

```
1          INSERT INTO Customer_Master
2          SELECT Source_Cust_ID, First_Name, Last_Name,
           Eff_Date, End_Date, Current_Flag
3          FROM
4            (  MERGE Customer_Master     CM
5               USING Customer_Source     CS
6               ON (CM.Source_Cust_ID = CS.Source_Cust_ID)
7               WHEN NOT MATCHED THEN
8                 INSERT VALUES (CS.Source_Cust_ID,
               CS.First_Name, CS.Last_Name,
               convert(char(10), getdate()-1, 101),
               '12/31/2199', 'y')
9               WHEN MATCHED AND CM.Current_Flag = 'y'
10                    AND (CM.Last_Name <> CS.Last_Name )   THEN
11             UPDATE SET CM.Current_Flag = 'n',
                   CM.End_date = convert(char(10),
                   getdate()-2, 101)
12             OUTPUT $Action Action_Out, CS.Source_Cust_ID,
                   CS.First_Name, CS.Last_Name,
                   convert(char(10),
                   getdate()-1, 101) Eff_Date,
                   '12/31/2199' End_Date, 'y' Current_Flag
13            ) AS MERGE_OUT
14         WHERE  MERGE_OUT.Action_Out = 'UPDATE';
```

Here are some additional comments about the code:

- Lines 1–3 set up a typical `INSERT` statement. What we will end up inserting are the new values of the type 2 rows that have changed.
- Line 4 is the beginning of the `MERGE` statement, which ends at line 13. The `MERGE` statement has an `OUTPUT` clause that will stream the results of the `MERGE` out to the calling function. This syntax defines a common table expression, essentially a temporary table in the `FROM` clause, called `MERGE_OUT`.
- Lines 4–6 instruct the `MERGE` to load customer source data into the customer master dimension table.
- Line 7 says when there is no match on the business key, we must have a new customer, so line 8 does the `INSERT`. You could parameterize the effective date instead of assuming yesterday's date.
- Lines 9 and 10 identify a subset of the rows with matching business keys, specifically, where it's the current row in the customer master and any one of the type 2 columns is different.
- Line 11 expires the old current row in the customer master by setting the end date and current row flag to 'n'.
- Line 12 is the `OUTPUT` clause, which identifies what attributes will be output from the `MERGE`, if any. This is what will feed into the outer `INSERT` statement. The `$Action` is a `MERGE` function that tells us what part of the merge each row came from. Note that the output can draw from both the source and the master. In this case, we are outputting source attributes because they contain the new type 2 values.
- Line 14 limits the output row set to only the rows that were updated in customer master. These correspond to the expired rows in Line 11, but we output the current values from customer source in Line 12.

The big advantage of the `MERGE` statement is being able to handle multiple actions in a single pass of the data sets, rather than requiring multiple passes with separate inserts and updates. A well-tuned optimizer could handle this extremely efficiently.

11.38 Creating and Managing Shrunken Dimensions

Warren Thornthwaite, Design Tip #137, *Aug 2, 2011*

This article is part of a series on implementing common ETL design patterns. These techniques should prove valuable to all ETL system developers, and, we hope, provide some product feature guidance for ETL software companies as well.

Recall that a shrunken dimension is a subset of a dimension's attributes that apply to a higher level of summary. For example, a Month dimension would be a shrunken subset of the Date dimension. The Month dimension could be connected to a forecast fact table whose grain is at the monthly level.

I recently ran across a good example of the need for a shrunken dimension from a Kimball Group enthusiast who works for a company that manages shopping mall properties. They capture some facts at the store level such as rent payments, and other facts at the overall property level such as shopper traffic and utility costs. Remember, a fundamental design goal is to capture data at the lowest grain possible. In this case, we would first attempt to allocate the property level data down to the store level. However, the company in question felt some of the property data could not be sensibly allocated to the store level, therefore, they needed fact tables at both the store and property levels. This means they also needed dimensions at the store and property level.

Create the Base Dimension

There are many ways to create a shrunken dimension, depending on how the data is structured in the source system. The easiest way is to create the base dimension first. In this case, build the Store dimension by extracting store and property level natural keys and attributes from the source, assigning surrogate keys and tracking changes to important attributes with type 2 change tracking.

The Store dimension will have several property level attributes including the property's natural key because users will want to roll up store facts by property descriptions. They will also ask questions that only involve the relationship between store and property, such as "What is the average number of stores per property?"

Create the Shrunken Dimension from the Base Dimension

Once the lowest level dimension is in place, creating the initial shrunken dimension, in this case the Property dimension, is essentially the same as creating the mini-dimension described in the next article. Identify the attributes you want to extract from the base dimension and create a new table with a surrogate key column. Populate the table using a SELECT DISTINCT of the columns from the base dimension along with an IDENTITY field or SEQUENCE to create the surrogate key. In the property example, the following SQL would get you started:

```
INSERT INTO Dim_Property
SELECT DISTINCT Property_Name, Property_Type, Property_SqFt,
MIN(Effective_Date), MAX(End_Date)
FROM Dim_Store
GROUP BY Property_Name, Property_Type, Property_SqFt;
```

The incremental processing is a bit more challenging. The easiest approach if you are working from an existing base dimension as we've described is to use the brute force method. Create a temporary shrunken dimension by applying the same SELECT DISTINCT to the newly loaded base dimension. Then process any type 2 changes by comparing the current rows of the temporary shrunken dimension (WHERE End_Date = '9999-12-31') to the current rows of the master shrunken dimension based on the shrunken dimension's natural key. This may sound inefficient, but a test run only took 10 seconds against a base dimension with over 1.1 million rows on a virtual machine on a laptop.

Alternative: Create the Base and Shrunken Dimensions Separately

If you have separate source tables for the shrunken dimension attributes, you could use them to create the shrunken dimension directly. Again, assign surrogate keys, and track changes using type 2 change tracking. The completed shrunken dimension can be joined back to the base dimension early in the ETL process to populate the current higher-level attributes. Then you can proceed with the base dimension change tracking. The hard part is creating the historical base and shrunken dimensions because you have to compare both the effective dates and end dates from both dimensions, inserting new rows into the base dimension when changes in the shrunken dimension occur.

Present the Dimensions to the Users

Once you have your historical dimensions populated and ETL processes in place, the final decision is how to represent these tables to the user. The shrunken dimension can be presented exactly as it exists, joining to higher level facts as needed. When users see the base dimension, they like to see the associated attributes from the shrunken dimension as well. This could be done in several ways: either through a view that joins the base dimension to the shrunken dimension via the shrunken dimension's surrogate key, or by defining the joins in your BI tool's semantic layer, or by actually joining the tables in the ETL process and physically instantiating the shrunken dimension columns in the base dimension.

All of these approaches should look exactly the same to the users. The only difference might be in performance, and you'd have to experiment with your system to see which works faster for most queries. We usually find we get the best performance and simplest semantic layer by pre-joining the tables in the ETL process and physically copying the columns, unless they are very large tables.

11.39 Creating and Managing Mini-Dimensions

Warren Thornthwaite, Design Tip #127, Sep 1, 2010

This article describes how to create and manage mini-dimensions. Recall that a mini-dimension is a subset of attributes from a large dimension that tend to change rapidly, causing the dimension to grow excessively if changes were tracked using the type 2 technique. By extracting unique combinations of these attribute values into a separate dimension, and joining this new mini-dimension directly to the fact table, the combination of attributes that were in place when the fact occurred are tied directly to the fact record. (For more information about mini-dimensions, see article 9.24, Slowly Changing Dimensions Are Not Always as Easy as 1, 2, and 3, and article 10.14, Dimension Embellishments.)

Creating the Initial Mini-Dimension

Once you identify the attributes you want to remove from the base dimension, the initial mini-dimension build is easily done using the brute force method in the relational database. Simply create a new table with a surrogate key column, and populate the table using a SELECT DISTINCT of the columns from the base dimension along with an IDENTITY field or SEQUENCE to create the surrogate key. For example, if you want to pull a set of demographic attributes out of the customer dimension, the following SQL will do the trick:

```
INSERT INTO Dim_Demographics
SELECT DISTINCT col 1, col2, ...
FROM Stage_Customer
```

This may sound inefficient, but today's database engines are pretty fast at this kind of query. Selecting an eight column mini-dimension with over 36,000 rows from a 26-column customer dimension with 1.1 million rows and no indexes took 15 seconds on a virtual machine running on my four year old laptop.

Once you have the Dim_Demographics table in place, you may want to add its surrogate key back into the customer dimension as a type 1 attribute to allow users to count customers based on their current mini-dimension values and report historical facts based on the current values. In this case, Dim_Demographics acts as an outrigger table on Dim_Customer. Again, the brute force method is easiest. You can join the Stage_Customer table which still contains the source attributes to Dim_Demographics on all the attributes that make up Dim_Demographics. This multi-join is obviously inefficient, but again, not as bad as it seems. Joining the same million plus row customer table to the 36 thousand row demographics table on all eight columns took 1 minute, 49 seconds on the virtual machine.

Once all the dimension work is done, you will need to add the mini-dimension key into the fact row key lookup process. The easy way to do this during the daily incremental load is to return both the Dim_Customer surrogate key and the Dim_Demographic surrogate key as part of the customer business key lookup process.

Ongoing Mini-Dimension Maintenance

Ongoing management of the dimension is a two-step process: First you have to add new rows to the Dim_Demographics table for any new values or combinations of values that show up in the incoming Stage_Customer table. A simple brute force method leverages SQL's set based engine and the EXCEPT, or MINUS, function:

```
INSERT INTO Dim_Demographics
SELECT DISTINCT Payment_Type, Server_Group, Status_Type,
  Cancelled_Reason, Box_Type, Manufacturer, Box_Type_Descr,
  Box_Group_Descr FROM BigCustomer
EXCEPT SELECT Payment_Type, Server_Group, Status_Type, Cancelled_Reason,
  Box_Type, Manufacturer, Box_Type_Descr, Box_Group_Descr FROM
  Dim_Demographics
```

This should process very quickly because the engine simply scans the two tables and hash matches the results. It took 7 seconds against the full source customer dimension in my sample data, and should be much faster with only the incremental data.

Next, once all the attribute combinations are in place, you can add their surrogate keys to the incoming incremental rows. The same brute force, multi-column join method used to do the initial lookup will work here. Again, it should be faster because the incremental set is much smaller.

By moving the type 2 historical tracking into the fact table, you only connect a customer to their historical attribute values through the fact table. This may not capture a complete history of changes if customer attributes can change without an associated fact event.

You may want to create a separate table to track these changes over time; this is essentially a fact-less fact table that would contain the customer, Dim_Demographics mini-dimension, change event date, and change expiration date keys. You can apply the same techniques we described in article 11.37, *Using the SQL MERGE Statement for Slowly Changing Dimensions*, to manage this table.

11.40 Creating, Using, and Maintaining Junk Dimensions

Warren Thornthwaite, Design Tip #113, Jun 3, 2009

A junk dimension combines several low cardinality flags and attributes into a single dimension table rather than modeling them as separate dimensions. There are good reasons to create this combined dimension, including reducing the size of the fact table and making the dimensional model easier to work with, as described in article 9.13, *De-Clutter with Junk Dimensions*. On a recent project, I addressed three aspects of junk dimension processing: building the initial dimension, incorporating it into the fact processing, and maintaining it over time.

Build the Initial Junk Dimension

If the cardinality of each attribute is relatively low, and there are only a few attributes, then the easiest way to create the dimension is to cross-join the source system lookup tables. This creates all possible combinations of attributes, even if they might never exist in the real world.

If the cross-join of the source tables is too big, or if you don't have source lookup tables, you will need to build your junk dimension based on the actual attribute combinations found in the source data for the fact table. The resulting junk dimension is often significantly smaller because it includes only combinations that actually occur.

We'll use a simple health care example to show both of these combination processes. Hospital admissions events often track several standalone attributes, including the admission type and level of care required, as illustrated in Figure 11-17 showing sample rows from the source system lookup and transaction tables.

Admit_Type_Source

Admit_Type_ID	Admit_Type_Descr
1	Walk-in
2	Appointment
3	ER
4	Transfer

Care_Level_Source

Care_Level_ID	Care_Level_Descr
1	ICU
2	Pediatric ICU
3	Medical Floor

Fact_Admissions_Source

Admit_Type_ID	Care_Level_ID	Admission_Count
1	1	1
2	1	1
2	2	1
5	3	1

Figure 11-17: Sample source data.

The following SQL uses the cross-join technique to create all 12 combinations of rows (4 x3) from these two source tables and assign unique surrogate keys:

```
SELECT  ROW_NUMBER()
  OVER(ORDER BY Admit_Type_ID, Care_Level_ID) AS Admission_Info_Key,
Admit_Type_ID, Admit_Type_Descr, Care_Level_ID, Care_Level_Descr
FROM Admit_Type_Source
CROSS JOIN Care_Level_Source;
```

In the second case, when the cross-join would yield too many rows, you can create the combined dimension based on actual combinations found in the transaction fact records. The following SQL uses outer joins to prevent a violation of referential integrity when a new value shows up in a fact source row that is not in the lookup table:

```
SELECT ROW_NUMBER()
  OVER(ORDER BY F.Admit_Type_ID) AS Admission_Info_Key,
  F.Admit_Type_ID,
  ISNULL(Admit_Type_Descr,
  'Missing Description') Admit_Type_Descr,
  F.Care_Level_ID,
  ISNULL(Care_Level_Descr,
  'Missing Description') Care_Level_Descr
      -- substitute NVL(0) for ISNULL() in Oracle
FROM Fact_Admissions_Source F
LEFT OUTER JOIN Admit_Type_Source C ON
      F.Admit_Type_ID = C.Admit_Type_ID
LEFT OUTER JOIN Care_Level_Source P ON
      F.Care_Level_ID = P.Care_Level_ID;
```

Our example Fact_Admissions_Source table only has four rows, which result in the following Admissions_Info junk dimension, shown in Figure 11-18. Note the missing description entry in row 4.

Admissions_Info Junk Dimension

Admission_Info_Key	Admit_Type_ID	Admit_Type_Descr	Care_Level_ID	Care_Level_Descr
1	1	Walk-In	1	ICU
2	2	Appointment	1	ICU
3	2	Appointment	2	Pediatric ICU
4	5	Missing Description	3	Medical Floor

Figure 11-18: Sample junk dimension rows.

Incorporate the Junk Dimension into the Fact Row Process

Once the junk dimension is in place, you will use it to look up the surrogate key that corresponds to the combination of attributes found in each fact table source row. Some of the ETL tools do not support a multi-column lookup join, so you may need to create a workaround. In SQL, the lookup query would be similar to the second set of code in the preceding section, but it would join to the junk dimension and return the surrogate key rather than joining to the lookup tables.

Maintain the Junk Dimension

You will need to check for new combinations of attributes every time you load the dimension. You could apply the second set of SQL code to the incremental fact rows and select out only the new rows to be appended to the junk dimension as shown here:

```
SELECT * FROM ( {Select statement from second SQL code listing} ) TabA
WHERE TabA.Care_Level_Descr = 'Missing Description'
OR TabA.Admit_Type_Descr = 'Missing Description'  ;
```

This example would select out row 4 in the junk dimension. Identifying new combinations could be done as part of the fact table surrogate key substitution process, or as a separate dimension-processing step prior to the fact table process. In either case, your ETL system should raise a flag and notify the appropriate data steward if it identifies a missing entry.

There are a lot of variations on this approach depending on the size of your junk dimension, your sources, and the integrity of your data, but these examples should get you started.

11.41 Building Bridges

Warren Thornthwaite, Design Tip #142, Feb 1, 2012

The relationship between a fact table and its dimensions is usually many-to-one. That is, one row in a dimension, such as customer, can have many rows in the fact table, but one row in the fact table should belong to only one customer. However, there are times when a fact table row can be associated with more than one value in a dimension. We use a bridge table to capture this many-to-many relationship, as described in article 10.3, Help for Dimensional Modeling.

Article 10.3 identifies two major classes of bridge tables. The first, and easiest to model, captures a simple set of values associated with a single fact row. For example, an emergency room admittance record may have one or more initial disease diagnoses associated with it. There is no time variance in this bridge table because it captures the set of values that were in effect when the transaction occurred.

The second kind of a many-to-many relationship exists independent of the transactions being measured. The relationship between Customer and Account is a good example. A customer can have one or more accounts, and an account can belong to one or more customers, and this relationship can vary over time.

This article covers the steps to create a simple static bridge table; this approach can be extended to support the more complex time-variant bridge table.

Historical Load

The steps involved in creating the historical bridge table depend on how the data is captured in the source system. Our assumption is the source captures data that associates the multi-valued set of dimension IDs with each transaction ID. In the diagnosis example, this would be a table with one row for each admission record transaction ID and diagnosis ID. Note that this table will have more rows than the number of individual admission transactions.

Create the Initial List of Groups

Since the source is normalized and has one row per dimension value, the first step is to create a unique list of the groups of diagnoses that occur in the transaction table. This involves grouping the sets of diagnoses together, de-duplicating the list of groups, and assigning a unique key to each group. This is often easiest to do in SQL by creating a new table to hold the list of groups. Using the diagnosis example, Figure 11-19 shows how the first few rows from the transaction system might be grouped and de-duplicated into the Diagnosis Group table.

ER_Admittance_Transactions

ER_Admittance_ID	Diagnosis_ Code
27	T41.201
27	Z77.22
28	K35.2
28	B58.09
28	I13.10
29	T41.201
29	Z77.22

Diagnosis_Group

Diagnosis_ Group_Key	Diagnosis_Code_List
1	B58.09, I13.10, K35.2
2	T41.201, Z77.22

Figure 11-19: Source transaction data and associated diagnosis group table.

There are many ways to do this in the various dialects of SQL. The following version uses a string aggregation approach based on SQL Server T-SQL, using the STUFF() string function to do the concatenation, the FOR XML PATH to collapse the rows into each transaction's set of codes, the SELECT DISTINCT to create the unique list of groups, and the Row_Number() function to assign the group key:

```
SELECT Row_Number() OVER ( ORDER BY Diagnosis_Code_List) AS
Diagnosis_Group_Key, Diagnosis_Code_List
INTO Diagnosis_Group
FROM(
SELECT DISTINCT Diagnosis_Code_List
FROM
(SELECT DISTINCT OuterTrans.ER_Admittance_ID,
STUFF((SELECT ', ' + CAST(Diagnosis_Code AS VARCHAR(1024))
FROM ER_Admittance_Transactions InnerTrans
WHERE InnerTrans.ER_Admittance_ID = OuterTrans.ER_Admittance_ID
ORDER BY InnerTrans.Diagnosis_Code
FOR XML PATH('')),1,2,'') AS Diagnosis_Code_List
FROM ER_Admittance_Transactions OuterTrans
) OuterList
) FinalList;
```

Make sure your version of this code keeps the group lists in consistent order; in some cases the group 'T41.201, Z77.22' is the same as the group 'Z77.22, T41.20'. In health care, the order is often important and both groups would be created; the source system must provide a sequence number which would be included in the inner sort order and passed through to the bridge table. Note that the Diagnosis Group table is much shorter than the original source data. This is partly because we've flattened the row set, but also because the number of combinations of values used in real life is often much smaller than the theoretically possible combinations.

Create the Bridge Table

Once we've done the work to create the Diagnosis Group table and assign the group keys, we need to unpivot it to create the actual Diagnosis Bridge table. This is the table that maps each group to the individual dimension rows from which it is defined. Figure 11-20 shows the Diagnosis Bridge table and the associated ICD10_Diagnosis dimension table based on our example data.

Again, there are many ways to accomplish this in SQL. The following version in SQL Server T-SQL uses a two-step process to unpivot the group table. The first step concatenates XML tags (<I> </I>) into the Diagnosis_Code_List and converts it to an XML datatype as part of a common table expression. The second step uses the CROSS APPLY command to parse out the XML tags and list the values on separate lines:

```
WITH XMLTaggedList AS (
SELECT Diagnosis_Group_Key,
CAST('<I>' + REPLACE(Diagnosis_Code_List, ', ', '</I><I>') + '</I>'
  AS XML)
AS Diagnosis_Code_List
FROM Diagnosis_Group
)
SELECT Diagnosis_Group_Key,
ExtractedDiagnosisList.X.value('.', 'VARCHAR(MAX)') AS
  Diagnosis_Code_List
FROM XMLTaggedList
CROSS APPLY Diagnosis_Code_List.nodes('//I') AS
  ExtractedDiagnosisList(X);
```

Diagnosis_Bridge

Diagnosis Group Key	Diagnosis _Key
1	1
1	3
1	5
2	4
2	5

ICD10_Diagnosis

Diagnosis _Key	Diagnosis _Code	Diagnosis_Description
1	B58.09	Other toxoplasma oculopathy
2	I13.10	Hypertensive heart and chronic kidney disease without heart failure
3	K35.2	Acute appendicitis with generalized peritonitis
4	T41.201	Poisoning by unspecified general anesthetics, accidental (unintentional)
5	Z77.22	Contact with and (suspected) exposure to environmental tobacco smoke

Figure 11-20: Diagnosis Bridge table and associated ICD10_Diagnosis dimension.

Incremental Processing

The incremental load process applies essentially the same code to the incoming fact rows. The first step generates a Diagnosis_Code_List column for each group of incoming fact rows at the grain of the fact table. This Diagnosis_Code_List value can then be used to join to the Diagnosis_Group table to map incoming fact rows to the appropriate group key. If a new group shows up, the ETL process will need to add it the Diagnosis_Group table, just like it does for mini-dimensions and junk dimensions.

We've used SQL to illustrate the design pattern used in creating a bridge table. The same logic could be implemented in the native syntax and control structures of most ETL tools. Of course, if would be ideal if the ETL tool developers built bridge table processing into their toolset rather than forcing us all to reinvent the wheel.

11.42 Being Offline as Little as Possible

Ralph Kimball, Design Tip #27, *Aug 28, 2001*

If you update your data warehouse each day, you have a characteristic scramble when you take yesterday's data offline and bring today's data online. During that scramble, your data warehouse is probably unavailable. If all your business users are in the same time zone, you may not be feeling much pressure, as long as you can run the update between 3 and 5 a.m. But, more likely, if your users are dispersed across the country or around the world, you want to be offline absolutely as little as possible, because in your case, the sun never sets on the data warehouse. So, how can you reduce this downtime to the bare minimum?

In this article, we describe a set of techniques that will work for all of the major relational DBMSs that support partitioning. The exact details of administering partitions will vary quite a bit across the DBMSs, but you will know what questions to ask.

A partition in a DBMS is a physical segment of a DBMS table. Although the table has a single name as far as applications are concerned, a partitioned table can be managed as if it is made up of separate physical files. In this article, I assume your partitioning allows:

- Moving a partition, but not the whole table, to a new storage device
- Taking a partition, but not the whole table, offline
- Dropping and rebuilding any index on the partition, but not the whole table
- Adding, deleting, and modifying records within a designated partition
- Renaming a partition
- Replacing a partition with an alternate copy of that partition

Your DBMS lets you partition a table based on a sort order that you specify. If you add data on a daily basis, you need to partition your fact tables based on the main date key in the fact table. In other articles I have mentioned that if you are using surrogate (integer) keys then you should make sure that the surrogate keys for your date dimension table are assigned in order of the true underlying dates. That way, when you sort your fact table on the date surrogate key, all the most current records cluster in one partition. Furthermore, it's acceptable to use a more meaningful surrogate date key, such as yyyymmdd, to simplify the partitioning task.

If your fact table is named FACT, you also need an unindexed copy called LOADFACT. Actually, in all the following steps we're only talking about the most current partition, not the whole table! Here are the steps to keep you offline as little as possible. We go offline at step 4 and come back online at step 7.

1. Load yesterday's data into the LOADFACT partition. Complete quality assurance pass.
2. When done loading, make a copy of LOADFACT named COPYLOADFACT.
3. Build indexes on LOADFACT.

4. Take FACT offline (actually just the most current partition).
5. Rename the most current FACT partition to be SAVEFACT.
6. Rename the LOADFACT (partition) to be most current FACT partition.
7. Bring FACT online.
8. Now clean up by renaming COPYLOADFACT to be the new LOADFACT. You can resume dribbling incoming data into this new LOADFACT.
9. If all is well, you can delete SAVEFACT.

So, we have reduced the offline interval to just two renaming operations in steps 5 and 6. Almost certainly, these renaming operations will be faster if the physical size of the most current partition is as small as possible.

There is no question that this scenario is an idealized goal. Your data warehouse will have additional complexities. The main complexities you will have to think through include:

- Limitations to the partitioning capability of your DBMS
- Need to load old, stale data into your fact table that would disrupt the "most current" assumption
- Handling associated aggregate fact tables

Supporting Real Time

These articles discuss the requisite ETL system modifications to satisfy user demands for more real-time data warehousing. Although the state of the art has obviously evolved since these articles were written, the basic approaches described here remain surprisingly relevant today, appreciating that the data volumes have grown by a factor of 100 or even 1000, and the expectations for real-time performance are even more exaggerated!

11.43 Working in Web Time

Ralph Kimball, Intelligent Enterprise, *Nov 16, 1999*

Web-created demands are drawing the data warehouse increasingly closer to the front line of operational reporting and operational response generation, forcing us to rethink our data warehouse architecture. Ten years ago we considered the data warehouse a kind of background resource for management, who queried it in a non-urgent, contemplative mode. But today's dramatically increased pace of business decision making requires not only a comprehensive snapshot of the business in real time, but simultaneously, answers to broad questions about customer behavior.

With this data warehouse evolution, we have managed to make three big technical design factors more difficult, all at once:

- **Timeliness.** Business results must now be available in real time. "As of the previous day" reporting, on the wish list two years ago, is no longer a sufficient pace. Increasingly more efficient delivery pipelines with smaller, just-in-time inventories, along with mass customization, force us to quickly understand and respond to demand.
- **Data volumes.** The big move to mass customization means we now capture, analyze, and respond to every transaction in the business including every gesture a customer makes, both before and after operational or sales transactions, and there seems to be no volume limit. For instance, the combined Microsoft-related websites on some busy days have captured more than a billion page events!
- **Response times.** The web makes fast response times critical. If something useful doesn't happen within 10 seconds, I'm on to another page. Those of us who run big data warehouses know that many queries will take more than 10 seconds. But our pleas to the users to be understanding of performance issues are falling on deaf ears.

As these design factors have become more difficult, we find ourselves supporting a broader continuum of users and requests. With the increased operational focus of the data warehouse, and the increased ability of many people worldwide to present themselves at our website doorstep, we must provide data warehouse services to a widely varying mix of external customers, business partners, and suppliers as well as internal salespeople, employees, analysts, and executives. We must deliver a mixture of query results, top line reports, data mining results, status updates, support answers, custom greetings, and images. Most of these things aren't nice rows from an answer set; they are messy, complex objects.

To address these issues, we need to adjust our data warehouse architecture. We can't just make our single database server increasingly powerful. We can't make it deliver all these complicated objects and hope to keep up with these escalating requirements.

One way to take pressure off the main database engines is to build a powerful hot response cache, shown in Figure 11-21, that anticipates as many of the predictable and repeated information requests as possible. The hot response cache adjoins the application servers that feed the public web server and the private firewall entry point for employees. A series of batch jobs running in the main application server creates the cache's data. Once stored in the hot response cache, the data objects can be fetched on demand through either a public web server application or a private firewall application.

The fetched items are complex file objects, not low level data elements. The hot response cache is therefore a file server, not a database. Its file storage hierarchy will inevitably be a simple kind of lookup structure, but it does not need to support a complex query access method.

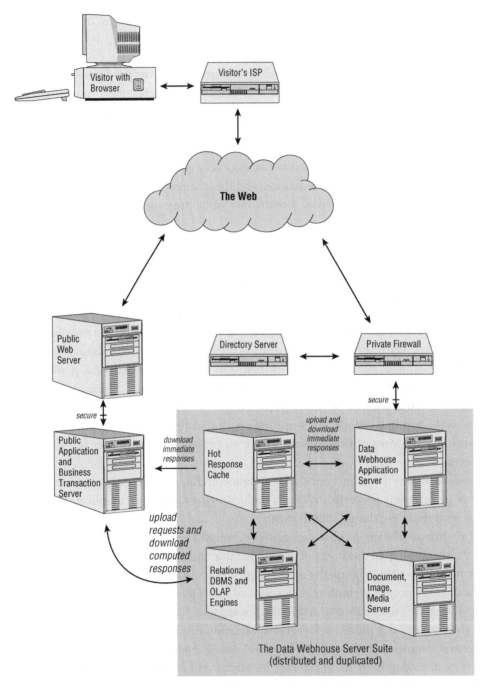

Figure 11-21: The web-intensive data warehouse architecture, showing the hot response cache and the application server that creates its contents.

Security is the requesting application server's responsibility, not the cache's. The application servers should be the only entities able to access the hot response cache directly, and they make their security decisions based on centrally administered, named roles.

The hot response cache is more than the ODS from the early 1990s. The ODS was built most often when legacy operational systems were incapable of responsively reporting status on individual accounts. The hot response cache not only provides this original ODS function, but also provides:

- Custom greetings to web visitors, consisting of both text and graphics
- Cross-selling and up-selling propositions to web visitors perhaps based on data mining applications looking for other cohort members of the web visitor's demographic cluster or behavior cluster
- Dynamically chosen promotion content to web visitors
- XML-based, structured-form content to business partners (what we used to call EDI) requesting delivery status, order status, hours' supply in inventory (our earlier interest in days' supply is becoming obsolete), and critical path warnings in the delivery pipeline
- Low level FAQ-like answers to problems and support requests
- Mid-line reports to customers and business partners in the delivery pipeline, needing a moderate amount of integration across time (such as last 10 orders or returns) or across business function (manufacturing, inventory, and so on)
- Top-line reports to management, needing significant integration across time (multiyear trends), customers, product lines, or geographies all delivered in three interchangeable formats including page-oriented report, pivot table, and graph, and frequently accompanied by images
- Downloadable precomputed OLAP cubes for exploratory analysis
- Data mining studies, both near term and long term, showing the evolution of customer demographic and behavior clusters, and the effects of decisions about promotion content and website content on business done through the web
- Conventional aggregations that enhance query performance when drilling up through standard hierarchies in the major dimensions such as customer, product, and time

The hot response cache's management must help it support the application servers' needs. Ideally, a batch job will have computed and stored in advance the information object that the application server needs. All applications need to be aware that the hot response cache exists and should be able to probe it to see if the answer they want is already there. The hot response cache has two distinct modes of use; the nature of the visitor session requesting the data determines which one to use.

The guaranteed response time request must produce some kind of answer in response to a page request that the web server is handling, usually in less than a second. If the requested object (such as a custom greeting, a custom cross-selling proposition, an immediate report, or an answer to a question) has not been precomputed and hence is not stored, a default response object must be delivered in its place, all within the guaranteed response time.

The accelerated response time request hopes to produce a response to the web visitor's request but will default to computing the response directly from the underlying data warehouse if the pre-computed object is not found immediately. The application server should optionally be able to warn the user that there may be a delay in providing the response in this case. The web server needs to be able to alert the application server if it detects that the user has gone on to another page, so the application server can halt the data warehouse process.

Note that this strategy of seeking a precomputed answer and defaulting if necessary to the base data is exactly the way conventional aggregates have always worked in the data warehouse. The data warehouse aggregate navigator has always searched for aggregates to answer portions of an overall report query. If the navigator finds the aggregate, it uses it. But if it doesn't find the aggregate, it grace-fully defaults to computing the answer slowly from the base data. Viewed this way, the hot response cache is a kind of supercharged aggregate navigator.

Any time you design something for the web, especially if it's used in conjunction with the pub-lic web server, you must pay special attention to scaling and explosive surges in demand. The hot response cache is, by its nature, an I/O engine, not a computing engine. It is, after all, a file server. The scalability bottleneck for the hot response cache, therefore, is not computing power, but I/O bandwidth. In periods of peak demand, the hot response cache must provide a flood of large file objects to the requesting application servers.

Building a hot response cache is not a panacea. It introduces another server in what is already a complex architecture. The hot response cache implies administrative support and a particular disci-plined application development style. But it is still worth it. The hot response cache takes enormous pressure off of the database management systems and the application systems when they are faced with the timeliness, data volume, and response time requirements so typical of the web.

11.44 Real-Time Partitions

Ralph Kimball, Intelligent Enterprise, *Feb 1, 2002*

In the past two years, a major new requirement has been added to the data warehouse designer's mental list. The data warehouse now must seamlessly extend its existing historical time series right up to the current instant. If the customer has placed an order in the last hour, you need to see this order in the context of the entire customer relationship. Furthermore, you need to track the hourly status of this most current order as it changes during the day.

Even though the gap between the production OLTP systems and the data warehouse has shrunk in most cases to 24 hours, the rapacious needs of our marketing users require the data warehouse to fill this gap with real-time data.

Most data warehouse designers are skeptical that the existing ETL jobs can simply be sped up from a 24-hour cycle time to a 15-minute cycle time. Even if the data cleaning steps are pipelined to occur in parallel with the final data loading, the physical manipulations surrounding the biggest fact and dimension tables simply can't be performed every 15 minutes.

Data warehouse designers are responding to this crunch by building a *real-time partition* in front of the conventional, static data warehouse.

Requirements for Real-Time Partitions

To achieve real-time reporting, we build a special partition that is physically and administratively separated from the conventional static data warehouse tables. Actually, the name partition is a little misleading. The real-time partition may not be a literal table partition, in the database sense. Rather, the real-time partition may be a separate table, subject to special rules for update and query.

The real-time partition, whether it is an actual partition or a separate table, ideally should meet the following tough set of requirements. It must:

- Contain all the activity that has occurred since the last update of the historical data warehouse (assume right now that the more static historical tables are updated each night at midnight).
- Link as seamlessly as possible to the grain and content of the static data warehouse fact tables.
- Be indexed so lightly that incoming data can continuously be "dribbled in".
- Support highly responsive queries.

In the dimensional modeling world there are three main types of fact tables: transaction grain, periodic snapshot grain, and accumulating snapshot grain, as described in article 8.5, Fundamental Grains. The real-time partition has a different structure corresponding to each type.

Transaction Grain Real-Time Partitions

If the historical data warehouse fact table has a transaction grain, then it contains exactly one record for each individual transaction in the source system from the beginning of "recorded history." If no activity occurs in a time period, there are no transaction records. Conversely, there can be a blizzard of closely related transaction records if the activity level is high. The real-time partition has exactly the same dimensional structure as its underlying more static fact table. It contains only the transactions that have occurred since midnight, when you loaded the regular data warehouse tables. The real-time partition may be completely unindexed, both because you need to maintain a continuously open window for loading, but also because there is no time series—because you keep only today's data in this table. Finally, you avoid building aggregates on this partition because you want a minimalist administrative scenario during the day.

Attach the real-time partition to your existing applications by drilling across from the historical fact table to the real-time partition, or if you can, make the real-time partition be a true database partition of your fact table. Time series aggregations (for example, all sales for the current month) will need to send identical queries in the case of two fact tables and add them together. If you can use a partition-based approach, then you need only a single query.

In a relatively large retail environment experiencing 10 million transactions per day, the historical fact table would be pretty big. Assuming that each transaction grain record is 40 bytes wide (seven dimensions plus three facts, all packed into 4-byte fields), you accumulate 400 MB of data each day.

Over a year, this would amount to about 150 GB of raw data. Such a fact table would be heavily indexed and supported by aggregates. But the daily slice of 400 MB (the real-time partition) could be pinned in memory. Forget indexes, except maybe a B-tree index on the primary key to support rapid data loading! Forget aggregations! Your real-time partition can remain biased toward very fast loading performance but at the same time provide speedy query performance.

Because you send identical queries to the more static fact table as well as the real-time partition, you can relax and let the aggregate navigator sort out whether either of the tables (or partitions) has supporting aggregates. In the case just described, only the big historical table needs them.

Periodic Snapshot Real-Time Partition

If the historical data warehouse fact table has a periodic grain (say monthly), then the real-time partition can be viewed as the current hot rolling month. Suppose you are a big retail bank with 15 million accounts. The historical static fact table has the grain of account by month. A 36-month time series would result in 540 million fact table records. Again, this table would be extensively indexed and supported by aggregates in order to provide good performance. The real-time partition, on the other hand, is just an image of the current developing month, updated continuously as the month progresses. Semi-additive balances and fully additive facts are adjusted as frequently as they are reported. In a retail bank, the "core" fact table spanning all account types is likely to be quite narrow, with perhaps four dimensions and four facts, resulting in a real-time partition of 480 MB. The real-time partition again can be pinned in memory.

Query applications drilling across from the static fact table to the real-time partition have slightly different logic compared to the transaction grain. Although account balances and other measures of intensity can be trended directly across the tables, additive totals accumulated during the current rolling period may need to be scaled upward to the equivalent of a full month to keep the results from looking anomalous.

Finally, on the last day of the month, the accumulating real-time partition can, with luck, just be loaded onto the historical data warehouse as the most current month, and the process can start again with an empty real-time partition.

Accumulating Snapshot Real-Time Partition

Accumulating snapshots are used for short-lived processes like orders and shipments. A record is created for each line item on the order or shipment. In the historical fact table, this record is updated repeatedly as activity occurs. You create the record for a line item when the order is first placed, then update it whenever the item is shipped, delivered to the final destination, paid for, and maybe returned. Accumulating snapshot fact tables have a characteristic set of date foreign keys corresponding to each of these steps.

In this case, it is misleading to call the historical data warehouse fact table static because this is the one fact table type that is deliberately updated, often repeatedly. But let's assume that for query performance reasons, this update occurs only at midnight when the users are offline. In this case, the real-time partition will consist of only those line items that have been updated today. At the end of the day, the records in the real-time partition will be precisely the new versions of the records that need to be written onto the historical fact table either by inserting the records if they are completely new or overwriting existing records with the same primary keys.

In many order and shipment situations, the number of line items in the real-time partition will be significantly smaller than the first two examples. For example, the biggest dog and cat food manufacturer in the United States processes about 60,000 shipment invoices per month. Each invoice may have 20 line items. If an invoice line has a normal lifetime of two months and is updated five times in this interval, then we would see about 7,500 line items updated on an average working day. Even with the rather wide 80-byte records typical of accumulating invoice fact tables, we only have 600 KB of data in our real-time partition. This will obviously fit in memory. Forget indexes and aggregations on this real-time partition.

Queries against an accumulating snapshot with a real-time partition need to fetch the appropriate line items from both the main fact table and the partition and can either drill across the two tables by performing a sort merge (outer join) on the identical row headers or perform a union of the rows from the two tables, presenting the static view augmented with occasional supplemental rows in the report representing today's hot activity.

In this article I have made what I hope is a strong case for satisfying the new real-time requirement with specially constructed, but nevertheless familiar, extensions of existing fact tables. If you drop nearly all the indexes and aggregations on these special new tables and pin them in memory, you should be able to get the combined update and query performance that you need.

11.45 The Real-Time Triage

Ralph Kimball, Design Tip #89, *Mar 20, 2007*

Asking business users if they want "real-time" delivery of data is a frustrating exercise for the BI system designer. Faced with no constraints, most users will say "that sounds good, go for it!" This kind of response is almost worthless. One is left wondering if the user is responding to a fad.

To avoid this situation we recommend dividing the real-time design challenge into three categories, which we call daily, frequently, and instantaneous. We use these terms when we talk to users about their needs, and we design our data delivery pipelines differently for each of these choices.

Instantaneous means that the data visible on the screen represents the true state of the source transaction system at every instant. When the source system status changes, the screen responds instantly and synchronously. An instantaneous real-time system is usually implemented as an EII (enterprise information integration) solution, where the source system itself is responsible for supporting the update of remote user's screens, and servicing query requests. Obviously such a system must limit the complexity of the query requests because all the processing is done on the operational application system. EII solutions typically involve no caching of data in the ETL pipeline, since EII solutions by definition have no delays between the source systems and the users' screens. EII technologies offer reasonable lightweight data cleaning and transformation services, but all these capabilities must be executed in software because the data is being continuously piped to the users' screens. Most EII solutions also allow for a transaction-protected write back capability from the users' screens to the transactional data. In the business requirements interviews, you should carefully assess the need for an instantaneous real-time solution, keeping in mind the significant load that such a solution places on the source application, and the inherent volatility of instantaneously updated data. Some situations are ideal candidates for an instantaneous real-time solution. Inventory status tracking may be a good example, where the decision maker has the right to commit inventory to a customer that is available in real time.

Frequently means that the data visible on the screen is updated many times per day but is not guaranteed to be the absolute current truth. Most of us are familiar with stock market quote data that is current to within 15 minutes but is not instantaneous. The technology for delivering frequent real-time data (as well as the slower daily real-time data) is distinctly different from instantaneous real-time delivery. Frequently delivered data is usually processed as micro-batches in a conventional ETL architecture. This means that the data undergoes the full gamut of change data capture, extract, staging to file storage in the ETL back room, cleaning and error checking, conforming to enterprise data standards, assigning of surrogate keys, and possibly a host of other transformations to make the data ready to load into a dimensional schema or OLAP cube. Almost all of these steps must be omitted or drastically reduced in an EII solution. The big difference between frequently and daily delivered real-time data is in the first two steps: change data capture and extract. In order to capture data many times per day from the source system, the data warehouse usually must tap into a high bandwidth communications channel such as message gram traffic between legacy applications, or an accumulating transaction log file, or low level database triggers coming from the transaction system every time something happens. As a designer, the principal challenge of frequently updated real-time systems is designing the change data capture and extract parts of the ETL pipeline. If the rest of the ETL system can be run many times per day, then perhaps the design of these following stages can remain batch oriented.

Daily means that the data visible on the screen is valid as of a batch file download or reconciliation from the source system at the end of the previous working day. A few years ago a daily update of the data warehouse was considered aggressive, but at the time of this article daily data would be the most conservative choice. There is a lot to recommend daily data! Quite often processes run on the source system at the end of the working day that correct the raw data. When this reconciliation becomes available, that is the signal that the data warehouse can perform a reliable and stable download of the data. If you have this situation, you should explain to the business users what compromises they will experience if they demand instantaneous or frequently updated data. Daily updated data usually involves reading a batch file prepared by the source system, or performing an extract query when a source system readiness flag is set. This, of course, is the simplest extract scenario because you take your time waiting for the source system to be ready and available. Once you have the data, then the downstream ETL batch processing is similar to that of the frequently updated real-time systems, but it only needs to run once per day.

The business requirements gathering step is crucial to the design process. The big decision is whether to go instantaneous, or can you live with frequently or daily. The instantaneous solutions are quite separate from the other two, and you would not like to be told to change horses in midstream. On the other hand, you may be able to gracefully convert a daily real-time ETL pipeline to frequently, mostly by altering the first two steps of change data capture and extract.

12 Technical Architecture Considerations

After spending the last seven chapters on data-related topics, we are moving on to technical and system architecture concerns. Some readers may be relieved, while perhaps others are disappointed that our immersion in the data itself is a thing of the past.

This chapter begins with several topics that impact the overall architecture of the DW/BI environment, including server oriented architecture (SOA), master data management (MDM), and packaged analytics. A new section in this second edition of the *Reader* takes a deep dive into the new world of big data, and features two major white papers written by Ralph. From there, we shift to the presentation server with a discussion of aggregate navigation, OLAP, and other performance tuning options. We briefly explore user interface issues in the data warehouse's front room, followed by several articles about metadata. Finally, the chapter wraps up with a discussion of information privacy, security, and other infrastructure issues.

Overall Technical/System Architecture

This section looks at a variety of system architecture topics, from the roles of service oriented architecture and packaged applications to master data management and integrated analytics for operational decision making.

12.1 Can the Data Warehouse Benefit from SOA?

Ralph Kimball, Design Tip #106, *Oct 10, 2008*

The service oriented architecture (SOA) movement has captured the imagination, if not the budgets, of many IT departments. In a nutshell, organizing your environment around SOA means identifying reusable services, and implementing these services as centralized resources typically accessed over the web. The appeal comes from the promised cost savings of implementing a service only once in a large organization, and making the service independent of specific hardware and operating system platforms because all communications take place via a neutral communications protocol, most often WSDL-SOAP-XML.

Well, pretty much all of these advantages of SOA can be realized, but early SOA pioneers have learned some valuable lessons that give one pause for thought. The names of these lessons are data quality, data integration, and governance. To make a long story short, SOA initiatives fail when they 1) sit on a platform of poor-quality data, 2) attempt to share data that is not integrated across the enterprise, and 3) are implemented with insufficient thought given to security, compliance, and change management. SOA architects have also learned to avoid the overly detailed use case. Services meet the goals of SOA architecture when they are simple, conservative in their scope, and not dependent on complex business rules of an underlying application.

So, does SOA have anything to offer data warehousing? Can we identify abstract services in the data warehouse world, commonly recognized, simply stated, and independent of specific data sources, business processes, and BI deployments? I think we can.

Consider the relationship between the dimension manager and fact provider. Remember that a dimension manager is the centralized resource for defining and publishing a conformed dimension to the rest of the enterprise. A master data management (MDM) resource is an ideal dimension manager but few of us are lucky enough to have a functioning MDM resource. More likely, the data warehouse team is a kind of downstream MDM function that gathers incompatible descriptions of an entity such as customer and publishes the cleaned, conformed, and deduplicated dimension to the rest of the data warehouse community. The subscribers to this dimension are almost always owners of fact tables who want to attach this high quality conformed dimension to their fact tables so that BI tools around the enterprise can perform drill-across reports on the conformed contents of the dimension.

Every dimension manager publisher needs to provide the following services to their fact table subscribers. For these services, *fetch* means that the fact table provider pulls information from the dimension manager, and *alert* means that the dimension manager pushes information to the fact providers.

- Fetch specific dimension member. We assume in this and the following steps that the dimension record has a surrogate primary key, a dimension version number, and that the information transmitted is consistent with the security and privacy privileges of the requester.
- Fetch all dimension members.
- Fetch dimension members changed since specific date/time with designated SCD types 1, 2, and 3.
- Fetch natural key to surrogate key correspondence table unique to fact table provider.
- Alert providers of new dimension release. A major dimension release requires providers to update their dimensions because type 1 or type 3 changes have been made to selected attributes.
- Alert providers to late-arriving dimension members. This requires fact table providers to overwrite selected foreign keys in fact tables.

These services are generic to all integrated data warehouses. In a dimensionally modeled data warehouse, we can describe the administrative processing steps with great specificity, without regard to the underlying subject matter of the fact or dimension tables. That is why, in SOA parlance, dimensional modeling provides a well-defined reference architecture on which to base these services.

These services seem pretty defensible as meeting SOA design requirements. An interesting question is whether a similar set of abstract services could be defined between the fact provider and the BI client. How about "Alert client to KPI change?" Maybe this is possible. In the meantime, I'd suggest reading *Applied SOA: Service-Oriented Architecture and Design Strategies* (Rosen, et al, Wiley 2008).

12.2 Picking the Right Approach to MDM

Warren Thornthwaite, Intelligent Enterprise, *Feb 7, 2007*

I admit I'm a little slow sometimes when it comes to embracing market trends. That's because I think many market trends end up being more hype than substance, but that's not always the case. Take master data management (MDM), a trend that has been at the top of the technology buzzwords list for the past few years. A decade ago, the idea of creating and maintaining a single source for information about customers, products, and other entities was considered a pipedream, but this is a trend that is increasingly real.

This article examines the problems addressed and the business value delivered by MDM. We also look at the three common approaches to creating and managing master data, detailing the pros and cons of each approach. Finally, we give you four solid recommendations on how to proceed with MDM no matter which approach makes the most sense for your organization.

Source System Disparities

The difficulties in creating a single view of the enterprise stem from the quality of source system data. One of the biggest challenges is that multiple source systems collect and maintain their own versions of the same data elements. We find entries for the same customer in separate systems when the web registration screen captures customer name and address, while the shipping system keeps another copy of the customer's name and address. When that customer calls for support, we create another customer record and capture another address. The same customer may even have duplicate entries within the same system, as when the customer registers twice on the same website.

One of the goals of enterprise resource planning (ERP) systems was to address this problem by creating a single, centralized transaction system with data elements that are shared across all transaction processes. The "E" stands for "enterprise," right? Most organizations have yet to reach this level of source system integration. They either have systems outside the ERP system or are using the ERP system independently. In other words, multiple divisions or business units may have separate customer sets that might even be kept in the same physical table. When it comes time to create an enterprise information resource, these "separate" divisions have usually been working with many of the same customers.

The problem gets worse when you have to include data from external sources. External customer demographic data, retail product sales data, and even product data from manufacturers or distributors almost never have the same customer or product keys as your internal systems.

The Need for Master Data

Clean master data can benefit the organization by increasing revenues and profits and improving productivity and customer satisfaction. The requirement for integrated data at the operational level has coalesced under the general term *master data management*. MDM is the idea that there should be a single source for information about a customer or product: the master source. Ideally, all transaction systems will interact with the master source to get the most current values for a particular attribute, like name or address. MDM solves the data disparity problem where it should be solved: once, at the source.

It's not enough to keep track of the correct current value of an attribute. Analytic needs and compliance reporting demand tracking of historical changes to the MDM function. This requirement makes MDM more complex but doesn't fundamentally change what needs to happen, or how.

There are three common approaches to creating MDM systems:

1. **Let the data warehouse do it.** This approach is the least disruptive to existing systems, but it has hidden costs and limitations.
2. **Create an operational MDM to integrate data from multiple sources on a transactional basis.** This approach surfaces the hidden costs and improves timing and accessibility to the master data, but it still leaves multiple, disparate copies of data in various transaction systems.
3. **Create an enterprise MDM system of record for transaction systems data and facilitate data sharing as needed.**

Let's take a closer look at each approach.

Approach 1: Master Data in the Conformed Data Warehouse

The goal of creating a true enterprise understanding of the business has forced the data warehouse to deal with disparate sources. In the 1990s, most transaction systems managers did not care about data integration because it was not a business priority. Their top priority was meeting the specific transaction needs as quickly as possible. The idea that the transaction systems should create and manage a centralized master data set was considered a grand vision at best, but not practical; more often, it was considered a good joke.

If data warehouse team members wanted a single master version of each dimension, we had to build it ourselves. We used the extract, transform, and load (ETL) process to pull data from multiple sources, clean, align, standardize, and integrate it in order to create what we call an *enterprise conformed dimension*, as shown in Figure 12-1.

Approach 1: Master Data in the Conformed Data Warehouse

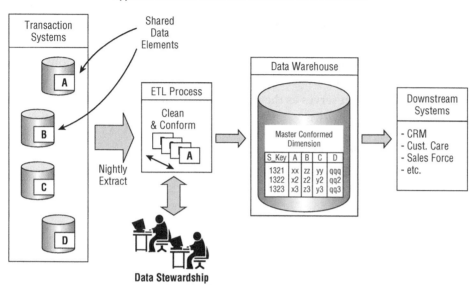

Figure 12-1: Approach 1: Managing master data in the data warehouse ETL.

The master conformed dimension contains attributes that are common across transaction systems, such as customer name, and attributes that are unique to individual systems, such as ship-to address. The master conformed dimension maps the source system keys to a single master surrogate key for each entry in the entity. This mapping is the Rosetta stone that ties data from one source system to another.

Once the master dimension is in place, the effort does not end. Changes and additions to the shared attributes from different source systems must be entered into the dimension. Also, the dimension management system is usually called upon to identify the best version of a shared attribute out of all possible versions that exist. This determination, known as *survivorship*, involves complex business rules and comparisons during the ETL pipeline.

To many, having the data warehouse create and manage master data feels wrong because it flies in the face of the fundamental tenets of quality. In the 1950s, Edward Deming and his counterparts taught us that you must fix quality problems at their source or you will be doomed to fix them forever. Every night, the ETL process will push its Sisyphean rock up to the top of the hill, only to have it knocked back down by the transaction systems the next day. Unfortunately, a majority of organizations have been unwilling to address the problem any other way, so we had to do it in the data warehouse.

Approach 2: The MDM Integration Hub

Most organizations have multiple customer touch points, and they often have a separate customer relationship management (CRM) system and a web-based customer interface that keeps some of its own customer data. Companies that want to address the problem of disparate data might begin by leaving each silo transaction data store in place while building a centralized master data store. A copy of all the attributes is placed in the MDM system, and all future updates are replicated into the MDM system from each source. As a result, the MDM system will contain multiple versions of the same attributes as they are collected by the various source systems. We call this the MDM *integration hub*, illustrated in Figure 12-2, because it serves as the point of integration for downstream systems (and in some cases for source systems as well).

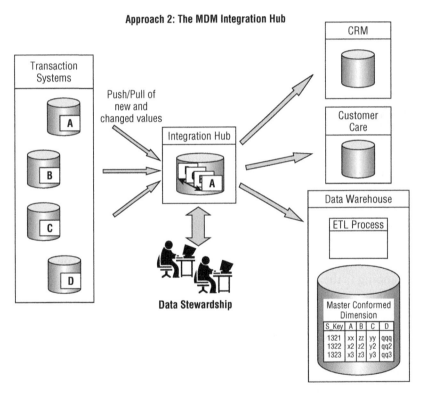

Figure 12-2: Approach 2: Implementing MDM via an integration hub.

This MDM approach usually generates the same valuable outputs as the data warehouse version: the source key mapping table, and the best, or master, value for each attribute (equivalent to the survivorship function in the ETL process) based on complex rules that assess the accuracy and validity of each source. These rules include an assessment of the relative accuracy of the different sources, how recently the source has been updated, where the update came from, and so on. The data steward is responsible for creating and maintaining these rules through the MDM interface.

The integration hub approach does not attempt to fix the problem at the source; it simply moves the cleaning, aligning, standardizing, and integration upstream a bit. The integration hub is better than the data warehouse approach because it can operate at transaction service levels, letting some of the operational systems make calls to the integration hub to get the most current value of an attribute. It also becomes a data provider for downstream systems, like the data warehouse. At last, the data warehouse can stop pushing the rock up the hill. Applying this approach to customer data is essentially what customer data integration (CDI) is all about.

Approach 3: The Enterprise MDM System

The third approach, shown in Figure 12-3, is to create a centralized database that holds the master version of all attributes of a given object along with the interface functions needed to tie this master data back to the transaction systems. In other words, the master database serves as the data store of record for all participating transaction processes. Rather than having each system maintain its own customer data, transaction systems all create, query, and update attributes in the centralized MDM. The user-facing portion of each system must first identify the exact customer or product involved in a given transaction and obtain its unique key from the MDM. The MDM must keep all attributes that are (or might be) required by more than one system and must also allow each system to define its own custom attributes. In addition, master data systems must have standard APIs available to all client systems.

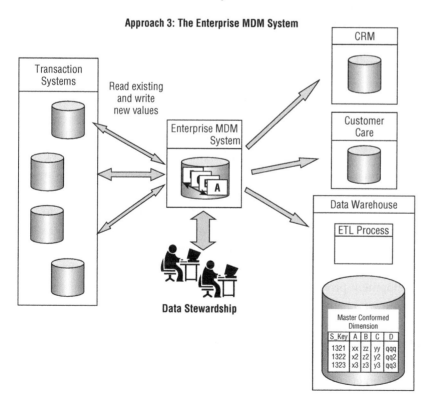

Figure 12-3: Approach 3: The enterprise MDM system.

The enterprise MDM does not solve the problem of disparate data by itself. One system can define an attribute that is the equivalent of an already existing attribute. The data steward must be responsible for each master data object, and have cross-system responsibility for uniquely defining each attribute and monitoring the usage of those attributes. As the Kimball Group has long espoused, strong, centralized data governance is the mandatory foundation for successfully creating information that's conformed across the enterprise.

This single, centralized database is obviously the ideal solution, but it requires every transaction system that shares data to give up ownership of shared data sets. This is not trivial because it requires rewriting core parts of each system, or at least redirecting the data requests to the external MDM system. On the other hand, the enterprise MDM is the ideal place to start a service oriented architecture (SOA) deployment because a large number of clients could take advantage of the obvious reusability of the service. From what we've seen, far fewer than 10 percent of organizations have an enterprise MDM system in place.

Four Steps toward MDM

Regardless of how far you go toward creating an enterprise MDM, there are several common steps you need to take:

- **Set up a data governance function.** First, create a permanent data governance function that includes, or is managed by, the business side. This group must drive agreement on names, definitions, systems of record, and business rules for every entity and attribute in question. Create an organizational process for ongoing review and enforcement to ensure correct usage and appropriate sharing of data.

- **Integrate existing data.** You must take a first pass at integrating data from the various sources in the organization. This may be fairly simple for some attributes, like product category, once the business rules are defined. However, it is a massive effort if you need to match and deduplicate more complex entities such as customer. You will never be 100 percent right. Remember that the resulting integrated data must be maintained. If this is as far as you get, consider yourself above average.

- **Work toward the ideal.** Rewriting existing systems and reworking business processes to use the master data system rather than local data sets is a massive undertaking. The organization must be committed to correcting the problem at the source. This effort involves data governance resources, development resources, purchased software, and an overall redesign of the core systems and the development process.

- **Enlist others.** If you are getting no help from the larger organization, remember that the results of integration have value to downstream systems such as CRM and customer service. Try to enlist them in the fight for creating an integration hub or enterprise MDM system. All organizations should have a data stewardship function to define shared data elements and monitor their usage. You should also practice MDM in the form of creating conformed dimensions in the data warehouse ETL process. Beyond this, the organization should be working on moving the MDM function upstream into the operational systems, initially as an integration hub, and ultimately as an enterprise master data management system.

12.3 Building Custom Tools for the DW/BI System

Joy Mundy, Design Tip #94, *Sep 4, 2007*

There is a large and diverse market for products to help build your DW/BI system and deliver information to your business users. These range from DBMSs (relational and OLAP) to ETL tools, data mining, query, reporting, and BI portal technologies. What role could there possibly be for custom tools in such a rich environment?

Most of the custom tools we've seen have supported back room operations, such as metadata management, security management, and monitoring. For example, you could be capturing information about who's logging in to the system, and how long queries are taking. The simplest custom monitoring tool would be a set of predefined reports to display historic trends and real-time activity.

But the best tools will let the users initiate an action. One recent client had an unusual requirement where business users performed complex analysis and then submitted jobs to the ETL system. Each job could take anywhere from a few minutes to a quarter hour to run, depending on how busy the system was. The business users submitted their jobs at the end of the day, and then hung around the office until they were certain their data processed correctly and was ready for the next morning. The DW/BI team developed a straightforward tool that monitored the jobs that were submitted to the system. Users could see where their jobs were in the processing queue, get a good idea of how long they might take, and—best of all—users could cancel their own jobs if they realized they made a mistake in the data preparation step. This tool was particularly nice and developed by a skilled programmer, but a less fancy tool could be pulled together in a matter of a few weeks.

Most DW/BI teams use a variety of products from multiple vendors. Custom tools will be most useful at the transition points between different technologies. This holds true even if your DW/BI system is built largely on a single platform; there are always gaps between the components. Metadata management is one place where we might need to write a bit of custom glue. In the absence of an integrated platform with complete and synchronized metadata between design, relational and OLAP databases, business intelligence layer, and standard reports—a platform we still hope to see some day—there will always be a place for a custom tool to bridge those metadata ponds. A very simple tool might consist of a few scripts to synchronize metadata stores. But we have seen customers with web-based applications that let a business analyst update and synchronize metadata, such as business descriptions.

Other examples of custom tools that we've seen at our clients include:

- **Report publishing workflow.** Manage the process for creating a new standard report, including ensuring the report's definition is approved by appropriate representatives from both business and IT.

- **Security management.** Programmatically issue the commands to add users to the system with a user interface for assigning them to specific roles. This is particularly valuable for data-driven security systems such as those driven from an organizational structure and for security systems that span multiple databases.
- **Dimension hierarchy management.** Enable business users to remap dimension hierarchies, such as which products roll up to a product subcategory and category, or which general ledger accounts are aggregated together.

Don't be overwhelmed! Many DW/BI teams build no custom tools, or only a few very primitive tools. But there are some very effective programming environments on the market, not to mention inexpensive software development houses that you can hire. Don't be afraid to be creative. It's often the case that a very modest investment in some custom tools can greatly improve the manageability of your DW/BI system. The best tools are the ones that make the business users happier, by giving them more control over the DW/BI system that is, by all rights, theirs rather than yours.

12.4 Welcoming the Packaged App

Ralph Kimball, Intelligent Enterprise, *Jun 5, 2000*

The tremendous rush toward CRM, electronic commerce, and BI has brought many business departments clamoring to the IT department. This demand is almost entirely great news for us data warehouse implementers. We have finally "gotten the order" to put a data foundation under nearly every business decision and business relationship. Business-to-customer (B2C) and business-to-business (B2B) relationships are both data intensive, and our user departments are very aware of this fact. In a sense, with the web providing a big push recently, business has at last committed heavily to managing by the numbers. Now all we IT folks need to do is build the infrastructure to support this revolution.

Our marketing, sales, finance, and operations business users are in a hurry to keep up with their marketplaces and competition, and they are buying packaged application solutions to satisfy their urgent needs. The heavyweight packaged applications are the ERP systems, many of which were installed prior to the year 2000 boundary. But by counting the sheer number of software license sales, the real growth has been at the lower end of the packaged applications market for processes such as sales pipeline and call center management, campaign management, and CRM.

The packaged application providers deliver a very useful service because they have already written the software. But at the same time, these providers may not emphasize the system and interfacing issues that make their applications function in the larger IT context, perhaps to avoid IT scrutiny and the longer sales cycles involved.

Avoid Stovepipe Data Marts

What happens if you fail to welcome the packaged application as a full member of your data warehouse? The packaged application will become a stovepipe data mart.

Those of us a little long in the tooth have seen this scenario before. Throughout the 1980s, grocery and drug store syndicated scanner data was sold on turnkey hardware directly to retail and manufacturing marketing departments without IT involvement. Back then, it was a little easier to get away with such a strategy because there were no networks to speak of. But for those of us building the first integrated data warehouses and trying to combine the syndicated data with internal shipments and finance data, it was a nightmare: None of the dimensions in the syndicated data conformed to the internal data.

In some syndicated data, the time dimension had the grain of quad weeks (four-week intervals unrelated to calendar months), the product dimension had a vendor-supplied rollup hierarchy, and the market dimension consisted of 54 specially constructed markets that did not align with state boundaries. The infamous 54th market was called All Other and comprised all the spaces in between the first 53 markets!

Conforming dimensions is the key to a successful distributed data warehouse, and you have to do so from the most granular data during the data preparation phase. For the packaged application data, this process occurs in the back room of the package provider, and for internal company data, it occurs in the back room ETL staging area.

Conforming at Query Time

Conforming dimensions on the fly—where the allocation factors between out-of-conformance data sources are applied at query time—has been a dream for many years, but is computationally intensive and slows down real-time queries. More seriously, this approach still requires the assignment of hundreds or possibly thousands of allocation factors. For example, you need to decompose time spans that overlap in awkward ways between two data sources to individual days, and then roll them up again. It is rarely satisfactory to assume each day of the week is equal; maybe you do much more business on weekdays than on weekends. We also need to make product hierarchies exactly equivalent between two data sources. The names of categories and departments must be drawn from the same domain, must have the same contents, and must be spelled consistently. Finally, you have to make geographic zones and regions identical in the same way. Conforming incompatible geographies accurately is very interesting because it may involve a sophisticated model of population densities and demographic patterns. Thus, beware of anyone claiming to conform separate data sources without your extensive involvement!

Even if we could conform on the fly, the architecture isn't correct; you would have to re-apply the allocations in each query, repeatedly. You will never have enough computing horsepower to make this goal the best solution.

Vendors Do Take Integration Seriously

Are vendors aware of these issues, and do they encourage their applications to be functioning components of a larger data warehouse? Remarkably, a whole movement known as *enterprise application integration* (EAI) is addressing this set of issues. Although the EAI vendors are mostly focused on transaction processing, they are defining exactly what we need to make the distributed data warehouse function. They are defining a framework, principally through extensible markup language (XML), for transmitting business results back and forth, whether for B2C or B2B. Customers ordering a book fill out a form on the web, and parts of the form, such as the book's ISBN number, title, author, price, tax, and the shipping charge, are all described in an accessible language that every customer and business observer can use. This arrangement allows "incompatible" applications to pick up the information and consume it locally. It also lets a data warehouse read the order form and populate its fact tables.

Besides supporting the common data interchange XML offers, what can a packaged application vendor do to make us take their integration responsibility seriously? Here's my list of recommendations:

- Offer to supply the package data in terms of the customer's dimensions, especially product (or service), customer, geography, calendar, status, and transaction. Charging more for this service is acceptable, provided it requires extra processing or special software development.
- Call on IT early in the sales cycle. If you handle this correctly, IT should be grateful that a business user department has recognized a need for a packaged application and has articulated the requirements seriously. But both the package provider and the business department must agree that IT will be responsible for running the hardware and software and integrating the information into the fabric of the organization.
- Publish the package data interface specifications so that the IT department can extract all the important dimensional and fact data into a remote data warehouse. In fact, give up all notions that the packaged application is itself the enterprise data warehouse. Admittedly, this recommendation is strongly worded, but in my experience, the concerns for most packaged application providers are transaction processing and expanding and protecting their proprietary interests. These goals rarely translate into genuinely effective support for data warehousing, which demands a profound level of integration among many data sources, simplicity of presentation, and no compromise speed.
- Allow the import of data from the rest of the organization or business partners, even if these third parties aren't using the packaged application.

Fortunately, powerful forces are pushing in the right direction to make application integration real. The whole move to distributed supply chain management requires an honest effort to share data. No vendor that thinks about the problem wants to create an objection to sales by being perceived as so proprietary that it defeats the idea of electronic commerce.

So what is the best strategy for IT, given the immense and sometimes undisciplined growth of packaged applications?

- Spend time with your business departments to see what they need, and be forewarned when they are looking at a packaged application solution. Credibility with the business users has always been the gold coin for IT, but now it is even more urgent. The world is really beginning to manage by the numbers over the web. IT is responsible for building the infrastructure for the data warehouse revolution.

- Be on the packaged application selection committee so you can ask the right questions early in the process. Have the provider respond to the list of interfacing responsibilities I described.
- Begin the process of integrating the packaged application into the rest of your information structure as quickly as possible.

12.5 ERP Vendors: Bring Down Those Walls

Ralph Kimball, Intelligent Enterprise, *Jun 26, 2000*

Now is a stressful time for data warehouse designers. In the past year or so (from the perspective of the year 2000), data warehousing has moved onto center stage. Everyone agrees that we need data warehouses; everybody wants to manage their businesses "by the numbers." But just when the world asks us to deliver, it has decided to undertake a major paradigm shift.

Setting the hype aside, it really is becoming a web world. Not only must we browser-enable our query tools and user interfaces, but we must also change the way we do business.

What Are the New Rules?

First, as Patricia Seybold states so clearly in her book *Customers.Com* (Times Books, 2010), we must redesign our customer-facing processes from the bottom up. In other words, our customers and business partners must be able to navigate smoothly through all of our business processes, from original order to final cash settlement. They should be able to access each step along the way with just one more click. Customers and business partners need to see the detailed status of an individual order or an individual delivery (perhaps placed five minutes ago) and also be able to switch to a historical summary immediately.

Second, as a company, we must embrace a very dynamic, web-oriented world where our supply chain is far more dynamic than it used to be. We will enter into short-lived partnerships with suppliers, based on web auctions. These partnerships will be project oriented and may have lifetimes of only weeks or months. Since the economics of inventory management are so compelling when we can source parts, products, and services at a lower cost and move them more quickly, we will feel huge pressure to move to the project-oriented view of the world.

As companies and vendors scramble to accommodate these new rules, the data warehouse designer must, paradoxically, take a long term view. By definition, the data warehouse defines a perspective that is stable over a multi-year period. The data warehouse designer must resist the intense pressures to lock into a particular vendor's technology if that means their company cannot follow the web evolution.

Let's try to summarize the data warehouse design criteria that have changed the most leading up to 2000. A web-intensive data warehouse must be:

- **Fully web deployed,** with every user and administrative capability usable through a standard web browser from any location.
- **Historically accurate up to the moment,** so that the longer view of history extends seamlessly to include the order a customer placed five minutes ago.
- **Profoundly distributed,** so that internal business processes, external data sources, and the databases of far-flung suppliers and customers are all part of the "enterprise" data warehouse.
- **Dynamically changing,** so that as we venture into new lines of business, and as we initiate contracts with new suppliers, the data warehouse smoothly accommodates the new data types and interfaces.

Any one of these changes would be sufficient cause for rethinking our data warehouse strategies, but all four together are definitely daunting. I think we are in a period of significant change in data warehousing and it will take another year or two before vendors and IT consumers agree upon clear product categories. As evidence of this creative turmoil, try to sort out the differences among business intelligence (BI), customer relationship management (CRM), business-to-customer (B2C), business-to-business (B2B), enterprise application integration (EAI), enterprise information portals (EIP), inter-enterprise application cooperation (IAC), virtual enterprises (VE), plug-and-play bondware (P&PB), wide-area workflow management (WAWM), and restructurable modeling of organization players (RMOP).

Role of ERP in the New Webhouse

I learned long ago never to do too good a job of describing a problem without also providing at least one solution. You don't get many points for leaving the boss (or the reader of this article) with unresolved frustration.

In thinking about these new data warehouse challenges over the past few months, I have become increasingly convinced that among all the players, the ERP system providers are best positioned to lead us to the solution, if these providers are willing to remake themselves in response to the demands of the web business revolution. ERP systems' fundamental goals have always been business process reengineering and replacing an organization's primary operational systems with a comprehensive and smoothly integrated suite of applications that implements a whole set of business processes. The most successful installations of ERP systems have been those where the customer has built their business processes around the ERP software, rather than the other way around.

ERP implementations have a reputation for being lengthy and difficult. Most ERP applications take years to install and require changes in data capture screens, detailed operational procedures, descriptive terminology, accounting rules, and final management reports. But this fact should not surprise you. Usually, those organizations most in need of adopting an ERP solution are trying for the first time in their histories to design a completely coherent set of business processes. In data warehouse terms, they are making serious efforts to *conform their dimensions* and *conform their facts* across their organizations. In many ways, ERP projects have been the most ambitious projects that large organizations have ever undertaken to create conformed data environments.

In spite of ERP systems' basic constructive approach, until now they have had a minor, disappointing effect on the data warehouse world, in my opinion, for several reasons:

■ ERP systems have been far more concerned with transaction processing than decision support. Data warehousing has been a late arrival and an afterthought for most ERP vendors. Many ERP vendors have a back room culture that doesn't validate the needs of front room business users.

■ ERP systems' primary database schemas are absurdly complex, including thousands of database tables. Although it is possible to extract data from an ERP system into a data warehouse, it requires specialized knowledge and powerful extraction software.

■ ERP vendors have introduced data warehouse environments within their product offerings, but have not until now convincingly demonstrated their willingness to openly import and export data when that is what the customer desires.

Within the past year, ERP vendors have begun to respond more effectively to these issues. After the run up to the year 2000 transition, ERP vendors have seen a pronounced flattening of their revenues. In order to respond to the web revolution, the IT marketplace is already wondering if ERP implementations are legacy applications that we need to augment with something more modern.

Although ERP vendors have always argued effectively that single vendor solutions eliminate interfacing nightmares among vendors, the IT marketplace for applications has been growing so fast that the ERP vendors realize that they cannot keep up. ERP vendors more or less completely missed the new customer-oriented developments, including call center management and CRM applications. And the marketplace is not going to wait for them to develop these applications in a proprietary way. We are now on web time, remember?

In the past year leading up to 2000, all the ERP vendors have seriously embraced the web revolution and have taken major steps to add customer-oriented functionality and better reporting facilities.

But I believe that the ERP vendors are only halfway there in terms of joining the new web business paradigm. An organization must be able to use its own ERP installation's solidity to define internal processes and data, and at the same time flexibly accommodate a constantly changing array of external partners and interfaces. The ERP vendors must be willing to participate much more openly and dynamically than they have in the past.

Given this fact, can we build a true enterprise data warehouse within a particular ERP vendor's walls?

Well, maybe.

I think any enterprise data warehouse we implement within an ERP environment can only be successful if the ERP vendor makes a full commitment to *open data warehousing* with:

■ Competitive level of query performance, equal to the best performance available from an extracted, independent, and aggregate-aware set of data warehouse tables

■ Competitive level of user interface excellence, and ease of use if the ERP vendor expects the application to use its own tools

- Full data import interfaces that encourage the easy integration of foreign data sources, including syndicated data suppliers, legacy applications, packaged applications, and competitor ERP systems
- Full data export interfaces that let the customer extract the ERP data to an independent data warehouse if that is what the customer wants to do
- Flexible attachment of third party query and reporting tools directly to the ERP vendor's data warehouse tables
- Flexible attachment of external transaction processing applications and other ERP systems to the vendor's operational and/or data warehouse data through extensible markup language (XML) interfaces, thereby sending the clear message that it is OK for us to view the ERP vendor's system as part of a larger system
- Seamless connection of current status reporting to historical record reporting
- Seamless transition between analysis (data warehousing) and update (transaction processing)
- Seamless integration of standardized facts and dimensions with local, user-defined facts and dimensions

ERP vendors have a profound natural advantage because of their success in reengineering the internal processes of many businesses. But they are poised on a cusp. Significant new forces are sweeping the marketplace that can either strengthen the ERP vendors' position or make them less important. In my opinion, the ERP vendors can grab the advantage in this complex new marketplace by aggressively pursuing the end customer, the business user, and above all, open systems.

12.6 Building a Foundation for Smart Applications

Joy Mundy, Intelligent Enterprise, Dec 1, 2006

Enterprise applications such as ERP and CRM systems are increasingly available with integrated analytic capabilities aimed at automating and improving operational decision making. That doesn't mean you can get away without the solid foundation of an enterprise DW/BI system.

No matter how customizable these applications may be and how extensive the analytic capabilities, your implementation team will still face the problem of integrating and cleaning data from multiple sources. Unless most or all of your transaction systems are part of the same integrated suite, tightly coupled with your smart applications, you'll eventually do much of the work that would otherwise be required to build a DW/BI system.

The best way to move beyond information silos and support multiple smart applications is to build an enterprise DW/BI system. You'll gain integrated and conformed information from across the enterprise, granular detail with attributes and hierarchies that can feed any smart application, and rich history and change tracking capabilities that can help you better predict customer behavior in any business process.

Organizations have two overarching drivers for their DW/BI system:

- Inform strategic and tactical decision making.
- Automate operational decisions.

The first goal is classic decision support: Executives and analysts use information to run the business. With an excellent data warehouse, executives know what's going on in their business and markets, and can steer a course for success. The second goal can be realized by smart enterprises with enhanced operational systems that make use of data to run more effectively based on informed suggestions or predictions.

The smart enterprise weaves the information platform into the operational application layer. The DW/BI system can add value wherever operational decisions could benefit from a historical context. Examples range from setting order fulfillment priorities based on customer value and personalizing product suggestions to improving fraud detection applications and manufacturing quality-monitoring systems.

Decision support is great, but a smart enterprise is even better. The smart enterprise is not new: We've talked about and even implemented such systems for decades. Even the oldest data warehousing architectural diagrams include a feedback or closed loop arrow. What's new is that the smart enterprise is moving into the mainstream, through both packaged analytics and custom applications.

The best way to get to the smart enterprise is to build an enterprise DW/BI system: an information platform that cleans, integrates, and conforms data from across your organization. With this solid foundation, the goal of a smart enterprise is much more attainable. We will help you reach the desired end goal by describing the architectural foundation of the smart enterprise.

The Quick but Risky Path

Building a data warehouse isn't absolutely necessary for delivering smart applications. The easiest way to get smart applications is to buy them. You can purchase CRM software, quality management software, and ERP systems that include BI and smart enterprise features. Why go to the trouble of building an enterprise data warehouse?

Many organizations have a few transaction systems that are either custom built or significantly customized packaged software, generally when off-the-shelf systems don't meet company needs. This most often occurs at the point where your organization is unique, and often that uniqueness is a key corporate asset. Organizations willing to be on the leading edge may find that packaged smart applications built for a broader market don't do as good a job as a custom application. We expect the market for packaged smart apps will evolve to support very flexible customization, but today these systems are, more often than not, black boxes over which you have little control.

Even if a purchased application is perfect, or perfectly customizable, your implementation team faces the problem of pulling data from multiple sources, cleaning and integrating it, and pumping it into the smart application. As you install your second or third packaged smart application, you're repeating a lot of ETL functionality, and you're doing it inefficiently and inconsistently. Unless most or all of your transaction systems are part of the same integrated suite, tightly coupled with your smart applications, you'll eventually do a lot of the same work necessary to build an enterprise data warehouse, but won't reap all of the benefits without actually building that warehouse.

The Right Way to Smart Apps

A better long term approach is to build on an enterprise data warehouse, an information infrastructure that:

- Is focused on the business users' requirements
- Is enterprise wide, containing integrated, conformed information from multiple business processes
- Contains data at the finest granularity possible
- Defines standard attributes, hierarchies, and structures that are used across multiple business processes
- Includes attributes, such as customer income levels, that can be used to predict behavior
- Implements change-tracking techniques on key attributes to associate behaviors such as purchases with the attribute's value at the time the behavior occurred
- Identifies data quality problems and works to fix them at the source or in the ETL process
- Delivers standard reports and analytic applications to the enterprise
- Includes a software, hardware, and infrastructure environment that can support all this data, transformation, reporting, and analysis at the enterprise level

The enterprise data warehouse directly meets the first goal we described: to support informed decision making. This is the information infrastructure that supports reports, ad hoc querying, analysis, and executive dashboards. Even if you stop here and never implement a smart enterprise application, you've already done a great thing.

However, with this solid information infrastructure in place, you're in a great position to build or buy smart applications. If you're a builder, your analysts will explore the data, build statistical models, evaluate the performance of those models, and work with your developers to define the smart features of your enterprise applications. You may implement something simple, like ranking and tagging customers who make a lot of purchases. Or, your analysts may delve into data mining and use sophisticated statistical techniques to score purchase decisions, product quality measures, or internet browsing behaviors. Whether your analytic techniques are simple or complex, you'll be working from clean, integrated, and consistent data. You can verify that analytic results are real and reproducible.

If your organization leans toward buying rather than building, you'll have enough familiarity with your data to better evaluate the off-the-shelf alternatives. It may be economically feasible to do a proof of concept to evaluate whether candidate products accurately predict the behavior of your customers or processes. Implementation will be an order of magnitude simpler than if you needed to build the complete ETL process to shoehorn the application into your architecture.

When the Infrastructure Falls Short

What if you don't have a data warehouse at all, or you're worried that your infrastructure doesn't measure up to the demands of the smart enterprise?

If you have no data warehouse or enterprise information infrastructure at all, you should follow the Kimball method to build one. The Kimball method presents a practical approach to specifying and building your system: Focus on business requirements, build and populate a dimensional model to support a high value yet solvable set of business processes, and use the bus matrix and conformed dimensions to incrementally grow the system to span the enterprise. It usually takes six to nine months to go live with the first Kimball dimensional model. If you're eager to get going on the smart applications, you may be able to explore the data and options well before the system goes live.

Most organizations have at least some sort of information infrastructure, often isolated data marts built by departments or simple reporting copies of transactional databases. These departmental solutions can be a barrier to your goals because at first glance they may appear to be, and are often called, data warehouses. Their key shortcoming is that they're stovepipes built without an enterprise focus, and it's difficult or impossible to combine the data with information outside their narrow subject area. To avoid this pitfall, you will need to build an enterprise data warehouse. Either start from scratch or choose the best available infrastructure and incrementally grow it into an enterprise-focused resource.

Some organizations have built an enterprise information infrastructure, but with flaws that make it difficult to evaluate, build, or implement smart enterprise applications. Hopefully, your enterprise data warehouse has a decent infrastructure and has already tackled some of the most challenging data integration issues. It's possible to add a dimensional data warehouse downstream of an existing data warehouse, and quickly roll out a solid, flexible, easy-to-use system.

The key flaw typically observed in existing enterprise data warehouses is a lack of historically accurate attributes. Almost all data warehouses track transaction history—what was sold, to whom, and for how much—but many do a poor job of associating the transaction with the attributes as they were at the time of the transaction. This attribute history is very important for data mining and other smart enterprise applications. Suppose, for example, that you want to build an application that will present product choices to a potential customer based on where he lives. If the data warehouse only keeps the customer's current address, then for the purposes of queries, analysis, and prediction, it looks as if the customer has always lived where he does now. We lose the vitally important information about how the customer's behavior changed when he moved from a cold climate to a warm climate. And once that history is gone from the data warehouse, it's difficult or impossible to reconstruct it.

Many enterprise data warehouses are backward looking to the transaction systems, rather than forward looking to the business users' requirements. As a result, they generally do an adequate job of serving up predefined reports but are often unwieldy for ad hoc use. The enterprise information infrastructure must be designed to support easy and consistent ad hoc analysis. This is especially true if you plan to build your own smart enterprise applications or customize a packaged system. If a statistician or business analyst can't explore the data at will, one of two things will happen; either the project will be abandoned or the analyst will pull off a chunk of data into a personal mart, which presents all sorts of challenges when it's time to develop and deploy the application.

Supporting Transactional Workloads

Let's say that you've designed the warehouse databases to support structured reports, as well as ad hoc query and analysis. Let's also assume that during the process of designing the smart enterprise apps, a statistician or analyst has made heavy use of the information infrastructure. Don't be surprised to see the model builder issuing queries that strain system resources. In production, however, most smart applications put a small load on the system. All the work has been done in advance; at transaction time all that's required is a simple query and some modest computation. This is good news, because it means that the same database used to support reports and analysis can serve up the information needed for the ongoing operation of the smart enterprise application.

However, just because the database can handle the load doesn't mean it's a good idea. This approach brings us back to one of the fundamental reasons we started building data warehouses in the first place: Analytic workloads are not compatible with transaction workloads—even the read-only workloads that are the BI portion of the smart enterprise application.

Smart designers will isolate the data needed to support the smart enterprise application in a managed environment that's not shared with the classic BI workload of reporting and analysis. This downstream database is usually much smaller than the data warehouse because it's focused on a particular problem. Queries are known in advance and can be carefully tuned. This new database is typically subject to a much higher level of service than the data warehouse since it's really part of the transaction system.

Some smart applications require that historical information be combined with very low-latency data. For example, a CRM application might present a call center screen that combines a customer's historical information with details about today. The majority of data warehouses include information up to yesterday, so how do you present a unified time series that includes both historical and real-time data?

The most common solution is to have the application query both the data warehouse and the transaction system and then combine the information for presentation. This approach works best if the transactional information requires little integration or transformation. A second popular approach is to add the low-latency data directly to the application database. Adding low-latency data to the more static warehouse database should be a last resort because it significantly complicates the architecture.

Pervasive BI: Spreading BI Everywhere

The promise of BI is that all decision makers in an organization, no matter how strategic, tactical, or operational, should have the information they need to do their jobs as well as possible. Data warehousing and BI started decades ago by focusing on the business analyst who advised senior management. We've done a pretty good job of reaching up to the executives and down to middle management by providing BI portals with rich reports and dashboards. The promise for the future is to reach throughout the enterprise, to make our operational systems use the information we've warehoused in an active and automated way.

12.7 RFID Tags and Smart Dust

Ralph Kimball, Intelligent Enterprise, *Jul 18, 2003*

This article speculates aggressively about the future. As you read it, think about the profound architectural impacts on the data warehouse, including the need to integrate thousands or even millions of separate data collection systems, and the corresponding flood of data that would be measured in petabytes.

A tidal wave of data is approaching the data warehouse that could easily deliver 10 to 100 times more data than we have ever seen. The data is incredibly potent, potentially tracking every tangible object, person, and location on the globe.

Is this some Big Brother scheme? No, it's an incremental revolution that's been quietly proceeding in manufacturing plants, retail stores, and development labs in many locations. The revolution consists of two related technologies: radio frequency identification (RFID) and "smart dust."

RFID is the next generation of bar coding technology. Instead of a series of bars simply printed on a label, an RFID tag is a miniature electronic circuit. The simplest RFID tag can be packaged in a label very similar to a bar code label. But instead of being scanned by a laser that must "see" the bar code, the RFID tag merely needs to pass near a specially equipped RFID transceiver. The transceiver bombards the tag with invisible radio waves, thereby activating the RFID tag's circuitry, which transmits its information back to the transceiver. The tag is entirely passive: It doesn't need to contain a power source. RFID tags typically store a 64-bit unique code. A standard printed bar code such as a universal product code may store only 11 digits, but the 64 bits—roughly equivalent to a 19-digit number—allow for vastly more combinations.

RFID tags will take advantage of this larger code storage to allow every instance of every product to be tracked. And because the RFID tag simply needs to pass near an RFID transceiver, every doorway can be equipped to detect the passage of an RFID tag on an object. Companies involved in supply chain management are already tracking the movement of individual products off an assembly line, onto a pallet, across the shipping room floor, onto a truck, and off the truck at a remote delivery location. Each of these physical locations is equipped with an RFID transceiver, and of course, this flood of data goes into a database.

At the retail end of the supply chain, RFID technology would let a shopper fill her shopping basket and then simply walk past an RFID-enabled doorway. The entire basket would be detected. The shopper would probably have a credit card with its own RFID device in it. The shopper would then approve the purchase and exit the store. A few little privacy and security details need to be worked out.

RFID tags come in many sizes and shapes. Livestock and pets have had implanted RFID devices for a number of years that allow easy tracking and identification. Don't even suggest that humans get these implanted. On the other hand, the special bracelets that parolees sometimes must wear are based on related technology.

RFID tags don't need to be completely static. The simplest RFID tags are write once devices that are configured with their unique codes at the time of manufacture. But more sophisticated RFID tags can be updated by an RFID transceiver in the field. One ambitious scheme being considered in Europe is the embedding of an updatable RFID tag in high value currency banknotes so that the history of their whereabouts can be determined. Supposedly this use would combat counterfeiting and money laundering.

The RFID revolution is well underway. In January of 2003, Gillette announced that it had placed an order for up to 500 million RFID tags to be used in its supply chain, including "smart shelves" in retail stores. Another major manufacturer is rumored to be preparing an order for several billion RFID tags. Avery Dennison, the well-known label maker, is deeply involved in developing RFID technology. Obviously these order volumes will drive the unit price of RFID tags down. The five cent price point is thought to be a threshold where the RFID tidal wave will really pick up.

Lifetime Employment

The biblical flood of data coming from all these RFID sources will dwarf our current databases. We have an insatiable desire to manage by the numbers, and someone, somewhere, is going to want to see all the detail. If we are routinely pushing the terabyte boundary in our larger databases today, it wouldn't surprise me to see 10 TB or even 100 TB fact tables before the end of this decade. Such large tables must be simple in order to be processed efficiently. Dimensional modeling provides the kind of simplicity to make these large tables queryable in a cost-effective way.

The nature of our applications will be increasingly operational, real time, and driven by the need to analyze sequential behavior. The operational and real-time demands will accelerate the design of hot partitions as extensions to our existing static fact tables. These hot partitions will be fed with new extract pipelines from the data sources that are capable of watching the RFID measurements as they occur. Enterprise application integration (EAI) vendors make their living by connecting separate operational systems together with EAI "message grams." The data warehouse hot partition can subscribe to this message gram traffic on the local area network, and dribble the RFID measurements directly into the hot extension of the regular fact table. I explored a number of these ideas in article 11.44, *Real-Time Partitions*.

Relatively few of our data warehouse applications do a proper job of analyzing sequential behavior. Rather, we usually stand at a point in a pipeline and monitor the flow at that point. But sequential behavior analysis changes the perspective to follow an item down the pipeline, past many different data collection points. Each of these data collection points is likely to appear in the data warehouse as a separate dimensional schema because the changing dimensionality of these sources as you move down the chain makes it logically impossible to combine the data collection points into a single schema. The increased emphasis on analyzing sequential behavior will increase the need for well-architected drill-across applications relying on conformed dimensions, as well as multipass querying.

The Assault on Privacy

We in the data warehouse industry are aware of the impact of ever increasing data collection on our personal privacy. But the widespread use of RFID technology is a really big jump toward tracking every person and every object. In my opinion, the technology is far ahead of our understanding of this impact, and even further ahead of properly written laws to protect our privacy. The toothpaste is out of the tube, and it won't be easily put back.

Given our increased security concerns stemming from terrorism and the SARS epidemic, the forces that argue for widespread data collection and the integration of these sources will be hard to resist, as I describe in article 12.24, *Watching the Watchers*.

Beyond RFID to Smart Dust

In many ways, the RFID revolution is past the scientific phase and into the engineering and deployment phase. The basic technology is well understood and the ongoing development is now focused on reducing the unit cost of the tags and perfecting manufacturing processes for embedding the tags in all the possible applications.

But another, even more astounding revolution is gathering momentum. *Smart dust* takes the concept of a simple RFID circuit replacing the bar code label, and extends it to embedding an entire computer in a microscopic package!

If that seems outlandish, consider the following: The Intel 8080 microprocessor, released in 1974, was a 2MHz device. By 1980, personal computers running DOS were built around this processor, and usually had 640 K of memory. In the intervening years, the size of our desktop machines has remained relatively constant, but the power of the CPU and the size of the real memory have both increased by a factor of more than 1,000.

Instead of holding the size of the box as a constant and allowing the power of the machine to increase, what if we hold the processing power constant and allow the size of the box to shrink? We end up with an 8080 class machine in a "box" just one millimeter in size! This is smart dust.

A number of research projects have demonstrated the ability to manufacture smart dust devices. These tiny computers can even be packaged with microscopic batteries. Really tiny computers can run on miniscule amounts of power, and it's possible to package a battery alongside the computer in a 1-mm package that will run the computer for years.

Smart dust can be used for environmental reporting. Scatter or even paint smart dust in an environment. The separate processors can self organize into a network that you can interrogate remotely. Security and military applications are just the tip of the iceberg.

I have always advised data warehouse people to stay in the center of the runway as they plan their careers. CRM, information portals, and EAI will come and go. But standing back from these short-lived themes, the real constant is the irresistible growth of data sources and the insatiable demand from our business users to see the data. Although the RFID and smart dust revolutions will change our vocabulary and our tools, our mission remains constant. Data warehousing in its many forms is guaranteed job security.

12.8 Is Big Data Compatible with the Data Warehouse?

Ralph Kimball, Design Tip #146, *Jun 5, 2012*

Big data gets a lot of press in technology and IT circles these days, both because it is a disruptive technology very different from traditional relational databases, and because it opens up many new forms of analysis. In this article, I'll tackle some questions many IT people may be worried about. Is big data a new IT theme that has nothing to do with the data warehouse? Do the data warehouse skills and perspectives we have developed over the years help us in any way with big data? And maybe does big data belong in end user departments outside the scope of IT altogether? For an in-depth treatment of big data, please see the extended article 12.9, *The Evolving Role of the Enterprise Data Warehouse in the Era of Big Data Analytics.*

Big data fits within the mission of the data warehouse. The mission of the data warehouse has always been to marshal the data assets of an organization and expose those assets in the most effective way to facilitate decision making by a broad range of business users. Big data clearly fits within this mission.

The dimensional modeling foundations of the data warehouse can be found in every big data use case. The dimensional modeling approach to data warehousing starts with measurement events (observations). In the relational world, these events are captured in fact tables, and these fact tables are linked to the natural entities of the organization which we structure as dimension tables. It is not a stretch to interpret virtually every big data use case as collecting a set of observations whose context requires linking to natural entities. The observations and entities don't need to be cast as literal relational fact tables and dimension tables. For example, a tweet coming from Twitter is itself an observation which carries with it a number of obvious dimension-like entities, including the sender, the recipients, the subject, the origin server, the date and time, and the causal factors in the environment that the tweet may be responding to. Digging out some of these dimensions is not unlike what we do when constructing causal promotion dimensions in the data warehouse.

Data integration requires conformed dimensions. If we agree that big data entities are just dimensions, and if we are committed to integrating diverse big data sources together, then we can't avoid the central step of integration: conforming. Stepping back from relational databases, conforming dimensions means that we establish common descriptive context for a given entity when that entity appears in more than one big data source. In other words, if we have a common User entity associated with Twitter, Facebook, and LinkedIn observations, then if we intend to tie these data sources together, we must have a common data thread consisting of descriptive attributes administered identically across these three data sources. In the data warehouse we know a lot about conformed dimensions. This knowledge is spot-on relevant to integrating big data sources.

Proper tracking of time variance in big data requires durable keys and probably surrogate keys. If a big data use case requires correct historical tracking, then a mechanism must be supplied for keeping the old versions of the dimensional entities. At the very least, an entity like User requires a durable identifier that remains constant across varying versions of the dimension member. And, sooner or later, big data practitioners will discover a lesson we learned in the data warehouse nearly twenty years ago: You need to create your own surrogate keys for the members of a dimension because natural keys created by source systems are plagued with operational problems. Thus, once again, fundamental lessons learned in the data warehouse can be applied to big data. Or, to put it more strongly, sooner or later these fundamental lessons MUST be applied in the big data world.

IT and big data must get married someday. A lot of the action in big data today is taking place outside of IT. "Data scientists" are building their own data analysis sandboxes, developing their own ad hoc analytic applications, and taking their results directly to senior management. As exciting as this is, this is not a sustainable model. Where do I start? No data governance, no sharing of IT resources across sandboxes, poor communication among data scientists, no culture for producing production hardened applications, no end user training or support, and the list goes on. For IT and big data to get married, a significant effort will have to be made by end user management in recognizing that the current model is at best a prototyping effort, and by IT who has to invest in big data technical skills and business content.

I am cautiously optimistic that big data is real and that it will grow to be a significant theme for the data warehouse and IT. This will happen sooner if big data users recognize the valuable legacy that the data warehouse brings to the party.

 ## 12.9 The Evolving Role of the Enterprise Data Warehouse in the Era of Big Data Analytics

Ralph Kimball, White Paper Excerpt, *Apr 29, 2011*

This article was originally a white paper written by Ralph in 2011 and sponsored by Informatica. It was written in the context of the Hadoop 1.0 environment which was dominated by the MapReduce architecture. In the intervening four years, Hadoop has evolved to version 2.0 and enormously expanded its capabilities, especially those relevant to data warehousing. This article has been shortened and extensively edited to reflect these new capabilities.

Executive Summary

In this white paper, we describe the rapidly evolving landscape for designing an enterprise data warehouse (EDW) to support business analytics in the era of big data. We describe the scope and challenges of building and evolving a very stable and successful EDW architecture to meet new business requirements. These include extreme integration, semi- and unstructured data sources, petabytes of behavioral and image data accessed through Hadoop as well as massively parallel relational databases, and then structuring the EDW to support advanced analytics. This paper provides detailed guidance for designing and administering the necessary processes for deployment. This white paper has been written in response to a lack of specific guidance in the industry as to how the EDW needs to respond to the big data analytics challenge, and what necessary design elements are needed to support these new requirements.

Introduction

What is big data? Its bigness is actually not the most interesting characteristic. Big data is structured, semi-structured, unstructured, and raw data in many different formats, in some cases looking totally different than the clean scalar numbers and text we have stored in our data warehouses for the last 30 years. Much big data cannot be analyzed with anything that looks like SQL. But most important, big data is a *paradigm shift* in how we think about data assets, where do we collect them, how do we analyze them, and how do we monetize the insights from the analysis. The big data revolution is about finding new value within and outside conventional data sources. An additional approach is needed because the software and hardware environments of the past have not been able to capture, manage, or process the new forms of data within reasonable development times or processing times. We are challenged to reorganize our information management landscape to extend a remarkably stable and successful EDW architecture to this new era of big data analytics.

In reading this white paper please bear in mind that my consistent view has always been that the "data warehouse" comprises the complete ecosystem for extracting, cleaning, integrating, and delivering data to decision makers, and therefore includes the ETL and business intelligence (BI) functions considered as outside of the data warehouse by more conservative writers. I have always taken the view that data warehousing has a very comprehensive role in capturing all forms of enterprise data, and then preparing that data for the most effective use by decision makers all across the enterprise. This white paper takes the aggressive view that the enterprise data warehouse is on the verge of a very exciting new set of responsibilities. The scope of the EDW will increase dramatically.

This white paper stands back from the marketplace as it exists in 2015 to highlight the clearly emerging new trends brought by the big data revolution. And a revolution it is. As James Markarian, Informatica's Executive Vice President and Chief Technology Officer, remarked: "the database market has finally gotten interesting again." Because much of the new big data tools and approaches are version 1 or even version 0 developments, the landscape will continue to change rapidly. However, there is growing awareness in the marketplace that new kinds of analysis are possible and that key competitors, especially e-commerce enterprises, are already taking advantage of the new paradigm. This white paper is intended to be a guide to help business intelligence, data warehousing, and information management professionals and management teams understand and prepare for big data as a complementary extension to their current EDW architecture.

Data Is an Asset on the Balance Sheet

Enterprises increasingly recognize that data itself is an asset that should appear on the balance sheet in the same way that traditional assets from the manufacturing age such as equipment and land have always appeared. There are several ways to determine the value of the data asset, including:

- Cost to produce the data
- Cost to replace the data if it is lost
- Revenue or profit opportunity provided by the data
- Revenue or profit loss if data falls into competitors' hands
- Legal exposure from fines and lawsuits if data is exposed to the wrong parties

But more important than the data itself, enterprises have shown that insights from data can be monetized. When an e-commerce site detects an increase in favorable click-throughs from an experimental ad treatment, that insight can be taken to the bottom line immediately. This direct cause-and-effect is easily understood by management, and an analytic research group that consistently demonstrates these insights is looked upon as a strategic resource for the enterprise by the highest levels of management. This growth in business awareness of the value of data-driven insights is rapidly spreading outward from the e-commerce world to virtually every business segment.

Use Cases for Big Data Analytics

Big data analytics use cases are spreading like wildfire. Here is a set of use cases reported recently, including a benchmark set of "Hadoop-able" use cases proposed by Jeff Hammerbacher, Chief Scientist for Cloudera. Note that none of these use cases can be satisfied with scalar numeric data, nor can any be properly analyzed by simple SQL statements. All of them can be scaled into the petabyte range and beyond with appropriate business assumptions.

> **Search ranking.** All search engines attempt to rank the relevance of a web page to a search request against all other possible web pages. Google's page rank algorithm is, of course, the poster child for this use case.
>
> **Ad tracking.** E-commerce sites typically record an enormous river of data including every page event in every user session. This allows for very short turnaround of experiments in ad placement, color, size, wording, and other features. When an experiment shows that such a feature change in an ad results in improved click-through behavior, the change can be implemented virtually in real time.
>
> **Location and proximity tracking.** Many use cases add precise GPS location tracking, together with frequent updates, in operational applications, security analysis, navigation, and social

media. Precise location tracking opens the door for an enormous ocean of data about other locations nearby the GPS measurement. These other locations may represent opportunities for sales or services.

Causal factor discovery. Point-of-sale data has long been able to show us when the sales of a product go sharply up or down. But searching for the causal factors that explain these deviations has been, at best, a guessing game or an art form. The answers may be found in competitive pricing data, competitive promotional data including print and television media, weather, holidays, national events including disasters, and virally spread opinions found in social media. See the next use case as well.

Social CRM. This use case is one of the hottest new areas for marketing analysis. The Altimeter Group has described a very useful set of key performance indicators for social CRM that include share of voice, audience engagement, conversation reach, active advocates, advocate influence, advocacy impact, resolution rate, resolution time, satisfaction score, topic trends, sentiment ratio, and idea impact. The calculation of these KPIs involves in-depth trolling of a huge array of data sources, especially unstructured social media.

Document similarity testing. Two documents can be compared to derive a metric of similarity. There is a large body of academic research and tested algorithms, for example, latent semantic analysis, that is just now finding its way to driving monetized insights of interest to big data practitioners. For example, a single source document can be used as a kind of multifaceted template to compare against a large set of target documents. This could be used for threat discovery, sentiment analysis, and opinion polls. For example: "Find all the documents that agree with my source document on global warming."

Genomics analysis: For example, commercial seed gene sequencing. In 2011 the cotton research community was thrilled by a genome sequencing announcement that stated in part "The sequence will serve a critical role as the reference for future assembly of the larger cotton crop genome. Cotton is the most important fiber crop worldwide and this sequence information will open the way for more rapid breeding for higher yield, better fiber quality and adaptation to environmental stresses and for insect and disease resistance." Scientist Ryan Rapp stressed the importance of involving the cotton research community in analyzing the sequence, identifying genes and gene families and determining the future directions of research. (SeedQuest, Sept 22, 2010). This use case is just one example of a whole industry that is being formed to address genomics analysis broadly, beyond this example of seed gene sequencing.

Discovery of customer cohort groups. Customer cohort groups are used by many enterprises to identify common demographic trends and behavior histories. We are all familiar with Amazon's cohort groups when they say other customers who bought the same book as you have also bought the following books. Of course, if you can sell your product or service to one member of a cohort group, then all the rest may be reasonable prospects. Cohort groups are represented logically and graphically as links, and much of the analysis of cohort groups involves specialized link analysis algorithms.

In-flight aircraft status. This use case as well as the following two use cases are made possible by the introduction of sensor technology everywhere. In the case of aircraft systems, in-flight status of hundreds of variables on engines, fuel systems, hydraulics, and electrical systems are measured and transmitted every few milliseconds. The value of this use case is not just the engineering telemetry data that could be analyzed at some future point in time, but the data drives real-time adaptive control, fuel usage, part failure prediction, and pilot notification.

Smart utility meters. It didn't take long for utility companies to figure out that a smart meter can be used for more than just the monthly readout that produces the customer's utility bill. By drastically cranking up the frequency of the readouts to as much as one readout per second per meter across the entire customer landscape, many useful analyses can be performed including dynamic load-balancing, failure response, adaptive pricing, and longer-term strategies for incenting customers to utilize the utility more effectively (either from the customers' point of view or the utility's point of view!).

Building sensors. Modern industrial buildings and high-rises are being fitted with thousands of small sensors to detect temperature, humidity, vibration, and noise. Like the smart utility meters, collecting this data every few seconds 24 hours per day allows many forms of analysis including energy usage, unusual problems including security violations, component failure in air-conditioning and heating systems and plumbing systems, and the development of construction practices and pricing strategies.

Satellite image comparison. Images of the regions of the earth from satellites are captured by every pass of certain satellites on intervals typically separated by a small number of days. Overlaying these images and computing the differences allows the creation of hot spot maps showing what has changed. This analysis can identify construction, destruction, changes due to disasters like hurricanes and earthquakes and fires, and the spread of human encroachment.

CAT scan comparisons. CAT scans are stacks of images taken as "slices" of the human body. Large libraries of CAT scans can be analyzed to facilitate the automatic diagnosis of medical issues and their prevalence.

Financial account fraud detection and intervention. Account fraud, of course, has immediate and obvious financial impact. In many cases fraud can be detected by patterns of account behavior, in some cases crossing multiple financial systems. For example, "check kiting" requires the rapid transfer of money back and forth between two separate accounts. Certain forms of broker fraud involve two conspiring brokers selling a security back-and-forth at ever increasing prices, until an unsuspecting third party enters the action by buying the security, allowing the fraudulent brokers to quickly exit. Again, this behavior may take place across two separate exchanges in a short period of time.

Computer system hacking detection and intervention. System hacking in many cases involves an unusual entry mode or some other kind of behavior that in retrospect is a smoking gun but may be hard to detect in real time.

Online game gesture tracking. Online game companies typically record every click and maneuver by every player at the most fine-grained level. This avalanche of "telemetry data" allows fraud detection, intervention for a player who is getting consistently defeated (and therefore discouraged), offers of additional features or game goals for players who are about to finish a game and depart, ideas for new game features, and experiments for new features in the games. This can be generalized to television viewing. Your DVR box can capture remote control keystrokes, recording events, playback events, picture-in-picture viewing, and the context of the guide. All of this can be sent back to your provider.

Big science including atom smashers, weather analysis, and space probe telemetry feeds. Major scientific projects have always collected a lot of data, but now the techniques of big data analytics are allowing broader access and much more timely access to the data. Big science data, of course, is a mixture of all forms of data: scalar, vector, complex structures, analog wave forms, and images.

Data bag exploration. There are many situations in commercial environments and in the research communities where large volumes of raw data are collected. One example might be data collected about structure fires. Beyond the predictable dimensions of time, place, primary cause of fire, and responding firefighters, there may be a wealth of unpredictable anecdotal data that at best can be modeled as a disorderly collection of name-value pairs, such as "contributing weather= lightning." Another example would be the listing of all relevant financial assets for a defendant in a lawsuit. Again such a list is likely to be a disorderly collection of name-value pairs, such as "shared real estate ownership =condominium." The list of examples like this is endless. What they have in common is the need to encapsulate the disorderly collection of name-value pairs, which is generally known as a "data bag." Complex data bags may contain both name-value pairs as well as embedded sub data bags. The challenge in this use case is to find a common way to approach the analysis of data bags when the content of the data may need to be discovered after the data is loaded.

The final two use cases are old and venerable examples that even predate data warehousing itself. But new life has been breathed into these use cases because of the exciting potential of ultra-atomic customer behavior data.

Loan risk analysis and insurance policy underwriting. In order to evaluate the risk of a prospective loan or a prospective insurance policy, many data sources can be brought into play ranging from payment histories, detailed credit behavior, employment data, and financial asset disclosures. In some cases the collateral for a loan or the insured item may be accompanied by image data.

Customer churn analysis. Enterprises concerned with churn want to understand the predictive factors leading up to the loss of a customer, including that customer's detailed behavior as well as many external factors including the economy, life stage, and other demographics of the customer, and finally real-time competitive issues.

Big Data Analytics System Requirements

Before discussing the exciting new technical and architectural developments of the 2010s, let's summarize the overall requirements for supporting big data analytics, keeping in mind that we are not requiring a single system or a single vendor's technology to provide a blanket solution for every use case. From the perspective of 2015, we have the luxury of standing back from all these use cases gathered in the last few years, and we are now in a position to surround the requirements with some confidence.

In the coming 2010s decade, the analysis of big data will require a technology or combination of technologies capable of:

- Scaling to easily support petabytes (thousands of terabytes) of data
- Being distributed across thousands of processors, potentially geographically unaware, and potentially heterogeneous
- Subsecond response time for highly constrained standard SQL queries
- Embedding arbitrarily complex user-defined functions (UDFs) within processing requests
- Implementing UDFs in a wide variety of industry-standard procedural languages
- Assembling extensive libraries of reusable UDFs crossing most or all of use cases
- Executing UDFs as "relation scans" over petabyte-sized data sets in a few minutes
- Supporting a wide variety of data types growing to include images, waveforms, arbitrarily hierarchical data structures, and data bags
- Loading data to be ready for analysis, at very high rates, at least gigabytes per second
- Integrating data from multiple sources during the load process at very high rates (GB/sec)
- Loading data before declaring or discovering its structure
- Executing certain "streaming" analytic queries in real time on incoming load data
- Updating data in place at full load speeds
- Joining a billion row dimension table to a trillion row fact table without pre-clustering the dimension table with the fact table
- Scheduling and execution of complex multi-hundred node workflows
- Being configured without being subject to a single point of failure
- Failover and process continuation when processing nodes fail
- Supporting extreme mixed workloads including thousands of geographically dispersed online users and programs executing a variety of requests ranging from ad hoc queries to strategic analysis, and while loading data in batch and streaming fashion

Two architectures have emerged to address big data analytics: extended RDBMS, and Hadoop. These architectures are being implemented as completely separate systems and in various interesting hybrid combinations involving both architectures. We will start by discussing the architectures separately.

Extended Relational Database Management Systems

All of the major relational database management system vendors are adding features to address big data analytics from a solid relational perspective. The two most significant architectural developments have been the overtaking of the high end of the market with massively parallel processing (MPP), and the growing adoption of columnar storage. When MPP and columnar storage techniques are combined, a number of the system requirements in the preceding list can start to be addressed, including:

- Scaling to support exabytes (thousands of petabytes) of data
- Being distributed across tens of thousands of geographically dispersed processors
- Subsecond response time for highly constrained standard SQL queries
- Updating data in place at full load speeds
- Being configured without being subject to a single point of failure
- Failover and process continuation when processing nodes fail

Additionally, RDBMS vendors are adding some complex user-defined functions (UDFs) to their syntax, but the kind of general-purpose procedural language computing required by big data analytics is not being satisfied in relational environments at this time.

In a similar vein, RDBMS vendors are allowing complex data structures to be stored in individual fields. These kinds of embedded complex data structures have been known as "blobs" for many years. It's important to understand that relational databases have a hard time providing general support for interpreting blobs since blobs do not fit the relational paradigm. An RDBMS indeed provides some value by hosting the blobs in a structured framework, but much of the complex interpretation and computation on the blobs must be done with specially crafted UDFs, or BI application layer clients. Blobs are related to "data bags" discussed earlier.

MPP implementations have never satisfactorily addressed the "big join" issue where an attempt is made to join a billion row dimension table to a trillion row fact table without resorting to clustered storage. The big join crisis occurs when an ad hoc constraint is placed against the dimension table resulting in a potentially very large set of dimension keys that must be physically downloaded into every one of the physical segments of the trillion row fact table stored separately in the MPP system. Since the dimension keys are scattered randomly across the separate segments of the trillion row fact table, it is very hard to avoid a lengthy download step of the very large dimension table to every one of the fact table storage partitions. To be fair, the Hadoop architecture has not been able to address the big join problem either.

Columnar data storage fits the relational paradigm, and especially dimensionally modeled databases, very well. Besides the significant advantage of high compression of sparse data, columnar databases allow a very large number of columns compared to row-oriented databases, and place little overhead on the system when columns are added to an existing schema. The most significant Achilles' heel, at least in 2015, is the slow loading speed of data into the columnar format. Although impressive load speed improvements are being announced by columnar database vendors, they have still not achieved the gigabytes-per-second requirement.

The extended RDBMS architecture to support big data analytics preserves the familiar data warehouse architecture with a number of important additions, shown in Figure 12-4 with **bold text**:

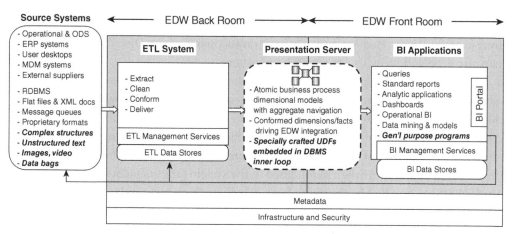

Figure 12-4: The extended RDBMS–based architecture for an enterprise data warehouse.

The fact that the high-level enterprise data warehouse architecture is not materially changed by the introduction of new data structures, or a growing library of specially crafted user-defined functions, or powerful procedural language-based programs acting as powerful BI clients, is the charm of the extended RDBMS approach to big data analytics. The major RDBMS players are able to marshal their enormous legacy of millions of lines of code, powerful governance capabilities, and system stability built over decades of serving the marketplace.

However, it is the opinion of this author that the extended RDBMS systems cannot be the only solution for big data analytics. At some point, tacking on non-relational data structures and non-relational processing algorithms to the basic, coherent RDBMS architecture will become unwieldy and inefficient. The Swiss Army knife analogy comes to mind. Another analogy closer to the topic is the programming language PL/1. Originally designed as an overarching, multipurpose, powerful programming language for all forms of data and all applications, it ultimately became a bloated and sprawling corpus that tried to do too many things in a single language. Since the heyday of PL/1 there has been a wonderful evolution of more narrowly focused programming languages with many new concepts and features that simply couldn't be tacked onto PL/1 after a certain point. Relational database management systems do so many things so well that there is no danger of suffering the same fate as PL/1. The big data analytics space is growing so rapidly and in such exciting and unexpected new directions that a lighter weight, more flexible and more agile processing framework in addition to RDBMS systems may be a reasonable alternative.

Hadoop

Hadoop is an open source, top-level Apache project, with thousands of contributors and a whole industry of diverse applications. Hadoop runs natively on its own Hadoop Distributed File System (HDFS) and can also read and write to Amazon S3 and others.

The key to understanding Hadoop and why it is a revolutionary alternative to existing RDBMS systems is to study how relational databases are implemented within HDFS. In Figure 12-5 we show how an RDBMS stack is implemented in conventional environments and within HDFS. In both architectures, the RDBMS consists of three layers: storage, metadata, and query. In the conventional RDBMS the storage layer consists of the database tables created by issuing CREATE TABLE SQL statements. These table definitions are then maintained in the system table metadata layer. All queries presented to the RDBMS are handled by the query layer, which implements standard SQL and special proprietary SQL extensions. The key understanding is that these three layers are glued together and are proprietary to the DBMS vendor, whether it is Oracle, IBM DB2, Sybase, Microsoft SQL Server, or others. The three layers are not separable, and one vendor's DBMS cannot directly access or control any of the layers in another vendor's DBMS.

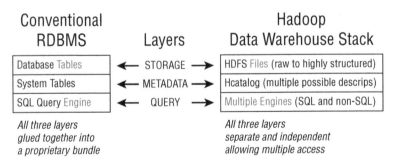

Figure 12-5: Comparison of the storage, metadata, and query layers between conventional RDBMSs and the Hadoop data warehouse stack.

The Hadoop data warehouse stack has the same three layers but they are decoupled from each other. The HDFS storage layer does not consist of precisely declared relational database tables, but rather is made up of much simpler HDFS files which range across the spectrum from raw files downloaded from original sources without any transformations, to highly structured files that have been prepared by ETL processing. Since the storage layer is independent from the other layers, any client application can read these HDFS files (with appropriate access rights), whether the client application is a relational database or some entirely different non-SQL analytic application. Any client wishing to access an HDFS file needs to read its description to understand the structure of the file. The descriptions are universally accessed through the HDFS metadata layer, HCatalog, also called the Hive Metastore. Again, with appropriate access rights, many different clients can simultaneously access HCatalog to interpret the file contents for their own purposes. It is entirely possible that an HDFS file could contain a complex mixture of text data, numerical data, and specially structured data. Each of the clients can pick out what makes sense. The third layer, query, now becomes a kind of marketplace where multiple SQL and non-SQL query engines can coexist. Two SQL query engines are available as open source (free) SQL query applications: Hive, an original component of the Hadoop project, which is generally more intended for very distributed "relation scan" kinds of queries, and Impala, contributed to the Hadoop project by Cloudera, which is intended for highly specific constrained queries that are returned with very short response times.

In Figure 12-6 we step back from the RDBMS stacks to the larger picture of HDFS.

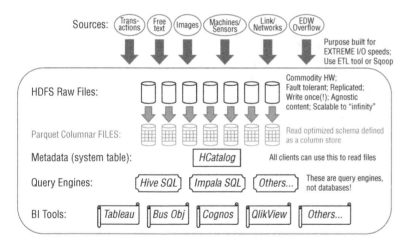

Figure 12-6: HDFS viewed as a data warehouse environment.

HDFS is built to support extreme I/O speeds. An actual HDFS implementation is a "cluster" of fairly normal server class machines each perhaps with a 3 GHz CPU, lots of RAM (100 GB and more), and lots of disk storage (30 TB or more). A cluster can be as little as one machine, but many of the mature clusters have hundreds of machines or even more, all connected to each other.

Typically, source data is loaded into HDFS using the utility SQOOP at up to gigabytes per second. Many environments prefer the data to be landed in unchanged raw format and simultaneously described in the HCatalog metadata. HDFS is completely agnostic. An HDFS file is a collection of bits downloaded from outside HDFS. There are no formatting restrictions on a raw HDFS file. A key feature of HDFS is that the base level HDFS files are write-once and redundantly stored in three independent locations (the default). Write-once means that an HDFS file is always guaranteed to be the original bits that were loaded into HDFS. The redundant storage on different files, different back planes, and different physical devices creates a very high level of protection against file loss.

Figure 12-6 shows two additional layers not shown in the RDBMS stack of Figure 12-5. The Parquet columnar files are a preferred format for mimicking the structure of conventional columnar databases such as Sybase IQ, Vertica (now owned by HP), ParAccel, or InfoBright, among others. Parquet columnar files are typically created by an ETL process that converts raw HDFS files into the Parquet format. The second additional layer is the set of familiar BI tools on the bottom row. Actually, these tools are basically unchanged from their deployments on conventional RDBMS machines. All that these query tools need to do is open a connection to a SQL applications programming interface (API) supported by a Hadoop query processor such as Hive or Impala, and the query tool can send normal SQL requests and receive back answer sets.

In order to execute an actual query against either HDFS raw files or structured Parquet files, the query tool must issue a kind of view declaration that declares the structure of the target file. It is at this point that the underlying file is interpreted as a database. Since this declaration occurs at query time, rather than at data load time, the approach is called "schema on read." Schema on read is profoundly different than "schema on load," which is required in all conventional RDBMSs. Schema on read defers many ETL issues until the moment of querying. Since this approach can be applied to HDFS raw files, it allows a prototyping style of exploratory BI where the original raw files can be queried by familiar query tools without any physical data transformation. This can be viewed as a powerful kind of data virtualization. The cost, of course, is that querying raw files will be slow compared to querying carefully curated files loaded into pre-designed target schemas in a conventional RDBMS. However, once this exploratory phase of querying is done with schema on read, a more conventional ETL data transfer step can take place to load the data into Parquet files where the query performance is comparable to a conventional RDBMS.

Finally, one obvious point is that HDFS, Sqoop, Hive, and Impala are all open source software components of the Hadoop project that can be downloaded and installed with no licensing charges. In fairness, relatively few organizations have opted for completely rolling their own, and instead purchase Hadoop "distributions" of software suites that have been tested to work together.

The preceding description has chosen a somewhat narrow path though the Hadoop ecosystem to emphasize the data warehouse–friendly configurations. There is a rich set of database engines and analytic tools that extend the power of the Hadoop environment while gracefully coexisting with the previously mentioned components, even while accessing the same data files. Leading non-SQL tools of interest to data analysts and business users as described by their web wikis include:

> **Spark.** Spark is a fast and general processing engine compatible with Hadoop data. It can run in Hadoop clusters through YARN or Spark's standalone mode, and it can process data in HDFS,

HBase, Cassandra, Hive, and any Hadoop input format. It is designed to perform both batch processing (similar to MapReduce) and new workloads like streaming, interactive queries, and machine learning.

MongoDB. MongoDB powers the online, real-time operational application, serving business processes and end users. Hadoop consumes data from MongoDB, blending this data with other operational systems to fuel sophisticated analytics and machine learning. Results are loaded back to MongoDB to serve smarter operational processes—i.e., delivering more relevant offers, faster identification of fraud, and improved customer experience.

Hunk from Splunk. Hunk is the big data analytics platform that lets you rapidly explore, analyze, and visualize data in Hadoop and NoSQL data stores, especially machine and sensor data.

Feature Convergence in the Coming Decade

It is safe to say that relational database management systems and Hadoop systems will increasingly find ways to coexist gracefully in the coming decade. But the systems have distinct characteristics, as depicted in Figure 12-7.

Relational DBMSs	Hadoop
Proprietary, mostly	Open source
Expensive	Much less expensive
Data requires structuring before loading	Data does not require structuring before loading
Great for speedy indexed lookups	Great for massive data scans and focused Parquet based queries
No RDBMS support for complex data structures	Deep support for complex data structures
NO RDBMS support for iteration, complex branching	Deep support for iteration, complex branching
Deep support for transaction processing	Little or no support for transaction processing

Figure 12-7: Capability comparison of conventional RDBMS and Hadoop systems.

In the upcoming decade RDBMSs will extend their support for hosting complex data types as "blobs," and will extend APIs for arbitrary analytic routines to operate on the contents of records. Hadoop systems, especially Hive and Impala, will deepen their support for SQL interfaces and fuller support of the complete SQL language. But neither will take over the market for big data analytics exclusively. As remarked earlier, RDBMSs cannot provide "relational" semantics for many of the complex use cases required by big data analytics. At best, RDBMSs will provide relational structure surrounding the complex payloads.

Similarly, Hadoop systems will never take over ACID-compliant transaction processing, although they will become competitive to RDBMSs for relation scans and indexed queries on row and column oriented tables, and superior on a cost/performance basis.

It will probably be difficult for IT organizations to sort out the vendor claims, which will almost certainly claim that their systems do everything. In some cases these claims are "objection removers," which means that they are claims that have a grain of truth to them, and are made to make you feel good, but do not stand up to scrutiny in a competitive and practical environment. Buyer beware!

Reusable Analytics

Up to this point we have begged the issue of where does all the special analytic software come from. Big data analytics will never prosper if every instance is a custom-coded solution. Both the RDBMS and the open source communities recognize this and two main development themes have emerged. High-end statistical analysis vendors, such as SAS, have developed extensive and proprietary reusable libraries for a wide range of analytic applications, including advanced statistics, data mining, predictive analytics, feature detection, linear models, discriminant analysis, and many others. The open source community has a number of initiatives, the most notable of which are Hadoop-ML and Apache Mahout.

Data Warehouse Cultural Changes in the Coming Decade

The enterprise data warehouse must absolutely stay relevant to the business. As the value and the visibility of big data analytics grows, the data warehouse must encompass the new culture, skills, techniques, and systems required for big data analytics.

Sandboxes For example, big data analysis encourages exploratory sandboxes for experimentation. These sandboxes are copies or segments of the massive data sets being sourced by the organization. Individual analysts or very small groups are encouraged to analyze the data with a very wide variety of tools, ranging from serious statistical tools like SAS, Matlab, or R, to predictive models, and many forms of ad hoc querying and visualization through advanced BI graphical interfaces. The analyst responsible for a given sandbox is allowed to do anything with the data, using any tool they want, even if the tools they use are not corporate standards. The sandbox phenomenon has enormous energy but it carries a significant risk to the IT organization and EDW architecture because it could create isolated and incompatible stovepipes of data. This point is amplified in the subsequent section on organizational changes.

Exploratory sandboxes usually have a limited time duration, lasting weeks or at most a few months. Their data can be a frozen snapshot, or a window on a certain segment of incoming data. The analyst may have permission to run an experiment changing a feature on the product or service in the marketplace, and then performing A/B testing to see how the change affects customer behavior. Typically, if such an experiment produces a successful result, the sandbox experiment is terminated, and the feature goes into production. At that point, tracking applications that may have been implemented in the sandbox using a quick and dirty prototyping language, are usually re-implemented by other personnel in the EDW environment using corporate standard tools. In several of the e-commerce enterprises interviewed for this white paper, analytic sandboxes were extremely important, and in some cases hundreds of the sandbox experiments were ongoing simultaneously. As one interviewee commented, "newly discovered patterns have the most disruptive potential, and insights from them lead to the highest returns on investment."

Architecturally, sandboxes should not be brute force copies of entire data sets, or even major segments of these data sets. In dimensional modeling parlance, the analyst needs much more than just a fact table to run the experiment. At a minimum the analyst also needs one or more very large dimension tables, and possibly additional fact tables for complete "drill across" analysis. If 100 analysts are creating brute force copy versions of the data for the sandboxes there will be enormous wasting of disk space and resources for all the redundant copies. Remember that the largest dimension tables, such as customer dimensions, can have 500 million rows! The recommended architecture for a serious sandbox environment is to build each sandbox using conformed (shared) dimensions which are incorporated into each sandbox as relational views, or their equivalent under Hadoop applications.

Low Latency An elementary mistake when gathering business requirements during the design of a data warehouse is to ask the business users if they want "real-time" data. Users are likely to say "of course!" Although perhaps this answer has been somewhat gratuitous in the past, a good business case can now be made in many situations that more frequent updates of data delivered to the business with lower and lower latencies are justified. Both RDBMSs and Hadoop systems struggle with loading gigantic amounts of data and making that data available within seconds of that data being created. But the marketplace wants this, and regardless of a technologist's doubt about the requirement, the requirement is real and over the next decade it must be addressed.

An interesting angle on low latency data is the desire to begin serious analysis on the data as it is streaming in, but possibly far before the data collection process even terminates. There is significant interest in streaming analysis systems which allow SQL-like queries to process the data as it flows into the system. In some use cases when the results of a streaming query surpass a threshold, the analysis can be halted without running the job to the bitter end. An academic effort, known as continuous query language (CQL), has made impressive progress in defining the requirements for streaming data processing including clever semantics for dynamically moving time windows on the streaming data. Look for CQL language extensions and streaming data query capabilities in the load programs for both RDBMSs and HDFS deployed data sets. An ideal implementation would allow streaming data analysis to take place while the data is being loaded at gigabytes per second.

Continuous Thirst for More Exquisite Detail Analysts are forever thirsting for more detail in every marketplace observation, especially of customer behavior. For example, every web page event (a page being painted on a user's screen) spawns hundreds of records describing every object on the page. In online games, where every gesture enters the data stream, as many as 100 descriptors are attached to each of these gesture micro-events. For instance, in a hypothetical online baseball game, when the batter swings at a pitch, everything describing the position of the players, the score, runners on the bases, and even the characteristics of the pitch, are all stored with that individual record. In both of these examples, the complete context must be captured within the current record, because it is impractical to compute this detailed context after the fact from separate data sources. The lesson for the coming decade is that this thirst for exquisite detail will only grow. It is possible to imagine thousands of attributes being attached to some micro-events, and the categories and names of these attributes will grow in unpredictable ways.

Light Touch Data Waits for Its Relevance to Be Exposed   Light touch data is an aspect of the exquisite detail data described in the previous section. For example, if a customer browses a website extensively before making a purchase, a great deal of micro-context is stored in all the web page events prior to the purchase. When the purchase is made, some of that micro-context suddenly becomes much more important, and is elevated from "light touch data" to real data. At that point the sequence of exposures to the selected product or to competitive products in the same space becomes possible to be sessionized. These micro-events are pretty much meaningless before the purchase event, because there are so many conceivable and irrelevant threads that would be dead ends for analysis. This requires oceans of light touch data to be stored, waiting for the relevance of selected threads of these micro-events to eventually be exposed. Conventional seasonality thinking suggests that at least five quarters (15 months) of this light touch data needs to be kept online. This is one instance of a remark made consistently during interviews for this white paper that analysts want "longer tails," which means that they want more significant histories than they currently get.

Simple Analysis of All the Data Trumps Sophisticated Analysis of Some of the Data   Although data sampling has never been a popular technique in data warehousing, surprisingly the arrival of enormous petabyte-sized data sets has not increased the interest in analyzing a subset of the data. On the contrary, a number of analysts point out that monetizable insights can be derived from very small populations that could be missed by only sampling some of the data. Of course this is a somewhat controversial point, since the same analysts admit that if you have 1 trillion behavior observation records, you may be able to find any behavior pattern if you look hard enough.

Another somewhat controversial point raised by some analysts is their concern that any form of data cleaning on the incoming data could erase interesting low-frequency "edge cases." Ultimately both the cases of misleading rare behavior patterns, and misleading corrupted data need to be gently filtered out of the data.

Assuming that the behavior insights from very small populations are valid, there is widespread recognition that micro-marketing to the small populations is possible, and doing enough of this can build a sustainable strategic advantage.

A final argument in favor of analyzing complete data sets is that these "relation scans" do not require indexes or aggregations to be computed in advance of the analysis. This approach fits well with the basic Hadoop distributed analysis architecture.

The EDW Supporting Big Data Analytics Must Be Magnetic, Agile, and Deep Cohen and Dolan in their seminal but somewhat controversial paper on big data analytics argue that EDWs must shed some old orthodoxies in order to be "magnetic, agile, and deep." A magnetic environment places the least impediments on the incorporation of new, unexpected, and potentially dirty data sources. Specifically, this supports the need to defer declaration of data structures until after the data is loaded. According to Cohen and Dolan, an agile environment eschews long-range careful design and planning! And a deep environment allows running sophisticated analytic algorithms on massive data sets without sampling, or perhaps even cleaning.

Here's the link to their paper: "MAD Skills: New Analysis Practices for Big Data," Cohen, Dolan et al., `http://db.cs.berkeley.edu/jmh/papers/madskills-032009.pdf`.

Data Warehouse Organization Changes in the Coming Decade

The growing importance of big data analytics amounts to something between a midcourse correction and a revolution for enterprise data warehousing. New skill sets, new organizations, new development paradigms, and new technology will need to be absorbed by many enterprises, especially those facing the use cases described in this paper. Not every enterprise needs to jump into the petabyte ocean, but it is this author's prediction that the upcoming decade will see a steady growth in the percentage of large enterprises recognizing the value of big data analytics.

Technical Skill Sets Required It is worth repeating here the message of the very first sentence of the introduction to this article. Petabyte scale data sets are of course a big challenge but big data analysis is often about difficulties other than data volume. You can have fast arriving data or complex data or complex analyses, which are very challenging even if all you have are terabytes of data!

The care and feeding of RDBMS-oriented data warehouses involves a comprehensive set of skills that is pretty well understood: SQL programming, ETL platform expertise, database modeling, task scheduling, system building and maintenance skills, one or more scripting languages such as Python or Perl, UNIX or Windows operating system skills, and business intelligence tools skills. SQL programming, which is at the core of an RDBMS implementation, is a declarative language, which contrasts with the mindset of the procedural language skills needed for Hadoop programming, at least in Java. The data warehouse team also needs to have a good partnership within other areas of IT including storage management, security, networking, and support of mobile devices. Finally, good data warehousing also requires an extensive involvement with the business community, and with the cognitive psychology of end users!

The care and feeding of Hadoop data warehouses, including any of the big data analytics use cases described in this paper, involves a set of skills that only partially overlap traditional RDBMS data warehouse skills. Therein lies a significant challenge. These new skills include lower-level programming languages such as Java, C++, Ruby, Python, and MapReduce interfaces most commonly available via Java. Although the requirement to program via procedural based lower-level programming languages will be reduced significantly during the upcoming decade in favor of Pig, Hive, and HBase, it may be easier to recruit Hadoop application developers from the programming community rather than the data warehouse community, if the data warehouse job applicants lack programming and UNIX skills. If Hadoop data warehouses are managed exclusively with open source tools, then orchestration tools like Zookeeper and Oozie skills will be needed too. Keep in mind that the open source community innovates quickly. Hive, Pig, and HBase are not the last word in high-level interfaces to Hadoop for analysis. It is likely that we will see much more innovation in this decade including entirely new interfaces.

Finally, the analysts whom we have described as often working in sandbox environments will arrive with an eclectic and unpredictable set of skills starting with deep analytic expertise. For these people it is probably more important to be conversant in SAS, Matlab, or R than to have specific programming language or operating system skills. Such individuals typically will arrive with UNIX skills, and some reasonable programming proficiency, and most of these people are extremely tolerant of learning new complex technical environments. Perhaps the biggest challenge with traditional analysts is getting them to rely on the other resources available to them within IT, rather than building their own extract and data delivery pipelines. This is a tricky balance because you want to give the analysts unusual freedom, but you need to look over their shoulders to make sure that they are not wasting their time.

New Organizations Required   At this early stage of the big data analytics revolution, there is no question that the analysts must be part of the business organization, in order to understand the microscopic workings of the business, and also to be able to conduct the kind of rapid turnaround experiments and investigations we have described in this paper. As we have described, these analysts must be heavily supported in a technical sense, with potentially massive compute power and data transfer bandwidth. So although the analysts may reside in the business organizations, this is a great opportunity for IT to gain credibility and presence with the business. It would be a significant mistake and a lost opportunity for the analysts and their sandboxes to exist as rogue technical outposts in the business world without recognizing and taking advantage of their deep dependence on the traditional IT world.

In some organizations we interviewed for this white paper, we saw separate analytic groups embedded within different business organizations, but without very much cross communication or common identity established among the analytic groups. In some noteworthy cases, this lack of an "analytic community" led to lost opportunities to leverage each other's work, and led to multiple groups reinventing the same approaches, and duplicating programming efforts and infrastructure demands as they made separate copies of the same data.

We recommend that a cross divisional analytics community be established mimicking some of the successful data warehouse community building efforts we have seen in the past decade. Such a community should have regular cross divisional meetings, as well as a kind of private LinkedIn application to promote awareness of all the contacts and perspectives and resources that these individuals collect in their own investigations, and a private web portal where information and news events are shared. Periodic talks can be given, hopefully inviting members of the business community as well, and above all, the analytics community needs T-shirts and mugs!

Whither EDW?

The enterprise data warehouse must expand to encompass big data analytics as part of overall information management. The mission of the data warehouse has always been to collect the data assets of the organization and structure them in a way that is most useful to decision makers. Although some organizations may persist with a box on the org chart labeled EDW that is restricted to traditional reporting activities on transactional data, the scope of the EDW should grow to reflect these new big data developments. In some sense there are only two functions of IT: getting the data in (transaction processing), and getting the data out. The EDW is getting the data out.

The big choice facing shops with growing big data analytics investments is whether to choose an RDBMS-only solution, or a dual RDBMS and Hadoop solution. This author predicts that the dual solution will dominate, and in many cases the two architectures will not exist as separate islands but rather will have rich data pipelines going in both directions. It is safe to say that both architectures will evolve hugely over the next decade, but this author predicts that both architectures will share the big data analytics marketplace at the end of the decade.

Sometimes when an exciting new technology arrives, there is a tendency to close the door on older technologies as if they were going to go away. Data warehousing has built an enormous legacy of experience, best practices, supporting structures, technical expertise, and credibility with the business world. This will be the foundation for information management in the upcoming decade as data warehousing expands to include big data analytics.

 ## 12.10 Newly Emerging Best Practices for Big Data

Ralph Kimball, White Paper, *Sep 30, 2012*

The big data revolution is well under way. We know that the sheer bigness of the data is not what is interesting. Rather, big data also departs severely from the familiar text and number data that we have stored in relational databases and analyzed with SQL for more than 20 years. The format and content of big data ranges from unstructured free text to highly structured relational tables, as well as vectors, matrices, images, and collections of name-value pairs.

The first big shock to the system is that standard relational databases and SQL simply can't store or process big data, and are reaching fundamental capacity and scaling limits. Not only are the data formats outside the scope of relational databases, but much of the processing requires iterative logic, complex branching, and special analytic algorithms. SQL is a declarative language with a powerful but fixed syntax. Big data generally needs procedural languages and the ability to program arbitrary new logic.

The second big shock to the system is the shift away from slice and dice reporting based on simple filters and aggregations to analytics. Reports, dashboards, and ad hoc queries will always be important, but big data is best exploited by combing across huge unfiltered data sets assembled by combining both historical and real-time data.

Finally, the third big shock to the system is the recognition that the value of big data increases sharply as latency decreases and the data is delivered faster. Tenfold and hundredfold performance improvements result in qualitatively different analysis opportunities, often translating into increased revenue and profit.

All of this has made for a very dynamic, technology-driven marketplace with two main development threads: extended relational databases and Hadoop. I described these architectures in depth in article 12.9, *The Evolving Role of the Enterprise Data Warehouse in the Era of Big Data Analytics*. Both of these architectures endeavor to address the big data challenges listed previously.

The big data marketplace is far from mature, but we now have several years of accumulated experience with a number of best practices specific to big data. This white paper captures these best practices, steering a middle ground between high level motherhood admonitions versus down in the weeds technical minutia specific to a single tool.

It's important to recognize we have a well-tested set of best practices developed for relationally based enterprise data warehouses (EDWs) that big data efforts should leverage. We list them briefly:

- Drive the choice of data sources feeding the EDW from business needs.
- Focus incessantly on user interface simplicity and performance.

The following lists EDW best practices especially relevant to big data:

- Think dimensionally: Divide the world into dimensions and facts.
- Integrate separate data sources with conformed dimensions.
- Track time variance with slowly changing dimensions (SCDs).
- Anchor all dimensions with durable surrogate keys.

In the remainder of this paper, we divide big data best practices into four categories: data management, data architecture, data modeling, and data governance.

Management Best Practices for Big Data

The following best practices apply to the overall management of a big data environment.

Structure big data environments around analytics, not ad hoc querying or standard reporting. Every step in the data pathway from original source to analyst's screen must support complex analytic routines implemented as user-defined functions (UDFs) or via a metadata-driven development environment that can be programmed for each type of analysis. This includes loaders, cleansers, integrators, user interfaces, and finally BI tools. This best practice does not recommend repudiating your existing environment, but rather extending it to support the new demands of analytics. See the section following this on architectural best practices.

Do not attempt to build a legacy big data environment at this time. The big data environment is changing too rapidly at this time to consider building a long-lasting legacy foundation. Rather, plan for disruptive changes coming from every direction: new data types, competitive challenges, programming approaches, hardware, networking technology, and services offered by literally hundreds of new big data providers. For the foreseeable future, maintain a balance among several implementation approaches including Hadoop, traditional grid computing, pushdown optimization in an RDBMS, on-premise computing, cloud computing, and even your mainframe. No one of these approaches will be the single winner in the long run. Platform as a service (PaaS) providers offer an attractive option that can help you assemble a compatible set of tools. Similarly, much of the system architecture and programming can be specified in a layer above the specific deployment choices, a distinct advantage of metadata-driven development environments.

> **Example:** Use HCatalog in the Hadoop environment to provide a layer of abstraction above the specific storage location and data format. This allows Pig scripts, for instance, to remain unchanged when locations and formats have been altered.

> **Example:** Think of Hadoop as a flexible, general-purpose environment for many forms of ETL processing, where the goal is to add sufficient structure and context to big data so that it can be loaded into an RDBMS. The same data in Hadoop can be accessed and transformed with Hive, Pig, HBase, and MapReduce code written in a variety of languages, even simultaneously.

Above all, this demands flexibility. Assume you will reprogram and re-host all your big data applications within two years. Choose approaches that can be reprogrammed and re-hosted. Consider using a metadata-driven codeless development environment to increase productivity and help insulate you from underlying technology changes.

Embrace sandbox silos and build a practice of productionizing sandbox results. Allow data scientists to construct their data experiments and prototypes using their preferred languages and programming environments. Then, after proof of concept, systematically reprogram and/or reconfigure these implementations with an "IT turn-over team."

> **Example:** Your production environment for custom analytic programming might be Matlab within PostgreSQL or SAS within a Teradata RDBMS, but your data scientists might be building their proofs of concept in a wide variety of preferred languages and architectures. The key insight here: IT must be uncharacteristically tolerant of the range of technologies the data scientists use, and be prepared in many cases to re-implement the data scientists' work in a standard set of technologies that can be supported over the long haul.

> **Example:** Your sandbox development environment might be a combination of ETL transformations and custom R code directly accessing Hadoop, but controlled by Informatica PowerCenter. Then when the data scientist is ready to hand over the proof of concept, much of the logic could immediately be redeployed under PowerCenter to run in a grid computing environment that is scalable, highly available, and secure.

Put your toe in the water with a simple big data application: backup and archiving. While getting started with your big data program and as you are searching for valuable business use cases with limited risk and assembling the requisite big data skills, consider using Hadoop as a low cost, flexible backup and archiving technology. Hadoop can store and retrieve data in the full range of formats from totally unstructured to highly structured specialized formats. This approach may also let you address the "sunsetting" challenge where original applications may not be available in the distant future (perhaps because of licensing restrictions), but you may dump data from those applications into your own documented format. Finally, remember that even Hadoop consumes resources and cost—so anytime data gets stored in Hadoop, data retention should be considered in advance such that HDFS folders and data sets can be purged or archived out of HDFS easily to even lower cost storage when the retention period expires.

Architecture Best Practices for Big Data

The following best practices affect the overall structure and organization of your big data environment.

Plan for a logical "data highway" with multiple caches of increasing latency. Physically implement only those caches appropriate for your environment. The data highway can have as many as five caches of increasing data latency, each with its distinct analytic advantages and tradeoffs:

- **Raw source applications:** credit card fraud detection, immediate complex event processing (CEP) including network stability and cyber attack detection
- **Real time applications:** web page ad selection, personalized price promotions, online games monitoring, various forms of predictive and proactive monitoring
- **Business activity applications:** low latency KPI dashboards pushed to users, trouble ticket tracking, process completion tracking, "fused" CEP reporting, customer service portals and dashboards, and mobile sales apps
- **Top line applications:** tactical reporting, promotion tracking, mid-course corrections based on social media buzz. "Top line" refers to the common practice by senior managers of seeing a quick top line review of what has happened in the enterprise over the past 24 hours.
- **EDW and long time series applications:** all forms of reporting, ad hoc querying, historical analysis, master data management, large scale temporal dynamics, Markov chain analysis

Each cache that exists in a given environment is physical and distinct from the other caches. Data moves from the raw source down this highway through ETL processes. There may be multiple paths from the raw source to intermediate caches. For instance, data could go to the real-time cache to drive a zero latency-style user interface, but at the same time be extracted directly into a daily top line cache that would look like a classic operational data store (ODS). Then the data from this ODS could feed the EDW. Data also flows in the reverse direction along the highway. See "implement backflows" later in this section.

Much of the data along this highway must remain in non-relational formats ranging from unstructured text to complex multi-structured data such as images, arrays, graphs, links, matrices, and sets of name-value pairs.

Use big data analytics as a "fact extractor" to move data to the next cache. For example, the analysis of unstructured text tweets can produce a whole set of numerical, trendable sentiment measures including share of voice, audience engagement, conversation reach, active advocates, advocate influence, advocacy impact, resolution rate, resolution time, satisfaction score, topic trends, sentiment ratio, and idea impact. Also, see Splunk, a technology for extracting features from and indexing many forms of unstructured machine data; Kapow, a technology for extracting many forms of web-based data from blogs, discussion forums, websites, and portals; and of course, Informatica's HParser, which can extract facts and dimensions from unstructured text documents, multi-structured XML documents and web logs, as well as industry standard structures such as market data, SWIFT, FIX, CDR, HL7, HIPAA, and many more.

Use big data integration to build comprehensive ecosystems that integrate conventional structured RDBMS data, paper-based documents, emails, and in-house business-oriented social networking. One of the potent messages from big data is the ability to integrate disparate data sources of very different modalities. We are getting streams of data from new data producing channels like social networks, mobile devices, and automated alert processes. Imagine a big financial institution handling millions of accounts, tens of millions of associated paper documents, and thousands of professionals both within the organization but in the field as partners or customers. Now set up a secure "social network" of all the trusted parties to communicate as business is being conducted. Much of this communication is significant and should be saved in a queryable way. Capture all this information in Hadoop, dimensionalize it (see the modeling best practices section following this), use it in the course of business, and then back it up and archive it.

Plan for data quality to be better further along the data highway. This is the classic tradeoff of latency versus quality. Analysts and business users must accept the reality that very low latency (i.e., immediate) data is unavoidably dirty because there are limits to how much cleansing and diagnosing can be done in very short time intervals. Tests and corrections on individual field contents can be performed at the fastest data transfer rates. Tests and corrections on structural relationships among fields and across data sources are necessarily slower. Tests and corrections involving complex business rules range from being instantaneous (such as a set of dates being in a certain order) to taking arbitrarily long times (such as waiting to see if a threshold of unusual events has been exceeded). And finally, slower ETL processes, such as those feeding the daily top line cache, often are built on fundamentally more complete data, for example, where incomplete transaction sets and repudiated transactions have been eliminated. In these cases, the instantaneous data feeds simply do not have the correct information.

Apply filtering, cleansing, pruning, conforming, matching, joining, and diagnosing at the earliest touch points possible. This is a corollary of the previous best practice. Each step on the data highway provides more time to add value to the data. Filtering, cleansing, and pruning reduces the amount of data transferred to the next cache and eliminates irrelevant or corrupted data. To be fair, there is a school of thought that applies cleansing logic only at analysis run time, because cleansing might delete "interesting outliers." Conforming takes the active step of placing highly administered enterprise attributes into major entities like customer, product, and date. The existence of these conformed attributes allows high value joins to be made across separate application domains. A shorter name for this step is "integration!" Diagnosing allows many interesting attributes to be added to data, including special confidence tags and textual identifiers representing behavior clusters identified by a data mining professional. Data discovery and profiling aids in the identification of data domains, relationships, metadata tags useful for search, sensitive data, and data quality issues.

Implement backflows, especially from the EDW, to earlier caches on the data highway. The highly administered master dimensions in the EDW, such as customer, product, and date, should be connected back to data in earlier caches. Ideally, all that is needed is unique durable keys for these entities in all the caches. The corollary here is that Job One in each ETL step from one cache to the next is to replace idiosyncratic proprietary keys with the unique durable keys so that analysis in each cache can take advantage of the rich upstream content with a simple join on the unique durable key. Can this ETL step be performed even when transferring raw source data into the real-time cache in less than a second? Maybe…

Dimension data is not the only data to be transferred back down the highway toward the source. Derived data from fact tables, such as historical summaries and complex data mining findings, can be packaged as simple indicators or grand totals—and then transferred to earlier caches on the data highway. And finally, reference links such as useful keys or codes can be embedded in the low latency data caches in order to allow an analyst to link to other relevant data with a single click.

Implement streaming data analytics in selected data flows. An interesting angle on low latency data is the desire to begin serious analysis on the data as it streams in, but possibly far before the data transfer process terminates. There is significant interest in streaming analysis systems that allow SQL-like queries to process the data as it flows into the system. In some use cases, when the results of a streaming query surpass a threshold, the analysis can be halted without running the job to the bitter end. An academic effort, known as continuous query language (CQL), has made impressive progress in defining the requirements for streaming data processing including clever semantics for dynamically moving time windows on the streaming data. Look for CQL language extensions and streaming data query capabilities in the load programs for both RDBMSs and HDFS deployed data sets. An ideal implementation would allow streaming data analysis to take place while the data is being loaded at gigabytes per second.

Implement far limits on scalability to avoid a "boundary crash." In the early days of computer programming, when machines had pathetically small hard drives and real memories, boundary crashes were common and were the bane of applications development. When the application runs out of disk space or real memory, the developer must resort to elaborate measures, usually requiring significant programming that adds nothing to the main content of the application. Boundary crashes for normal database applications have more or less been eliminated, but big data raises this issue once again. Hadoop is an architecture that dramatically reduces programming scalability concerns because one can, for the most part, add commodity hardware indefinitely. Of course, even commodity hardware must be provisioned, plugged in, and have high bandwidth network connections. The lesson is to plan very far ahead for scaling out to huge volumes and throughputs.

Perform big data prototyping on a public cloud and then move to a private cloud. The advantage of a public cloud is that it can be provisioned and scaled up instantly. Examples include Amazon EMR and Google BigQuery. In those cases where the sensitivity of the data allows quick in-and-out prototyping, this can be very effective. Just remember not to leave a huge data set online with the public cloud provider over the weekend when the programmers have gone home! However, keep in mind that in some cases where you are trying to exploit data locality with rack-aware MapReduce processes, you may not be able to use a public cloud service because they may not give you the data storage control you need.

Search for and expect 10x to 100x performance improvements over time, recognizing the paradigm shift for analysis at very high speeds. The openness of the big data marketplace has encouraged hundreds of special-purpose tightly coded solutions for specific kinds of analysis. This is a giant blessing and a curse. Once free from being controlled by a big vendor's RDBMS optimizer and inner loop, smart developers can implement spot solutions that are truly 100 times as fast as standard techniques. For instance, some impressive progress has been made on the infamous "big join" problem where a billion row dimension is joined to a trillion row fact table. For example, see Yahoo's approach for handling sparse joins on huge data sets as well as Google's Dremel and BigQuery projects. The curse is that these individual spot solutions are not yet part of a unified single architecture.

One very visible big data theme is visualization of data sets. "Flying around" a petabyte of data requires spectacular performance! Visualization of big data is an exciting new area of development that allows both analysis and discovery of unexpected features and data profiling.

Another exciting application that imposes huge performance demands is semantic zooming without pre-aggregations, in which the analyst descends from a highly aggregated level to progressively more detailed levels in unstructured or semi-structured data, analogous to zooming in on a map.

The important lesson behind this best practice is that revolutionary advances in our power to consume and analyze big data will result from 10x to 100x performance gains, and we have to be prepared to add these developments to our suite of tools.

Separate big data analytic workloads from the conventional EDW to preserve EDW service level agreements. If your big data is hosted in Hadoop, it probably doesn't compete for resources with your conventional RDBMS-based EDW. However, be cautious if your big data analytics run on the EDW machine since big data requirements change rapidly and inevitably in the direction of requiring more compute resources.

Exploit unique capabilities of in-database analytics. The major RDBMS players all invest significantly in in-database analytics. Once you pay the price of loading data into relational tables, SQL can be combined with analytic extensions in extremely powerful ways. Recent notable in-database developments include IBM's acquisition of Netezza and SPSS, Teradata and Greenplum's embedding of SAS, Oracle's Exadata R Enterprise, and PostgreSQL's syntax for programming analytics and other arbitrary functions with the database inner loop. All of these options make available tested libraries of hundreds of analytic routines. Some data integration platforms provide pushdown optimization to leverage in-database analytics as part of a data flow or ELT process.

Data Modeling Best Practices for Big Data

The following best practices affect the logical and physical structures of the data.

Think dimensionally: Divide the world into dimensions and facts. Business users find the concept of dimensions to be natural and obvious. No matter what the format of the data, the basic associated entities such as customer, product, service, location, or time can always be found. In the following best practice we will see how, with a little discipline, dimensions can be used to integrate data sources. But before we can get to the integration finish line, we must identify the dimensions in each data source and attach them to every low level atomic data observation. This process of dimensionalization is a good application for big data analytics. For example, a single Twitter tweet "Wow! That is awesome!" may not seem to contain anything worth dimensionalizing, but with some analysis we often can get customer (or citizen or patient), location, product (or service or contract or event), marketplace condition, provider, weather, cohort group (or demographic cluster), session, triggering prior event, final outcome, and the list goes on. Some form of automated dimensionalizing is required to stay ahead of the high velocity streams of data. As we point out in a subsequent best practice, incoming data should be fully dimensionalized at the earliest extraction step.

Integrate separate data sources with conformed dimensions. Conformed dimensions are the glue that holds together separate data sources, and allow them to be combined in a single analysis. Conformed dimensions are perhaps the most powerful best practice from the conventional EDW world that should be inherited by big data.

The basic idea behind conformed dimensions is the presence of one or more enterprise attributes (fields) in the versions of dimensions associated with separate data sources. For instance, every customer-facing process in an enterprise will have some variation of a customer dimension. These variations of the customer dimension may have different keys, different field definitions, and even different granularity. But even in the worst cases of incompatible data, one or more enterprise attributes can be defined that can be embedded in all the customer dimension variations. For instance, a customer demographic category is a plausible choice. Such a descriptor could be attached to nearly every customer dimension, even those at higher levels of aggregation. Once this has been done, analyses of that group on this customer demographic category can cross every participating data source with a simple sort-merge process after separate queries are run against the different data sources. Best of all, the step of introducing the enterprise attributes into the separate databases can be done in an incremental, agile, and non-disruptive way as described in detail in my Informatica-sponsored white paper on this subject. All existing analysis applications will continue to run as the conformed dimension content is rolled out.

Anchor all dimensions with durable surrogate keys. If there is one lesson we have learned in the EDW world, it is not to anchor your major entities such as customer, product, and time with the "natural keys" defined by a specific application. These natural keys turn out to be a snare and a delusion in the real world. They are incompatible across applications and are poorly administered. The first step in every data source is to augment the natural key coming from a source with an enterprise-wide durable surrogate key. Durable means that there is no business rule that can change the key. The durable key belongs to IT, not to the data source. Surrogate means that the keys themselves are simple integers either assigned in sequence or generated by a robust hashing algorithm that guarantees uniqueness. An isolated surrogate key has no applications content. It is just an identifier.

The big data world is filled with obvious dimensions that must possess durable surrogate keys. Earlier in this paper when we proposed pushing data backwards down the data highway, we relied on the presence of the durable surrogate keys to make this process work. We also stated that Job One on every data extraction from a raw source was to embed the durable surrogate keys in the appropriate dimensions.

Expect to integrate structured and unstructured data. Big data considerably broadens the integration challenge. Much big data will never end up in a relational database; rather it will stay in Hadoop or a grid. But once we are armed with conformed dimensions and durable surrogate keys, all the forms of data can be combined in single analyses. For example, a medical study can select a group of patients with certain demographic and health status attributes, and then combine their conventional EDW-style data with image data (photographs, x-rays, EKGs), free form text data (physician's notes), social media sentiments (opinions of treatment), and cohort group linkages (patients with similar situations).

Architecturally, this integration step needs to take place at query time, not at data load and structure time. The most flexible way to perform this integration is through data virtualization, where the integrated data sets appear to be physical tables but are actually specifications similar to relational views where the separate data sources are joined at query time. If data virtualization is not used, then the final BI layer must accomplish this integration step.

Track time variance with slowly changing dimensions (SCDs). Tracking time variance of dimensions is an old and venerable best practice from the EDW world. Basically, it makes good on the pledge we take to track history accurately. It is unacceptable to associate a current profile of a customer (or citizen, or patient, or student) with old history. In the worst case, the current profile is ridiculously wrong when applied to old history. Slowly changing dimension (SCD) processing comes in three flavors. The type 1 SCD overwrites the profile when a change takes place, thereby losing history. We may do this when we correct a data error. The type 2 SCD is the most often used technique that generates a revised dimension record when a change takes place. The type 2 SCD requires that when we generate the new dimension record, we retain the durable surrogate key as the glue that binds the new record to the old records, but we must also generate a unique primary key for the particular snapshot of the dimension member. Like conformed dimensions, this process has been described and vetted extensively. Finally the type 3 SCD, which is not as common as the other two types, covers the situation where an "alternate reality" is defined that coexists with the current reality. Please see my introductory articles on SCDs, as well as extensive coverage of SCDs in my books. But the point as far as big data is concerned is that it is just as important to associate the correct contemporary profile of a major entity with history as it has proven to be in the EDW world.

Get used to not declaring data structures until analysis time. One of the charms of big data is putting off declaring data structures at the time of loading into Hadoop or a data grid. This brings many advantages. The data structures may not be understood at load time. The data may have such variable content that a single data structure either makes no sense or forces you to modify the data to fit into a structure. If you can load data into Hadoop, for instance, without declaring its structure, you can avoid a resource-intensive step. And finally, different analysts may legitimately see the same data in different ways. Of course, there is a penalty in some cases, because data without a declared structure may be difficult or impossible to index for rapid access as in an RDBMS. However, most big data analysis algorithms process entire data sets without expecting precise filtering of subsets of the data.

This best practice conflicts with traditional RDBMS methodologies, which puts a lot of emphasis on modeling the data carefully before loading. But this does not lead to a deadly conflict. For data destined for an RDBMS, the transfer from a Hadoop or data grid environment and from a name-value pair structure into RDBMS named columns can be thought of as a valuable ETL step.

Build technology around name-value pair data sources. Big data sources are filled with surprises. In many cases, you open the fire hose and discover unexpected or undocumented data content which you must nevertheless load at gigabytes per second. The escape from this problem is to load such data as simple name-value pairs. For example, if an applicant were to disclose their financial assets, they might declare something unexpected like "rare postage stamp = $10,000." In a name-value pair data set, this would be loaded gracefully even though you had never seen "rare postage stamp" and didn't know what to do with it at load time. Of course, this practice meshes nicely with the previous practice of deferring the declaration of data structures until past load time.

The MapReduce programming framework requires data to be presented as name-value pairs, which makes sense given the complete possible generality of big data.

Use data virtualization to allow rapid prototyping and schema alterations. Data virtualization is a powerful technique for declaring different logical data structures on underlying physical data. Standard view definitions in SQL are a good example of data virtualization. In theory, data virtualization can present a data source in any format the analyst needs. But data virtualization trades off the cost of computing at run time with the cost of ETL to build physical tables before run time. Data virtualization is a powerful way to prototype data structures and make rapid alterations or provide distinct alternatives. The best data virtualization strategy is to expect to materialize the virtual schemas when they have been tested and vetted and the analysts want the performance improvements of actual physical tables.

Data Governance Best Practices for Big Data

The following best practices apply to managing your data as a valuable enterprise asset.

There is no such thing as big data governance. Now that we have your attention, the point is that data governance must be a comprehensive approach for your entire data ecosystem, not a spot solution for big data in isolation. Data governance for big data should be an extension of your approach for the governance of all your enterprise data. We have introduced a compelling case for how big data must be enhanced by integration with other existing forms of data, especially data from your EDW. But successful integration while establishing (or ignoring) data governance for big data in isolation leads to significant risk. At a minimum, data governance embraces privacy, security, compliance, data quality, metadata management, master data management, and the business glossary that exposes definitions and context to the business community. This is an imposing and daunting list of responsibilities and competencies, and IT should not attempt to define these without significant and sophisticated support from management—who must understand the scope of the effort, and support the cross-organizational cooperation required.

Dimensionalize the data before applying governance. Here is an interesting challenge big data introduces: You must apply data governance principles even when you don't know what to expect from the content of the data. You will receive data arriving at up to gigabytes per second, often as name-value pairs with unexpected content. Your best chance at classifying data in ways that are important to your data governance responsibilities is to dimensionalize it as fully as possible at the earliest stage in your data pipeline. Parse it, match it, and apply identity resolution on the fly. We made this same point when arguing for the benefits of data integration, but here we advocate against using the data before this dimensionalizing step.

If analyzing data sets including identifying information about individuals or organizations, privacy is the most important governance perspective when working with any big data set incorporating information about individuals or organizations. Although every aspect of data governance looms as critically important, in these cases privacy carries the most responsibility and the most business risk. Egregious episodes of compromising the privacy of individuals or groups can damage your reputation, diminish marketplace trust, expose you to civil lawsuits, and get you in trouble with the law. These compromises can also be a barrier to sharing rich data sets between companies, institutions, third parties, and even within organizations, severely limiting the power of big data in industries such as healthcare, education, and law enforcement. The flood of personal data to which we have access threatens to dull our senses and lower our guards. At the very least, for most forms of analysis, personal details must be masked, and data aggregated enough to not allow identification of individuals. Note that at the time of this writing special attention must be paid when storing sensitive data in Hadoop since once data gets written to Hadoop, Hadoop doesn't manage updates very well—so data should either be masked or encrypted on write (i.e., persistent data masking) or data should be masked on read (i.e., dynamic data masking).

Don't put off data governance completely in your rush to use big data. Even for your exploratory big data prototype projects, maintain a checklist of issues to consider as you go forward. You don't want an ineffective bureaucracy, but maybe you can strive to deliver an agile bureaucracy! Your checklist, which you maintain discretely, should:

- Verify there is a vision and a business case that is providing direction and priorities.
- Identify people roles including data stewards, sponsors, program drivers, and users.
- Verify organization buy-in and cross-organization steering committees and sponsorship to support escalations and prioritization.
- Qualify existing and required tools and architecture that will support the big data lifecycle being managed.
- Incorporate some notion of data usage policies and data quality standards.
- Embrace lightweight organizational change management for all other points on this list.
- Measure results, operational as well as business value ROI.
- Assess and influence dependent processes, upstream and downstream to minimize the ever-present garbage in/garbage out dilemma.

Summary

Big data brings a host of changes and opportunities to IT, and it is easy to think that a whole new set of rules must be created. But with the benefit of almost a decade of experience, many best practices have emerged. Many of these practices are recognizable extensions from the EDW/BI world, and admittedly quite a few are new and novel ways of thinking about data and the mission of IT. But the recognition that the mission has expanded is welcome and is in some ways overdue. The current explosion of data-collecting channels, new data types, and new analytic opportunities means that the list of best practices will continue to grow in interesting ways.

12.11 The Hyper-Granular Active Archive

Ralph Kimball, Design Tip #165, *Apr 2, 2014*

Data warehouse archiving has traditionally been a low priority topic for data warehouse architects, but the landscape is changing rapidly. The passive, off-line archive of carefully selected data sets is being replaced by an active, online archive of all possible data assets, including hyper-granular data previously not even considered for long term retention.

Technically, the big story is the continuing drop in the cost of online storage on spinning disk drives. It is not unusual to configure individual nodes of a local Hadoop cluster with 24 to 36 terabytes of disk storage, and the cost of cloud storage is dropping spectacularly these days with a price war going on between Google and Amazon.

Legally, the requirements for retaining data for very long periods are increasing. Intellectual property data, drug trial data, safety records, and financial records of all types need to be retained for decades. I was surprised when my father, an orthopedic surgeon, retired and was told that he had to maintain detailed patient treatment records for all former patients who had not yet turned 21 years of age. Since he had treated infants, that meant keeping these records for almost 21 years!

Operationally, moving all archiving to online spinning disk drives, and away from other "permanent" media such as CDs, DVDs, and tape systems means avoiding all the discussions of whether these media will be viable at various points in the future. I have an 8-inch floppy disk in my desk drawer that reminds me of this issue every time I look at it.

Migrate and Refresh

Keeping archived data continuously available online makes the tried and true migrate-and-refresh archiving strategy particularly simple. The idea behind migrate-and-refresh is every few years to verify that the data is physically available on modern media (migrate) and that the data can be interpreted in a usable way (refresh).

Active Archiving

Traditional archiving has often meant that the data is stored in a more or less inaccessible location, to be restored only if there is a legitimate request. Obviously this creates a barrier and a delay in restoring the data, and the data cannot be used until the restore process is complete. An active archive, by contrast, not only serves legal and operational archiving requirements, but keeps the data continuously usable. When the barriers and delays in accessing the archived data go away, all sorts of analyses become feasible that would otherwise not be considered.

Hyper-Granular Data

As the cost of spinning disk storage continues to drop, the whole notion of what can be archived changes. In the past, only carefully chosen subsets of the data were archived, and frequently the most atomic hyper-granular data was discarded. For example, in a communications switching network, each switch generates an enormous amount of detailed data that may not be archived. Similarly, every commercial airplane flight generates gigabytes of operational data. When the cost of active archiving of these data sets approaches zero, our thinking changes fundamentally. We can think of lots of reasons to keep this data.

Raw Data Formats

Finally, most data currently being collected does not start out as highly curated and well behaved relational data. All of us are aware that the big data revolution embraces a much wider gamut of unstructured, semi-structured, and uniquely structured data. Rather than carefully preparing this data in advance for archiving, it makes much more sense to capture the data in the original formats, and then make the data continuously available for later analysis. Certainly we can expect ongoing advances in image processing and complex event processing (as two examples) where future more sophisticated analyses of the original raw data would be valuable.

In summary, the archiving landscape has already changed. In particular, the Hadoop open source project and Hadoop Distributed File System (HDFS) has opened the door to many of these ideas.

Presentation Server Architecture

The first two articles in this section describe the importance of aggregate navigation in the data warehouse's presentation server. Somewhat surprisingly, both articles were written shortly after Ralph became a columnist for *DBMS* in the mid-1990s, but the concepts still hold true today. From there, OLAP cubes are discussed, with a deeper dive into the specifics of Microsoft's offering. The final article focuses on the role of compression, partitioning, and star schema optimization in performance tuning.

12.12 Columnar Databases: Game Changers for DW/BI Deployment

Ralph Kimball, Design Tip #121, *Mar 3, 2010*

Although columnar RDBMSs have been in the market since the 1990s, the recent BI requirements to track rapidly growing customer demographics in enormous terabyte databases have made some of the advantages of columnar databases increasingly interesting.

Remember that a columnar RDBMS is a "standard" relational database supporting the familiar table and join constructs we are all used to. What makes a columnar RDBMS unique is the way data is stored at the physical level. Rather than storing each table row as a contiguous object on the disk, a columnar RDBMS stores each table column as a contiguous object on the disk. Typically, these column-specific data objects are sorted, compressed, and heavily indexed for access. Even though the underlying physical storage is columnar, at the user query level (SQL), all tables appear to be made up of familiar rows. Applications do not have to be recoded to use a columnar RDBMS. The beneath-the-cover twist from a row orientation to a column orientation is the special feature of a columnar RDBMS.

A columnar RDBMS offers the application designer and the DBA some design advantages, including:

- **Significant database compression.** Dimension tables filled with many low cardinality repeated attributes compress significantly, sometimes by 95 percent or even more. Fact tables with numeric measurement values also compress surprisingly well, often by 70 percent or more. Columnar databases are very supportive of the dimensional modeling approach.
- **The query and storage penalties for very wide tables with many columns are greatly reduced.** A single column, especially one with low cardinality, adds very little to the overall storage of

a table. More significantly, when a table row is fetched in a query, only the named columns are actually fetched from the disk. Thus if three columns are requested from a 100 column dimension, only about 3 percent of the row content is retrieved. In a conventional row oriented RDBMS, typically the entire row must be fetched when any part of the row is needed. (More exactly, the disk blocks containing the requested data are fetched into the query buffer and much un-requested data in these blocks comes along for the ride.)

■ **Adding a column to a fact or dimension table in a columnar RDBMS is not an especially big deal since the system doesn't care about row widths.** There are no more block splits when you expand a "row." Now the designer can be much more profligate about adding columns to an existing table. For instance, you can now be comfortable with wider fact table designs, where many of the fields in a "row" have null values. In this way, the designer can regularly add new demographics columns to a customer dimension because each column is an independent compressed object in the physical storage. Be aware, however, that as you add more columns to your fact and dimension tables, you have increased responsibility to keep the BI tool user interfaces simple. A tried and true way to keep the user interfaces simple is to deploy multiple logical views for different BI use cases, where each view exposes a set of relevant fields used together. And, we should point out that adding more columns to a table is not an excuse for adding data to a table that violates the grain!

■ **Columnar databases allow complex constraints and computations across records, which is generally difficult or impossible in relational databases.** Columnar RDBMSs remove some of this applications pressure, not only because they encourage far wider table designs (thereby exposing many fields within the same row to SQL), but also because columnar RDBMSs specialize in cross column access through bitmap indexes and other special data structures. BI tool designers welcome the extended width of fact and dimension tables because within-row constraints and computations are a hundred times easier to set up than the corresponding cross-row versions.

Columnar databases pose provocative tradeoffs for IT. In particular, these databases have had a reputation for slow loading performance, which the vendors have been addressing. Before investing in a columnar database, make sure to carefully prototype loading and updating back room tasks. But in any case, these databases offer some interesting design alternatives.

12.13 There Is No Database Magic

Joy Mundy, Design Tip #175, *Jun 8, 2015*

An ever-growing set of data storage technologies offers advantages to the data warehouse architect that look pretty magical. How can you figure out what to do? Should you stick to the tried-and-true relational databases to host your data warehouse? Should you use cubes? Or should you move to the latest and greatest data management solutions like the massively parallel processing (MPP) or columnar solutions? Or to the cloud?

First, let's talk about the data warehouse database, the main store in which the atomic grain dimensional models are maintained. Everyone who follows the Kimball Method will have one; its design, care, and feeding are the focus of the Kimball Method. You may additionally have downstream cubes or other structures, but for now let's talk about the atomic data warehouse database.

Most of the organizations we've worked with use an RDBMS to host the atomic grain dimensional star schemas for their conformed data warehouses. We observe many SQL Server and Oracle implementations, a smaller number of DB2, and a growing minority of other platforms and technologies. And it's these alternative technologies that are generating the most questions among our clients.

For most organizations, the plain old RDBMS approach works just fine. You get yourself a server or an internal cloud virtualized environment, install and configure the RDBMS for a data warehouse load, implement and populate your dimensional models, hook up your BI tools, and off you go. The overwhelming majority of sub-terabyte data warehouses use one of the big three RDBMSs to host the atomic dimensional models. These BI systems, if they fail, do not fail because of their choice of database technology.

The landscape is markedly different for very large data warehouse systems. At 10 TB and certainly 100 TB and above, you are far more likely to encounter the alternative technologies.

Alternative Atomic Database Technologies

Generally speaking, there are two main types of database technologies that garner a lot of interest today:

- Massively parallel processing (MPP) solutions, which scale out across many small servers rather than scale up one large SMP machine. Available MPP appliances include Teradata, IBM's Netezza, EMC's Greenplum, Oracle's Exadata, and Microsoft's PDW, among others. We include the open source Hadoop solutions, such as Hive and Impala, in this category of massively distributed deployments.
- Columnar databases, which turn some or all of your tables on their heads by storing data by column rather than by row. Some of the columnar solutions are also massively parallel. The most popular columnar databases include SAP Sybase IQ, InfoBright, HP Vertica, ParAccel (which hosts Amazon's RedShift), and EXASOL, among others. A data storage structure in Hadoop is the Parquet columnar format, which can be effectively deployed with both Hive and Impala, and provides equivalent benefits to the non-Hadoop columnar database solutions.

Most of the technologies are long out of the experimental stage: Teradata has been around 35 years, SAP Sybase IQ 20+ years, and most of the others from 10 to 15 years.

What Do These "New" Technologies Offer?

These technologies offer substantial scalability and query performance improvements for analytic workloads compared to the standard RDBMSs. What they do not offer is magic. There is no magic! You pay for the improved query performance and scalability first through currency: These products are typically more expensive than the corresponding standard RDBMS license plus server cost. You pay for the benefits through a somewhat more complex ETL system. I observe as many people swearing at these technologies as I see swearing by them. Each technology has its own foibles, but updates and deletes seem particularly problematic for many. Nonetheless, if you have a large system—measured both by data volumes and the complexity of usage—you will figure it out and make it work. This becomes just one more in a long string of decisions where we place a burden on ETL in order to deliver a great user experience.

For the very largest data warehouses, these MPP and/or columnar technologies are de rigueur. For the vast majority of small to mid-sized BI environments, they may simply be too expensive in terms of currency, expertise, or system complexity, to be worth spending much time worrying about. Medium to large systems, say 750 GB to 10 TB, have the hardest decision. The factors that would indicate the newer technologies include:

- High data volume
- Rapid planned growth (MPP systems scale more easily)
- Simpler ETL requirements with minimal fact table updates (which tend to be more problematic for these technologies)
- An architecture that uses little or no OLAP or cube technology, and hence has a large and diverse query load directly on the atomic data warehouse database

What about Cubes?

Architectural decisions can never be made in isolation. Your decision about the atomic data warehouse database technology influences, and is influenced by, your downstream architecture including how you will use cubes. The more you plan to use cubes—whether older OLAP cubes or newer in-memory structures—the less you will need direct ad hoc access to the atomic data warehouse database. In the unusual extreme, where 100 percent of user access comes through cubes, the DW database is relegated to a purely back room existence.

Your business users often love cubes. They offer a nice user experience for ad hoc querying because they are fundamentally designed for dimensional data. They provide a place to centrally define and share complex calculations. And they usually deliver very good query performance.

As we discuss in article 13.7, *Leverage Data Visualization Tools, But Avoid Anarchy*, the atomic relational data warehouse database is the required piece of the architecture. Cubes, much as we love them, are optional. But their inclusion in your architecture does affect your decision about technology for the data warehouse database, as well as some of the physical implementation decisions such as indexing strategies.

And What about the Cloud?

This article made mention of the cloud in its first paragraph, so it's fitting that we end there. The tool and database vendors have been making substantial investments in cloud hosting of their tools and services. But among the data warehouse/business intelligence implementations that we work with, we've seen little adoption. First, there is the inevitable letdown when people realize that a tool in the cloud is just that: pretty much the same old tool, now in the cloud. No, there's no magic, you still have to write the ETL.

The earliest adopters are organizations who have already made an investment to hosting their operational systems in the cloud. Assuming reasonable data volumes, using the cloud to host their DW/BI environment is sensible and probably cost effective. Some organizations and industries will not adopt the cloud any time soon, because they are forbidden by law or policy to move their data to a cloud environment. But I'm reasonably confident that what today is a trickle will become more of a flood. The pricing models will grow more appealing, and the notion of managing servers and databases in-house will seem old fashioned. But I don't have a magic ball that will tell me when that transition will occur.

12.14 Relating to OLAP

Joy Mundy, Intelligent Enterprise, *Oct 8, 2002*

Joy wrote this article in 2002, and while most of her concerns in this article are still important, the historical context should be kept in mind!

Virtually all data warehouses use a relational data store. As a relational designer until a few years ago, I assumed that online analytic processing (OLAP) was merely a technology for small-scale applications. I now believe that perception is outdated and will become only more so as OLAP servers evolve to be a major component of the data warehouse.

Desktop versus Server OLAP

In desktop OLAP, a SQL query executes against the database and returns a result set to the desktop as a cube, which you can then pivot and manipulate locally. Desktop OLAP is useful but not very scalable. Server OLAP, where the tool issues a non-SQL query against a much larger remote data store, is more scalable and supports deeper analytics than its desktop cousins.

An OLAP server enables intuitive data browsing and querying, supports analytic complexity, and provides great query performance through transparent navigation of precomputed aggregations. The requirement to support analytic complexity on the server implies a language other than SQL, such as MDX or Calc Scripts. The most effective designs store the definition of these complex calculations on the server, where they're transparently available to all users. The recommended architecture for most purposes feeds the OLAP server from a dimensional data warehouse in the relational DBMS.

If OLAP technology delivers complex analytics and great query performance, why doesn't it dominate the market? The main reasons are market fragmentation, scalability, price, and flexibility. Market fragmentation has ill-served the customer. Until recently there has been no agreement even on client-access APIs. This situation is changing with the recent widespread adoption of XML for Analysis by most of the OLAP server market.

Historically, OLAP systems haven't been as scalable as relational systems. Concern about scalability remains, but it's become more a matter of perception than reality; terabyte-scale OLAP case studies and references are available from several vendors. Price is a harder objection to refute because an OLAP server is almost always *added* to a relational environment. OLAP systems are indeed flexible, as long as you're willing to adjust your relational thinking a little. I will probe these flexibility issues in a little more depth in the following paragraphs.

Dimensional Similarities

An experienced dimensional data modeler should feel comfortable reading the documentation for any of the OLAP server products. They all talk about dimensions, hierarchies, and facts or measures. Most use the concept of a cube, which is directly analogous to a relational fact table schema with associated dimensions and aggregate tables.

OLAP dimensions consist of hierarchies, or summarization paths. The relationship between a data hierarchy and an OLAP dimension is very important. Many OLAP products will let you define multiple hierarchies on a dimension, such as a fiscal and standard calendar. If you've built your OLAP application from a relational dimensional data warehouse, you should have already implemented surrogate keys, which provide the same benefits for OLAP as for relational processing.

Like the relational database, OLAP servers have physical and calculated facts. However, the analytic engine in OLAP servers supports a much wider variety of complex calculated facts defined in the server, and this is often the key defining benefit of an OLAP implementation.

Dimensional Differences

The key difference between OLAP dimensions and simple relational (ROLAP) dimensions is the central role played by hierarchies in OLAP implementations. An OLAP dimension is strongly structured around its hierarchies, and the metadata of a cube definition includes the hierarchical levels. This is one of the great strengths of an OLAP implementation. An OLAP query tool picks up the information about the hierarchical structure from the OLAP server and presents the structure to the user in an intuitive way.

Equally important, OLAP tools use strong hierarchies to define aggregations. An OLAP server enforces a kind of referential integrity between hierarchical levels in a dimension.

Another difference between OLAP and relational deployments is the ease of implementation of different types of changing dimensions. Type 2 dimensions (tracking history by adding a new dimension member) are very easy to leverage in an OLAP system, assuming you have already implemented them in the relational database. By contrast, type 1 dimensions (restating history by updating in place) are a difficult problem for OLAP. If you've ever built and maintained an aggregate table on a relational schema with a type 1 dimension, you'll identify the problem immediately. When a customer moves from the West to the East, aggregates need to be updated. You'll either have to drop and re-create all aggregate tables, or figure out which sections of which aggregates are affected and fix them. OLAP servers tackle this problem for you, but there's no getting around the fact that significant processing is required. Type 1 changing dimensions can be expensive in an OLAP server.

There are some things that are utterly trivial to accomplish on a pure relational schema, yet are tricky in the OLAP world. An example is to issue a query that returns a total over an arbitrary time span. A query such as total sales for Q1 2002 is simple to formulate and should return from an OLAP server nearly instantaneously.

But woe betides the user who wants total sales for an arbitrary period such as January 3 through March 12, 2002, for which no predefined hierarchy exists. Part of the blame belongs to the client query tools, some of which won't even let you formulate the query except by bringing back daily data for January, February, and March.

OLAP's Strengths

I just discussed some things that are really easy in the pure relational world but are difficult for some OLAP servers to handle. But OLAP is brimming with advantages compared to relational systems. Here's my list of OLAP's advantages:

- It provides an intuitive user interface for browsing data.
- It gives you spectacular query performance, primarily owing to the intelligent navigation of aggregates and partitions.
- Parent-child dimension structures are easy and intuitive to implement.
- It gives you server-defined rules for handling semi-additive and non-additive measures.

As a simple example, consider inventory balances: The inventory balance for January and February is certainly not the sum of inventories in January and February. You can train users not to sum inventory balances over time, but will they always remember? Will all users use the same aggregation method, such as ending or average balance? OLAP systems can handle this problem transparently.

An OLAP system lets you have server-defined calculations of great complexity. SQL's limitations as an analytic language are outlined in the "Dealing with SQL" section of Chapter 13. SQL is not an analytic or report writing language: You need an analysis server to support statistics, data mining algorithms, or even simple rule-based business calculations such as allocations and distributions. The OLAP server acts as a friendly interface to the data cube, letting users consume server-defined analytics without worrying about how and where they are defined and computed.

Server defined, high performance queries and calculations can be performed over multiple fact tables or cubes. Combining data from multiple fact tables is a difficult problem in the pure relational world, but can be made easy and intuitive in certain OLAP servers.

Calculations can be defined once and used many times. The more calculations you can define on a central server, the more flexibility your users have in accessing the data. Even a simple slice-and-dice tool can use complex analytics previously defined on the OLAP server. This capability is not generally found in relational environments. And of course, power users can define complex calculations on the server so all users benefit.

Recent trends in the OLAP market are toward lower cost, improved performance and scalability, increased functionality in the core analytic space, and extensions to neighboring spaces such as data mining. These trends will continue over the next few years as the major database vendors bet more heavily on OLAP servers and more tightly integrate those servers with other data management and analytic software.

OLAP servers present dimensional data in an intuitive way, enabling a broad range of analytic users to slice and dice data to uncover interesting information. OLAP is a sibling of ROLAP (dimensional models in a relational database), with intelligence about relationships and calculations defined on the server, which enables faster query performance and interesting analytics from a broad range of query tools. You shouldn't think of an OLAP server as a competitor to a relational data warehouse, but rather an extension. Let the relational database do what it does best: provide storage and management. Don't torture yourself forcing the RDBMS, and its clunky query language SQL, to do something they were not designed for: analysis.

12.15 Dimensional Relational versus OLAP: The Final Deployment Conundrum

Ralph Kimball, Intelligent Enterprise, *Apr 27, 2007*

It has become fashionable to regard the final deployment step of building an ETL system as a mere tactical choice between delivering dimensional relational tables (ROLAP) or OLAP cubes into the user environment. But is this choice quite so superficial? Should we defer thinking about this choice until just before rollout? In this article we take a hard look at this final deployment conundrum and urge you to resolve this question very early in the design process.

BI developers have largely accepted the premise that data is most user friendly when delivered in a dimensional format. If you define the data warehouse as the *platform* for all forms of BI, then the last step of the ETL process in the data warehouse is exposing the data in a dimensional format. Many BI developers have recognized that a properly designed set of dimensional relational tables can be transformed into an OLAP cube in a virtual one-to-one mapping. For various reasons explained in this article, I recommend that all OLAP cubes be built directly from dimensional models. The dimension tables in such a relational schema become the OLAP cube dimensions, often referred to as the *edges* of the cube. The fact tables from the relational schema provide the content of the OLAP cube cells.

While there can be some semantic differences between relational dimensions and OLAP cube dimensions, the profound overlap between these two approaches has made it tempting to regard the final deployment choice as a tactical maneuver executed at the very end of the data warehouse development. Worse yet, the argument is sometimes made that BI applications can be switched between relational and OLAP implementations because of this similarity.

Not so fast! Under the right circumstances, the ETL pipeline can be mostly insulated from the final deployment choice, but the relational versus OLAP choice is a multi-faceted decision with lots of issues to consider. Let's look at the advantages and disadvantages of both choices before we jump on either bandwagon.

Dimensional Relational Advantages

First, we'll consider the advantages of deploying a dimensional model on a relational DBMS:

- Relational database structures are largely vendor independent, and dimensional structures especially are pretty easily ported. However, ETL command line scripts and proprietary code like PL/SQL may not be very portable.
- All the main relational DBMSs have high volume bulk data loaders, and they're especially effective if you turn off transaction logging.
- A wide variety of SQL generating BI tools from many vendors are able to directly access the data. Usually these tools can be repurposed to point at a new relational DBMS.
- SQL expertise is widely available in the marketplace, because the main features of SQL have long been standardized, and SQL is routinely taught at the college level.
- Hand-coded SQL is generally readable, although the SQL emitted by high end BI tools is overwhelming and cannot reasonably be changed by the BI applications development staff.
- There are many different ways to control DBMS performance, including schema designs, indexes, aggregates, and materialized views. Dimensional relational structures, because of their predictable characteristics, have well understood performance-tuning techniques, although these techniques vary somewhat by vendor.
- Relational databases are extremely stable and are suitable for serious archiving and backup.
- Relational database structures are not vulnerable to catastrophic invalidation, unlike OLAP cubes that may involuntarily rebuild themselves if an SCD type 1 change is made to a dimension.
- Database sizes are pretty much unlimited, and individual fact tables in the multi-terabyte range are increasingly common.
- High end relational databases can join many large tables.
- Hybrid (mixed workload) applications involving both querying and updating are usually easy to construct.

Relational Disadvantages

And the downsides of deploying the dimensional model on a relational platform:

- SQL is a truly horrible language for powerful analysis and complex applications.
- SQL is severely asymmetric: You can perform complex constraints and calculations generally only within records, not across records.
- In spite of performance-tuning capabilities, it is still too easy to lose control of performance.

OLAP Advantages

On to the benefits of an OLAP cube deployment:

- OLAP generally provides much better performance than relational when the cubes are designed correctly, with less need to play complex performance tuning games compared to relational.
- OLAP has much more powerful analytic capabilities than relational. MDX, for example, has more powerful semantics for traversing ragged unbalanced hierarchies, such as organization charts, than does SQL.
- Vendor-supplied OLAP tools for reporting and querying have historically been superior to relational tools, although I'm impressed by the steady investment relational tool vendors have made in improving ease of use and feature sets.
- OLAP doesn't suffer from the row versus column symmetry problem that limits SQL.
- The decision to load OLAP directly from dimensional relational tables doesn't affect the ETL backroom very much: The deployment step occurs at the very end.
- Certain loading scenarios can be very fast.
- Certain vertical industries, especially financial services, have developed awesome OLAP solutions.
- OLAP encourages more complex security scenarios, especially for ad hoc access. By comparison, it's difficult to set up a relational database to protect detailed data (sales by sales rep), but provide more open access to summarized data (sales by region). This is especially true for ad hoc access on the relational side. Security is significantly more powerful on OLAP because of the semantics about parents and children inherent in the access languages.

OLAP Disadvantages

And last but not least, the disadvantages of an OLAP cube deployment:

- The big objection to OLAP is the proprietary, non-standard character of each vendor's OLAP offering.
- Don't expect to port an OLAP implementation to another vendor's product. Discard everything including all your application development.
- There is no accepted, universally implemented access language for OLAP, although Microsoft's MDX is the closest thing to a standard access language. Significantly, Oracle has not embraced MDX, preferring to rely on SQL for all forms of database access.
- MDX in its full glory may be too complex for IT personnel to write by hand, or understand a complex application. But to be fair, I have looked at incomprehensible SQL many times!

- Historically there has been much less industry expertise in MDX than in SQL, although Microsoft has successfully sponsored a cottage industry of training organizations.
- OLAP application development expertise is fragmented by vendor.
- OLAP cubes can be catastrophically invalidated if you are not careful, i.e., a type 1 or type 3 SCD change to a dimension may cause all the cubes using that dimension to rebuild!
- OLAP cubes are not considered stable enough for serious archiving and backup: This is a strong reason for creating a set of dimensional relational tables duplicating the content of the cube for those purposes.
- OLAP vendors have certain size limits not present in relational implementations, including possibly the number of members in a dimension, the number of distinct values at various levels in a hierarchy, and the overall size of the cube.
- When you must rebuild a cube, it may be a very time-consuming process.

Equally Easy in Either Approach

The basic foundations of dimensional modeling, including slowly changing dimensions, the three fundamental grains of fact tables, and achieving integration through conformed dimensions, are equally easy to deliver with either approach, especially since these dimensional structures are carried to the very last step of the ETL pipeline.

Making the Final Choice

So how do senior management and the enterprise BI system designers resolve the final deployment conundrum: dimensional relational or OLAP? As I hope you appreciate, there is no slam dunk answer because there are significant advantages and disadvantages for both approaches. But let's consider two extremes. If you are a large distributed enterprise with a number of different database vendors and you are struggling to establish more commonality across your BI deployments, as well as creating an enterprise-wide pool of BI development expertise without being beholden to any single vendor, then I recommend dimensional relational. On the other hand, if you are looking for the most potent single-subject solution with high performance and killer analytics, and you are confident that you can source the development expertise you need, then I recommend OLAP supported by underlying dimensional relational schemas. Otherwise, it depends.

12.16 Microsoft SQL Server Comes of Age for Data Warehousing

Warren Thornthwaite, Intelligent Enterprise, Jun 23, 2008

Warren wrote this article in 2008. Please keep this historical context in mind!

Microsoft's upcoming SQL Server 2008 release includes several new features and enhancements that are extremely valuable in DW/BI systems, as those already leveraging these capabilities on other database platforms will attest. The key performance enhancements include database compression, partitioning, and star schema optimization. In this article, I briefly describe the benefits of these three features in any DW/BI deployment.

Joy Mundy and I wrote *The Microsoft Data Warehouse Toolkit* (Wiley, 2011) to describe how to apply our data warehouse design principles and techniques specifically on the Microsoft platform, but it should be noted that we have always been and we remain vendor independent. Whether you're using Microsoft SQL Server or another platform, we encourage you to explore the potential of these three broadly available features in your environment.

Speed the Queries with Database Compression

Database compression is exactly what it sounds like: compressing the data before it is stored on disk. While this sounds mundane because we've been using zip utilities to reduce file size for decades, moving compression into the database can make a significant difference in storage and performance.

The storage advantages of compression are obvious: Smaller data size means you need less disk space. In SQL Server 2008, you should expect about a 50 percent reduction in storage requirements thanks to compression. This advantage passes through to the backup process, which should complete much faster with less data to back up. It's also possible to compress the backup without compressing the data in the database.

On the performance side, the DW/BI system is often constrained by disks, which are the slowest performing component in the environment. By compressing data you reduce the amount of disk space used and therefore the number of disk reads required, in some cases by 50 percent or more. The trade-off is that more CPU cycles are needed to decompress the data before it is delivered to the application, but as CPU speeds have increased, the penalty of this trade-off has been reduced. As a result, compression can cut query time significantly for certain kinds of queries. Since compression happens at the data definition level, database components, like the storage manager, can handle the compression process without changes in your BI applications.

There are many different types of compression, with the general rule being the greater the compression, the more CPU time required. Compression techniques can be applied within a row, across all rows on a page, or at the table, file, or database level. One form of row-level compression involves applying the variable length concept we already have in the VARCHAR data type to all fields where it might make a difference. For example, we might define a column like `OrderDollars` as `Decimal(20, 5)`, which would take 13 bytes in SQL Server 2005. The scale and precision of this might be necessary to support the few very large orders you get every year, but it leaves a lot of unused space in every row for most records in the fact table.

There are several forms of compression that can be applied at the page level. One technique used in SQL Server 2008 is called *dictionary compression*. This involves looking for repeated values anywhere on the page and storing them in a special compression information structure kept on each page after the page header. For example, a customer dimension may have a region attribute that only has 10 possible values. Storing a distinct list of these values in the compression information structure and only keeping small pointers to the structure at the row level can reduce the overall size of the data dramatically. Note that this technique is conceptually the same as normalizing the data into a region table at the page level behind the scenes. You get the benefits of the dimensional model and reduced storage requirements all in one!

The biggest benefit of compression is realized on queries that require reading many pages from disk. Queries that do distinct counts of the top N customers or that require full table scans, such as creating data mining sets, are good examples. To give you a sense of the potential impact of compression, I did a simple test with a customer dimension with more than 3 million rows and 44 columns. The following table compares data size and query results before and after compression.

Impact of Compression on Data Size and Query Performance

	Base Table	Compressed Table	Percent Reduction
Data size	1,115,408 KB	465,352 KB	58.30%
Total rows	3,068,505	3,068,505	—
Query times (min:sec):			
Select Count(*)	04:35.9	00:43.4	84.30%
Select CustType, AVG(CustValueScore)	04:26.3	00:05.1	98.10%
Select Distinct Region	04:20.1	00:04.9	98.10%

The table also shows how compression leverages another DW/BI system performance principle: More memory is better. In this case, SQL Server 2008 keeps the compressed structure after it is read from disk. As a result, the compressed table now fits completely in memory, so the second and third queries were dramatically faster than the first. This advantage of having more available memory is a major driver for the adoption of 64-bit machines. Note that the queries used for this table were designed to demonstrate the best case. Overall, you should expect more modest performance gains of 15 percent to 20 percent, as long as you have available CPU cycles. If your system is already CPU bound, compression will worsen performance.

The CPU cost of compression comes at both ends of the data management process. The CPU must do more work to compress the data before it is written to disk. This raises the question: How does compression impact data load times? The answer depends on the type of compression used, but I tried a simple insert of 30,205 new rows into compressed and uncompressed versions of the customer dimension and found that the compressed insert required about 25 percent more CPU time. Compressed index builds also require more CPU time, but the resulting indexes are faster to traverse.

If the time it takes to load and index data in your ETL process is already substantial and your server is CPU bound, this increase could hurt. If the load and index times are relatively small, the increase is bearable. Before you commit to compression, test its impact on your disk usage and backups, as well as your query and load times.

Divide and Conquer with Table Partitioning

Table partitioning involves dividing a large table into multiple sub-tables that can be managed independently while retaining, from a query perspective, the appearance of a single table. Table partitioning isn't a new concept; what is new in recent years is that it's available on most relational database platforms (although it often requires an "enterprise" license). Partitioning enables you to handle much larger tables by allowing you to segment the workload and distribute its processing. Implementing table partitioning requires additional management work in the ETL process, but should not require any changes in your BI applications.

In data warehousing, you typically partition your fact tables to support loading current data into a single partition that is set up (perhaps as an empty partition or without indexes) to support fast-as-possible loading. Usually this means partitioning at some level in the transaction date hierarchy, such as month, week, or even day.

While you're at it, you can set up a separate load partition in a parallel structure so users can query yesterday's fact table while you load into this "shadow" partition. When the load is finished, simply swap the shadow partition into the main table with an ALTER TABLE command. This lets you provide 24 × 7 availability by duplicating only a small portion of the fact table.

The shadow table concept also makes it easier to prune old data from a table. For example, if you have a table with the last five years of data partitioned by month, you can swap out the oldest month with an empty shadow partition. You can then archive or drop this separate partition as needed.

Partitioning will impact your indexing strategies. In general, DW/BI systems work best with indexes limited to the partition level. An index that spans partitions will require significantly more maintenance time when inserting new rows or dropping historical rows.

If you are having data load or management problems with large tables, you need to investigate table partitioning.

Go Dimensional with Star Schema Optimization

The basic structure of the dimensional model is different from a normalized transaction model. The database optimizer employs a detailed set of statistics about row counts, indexes, and cardinality to determine the most efficient starting point for a query. It then follows the join paths, creating temporary intermediate results sets that ultimately lead to the desired results set. If the database optimizer applies a traditional strategy to a dimensional model, it usually picks a small or tightly constrained dimension as the starting point, but the second table, the fact table, is always the largest one in the query. This can lead to highly inefficient queries with large temporary results sets.

Star schema optimization, also known as *star join optimization*, takes advantage of the unique symmetry of the dimensional model: one fact table joining to many dimension tables. Leveraging this symmetry, the optimizer generally identifies the set of primary keys from each dimension involved in a given query, then, as a last step, queries the fact table with this key list.

Different database products approach this challenge in different ways, but all the major players leverage the dimensional model in generating a better query strategy. Microsoft SQL Server 2008 has improved its star schema optimization by building a hash table and bitmap filter for each participating dimension. These bitmap filters are applied to the fact table, filtering out almost all of the rows that don't apply to the query. The remaining rows are then joined to the dimension hash tables.

Early usage of SQL Server 2008 indicates it will generate star schema performance improvements of 15 percent to 25 percent across the entire DW/BI relational query load. Oracle uses bitmapped indexes on each of the foreign keys in the fact table as the core of its star join strategy. Make sure you have all the prerequisites and conditions in place to allow your database to generate the best query plans for your DW/BI system.

Up and Coming Opportunities

If you have already pushed your relational database to its limit, there are other technologies you might consider. Column-oriented databases are not new to the market, with commercial products available since at least 1995; however, they are making inroads in the DW/BI space. True to their name, these databases store data in a column-oriented rather than row-oriented form. This naturally supports compression techniques and fits well with the selective nature of analytic queries. The column-oriented approach is not well suited to transaction processing, but that's not the problem we're trying to solve.

Compression, partitioning, and star schema optimization are some of the core features you can use to improve your DW/BI system's query performance. If you are not already using them, we encourage you to explore these capabilities on your platform. If you are using them and you still need better performance, you may need to explore alternative database platforms or bigger, more balanced hardware systems.

12.17 The Aggregate Navigator

Ralph Kimball, DBMS, *Nov 1995*

One of the most exciting new developments in data warehousing is the emergence of aggregate navigation, a capability that changes the architecture of all user applications. Aggregate navigation is a technique that enables DBAs to optimize performance by storing aggregate values in the database, without requiring users to know about the existence of those aggregates. Several vendors offer aggregate navigation in their current products. In this article, I explain why aggregate navigation is so important.

The rapid growth of data warehousing has been accompanied by the creation of huge databases of fine-grained detail. Increasingly, the trend has been to lay the foundation of the data warehouse with operational or even transaction level data. It is generally necessary to start at such a level, not because an executive or analyst will want to look at individual low level records, but because the data must often be sliced very precisely. If you want see how many customers renewed their cable TV subscriptions each day following a particular media promotion, you need very fine-grained data.

Our data warehouse foundation layers consist of hundreds of millions of records in large fact tables, surrounded by a small set of dimension tables that serve as entry points into the fact tables. If database engines were infinitely fast, this design would be satisfactory, and we could concentrate on other issues such as application programming and front end tools. However, we all know that we need to "cheat" and calculate some values in advance, such as totals, and store them in the database in order to improve performance. In our cable TV example, we would probably also be asking for the comparison of the renewal subscription rate against the monthly average renewal rate over the past year. If we use this baseline measure in our business often, we certainly do not want to process an entire year's worth of transactions every time we ask for this denominator. Every good DBA should build a set of aggregates to accelerate performance.

The building of aggregates is a huge double-edged sword in a big data warehouse environment. On the positive side, aggregates have a stunning effect on performance. The highest level aggregates, such as yearly national sales totals, frequently offer a 1000-fold improvement in run time, compared to processing the daily transactions. Other than ensuring that the database optimizer is working correctly, the addition of aggregates to a data warehouse is the most effective tool that the DBA can bring to bear on performance.

But aggregates have two big negative impacts. First, they obviously take up space. If you build aggregates in three primary dimensions, such as product (brand level, category level, and department level), market (district level and region level), and time (week level, month level, and year level), these aggregates can multiply geometrically to overwhelm the database. A bizarre effect called *sparsity failure* can cause the number of aggregate records to exceed the number of base-level records!

The second problem, and the one directly addressed by the aggregate navigators, is that a user's query tool must specifically call for an aggregate in the SQL or it won't be used. This leaves the DBA with a nightmarish administrative challenge. If the users' tools have to be hardcoded with knowledge of the aggregates, then the DBA doesn't have the flexibility to change the aggregate profile in the data warehouse. Aggregates can't be added or subtracted because all the user applications would have to be recoded. Until recently, DBAs responded to this problem by building every conceivable aggregate "for a rainy day," which leads to the over-proliferation of aggregates.

The aggregate navigator addresses the problem of hardcoded user applications by sitting between the application and the DBMS, and intercepting the user's SQL, as illustrated in Figure 12-8. With an aggregate navigator, the user application now speaks "base-level" SQL and never attempts to call for an aggregate directly. Using metadata describing the data warehouse's portfolio of aggregates, the aggregate navigator transforms the base-level SQL into "aggregate-aware" SQL. The business user and application designer can now proceed to build and use applications, blissfully unaware of which aggregates are available. To tune system performance, the DBA can adjust the warehouse's portfolio of aggregates on a daily or weekly basis. This unhooks the dependence of user applications on the back room physical aggregates.

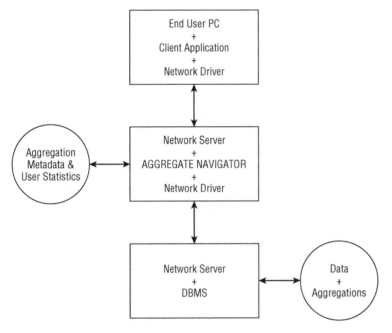

Figure 12-8: The aggregate navigator sits between the user application and DBMS.

There are two main ways to store aggregates: in the original fact and dimension tables as extra records, or in separate fact and dimension tables. In both cases, you store exactly the same number of records; it is just a question of where to put them. The separate fact and dimension table approach is the recommended technique, even though it proliferates quite a few tables. The problem with storing the aggregates in the original fact and dimension tables is that, in order to distinguish the aggregate records from the base-level records, you must introduce a special level field in each of the affected dimensions, as shown in Figure 12-9. This makes for rather complex table administration because now the dimension tables have many null entries for individual attributes that no longer make sense at the aggregated levels.

The recommended technique is to take each kind of aggregate (such as product category by market region by month) and place it in a separate table. Such a derivative fact table is now joined to a set of shrunken dimension tables that contain only the attributes that make sense at the aggregate levels, as illustrated in Figure 12-10. Note that in going from Figure 12-9 to Figure 12-10, you lost the SKU and package columns because they make sense only for the base-level data; they are not defined at the category level.

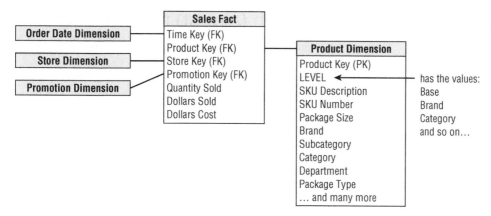

Figure 12-9: Aggregate records identified by the level attributes, which is not recommended.

Figure 12-10: Aggregate records stored in separate fact and shrunken dimension tables is recommended.

Some front end tool vendors embed the aggregate navigation in their tool suites in such a way that third party tools cannot take advantage of aggregate navigation directly, even though these vendors allow open access to all the metatables on the DBMS that describe the aggregate portfolio. Other vendors offer aggregate navigation as a separate network resource that any ODBC-compliant front end tool can use transparently. As far as I'm concerned, Hewlett Packard (HP) deserves the credit for inventing aggregate navigation and for being the first to think through the client/server architecture for aggregates.

In thinking about the approach taken by various vendors, I believe that the future lies in network server-based aggregate navigators. The DBAs of the world will appreciate a solution that provides the aggregate navigation benefit transparently to all end user tools. I suspect that the proprietary tool providers will find a way to unhitch their aggregate navigator modules from their tools and provide the capability as a networked, ODBC-compliant resource. Clearly, these vendors understand aggregate navigation. It will also be interesting to see how soon the big DBMS players notice this new development and add aggregate navigation to their bundles.

12.18 Aggregate Navigation with (Almost) No Metadata

Ralph Kimball, DBMS, Aug 1996

The single most dramatic way to affect performance in a large data warehouse is to provide a proper set of aggregate (summary) records that coexist with the primary base records. Aggregates can have a very significant effect on performance, in some cases speeding queries by a factor of one hundred or even one thousand. No other means exist to harvest such spectacular gains. Certainly the IT owners of a data warehouse should exhaust the potential for performance gains before investing in new hardware. The benefits of a comprehensive aggregate-building program can be realized with almost every data warehouse hardware and software configuration, including all of the popular relational DBMSs, as well as uniprocessor, SMP, and MPP architectures.

The basics of aggregate navigation were discussed in detail in article 12.17, *The Aggregate Navigator*. In this article, I describe how to structure a data warehouse to maximize the benefits of aggregates, and how to build and use those aggregates without requiring complex accompanying metadata.

High Level Goals and Risks

The goal of an aggregate program in a large data warehouse must be more than just improving performance. A good aggregate program should:

- Provide dramatic performance gains for as many categories of user queries as possible.
- Add only a reasonable amount of extra data storage to the warehouse; reasonable is in the eyes of the DBA, but many data warehouse DBAs strive to increase the overall disk storage for the data warehouse by a factor of two or less.
- Be completely transparent to users and application designers except for the obvious performance benefits; in other words, no user application SQL should reference the aggregates directly.
- Benefit all users of the data warehouse, regardless of which query tool they use.
- Impact the cost of the data extract system as little as possible; it is inevitable that aggregates must be built every time data is loaded, but the specification of these aggregates should be as automated as possible.
- Impact the DBA's administrative responsibilities as little as possible; the metadata supporting aggregates should be very limited and easy to maintain.

A well-designed aggregate environment can achieve all of these objectives. A poorly designed aggregate environment can fail on all of the objectives. In the remainder of this article, I provide four design requirements that, if followed, will achieve all of your desired objectives:

- **Design requirement #1.** Aggregates must be stored in their own fact tables, separate from the base-level data, as shown in Figure 12-11. In addition, each distinct aggregation level must occupy its own unique fact table.

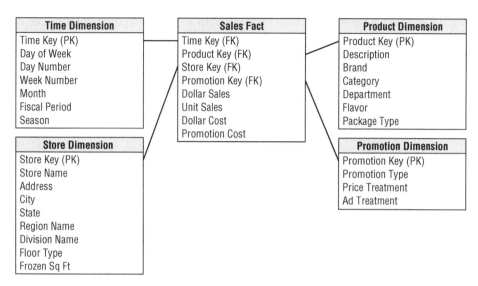

Time Dimension
Time Key (PK)
Day of Week
Day Number
Week Number
Month
Fiscal Period
Season

Sales Fact
Time Key (FK)
Product Key (FK)
Store Key (FK)
Promotion Key (FK)
Dollar Sales
Unit Sales
Dollar Cost
Promotion Cost

Product Dimension
Product Key (PK)
Description
Brand
Category
Department
Flavor
Package Type

Store Dimension
Store Key (PK)
Store Name
Address
City
State
Region Name
Division Name
Floor Type
Frozen Sq Ft

Promotion Dimension
Promotion Key (PK)
Promotion Type
Price Treatment
Ad Treatment

Figure 12-11: A base-level dimensional model.

The separation of aggregates into their own fact tables is very important. First, the aggregate navigation scheme I describe is simpler when the aggregates occupy their own tables because the aggregate navigator can learn almost everything it needs from the DBMS's ordinary system catalog, rather than requiring additional metadata. Second, a user is less likely to double-count additive fact totals accidentally when the aggregates are in separate tables because every query against a given fact table will by definition go against data of a uniform granularity. Third, the small number of giant numerical entries representing, for instance, national sales totals for the entire year do not have to be shoehorned into the base table. Often the presence of these few giant numbers forces the database designer to increase the field widths of all entries in the database, thereby wasting disk storage. Because the base table is a huge table occupying perhaps half of the entire database, it is very helpful to keep its field widths as tight as possible. Fourth, the administration of aggregates is more modular and segmented when the aggregates occupy separate tables. Aggregates can be built at separate times, and, with an aggregate navigator, individual aggregates can be taken offline and placed back online throughout the day without impacting other data.

■ **Design requirement #2.** The dimension tables attached to the aggregate fact tables must, wherever possible, be shrunken versions of the dimension tables associated with the base fact table.

In other words, using the base-level fact table in Figure 12-11, you might wish to build category-level aggregates, representing the product dimension rolled up from the individual product to the category. Notice that in this example you have not requested aggregates in either the time or store dimension. The central sales fact table in Figure 12-12 represents how much of a category of product was sold in each store each day. Your design requirement tells you that the original product table must now be replaced with a shrunken product table called category. A simple way to look at this shrunken product table is to think of it as containing only those fields that survive the aggregation from individual product up to the category level. For example, both the category description and department description would be well defined at the category level, and these must have the same field names they have in the base product dimension table. However, the individual UPC number, package size, and flavor would not exist at this level, and must not appear in the category table.

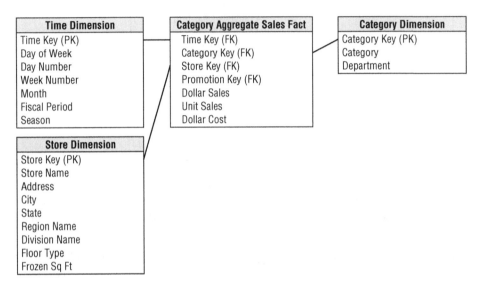

Figure 12-12: An aggregated dimensional schema derived from Figure 12-11 by aggregating to the category level.

Shrunken dimension tables are extremely important for aggregate navigation, because the scope of any particular aggregation level can be determined by looking in the system catalog description of the shrunken table. In other words, when you look in the category table, all you find is category description and department description. If a query asks for product flavor, you know immediately that this aggregation level cannot satisfy the query, and thus the aggregate navigator must look elsewhere.

Shrunken dimension tables are also attractive because they let you avoid filling the original dimension tables with weird null values for all of the dimension attributes that are not applicable at the higher levels of aggregation. Because you don't have flavor and package size in the category table, you don't have to dream up null values for these fields, and you don't have to encode user applications with tests for these null values.

Although I have focused on shrunken dimension tables, it is possible that the width of the fact table will also shrink as you build ever higher levels of aggregation. Most of the basic additive facts such as dollar sales, unit sales, and dollar cost will survive at all levels of aggregation, but some dimensions such as promotion and facts such as promotion cost may only make sense at the base level and may need to be dropped in the aggregate fact tables.

■ **Design requirement #3.** The base fact table and all of its related aggregate fact tables must be associated together as a "family of schemas" so that the aggregate navigator knows which tables are related to one another.

   Any single schema in the family consists of a fact table and its associated dimension tables. There is always exactly one base schema that is the unaggregated data, and there will be one or more aggregate schemas, representing computed summary data. Figure 12-11 is a base schema and Figure 12-12 is one of perhaps many aggregate schemas in your family. The registration of this family of fact tables, together with the associated base and shrunken dimension tables, is the sole metadata needed in this design.

■ **Design requirement #4.** Force all SQL created by any user or application to refer exclusively to the base fact table and its associated dimension tables.

   This design requirement pervades all user interfaces and applications. When users examine a graphical depiction of the database, they should only see the equivalent of Figure 12-11. They should not be aware that aggregate tables even exist. Similarly, all hand-coded SQL embedded in report writers or other complex applications should only reference the base fact table and its associated dimension tables. In those environments in which ad hoc query tools let the end users see every table in the system, it is a good idea to place the aggregate tables in a separate database to hide them from users. Because the aggregate navigator is maintaining its own connections to the DBMS, this should not present a technical problem.

Aggregate Navigation Algorithm

Assuming that you built your dimensional data warehouse according to these four design requirements, you are now in a position to understand how aggregate navigation works. The aggregate navigation algorithm is very simple. It consists of only three steps:

1. **For any given SQL statement presented to the DBMS, find the smallest fact table that has not yet been examined in the family of schemas referenced by the query.** Smallest in this case means the least number of rows. Finding the smallest unexamined schema is a simple lookup in the aggregate navigator metadata table. Choose the smallest schema and proceed to step 2.

2. **Compare the table fields in the SQL statement to the table fields in the particular fact and dimension tables being examined.** This is a series of lookups in the DBMS system catalog. If all of the fields in the SQL statement can be found in the fact and dimension tables being examined, alter the original SQL by simply substituting destination table names for original table names. No field names need to be changed. If any field in the SQL statement cannot be found in the current fact and dimension tables, then go back to step 1 and find the next larger

fact table. This process is guaranteed to terminate successfully, because eventually you arrive at the base schema, which is always guaranteed to satisfy the query.

3. **Run the altered SQL.** It is guaranteed to return the correct answer because all of the fields in the SQL statement are present in the chosen schema.

The beauty of this algorithm is that almost no metadata is required to support general navigation. The metadata amounts to only one row for each fact table and dimension table in the aggregate schemas. The maintenance of the metadata does not require complex logical modeling. Only the existence of the shrunken fact and dimension tables must be recorded.

In actually implementing this algorithm, several points are worth noting. In step 2, only the shrunken dimension tables and fact table must be examined. If a given schema uses a base-level dimension table, then its fields do not need to be searched because a match is guaranteed. For example, in our aggregate schema shown in Figure 12-12, the time and store dimension tables are not shrunken. Any SQL reference to a field in one of these tables does not need to be checked. Only references to fields in the product table and the fact table itself must be checked. In the case of Figure 12-12, the check will be successful only if the references to the product table are restricted to the category description, department description, or both. In a successful match, the final SQL differs from the original SQL only by the substitution of "category" for the table name, "product" for the dimension, and "sales_fact_ agg_by_category" for the fact table name. The original SQL is:

```
select p.category, sum(f.dollar_sales), sum(f.dollar.cost)
from sales_fact f, product p, time t, store s
where f.product_key = p.product_key
and f.time_key = t.time_key
and f.store_key = s.store_key
and p.category = 'Candy'
and t.day_of_week = 'Saturday'
and s.floorplan_type = 'Super Market'
group by p.category
```

The preceding query asks for the total dollar sales and total dollar cost of all candy sold in supermarket stores on Saturdays. The aggregate navigator scans this SQL and first looks at a highest level aggregate, perhaps called "agg_by_all" because that aggregate is the smallest, having approximately 200 fact table rows. However, this aggregate fails because the constraints on time (day of week) and store (floor plan type) both violate the agg_by_all schema. Day of week cannot be found in the month aggregate dimension table, and floor plan type cannot be found in the region aggregate dimension table.

Then the aggregate navigator tries the next larger schema, namely "agg_by_category." This time it is successful. All of the fields in the SQL query match. In particular, the product references to "category" are found in the shrunken product table named "category." Now the aggregate navigator replaces the table references and produces the following SQL. Only the italicized items are different:

```
select p.category, sum(f.dollar_sales), sum(f.dollar.cost)
from sales_fact_agg_by_category f, category p, time t, store s
```

```
where f.product_key = p.product_key
and f.time_key = t.time_key
and f.store_key = s.store_key
and p.category = 'Candy'
and t.day_of_week = 'Saturday'
and s.floorplan_type = 'Super Market'
group by p.category
```

The most straightforward implementation of the aggregate navigation algorithm would decompose the SQL query and look up each field name in step 2 of the algorithm. Each such lookup would be a SQL call to the DBMS's system tables. This is not a crazy approach because such calls are quite efficient and should run in a few hundred milliseconds each. However, in a large and complex data warehouse environment, a practical consideration arises. Calls to the DBMS system tables may take several seconds each, rather than several hundred milliseconds. If six or eight layers of aggregate tables exist, the aggregate navigator may take 20 seconds to determine the correct choice. This is an example of snatching defeat from the jaws of victory.

A better approach is to cache the system tables in the aggregate navigator so that the lookup of prospective field names does not require a SQL call to the DBMS. This approach is wonderful from a performance point of view, but it makes the aggregate navigator somewhat more difficult to design. First, the navigator must be able to read and store complicated system table configurations including, in the worst case, those with potentially thousands of fields scattered across hundreds of tables. Of course, you restrict your readout of the system tables to only those fields named in your aggregate navigator metadata table. Second, the navigator must have some idea of when to return to the real DBMS system tables to refresh its representation.

The aggregate navigation algorithm has certain limitations. Note that I am assuming that Kimball's law for dimensional queries is being obeyed. Kimball's law states that "no dimensional query will ever mention more than one fact table in the from clause." The basis of this law is the presumption that any DBMS that attempts to join multiple huge fact tables together in a single query will lose control of performance. Fortunately, few, if any, query tools let users easily combine multiple fact tables. In the vast majority of cases, the query is a simple set of joins between a single fact table and a suite of dimension tables. So this is not a serious restriction.

A second limitation is that each aggregation is "complete." For example, our category aggregate table in Figure 12-12 contains summaries for every possible aggregate. The aggregate tables are not restricted to a subset of values. Suppose the complete list of categories had 10 names. Our category table must always contain entries for all 10. You could not build a category table for just the snacks and candy categories. It would be difficult to generalize the algorithm to handle a subset of values, because there is no obvious representation of a subset of values that could be quickly stored and that it could be compared against. For example, with snacks and candy, do you store the text names of the categories, their underlying key values, or a more complex criterion such as "in the Convenience Department, but not including Hardware"? And how would you handle very, very long lists with hundreds or even thousands of entries?

My design approach has one major and unexpected benefit. As you ascend the various dimension hierarchies, you are likely to intersect the natural levels at which corporate planning and budgeting occur. For instance, the fact table in Figure 12-13 shows sales at the category by region by month level. In Figure 12-13, all three of the dimensions are shrunken. Although this is a small table physically, it may be accessed frequently for high level analyses. For completely coincidental reasons, it is likely that the corporate planning or budgeting process is producing plans at the same level, namely category by region by month.

Figure 12-13: The three-way aggregate table formed by aggregating time to month, product to category, and store to region.

A goal of most data warehouses is to compare plans to actuals. This is very efficient if these comparisons are intra-record computations. When you notice the serendipitous correspondence between your aggregate fact table at the category by region by month level and the planning table at the same level, take the opportunity to combine these two tables. You should add the italicized fields in Figure 12-13. At a certain high level of the aggregate hierarchy, planning or budgeting data "snaps in" and resides in the same table.

The addition of planning or budgeting data at high levels of aggregation requires generalizing your algorithm somewhat. You now have fields that don't exist at the base level. The search for tables that match all of the fields in the query becomes more complicated. The user's interfaces now must know about planning or budgeting fields. However, these fields can only be used successfully in the example at the category by region by month level and above. The aggregate navigator must now be able to detect when its search for fields in successively lower-level fact tables fails. For instance, if a user tries to compare planned and actual results at the level of product flavor, the system will deny the request because planning is not performed at the flavor level.

Aggregates for Everyone

The aggregate architecture described in this article allows for a very flexible administration. Aggregates are always behind the scenes. Neither the users nor the application developers need ever be aware that specific aggregations have been built. Aggregates can be added or removed by the DBA, even on an hourly basis. A good aggregate navigator should be accompanied by query usage statistics that guide the DBA in building new aggregates. If a group of queries are observed running slowly and all of them are requesting sales summaries by calendar quarter, then the DBA should be alerted to this pattern and begin thinking about building quarterly aggregates. Note that quarterly aggregates would almost never be needed if a "close by" aggregate, such as month aggregates, already exists. There would be little advantage in providing a new level of aggregate that only represented a rollup of a factor of three from an existing aggregate. A quarterly aggregate would make much more sense if the next lower time aggregate was by week, in which case the quarterly aggregate would offer a 13-fold advantage.

It is very important that the aggregate navigator benefit is available to all clients of the data warehouse. It is not acceptable to have aggregate navigation built into only a single client tool. In such a case, only some of the users would experience the benefits of navigation. Because it is practically impossible to restrict a large corporate environment to using one user tool, an embedded navigator approach would be an administrative headache. The worst scenario would involve two or more incompatible navigator schemes, potentially with different aggregate table structures and different metadata. The aggregate navigator must be a corporate network resource and must be a uniform DBMS front end for all query clients.

This article describes a simple but powerful architecture for aggregate navigation. If DBAs would adhere to the design requirements I've outlined, and if one or more DBMS or middleware vendors would market an aggregate navigator similar to the one I describe, your databases would speed up, your DBAs would spend their time on activities other than fighting with aggregates, and your metadata maintenance responsibilities would drop drastically. This approach requires almost no metadata.

If the vendors don't provide this benefit, perhaps you should build the navigator yourself. It should take approximately two weeks of competent C programming plus some testing. I built a navigator that does everything described in this article in three days of Visual Basic programming. Anyone game?

Front Room Architecture

This section contains two articles on user interface design in the front room. More recommendations concerning the data warehouse's front room can be found in Chapter 13.

12.19 The Second Revolution of User Interfaces

Ralph Kimball, Intelligent Enterprise, *Aug 24, 1999*

This article was written in 1999. Please keep the historical context in mind!

Data warehousing is increasingly being delivered via the web. And, conversely, the web is increasingly inviting the data warehouse to share its treasure trove of high quality data, in the same way that other kinds of data are already shared on the web. As a result, mainline data warehousing is now inexorably linked with that which stands between the data store and the human source and destination of the data: the web interface.

In this article, I return to my roots as a user interface designer. Twenty five years ago in the 1970s, when I was working at Xerox PARC, I had the great fortune to participate in the birth of the modern computer user interface. Inspired by the demonstrations of Alan Kay and his Learning Research Group at Xerox, a whole generation of user interfaces based on bitmapped displays, mice, windows, and icons flowed forth in a great burst of creativity from PARC in the early 1970s. My job, in the Systems Development Department of Xerox, was as part of a team that adapted and refined this creative work from PARC and made actual products. Our baby, the Xerox Star workstation launched in 1981, was the first commercial product to employ mice, windows, and icons. Apple's Lisa and Macintosh, and Microsoft's Windows all came later and, like the Star, were based on the demonstrations performed at Xerox PARC.

Of course, the real cognoscenti among you know that even PARC's ideas had their origins in yet earlier creative work by Doug Englebart at Stanford Research Institute and Ivan Sutherland at the University of Utah in the 1960s. But that's a story that will have to wait until another time.

The story in 1999 is that we are poised to undergo a second major revolution in user interface design. This second revolution, propelled by the inexorable forces of the web, builds on the first revolution, but defines the user interface in ways not envisioned by the designers of the 1960s and '70s. The goal for user interfaces we're building as we turn the millennium is no longer to make the computer useful. Our new goal is to make the web useful.

How the Second Revolution Differs from the First

The first revolution was based on a new medium that allowed a personal relationship with the computer. This new medium was called, appropriately, the personal computer (PC). Although early PCs had character displays, the revolution really caught fire when the personal computer became equipped with a bitmap screen, mouse, windows, and icons. This new interface was described as WYSIWYG ("what you see is what you get"). It emphasized recognizing rather than remembering, and pointing rather than typing.

The second revolution is based on an even newer medium; one that allows people access to the services of the web. Although early uses of the internet were based on character interfaces, the revolution really caught fire with the adoption of a standard format for hypertext links that allowed the development of a vast interconnection of information consisting of text, graphics, and other media. The impact and importance of the web is difficult to overstate. It is a force like a tidal wave. Within the next few years, most of the human beings on the planet will probably have some kind of access to the web. It is the great homogenizer, the great communicator, and it is also chaos.

The new web user interface no longer promotes WYSIWYG; it promotes IWIN ("I want it now"). It is based on gathering information, recognizing the choices that one expects, and getting the results instantly.

The User Interface Is Now More Urgent

During the first user interface revolution, we all marveled at the PC, but strangely, we have not put effective pressure on the user interfaces to improve. The computer marketplace still has not provided a good feedback loop for improving user interface design. User needs and dissatisfaction have not been communicated directly to the developers responsible for the design. Product evolution has been driven either by marketing, which wants more features, or by development, which wants more robust infrastructure. How often have we waited a complete release cycle during which a computer product was being rearchitected without feature additions? Lost in all of this have been the users' concerns. Advances in usability can come only from a thousand tiny improvements. Until now, when each of the improvements needed to compete in the vendor's annual release planning meeting, they often didn't have a powerful spokesperson or a critical mass of visible supporters.

Although for the moment the web is delivered through the first generation user interfaces, make no mistake about it—this medium is new. The rules are changing, and most of these changes never could have happened without the constantly pushing force of the web. The push is real and much more urgent for the following reasons:

- **User interface feedback from the web is personal.** website logs allow us to see gestures of the individual customer. We usually know who the customer is, what the customer was trying to do on the web, and whether that customer was successful. Developers in the first generation PC world could go their entire careers without ever analyzing user protocols.
- **User interface feedback from the web is immediate.** Headquarters can detect individual web user sessions' success or failure within seconds and analyze the sessions at leisure by the next day. In the personal computer world, user gripes and usability issues could take a year to accumulate, only to have to survive the political, release planning process.
- **User interface effectiveness on the web is now tied directly to profit.** The user interface is no longer the product; it is the portal to the product. By the time the customer used a product on a personal computer, the producer had received payment for it. Now, on the web, the user interface stands between the customer and the purchase. Corporate revenue may be tied directly to the effectiveness of the user interface. We are in the unprecedented situation where the CEO is pounding the table and demanding a better user interface!

Second Generation User Interface Guidelines

Having made the case for better user interfaces, is that all there is? What is different about what the web demands from the user interface? A list of user interface criteria has emerged as a kind of standard checklist for web user interface design. Be sure to read article 12.20, *Designing the User Interface*, where I apply these interface guidelines specifically to the mainline data warehouse activities of ad hoc querying, reporting, and data mining.

12.20 Designing the User Interface

Ralph Kimball, Intelligent Enterprise, *Sep 14, 1999*

Here's another article Ralph wrote in 1999. Unlike some of the others that expose a nostalgic view how the "old days" were, this one remains maddeningly accurate in 2015!

As promised in article 12.19, *The Second Revolution of User Interfaces,* in this article I identify 10 guidelines for user interface design that meet the web's unique demands, along with recommendations for applying them to the needs of the web-oriented data warehouse which I refer to as the *data webhouse.*

- **Near instantaneous performance.** Achieving near instantaneous performance requires a systemwide attack on all the parts of the data webhouse pipeline that can slow performance. You can also do some useful cosmetic procedures that improve perceived performance. The most effective data webhouse performance enhancers, starting with the most important, are:

    - **Choose DBMS software that is purpose-built for query performance.** Increasingly, this guideline means choosing a dimensionally-aware DBMS that thrives on join-rich queries either on online analytical processing (OLAP) cubes or dimensional schemas. Of course with OLAP, you must build simple dimensional schemas to begin with.
    - **Use your DBMS indexes effectively.** Choose a DBMS that lets you index every access path in a dimensional schema. Some vendors offer separate bitmap indexes on each of a fact table's foreign keys. With eight dimensions, you have eight indexes, but you can combine them to handle any combination of user constraints (the so-called ad hoc attack).
    - **Use aggregations effectively.** Aggregations behave like indexes; they consume disk space and require back room administration. You should have an aggregate navigator invoke them, transparently. But, perhaps even more than indexes, an appropriately used aggregation can harvest huge performance gains.
    - **Increase real memory.** Real RAM almost always improves performance, because it increases the in-memory working set size and reduces the need to swap data to and from the disk. RAM access is roughly 100 times faster than normal disk access. A big data webhouse engine can often use gigabytes of RAM.
    - **Exploit parallel processing, which can directly speed up many activities in the data webhouse.** Once you choose parallel-enabled hardware and software, pursue parallelism at the applications level also. Drill-across SQL is a technique for decomposing reports and complex comparisons into several separate queries, each of which is simple and fast. In almost all applications of drill-across SQL, the separate queries are executable in parallel, on the same machine or different ones.
    - **Use progressive disclosure.** Design your webhouse user interfaces to paint useful content, especially navigation buttons, immediately. Remember, in the data webhouse, everything is a web page. The user can begin reading the text to understand the content of the page before other items, such as graphic images, finish painting. Large graphic

images should be painted progressively at increasing resolutions so that users can recognize them before they finish painting. Information appearing off screen should paint after all the main useful information on the first screen appears.

- **Use caching at all levels.** Three kinds are useful to the webhouse. Web page caching works for static pages, the content of which is known in advance. Its objective is to allow a local server on your high speed network to give you the page rather than reaching across the web to the original host. Data caching is distinct from page caching; you can think of it as a kind of precomputed query stored for rapid retrieval. Data caching includes the use of aggregations. Report caching is a larger form of data caching and involves more. Full report generation may involve merging data from multiple sources, or perhaps running complex analytic models. If the report can be anticipated in advance, and especially if more than one user will access it, fetching it from a cache always, obviously, improves performance.

- **Expected choices.** Every web user interface provides all the natural choices the user expects and makes them immediately visible and recognizable. The designer needs to carefully list all the choices a user might expect when opening a particular page. The categories include sets of predictable navigation, application-specific, help, and communication choices.

  - **Navigation choices determine user interface design.** You must pay attention to the conventions of the web itself, not the individual website. The user's perception of the web is that it is a seamless whole, not a collection of independent media. Basic site navigation must be possible from every web page in a standard and predictable way. Site navigation buttons include drill-down choices from the current page, a direct link to the home page, major site subject choices, site map button, site search box, alternate language versions of the site, and a trouble resolution button.

  - **Application-specific choices.** Users expect to navigate available reports to choose the one they want. An explanation of the report's meaning should be available to the user reviewing the choices. It's a good idea to provide an instantly available, precomputed sample of the report, especially if the report itself takes a long time to return to the user's screen. If the report does take a long time, it should be emailed to the user, so the user can close the browser window or log off the computer.

  - **Help choices.** Besides links to tool documentation and frequently asked questions, every webhouse environment needs a metadata interface that allows the user to understand the organization's data assets. The metadata interface should display the names and definitions of all the available data elements in the webhouse. The definitions should be organized into brief introductions, detailed technical derivations, and current extract status reports.

  - **Communication choices.** Webhouse user interfaces need links at the bottom of every window to data webhouse technical support, sponsoring department business support, and higher level management both in IT and the sponsoring department. However, these communication interfaces must be supported with very responsive follow up. If the user sends an email to one of these functions, an automatic response should arrive within minutes, together with a promise that a real human being will follow up within a specified time frame. The expected follow up needs to occur as promised.

- **No gratuitous distractions.** This guideline perhaps should be phrased "make every page view a pleasant experience." There are many techniques you can use to improve the page viewing experience, and a lot of them are issues of good taste. The ones I think are most important include:

  - **Use fonts and colors only to communicate effectively.** Typographers learned hundreds of years ago that less is more when it comes to laying out a book, magazine, or newspaper. When the font draws attention to itself, it has failed in its mission to convey the content effortlessly and pleasantly to the reader. Similarly, avoid gimmicks such as blinking objects on the screen and the excessive use of exclamation points.
  - **Simplify your reporting interfaces.** The message consistently resounding from the web is that simplicity wins. The best simple interfaces get exponentially more use. Simple means uncluttered and direct. In some sense the best interface is a nearly blank screen with only two or three buttons in the middle that say, for example, "Push me for report #1" and "Push me for report #2."
  - **Provide convenient capture.** The webhouse reporting tools need to provide convenient capture of the results on the screen for use in all the other tools. Selected rows and columns of reports should be selectable and copyable to spreadsheets and documents.

- **Streamlined processes.** As the webhouse architect, you must design your business processes from the ground up to work seamlessly on the web. For example:

  - Work with legacy system designers to architect a seamless application suite with uniform web interfaces.
  - Remove barriers to accessing a page. An important page on your website should be easy to reach.
  - Count the clicks and count the windows to judge whether the process is streamlined.
  - Resume sessions; park reports to work on later.
  - Build an explicit value chain for reporting and analysis around the application suite, using conformed dimensions and facts.
  - Provide easy drill-across reporting.
  - Provide complete report library descriptions and frequently asked questions (FAQs).

- **Reassurance.** Users are more comfortable with a website when they can visualize where they are in the process and see that everything is all right. In a linear process that is hard to visualize, the status of the process should be carried along from page to page:

  - Provide a map of the processes.
  - Provide status and lineage of data.
  - Provide status of running reports.

- Actively notify users when new data is available or when reports are complete.
- Time stamp your dimensions and your reports.

- **Trust.** General website trust comes from respecting the user's privacy and communicating the intended uses of any personal information clearly with the user. Data webhouse trust includes these elements but also implies that the information it presents to the webhouse's business user is secure.

  - **Implement two-factor security everywhere.** Two-factor security involves verifying what you know (a password) and showing what you possess (a piece of plastic or maybe your thumb).
  - **Track human resource changes for employees and contractors.** Ideally, the data webhouse manager works closely and continuously with the human resource manager to make sure these changes of status are reflected in the information access privileges of the webhouse.
  - **Manage information boundaries among employees, contractors, and customers.** Much of the data in the webhouse must be carefully partitioned so that only the right people have access to it. A breakdown in the authorization system for accessing data will scare business partners and can easily provoke lawsuits.
  - **Manage webhouse security directly.** No one is better qualified to marry the data with the users from a security perspective than the data webhouse manager. The security responsibility for the webhouse must not be ignored, and it must not be handed to a service organization that has no way of understanding the content of the webhouse data or the legitimate access needs of all the users. A large webhouse environment requires a full-time security manager.

- **Problem resolution.** The data webhouse needs the same attention to problem resolution as the general website.

  - **Allow backtracking and play forward.** Backtracking means returning to a previous step in the process, maybe because the user realized that different information was required. Then the process is resumed from that point forward.
  - **Make it easy for users to report errors.** Users can be very helpful in reporting quality problems. But it must be a positive and easy action for them. A corollary is to provide a user survey capability that lets users describe how well their needs have been served.
  - **Religiously acknowledge, track, and follow up all user inputs.** User inputs will dry up quickly if significant energy is not put into acknowledging the inputs, tracking the status of the inputs, effectively addressing the inputs, and always communicating these steps to the original user who provided the input.
  - **Provide adequate end user support.** The use of a data webhouse, and the use of data in general, requires a significant commitment to direct support. At the beginning of a data webhouse rollout, it is reasonable to plan for one MBA-class support person for every 20 business users at first, maybe gravitating to one for every 50 users eventually.

- **Communication hooks.** Part of the expected choices I discussed earlier was a set of communication links to key individuals supporting functions behind the website. These links included the technical support for help with the website or database access, business support for help with report content and the location of data, and management for general questions and information.
- **International transparency.** The webhouse architect needs to be concerned with multinational reporting requirements. In multinational organizations there is a complex trade-off between expressing business results in local terms in a single central language or style. The key differences revolve around the choice of dates, times, currencies, languages, and collating sequences. You want the sales manager from Sweden and the sales manager from Spain to have similar-looking reports that they can compare.
- **Common denominator compatibility.** The general website must try to accommodate multiple browser types, old browser versions, slow phone lines, and tiny displays. Perhaps you have a little more freedom when designing the user interfaces for employees and business partners. It seems reasonable to ask that all participants use the same browser software and that all of this software be at a common revision level. You can also deploy specific ActiveX or JavaBean applets to every user that assists in the analysis or the presentation.

The web makes the user interface more urgent and more important. Increasingly, as we expose our data warehouses through the web, we are subject to the same user interface pressures. Ultimately, we webhouse designers must attack all 10 of the user interface guidelines. Doing so is certainly a significant effort. But as with many aspects of the web, we are being swept along. Welcome to the web.

Metadata

This section begins with an article that identifies the vast breadth of metadata in an end-to-end DW/BI system. The second article suggests a practical approach that focuses on the metadata most critical to the business users first.

12.21 Meta Meta Data Data

Ralph Kimball, DBMS, Mar 1998

Metadata is an amazing topic in the data warehouse world. Considering that we don't know exactly what it is, or where it is, we spend more time talking about it, worrying about it, and feeling guilty we aren't doing anything about it than any other topic. Several years ago we decided that metadata is any data about data. This wasn't very helpful because it didn't paint a clear picture in our minds. This fuzzy view gradually cleared up, and recently we have been talking more confidently about the "back room metadata" that guides the extraction, cleaning, and loading processes, as well as the "front room metadata" that makes our query tools and report writers function smoothly.

The back room metadata presumably helps the DBA bring the data into the warehouse and is probably also of interest to business users when they ask where the data came from. The front room metadata is mostly for the benefit of the business user, and its definition has been expanded not only to include the oil that makes our tools function smoothly, but also a kind of dictionary of business content represented by all the data elements.

Even these definitions, as helpful as they are, fail to give the data warehouse manager much of a feeling for what it is he or she is supposed to do. It sounds like whatever this metadata stuff is, it's important, and we had better:

- Make a nice annotated list of all of it.
- Decide just how important each part is.
- Take responsibility for it.
- Decide what constitutes a consistent and working set of it.
- Decide whether to make it or buy it.
- Store it somewhere for backup and recovery.
- Make it available to the people who need it.
- Assure its quality and make it complete and up to date.
- Control it from one place.
- Document all of these responsibilities well enough to hand this job off (and soon).

Now there is a good, solid IT set of responsibilities. So far, so good. The only trouble is, we haven't really said what it is yet. We do notice that the last item in this list really isn't metadata, but rather, data about metadata. With a sinking feeling, we realize we probably need meta meta data data.

To get this under control, let's try to make a complete list of all possible types of metadata. We surely won't succeed in this first try, but we will learn a lot. First, let's go to the source systems, which could be mainframes, servers, users' desktops, third party data providers, or even online sources. We will assume that all we do here is read the source data and extract it to an ETL data staging area. Taking a big swig of coffee, we start the list:

- Repository specifications
- Source schemas
- Copy book specifications
- Proprietary or third party source specifications
- Print spool file source specifications
- Old format specifications for archived mainframe data
- Relational, spreadsheet, and Lotus Notes source specifications
- Presentation graphics source specifications (for example, PowerPoint)
- URL source specifications
- Ownership descriptions of each source
- Business descriptions of each source
- Update frequencies of original sources
- Legal limitations on the use of each source

- Mainframe or source system job schedules
- Access methods, access rights, privileges, and passwords for source access
- COBOL/JCL, C, or Basic to implement extraction
- Automated extract tool settings, if we use such a tool
- Results of specific extract jobs including exact times, content, and completeness

Now let's list all the metadata needed to get the data into an ETL staging area and prepare it for loading into one or more dimensional models. We may do this with hand coding, or by using an automated extract tool. Or we may bring the flat file extracts more or less untouched into a separate data staging area on a different machine. In any case, we have to be concerned about metadata describing:

- Data transmission scheduling and results of specific transmissions
- File usage in the data staging area including duration, volatility, and ownership
- Definitions of conformed dimensions and conformed facts
- Job specifications for joining sources, stripping out fields, and looking up attributes
- Slowly changing dimension policies for each incoming descriptive attribute (for example, overwrite, create new record, or create new field)
- Current surrogate key assignments for each production key, including a fast lookup table to perform this mapping in memory
- Yesterday's copy of a production dimension to use as the basis for diff compare (change data capture)
- Data cleaning specifications
- Data enhancement and mapping transformations (for example, expanding abbreviations and providing more detail)
- Transformations required for data mining (for example, interpreting nulls and scaling numerics)
- Target schema designs, source to target data flows, target data ownership, and DBMS load scripts
- Aggregate definitions
- Aggregate usage statistics, base table usage statistics, potential aggregates
- Aggregate modification logs
- Data lineage and audit records (where exactly did this record come from and when)
- Data transform runtime logs, success summaries, and time stamps
- Data transform software version numbers
- Business descriptions of extract processing
- Security settings for extract files, software, and metadata
- Security settings for data transmission (passwords, certificates, and so on)
- Data staging area archive logs and recovery procedures
- Data staging archive security settings

Once we have finally transferred the data to the target data warehouse DBMS, then we must have metadata, including:

- DBMS system tables
- Partition settings
- Indexes
- Disk striping specifications
- Processing hints
- DBMS-level security privileges and grants
- View definitions
- Stored procedures and SQL administrative scripts
- DBMS backup status, procedures, and security

In the front room, we have metadata extending to the horizon, including:

- Precanned query and report definitions
- Join specification tool settings
- Pretty print tool specifications (for relabeling fields in readable ways)
- Business user documentation and training aids, both vendor supplied and IT supplied
- Network security user privilege profiles, authentication certificates, and usage statistics, including logon attempts, access attempts, and user ID by location reports
- Individual user profiles, with links to human resources to track promotions, transfers, and resignations that affect access rights
- Links to contractor and partner tracking where access rights are affected
- Usage and access maps for data elements, tables, views, and reports
- Resource charge back statistics

Now we can see why we didn't know what this metadata was all about. It is everything! Except for the data itself. Suddenly, the data seems like the simplest part.

With this perspective, do we really need to keep track of all this? We do, in my opinion. This list of metadata is the essential framework of your data warehouse. Just listing it as we have done seems quite helpful. It's a long list, but we can go down through it, find each kind of metadata, and identify what it is used for and where it is stored.

There are some sobering realizations, however. Much of this metadata needs to reside on the machines close to where the work occurs. Programs, settings, and specifications that drive processes have to be in certain destination locations and in very specific formats. That isn't likely to change soon.

We are going to need a tool for cataloging metadata and keeping track of it at the very least. The tool probably can't read and write all the metadata directly, but at least it should help us manage the metadata that is stored in so many locations. Once we have taken the first step of getting our metadata corralled and under control, can we hope for tools that will pull all the metadata together in one place and be able to read and write it as well? With such a tool, not only would we have a uniform user interface for all this disparate metadata, but on a consistent basis we would be able to snapshot all the metadata at once, back it up, secure it, and restore it if we ever lost it.

Don't hold your breath. As you can appreciate, this is a very hard problem, and encompassing all forms of metadata will require a kind of systems integration that we don't have today. I believe the Metadata Coalition (a group of vendors trying seriously to solve the metadata problem) will make some reasonable progress in defining common syntax and semantics for metadata, but (in 1998) it has been two years and counting since they started this effort. (Note added in 2010: The Metadata Coalition ceased publishing standards in 2000.) Unfortunately, Oracle, the biggest DBMS player, has chosen to sit out this effort and has promised to release its own proprietary metadata standard. Other vendors are making serious efforts to extend their product suites to encompass many of the activities listed in this article and simultaneously to publish their own framework for metadata. In any case, these vendors will have to offer significant business advantages in order to compel other vendors to write to their specifications. Meanwhile, get started entering your meta meta data data.

12.22 Creating the Metadata Strategy

Warren Thornthwaite, Design Tip #75, Jan 13, 2006

In most cases, metadata is a neglected area of the DW/BI system; in a few cases, it's an over-engineered monstrosity. In this article, we offer an approach to dealing with metadata that we believe is a reasonable compromise between having little or no managed metadata and building an enterprise metadata system.

Our recommendation concentrates on business metadata first, making sure it is correct, complete, maintained, and accessible to the business users. Once that's done, you can focus on viewing the other major metadata stores. Here's a straightforward, business value based approach:

1. Use whatever tools you have to survey your system to identify and list the various locations, formats, viewers, editors, owners, and uses of metadata. Where there aren't any tools, you will need to create query or programmatic access to the metadata sources so you can explore and track them.

2. Identify and/or define missing metadata elements that need to be captured and managed. These are typically business elements that will be used more broadly and therefore need to be updated and distributed throughout the system.

3. Once you have a solid list of metadata elements in place, decide on the master location for each. This is the location where the element will be stored and edited. It is the source for any copies needed by other parts of the system. It might be in the relational database for some elements, in the front end tool for others, or even in your organization's repository tool. Try

to use all available preexisting metadata structures like description fields before adding your own metadata tables.

4. Create systems to capture and maintain any business or process metadata that does not have a home. These can be simple front ends that let the user directly edit metadata in its master location. You'll want some data quality checks and a good metadata backup system in place, just in case.

5. Create programs or tools to share and synchronize metadata as needed. This primarily involves copying metadata from its master location to whatever subsystem needs it. The goal is to use the metadata in the master locations to fill in the description, source, business name, and other fields in all the tables and object models all the way out to the front end BI tools. If the master location is populated right from the start as part of the design and development process, the metadata will be easier to synchronize and maintain on an ongoing basis. Note that copying the metadata from one location to another is an ideal task for your ETL system.

6. Educate the DW/BI team and key business users about the importance of metadata and the metadata strategy. Work with the data steward to assign metadata creation and updating responsibilities.

7. Design and implement a delivery approach for getting business metadata to the user community. Typically, this involves sourcing your front end tool's metadata structures from the master metadata locations. Often, it helps to create a simple metadata repository for business metadata and provide users with a way to browse the repository to find out what's available in the DW/BI system.

8. Manage the metadata and monitor usage and compliance. Make sure people know the information is out there and are able to use it. Make sure the metadata is complete and current. A large part of the baseline metadata effort is spent building reports and browsers so people can look at the metadata. Managing the metadata means looking at it regularly and making sure it is complete and current.

Even though this is the balanced strategy between nothing and too much, it is still a fair amount of work. Make sure there's time in your project plan's development tasks to capture and manage metadata, including separate tasks for the preceding steps. And finally, make sure someone on the DW/BI team is assigned the role of metadata manager and owns the responsibility for creating and implementing the metadata strategy.

12.23 Leverage Process Metadata for Self-Monitoring DW Operations

Bob Becker, Design Tip #170, Nov 5, 2014

In most cases, metadata is a neglected area of the DW/BI system; however, an increasing number of DW/BI teams have made positive strides in delivering business metadata to their users. This article looks beyond the business metadata to suggest several opportunities for leveraging ETL process metadata to improve data warehouse operations. The goal is to apply dimensional modeling principles and leverage your BI tool's capabilities to enable a suite of scheduled, exception-driven BI applications that proactively alert DW/BI team members to inconsistencies in the data warehouse environment before they surface to users.

As Warren Thornthwaite described in *The Data Warehouse Lifecycle Toolkit, Second Edition* (Wiley, 2008), metadata is the DNA of the data warehouse, defining its elements and how they work together. Metadata drives the warehouse and provides flexibility by buffering the various components of the system from each other. Metadata lives in various repositories created by the tools, programs, and utilities that make the DW/BI system work. There are three key categories of metadata:

- **Business metadata** describes the contents of the data warehouse in more user accessible terms. It identifies what data you have, where it comes from, what it means, and what its relationship is to other data in the warehouse. The display name and content description fields are basic examples of business metadata. Business metadata often serves as documentation for the data warehouse. When users browse the metadata to see what's in the warehouse, they are primarily viewing business metadata. Our recommended metadata approach, described in article 12.22, *Creating the Metadata Strategy*, suggests concentrating on business metadata first, making sure it is correct, complete, maintained, and accessible to the business users.

- **Technical metadata** defines the objects and processes that make up the DW/BI system from a technical perspective. This includes the system metadata that defines the data structures themselves, like tables, fields, data types, indexes, and partitions in the relational engine, and databases, dimensions, measures, and data mining models. In the ETL process, technical metadata defines the sources and targets for a particular task, the transformations (including business rules and data quality screens), and their frequency. Technical metadata does the same kinds of things in the front room; it defines the data model and how it is to be displayed to the users, along with the reports, schedules, distribution lists, and user security rights.

- **Process metadata** describes the results of various operations in the warehouse. In the ETL process, each task logs key data about its execution, such as start time, end time, CPU seconds used, disk reads, disk writes, and rows processed. Similar process metadata is generated when users query the warehouse. This data is initially valuable for troubleshooting the ETL or query process. After people begin using the system, this data is a critical input to the performance monitoring and improvement process.

Process metadata presents a number of interesting opportunities for the DW/BI team to more proactively manage the data warehouse environment. Three particularly interesting types of process metadata include:

- ETL operations statistics generated by the workflow monitor including start times, end times, durations, CPU utilization, incoming and loaded row counts, buffer utilization, and fail-over events

- Error events captured via the data quality architecture described in article 11.19, *An Architecture for Data Quality*
- Query statistics and aggregate usage statistics captured by the BI tool or query monitor

Each of these process metadata categories can easily be captured in most data warehouse environments. Imagine applying our knowledge of dimensional modeling toward these different types of metadata. We can quickly envision at least one schema for each type of process metadata including a fact table capturing every detailed measurement.

The ETL operations statistics will result in one fact table row for each ETL process run with its associated metrics; this fact table might be surrounded by dimensions that describe the date, time, ETL process, source system, target schema, and job status. In Ralph's aforementioned article, he describes an error event fact table that captures detailed metadata about each error encountered during the ETL processing. This fact table links to dimensions such as date, time, ETL process, source table/column, and target table/column. Likewise, we can imagine a similar schema for the query statistics metadata. Once we've designed and populated these schemas, we can begin to leverage this metadata.

For example, we can use the BI tool available in our technology stack to evaluate each ETL job's operations statistics against its recent history. We'll not only report on the operations statistics, but also leverage the BI tool's exception reporting capabilities. Perhaps we'd like to see all ETL jobs that took plus or minus two standard deviations longer or shorter than normal or handled plus or minus two standard deviations more or less rows. We're looking for ETL jobs that have most likely encountered some sort of processing error which is causing more or less work than normal. Clearly we'll want to investigate these outlier situations and take corrective actions.

Similarly, we can utilize our BI tool against the error event schema. One of the advantages of the error event schema is that it provides a basis for managing data quality initiatives over time. The dimensionality of the error event data allows us to study the evolution of data quality by source, software module, key performance indicator, and type of error. In addition, we can develop BI analyses that evaluate the daily error events and utilize them to help identify other types of ETL operations challenges similar to those we described against the ETL operations schema. The error event schema allows the team to identify soft errors where data is not manifestly wrong but falls outside the expected variation around the mean. We encapsulate the data from the error event fact table and publish it all the way to the BI layer in the form of the audit dimension. The audit dimension elevates metadata to being real data.

In order to leverage our query statistics metadata, a standard set of test BI queries will be scheduled to run against the presentation area upon completion of the ETL processes. The query stats fact table will be populated by the results of this standard suite of test queries to develop a history of performance statistics. We can then build another similar set of BI analyses against this schema looking for any queries that run plus or minus two standard deviations faster or slower today than they have over the last 90 days. This will help us identify empty tables, missing indexes, and aggregate table opportunities.

From basic process metadata, we can develop capabilities to enable our data warehouse to be self-monitoring. We can package the BI analyses developed against our process metadata schemas and schedule them to run at appropriate points during the ETL processing. Should any of our exception conditions hit, the BI tool can be directed to fire off an alert to the appropriate person on the DW team. Far better to learn of a bad load or missing index from our monitoring environment than from a slew of hostile emails and phone calls when our business users are unable to retrieve their reports and analyses.

Enabling process metadata reporting and analysis may sound like a lot of work, but the payback is a self-monitoring data warehouse environment with capabilities that enable the DW team to be more proactive in managing the environment. Most data warehouse teams have the skills and technologies available to them to leverage this type of ETL/DW monitoring.

Infrastructure and Security Considerations

This final section deals with several infrastructure issues, from information privacy and security to digital preservation, server configurations, and storage area networks.

12.24 Watching the Watchers

Ralph Kimball, Intelligent Enterprise, *Jul 17, 2000*

I have been increasingly concerned in recent months over an ethical dilemma that I face in my data warehouse consulting and education business regularly: privacy. I'm certain you, as designers and implementers of data warehouses, face that dilemma as well. We are building the infrastructure for effectively sharing information. We are tying far-flung databases together. We are analyzing customer behavior, and evaluating credit risks, investment risks, and health risks. At the same time, we are building integrated, accessible data warehouse profiles on most of our fellow citizens. When we talk about the technical details of "conforming the customer dimension," it is too easy to focus on the minutiae and lose sight of the larger system we are building.

The issue of personal information privacy has become a national debate. Web users are alarmed at revelations of how the websites we visit collect personal dossiers on each of us. The Clinton-Gore administration has begun to push hard for new federal legislation that would substantially define and limit the sharing of personal information. On April 21, 2000, a very tough new set of privacy laws known as COPPA (Child's On-Line Privacy Protection Act) went into effect. COPPA provides substantial penalties for websites that inappropriately gather personal information from minors.

To be honest, I am ambivalent about the role we play in all of this. There are powerful positive and negative arguments for gathering personal information. There is also a certain unstoppable momentum that data warehouse professionals cannot ignore because of the fast pace of technology and the slow pace of legislative action. Even if the Clinton-Gore proposals turn out to be fundamentally reasonable, it will be at least two years before we'll see any serious debate about this legislation given election year realities.

I do not intend this article as a call to arms for a particular view. But I think we can make a number of predictions about the impact of the privacy debate on all of us, and it is time we added the term "privacy architecture" to our vocabularies.

Beneficial Uses and Insidious Abuses

In my opinion, the core of the privacy dilemma is the conflict between the beneficial uses and insidious abuses of personal information. We often allow corporations to gather our personal information when we only consider the beneficial uses. And we usually don't understand or anticipate companies' abuses of that same gathering of information when we approve it. Consider the following examples:

- **Personal medical information.** The beneficial uses are obvious and compelling. We want our doctors to have complete information about us so that they can provide the most informed care. We recognize that insurance companies need access to our medical records so that they can reimburse the health care providers. Most of us agree that aggregated data about symptoms, diagnoses, treatments, and outcomes is valuable for society as a whole. Furthermore, we see the need to tie these medical records to fairly detailed demographic and behavioral information. Is the patient a smoker? How old is the patient? But the insidious abuses are nearly as riveting as the benefits. I don't want my personal medical details to be available to anyone other than my doctor. I would prefer that the insurance claims processing clerk did not see my name, but that is probably unrealistic. I certainly don't want marketing-oriented third parties buying my personal medical information. I don't want anyone discriminating against me because of my health status, age, or genetic predispositions.
- **Purchase behavior.** Retailers' beneficial uses of my purchase behavior let them give me personalized service. In fact, when I trust a retailer, I am quite happy to provide a customization profile listing my interests, if that focuses the choices down to a manageable number and alerts me to new products that might interest me. I want the retailer to know me well enough to handle questions, payment issues, delivery problems, and product returns in a low stress way. But insidious abuses of my purchase behavior drive me ballistic. I do not wish any third party to solicit me through junk mail, email, or over the telephone; they also ignore my requests to opt out.
- **Safety and security in public facilities.** In this day and age, most of us are grateful for a feeling of security in airports, in front of bank teller machines, and in parking garages. We wish the people who deliberately run red traffic lights would stop endangering the rest of us. Most of us accept the presence of cameras and license plate recognition systems in these public places as an effective compromise that increases our safety and security. The legal system, which ultimately reflects our society's values, has solidly supported the use of these kinds of surveillance technologies. But the insidious abuses of cameras and citizen tracking systems

are scary and controversial. We have the technical ability to create a national image database of every citizen and identify most of the faces that cross through airport security gates. How is the accumulated record of my travels going to be used, and by whom? Systems that track this type of information are being tested in Europe already. Ironically, a mandate from the U.S. Federal Aviation Administration that states that individual airports cannot introduce technology that allows them a "marketing advantage" related to safety is one of the main impediments to implementing such systems in the United States. So the entire U.S. airport system would have to adopt this technology all at once.

Who Owns Your Personal Data?

We all have a natural inclination to believe that we own and have an inalienable right to control all of our personal information. But let's face the harsh reality. This view is naive and impractical in today's society. The forces that collect and share personal information are so pervasive and growing so quickly that we can't even make comprehensive lists of the information gathering systems, much less define what kinds of collecting and sharing is acceptable.

Think about the three examples I've just discussed. We all routinely sign the waivers that allow providers and insurance companies to share our medical records. Have you read one of these waivers? Usually they allow companies to use all forms of records for any purpose for an indefinite period. Just try objecting to the wording on the waiver, especially if you are in the emergency room. And, honestly, the providers and the insurance companies have a right to own the information because they have committed their resources and exposed themselves to liability on your behalf.

Similarly, the retailer has a right to know who you are and what you bought if you expect any form of credit or delivery relationship with it. If you don't want personalized service, then engage only in anonymous cash transactions at traditional brick and mortar stores.

And finally, if you use airports, teller machines, or roads, you implicitly agree to accept the surveillance compromise. Any images collected belong to the government or the bank, at least as far as current law is concerned. An odd corollary of being filmed in a public place is the experience we all have had of walking through a "scene" an amateur photographer is filming. Because a third party has innocently captured our image, do we have any rights of ownership to that image?

What Is Likely to Happen?

In my opinion, there are two major ways in which privacy laws and practices will be developed. Either our lawmakers will lead the way with such innovative and insightful legislation as COPPA, or the marketplace and media will force organizations to adapt to our citizens' perceived privacy concerns. Neither method is likely to produce a perfect solution; however, because we are in an election year, the marketplace and the media seem the likely leaders for the next round of innovation, and the Clinton-Gore privacy initiatives are already engendering a partisan standoff.

David Brin presents a pragmatic and compelling perspective on the threats to privacy and the impact of new technologies in *The Transparent Society: Will Technology Force Us to Choose Between Privacy and Freedom?* (Perseus Books, 1999). Brin argues that we can strike an effective compromise between freedom and privacy by "watching the watchers." In other words, we can insist on very visible notifications of information gathering wherever it occurs; honesty and ethical consistency in following the stated policies; and, significantly, on being notified whenever anyone uses our personal information.

The Impact on Warehouse Architecture

The privacy movement is a potent force that may develop quickly. As data warehouse designers, management may suddenly ask us to respond to an array of privacy concerns. How would privacy issues affect our data warehouse? Here are my predictions:

- We will need to consolidate and centralize all the personal information scattered across our organization into a single database. There should only be one consistent, clean set of data about individuals, and we should remove all data that no one is using for any identified purpose from all databases.

- We'll need to define, enforce, and audit security roles and policies surrounding this centralized personal information database.

- We'll need to physically isolate the server containing the centralized personal information database on its own segment of the local area network behind a packet filtering gateway that only accepts packets from trusted application servers on the outside.

- We'll need strong forms of physical and logical security for the backup and recovery of the centralized personal information server.

- We'll need to define at least two levels of security sensitivity to implement a new privacy standard in our organization. We'll assign general demographic information a lower level of security; we'll assign names, account numbers, and selected financial and health related information a higher level of security.

- An audit database that tracks every use of the personal information must accompany the main database. This audit database must notify every individual of all uses of their personal information, including who requested the information and the type of application. The audit database may have different access requirements from those of the main database. If the audit database is used in a batch mode, it pumps out usage reports that it emails (or mails via post) to the individual whose information is being used. If the audit database can be queried online, then it is inherently less secure than the main database and probably needs to sit on a different, more public server. It is important that the audit database contain as little compromising content as possible, and focus on simply disclosing the final uses of information.

- We must provide an interface that authenticates the individual requestor and then provides a copy of all of their personal information stored on the database. A second interface must allow the individual to challenge, comment on, or correct the information.
- We must create a mechanism for effectively expunging information that we deem incorrect, legally inadmissible, or outdated.

Although the data warehouse community hasn't traditionally led the way in advocating social change, I think that it may be a canny look into the future if we each consider whether we could implement any of the changes I've mentioned into our organizations. Consider it a "reasonable future scenario" that merits a little advanced planning. If you are more daring, and if you think the privacy debate will end up as the kind of compromise Brin describes in his book, then have a talk with your CIO and your marketing management about some of these ideas.

I am indebted to my son, Brian, for urging the old man to think about some of these issues and for recommending David Brin's book.

12.25 Catastrophic Failure

Ralph Kimball, Intelligent Enterprise, Nov 12, 2001

This article was written in the immediate aftermath of the September 11, 2001 disaster.

The tragic events of September 11 have made all of us reexamine our assumptions and priorities. We are forced to question our safety and security in ways that would have seemed unthinkable just weeks before. We have been used to thinking that our big, important, visible buildings and computers are intrinsically secure, just because they are big, important, and visible. That myth has been shattered. If anything, these kinds of buildings and computers are the most vulnerable.

The devastating assault on our infrastructure has also come at a time when the data warehouse has evolved to a near production-like status in many of our companies. The data warehouse now drives CRM and provides near real-time status tracking of orders, deliveries, and payments. It is often the only place where a view of customer and product profitability can be assembled. The data warehouse has become an indispensable tool for running many of our businesses.

Is it possible to do a better job of protecting our data warehouses? Is there a kind of data warehouse that is intrinsically secure and less vulnerable to catastrophic loss?

I have been thinking about writing on this topic for some time, but suddenly the urgency is crystal clear. The following are some important threats that can result in a sustained catastrophic failure of a data warehouse, and possible practical responses.

Catastrophic Failures

Here are several categories of potential catastrophic failure:

- **Destruction of the facility.** A terrorist attack can level a building or damage it seriously through fire or flooding. In these extreme cases, everything on site may be lost, including tape vaults and administrative environments. Painful as it is to discuss, such a loss may include the IT personnel who know passwords and understand the structure of the data warehouse.

■ **Deliberate sabotage by a determined insider.** The events of September 11 showed that the tactics of terrorism include the infiltration of our systems by skilled individuals who gain access to the most sensitive points of control. Once in the position of control, the terrorist can destroy the system, logically and physically.

■ **Cyber warfare.** It's not news that hackers can break into systems and wreak havoc. The events of September 11 should remove any remaining naive assumptions that these incursions are harmless, or constructive because they expose security flaws in our systems. There are skilled computer users among our enemies, who, today, are actively attempting to access unauthorized information, alter information, and disable our systems. How many times in recent months have we witnessed denial-of-service attacks from software worms that have taken over servers or personal computers? I don't believe for a minute that these are solely the work of script kiddies. I suspect that some of these efforts are practice runs by cyber terrorists.

■ **Single point failures (deliberate or not).** A final general category of catastrophic loss comes from undue exposure to single point failures, whether the failures are deliberately caused or not. If the loss of a single piece of hardware, a single communication line, or a single person brings the data warehouse down for an extended period of time, then there is a problem with the architecture.

Countering Catastrophic Failures

Here are ways we can protect our data warehouses and make them less vulnerable to catastrophic failure:

■ **Distributed architecture.** The single most effective and powerful approach for avoiding catastrophic failure of the data warehouse is a profoundly distributed architecture. The enterprise data warehouse must be made up of multiple computers, operating systems, database technologies, analytic applications, communication paths, locations, personnel, and online copies of the data. The physical computers must be located in widely separated locations, ideally in different parts of the country or across the world. Spreading out the physical hardware with many independent nodes greatly reduces the vulnerability of the warehouse to sabotage and single point failures. Implementing the data warehouse simultaneously with diverse operating systems (such as Linux, UNIX, and NT) greatly reduces the vulnerability of the warehouse to worms, social engineering attacks, and skilled hackers exploiting specific vulnerabilities.

Although building and administering a profoundly distributed data warehouse sounds difficult, I have been arguing for many years that we all do that anyway! Very few of our enterprise data warehouses are centralized on a single, monolithic machine. Although there are a number of approaches to building distributed decision support systems, in my books and articles I have described a complete view of a data warehouse bus architecture that relies on a framework of conformed dimensions and facts to implement a profoundly distributed system in the sense of this column.

- **Parallel communication paths.** Even a distributed data warehouse implementation can be compromised if it depends on too few communication paths. Fortunately, the internet is a robust communication network that is highly parallelized and continuously adapts itself to its own changing topography. My impression is that the architects of the internet are very concerned about system-wide failures due to denial-of-service attacks and other intentional disruptions. Collapse of the overall internet is probably not the biggest worry. The internet is locally vulnerable if key switching centers (where high performance web servers attach directly to the internet backbone) are attacked. Each local data warehouse team should have a plan for connecting to the internet if the local switching center is compromised. Providing redundant multimode access paths such as dedicated lines and satellite links from your building to the internet further reduces vulnerability.

- **Extended storage area networks (SANs).** A SAN is typically a cluster of high performance disk drives and backup devices connected together via very high speed fiber channel technology. Rather than being a file server, this cluster of disk drives exposes a block-level interface to computers accessing the SAN that make the drives appear to be connected to the backplane of each computer.

  SANs offer at least three huge benefits to a centralized data warehouse. First, a single physical SAN can be 10 kilometers in extent. This means that disk drives, archive systems, and backup devices can be located in separate buildings on a fairly big campus. Second, backup and copying can be performed disk-to-disk at extraordinary speeds across the SAN. And third, because all the disks on a SAN are a shared resource for attached processors, you can configure multiple application systems to access the data in parallel. This design is especially compelling in a true read-only environment.

- **Daily backups to removable media taken to secure storage.** We've known about this one for years, but now it's time to take all of this more seriously. No matter what other protections we put in place, nothing provides the bedrock security that offline and securely stored physical media provide. But before rushing into buying the latest high density device, give considerable thought as to how hard it will be to read the data from the storage media one, five, and even 10 years into the future.

- **Strategically placed packet filtering gateways.** We need to isolate the key servers of our data warehouse so that they're not directly accessible from the local area networks used within our buildings. In a typical configuration, an application server composes queries that are passed to a separate database server. If the database server is isolated behind a packet filtering gateway, the database server can receive packets from the outside world only if they come from the trusted application server. Therefore, all other forms of access either are prohibited or must be locally connected to the database server behind the gateway. Consequently, DBAs with system privileges must have their terminals connected to this inner network, so that their administrative actions and passwords typed in the clear can't be detected by packet sniffers on the regular network in the building.

■ **Role-enabled bottleneck authentication and access.** Data warehouses can be compromised if there are too many different ways to access them and if security is not centrally controlled. Note that I didn't say centrally located; rather, I said centrally controlled. An appropriate solution would be a lightweight directory access protocol (LDAP) server controlling all outside-the-gateway access to the data warehouse. The LDAP server allows all requesting users to be authenticated in a uniform way, regardless of whether they are inside the building or coming in over the internet from a remote location. Once the user is authenticated, the directory server associates the user with a named role. The application server then makes the decision on a screen-by-screen basis as to whether the authenticated user's role entitles that user to see the information. As our data warehouses grow to thousands of users and hundreds of distinct roles, the advantages of this bottleneck architecture become significant.

There is much we can do to secure our data warehouses. In the past few years our data warehouses have become too critical to the operations of our organizations to remain as exposed as they have been. We have had the wakeup call.

12.26 Digital Preservation

Ralph Kimball, Intelligent Enterprise, *Mar 1, 2000*

One of the oaths we take as data warehouse managers is that we will preserve history. In many ways we have become the archivists of corporate information. We don't usually promise to keep all old history online, but we often claim that we will store it somewhere for safekeeping. Of course, storing it for safekeeping means that we will be able to get the old history back out again when someone is interested in looking at it.

Most of us data warehouse managers have been so busy bringing up data warehouses, avoiding stovepipe data marts, adapting to new database technologies, and adapting to the explosive demands of the web, that we have relegated our archiving duties to backing up data on tapes and then forgetting about the tapes. Or maybe we are still appending data onto our original fact tables, and we haven't really faced what to do with old data yet.

But across the computer industry there is a growing awareness that people are not yet preserving digital data, and that it is a serious and difficult problem.

Does a Warehouse Even Need to Keep Old Data?

Most data warehouse managers are driven by the urgent needs of business departments such as marketing, which have very tactical concerns. Few marketing departments care about data that is more than three years old because our products and markets are changing so quickly. It is tempting to think only of these marketing clients and to discard data that no longer meets their needs.

But with a little reflection, we realize we are sitting on a lot of other data in our warehouses that we absolutely must preserve. This data includes:

- Detailed sales records, for legal, financial, and tax purposes
- Trended survey data in which long term tracking has strategic value
- All records required for government regulatory or compliance tracking
- Medical records that in some cases must be preserved for 100 years!
- Clinical trials and experimental results that may support patent claims
- Documentation of toxic waste disposal, fuel deliveries, and safety inspections
- All other data that may have historical value to someone, sometime

Faced with this list, we have to admit that we need a plan for retrieving these kinds of data five, 10, or maybe even 50 years in the future. It begins to dawn on us that maybe this will be a challenge. How long do mag tapes last? Are CD-ROMs or DVDs the answer? Will we be able to read the formats in the future? I have some eight-inch floppies from just a few years ago that are absolutely unrecoverable and worthless. All of a sudden, this is sounding like a difficult project.

Media, Formats, Software, and Hardware

As we begin to think about really long term preservation of digital data, our world begins to fall apart. Let's start with the storage media. There is considerable disagreement about the practical longevity of physical media such as mag tapes and CD-ROM disks, with serious estimates ranging from as few as five years to many decades. But of course, our media may not be of archival quality, and they may not be stored or handled in an optimum way. We must counterbalance the optimism of vendors and certain experts with the pragmatic admission that most of the tapes and physical media we have today that are more than 10 years old are of doubtful integrity.

Any debates about the physical viability of the media, however, pale when we compare them to the debates about formats, software, and hardware. All data objects are encoded on physical media in the format-of-the-day. Everything from the density of the bits on the media, to the arrangement of directories, and finally to the higher level application-specific encoding of the data, is a stack of cards waiting to fall. Taking my eight-inch floppies as examples, what would it take to read the embedded data? Well, it would take a hardware configuration sporting a working eight-inch floppy drive, the software drivers for an eight-inch drive, and the application that originally wrote the data to the file.

Obsolete Formats and Archaic Formats

In the lexicon of digital preservationists, an obsolete format is a format that is no longer actively supported, but there is still working hardware and software extant that can read and display the content of the data in its original form. An archaic format is one that has passed on to the nether realm. My eight-inch floppies are, as far as I am concerned, archaic formats. I will never recover their data. The

Phoenician writing system known as Linear A is also an archaic format that has apparently been lost forever. My floppies may be only slightly easier to decipher than Linear A.

Hard Copy, Standards, and Museums

A number of proposals have been made to work around the format difficulties of recovering old data. One simple proposal is to reduce everything to hard copy. In other words, print all your data onto paper. Surely this action will sidestep all the issues of data formats, software, and hardware. While for tiny amounts of data this approach has a certain appeal, and is better than losing the data, it has a number of fatal flaws. In today's world, copying to paper doesn't scale. A gigabyte printed out as ASCII characters would take 250,000 printed pages at 4,000 characters per page. A terabyte would require 250,000,000 pages! Remember that we can't cheat and put the "paper" on a CD-ROM or a mag tape because that would just reintroduce the digital format problem. And finally, we would be seriously compromising the data structures, the user interfaces, and the behavior of the systems originally meant to present and interpret the data. In many cases, a paper backup would destroy the data's usability.

A second proposal is to establish standards for the representation and storage of data that would guarantee that everything can be represented in permanently readable formats. In the data warehouse world, the only data that remotely approaches such a standard is relational data stored in an ANSI standard format. But almost all implementations of relational databases use significant extensions of the data types, SQL syntax, and surrounding metadata to provide needed functionality. By the time we have dumped a database with all its applications and metadata onto a mag tape, even if it has come from Oracle or DB2, we can't be very confident that we will be able to read and use such data in 30 or 50 years. Other data outside of the narrow ANSI standard RDBMS definition is hopelessly fragmented. There is no visible market segment, for instance, that coalesces all possible OLAP data storage mechanisms into a single physical standard that guarantees lossless transfer to and from the standard format.

A final, somewhat nostalgic proposal is to support museums, where ancient versions of hardware, operating systems, and applications software would be lovingly preserved so that people could read old data. This proposal at least gets to the heart of the issue in recognizing that the old software must really be present in order to interpret the old data. But the museum idea doesn't scale and doesn't hold up to close scrutiny. How are we going to keep a Datawhack 9000 working for 50 years? What happens when the last one dies? And if the person walking in with the old data has moved the data to a modern medium like a DVD ROM, how would a working Datawhack 9000 interface to the DVD? Is someone going to write modern drivers for ancient pathetic machines? Maybe it has an 8-bit bus.

Refreshing, Migrating, Emulating, and Encapsulating

A number of experts have suggested that an IT organization should periodically refresh the data storage by moving the data physically from old media onto new media. A more aggressive version of refreshing is migrating, where the data is not only physically transferred but is reformatted so that contemporary applications can read it. Refreshing and migrating do indeed solve some of the short-term preservation crises because if you successfully refresh and migrate, you are free from the problems of old media and old formats. But taking a longer view, these approaches have at least two very serious problems. First, migrating is a labor-intensive, custom task that has little leverage from job to job and may involve the loss of original functionality. A second and more serious problem is that migrating cannot handle major paradigm shifts. We all expect to migrate from version 8 of an RDBMS to a version 9, but what happens if heteroschedastic database systems (HDSs) take over the world? The fact that nobody, including me, knows what an HDS is, illustrates my point. After all, we didn't migrate very many databases when the paradigm shifted from network to relational databases, did we?

Well, we have managed to paint a pretty bleak picture. Given all these facts, what hope do the experts have for long term digital preservation? If you are interested in this topic and a serious architecture for preserving your digital data warehouse archives for the next 50 years, you should read Jeff Rothenberg's 1998 treatise *Avoiding Technological Quicksand, Finding a Viable Technical Foundation for Digital Preservation* (http://www.clir.org/pubs/reports/rothenberg/pub77.pdf), a report to the Council on Library and Information Resources (CLIR). It is very well written and I recommend it very highly.

As a hint of where Rothenberg goes with this topic, he recommends the development of emulation systems that, although they run on modern hardware and software, nevertheless faithfully emulate old hardware. He chooses the hardware level for emulation because hardware emulation is a proven technique for re-creating old systems, even ones as gnarly as electronic games. He also describes the need to encapsulate the old data sets along with the metadata we need in order to interpret the data set, as well as the overall specifications for the emulation itself. By keeping all these together in one encapsulated package, the data will travel along into the future with everything that we need to play it back out again in 50 years. All we need to do is interpret the emulation specifications on our contemporary hardware.

The library world is deeply committed to solving the digital preservation problem. Look up "embrittled documents" on the Google search engine. We need to study their techniques and adapt them to our data warehouse needs.

12.27 Creating the Advantages of a 64-Bit Server

Joy Mundy, Design Tip #76, Feb 9, 2006

Joy wrote this article 10 years ago. Please keep this historical context in mind!

DW/BI systems love memory. This has been true for decades, since 64 MB was a lot of system memory. It remains true today, when 64 GB is a lot of system memory.

Memory is the most common bottleneck affecting the performance of a DW/BI system. Adding more memory is often the easiest way to improve system performance. DW/BI systems have a strong affinity for 64-bit hardware. The improved processing performance is nice, but 64-bit is particularly important to us because of the vastly larger addressable memory space. In-memory operations are orders of magnitude faster than operations that need to access a lot of disk.

All components of the DW/BI system benefit from additional memory. Memory helps the relational engine answer queries and build indexes much faster. The ETL system can be a significant memory hog. Good design for an ETL system performs transformations in a pipeline and writes data to disk as seldom as possible. OLAP technology uses memory during processing when the cube is computing aggregations and during query time. Even the reporting application can use significant memory. The query that underlies a report uses the memory of the underlying relational or OLAP engine. And if you're using a reporting server to manage and render reports, you may be surprised at how much memory it can consume.

High end hardware for both Windows and UNIX systems are dominated by 64-bit, as you can see by reviewing the TPC-H benchmark results. But 64-bit is a no-brainer for DW/BI systems of any size. You can buy a commodity server in 2006 with four dual core 64-bit processors, 16 GB of memory, and 700 GB of storage for about $25,000. That kind of hardware should easily support a smallish DW/BI system of several billion fact rows and dozens of users.

Although we've characterized the 64-bit hardware as a no-brainer even for small to medium systems, there are some things you need to worry about. The first question is the chip architecture. Those of us who've grown comfortable with the simplicity of the "Wintel" world are faced with new decisions: Itanium, x64, or AMD64? These are fundamentally different chips, and the operating system and application code must be separately compiled, tested, and supported. You're betting that the operating system and database software will continue to support your chosen chipset for the expected life of your hardware. Consider software requirements beyond the core server software, such as specialized ETL functionality or database management tools.

A secondary issue is the architecture of your development and test environments. Your DW/BI test system must use the same architecture as your production system. In an ideal world, the development database servers would also use the same architecture, but it's common to use cheaper systems for development. As an aside, it's amazingly common to use a different architecture for the test system—including not having a test system at all—but that's just asking for trouble.

For a large DW/BI system, 64-bit is the only way to go. But even for smaller systems, a modest investment in a 64-bit server and a decent amount of memory will pay for itself in system performance. We used to make fun of people who'd buy bigger hardware so they don't have to tune their DW/BI system. But in the case of 64-bit and large memory, it's a sensible thing to do.

12.28 Server Configuration Considerations

Warren Thornthwaite, Design Tip #102, Jun 3, 2008

"How many servers do I need?" is a frequently asked question by our students. The only right answer is the classic "it depends." While this may be true, it's more helpful to identify the factors upon which it depends. In this article, I briefly describe these factors, along with common box configurations.

Factors Influencing Server Configurations

Not surprisingly, the three major layers of the DW/BI system architecture (ETL, presentation server, and BI applications) are the primary drivers of scale. Any one of these may need more horsepower than usual depending on your circumstances. For example, your ETL system may be particularly complex with lots of data quality issues, surrogate key management, change data detection, data integration, low-latency data requirements, narrow load windows, or even just large data volumes.

At the presentation server layer, large data volumes and query usage are the primary drivers of increased scale. This includes the creation and management of aggregates, which can lead to a completely separate presentation server component like an OLAP server. At the query level, factors such as the number of concurrent queries and the query mix can have a big impact. If your typical workload includes complex queries that require leaf-level detail, like COUNT(DISTINCT X), or full table scans such as the queries required to create a data mining case set, you will need much more horsepower.

The BI applications are also a major force in determining the scale of your system. In addition to the queries themselves, many BI applications require additional services including enterprise report execution and distribution, web and portal services, and operational BI. The service-level requirements also have an impact on your server strategy. If it's OK to lock out user queries during your load window, you can apply most of your resources to the ETL system when it needs it, and then shift them over to the database and user queries once the load is finished.

Adding Capacity

There are two main approaches to scaling a system. Separating out the various components onto their own boxes is known as *scaling out*. Keeping the components on a single system and adding capacity via more CPUs, memory, and disk is known as *scaling up*.

Start with the basic design principle that fewer boxes is better, as long as they meet the need from a data load, query performance, and service level perspective. If you can keep your DW/BI system all on a single box, it is usually much easier to manage. Unfortunately, the components often don't get along. The first step in scaling is usually to split the core components out onto their own servers. Depending on where your bottlenecks are likely to be, this could mean adding a separate ETL server or BI application server, or both. Adding servers incrementally is usually cheaper up front than a single large server, but it requires more work to manage, and it is more difficult to reallocate resources as needs change. In the scale-up scenario, it is possible to dedicate a portion of a large server to the ETL system, for example, and then reallocate that portion on the fly. At the high end, you can actually define independent servers that run on the same machine, essentially a combination of scaling up and scaling out.

Clustering and server farms offer ways to add more servers in support of a single component. These techniques usually become necessary only at the top end of the size range. Different database and BI products approach this multi-server expansion in different ways, so the decision on when/if is product dependent.

Just to make it more interesting, your server strategy is also tightly integrated with your data storage strategy. The primary goal in designing the storage subsystem is to balance capacity from the disks through the controllers and interfaces to the CPUs in a way that eliminates any bottlenecks. You don't want your CPUs waiting idly for disk reads or writes.

Finally, once you get your production server strategy in place, you need to layer on the additional requirements for development and test environments. Development servers can be smaller scale; however, in the ideal world, your test environment should be exactly the same as your production system. We have heard from folks who have had some success using virtual servers for functional testing, but not so much with performance testing.

Getting Help

Most of the major vendors have configuration tools and reference systems designed specifically for DW/BI systems based on the factors we just described. They also have technical folks who have experience in DW/BI system configuration and understand how to create a system that is balanced across the various factors. If you are buying a large system, they also offer test labs where they can set up full-scale systems to test your own data and workloads for a few weeks. Search your vendor's website for "data warehouse reference configuration" as a starting point.

Conclusion

Hardware has advanced rapidly in the past decade to the point that many smaller DW/BI systems can purchase a server powerful enough to meet all their needs for relatively little money. The rest of you will still need to do some careful calculations and testing to make sure you build a system that will meet the business requirements.

This article focuses on the tangible decision of how much hardware to buy, and how to configure that hardware for the widely varying requirements of ETL, database querying, and BI. This is an exciting time to make hardware decisions because of the explosive growth of server virtualization and the eventual promise of cloud computing. However, on reflection it is clear that neither of these approaches makes the problem of hardware configuration go away. DW/BI systems are so resource intensive, with highly specific and idiosyncratic demands for disk storage, CPU power, and communications bandwidth, that you cannot "virtualize it and forget it." Certainly, virtualization is appropriate in certain cases, such as flexing to meet increased demands for service. But those virtual servers still have to sit on real hardware that is configured with the right capacities.

Cloud computing is an exotic possibility that may one day change the DW/BI landscape. But we are still in the "wild ideas" stage of using cloud computing. Only the earliest adopters are experimenting with this new paradigm, and as an industry, we haven't learned how to leverage it yet. Thus far, a few examples of improved query performance on large databases have been demonstrated, but this is just a piece of the DW/BI pie.

12.29 Adjust Your Thinking for SANs

Ralph Kimball, Intelligent Enterprise, *Mar 8, 2001*

This article was written 14 years ago. Please keep this historical context in mind!

In the past three or four years, a segment of the data storage industry has been quietly building a new architecture that has real potential for our larger, busier data warehouses. This new architecture is called the storage area network (SAN). Think of a SAN as a way to take all the disk drives off all your mainframes and servers, concentrate the drives in a single location, and then allow all the servers to read and write to any combination of the drives simultaneously.

If you could concentrate all your storage technology in one location, together with universal access, you could realize some interesting economies of scale. You could also eliminate redundant costs, compared with the conventional "processor controls its own storage" architecture that you are probably using with most of your systems.

Let's take a quick look at a typical SAN configuration, which Figure 12-14 illustrates. As its name implies, a SAN is its own network, almost always based on fiber channel technology. Fiber channel technology is capable of very high bandwidths, matching the ability of high performance disk drives to transfer data at their highest sustained rates. But unlike computer buses and SCSI chains, fiber channel can be extended to very large campuses. A SAN based on 9mm fiber optics can extend to a 10km diameter. Keep this thought in mind when I discuss backup and disaster recovery.

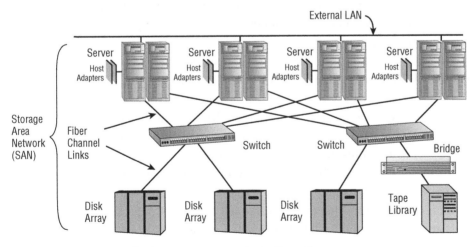

Figure 12-14: A typical storage area network configuration.

SANs normally contain storage devices, servers, and switches. A server can be any of the familiar server types, including online transaction processing (OLTP) servers, data staging servers for your data warehouse back room, presentation servers for your data warehouse front room, and a wide variety of other servers. Other servers include those devoted to data administration and functions such as data mining, multimedia servers, conventional file servers, and hot response caches found in more real-time data warehouses.

Every server that is part of the SAN normally has a fiber channel interface to connect inward to the SAN and a local network interface to connect outward to a conventional local area network (LAN). The SAN switches are capable of connecting every server to every storage device on the SAN, at fiber channel speeds.

At this point, you are probably thinking of a number of advantages that a SAN could bring to a large, busy data warehouse. Here's an attempt to list all the ways a SAN could be interesting to a data warehouse:

- **High performance disk access.** Above all, a SAN offers very high data transfer rates from disk to server and directly from disk to disk. SANs transfer data at 100 MBps, with promises in the near future ranging up to 400 MBps. The current speed of 100 MBps is comparable to the speed of a gigabit Ethernet but has the immense advantage (compared to a LAN) that every server has intimate access to every storage device. Some people have described the SAN as "SCSI on steroids."
- **High performance transfer between applications.** A typical data warehouse operation is bottlenecked by two, or possibly three, major data transfer steps. The OLTP system must transfer the primary production data to the back room ETL staging area of the data warehouse. Or maybe this first step transfers data to an operational data store (ODS). In either case, a lot of very granular data must be physically copied from one storage device to another. A large retailer could transfer 50 million sales transaction records per day to the staging area. A large telephone company could transfer 200 million call detail records to the staging area each day. And finally, a huge internet site could transfer several billion page event records from production web servers to a staging area each day. The secret is to have both the production servers and the components of the data warehouse back rooms and front rooms all on the same SAN.

A second transfer in the data warehouse must take place after the data goes through all the cleaning steps in the ETL data staging area. In this second step, a dimension manager replicates conformed dimensions to many distributed business process dimensional models. Because an entire enterprise can use a single SAN, the separate dimensional models can all be resident on the SAN and can receive the conformed dimensions at high data rates. This possibility raises an interesting, subtle point. The data warehouse can still be a highly distributed affair with separate subject areas organized around primary business process data sources. Having a SAN does not require you to build a monolithic, centralized data warehouse!

A third data transfer step might take place for certain kinds of data warehouse clients, such as data miners, who need to transfer very large observation sets from the normal presentation services of the data warehouse into their specialized tools, such as decision tree, neural network, and memory-based reasoning tools. These same specialized users may also transfer large data sets back into the data warehouse after they have run what-if scenarios or after they have computed behavior scores for all the enterprise's customers.

A Postscript

It has been more than a decade since this article was written, and now in 2015, SAN technology has advanced enormously, with significant increases in transfer speeds and physical network size. And, just as important, IT shops have moved storage planning nearly to the top of the priority list. The tape library shown in Figure 12-14 is in the process of disappearing altogether, as the advantages of keeping all data online forever are trumping other storage technologies. Finally, the recent advent of monstrous databases in the petabyte range is forcing IT to pay attention to the objectionable over-head of moving these huge volumes of data across slower communication paths, thus increasing the attractiveness of SAN approaches.

13 Front Room Business Intelligence Applications

For most business users, the data warehouse's front room with its business intelligence (BI) reports and analytic applications is the only visible layer of the data warehouse. We need to ensure it effectively answers the users' questions if we stand any chance of real business acceptance and return on the DW/BI investment.

This chapter begins with an introduction to the thought process and approach used by many analysts as they embark on a new analysis of business performance. They start with a report of historical metrics, but that's just the beginning of the typical analysis lifecycle, not the end state goal. Hopefully, deeper understanding of this process and associated activities will encourage DW/BI teams to go beyond merely publishing reports. We then make a case for behavior analysis to highlight a low hanging analytic opportunity.

From there, we turn our attention to the more mundane tasks of producing the starter set of standard BI reports, along with a BI portal. We also warn you about the dangers of committing to a dashboard too early. Next we shift gears to focus on data mining, from what it is, to how it might impact the data warehouse, and finally, how to jump on the bandwagon. The final section in this chapter deals with SQL; although it is the fundamental language used by application developers and query tools to access the data warehouse, it has serious limitations for conducting analysis.

Delivering Value with Business Intelligence

Delivering value to the business users must be a nonnegotiable objective for DW/BI teams. This section begins with two articles describing the typical analytic lifecycle. Hopefully this framework helps you appreciate that there's more to life than just producing reports. We also discuss the demands of compliance and behavior analysis as prime opportunities to deliver the requisite business value.

13.1 The Promise of Decision Support

Bill Schmarzo, Intelligent Enterprise, *Dec 5, 2002*

Most data warehouse implementations start by servicing the reporting needs of their business communities. They focus on providing a rearview mirror perspective on their business operations, but stop there and declare success. These projects fail to go beyond merely providing a bunch of prebuilt reports. Instead, they need to go further, to entwine analytic applications into the very fiber of an organization's decision making processes.

When you study the most successful data warehouses and their approaches to business analysis, several common themes emerge: Decision makers in these organizations typically use exception-based analysis to identify opportunities, then dig deeper into the data to understand the causes of those opportunities. From there, they model the business situation (perhaps using a spreadsheet or statistical tool) so that they have a framework against which to evaluate different decision alternatives. Finally, they track the effectiveness of their decisions in order to continuously refine their decision making capabilities.

Analytic Applications Lifecycle

The best of the new breed of analytic applications support this thoughtful, textured use of the data warehouse. A comprehensive analytic application environment needs to support a multistep framework that moves users beyond standard reports. The environment needs to proactively guide users through the analysis of the business situation, ultimately helping them make an insightful and thoughtful decision. The goals of this analytic application lifecycle are to:

- Guide business users beyond basic reporting.
- Identify and understand exceptional performance situations.
- Capture decision making best practices for each exceptional performance situation.
- Share the resulting best practices or intellectual capital across the organization.

The analytic application lifecycle, shown in Figure 13-1, comprises five distinct stages:

1. **Publish reports.** Provides standard operational and managerial report cards on the current state of the business
2. **Identify exceptions.** Reveals exceptional performance (over- and under-performance) on which to focus attention
3. **Determine causal factors.** Seeks to understand the root causes behind the identified exceptions
4. **Model alternatives.** Aggregates what's been learned to model the business, providing a backdrop to evaluate different decision alternatives
5. **Track actions.** Analyzes the effectiveness of the recommended actions and feeds the decisions back to the operational systems and data warehouse (against which stage 1 reporting will be conducted), thereby closing the loop

Let's walk through each of these stages in a bit more detail to understand their objectives and the ramifications on the data warehouse architecture.

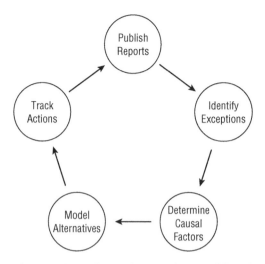

Figure 13-1: The analytic application lifecycle.

Publish Reports

Standard operational and managerial reports are the necessary starting points for the five-step life-cycle. These reports look at the current results versus plan or previous periods to provide a report card on the state of the business, such as, "Market share is up two points, but profitability is down 10 percent."

Data warehouse requirements in the publish reports stage focus on improving the presentation layer and include presentation technologies such as dashboards, portals, and scorecards.

Although many data warehouse implementations successfully deliver reports, they stop there. Reports that are only electronic versions of the preexisting hardcopy reports just pave the cow path instead of building a new highway. A well done analytic application needs to elevate the data warehouse efforts beyond just reporting to support more valuable analytics that provide significant business returns. Data warehouse designers should carefully study the work done in recent years on balanced scorecards, key performance indicators, classical exception tracking, and data mining in order to suggest new categories of powerful report metrics.

Also, many marketing and finance departments have a small staff of expert analytic users who may have creative ideas about report metrics. Don't let these highly trained, computer friendly business users spend all their time developing their own applications! Spend some time with them to elicit suggestions for your standard reports. Your goal is to entwine the data warehouse and analytic applications even more effectively into the fiber of your organization's decision making processes.

Identify Exceptions

The exceptions identification stage focuses on answering "What's the matter?" or "Where are the problems?" This stage involves identifying both upside and downside exceptions to normal performance. Most business managers have asked the data warehouse team to replicate a stack of reports in the data warehouse, when in reality they just want the parts of the reports marked with highlighters and yellow stickies. The exceptions stage is essential in helping users wade through the deluge of data to focus on the opportunities offering the best business return and those deserving the most attention. The ability to identify exceptions is especially important now that multi-terabyte databases are the norm.

Most exceptions are identifiable along key dimensions such as time, geography, store, customer, promotion, or product. Consequently, the more robust your dimensions and their attributes, the more comprehensive the exception identification processes.

The implications of the identify exceptions stage on your data warehouse architecture include new capabilities such as broadcast servers that distribute alerts to users' devices of choice based upon exception triggers, and visualization tools to view the data in new and more creative ways, such as trend lines, geographical maps, or clusters.

Determine Causal Factors

This stage tries to understand the root causes of the identified exceptions. Key to this stage is the ability to identify reliable relationships and interactions between variables that drive exceptional performance.

Successfully supporting users' efforts in the determine causal factors stage means your data warehouse architecture must include additional software such as statistical tools and data mining algorithms that enable association, sequencing, classification, and segmentation to quantify cause and effect. You may also need to incorporate unstructured data, such as press releases or news feeds, which can help determine the causes of certain exceptional performance situations.

Data warehouse managers must think carefully about how data mining efforts relate to their core activities. Data mining is a fascinating and intricate extension of normal data reporting and analysis. The simpler data mining tools, such as classical statistics and decision trees, are reasonable extensions to the current skills list of the data warehouse staff. But the high end data mining tools, such as neural nets, cluster identification tools, genetic algorithms, and case-based reasoning tools, probably require a dedicated expert. Such an expert may be part of the data warehouse staff or may be a business user who ideally is an intense client of the data warehouse.

Model Alternatives

The model alternatives stage builds on cause and effect relationships to develop models for evaluating decision alternatives.

The ability to perform what-if analysis and simulations on a range of potential decisions is considered the final goal when following the analytic application lifecycle. The payoff is when you can successfully answer strategic questions, such as "What happens to my market share, revenue, and units sold if I achieve a greater than 10 percent price differential versus my top two competitors?" Or "What are the effects on my inventory costs if I can achieve five percent sales forecast accuracy instead of my usual 10 percent?"

Answering these questions from the existing data warehouse is often possible by filtering the data to mimic (that is, model) the desired condition. Data warehouses have long supported this kind of modeling by calculating baselines for promotions analysis and selecting test markets with particular demographics.

Your data warehouse architecture may need to accommodate additional technologies in the model alternatives stage, including statistical tools and algorithms for model evaluation, such as sensitivity analysis, Monte Carlo simulations, and goal seeking optimizations.

Track Actions

The objective of the track actions stage is to monitor the effectiveness of the decisions that the model alternatives stage recommends. Ideally, you can then implement a closed-loop process and feed the recommended actions back into the operational system. The effectiveness of the decisions should be captured and analyzed in order to continuously fine tune the analysis lifecycle, business rules, and models.

The track actions stage places additional demands on the data warehouse architecture. Besides implementing closed-loop capabilities back into the operational systems and the data warehouse, I also recommend enhancing existing dimensional models and building performance management tracking schema to determine which decisions worked and which didn't. Emerging technologies applicable in this area include broadcast servers, which will soon enable users to respond with recommended actions from their device of choice (email, PDAs, pagers, and WAP phones, for example), not just deliver alerts.

Stepping Back

Implementing a decision guiding structure to proactively move data warehouse projects beyond today's focus on reporting is critical if the data warehouse is to materially affect an organization's decision making capabilities. The implementation of an analytic applications lifecycle is instrumental to achieving that vision. It enables capturing, sharing, and reusing the intellectual capital that's a natural byproduct of the organization's decision making process. I envision a flexible, rather than a rigid, environment that provides guard rails, not railroad tracks, to an organization's analysis processes.

13.2 Beyond Paving the Cow Paths

Bill Schmarzo, Intelligent Enterprise, *Nov 18, 2003*

Some data warehouse designers want to declare victory after merely replicating the organization's top five reports. They're satisfied with this level of deliverable because "that's what the users asked for." However, this approach is akin to paving the cow paths. In some communities, the roadways resemble a tangled web because early roads were built on preexisting cow paths. Unfortunately, the cows didn't meander along straight grid lines. Similarly, merely using the data warehouse to pave reporting "cow paths" doesn't push the organization beyond what it has today. This is where the analytic lifecycle can help.

In article 13.1, *The Promise of Decision Support*, I introduced the five-stage analytic lifecycle. To move beyond the first stage of publishing reports, the analytic lifecycle provides a framework for collaborating with users to better understand their analytic processes and gather more in-depth business requirements. It forces data warehouse designers to ask the second- and third-level questions, the "hows" and "whys," to understand how the organization could leverage the data warehouse for analysis.

Begin with Reported Results

Let's walk through a real-world experience, buying a house, to understand how the analytic lifecycle guides the requirements gathering process. Let's say that you've been transferred to a new city, and you have to find a new house. What sort of process do you use to find that ideal house? You might start with a couple of real estate listings (and the guidance of a knowledgeable real estate agent) and begin asking a lot of questions:

- What neighborhoods have the best schools?
- What neighborhoods are closest to my job?
- What can I afford?

For the data warehouse designer, reporting requirements are the starting point. You need to take the time to identify and understand which reports the business relies on to monitor their performance. However, users can't possibly look at all the data. You need to take the analysis process to the next level.

Identify Criteria and Threshold Tolerances

When house hunting, you need to limit your search; otherwise you'll be inundated by all the housing options (especially considering that houses are constantly moving on and off the market). You can reduce the number of housing options by identifying only those properties that meet a certain set of criteria. You've now moved to stage 2: Identify exceptions. In the housing example, these critical criteria might include:

- Price range
- Quality of schools
- Safety of neighborhood
- Square footage of the house

Stage 2 guides the data warehouse designer to look for requirements that focus on identifying the factors and thresholds that identify unusual situations worthy of further analysis. The exception identification factors typically manifest themselves as new facts and dimension attributes.

Understand Cause and Effect

After identifying those factors that you'll use to scope your search, you need to understand why these drivers are critical to your housing decision. You need to understand the relationship between these driving factors, what makes them important, and the ultimate housing choice. You have now moved into stage 3: Determine causal factors. Here you refine your selection criteria, being more detailed in their definition and corresponding acceptance criteria, such as:

- Top 5 school ranking in the city over the past year (because you have three school-age children)
- Minimum of 3,200 square feet with four bedrooms and two bathrooms
- One half acre of a usable, mostly flat lot (room to play catch with the kids)
- No more than a 30-minute drive to work (You don't want to spend more than five hours a week driving to work.)
- No more than a 20-minute drive to downtown shopping
- In the price range of $350,000 to $400,000

During stage 3, the data warehouse designer focuses on understanding why these variables are important, how they interrelate with each other, and how they'll be used in making the final decision. The results of this phase typically result in even more detailed dimension tables, new data sources (typically third party or causal data), and statistical routines to quantify the cause and effect of the relationships.

Evaluate the Options

After doing all the research and house tours, you can now create some sort of model to help you with the inevitable trade-offs in your final housing decision. You have now moved into stage 4: model alternatives.

Models can be quite advanced statistical or spreadsheet algorithms or simple heuristics, rules of thumb, or gut feelings. Whatever type of model is used, its basic purpose is to provide a framework against which these different trade-off decisions can be evaluated. The model doesn't make the simple decision mundane, but helps make the seemingly impossible decision manageable.

You can employ your housing "model" to help you with the following types of housing trade-off decisions, perhaps using weighted averages in a spreadsheet to make the decision more quantitative versus entirely qualitative:

- Price of the house versus the average neighboring prices
- Price per square foot of the house versus the neighborhood average

- Price of the house versus ranked quality of the school
- Ranked quality of the school versus number of minutes to work
- Number of bedrooms versus extra rooms (dens or sun rooms)
- Square footage of the house versus usability of the lot

For the data warehouse designer, the analytics requirements gathering process focuses on the model that will be used in evaluating the different decision alternatives. This includes the metrics that will drive the ultimate decision (independent variables) and their relationships to the ultimate decision (dependent variable).

Track Actions for Future Optimization

And finally, once a decision has been made, you need to track the effectiveness of that decision to fine tune the future decision process. That's the goal of the stage 5: Track actions.

This stage is often skipped in the analytics process. Few people or organizations seem willing to spend the time to examine the effectiveness of their decisions. In our housing example, the same probably holds true. I'm not sure how many folks really consciously examine the effectiveness of their decision, until it comes time to sell their house. Then you quickly learn if the general marketplace values the factors that you valued.

- Did I get the price appreciation that other neighborhoods got?
- Was the quality of school what I thought it would be?
- Did I have the access to work that I thought I would have?

For the data warehouse designer, the analytics requirements gathering process needs to capture the decision or actions taken, ideally in the data warehouse. With this information captured, the business user can see if an action had the desired impact upon the key driving business metrics (such as revenue, share, profitability, or customer satisfaction).

As you can see, reporting is typically the starting point for the analysis, but it isn't the end state goal. Only when an organization is able to move beyond just reporting do you start to see the business returns associated with better decisions.

13.3 BI Components for Business Value

Warren Thornthwaite, Design Tip #151, *Jan 8, 2013*

Each DW/BI lifecycle iteration delivers a coherent, incremental data set that provides value to the organization and can be implemented in a relatively short time frame. All too often, DW/BI teams lose their business focus during the project and concentrate on selecting a BI tool rather than providing full end-to-end solutions. Every lifecycle iteration should consider delivering at least three BI layer components: standard reports, self-service access, and targeted BI applications. Obviously, tools are important, but business needs come first. Let's examine the three required BI components.

Standard Reports

The DW/BI system should become the source for the organization's preferred business process measures. To accomplish this, each lifecycle pass should include the creation of standard reports that provide business process monitoring capabilities. For example, the customer service call process should have standard reports with basic customer service metrics, such as the number of new calls by day, week, or month over a significant time period.

The metrics on these standard reports must be accurate. The BI team needs to work with representatives from the business to test and validate them. This validation includes documenting any differences between the DW/BI numbers and legacy versions of similar reports. The BI team will refer to this documentation repeatedly to help business users understand that the new DW/BI system reports are both correct and improved because they usually fix data quality and business rule problems in the old reports.

These standard reports are critical to a broad category of users who monitor the business at a relatively high level. They need simple, pre-defined report structures, perhaps with the ability to change parameters or drill down a level or two. They often want the same report emailed to them and viewable from a mobile device.

Self-Service Access

Beyond the foundation of standard reporting, the DW/BI team must also provide direct access to the data. This BI component used to be called ad hoc query tools, but the category has split over the last few years into BI tools and visualization tools with significant overlap in functionality.

BI tools generally provide access through a semantic model that captures the dimensional definitions and relationships to help translate the user selections into the underlying SQL or MDX language. This access is usually drag-and-drop at the column level and the output layout and formatting is determined by the user. The best BI tools allow drilling down, drilling across, setting constraints, browsing attribute values, and choosing various tabular and graphical output formats. Often these ad hoc explorations evolve into additional standard reports.

Visualization tools also use a model-based intermediate layer, but they tend to guide and control the look of the resulting reports and graphs. Visualization tools attempt to provide instant feedback to the analytic design process by making assumptions about the appropriate graphical output format. The graphing or visualization capabilities of these tools have moved beyond basic line and bar charts to include scatter charts, small multiples, animated time series, network representations, spatial maps, heatmaps, and treemaps.

Note that self-service access does not mean access for everyone. These tools are appropriate for the core DW/BI system users. Known as power users, super users, or business analysts, they understand the data, the tools, and the business well enough to successfully serve themselves; self-service isn't viable without this prerequisite knowledge. There is a relatively small percentage of these core users in any given organization.

Targeted BI Applications

Above all else, the DW/BI system must deliver measurable value to the organization with each lifecycle iteration. This value should be tied to a specific analytic opportunity that was identified during the gathering of business requirements and is part of the justification for loading the given data set. This could be standard reports if the information they contain has not been readily available, but more often, it is a specific set of analytic capabilities.

For example, a friend who works in an investment related firm found his organization needed to understand how their products were being sold through various channels. The problem was their products were sold through third parties, and they did not have this sales data. He found a source that collected certain descriptions about the sale and applied a complex set of data cleansing steps and business rules that extracted a channel dimension from the descriptions. The business folks were then able to determine where to focus their sales resources, and negotiate more effective agreements and pricing based on this channel information.

The tools for delivering these specific capabilities could be standard reports, or self-service tools, or dashboards, or predictive analytics, or even a .NET or Java application. The BI team should be prepared to do whatever it takes to deliver the value all the way to the user.

It's Harder than You Expect

Every DW/BI team must accept the responsibility of delivering end-to-end value to the organization. Once you understand you are serving multiple user communities with different analytic requirements and different levels of analytic skill and maturity, you realize there is no such thing as a single BI tool that solves all the problems; that is, there is no best BI tool. But there is a single architecture that should serve as the foundation for all the BI components. Your most direct path to success is to build a solid, enterprise-conformed, atomic level dimensional data warehouse, which becomes the platform for all forms of BI. This platform delivers the greatest flexibility and will perform well with almost all BI tools. Then focus your BI resources on delivering business value using the appropriate BI components for the job.

13.4 Big Shifts Happening in BI

Ralph Kimball, Design Tip #60, Oct 8, 2004

At last week's Business Intelligence Perspectives Conference hosted by *Computerworld* magazine in Palm Springs, two interesting themes were very evident that signaled some big shifts in the BI world.

Compliance Is a Free Pass for BI

A number of speakers marveled at how the new regulatory compliance requirements for financial disclosures, especially the Sarbanes-Oxley Act, were opening the pocketbooks of companies to upgrade their BI environments. One speaker said, "All you have to do is mention compliance and the funding proposal is approved." But most of the speakers expressed simultaneous concern that no one knows just what the compliance requirements really mean. Not only are the requirements not spelled out in concrete database technical terms, but it appears that the practical impact of the compliance requirements may have to be played out in the courts, with IT departments defending their practices as "commercially diligent" and responsible.

Obviously, most IT departments interested in meeting the compliance requirements will try to err on the conservative side. And, of course, Sarbanes-Oxley is not the only game in town. There are probably a dozen overlapping financial reporting statutes with similar requirements, depending on where you do business.

A conservative approach to meeting most compliance requirements would suggest the ability to:

- Prove (backward) lineage of each final measure and KPI appearing in any report.
- Prove (forward) impact of any primary or intermediate data element on a final report.
- Prove input data has not been changed.
- Prove final measures and KPIs are derived from original data under documented transformations.
- Document all transforms, present and past.
- Maybe re-run old ETL pipelines.
- Maybe show all business user and administrative accesses of selected data.

Sequential Behavior Analysis Is BI's Mount Everest

Some of the most interesting and scary case studies at the BI conference were descriptions of trolling huge databases to answer customer behavior questions. Andreas Weigend, Stanford Professor and former Chief Scientist at Amazon, described a study done at Amazon finding the delay (in days) between a customer first clicking on a product and then eventually buying that product. This is immensely difficult. Since most clicks do not result in purchases, you have to wait until a purchase is made and then look backward hours, days, or weeks in the blizzard of records in the clickstream to find the first click by that customer on that product.

The potential volume of data that entities like Amazon want to look through is staggering. Amazon stores every link exposure in its historical data. A link exposure is the presence of a link on a displayed page. It doesn't mean the user clicked the link. Amazon is capturing terabytes of link exposure data each day!

Link exposures are just the beginning of a biblical flood of data, which will really get serious when RFIDs are deployed down to the individual stock item level. Not only is the volume of data horrifying, but the data is often captured in different servers, each representing "doorways" at different locations and times. These challenges raise the question whether the relational model and the SQL language are even appropriate. Yet the ad hoc questions people want to ask of this data demand the same kind of access that relational databases have been so successful in providing against much smaller data sources.

These two big shifts in BI have different personalities. The first (compliance) is like ballast, and the second (behavior) is like a balloon. But in my opinion, both are real and permanent. They will keep us busy.

13.5 Behavior: The Next Marquee Application

Ralph Kimball, Intelligent Enterprise, *Apr 16, 2002*

The focus of data warehousing has evolved along a steady and inexorable progression since the early 1980s. Competitive pressures and new generations of management have brought us over time to the threshold of a new era of analytics.

The 1980s and '90s each had their distinctive "marquee" applications. In the early '80s, a 50 MB database was pretty large. But we were happy to be able to analyze the basic sales numbers of an organization. The marquee data warehousing application of the '80s was shipments and share. We were delighted to see how much product we shipped each month and, if we were lucky, we could see what fraction of the total market that represented. In a sense, these early data warehousing applications represented the first time we could drill down from the annual report to start analyzing the components of our businesses. In the '80s, our analytics were simple: this month versus last month or a year ago. And perhaps the most difficult calculation was our share of a market this month versus the same share metric a year ago.

By the early '90s, our capacities, techniques, and analytic expectations had progressed beyond simple shipments and share numbers to demand a full analysis of profitability at an individual customer level. At the beginning of the '90s, the most sophisticated data warehouses were already analyzing revenue at the individual store or branch level. Certainly by the end of the '90s we were able to capture and store the most atomic transactions of our businesses in the data warehouse. The marquee data warehouse application of the '90s was customer profitability. We developed techniques for tying together the disparate revenue and cost data sources in order to assemble a complete view of profitability. The extreme atomic detail of the data allowed us to tag each transaction with the exact product and customer. In this way, we could roll up a full P&L perspective for each customer and product line.

Curiously, although the quantity of data available for analysis increased by at least a factor of 1,000 between the '80s and '90s, we didn't see a significant increase in the sophistication of our analytic techniques. We had our hands full just wrangling the huge databases. While there was some modest increase in the use of data mining techniques, these advanced analytic approaches remained a tiny fraction of the data warehouse marketplace. However, we did see a significant improvement in the ease of use of querying and reporting tools. The explicit SQL user interfaces of the '80s mercifully gave way in the '90s to much more powerful user interfaces for combining data from multiple sources, highlighting exceptions, and pivoting the data at the user's desktop to make the numbers jump out.

The relatively slow adoption of advanced analytic techniques in the '90s, in my opinion, was also due to a cultural resistance. Business management has always been reluctant to trust something it doesn't really understand. I'll argue in a moment that we are finally ready for the cultural doors to open, and for advanced analytic techniques to be more visible and important, but we need to be patient.

When I began my data warehousing career in the late 1970s as the Xerox Star Workstation product manager, I remember that at least half of our prospective Fortune 500 clients really didn't use computers or numbers of any kind to manage their businesses. They managed literally by walking the aisles and "gut feel." The transition since then to an absolute demand for managing by the numbers is both the result of technology advances, as well as a generational shift in the business world as younger managers arrive with computer training and familiarity. Thus, looking forward, we need to be patient as we wait for an even more analytic culture to assert itself. I'll also argue in the following section that the demands of the next marquee data warehousing application will force us to upgrade our analytic sophistication because this next marquee application is a lot more difficult.

CRM: The Stepping Stone to Behavior

At the end of the '90s, customer relationship management (CRM) emerged as an important new data warehousing application. CRM extended the notion of customer profitability to include understanding the complete customer relationship. Patricia Seybold captured the CRM perspective beautifully in her book *Customers.Com* (Random House, 2010). A data warehouse designer can read her book as a set of business requests that can be translated directly into a system design for a data warehouse. One of Seybold's most powerful points is the need to capture all the customer-facing processes in the business. Much of my own writing about conformed dimensions and the data warehouse bus architecture has been with the issues Seybold raised in my mind.

But CRM as implemented in the '90s is still just a transactional perspective on the customer. We count the number of times the customer visited our store or website. We measure customer satisfaction by the ratio of successful product deliveries to the total or by the change in the number of complaints. Our analytic techniques are still the kinds of counts and comparisons we used for shipments and share calculations in the early '80s.

But marketing managers are constantly looking for new competitive angles. Many organizations now have a pretty good understanding of customer profitability. They know which customers turn out to be profitable. They know which campaigns yield the best customers. But marketing managers are thirsting for a deeper understanding of how to recognize and develop good customers, and conversely how to recognize and discourage bad customers. Marketing managers will get the next competitive edge when they can understand, predict, and influence individual customer behavior.

At the same time, our data sources have descended to the subtransactional level. It seemed in the late '90s that if we captured every atomic sales transaction, we had somehow arrived at a fundamental foundation for all possible data. But the development of CRM and the capture of presales customer behavior has opened up potentially another factor of 1,000 in the amount of data we can collect about our customers. These new data sources include individual page requests tracking visitors on the web, call center logs relating to product information and customer support, market basket information from retail and financial companies, and promotion offer and response tracking. We are just in the beginning of explosive growth of these subtransactional data sources. Soon we will have global positioning systems embedded in our cars, our passports, and our credit cards. At the same time, our increased security needs will allow us to see customers coming and going from many of our stores and offices. I'll sidestep the legitimate issues of privacy raised by these technologies.

The marquee data warehousing application in the 2000s, in my opinion, will be customer behavior. We will analyze both individual and commercial customer behavior. But what is behavior, exactly? It certainly doesn't seem to be as simple as shipments, share, or profit. What does it mean to add up behavior? Is behavior even numeric?

The New Analytics of Behavior

Although Michael Berry and Gordon Linoff haven't used the word "behavior" in the titles of their books, it's easy to cast what they've written as a foundation for the large topic of behavior. In their latest book, *Data Mining Techniques, The Art and Science of Customer Relationship Management* (Wiley, 2011), they show how the simple progression of clustering, classification, and prediction takes subtransactional data sources and turns them into actionable descriptions of behavior.

Briefly, clustering is the recognition of discrete cohort groups (typically of customers) from the ocean of all customers. Clustering can be accomplished with a number of different advanced data mining techniques described by Berry and Linoff. Note the cultural jump required here: You have to trust the clustering algorithms.

Classification is possible once you have clusters. If a new customer prospect can be associated with one of your existing clusters, you can reasonably infer that this customer will behave like the other members of that cohort group. Note the word "behave." You have classified the customers by their behavior. We need some more advanced analytics here in order to understand how close the prospect is to the centroid of the existing cohort group, another step up the analytic ladder.

Prediction is the highest art form. You can associate a numeric metric with each known member of a cohort group and then use that metric together with the "distance" to the new prospect to derive a numeric prediction of lifetime value, or likelihood to default.

At any given point in time, the behavior of a customer can be summarized by a textual tag, such as regular high margin customer or unproductive window shopper. One of the chief goals of the marketing manager is how to convert customers from this second group into the first group. Lately I have been helping a number of data warehouse designers create schemas for tracking and reporting exactly this kind of label transition over time in their customer-oriented data warehouses, as I describe in article 10.15, *Wrangling Behavior Tags*. Although the final reports are pretty straightforward, I hope you can appreciate the significant analytic foundation they require.

Finally, a tricky but very compelling form of behavior is understanding the paths taken by customers as they visit your website or otherwise access all the customer communication points of your organization. Data miners call this *link analysis*. Again, once you diagnose the path's significance, you can assign it a behavioral label, and then use the techniques I just described to boil it down to an actionable report for the marketing manager.

Implementing the Business Intelligence Layer

For many business users, the standardized BI reports and applications are the only data warehouse deliverables they'll ever see. This section provides detailed tips and techniques for designing and constructing these key elements in the data warehouse's front room.

13.6 Three Critical Components for Successful Self-Service BI

Joy Mundy, Design Tip #153, Mar 4, 2013

The business intelligence industry has been using the phrase self-service BI for several years. Self-service BI means enabling the business user community to create their own reports and analyses from scratch. Self-service business intelligence is nothing new. The Kimball method has focused on delivering ad hoc access as an integrated—even integral—component of the DW/BI system for over 20 years. But self-service BI is a good name for an old concept, and one that may capture the attention of your business user community. Old name or new, let's review what you need to have in place to support your business users' information self-service. These three components are the foundation of a self-service BI environment: a solid dimensional model, a good user support system, and an effective BI tool.

Solid Dimensional Data Model

The first key to success is a dimensional data model. The benefits of dimensional models are widely known and documented in all the Kimball Group books. In brief, the dimensional model delivers:

- Simplified structure that business users have some hope of understanding
- Simplified structure that works seamlessly with the best self-service BI tools
- Consistent attribute change management
- Excellent query performance, which comes from several directions:
    - Fewer table joins because decodes and hierarchical structures are collapsed into a simple flat dimension table
    - Simple table joins because an efficient single column surrogate key always joins facts and dimensions
    - Database engine optimizations that recognize dimensional structures
    - Where possible, pre-calculation of metrics or attributes during the ETL process rather than at query time

Good User Support System

Many of the organizations I've spoken with expect that self-service BI means they can reduce the size of IT staff who develop reports. That may be true. You may have fewer report writers in IT, but you'll almost certainly replace them (or change their duties) with folks tasked with a broader set of service bureau responsibilities.

Effective self-service or ad hoc use of your organization's data requires some services. The provision of these services should be coordinated centrally, even if the BI "front room service bureau" is staffed and funded locally. The services that are absolutely necessary for successful self-service BI include:

- **Documentation and metadata.** In order for business users to successfully use the tools and data you provide, they need to know what data elements mean, where they came from, how they're organized, and what to watch out for. In the Kimball Group, we are fans of having the business users actually see a simple representation of the dimensional model, ideally in the BI tool. After all, many of them participated in the collaborative design sessions, right? In this way, all three components of self-service BI come together.
- **Metadata delivery.** Developing and maintaining the metadata and descriptions are only part of the battle. You also need to make them available to the user community. The descriptive metadata is the most important, and if possible, should be exposed to users from within their BI tool.
- **Training.** It would be nice if your data model, documentation, and tools were so fabulous that your smart users could walk up to them and be effective right away. It just doesn't work that way; you need to teach people how to use the environment safely and effectively. Users need to learn how to use the data as much as how to use the tool.
- **Assistance.** The dream of self-service BI is no assistance required. Realistically, there are always going to be questions, queries, and analyses that your users will need help with. Users can and will help each other, but it's most effective to have a few people on the BI team to help with the really tough problems.
- **Rich standard reports.** The ability to "lightly customize" a standard report by choosing parameters is enough self-service for many users.

Effective Self-Service BI Query/Analysis Tool

Of course, you need a tool or tools for self-service BI. These are different tools than the standard report development and delivery software, although they may be provided by the same vendor. There are two main kinds of self-service BI tools, which for lack of better names, I'll call conventional and visualization.

Conventional tools include the flagship offerings by many vendors, including from the venerable SAP (Business Objects), IBM (Cognos), MicroStrategy, and many others. These tools are venerable because they work. They provide a semantic layer that enables users to construct queries by dragging and dropping. Once the data set is defined, users have a variety of options to construct a report or export the data to Excel. Most of the vendors provide a version of their tool with a simplified user interface for report layout, aimed at business users who want to rapidly prototype rather than report developers who aim to be pixel-perfect. IT organizations appreciate how easy it is to turn a business user's analysis built in a conventional tool into a standard report.

Visualization tools are newer, but they've still been around for nearly a decade. Examples in this category include IBM (Cognos Insight), Tableau, and QlikView. These tools tend to have the words visual or insight (or both) in their names. The visualization tools provide a more bounded or guided user experience. This guided query experience makes it easier to color inside the lines, but harder to break out of the box. Of course, the visualization tools really shine when it comes to analysis, particularly graphical representation of data. Visualization tools retain a close link between display and the underlying query, so it's really easy for users to drill up, down, and across, and experiment with different presentation types such as spatial maps, animated time series, and heatmaps.

In my experience, the visualization tools do a better job of keeping the users inside the BI tool environment. With the conventional tools, there's a strong tendency to construct the query in the tool, then export to Excel for analysis and display. I love Excel as much as the next person, but it can be very difficult to reverse engineer what the analyst has done, if we want to productionalize that analysis.

Self-Service BI: It's Not Just a Tool

The BI tool vendors imply that if you buy their product, your business community will reap the benefits of self-service BI. There are many great BI tools out there; some of them are very fun to use, but don't kid yourself (or let the vendors kid you). There's a bunch of work that has to get done before your business users can leverage this fabulous capability. Don't let the effort stand in your way, but be realistic about how much work there is, and how much time and resources it'll take to deliver great self-service BI to your user community.

13.7 Leverage Data Visualization Tools, But Avoid Anarchy

Joy Mundy, Design Tip #162, *Jan 7, 2014*

The increasingly popular data visualization tools deliver an environment that business analysts love. They provide the ability to define calculations, and more importantly, to explore and experiment with the data. The products have finally innovated away from the old standbys of tables, bar charts, and pie charts, making it easier for users to draw visual insights from their data. Business users can even create nice dashboard elements with drill downs and interactivity to share with their colleagues.

I love these newly mainstream tools. If I were a business analyst, I'd relentlessly request a license purchase from my management. I'd promise a huge return on investment, and the odds are pretty good that I'd be able to deliver. From a user's perspective, one of the most valuable features of these tools is the ability to hook together disparate data, including data from outside the data warehouse or even outside the company. From the Cloud. From Google Analytics. From Excel.

However, if I were an IT person, I would be ambivalent. On the one hand: Give the users what they want. They can pull data from multiple sources, combine it as they wish, create their own analyses. The previous article 13.6, *Three Critical Components for Successful Self-Service BI,* moves from dream to reality. Hurray! On the other hand: anarchy. Each analyst creates her own data sets in the data visualization tool, naming elements as she wishes, burying transformations and calculations within tool-specific "code." It's stovepipe data marts or spreadmarts all over again. We end up with inconsistent definitions, inconsistent names, and inconsistent data moved and transformed multiple times the-same-but-different.

Stepping aside from the exciting analyst-geek perspective to the less fun auditing and compliance perspective, the sprinkling of constraints and integration logic deep within individual data visualization tools can turn into a nightmare. What if the analyst claims to demonstrate a $10 million profit opportunity from looking at the marketplace through a half dozen data feeds stitched together with hand crafted integration rules in the data visualization tool? Are these integration rules documented? Where do you look in the tool to see what the analyst did? Are other analysts using exactly the same rules?

The salespeople from these data visualization tool vendors sell a dream to the business user. They tell users they don't need to wait for IT to build a star schema—you can hook the tool right up to the source system or operational data store and build your in-memory cube structure yourself (or maybe get some cheap consulting assistance for the geeky bits). And in the short to medium term, they're correct. But they don't talk about what this environment is going to look like in a year or two, when the user community's uncoordinated analytic demands are straining the IT infrastructure. Or when the users get tired of maintaining the baroque code underlying their mission-critical dashboard and try to pass it off to IT. Not to mention the multiple versions of the truth problem that is the inevitable consequence of such anarchy. Those of us who have been building data warehouses for a long time have seen this algae bloom of "desktop databases" several times, first with 4GL languages in the 1980s, then with the proliferation of data marts in the 1990s, and now again with the amazing power of the new data visualization tools. Let's be clear: We love the data visualization tools. We just want the business insights from these tools to be understandable, consistent, and trustworthy.

In some cases it may be possible to implement your entire BI solution in a data visualization tool, skipping the costly step of planning, designing, and building a data warehouse first. It is almost certainly not a good idea. A Kimball style data warehouse/business intelligence system is more than just star schemas. The most important component of the Kimball method is the focus on conformance: Let's all get together and agree on the names, definitions, and attribute change management techniques for every data element. Define it once, use a real ETL tool to plan and implement that data movement, and store that transformed data in a durable, manageable format (the data warehouse).

If anarchy isn't the answer, what does the Kimball Group recommend? First, find a place in your architecture for a data visualization tool. Your business users are going to want them, and if the IT organization doesn't plan an effective architecture, you will find an ineffective architecture evolving under your feet.

An effective architecture relies on a Kimball data warehouse, and the data management implied and required by conformed dimensions. The business users must agree to the concept of one name for one thing, and make that an integral part of the way they communicate and do business. This is a business problem, not an IT problem, though IT should advocate for and enable effective data management. With any kind of self-service BI, it's not possible to forbid users to change the name or calculation of an object once it's in their analysis, so we need to help them understand why they shouldn't.

With a well designed and implemented Kimball data warehouse in place, business users can hook the data visualization tools directly to the relational data warehouse, or to centrally managed cubes. The tools will be used primarily as the label implies: for analysis and visualization. Some users will need to bring in external data—there's always something that hasn't yet been acquired by the central data warehouse—but it should be at the periphery. IT needs to maintain good communication with the users to see the external data they're using, and evaluate whether it should be acquired centrally. Similarly, it will be appropriate to promote some calculations defined by the users into a centrally managed cube or semantic layer.

If your data warehouse is planned but not yet live, you may need to support interim use against an operational data store or even the source system. It'll work better in the long run if you're proactively helping the user community use the visualization tools effectively. By creating a partnership, you'll gain insight into how they're using the tools. You may even gain some influence over what they do and how they do it. You should be very clear that anything done directly against a source system or ODS is a candidate for re-factoring against a data warehouse once it's available.

Finally, there are organizations that don't have a data warehouse, aren't planning to build one, aren't working on data management, or have an antagonistic rather than collaborative relationship between IT and the users. If this describes your organization, self-service BI anarchy may be an inevitable outcome.

13.8 Think Like a Software Development Manager

Warren Thornthwaite, Design Tip #96, Oct 31, 2007

For most organizations, the vast majority of users access the DW/BI system through the BI applications, including standard reports, analytic applications, dashboards, and operational BI; all these applications provide a more structured, parameter-driven, relatively simple means for people to find the information they need. The BI applications are the final product of the DW/BI system; they must be valuable, usable, functional, high quality, and perform well.

Most of these characteristics are formed in the BI application design and development process. Throughout application development, testing, documenting, and rollout, it is very helpful to pretend to be a professional development manager from a consumer software product company. Actually, it's not pretending. Real software development managers go through the same steps as the folks responsible for delivering the BI applications. The best software development managers have learned the same lessons:

- The project is 25 percent done when your developer gives you the first demonstration of the working application. The first demo from a proud developer is an important milestone that you should look forward to, but seasoned software development managers know that the developer has only passed the first unit test. The second 25 percent is making the application pass the complete system test, where all the units are working. The third 25 percent is validating and debugging the completed system in a simulated production environment. The final 25 percent is documenting and delivering the system into production.
- Don't believe developers who say their code is so beautiful that it is self-documenting. Every developer must stay on the project long enough to deliver complete, readable, high quality documentation. This is especially true for any interactions or algorithms that are directly exposed to the users.
- Use a bug tracking system. Set up a branch in your bug tracking or problem reporting system to capture every system crash, every incorrect result, and every suggestion. A manager should scan this system every day, assigning priorities to the various problems. An application cannot be released to the user community if there are any open priority 1 bug reports.
- Place a very high professional premium on testing and bug reporting. Establish bug finding awards. Have senior management praise these efforts. Make sure that the application developers are patient with business users and testers.
- Be proactive with the bug reports you collect from business users and testers. Acknowledge receipt of every reported bug, allow the users and testers to see what priority you have assigned to their reports and what the resolution status of their reports is, and then fix all the bugs.

These lessons are especially important in organizations with large user communities. The same is true when creating operational BI applications that will be used by a large number of operational users. You will probably not meet everyone individually in these user communities, so your product had better be great.

13.9 Standard Reports: Basics for Business Users

Joy Mundy and Warren Thornthwaite, Intelligent Enterprise, Feb 1, 2006

Business people should be eager to dive in and explore the data that represents their business. After all, who knows better what information is needed? Unfortunately, few business people seem to agree. Consider yourself lucky if 10 percent of your users actually build their own reports from scratch. As for the other 90 percent of the user community, it's up to the DW/BI team to provide an easier way to access the data. Here's a process for designing a starter set of BI application standard reports.

What Are BI Applications?

There's no commonly accepted definition of BI or a BI application, so we're offering our own: BI applications are the delivery vehicles of business intelligence—the reports and analyses that provide usable information to the business. BI applications include a broad spectrum of reports and analyses, ranging from simple fixed-format reports to sophisticated analytics with complex embedded algorithms and domain expertise. It helps to divide this spectrum based on the level of sophistication. We call the simple side *standard* reports and the complex side *analytic applications*.

It's possible to build BI applications without the benefit of a data warehouse, but this rarely happens. A well-built data warehouse adds value through the dimensional model and ETL process, so it makes no sense to replicate this effort to build a standalone BI application. Most successful BI applications are an integral part of the user-facing portion of the data warehouse.

Standard reports usually have a fixed format, are parameter driven and, in their simplest form, are pre-run. Standard reports provide a core set of information about what's going on in a particular business area—sounds dull, but these reports are the backbone of BI applications. Examples from different industries include year-to-date sales versus forecast by sales rep, monthly churn rate by service plan, and direct mail response rates by promotion by product.

The standard reporting system consists of several technology components. You must have a tool for the report designer, either someone in IT or a skilled business user, to define reports. You need management services for report storage, execution, and security. Finally, your reporting system should have a navigation portal that helps users find the report they want.

Analytic applications are more complex than standard reports. They center on a specific business process and encapsulate domain expertise about how to analyze and interpret that process. They may include complex algorithms or data mining models. Some analytic applications give users the advanced capability to feed changes back into the transaction systems based on insights gained using the application; some are sold as black box or hosted systems. Common examples of analytic applications include budgeting and forecasting systems, promotion effectiveness and category management applications, fraud detection, and web path analysis.

Build versus Buy

Most organizations build their own standard report set, using a purchased reporting tool to design and publish the reports on the corporate intranet, usually in an accompanying reporting portal. There are many popular tools that make it easy to define and publish reports and to customize the bundled portal.

The build versus buy decision for analytic applications is more complex. The market for packaged applications is growing both in quantity and quality, and it's increasingly common for organizations to buy them. However, almost every implementation of a packaged analytic application requires significantly more customization than is required for a prebuilt transaction system. Evaluate a packaged application for its flexibility and ease of customization. Is it based on a well-designed dimensional model? If so, it might be relatively easy to map your data model to that of the application. If the data model is tightly tied to the application itself, implementation may require significant effort, even if the application is sourced from your dimensional data warehouse.

Some organizations still build custom analytic applications, using a combination of standard tools and custom code to capture and apply best practice business rules. Organizations with particular expertise in analyzing their business processes or that have unusual systems and business models are more likely to build their own analytic applications.

Designing the Reporting System

You can't build reports until you near the deployment of the DW/BI project, but you can and should start the design process much earlier. As soon as you've finished interviewing business users about their information and analytic requirements, you can create the report specifications—the longer you wait, the harder it will be to remember the details. This step includes the following tasks:

- **Create the target report list.** It's important to deliver value to business users as quickly as possible; don't wait for hundreds of reports to be developed and tested before letting users into the system. Identify 10 to 15 reports you'll create for the first round.

  The best way to create the target report list is to start with a full list of candidate reports by reviewing the business requirements for every information request, desire, or fantasy that anyone expressed. Give each report a name and description, and on a scale of one to 10, rate its business value and the effort it will take to build.

  Once you have a complete list of candidates, prioritize them, group related reports, and review the priorities with a small group of competent, interested business users. Negotiate a cutoff point for the initial delivery at 10 to 15 reports. Remind users that many of the lower priority reports can be handed off to the departmental experts who were most interested in them.

- **Create the standard template.** Think of the reporting system as a publication and yourself as the editor. To communicate effectively, you need consistent format and content standards. Create a template identifying the standard elements that will appear on every report, as shown in the report mockup in Figure 13-2. The basics include:

  - Report name and title
  - Report body:

    - Data justification, data precision, and data format
    - Column and row heading format
    - Background fills and colors
    - Formatting of totals and subtotals

  - Header and footer:

    - Report name and navigation category
    - Report run date and time
    - Data source(s) and parameters used

- Report notes, including important exceptions, such as "excludes intracompany sales"
- Page numbering
- Confidentiality statement
- DW/BI reference (name and logo of the DW/BI system)
- Report file name

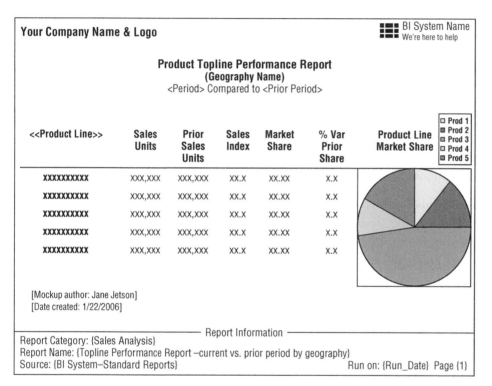

Figure 13-2: A sample report mockup.

Not all report information is displayed on the report itself. Use a specification document or repository to collect the following report metadata:

- User variables and other user interactions, such as drill downs
- Report calculations, derivations, author, and date created
- Security requirements
- Execution cycle or trigger event, if the report runs automatically
- Delivery mechanisms, such as email, website, file directory, or printer
- Standard output format, such as HTML, PDF, or Excel
- Page orientation, size and margin settings

- **Create report specifications and documentation.** For each report on the target list, create a specification that includes the following components:

  - Report template information as outlined earlier
  - Report mockup
  - User interaction list
  - Detailed documentation

  Report mockups are a great way to communicate the content and purpose of the reports. Use symbols to denote functions, such as:

  < > to indicate a user-entered variable
  < < > > to indicate a drillable field
  {} to indicate an application-entered variable
  \\ \\ to indicate a link to another report or documentation source
  ( ) to indicate a page or section break field
  [ ] to indicate report template comments

  The function symbols tell you what kind of interaction is possible, but they don't specify how that interaction works. Create a user interaction list to identify the nature and degree of interaction a user may have with each report, including variable specification, pick list descriptions, drill down, and field addition or replacement.

  Document required information not directly associated with the report display, such as the report category, sources of the data, calculations for each column and row, and any exceptions or exclusions to build into the query. You can append this document to the user interaction list.

  The mockup, user interaction list, and additional documentation must provide enough information so that a developer can build the report.

- **Design the navigation framework.** Once you know which reports to build, categorize them. This structure should enable anyone who knows something about your business to find what they want quickly. The best approach is to organize the reports by business process, just like the data warehouse bus matrix. This navigation framework is the primary entry point into the BI system, which we call the BI portal.

- **Conduct a user review.** Review the report specifications with the business community to:

  - Validate the choice of high priority reports and test the clarity of the specifications.
  - Validate the navigation hierarchies in the BI portal.
  - Involve users in the process, emphasizing their roles and developing their commitment.
  - Give users a sense of what will be possible in just a few months' time.

Once the specs have been reviewed, you can put them on the shelf until it's time to develop the reports. They'll be useful if you evaluate front end tools, as the candidates should be able to easily handle the range of reports in the initial report set.

In a Nutshell

BI applications, whether standard reports or advanced analytic applications, are typically the only access to your DW/BI system for 90 percent of business users. Standard reports are the backbone of the system, so you need to do a great job designing them and creating a navigation framework. Do this work early in the project, when business users' requirements are fresh in your mind.

When the hard work of building and populating the data warehouse nears completion, it's time to think about the BI applications again. That's when you'll pull your target list specs off the shelf and build the standard reports and BI portal, including plans for maintaining, extending, securing, and tuning the reports.

QUICK STUDY

It is common for a DW/BI team to replicate a set of reports from an old system into the new reporting environment. Although this may be necessary and justified because it will let you turn off the old environment, the replication of existing reports rarely brings much perceived value. All you are giving users is what they already had. It is also risky since the old reports often have embedded business rules that are complex and undocumented. Accurately replicating reports will be much harder than you think.

If you must replicate a set of existing reports, work with your business users to identify the most important legacy reports, but also incorporate new reports into the release that stimulate interest and offer more business value.

13.10 Building and Delivering BI Reports

Warren Thornthwaite, Intelligent Enterprise, *Apr 1, 2006*

In article 13.9, *Standard Reports: Basics for Business Users*, we laid out a process for identifying, prioritizing, and specifying the core set of BI standard reports. In this article, we describe the BI application development tasks that begin much later in the project lifecycle, once real data is available in its final dimensional structure and the BI tool has been selected.

Set Up Development

It's hard to resist the temptation to dive in and start building reports once real data is available. Be strong! Take a few days to set up your reporting environment. If this is the first time you're using your front end tool, be warned that installation and configuration can take more work than you might expect. Many reporting environments have several components, including developer tools, report viewers, an administrator tool, and a report server. Adding to the complexity, the report server often works best when installed on its own machine and usually must work closely with a web server. In some cases, the report server needs a database or file directory to hold metadata about reports, schedules, events and distribution lists; make sure you include this database in a regular backup routine. Depending on the size and complexity of your BI environment, you may want to set up a separate test report server to support the testing process.

The best practice for new ETL projects is to develop them against a test system to protect the production environment from problems such as table locks and disappearing data. In the BI report development process, on the other hand, it usually makes sense to develop reports directly against the production DW/BI database. The risk of a negative impact on the production system is relatively small. Reports are read-only and are generally similar to any other ad hoc usage of the database. If the DW/BI database is designed to support ad hoc queries, it should support report development. Building reports against the production database gives you an early opportunity to assess performance and validate the reports. It also makes it easier to move the reports into production, since they already point at the production database.

In addition to installing the tool components, you may need to take other steps before you can get started. Some front end tools may require you to define the metadata layer that insulates users from the database, set up delivery and notification metadata and processes, and a usage tracking system.

Create the Reports

Figuring out which report to start with is easy, if you've done your homework. The specifications from the BI application design phase include a prioritized list of the standard reports, along with mockups and documentation on the definitions and contents of the reports.

The first step in creating the report is to define the query (or queries) that populate the contents of the report. Report specs often require user-provided query constraints, most of which should leverage the pick lists and parameters already included in your standard template. In some cases, the report may require multiple data sets. For example, you may have revenue data in one fact table and costs in another. To show product profit contribution, you may need two separate queries to combine these two sources.

Once the data set is defined, the next step is to lay out the report contents according to the specifications. That means deciding what goes into the rows and columns, what calculations will take place in the report, and how the report should be formatted. Getting the report exactly right takes a lot longer than you might expect. Make sure you preview the report in all its possible delivery forms such as spreadsheet, PDF, web, email, and print.

The guiding philosophy in formatting reports is that they should be as clear and self-explanatory as possible. Users will not take the time to look elsewhere for report documentation, nor should they be expected to. Clarity is one of the major challenges the DW/BI team takes on when they include standard reports as part of their responsibilities. It's helpful to involve someone with solid graphic design expertise while designing the template and initial report set. Experiment with alternatives and get feedback from users as to which one works best. A bit of extra work at this point will pay off massively in the long run.

Test Accuracy and Performance

The development process includes testing various combinations of parameters and ensuring the report returns appropriate results. Test the contents of the report to make sure the calculations and constraints are correct. Check the numbers as carefully as possible, comparing them to any known alternative sources for the same information. If the numbers should be the same and aren't, figure out why. If the numbers are supposed to be different because they have been improved or corrected in the ETL process, carefully document the reasons for the differences. If possible, show how a user or auditor can get from the data warehouse numbers back to the original source numbers. This documentation should be available in the BI portal, and the report description should refer to it.

In large organizations, with hundreds or thousands of users pounding on the standard report set, it makes sense to deploy the reports to a test server environment that is as similar to the production environment as possible. A test server lets the reporting team stress test the new reports to ensure they don't reduce the performance of other reports before moving them into production. In midsize and smaller organizations, you may not need a full test server environment. The reporting team could deploy the reports to the production report server and test them there. You can minimize the risk by limiting access to the test report directories and by not publishing the new reports in the BI portal until testing is completed.

There are several testing steps, starting with deploying the project to the test or production report server. Next, the reports need to be reviewed to ensure proper display and printing. If they are not working as expected, try performance enhancement techniques such as tuning the query, creating report snapshots, or changing the server configurations. Carefully retest, because reports are the only experience most users have with the DW/BI system; they'd better work and they better be right.

Deploy to Production

The next step is to integrate the new reports into the production process. The report specifications should indicate whether the report is executed on demand or cached on a time-based or event-based schedule. Exactly how you set up these procedures depends on your report operations environment. As part of the deployment process, you should develop instructions on how the system should distribute the report: caching the results to quickly serve future requests, emailing the report to a distribution list, or saving the report to the file system or database. You may need to set up a subscription process to let users select reports they would like to receive on a regular basis. If you are providing reports through a BI portal, you'll need to integrate this new set of reports into the portal as part of the production deployment.

Whenever there's a deployment to the production server, you'll need to repeat many of the steps you went through to move the reports into test, including schedules, snapshots, subscriptions, and email distribution lists. However, in most cases, the deployment to production took place in the test step, so this step is more of an unveiling, especially when the primary report interface is through a website or portal. For this situation, deployment is a matter of changing the security settings to make the reports accessible through the portal.

Manage and Maintain

Once BI applications are in use, the DW/BI team must keep them current and in good working order. Individual reports often go stale as the business evolves. The reports created to track a new product are no longer interesting once the product has been discontinued. Reports may fail for technical reasons; for example, you may make enhancements to a database that causes a report to fail but not realize it unless you are monitoring the report server logs and regularly inspecting the results.

The DW/BI team must add and delete data-driven subscriptions that involve individual users and email lists as people come and go. The same goes for other distribution mechanisms, such as file shares. Computers and networks change. The accounting department may have requested a set of reports distributed to its file server. Then it gets a new file server and turns off the old one without telling you, so you have a group of users not receiving their requested reports.

Extend the Applications

The DW/BI team also must provide ongoing report development resources expecting that the initial reports and BI applications for a new business process will soon be modified and augmented. Users don't always know what reports and analyses they want until you show them something close. Then they'll tell you what they don't want—the report you just created—and hopefully give you clearer guidance about what they now think they need.

Data mining applications and other closed-loop systems are seldom implemented in the first phase of a DW/BI system (unless they generate the return in the return on investment analysis). The process of developing a closed-loop BI system requires close partnership between the business people, who can effectively develop the business rules and analytic models, and the DW/BI team, who will write the system specifications and formalize the models. The majority of the application development effort requires a standard skill set, which is often met by the same developers who work on the operational systems. The developer needs a relatively small amount of specialized knowledge, the object model for the data mining system, to implement the calls into the databases or data mining model.

Every 12 to 18 months, review the entire business intelligence system. Evaluate what's working well for users and what should change. Remember, change is inevitable and is a sign of a healthy system. As part of this periodic evaluation, consider refreshing the look, layout, and content of the BI portal.

QUICK STUDY

If you have users who know the front end tool or are capable of learning it quickly, the BI application development process is a great opportunity to get them directly involved in the DW/BI system implementation. There are several good reasons to get key users to participate. First, it gives these users an opportunity to learn the tools, techniques, and data as early as possible. Second, working together helps build stronger relationships, especially if you physically bring the group together. If it's at all possible, set up a development lab with as many workstations as you need. Schedule a week or two for the group to meet daily for a half day (or all day if your organization can handle it). Bring food and maybe even some kind of gift to show your appreciation. The early involvement of these key users emphasizes their special status and it builds their ownership of the reports and the overall DW/BI system.

13.11 The BI Portal

Warren Thornthwaite, Design Tip #58, Aug 26, 2004

The success of a DW/BI system depends on whether or not the organization gets value out of it. Obviously, people have to use the environment for the organization to realize value. Since the BI portal is the primary point of interaction (the only interaction in many cases), the BI team needs to ensure it's a positive experience.

Too often, BI portal home pages focus largely on the history of the data warehouse, the current status of the load process, or who's on the data warehouse team. These are interesting bits of information, but typically not what BI users are looking for. The BI portal is the user interface to the data warehouse. It must be designed with the user community's needs foremost in mind. There are two basic web design concepts that help: density and structure.

Density

The human mind can take in an incredible amount of information. The human eye is able to resolve images at a resolution of about 530 pixels per inch at a distance of 20 inches (Roger N. Clark, http://www.clarkvision.com/articles/human-eye/index.html). Compare this with the paltry 72 pixels per inch resolution of the typical computer screen. Our brains rapidly process information looking for the relevant elements. This combination of visual acuity and mental capacity is what kept our ancestors from being removed from the gene pool by various threats; from predators to low hanging branches to a knife in a bar fight. The browser gives us such a low resolution platform that we have to use it as carefully and efficiently as possible. This means we should fill the BI portal pages with as much information as possible. But we can't just load it with hundreds of unordered descriptions and links.

Structure

Our brains can handle all this information only if it is accompanied by an organizing structure. Since the primary reason users come to the BI portal is to find information, a great percentage of the home page should be dedicated to categorizing standardized reports and analyses in a way that makes sense to people. Generally we've found the best way to organize the BI portal is around the organization's core business processes. The business process categories allow users to quickly identify the relevant choice. Within each category, there are detailed subcategories, allowing users to quickly parse through the home page to find information that is interesting to them.

For example, a website for a university DW/BI system might have the following report (business process) groupings on its home page:

> Admissions
> Employee Tracking
> Finance
> Alumni Development
> Enrollment
> Research Grants

Each of these might link to another page that provides additional descriptions and links to pages with reports on them. We can increase the information density by pulling some of the lower level categories up to the home page:

> Admissions: Applications Stats, Offers and Acceptances, Financial Aid
> Employee Tracking: Headcount, Benefits, Affirmative Action
> Enrollment: Registration, Instructors & Classes, Degrees & Majors

Increasing the density in this manner helps define each category and refine the choices before the user has to click. One way to test your BI portal home page is to measure the percentage of the visible page (full screen browser on an average sized monitor) dedicated to providing users with access to information. It should be at least 50 percent. Some information design folks believe the target should be closer to 90 percent "substance."

More Structure and Content

Categories help structure the content, but the website needs a physical structure as well. The website needs to have a standard look and feel, typically based on the organization's overall page layout, so people can navigate the site with ease.

Although the main point of the BI portal is to provide access to the standardized reports, it must offer much more than just reports. In addition to the categories and reports lists, we need to provide access to a whole range of tools and information, including:

- Search tool that indexes every report, document, and page on the BI website
- Metadata browser
- Online training, tutorials, example reports, and help pages
- Help request system and contact information
- Status, notices, surveys, installs, and other administrative info
- Perhaps a support-oriented news/discussion group
- Personalization capabilities that allow users to save reports or report links to their own page

This information all goes in the lower-right corner, the least valuable real estate on the screen (at least in English where we read from left to right and top to bottom).

Building an effective BI portal is an incredible amount of work, but it is a key link in the data warehouse value chain. Every word, header, description, function, and link included on the portal needs to communicate the underlying DW/BI content. You should do a design review and test the BI portal with users, asking them to find certain reports and other information. Make sure you don't build a weak link.

13.12 Dashboards Done Right

Margy Ross, Design Tip #88, Feb 21, 2007

With their graphically appealing user interfaces, dashboards and their scorecard cousins are demonstration superstars. Dashboards have grabbed the attention of senior management because they closely align with the way these people operate. What's not to like about the promise of performance feedback on every customer or supplier-facing process in the organization at a glance? It's no wonder execs are enthused.

But there's a dark side to dashboard projects. They're extremely vulnerable to runaway expectations. They're risky due to the cross-organizational perspective inherent in most dashboard designs. And they can be a distraction to the DW/BI team; rather than focusing on the development of an extensible infrastructure, dashboard projects often encourage a data triage where key performance indicators from a multitude of processes are plucked and then pieced together using the systems equivalent of chewing gum and duct tape.

Dashboards and scorecards done right are layered on a solid foundation of detailed integrated data. Anything less is ill advised. Dashboards based on manually collected, pre-aggregated, standalone subsets of data are unsustainable in the long run.

If you have an existing data warehouse that's populated with the requisite detailed, integrated data, you should tackle the proposed dashboard development project with gusto. Dashboards present a tangible opportunity to deliver on the promise of business value derived from your data warehouse. The dashboard interface appeals to a much broader set of users than traditional data access tools. In addition, dashboards provide a vehicle for going beyond rudimentary, static reporting to more sophisticated, guided analytics.

But what do you do when your executives are clamoring for a sexy dashboard, but there's no existing foundation that can be reasonably leveraged? Facing a similar predicament, some of you have bootstrapped the dashboard development effort. And it may have been initially perceived as a success. But then middle managers start calling because their bosses are monitoring performance via the dashboard, yet there's no ability for them to drill into the details where the true causal factors of a performance problem are lurking. Or management starts to question the validity of the dashboard data because it doesn't tie to other reports due to inconsistent transformation/business rules. Or the users determine they need the dashboard updated more frequently. Or your counterpart who supports another area of the business launches a separate, similar but different dashboard initiative. The bootstrapped dashboard will be seriously, potentially fatally, stressed from the consequences of bypassing the development of an appropriate infrastructure. Eventually you'll need to pay the price and rework the initiative.

While it's perhaps less politically attractive at first, a more sustainable approach would be to deliver the detailed data, one business process at a time, tied together with conformed dimensions. As the underlying details become available, the dashboard would be incrementally embellished to provide access to each deployment of additional information. We understand this approach doesn't deliver the immediate "wow" factor and requires executive patience. While executives may not naturally exhibit a high degree of patience, most are also reluctant to throw away money on inevitable rework caused by taking too many shortcuts. Having an honest conversation with business and/or IT management so they fully understand the limitations and pitfalls of the quick and dirty dashboard may result in staunch converts to the steadier, more sustainable approach.

Those of us longer in the tooth remember the executive information systems (EIS) that blossomed briefly in the 1980s. EIS suffered from exactly the same problem we are discussing here. The carefully prepared executive KPIs were not supported by solid detailed data that could withstand drill down. Any good executive is going to ask "why?" And that's when the data warehouse and its dashboards need to sit on a solid foundation.

13.13 Don't Be Overly Reliant on Your Data Access Tool's Metadata

Bob Becker, Design Tip #44, Mar 14, 2003

"Oh, we'll handle that in the front end tool" is the refrain we sometimes hear from data warehouse designers. Instead, whenever possible, we suggest you invest the effort to architect as much flexibility, richness, and descriptive information directly into your dimensional schemas as possible rather than leaning on the capabilities of the tool's metadata as a crutch.

Today's business intelligence tools provide robust metadata to support a wide range of capabilities, such as label substitution, predefined calculations, and aggregate navigation. These are useful features for your business community. But we need to be judicious in the use of features the tools provide. Too often design teams take shortcuts and rely on the data access tool metadata to resolve issues that are better handled in dimensional models. The end result is business rules that become embedded in the tool metadata rather than in schemas. We also see design teams utilize tool metadata to provide code lookups and indicator descriptors in a misguided effort to keep their schema smaller and tighter.

The biggest drawback to these shortcuts is the dependence on the front end tool metadata to enforce business rules. If we rely on the tool metadata to implement business rules, every user must access the data via the supported tool to guarantee business users are presented with "correct" data. Users that want or need to use another access method are forced to precisely re-create the business rules buried in the tool's metadata to be assured of consistent results.

As data warehouse developers, we need to protect against situations where business users might see different results depending on the tool they elect to use. Regardless of how they access the data warehouse data, users should get the same high quality, consistent data.

You may be thinking, "Fine, then we'll force all users to access the data warehouse through our supported tool." However, this approach will inevitably fall apart. There are a number of reasons an individual may need to access the data warehouse through some other means, bypassing the supported tool and therefore any business rules enforced via its metadata. These scenarios may not exist in your organization at the time you are developing your schema, but rest assured that one of them will arise during your watch:

- An IT professional (perhaps you) may elect to use SQL directly against the data warehouse data to resolve a complex query or audit data.
- Your organization may develop analytic applications based on custom-written SQL-based queries directly against the data warehouse.
- Statistical modeling tools and/or data mining tools may need to directly access the data warehouse data.
- A sophisticated user armed with Microsoft Access (or another non-supported tool) may be granted direct access to the data warehouse.
- There may become a need to supplement the data warehouse with OLAP cubes drawn directly from the data warehouse.
- Your organization may select another user tool, yet not replace the current tool.

None of this should be construed as an argument against leveraging the capabilities of your data access tool. Rather the key is that when in doubt or confronted with a choice, we prefer the design choice that places a capability as close to the data as possible to assure that the capability is available to as wide an audience as possible.

13.14 Making Sense of the Semantic Layer

Joy Mundy, Design Tip #158, Aug 5, 2013

One of the key components of the business intelligence architecture is a semantic layer. The semantic layer provides a translation of the underlying database structures into business user oriented terms and constructs. It is usually part and parcel of the query and reporting tool. OLAP or cube databases also include a BI semantic layer.

Some BI layers are microscopically thin, others are rich and robust. The very minimum functionality that would qualify as a semantic layer includes:

- **An organizing structure that presents the data elements in a way that's intuitive to business people.** In most tools, you will organize tables and columns in folder structures. The Kimball method tells you to dimensionally structure your data warehouse, which sets you miles ahead of those who try to deliver BI directly on top of transactional database structures. But even if you're working atop a clean dimensional model, a semantic layer will provide opportunities to improve navigability and find-ability.
- **An opportunity to rename data elements so they make sense to the business users.** Of course, the Kimball method strongly recommends that the data warehouse tables and columns be named as the users would like to see them, but this functionality is sometimes implemented in the semantic layer.
- **An interface to hold business-oriented descriptions of data elements.** Ideally, you'd store and expose multiple flavors of metadata: business description, example values, and dimension attribute change policy. In a perfect world, the BI semantic layer would expose the full lineage of each data element: which transaction system data element was the source, which ETL jobs touched this attribute, and when was it loaded into the data warehouse. Realistically, few semantic layers support more than a single description for each data element. In my experience, most DW/BI teams don't even bother to populate that single description.
- **A mechanism to define calculations and aggregation rules.** For example, you might define in the semantic model that inventory balances are additive across most dimensions, but when aggregating across time, you want to take the period ending balance or divide the sum of the balances by the number of time periods.

Is the semantic layer a mandatory component of a DW/BI architecture? The answer is yes, if you plan to open the doors to your DW/BI system for ad hoc use. Every hour you spend on building a rich semantic layer will pay off in improved adoption and success in the user community. Don't simply run the wizard for your BI tool and generate a semantic layer that's equivalent to the underlying tables (even if they're dimensional). Spend the time to make it as rational and polished as you can.

The downside of investing in a semantic layer is that you can expect to make that investment multiple times. Most organizations find they need several BI tools to meet the diverse needs of their user communities. Each tool has its own semantic layer, which can seldom be copied from one tool to another (even tools sold by the same vendor). One of the many challenges for the BI team is to keep a similar look and organizational structure across the BI tools. Once again, the Kimball method's focus on getting the relational dimensional data model right will considerably ease that task by slimming down the BI tools' semantic layers, as discussed in article 13.13, *Don't Be Overly Reliant on Your Data Access Tool's Metadata*.

There's only one scenario where I might buy the argument that you can get away without a semantic layer. If the doors to your DW/BI system are closed to all ad hoc users, and all access is mediated by professional report developers, you can make it work without a BI semantic layer. This is a lukewarm recommendation on several fronts. Most importantly, how can you close the doors to ad hoc users? That's crazy. Additionally, developers are people too and even if they can write SQL by hand and look up definitions in an external data dictionary, why torture them?

If you buy the argument that you need a semantic layer, your next question may be whether you need a dimensional data warehouse. Some observers, especially some BI tool vendors, argue that you can skip the relational data warehouse and deliver the dimensional experience virtually. This sounds appealing—no one really wants to build an ETL system—but it's a chimera. No semantic layer tool provides the transformation and integration functionality of an ETL tool. Most BI tools are great at what they do; don't break them by attempting to do ETL in the semantic layer. And don't forget that the ETL back room adds value to the data by cleaning, standardizing, conforming, and deduplicating, all steps that a BI tool cannot do.

That said, I have worked with clients who have succeeded in hooking up a BI tool directly to the normalized (transactional or ODS) data model. The most common scenario is a prototype: let's show people what a Business Objects universe or Tableau interface might look like to generate excitement and financial support for an enterprise data warehouse. Another scenario is to meet operational reporting requirements by building a semantic layer atop the transaction system. But in most cases, this operational semantic layer is a relatively minor component of an enterprise analytic environment that includes a real data warehouse. I'm immediately skeptical of any organization that claims its transaction systems are sufficiently clean, and analytic needs simple enough, that they don't need to instantiate their dimensional models. I'm not opposed to the idea in theory, but in practice I still don't see it working.

I don't think I've ever seen an organization over-invest in a semantic layer, but I've seen lots of data warehouses fail because of under-investment. Buy a decent BI tool (there are dozens), and spend time developing the semantic layer. Otherwise you're selling short your very substantial investment in design and development of a technically solid data warehouse.

Mining Data to Uncover Relationships

The four articles in this section do a deep dive into data mining, starting with what it is, to the implications on data warehouse design, and recommendations on a business-centric approach to help DW/BI teams get started with data mining.

13.15 Digging into Data Mining

Ralph Kimball, DBMS, Oct 1997

Data mining is one of the hottest topics in data warehousing. Virtually every IT organization believes that data mining is part of its future and that it is somehow linked to the investment the organization has already made in the data warehouse. But behind all of the excitement is a lot of confusion. Just exactly what is data mining? Is data mining just a generic name for analyzing my data, or do I need special tools and special knowledge in order to do it? Is data mining a coherent body of knowledge or is it an eclectic set of incompatible techniques? Once I have a basic understanding of data mining, can I automatically use my data warehouse to mine my data or do I have to perform yet another extraction to a special platform?

In this article, I define the main categories of data mining; in article 13.16, *Preparing for Data Mining*, I show what transformations need to be done on your data warehouse data to make it ready for data mining.

Before descending into the details, let's paint the big picture:

- Data mining is a collection of powerful analysis techniques for making sense out of very large data sets. In the right situations, data mining can be extraordinarily valuable.
- There is no one data mining approach, but rather a set of techniques that often can be used in combination with each other to extract the most insight from your data. If you invest in data mining, you will probably end up with several data mining tools from several different vendors.
- Each data mining tool can be viewed logically as an application that is a client of the data warehouse. Like a query tool or report writer, the data mining tool often sits on a separate machine, or in a separate process, requesting data from the data warehouse, and occasionally using the data warehouse as a convenient resource to house and store results from running the data mining tool.
- An interesting growth area for RDBMSs and proprietary OLAP systems is to physically embed data mining capabilities deeply within their engines to improve the efficiencies of data access and offer useful analytic extensions on top of their base product capabilities.

The Roots of Data Mining

Although the marketplace for data mining currently features a host of new products and companies, the underlying subject matter has a rich tradition of research and practice that goes back at least 50 years. The first name for data mining, beginning in the 1960s, was *statistical analysis*. The pioneers of statistical analysis, in my opinion, were SAS, SPSS, and IBM. Originally, statistical analysis consisted of classic statistical routines such as correlation, regression, chi-square, and cross tabulation. SAS and SPSS in particular still offer these classical approaches, but they, and data mining in general, have moved beyond these statistical measures to more insightful approaches that try to explain or predict what is going on in the data.

In the late 1980s, classical statistical analysis was augmented with a more eclectic set of techniques with names such as fuzzy logic, heuristic reasoning, and neural networks. This was the heyday of artificial intelligence (AI). Although perhaps a harsh indictment, we should admit that AI was a failure as packaged and sold in the 1980s. Far too much was promised. The successes of AI turned out to be limited to special problem domains and often required a complicated investment to encode a human expert's knowledge into the system. And perhaps most seriously, AI forever remained a black box to which most of us normal IT people couldn't relate. Try selling the CEO on an expensive package that performs "fuzzy logic."

Now in the late 1990s, we have learned how to take the best approaches from classical statistical analysis, neural networks, decision trees, market basket analysis, and other powerful techniques, and package and talk about them in a much more compelling and effective way. Additionally, I believe that the arrival of serious data warehouse systems is the necessary ingredient that has made data mining real and actionable.

The Categories of Data Mining

The best way to talk about data mining is to talk about what it does. A useful breakdown of data mining activities includes: clustering, classifying, estimating and predicting, and affinity grouping. For the discussion of this taxonomy, I am indebted to Michael Berry and Gordon Linoff for their series of books from Wiley Publishing on data mining. See especially their book *Data Mining Techniques, The Art and Science of Customer Relationship Management* (Wiley, 2011).

An example of *clustering* is looking through a large number of initially undifferentiated customers and trying to see if they fall into natural groupings. This is a pure example of "undirected data mining" where the user has no preordained agenda and is hoping that the data mining tool will reveal some meaningful structure. The input records to this clustering exercise ideally should be high quality verbose descriptions of each customer with both demographic and behavioral indicators attached to each record. Clustering algorithms work well with all kinds of data, including categorical, numerical, and textual data. It is not even necessary to identify inputs and outputs at the start of the job run. Usually the only decision the user must make is to ask for a specific number of candidate clusters. In our example, the clustering algorithm will find the best partitioning of all the customer records and will provide descriptions of the "centroid" of each cluster in terms of the user's original data. In many cases, these clusters have an obvious interpretation that provides insight into the customer base. Specific techniques that can be used for clustering include standard statistics, memory-based reasoning, neural networks, and decision trees.

An example of *classifying* is to examine a candidate customer and assign that customer to a pre-determined cluster or classification. Another example of classifying is medical diagnosis. In both cases, a verbose description of the customer or patient is fed into the classification algorithm. The classifier determines to which cluster centroid the candidate customer or patient is nearest or most similar. Viewed in this way, we see that the previous activity of clustering may well be a natural first step that is followed by the activity of classifying. Classifying in the most general sense is immensely useful in many data warehouse environments. A classification is a decision. We may be classifying customers as credit worthy or credit unworthy, or we may be classifying patients as either needing or not needing treatment. Techniques that can be used for classifying include standard statistics, memory-based reasoning, genetic algorithms, link analysis, decision trees, and neural networks.

Estimating and *predicting* are two similar activities that normally yield a numerical measure as the result. For example, we may find a set of existing customers that have the same profile as a candidate customer. From the set of existing customers we may estimate the overall indebtedness of the candidate customer. Prediction is the same as estimation except that we are trying to determine a result that will occur in a future time. Estimation and prediction can also drive classification. For instance, we may decide that all customers with more than $100,000 of indebtedness are to be classified as poor credit risks. Numerical estimates have the additional advantage that the candidates can be rank ordered. We may have enough money in an advertising budget to send promotion offers to the top 10,000 customers ranked by an estimate of their future value to the company. In this case, an estimate is more useful than a simple binary classification. Specific techniques that can be used for estimating and predicting include standard statistics and neural networks for numerical variables, as well as all the techniques described for classifying when only predicting a discrete outcome.

Affinity grouping is a special kind of clustering that identifies events or transactions that occur simultaneously. A well-known example of affinity grouping is market basket analysis. Market basket analysis attempts to understand what items are sold together at the same time. This is a hard problem from a data processing point of view because in a typical retail environment there are thousands of different products. It is pointless to enumerate all the combinations of items sold together because the list quickly reaches astronomical proportions. The art of market basket analysis is to find the *meaningful* combinations of different levels in the item hierarchy that are sold together. For instance, it may be most meaningful to discover that the individual item "Coca Cola 12 oz." is very frequently sold with the "Frozen Pasta Dinners" category. Specific techniques that can be used for affinity grouping include standard statistics, memory-based reasoning, link analysis, and special-purpose market basket analysis tools.

13.16 Preparing for Data Mining

Ralph Kimball, DBMS, Nov 1997

In article 13.15, *Digging into Data Mining*, I discussed the most common set of data mining activities, including clustering, classification, predicting, and affinity grouping. I hope I whetted your appetite and you are anxious to begin doing some actual data mining. But are you ready? Does anything have to be done to your data, or can any data warehouse automatically be used for data mining? The answer is that often a significant amount of work needs to be done to prepare your data for data mining. In fact, you may spend more effort getting the data ready for data mining than you will spend actually doing the data mining. I explore many of the data transformations you will need to perform in this article.

General Data Transformations

There is a set of basic data transformations you are probably already doing if you have a data warehouse. You are performing these transformations in your ETL system that pulls data from your legacy system, and houses the data in the back room for cleaning and reformatting. The cleaned data is then exported from the back room into one or more of business process dimensional models. Although there may be many transformation steps in your data extract system, the ones of particular interest to data mining are:

- **Resolving inconsistent legacy data formats, such as ASCII and EBCDIC, and resolving inconsistent data encoding, geographic spellings, abbreviations, and punctuation.** I hope you are already cleaning your data at this level, because if you aren't, then you can't even ask for SQL groupings or produce simple reports with meaningful row and column headers.

- **Stripping out unwanted fields.** Legacy data contains many fields that are meaningless from an analysis point of view, such as version numbers and formatted production keys. If you haven't stripped these out, the data mining tool may waste cycles trying to find patterns in these fields or trying to correlate these fields to real data. A data mining tool may attempt to interpret these fields as measurements or magnitudes, especially if the fields are numeric.

- **Interpreting codes into text.** A classic form of data cleaning that should be done in all data warehouses is augmenting or replacing cryptic codes with textual equivalents written in recognizable words. These codes should already be in your dimension tables (not your fact tables) so that adding the explanatory text is an easy, graceful change to the dimension table.

- **Combining data from multiple sources under a common key.** I hope you have several rich sources of descriptions of your customers (or products or locations) and you are merging these data sources under a common enterprise-wide customer key in your ETL back room.

- **Finding fields that have been used for several different purposes in your legacy data, where you must interpret the field's value based on the context of the legacy record.** In some cases you may not even realize that you have a legacy field that is hiding multiple uses. Your data mining tool will almost certainly figure this out. Perhaps "go crazy" is a better description than "figure this out." A good way to find multiple used fields is to count and perhaps list all the distinct values residing in a field. My clients have been surprised many times by this exercise.

Transformations for All Forms of Data Mining

This group of data transformations may not be needed for standard reporting and analysis functions in a data warehouse but is required for just about every data mining application. Many of these transformations affect the numeric, additive facts in the central fact tables of your dimensional models:

- **Flag normal, abnormal, out of bounds, or impossible facts.** Marking measured facts with special flags may be extremely helpful. Some measured facts may be correct but highly unusual. Perhaps these facts are based on a small sample or a special circumstance. Other facts may be present in the data but must be regarded as impossible or unexplainable. For each of these circumstances, it is better to mark the data with a status flag so that it can be optionally constrained into or out of the analysis than it is to delete the unusual value. A good way to handle these cases is to create an audit dimension for the fact record. You can use this dimension as a constraint and to describe the status of each fact.

- **Recognize random or noise values from context and mask out.** A special case of the previous transformation is to recognize when the legacy system has supplied a random number rather than a real fact. This can happen when no value is meant to be delivered by the legacy system, but a number left over in a buffer has been passed down to the data warehouse. When this case can be recognized, the random number should be replaced with a null value, as described in the next transformation.

- **Apply a uniform treatment to null values.** Null values can often cause a data mining tool to hiccup. In many cases the null value is represented by a special value of what should be a legitimate fact. Perhaps the special value of −1 is understood to represent null. Null dates are often represented by some agreed upon date like January 1, 1900. (I hope you haven't been using January 1, 2000.) The first step in cleaning up nulls is to use a DBMS that represents nulls explicitly. Replace the specific data values with true nulls in the database. The second step is to use a data mining tool that has specific options for processing null data.

  Your fact table records likely contain date fields being used as foreign keys to date dimension tables. In this case you have no good way to represent null dates in your fact table record. You cannot use a null-valued foreign key in the fact table because null in SQL is never equal to itself; in other words, you cannot use a null value in a join between a fact and dimension table. What you should do is implement the join with an anonymous integer key and then have a special record in the dimension table to represent the null date.

  Null values in data are tricky because philosophically there are at least two kinds of nulls. A null value in the data may mean that at the time of the measurement, the value literally did not exist and could not exist. In other words, any data value at all is wrong. Conversely, a null value in the data may mean that the measurement process failed to deliver the data, but the value certainly existed at some point. In this second case, you might argue that to use an estimated value would be better than to disqualify the fact record from the analysis. Some data mining professionals assign a most probable or median value in this case so that the rest of the fact table record can participate in the analysis. This could either be done in the original data by overwriting the null value with the estimated value, or it could be handled by a sophisticated data mining tool that knows how to process null data with various analysis options.

■ **Flag fact records with changed status.** A helpful data transformation is to add a special status indicator to a fact table record to show that the status of that account (or customer or product or location) has just changed or is about to change. The status indicator is implemented as a status dimension. Useful statuses include new customer, customer defaulted, customer about to cancel, or changed order. The customer about to cancel status is especially valuable because without this flag the only evidence that the customer canceled may be the absence of account records beginning the next billing period. Finding such an absence by noticing that records don't exist is impractical in most database applications.

■ **Classify an individual record by one of its aggregates.** In some cases, it may be desirable to identify the sale of a very specific product, such as a garment in a particular color and size combination, by one of the garment's aggregates, such as its brand. Using the detailed color and size description in this case might generate so much output in the market basket report that the correlation of the clothing brand with say, a shoe style, would be hard to see. One of the goals of using an aggregate label in this way is to produce reporting buckets that are statistically significant.

Special Tool-Dependent Transformations

This group of transformations will depend on the specific requirements on your chosen data mining tool.

■ **Divide data into training, test, and evaluation sets.** Almost all data mining applications require that the raw input data be separated into three groups. Perhaps the data should be separated randomly into three control groups, or perhaps the data should be separated by time. The first data group is used for training the data mining tool. A clustering tool, neural network tool, or decision tree tool absorbs this first data set and establishes parameters from which future classifications and predictions can be made. The second data set is then used to test these parameters to see how well the model performs. When the data mining tool has been properly tuned on the first and second data sets, it is then applied to the third evaluation data set, where the clusters, classifications, and predictions coming from the tool are to be trusted and used.

■ **Adding computed fields as inputs or targets.** A data mining exercise can be greatly leveraged by letting the data mining tool operate on computed values, as well as on base data. For instance, a computed field such as profit or customer satisfaction that represents the value of a set of customer transactions may be required as a target for the data mining tool to pick out the best customers, or to pick out behavior that you want to encourage. You may not have to modify your base schemas with these computed values if you can present the data mining tool with a view containing these computed values. However, in other cases where the added information is too complicated to compute at query time in a view, you have to add the values to the base data itself before you can perform data mining.

■ **Map continuous values into ranges.** Some data mining tools such as decision trees encourage you to band continuous values into discrete ranges. You may be able to do this by joining your fact table to a little "band values" dimension table, but this may be an expensive join against millions or billions of unindexed numeric facts. In such a case, you may have to add a textual bucket fact or even a bucket dimension to your fact table if the fact in question is important enough to be used as a frequent data mining target.

■ **Normalize values between 0 and 1.** Neural network data mining tools usually require that all numeric values be mapped into a range of zero to one. You should make your data range a little larger than the observed data for this normalization calculation so that you can accommodate new values that fall outside the actual data you have on hand in your training set.

■ **Convert from textual to numeric or numeral category.** Some data mining tools may only operate on numeric input. In these cases, discrete text values need to be assigned codes. You should only do this process when the data mining tool is smart enough to treat such information categorically, and does not infer an ordering or a magnitude to these numbers that is unwarranted. For instance, you can convert most locations in the United States into a ZIP code. However, you can't compute on these ZIPs!

■ **Emphasize the unusual case abnormally to drive recognition.** Many times a data mining tool is used to describe and recognize unusual cases. Perhaps you are looking for fraud in a series of sales transactions. The problem is that your training set data may not contain enough instances of the target fraud behavior to extract meaningful predictive indicators. In this case you may have to artificially replicate or seed the training data with the desired target patterns in order to make the data mining tool create a useful set of parameters.

Writing this article was an eye opener for me. I had not really appreciated the full extent of the data preparation that is required for full-fledged data mining. Although many of the data transformations I have described probably should be done in a general data warehouse environment, the demands of data mining really force the data cleaning issue. The purpose of data mining should be to discover meaningful patterns in your data, not to stumble over data cleanliness problems.

13.17 The Perfect Handoff

Ralph Kimball, Intelligent Enterprise, Dec 21, 1999

The web is having a profound effect on the content and structure of the data warehouse. For instance, the web provides many new data sources, mostly related to customer behavior; such information is essential to customer relationship management, which is gaining popularity. Behavior analysis is the province of data mining, which is essentially a complex analytic client that seeks patterns in behavioral data. You can discover such things as:

- Which characteristics of individual customers predict whether they will be good or bad customers?
- Does the way people tour your site reveal their interest in your products?
- How to dynamically modify the website experience, based on the data warehouse's assessment of the viewer's behavioral similarity to thousands of other customers.
- Which pages on the site attract visitors or are session killers?

Although data warehousing and data mining have coexisted in various forms since the mid 1980s, the two communities have not frequently collaborated. All too often, the data miners have end-run the data warehouse and directly sourced the data, usually because they want extremely granular data, which they call *observations*. Any aggregations built in the data warehouse were poison to data mining.

For some time, the data warehouse, especially when sourced from the web, has routinely stored atomic level data describing detailed behavior of our customers. We data warehouse teams must stand up and say *we are the source* of data for all forms of reporting, analysis, forecasting, scoring, and data mining. We have teased the data out of its hiding places, built data extract and transformation pipelines, know how to conform data from multiple sources, and are a professional platform for storing used data for all kinds of purposes. The data mining community needs to use our data rather than source it independently. The data miner's job is analysis; we are data wranglers.

The Perfect Observation

Consider the meta-SQL shown in Figure 13-3. Imagine that this data specification was able to deliver millions of records with this content. Each record is an elaborate description of customer behavior with one record for each customer.

```
SELECT Customer Identifier, Census Tract, City, County, State, Postal Code, Demographic Cluster, Age, Sex, Marital Status, Years of
Residency Number of Dependents, Employment Profile, Education Profile, Sports Magazine Reader Flag, Personal Computer Owner
Flag, Cellular Telephone Owner Flag, Current Credit Rating, Worst Historical Credit Rating, Best Historical Credit Rating, Date First
Purchase, Date Last Purchase, Number Purchases Last Year, Change in Number Purchases vs. Previous Year, Total Number Purchases
Lifetime, Total Value Purchases Lifetime, Number Returned Purchases Lifetime, Maximum Debt, Average Age Customer's Debt
Lifetime, Number Late Payments, Number Fully Paid, Times Visited Website, Change in Frequency of Website Access, Number of
Pages Visited Per Session, Average Dwell Time Per Session, Number Web Product Orders, Value Web Product Orders, Number Website
Visits to Partner Websites, Change in Partner Website Visits
FROM *** WHERE *** ORDER BY *** GROUP BY ***
```

Figure 13-3: Sample SQL to hand off data from the warehouse to a data mining application.

Most data miners would kill for a set of observations with this content. Believe me, a data miner would much rather analyze this data than prepare it! In my experience, data miners often do very limited data extracts by data warehouse standards, ending up with much less than Figure 13-3 shows.

Study Figure 13-3 closely. This data couldn't possibly come from one source; it must be conformed from multiple sources, probably by implementing fuzzy matches on the customer's name, address, and other fields. Even when you conform the separate sources of data, the resulting drill-across application runs too slowly for a data miner, whose tools can analyze thousands of these observations per second!

We are now beginning to see our destiny as data warehousers.

The purpose of the data warehouse is to gather, store, and present data in the best possible way to the data mining tool, and not to actually perform the data mining. Data mining is more of an analytic application than a database. Historically, we have duplicated too much effort and lost too many opportunities because the responsibilities of the data warehouse and data mining operation were inadequately defined.

In the overall flow of data from its original source to the final step of data mining, I recommend the following division of responsibilities. Data warehouse responsibilities for supporting data mining include:

- Original extraction from all internal legacy sources and third party sources
- Data content validation and cleaning
- Combining of disparate data sources into fact and dimension tables of uniform granularities
- Creation of derived facts and attributes of interest to data mining tools
- Assignment of all foreign and primary keys in fact and dimension tables
- Creation of complex drill-across reports that are ready to go observation sets
- Storage of the observation sets for high performance access by the data mining tools
- Optionally accepting and storing the results of data mining tool runs

Data mining's responsibilities include:

- Reading the ready to go observation sets, perhaps repetitively, directly into the data mining tools
- Providing on the fly data transformation steps where not provided by the data warehouse
- Performing the data mining analyses
- Handing off the results from data mining tool runs to the data warehouse for storage

The creation of the complex drill-across reports is the most valuable step in the process because it draws upon the strengths of the data warehouse and is what the data miners are least prepared to do.

Many data warehouse developers are inwardly focused on data available from their organizations' production systems, perhaps unaware of the rich sources of data available from third party data providers. With the increased focus on customer behavior and demographics, the data warehouse team needs to become more familiar with the data sources and companies providing this data. It would be a mistake to turn this data sourcing over to the data mining group because that leaves all the issues of sourcing data, conforming keys, combining tables, representing time series, and providing data access to the business users whose main interest is analyzing the data. These jobs, and hence demographics data acquisition, belong to the data warehouse team.

Referring back to Figure 13-3, you can see that the various behavioral measures come from many different data warehouse tables and are expressed in different granularities. A data warehouse producing this set of applications might consist of more than a dozen separate queries to different fact tables, all of which are combined under the customer identifier row heading. The warehouse could not provide this set of observations directly from the original data sources with the speed the data mining tool requires.

The data warehouse needs to produce this set of observations once and then store it for high-performance, repeated access by the data mining tools. A decision tree or a neural net might read the data only once, but a memory-based reasoning tool may want to read it repeatedly.

The highest performance access may well be through a flat file. It would be reasonable for the data warehouse to hand off the ready to go observation set as one or more flat files, which can be read repeatedly. The data warehouse then steps back and lets the data mining tool process the observations at high speed.

All data mining is a repetitive cycle of cutting and trying. It would be very typical of the data mining project to want more behavioral data measurements, or desire numerical or categorical transformations of existing measurements. In some cases, the data mining tool will provide the final transformations efficiently, but it is very likely the data warehouse's data delivery environment will augment and extend the observation sets. Most data warehouse tool suites can easily take the flat file outputs described previously and augment them with further columns of data for each customer.

The data warehouse team can work with the data miners to reduce the amount of data handed across. After all, not every demographic indicator provides useful insight or has useful predictive value. Some data inputs the data warehouse provides may be expensive to compute or buy. It would be helpful to eliminate these variables. By using a neural network tool in auto-associative mode, the data miners can test to see whether the data inputs describing the customer can predict themselves.

This technique can eliminate some data elements because they literally are not consistent with the rest of the customer profile information. Similarly, a neural network tool can eliminate other variables when it is configured in the normal mode of predicting or recognizing desired output variables from the input variables. In this case, the data miner compares the changes in neuron weights from the beginning to the end of the neural network training phase. Input variables with neuron weights that change very little in the training phase clearly have not affected the model very much and the data miner may choose to drop them from consideration.

Implications for Database Architecture

I used to think that database vendors would absorb data mining by providing data mining in the inner loop of the DBMS answer set generator, but have since changed my mind. Figure 13-3 is not the inner loop of a query, but the final result of a complex drill-across application, probably generated well above the DBMS's inner loop. Maybe the way to say it is that detailed behavior needs to be described within a comprehensive context, not within a narrow query. In any case, I think the architecture is shaking out to be more of a handoff. The data warehouse produces the observations at a very granular level and embellishes them with detail, then hands them off to the data miner as a flat file for high-performance, repeated access.

13.18 Get Started with Data Mining Now

Warren Thornthwaite, Intelligent Enterprise, *Oct 1, 2005*

Data mining has come into its own, taking a central role in many businesses. We're all the subject of data mining dozens of times a day, from the direct mail we receive to the fraud detection algorithms that scrutinize our every credit card purchase. Data mining is widespread because it works. Its popularity is also rising because the tools are better, more broadly available, cheaper, and easier to use.

However, many DW/BI teams aren't sure how to get started with data mining. This article presents a business-based approach that will help you successfully add data mining to your DW/BI system. Figure 13-4 shows the three phases of the data mining process, major task areas within those phases, and common iteration points.

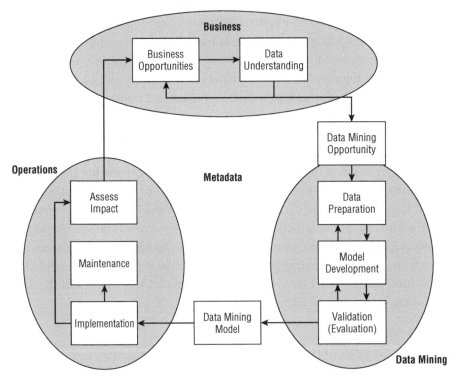

Figure 13-4: The overall data mining process.

The Business Phase

This first phase is a more focused version of the overall DW/BI requirements gathering process. Identify and prioritize a list of opportunities that can have a significant business impact. The business opportunities and data understanding tasks in the diagram connect because identifying opportunities must be connected to the realities of the data world. By the same token, the data itself may suggest business opportunities.

As always, the most important step in successful BI isn't about technology, it's about understanding the business. Meet with business people about potential opportunities and the associated relationships and behaviors captured in the data. The goal of these meetings is to identify several high value opportunities and carefully examine each one. First, describe business objectives in measurable ways. "Increase sales" is too broad; "reduce the monthly churn rate" is more manageable. Next, think about what factors influence the objective. What might indicate that someone is likely to churn? How can you tell if someone would be interested in a given product? While you're discussing these factors, try to translate them into specific attributes and behaviors that are known to exist in a usable, accessible form.

After several meetings with different groups to identify and prioritize a range of opportunities, take the top-priority business opportunity and its associated list of potential variables back to the DW for further exploration. Spend a lot of time exploring the data sets that might be relevant to the business opportunities discussed. At this stage, the goal is to verify that the data needed to support the business opportunity is available and clean enough to be usable.

You can discover many of the content, relationship, and quality problems firsthand through data profiling, using query and reporting tools to get a sense of the content under investigation. While data profiling can be as simple as writing some SQL SELECT statements with counts and distinct counts, many data profiling tools can provide complex analysis that goes well beyond simple queries.

Once you have a clear, viable opportunity identified, document the following:

- Business opportunity description
- Expected data issues
- Modeling process description
- Implementation plan
- Maintenance plan

Finally, review the opportunity and documentation with businesspeople to make sure you understand their needs and they understand how you intend to meet them.

The Data Mining Phase

Now you get to build some data mining models. The three major tasks in this phase involve preparing the data, developing alternative models and comparing their accuracy, and validating the final model. As shown in Figure 13-4, this is a highly iterative process.

The first task in this phase is to build the data mining case sets. A case set includes one row per instance or event. For many data mining models, this means a data set with one row per customer. Models based on simple customer attributes, such as gender and marital status, work at the one row per customer level. Models that include repeated behaviors, such as purchases, include data at the one row per event level.

A well designed and built dimensional data warehouse is a perfect source for data mining case data. Ideally, many variables identified in the business opportunity already exist as cleaned dimension attributes. The data miner's world gets even better when demographics and other external data are already loaded into the data warehouse using conformed dimensions. Warning: Accurately tracking history using type 2 slowly changing dimensions is critical to successful data mining. If your data warehouse or external sources overwrite changes in a type 1 fashion, your model will be associating current attribute values with historical behavior.

While descriptive data is important, the most influential variables in a data mining model are typically behavior based. Behaviors are generally captured in the dimension model as facts detailing what customers did, how often, how much, and when.

The process of building the case sets usually involves queries and transformations that generate a data structure made up of individual observations, or cases, often with repeating nested structures that will be fed into the data mining service. The process is typically similar to the conventional ETL process used to build the data warehouse itself. Writing the data mining case sets to a separate database (or machine) lets you manage these tables independently from the data warehouse. ETL tools are well suited to creating case sets because you can encapsulate all the selection and cleaning components in a single ETL job.

Depending on the business opportunity and data mining algorithms used, developing the initial data sets often involves creating separate data subsets for different purposes. Figure 13-5 lists four common sets used for data mining. Your ETL tool should have simple transformations that let you grab a random sample of 10,000 rows from a large data set and then send 80 percent of the those rows to a training set and 20 percent to a test set.

After developing the data sets, start to build some data mining models. Build as many different mining models and versions as time allows; try different algorithms, parameters, and variables to see which yields the greatest impact or the most accuracy. You can return to the data preparation task to add new variables or redefine existing transformations. The more variations tested, the better the final model.

Creating the best data mining model is a process of triangulation. Attack the data with several algorithms such as decision trees, neural nets, and memory-based reasoning. The best-case scenario is when several models point to similar results. This is especially helpful when the tool spits out an answer but doesn't provide an intuitive explanation for it, a notorious problem with neural nets. Triangulation gives all observers (especially business users and management) confidence that the predictions mean something.

Data Set	Purpose
Training	Used as input to the algorithm to develop the initial model
Validation	Used to make sure the algorithm has created a model that is broadly applicable rather than tightly tied to the training set. Used only in certain circumstances
Test	Data not included in the training set—often called holdout data. Used to verify the model's accuracy and effectiveness
Evaluation	The intended target data to be analyzed

Figure 13-5: The primary data sets used by data mining tools.

There are two kinds of model validation in data mining. The *technical approach* compares the top models to see which is most effective at predicting target variables. Your data mining tool should provide utilities for comparing the effectiveness of certain types of data mining models. Lift charts and classification (or confusion) matrices are common examples. These utilities run the test data sets through the models and compare the predicted results with the actual, known results.

The *business approach* to validation involves documenting the contents and performance of the best model and conducting a business review to examine its value and verify that it makes sense. Ultimately, model choice is a business decision. The next step is to move the model into the real world.

The Operations Phase

The operations phase is where the rubber meets the road. At this point, you have the best possible model (given time, data, and technology constraints) and business approval to proceed. The operations phase involves three main tasks: implementation, impact assessment, and maintenance.

At one end of the spectrum, a customer-profiling data mining model that runs once a quarter may only involve the data miner and ETL developer. At the other end of the spectrum, making online recommendations will require the involvement of applications developers and production systems folks, which is usually a big deal. If you're working on a big deal project, include these people as early as possible, preferably during the business phase, so they can help determine appropriate time frames and resources. It's best to roll out the data mining model in phases, starting with a test version, to make sure the data mining server doesn't affect the transaction process.

Assessing the impact of the data mining model can be high art. In some fields, such as direct mail, the process of tuning and testing marketing offers, collateral, and target prospect lists is full time work for a large team. These teams perform tests on small subsets before they send mass mailings. Even in full campaigns, there are often several phases with different versions and control sets built in. The results of each phase help teams tweak subsequent phases for improved returns. Adopt as much of this careful assessment approach as possible.

Keep in mind that as the world changes, behaviors and relationships captured in the model become outdated. Almost all data mining models must be retrained or completely rebuilt at some point. A recommendation engine that doesn't include the latest products would be less than useful, for example.

Role of Data Mining Metadata

In the best of all worlds, the final data mining model should be documented with a detailed history. A professional data miner will want to know exactly how a model was created in order to explain its value, avoid repeating errors, and re-create it if necessary.

Modern data mining tools are so easy to use; it often takes more time to document each iteration than it does to do the work. Nonetheless, you must keep track of what you have and where it came from. Keep a basic set of metadata to track the contents and derivation of all the transformed data sets and resulting mining models you decide to keep. Ideally, your data mining tool will provide the means for tracking these changes, but the simplest approach is to use a spreadsheet.

For every data mining model you keep, your spreadsheet should capture at least the following: model name, version, and date created; training and test data sets; algorithm(s), parameter settings, input and predicted variables used; and results. Your spreadsheet should also track the definitions of the input data sets, the data sources they came from, and the ETL modules that created them.

This approach will help you successfully integrate data mining into your DW/BI system. Remember, the easiest path to success begins with understanding business requirements and ends with delivering business value.

13.19 Leverage Your Dimensional Model for Predictive Analytics

Ralph Kimball, Design Tip #172, *Feb 2, 2015*

Predictive analytics is the name for a broad range of analysis techniques used for making predictions about future behavior. Credit scoring, risk analysis, and promotion selection are among the many applications that have proven to drive revenue and profit. It is worth taking a look at the "predictive analytics" section of Wikipedia to appreciate the broad scope of these techniques.

In spite of the significant differences among predictive analytic techniques, almost all of them can ingest data as a series of "observations" usually keyed by a familiar data warehouse key such as customer. For the sake of discussion let us assume that we have 10 million customers and we wish to predict future behavior by running a series of predictive analytic applications against these customers' histories.

The desired input data to the predictive analytic application is a 10 million row table whose primary key is the durable and unique customer key, and whose columns are an open ended number of descriptive attributes, including the usual descriptive fields and demographic fields, *but also including indicators, counts, and amounts purposely prepared for the particular run of the predictive analytic application.* It is this italicized requirement that makes all this so interesting.

Our input data to the predictive analytics model looks a lot like a very wide table, but it is much more volatile and complex than a normal fairly stable dimension table. Some of the attributes already exist in a normal customer dimension, but many of the interesting attributes are chosen at analysis time by searching fact tables describing customer history and then summarizing that history with a tag, score, or amount. Some predictive analytic applications may want to update the input data in real time, and the analyst may wish to dynamically add new calculated attributes to the input data at any time. Finally, a given snapshot of this input data may well be a useful customer dimension in its own right.

If these customer tags, scores, and amounts are stable and regularly used for query filtering and grouping beyond predictive analysis, then they could become permanent members of the customer dimension. The observation data that's fed into a predictive analysis application from a dimensional model is pretty simple. But how do we populate the table? Is it done in ETL with a complex backroom application that writes this final table in a conventional format? Is it done entirely in SQL at run time where each field in each column is populated by a correlated SELECT statement accessing remote fact tables? Can the data for the observation attributes be stored in an actual dimension, rather than separate fact tables, where the multiple values are stored as a SQL ARRAY of STRUCTS, even as a time series? Are there tools in the Hadoop environment such as Spark or HBase that provide a more natural and efficient way to build the observation data set that's handed off for predictive analytics?

Part of my role in this retirement year for the Kimball Group is to describe the enduring relevance of our well-proven dimensional modeling techniques, and at the same time challenging you readers in the data warehouse community to be thinking about new directions for data warehousing in the future. To be honest, I don't have all the answers to the preceding questions, but between now and the end of the year I will at least describe the challenges and my thinking on these approaches as best I can.

13.20 Does Your Organization Need an Analytic Sandbox?

Bob Becker, Design Tip #174, May 6, 2015

Countless organizations have created mature dimensional data warehouses that are considered tremendous successes within their organizations. These data warehouse environments support key reporting and analysis requirements for the enterprise. Many are capable of supporting self-serve data access and analysis capabilities for disparate business users.

Nonetheless, regardless of the success achieved by these dimensional data warehouses, they are sometimes criticized as being too slow to react to new requirements, implement new data sources, and support new analytic capabilities. Sometimes these concerns are overstated as it clearly takes a certain amount of time to react to any new requirements, but sometimes these criticisms are true. Many data warehouses have grown and evolved to become mission-critical environments supporting key enterprise reporting, dashboards/scorecards, and self-serve data access capabilities. Due to the mission-critical nature, the data modeling, governance, ETL rules development, and change management requirements result in lengthy approval, design, and development cycles for new requirements and changes. In many ways, these challenges are the price of success.

The data warehouse is likely to be very structured, heavily designed, subject to well-defined business rules, and tightly governed by the enterprise. Much of the data warehouse data is extensively cleansed and transformed to ensure it represents the true picture of what actually happened in the business. In addition, data warehouse data is frequently synchronized with the production environments via regularly scheduled loads. Thus, in the end, it is fairly rigid; it simply takes time to react to new data and analytic requests.

Yet, in today's competitive world, organizations need to be more nimble. They want to quickly test new ideas, new hypotheses, new data sources, and new technologies. The creation of an analytic sandbox may be an appropriate response to these requirements. An analytic sandbox complements your dimensional data warehouse. It is not intended to replace the data warehouse, but rather stand beside it and provide an environment that can react more quickly to new requirements. The analytic sandbox is not really a new concept, but the recent big data discussions have brought the concept back to the forefront. Typically an analytic sandbox is thought of as an area carved out of the existing data warehouse infrastructure or as a separate environment living adjacent to the data warehouse. It provides the environment and resources required to support experimental or developmental analytic capabilities. It's a place where these new ideas, hypotheses, data sources, and tools can be utilized, tested, evaluated, and explored. Meanwhile, the data warehouse stands as the prerequisite data foundation containing the historically accurate enterprise data that the analytic sandbox efforts spin around and against.

Sometimes key data is fed from the existing data warehouse environment into the analytic sandbox and aligned with other non-data warehouse data stores. It is a place where new data sources can be tested to determine their value to the enterprise. Examples of these new data sources might be externally acquired market intelligence; externally acquired customer attributes; or sources such as social media interactions, mobile app interactions, mobile dust, and website activity. Often it may be too onerous to bring these new data sources into the existing data warehouse environment unless or until their value has been proven. Data in the analytic sandbox typically does not need to be synchronized on a recurring basis with production environment and these data sets expire after the passage of time.

A key objective of the analytic sandbox is to test a variety of hypotheses about data and analytics. Thus, it shouldn't be a huge surprise that most analytic sandbox projects result in "failure." That is, the hypothesis doesn't pan out as expected. This is one of the big advantages of the analytic sandbox. The data utilized in these "failures" didn't and won't need to be run through the rigor expected of data contained in the data warehouse. In this case, failure is its own success; each failure is a step toward finding the right answer.

Most business users will rightfully view the data warehouse as the go-to source for enterprise data. Their reporting, dashboards/scorecards, and "self-serve" ad hoc requests will be readily supported by the data warehouse. The target users of the analytic sandbox are often called "data scientists."

These individuals are the small cadre of business users technologically savvy enough to identify potential sources of data, create their own "shadow" databases, and build special-purpose analyses. Often these individuals have to work "off the grid." They have crafted and created their own shadow analytic environments in spreadsheets, local data sets, under the desk data marts, or whatever it takes to get the job done. The analytic sandbox recognizes that these individuals have real requirements. It provides an environment for them to work "on the grid" in an environment that is blessed, supported, funded, available, performant and, to some light extent, governed.

Having the right skills in house is critical to the success of the analytic sandbox. The users of the analytic sandbox need to be able to engage with the data with far fewer rules of engagement than most business users. They are users capable of self-provisioning their required data whether it comes from the data warehouse or not. They are capable of building the analytics and models directly against this data without assistance.

The analytic sandbox should be minimally governed. The idea is to create an environment that lives without all the overhead of the data warehouse environment. It should not be used to support the organization's mission-critical capabilities. It shouldn't be used to directly control or support any core operational capabilities. Likewise, it is not intended to be utilized for ongoing reporting or analytics required by the business on an ongoing basis, especially any reporting that supports external reporting to meet financial or government regulations.

An important characteristic of the analytic sandbox is that it is transient in nature. Data and analysis come and go as needed to support new analytic requirements. The data does not persist and it is not regularly updated via ongoing ETL capabilities. Data in the analytic sandbox typically has an agreed upon expiration date. Thus, any new findings or capabilities identified as important to the organization and critical for supporting ongoing capabilities will need to be incorporated into the enterprise operation or data warehouse environments.

Dealing with SQL

This section begins with an article that illustrates drill-across queries using SQL. From there, we move to a series of articles written by Ralph in the 1996 to '97 time frame that point out the limitations of SQL for analysis. We believe the Kimball Group was instrumental in alerting the SQL standards committees to extend the semantics of SQL in the SQL-99 release, as described in article 13.27, *Smarter Data Warehouses*.

13.21 Simple Drill Across in SQL

Warren Thornthwaite, Design Tip #68, Jun 3, 2005

Drill across refers to the process of querying multiple fact tables and combining the results into a single data set. A common example involves combining forecast data with actual data. The forecast data is typically kept in a separate table, captured at a different level of detail than the actual data.

When a user wants a report that compares actual and forecast by customer, the query needs to go against two fact tables. Of course, data from the two fact tables can only be combined if they are built using conformed dimensions. The customer, date, and any other shared dimension fields must be exactly the same in both dimensional models.

The most efficient way to combine data from the two fact tables is to issue separate queries against each fact table, then combine the two results sets by matching up their shared attributes. This tends to work best because most database optimizers recognize simple star join queries and quickly return the two results sets.

The following SQL is used to drill across two dimensional models, actual sales and forecast, both with customer and date dimensions. The query uses SELECT statements in the FROM clause to create two subqueries and join their results together, exactly as we'd like. Even if you don't have to write the SQL yourself, you'll get a sense for what your BI tool might be doing behind the scenes.

```
SELECT Act.Customer, Act.Year, Act.Month, Actual_Amount, Forecast_Amount
FROM
```

Subquery "Act" returns Actuals:

```
(SELECT Customer_Name AS Customer, Year, Month_Name AS Month,
    SUM(Sale_Amount) Actual_Amount
    FROM Sales_Facts A
    INNER JOIN Customer C
    ON A.Customer_Key = C.Customer_Key
    INNER JOIN Date D
    ON A.Sales_Date_Key = D.Date_Key
  GROUP BY Customer_Name, Year, Month_Name) Act
INNER JOIN
```

Subquery "Fcst" returns Forecast:

```
(SELECT Customer_Name AS Customer, Year, Month_Name AS Month,
    SUM(Forecast_Amount) Forecast_Amount
    FROM Forecast_Facts F
    INNER JOIN Customer C
    ON F.Customer_Key = C.Customer_Key
    INNER JOIN Date D
    ON F.Sales_Date_Key = D.Date_Key
  GROUP BY Customer_Name, Year, Month_Name) Fcst
```

Join condition for our small result sets:

```
ON Act.Customer = Fcst.Customer
AND Act.Year = Fcst.Year
AND Act.Month = Fcst.Month
```

This should perform almost as fast as doing the two individual queries against the separate fact tables because the join is on relatively small subset of data that's already in memory. The interim and final results from this SQL statement would look like Figure 13-6.

For relational-based star schemas, many front end BI tools can be configured to issue the separate SQL queries through their metadata, or at least in their user interface. Many OLAP engines do this through a "virtual cube" concept that ties the two underlying cubes together based on their shared dimensions. Remember, if you do not have rigorously enforced conformed dimensions, you will not be comparing apples to apples when you drill across!

Act subquery results:

Customer	Year	Month	Actual_Amount
Big Box	2005	May	472,394
Small Can	2005	May	1,312,034

Fcst subquery results:

Customer	Year	Month	Forecast_Amount
Big Box	2005	May	435,000
Small Can	2005	May	1,257,000

Final drill-across query results:

Customer	Year	Month	Actual_Amount	Forecast_Amount
Big Box	2005	May	472,394	435,000
Small Can	2005	May	1,312,034	1,257,000

Figure 13-6: Sample data from the two subqueries and the final drill-across results.

13.22 An Excel Macro for Drilling Across

Ralph Kimball, Design Tip #156, Jun 2, 2013

Drilling across separate business processes is one of the most powerful applications in a data warehouse. We often describe drilling across as magic: Separately open connections to the dimensional models for each business process, fetch answer sets from each process labeled identically with row headers drawn from specially conformed dimensions, then deliver the result by sort-merging these answer sets over the row headers. It is magic because the original data for each business process can be profoundly distributed on different machines, perhaps even running different styles of DBMSs.

In our classes we introduce drilling across with the following simple example. Suppose we have three processes: manufacturing shipments, warehouse inventory, and retail sales. We have carefully administered the product dimension associated with each of these processes so the product descriptions are exactly consistent. We call this a conformed dimension. In our simple example, there are three products named Framis, Toggle, and Widget.

When we query each process separately, we get the following three answer sets:

Product	Mfg Shipments
Framis	100
Toggle	200
Widget	300

Product	Warehouse Inventory
Framis	300
Toggle	400
Widget	500

Product	Retail Sales
Framis	50
Toggle	75
Widget	125

The challenge of drilling across is to take these three answer sets and sort-merge them on the Product row header, hopefully getting the following result:

Product	Mfg Shipments	Warehouse Inventory	Retail Sales
Framis	100	300	50
Toggle	200	400	75
Widget	300	500	125

Seems simple, doesn't it? But in real life, if the three business processes are on different machines, where do you perform the drill across? Cognos, Business Objects, and the server layer of OBIEE all can perform their own versions of drilling across if you can find the feature under a different name! But how do you open arbitrary connections to random remote data sources and then perform this sort-merge, especially if you don't have one of these tools?

In the past, I have told students to study their BI applications and "figure out" what to do. This is unsatisfactory, and I suspect many students have never actually implemented drill-across applications.

I decided to try implementing drill across in Excel, where within a single master spreadsheet, each process's results would be stored in a separate worksheet. I hoped that I could just use the Pivot command to accomplish the sort-merge, but Pivot by itself is not nearly powerful enough. The sort-merge across many simultaneous data sources is actually a sophisticated series of steps, which in relational parlance is a highly parallelized full symmetric outer join across all the sources. But in general we can't use an RDBMS because we are pulling from multiple diverse sources, perhaps including OLAP systems or Hive tools in Hadoop environments. Actually, any results set that has the requisite format is fair game for drilling across.

Fortunately I am very comfortable with Visual Basic so I wrote an Excel macro in VB to do drilling across. Once you store the various results into separate worksheets, you run the macro and Presto!

The code for the macro is available at www.kimballgroup.com/data-warehouse-business-intelligence-books/kimball-reader/. You can also download the complete spreadsheet with sample data and the macro at this link. In the code, worksheets for each process are called Process1, Process2, and so forth. Open the worksheet named StartHere to begin. The worksheet for the final result is called DrillAcrossResult.

Coding and debugging this macro took me about six hours over a two-day period. I have made it fairly robust. You can drill across 20 processes, where each process can have hundreds or even thousands of rows. The results sets can be labeled with multi-level row headers, and each process can have up to 20 unique associated facts. Because it implements an outer join of the results sets, the final answer is allowed to have blank cells.

Each process is fully sorted by the macro before the drill-across operation. Thus you can even manually add new rows anywhere without requiring that each process be sorted.

13.23 The Problem with Comparisons

Ralph Kimball, DBMS, Jan 1996

The concerns Ralph raised in 1996 in this article and in article 13.24, SQL Roadblocks and Pitfalls, were partly addressed in the SQL-99 release as described in article 13.27, Smarter Data Warehouses. SQL has advanced significantly since this article and the next were written, but they still serve as useful motivation. Please study the RANK and WINDOWING functions in the current definition of the SQL standard for how the industry has (partly) provided useful functionality. Also, think carefully about how (or if) your BI tool can generate such SQL.

The most difficult area of data warehousing is the translation of simple business analyses into SQL. SQL was not designed with business reports in mind. SQL was really an interim language designed to allow relational table semantics to be expressed in a convenient and accessible form, and to enable researchers and early developers to proceed with building the first relational systems in the mid 1970s.

How else can you explain the fact that there is no direct way in SQL to compare this year to last year? Or to compare one group of customers to another? Or to number the answer set? Very simple business questions require complex and daunting SQL.

The early days of relational systems were marked by arguments at conferences between the academics at Berkeley and members of the more traditional COBOL camp. When the COBOL camp withdrew, some of the standard techniques that had been learned from data processing were lost in the shuffle. This situation would not have been too bad if SQL had been more dynamic and alive as a language over the intervening 20 years, but the efforts of the language committees for both SQL-89 and SQL-92 were concerned with extending the relational semantics of SQL, rather than with adding simple business data analysis capabilities. Therefore, the industry is struggling today with a 1970s interim relational processing language that was invented by kindly academic professors, rather than by business people.

Let me present some examples from common business reports to show what is so hard in SQL. The first, and most glaring, problem is the difficulty of performing simple comparisons. Suppose you want to show this year's sales versus last year's sales, as illustrated in Figure 13-7.

Product	4Q09 Sales	4Q08 Sales
Doodads	57	66
Toggles	29	24
Widgets	115	89

Figure 13-7: A sample report comparing this year's sales to last year.

This little report is the bedrock of business analysis. A number in the business world rarely makes much sense unless it is compared to some other number. In this report, the comparison numbers are side by side, but you could just as well have used them together in a ratio to show the growth in sales from last year to this year. This year versus last year is the standard example. You can see that sales of Widgets and Toggles are up substantially from last year, and the sales of Doodads are down. This immediately suggests further analysis and perhaps even management action.

Amazingly, it is very difficult in SQL to get an answer set that looks like this. The usual SQL template fails you. You start by writing a fragment of the SQL needed for the fourth quarter 2009 sales (4Q09):

```
SELECT Product.Product_Name, SUM(Sales.Dollars)
FROM Sales, Product, Time
WHERE . . . Time.Quarter = '4Q09'
AND Product.Product_Name in ('Doodads', 'Toggles', 'Widgets')
GROUP BY Product.Product_Name
```

As expected, the underlying dimensional model consists of a large central fact table (sales) joined to a few dimension tables (including product and time). To keep this article focused, I have omitted some of the bookkeeping required in the SQL, such as listing all the join constraints in the WHERE clause required to hook the tables together.

Now, how do you get the sales numbers for 4Q08? SQL leaves you with no good alternatives. If you expand the Time constraint to include both quarters, as in

WHERE . . . Time.Quarter IN ('4Q09', '4Q08'), then the sum expression adds up the sales from both quarters, which you do not want.

SQL-92 provided a case expression that would seem to offer a way out. Put both quarters' data into the query, and then sort out the two quarters in the select list. This is a kind of if-then logic:

```
SELECT Product.Product_Name,
SUM(CASE(Time.Quarter = '4Q09', Sales.Dollars, 0)),
SUM(CASE(Time.Quarter = '4Q08', Sales.Dollars, 0))
```

```
FROM Sales, Product, Time
WHERE . . . Time.Quarter IN ('4Q09', '4Q08')
AND Product.Product_Name in ('Doodads', 'Toggles', 'Widgets')
GROUP BY Product.Product_Name
```

The first CASE expression tests each record in the candidate answer set. If the Time.Quarter is 4Q09, then Sales.Dollars is added to the accumulating sum. If Time.Quarter is something else, zero is added. The same logic applies to the second case statement, except that the time period is 4Q08. This logic allows the two Sales.Dollar columns to be computed.

Unfortunately, several things are wrong with this scenario. First, I don't know of a query tool that supports building this kind of logic. The case construct would have to be hand coded at the SQL level into applications. Second, the approach doesn't scale to more realistic examples. Suppose you wanted a more interesting set of comparisons, as shown in Figure 13-8.

Product	4Q09 Sales	4Q08 Sales	2009 Sales	2008 Sales	4Q09 Sales % of All Products
Doodads	57	66	210	213	16%
Toggles	29	24	110	93	8%
Widgets	115	89	409	295	32%

Figure 13-8: A more interesting and challenging set of comparison metrics versus Figure 13-7.

This example turns into a mind-boggling set of case statements. Notice the little trap in the last column, where "All Products" represents a larger scope than just Doodads, Toggles, and Widgets.

The third problem with the CASE approach is that the SQL gets so complicated that the optimizer can't really tell what is going on. The proliferation of CASE statements obscures the original simple goal. As you add more comparisons, there is a real possibility that the optimizer will "lose it" and do something zany (like a full table scan of Sales), resulting in disastrous effects on performance. A language designer would look at the SQL and say that it "lacks intentionality." In other words, it doesn't say clearly what it is trying to do.

A fourth problem with the CASE approach in this last example is that the WHERE clause must be emasculated to such a point that it lets almost the entire database into the query. Because the CASE approach defers the issue of constraining the records until they arrive in the answer set, the WHERE clause is forced to let through all the Sales records for all products sold both this year and the previous year. If you had hoped to use a speedy aggregate record, you will be disappointed, because the use of the All Products aggregate is hopelessly embedded in the query using the CASE approach.

Stepping back from the details, how do you program comparisons using a relational database? Historically, you have had only four choices: CASE statements, SQL self-joins, SQL correlated subselects, and separate queries combined in the client application.

The second and third approaches (self-joins and correlated subselects) are older techniques that are even uglier than the CASE statement. Neither approach is viable for data warehouse comparisons. Note that the SQL UNION operator does not address the issues of comparisons within a row, because UNION appends rows, not columns, from multiple queries.

Thus, you are left with the fourth choice: separate queries combined in the client application. In other words, in the Figure 13-8 example, you would send the following five separate queries to the database:

> 4Q09 sales for Doodads, Toggles, and Widgets
>
> 4Q08 sales for Doodads, Toggles, and Widgets
>
> 2009 sales for Doodads, Toggles, and Widgets
>
> 2008 sales for Doodads, Toggles, and Widgets
>
> 4Q09 sales for All Products

Your client application must then combine these results outside of the database. Although this approach obviously increases the complexity of the client application, there are some valuable benefits. First, each of the five SQL statements is extremely simple SQL (which all query tools are good at producing). Second, the optimizer can easily analyze these simple SQL statements in order to choose appropriate evaluation plans. Third, the aggregate navigator will process each of these separate queries smoothly, jumping to the yearly aggregates for queries 3 and 4, and jumping to the All Products aggregate for query 5.

The only real glitch is that the client application must perform an outer join on the five answer sets. Keep in mind that there is no guarantee that Doodads, Widgets, and Toggles are all sold in the various time periods requested. If Doodads had not been sold in 2008, you would be forced to enter null data elements into the appropriate cells of your report. Fortunately, outer join is just a fancy name for sort-merge from the old COBOL data processing days. Building the answer set from the five queries requires only that the five answer sets be sort-merged on the set of sorted row headers ("Doodads," "Toggles," and "Widgets").

The separate query approach is extremely simple and general. You can build very complicated reports from separate queries, and the database performance is controllable and scales linearly in the number of queries. I believe that the separate query approach is the only viable approach for standard business reports.

In thinking about how the database industry should attack the problem of building these standard reports, DBMS vendors should address part of the problem and the tool vendors should address the rest. DBMS vendors should extend the concept of the SQL answer set so that multiple queries with the same row headers can be "accreted" column by column into an answer set with symmetric outer join (sort-merge on the row headers). Once this master answer set has been assembled, it can be fetched back to the requesting application for final analysis and presentation.

Tool vendors should make it possible to create comparisons like those in this article. Initially, tool vendors will have to do the sort-merge in the client; later, DBMS vendors can evolve this capability on the server side.

13.24 SQL Roadblocks and Pitfalls

Ralph Kimball, DBMS, Feb 1996

Please see the editorial comment at the beginning of the previous article.

In article 13.23, *The Problem with Comparisons*, I discussed the first of two glaring problems in SQL that make even simple business analyses frustratingly difficult. This article takes up the second big problem: the lack of sequential operations. While you can attempt to program comparisons using existing SQL syntax, you are out of luck in the case of sequential operations. There is no way to perform simple sequential operations using standard SQL.

Let's review the really useful sequential operations. All sequential operations process the answer set in order, from the first record to the last, accumulating some kind of calculation along the way. In many of these cases, the answer set represents a time series, and the records are presented in time series order.

The simple report in Figure 13-9 shows a number of useful sequential operations applied to a time series. Only the first column can be produced in SQL. The day number column is a numbering of the answer set starting with the first record. The cumulative total and the three-day moving average are equally simple. Amazingly, SQL does not provide any of these functions. It is left up to the client application to provide the ability to perform these calculations. However, it is extremely important not to defer these calculations to the client application.

Date	Dollar Sales	Day Number	Cumulative Total	Three Day Moving Avg
February 1	20	1	20	20
February 2	24	2	44	22
February 3	16	3	60	20
February 4	32	4	92	24
February 5	21	5	113	23

Figure 13-9: Sample report illustrating several sequential operations.

Consider a variation of the preceding report, shown in Figure 13-10. SQL can calculate the average unit price easily by dividing the dollar sales by a hidden unit sales value in the data. But if the two sequential computations in columns 3 and 4 are deferred until the data arrives at the client application, it is very difficult for the tool to calculate the correct answer. The unit sales data has been lost. Most non-additive business calculations, such as average price, exhibit this problem. The calculations must be performed in the SQL engine where all the components of the calculations are available.

Another very useful sequential computation is the rank. Many companies base their business analysis around ranking reports, such as the one shown in Figure 13-11. Creating this report using standard SQL and spreadsheet manipulation is a mind-boggling exercise. Only the actual sales numbers are returned from SQL. The rest of the application consists of a complicated series of sorts and macros in the spreadsheet. A simple ranking function in SQL would make this application a breeze. Note that "serious" ranking functions must assign ties and skip the next ranking numbers where the ranks are the same.

Date	Dollar Sales	Average Unit Price	Cumulative Unit Price	Three Day Moving Price
February 1	20	2.00	2.00	2.00
February 2	24	2.40	2.20	2.20
February 3	16	2.00	2.20	2.00
February 4	32	1.60	1.90	1.80
February 5	21	1.70	1.70	1.60

Figure 13-10: Non-additive calculations, like average price, must be performed where all the underlying calculation components are available.

Region	Doodad Sales Rank	Toggle Sales Rank	Widget Sales Rank	Total Sales Rank
East	1	2	3	1
Atlantic	3	5	2	4
Southeast	4	3	7	5
Midwest	5	4	1	3
Southwest	7	7	5	7
Pacific	2	2	4	2
Northwest	6	6	6	6

Figure 13-11: Sample report with rankings.

A variant of ranking is N-tiling. Tertiles divide the ranks into three categories: high, medium, and low. Quartiles divide the ranks into four categories, and so on. Advanced analytics may implement smart tertiling where the boundaries between high and medium, and between medium and low, are adjusted automatically to accommodate clumping of the data values.

Another sequential computation related to ranking is top N, and, of course, bottom N. Top N can be implemented in terms of rank if the ranking function is allowed in the SQL WHERE clause: WHERE . . . rank(sales) <= 10. This is the same as "top 10." You want several flavors of top N, including top N by value, top N percent of a list, and top N percent of contribution in a column with an additive measure.

A quite different kind of sequential operation is the break row. In this case, you accumulate the computation in every column until the row header changes value. Then you insert a break row (shown in Figure 13-12) with the correct values.

Product	Region	Sales	Average Unit Price
Doodads	Atlantic	72	$2.00
Doodads	East	46	$2.20
Doodads	Southeast	28	$2.16
TOTAL DOODADS		146	$2.09
Toggles	Atlantic	66	$3.95
Toggles	East	56	$3.85
Toggles	Southeast	32	$4.02
TOTAL TOGGLES		144	$3.92

Figure 13-12: Sample report with product break rows.

Once again, you dare not compute the break row in the client application because non-additive computations such as average unit price, in general, cannot be calculated correctly outside of the database. This means that you need BREAK BY syntax to go along with GROUP BY and ORDER BY, as follows:

```
SELECT prod_description, region, SUM(sales),
SUM(sales)/SUM(units)
FROM sales_fact, product, market, time
WHERE . . . <join constraints> AND <application constraints>
GROUP BY prod_description, region
ORDER BY prod_description, region
BREAK BY prod_description
SUMMING 3, 4 DISTRIBUTED
RESET BY prod_description
```

The SUMMING 3, 4 DISTRIBUTED phrase means sum column 3 directly, and sum column 4's components before doing the division.

A further refinement of BREAK BY adds a RESET BY clause that restarts the sequential computation at specified breakpoints. This is required in this example because it is meaningless to accumulate the average unit price computation across the product break. However, in time series computations, the sequential computation often continues across the break even though the report includes a monthly break row.

Sequential computations can be added gracefully to existing SQL because the syntax extensions are compatible with the existing language. Several DBMS vendors have added bits and pieces of sequential processing to their SQL implementations; however, most are incomplete and do not address the important issues of distributed computations in sequential functions and break rows or sequential computations in WHERE clauses.

Fixing the SQL Problem

Application developers and business users of the world are wasting enormous amounts of valuable time implementing simple comparisons and sequential computations in their client applications. If they are not wasting their valuable time, they are probably not even trying to provide the comparisons or sequential computations.

Sequential operations are all examples of post-processing the answer set; application designers should think that way. Numbering, ranking, tiling, and break row processing are all performed after the answer set is ready to be shipped to the user. Comparisons and sequential operations can coexist harmoniously. First you accrete the comparisons; then you perform the sequential processing on the generalized answer set.

13.25 Features for Query Tools

Ralph Kimball, DBMS, Feb 1997

As a reminder to the reader, this article was written 18 years ago.

Data warehousing is beginning to develop a rich set of facilities and tools that distinguish it from its older cousin, transaction processing. As we in the data warehouse segment of the market understand more deeply what we are trying to coax out of our databases, a set of themes has begun to emerge in our query and analysis tools that has quite a different texture from the old transaction processing report writers of five years ago.

In this article, I discuss a selected set of new high end query tool capabilities appearing in various tools that I think are important to getting the data warehousing job done. This list of capabilities is by no means complete! Consider it Ralph Kimball's idiosyncratic view of the data warehouse market. All of these features are deep and powerful. It would be wonderful if members of the query tool vendor community would raise the bar and begin competing with each other on these types of features.

Here are my serious query tool features:

■ **Cross-browsing of dimension attributes.** Almost every use of a query tool against a data warehouse involves a characteristic two-step dance: First, you visit some or all of the dimension tables in your dimensional model in order to set the constraints, and second, after setting the constraints, you launch the multi-table join involving several of the dimension tables together with the large central fact table. Cross-browsing is needed to perform the first step. It is absolutely mandatory for a query tool to present, in real time, a list of the valid values in a dimension attribute (for example, product brand) and let the user choose one or more of the values to set a constraint. This basic browsing capability is now fairly standard in sophisticated query tools.

Cross-browsing, on the other hand, refers to the capability of a query tool to present the valid values of the product brand, subject to a constraint elsewhere on that dimension table. In other words, you only want to browse the brand names of products in the salad dressing category. This ability to cross-browse distinguishes showroom demos from query tools used for serious querying in large data warehouse environments. If you can't cross-browse, you may ask for the descriptions of all of the salad dressings and get 16,000 of them (as I did a few years ago).

- **Open aggregate navigation.** Aggregate navigation is the ability to automatically choose pre-stored summaries, or aggregates, in the course of processing a user's SQL requests. Aggregate navigation must be performed silently and anonymously, without the user or application developer being aware that the aggregations even exist. Open aggregate navigation occurs when the aggregate navigation facility is a separate module that is available for all query tool clients simultaneously. In my opinion, nothing is worse, or more shortsighted, than an aggregate navigation facility embedded in a proprietary query tool and unavailable to other user clients. Unless the current proprietary aggregate navigators embedded in query tools are made into openly accessible modules, big DBMS vendors may take this business away from query tool providers.

- **Query decomposition.** To calculate comparisons or to correctly calculate non-additive measures in report break rows, the query tool must break the report down into a number of simple queries that are processed separately by the DBMS. The query tool then automatically combines the results of the separate queries in an intelligent way. This approach also allows drilling across several conformed business process dimensional models in different databases where the processing of a single galactic SQL statement would otherwise be impossible. Finally, query decomposition gives the aggregate navigator a chance to speed up the report, because each atomic SQL request is simple and easily analyzed by the aggregate navigator.

- **Semi-additive summations.** There is an important class of numeric measures in common business fact tables that are not completely additive. Anything that is a measure of intensity is generally not additive, especially across the time dimension. For example, inventory levels and account balances are not additive across time. These facts are called *semi-additive*. Everyone is familiar with the idea of taking one of these semi-additive facts, such as a bank balance, and creating a useful summary at the end of the month by averaging across time. Unfortunately, you cannot use the basic SQL AVG function to calculate this kind of average across time. AVG averages across all of the dimensions, not just time. If you fetch five accounts and four time periods from the DBMS, AVG will divide the total account balance by 20 (five times four) rather than doing what you want, which is to divide by four. It isn't difficult to divide by four, but it is a distraction for the user or application developer, who must stop and store the number four in the application explicitly. What is needed is a generalization of the sum operator to become AVGTIMESUM. This function automatically performs a sum, but also automatically divides by the cardinality of the time constraint in the surrounding query. This feature makes all applications involving inventory levels, account balances, and other measures of intensity significantly simpler.

■ **Show me what is important.** The growth in the power and capacities of data warehouses is a good news/bad news story in some respects. The good news is that you can now store mind-boggling amounts of low level data in your databases: Fact tables with a billion records are fairly commonplace. The bad news is that you are in much more danger of getting back too much data to comprehend usefully. Increasingly, your query tools must help you automatically sift through the data to show you only what is important. At the low end, you simply need to show data rows in your reports that meet certain threshold criteria. This process involves more than just adding a HAVING clause to the SQL. In an aggregate navigated, drill-across environment, the criteria for including or excluding a record from the user's view may not be known until after the DBMS has long since passed back all the results. Thus, this filtering function is rightfully the responsibility of the query tool. The high end of showing what is important is the exciting new area of data mining. Increasingly, query tools need to embed data mining capabilities into their user interfaces and underlying architectures.

■ **Behavioral studies.** An interesting class of applications involves taking the results of a previous report or set of reports and then using these results over and over again at a later time. A manufacturer might run a series of reports analyzing customer ordering behavior. From the original group of 50,000 customers, a subset of 2,000 problem customers might be derived. At this point, the user wants to run a whole series of follow up reports on these 2,000 customers. The problem is that it is very difficult to constrain on the set of 2,000 customers. They almost certainly are not defined by any reasonable constraint on the customer dimension table. They are really only defined by the complex outcome of the original analysis. What is needed is a two-step capability in the query tool. First, when the original defining report is run that shows the 2,000 problem customers, it must be possible with a single command to capture directly the underlying customer keys in a special separate behavioral study table. This table then gets a permanent name and is independent from the original defining report. Second, the user must be able to attach this special table of customer keys to any fact table as a direct constraint on the customer key. This process then automatically constrains all subsequent analysis to the 2,000 problem customers. In this way, a full range of follow up reports can be run on the behaviorally defined group.

13.26 Turbocharge Your Query Tools

Ralph Kimball, DBMS, Sep 1997

As a reminder to the reader, this article was written 18 years ago.

SQL is very seductive. Simple SQL statements seem to read like English language requests for information from a database. After all, almost anyone can figure out the intent of a simple SQL request such as this one that asks for the September sales of each of our products:

```
Select Product_Description, Sum(dollars)
```
all the columns in the final output

```
From Product, Time, Sales
```
the tables needed in the query

```
Where Sales.Product_key = Product.Product_key
```
joining the sales table to the product table

```
And Sales.Time_key = Time.Time_key
```
joining the sales table to the time table

```
And Time.Month = 'September, 1997'
```
the "application" constraint

```
Group by Product_Description
```
the row header in the final output.

Unfortunately, in most cases a more ambitious business request begins to make the SQL complex to write and read. For too long, query tool vendors did not venture far beyond the safe havens of simple SQL requests, like our example. In the early days, most query tools automated the construction of simple SQL requests, sometimes even showing the SQL clauses as they were being built. Only in the past two or three years have query tool vendors tackled how to issue the complex SQL needed for serious business questions. Some vendors have deepened their tools by allowing the user to construct embedded subqueries. Some vendors have also implemented query decomposition where complex requests are broken into many separate queries whose results are combined after the database has completed processing all of them.

Are these approaches sufficient? Are we able to pose all the business questions we want? Are there some business results that beg to be recognized but are trapped in the database because we just can't "speak" clearly enough? Should the SQL language committee give us more power to ask difficult business questions, and could the database vendors implement these language extensions, all before the next millennium? (Only 935 days from the creation of this article!)

To get some perspective on these issues, let me propose seven categories of business questions. These are ordered from the most simple to the most complex, in terms of the logical complexity of isolating the exact records in the database needed to answer the question. This taxonomy isn't the only one possible for business questions or SQL queries, but it is useful as a scale to judge SQL and SQL-producing tools. As you read the following seven categories of queries, try to imagine whether SQL could pose such a query and whether your query tool could produce such SQL. The seven categories of queries are:

1. **Simple constraints**: Constraints against literal constants, such as "Show the sales of candy products in September 1997."

2. **Simple subqueries**: Constraints against a global value found in the data, such as "Show the sales of candy products in September 1997 in those stores that had above average sales of candy products."

3. **Correlated subqueries**: Constraints against a value defined by each output row, for example, "Show the sales of candy products for each month of 1997 in those stores that had above average sales of candy in that month."

4. **Simple behavioral queries**: Constraints against values resulting from an exception report or a complex series of queries that isolate desired behavior, such as "Show the sales of those candy products in September 1997 whose household penetration for our grocery chain in the 12 months prior to September were more than two standard deviations less than the household penetration of the same products across our 10 biggest retail competitors." This query is a variation of the classic opportunity gap analysis.

5. **Derived behavioral queries**: Constraints against values found in set operations (union, intersection, and set difference) on more than one complex exception report or series of queries, such as "Show the sales of those candy products identified in the example from category 4, and which also experienced a merchandise return rate more than two standard deviations greater than our 10 biggest retail competitors." This request is a set intersection of two behavioral queries.

6. **Progressive subsetting queries**: Constraints against values, as in the example in category 4, but temporally ordered so that membership in an exception report is dependent on membership in a previous exception report: "Show the sales of those candy products in the example from category 4 that were similarly selected in August 1997 but were not similarly selected in either June or July 1997." A health care example of a progressive subsetting query would be "Show the oldest 100 patients who initially complained of chest pain, then had either treatment A or treatment B, then did not have surgery, and are still alive today."

7. **Classification queries**: Constraints on values that are the results of classifying records against a set of defined clusters using nearest neighbor and fuzzy matching logic: "Show the percentage of low-calorie candy sales contained in the 1,000 market baskets whose content most closely matches a young, health-conscious family profile."

The business questions in these seven categories grow progressively more interesting as we move down the list. The questions in categories 4 through 7 lead almost directly to decisions made and actions taken. Decisions made and actions taken are the true outputs of a data warehouse, and in that sense we should devote a large part of our creative energy to making these kinds of difficult queries possible.

How did you do in comparing these business questions to SQL and industry standard tools? Not too well, I assume. Most query tools can really only do category 1 (simple constraints) easily. Nearly all the seasoned tools that I am aware of can also do category 2 (simple subqueries), although the user interface commands for doing these subqueries may be cumbersome. A few tools are aggressively selling their ability to perform category 3 queries (correlated subqueries). As far as I know, none of the standard query or reporting products has direct user interfaces for categories 4 through 7. If you are trying to support queries in these categories, you are faced with an architectural dilemma: These business questions are getting too complex to express in a single request. Not only should the user partition these queries into sequential processing steps in order to think more clearly about the problem, but the underlying algorithms may be more stable and controllable if they are doing less in each step. So how do you attack these difficult problems in categories 4 through 7, and can you use your current tools to get you part way or all the way to useful answers?

In article 13.25, *Features for Query Tools*, I briefly described a technique for handling behavioral queries. Since then, I have been discussing this technique with many groups, and I am becoming convinced that this approach could be an important step forward for query tools that would extend their reach across categories 4, 5, and 6 (simple and derived behavioral queries and progressive sub-setting queries). The technique partitions the problem into two steps:

1. Run an exception report or series of queries that defines the complex behavior you wish to label. For instance, "Define the candy products in September 1997 whose household penetration for our grocery chain in the 12 months prior to September were more than two standard deviations less than the household penetration of the same products across our 10 biggest retail competitors." Although this is a complex request, most of the good report and analysis systems on the market should be able to handle it. After running the exception report (in this case yielding a list of products), capture the product keys of the products identified in the exception report as an actual physical table, consisting of a single product key column, taking care to use the product's natural key.

2. Now, use the special behavior dimension table of product keys, shown in Figure 13-13, whenever you wish to constrain any analysis on any table to that set of specially defined products. The only requirement is that the target fact table must contain a product dimension.

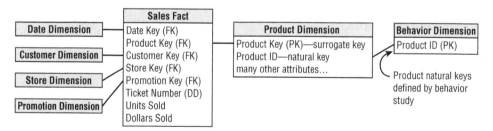

Figure 13-13: A special behavior dimension is added to a normal dimensional model to restrict the schema to the context of a behaviorally defined group of products.

The special behavior dimension is attached only with an equijoin to the natural key field in the product. This can even be done in a view that hides the explicit join to the special behavior dimension so it looks and behaves like a regular, uncomplicated dimensional model. If the special dimension table is hidden under a view and we call this view "Special Product Sales" instead of "Sales," then virtually every query tool and report writer should be able to analyze this specially restricted schema smoothly, without paying a syntax or user interface penalty for the complex processing that defined the original exception report.

Like any design decision, this one involves certain compromises. First, this approach requires a user interface for capturing, creating, and administering real physical tables in the data warehouse. We can imagine building a simple applet in Visual Basic (or another capable application development tool) that sits outside of your favorite query tool or report writer. Whenever a complex exception report has been defined on the screen, you make sure that the appropriate set of keys is displayed and then capture them into the applet with cut and paste. This applet then creates the special behavior dimension table.

A second reality is that these tables must live in the same database space as the primary fact table because they are going to be joined to the fact table directly, thus affecting the DBA's responsibilities.

Third, the use of a random set of product keys, as in our example, will affect aggregate navigation on the product dimension. A sophisticated approach could build custom aggregations on the special behavior set for all those queries that summed over the whole set rather than enumerating the individual members. Aggregate navigation on all the other dimensions should be unaffected.

By storing the keys in the special behavior dimensions in sorted order, set operations of union, intersection, and set difference can be handled in a single pass, thus allowing us to construct derived behavior dimensions that are the combinations of two or more complex exception reports or series of queries.

Finally, by generalizing the behavior dimension to include a time key in each record along with the product key (in the example), the time key can be used to constrain records in the master fact table that occurred after the behaviorally defined event. In this way, we can search for behaviors in a sequential order.

This approach offers the hope that we can use our existing tools to extend our queries beyond simple constraints and subqueries.

13.27 Smarter Data Warehouses

Joy Mundy, Intelligent Enterprise, *Feb 16, 2001*

Few queries and reports perform any calculation fancier than summing or counting, with the occasional ratio thrown in for excitement. Query and reporting tool vendors have done an excellent job of making the simple things easy. They do a nice job of providing functionality that is missing from SQL, such as subtotals and market contributions. Some can perform more complex calculations, but doing so requires extracting data from the database onto a client desktop or middle-tier server.

In a lot of cases, this multi-tiered design is not a problem. Many companies have good internal network bandwidth, and power analysts seem to prefer having local data sets that they can play with as they wish. Yet to make greatest use of the power analysts' efforts, the output from their work must be fed back into the operations of the enterprise systems. Such closed-loop systems are becoming increasingly common in CRM, web-oriented data warehouses, system operations, and many other applications.

We are led down this path by the predictable choice of SQL as the query and analysis language for the data warehouse. But SQL is not rich and flexible enough to do analysis on its own, so our best analysts use it to pull data out of the warehouse and into their preferred tools. This creates the multi-tiered architecture.

The OLAP extensions to SQL-99 reduce this problem, but SQL is fundamentally not an analytic language. We need an analytic engine and language that are tightly integrated with the data store, yet robustly designed for scalability and programmability.

SQL Scrutinized

Can SQL do the job for production reporting applications? Is SQL an analytic language? Not really. It requires convoluted syntax to perform trivial analytics, such as market share, moving average, rank, percentile, delta, or standard deviation. SQL, as its name (Structured Query Language) says, is a query language.

SQL-92 is fairly flexible, and can perform more computations than most people realize. As I describe later, a SQL expert could write a query that computes market share and moving averages. However, it seems highly unlikely that this is something you'd really choose to do, and you'd have to write the query by hand, because no query tool is going to provide much help.

Let's choose a simple example. As everyone who has looked at an investment website must know, moving averages are a common tool in financial analysis. A moving average, very simply, is the average of a measure over a rolling window. For example, to calculate a three-day moving average of a stock price you'd average the price for today, yesterday, and the day before. Standard deviation, a measure of volatility, is also a common measure in investment analysis. As a starting point for our discussion, assume you want to compute the moving average and standard deviation of stock prices over appropriate time intervals from the schema shown in Figure 13-14.

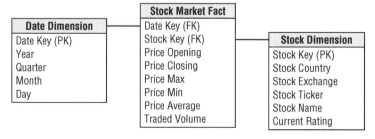

Figure 13-14: A sample schema with stock prices.

A fundamental characteristic of a relational database is that the order of rows in a table has no meaning. SQL can order rows on output, but there is no syntax for ordering rows so as to operate on them in a query. To perform a moving average calculation in SQL-92, you'd need to join the fact table to itself three times. A 200-day moving average would require a 200-way self join, which is ridiculous.

SQL-99 OLAP Extensions

What about the much anticipated OLAP extensions to SQL-99? They are a genuine improvement to the query language. The primary feature of the OLAP extensions is the WINDOW clause. The WINDOW clause is designed to solve exactly this sort of problem: It's a way to specify in the query that you want to perform an action over the set of rows {today, yesterday, day before}.

Here is the basic query drawn from the schema shown in Figure 13-14 using SQL-99 syntax:

```
SELECT d.day_date,
s.stock_ticker,
F. price_close,
avg(F. price_close) over Window1 AS MovAvg,
STD(f.price_close) OVER Window1 AS StDev
From market_facts f, dates d, stocks s
WHERE f.date_key = d.date_key and f.stock_key = s.stock_key
WINDOW Window1 As (PARTITION BY (s.stock_ticker)
ORDER BY (d.day_date ASC)
ROWS 2 PRECEDING) ;
```

The PARTITION BY clause is similar to a GROUP BY clause. It tells the "window" to start over when it sees a new stock. Without this clause, you'd be intermingling data from different companies. The ORDER BY clause ensures that you include the correct rows in the window. Remember that the relational database is inherently agnostic about the ordering of rows.

The ROWS 2 PRECEDING clause specifies that you want to perform some action on the current row and the two previous rows. A 200-day window, then, would simply replace the ROWS phrase with ROWS 199 PRECEDING. Finally, it's the AVG and STD functions in the SELECT list that indicate what action you want to perform on sets of rows you've grouped together in the window.

The SQL-99 syntax supports multiple windows in a query. Extending this query to compute a moving average over one range, and standard deviation over a second range, would be as straightforward as defining a second WINDOW clause.

Just because your database engine implements the SQL-99 OLAP extensions doesn't mean it does so well. All it means to conform to the ANSI syntax standards is that your database engine accepts the syntax and returns correct results. Underneath the covers, the engine might be joining the fact table to itself.

More Advanced Queries

What if you wanted to look at investment returns rather than prices? The desired output is a series of each stock's daily return and standard deviation, computed relative to the beginning of the year.

Consider the following query, derived from Figure 13-14, which employs a subquery to get the starting price used to calculate the investment return:

```
SELECT d.day_date,
s.stock_ticker,
(f.price_close / sq.price_Jan - 1.0) AS InvRtn,
AVG(f.price_close) OVER Window1 / sq.price_Jan AS MovAvg,
STD(f.price_close) OVER Window1 AS StDev
FROM market_facts f, dates d, stocks s,
(SELECT f1.stock_key, f1.price_open AS price_Jan
FROM market_facts f1, dates d1
WHERE d1.day_date = 'Jan-01-2000') AS sq
WHERE f.date_key = d.date_key and f.stock_key = s.stock_key
AND f.stock_key = sq.stock_key
AND d.day_date >= 'Jan-01-2000'
WINDOW Window1 AS ( PARTITION BY (s.stock_ticker)
ORDER BY (d.day_date ASC)
ROWS 49 PRECEDING) ;
```

There are several additional common computations that the new SQL-99 OLAP extensions support. The following items are excruciatingly difficult to generate without the WINDOW clause:

- **Cumulative totals.** It is straightforward to accumulate an additive measure, using the ROWS UNBOUNDED PRECEDING clause.
- **Deltas.** With some creativity, you could define a query that compares a measure for today with the same measure for yesterday, last week, or last year.
- **Market share.** You could express this query in a single statement with multiple windows. This is a very common requirement in reporting.
- **Rank.** The RANK windowing function returns an integer that indicates a rank within a partition. Ranks are typically used as alternative sort orders or filters in a report. In our investment example, you may rank stocks on investment return, volatility, and on trading volume.

It's important to note that neither example illustrated in this article is what I would call a complex question; these are complex queries that answer simple questions.

The Extension Problem

The addition of the WINDOW clause to the SQL standard greatly increases the usefulness of the SQL language for numerical analysis. Analysts will receive the syntax gratefully, and I expect the burden of computation to shift somewhat toward the database engine and away from the front end tool. But there are several types of analytic problems that are not addressed by the standard, including:

- Aggregations using multiplication
- Applying different rules to different branches of a hierarchy (such as computing returns in Europe using a different formula than for returns in the United States)

These are second order issues. The fundamental problem with using SQL, even SQL-99, to perform complex computations is that it is just too hard to formulate the queries. Subqueries and HAVING clauses have been part of SQL for many years, yet the syntaxes are poorly supported by query tools. Unfortunately, I suspect it will be several years before we see many products with an intuitive interface for building ad hoc queries that use the new SQL-99 OLAP extensions.

OLAP Is an Answer

One answer is to place an analytic tier between the data store and the users. This analytic tier will provide the kinds of functionality described in article 7.12, *Rating Your Dimensional Data Warehouse*. For the purposes of the current discussion, I'm agnostic about whether the underlying data store is in the relational database or another format, although if the underlying database is relational, it should support the OLAP extensions. The analytic criteria should include:

- Performing effective and consistent analysis at multiple levels of aggregation
- Exploring the relationships among multiple attributes of the data
- Predefining analytic expressions in a flexible way
- Natively supporting a wide variety of analytics
- Leaving the analytic door open: Use APIs to seamlessly integrate external computation engines for special purpose analytics that are beyond the scope of the OLAP engine.

The OLAP products on the market today address these criteria with varying, but generally good, success. OLAP technology is most widely known for solving the "aggregate navigation" problem, but it also provides an effective platform for interesting analytics. All OLAP products provide significantly greater flexibility for analysis than SQL does, but at a cost: Each uses its own proprietary query or calculation language.

For example, Microsoft's analytic language MDX (from "multidimensional expressions") provides a facility for the power analyst to store an analytic expression in the Analysis Services database. The *computed member*, as these stored expressions are called, can be staggeringly complex. They can even be defined to call out to an external module that would perform multivariate time series analysis. All the functionality I discuss in this article is natively supported.

Returning to the business problem at the beginning of this article, the power analyst would define the moving average for a stock price as a computed member:

```
Avg(Time.CurrentMember.Lag(2):Time.
CurrentMember, [Closing Price])
```

The casual user of the system can drag this measure into a query. It will work correctly regardless of the requested level of aggregation and no matter which dimensions are displayed. You could create a more complex expression, transparently creating a 50-day moving average if the measure is viewed on the day level; a 10-week moving average at the week level; and a three-month moving average for data viewed by month.

Here is a full query that uses this predefined measure:

```
SELECT {[Closing Price],
[Price Moving Average], -- computed member
[Price StDev]} -- computed member
ON COLUMNS,
{[Time].[2000].Members} ON ROWS,
{[Stocks].[USA].Members} ON PAGES
FROM [Stock Price Cube]
```

No matter how complex the MDX of the computed measure, its use is straightforward. The MDX-enabled query and reporting tool can be designed to graphically present elements on rows, columns, and pages; the numeric measures that fill in the grid are computed by the Analysis Services code.

I don't mean to trivialize the complexity of MDX and the other analytic languages. They are difficult syntaxes to master. I have seen MDX that is breathtakingly complex, and there are few tools to help develop analytic measures. Again, the saving grace is that the difficult work needs be done only once, and is easily shared with many.

Looking to the future, we can expect to see a broader use of analytic systems in closed-loop applications. Query and reporting requirements are well served by languages and programming interfaces that were designed to support ad hoc analysis. Similarly, the graduate-level statistical requirements of closed-loop systems call for analysis systems vendors to incorporate data mining APIs into their products. And the data mining algorithm developers must take this movement seriously, or risk having their tool set dismissed as too difficult to use and too awkward to integrate into operational systems.

14 Maintenance and Growth Considerations

ongratulations! You've just about reached the goal line. But don't start celebrating quite yet. You still need to keep your eye on the ball as you deploy and then enter the maintenance end zone. This chapter is divided into two sections. The first provides recommendations surrounding deployment. Then we turn our attention to maintenance issues, starting with checkups to assess the health of your DW/BI system, followed by prescriptive plans to address common sponsorship, usage, architecture, and data maladies. We finish by dealing with the orderly "sunsetting" or preserving of data from legacy applications that are no longer being used by IT.

Deploying Successfully

Deployment demands significant upfront planning prior to the big event. In this section, we discuss the advance preparation required for operations and marketing, as well as considerations when rolling out subsequent projects focused on new business processes.

14.1 Don't Forget the Owner's Manual

Joy Mundy, Intelligent Enterprise, *Jul 1, 2005*

Data warehouse teams often postpone thinking about the ongoing operations of their new DW/BI systems until they're nearly in production. It's too late to start designing your operating procedures when deployment deadlines are looming and users are clamoring for data and reports. The train has already left the station. You'll be making stuff up as you go along, inevitably making mistakes.

Think about two sets of considerations with respect to the ongoing operations of your production DW/BI systems. The first set revolves around users: What information do they need to use the system successfully? And after the initial launch, how will the system improve and evolve to meet their needs? Second and equally important are the planning considerations for technical systems management: the procedures to ensure the system operates trouble free, or at least crisis free.

Front Room Operations

When a new DW/BI system is deployed, business users focus on the front room: the interface they see and use every day. In fact, user communities sometimes refer to the data warehouse by the BI tool vendor's name or the "reporting portal." Little do they realize that building and deploying reports is only a fraction, typically less than 10 percent, of the effort required to create a DW/BI system. But people focus on what they can see. If the reporting portal is ugly, uninformative, or slow, the entire warehouse/BI system looks bad.

When launching the BI environment, you'll publish an initial set of reports, charts, and analyses that meet the requirements identified through business user interviews at the beginning of your project. Let's assume these deliverables are meaningful, attractive, parameterized as appropriate, and allow drill-down where useful. You must train the business users on the system you've built: not just where to click, but also how the analyses should be used and why. Here are some typical user questions you must be prepared to answer:

- How do I access the BI system?
- How do I request broader system access?
- How do I find the report I need?
- When was the data in the system last refreshed?
- Where can I get help?
- How do I customize a report?
- How do I build a completely new report?
- How do I add my report to the system so others in the organization can use it?
- How do I customize my portal view?
- How do I build a more complex analysis?

You might be able to build such an intuitive reporting environment that the answers to some of these questions are obvious, but you're fooling yourself if you think you can avoid documenting the system and providing rollout training.

You must establish (and maintain) a web site with fresh information about how to use the system, data currency, and where to get help. If your reporting tool has a web-based launch page, think about customizing that page to add this important information. Otherwise, train users to go to your page first and link from there to the reports and/or tool page.

You must also develop plans for training after the system is in production. New hires will need training and a surprisingly large percentage of the initial users will benefit from more instruction. Perhaps you'll need to offer new types of training, for superpower users or very occasional users. Online instruction materials are useful, but there are significant benefits to getting business users in a room where you can talk to them, and they can talk to each other, face to face.

Your front room rollout and operations plan should include a plan for the help desk. If your organization has a centralized IT help desk, use the same infrastructure for first-tier support. Even though connectivity is a lot simpler than it was a decade ago, the majority of user issues are still about how to connect. A centralized help desk can help on this front, but plan for a large percentage of questions to get escalated to specialists, probably someone on the data warehouse team.

Many query and reporting tools let business users customize their system views, often by creating "My Reports" folders on the portal. This functionality is great, but you should develop policies and procedures for personal reports warranting higher visibility. It often makes sense for central BI team members to put reports through quality assurance and tweak them before publishing to a broad audience. It's not only a matter of ensuring that new or revised reports are accurate; you must also ensure that they perform well and that modifications won't adversely affect existing users.

Back Room Operations

The second set of considerations focuses on technical systems management. Long before you go into production, you must think about a host of operational concerns because your decisions will affect the system configuration and design. If you don't create a sound operations plan before you deploy, the data warehouse team will end up patching things together in crisis mode, which inevitably leads to crises of confidence within the user community.

The back room operations plan should address at least the following questions:

- How will you monitor resource usage?
- How will you report on usage?
- How will you automate your operations, especially the extract, transformation, and load (ETL) processing?
- How will you know when your ETL processing has encountered a problem?
- How will you notify users of data problems?
- How will you monitor system performance?
- How will you kill relational database and OLAP system queries?
- How will you identify and solve performance bottlenecks?
- How can you tune the system to prevent bottlenecks?
- How will you ensure your system never runs out of disk space?
- Do you need to modify your ongoing ETL process to accommodate data partitioning?

Most important, you need to plan, implement, and test your backup and recovery strategy. A backup and recovery plan that's not tested regularly isn't a plan. It's a wish, and it's unrealistic of you to expect that wish to come true.

There are no easy answers to these questions. The best solutions are intertwined with your ETL system design. You can prevent a lot of problems by designing your ETL system to proactively check for conditions, such as the successful completion of an operational process, before starting work. As described in article 11.2, *The 34 Subsystems of ETL*, a robust ETL system checks for exceptions and whether the data volume and contents are reasonable. Keep track of how much disk space a daily load requires and verify that plenty of disk space is available and allocated.

Monitor Operations

Plan to monitor the operations of all the software components in your DW/BI environment: operating systems, relational databases, OLAP and data mining systems, query and reporting software, and any web portals. Developing a robust monitoring system usually requires combining features of your operating systems with features of your database engines and front end tools. Even if you use a single vendor for your BI technology, you should expect to combine several kinds of monitoring. Plan to create a relational database to store the monitoring performance data. You may populate the results of monitoring traces directly into the relational database, or it may make more sense to trace into files and then load those files periodically.

Monitor the systems at all times. Set up the "always on" monitoring to include important events such as user logons and ETL process completions, in addition to all error events. This "always on" monitoring should periodically record statuses such as memory usage, perhaps at 15-minute intervals. Because this basic monitoring is continuous, you should justify the inclusion of every element you're tracing.

Periodically, perhaps once a month, ratchet up the monitoring to capture more events and statuses. This monthly detailed baseline can be invaluable in diagnosing performance problems, and you can often catch these problems before they're perceptible to business users. You may trace statuses at five- or 15-second intervals and keep detailed track of the processes occurring. Detailed monitoring usually affects system performance, so avoid doing it during system usage peak times. On the other hand, if you monitor the reporting system in the middle of the night, you probably won't learn anything.

These operational issues aren't sexy. You're not going to fire up the imagination of business users by talking about them. But if you don't think about these problems early on and build an operations plan into your procedures, your DW/BI system will fail. Business users won't know how to use the system and they won't know where to go to get information and assistance. Their confidence in the system, the data, and your efforts will be shaken. All they'll see is the bad, and the 98 percent of the system that's good will go to waste.

QUICK STUDY: DOS AND DON'TS FOR DW/BI SYSTEM OPERATIONS PLANNING

- Do test the system and operations thoroughly before moving into production.
- Do develop user training that's customized to your data and environment.
- Do publish a web site or portal with fresh information about the system, including when data was last updated.
- Do publish information about how to access the system.
- Do monitor the processing and query operations at all times at a nonintrusive level.

- Do develop a procedure for killing a query (and then follow it).
- Do ratchet up monitoring occasionally to develop a detailed performance baseline before you encounter performance problems.
- Do develop a backup and recovery strategy.
- Do inform business users as quickly as possible about any processing or data issues in the system, such as failed loads or (horrors!) inaccurate data.
- Don't expect a centralized IT help desk to provide much assistance beyond troubleshooting connectivity.
- Don't assume recovery is going to work unless you've tested it.

14.2 Let's Improve Our Operating Procedures

Joy Mundy, Design Tip #52, *Mar 4, 2004*

In my career I've been able to review a lot of data warehouses in various stages of their lifecycles. I've observed that, broadly speaking, we are not very good about operating the data warehouse system with anything like the rigor that the transaction system folks expect of their systems. In all fairness, a data warehouse is not a transaction system, and few companies can justify a 24 × 7 service level agreement for data warehouse access. But come on guys, do we have to look like Keystone Kops in an emergency? As we all know, bad things happen, especially in data warehouses, which are downstream from every other system in your company.

Operating a data warehouse in a professional manner is not much different than any other systems operations: Follow standard best practices, plan for disaster, and practice. Here are some basic suggestions, based on my observations from actual deployments.

- **Negotiate a service level agreement (SLA) with the business users.** The key here is to negotiate, and then to take that SLA seriously. The decision about service level must be made between the executive sponsor and data warehouse team leader, based on a thoughtful analysis of the costs and benefits of ratcheting up the SLA toward high availability. The basic outlines of the SLA need to be negotiated early in the project, as a requirement for high availability may significantly change the details of your physical architecture. Remember that an SLA is meant to be a reasonable compromise between both parties: IT and the business users. Signing up for "five 9's" of uptime reliability means your data warehouse can only be down for five minutes and 15 seconds *per year.*
- **Use service accounts for all data warehouse operations.** You'd think it would go without saying that all production operations should use a specified service account with appropriate permissions. But I've long lost count of how many times I've seen production loads fail because the DBA left the company and his personal account became inactive.

■ **Isolate development from testing from production.** Again, it should go without saying. Again, apparently it doesn't. I've observed two main barriers against teams being rigorous about dev/test/prod procedures: cost and complexity.

The hardware and software costs can be significant, because the best practice is to configure a test system identically to its corresponding production system. You may be able to negotiate reduced software licensing costs for the test system, but the hardware vendors are seldom so accommodating. If you have to skimp on hardware, reduce storage first, testing with a subset of historical data. Next I'd reduce the number of processors. As a last resort, I'd reduce the memory on the test machine. I really hate to make these compromises, because processing and query characteristics might change in a discontinuous fashion. In other words, the test system might behave substantially differently with reduced data, processors, or memory.

The development hardware systems are usually normal desktop machines, although their software should be virtually identical to test and production. Coerce your software vendors to provide as many development licenses as you need at near zero cost. I think all development licenses should cost less than $100. (Good luck!)

Everything that you do to the production system should have been designed in the development machine and the deployment script tested on the test system. Every operation in the back room should go through rigorous scripting and testing, whether deploying a new dimensional model, adding a column, changing indexes, changing your aggregate design, modifying a database parameter, backing up, or restoring. Centrally managed front room operations like deploying new query and reporting tools, deploying new corporate reports, and changing security plans, should be equally rigorously tested, and scripted if your front end tools allow it.

Data warehouse software vendors do not make it easy for you to do the right thing. The front end tools and OLAP servers are particularly bad about helping, or even permitting, the development of scripts for incremental operations. It is very challenging to coordinate the rollout of a new subject area across RDBMS, ETL system, analysis, and reporting systems. Be very careful, and practice, practice, practice!

■ **As much as possible, make a data warehouse release be like a commercial software release** with a well defined release number and an accurate list of all the components that implement the release. Make it possible to back out a release in order to restore the previous version if the release contains a catastrophic error, such as calculating division profitability incorrectly(!).

■ **Develop playbooks for all operations.** A playbook contains step-by-step instructions for performing an operation, such as restoring a database or table, or deploying a new dimensional model, or adding a new column to a table. You should develop generic playbooks, and then customize that playbook for each operation you plan to perform in production. For example, if you are changing a database parameter, write down, in reasonable detail, the steps to follow.

Then test the playbook on the test system before applying it to the production environment. The playbook is particularly vital if you are performing an operation through a tool's user interface rather than via a script.

Operations is not the fun part of data warehousing. But with good planning and practice, you can meet the inevitable snafus with calm and deliberation, rather than hysteria.

14.3 Marketing the DW/BI System

Warren Thornthwaite, Design Tip #91, *May 30, 2007*

Marketing is often dismissed by technical folks. When someone says "oh, you must be from marketing," it's rarely meant as a compliment. This is because we don't really understand what marketing is and why it's important. In this article, we review classic marketing concepts and explore how we can apply them to the DW/BI system.

It might be more palatable to think of marketing as education. Marketers educate consumers about product features and benefits, while generating awareness of a need for those features and benefits. Marketing gets a bad name when it's used to convince consumers of a need that isn't real, or sell a product that doesn't deliver its claimed features and benefits. But that is a different article. Really great marketing, when effectively focused on the value delivered, is hugely important.

Before you start creating your marketing program, you should have a clear understanding of your key messages: What are the mission, vision, and value of your DW/BI system? Marketing 101 has focused on the four Ps (product, price, placement, and promotion) for at least the past 30 years or so. We'll look at each of these factors in the context of the DW/BI system and direct you to additional information where it is available.

Product

As far as the business community is concerned, the DW/BI products are the information needed for decision making and the BI applications and portal through which the information is delivered. Our products must excel in the following five areas:

- **Value.** Meet the business needs identified in the requirements process.
- **Functionality.** Product must work well.
- **Quality.** Data and calculations have to be right.
- **Interface.** Be as easy as possible to use and look good.
- **Performance.** Deliver results in a reasonable time frame as defined by the users.

Price

Most users don't pay for the DW/BI system directly. The price they pay is the effort it takes to get the information from the DW/BI system compared to other alternatives. There is an upfront cost of learning how to use the BI tool or applications, and an ongoing cost of finding the right report or building the right query for a particular information need. You must lower the price as much as possible by first creating excellent products that are as easy to use as possible. Then offer a full set of training, support, and documentation, including directly accessible business metadata, on an ongoing basis.

Placement

In consumer goods, placement is obvious: The product has to be on the store shelf or the customer can't buy it. For the DW/BI system, placement means our customers are able to find the information they need when they need it. In other words, you must build a navigation structure for the BI applications that makes sense to the business folks. Additionally, tools like search, report metadata descriptions and categories, and personalization capabilities can be extremely helpful. For additional information, take a look at article 13.11, *The BI Portal*.

Promotion

Every customer contact you have is a marketing opportunity. TV ads are not an option, not counting YouTube, but you do have several promotion channels for the DW/BI system:

- **BI applications.** These are what people use the most. Names are important; having a good acronym for the DW/BI system can leave a good impression. Every report and application should have a footer indicating that it came from the DW/BI system and a logo in one of the upper corners. Ultimately, if you create a good product, the name and logo of your DW/BI brand will become marks of quality.
- **BI portal.** This is the main entry point for the DW/BI system. It has to meet the same requirements as the BI applications.
- **Regular communications.** Know who your stakeholders are and which communications vehicle works best for each. Your ongoing communications plan will include status reports, executive briefings, and user newsletters. Consider webcasts on specific topics if that's an option in your organization.
- **Meetings, events, and training.** Any public meeting where you can get a few minutes on the agenda is a good thing. Briefly mention a recent successful business use, remind people of the nature and purpose of the DW/BI system, and tell them about any upcoming plans or events. Host your own events, like user forum meetings, every six to nine months or so.

Ongoing marketing is a key element of every successful DW/BI system. The more you keep people informed about the value you provide them, they more they will support your efforts.

14.4 Coping with Growing Pains

Joy Mundy, Intelligent Enterprise, May 1, 2004

So you've deployed your first dimensional model. Fortunately, the business loves it and is clamoring for more! They want to query and analyze integrated data from additional enterprise data sources.

For some of you, this demand is a dream come true. For others, it may be the start of a slow motion nightmare.

In this article, I'll use a case study to discuss the challenges you'll likely encounter when it's time to roll your next business process dimensional model into production. Sadly, there's no magic. Putting your next business process subject area into production is a difficult, though not intractable, problem. It's a good place to focus any fastidious tendencies you might have.

Recognize the Target

Let's start at the end state goal. Your target enterprise information architecture consists of multiple interconnecting business process dimensional models sharing conformed dimensions as advocated by the enterprise data warehouse bus architecture approach. Using shared conformed dimensions has several important implications. Durable keys in the dimensions must be identical. How else can you join across subject areas? Additionally, you must have corporate agreement about which attributes are tracked through history and which are updated in place. How else can dimension keys be identical?

Case Study Scenario

Let's imagine you launched your enterprise information infrastructure with a successful retail sales dimensional model. The retail sales information is used daily by store management, as well as by many corporate users in marketing and finance. It captures data at the correct transactional grain, its daily update process is smooth, and system downtime is well within the service level agreement (SLA). The retail sales schema is a thing of grace and beauty.

The success of the retail sales project has emboldened management to extend the enterprise data warehouse to support additional CRM requirements, namely customers' calls into the call center. In theory, this decision is no problem: You'll reuse the date and customer dimensions from the first project, add some new dimensions and new facts, and you're done, right? In practice, there will be a few wrinkles.

Not So Fast

Obviously, you'll need to figure out how to modify the ETL process to also populate the new tables in the call center schema. But there may be some more complex implications.

Let's think a bit more about the customer dimension in the original retail sales schema. First, the definition of a sales customer is actually a subset of all customers; the only customers you know anything about are those with loyalty cards and corresponding account numbers. When you add the call center information, you can expect to get information about a whole group of customers you've never seen before. The customer dimension ETL process is going to have to change to accommodate the new source, as I'll discuss later. Adding new customers to the customer dimension shouldn't affect the existing dimensional model. The new customer rows won't join to any existing retail sales fact rows because there's no way to link a "nonloyalty" caller to a sales transaction. The existing sales schema should behave the same, or almost the same, as it always has.

What if the business users want to track more information for call center customers than was necessary or available for retail sales? For example, what if the caller's phone number is important? You need to add that new attribute to the customer dimension, again modifying the customer dimension ETL process. As was the case with the new customers, adding the phone number shouldn't disrupt the original dimensional model; existing reports and analyses will continue to work as before.

Finally, let's tackle a harder problem. What if the business users of the call center data have a compelling need to track history for the customer's address? In other words, they want to be able to know that when a customer called last year she lived in Montana, but now lives in Hawaii. Dimensional modeling can handle this requirement with the type 2 slowly changing dimension (SCD) technique. The issue is that you're changing a fundamental characteristic of the customer dimension in a way that could affect the existing retail sales dimensional model. I'll return to this dilemma in a bit.

Plan Before You Build

Not surprisingly, the first thing you need to do to deploy the call center data is develop a plan. I hope you already have policies for managing the development cycle: checking in code to source control; using separate development, test, and production environments; having specifications and test plans; deploying SLAs for system availability, and so on. If not, now is a good opportunity to put that infrastructure in place.

The call center schema design specifies the new tables and modifications to the existing tables, such as customer. The designers should also provide a reasonable specification for the ETL process. You need to drill down on those specifications to a finer detail, discussing what the designs mean within the context of modifications to a system in production. In other words, you need to think through, at a high level, how you're going to modify the existing ETL system to incorporate the new workload. You also need to consider whether you're going to alter the existing customer table or rebuild it. In either case, you must think about any implications on the SLA.

One of the most important issues to resolve during the planning phase is how to handle the modification of the customer dimension to track history. By far the easiest approach is to start tracking history now. All existing historical data gets associated with the customer's attributes as they are today. New facts get correctly associated with future changes in customer attributes. Often it's the only feasible approach because the history of customer attributes, address in our example, is simply unavailable. Note that even with this simple approach, you might need to modify the ETL process for retail sales so that you're propagating the correct customer key into the fact table. In practice, the retail sales ETL process likely picks up the most current customer key, but you'd be foolish to exclude verification of this point from your test plan.

A more challenging approach is to re-create history for a customer. You may be able to build a version of the customer dimension that includes the history of customer address changes. This is seldom easy, but may be possible. If it's possible, it's the job of the data warehouse team leader to present management with a cost benefit analysis of the effort. If you decide to take on this challenge, you have a second decision: whether or not to re-create history for the retail sales schema. The process of re-creating history in the fact table is conceptually simple because you know the sales transaction dates and the dates for which a customer's address is valid. However, performing this simple action requires updates on a significant number of fact table rows, which is an expensive operation. A second cost benefit analysis is required. And don't forget to develop a test plan to ensure you didn't mess things up!

Finally, your plan should discuss how to handle the proliferation of these changes to aggregate tables and OLAP cubes. If these structures are affected at all, they probably need to be rebuilt from scratch. Adjust your schedule accordingly, and don't forget your test plan.

Develop, Test, Deploy

The development of the new database elements and ETL processes is typically done against a small subset of data. This approach is only sensible. But developers need to remain constantly aware that they're adding new elements to an existing production system with potentially significant data volumes. A technique such as dropping and re-creating a table might work just fine in the development environment, but could be a complete disaster in the real world.

The test environment is the place to verify that the database can be upgraded, new data sources added, and new transformations processed without adversely affecting the existing operations. The first thing you need to do in the test environment is back up the entire system: data structures, data, and ETL processes. You need to test these main things: the new database structures, the ETL processes, and the process of migrating to the new structures and processes. Each test iteration should start from a clean system that hasn't had any of the migration changes applied to it (in other words, a system just restored from backup). Although early testing can be performed against a subset of data, your final set of tests should operate against a comprehensive environment, ideally an exact copy of the production system that you'll be modifying.

It's difficult to determine how to test the migration process. People often use this time as an opportunity to migrate the data warehouse to new hardware, which they've been testing as a shadow system. If you're running your data warehouse on commodity hardware, it's not terribly difficult to justify this approach. But if you have huge data volumes in production, you probably have no choice but to invest some serious planning and testing time to "doing it right."

Some Final Thoughts

Much of the pain discussed in this article can be avoided if the initial design for retail sales thinks a few steps ahead to anticipate the need for address change tracking. One of the elements of art in data warehouse design is to think just broadly enough without being sucked into getting all requirements from all users. Realistically, it's a characteristic of a successful data warehouse to change over time, and the data warehouse team should be prepared to accommodate those changes.

In general, my recommendations are: Plan, plan, plan. Communicate. Develop. Test, test, test.

Sustaining for Ongoing Impact

In this final section, we focus on doing the right things to keep your DW/BI system on the right track. Since staying on course is directly related to establishing that path in the first place, you'll find quite a few pointers to earlier *Reader* articles.

We begin this section with a recommendation to conduct periodic checkups to verify that your DW/BI implementation is in good health. Subsequent articles address the sponsorship, business acceptance, architecture, and data "illnesses" typically uncovered during a health assessment. We finish with a responsibility you may not have planned for: preparing for the shut down of production applications and their associated data sources.

14.5 Data Warehouse Checkups

Margy Ross, Intelligent Enterprise, Jun 12, 2004

It's human nature to resist visiting a doctor for periodic checkups. Generally, we'd prefer to avoid being poked and prodded, having our vital signs taken, and then being told that we need to quit smoking, exercise more, or change our lifestyle habits in some fashion. However, most of us are mature enough to realize that these regular checkups are critical to monitor our health against conventional and personal norms.

Similarly, it's critical to conduct regular checkups on your DW/BI environment. It's less invasive to just keep doing what you've grown accustomed to in your DW/BI environment, but it pays to regularly check its weight and blood pressure, as well as the pulse of the business community.

Just like the assortment of health guides available in your doctor's office, we'll describe the most common disorders encountered when performing DW/BI checkups. For each malady, we'll then discuss the telltale symptoms to watch for, as well as prescribed treatment plans.

This article is pertinent to anyone with a maturing (dare we say "graying") DW/BI system. Those of you just getting started should also watch for these warning signs to nip any disorder in the bud before it takes hold and spreads within your environment.

Business Sponsor Disorder

One of the most common, yet potentially fatal disorders involves the sponsorship of the DW/BI environment. A business sponsor disorder is often the key contributor to data warehouse stagnation.

Symptoms   Organizations are most vulnerable to this disorder when the original sponsor moves on either internally or externally. Even though someone will ultimately fill the job or assume the title, the new person likely isn't as zealous as the original sponsor. If the original sponsor left under somewhat negative circumstances, many of the assumptions concerning the data warehouse effort may be at risk, including tool selection, identity of trusted vendors, and even the chosen business process subject area. The political winds at the moment of such a transition can be especially turbulent.

Even if the sponsor hasn't changed jobs, he or she may mentally abdicate sponsorship duties. Newly formed data warehouse teams are especially susceptible. Once the team gets approval to proceed with the DW/BI initiative, it turns its complete attention to building the new environment as promised. In the meantime, another hot issue distracts the business sponsor (who potentially suffers from attention deficit disorder).

Another warning sign is if IT is the primary sponsor of the DW/BI program, establishing priorities and driving the development plan. Finally, if you find DW/BI funding suddenly coming under intense scrutiny, you're likely suffering from sponsorship disorder.

Treatment Plans The first step to treat this disorder is to identify and recruit a business sponsor. An ideal business sponsor visualizes the potential impact of the DW/BI environment on the business, which empowers the sponsor with enthusiasm to ensure that the larger business community embraces the DW/BI deliverable. If the sponsor isn't engaged and passionate about the cause, then it's tough to convey that to the rank and file. Effective sponsors often face a compelling problem that they're trying to address. Good sponsors are able to leverage this compelling problem to provide the project with momentum by insisting the organization can't afford not to act.

We look for business sponsors who are influential within their organizations, both in terms of hierarchical and personal power. DW/BI sponsors need to be politically astute and understand the culture, players, and processes. Because neither the business nor IT communities can effectively construct the DW/BI world independently, business sponsors should be realistic and willing to partner with IT. A business sponsor should be a thoughtful observer of the IT development cycle, knowing when in that cycle to ask for new capabilities.

The most obvious way to find a business sponsor is to conduct a high level assessment of the business requirements. Likely sponsor candidates will rise to the top of the surface as a result of this process. Another approach is to conduct a demonstration proof of concept, presuming expectations can be realistically managed.

If no one emerges as a potential willing and able sponsor, then the project team should seriously reconsider moving ahead. You absolutely need someone high in the business to champion the cause. Otherwise, you'll suffer from chronic business sponsor disorder. The estimated lifespan of a DW/BI environment plummets without strong business sponsorship.

Your work isn't done once you've identified and recruited a single sponsor. Given the never-ending nature of the DW/BI program, sponsorship needs to be institutionalized with a steering committee or governance group of senior business and IT representatives. Clearly, you don't want to put all your sponsorship eggs in one basket.

One of our favorite tools for working with business sponsors is the prioritization quadrant, described in article 4.10, *The Bottom-Up Misnomer*. This technique is used in the early stages of a data warehouse to align business and IT priorities, resulting in a program roadmap for the enterprise. On an ongoing basis, perhaps every six months to a year, the DW/BI sponsorship or governance group should review progress to date and revisit the prioritization quadrant to queue up subsequent projects balancing business value and feasibility.

You need to establish a "care and feeding" program for the DW/BI sponsors. Business sponsors are highly experienced and respected businesspeople, however, they may not be highly experienced in the organizational culture change often required for an analytic initiative. They may need some coaching on their new roles and responsibilities. Take a look at article 3.11, *Habits of Effective Sponsors*, for more details.

Never take your sponsors for granted. It's certainly not safe to rest on your laurels. You need to constantly communicate, feeding constructive, realistic, and solution-oriented feedback to the sponsors, while listening to stay abreast of sponsors' hot buttons. Communication is also critical to continually build bridges with other business leaders in the organization. Lastly, you should actively convey what the DW/BI world has done for them lately. You can't afford to wait until someone's scrutinizing expenditures to inform them of your successes. As uncomfortable as it may seem, you need to market the DW/BI environment. Enthusiastic business users typically deliver the most effective commercials.

Data Disorder

Accessing good data is one of the two pillars of the data warehouse. (The other is addressing the right business problems.) The most serious and common data disorders are poor quality data, incomplete data, and late data.

Symptoms   One of the key indicators of a data disorder is the degree of data reconciliation happening across the organization because the data is inconsistent or not trusted. Data disorders are often blurred with business acceptance shortfalls when the real underlying issue is that the data is irrelevant or overly complex.

Treatment Plans   The initial treatment for data disorders requires drafting an enterprise data warehouse bus matrix. The matrix establishes a blueprint for enterprise integration by identifying the core business processes and common, conformed dimensions. After the matrix is developed, it should be communicated and "sold" up, down, and across the organization to establish enterprise buy-in. If you already have a slew of disconnected analytic data repositories, you can embellish the bus matrix by cataloging the "as is" environment prior to developing action plans for your longer term data strategy.

While the bus matrix identifies the links between core business process subject areas in the data warehouse, it also highlights opportunities for ETL processing. Like the overall technical architecture, the back room ETL architecture is often created implicitly rather than explicitly, evolving as data profiling, quality, and integration needs grow. You may need to rethink the staging and ETL architecture to ensure consistency and throughput at acceptable costs.

You should preface the DW/BI project with a comprehensive data profiling task to confirm that the data is what it's advertised to be. During the production phase, you must continuously monitor the data for quality glitches and omissions. Finally, you should carefully examine whether you need to go to a streaming real-time architecture to deliver the data to decision makers within their "sweet spot" time window for affecting the business.

Data disorders often result when data is irrelevant, incomprehensible, or otherwise difficult to use. Review your existing data schemas for potential improvements. We identified guidelines for reviewing presentation dimensional models in article 7.11, *Fistful of Flaws*.

Finally, if you've invested a lot of time and resources to develop an atomic, normalized data warehouse but the business users complain that it's too complicated and slow, you can leverage that existing investment by creating complementary dimensional models to address ease of use and query performance, while also boosting your chances of business acceptance.

Business Acceptance Disorder

Here's another critical disorder affecting data warehouse mortality rates. If the business community doesn't accept the DW/BI environment to support decision making processes, then you've failed. Sorry to be so blunt, but it's a harsh reality. The business must be engaged if you're to stand any chance of DW/BI acceptance. Unfortunately, business engagement is often outside our comfort zones; we may be unsure about techniques for ensuring their engagement, plus there are typically no incentives in place for mastering this domain.

Symptoms   There are some strong indications of business acceptance disorder. Are the business users simply not using the data warehouse like you expected they would? Do the number of BI tool licenses greatly exceed the number of active users? Do the number of trained users greatly exceed the number of active users? Are the prime targeted beneficiaries of the DW/BI environment turning their attention to a different analytic platform, independent of the data warehouse? Do the business users make requests like "just give me a report with these three numbers on it" because they're loading the report into Excel where they're building their own personal data warehouse? Does the business community perceive a legacy of disappointment when it comes to IT's ability to address their requirements? Did the DW/BI project team focus on data and technology, presuming they understand the business's requirements better than the business does?

Treatment Plans   Your mission is to engage, or reengage, the business. Talking to users about their requirements is an obvious place to start. The DW/BI environment is supposed to support and turbocharge their decision making. Given this mission, distributing surveys or reviewing entity-relationship diagrams are ineffective tools for gathering business requirements. Put yourself in their shoes to understand how they currently make decisions and how they hope to make decisions in the future. Obviously, you need to have the right attitude, listen intently, and strive to capture their domain expertise.

It's important that you engage business folks across a vertical span of the organization. It's not enough to merely speak with pseudo IT power analysts who can make data jump through hoops. We need to talk to their peers who aren't so empowered, plus speak with middle and upper management to better understand where the organization is going. If you spend all your time in the trenches, you're vulnerable to being shortsighted by focusing solely on today's problems while ignoring the bigger issues looming in the future. It's highly beneficial to have relationships with all levels of the business organization, including executives, middle management, and individual contributors.

Of course, you're more likely to successfully engage the business when you have a strong business sponsor with a powerful ability to influence the organization. A strong, committed business sponsor can significantly affect the organization's culture. Conversely, if you suffer from a sponsorship disorder, it's even harder to obtain business acceptance. These two disorders often go hand in hand.

As previously discussed, one size doesn't fit all when it comes to analytic capabilities. You need to acknowledge the range of usage requirements and institutionalize a strategy to address the spectrum, as discussed in article 13.2, *Beyond Paving the Cow Paths*.

Similar to our discussion about business sponsor care and feeding, you need to establish a comparable program for the rest of the business community. Care and feeding commonly occurs with the initial deployment, but then we often quickly turn our attention to the next project iteration. You need to proactively conduct ongoing checkpoint reviews to remain engaged with the business. In addition, you should help the business users understand their shared responsibility for a healthy DW/BI program.

Education is a key component of deployment, but it isn't a one-time event. You need to consider ongoing needs for tool, data, and analysis education. We've worked with some organizations that include DW/BI training as part of their new hire orientation because information is a fundamental part of their culture. Not surprisingly, the DW/BI environment is broadly accepted in these companies; it's part of the way they do business.

Finally, as we described with the sponsorship disorder, communication is critical. You can't rely solely on traditional project documentation tools to communicate with all your constituencies. You need to concentrate on what's in it for them, marketing successes while managing expectations.

Infrastructure Disorder

Contrary to popular opinion, infrastructure disorders are seldom fatal. There's often room for improvement, but it's usually an elective procedure. Despite our personal interests in this disorder, it usually doesn't warrant the attention due the others.

Symptoms   Are the DW/BI systems slow or is the data late? Is the DW/BI environment commonly described as a bundle of technical bells and whistles? Are there tool overlaps and/or voids? What about performance concerns? Performance covers a gamut of potential underlying problems: ETL processing time to get the data loaded, query result time lags, and the DW/BI development cycle time to deliver new functionality.

Treatment Plans Every DW/BI environment is based on an architectural foundation; however, it may be time to revisit your overall architecture plan. The question is whether your plan was explicitly developed, or whether it just implicitly occurred. A well thought out plan facilitates communication, minimizes surprises, and coordinates efforts.

Revisiting your technical architecture doesn't mean going out and buying all the latest, greatest technology. You need to understand the business's needs and determine the associated implications on the technical architecture in terms of the required ETL services, BI access/analysis services, infrastructure, and metadata. The drive toward more real-time data warehousing is a prime example of the translation from business needs into architectural requirements. Some organizations have made poor technology choices in the past. It takes courage to unload that baggage to enhance the DW/BI environment going forward.

Cultural/Political Disorder

Unfortunately, DW/BI environments aren't immune to cultural or political disorders, and there's no vaccine in development on the research horizon.

Symptoms Symptoms of this disorder are fuzzier to articulate, especially because they typically transcend more than the DW/BI environment. Organizations with cultural and political disorders may be stymied by conflicting priorities of "doing it fast" versus "doing it right." Similarly, they often struggle to reach consensus on tough issues, such as data standardization and process changes. Be especially watchful when it comes time to reach agreement on the rollout of conformed dimensions since that is when talking ends and action begins. Finally, more specifically related to DW/BI, many organizational cultures aren't poised to embrace analytic decision making, especially when decisions have traditionally been based on gut feelings or intuition. Do the business users currently manage by the numbers? There's often a lack of recognition and/or willingness to champion a culture shift to more fact-based decision making.

Treatment Plans When dealing with cultural and political disorders, you can't just duck them, much as you would like. You need to be courageous, while understanding that these disorders are difficult to overcome with trench warfare. Now is the time to call in your support group: IT management, business sponsors, and the business community. If the support group doesn't recognize the need and assume accountability for treating these disorders, then the DW/BI team is in for a long, uphill struggle. Senior business and IT management must accept its fiduciary responsibility for handling information and analytics as corporate assets. Finally, actions speak louder than words. The organization will easily see through a veil of verbal commitment if management doesn't exhibit reinforcing behaviors.

Early Detection

With many maladies, early detection is essential to mounting a strong defense. Similarly, proactively monitoring your data warehouse and business intelligence environment is the best method of ensuring its long term health. It's tough to prescribe a remedy if you don't know what you're suffering from. As a student commented recently, thinking about common disorders and alternative treatment plans is a "shot in the arm" for anyone who's trying to rescue a failing data warehousing project. The metaphor lives on.

Finally, remember there's nothing wrong with having a checkup and learning that you're in perfect health. In fact, that's the optimal outcome!

14.6 Boosting Business Acceptance

Bob Becker, Intelligent Enterprise, *Aug 7, 2004*

Article 14.5, *Data Warehouse Checkups,* discussed the importance of regularly casting a critical eye over your DW/BI program. Checkups identify early warning signs and symptoms so appropriate treatment can occur before more serious consequences are encountered down the road.

One of the more troubling DW/BI maladies is the business acceptance disorder. In layperson's terms, the business community isn't using the DW/BI environment; it's just not a critical component of the business decision making process. Frankly, this is a frightening diagnosis for project teams. It's impossible to declare DW/BI success if no one in the business has embraced the results of your hard work and best intentions.

Business acceptance shortfalls must be rectified quickly once the symptoms are recognized to get the DW/BI effort back on track. The Kimball Group has talked and written extensively in the *Toolkit* books about the importance of embracing business users early in a new DW/BI initiative to understand their requirements and garner their buy-in. We use a similar approach for reengaging the business community. This article describes the fundamental techniques so you can comfortably and confidently get back in sync with the business to ensure ongoing involvement and acceptance.

DW/BI Business Realignment

Viewing the DW/BI project through the business users' eyes is an effective method to realign with the user community. In cooperation with the business sponsor, DW/BI team representatives should talk with the business community about the ability of the environment to effectively support their needs. Results of this process are then analyzed and presented back to the business with appropriate recommendations.

The most important aspect of the realignment process is meeting with the business community to solicit their feedback. We talk to them about what they do, why they do it, how they make decisions, and how they hope to make decisions in the future. Along the way, we also need to understand how the current DW/BI efforts support this process as well as any issues and concerns regarding the DW/BI environment. Like organizational therapy, we're trying to detect the issues and opportunities.

Choose the Forum

Before meeting with the business community, determine the most appropriate forum for a productive session. There are two primary techniques for gathering feedback: interviews and facilitated sessions. For a realignment project, interviews are preferable to facilitated sessions. Because lack of business acceptance is suspected, it's reasonable to expect some negative reactions to the existing environment. You should avoid facilitated group sessions, which may disintegrate into finger pointing, blame casting complaint sessions counterproductive to your mission of reinvigorating business acceptance. Besides, interviews encourage a lot of individual participation and are easier to schedule.

Surveys aren't a reasonable tool for gathering realignment feedback. Business users are unlikely to feel their issues have really been heard through a survey. Most won't bother to respond. Surveys are flat and two dimensional; those who do respond will only answer the questions you've asked in advance. There's no option to probe more deeply like you can when you're face to face. A key outcome of the realignment process is to create a bond between users and the DW/BI initiative. This outcome just doesn't happen with surveys.

Identify and Prepare the Interview Team

It's important to identify and prepare the involved project team members, especially as some of the interviews could become contentious. The lead interviewer must ask great open-ended questions, but also needs to be calm and mature, capable of receiving negative feedback without taking it personally and becoming defensive or combative. The interview scribe needs to take copious notes, pages of them from each session. A tape recorder isn't appropriate for the realignment effort because it may cause interviewees to hold back on key organizational issues. Although we often suggest inviting one or two additional project members as observers in an initial requirements gathering effort, this practice is less desirable in a realignment project because you'll want the interviewees to be as open and honest as possible.

Before sitting down with the participants, make sure you're approaching the sessions with the right mindset. Don't presume that you already know it all; if done correctly, you'll definitely learn during these interviews. Prepare yourself to listen effectively without becoming defensive. These sessions are the business community's opportunity to share their perspective of the DW/BI project. They aren't intended for you to try to explain how or why the situation developed.

Select, Schedule, and Prepare Business Representatives

The businesspeople involved should represent the horizontal breadth of the organization. Obviously, you'll schedule individuals from groups currently served (or meant to be served) by the DW/BI environment. In addition, you should include groups that are potential DW/BI candidates. You want to uncover any issues that may be constraining the DW/BI project's ability to serve these needs.

You also want to be sure to cover the organization vertically. Project teams naturally gravitate toward the superpower business analysts who are the most frequent and capable DW/BI users. While their insight is obviously valuable and important, don't ignore senior executives and middle management. Otherwise, you're vulnerable to being overly focused on the tactical here and now but losing sight of the real reasons for flagging business acceptance.

Scheduling the business representatives can be an onerous task. Be especially nice to any assistants as calendars are juggled. We prefer to meet with executives on their own, whereas we can meet with a homogeneous group of two to three people for those lower on the organization chart. We allow one hour for individual meetings and one and a half hours for the small groups. The scheduler needs to allow a half hour between meetings for debriefing and other necessities. Interviewing is extremely taxing because you must be completely focused for the session's duration. Consequently, we only schedule three to four sessions in a day because our brains turn mushy after that.

When it comes to preparing the interviewees, the optimal approach is to conduct a launch meeting with the participants. Business sponsors play critical roles, stressing their commitment and the importance of everyone's participation. The launch meeting disseminates a consistent message about the realignment effort. It also generates a sense of the business's project ownership. Alternately, if the launch meeting is a logistical nightmare, sponsors should communicate the same messages via launch memos.

Conduct the Interviews

It's time to sit down face to face to gather feedback. Responsibility for introducing the interview should be established prior to gathering in a conference room. The designated kickoff person should script the primary points to be conveyed in the first couple of minutes when the meeting tone is established. This introduction should convey a crisp, business-centric message focused on the realignment project and interview objectives. Don't ramble on about the hardware, software, and other technical jargon.

The goal of the interview is to get business users to talk about what they do and why they do it. Although in the long run you want to understand how well the existing DW/BI environment aligns with decision making processes, you don't want to be singularly focused on the DW/BI project's current state too early in the interview. You're most interested in how the organization uses information to make decisions so that you can align your efforts.

A simple, nonthreatening place to begin is to ask about job responsibilities and organizational fit. This is a lob ball that interviewees respond to easily. From there, we typically ask about their key performance metrics and how they use information in support of decision making. Ultimately, we ask about their experience with the DW/BI project and its ability to support their requirements. If the interviewee is more analytic and hands on, we ask about the types of analyses currently performed, how easily they're developed, and how well they deliver. When meeting with business executives, ask them about their vision for better leveraging information in the organization. You're seeking opportunities to align future data warehouse deliverables with business demand.

As the interview comes to a conclusion, we ask interviewees about their success criteria for the DW/BI environment. Of course, each criterion should be measurable. Easy to use and fast mean something different to everyone, so you need to get the interviewees to articulate specifics. At this point in the interview, we make a broad disclaimer. The interviewees must understand that just because an opportunity was discussed doesn't guarantee that it will be resolved immediately. You need to take advantage of this opportunity to manage expectations. Finally, thank interviewees for their insights and let them know what's happening next.

Document, Prioritize, and Reach Consensus

Now it's time to write down what you heard. While documentation is everyone's least favorite activity, it's critical for both user validation and project team reference materials.

Two levels of documentation typically result from the interview process. The first is to write up each individual interview. This activity can be quite time consuming because the write-up shouldn't be merely a stream of consciousness transcript, but should make sense to someone who wasn't in the session. The second level is a consolidated findings document. We typically begin with an executive summary, followed by a project overview that discusses the process used and participants involved. The bulk of the report centers on the findings, including specific opportunities for improving, enhancing, and expanding the existing DW/BI environment to better address business needs and expectations.

The realignment findings document serves as the basis for presentations back to senior management and other business representatives who participated. Inevitably, you've uncovered more opportunities than can be tackled immediately, so you need to develop consensus regarding priorities. Prioritization of efforts is an important step in leveraging and fostering an improved partnership to ensure the DW/BI effort aligns with the business. A highly effective tool for reaching agreement on a DW/BI roadmap and action plan is the prioritization quadrant, discussed in article 4.10, *The Bottom-Up Misnomer.*

At this point, the DW/BI team has a solid understanding of what needs to be accomplished to better support the business community's requirements and expectations. Delivering on the opportunities identified during the realignment process will establish an improved DW/BI environment that's embraced and accepted across the organization.

14.7 Educate Management to Sustain DW/BI Success

Warren Thornthwaite, Intelligent Enterprise, Aug 27, 2007

Most large organizations have fairly mature DW/BI systems in place, and many of these have met with some measure of success. Unfortunately, in this "what have you done for me lately" world, success is not a single event you can gloat about as you kick back with your feet on the desk. Continued success is a constant process of building and maintaining a solid understanding of the value and purpose of the DW/BI system across the organization. We call this education, but many of the techniques involve marketing and organizational strategies. Call it what you will, you must actively and constantly promote the DW/BI system.

First, you need to know who your stakeholders are and make sure you have standard communications tools in place, like status notes, newsletters, and quantitative usage reports. There are also a few qualitative and organizational tools you can use to educate management about the value and purpose of the DW/BI system.

Gathering Evidence

While usage statistics are interesting, they show only activity, not business value. Simple query counts tell you nothing about the content or business impact of those queries. Unfortunately, there's no automated way of capturing the value of each analysis from the DW/BI system. You still have to get this information the old fashioned way, by talking to people. Someone on the DW/BI system team has to go out into the user community on a regular basis and ask people to describe what they are doing, assess the business impact it has had, and document it.

Most of the time, the impact of any given analysis isn't all that stunning. People do useful things that make a big difference in their work, but it's not a multi-million dollar hit. Every so often, you will find an analysis or operational BI application that has had a significant impact. For example, the analyst may have identified a pattern of calls in the customer care data that led to a simple change in the documentation and reduced the call volume by 13 percent (at $6 per call, that's over $140,000 per year for a company that takes 500 calls per day). Or they may have analyzed the donor database in a small nonprofit organization and identified donors who had dropped out. This led to a special program to reconnect with these people that yielded a 22 percent response rate and close to $200,000. Or the operational BI application may offer ring tone recommendations on a web site based on customer purchase history. Each ring tone may fetch only $1, but a 30 percent increase in ring tone downloads could add up to real money. You get the idea.

Educating the Business: The User Forum

Finding high impact examples requires a bit of work. One effective technique the Kimball Group has used to identify and leverage qualitative examples of value is called a user forum. The user forum is a DW/BI event designed for the business community. Your main business sponsor should kick off this 90 minute meeting with a short speech about how important the DW/BI system is to the organization's success. The first agenda item is a brief presentation from the team about the recent accomplishments, current state, and short term plans of the DW/BI system. The bulk of the meeting is dedicated to two presentations from business analysts who used the BI system to generate significant value for the organization. They talk about what they did, how they did it, and what kind of impact it had.

Senior managers like these events because they see the impact. Often the head of one department will see what another department has done and realize his group is missing an opportunity. Middle management and analysts like the presentations because they include enough detail so people can see exactly how the analysis was accomplished. They learn new techniques and approaches to the analytic process. The three examples of business value described in the preceding section would be great feature presentations at a user forum.

A good meeting doesn't happen by accident. Find good presentation candidates with high business value by canvassing users on a regular basis. Once you find a good example, work with the user to create a clear, compelling presentation with lots of screen captures and a summary page that shows the dollar impact of the analysis. Rehearse the presentation with them, especially if they are not experienced presenters. This helps you, and them, get the timing down so your audience doesn't miss the punch line because the meeting went too long. Email a reminder a day or two ahead of time, and call everyone you'd like to be there to make sure they are going to make it to the meeting. If key folks, like the CEO or VP of Marketing, can't make it, consider rescheduling rather than have them miss out. If they are already on your side, it's good to have the show of support; if they are not converts yet, they could learn something by being at the meeting.

Schedule user forum meetings on a regular basis, about every six months or so. Don't be too proud to employ blatant marketing techniques to promote the meeting. The basics almost go without saying: food and drink are a must. Consider offering marketing swag as prizes. Since most BI teams are friendly with the marketing group, see if they'll let you raid their goodies closet.

It's a great idea to keep the presentations on file. After a year or two, you will have a library of powerful business value examples. Put a link to them on your BI portal. Print them out and make a welcome packet you can present to every new executive.

Educating Senior Staff

Your top educational priority in the long term should be to continuously and consistently inform senior management about what the DW/BI system is, why it's important, how it should be used, and what it takes to make it happen. The user forum helps achieve this objective, but the greater your access to senior management, the easier this education process will be.

Ideally, the head of the DW/BI system is part of senior staff and participates in their planning meetings. If not, try to get a regular slot on their meeting schedule to present success stories and plans and to hear about potential changes in business priorities.

Often, senior management will want to explore an idea to see if it's viable before launching any major new initiatives. Having a direct line to the DW/BI team can help senior management quickly triage ideas that should be abandoned and those that should be developed further. Once an idea begins to gain traction, the DW/BI team should make sure its development is accompanied by appropriate measurement and analytical systems. All too often, we've seen new initiatives taken on by senior management with no means to measure impact or value. If the data is not collected, you can't analyze it.

Bottom line: However you make it happen, you need to make sure someone on the DW/BI team is involved with senior management and understands where the business is headed so you can be prepared to support it.

Working with Steering Committees

If it's not politically possible for the DW/BI team leader to be part of senior staff, another way to get the information you need is to establish an ongoing steering committee for the DW/BI system made up of senior-level business representatives. If you don't have a steering committee, try to recruit people who you know will be able to work together, give you the information you need, and wield some influence in the organization. You might call this group the Business Intelligence Directorate (BID), or some other important sounding name with a nice acronym. It may seem trivial, but naming is a big part of the marketing process.

You may also have a different kind of business user steering committee made up of analysts and power users who help prioritize lower level tasks and identify technical opportunities for the BI system. You might call this the BI Technical Experts (BITE) group.

Conclusion

You may feel that because you've done a good job, you shouldn't have to continually market the DW/BI system, or educate the business community. Unfortunately, that's not the case. You need to continually gather concrete evidence of success and use that to educate senior management. You also need to be informed of and have some influence over the decision making process at the senior staff level, either through direct participation or via a steering committee. This may sound like a burden, but one positive result is that as senior management understands the business value of the DW/BI system, they no longer question your budget.

14.8 Getting Your Data Warehouse Back on Track

Margy Ross and Bob Becker, Design Tip #7, Apr 30, 2000

During the past year, we've repeatedly observed a pattern with maturing data warehouses. Despite significant effort and investment, some data warehouses have fallen off course. Project teams, or their user communities, are dissatisfied with the warehouse deliverables. The data's too confusing, it's not consistent, queries are too slow, and the list goes on. Teams have devoured the data warehousing best sellers and periodicals, but are still unsure how to right the situation, short of jumping ship and finding new employment.

If this situation sounds familiar, take the following self-check test to determine if the four leading culprits are undermining your data warehouse. Consider each question carefully to honestly critique your warehouse situation. In terms of corrective action, we recommend tackling these fundamental concerns in sequential order, if possible.

1. **Have you proactively gathered requirements from the business users for each iteration of the data warehouse development and aligned the implementation effort with their top priorities?**

    This is the most prevalent problem for aging data warehouses. Somewhere along the line, perhaps while overly focused on data or technology, the project lost sight of the real goal to serve the information needs of business users. As a project team, you must always focus on the users' gain. If the team's activities don't provide benefit to the business users, the data warehouse will continue to drift. If you're not actively engaged in implementing solutions to support users' key business requirements and priorities, why not? Revisit your plans to determine, and then focus on delivering to, the users' most critical needs.

2. **Have you developed an enterprise data warehouse bus matrix?**

   The matrix is one of the data warehouse team's most powerful tools. See article 5.5, *The Matrix*. Use it to clarify your thinking, communicate critical points of conformance, establish the overall data integration roadmap, and assess your current progress against the long term plan.

3. **Is management committed to using standardized conformed dimensions?**

   Conformed dimensions are absolutely critical to the viability of a data warehouse. We find many warehouse teams are reluctant to take on the socio-political challenges of defining conformed dimensions. In all honesty, it's extremely difficult for a data warehouse team to establish and develop conformed dimensions on its own. Yet the team can't ignore the issue and hope it will resolve itself. You'll need management support for conformed dimensions to help navigate the organizational difficulties inherent in the effort.

4. **Have you provided atomic data in dimensional models to users?**

   Data shortcomings, whether it's the wrong data, inappropriately structured, or prematurely summarized, are often at the root of data warehouse course adjustments. Focusing on business requirements will help determine the right data; then the key is to deliver the most atomic data dimensionally. Unfortunately, it's tough to gracefully migrate from data chaos to this nirvana. In most cases, it's best to bite the bullet and redeploy. Teams sometimes resort to the seemingly less drastic approach of sourcing from the current quagmire; however, the costs are inevitably higher in the long run. Often the granularity of the existing data precludes this alternative due to premature summarization.

In summary, if your data warehouse has fallen off course, it won't magically right itself. You'll need to revisit the basic tenets of data warehousing: Listen to users to determine your target destination, get a map, establish a route, and then follow the rules of the road to get your data warehouse back on track.

14.9 Upgrading Your BI Architecture

Joy Mundy, Design Tip #104, Aug 7, 2008

Article 13.1, *The Promise of Decision Support,* described the typical lifecycle of a business analysis:

1. **Publish standard reporting and scorecards.** How's my business doing?
2. **Identify exceptions.** What's unusually good or bad?
3. **Determine causal factors.** Why did something go well or poorly?
4. **Model predictive or what-if analysis.** How will business look next year?
5. **Track actions.** What's the impact of the decisions that were made?

What do you do if you're stuck at step 1? What if you have an infrastructure that supports basic reporting, but is the wrong architecture to enable complex analytics or business user self-service? How do you get to where you want to go? In some ways it's easier to start from a blank slate and do it right the first time; it's easy to be a hero when you're starting from zero. But large companies, and a growing number of medium and even small companies, already have some kind of DW/BI system in place. There are additional challenges in moving to a new architecture while maintaining the existing system at the same time.

There are three common unsuccessful DW/BI architectures:

- **Normalized data warehouse with no user-focused delivery layer.** The organization has invested in a data warehouse architecture, but stopped short of the business users. The data warehouse is normalized, which means it may be simple to load and maintain, but not easy to query. Reports are written directly on the normalized structures, and often require very complex queries and stored procedures. In most cases, only a professional IT team can write reports.
- **Normalized data warehouse with mart proliferation.** A common approach to solving the problem of data model complexity is to spin off data marts to solve specific business problems. Usually these marts are dimensional (or at least can pass as dimensional in the dark with your glasses off). Unfortunately, they are limited in scope, contain only summary data, and are un-architected. A new business problem requires a new mart. Users' ad hoc access is limited to the scenarios that have been cooked into the standalone marts.
- **Mart proliferation directly from transaction systems.** The least effective architecture is to build standalone data marts directly from OLTP systems, without an intermediate DW layer. Each mart has to develop complex ETL processes. Often, we see marts chained together as one mart feeds the next.

In any case, the appropriate solution is to build a conformed, dimensional data warehouse delivery area.

If you already have a normalized enterprise data warehouse, analyze the gap between the business requirements and the existing data warehouse's contents. You might be able to build relatively simple ETL processes to populate the dimensional data warehouse from the normalized one. For any new business processes and data, determine whether the normalized DW provides value in your environment. If so, continue to integrate and store data there, then dimensionalize and store it again in the dimensional structure. Alternatively, you may find that it makes more sense to integrate and dimensionalize in one ETL process, and phase out the normalized data warehouse. Once the data is in the conformed dimensional model, you'll find that business users have much greater success self-servicing and developing ad hoc queries. Some of those ad hoc queries will push up into exception, causal, and even predictive analysis, and will evolve into BI applications for the broader audience.

If you don't have a normalized data warehouse in place, you probably won't build one. This scenario is more like the "starting from scratch" approach using the Kimball Lifecycle method. You'll need to gather business requirements, design the dimensional model, and develop the ETL logic for the enterprise dimensional data warehouse.

Arguably the biggest challenge in building an upgraded architecture is that your users' expectations are higher. You'll need to keep the existing environment in place and provide modest improvements while the new system is being developed. If you're starting from scratch, you can make users happy by rolling out the new system a little bit at a time. With a BI upgrade or replacement project, your phase 1 scope is likely going to have to be bigger than we normally recommend to make a splash.

You need to plan for people and resources to maintain the existing environment as well as to perform the new development. We recommend that you devote a team to the new development; if the same people are trying to do the old and the new, they'll find their energies sucked into the constant operational demands of the user community. The entire group will have to expand, and the old team and new team both need business expertise and technical skills.

Once you roll out a core set of data in the upgraded environment, there are two paths you can take. You can go deeper into the initial set of data by building analytic applications that go beyond just publishing basic reports. Or, you can bring in data from additional business processes. With enough resources, you can do both at the same time.

 ## 14.10 Four Fixes for Legacy Data Warehouses

Margy Ross, Intelligent Enterprise, *Oct 1, 2006*

Few designers have the luxury of working with a blank slate when it comes to the development of their DW/BI environment anymore. Instead, many of us deal with the decisions, and potentially the sins, of our predecessors. Your DW/BI environment would likely look very different if you were to build it from scratch, but a complete toss-and-rebuild is seldom a viable alternative. More often, DW/BI professionals are tasked with making evolutionary upgrades and improvements to minimize cost and upheaval of the current analytic environment. The following four upgrades can breathe new life into legacy data warehouses.

Conform the Nonconformed Dimensions

Master conformed dimensions contain the descriptive attributes and corresponding names, meanings, and values that have been agreed to across the enterprise. Using conformed dimensions ensures that the data warehouse is delivering consistently defined attributes for labeling, grouping, filtering, and integrating data from multiple business processes.

Unfortunately, many data warehouses and marts were developed without regard for this critical master data. Standalone data stores with independently defined dimensions are often constructed because it's the path of least resistance when deadlines loom. Rather than attempt to reach consensus on common reference data, isolated teams believe it's quicker and easier to just build autonomous dimensions. This approach may let these teams declare victory, but it doesn't support the business' desire for integration and consistency.

Some organizations wind up with independent data stores because developers purposely focused on delivering a departmental solution, likely due to the funding available. Without the vision and acknowledged need for an enterprise perspective, teams are often chartered to build with blinders on to meet a limited set of goals.

So what do you do if you're confronted with an environment that's been built without a foundation of common conformed dimensions? Can these stovepipes be rescued? In spite of the vendor hype, there's no magic elixir that miraculously delivers master dimensions. Technology can facilitate and enable data integration, but there's no silver bullet. The first step toward integration nirvana is to assess the state of the data, as well as requirements, expectations, and buy-in from the business. You can self-diagnose the issues related to nonconforming dimensions, but keep in mind that you're likely to face a long, uphill internal struggle and resistance to change if the business community doesn't perceive the need or incremental value in the project.

As we described in article 5.14, *Data Stewardship 101: The First Step to Quality and Consistency*, one of the most crucial steps in conforming nonconformed dimensions is to organize the appropriate resources to tackle this vexing problem. Data stewards must be identified and assigned responsibility and authority to determine common dimension attributes, define domain values and transformation business rules, and establish ongoing processes to ensure data quality. Obviously, that's no small feat, so it's critical to identify the right leader. Ideally, you want someone from the business community who is respected by senior management and who has knowledge and skills to achieve organizational consensus. Navigating the unavoidable cross-functional challenges requires experience, widespread respect, political acumen, and strong communication skills.

Not everyone is cut out to be a data steward. It's feasible for folks on the data warehouse team to serve as stewards, but they need to demonstrate all the traits and characteristics just described. Most important, they need the support of business management and the authority to push cross-enterprise agreement and adoption, even when unpopular compromise is required. Without this power, stewards face the prospect of endless tire spinning as they try to rationalize diverse perspectives.

Once the data stewards produce the specifications for a conformed master dimension, the skilled ETL staff builds the master dimension. Depending on the existence and/or quality of reference data in the operational source systems, this may require intricate record matching and deduplication. When merging multiple source systems, clearly defined rules of survivorship are needed to identify which data source takes precedence for each attribute.

With master dimensions built, it's then time to retrofit the existing data warehouse subject areas with standardized data. New surrogate key mapping tables for each dimension are used to recast existing fact table rows. In addition, aggregate summary tables and cubes will likely need to be reconstructed. While the implications for the ETL system are inevitably significant, hopefully the impact on the business intelligence layer of these underlying physical table changes can be minimized with an abstraction layer using views, synonyms, or your BI tool's metadata, depending on your platforms.

Create Surrogate Keys

Another data warehousing best practice is to create surrogate keys, typically a meaningless simple integer, for the primary key in each dimension table. The associated fact table rows use this same surrogate as a foreign key reference to the dimension tables.

Establishing, managing, and using surrogate keys may initially feel like an unnecessary burden on the ETL system, so many data warehouses have been constructed based on the operational natural keys, sometimes referred to as *smart keys* because of their embedded meaning, rather than using surrogates. At first blush, these natural keys may not present any obvious problems. But as the environment matures, teams often wish things had been done differently when the following situations arise:

- **The natural keys in the operational system get recycled after a product has been discontinued or an account closed for more than a specified length of time.** Two years of dormancy may seem like a lifetime to an operational system, but relying on reassigned natural keys can wreak havoc in the data warehouse where data is retained for extended periods.
- **The business decides it's important to track dimension attribute changes after all.** While this need may not have been envisioned up front, as the business develops expertise with the data, team members often want to see the impact when descriptive dimension attributes change. Naturally gravitating to the least onerous route, they may have developed the initial data warehouse with the premise that dimension tables would reflect the most current attribute values, overwriting any previous descriptors when they change using the SCD type 1 technique. But the rules may now be maturing, requiring the insertion of new rows into the dimension table to capture new profiles via SCD type 2 methods. Relying on the natural key as the primary key of the dimension table obviously doesn't allow for multiple profile versions, while using a concatenated key based on the natural key and effective dates has a negative impact on both query performance and usability.
- **Performance has been negatively impacted by an inefficient natural key.** In contrast to a tight integer, natural keys are often bulky alphanumeric fields that result in suboptimal dimension/fact table join performance and unnecessarily large indexes.
- **You must create conformed dimensions to integrate reference data from multiple sources, each with its own unique natural key.** You may need a default dimension primary key to represent the condition when a dimension value is unknown or not applicable to a given measurement event.

Each of these situations can be addressed by using surrogate keys as the primary keys for the dimension tables. So how do you implement surrogates when you're already working with a system that was built without them? In the simplest scenario, you would add the sequential surrogate key to the dimension table, leaving the existing natural key intact as an attribute, and recast the fact rows to reference the new surrogate key values. Depending on your BI tool, you may need to update the tool's metadata to reflect the change in join fields. If you need to support type 2 attribute change tracking, additional work would be required to source the historical attribute profiles and then repopulate the fact table with the surrogate key values that were valid and in effect when the fact row occurred.

Deliver the Details

Some people believe dimensional models are only appropriate for summarized information. They maintain that dimensional structures are intended for managerial, strategic analysis and therefore should be populated with summarized data, not operational detail. The Kimball Group vehemently disagrees; in our view, dimensional models should be populated with the most detailed, atomic data captured by the source systems so business users can ask the most detailed, precise questions possible. Even if users don't care about the particulars of a single transaction or subtransaction, their question of the moment may require rolling up or drilling down in these details in unpredictable ways. Of course, database administrators may opt to presummarize information to avoid on the fly summarization in every case, but these aggregate summaries are performance-tuning complements to the atomic level, not replacements.

Restricting your dimensional models to summarized information imposes serious limitations. Summary data naturally presupposes the typical business questions so when business requirements change, as they inevitably will, both the data model and ETL system must change to accommodate new data. Summary data alone also limits query flexibility. Users run into dead ends when the presummarized data can't support an unanticipated inquiry. While you can roll up detailed data in unpredictable ways, the converse is not true; you can't magically explode summary data into its underlying components. Delivering dimensional models populated with detailed data ensures maximum flexibility and extensibility.

So what do you do if you've inherited a data warehouse filled with preaggregated information, but the details are missing in action? The solution is straightforward: You need to source and populate the bedrock atomic detail. Because more detailed data is naturally more dimensional, this will almost inevitably require that new dimension tables be constructed as well.

As you're delivering the details, don't be lulled into thinking that summary data should be dimensionalized but that atomic details are better handled in a normalized schema. Business users need the ability to seamlessly and arbitrarily traverse up, down, and across both the detailed and summary data in a single interface. While normalization may save a few bytes of storage space, the resulting complexity creates navigational challenges and typically slower performance for BI reports and queries.

Reduce Redundancies

Many organizations take a piecemeal approach to their data warehouse design and deployment, so it's common for the same performance metrics to reside in numerous analytic environments, often segregated by business department or function. The multiple, uncoordinated extracts from the same operational source systems required to populate these redundant data stores are inefficient and wasteful. Variations of similar, but different, information result from inconsistent business rules and naming conventions, causing unnecessary confusion and requiring reconciliation throughout the enterprise. Obviously, conflicting databases that perpetuate incompatible views of the organization are distracting resource drains.

Take a more enterprise-centric approach, storing core performance metrics once to support the analytic needs of multiple departments or groups. The enterprise framework is defined and communicated via the data warehouse bus matrix. The matrix rows represent the business events or processes of the organization, while the columns reflect the common, conformed dimensions. The bus matrix provides the macro point of view for architecting the data warehouse environment, regardless of database or technology preferences.

But what do you do if you've discovered that your organization's key performance metrics and indicators are currently available in many different analytic environments? The first step is to assess the damage. You can create a detailed implementation bus matrix, described in article 5.6, *The Matrix: Revisited*, to gather information and document your current state. With these details in hand, you're ready to help senior executives understand the quagmire resulting from uncontrolled, standalone development. Because they're often the ones demanding more information (and by the way, they want it delivered yesterday), it's important that they comprehend the consequences of piecemeal development, which can significantly hinder the organization's decision making capabilities.

If the business appreciates the inefficiencies and obstacles of the current environment, they are much more likely to support a migration strategy to reduce the unnecessary redundancies. Unfortunately, this rationalization often has serious ramifications on the BI application layer when the underlying data stores are removed or consolidated.

Face the Realities

We've described four of the most common data fixes for more mature warehouses. It's worth noting that regardless of the opportunities for improvement with your existing environment, it's important to evaluate the costs versus benefits of taking any corrective action. It's similar to the decision process when confronted with maintenance of an aging automobile; sometimes it makes sense to spend the money, but other times you may opt to merely live with the dents or dump the heap of junk altogether.

Keep your eyes open for occasions when the impact of the corrective action is either less noticeable or less painful. For example, if your organization is implementing a new operational source system or migrating to a new ETL or BI tool platform, the upheaval with your existing transformation or analytic processes presents an opportunity for other corrections. Using the automobile maintenance analogy, if your car is already in the shop and the mechanic has lifted the hood to change the oil, he might as well check the windshield wiper fluid while he's in there.

14.11 A Data Warehousing Fitness Program for Lean Times

Bob Becker and Joy Mundy, Intelligent Enterprise, *Mar 16, 2009*

It's no secret that the U.S. and global economies are facing difficult times. If the economic pundits are correct, we are now working through the most challenging economic decline of most of our lifetimes.

Many organizations have already made significant reductions in staffing and spending. The DW/BI sector seems to be faring somewhat better than others; in bad times as in good times, organizations desire better visibility into their business and improved decision making capabilities. Even so, many DW/BI teams are facing staff reductions or at least hiring freezes coupled with significant reductions in budgets for new hardware, software, training, and consulting. Perhaps your organization had grander plans, but now you find those plans on hold.

No astute DW/BI manager would be so shortsighted as to ignore these realities in the face of today's economic environment. But rather than just putting current activities on a budgetary crash diet, it's time to institute a proactive fitness program that will yield a leaner, more efficient and effective

DW/BI program for the long haul. How can you do more in an environment where staffing and funding are constrained? You need to focus on three key opportunities:

- Cost savings
- Cost avoidance
- Growth

Cut the Flab

In tough times, most organizations try to identify opportunities for cost savings. This often means significant reductions in budgets as well as possible staff reductions. We'll assume you are already running very lean; your budgets and staffing have already been evaluated and trimmed. After these obvious cuts, you'll want to look for other avenues to achieve cost savings.

Revisit the original justification for your DW/BI effort; often a number of cost savings goals were identified during the project justification effort. Have these goals been realized? If not, why not? Are the savings still available? If so, look for inexpensive methods that would help you achieve these goals.

Often the most significant cost savings assigned to a DW/BI effort are related to sunsetting older analytic environments, resulting in significant savings on hardware, software licenses, maintenance, and support resources. Try to determine why these savings have yet to be realized. We can often point the finger of blame at office politics. The new DW/BI environment may be well positioned to support the requirements of the existing analytic environment, yet a group of business users lacks the motivation to make the move. A mandate is required to force these stragglers to migrate to the new environment, and the current economic environment may provide just the incentive you need.

It's easy to just blame politics, but you need to talk to the holdout business users to understand their perspectives. The new solution may be almost everything these users need, but some vital component might still be missing. It could be very easy to solve the issue, perhaps with user training, a little applet or macro, modifications to reports, or possibly a minor change in the data or model.

Even in the best of times we want to sunset old applications, not only because of the operating costs but also because we want a single version of the truth. In these worst of times, we should be able to entice or force the stragglers to migrate away from the legacy environment to the new DW/BI solution and finally achieve the cost savings initially envisioned.

Monitor and Tune to Defer Spending

Organizations are also looking to defer planned costs. Perhaps in your surviving budget you have financial resources available to invest in additional hardware or software. Often, with a bit of creative thinking and hard work, these costs can be deferred or in some cases avoided altogether.

Inventory the software licenses you already have in place. Are they all being effectively used? Pay special attention to your BI tool licenses and how they are deployed. Many organizations find that the actual number of licenses in use is far below the number that have been deployed.

- First, understand why the deployed licenses aren't being utilized. Perhaps there are low cost training or support investments that will help users become more effective, leverage the existing licenses, and enable your organization to achieve the anticipated benefits.
- Second, if the licenses are not required where they were deployed, they should be shifted to other users. This realignment of licenses may allow you to defer a planned investment.
- Worst case, if there is no current or future need for the licenses the maintenance can be discontinued and some cost savings achieved.

Similarly, cast a critical eye over the overall performance of your DW/BI environment. Often an investment in performance tuning can push a planned hardware upgrade a number of months into the future, ideally out of the current budget cycle. Query performance is highly visible, so start there:

- Develop a log of system performance characteristics, if you're not already doing so. Your database systems and operating systems have features that enable you to capture a history of memory, disk, CPU usage, and other characteristics. You cannot tune performance if you don't understand performance.
- Tune the SQL for all standard reports and other BI applications. This is the lowest hanging fruit because you can usually modify the query syntax, such as adding a hint, without changing the report's fundamental design.
- Analyze the queries run in your environment looking for opportunities to improve your indexing and aggregation strategies. Tuning for ad hoc use continues to be something of an art form; you need to balance the value of an additional index against the cost of maintaining that index.
- Work with your hardware/software vendors to ensure that you are leveraging the capabilities already available to you. Ask your vendors to provide known DW/BI best practices and tips.

After you've done what you can to squeeze every ounce of performance from the existing environment, consider whether moderate changes to your system design might provide substantial performance benefits. Your fact tables and their associated indexes and aggregates consume the most resources in your DW/BI environment. You may be surprised by how much query performance can be improved by reducing fact table and index size. Review your fact table designs and consider the following:

- Replace all natural foreign keys with the smallest integer (surrogate) keys possible.
- Combine correlated dimensions into single dimensions where possible.
- Group tiny, low cardinality dimensions together, even if uncorrelated.
- Take all text fields out of the fact table and make them dimensions, especially comment fields. It seems counterintuitive to make a dimension out of a high cardinality, analytically insignificant field like a comment, but the comment field is omitted from most queries. Removing the

large character field from the fact table and replacing it with an integer key can make the fact table perform much more nimbly.

- Replace long integer and floating point facts with scaled integers wherever possible.
- If, contrary to our longstanding advice, your dimensions are normalized into snowflakes, collapse each into a denormalized, single table flat dimension table. You can often implement this as an additional step at the end of the ETL process.

Review your ETL system. Look for performance bottlenecks and identify ways to remove them. ETL teams often overlook indexing approaches in staging tables that might improve overall ETL performance. In addition, revisit the ETL logic from the early days of your DW/BI effort. The ETL team is now more experienced than it was in the beginning. Inevitably your team has identified more efficient and effective techniques than those initially implemented.

Bulk Up the Bottom Line

Most organizations initially justify their DW/BI initiatives citing opportunities to grow the business and improve productivity. The benefits identified are real and tangible, but they're often hard to quantify. It can be challenging to measure enhanced business results, such as increased revenue growth, improved profitability, greater customer acquisition/retention rates, or improved customer satisfaction.

Now's the time to revisit the proposed growth opportunities to evaluate whether the DW/BI environment has actually helped attain the benefits promised. If the benefits are being achieved, be sure to let the world know! There's nothing wrong with taking credit for a job well done. Your recent budget negotiations might have gone more smoothly if you had better records of the business value resulting from the DW/BI system. Start keeping those records now, even if they are just DBMS usage logs.

Most of us will recognize desired benefits that have not yet been fully realized. Investigate why these benefits continue to elude you. This analysis will require the DW/BI team to cast a critical eye over activities and results. Be brutally honest with yourself. Have you done everything required to help the organization achieve these benefits?

DW/BI teams often lose sight of the ultimate goal. They get so focused on getting the data into the data warehouse they forget about making it all the way to the finish line—enabling the business users to easily use the data for decision making. Consider refocusing some of your resources on achieving those benefits that provide significant value to the organization.

Look for low cost, incremental improvements you can make that offer substantive value to the organization:

- Make sure you have documentation and training in place to help business people use the DW/BI system effectively.
- Look for areas where the addition of a few dimension attributes or additional metrics to existing schema will enable valuable new analyses.

- Look for opportunities to expose the existing portfolio of data and BI applications to a wider audience, perhaps tapping available software licenses identified as discussed earlier.
- Work with key, analytic business users to evaluate the effectiveness of BI applications that have already been deployed. Look for opportunities to improve these existing BI applications to provide keener insights into the business. Seek out ways to better understand the analytic processes utilized by the savviest users in order to capture and extend these benefits to additional BI applications.
- Enrich your data warehouse with new fact tables supporting additional business processes and new analytics.

It's unfortunate that the downturn in the economy has put many of us on an unwelcome budgetary diet, but we can also get lean and mean by hitting the gym and working out, figuratively speaking. We can focus carefully on our DW/BI environment's overall health and fitness and become far stronger and healthier for the long run.

14.12 Enjoy the Sunset

Bob Becker, Design Tip #143, Mar 1, 2012

Most organizations implementing a new data warehouse/business intelligence environment are replacing or "sunsetting" a legacy analytic/reporting system. This environment may be an older data warehouse, a single or series of departmental data marts, or a collection of analytic/reporting environments cobbled together using tools such as Access and Excel. Some may be officially sanctioned platforms; often they are shadow reporting environments crafted by a business unit. Regardless of the flavor, many business users rely on these environments for their reporting and analytic needs. Elimination of these disparate systems is a common goal of new DW/BI initiatives.

Elimination of these legacy/shadow systems often provides a significant amount of the hard dollar justification for the new DW/BI world. These savings result from the proposed elimination of hardware, software licenses, and associated maintenance and support costs. The hard dollar savings often include the manpower costs involved in reconciling data across multiple analytic platforms. In addition, there is often soft dollar justification based on the value of better integrated data, greater management confidence, and improved ease of use associated with replacing the legacy environments.

Unfortunately, sunsetting the legacy environments seldom occurs in a timely manner or often not at all, placing these justification dollars at risk. It's not uncommon to see an older legacy reporting environment running side by side with the new DW/BI environment far longer than was ever intended. Clearly, this is undesirable; if both environments continue to run, the hard dollar justification will never be recognized. At some point, management is going to look askew at this situation and begin questioning the integrity of the team responsible for the new DW/BI environment, potentially putting future funding at risk. In addition, most users will never embrace the new environment as long as the old environment continues to be available. Why change if you don't have to? As a result, there will continue to be data reconciliation challenges due to the multiple, inconsistent analytic and reporting platforms.

It is vital to the ongoing success of the new environment to avoid this situation. The DW/BI team needs to keep its eye on the goal, ensuring that each iteration helps move closer to sunsetting some portion of the legacy environment. At some point, it is often just a matter of having the courage to actually turn something off that is no longer needed. Before sunsetting an older environment you must completely understand the requirements that must be supported by the replacement DW/BI system:

- Are all of the data and capabilities in place to support the current reports/analyses?
- Are there other non-analytic functions that the older environment is supporting?
- Does the existing system provide certain capabilities, such as auditing and compliance, which are not available elsewhere?
- Are there downstream environments dependent on data from the legacy environment?

All of these requirements have a valid claim against the existing environment. Thus, you can't sunset the environment until you can support these requirements. At a recent client, the old analytic platform included a series of daily replicated copies of the production source. The primary purpose of these tables was to support the ETL change data capture process required to populate the environment. However, unbeknownst to the DW/BI team, some key users had obtained access to the replicated tables. They included these tables as a critical component of several data governance, data quality, and internal audit processes. When the DW/BI team attempted to shut down the old system, they found they couldn't as they had no alternate capability for supporting these requirements. Similarly, an analytic platform may find itself feeding other downstream purposes it may be totally unaware of. Again, be sure you have alternate solutions in place to support these requirements.

Once you are confident you have addressed the legacy system's support of analytics and reporting, non-DW/BI usage, and downstream application requirements, it's time to turn that system off! Of course, you may want to keep it processing for a few weeks while you shut off all external access and feeds from the system just to make sure you've got everything covered. Clearly, you'll want to get past a month end close to see if anything breaks.

A final technical/legal issue is whether you have full rights to expose the data from the old system once you have terminated its license. While you can probably argue that the data itself belongs to you, you may not be able to use the old system any more to generate reports on the old data. In such a case, you may have to dump your data into a neutral format before your right to use the underlying application terminates.

Once you're comfortable you've got all your bases covered, it's time—mix up some margaritas, pull the plug, and enjoy the sunset!

15 Final Thoughts

This chapter consists of just four articles: the final *Design Tips* written by Margy, Bob, Joy, and Ralph.

We begin with guidance regarding the keys to success for DW/BI initiatives. Margy, Bob, and Joy marshal more than 80 years of cumulative experience to share the critical insights they gained while helping literally hundreds of clients create successful DW/BI environments. Ralph finishes by turning to the future to make some fearless predictions about big opportunities that lie ahead.

Key Insights and Reminders

Margy, Bob, and Joy share the essential "must dos" that they've relied on throughout their careers. Following this guidance is sure to position you for similar successes in your careers.

15.1 Final Word of the Day: Collaboration

Margy Ross, Design Tip #177, Sep 1, 2015

For my final *Design Tip*, I'm returning to a fundamental theme that's not rocket science, but too often ignored: business-IT collaboration. If you buy into the proposition that the true measure of DW/BI success is business acceptance of the deliverables to improve their decision making, then buying into the importance of collaboration should be easy. Achieving business adoption is a pipedream if the IT resources on a DW/BI team don't collaborate with their business counterparts. Likewise, the business needs to be willing to collaborate with IT.

Collaborative multi-disciplinary teams create successful DW/BI programs. Every major juncture of the Kimball Lifecycle approach lends itself to joint activities that bolster business-IT alignment:

- **Program/project planning.** Drive priorities based on business goals and objectives, balanced with delivery feasibilities.
- **Program/project management.** Communicate openly regarding checkpoint updates and solicit joint input regarding scope modifications.

- **Business requirements.** Focus on what the business does and why, plus how the business hopes to make decisions in the future, rather than asking "what do you want in a DW/BI system?"
- **Technical architecture and product selection.** Involve business representatives to select their tools. As a friendly reminder to the technologists: Technology is a prerequisite enabler, but should not be the DW/BI team's primary focus! Don't bother educating (or perhaps overeducating) the business about infrastructure and plumbing.
- **Dimensional modeling.** Derive dimensional models from interactive workshops with business and IT representatives rather than from an isolated designer sitting in an ivory tower. Engaging subject matter experts from the business is absolutely critical to designing appropriate dimensional models. They should also be included in the data discovery and associated data governance decisions.
- **ETL design and development.** Enlist business subject matter experts to appropriately address data quality issues with IT representatives; IT shouldn't make these decisions in a vacuum.
- **BI application design and development.** Prototype BI reports and analytics with the business.
- **Deployment.** Solicit business input on the initial and ongoing education/support needs.

Since many *Design Tip* subscribers reside in the IT organization, I've focused on the importance of IT breaking down barriers with the business so they're viewed as partners instead of bottlenecks. But collaboration is a two-way street. It's equally important that business representatives collaborate with their IT counterparts by considering the following guidance:

- Invite IT to sit alongside you during business strategy sessions.
- Invest the time to educate IT about the business. The more IT knows, the better they can support your needs. It's insufficient and ineffective to merely provide IT with a report or data set specification.
- Engage IT at the beginning of an initiative rather than involving them mid-project (or after your consultants are gone).
- Appreciate IT's need to think about the enterprise, not just your individual department. Their concerns regarding data governance and master data are real.
- Strive to avoid re-creating the wheel with a proliferation of similar, but often slightly different, data sets, reports, and analyses. This proliferation typically results in significant hard and soft costs for the organization.
- Tap into IT's expertise. Don't make technology decisions in a vacuum without their involvement. And ask yourself whether you really want to maintain silo data sets, applications, and supplier relationships without IT's help.

The Kimball Lifecycle approach discourages a customer-vendor mindset where the business provides IT with an order which IT then attempts to fulfill. Our approach has always advocated for a partnership between IT and business stakeholders. Collaboration is far more than scheduling a meeting with interested parties; collaboration means working differently to actively engage both sides in joint decisions. Unfortunately, collaboration between the business and IT doesn't come naturally in some organizations. People may think differently, communicate using different vocabulary, and be incented differently. The goal is mutual engagement and understanding which typically requires strong cross-organizational support at leadership levels, especially if business and IT resources need to be nudged out of their "same as always" attitudes. Ultimately, the line between the camps will blur with resources who comfortably straddle both worlds.

Finally, this is my last chance to speak with all of you. I want to express my gratitude and appreciation for the countless people who've crossed my path during the last 34 years. Thanks to my husband and daughter for your unwavering patience and support. Thanks to my Metaphor colleagues whose influence has persisted throughout my career. Thanks to my DecisionWorks and Kimball Group partners for your intelligence and inspiration. And most importantly, thanks to my clients, students, and readers; you've made it an amazing journey! Breaking up the band is always hard. While the Kimball Group is shutting its doors, our methods will live on through all of you. Good luck! Just remember: focus on the business and be dimensional!

15.2 Tried and True Concepts for DW/BI Success

Bob Becker, Design Tip #178, Oct 1, 2015

Time marches on and soon the collective retirement of the Kimball Group will be upon us. At the end of 2015 we will all retire. In my final *Design Tip*, I would like to share the perspective for DW/BI success I've gained from my 26 years in the data warehouse/business intelligence industry.

While data warehousing has been around now for a long while, there continue to be significant opportunities for organizations to leverage information for more effective decision making. New technologies consistently emerge that create and allow us to gather increasingly more granular data from the world that surrounds us. The data and the analytics surrounding it are as interesting and important as ever—perhaps more so. New and improved DW/BI solutions will continue to be deployed. There will be no future shortage of opportunities to apply the lessons learned about creating a successful DW/BI environment.

By now, we all recognize that data warehousing is a mature industry. We are long past the pioneering stage of DW/BI evolution. We are working with proven, capable hardware and software technologies with new and more capable technologies evolving all the time. As an industry, we have been implementing data warehouse and business intelligence capabilities for a long time—decades in fact. Lessons have been learned, technologies improved, techniques honed, and methodologies matured. Countless individuals have been trained, baptized by the fire of experience, and have proven capable of building successful DW/BI solutions. Clearly, there will always be newbies to be trained, mentored, and seasoned. Yet, as an industry, we know what it takes to be successful. There are no excuses for failure.

My suggestion for ongoing success is to keep your eyes wide open and constantly focus on the basics—the fundamental blocking and tackling of data warehousing. Embrace these tried and true concepts that years of experience have revealed to be true:

- **Focus on the business and business requirements.** Never forget to maintain a laser-like focus on achieving business value. The success of a DW/BI effort is totally dependent on business user engagement; keeping the business users involved and meeting their requirements dramatically increases the probability of success. In fact, it ensures it.

- **Obtain strong senior management sponsorship.** Lack of organizational support undermines the success of a DW/BI effort. Senior management must accept, support, manage, and fund these efforts as long term programs.

- **Organize for success.** Successful DW/BI initiatives are undertaken as a partnership between the IT team and the business units. The DW/BI effort cannot be identified as just an IT effort. The business community (not IT) needs to take ownership of the vision, strategy, roadmap (priorities), scope, timelines, governance, and quality of the DW/BI environment.

- **Integration is critical.** Leverage conformed dimensions as the basis for integration. Understand and embrace the discipline of dimensional design as the organizing theme for the data within the DW/BI environment.

- **Establish and enforce common vocabulary.** The first step to eliminating data inconsistency issues is to establish and enforce common names, definitions, and descriptors across the DW/BI environment. Again, embracing the discipline of dimensional modeling is the secret to victory.

- **Focus on data quality.** At its foundation, the DW/BI environment must be a repository of high quality data. The biggest challenges for most DW/BI efforts are data-related. In general, the effort to develop the ETL processes required to provide high quality data is typically more demanding than anticipated. Adequate time and resources, including key subject area experts, must be allocated to these tasks.

- **Establish a phased design, development, and deployment plan.** Constructing a DW/BI environment is a significant effort. It is nearly impossible to tackle everything at once. Embrace an iterative development plan that avoids an overly ambitious scope. Project iterations need to be identified to phase-in the overall design, development, and deployment effort. The environment should grow by tackling new and additional business processes (i.e., fact tables).

- **Exhibit patience.** The initial phase of a DW/BI initiative usually takes a disproportionately long time; I call this the "big gulp." This is necessarily true. While the initial phase corresponds to deploying a single business process (i.e., fact table) the bulk of the time in this phase is committed to designing, developing, and deploying the critical, core set of conformed dimensions that will be leveraged throughout the DW/BI environment in later phases. This is normal and to be expected.

Finally, on a personal note—I would like to thank my clients, students, partners, family, and friends for your support all these years. I have learned more from all of you than you will ever appreciate. Each of you has my deepest gratitude.

Thank you and good luck!

15.3 Key Tenets of the Kimball Method

Joy Mundy, Design Tip #179, *Nov 3, 2015*

Most of the guidance in the Kimball method for designing, developing, and deploying a DW/BI system is just that: guidance. There are hundreds or thousands of rules in the Kimball Group's many books, and I confess to having bent many of those rules over the decades, when faced with conflicting goals or unpleasant political realities.

There are several tenets to the Kimball method that I am passionate about. This article lists the things I say over and over, to audiences experienced and new. Any reader who has attended a class that I've taught, or hired me as a consultant, has heard me discourse on most or all of the items on this list.

1.   **The dimensional model is the key asset.**

     The Kimball method, as outlined in *The Data Warehouse Lifecycle Toolkit, 2nd Edition,* (Wiley, 2008) is centered on the dimensional model. Dimensional modeling principles are Ralph Kimball's and the Kimball Group's most widely known contribution to the world of business intelligence. It's our focus because a good dimensional model is absolutely vital to the success of your DW/BI endeavor. If you get the model right, and populate it with integrity, the rest is straightforward.

2.   **Dimensional modeling is a group activity.**

     Even the best dimensional modeler will create a poor dimensional model if she works solo. Not only is dimensional modeling a group activity, it is a group activity that must involve the business user community. Over the years, we have turned down countless consulting requests to design a model without business input. Or, worse, struggled through painful projects where the promised business user participation did not materialize.

     It is undoubtedly a huge request of the user community. Our design process usually requires 50 to 60 hours of sessions over a 4 to 6 week period (or vastly more, depending on project complexity). The people whom we want to participate in the design sessions are always valuable and in demand. But if they can't be convinced to put in the time and energy, the resulting system will fail.

     We've talked about this many times over the years, from Margy's article 7.2, *Practical Steps for Designing a Dimensional Model,* to a discussion by Bob in article 7.4, *Involve Business Representatives in Dimensional Modeling.* It's an element of the Kimball method that I am unwaveringly passionate about.

3. **The dimensional model is the best specification for the DW/BI system.**

    The majority of clients that I work with don't have a written specification for the DW/BI system, certainly no document that reflects reality in a meaningful way. The most common specification format includes mind-numbing lists of what users want to filter and drill on, as well as the demand that all 2000 of the existing reports be supported by the new system. If all we've accomplished with our new DW/BI system is re-platforming the existing canned reports, we have failed.

    We ask the business users at the end of the design process to think about the analyses they've recently done, tried to do, or would have liked to do, from the information contained in the current design scope. We want them to say "Yes, this model meets our needs." At the same time, the IT people on the team have been watching the discussion of data sources, transformations, and other technical details. We ask them to affirm "Yes, we can populate this data model." The dimensional model design write up is a meaningful and actionable specification of the requirements.

    Bob wrote eloquently on this topic in article 4.12, *Using the Dimensional Model to Validate Business Requirements*.

4. **The dimensional model should add value beyond restructuring.**

    Some of the most valuable improvements that you can deliver in your DW/BI system are to add improved descriptors and groups to frequently used data. Yet, these opportunities are often missed by the design team. I've even encountered teams with an explicit policy to add nothing beyond what is in the source system.

    Examples of valuable data model additions include:

    - Making it easy for users to filter out the seldom used transaction codes
    - Providing attractive sort columns for pick lists and reports
    - Precompute banding, such as age ranges or transaction quality measures
    - Supporting different or deeper hierarchies than are managed in the source systems, such as marketing versus manufacturing views of the product dimension

5. **Master data management systems are a great source.**

    Deduplication is one of the most difficult tasks facing a data warehouse team. Since the earliest days of data warehousing, the back room team has struggled to design ETL processes that deduplicate entities such as customer. The increasing popularity and functionality of master data management (MDM) technology and programs provides a much better solution than within the ETL flow. And not just because it's hard! The rhythm of the ETL process, which on an ongoing basis we want to be bullet proof and hands free, is fundamentally at odds with the deduplication process. No matter how great our tools, how clever our code, how complete our business rules, the automated deduplication process cannot achieve 100 percent accuracy. A person is required to make a judgment on the questionable cases. This works much better if it is a job responsibility during the business day, rather than waiting for the ETL load.

Warren wrote about how to set up an MDM program way back in article 12.2, *Picking the Right Approach to MDM*. His advice is still good, and I have been seeing increasing success in MDM implementations. One recent client requires that all dimension attributes come from the MDM system, where they are actively managed by assigned business owners. ETL is basically just a consumer.

Most organizations will not be quite so zealous, but a simple MDM system can be used to build the value-added data elements discussed previously in this Design Tip. Dimension hierarchies are notorious for being imperfectly structured if sourced from users' desktops; the MDM tools deliver a simple platform to manage this information, as discussed in my article 10.9, *Maintaining Dimension Hierarchies*.

6. **Don't skip the relational data warehouse.**

Designing and populating an enterprise conformed data warehouse is hard. Everyone would like to skip this step. Throughout the 23-plus years of my career in data warehousing, I have observed any number of technological attempts to simplify the process, from building the BI layer directly on the transaction system, to so-called virtual data warehouses, back full circle to the current flavor of visualization tool build scripts.

As I discussed in article 13.7, *Leverage Data Visualization Tools, But Avoid Anarchy*, just say no! Unless you completely control all of your source data, you should leave ETL to the ETL tool, leave data storage and management to a relational database engine, and let the BI tools shine at what they do best: great visualizations and user experience.

7. **It's all about the business.**

I say this many times during classes and consulting. It's the most important characteristic of the Kimball Lifecycle method: practical, uncompromising focus on the business. It infuses everything we do, and it's the single most important message to carry forward.

A Look to the Future

Ralph paints a decidedly optimistic view of the future for data warehousing.

15.4 The Future Is Bright

Ralph Kimball, Design Tip #180, *Dec 1, 2015*

Data warehousing has never been more valuable and interesting than it is now. Making decisions based on data is so fundamental and obvious that the current generation of business users and data warehouse designers/implementers can't imagine a world without access to data. I'll resist the urge to tell stories about what it was like before 1980.

But this is a time of change for the practice of data warehousing. It is essential that "data warehousing" always encompasses the gathering of business needs and the enumeration of all the data assets of an organization in the broadest possible senses. If data warehousing is ever relegated to just reporting text and number data out of transaction systems of record, then huge opportunities will be lost.

Data warehousing has defined an architecture for *Publishing the Right Data* to decision makers, and that architecture has names: dimensional modeling, fact tables, dimension tables, surrogate keys, slowly changing dimensions, conformed dimensions, and many more.

Big changes are occurring today in the business world, with new torrents of data from social media, free text, sensors and meters, geo-positioning devices, satellites, cameras, and other recording devices. Business users are expecting to make decisions based on these data sources. Marketing, the traditional driver of data warehousing, is now competing with manufacturing, operations, and research. Many of these departments new to data analysis are building their own systems, often in good faith, but ignorant of the deep legacy and accumulated architectural skills of data warehousing. It is incumbent on the data warehouse community to meet these new business users half way, not only to offer our useful perspectives, but for us to learn about these new business areas.

In this, my final Kimball Group *Design Tip*, I'll describe how I think the main components of data warehousing are changing and will change in the near future. It's an exciting and challenging time to be a data warehouse professional!

The Future of ETL

If data warehousing is going to encompass all the data assets of an organization, then it must deal with the immense new torrents of strangely structured data. Several big changes must take place in the ETL environment. First, the data feeds from original sources must support huge bandwidths, at least gigabytes per second. Learn about Sqoop loading data into Hadoop. If these words mean nothing to you, you have some reading to do! Start with Wikipedia. Second, many of the analytic clients for these new data streams insist that no transformations be applied to the incoming data. In other words, the ETL landing zone must be able to store files consisting of un-interpreted bits with no assumptions made about how that file will be stored in a database or analyzed. Third, the storage architecture must be open so that multiple diverse decision support tools and analytic clients can access the data through a universal metadata layer. And fourth, the metadata descriptions of data files of all types must be much more extensible, customizable, and powerful as new complex data sources are made available. We have gone far too long with simple text-and-number RDBMS files where the metadata contained in RDBMS system files has little or no semantics.

The proprietary stacks of mainline RDBMSs will be challenged to be pried apart into separate storage, metadata, and query layers. This has already happened in the Hadoop open source environment under the Hadoop Distributed File System (HDFS). This means that ETL processing in some cases can be delayed until a point in time after the data is loaded into accessible files. Query and analysis tools, through the metadata, may wish to declare the target schema at query time as a kind of powerful "view" at query time, not at load time. As exotic as this "schema on read" sounds, this is just another form of data virtualization which we have used for more than a decade. The tradeoff in all these forms of data virtualization is that by substituting computation for ETL data restructuring, one pays a significant performance penalty. At some point after an exploratory query phase, the designer will usually loop back and do normal ETL processing to prepare more performant file structures.

The Future of Database Technology

Relational databases are the bedrock of data warehousing and will always be such. But RDBMSs will never be extended to natively process all the new data types. Many specialty analytic tools will compete with each other to analyze the data, and gracefully coexist with RDBMS databases that will cherry pick the parts of the incoming data streams that relational databases can handle.

On a related topic, archiving will never be the same. Disk storage has won the war for the long term archiving choice for many reasons, but the biggest factor is the amazing low cost per petabyte. Additionally disk storage is always online, thus the archived data remains active and accessible, awaiting new analysis modes, and new retrospective questions. This is called "active archiving."

The Future of Dimensional Modeling

Even in the brave new world of strange data types and non-relational processing, dimensional modeling is enormously relevant. Even the most bizarre data types can be thought of as a set of observations recorded in the real world. These observations always have context: date, time, location, customer/person/patient, action, and the list goes on. These, of course, are our familiar dimensions. When we realize this, suddenly all the familiar dimensional machinery kicks in. We can attach high quality curated dimensions from our EDW to any data source. Expand your minds: This attachment doesn't have to be through a conventional relational database join, because the correspondence can be made in other ways.

Dimensions, of course, are the soul of the data warehouse. Facts are merely observations that always exist in a dimensional context. Going forward, we can expect dimensions to become more powerful in order to support more sophisticated behavior based queries and predictive analytics. Already there have been proposals for generalizing the star schema to a supernova schema. In a supernova schema, dimensional attributes are allowed to become complex objects rather than simple text. Supernova dimensions also become much more malleable and extensible from one analysis to another. Contrast the traditional customer dimension with the supernova customer dimension in Figure 15-1. Note that much of this is not future pie-in-the-sky. You can generalize a single dimension attribute today with an ARRAY of STRUCTS. Time to read the SQL reference manual.

The Future of BI Tools

The space of BI tools will grow to include many non-SQL kinds of analysis. Of course this has already happened, especially in the open source Hadoop environment, and we have always relied on powerful non-SQL tools such as SAS. So in some ways this is a matter of definition of what is a BI tool. I am arguing this point mainly to prod data warehouse teams to expand their scope and not get left out of the new data sources and new kinds of analysis.

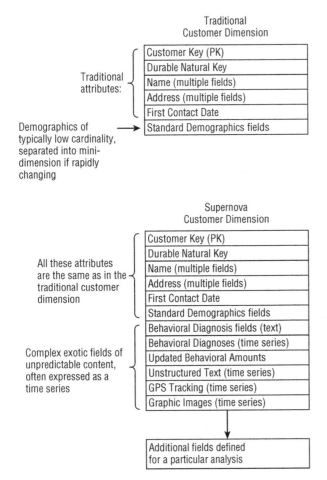

Figure 15-1: Traditional and Supernova Customer Dimensions.

The Future of Data Warehouse Professionals

I have remarked many times that a successful data warehouse professional must be interested in three things: the business, the technology, and the business users. This will always be true in the future. If you want to spend your time coding and not talking to business users, that's great but you don't belong on the data warehouse team. Having said that, data warehouse professionals going forward need to have Unix and Java skills at a minimum, and familiarity with some of the principal non-SQL analytic environments such as Spark, MongoDB, and HBase, as well as data transfer tools such as Sqoop.

I think the big exciting challenge going forward is the expansion of the data warehouse professional's job description. New departments are suddenly appearing who are trying to grapple with torrents of data, and are probably reinventing the data warehouse wheel. Find out who these departments are and educate them about the power of conformed dimensions and surrogate keys. Offer to attach your high quality EDW dimensions to their data.

And as Margy says: Go forth and be dimensional!

Article Index

Index